CW00822015

TRANSPORT FOR LONDON

UNDERGROUND

EVERY JOURNEY MATTERS

Version A TfL 3.2017   Correct at time of going to print

STREET ATLAS
London

Contents

II Key to map pages

IV Administrative and Postcode boundaries

VI Key to map symbols

1 Street maps

77 Central London

77 Key to map pages and key to symbols

78 Large-scale street maps

174 Index

292 List of numbered locations

312 London Underground map

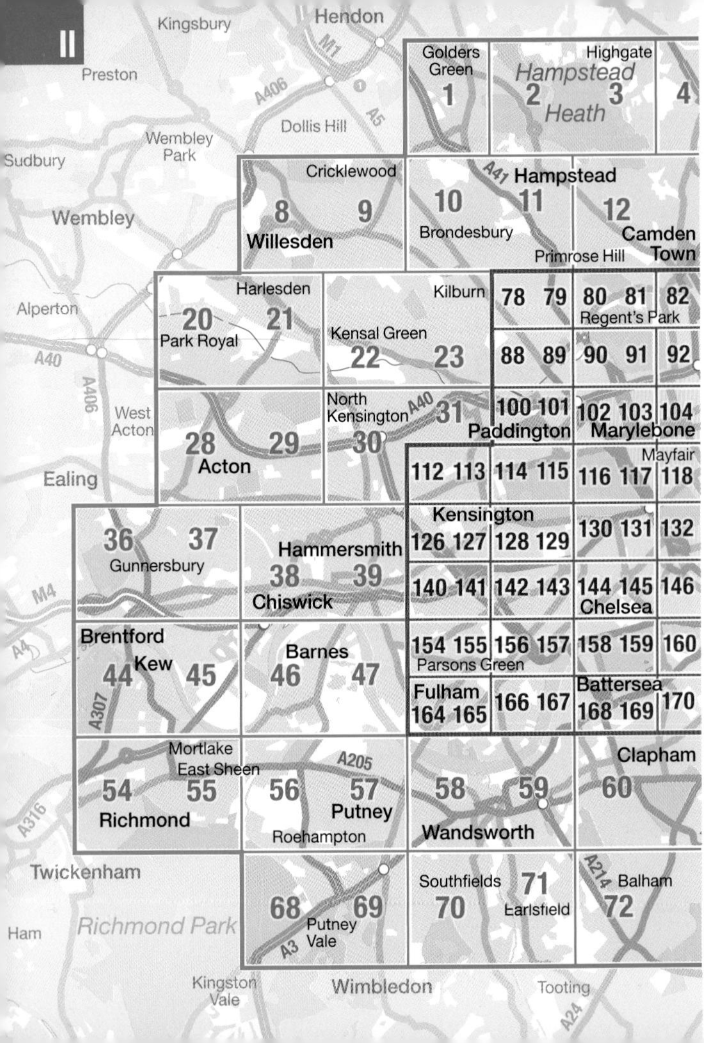

Kingsbury

Hendon

Preston

Golders Green **1**

Highgate

Hampstead

2 **3** **4**

Heath

A406

M1

Dollis Hill

A5

Wembley Park

Cricklewood

Sudbury

Willesden **8** **9** **10** Brondesbury

A41 **Hampstead 11**

Wembley

12 Camden Town

Primrose Hill

Alperton

Harlesden

20 **21**

Park Royal

Kensal Green **22**

Kilburn **23**

78 79 **80 81** **82**

Regent's Park

A40

88 89 **90 91** **92**

West Acton

28 **29**

Acton

North Kensington **30** A40 **31**

100 101

Paddington

102 103 104

Marylebone

Ealing

112 113 **114 115**

116 117 Mayfair **118**

M4

36 **37**

Gunnersbury

Hammersmith

38 **39**

Chiswick

Kensington

126 127 **128 129**

130 131 **132**

140 141 **142 143**

144 145 **146**

Chelsea

Brentford

Kew

44 **45**

Barnes

46 **47**

154 155 **156 157**

Parsons Green

158 159 **160**

A307

Fulham

164 165 **166 167**

168 169 **170**

Battersea

Mortlake

East Sheen

54 **55**

Richmond

56 **57**

Putney

Roehampton

A205

58 **59**

Wandsworth

Clapham

60

A316

Twickenham

Richmond Park

68 **69**

Putney Vale

A3

Southfields

70 **71** Earlsfield

A24

Balham

72

Ham

Kingston Vale

Wimbledon

Tooting

A24

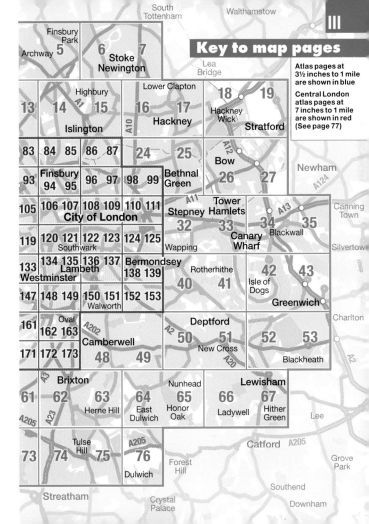

III

Key to map pages

Atlas pages at 3½ inches to 1 mile are shown in blue

Central London atlas pages at 7 inches to 1 mile are shown in red (See page 77)

South Tottenham

Walthamstow

Finsbury Park

Archway **5**

6 Stoke Newington **7**

Lea Bridge

Highbury

13 **14** A1 **15**

Islington

Lower Clapton

16 A10 **17** Hackney

18 Hackney Wick

19

Stratford

Newham A124

83 **84** **85** **86** **87** **24** **25** Bow A12

93 Finsbury **94** **95** **96** **97** **98** **99** Bethnal Green **26** **27**

105 **106** **107** **108** **109** **110** **111** City of London

A11 Tower Stepney Hamlets

32 **33** **34** A13 **35**

Canary Wharf Blackwall

Canning Town

Silvertown

119 **120** **121** **122** **123** **124** **125** Southwark

Wapping

133 **134** **135** **136** **137** Bermondsey Lambeth

Westminster **138** **139**

Rotherhithe **40** **41**

42 Isle of Dogs

43

Greenwich

147 **148** **149** **150** **151** **152** **153** Walworth

Charlton

161 Oval **162** **163** A202 Camberwell

171 **172** **173** **48** **49**

Deptford A2 **50** **51** New Cross A20

52 **53**

Blackheath

A2

61 **43** Brixton **62** A23 **63** Herne Hill

64 East Dulwich

Nunhead **65** Honor Oak

Lewisham **66** Ladywell **67** Hither Green

Lee

73 **74** Tulse Hill **75** A205 **76** Dulwich

Forest Hill

Catford A205

Grove Park

Streatham

Crystal Palace

Southend

Downham

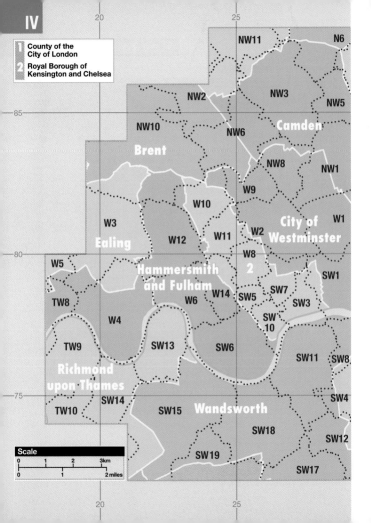

IV

1 County of the
City of London

2 Royal Borough of
Kensington and Chelsea

NW11   N6

NW2   NW3   NW5

NW10   NW6

Camden

NW8   NW1

Brent

W9

W10

W3   W12   W11   W2   **City of Westminster**   W1

Ealing

W8

W5

2

TW8   SW1

Hammersmith and Fulham

W4   W6   W14   SW5   SW7   SW3

SW10

TW9   SW13   SW6   SW11   SW8

Richmond upon Thames

SW14   SW4

TW10   SW15   **Wandsworth**   SW12

SW18   SW17

SW19

Scale

0   1   2   3km

0   1   2 miles

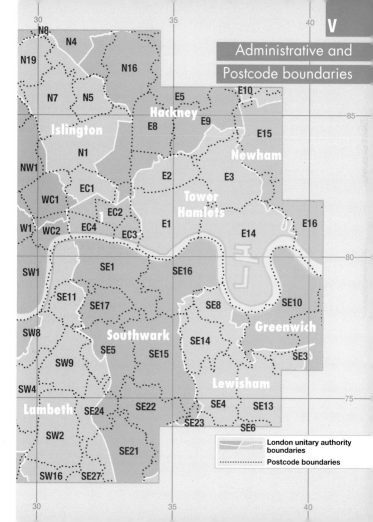

Administrative and Postcode boundaries

V

London unitary authority boundaries

Postcode boundaries

Key to map symbols

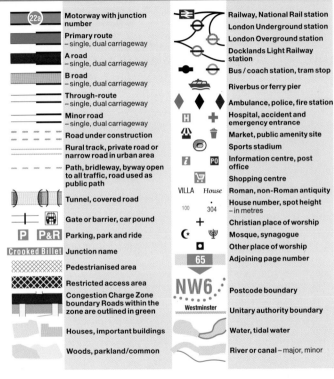

Motorway with junction number	Railway, National Rail station
Primary route – single, dual carriageway	London Underground station
A road – single, dual carriageway	London Overground station
B road – single, dual carriageway	Docklands Light Railway station
Through-route – single, dual carriageway	Bus / coach station, tram stop
Minor road – single, dual carriageway	Riverbus or ferry pier
Road under construction	Ambulance, police, fire station
Rural track, private road or narrow road in urban area	Hospital, accident and emergency entrance
Path, bridleway, byway open to all traffic, road used as public path	Market, public amenity site
Tunnel, covered road	Sports stadium
Gate or barrier, car pound	Information centre, post office
Parking, park and ride	Shopping centre
Junction name	Roman, non-Roman antiquity
Pedestrianised area	House number, spot height – in metres
Restricted access area	Christian place of worship
Congestion Charge Zone boundary Roads within the zone are outlined in green	Mosque, synagogue
	Other place of worship
Houses, important buildings	Adjoining page number
Woods, parkland/common	Postcode boundary
	Unitary authority boundary
	Water, tidal water
	River or canal – major, minor

VILLA *House*

100   304

65

NW6

Westminster

The map scale on the pages numbered in blue is 3½ inches to 1 mile
5.52 cm to 1 km • 1 : 18 103

0	¼ mile	½ mile
0	250m	500m 750m 1km

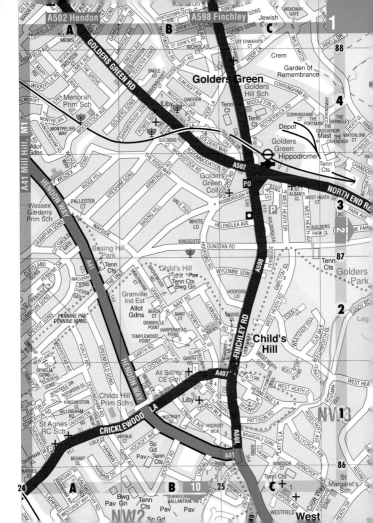

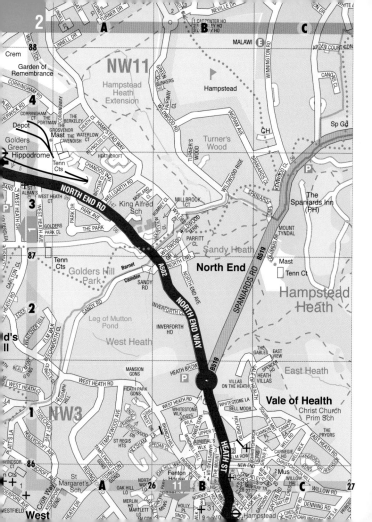

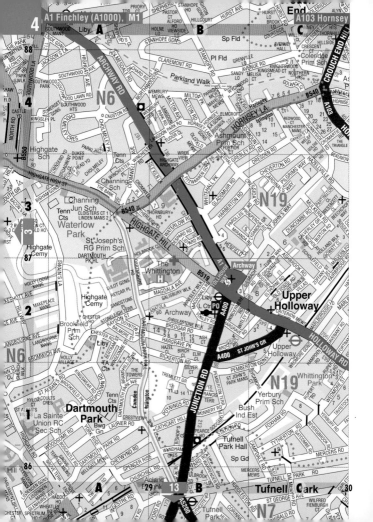

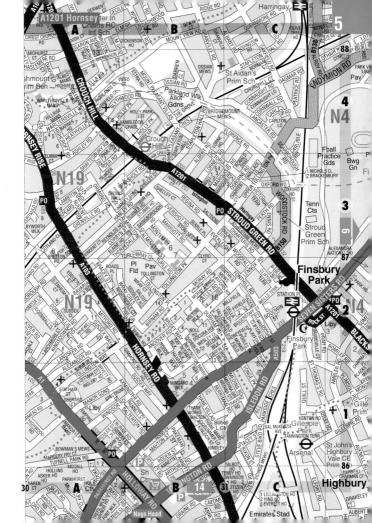

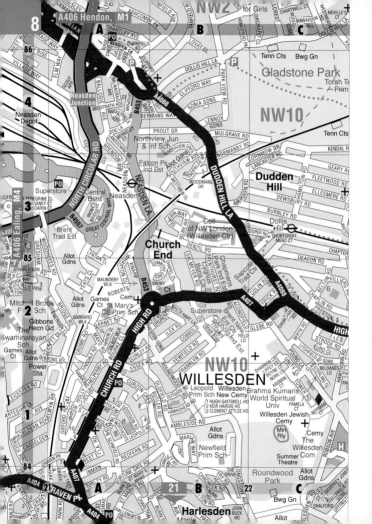

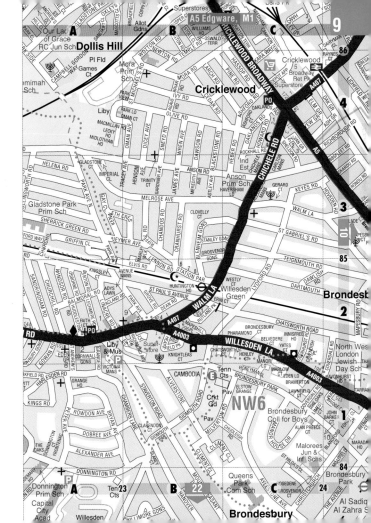

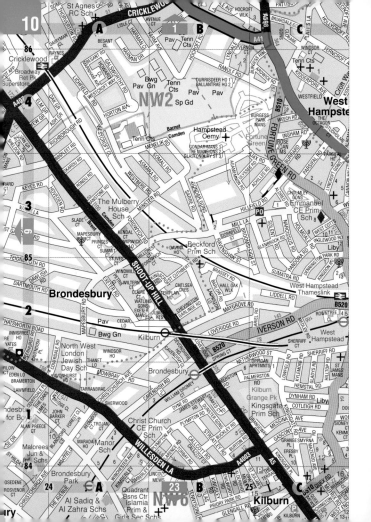

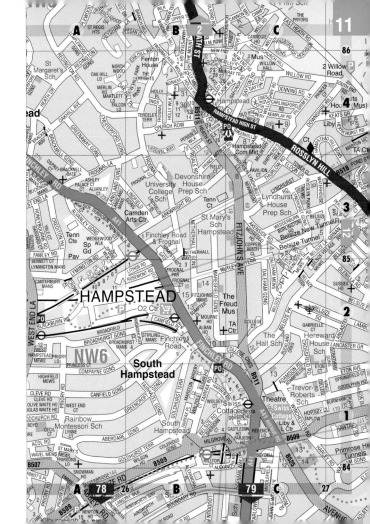

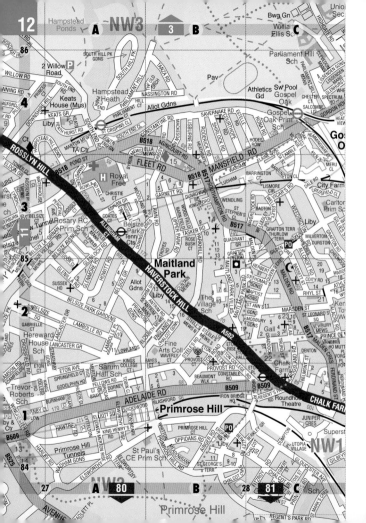

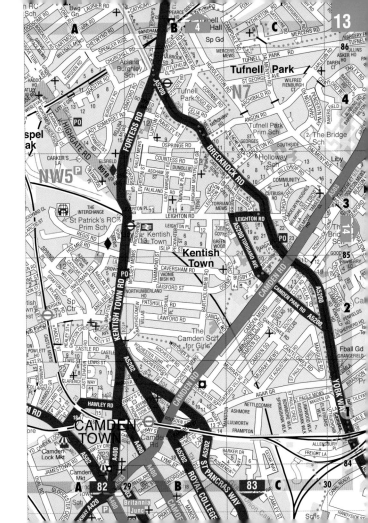

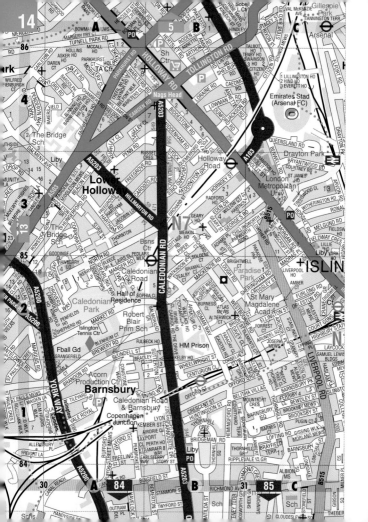

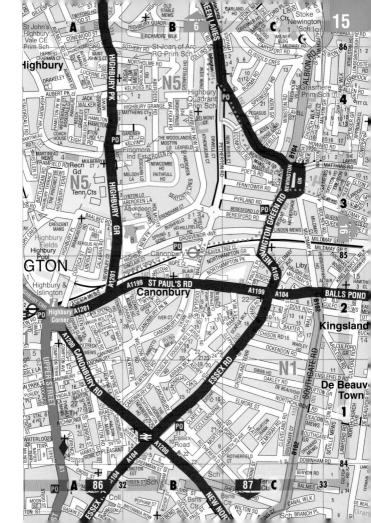

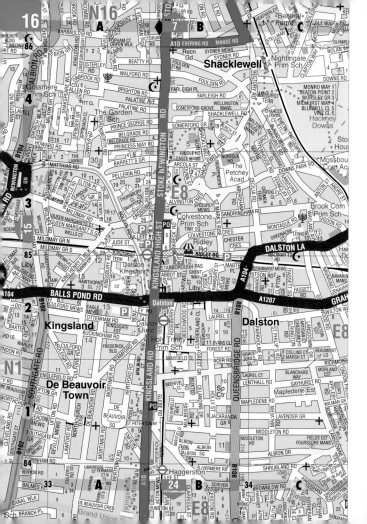

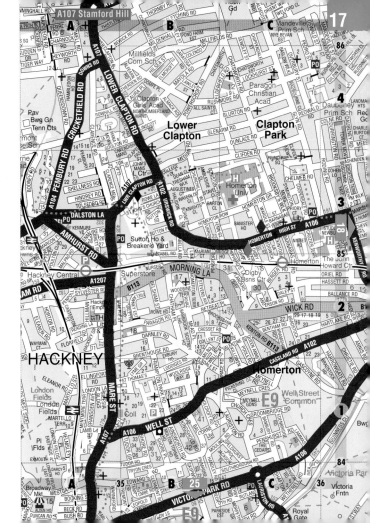

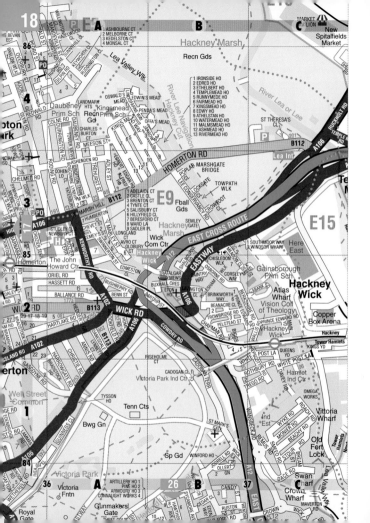

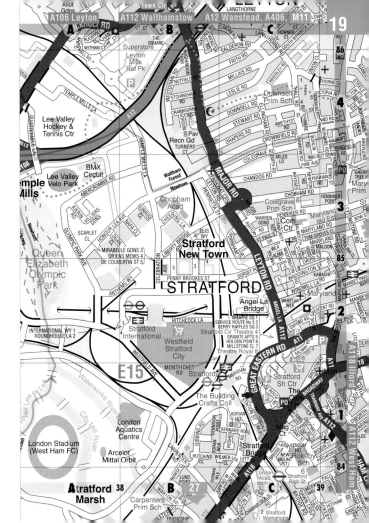

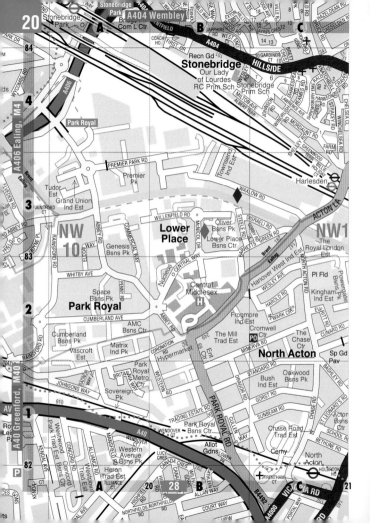

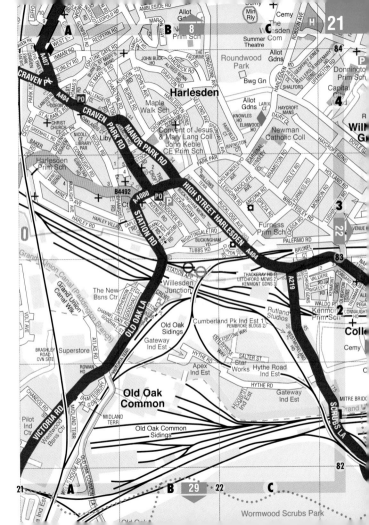

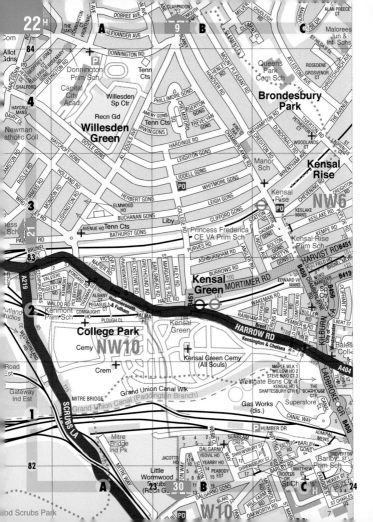

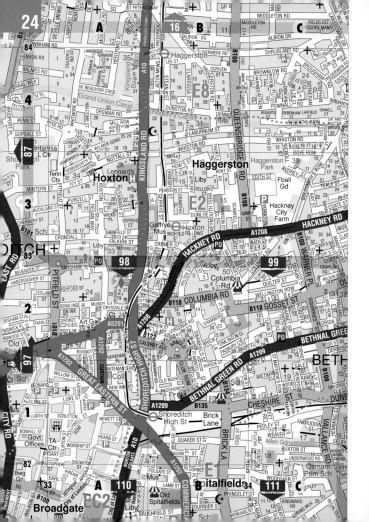

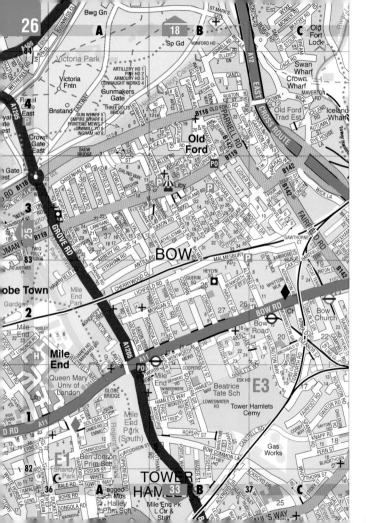

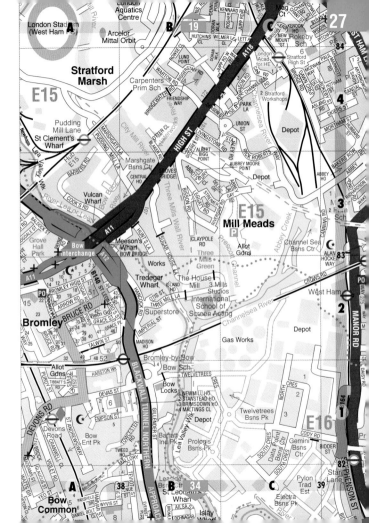

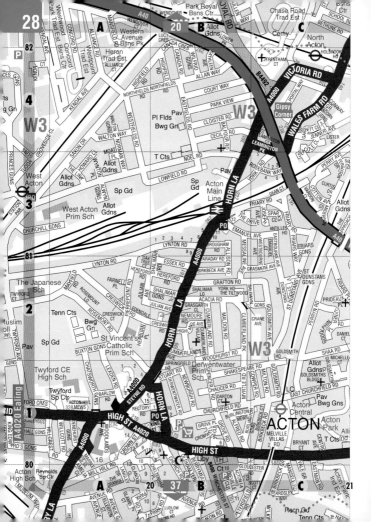

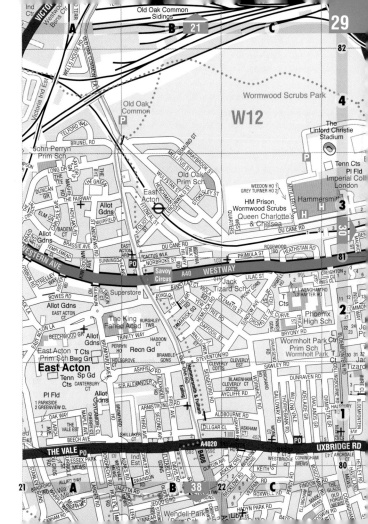

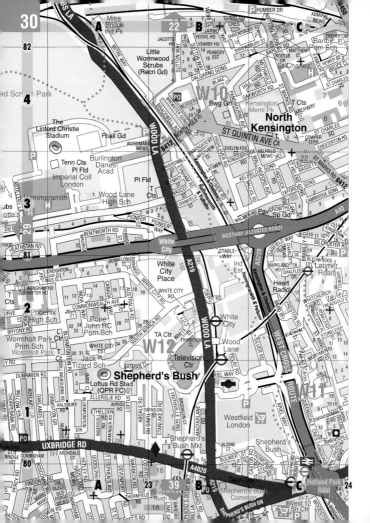

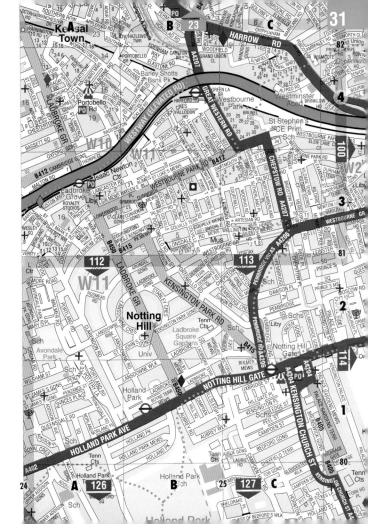

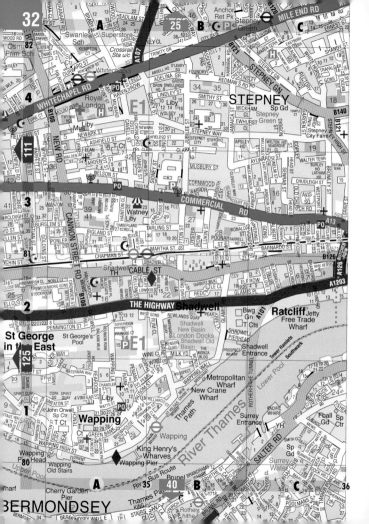

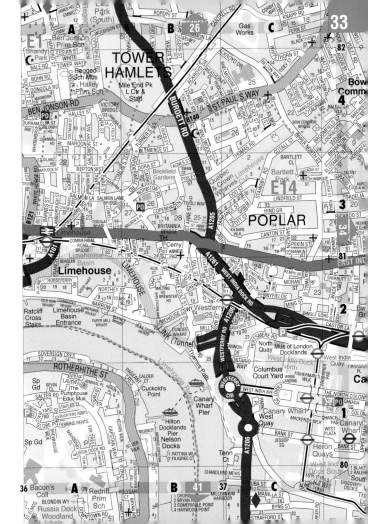

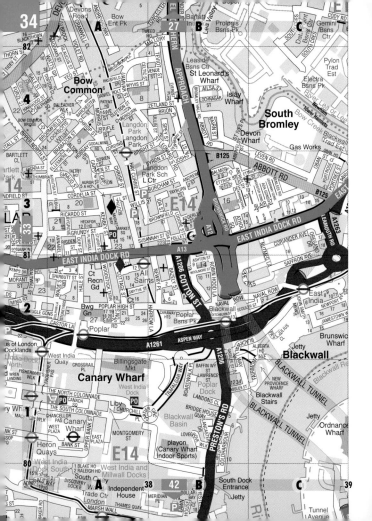

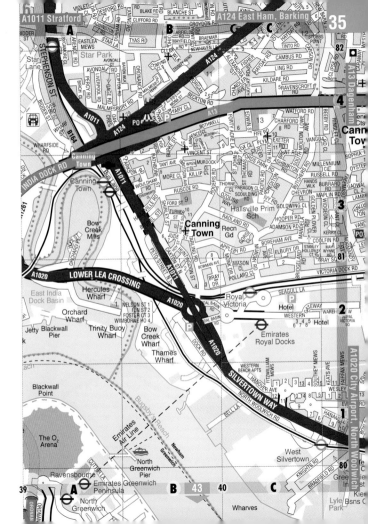

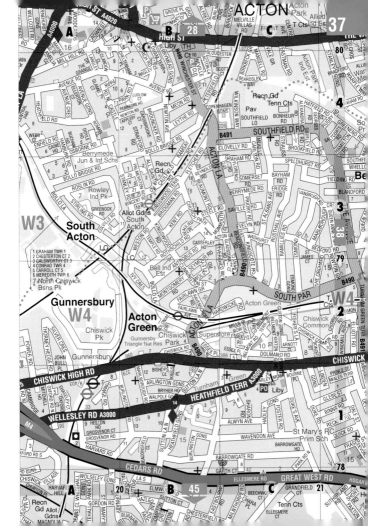

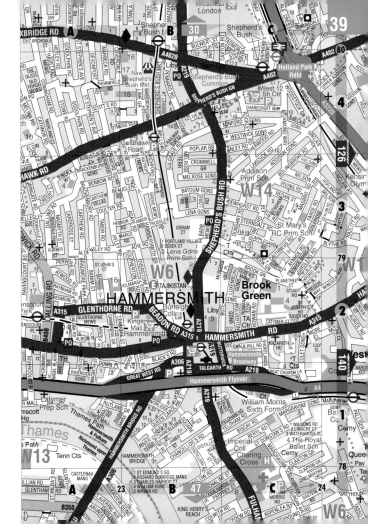

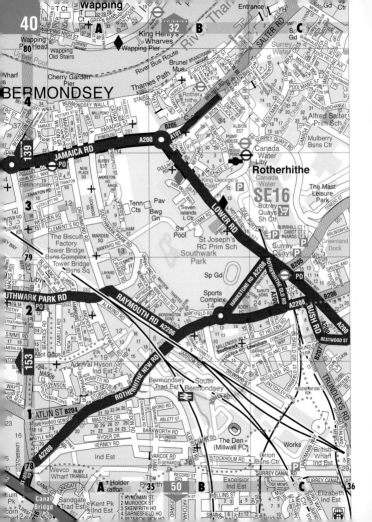

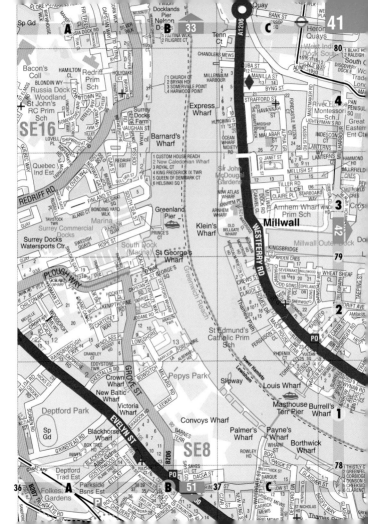

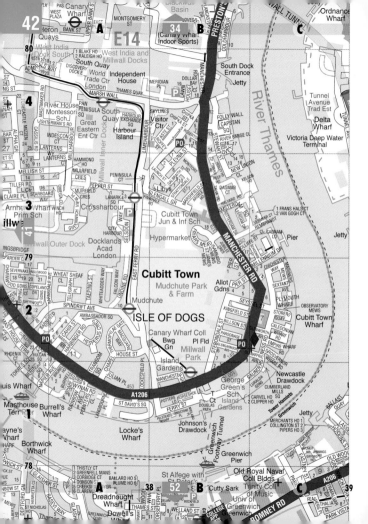

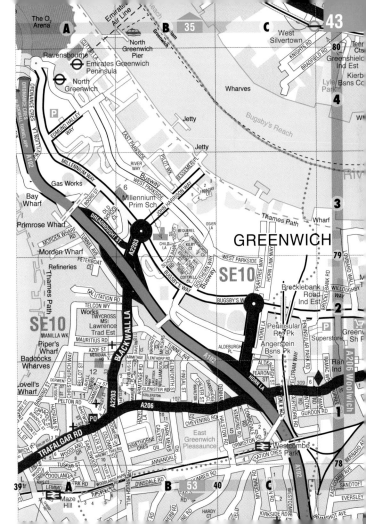

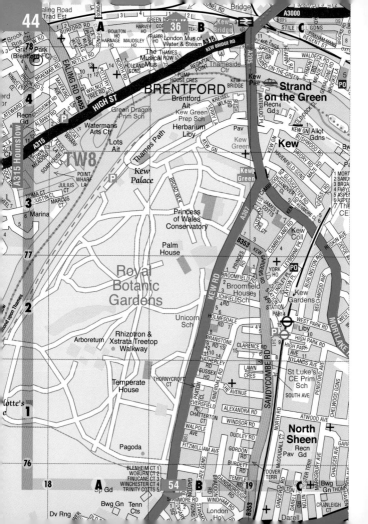

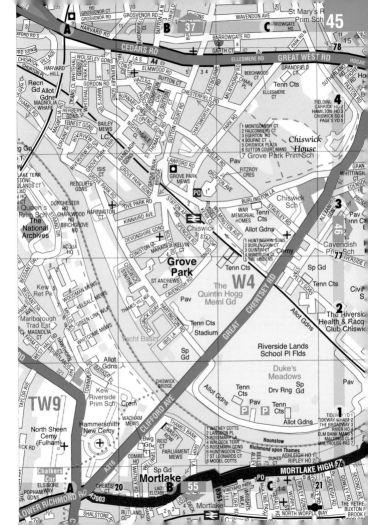

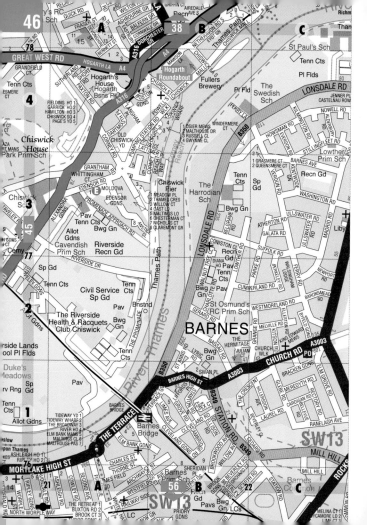

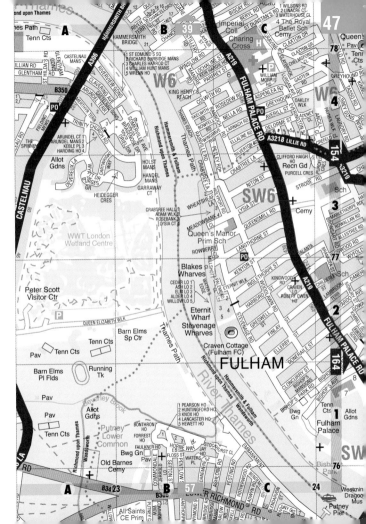

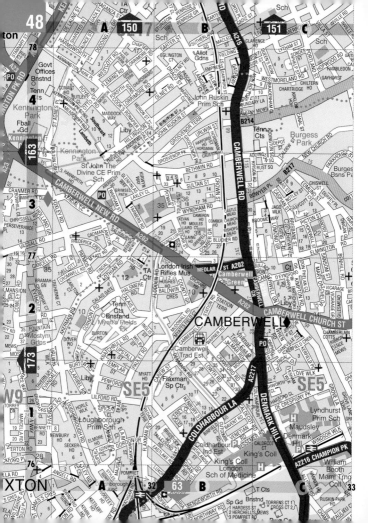

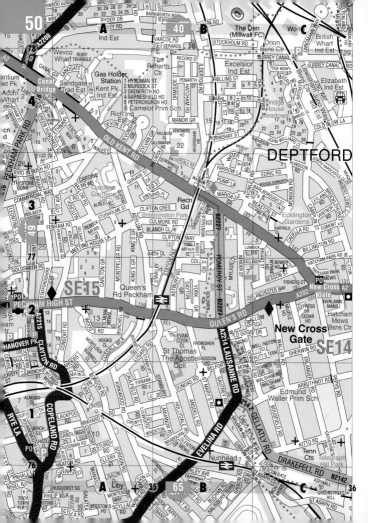

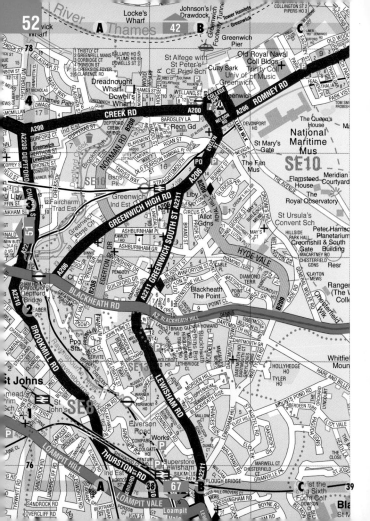

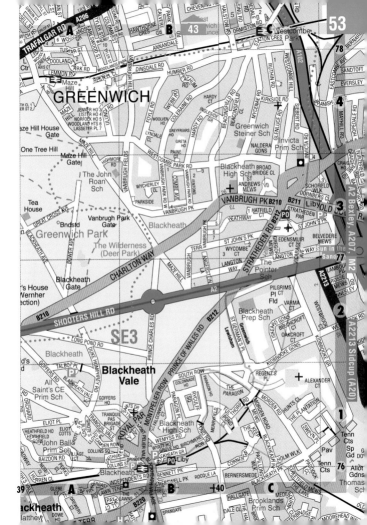

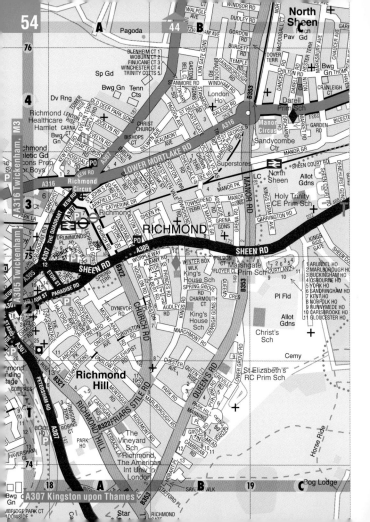

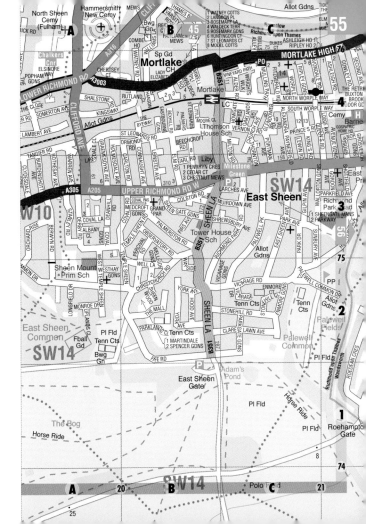

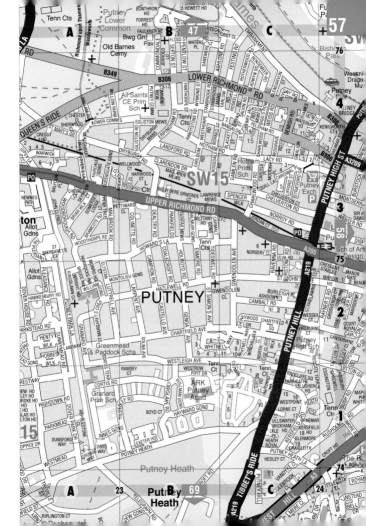

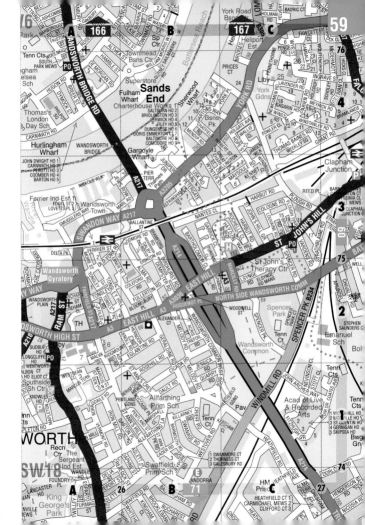

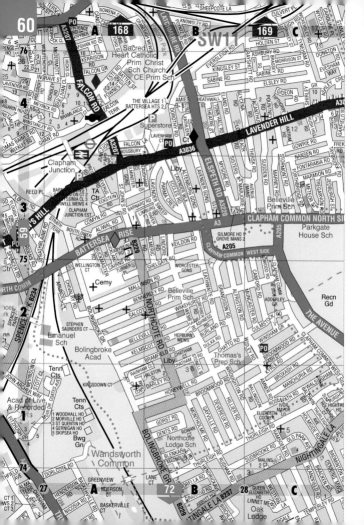

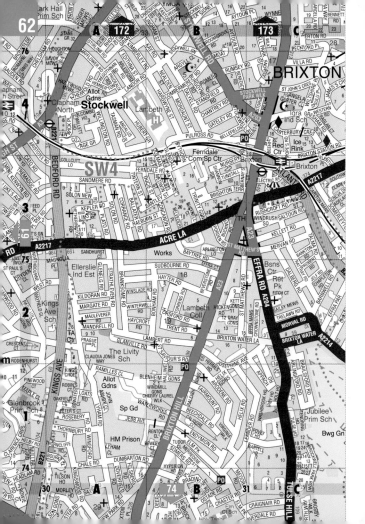

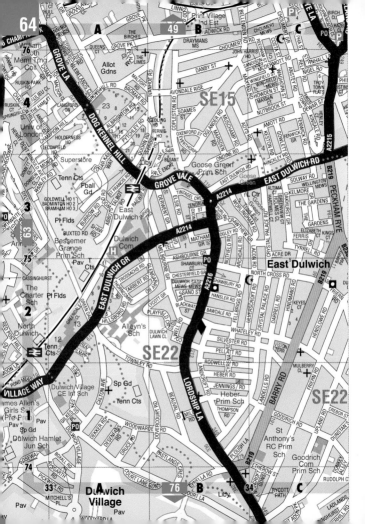

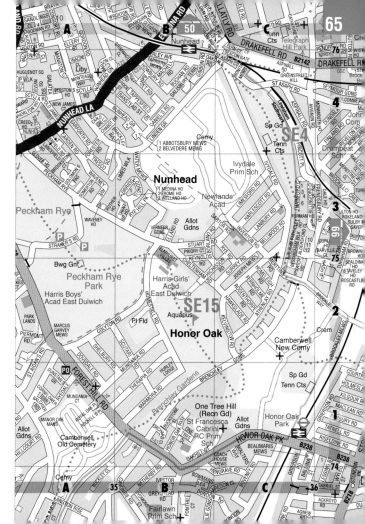

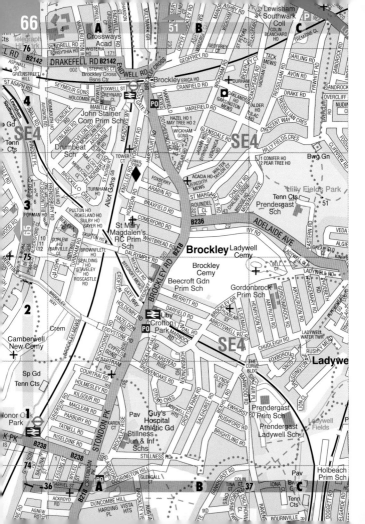

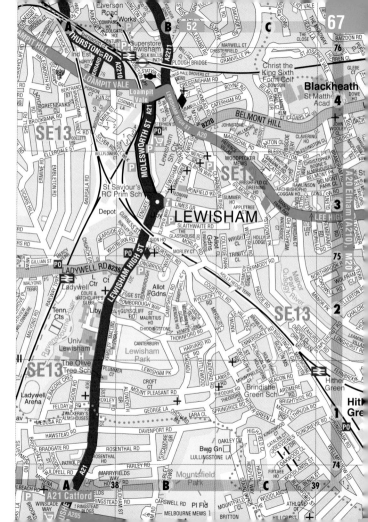

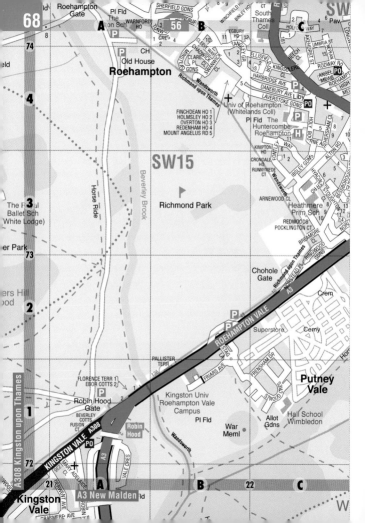

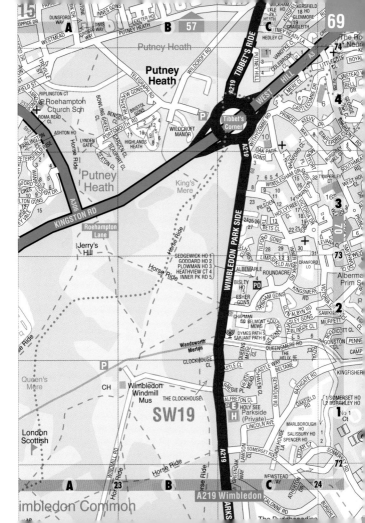

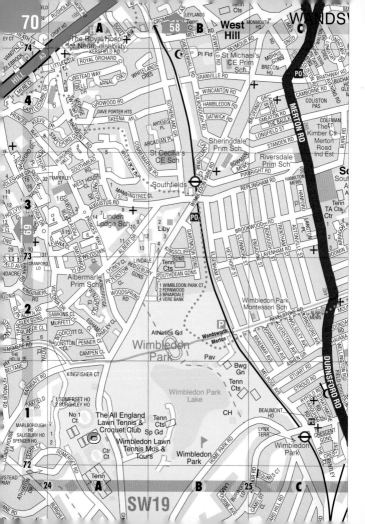

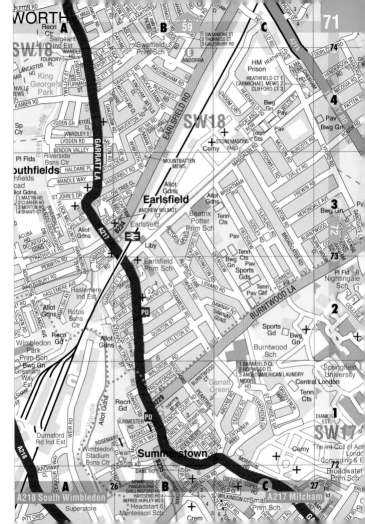

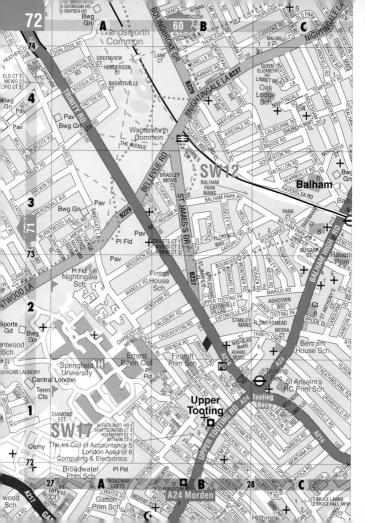

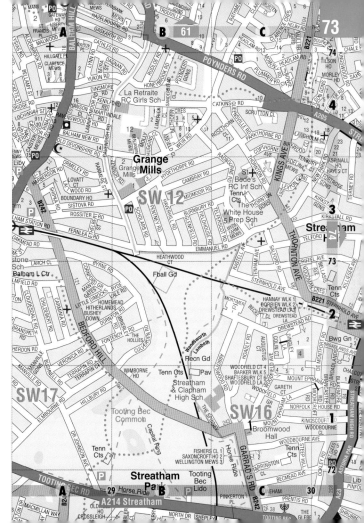

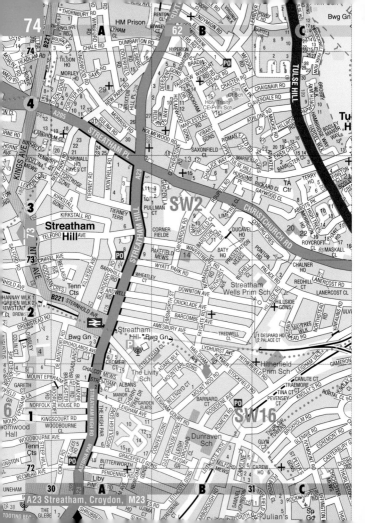

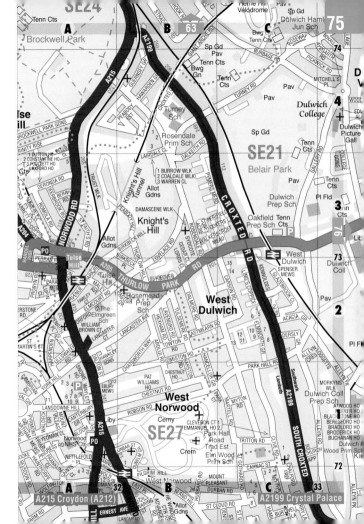

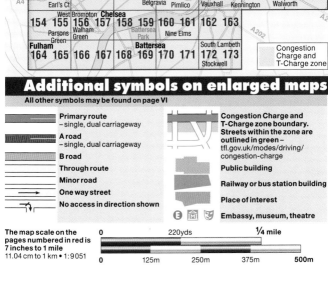

77

Key to central London map pages

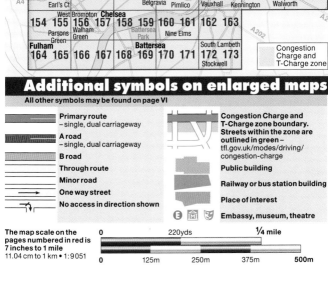

78 79 St John's Wood	Primrose Hill 80 81 Regent's Park	82 83 Somers Town	Islington 84 85 King's Cross	86 87	A10
Maida Vale 88 89 Westbourne Green	90 91 Lisson Grove	92 93	St Pancras 94 95 Bloomsbury	Finsbury Shoreditch 96 97	Bethnal 98 99 Green Spitalfields
Paddington 100 101	Marylebone 102 103	Fitzrovia 104 105	Holborn 106 107 St Giles Strand	City 108 109	110 111 Whitechapel
Notting Hill 112 113	Bayswater 114 115 Kensington Gardens	Mayfair 116 117 Hyde Park	118 119 St James	120 121 South Bank	124 125 St George in the East
Kensington 126 127 Holland Pk West	128 129 Knightsbridge Brompton	Green Park 130 131	132 133	Waterloo 134 135 Southwark The Borough 136 137	138 139 Bermondsey
Kensington 140 141 Earl's Ct	South Kensington 142 143 Westminster	144 145 Belgravia	Victoria 146 147 Pimlico	Lambeth 148 149 Vauxhall Kennington	Newington 150 151 Walworth 152 153
West Brompton 154 155 Parsons Green Fulham 164 165	Chelsea 156 157 Walham Green 166 167	158 159 Battersea Park Battersea 168 169	160 161 Nine Elms 170 171	162 163 South Lambeth 172 173 Stockwell	A2 A202

Congestion Charge and T-Charge zone

Additional symbols on enlarged maps

All other symbols may be found on page VI

▬▬	Primary route – single, dual carriageway
▨▨	A road – single, dual carriageway
═══	B road
═══	Through route
───	Minor road
→──	One way street
⇥──	No access in direction shown

Congestion Charge and T-Charge zone boundary. Streets within the zone are outlined in green – tfl.gov.uk/modes/driving/congestion-charge

Public building

Railway or bus station building

Place of interest

Ⓔ 🏛 🎭 Embassy, museum, theatre

The map scale on the pages numbered in red is 7 inches to 1 mile
11.04 cm to 1 km • 1: 9051

| 0 | 220yds | ¼ mile |
| 0 | 125m | 250m | 375m | 500m |

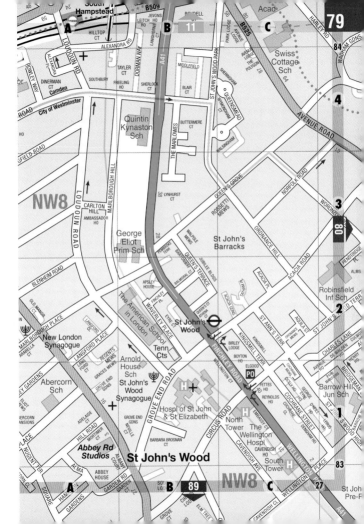

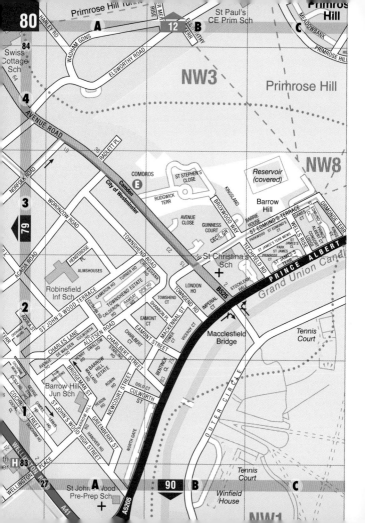

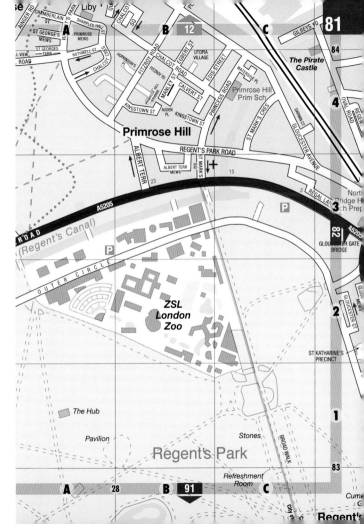

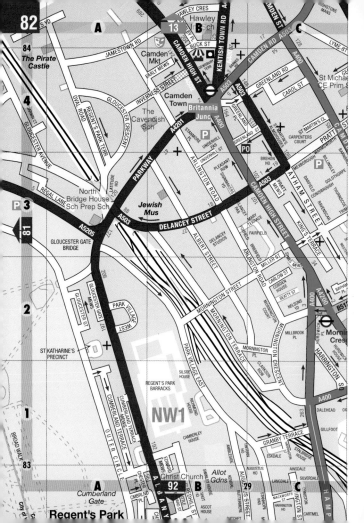

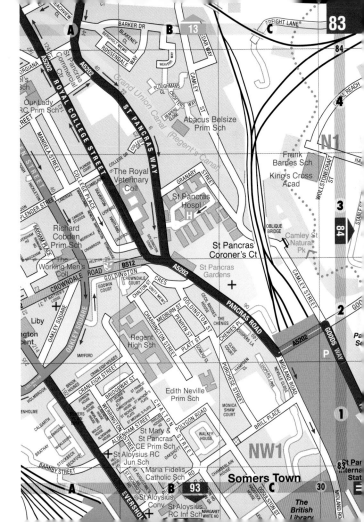

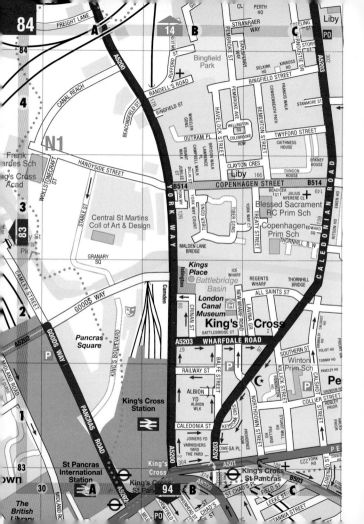

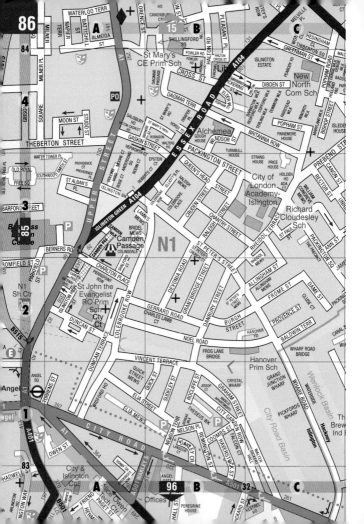

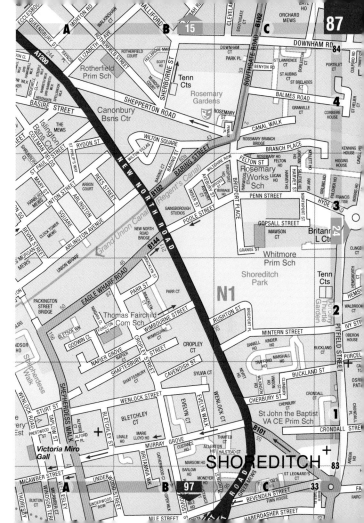

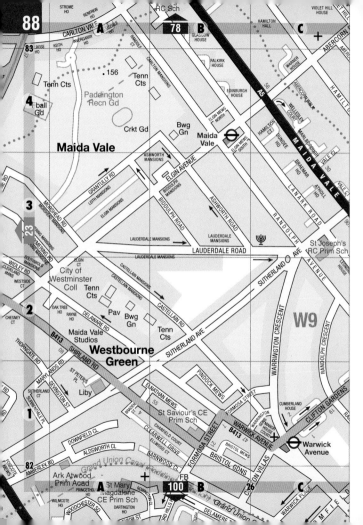

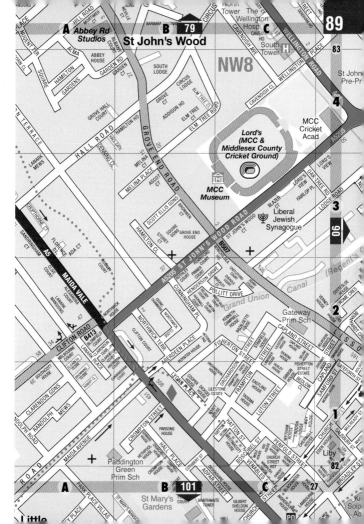

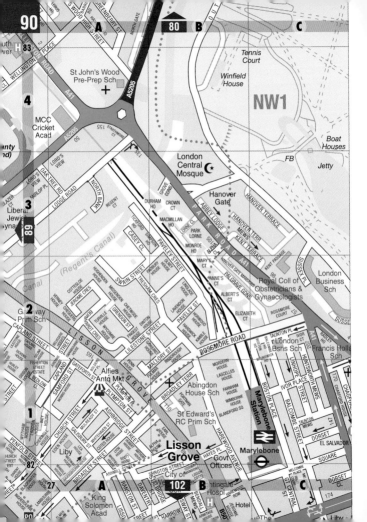

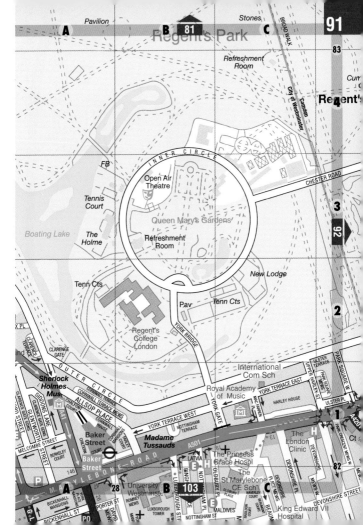

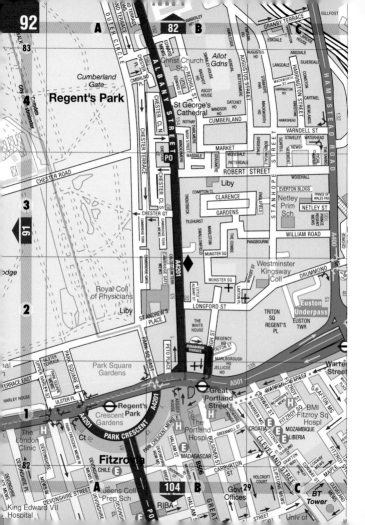

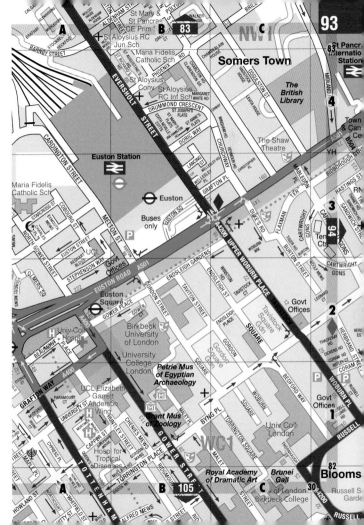

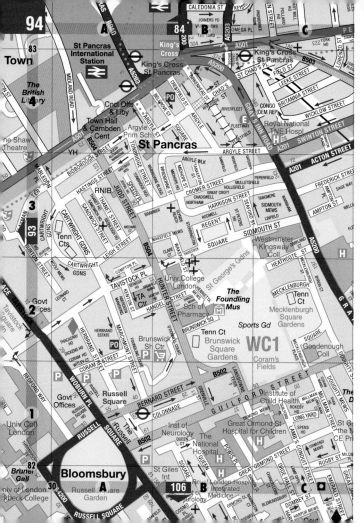

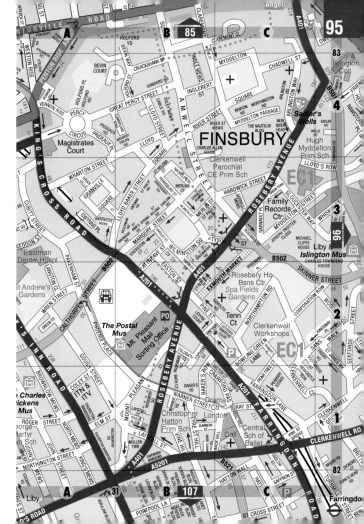

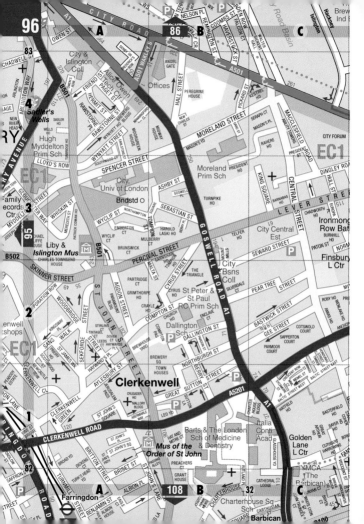

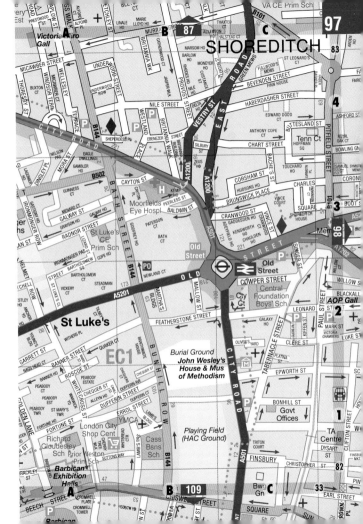

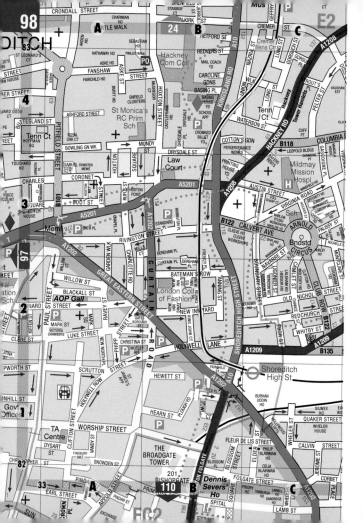

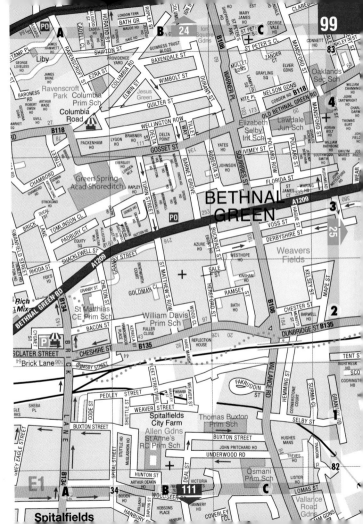

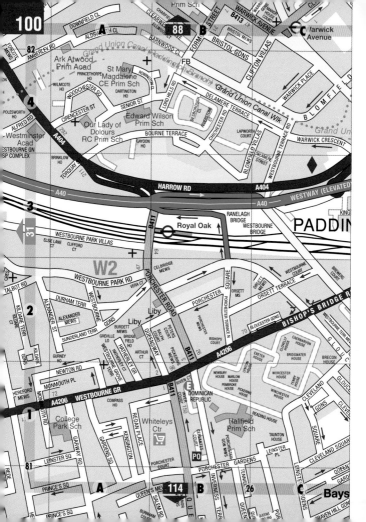

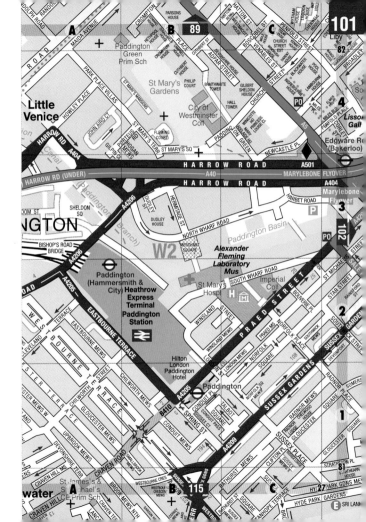

A   B   **89**   C

Liby

82

BRADLEY

MAIDA AVENUE

Paddington
Green
Prim Sch

PARSONS
HOUSE

4

Lisso
Gall

Edgware Ro
(Bakerloo)

Little
Venice

St Mary's
Gardens

PHILIP
COURT

BRAITHWAITE
TOWER

City of
Westminster
Coll

GILBERT
SHELDON
HOUSE

HALL
TOWER

CHURCH

PADDINGTON GREEN

NEWCASTLE PL

HARROW RD

A404

Canal

JOHN AIRD CT

PORTEUS RD

ST MARY'S TER

ST MARY'S SQ

FLEMING
CONRD

A5

HARROW ROAD   A501   MARYLEBONE FLYOVER

HARROW RD (UNDER)   A40   MARYLEBONE FLYOVER

HARROW ROAD   A404

OOM ST

SHELDON
SQ

NGTON

A4206

DUDLEY
HOUSE

DUDLEY ST

HERMITAGE ST

NORTH WHARF ROAD

MERCHANT
SQUARE

Paddington Basin

HARBET ROAD

3

Marylebone
Flyover

102

PO

BISHOP'S ROAD
BRIDGE

A4206

W2

Paddington
(Hammersmith &
City) Heathrow
Express
Terminal
Paddington
Station

EASTBOURNE TERRACE

Alexander
Fleming
Laboratory
Mus

St Mary's
Hosp

SOUTH WHARF ROAD

Imperial
Coll

BOUVERIE PL

PRAED STREET

ST MICHAEL'S

STAR STREET

2

WINSLAND STREET

WINSLAND MEWS

PRAED ST

NORFOLK PLACE

SOUTHWICK
MEWS

LONDON MEWS

NORFOLK
SQUARE

108

SUSSEX

Hilton
London
Paddington
Hotel

Paddington

A4205

CONDUIT PL

SPRING ST

CONDUIT MEWS

SUSSEX GARDENS

RADNOR MEWS

RADNOR
PLACE

SUSSEX PLACE

1

EASTBOURNE MEWS

CHILWORTH MEWS

GLOUCESTER MEWS

SMALLBROOK

A410

CLIFTON
MEWS

STRATHEARN PL

81

WESTBOURNE CRES

A   St James's &
St Michael's
C Prim Sch

water

CRAVEN HILL

CRAVEN HILL GDNS

B   **115**   WESTBOURNE
CRESCENT
MEWS

BATHURST
MEWS

C   HYDE PARK GARDENS

STANHOPE TERRACE

E SRI LANK

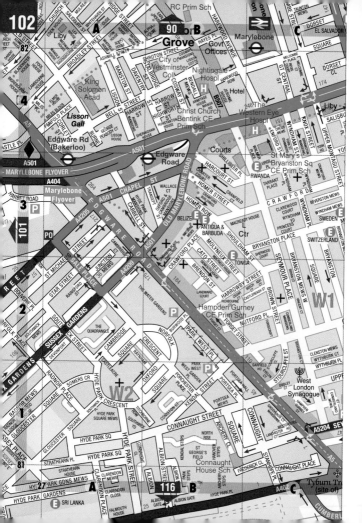

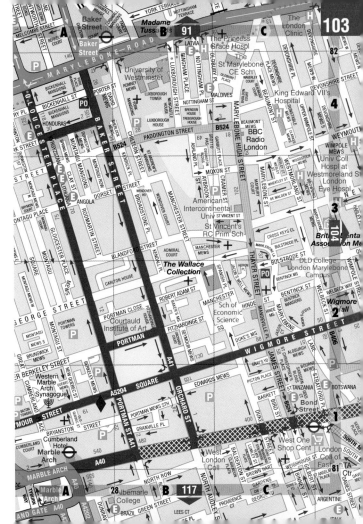

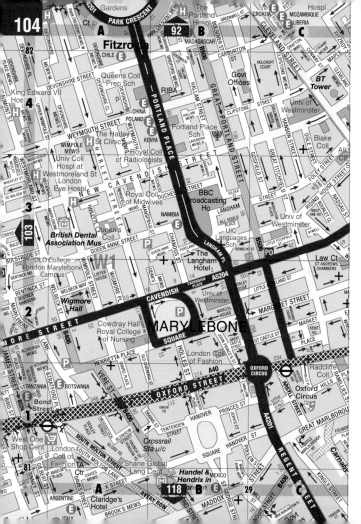

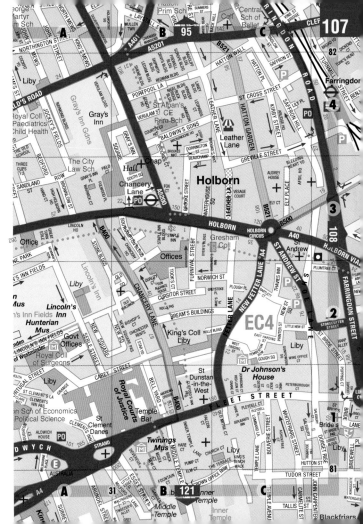

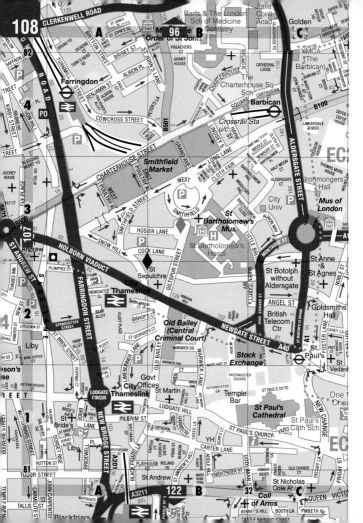

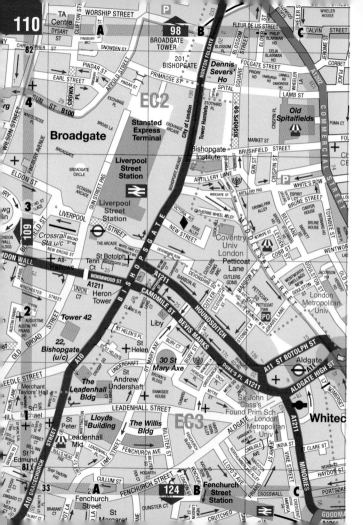

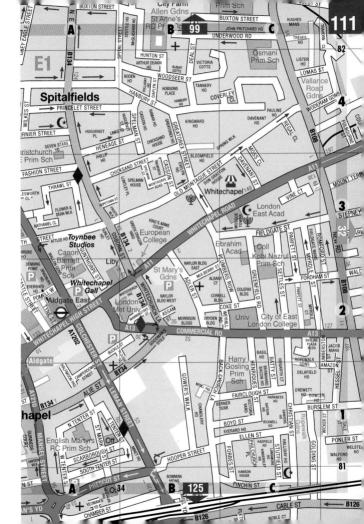

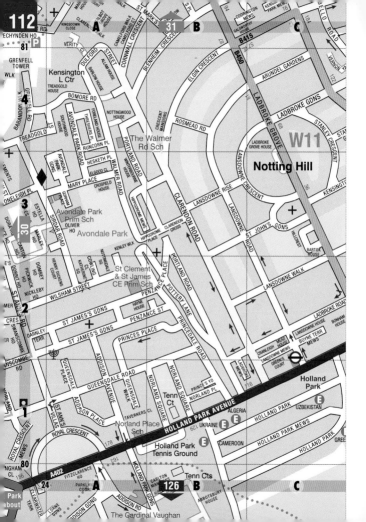

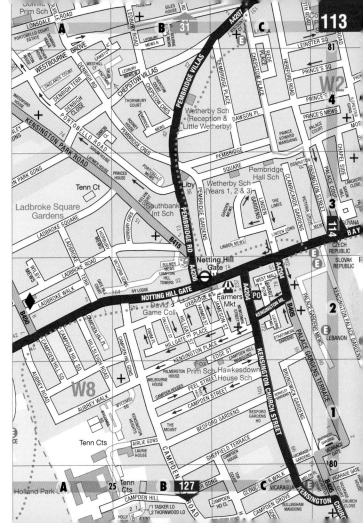

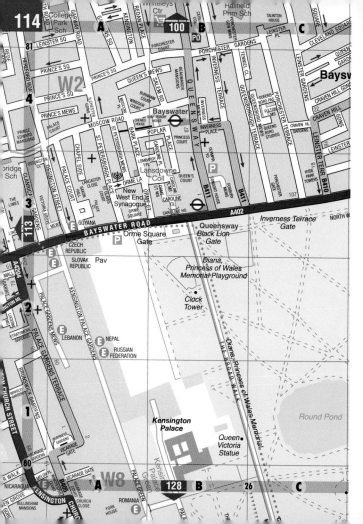

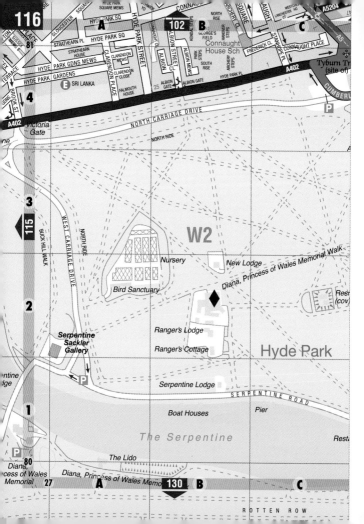

A

B

102

C

Tyburn Tree
(site of)

CONNAUGHT

SQUARE

NORTH
RISE

HANOVER
STEPS

GEORGE'S
FIELD

SOUTH
RISE

ARCHERY STEPS

Connaught
House Sch

LANCHESTER HO
WESTOVER
CT

A5204

A5

HYDE PARK SQUARE MEWS

HYDE PARK SQ

STRATHEARN PL

HYDE PARK SQ

HYDE PARK STREET

ALBION STREET

ALBION MEWS

ALBION ST

ALBION MEWS

FREDERICK CL

STANHOPE PL

CONNAUGHT PLACE

A402

STRATHEARN
HOUSE

HYDE PARK GDNS MEWS

CLARENDON
MEWS

CLARENDON PLACE

CLARENDON
CLOSE

HYDE PARK GARDENS

FALMOUTH
HOUSE

E Sri Lanka

81

TERRACE

BROOK ST

4

ALBION
GATE

ALBION GATE

25

HYDE PARK PL

CUMBERLAND

P

A402

Victoria
Gate

ne

NORTH CARRIAGE DRIVE

NORTH RIDE

3

115

2

1

BUCK HILL WALK

WEST CARRIAGE DRIVE

NORTH RIDE

Nursery

Bird Sanctuary

W2

New Lodge

Diana, Princess of Wales Memorial Walk

Resr
(cov)

Serpentine
Sackler
Gallery

Ranger's Lodge

Ranger's Cottage

Hyde Park

P

Serpentine Lodge

SERPENTINE ROAD

rpentine
dge

Boat Houses

Pier

The Serpentine

Resta

P

80

Diana,
cess of Wales
Memorial

27

The Lido

Diana, Princess of Wales Memo

A

130

B

C

ROTTEN ROW

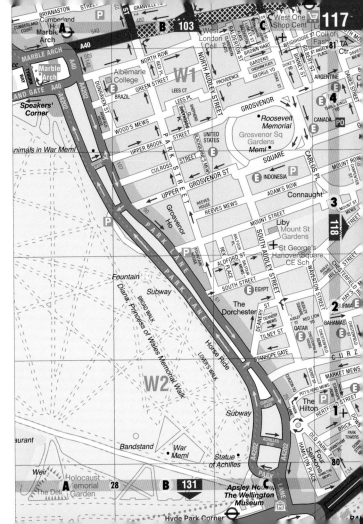

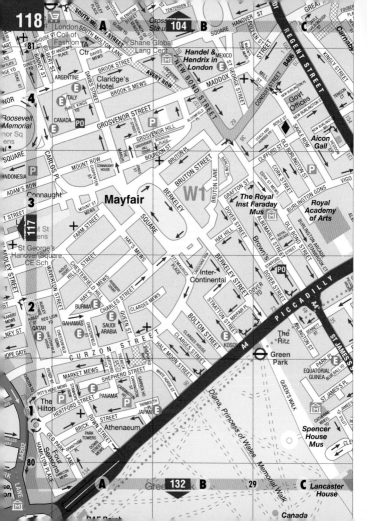

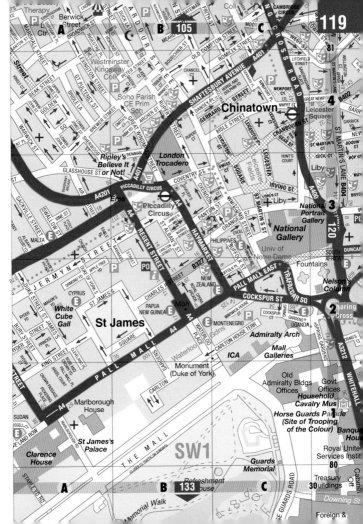

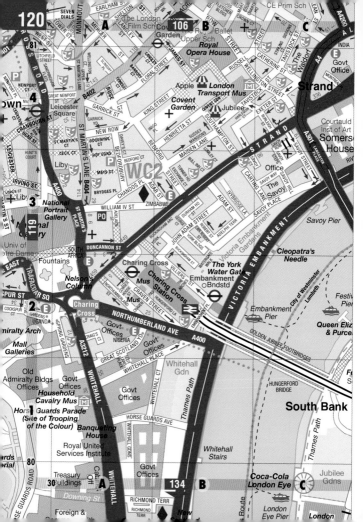

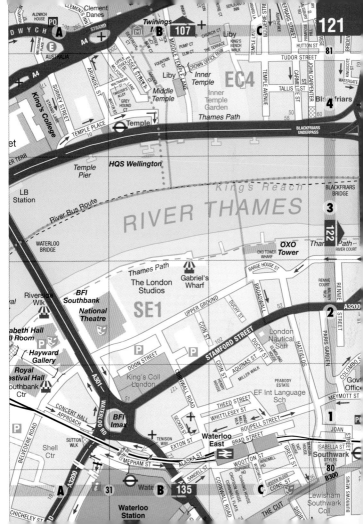

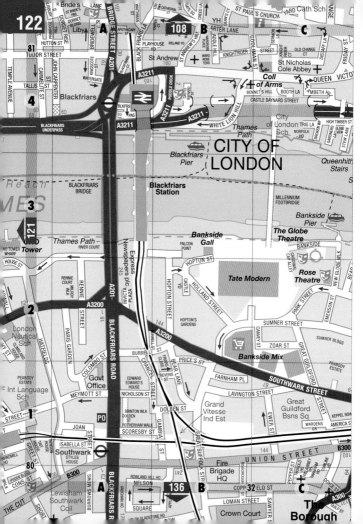

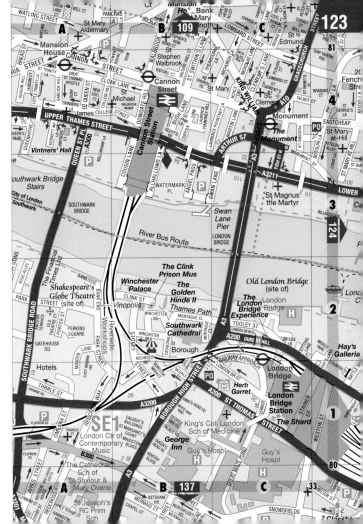

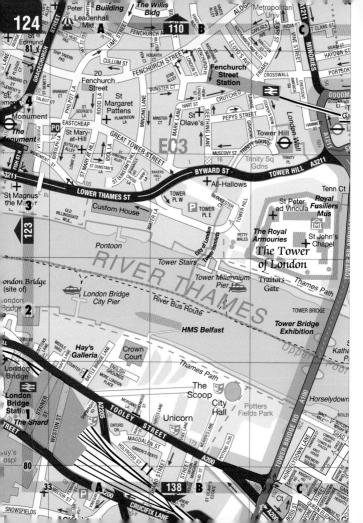

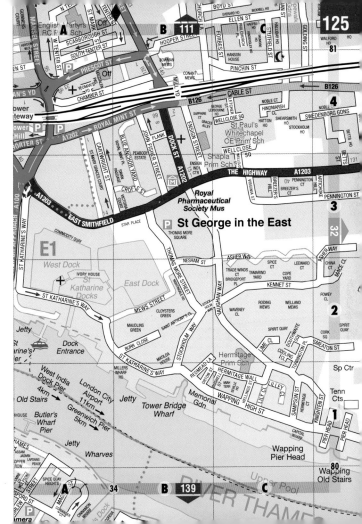

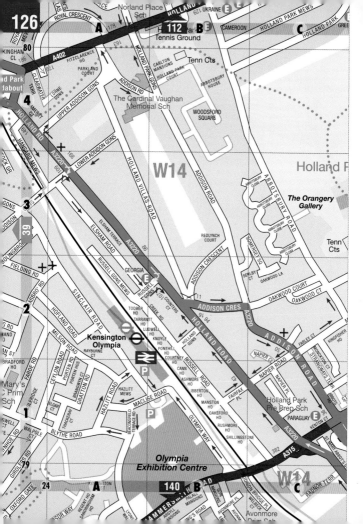

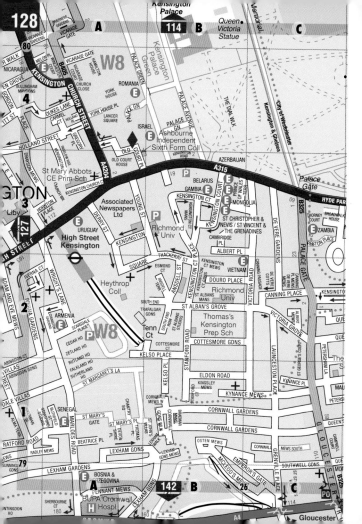

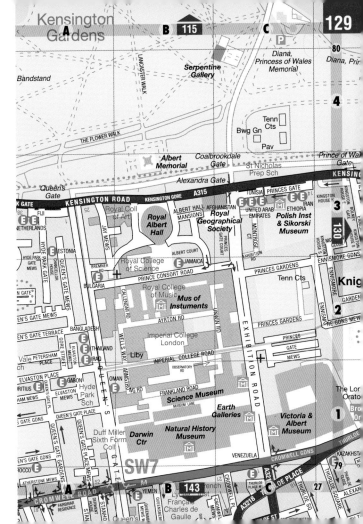

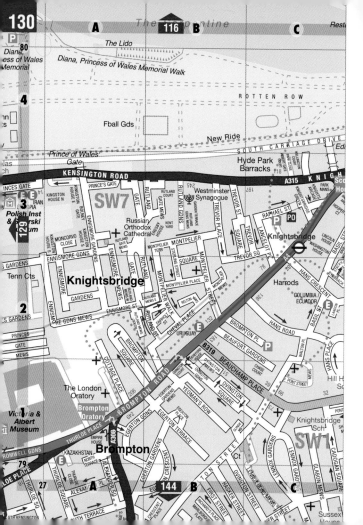

A   116   B   C   Resta

P
80
Diana,
ess of Wales
Memorial

The Lido

Diana, Princess of Wales Memorial Walk

4

ROTTEN ROW

Fball Gds

New Ride

SOUTH CARRIAGE DRIVE   Ed

Prince of Wales
Gate

Hyde Park
Barracks

KENSINGTON ROAD   A315   KNIGH

INCES GATE   E   E

KINGSTON   PRINCE'S GATE
HOUSE N   IRAN
Polish Inst   MPIA   KINGSTON
& rski   HOUSE S
um   129   MONCORVO
CLOSE

RAPHAEL ST   P   PO

Westminster
Synagogue

SW7

RUTLAND
GATE MEWS
RUTLAND GATE
RUTLAND GATE   RUTLAND   GATE
GATE   MEWS
KENT   YARD   Russian
Orthodox
Cathedral   TREVOR ST
TREVOR PLACE

TREVOR
SQUARE

Knightsbridge

LANCELOT PL

S GARDENS

ENNISMORE GARDENS   ENNISMORE GDNS
Tenn Cts

ENNISMORE
GARDENS
Knightsbridge

ENNISMORE   GATE
MEWS
ENNISMORE ST

MONTPELIER TERR   MONTPELIER
STIRLING STREET
MONTPELIER
SQUARE
MONTPELIER PLACE
MONTPELIER WALK
MELTON CT
MONTPELIER
STREET
ENNISMORE MEWS   RUTLAND MEWS
RUTLAND STREET   FAIRHOLT
ST

TREVOR SQ

Harrods

HANS CRESCENT

COLUMBIA
ECUADOR   E

BASIL ST

2

S GARDENS

PRINCES
GATE
MEWS

ENNISMORE GDNS MEWS

CHEVAL PLACE
URUGUAY   E

HANS ROAD

BROMPTON PL   BEAUFORT GARDENS
B319   BEAUCHAMP PLACE   P
OVINGTON
GARDENS   WALTON PL

COTTAGE PLACE

BROMPTON
SQUARE

BROMPTON ROAD

OVINGTON
GARDENS MEWS
YEOMAN'S ROW   OVINGTON
SQUARE

PONT STREET   Hill H
Sc

1

The London
Oratory   EGERTON GDNS   OVINGTON STREET   LENNOX GARDENS

Brompton
Oratory   EGERTON GARDENS   LENNOX GDNS MEWS   CLABON MEWS
EMPIRE HOUSE   B308

Victoria &
Albert
Museum   THURLOE PLACE   Brompton   EGERTON TERRACE   Knightsbridge
Sch
SW1

79
ROMWELL GDNS   E   KAZAKHSTAN   NORTH
TERRACE

27   THURLOE SQUARE   A   ALEXANDER PL   144   B   FIRST STREET   C   CADOGAN GDNS

HLOE PLACE
ALEXANDER SQ   EGERTON CRESCENT   HASKER STREET   OVINGTON GARDENS MEWS
CRESCENT
PLACE   RICHARD'S
PLACE   MARLBOROUGH
STREET   Sussex
R KENSINGTON   SOUTH TERRACE   ER STREET

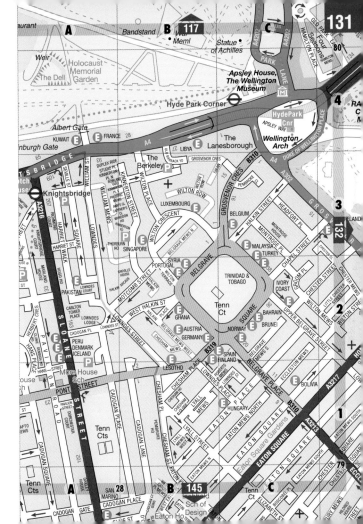

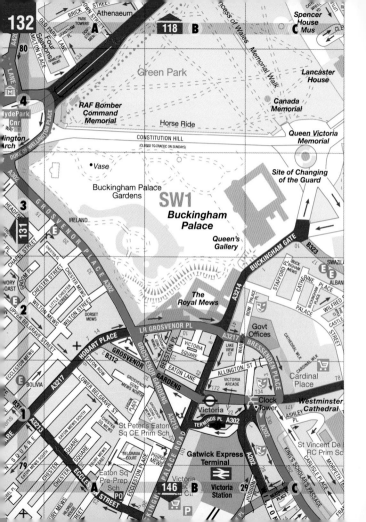

118 B

C

80

Athenaeum

Spencer House Mus

Green Park

Lancaster House

RAF Bomber Command Memorial

Canada Memorial

HydePark Cnr

Horse Ride

CONSTITUTION HILL
(CLOSED TO TRAFFIC ON SUNDAYS)

Queen Victoria Memorial

Ellington Arch

• Vase

Buckingham Palace Gardens

Site of Changing of the Guard

SW1

Buckingham Palace

IRELAND

131

Queen's Gallery

BUCKINGHAM GATE

B323

SWAZIL

GROSVENOR PLACE

CHESTER STREET

LITTLE CHESTER STREET

WILTON MEWS

DORSET MEWS

The Royal Mews

STAFFORD PL

BUCK INGHAM MEWS

CAXTON

PALACE PLACE

ALBAN

WILFRED

CASTLE

STREET

UPPER BELGRAVE STREET

2

LR GROSVENOR PL

A3214

Govt Offices

CATHEDRAL WALK

CARDINAL WALK

Cardinal Place

HOBART PLACE

GROSVENOR

BEESTON PL

VICTORIA SQUARE

LAKE VIEW CT

WARWICK ROW

BRESSENDEN PLACE

78

BOLIVIA

B312

EATON ROW

GROSVENOR GARDENS

EATON LANE

ALLINGTON ST

VICTORIA ARCADE

134

ASHLEY PL

Westminster Cathedral

ECCLESTON MEWS

A3217

LOWER BELGRAVE ST

GARDENS

VICTORIA ST

St Vincent De RC Prim Sch

1

A3213

EATON MEWS SOUTH

CHESTER SQUARE

St Peters Eaton Sq CE Prim Sch

TERMINUS PL

A302

Clock Tower

KING'S SCHOLARS PASSAGE

MORPETH

CHESTER SQUARE

BELGRAVIA COURT

PHIPPS MEWS

Victoria

Gatwick Express Terminal

HUDSON

S Q U A R E

79

ECCLE

Eaton Sq Pre-Prep Sch

PO

146 B

Victoria Station

29

C

STREET

P

FRAN

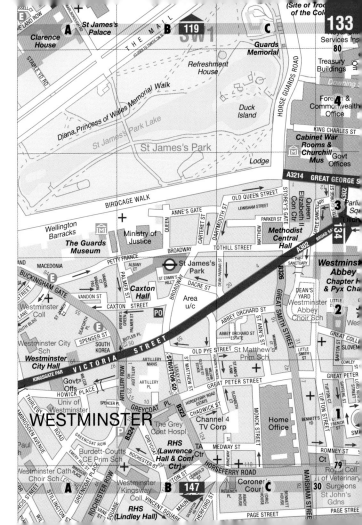

(Site of Troo
of the Col

E A St James's B 119 C SW1
Palace

RUSSELL

LANE/LONDON ROW

LANEBRIDGE ROW

Clarence
House
THE MALL
CLEVELAND ROW
CLOSED TO TRAFFIC ON S
Guards
Memorial

STABLE YD RD

Refreshment
House

Services Ins
80
Treasury
Buildings

HORSE GUARDS ROAD
Downing

Diana, Princess of Wales Memorial Walk
Fore
Commonwealth
Office
4

KING CHARLES ST

St James's Park Lake
Duck
Island
Cabinet War
Rooms &
Churchill
Mus
Govt
Offices

St James's Park
Lodge

A3214 GREAT GEORGE S

BIRDCAGE WALK
OLD QUEEN STREET
Queen
Elizabeth II
Con Cen
Parli
Sq
134
3

ANNE'S GATE
LEWISHAM STREET

STOREY'S GATE

LITTLE GEORGE ST
SW2

Wellington
Barracks
Ministry of
Justice
PARKER ST
Methodist
Central
Hall
Westmins
Abbey

QUEEN

CARTERET ST

DARTMOUTH ST

MATTHEW

A302

LITTLE SANCTUARY

BROAD SANCTUARY

The Guards
Museum
BROADWAY
TOTHILL STREET
THE SANCTUARY
Chapter H
& Pyx Cha

MACEDONIA
PETTY FRANCE

BUCKINGHAM GATE
ALBANY
CT
St James's
Park
DEAN FARRAR ST
DEAN'S
YARD
Westminster
Abbey
Choir Sch
2
We

ST ERMIN'S
HILL
Caxton
Hall
Area
u/c

VANDON ST

PALMER ST

BROADWAY

DACRE ST

GREAT SMITH STREET

GREAT COLL

SLOVEN

LITTLE DE

VANDON ST
CAXTON STREET
PO
ABBEY ORCHARD ST
ST ANN'S ST

Westminster
Coll

SEAFORTH PL
SPENSER ST
BUTLER PL

SOUTH BLDGS

SOUTH KOREA

ABBEY ORCHARD
ESTATE

LITTLE
SMITH ST
GREAT COLL

COWLEY

Westminster City
Sch
SPENSER ST
OLD PYE STREET St Matthew's
Prim Sch
GREAT PETER
Westminster
City Hall

VICTORIA STREET

KINGSGATE PAR

ARTILLERY
MANS
ST MATTHEW ST
ST ANN'S
LANE
GREAT PETER STREET
TUFTON ST
SAFFIRE ST
LORD NORTH
1

Govt
Offs
HOWICK PLACE
ARTILLERY
HO
ARTILLERY
PL
BENNETT'S
YD

THIRLEBY RD

ARTILLERY ROW

GREYCOAT PL

B323

LESLEY CT

STRUTTON GD

HORSEFERRY ROAD
ESTATE

ELIZABETH ST

MONCK STREET

TUFTON STREET

SPENCER PL
CHADWICK ST
Home
Office

WESTMINSTER
Univ of
Westminster
P
The Grey
Coat Hosp
Channel 4
TV Corp
79

AMBROSDEN AVENUE

GREENCOAT PLACE

B324

GREYCOAT ST

MEDWAY ST
TA
Ctr

Royal Coll
of Veterinary
Surgeons
30

Paul
Burdett-Coutts
CE Prim Sch
RHS
(Lawrence
Hall & Conf
Ctr)
HORSEFERRY ROAD
Coroner's
Court
St John's
Gdns

EMERY HILL ST

ROCHESTER ROW

ROCHESTER ST

Westminster Cath
Choir Sch
A St James's
Westminster
Kingsway
Coll
B 147 C

STILLINGTON ST

WINDSOR PLACE

GREENCOAT ROW

VINCENT SQUARE

MAUN

REGENCY

ABADY
HOUSE

CEDRIC
HOUSE

BENNETT
HOUSE

PAGE STREET
PAGE STREE

VANE ST

VINCENT SQUARE

HERFORD ST

RHS
(Lindley Hall)

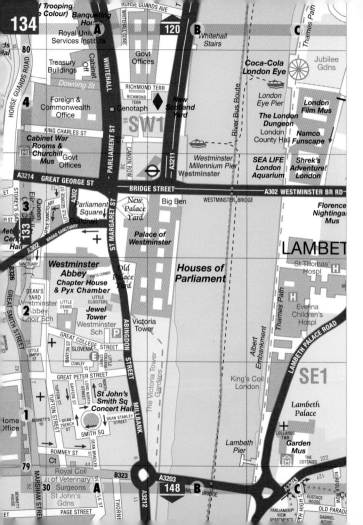

(of Trooping
the Colour)
**Banqueting
House**
A
HORSE GUARDS AVE
WHITEHALL PLACE
B
120
Whitehall
Stairs
C
Thames Path

Royal Unit...
Services Institute

80

WHITEHALL

Treasury
Buildings

Cabinet
Off

Govt
Offices

Jubilee
Gdns

**Coca-Cola
London Eye**

Downing St

RICHMOND TERR

RICHMOND
TERR

Cenotaph

**New
Scotland
Yard**

London
Eye Pier

**London
Film Mus**

4

Foreign &
Commonwealth
Office

SW1

**The London
Dungeon**

London
County Hall

**Namco
Funscape**

KING CHARLES ST

**Cabinet War
Rooms &
Churchill
Mus**

Govt
Offices

CANNON ROW

38

**Westminster
Millennium Pier**
Westminster

**SEA LIFE
London
Aquarium**

**Shrek's
Adventure!
London**

A3214

GREAT GEORGE ST

BRIDGE STREET

A302 WESTMINSTER BR RD

A3211

River Bus Route

A3206

STOREY'S GATE

Queen
Elizabeth II
Centre

3

Hall

LITTLE GEORGE ST

A302

**Parliament
Square**

**New
Palace
Yard**

Big Ben

WESTMINSTER BRIDGE

**Florence
Nightingale
Mus**

133

BROAD SANCTUARY

THE SANCTUARY

Guildhall

ST MARGARET ST

**Palace of
Westminster**

LAMBET

**Westminster
Abbey**
**Chapter House
& Pyx Chamber**

POETS CORNER

Old
Palace
Yard

**Houses of
Parliament**

St Thomas'
Hospl

H

DEAN'S
YARD

Westminster
Abbey Choir Sch

LITTLE CLOISTERS

LITTLE DEAN'S
YD

2

**Jewel
Tower**

Westminster
Sch

Victoria
Tower

**Evelina
Children's
Hospl**

H

GREAT SMITH STREET

LITTLE
SMITH
ST

GREAT COLLEGE STREET

ABINGDON STREET

BARTON ST

COWLEY

SLOVENIA
STREET

LITTLE
COLLEGE
STREET

E

SE1

Albert Embankment

Thames Path

King's Coll
London

GREAT PETER STREET

TUFTON STREET

GAYFERE ST

LORD NORTH
STREET

**St John's
Smith Sq
Concert Hall**

MILLBANK

**Lambeth
Palace**

1

DEAN
TRENCH
ST

SMITH SQ

DEAN STANLEY STREET

The Victoria Tower Gardens

**LOLLARDS
TWR**

**Garden
Mus**

Lambeth
Pier

Home
Office

BENNETT'S
YD

ROMNEY ST

DEAN BRADLEY
STREET

THE COTTAGES

222

79

MARSHAM STREET

Ct

**Royal Coll
of Veterinary
Surgeons**

A

B323

A3212

THORNE

A3203

148

LAMBETH BRIDGE

B

A3203

LAMBETH HIGH ST

EUSTACE
HOUSE

OLD PARADI

C

30

St John's
Gdns

PAGE STREET

PARLIAMENT
VIEW
APARTMENTS

GABRIEL

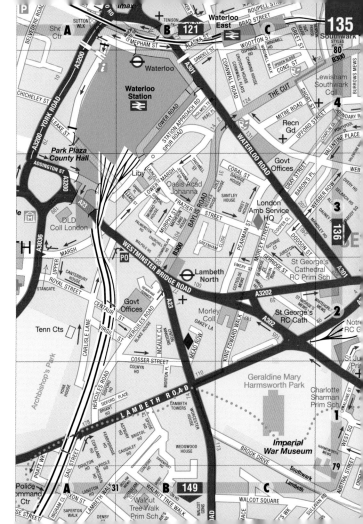

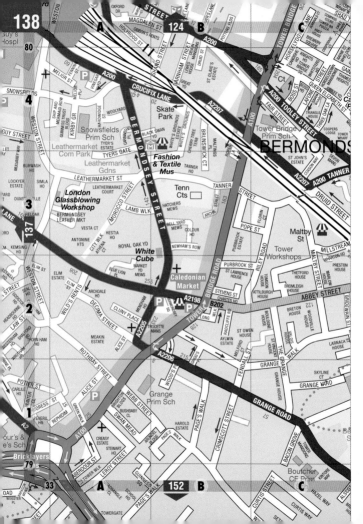

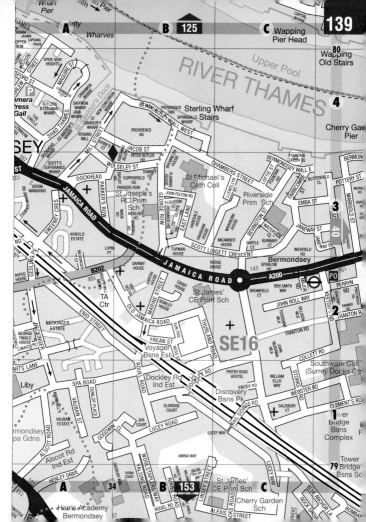

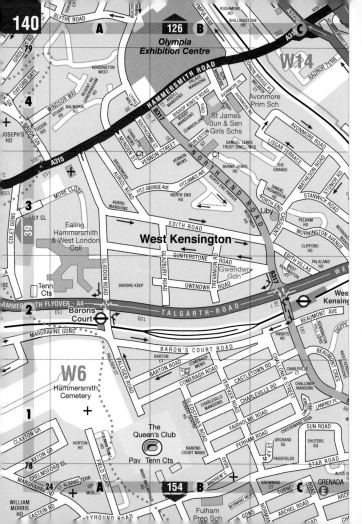

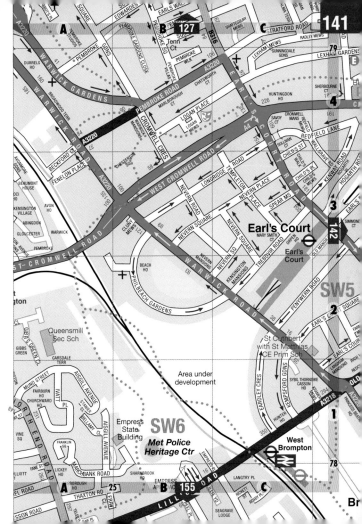

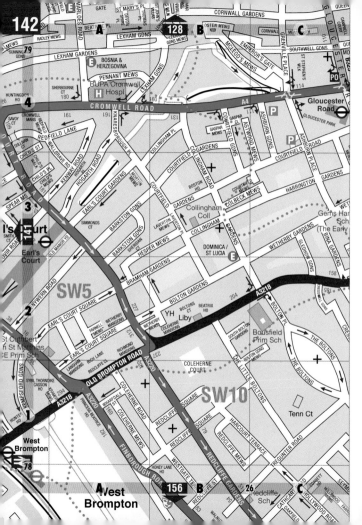

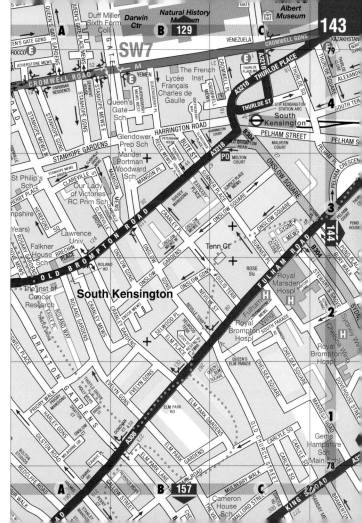

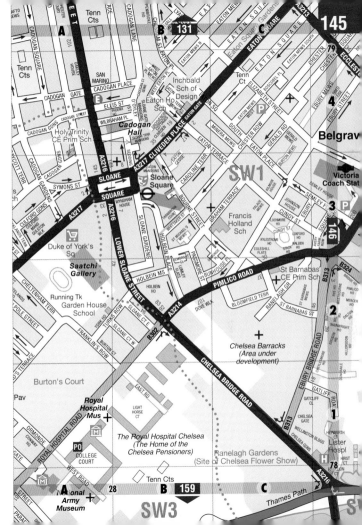

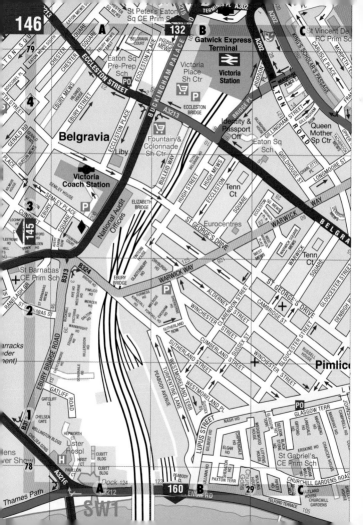

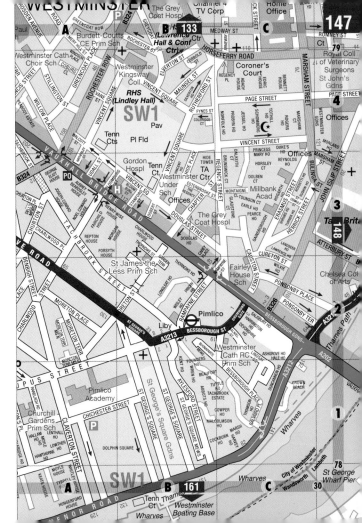

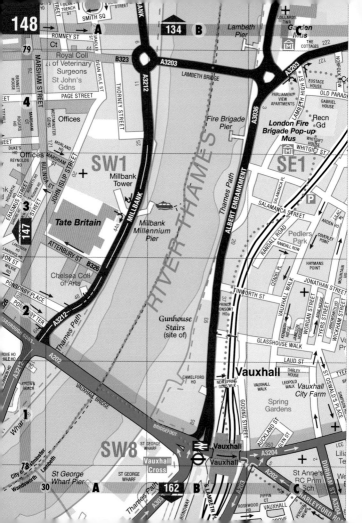

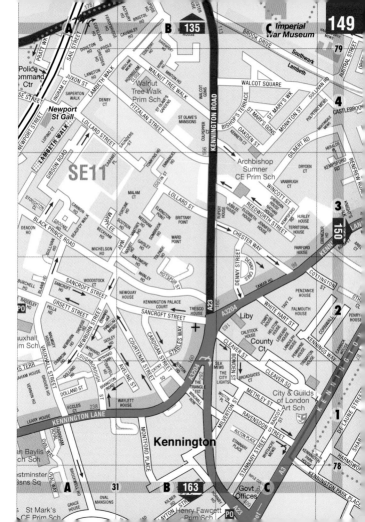

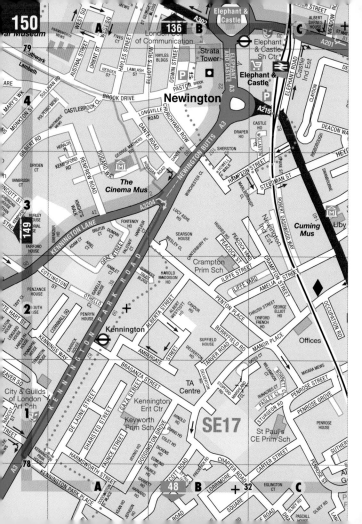

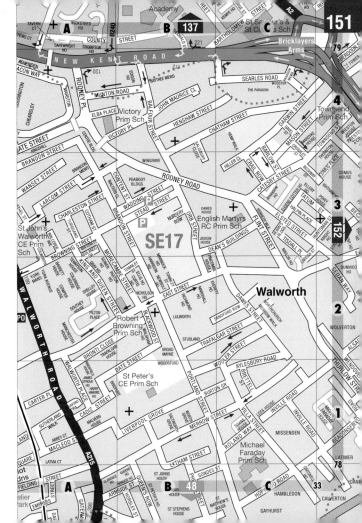

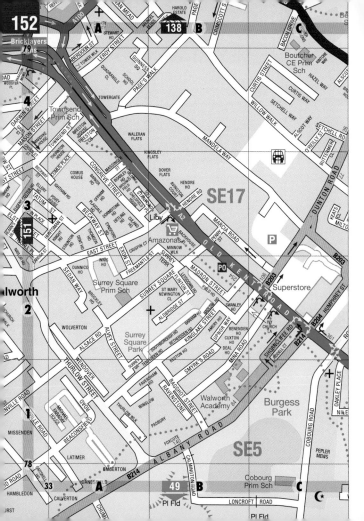

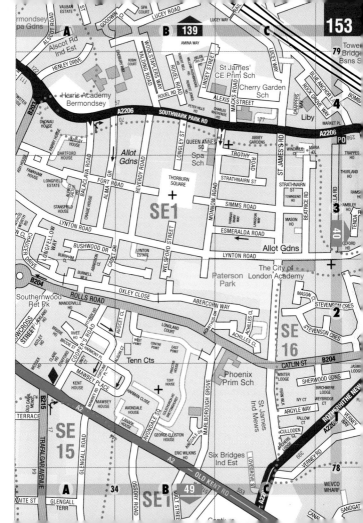

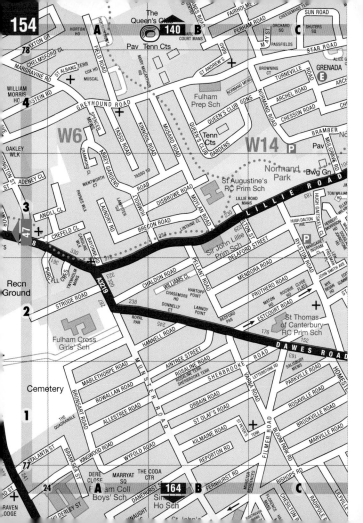

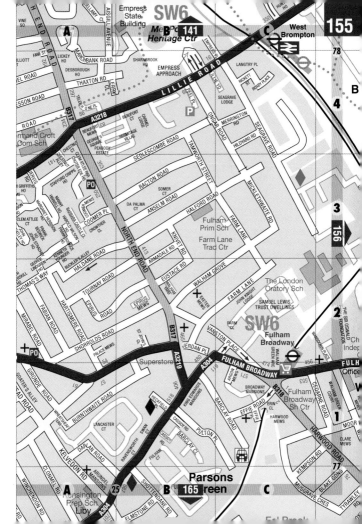

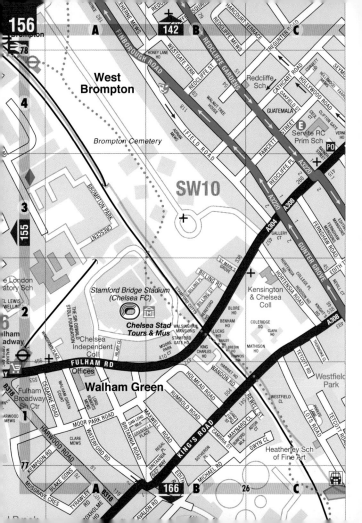

156

Brompton

A 142 **B** HARCOURT TERRACE **C**

WESTGATE TERR

Redcliffe Sch

GUATEMALA

Servite RC Prim Sch

PO

West Brompton

FINBOROUGH ROAD

HONEY LANE HO

REDCLIFFE ST

REDCLIFFE GARDENS

CATHCART ROAD

HOLLYWOOD ROAD

CLIFTON GATE

TREGUNTER ROAD

WALNUT TREE HOUSE

IFIELD ROAD

ADINA MEWS

FAWCETT

REDCLIFFE PL

A3220

A308

E

4

Brompton Cemetery

SW10

BROMPTON PARK

GALLERY CT

FERNSHAW ROAD

EDITH GROVE

3 155

BROMPTON PARK CRESCENT

ST MARK'S RD

COLLEGE PL

A304

GUNTER GROVE

HORTENSIA RD

EDITH

e London atory Sch

EL LEWIS WELLING

2

THE SIR OSWALD STOLL FOUNDATION

BILLING RD

BILLING ST

BLORE HO

BENHAM HO

HORTENSIA ROAD

Kensington & Chelsea Coll

A308

Stamford Bridge Stadium (Chelsea FC)

Chelsea Stad Tours & Mus

Chelsea Independent Coll

WALSINGHAM MANSIONS

STAMFORD GATE HO

LUCAS HO

BAILEY HO

KING CHARLES HO

BREDIN HO

FRANCIS HO

COLERIDGE SQ

CLARK HO

MATHISON HO

lham adway

WARSPITE ROAD

HARTLEY CL

MOORE PARK RD

410 CL

HARRIET RD

WANDON RD

TETCOTT RD

6

466

FULHAM RD Offices

HOLMEAD ROAD

WESTFIELD CL

Westfield Park

1

659

Fulham Broadway Sh Ctr

B318

CEDARNE ROAD

WALHAM GREEN COURT

LORD ROBERTS MEWS

MOOR PARK ROAD

WATERFORD RD

BRITANNIA RD

MAXWELL RD

GRANVILLE PLACE

DAN LENO WALK

REGAL

RUMBOLD ROAD

MAYNARD CL

GRANVILLE WALK

CAMBRIA ST

ASTOR CT

GWYN CL

PENFOLD ST

RENFELT

WESTFIELD CL

LOTS ROAD

TELCOTT ROAD

HARWOOD MEWS

Walham Green

CLARE MEWS

BRITANNIA WAY

SOTHERON PL

MICHAEL RD

EDITH YD

KING'S ROAD

Heatherley Sch of Fine Art

77

KEMPSON RD

BLAKE GDNS

MUSGRAVE CRES

HARWOOD ROAD

TYRAWLEY RD

RYLSTON RD

B318

A 166 **B** 26 **C**

AVALON RD

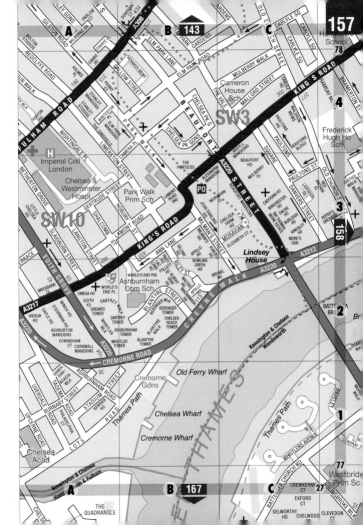

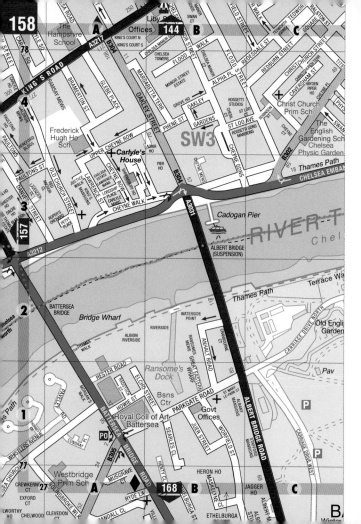

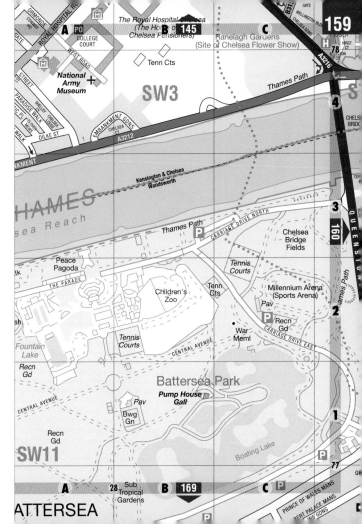

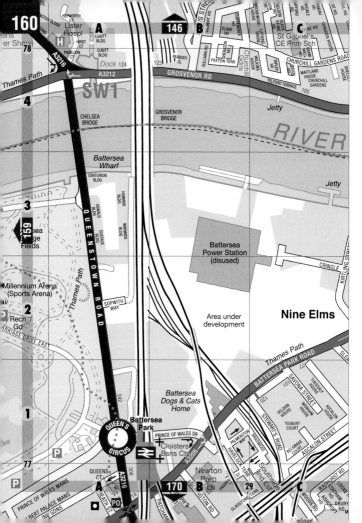

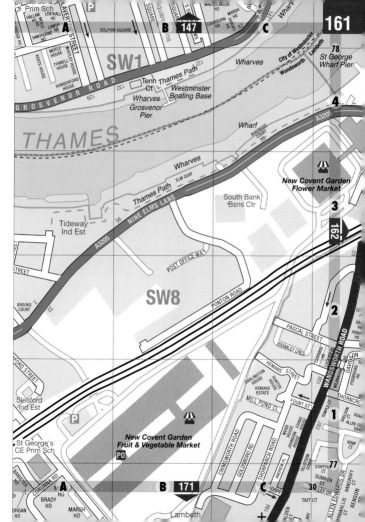

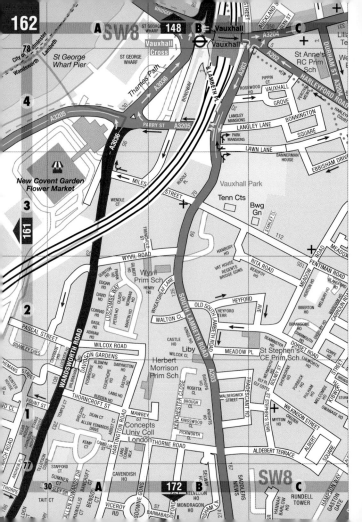

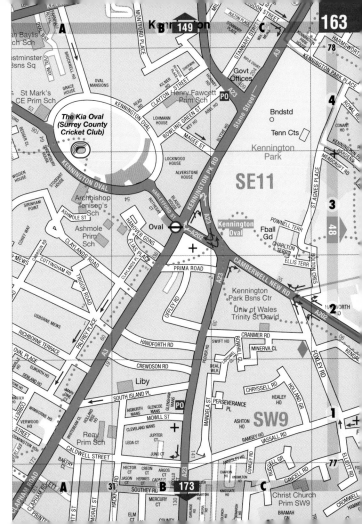

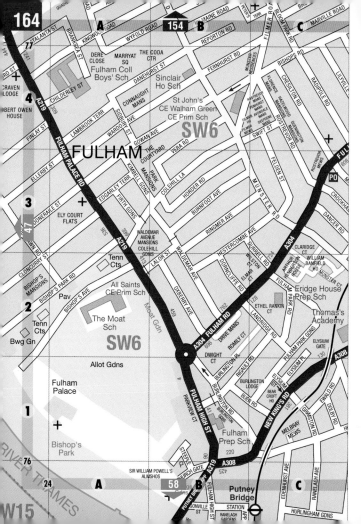

A KINGWOOD RD
154 **B** MAINE ROAD **C** MARVILLE ROAD

77
ATALANTA'S ST
BRANSEY ST
WYFOLD ROAD
REPORTON RD
PETER'S TERR
BLOOM PARK RD
FILMER ROAD

DERE CLOSE
MARRYAT SQ
THE CODA CTR
FERNHURST RD
BISHOPS RD
CHESILTON RD
RADIPOLE RD
LILYVILLE

CRAVEN LODGE
Fulham Coll Boys' Sch
DANEHURST ST
Sinclair Ho Sch
MINISTER RESIDENCES
FLORENCE MANS
HAZELBURY RD
QUARRENDON ST

4 **A219**
CHILDERLEY ST
CONNAUGHT MANS
St John's CE Walham Green CE Prim Sch
SWIFT ST
RESTREVOR MANS
ROSTREVOR RD
DESPENDE MEWS

BERT OWEN HOUSE
LAMBROOK TERR
SUBURB AVE
WARDO AVE
SW6
+
FUL

FINLAY ST
GOWAN AVE
FELDEN ST
ROSTREVOR MEWS

FULHAM
FULHAM PALACE RD
THE COURTYARD
VERA RD
PO
A308

ELLERBY ST
KIMBELL GDNS
PARK MANSIONS
COLHILL LA
HORDER RD
MUNSTER RD
CROOKHA

3
EDGARLEY TERR
FIRTH GDNS
BURNFOOT AVE
DANCER RD

JONERALE ST
ELY COURT FLATS
WALDEMAR AVENUE MANSIONS
COLEHILL GDNS
RINGMER AVE
HESTERCOMBE AVE
BURBELL RD
WILTON

47
CLONCURRY ST
A29
LALOR ST
WALDEMAR AVE
DORNCLIFFE RD
ELMAR
CLARIDGE CT
WILLIAM BANFIELD HO

Tenn Cts
All Saints CE Prim Sch
OXBERRY AVE
Eridge House Prep Sch

BISHOP'S MANSIONS
BISHOP'S PARK RD
Pav
BISHOP'S AVE
FULHAM RD
ETHEL RANKIN CT
FULHAM PARK RD
Thomas's Academy

2
Tenn Cts
The Moat Sch
Moat Gdn
A304
DRIVE MANS
LANDRIDGE RD
ROMILY CT
ELYSIUM GATE

Bwg Gn
SW6
DWIGHT CT
BURLINGTON PL
RIGAULT RD
ELYSIUM PL
A308

Allot Gdns
BURLINGTON LODGE
BEAR CROFT HO
MELBRAY MEWS

1
Fulham Palace
PARKVIEW CT
FULHAM HIGH ST
BURLINGTON RD
BUER RD
NEW KINGS RD
EDENHURST AVE
RANELAGH AVE

+
Bishop's Park
Fulham Prep Sch
220

76
STEERE
SIR WILLIAM POWELL'S ALMSHOS
CHURCH GATE
A308
A219

24 **A** 58 **B** **C**
PUTNEY BR RD
SONVILLE ST
RANELAGH GARDENS
Putney Bridge
STATION
HURLINGHAM GDNS

W15
RIVER THAMES

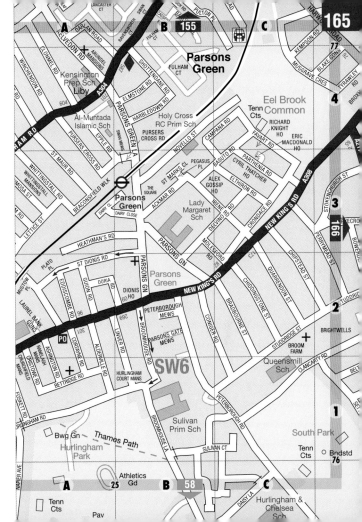

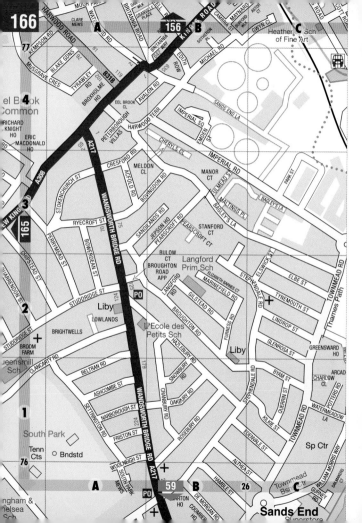

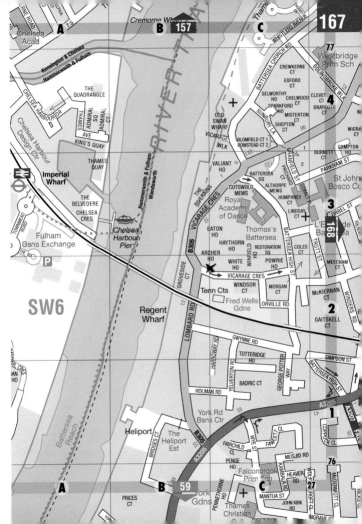

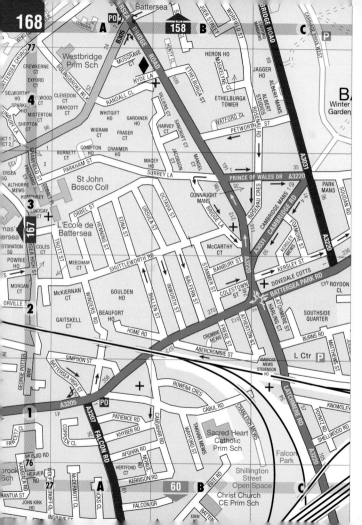

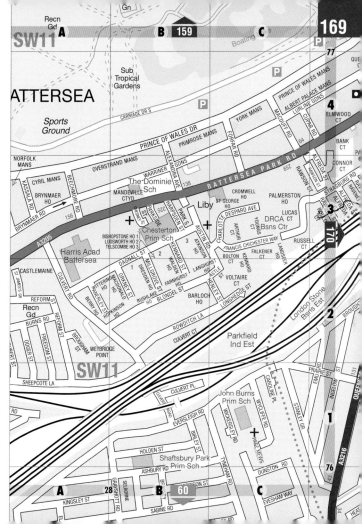

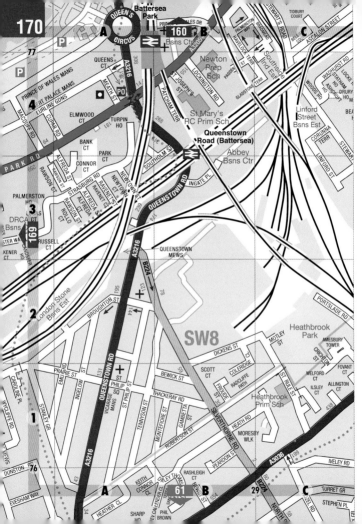

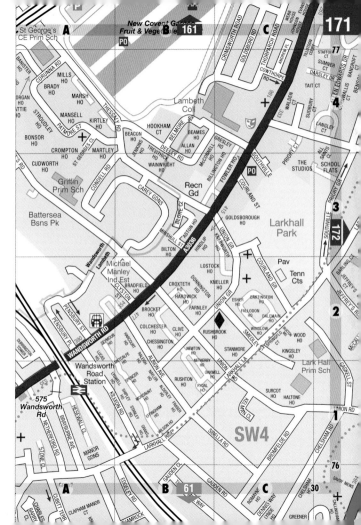

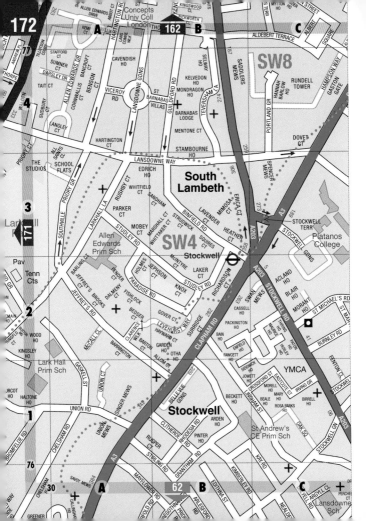

Index

Church Rd **6** Beckenham BR2..........**53** C6 **228** C6

Place name	Location number	Locality, town or village	Postcode district	Standard scale reference	Enlarged scale reference
May be abbreviated on the map	Present when a number indicates the place's position in a crowded area of mapping	Shown when more than one place (outside London postal districts) has the same name	District for the indexed place	Page number and grid reference for the standard mapping	Page number and grid reference for the central London enlarged mapping, underlined in red

Public and commercial buildings are highlighted in magenta.
Places of interest are highlighted in blue
Cities, towns and villages are listed in CAPITAL LETTERS

Abbreviations used in the index

Acad	**Academy**	Ct	**Court**	Int	**International**	Prom	**Promenade**
App	**Approach**	Ctr	**Centre**	Intc	**Interchange**	RC	**Roman Catholic**
Arc	**Arcade**	Crkt	**Cricket**	Jun	**Junior**	Rd	**Road**
Art Gall	**Art Gallery**	Ctry Pk	**Country Park**	Junc	**Junction**	Rdbt	**Roundabout**
Ave	**Avenue**	Cty	**County**	La	**Lane**	Ret Pk	**Retail Park**
Bglws	**Bungalows**	Ctyd	**Courtyard**	L Ctr	**Leisure Centre**	Sch	**School**
Bldgs	**Buildings**	Dr	**Drive**	Liby	**Library**	Sec	**Secondary**
Bsns Ctr	**Business Centre**	Ent Ctr	**Enterprise Centre**	Mans	**Mansions**	Sh Ctr	**Shopping Centre**
Bsns Pk	**Business Park**	Ent Pk	**Enterprise Park**	Mdw/s	**Meadow/s**	Sp	**Sports**
Bvd	**Boulevard**	Est	**Estate**	Meml	**Memorial**	Specl	**Special**
Cath	**Cathedral, Catholic**	Ex Ctr	**Exhibition Centre**	Mid	**Middle**	Sports Ctr	**Sports Centre**
CE	**Church of England**	Ex Hall	**Exhibition Hall**	Mix	**Mixed**	Sq	**Square**
Cemy	**Cemetery**	Fst	**First**	Mkt	**Market**	St	**Street, Saint**
Cir	**Circus**	Gdn	**Garden**	Mon	**Monument**	Sta	**Station**
Circ	**Circle**	Gdns	**Gardens**	Mus	**Museum**	Stad	**Stadium**
Cl	**Close**	Gn	**Green**	Obsy	**Observatory**	Tech	**Technical Technology**
Cnr	**Corner**	Gr	**Grove**	Orch	**Orchard**		
Coll	**College**	Gram	**Grammar**	Par	**Parade**	Terr	**Terrace**
Com	**Community**	Her Ctr	**Heritage Centre**	Pas	**Passage**	Trad Est	**Trading Estate**
Comm	**Common**	Ho	**House**	Pav	**Pavilion**	Twr/s	**Tower/s**
Comp	**Comprehensive**	Hospl	**Hospital**	Pk	**Park**	Univ	**University**
Con Ctr	**Conference Centre**	Hts	**Heights**	Pl	**Place**	Wlk	**Walk**
Cotts	**Cottages**	Ind Est	**Industrial Estate**	Prec	**Precinct**	Yd	**Yard**
Cres	**Crescent**	Inf	**Infant**	Prep	**Preparatory**		
Cswy	**Causeway**	Inst	**Institute**	Prim	**Primary**		

2 Willow Rd NW3....12 A4
3 Mills Studios
E16..................27 B2
22, Bishopgate
EC2.................110 A3
30 St Mary Axe (The
Gherkin) EC3.....110 A3
176 Gall NW5......12 C2
201 Bishopgate
EC2.................110 A3
575 Wandsworth Rd
SW8................171 A1

A

Abacus Belsize Prim
Sch NW1...........83 B4
Abady Ho SW1......110 A1
Aberley Mews ⁵
SW8.................61 A4
Abbess Cl SW2 ⁷...75 A3
Abbeville Mews ⁵
SW4.................61 C3
Abbeville Rd SW4...61 B2
Abbey Bsns Ctr
SW8................170 B4
Abbey Ct
⁶ Bedford Pk
W12.................38 A3
Camberwell SE17...151 A1
St John's Wood
NW8.................78 C2
Abbeyfield Rd
SE16................40 B2
Abbey Gdns
⑱ Bermondsey
SE16................153 C4
St John's Wood
NW8.................79 A1
West Kensington
W6.................154 A3
Abbey Ho NW8......89 A4
Abbey La E15........27 C3
Abbey Lo NW8.......90 B3
Abbey Orchard St
SW1................133 C2
Abbey Orchard Street
Est SW1...........133 C2
Abbey Rd
St John's Wood
NW8.................78 C2
Wembley NW10.....20 A4
Abbey Rd Studios
NW8.................79 A1
Abbey St SE1.......138 C2
Abbot Ct SW8......162 A1
Abbot Ho E14 ¹⁴...34 A2
Abbotsbury Cl
Kensington W14...126 C3
Mill Meads E15......27 B3
Abbotsbury Ho
W14................126 C3
Abbotsbury Mews
SE15................65 B4
Abbotsbury Rd
W14................126 C3
Abbotshade Rd ¹⁵
SE16................32 C1
Abbots Ho
Kensington W14...126 C1
Pimlico SW1.......147 B1
Abbots La SE1.....124 B1
Abbots Pk SW2......74 C3
Abbot's Pl NW6.....78 A4
Abbot St E8.........16 B2

Abbotstone Ho ⁴
E5...................7 C2
Abbotstone Rd
SW15................57 B4
Abbotswell Rd
SE4.................66 B2
Abbotswood Rd
London SE22..........64 A3
Streatham SW16....73 C1
Abbott Ho SW12....72 B4
Abbott Rd E14......34 C3
Abbotts Cl N1......15 B2
Abbotts Wharf ⁴
E14.................33 C3
Abchurch La EC2,
EC4................123 C4
Abchurch Yd EC4...123 B4
Abdale Rd W12......30 A1
Abel Ho ⁸ SE11....163 B4
Aberavon Rd E3....26 A2
Abercorn Cl NW8...88 C4
Abercorn Mans
NW8.................79 A1
Abercorn Mews ⑩
TW10................54 B3
Abercorn Pl NW8...78 C1
Abercorn Sch
NW8.................79 A1
Abercorn Wlk
NW8.................79 A1
Abercorn Way
SE1.................153 B2
Abercorn Wlk
NW8.................79 A1
Abercrombie Ho ¹
W12.................30 A2
Abercrombie Rd
E15.................19 C1
Abercrombie St
SW11...............168 B2
Aberdale Ct ²²
SE16................40 C4
Aberdare Gdns
NW6.................11 A1
Aberdeen Ct
Canonbury N5......15 B3
Paddington W2 ²....89 B1
Aberdeen Ctr N5...15 B3
Aberdeen La N5.....15 B3
Aberdeen Mans
WC1.................94 A2
Aberdeen Pk N5....15 B3
Aberdeen Pl NW8...89 B2
Aberdeen Rd
Canonbury N5......15 B4
Dudden Hill NW10...8 B3
Aberdeen Terr
SE3.................52 C1
Aberdour St SE1...152 A4
Aberfeldy Ho SE5...48 A3
Aberfeldy St E14...34 B3
Abersham Rd E8....16 B3
Ability Plaza ⁸ E8...16 B1
Ability Twrs EC1....96 C4
Abingdon W14.....141 A3
Abingdon Cl
Fulham SE1.........153 A2
Kentish Town NW1..13 C2
Abingdon Gdns
W8.................127 C1
Abingdon Ho
E2...............24 B1 98 C2
Abingdon House Sch
NW1.................90 B1
Abingdon Mans
W8.................127 C2
Abingdon Rd W8...127 C1

Abingdon St SW1..134 A2
Abingdon Villas
W8.................127 C1
Abinger Gr SE8.....51 B4
Abinger Ho SE1...137 B3
Abinger Mews W9...23 C1
Abinger Rd W4......38 A3
Ablett St SE16......40 B1
Abney Park Cemetery
N16...................6 C2
Abney Park Ct N16..7 A3
Aborfield ⁶ NW5...13 B3
Aboyne Rd SW17...71 C1
Abyssinia Cl SW11..60 A3
Abyssinia Rd
SW11................60 A3
Acacia Cl SE8.......41 A2
Acacia Gdns NW8...79 C2
Acacia Gr SE21.....75 C2
Acacia Ho
Brockley SE4.......66 B3
Stoke Newington
N16...................6 C2
Acacia Pl NW8......79 C2
Acacia Rd
Acton W3...........28 B2
St John's Wood
NW8.................79 C2
Acacia Wlk SW10..157 A1
Academy Gdns
W8.................127 B4
Academy Sch The ⁹
NW3.................11 C4
Academy The ²
N19...................4 B3
Acad of Live &
Recorded Arts
SW18................59 C1
Acanthus Dr SE1..153 B2
Acanthus Rd
SW11................60 C4
Accommodation Rd
NW11..................1 B3
Acer Ct ⁸ NW2......9 C4
Acer Rd E8.........16 B1
Acfold Rd SW6.....166 A3
Achilles Cl SE1....153 C2
Achilles Ho ⑱ E2...25 A3
Achilles Rd NW6...10 C3
Achilles St SE14...51 A3
Achilles Way W1...117 C1
Acklam Rd W10....31 B4
Ackmar Rd SW6....165 B3
Ackroyd Dr E3.......33 C4
Acland Burghley Sch
NW5.................13 A4
Acland Cres SE5....63 C4
Acland Ho SW9....172 C2
Acland Rd NW2......9 A2
Acol Ct ³ NW6......10 C1
Acol Rd NW6.......11 A1
Acorn Ct ⁵ E3.......26 C3
Acorn Gdns W3.....28 C4
Acorn Par ⁷ SE15...50 A3
Acorn Production Ctr
N7..................14 A1
Acorns The ²¹
SW19................69 C3
Acorn Wharf SE15..49 C4
Acorn Wlk SE16....33 A1
Acqua Ho TW9......45 A3
Acre Dr SE22.......64 C3
Acre La SW2........62 B3
Acris St SW18......59 B2

ACTON..............28 C1
Acton Bsns Ctr
NW10................20 C1
Acton Central Ind Est
⁴ W3................38 C1
Acton Central Sta
W3...................28 C1
ACTON GREEN.....37 B2
Acton High Sch
W3...................36 C4
Acton Hill Mews
W3...................28 A1
Acton Ho
⁵ Acton W3......28 B3
⑱ Haggerston E8....24 B4
Acton La
Acton Green W4.....37 B1
Harlesden NW10....20 C3
Acton Main Line Sta
W3...................28 B3
Acton Mews E8.....24 B4
Acton Park Ind Est
W3...................37 C4
Acton St WC1.......94 C3
Acton Town Sta
W3...................36 C4
Acton Vale Ind Pk
W3...................29 B1
Acuba Ho SW18.....71 A3
Acuba Rd SW18.....71 A2
Ada Ct
Islington N1.........86 C3
St John's Wood W9..89 A3
Ada Gdns E14......34 C3
Ada Ho ²⁶ E2.......24 C4
Adair Ho SW3.....158 B4
Adair Rd W10.......23 A1
Adair Twr ⁷ W10...23 A1
Ada Kennedy Ct ⁶
SE10................52 B3
Adam Ct SE11.....150 A3
Adam & Eve Ct
W1.................105 A2
Adam & Eve Mews
W8.................127 C2
Adamfields NW3...11 C1
Adams Gardens Est ⁵
SE16................40 B4
Adams Ho ³ E14...34 C3
Adams Mews
SW17................72 B2
Adamson Rd
Hampstead NW3....11 C1
Newham E16.......35 C2
Adams Pl N7........14 B3
Adam's Row W1...117 C3
Adam St ⑳ WC2...120 B3
Adam Wlk SW6....47 B3
Ada Pl E2...........24 C4
Ada Rd SE5.........49 A3
Adare Wlk SW16,
SW2.................74 B2
Ada St E8...........25 A4
Adderley Gr SW11..60 C2
Adderley St E14.....34 B3
Addey Ho SE8......51 B3
Addey & Stanhope
Sch ⁴ SE14........51 C2
Addington Ct ⁷
SW14................55 C4
Addington Ho ⑱
SW9................173 A1
Addington Rd E3...26 C2
Addington Sq SE5..48 C3
Addington St SE1..135 A3

ACTON..............28 C1
Addis Ho ⁵ E1......32 B4
Addison Ave
W11.............31 A1 112 A1
Addison Bridge Pl
W14................140 C4
Addison Cres
W14................126 B2
Addison Gdns
W14.................39 C3
Addison Gr W4......38 A3
Addison Ho NW8...89 B4
Addison Park Mans ⁷
W14.................39 C4
Addison Pl
W11.............31 A1 112 A1
Addison Prim Sch
W14.................39 C3
Addison Rd W14...126 C2
Addle Hill EC4......108 B1
Addlestone Ho ⑷
W10.................30 B4
Addy Ho SE16......40 B2
Adela Ho ⁶ W6......39 B1
Adelaide Ave SE4...66 C3
Adelaide Cl SW9...62 C3
Adelaide Ct
Hackney E5..........18 A3
St John's Wood
NW8.................79 A1
Adelaide Gr W12...29 C1
Adelaide Rd
Primrose Hill
NW3.................12 A1
Richmond TW9......54 B3
⁷ Wandsworth
SW18................58 C2
Adelaide St ⑳ WC2..120 A3
Adela St W10.......23 A1
Adelina Gr E1.......32 B4
Adelina Mews
SW12................73 C3
Adeline Pl WC1....105 C3
Adelphi Ct ⁵
SE16................40 C4
Adelphi Terr WC2..120 B3
Adeney Cl W6......47 C4
Aden Gr N16........15 C4
Aden Ho ⑴ E1......32 C4
Aden Lo N16.......15 C4
Adeyfield Ho EC1...97 C3
Adie Rd W6.........39 B3
Adisham Ho E5 ⁴...17 A3
Adler St E1.........111 B2
Adley St E5.........18 A3
Admiral Ct
Chelsea SW10.....167 A4
Marylebone W1....103 B3
Admiral Hyson Ind Est
SE16................40 A1
Admiral Mews
W10.................22 C1
Admiral Pl SE16....33 A1
Admirals Ct
Bermondsey SE1...124 C1
⁶ Putney SW19.....69 C3
Admirals Gate
SE10................52 A2
Admiral Sq SW10..167 A4
Admiral St SE8.....51 C2
Admirals Way E14..41 C4
Admiral's Wlk NW3..2 B1
Admiralty Arch
SW1................119 C2

Admiralty Cl 1
SE8 . . . . .51 C2
Admiral Wlk W9 . .31 C4
Adolphus Rd N4 . . . . .6 A3
Adolphus St SE8 . . . .51 B3
Adpar St W1 . . . . . . .101 B4
Adrian Bolt Ho 2
E2 . . . . .25 A2
Adrian Ho
Islington N1 . . . . .85 A3
South Lambeth
SW8 . . . . .162 A2
Stratford E15 . . . . . . .19 C1
Adrian Mews
SW10 . . . . .156 B4
Adriatic Bldg 18
E14 . . . . .33 A2
Adriatic Ho 19 E1 . . . .25 C1
Adron Ho 15 SE16 . . .40 B2
Adstock Ho 5 N1 . . .15 A1
Adventurers Ct 17
E14 . . . . .34 C2
Adys Lawn NW2 . . . . .9 A2
Adys Rd SE15 . . . . . .64 B4
Aegean Apts 7
E16 . . . . .35 C2
Aegon Ho 3 E14 . . . .42 A3
Affleck St N1 . . . . . . .85 A1
Afghan Rd SW11 . . .168 A1
Africa Ho WC2 . . . . .106 C2
Afsil Ho EC1 . . . . . .107 C3
Aga Khan Univ
WC1 . . . . .105 C2
Agamemnon Rd
NW6 . . . . .10 B3
Agar Gr NW1 . . . . . . .13 C1
Agar Pl NW1 . . . . . . .13 C1
Agar St WC2 . . . . . .120 B3
Agate Rd W6 . . . . . . .39 B3
Agatha Cl E1 . . . . . . .32 B1
Agave Rd NW2 . . . . . .9 B4
Agdon St EC1 . . . . . .96 A2
Agincourt Rd NW3 . . .12 B4
Agnes Ct 11 SW18 . .59 C3
Agnes Ho 13 W11 . . .30 C2
Agnes Rd W3 . . . . . . .38 B4
Agnes St E14 . . . . . . .33 B3
Aicon Gall SW1 . . . .118 C4
Aigburth Mans 5
SW9 . . . . .163 B1
Ailsa St E14 . . . . .34 B4
Ainger Mews 3
NW3 . . . . .12 B1
Ainger Rd NW3 . . . . .12 B1
Ainsdale NW1 . . . . . .92 C4
Ainsdale Dr SE1 . . . .153 B1
Ainsley St 2
E2 . . . . .25 A2
Ainslie Wlk 8
SW12 . . . . .73 A4
Ainsty St 20 SE16 . . .40 B4
Ainsworth Cl SE5 . . .49 A1
Ainsworth Est
NW8 . . . . .78 C4
Ainsworth Ho NW8 . .78 B3
Ainsworth Rd E9 . . . .17 B1
Ainsworth Way
NW8 . . . . .78 C4
Aintree St SW6 . . . .154 B2
Aird Ho SE11 . . . . . .136 C1
Airdrie Cl N1 . . . . . . .14 B1
Airedale Ave W4 . . . .38 B1
Airedale Ave S W4 . . .38 B1
Airedale Rd SW12 . . .72 B4
Airlie Gdns
W8 . . . . . .31 C1 113 B1
Air St W1 . . . . .119 A3

Aisgill Ave SW5 . . . .141 A1
Aiten Pl W6 . . . . .38 C2
Aithan Ho 15 E14 . . .33 B3
Aitken Cl E8 . . . . .24 C4
Ajax Ho 15 E2 . . . . . . .25 A3
Ajax Rd NW6 . . . . . . .10 C3
Akbar Ho 7 E14 . . . . .42 A2
Akehurst St SW15 . . .68 C4
Akenside 3
NW3 . . . . .11 C3
Akenside Rd NW3 . . .11 C3
Akerman Rd SW9 . . .48 A2
Akintaro Ho 7
SE8 . . . . .51 B4
Alamaro Lo 5
SE10 . . . . .43 B3
Aland Ct SE16 . . . . . .41 A3
Alan Preece Ct
NW6 . . . . .9 C1
Alaska Bldg 12
SE13 . . . . .52 A2
Alaska St SE1 . . . . . .121 B1
Alastor Ho 10 E14 . . .42 B3
Albacore Cres
SE13 . . . . .67 A1
Alba Mews SW18,
SW19 . . . . .70 C2
Alban Ho
Hampstead NW3 . . . .11 B2
New Cross SE14 . . . .51 B2
Albans Cl SW16 . . . . .74 A1
Albany W1 . . . . .118 C3
Albany Cl SW14 . . . . .55 A3
Albany Ct
College St NW10 . . . .22 A2
NW8 . . . . .79 B1
Westminster SW1 . . .133 B2
8 Whitechapel E1 . . .111 B2
Albany Ctyd W1 . . . .119 A3
Albany Ho 6 TW8 . . .44 A4
Albany Mans
SW11 . . . . .158 B1
Albany Mews
Camberwell SE5 . . . .48 B4
Islington N1 . . . . .14 C1
Albany Par 4
TW8 . . . . .44 A4
Albany Pas 12
TW10 . . . . .54 A2
Albany Rd
Camberwell SE5 . . . .49 A4
Richmond TW10 . . . .54 A2
Albany St NW1 . . . . . .92 B4
Albany Terr 6
TW10 . . . . .54 A2
Alba Pl W11 . . . . .31 B3
Albemarle SW19 . . . .69 C2
Albemarle Coll
W1 . . . . .117 A4
Albemarle Ho
2 Brixton SW2 . . . . . .62 C1
Rotherhithe SE8 . . . .41 B2
Albemarle Mans
NW3 . . . . .11 A4
Albemarle Prim Sch
SW19 . . . . .70 A2
Albemarle St W1 . . . .118 C3
Albemarle Way
EC1 . . . . .96 A1
Alberta Ct 1
TW10 . . . . .54 B2
Alberta Ho E14 . . . . .34 B1
Alberta St SE17 . . . .150 B2
Albert Ave SW8 . . . .162 C1
Albert Barnes Ho
SE1 . . . . .136 C1

Albert Bigg Point
E15 . . . . .27 B4
Albert Bridge Rd
SW11 . . . . .158 C1
Albert Cl 11 E9 . . . . . .25 A4
Albert Cotts 2
E1 . . . . .111 B4
Albert Ct
Knightsbridge
SW7 . . . . .129 B3
9 Putney SW19 . . . . .70 A3
Albert Dr SW19 . . . . .70 A3
Albert Emb SE1 . . . .148 B3
Albert Gate Ct
SW1 . . . . .130 C3
Albert Gdns E1 . . . . . .32 C3
Albert Gray Ho
SW10 . . . . .157 B2
Albert Hall Mans
SW7 . . . . .129 B3
Albert Mans
Battersea SW11 . . . .168 C4
Hornsey N8 . . . . .5 A4
Albert Meml SW7 . . .129 B3
Albert Mews W8 . . . .128 C2
Albert Palace Mans
SW11 . . . . .169 C4
Albert Pl W8 . . . . . . .128 B3
Albert Rd
Finsbury Pk N4 . . . . . .5 B4
Kilburn NW6 . . . . . . .23 B3
Richmond TW10 . . . .54 B2
Albert's Ct NW1 . . . .90 B2
Albert Sq SW8 . . . . .162 C1
Albert St NW1 . . . . . .82 B3
Albert Starr Ho 7
SE8 . . . . .40 C2
Albert Studios
SW11 . . . . .168 C4
Albert Terr
Camden Town
NW1 . . . . .81 B3
Stonebridge NW10 . . .20 B4
Albert Terr Mews
NW1 . . . . .81 B3
Albert Way SE15 . . . .50 A3
Albert Westcott Ho
SE17 . . . . .150 B2
Albion Ave SW8 . . . .171 B1
Albion Cl W2 . . . . . . .116 B4
Albion Ct 7 W6 . . . . .39 A2
Albion Dr E8 . . . . .16 C1
Albion Est SE16 . . . . .40 B4
Albion Gate W2 . . . .116 B4
Albion Gdns 1
W6 . . . . .39 A2
Albion Gr N16 . . . . . . .16 A4
Albion Ho
17 Deptford SE8 . . . .51 C3
EC1 . . . . .108 A4
Albion Mews
Bayswater W2 . . . . .116 B4
6 Hammersmith
W6 . . . . .39 A2
Islington N1 . . . . .85 B4
Albion Pl
Broadgate EC2 . . . . .109 C3
Clerkenwell EC1 . . . .108 A4
Hammersmith W6 . . .39 A2
Albion Prim Sch 34
SE16 . . . . .40 B4
Albion Rd N16 . . . . . .15 C4
Albion Riverside
SW11 . . . . .158 A2
Albion Sq E8 . . . . . . .16 B1

Albion St
Bayswater W2 . . . . .116 B4
Rotherhithe SE16 . . . .40 B4
Albion Terr E8 . . . . . .16 B1
Albion Way
Barbican EC1 . . . . . .108 C3
Lewisham SE13 . . . . .67 B3
Albion Wlk N1 . . . . . .84 B1
Albion Works Studios
16 E8 . . . . .16 C3
Albion Yd N1 . . . . . . .84 B1
Albon Ho SW18 . . . . .59 A1
Albrighton Rd SE5,
SE22 . . . . .64 A4
Albury Bldgs SE1 . .136 B3
Albury Ct SE8 . . . . . .51 C4
Albury Lo 7 SW2 . . .74 B4
Albury St SE8 . . . . . . .51 C4
Albyn Rd SE8 . . . . . . .51 C2
Alconbury Rd E5 . . . .7 C2
Aldbourne Rd
W12 . . . . .29 C1
Aldbridge St SE17 . .152 B2
Aldburgh Mews
W1 . . . . .103 C2
Aldbury Ho SW3 . . .144 A3
Aldebert Terr
SW8 . . . . .162 C1
Aldeburgh Pl SE10 . .43 C1
Aldeburgh St SE10 . .43 C1
Aldenham Ho NW1 . . .83 B1
Aldenham St NW1 . . .83 B1
Alden Ho E8 . . . . .25 A4
Aldensley Rd W6 . . .39 A3
Alderbrook Prim Sch
12 SW12 . . . . .73 A4
Alderbrook Rd
SW12 . . . . .61 A1
Alderbury Rd
SW13 . . . . .46 C4
Aldergrove Ho 3
E5 . . . . .7 C2
Alder Ho
Camberwell SE15 . . .49 B4
1 Maitland Pk
NW3 . . . . .12 B2
St Johns SE4 . . . . . . .66 C4
Alderley Ho 33
SW8 . . . . .171 B1
Alder Lo SW6 . . . . . .47 C2
Aldermanbury
EC2 . . . . .109 A2
Aldermanbury Sq
EC2 . . . . .109 A3
Alderman's Wlk
EC2 . . . . .110 A3
Alder Mews 13 N19 . . .4 B2
Alderney Ho 20
N1 . . . . .15 B2
Alderney Mews
SE1 . . . . .137 B2
Alderney Rd E1 . . . . . .25 C1
Alderney St SW1 . . . .146 B2
Alders, The N16 . . . . . .6 C3
Aldersford Cl SE4 . . .65 C3
Aldersgate St
EC1 . . . . .108 C3
Aldersgate St EC1 . .108 C3
Aldershot Rd NW6 . . .23 B4
Alderson St W10 . . . .23 A1
Alderton Rd SE24 . . .63 B4
Alderville Rd
SW6 . . . . .165 A2

Alderwick Ct N7 . . . .14 B2
Aldford St W1 . . . . . .117 C2
Aldgate EC3 . . . . . . .110 B1
Aldgate East Sta
E1 . . . . .111 A2
Aldgate High St
EC3 . . . . .110 C1
Aldgate Sta EC3 . . . .110 C1
Aldham Ho SE4 . . . . .51 B2
Aldine Ct W12 . . . . . .30 B1
Aldine St W12 . . . . . .39 B4
Aldington Ct 1
E8 . . . . .16 C1
Aldred Rd NW6 . . . . .10 C3
Aldren Rd SW17 . . . .71 B1
Aldrich Terr SW18 . . .71 B2
Aldrick Ho N1 . . . . . . .85 A2
Aldridge Ct W11 . . . .31 A4
Aldridge Rd Villas
W11 . . . . .31 B4
Aldsworth Cl W9 . . . .88 A1
Aldwich Ho WC2 . . . .107 A1
Aldworth Gr SE13 . . .67 B1
Aldwych WC2 . . . . . .107 A1
Aldwych Bldgs
WC2 . . . . .106 B2
Aldwyn Ho SW8 . . . .162 A1
Alexander Ave
NW10 . . . . .9 A1
Alexander Ct
SW18 . . . . .59 B2
Alexander Fleming
Laboratory Mus
W2 . . . . .101 C2
Alexander Ho 16
E14 . . . . .41 C3
Alexander Mews 2
W2 . . . . .100 A2
Alexander Pl SW7 . . .144 A4
Alexander Rd N19 . . . .5 A2
Alexander Sq
SW3 . . . . .144 A4
Alexander St W2 . . . .31 C3
Alexandra Ave
SW11 . . . . .169 B3
Alexandra Cl 8 SE8 . .51 B4
Alexandra Cotts
SE14 . . . . .51 B2
Alexandra Gdns
W4 . . . . .46 A3
Alexandra Gr N4 . . . . .6 A3
Alexandra Ho 1
W6 . . . . .39 B1
Alexandra Mans
Chelsea SW3 . . . . . .157 B3
Cricklewood NW2 . . . .9 C3
1 Hampstead
NW6 . . . . .10 C3
9 Shepherd's Bush
W12 . . . . .38 C4
Alexandra National
Ho N4 . . . . .6 A2
Alexandra Pl NW8 . . .79 A4
Alexandra Rd
Acton W4 . . . . .37 C4
Hampstead NW8 . . . .11 C1
Mortlake SW14 . . . . .55 C4
Richmond TW9 . . . . .44 B1
Alexandra St
5 Deptford SE14 . . . .51 A3
Newham E16 . . . . . . .35 C4

Alex Gossip Ho
SW6 . . . . **165** B3
Alexis St SE16 . . . . . **153** C4
Alfearn Rd E5 . . . . . . **17** B4
Alfies Antique Mkt
NW8 . . . . **90** A1
Alford Ct N1 . . . . **87** A1
Alford PI N1 . . . . **87** A1
Alfreda Ct SW11 . . . **170** A3
Alfreda St SW11 . . . **170** A3
Alfred Butt Ho
SW17 . . . . **72** B1
Alfred Cl W4 . . . . **38** A2
Alfred Rd E9 . . . . **18** A3
Alfred Mews W1,
WC1 . . . . **105** B4
Alfred Nunn Ho
NW10 . . . . **21** B4
Alfred PI WC1 . . . . . **105** B4
Alfred Rd
Acton W3 . . . . **28** B1
Paddington W2 . . . **31** C4
Alfred Salter Ho
SE1 . . . . **153** A3
Alfred Salter Prim
Sch SE16 . . . . **40** C4
Alfred St E3 . . . . **26** B2
Alfreton Rd SW11 . . . **69** C1
Algar Rd SE1 . . . . . . **136** A3
Algarve Rd SW12 . . . **73** A3
Algernon Rd
Kilburn NW6 . . . . . . **23** C4
Lewisham SE13 . . . **67** A3
Algiers Rd SE13 . . . . **66** C3
Alice Gilliott Ct
W14 . . . . **155** A4
Alice La E3 . . . . **26** B3
Alice Owen Tech Ctr
EC1 . . . . **96** A4
Alice Shepherd Ho ⓰
E14 . . . . **42** B4
Alice St SE1 . . . . . . **138** A1
Alice Walker Cl ⓫
SE24 . . . . **63** A3
Alie St E1 . . . . **111** A1
Aliwal Rd SW11 . . . . **60** A3
Alkerden Rd W4 . . . . **38** A1
Alkham Rd N16 . . . . . **7** B2
Allam Ho
W11 . . . . **31** A2 **112** A4
Allanbridge N16 . . . . . **7** A4
Allan Ho SW8 . . . . . **171** B4
Allan Way W3 . . . . . . **28** B4
Allard Gdns SW4 . . . **61** C2
Allardyce St SW4,
SW9 . . . . **62** B3
Allbrook Ho ⓳
SW15 . . . . **68** C4
Allcroft Rd NW5 . . . . **12** C2
Allendale CI SE5 . . . . **48** C2
Allen Edwards Dr
SW8 . . . . **172** A4
Allen Edwards Prim
Sch SW4 . . . . **172** A3
Allenford Ho
SW15 . . . . **56** B1
All England Lawn
Tennis & Croquet
Club The SW19 . . . **70** A1
Allen Ho W8 . . . . . . **127** C2
Allen Mans W8 . . . . **127** C2
Allen Rd
Old Ford E3 . . . . . . **26** B3
Stoke Newington
N16 . . . . **16** A4

Allensbury PI
⓻ Camden Town
NW1 . . . . **13** C1
Camden Town NW1 . . **14** A1
Allen St W8 . . . . . . **127** C1
Allenswood ⓲
SW19 . . . . **70** A3
Allerdale Rd ⓷ N4 . . . **6** A4
Allerton Ho N1 . . . . . **87** C1
Allerton Rd N16 . . . . . **6** C2
Allerton St N1 . . . . . . **97** C4
Allestree Rd SW6 . . **154** A1
Alleyn Cres SE21 . . . **75** C2
Alleyn Ho
Bermondsey SE1 . . **137** B1
St Luke's EC1 . . . . . **97** A1
Alleyn Pk SE21 . . . . . **76** A1
Alleyn Rd SE21 . . . . . **76** A1
Alleyn's Sch SE22 . . . **64** A2
Allfarthing La
SW18 . . . . **59** B1
Allfarthing Prim Sch
SW18 . . . . **59** B1
Allgood St ⓱ E2 . . . . **24** B3
Allhallows La EC4 . . **123** B3
Alliance Ct W3 . . . . . **28** A4
Alliance Rd W3 . . . . . **20** A1
Allied Ind Est W3 . . . . **37** B3
Allied Way W3 . . . . . . **38** A4
Allingham Ct NW3 . . . **12** A3
Allingham Mews
N1 . . . . **86** C2
Allingham St N1 . . . . . **86** C2
Allington Ct ⓺
SW8 . . . . **170** C1
Allington Rd W10 . . . **23** A3
Allington St SW1 . . . **132** B1
Allison Cl SE10 . . . . . **52** B2
Allison Gr SE21 . . . . . **76** A3
Allison Rd W3 . . . . . . **28** B2
Alliston Ho ⓰
E2 . . . . **24** B2 **99** A3
Allitsen Rd NW8 . . . . **80** A2
All Nations Ho ⓰
E8 . . . . **17** A1
Allnutt Way SW4 . . . . **61** C2
Allom Ct ⓫ SW4 . . . **172** B1
Allonby Ho E14 . . . . . **33** A4
Alloway Rd E3 . . . . . . **26** A2
Allport Ho SE5 . . . . . **63** C4
Allport Mews ⓶
E1 . . . . **25** B1
All Saints CE Prim
Sch
⓼ Fulham SW6 . . . **164** A2
Putney SW15 . . . . . **57** B4
All Saints' CE Prim
Sch SE3 . . . . **53** A1
All Saints CE Sch
NW2 . . . . **1** C2
All Saints Church
N19 . . . . **4** C1
All Saints Ct
Lower Clapton E5 . . **17** B4
⓵ Shadwell E1 . . . **32** B2
All Saints Dr SE3 . . . **53** B1
All Saints Ho ⓶
W11 . . . . **31** B4
All Saints Pas
SW18 . . . . **58** C2
All Saints Rd W11 . . . **31** B3
All Saints' Rd W3 . . . **37** B3
All Saints St N1 . . . . . **84** C2
All Saints Sta E14 . . . **34** A2
Allsop PI NW1 . . . . . . **91** A1

All Souls Ave
NW10 . . . . **22** A4
All Souls CE Prim Sch
W1 . . . . **104** C4
All Souls PI W1 . . . . **104** B3
Alma Birk Ho ⓵
NW6 . . . . **10** B1
Almack Rd E5 . . . . . . **17** B4
Alma Gr SE1 . . . . . . **153** A3
Alma Ho ⓻ TW8 . . . . **44** A4
Alma PI NW10 . . . . . . **22** A2
Alma Rd SW18 . . . . . **59** B3
Alma Sq NW8 . . . . . . **89** A4
Alma St
Camden Town
NW5 . . . . **13** A2
Stratford New Town
E15 . . . . **19** C2
Alma Terr
Earl's Ct W8 . . . . . **127** C1
Wandsworth SW18 . **71** C4
Almeida St ⓰ N1 . . . **15** A1
Almeric Rd SW11 . . . **60** B3
Almington St N4 . . . . . **5** B3
Almond Ave W5 . . . . . **36** A3
Almond CI SE15 . . . . **49** C1
Almond Ho SE4 . . . . . **51** B1
Almond Rd SE16 . . . . **40** A2
Almorah Rd N1 . . . . . **15** C1
Al-Muntada Islamic
Sch SW6 . . . . **165** A4
Alperton St W10 . . . . **23** B1
Alphabet Sq E3 . . . . . **33** C4
Alpha CI NW8 . . . . . . **90** B3
Alpha Ct ⓺ NW5 . . . . **13** A2
Alpha Gr E14 . . . . **41** C4
Alpha Ho
⓳ Brixton SW4 . . . **62** B3
Kilburn NW6 . . . . . . **23** C3
Lisson Gr NW8 . . . . **90** B1
Alpha PI
Chelsea SW3 . . . . **158** B4
Kilburn NW6 . . . . . . **23** C3
Alpha Rd SE14 . . . . . **51** B2
Alpha St SE15 . . . . . . **49** C1
Alpine Gr ⓻ E9 . . . . . **17** B1
Alpine Rd SE16 . . . . . **40** C1
Alroy Rd N4 . . . . **5** C4
Alsace Rd SE17 . . . . **152** A2
Al Sadiq & Al Zahra
Schs NW6 . . . . **23** A4
Alscot Rd SE1 . . . . . **139** A1
Alscot Road Ind Est
SE1 . . . . **139** A1
Alscot Way SE1 . . . . **152** C4
Altair Ct N1 . . . . **15** C2
Altenburg Gdns
SW11 . . . . **60** B3
Althea St SW6 . . . . . **59** A4
Althorpe Mews
SW11 . . . . **167** C3
Althorp Rd SW17 . . . **72** B3
Altima Ct SE22 . . . . . **64** C3
Alton Ho ⓷ E3 . . . . . **27** A2
Alton Rd
Richmond TW10,
TW9 . . . . **54** A3
Roehampton SW15 . **68** C3
Alton St E14 . . . . **34** A4
Alton St SE14 . . . . . . **34** A4
Alumni Ct SE1 . . . . . **139** A4
Alvanley Ct NW3 . . . . **11** A3
Alvanley Gdns
NW6 . . . . **11** A3

Alvanley Ho ⓮
SW9 . . . . **173** B4
Alverstone Ave SW18,
SW19 . . . . **70** C2
Alverstone Ho ⓫
SE11 . . . . **163** B3
Alverstone Rd NW2 . . **9** B1
Alverton St SE8 . . . . . **51** B4
Alvey St SE17 . . . . . **152** A2
Alvington Cres E8 . . . **16** B3
Alwyne Ave W4 . . . . . **37** C1
Alwyne La N1 . . . . . . **15** A1
Alwyne PI N1 . . . . . . **15** B1
Alwyne Rd N1 . . . . . . **15** B1
Alwyne Sq N1 . . . . . . **15** B2
Alwyne Villas N1 . . . . **15** A1
Alwyn Gdns W3 . . . . . **28** A3
Alzette Ho ⓱ E2 . . . . **25** C3
Aman Dalvi Ho ⓶
SW18 . . . . **70** A4
Amazonas SE1 . . . . **152** B3
Amazon St E1 . . . . . . **32** A3
Ambassador Ct ⓹
NW6 . . . . **10** C3
Ambassador Ho
NW8 . . . . **79** A3
Ambassador Sq
E14 . . . . **42** A2
Amber Ct N7 . . . . **14** C2
Ambergate St
SE17 . . . . **150** B2
Amberley Ct ⓶
SW9 . . . . **63** A4
Amberley Rd W9 . . . . **31** C4
Amber Wharf ⓯
E2 . . . . **24** B4
Ambler Prim Sch ⓶
N4 . . . . **6** A2
Ambler Rd N4 . . . . **6** A1
Ambleside
⓯ Putney SW15 . . . **57** C1
Regent's Pk NW1 . . . **82** B1
Ambleside Ct ⓳ E9 . . **17** B3
Ambleside Point ⓵
SE15 . . . . **50** B3
Ambleside Rd
NW10 . . . . **8** B1
Ambrosden Ave
SW1 . . . . **133** A1
Ambrose Ho ⓹
E14 . . . . **33** C4
Ambrose Mews ⓻
SW11 . . . . **168** C2
Ambrose St SE16 . . . **40** A2
Ambrose Wlk E3 . . . . **26** C3
AMC Bsns Ctr
SW9 . . . . **62** A3
Amelia Ho ⓻ W6 . . . . **39** B1
Amelia Ho ⓹ W6 . . . . **39** C1
Amelia St SE17 . . . . **150** C2
Amen Cnr EC4 . . . . . **108** B1
Amen Ct EC4 . . . . . . **108** B1
American
Intercontinental
Univ W1 . . . . **103** C3
American Sch in
London The W8 . . . **79** B2
America Sq EC3 . . . **124** C4
America St SE1 . . . . **122** C1
Amerland Rd
SW18 . . . . **58** B1
Amersham Gr
SE14 . . . . **51** B3
Amersham Rd
SE14 . . . . **51** B2

Amersham Vale SE14,
SE8 . . . . **51** B3
Amery Gdns NW10 . . **22** A4
Amery Ho SE17 . . . . **152** B2
Amesbury Ave
SW2 . . . . **74** B2
Amesbury Twr ⓸
SW8 . . . . **170** C2
Ames Cotts ⓓ E3 . . . **33** A4
Ames Ho ⓰ E2 . . . . . **25** C3
Amethyst Rd E15 . . . . **19** C4
Amhurst Ct N4 . . . . **6** C4
Amhurst Par N16 . . . . **7** B4
Amhurst Rd N4, N16 . **7** A4
Amhurst Rd E8,
N16 . . . . **16** C4
Amhurst Terr E8 . . . . **16** C4
Amias Ho EC1 . . . . . . **96** C2
Amiel St ⓼ E1 . . . . . . **25** B1
Amies St SW11 . . . . . **60** B4
Amigo Ho SE1 . . . . . **135** C2
Amina Way SE16 . . . **139** B1
Amner Rd SW11 . . . . **60** C1
Amor Rd W6 . . . . **39** B3
Amory Ho N1 . . . . **85** A2
Amott Rd SE15 . . . . . **64** C4
Amoy PI E14 . . . . **33** C2
Ampton PI WC1 . . . . . **94** C3
Ampton St WC1 . . . . . **94** C3
Amstel Ct ⓱ SE15 . . . **49** B3
Amsterdam Rd
E14 . . . . **42** B3
Amundsen Ct ⓻
E14 . . . . **41** C1
Amwell St EC1 . . . . . . **95** B4
Amyruth Rd SE4 . . . . **66** C2
Anatola Rd N19 . . . . . . **4** A2
Anchorage Point ⓱
E14 . . . . **41** C4
Anchor Ho EC1 . . . . . **96** C2
Anchor Mews
SW12 . . . . **61** A1
Anchor Ret Pk E1 . . . **25** B1
Anchor St SE16 . . . . . **40** A2
Anchor Terr SE1 . . . **123** A2
Anchor Yd EC1 . . . . . **97** A2
Ancona Rd NW10 . . . **21** C3
Andalus Rd SW9 . . . . **62** A4
Andaman Ho ⓷
E1 . . . . **33** A4
Andersens Wharf ⓵
E14 . . . . **33** B3
Anderson Cl W3 . . . . **28** C3
Anderson Ho ⓾
E14 . . . . **34** B2
Anderson Rd E9 . . . . **17** C2
Andersons Sq N1 . . . **86** A3
Anderson St SW3 . . **144** C2
Anderton Cl SE5 . . . . **63** C4
Andover Ho ⓹ N7 . . . . **5** B2
Andover PI NW6 . . . . **78** A1
Andover Rd N7 . . . . . . **5** B2
Andoversford Ct ⓶
SE15 . . . . **49** A4
Andre St E8 . . . . **16** C3
Andrew Borde St
WC2 . . . . **105** C2
Andrewes Ho EC2 . . **109** A3
Andrew Ho
New Cross SE4 . . . . **51** B1
Putney SW15 . . . . . **56** C2
Andrew Marvell Ho ⓲
N16 . . . . **16** A4

Andrew Pl SW8.... 171 C4
Andrew Reed Ho **8**
  SW18 ....70 A4
Andrews Crosse
  WC2 ....107 B1
Andrew's Rd E8...25 A4
Andrew St E14 ....34 B3
Andrew Wharf **14**
  E8 ....25 A3
Andrews Wlk SE17..48 A4
Andrew Wilmot Ct
  SW18 ....71 B3
Anerley St SW11.. 169 C4
Anfield Cl SW12...73 B4
Angel EC1............86 B1
Angela Carter Cl
  SW9 ....62 C4
Angela Davis Ind Est
  20 SW9 ....63 A3
Angel Ct
  Broadgate EC2 ... 109 C2
  St James SW1 .... 119 A1
  5 Willesden NW2 ...9 A3
Angel Gate EC1.... 96 B4
Angel Ho N1 ....85 C1
Angelina Ho **2**
  SE15 ....49 C2
Angelis Appartments
  N1 ....86 B1
Angel La E15 ......19 C2
Angell Park Gdns **4**
  SW9 ....62 C4
Angell Rd SW9 ....63 A4
Angel Mews
  Finsbury N1 ....85 C1
  Putney SW15 ......57 C4
  Stepney E1 ....32 A2
Angel Oak Acad
  SE15 ....49 B3
Angel Pas EC4..... 123 B3
Angel Pl SE1 ...... 137 B4
Angel Sq N1 ......85 C1
Angel St EC1 ...... 108 C2
Angel Wlk W6.......39 B2
Angerstein Bsns Pk
  SE10 ....43 C2
Angerstein La SE3..53 B2
Anglebury **5** W2...31 C3
Anglers La NW5 ...13 A2
Anglesey Ho **11**
  E14 ....33 C3
Anglia Ho **13** E14...33 A3
Anglo American
  Laundry SW17....71 B1
Anglo Rd **10** E3.....26 B3
Angrave Ct **8** E8..24 B4
Angrave Pas **5** E8..24 B4
Angus Ho **12**
  SW12 ....73 C4
Angus St SE14 ....51 A3
Anhalt Rd SW11.. 158 B2
Animals in War Meml
  W1 ....117 A4
Anley Rd **6** W14...39 C4
Annabel Cl E14....34 A3
Anna Cl E8 ....24 B4
Annandale Rd
  Chiswick W4.......38 A1
  Greenwich SE10....43 B1
Anne Goodman Ho **8**
  E1 ....32 B3
Anne Kerr Ct **18**
  SW15 ....57 C1

Anne's Ct NW8.... 90 B2
Annesley Ho **15**
Annesley Wlk N19..4 B2
Annette Cres **16**
  N1 ....15 B1
Annette Ct N7 .....5 B1
Annette Rd N7 ....14 B4
Annie Besant Cl
  E3 ....26 B4
Anning St
  EC2..............24 A1 98 B2
Annis Rd E9 ....18 A2
Ann La SW10 ..... 157 B3
Ann Moss Way
  SE16 ....40 B3
Ann's Cl SW1..... 131 B3
Ann's Pl E1 ...... 110 C3
Ansdell Rd SE15...50 B1
Ansdell St W8 .... 128 B2
Ansdell Terr W8 .. 128 B2
Ansell Ho E1 ......32 B4
Ansell Rd SW17 ...72 B1
Anselm Rd SW6 .. 155 B3
Ansleigh Pl W11...30 C2
Anson Ho
  3 Tower Hamlets
    E1 ....26 A1
  5 West Kensington
    SW10 ....160 C4
Anson Prim Sch
  NW2 ....9 C3
Anson Rd
  Cricklewood NW2....9 B3
  Tufnell Pk N7 .....13 C4
Anstey Ct **6** W3...37 A4
Anstey Ho **7** E9..25 B4
Anstey Rd SE15 ...64 C4
Anstice Cl W4 .....46 A3
Antenor Ho **11** E2..25 A3
Anthems Way Ct E6..1 C4
Anthony Cope Ct
  N1 ....97 C4
Anthony Ho NW8...90 A1
Antilles Bay **19**
  E14 ....42 B4
Antilles Ho W3 ...28 C3
Antill Rd E3 ....26 A2
Antill Terr **5** E1 ...32 C3
Antonine Hts SE1 138 A3
Anton St E8 ....16 C3
Antony Ho
  4 Deptford SE14 ..50 C3
  3 Rotherhithe
    SE16 ....40 B2
Antrim Gr NW3....12 B2
Antrim Ho SW11...60 C4
Antrim Mans NW3..12 B2
Antrim Rd NW3 ...12 B2
Antrobus Rd W4...37 B3
AOP Gall EC2.......98 A2
Apex Ind Est
  NW10 ....21 B1
Aphrodite Ct **11**
  E14 ....41 C2
Apollo Bldg **2**
  E14 ....41 C2
Apollo Ho
  Chelsea SW10 .... 157 B3
  32 Hackney E2 ...25 A3
  Highgate N6 ......3 B4
Apollo Ind Bsns Ctr **20**
  SE8 ....50 C4
Apollo Pl SW10.... 157 B2

Apollo Studios **16**
  NW5.............13 C3
Apothecary St
  EC4..............108 A1
Appach Rd SW2....62 C1
Appleby Ct W3 ....37 B4
Appleby Rd
  Hackney E8.......16 C1
  Newham E16 .....35 C3
Appleby St E2 .....24 B3
Appledore Cl SW12,
  SW17 ....72 B2
Appleford **6** NW5..13 B3
Appleford Ho **6**
  W10 ....23 A1
Appleford Rd W10..23 A1
Applegarth Ho
  Borough The SE1 .. 136 B4
  6 Camberwell
    SE15 ....49 C3
Applegarth Rd
  W14 ....39 C3
Apple Mkt WC2... 120 B4
Appleshaw Ho **4**
  SE5 ....64 A4
Appleton Ct **30** E8..17 A3
Appletree Ct SE13..67 C3
Apple Tree Yd
  SW1 ....119 A2
Appold St SE1 .... 110 A4
Appollo Ct **7**
  SW9 ....62 C4
Apprentice Way **5**
  E5 ....17 A4
Approach Cl N16 ..16 A4
Approach Rd E2 ...25 B3
Approach The W3..28 C3
April Ct **20** E2 .....24 C3
April St E8 ....16 B4
Apsley Ho
  Stepney E1 ....32 B4
  St John's Wood
    NW8 ....79 B2
Apsley Ho, The
  Wellington Mus
  SW1 ....131 C4
Apsley Way NW2....1 A2
Aquila St NW8 .....79 C2
Aquinas St SE1 ... 121 C1
Arabella Ct NW8...79 A2
Arabella Dr SW15..56 A3
Arabian Ho **13** E1..26 A1
Arabin Rd SE4.....66 B3
Aragon Twr SE8 ...41 B2
Arakan Ho **4** N16..15 C4
Aral Ho **4** E1 ......25 C1
Arapiles Ho **6**
  E14 ....34 C3
Arbery Rd E3.......26 A2
Arbon Ct N1.......87 A3
Arbor Ct N16.......6 C2
Arborfield Cl SW2..74 B3
Arborfield Ho **7**
  E14 ....33 C2
Arbour Ho **3** E1...32 C3
Arbour Sq E1 .....32 C3
Arbuthnot Rd
  SE14 ....50 C1
Arbutus St E8 .....24 B4
Arcade The
  Broadgate EC2 ... 110 A3
  1 Tufnell Pk N7 ...14 A2
Arcadian Ho SW6 167 A1
Arcadian Pl SW18..70 B4
Arcadia St E14 ....33 C3

Arcelor Mittal Orbit
  E15 ....19 A1
Archangel St SE16..40 C4
Archbishop Coggan
  Ho SE13...........67 C3
Archbishop's Pl **1**
  SW2 ....74 B4
Archbishop Sumner
  CE Prim Sch
  SE11 ....149 C3
Archbishop Tenison's
  Sch SE11.........163 A3
Archdale Ct W12...30 A1
Archdale Ho SE1...138 A2
Archdale Rd SE22..64 B3
Archel Rd W14 ... 154 C4
Archer Ho
  1 Battersea
    SW11 ....167 C2
  Hoxton N1 ....24 A4
  8 New Cross SE14..51 A2
  Notting Hill
    W11 ....31 B2 113 A4
Archers Lo **22**
  SE16 ....153 C1
Archer Sq SE14... 51 A4
Archer St W1.......119 B4
Archer Cl W2 ......102 B1
Archery Fields Ho
  WC1 ....95 B4
Arches The SE4... 120 B2
Archibald Mews
  W1 ....118 A3
Archibald Rd N7...13 C4
Archibald St E3 ...26 C2
Archie St SE1 .... 138 B3
Arch St SE1 ...... 136 C1
Archway N19......4 B2
Archway Bsns Ctr **8**
  N19 ....4 C1
Archway Cl
  North Kensington
    W10 ....30 C4
  2 Upper Holloway
    N19 ....4 B2
Archway Hts **5** N19..4 B3
Archway L Ctr N19 .4 B2
Archway Mews
  SW15 ....58 A3
Archway Rd N6.....4 A4
Archway St SW13,
  SW14 ....56 A4
Archway Sta N19 ...4 B2
Arcola St E8 ....16 B3
Arctic St NW5 .....13 A3
Arden **19** SE19 ....63 C2
Arden Cres E14 ...41 C2
Arden Ho
  20 Hoxton N1 ....24 A3
  20 Stockwell SW9 172 B1
  Vauxhall SE11..... 148 C3
Ardent Ho **30** E3...26 A3
Ardilaun Rd N5....15 B4
Ardleigh Rd N1....16 A2
Ardlui Rd SE27 ....75 B2
Ardmere Rd SE13..67 C1
Ardshiel Cl **6**
  SW15 ....57 C4
Ardwell Rd SW2...74 A2
Ardwick Rd NW2...10 C4
Ares Ct **16** E14.....41 C2
Arethusa Ho **8**
  E14 ....42 A2

Argo Bsns Ctr **7**
  NW6.............23 C2
Argon Mews SW6 155 C1
Argos Ct **8** SW9 .. 173 B4
Argos Ho **8** E2.....25 A3
Argosy Ho
  Fitzrovia W1.......92 B1
  Rotherhithe SE8 ...41 A2
Argyle Ho E14.....42 B3
Argyle Mans **4**
  NW6.............10 C3
Argyle Pl W6.......39 A2
Argyle Prim Sch
  WC1 ....94 A4
Argyle Rd E1 ......25 C1
Argyle Sq WC1 ....94 B4
Argyle St WC1 ....94 B4
Argyle Way SE16 153 C1
Argyle Wlk WC1 ...94 B3
Argyll Cl SW9 .....62 B4
Argyll Ct **32** SW2 ..74 A4
Argyll Mans
  Chelsea SW3 .... 157 C4
  West Kensington
    W14 ....140 B4
Argyll Rd W8 ..... 127 C3
Argyll St W1...... 104 C1
Arica Ho SE16 .....40 A3
Arica Rd SE4......66 A4
Ariel Ct
  5 Hammersmith
    W12 ....38 C3
  Newington SE11... 150 A3
Ariel Rd NW6......10 C2
Ariel Way W11,
  W12 ....30 B2
Aristotle Rd SW4..61 C4
Arizona Bldg **10**
  SE13 ....52 A2
Ark All Saints Acad **5**
  SE5 ....48 B3
Arkansas Ho **21**
  N19 ....4 C4
Ark Atwood Primary
  Acad W9 .... 100 A4
Ark Ct N16 .... 23 A1
Ark UK C1 N16 ....7 B2
Ark Globe Acad
  SE1 ....137 C1
Arklow Ho **17**
  SE17 ....48 C4
Arklow Rd SE14 ...51 B4
Arklow Road Trad Est
  SE14 ....51 B4
Ark Priory Prim Acad
  13 W3............37 B4
ARK Putney Acad
  SW15 ....57 B3
Arkwright Ho **22**
  SW2 ....74 A4
Arkwright Mans **1**
  NW3 ....11 B3
Arkwright Rd NW3 11 B3
Arlesey Cl SW15...58 A2
Arlesford Rd SW9 .62 A4
Arlidge Ho EC1.... 107 C4
Arlingford Rd
  SW2 ....62 C1
Arlington Ave N1 .87 A3
Arlington Cl SE13..67 C2
Arlington Ct **13**
  W3 ....28 A1
Arlington Gdns
  W4 ....37 B1
Arlington Ho
  3 Deptford SE8 ...51 B4

Arlington Ho *continued*
Finsbury EC1 ....95 C4
[1] Shepherd's Bush
W12 ....30 A1
Arlington Lo SW2 ....62 B3
Arlington Park Mans
[1] W4 ....37 B1
Arlington Pl
[19] Greenwich
SE10 ....52 B3
SE10 ....52 B3
Arlington Rd NW1 ..82 B3
Arlington Sq N1 ......87 A3
Arlington St SW1 ..118 C2
Arlington Way EC1 ..95 C4
Armada Ct [11] SE8 ..51 C4
Armadale Rd
SW6 ....155 B3
Armada St SE8 ......51 C4
Armagh Rd E3 ....26 B4
Arminger Rd W12 ..30 A1
Armitage Ho
NW1 ....102 B4
Armitage Rd
Golders Green
NW11 ....1 B3
Greenwich SE10 ....43 B1
Armour Cl N7 ....14 B2
Armoury Ho E3 ......26 A4
Armoury Rd SE8 ....52 A1
Armoury Way
SW18 ....58 C2
Armsby Ho [17] E1 ..32 B4
Armstrong Ho [8]
SW15 ....57 C1
Armstrong Rd
East Acton W3 ......29 B1
Knightsbridge
SW7 ....129 B1
[10] Willesden NW6 ..8 C1
Arnal Cres SW18 ....70 A4
Arncliffe NW6 ....78 B3
Arndale Wlk [6]
SW18 ....59 A2
Arne Ho SE11 ......148 C2
Arne St WC2 ....106 B1
Arneway St SW1 ..133 C1
Arnewood Cl
SW15 ....68 C3
Arnhem Pl E14 ......41 C3
Arnhem Way [3]
SE22 ....64 A2
Arnhem Wharf
E14 ....41 C3
Arnhem Wharf Prim
Sch E14 ....41 C3
Arnold Cir
E2 ....24 B2 98 C3
Arnold Est SE1 ....139 A3
Arnold Ho
Newington SE11 ..150 B1
[1] Stoke Newington
N16 ....7 A1
Arnold House Sch
NW8 ....79 B1
Arnold Rd E3 ....26 C2
Arnot Ho [27] SE5 ..48 B3
Arnott Cl W4 ....37 C2
Arnould Ave SE5 ..63 C3
Arnside Ho [2]
SE17 ....48 C4
Arnside St SE17 ....48 C4
Arodene Rd SW2 ..62 B1
Arragon Rd SW18 ..70 C3

Arran Ho
[5] Canary Wharf
E14 ....34 B1
Stoke Newington
N16 ....7 B3
Arran Wlk N1 ....15 B1
Arrol Ho SE1 ......137 A1
Arrowe Ct [6] E5 ..17 A4
Arrow Ho [20] N1 ..24 A4
Arrow Rd E3 ....27 A2
Arrowsmith Ho
SE11 ....148 C2
Arsenal Sta N5 ......5 C1
Arta Ho [22] E1 ....32 B3
Artemis Ct [4] E14 ..41 C2
Artemis Pl SW18 ..70 B4
Artesian Rd W2 ....31 C3
Arthur Ct
Battersea SW11 ..169 C3
[3] Kensington
W10 ....30 C3
Paddington W2 ....100 A3
Arthur Deakin Ho [1]
E1 ....111 B4
Arthur Henderson Ho
[1] Crouch End N19 ..4 C4
[3] Fulham SW6 ..164 C2
Arthur Newton Ho [6]
SW11 ....59 C4
Arthur Rd N7 ....14 B4
Arthur St EC4 ......123 C4
Arthur Wade Ho [7]
E2 ....24 B2 99 A4
Artichoke Hill [8]
E1 ....32 A2
Artichoke Mews [5]
SE5 ....48 C2
Artichoke Pl SE5 ..48 C2
Artillery Ho
Bow E3 ....26 A4
Westminster SW1 ..133 B1
Artillery La
Broadgate E1 ......110 B3
North Kensington
W12 ....29 C3
Artillery Pas E1 ..110 B3
Artillery Pl SW1 ..133 B1
Artillery Row
SW1 ....133 B1
Artisan Ct E8 ......16 C2
Artisan Mews [9]
NW10 ....22 C2
Artisan Quarter [10]
NW10 ....22 C2
Arton Wilson Ho [12]
SW15 ....56 C2
Arts Educational
Schools London [14]
W4 ....38 A2
Arts La SE16 ......139 A1
Arundel Bldgs
SE1 ....138 B1
Arundel Cl SE11 ..60 A2
Arundel Ct
Barnes SW13 ......47 A4
Chelsea SW3 ......144 B2
Putney SW15 ......57 C2
Arundel Gdns
W11 ....31 B2 112 C4
Arundel Gr N16 ....16 A3
Arundel Ho
Islington N1 ....86 B4
Richmond TW10 ..54 C2
[3] South Acton W3 ..37 A4

Arundel Lo [9] N19..5 A2
Arundel Mans
Barnes SW13 ......47 A4
Fulham SW6 ......165 A4
Arundel Pl N1 ......14 C2
Arundel Sq N7 ......14 C2
Arundel St WC2 ..121 A4
Arundel Terr
SW13 ....47 A4
Arungford Mews [2]
SW2 ....62 C2
Arvon Rd N5 ....14 C3
Asaph Ho SE14 ....51 B2
Ascalon Ct [12] SW2..62 B1
Ascalon Ho SW8 ..160 C1
Ascalon St SW8 ..160 C1
Ascham St NW5 ..13 B3
Ascot Ct
[8] Brixton SW4 ..62 A3
St John's Wood
NW8 ....89 B3
Ascot Ho
[9] Acton Green
W4 ....37 B1
[1] Paddington W9 ..31 C4
Regent's Pk NW1 ..92 B4
Ascot Lo NW6 ......78 B2
Ascot Par [2] SW4 ..62 A3
Ascott Ave W5 ....36 A4
Ashbourne Ct [5] E5..18 A3
Ashbourne Gr
Chiswick W4 ....38 A1
East Dulwich SE22 ..64 B3
Ashbourne
Independent Sixth
Form Coll W8 ....127 C3
Ashbridge Ct [4]
W6 ....39 A3
Ashbrook Rd N19 ..4 C2
Ashburn Gdns
SW7 ....142 C4
Ashburnham Com Sch
SW10 ....157 B2
Ashburnham Gr
SE10 ....52 A3
Ashburnham Pl
SE10 ....52 A3
Ashburnham Rd
Chelsea SW10 ..157 A1
Kensal Rise NW10 ..22 B3
Ashburnham Retreat
[4] SE10 ....52 A3
Ashburnham Twr
SW10 ....157 B2
Ashburn Pl SW7 ..143 A3
Ashburton Mans
SW10 ....157 A2
Ashburton Ho [35] W9..23 B1
Ashbury Rd SW11 ..60 C4
Ashby Ct NW8 ......89 C2
Ashby Gr N1 ....15 B1
Ashby Ho
[6] Brixton SW9 ..48 A1
[1] Islington N1 ....15 B1
Ashby Mews
[5] Clapham Pk
SW2 ....62 A2
New Cross SE4 ....51 B1
Ashby Rd SE4 ......51 B1
Ashby St EC1 ......96 B3
Ashchurch Ct [2]
W12 ....38 C3
Ashchurch Gr
W12 ....38 C3

Ashchurch Park Villas
W12 ....38 C3
Ashchurch Terr
W12 ....38 C3
Ashcombe Ct [4]
SW15 ....58 A2
Ashcombe Ho [39]
E3 ....27 A2
Ashcombe St
SW6 ....166 A1
Ashcroft Ho SW8 ..170 C4
Ashcroft Rd E3 ....26 A2
Ashcroft Sq [8] W6..39 B2
Ashcroft Tech Acad
SW15 ....58 A2
Ash Ct
Clapham SW11 ..60 C2
Marylebone W1 ..102 C2
[6] Rotherhithe
SE16 ....33 A1
Upper Holloway N19..4 B2
Ashdale Ho N4 ......6 C4
Ashdene [5] SE15 ..50 A3
Ashdon Rd NW10 ..21 B4
Ashdown SW15 ....57 C2
Ashdown Cres
NW5 ....12 C3
Ashdown Ct SE22 ..76 C3
Ashdown Ho [5] N7..14 A4
Ashdown Way
SW17 ....72 C2
Ashdown Wlk [20]
E14 ....41 C2
Ashenden SE17 ..151 A4
Ashenden Rd E5 ..18 A3
Ashen Gr SW19 ....70 C2
Ashentree Ct EC4 ..107 C1
Asher Way [1] E1 ..125 C3
Ashfield Ho [5] N5..15 B3
Ashfield Rd W3 ....29 B1
Ashfield St
E1 ....32 B4
[4] Whitechapel E1 ..32 A4
Ashfield Yd [2] E1 ..32 B4
Ashford Ct NW2 ....9 C4
Ashford Ho
[4] Brixton SW9 ..63 A3
[1] Deptford SE8 ..51 B4
Ashford St
N1 ....24 A2 98 A4
Ash Gr
Cricklewood NW2 ..10 A4
Ealing W5 ....36 A3
Hackney E8 ....25 A4
Ashgrove Ct [2]
W9 ....31 C4
Ashgrove Ho SW1 ..147 C2
Ash Ho
[4] Canary Wharf
E14 ....42 B4
Fulham SE1 ......153 A3
Ashington [1] NW5..13 A2
Ashington Ho [16]
E1 ....25 A1
Ashington Rd
SW6 ....165 A1
Ashland Pl W1 ....103 B4
Ashleigh Ho SW14..56 A4
Ashleigh Rd SW14..56 A4
Ashley Cres SW11 ..60 C4
Ashley Ct
Hampstead NW3 ..11 A3
[19] Kensington N16..16 A4
Ashley Pl SW1 ....132 C1

Ashley Rd
Hornsey N19......5 A4
Richmond TW9 ....54 A4
Ashlin Rd E15 ......19 C4
Ash Lo SW6 ....47 C2
Ashlone Rd SW15..57 C4
Ashmead Bsns Ctr [2]
E16 ....27 C1
Ashmead Ho E9 ..18 A3
Ashmead Mews [1]
SE8 ....51 C1
Ashmead Prim Sch
SE8 ....51 C1
Ashmead Rd SE8 ..51 C1
Ashmere Gr [11] SW2,
SW4 ....62 A3
Ashmere Ho [10]
SW2 ....62 A3
Ashmill St NW1 ..102 A3
Ashmole Prim Sch
SW8 ....163 A3
Ashmole St SW8 ..163 A3
Ashmore NW1 ......83 A3
Ashmore Cl SE15 ..49 B3
Ashmore Ho W14..126 B1
Ashmore Rd W9 ..23 B2
Ashmount Prim Sch
London N19 ....4 C4
Upper Holloway N19..5 A4
Ashmount Rd N19 ..4 C4
Ashness Rd SW11 ..60 B2
Ashpark Ho [4]
E14 ....33 B3
Ashstead Ct [15]
SW19 ....69 C3
Ashtead Rd E5 ......7 C4
Ashton Ho
[3] Kennington
SW9 ....163 C1
Roehampton SW15..69 A4
Ashton Rd E15 ....19 C3
Ashton St E14 ......34 B2
Ashurst Lo [4] N5..15 A3
Ashwin St E8 ......16 B2
Ashworth Cl SE5 ..48 C1
Ashworth Mans
W9 ....88 B3
Ashworth Rd W9 ..88 B3
Aske Ho [2]
N1 ....24 A2 98 A4
Asker Ho N7 ....14 A4
Aske St N1 ....24 A2 98 A4
Askew Cres W12 ..38 C4
Askew Mans [14]
W12 ....38 C4
Askew Rd W12 ....29 C1
Askham Ct W12 ..29 C1
Askham Rd W12 ..29 C1
Askill Dr SW15 ....58 A2
Asland Rd E15 ....27 C4
Aslett St SW18 ....71 B4
Asmara Rd NW2 ..10 A3
Asolando Dr SE17 ..151 A3
Aspect Ho [7] E14..42 B4
Aspen Ct
Ealing W5 ....36 A4
[13] Upper Holloway
N19 ....4 B2
Aspen Ct
[10] Acton W3 ....28 B3
[12] Hackney E8 ..16 C3
Richmond TW9 ..44 C3
Aspen Gdns [2]
W6 ....39 A1

Aspen Ho
[8] Deptford SE15 ...50 B4
[4] Maitland Pk
NW3 ....12 B2
Richmond TW9 .....44 C2
Aspenlea Rd W6...47 C4
Aspen Way E14.....34 B2
Aspern Gr SE13.....12 A3
Aspinall Ho SW12 ..74 A3
Aspinall Rd SE6 ....7 C1
Aspinden Rd SE16 .40 A2
Aspire Bld [10]
SW15 ....58 B2
Aspley Rd SW18 ...59 A2
Assam SE1 ....125 A1
Assam St E1 ......111 B2
Assata Mews N1....15 A2
Assembly Pas E1...32 B4
Assisi Ct SW12 .....72 B3
Astbury Bsns Pk [5]
SE15 ....50 B2
Astbury Ho SE11. .135 B1
Astbury Rd SE15...50 B2
Astell St SW3 .....144 B2
Aster Ho [3] SE13 ..52 B1
Aste St E14 ....42 B4
Astey's Row [6] N1.15 B1
Astle St SW11 ....169 C2
Astley Ave NW2 ....9 B3
Astley Ho
Fulham SE1 ......153 A2
[39] Paddington W2 ..31 C4
Aston Ct N4 ....6 B2
Aston Ho
Notting Hill
W11 ....31 B2 113 A4
South Lambeth
SW8 ....171 B3
Aston St E14 ....33 A4
Astonville St
SW18 ....70 C3
Astor Ct SW6 .....156 C1
Astoria Mans [18]
SW16 ....74 A1
Astoria Par SW16...74 A1
Astoria Wlk SW9 ...62 C4
Astra Ho
[4] Bow E3 ....26 B2
Hornsey N4 ....5 B4
Astrop Mews W6 ...39 B3
Astrop Terr W6 .....39 B4
Astwood Mews
SW7 ....142 C4
Asylum Rd SE15 ...50 B3
Atalanta St
SW6 ......47 C3 154 A1
Atheldene Rd
SW18 ....71 B3
Athelstane Gr [3] ...26 B3
Athelstane Mews
N4. ....5 C3
Athelstan Gdns [8]
NW6. ....10 C1
Athelstan Ho
Hackney Wick E9 ..18 B3
Stoke Newington
N16. ....16 A4
Athena Ct
Bermondsey SE1 ..138 A3
St John's Wood
NW8 ....79 B2
Athenia Ho [7] E14 .34 C3
Athenlay Rd SE15 ..65 C2
Athenoeum Ct N5 ..15 B4

Athens Gdns W9...23 C1
Atherden Rd E5 ....17 B4
Atherfield Ct
SW18 ....59 A1
Atherfold Rd SW9 .62 A4
Atherstone Ct W2 100 B4
Atherstone Mews
SW7 ....143 A4
Atherton Rd SW13 .46 C3
Atherton St SW11 168 B2
Athlone Cl [21] E5 ..17 A4
Athlone Gate [18]
W10 ....31 A4
Athlone Ho
[16] Camden Town
NW5. ....12 C2
[9] Stepney E1 ....32 B3
Athlone Rd SW2 ...74 C4
Athlone St NW5 ...12 C2
Athol Cl [6] N4 .....5 B2
Atholl Ho W9 .....88 C3
Athol Sq E14 ......34 B3
Atkins Ct [3] E3....26 B4
Atkins Lo W8 .....127 B4
Atkinson Ho
Battersea SW11 ..169 B3
[3] Hackney E2 ....24 C3
Walworth SE17. ...151 C3
Atkins Rd SW4,
SW12 ....73 C4
Atlanta Bldg [8]
SE13 ....52 A1
Atlantic Ct [19] E14 .34 C2
Atlantic Ho
[5] Putney SW15 ...58 B2
[4] Tower Hamlets
E1 ....33 A4
Atlas Mews
Dalston E8 ....16 B2
Islington N7 ....14 B2
[1] Lewisham SE14 .51 A2
Atlas Rd NW10 ....21 A2
Atney Rd SW15....58 A3
Atterbury St SW1 .148 A3
Attilburgh Ho SE1 .138 C2
Attlee Ho E1 ......111 A3
Attneave St WC1...95 B3
Atwater Cl SW2 ...74 C3
Atwell Rd [6] SE15 .49 C1
Atwood Ave TW9 ..44 C1
Atwood Ho SE21...76 A1
Atwood Rd W6.....39 A2
Aubert Ct N5 ......15 A4
Aubert Pk N5 .....15 A4
Aubert Rd N5 .....15 A4
Aubrey Beardsley Ho
SW1 ....147 A3
Aubrey Mans
NW1. ....102 A4
Aubrey Moore Point
E15 ....27 B3
Aubrey Pl NW8 ...78 C1
Aubrey Rd
W14 ......31 B1 113 A1
Aubrey Wlk
W14 ......31 B1 113 A1
Auburn Cl SE14....51 A3
Aubyn Sq SW15...56 C2
Auckland Ho [11]
W12 ....30 A2
Auckland Rd
SW11 ....60 A3
Auckland St SE11 148 C1
Auden Pl NW1.....81 B4

Audley Cl [8] SW11...60 C4
Audley Ct E1 ......118 A2
Audley Rd TW10 ...54 B2
Audley Sq W1 ....117 C2
Audley St W1 .....117 C2
Audrey Ho EC1 ...107 C3
Audrey St E2 ......24 C3
Augusta St E14....34 A3
Augustine Ho
Broadgate EC2....109 C2
New Cross SE4....51 B2
Augustine Rd W14 .39 C3
Augustines Ct E9 ..17 B3
Augustus Cl W12 ..39 A3
Augustus Ct
[8] Putney SW19 ...70 A3
Streatham SW16 ...73 C2
Augustus Ho NW1 .92 C4
Augustus Rd
SW19 ....69 C3
[8] Putney SW19 ...70 A3
Augustus St NW1 .92 B4
Aulton Pl SE11 ....149 C1
Aura Ho [3] TW9 ...45 A2
Auriga Mews N1 ...15 C3
Auriol Mans W14 .140 A3
Auriol Rd W14.....140 A3
Aurora Bldg [4]
E14 ....34 B1
Austen Ho [5] NW6 .23 C2
Austin Friars EC2 109 C2
Austin Friars Ho
EC2. ....109 C2
Austin Friars Sq
EC2. ....109 C2
Austin Ho
[5] Brixton SW2 ...62 B2
[4] New Cross SE14 .51 B3
Austin Rd SW11 ..169 B3
Austins Ct SE15 ...64 C4
Austin St E2. ...24 B2 98 C3
Australia Rd W12...30 A2
Austral St SE11 ...150 A4
Autumn Rise [9]
W4 ....37 C1
Autumn St E3 .....26 C4
Avalon Rd SW6 ...166 A4
Avebury Ct N1 .....87 B3
Avebury St N1. ....87 B3
Aveline St SE11 ...149 B1
Aveling Ho [12] N19 ..4 B1
Ave Maria La EC4 108 B1
Avenell Mans N5 ...15 A4
Avenell Rd N5 ......6 A1
Avenfield Ho W1 ..117 A4
Avening Rd SW18 ..70 C4
Avening Terr
SW18 ....70 C4
Avenue Cl NW8 ....80 B3
Avenue Cres W3 ...37 A4
Avenue Ct
Chelsea SW3 .....144 C3
Cricklewood NW2 ..1 A1
Avenue Gdns
Mortlake SW14 ....56 A4
South Acton W3 ...36 C4
St John's Wood
NW8 ....80 A1
Upper Clapton N16...7 C2
Willesden Green
NW10 ....22 A3
Avenue Lo [12]
NW8 ....11 C1

Avenue Mans
Clapham SW11....60 C3
Hampstead NW3 ...11 A3
Willesden NW2 .....9 A2
Avenue Park Rd SE21,
SE27 ....75 A2
Avenue Rd
Crouch End N6 .....4 C4
Harlesden NW10 ..21 B3
Primrose Hill NW8 ..80 A4
South Acton W3 ...37 A4
Avenue The
Bedford Pk W4.....38 A3
Brondesbury Pk
NW6. ....23 A4
Clapham SW4 .....60 C2
Greenwich SE10 ...52 C3
Richmond TW9 ....44 B1
Wandsworth SW18,
SW12 ....72 A4
Averill St W6 ......47 C4
Avery Farm Row
SW1 ....146 A3
Avery Row W1 ....118 B4
Aviary Ct E16 .....35 B4
Avignon Rd SE4 ...65 C4
Avingdor Ct [10]
W3 ....28 B1
Avington Ct SE1 ..152 B3
Avis Sq E1 ....32 C3
Avocet Cl SE1 ....153 B2
Avon Ct
[1] Acton W3 ......28 B3
[10] Putney SW15 ..58 A2
Avondale Cl E16...35 C4
Avondale Ho
[1] Bermondsey
SE1 ....153 B1
[6] Mortlake SW14...55 C4
Avondale Mans
SW6 ....164 C4
Avondale Park Gdns
W11 ......31 A2 112 A3
Avondale Park Prim
Sch W11 ..31 A2 112 A3
Avondale Park Rd
W11 ......31 A2 112 A4
Avondale Rd
Mortlake SW14 ....55 C4
Newham E16 ......35 A4
Avondale Rise
SE15 ....64 B4
Avondale Sq SE1 .153 B1
Avon Ho
[2] Islington N1 ....14 C1
[14] Stoke Newington
N16. ....7 A3
West Kensington
W14 ....141 A3
Avonhurst Ho
NW6. ....10 A1
Avonley Rd SE14...50 B3
Avonmore Gdns
W14 ....141 A3
Avonmore Pl
W14 ....140 B4
Avonmore Prim Sch
W14 ....140 B4
Avonmore Rd
W14 ....140 C4
Avonmouth St
SE1 ....136 C2
Avon Pl SE1 ......137 A3
Avon Rd SE4 ......66 C4
Avriol Ho W12.....30 A1
Avro Ct E9 ....18 A3

Axford Ho SW2....75 A3
Axis Ct SE10. .....53 A4
Axminster Rd N7 ...5 B1
Aybrook St W1 ...103 B3
Aycliffe Rd W12 ...29 C1
Aylesbury Ho [15]
SE15 ....49 C4
Aylesbury Rd
SE17 ....151 C1
Aylesbury St EC1 ..96 A1
Aylesford Ho SE1 137 C3
Aylesford St SW1 147 B1
Aylesham Sh Ctr
SE15 ....49 C2
Aylestone Ave
NW6. ....22 C4
Aylmer Ho SE10 ..42 C1
Aylmer Rd W12....38 B4
Aylton Est [20] SE16 .40 B4
Aylward St E1 .....32 C3
Aylwin Est SE1 ...138 B2
Aynhoe Mans W14 .39 C2
Aynhoe Rd W14 ...39 C3
Ayres St SE1 .....137 A4
Ayrsome Rd N16 ...7 A1
Ayrton Gould Ho [9]
E2 ....25 C2
Ayrton Rd SW7 ...129 B2
Aysgarth Rd SE21..76 A4
Ayshford Ho E1. ...25 A2
Ayston Ho [10] SE8...40 C2
Aytoun Ct SW9 ..173 A1
Aytoun Pl SW9 ...173 A1
Aytoun Rd SW9 ..173 A1
Azalea Ho SE14....51 B3
Azania Mews NW5..13 A2
Azenby Rd SE15 ...49 B1
Azof St SE10 ......43 A2
Azov Ho [6] E1 .....26 A1
Aztec Ct [3] E8.....16 C3
Azure Ho [8]
E2 ....24 C2 99 B3

B

Baalbeck Rd N5 ...15 A3
Babington Ct
WC1 ....106 B4
Babington Ho
SE1. ....137 A4
Babmaes St SW1 119 B3
Bacchus Wlk [2]
N1. ....24 A3
Bache's St N1 ....97 C3
Back Church La
E1 ....111 B1
Back Hill EC1. .....95 C1
Backhouse SE1 ..152 B3
Back La NW3 ......11 B4
Bacon Gr SE1 ....138 C1
Bacon's Coll SE16 .41 A4
Bacon's La N16.....3 C3
Bacon St E2. ..24 B1 99 A2
Bacton NW5. ......12 C2
Bacton St E2 ......25 B2
Baddeley Ho
SE11 ....149 A2
Baden Pl SE1 .....137 B4
Baden Wlk N1. ....86 C4
Baden St N16. .....3 A3
Baden St SE1 .....137 B4
Bader Wy [2]
SW15 ....56 C1
Badminton Ct [5]
N4. ....6 B4

Badminton Ho
SE22 . . . . .64 A3
Badminton Mews 9
E16 . . . . .35 C1
Badminton Rd
SW12 . . . . .60 C1
Badric Ct SW11 . . . . .167 C1
Badsworth Rd 3
SE5 . . . . .48 B2
Bagley's La SW6 . . . .166 B3
Bagnigge Ho WC1 . . 95 B3
Bagshot Ho NW1 . . . .92 B4
Bagshot St SE17 . . .152 B1
Baildon 27 E2 . . . . . .25 B3
Baildon St SE8 . . . . .51 B3
Bailey Ct 9 W12 . . . .38 C4
Bailey Ho SW10 . . . .156 B2
Bailey Mews
  Brixton SW2 . . . . . .62 C2
  Chiswick W4 . . . . . .45 A4
Bainbridge St
WC1 . . . . .105 C2
Bain Ho 3 SW9 . . . .172 B2
Baird Ho 22 W12 . . . .30 A2
Baird St EC1 . . . . . . .97 A2
Baizdon Rd SE3 . . . . .53 A1
Baker Ho 12 E3 . . . . .27 A2
Baker Rd NW10 . . . . .21 A4
Bakers Field N7 . . . . .14 A4
Bakers Hall Ct
EC3 . . . . .124 B3
Baker's Mews 1 W1 .103 B2
Bakers Pas 22
NW3 . . . . .11 B4
Bakers Rents 13
E2 . . . . .24 B2 98 C3
Baker's Row EC1 . . . .95 B1
Baker St W1 . . . . . . .103 A4
Baker Street W1 . . . .103 A4
Baker Street Sta
NW1 . . . . .91 A1
Baker's Yd EC1 . . . . .95 B1
Balaclava Rd SE1 . . .153 A3
Balchier Rd SE22 . . . .65 A1
Balcombe Ho
  Lisson Gr NW1 . . . . .90 C2
  3 Streatham SW2 . . .74 B3
Balcombe St NW1 . . .90 C1
Balcorne St E9 . . . . .17 B1
Balderton Flats
W1 . . . . .103 C1
Balderton St W1 . . . .103 C1
Baldock Ho 31
SE5 . . . . .48 B1
Baldock St E3 . . . . . .27 A3
Baldrey Ho 1
SE10 . . . . .43 B1
Baldwin Cres SE5 . . . .48 B2
Baldwin Ho 15
SW2 . . . . .74 C3
Baldwin Rd SW12 . . . .60 C1
Baldwin's Gdns
EC1 . . . . .107 B4
Baldwin St EC1 . . . . .97 B3
Baldwin Terr N1 . . . . .86 C2
Baldwyn Gdns W3 . . .28 C2
Baldwin's Apts 3
E16 . . . . .35 C2
Bale Rd E1 . . . . .33 A4
Bales Coll W10 . . . . .22 C2
Balfern Gr W4 . . . . . .38 A1
Balfern St SW11 . . . .168 B2
Balfe St N1 . . . . .84 B1

Balfour Ho 4
W10 . . . . .30 C4
Balfour Mews W1 . . .117 C2
Balfour Pl
  Mayfair W1 . . . . . . .117 C3
  Putney SW15 . . . . . .57 A3
Balfour Rd
  Highbury N5 . . . . . .15 B4
  North Acton W3 . . . .28 B3
Balfour St SE17 . . . .151 B4
Balfron Twr 4
E14 . . . . .34 B3
BALHAM 72 C3
Balham Gr SW12 . . . .72 C4
Balham High Rd SW12,
SW17 . . . . .72 C2
Balham Hill SW12 . . .61 A1
Balham L Ctr
SW12 . . . . .73 A2
Balham New Rd
SW12 . . . . .73 A4
Balham Park Mans
SW12 . . . . .72 C3
Balham Park Rd SW12,
SW17 . . . . .72 C3
Balham Sta SW12 . . .73 A3
Balham Station Rd
SW12 . . . . .73 A3
Balin Ho SE1 . . . . . .137 B4
Balkan Wlk 1 E1 . . . .32 A2
Balladier Wlk E14 . . .34 A4
Ballance Rd E9 . . . . .18 A2
Ballantine St
SW18 . . . . .59 B3
Ballantrae Ho
NW2 . . . . .10 B4
Ballard Ho SE10 . . . .52 A4
Ballast Quay SE10 . . .42 C1
Ballater Rd SW2,
SW4 . . . . .62 A3
Ball Ct EC3 . . . . . . .109 C1
Ballin Ct 14 E14 . . . .42 B4
Ballingdon Rd
SW11 . . . . .60 C1
Ballinger Point 18
E3 . . . . .27 A2
Balliol Ho 11
SW15 . . . . .57 C1
Balliol Rd W10 . . . . . .30 C3
Ballogie Ave NW10 . .8 A4
Ballow Cl 13 SE5 . . . .49 A3
Ball's Pond Pl 3
N1 . . . . .15 C2
Ball's Pond Rd N1 . . .16 A2
Balman Ho 3
SE16 . . . . .40 C2
Balmer Rd E3 . . . . . .26 B3
Balmes Rd N1 . . . . . .87 C4
Balmoral Cl 1
SW15 . . . . .57 C1
Balmoral Ct
  21 Rotherhithe
  St John's Wood 79 B2
Balmoral Gr N7 . . . . .14 B2
Balmoral Ho
  2 Isle of Dogs 42 A3
  Stoke Newington N4 .6 B3
  West Kensington
  W14 . . . . .140 A4
Balmoral Mews
W12 . . . . .38 B3
Balmoral Rd NW2 . . . .9 A2
Balmore Cl E14 . . . . .34 B3

Balmore St N19 . . . . .4 A2
Balmuir Gdns
SW15 . . . . .57 B3
Balnacraig Ave
NW10 . . . . .8 A4
Balniel Gate SW1 . . .147 C2
Balsam Ho 8 E14 . . . .34 A2
Baltic Apts 5 E16 . . . .35 C2
Baltic Ho 7 SE5 . . . . .48 B1
Baltic St E EC1 . . . . . .96 C1
Baltic St W EC1 . . . . .96 C1
Baltimore Ho
  Clapham SW18 . . . . .59 B3
  Kennington SE11 . . .149 B2
Balvaird Pl SW1 . . . .147 C1
Balvernie Gr SW18 . .70 C4
Bamber Rd 6
SE15 . . . . .49 B2
Bamborough Gdns 12
W12 . . . . .39 B4
Banbury Ct WC2 . . . .120 A4
Banbury Ho 5 E9 . . . .17 C1
Banbury Rd E9 . . . . . .17 C1
Banbury St 3
SW11 . . . . .168 B2
Bancroft Ho 11
E1 . . . . .25 B1
Bancroft Rd E1 . . . . . .25 C1
Banff Ho 1 NW3 . . . . .12 A2
Banfield Rd SE15 . . . .65 A4
Bangabandhu Prim
Sch 82 E2 . . . . .25 A2
Bangalore St
SW15 . . . . .57 B4
Banim St W6 . . . . . . .39 A2
Banister Ho
  Hackney E9 . . . . . . .17 C3
  Nine Elms SW8 . . . .171 A4
  9 West Kilburn
  W10 . . . . .23 A2
Banister Rd W10 . . . .22 C2
Bank Ct SW11 . . . . .170 A4
Bank End SE1 . . . . . .123 A2
Bank La SW15 . . . . . .56 A2
Bank of England
EC2 . . . . .109 B1
Bank of England Mus
EC2 . . . . .109 B1
Banks Ho SE1 . . . . . .136 C1
Bankside
  Borough The SE1 . . .122 C3
  Borough The SE1 . . .123 A2
Bankside Ave 1
SE13 . . . . .67 B4
Bankside Gall
SE1 . . . . .122 C3
Bankside Ho EC3 . . .110 B1
Bankside Lofts SE1 . .122 B2
Bankside Pier
SE1 . . . . .122 C3
Bank St E14 . . . . .34 A1
Bank Sta EC3 . . . . . .109 C1
Bank The N6 . . . . .4 A3
Bankton Rd SW2 . . . .62 C3
Banner Ct 5 SE16 . . .40 B2
Banner Ho 3 EC1 . . . .97 A1
Bannerman Ho
SW8 . . . . .162 C3
Banning Ho 4
SW19 . . . . .69 C3
Banning St SE10 . . . .43 A1
Bannister Cl SW2 . . .74 C3
Bannister Ho 28
SE14 . . . . .50 C4

Banqueting Ho
SW1 . . . . .120 A1
Banstead Ct
  East Acton W12 . . . . .29 B2
  Stoke Newington N4 .5 A3
Banstead St SE15 . . . .65 B4
Bantock Ho 8
W10 . . . . .23 A2
Bantry Ho 15 E1 . . . . .25 C1
Bantry St SE5 . . . . . .48 C3
Banville Ho SW8 . . . .163 A1
Banyan Ho 8
NW3 . . . . .11 A2
Banyard Rd SE16 . . . .40 A3
Baptist Gdns NW5 . . .12 C2
Barandon Wlk 6
W11 . . . . .30 C2
Barbanel Ho 20 E1 . . .25 B1
Barbara Brosnan Ct
NW8 . . . . .79 B1
Barbara Castle Cl
SW6 . . . . .155 A3
Barbara Rudolph Ct
5 N19 . . . . .5 A4
Barbauld Rd N16 . . . . .7 A1
Barber Beaumont Ho
21 E1 . . . . .25 C2
Barbers Rd E15 . . . . .27 A3
BARBICAN 109 A3
Barbican Ctr EC2 . . .109 A4
Barb Mews W6 . . . . .39 B3
Barbon Alley EC3 . . .110 B2
Barbon Cl WC1 . . . . .106 C4
Barbrook Ho E9 . . . . .17 B2
Barchard St SW18 . . .59 A2
Barchester St E14 . . .34 A4
Barclay Cl SW6 . . . . .155 B1
Barclay Ho 20 E9 . . . .17 B1
Barclay Rd SW6 . . . .155 C1
Barcombe Ave
SW2 . . . . .74 B2
Bardell Ho 17 SE1 . . .139 B3
Bardolph Rd
  Richmond TW9 . . . . .54 B4
  Tufnell Pk N7 . . . . . .14 A4
Bard Rd W10 . . . . . . .30 C2
Bardsey Pl 41 E1 . . . .25 B1
Bardsey Wlk 2
N1 . . . . .15 B2
Bardsley Ho 5
SE10 . . . . .52 B4
Bardsley La SE10 . . . .52 B4
Barents Ho 10 E1 . . . .25 C1
Barfett St W10 . . . . . .23 B1
Barfleur La SE8 . . . . .41 B2
Barford Ho 20 E3 . . . .26 B3
Barford St N1 . . . . . . .85 C3
Barforth Rd SE15 . . . .65 A4
Barge House St
SE1 . . . . .121 C2
Barge La 15 E3 . . . . .26 B4
Barham Ho SE17 . . . .152 B2
Baring Ct N1 . . . . .87 B3
Baring Ho 15 E14 . . . .33 C3
Baring St N1 . . . . .87 B3
Barker Cl TW9 . . . . . .45 A1
Barker Dr NW1 . . . . . .13 C1
Barker Ho
  Walworth SE17 . . . . .76 A1
  Walworth SE17 . . . .152 A3
Barker Mews SW4 . . .61 A3
Barker St SW10 . . . . .156 C4
Barker Wlk SW16 . . . .73 C1
Bark Pl W2 . . . . .114 A4
Barkston Gdns
SW5 . . . . .142 A3

Barkway Ct N4 . . . . . . .6 B2
Barkwith Ho 27
SE14 . . . . .50 C4
Barkworth Rd
SE16 . . . . .40 B1
Barlborough St
SE14 . . . . .50 B3
Barlby Gdns W10 . . . .22 C1
Barlby Prim Sch
W10 . . . . .22 C1
Barlby Rd W10 . . . . . .30 C4
Barleycorn Way
E14 . . . . .33 B2
Barley Mow Pas
  Chiswick W4 . . . . . .37 C1
  Clerkenwell EC1 . . .108 B3
Barley Shotts Bsns Pk
W10 . . . . .31 B4
Barling 6 NW1 . . . . . .13 A1
Barling Ct 1
SW4 . . . . .172 A2
Barlings Ho 2
SE4 . . . . .65 C3
Barloch Ho 14
SW11 . . . . .169 B2
Barlow Ho
  14 Bermondsey
  SE16 . . . . .40 A2
  Notting Hill
  W11 . . . . .31 A2 112 A4
  Shoreditch N1 . . . . . .97 B4
Barlow Pl W1 . . . . . .118 B3
Barlow Rd
  Acton W3 . . . . .28 A1
  Brondesbury NW6 . . .10 C2
Barlow St SE17 . . . . .151 C3
Barmouth Ho 6 N7 . . .5 B2
Barmouth Rd
SW18 . . . . .59 B1
Barnabas Ho EC1 . . . .96 C3
Barnabas Lo SW8 . . .172 B4
Barnabas Rd E9 . . . . .17 C3
Barnaby Pl SW7 . . . .143 B3
Barnado Gardens 20
E1 . . . . .32 B2
Barnard Ct SW16 . . . .74 B1
Barnard Ho 12 E2 . . . .25 A2
Barnard Lo 10 W9 . . .31 C4
Barnard Mews
SW11 . . . . .60 A3
Barnardo Gdns 1
E1 . . . . .32 C2
Barnardo St E1 . . . . . .32 C3
Barnard Rd SW11 . . . .60 A3
Barnard's Inn EC4 . . .107 C2
Barnbrough NW1 . . . .82 C3
Barnby St NW1 . . . . . .93 A4
Barn Cl 6 NW5 . . . . . .13 C3
Barn Elms Sp Ctr
SW15 . . . . .47 B2
Barnersbury Ho
N7 . . . . .14 A4
BARNES 46 B2
Barnes Ave SW13 . . . .46 C3
Barnes Bridge Sta
SW13 . . . . .46 A1
Barnes Common
SW13 . . . . .56 C4
Barnes Ct N1 . . . . . . .14 C1
Barnes High St
SW13 . . . . .46 B1
Barnes Ho
  14 Bethnal Green
  E2 . . . . .25 B3

Barnes Ho continued
Camden Town NW1 .... **82** B4
26 Deptford SE14 .... **50** C4
Hornsey N19 .... 5 A3
Barnes Hospl
SW14 .... **56** A4
Barnes Prim Sch
SW13 .... **56** B4
Barnes St E14 .... **33** A3
Barnes Terr SW13 .... **56** C4
Barnet Gr
E2 .... **24** C2 **99** B3
Barnet Ho **5** SE5 .... **48** B1
Barnett Ho **1** E1 .... **110** C3
Barnett St **1** E1 .... **32** A3
Barn Field N18 .... **12** B3
Barnfield Cl
London N4 .... 5 A4
Wandsworth SW17 .... **71** B1
Barnfield Pl E14 .... **41** C2
Barnham St SE1 .... **138** B4
BARNSBURY **14** A1
Barnsbury Gr N7 .... **14** B1
Barnsbury Ho 12
SW4 .... **61** C1
Barnsbury Pk N1 .... **14** C1
Barnsbury Rd N1 .... **85** B3
Barnsbury Sq N1 .... **14** C1
Barnsbury St N1 .... **14** C1
Barnsbury Terr N1 .... **14** B1
Barnsdale Ave
E14 .... **41** C2
Barnsdale Rd W9 .... **23** B1
Barnsley St E1 .... **25** A1
Barn St N16 .... 7 A2
Barnstaple La
SE13 .... **67** B3
Barnston Wlk N1 .... **86** C4
Barnwell Ho 1
SE5 .... **49** A2
Barnwell Rd SW2 .... **62** C2
Barnwood Cl W9 .... **88** B1
Baron Cl N1 .... **85** B2
Baroness Rd 5
E2 .... **24** B2 **99** A4
Barons Court Mans
W14 .... **140** B1
Baron's Court Rd
W14 .... **140** B2
Barons Court Sta
W14 .... **140** A1
Barons Gate 13
W4 .... **37** B3
Baronsmede W5 .... **36** B4
Baron's Pl SE1 .... **135** C3
Baron St N1 .... **85** B2
Barque Mews SE8 .... **51** C4
Barradell Ho 16
W14 .... **39** C3
Barratt Ho **16** N1 .... **15** A1
Barratt Ind Pk E3 .... **27** B1
Barret Ho NW6 .... **23** C4
Barrett Ct 2
NW10 .... **21** A3
Barrett's Gr N16 .... **16** A3
Barretts Green Rd
NW10 .... **20** C3
Barrett St W1 .... **103** C1

Barrhill Rd SW2 .... **74** A2
Barriedale SE14 .... **51** A1
Barrie Ho
Acton W3 .... **37** B4
Bayswater W2 .... **115** A3
Primrose Hill NW8 .... **80** B3
8 Stoke Newington
N16 .... 7 A1
Barrington Cl
NW5 .... **12** C3
Barrington Ct
3 Acton W3 .... **37** A4
Kentish Town NW5 .... **12** C3
13 South Lambeth
SW9 .... **172** B1
Barrington Rd
SW9 .... **63** A4
Barrowgate Ho
W4 .... **37** C1
Barrowgate Rd
W4 .... **37** C1
Barrow Hill Est
NW8 .... **80** A1
Barrow Hill Jun Sch
NW8 .... **80** A1
Barrow Hill Rd
NW8 .... **80** A1
Barry Ct SW4 .... **61** B1
Barry Ho **2** SE16 .... **40** A1
Barry Lo N4 .... 5 A4
Barry Par SE22 .... **64** C3
Barry Rd SE22 .... **64** C2
Barset Rd SE15 .... **65** B4
Barston Rd SE27 .... **75** B1
Barstow Cres SW2 .... **74** B3
Bartell Ho SW2 .... **62** C1
Barter St WC1 .... **106** B3
Bartholomew Cl
Barbican EC1 .... **108** C3
16 Wandsworth
SW18 .... **59** B3
Bartholomew Ct
16 Blackwall E14 .... **34** C2
St Luke's EC1 .... **97** A2
Bartholomew Ho 22
SE5 .... **48** B1
Bartholomew La
EC2 .... **109** C1
Bartholomew Pas
EC1 .... **108** B3
Bartholomew Pl
EC1 .... **108** C3
Bartholomew Rd
NW5 .... **13** B2
Bartholomew Sq
18 Bethnal Green
E1 .... **25** A1
St Luke's EC1 .... **97** A2
Bartholomew St
SE1 .... **137** C1
Bartholomew Villas
NW5 .... **13** B2
Bartle Rd W11 .... **31** A3
Bartlett Cl E14 .... **33** C3
Bartlett Ct EC4 .... **107** C2
Bartok Ho
W11 .... **31** B2 **112** C3
Barton Cl
Hackney E9 .... **17** B3
Peckham SE15 .... **65** A4
Barton Ct
10 South Lambeth
SW4 .... **172** A2
West Kensington
W14 .... **140** B2
Barton Ho
8 Bromley E3 .... **27** A2

Barton Ho continued
Islington N1 .... **15** A1
Sands End SW6 .... **59** A4
Barton Rd W14 .... **140** B1
Barton St SW1 .... **134** A2
Bartonway NW8 .... **79** B2
Bartram Rd SE4 .... **66** A1
Bartrip St E9 .... **18** B2
Barts & The London
Sch of Medicine &
Dentistry EC1 .... **96** B1
Barville Cl SE4 .... **66** A3
Barwell Ho 7
E2 .... **24** C1 **99** C2
Barwick Ho **7** W3 .... **37** B4
Bascome St **13**
SW2 .... **62** C1
Base Apartments **8**
N1 .... **15** B1
Baseline Business
Studios **11** W11 .... **30** C2
Basevi Way SE8 .... **52** A4
Bashley Ho NW10 .... **20** C2
Basildon Ct W1 .... **103** C4
Basil Ho
South Lambeth
SW8 .... **162** A2
22 Whitechapel E1 .... **111** C2
Basil Mans SW1 .... **130** C3
Basil St
Knightsbridge
SW1 .... **130** C3
Knightsbridge SW1,
SW3 .... **130** C2
Basin App **20** E14 .... **33** A3
Basing Ct **13** SE15 .... **49** B2
Basing Hill NW11 .... 1 B3
Basing House Yd 2
E2 .... **24** A2 **98** B4
Basing Pl E2 .... **24** A2 **98** B4
Basing St W11 .... **31** B3
Basire St N1 .... **87** A4
Baskerville Ct
SW18 .... **72** A4
Baskerville Gdns
NW10 .... 8 A4
Baskerville Rd
SW18 .... **72** A4
Baslow Wlk E5 .... **17** C4
Basnett Rd 9
SW11 .... **60** C4
Basque Ct **21** SE16 .... **40** C4
Bassano St SE22 .... **64** B2
Bassein Park Rd
W12 .... **38** B4
Bassett House Sch **22**
W10 .... **30** C3
Bassett Rd W10 .... **30** C3
Bassett St NW5 .... **12** C2
Bassingbourn Ho **5**
N1 .... **15** A1
Bassingham Rd
SW18 .... **71** B4
Bassshaw Highwalk
EC2 .... **109** B3
Basswood Cl **5**
SE15 .... **65** A4
Basterfield Ho **6**
EC1 .... **96** C1
Bastion Highwalk
EC2 .... **108** C3
Bastwick St
EC1 .... **96** C2

Basuto Rd SW6 .... **165** C3
Batavia Ho 5
SE14 .... **51** A3
Batavia Mews **3**
SE14 .... **51** A3
Batavia Rd SE14 .... **51** A3
Batchelor St N1 .... **85** C3
Bateman Ho 8
SE17 .... **48** A4
Bateman Mews
SW4 .... **61** C1
Bateman's Bldgs
W1 .... **105** B1
Bateman's Row
EC2 .... **24** A1 **98** B2
Bateman St W1 .... **105** B1
Bate St **10** E14 .... **33** B2
Bath Cl SE15 .... **50** A3
Bath Ct
Finsbury EC1 .... **97** B3
17 Forest Hill SE26 .... **76** C1
Holborn EC1 .... **95** B1
Bathgate Ho 8
SW9 .... **48** A2
Bathgate Rd SW19 .... **69** C1
Bath Gr E2 .... **24** C3
Bath Ho
Bethnal Green
E2 .... **24** C1 **99** C2
Borough The SE1 .... **137** A2
Bath Pl
14 Hammersmith
W6 .... **39** B1
11 Shoreditch
EC2 .... **24** A2 **98** A3
Bath Rd W4 .... **38** A2
Bath St EC1 .... **97** B3
Bath Terr SE1 .... **136** C2
Bathurst Gdns
NW10 .... **22** A3
Bathurst Ho 7
W12 .... **30** A2
Bathurst Mews
W2 .... **115** C4
Bathurst St W2 .... **115** C4
Batley Pl 3 N16 .... 7 B1
Batley Rd N16 .... 7 B1
Batman Cl W12 .... **30** A1
Batoum Gdns W6 .... **39** B3
Batson Ho **21** E1 .... **111** C1
Batson St W12 .... **38** C4
Batten Ho
17 London SW4 .... **61** B2
10 West Kilburn
W10 .... **23** A2
Batten St SW11 .... **60** A4
BATTERSEA **169** A4
Battersea Bridge Rd
SW11 .... **158** A1
Battersea Bsns Ctr
SW11 .... **60** C4
Battersea Bsns Pk
SW8 .... **171** A3
Battersea Church Rd
SW11 .... **167** C4
Battersea Dogs &
Cats Home SW8 .... **160** B1
Battersea High St
SW11 .... **167** B1
Battersea Hts
SW11 .... **60** B4
Battersea Park **159** B1
Battersea Park Rd
SW11, SW8 .... **169** A3

Battersea Park Sta
SW8 .... **160** A1
Battersea Power
Station(dis)
SW8 .... **160** B1
Battersea Rise
SW11 .... **60** A3
Battersea Sq
SW11 .... **167** C3
Battishill St **9** N1 .... **15** A1
Battlebridge Ct
NW1 .... **84** B2
Battle Bridge La
SE1 .... **124** A2
Battledean Rd N5 .... **15** A3
Battle Ho **8** SE15 .... **49** C4
Batty St E1 .... **111** C2
Baty Ho SW2 .... **74** B3
Baulk The SW18 .... **70** C4
Bavaria Rd N19 .... 5 A2
Bavent Rd SE5 .... **48** B1
Bawdale Rd SE22 .... **64** B2
Bawtree Rd SE14 .... **51** A3
Baxendale St
E2 .... **24** C2 **99** B4
Baxter Ho **11** E3 .... **27** A2
Baxter Rd N1 .... **15** C2
Baycliffe Ho **8** E9 .... **17** C2
Bay Ct
Ealing W5 .... **36** A3
17 Stepney E1 .... **25** C1
Bayer Ho EC1 .... **96** C1
Bayes Ct NW3 .... **12** B1
Bayfield Ho 8
SE4 .... **65** C3
Bayford Ho SW2 .... **62** A2
Bayford St Ind Ctr **4**
E8 .... **17** A1
Bayford St **18** E8 .... **17** A1
Bayham Pl NW1 .... **83** A3
Bayham Rd W4 .... **37** C3
Bayham St NW1 .... **82** C3
Bayhurst Ho N4 .... 6 B4
Bayley St WC1 .... **105** B3
Baylis Rd SE1 .... **135** B3
Baynes Mews 2
NW3 .... **11** C2
Baynes St NW1 .... **13** B1
Bayon Ho **20** N19 .... 4 C4
Bayonne Rd W6 .... **154** A3
Bayston Rd N16 .... 7 B1
BAYSWATER **114** C3
Bayswater Rd W2 .... **115** A4
W2 .... **115** A3
Bayswater Sta
W2 .... **114** B4
Bayton Ct **2** E8 .... **16** C1
Baytree Ho 6
SE17 .... **151** B4
Baytree Rd SW2 .... **62** B3
Bazalgette Ho
NW8 .... **89** C2
Bazeley Ho SE1 .... **136** A3
Bazely St E14 .... **34** B2
Beach Ho SW5 .... **141** B2
Beachy Rd E3 .... **18** C1
Beaconfield Terrace
Rd W14 .... **126** A1
Beacon Gate SE14 .... **65** C3
Beacon Hill N7 .... **14** A3
Beacon Ho
11 Camberwell
SE5 .... **49** A3
7 Isle of Dogs
E14 .... **42** A1

Beacon Ho continued
South Lambeth
SW8 . . . . 171 B4
Beacon Rd SE13 . . . 67 C1
Beaconsfield Cl
Acton Green W4 . . . . 37 B1
Greenwich SE3 . . . . 53 C4
Beaconsfield Rd
Acton W4 . . . . 37 C3
Greenwich SE3 . . . . 53 C3
Walworth SE17 . . . . 152 A1
Willesden NW10 . . . . 8 B2
Beaconsfield Wlk
SW6 . . . . 165 A3
Beadon Rd W6 . . . . 39 B2
Beak St W1 . . . . . . 119 A4
Beale Ho 🔢 SW9 172 C1
Beale Pl E3 . . . . . . 26 B3
Beale Rd E3 . . . . . . 26 B4
Beames Ho SW8 . . 171 B4
Beames Rd NW10 . . 20 C4
Beaminster Ho 🔢
SW8 . . . . 162 C2
Beamish Ho 🔢
SE16 . . . . 40 B2
Beanacre Cl E9 . . . 18 B2
Bear Alley EC4 . . . . 108 A2
Bear Croft Ho 🔟
SW6 . . . . 164 C1
Beardsley Way
W3 . . . . 37 C4
Bear Gdns SE1 . . . 122 C2
Bear La SE1 . . . . . . 122 B1
Bear St WC2 . . . . . 119 C4
Bearstead Rise
SE4 . . . . 66 B2
Beaton Cl SE15 . . . 49 B2
Beatrice Ho
🔟 Brixton SW2 . . . 62 B2
🔟 Hammersmith
W6 . . . . 39 B1
🔟 Stepney E1 . . . . 32 C4
Beatrice Pl W8 . . . 128 A1
Beatrice Rd
Bermondsey SE1 . . 153 C3
Finsbury Pk N4 . . . . 5 C4
🔟 Richmond TW10 . 54 B1
Beatrice Tate Sch
Bow E3 . . . . 26 B1
🔟 E2 . . . . 25 A2
Beatrice Webb Ho 🔢
E3 . . . . 26 A3
Beatrix Ho SW5 . . . 142 B2
Beatrix Potter Prim
Sch SW18 . . . . 71 B3
Beatson Wlk 🔢
SE16 . . . . 32 C1
Beattie Ho SW8 . . . 171 A4
Beatty Ho 🔢 E14 . . 41 C4
Beatty Rd N16 . . . . 16 A4
Beatty St NW1 . . . . 82 C2
Beauchamp Cl 🔢
W4 . . . . 37 B3
Beauchamp Pl
SW3 . . . . 130 B1
Beauchamp Rd
SW11 . . . . 60 B3
Beauchamp St
EC1 . . . . 107 B3
Beauchamp Terr
SW15 . . . . 57 A4
Beauclerc Rd W6 . . 39 A3
Beauclerk Ho 🔟
SW16 . . . . 74 A1

Beaufort Cl SW19 . . 69 A4
Beaufort Ct SW6 . . 155 B4
Beaufort Gdns
SW3 . . . . 130 B2
Beaufort Ho
Battersea SW11 . . . 168 A2
Chelsea SW3 . . . . . 157 C3
🔟 Millwall E14 . . . . 41 C4
Pimlico SW1 . . . . . . 147 B1
Beaufort Mans
SW3 . . . . 157 C3
Beaufort Mews
SW6 . . . . 155 A4
Beaufort St SW3 . . 157 B4
Beaufoy Ho
South Lambeth
SW8 . . . . 162 C2
🔟 West Norwood
SE27 . . . . 75 A1
Beaufoy Rd 🔢
SW8 . . . . 61 A4
Beaufoy Wlk
SE11 . . . . 149 A3
Beaulieu Cl SE5 . . . 63 C4
Beaulieu Pl W4 . . . 37 B3
Beaumanor Mans
W2 . . . . 114 B4
Beaumaris Mews
SE23 . . . . 65 C1
Beaumaris Twr 🔢
W3 . . . . 37 A4
Beaumont Ave
Richmond TW9 . . . . 54 B4
West Kensington
W14 . . . . 140 C2
Beaumont Bldgs
WC2 . . . . 106 B1
Beaumont Cres
W14 . . . . 140 C1
Beaumont Ct
🔢 Acton Green
W4 . . . . 37 B1
Marylebone W1 . . . 103 C4
🔟 Mile End E1 . . . . 26 A2
Beaumont Gdns
NW3 . . . . 1 C1
Beaumont Gr E1 . . . 25 C1
Beaumont Ho
🔟 Streatham
SW2 . . . . 74 A3
West Kensington
W14 . . . . 141 A3
Wimbledon SW19 . . 70 C1
Beaumont Lo E8 . . . 16 C2
Beaumont Pl NW1, WC1,
W1 . . . . 93 A2
Beaumont Rd
Putney SW15,
SW19 . . . . 70 A4
🔟 South Acton W4 . 37 B3
Beaumont Rise N19 . 4 C3
Beaumont Sq E1 . . . 32 C4
Beaumont St W1 . . 103 C4
Beaumont Wlk
NW3 . . . . 12 B1
Beauvale 🔟 NW1 . . 12 C1
Beauval Rd SE22 . . 64 B1
Beavis Ho N16 . . . . 7 A1
Beavor La W6 . . . . . 38 C1
Beccles St E14 . . . . 33 B2
Beck Cl SE13 . . . . . 52 A2
Beckers The N16 . . . 16 C4
Becket Ho SE1 . . . . 137 B3
Becket St SE1 . . . . 137 B2

Beckett Cl
Streatham SW16 . . . 73 C2
Willesden NW10 . . . . 8 A2
Beckett Ho
🔢 London SW9 . . . 172 B1
🔟 Stepney E1 . . . . 32 B4
Beckfoot NW1 . . . . . 83 A1
Beckford Cl W14 . . 141 A3
Beckford Ho 🔢
N16 . . . . 16 A3
Beckford Pl SE17 . . 151 A1
Beckford Prim Sch
NW6 . . . . 10 B3
Beckham Ho
SE11 . . . . 149 A3
Beck Ho N16 . . . . . . 7 A1
Beckington 🔟
NW5 . . . . 12 C2
Beckley Ho E3 . . . . 26 B1
Becklow Gdns
Chiswick W12 . . . . . 38 B4
🔟 Shepherd's Bush
W12 . . . . 38 A4
Becklow Mews 🔢
W12 . . . . 38 A4
Becklow Rd W12 . . . 38 C4
Beck Rd E8 . . . . . . 25 A4
Beckton Rd E16 . . . 35 B4
Beckway St SE17 . . 152 A3
Beckwith Ho 🔢
E2 . . . . 25 A3
Beckwith Rd SE24 . . 63 C2
Bective Pl SW15 . . . 58 B3
Bective Rd SW15 . . 58 B3
Bedale St SE1 . . . . 123 B1
Bedefield WC1 . . . . 94 B3
Bede Ho
London SE14 . . . . . 51 B2
🔟 Putney SW15 . . . 57 C1
Bedford Ave WC1 . . 105 C3
Bedford Cnr 🔢
W4 . . . . 38 A2
Bedford Court Mans
WC1 . . . . 105 C3
Bedford Ct
🔟 Richmond
TW9 . . . . 54 B3
St James WC2 . . . . 120 A3
Bedford Gardens Ho
W8 . . . . 31 C1 113 C1
Bedford Gdns
W8 . . . . 31 C1 113 C1
Bedford Hill SW12 . . 73 A2
Bedford Ho
🔢 Acton W4 . . . . . 38 A2
🔢 Stockwell SW4 . . 62 A3
BEDFORD PARK . . . 38 A3
Bedford Park Cnr 🔢
W4 . . . . 38 A2
Bedford Park Mans 🔢
W4 . . . . 37 C2
Bedford Pas SW6 . . 154 B2
Bedford Pl WC1 . . . 106 A4
Bedford Rd
Acton W4 . . . . 38 A3
Stockwell SW2,
SW4 . . . . 62 A3
Bedford Row
WC1 . . . . 107 A3
Bedford Sq WC1 . . 105 C3
Bedford St WC2 . . . 120 B3
Bedford Way WC1 . . 93 C1
Bedgebury Gdns
SW19 . . . . 70 A2

Bedlam Mews 🔢
SE11 . . . . 149 B4
Bedlow Cl NW8 . . . . 89 C1
Bedser Cl 🔢 SE11 . 163 A4
Bedser Ct 🔢 SW4 . 172 A2
Bedwell Ho 🔢
SW9 . . . . 173 B1
Beech Ave W3 . . . . 29 A1
Beech Cl
Deptford SE8 . . . . . 51 B4
Putney SW15 . . . . . 68 C4
Beechcroft Ave
NW11 . . . . 1 B4
Beechcroft Ct
🔢 Golders Green
NW11 . . . . 1 C4
Greenwich SE3 . . . . 53 C2
Beech Croft Ct N5 . . 15 A4
Beechcroft Rd
Mortlake SW14 . . . . 55 B4
Upper Tooting
SW17 . . . . 72 A2
Beechcroft Way
N19 . . . . 4 C3
Beechdale Rd
SW2 . . . . 62 B1
Beechdene 🔢
SE15 . . . . 50 A2
Beeches Rd SW17 . . 72 B1
Beeches The 🔢
N19 . . . . 5 A3
Beechey Ho 🔢 E1 . 32 A1
Beech Gdns W5 . . . 36 A3
Beech Ho
🔢 Maitland Pk
NW3 . . . . 12 B2
🔟 Rotherhithe
SE16 . . . . 40 B4
🔟 Stoke Newington
N16 . . . . 6 C2
Beechmore Rd
SW11 . . . . 169 A3
Beech St EC2 . . . . . 109 A4
Beech Tree Cl N1 . . 14 C1
Beechwood Ave
TW9 . . . . 44 C2
Beechwood Ct
Chiswick W4 . . . . . 45 C4
Stamford Hill N16 . . . 7 A4
Beechwood Gr
W3 . . . . 29 A2
Beechwood Ho 🔢
E2 . . . . 24 C3
Beechwood Rd E8 . . 16 B2
Beechworth Cl
NW3 . . . . 1 C2
Beecroft Garden Prim
Sch SE4 . . . . 66 A2
Beecroft La SE4 . . . 66 A2
Beecroft Mews
SE4 . . . . 66 A2
Beecroft Rd SE4 . . . 66 A2
Beehive Cl E8 . . . . 16 B1
Beehive Pl SW9 . . . 62 C4
Beeston Cl 🔢 E8 . . 16 C3
Beeston's Ho SE15 . 65 B3
Beethoven St W10 . . 23 A2
Begbie Ho SW9 . . . 173 A2
Begonia Wlk W12 . . 29 B3

Beira St SW12 . . . . 73 A4
Beis Chinuch Lebonos
Girls Sch N4 . . . . . . 6 B4
Beis Malka Girls Sch
N16 . . . . 7 B4
Beis Rochel d'Satmar
Girls Sch 🔢 N16 . . . 7 A4
Beis Trana Girls Sch
N16 . . . . 6 C2
Beis Yaakov Girls Sch
N16 . . . . 6 C2
Bekesbourne St 🔟
E14 . . . . 33 A3
Beldanes Lo NW10 . . 8 C1
Belenoyd Ct SW16 . 74 B1
Belfast Rd N16 . . . . 7 B2
Belfont Wlk N7 . . . . 14 A4
Belford Ho 🔢 E8 . . 24 B4
Belfort Rd SE15 . . . 50 B1
Belfry Cl 🔢 SE16 . . 40 A1
Belgrade Ho N16 . . 16 A4
Belgrade Rd N16 . . 16 A4
Belgrave Cl 🔢 W3 . 37 B4
Belgrave Ct
🔢 Acton Green
W4 . . . . 37 B1
🔢 Limehouse E14 . 33 B2
🔟 South Lambeth
SW8 . . . . 160 C1
Belgrave Gdns
Kilburn NW8 . . . . . 78 C3
St John's Wood
NW8 . . . . 78 C3
Belgrave Mews N
SW1 . . . . 131 B3
Belgrave Mews S
SW1 . . . . 131 C2
Belgrave Mews W
SW1 . . . . 131 B2
Belgrave Pl SW1 . . 131 C2
Belgrave Rd
Barnes SW13 . . . . . 46 B3
Westminster SW1 . . 146 C3
Belgrave Sq SW1 . . 131 B2
Belgrave St E1 . . . . 32 C3
Belgrave Yd SW1 . . 132 A1
BELGRAVIA 146 A4
Belgravia Ct SW1 . . 132 A1
Belgravia Ho 🔢
SW4 . . . . 61 C1
Belgrave W WC1 . . 94 B4
Belham Wlk 🔟
SE5 . . . . 48 C2
Belinda Rd 🔢
SW9 . . . . 63 A4
Belitha Villas N1 . . 14 C1
Bellamy Cl
🔟 Millwall E14 . . . 41 C4
🔟 West Kensington
SW5 . . . . 141 A1
Bellamy's Ct 🔟
SE16 . . . . 32 C1
Bellamy St SW12 . . 73 A4
Bellasis Ave SW2 . . 74 A2
Bell Ct SE13 . . . . . 66 C2
Bell Dr SW18 . . . . . 70 A4
Bellefields Rd
SW9 . . . . 62 B4
Bellenden Prim Sch
🔟 SE15 . . . . 64 C4
Bellenden Rd
SE15 . . . . 49 B1
Bellenden Rd Ret Pk
SE15 . . . . 49 C2

Bellendon Road Bsns
Ctr SE15 ....49 B1
Bellerbys Coll SE8 ..51 C4
Belleville Primary Sch
SW11 ....60 C3
Belleville Prim Sch
SW11 ....60 B2
Belleville Rd SW11 ..60 B2
Belle Vue Gdns
SW11 ....172 B1
Bellevue Pl E1 ....25 B1
Bellevue Rd
Barnes SW13 ......46 C1
Upper Tooting
SW17 ....72 B3
Bellew St SW17 .....71 B1
Bell Flats E4 NW2 .....8 C2
Bellflower Ct SE13 ..67 A3
Bellgate Mews
NW5 ....4 A1
Bellgrave Lo E9 ......
W4 ....37 A1
Bell Ho
Greenwich SE10 ....52 B4
15 Streatham SW2 ..74 C4
Bellina Mews NW5 ...13 B4
Bell Ind Est E4 W4 ...37 B2
Bell Inn Yd EC3 .....109 C1
Bell La
Newham E16 ....35 C1
Spitalfields E1 .....110 C3
Bellmaker Ct 13
E3 ....33 C4
Bell Moor NW3 ....2 B1
Bello Cl SE24, SW2 ..75 A3
Bellot Gdns 1
SE10 ....43 A1
Bellot St SE10 ....43 A1
Bell St NW1 ....102 A4
Bell Wharf La
EC4 ....123 A4
Bellwood Rd SE15 ...65 C3
Bell Yard Mews
SE1 ....138 B3
Bell Yd WC2 ....107 B1
Belmont Ct 4
NW11 ....1 C4
Belmont Gr
Chiswick W4 ....37 C2
Lewisham SE13 .....67 C4
Belmont Hall Ct
SE13 ....67 C4
Belmont Hill SE13 ..67 C4
Belmont Mews
SW19 ....69 C2
Belmont Prim Sch 10
W4 ....37 C2
Belmont Rd
Clapham SW4 ......61 B4
London W4 ....37 C2
Belmont St NW1 .....12 C1
Belmont Terr W4 ....37 C2
Belmore Ho N7 .....13 C3
Belmore La N7 ......13 C3
Belmore St SW8 ...171 B4
Beloe Cl SW15 ......56 C2
Belper Ct 11 E5 .....17 C4
Belsham St E9 ......17 B2
Belsize Ave NW3 ....12 A3
Belsize Court Garages
1 NW3 ....11 C3
Belsize Cres NW3 ...11 C2

Belsize Ct NW3 ......11 C3
Belsize Gr NW3 .....11 C2
Belsize La NW3 .....11 C3
Belsize Mews
NW3 ....11 C3
Belsize Park Gdns
NW3 ....12 A2
Belsize Park Mews 1
NW3 ....11 C2
Belsize Park Sta
NW3 ....12 A3
Belsize Pk NW3 .....11 C2
Belsize Pl NW3 .....11 C3
Belsize Rd NW6 .....78 B4
Belsize Sq NW3 .....11 C2
Belsize Terr NW3 ...11 C2
Beltane Dr SW19 ...69 C1
Belthorn Cres
SW12 ....73 B4
Belton Rd NW2 ......8 C2
Belton Way E2 ......33 C4
Beltran Rd SW6 ....166 A1
Belvedere Bldgs
SE1 ....136 B3
Belvedere Htss
NW8 ....90 A2
Belvedere Mews
SE15 ....65 B4
Belvedere Pl
Brixton SW2 ....62 B3
Lambeth SE1 .....136 B3
Belvedere Rd SE1 ..121 A1
Belvedere The
Belvoir Lo SE22 .....76 C4
Belvoir Rd SE22 .....76 C4
Bembridge Cl
NW6 ....10 A1
Bembridge Ho
5 Deptford SE8 ....41 B2
Wandsworth SW18 ..59 A1
Bemerton St N1 .....84 C4
Bemish Rd SW15 ....57 C4
Benabo Ct E8 E8 ....16 C3
Benbow Ct W6 ......39 A3
Benbow Ho 12
SE8 ....51 C4
Benbow Rd W6 .....39 A3
Benbow St SE8 .....51 C4
Bence Ho 15 SE8 ...41 A2
Bendall Mews
NW1 ....102 B4
Bendemeer Rd
SW15 ....57 C4
Benden Ho SE13 ....67 B2
Bendon Valley
SW18 ....71 A4
Benedict Rd SW9 ..62 B4
Benenden Ho
SE17 ....152 B2
Benenden Ho
SE17 ....152 B2
Ben Ezra Ct SE17 ..151 A3
Benfleet Ct 8 E8 ...24 B4
Bengal Ct EC3 .....109 C1
Bengal Ho E1 ......32 C4
Bengeworth Rd
SE5 ....63 B4
Benham Cl 27
SW11 ....59 C4
Benham Ho 11 SW10 156 B2

Benham's Pl 11
NW3 ....11 B4
Benhill Rd E5 ....48 C2
Benington Ct N4 ....6 B2
Benjamin Cl E8 .....24 C4
Benjamin Franklin
House NW1 ......120 A2
Benjamin Ho 12
W3 ....28 A1
Benjamin Mews
SW12 ....73 B4
Benjamin St EC1 ...108 A4
Ben Jonson Ct 30
N1 ....24 A3
Ben Jonson Prim Sch
E1 ....25 C1
Ben Jonson Rd E1 ..33 A4
Benkart Mews 6
SW15 ....56 C1
Benledi Rd E14 .....34 C3
Bennelong Cl SW9 ..173 B4
Bennerley Rd
SW11 ....60 B2
Bennet's Hill EC4 ..122 B4
Bennett Ct
Hampstead NW6 ...11 A2
Lower Holloway N7 ..5 B1
7 South Acton W3 ..37 A4
Bennett Ho SE13 ...52 A2
Bennett Ho
2 Streatham
SW2 ....74 B4
Westminster SW1 ..147 C4
Bennett St
Chiswick W4 ....38 A1
St James SW1 .....118 C2
Bennett's Yd SW1 ..133 C1
Benn Ho E2 ....25 B2
Benns Wlk 8 TW9 ...54 A3
Bensbury Cl SW15 ..69 B4
Ben Smith Way 1
SE16 ....139 C2
Benson Ct
South Lambeth
SW8 ....172 A4
7 Tufnell Pk N19 ...13 B4
Benson Ho
Lambeth SE1 .....121 C1
Shoreditch
E2 ....24 B1 98 C2
Benson Quay E1 ....32 B2
Benthal Ct N16 .....7 C1
Benthal Prim Sch
N16 ....7 C1
Benthal Rd N16 .....7 C1
Bentham Ct 11 N1 ..15 B1
Bentham Ho SE1 ...137 B2
Bentham Rd E9 .....17 C2
Bentinck Cl NW8 ...80 B1
Bentinck Ho 5
W12 ....30 A2
Bentinck Mans
W1 ....103 C2
Bentinck Mews
W1 ....103 C2
Bentinck St W1 ....103 C2
Bentley Cl SW19 ....70 C1
Bentley Ct SE13 ....67 B3
Bentley Dr NW2 ....10 B1
Bentley Ho
8 Bow E3 ....26 C1
5 Camberwell SE5 ..49 A2
Bentworth Ct 1
E2 ....24 C1 99 B2

Bentworth Prim Sch
W12 ....30 A3
Bentworth Rd
W12 ....30 A3
Benwell Rd N7 .....14 C3
Benwick Cl SE16 ....40 A2
Benworth St E3 .....26 B2
Benyon Ho EC1 .....95 C4
Benyon Rd N1 ......87 C4
Benyon Wharf 81
E8 ....24 A4
Beormund Prim Sch
SE1 ....137 C3
Bequerel Ct SE10 ...43 B3
Berberis Ho 17 E3 ..33 C4
Berber Pl 2 E14 ....33 C2
Berber Rd SW11 ....60 B2
Berebinder Ho 11
E3 ....26 B3
Berenger Twr
SW10 ....157 B2
Berenger Wlk
SW10 ....157 B2
Berens Rd NW10 ...22 C2
Beresford Ct E9 ....18 A3
Beresford Ho
Dulwich SE21 ......76 A1
15 Stockwell SW4 ..62 A3
Beresford Lo N4 ....15 C3
Beresford Rd N5 ...15 C3
Beresford Terr 3
N5 ....15 B3
Berestede Rd 4
W6 ....38 B1
Bergen Ho 1 SE5 ..48 B1
Bergen Sq SE16 ....41 A3
Berger Prim Sch 30
E9 ....17 C2
Berger Rd E9 ......17 C2
Berghem Mews
W14 ....39 C3
Bergholt Cres N16 ..7 A4
Bergholt Mews 4
NW1 ....13 C1
Berglen Ct E14 .....33 A2
Bering Sq E14 ......41 C1
Berisford Mews
SW18 ....59 B1
Berkeley Ct
1 Golders Green
NW11 ....1 B4
Marylebone NW1 ...91 A1
Willesden NW10 ....8 A4
Berkeley Gdns
W8 ....31 C1 113 C1
Berkeley Ho
12 Bow E3 ....26 C2
6 Deptford SE8 ....41 B1
Berkeley Mews
W1 ....103 A1
Berkeley Rd SW13 ..46 C2
Berkeley Sq W1 ...118 B3
Berkeley St W1 ....118 B2
Berkeley The NW11 ..2 A4
Berkeley Wlk 1 N7 ..5 B2
Berkley Gr NW1 ....12 C1
Berkley Rd NW1 ....12 C1
Berkshire Ho
WC2 ....106 A2
Berkshire Rd E9 ....18 B2
Bermans Way
NW10 ....8 B4
BERMONDSEY 40 A4
Bermondsey Leather
Mkt SE1 ....138 A3

Bermondsey Sq
SE1 ....138 B2
Bermondsey St
SE1 ....138 B2
Bermondsey Sta
SE16 ....40 A3
Bermondsey Trad Est
SE16 ....40 B1
Bermondsey Wall E 1
SE16 ....40 A4
Bermondsey Wall W
SE1, SE16 ....139 B4
Bernard Angell Ho 4
SE10 ....52 C4
Bernard Cassidy St 2
E16 ....35 B4
Bernard Ho 1 E1 ..110 C3
Bernard Shaw Ct 5
NW1 ....13 B1
Bernard St WC1 ....94 B1
Bernay's Gr SW9 ...62 B3
Berners Ho N1 .....85 B2
Berners Mews
W1 ....105 A3
Berners Pl W1 .....105 A2
Berners Rd N1 .....86 A3
Berners St W1 .....105 A2
Berner Terr 2 E1 ..111 C1
Bernhard Baron Ho 28
E1 ....111 C1
Bernhardt Cres
NW8 ....90 A2
Bernie Grant Ho 40
E9 ....17 B1
Bernwood Ho
N4 ....6 C4
Berridge Mews
NW6 ....10 C3
Berriman Rd N7 ....5 B1
Berry Cotts 2 E14 ..33 A3
Berryfield Rd
SE17 ....150 B2
Berry Ho
10 Battersea
SW11 ....169 A2
22 Bethnal Green
E1 ....25 A1
Berrymead Gdns
W3 ....37 B4
Berrymede Inf Sch
W3 ....37 A4
Berrymede Jun Sch
W3 ....37 A4
Berrymede Rd W4 ..37 C3
Berry Pl EC1 ....96 B3
Berry St EC1 ....96 B1
Berry Way W5 ......36 A3
Bertha Neubergh Ho
1 SE5 ....48 B2
Berthon St SE8 ....51 C3
Bertie Rd NW10 ....8 C2
Bertram St N19 ....4 A2
Bertrand Ho 11
SW16 ....74 A1
Bertrand St SE13 ..67 A4
Bertrum House Sch
SW17 ....72 C2
Berwick St W1 .....105 A1

Berwick Street Mkt
W1 ....105 A1
Berwyn Ho 3 N16 ..7 B3
Berwyn Rd
Mortlake SW14,
TW10 ....55 A3

Berwyn Rd *continued*
Streatham SE24 . . . . .**75** A3
Beryl Rd W6 . . . .**39** C1
Besant Cl NW2 . . . .**1** A1
Besant Ct N1 . . . .**15** C3
Besant Ho NW8 . . . . . .**78** C3
Besant Pl SE22 . . . .**64** B3
Besant Rd NW2 . . . . . .**10** A4
Besant Wlk N7 . . . .**5** B2
Besford Ho E2 . . . .**24** C3
Bessant Dr TW9 . . . . . .**45** A2
Bessborough Gdns
SW1 . . . .**147** C2
Bessborough Pl
SW1 . . . .**147** C2
Bessborough Rd
SW15 . . . .**68** C3
Bessborough St
SW1 . . . .**147** B2
Bessemer Ct ⁊
NW1 . . . .**13** B1
Bessemer Grange
Prim Sch SE5 . . . . .**64** A3
Bessemer Park Ind
Est ⁊ SE24 . . . .**63** B2
Bessemer Rd SE5 . . . .**48** B1
Bessingham Wlk
SE4 . . . .**65** C2
Besson St SE14 . . . . . .**50** C2
Bessy St E2 . . . .**25** B2
Bestwood St SE8 . . . . .**40** C2
Beswick Mews ⁊
NW6 . . . .**11** A2
Beta Pl ⁊ SW4 . . . . . .**62** B3
Betchworth Ho ⁊
N7 . . . .**13** C3
Bethersden Ho
SE17 . . . .**152** B2
Bethlehem Ho ⁊
E14 . . . .**33** B2
BETHNAL GREEN . .**25** A2
Bethnal Green Rd
Bethnal Green
E2 . . . .**24** C2 **99** B3
Shoreditch E1,
E2 . . . .**24** B1 **99** A2
Bethnal Green Sta
Bethnal Green E1 . .**25** A1
Bethnal Green E2 . .**25** B2
Bethune Rd
North Acton
NW10 . . . .**20** C1
Stamford Hill N16 . . .**7** A4
Bethwin Rd SE5 . . . . .**48** B3
Betsam Ho SE1 . . . .**137** B4
Betterton Ho
WC2 . . . .**106** B1
Betterton St WC2 . .**106** B1
Bettridge Rd SW6 . .**165** A1
Betts Ho E1 . . . .**32** A2
Betts St E1 . . . .**32** A2
Betty Layward Prim
Sch ⁊ N16 . . . .**6** C1
Betty May Gray Ho ⁊
E14 . . . .**42** B2
Bevan St N1 . . . .**87** A3
Bev Callender Cl ⁊
SW8 . . . .**61** A4
Bevenden St N1 . . . . .**97** C4
Beveridge Rd ⁊
NW10 . . . .**8** A1
Beverley Cl
Barnes SW13 . . . . . .**46** C1
⁊ Wandsworth
SW11 . . . .**59** C3

Beverley Cotts
SW15 . . . .**68** A1
Beverley Ct
⁊ Acton Green
W4 . . . .**37** B1
⁊ Acton W12 . . . . . .**38** A4
Brockley SE4 . . . .**66** B4
Islington N5 . . . .**15** A2
Beverley Gdns
Barnes SW13 . . . . . .**56** B4
Hendon NW11 . . . .**1** A4
Beverley Lo ⁊
E2 . . . .**54** A2
Beverley Path ⁊
SW13 . . . .**46** B1
Beverley Rd
Barnes SW13 . . . . . .**56** B4
Chiswick W4 . . . .**38** B1
Beverstock Rd
N19 . . . .**5** A2
Beverstone Rd
SW2 . . . .**62** B2
Beverstone Mews
NW1 . . . .**102** C3
Bevin Cl SE16 . . . .**33** A1
Bevin Ct WC1 . . . .**95** A4
Bevington Prim Sch
⁊ W10 . . . .**31** A4
Bevington Rd W10 . .**31** A4
Bevington St
SE16 . . . .**139** C3
Bevin Ho
⁊⁊ Bethnal Green
E2 . . . .**25** B2
⁊ Bow E3 . . . .**26** C2
Bevin Sq SW17 . . . . . .**72** B1
Bevin Way WC1 . . . . . .**95** B4
Bevis Marks EC3 . .**110** B2
Bew Ct SE21 . . . .**76** C4
Bewdley Ho N4 . . . .**6** B4
Bewdley St N1 . . . .**14** C1
Bewick Mews
SE15 . . . .**50** A3
Bewick St SW8 . . . .**170** B1
Bewley Ct SW2 . . . . . .**62** B1
Bewley Ho ⁊ E1 . . . . .**32** A2
Bewley St E1 . . . .**32** A2
Bexhill Rd
Catford SE4 . . . .**66** B1
Mortlake SW14 . . . . . .**55** B4
Bexley Ho SE4 . . . .**66** A3
BFI Imax (Cinema)
SE1 . . . .**121** B1
BFI Southbank
SE1 . . . .**121** A2
Bianca Rd SE1,
SE15 . . . .**49** C4
Bibury Cl SE15 . . . .**49** A4
Bicester Rd TW9 . . . . .**55** A4
Bickenhall Mans
W1 . . . .**103** A4
Bickenhall St W1 . .**103** A4
Bickerton Rd N19 . . . . .**4** B2
Bicknell Ho ⁊ E1 . .**111** C1
Bicknell Rd SE5 . . . . . .**63** B4
Bicknor Ho ⁊ E5 . . . . .**17** A3
Bicycle Mews ⁊⁊
SW4 . . . .**61** C4
Bidborough St N1,
WC1 . . . .**94** A3
Biddenham Ho ⁊⁊
SE16 . . . .**40** C2
Bidder St E16 . . . .**35** A4
Biddesden Ho
SW3 . . . .**144** C3
Biddestone Rd N7 . . . .**14** B4

Bidulph Mans
W9 . . . .**88** B3
Biddulph Rd W9 . . . . .**88** B3
Bidwell St SE15 . . . . . .**50** A2
Big Ben SW1 . . . .**134** B3
Biggerstaff Rd
E15 . . . .**27** B4
Biggerstaff St N4 . . . . .**5** C2
Bigg's Row SW15 . . . .**57** C4
Biggs Sq ⁊⁊ E9 . . . . . .**18** B2
Bigland Green Prim
Sch ⁊⁊ E1 . . . .**32** A3
Bigland St E1 . . . .**32** A3
Bilberry Ho ⁊⁊ E3 . . . .**33** C4
Billie Holiday Ct
NW10 . . . .**20** C3
Billingford Cl SE4 . . . .**65** C3
Billing Ho ⁊ E1 . . . . . .**32** C3
Billingley NW1 . . . .**82** C3
Billing Pl SW10 . . . .**156** B2
Billing Rd SW10 . . . .**156** B2
Billingsgate Mkt
E14 . . . .**34** A1
Billing St SW10 . . . .**156** B2
Billington Ho
SW8 . . . .**171** C3
Billington Rd SE14 . . .**50** C3
Billiter Sq EC3 . . . . .**110** B1
Billiter St EC3 . . . . .**110** B1
Billson St E14 . . . .**42** B2
Bilton Ho SW8 . . . . .**171** B3
Bilton Twrs W1 . . . . .**103** A1
Bina Gdns SW5 . . . .**142** C3
Binbrook Ho ⁊⁊
W10 . . . .**30** B4
Binden Rd W12 . . . .**38** B3
Binfield Ct SE5 . . . . . .**48** B1
Binfield Rd SW4 . . . .**172** B3
Bingfield St N1 . . . . . .**84** C4
Bingham Pl W1 . . . .**103** B4
Bingham St N1 . . . . . .**15** C2
Binley Ho SW15 . . . . . .**56** B1
Binney St W1 . . . . . .**103** C1
Binnie Ct SE10 . . . .**52** A3
Binnie Ho SE1 . . . . .**136** C1
Binns Rd W4 . . . .**38** A1
Binns Terr ⁊ W4 . . . . .**38** A1
Binstead Ho SW18 . . . .**59** C3
Binyon Ho ⁊ N16 . . . . .**16** A4
Birbeck Ho ⁊⁊ N19 . . . .**4** C3
Bircham Path SE4 . . . .**65** C3
Birch Cl
Newham E16 . . . .**35** A4
Peckham SE15 . . . . . .**49** C1
Upper Holloway N19 . .**4** B2
Birchdown Ho ⁊⁊
E3 . . . .**27** A2
Birches The SE5 . . . . . .**49** A1
Birchfield Ho ⁊
E14 . . . .**33** C2
Birchfield St E14 . . . . .**33** C2
Birchgrove Ho
TW9 . . . .**45** A3
Birch Ho
New Cross Gate
SE14 . . . .**51** B2
⁊⁊ Tulse Hill SW2 . .**62** C1
Birchington Ct ⁊⁊
NW6 . . . .**78** A4
Birchington Ho ⁊⁊
E5 . . . .**17** A3
Birchington Rd
NW6 . . . .**23** C4
Birchin La EC3 . . . . .**109** C1
Birchlands Ave
SW12 . . . .**72** B4

Birchmere Lo ⁊⁊
SE16 . . . .**40** A1
Birchmere Row
SE3 . . . .**53** B1
Birchmore Wlk N5 . . . .**6** B1
Birch Vale Ct NW8 . . .**89** C2
Birchwood Dr NW3 . . . .**2** A1
Birch Yd ⁊⁊ SW13 . . . .**46** B1
Birdcage Wlk
SW1 . . . .**133** B3
Birdhurst Rd
SW18 . . . .**59** B2
Bird In Bush Rd
SE15 . . . .**49** C3
Bird In Hand Yd ⁊⁊
NW3 . . . .**11** B4
Birdsall Ho ⁊⁊ SE5 . . .**64** A4
Birdsfield La ⁊⁊
E3 . . . .**26** B4
Bird St W1 . . . .**103** C1
Birdwood Ave ⁊
SE13 . . . .**67** C1
Birkbeck Ave W3 . . . . .**28** B2
Birkbeck Coll W1 . . .**105** C2
Birkbeck Gr W3 . . . . . .**37** C4
Birkbeck Hill SE21 . . . .**75** A3
Birkbeck Mews ⁊⁊
E8 . . . .**16** B3
Birkbeck Pl SE21 . . . . .**75** B2
Birkbeck Rd
Acton W3 . . . .**28** C1
Dalston E8 . . . .**16** B3
Stratford New Town
E15 . . . .**76** C4
Birkbeck St E2 . . . .**25** A2
Birkbeck Univ of
London W1 . . . .**93** B2
Birkdale Cl ⁊⁊
SE16 . . . .**40** A1
Birkenhead Ho ⁊⁊
N7 . . . .**14** C3
Birkenhead St
WC1 . . . .**94** B4
Birkwood Cl SW12 . . . .**73** C4
Birley Lo NW8 . . . .**79** C2
Birley St SW11 . . . . .**169** B1
Birnam Rd N4 . . . .**5** B2
Birrell Ho ⁊⁊ SW9 . . .**172** C1
Birse Cres NW10 . . . . . .**8** A4
Birtwhistle Ho ⁊
E3 . . . .**26** B4
Biscay Ho ⁊⁊ E1 . . . . .**25** C1
Biscay Rd W6 . . . .**39** C1
Biscoe Way SE13 . . . . .**67** C4
Biscott Ho ⁊ E3 . . . . . .**27** A1
Biscuit Factory The
SE16 . . . .**40** A3
Bisham Gdns N6 . . . . . .**3** C3
Bishop Challoner
Catholic Federation
of Schools ⁊⁊ E1 . .**32** B3
Bishop Ct ⁊⁊ SW2 . . . .**62** C1
Bishop Duppa's
Almshouses ⁊
TW10 . . . .**54** A2
Bishop King's Rd
W14 . . . .**140** B4
Bishop's Ave SW6 . .**164** A2
Bishop's Bridge Rd
W2 . . . .**100** C2
Bishops Cl W4 . . . .**37** B1
Bishop's Cl N19 . . . .**4** B1
Bishops Ct
⁊⁊ Bayswater
W2 . . . .**100** A2
Richmond TW9 . . . . . .**54** A4
Bishop's Ct
Holborn EC4 . . . . . .**108** A2

Bishop's Ct *continued*
Holborn WC2 . . . . . .**107** B2
Bishopsdale Ho ⁊⁊
NW6 . . . .**23** C4
Bishopsgate EC2 . . .**110** A2
Bishopsgate Arc
E1 . . . .**110** B3
Bishopsgate
Churchyard EC2 . .**110** A2
Bishopsgate Inst
EC2 . . . .**110** B3
Bishops Ho SW8 . . .**162** B1
Bishop's Mans
SW6 . . . .**47** C1
Bishops Mead SE5 . . . .**48** B3
Bishop's Park Rd
SW6 . . . .**47** C1
Bishops Rd SW6 . . .**164** C4
Bishops Sq E1 . . . . .**110** B4
Bishop St N1 . . . .**86** C4
Bishop's Terr
SE11 . . . .**149** C4
Bishopstone Ho ⁊⁊
SW11 . . . .**169** B2
Bishop's Way E2 . . . . .**25** B3
Bishopswood Rd
N6 . . . .**3** B4
Bishop Wilfred Wood
Cl SE15 . . . .**49** C1
Bisley Ho SW19 . . . . . .**69** C2
Bissextile Ho SE13 . . .**52** A1
Bisson Rd E15 . . . .**27** B3
Bittern Ct ⁊⁊ SE8 . . . .**51** C4
Bittern Ho SE1 . . . . .**136** C3
Bittern St SE1 . . . . .**136** C3
Blackall St
EC2 . . . .**24** A1 **98** A2
Blackburn Ct ⁊⁊
SW2 . . . .**62** C1
Blackburne's Mews
W1 . . . .**117** B3
Blackburn Rd
NW6 . . . .**11** A2
Blackdown Ho E8 . . . .**16** C4
Blackett St SW15 . . . . .**57** C4
Blackfriars Bridge
EC4 . . . .**122** A3
Blackfriars Ct
EC4 . . . .**122** A4
Black Friars La
EC4 . . . .**108** A1
Blackfriars Pas
EC4 . . . .**122** A4
Blackfriars Pier
EC4 . . . .**122** A4
Blackfriars Rd
SE1 . . . .**122** B1
Blackfriars Underpass
EC4 . . . .**121** C4
Blackheath SE3 . . . . . .**53** A2
Blackheath Ave
SE3 . . . .**53** A3
Blackheath Bsns Est
SE10 . . . .**52** B2
Blackheath Gr SE3 . . . .**53** B2
Blackheath High Sch
Blackheath SE3 . . . . .**53** B1
Greenwich SE3 . . . . . .**53** C3
Blackheath Hill
SE10 . . . .**52** B2
Blackheath Prep Sch
SE3 . . . .**53** C2
Blackheath Rd
SE10 . . . .**52** A2

Blackheath Rise
SE13 . . . . .52 B1
**BLACKHEATH
VALE** 53 B1
Blackheath Vale
SE3 . . . . .53 A1
Blackheath Village
SE3 . . . . .53 B1
Black Horse Ct
SE1 . . . . .137 C2
Blackhorse Rd
SE8 . . . . .51 A4
Blacklands Terr
SW3 . . . . .145 A3
Black Lion La W6 . .38 C2
Black Lion Mews 4
W6 . . . . .38 C2
Blackmore Ho
Islington N1 . . . . . .85 A3
2 Wandsworth
SW18 . . . . .59 A4
Blackmore Twr 1
W3 . . . . .37 B3
Blackpool Rd
SE15 . . . . .50 A1
Black Prince Rd SE1,
SE11 . . . . .148 C4
Black Roof Ho 9
SE5 . . . . .48 A2
Black's Rd W6 . . . .39 B2
Blackstock Ho 5
N5 . . . . .6 A1
Blackstock Mews
N4 . . . . .6 A1
Blackstock Rd N4,
N5 . . . . .6 A1
Blackstone Ho
Dulwich SE21 . . . . .76 A1
Pimlico SW1 . . . .146 C1
Blackstone Rd NW2 .9 B4
Black Swan Yd
SE1 . . . . .138 A4
Blackthorn Ct
20 Camberwell
SE15 . . . . .49 B3
4 Leyton E15 . . . . .19 C4
Blackthorn St E3 . .26 C1
Blacktree Mews 11
SW9 . . . . .62 C4
BLACKWALL 34 C2
Blackwall Sta E14 . .34 B2
Blackwall Trad Est
E14 . . . . .34 C2
Blackwall Tunnel E14,
SE10 . . . . .43 A4
**Blackwall Tunnel
Northern Approach**
E14, E3 . . . . .27 B1
Blackwall Way
E14 . . . . .34 B2
Blackwater Ho
NW8 . . . . .101 C4
Blackwell Cl 10
E5 . . . . .17 C4
Blackwood Ho 1
E1 . . . . .25 A1
Blackwood St
SE17 . . . . .151 B2
Blade Mews SW15 .58 B3

Bladen Ho 4 E1 . .32 C3
Blades Ct
6 Hammersmith
W6 . . . . .39 A1
Putney SW15 . . . . .58 B3
Blades Ho 12
SE11 . . . . .163 B3
Blades Lo 6 SW2 . .62 C1
Blagdon Rd SE13 . .67 A1
Blagrove Rd 1
W10 . . . . .31 B4
Blair Cl N1 . . . . . . .15 B2
Blair Ct NW8 . . . . . .79 B4
Blairderry Rd SW2 .74 A2
Blairgowrie Ct 13
E14 . . . . .34 C3
Blair Ho SW9 . . . .172 C2
Blair St E14 . . . . . .34 C3
Blake Coll W1 . . .104 C4
Blake Ct
8 Bermondsey
SE16 . . . . .40 A1
Kilburn NW6 . . . . .23 C2
Blake Gdns SW6 . .166 A4
Blake Ho
2 Deptford SE8 . . .51 C4
Isle Of Dogs E14 . .42 A4
1 Kentish Town
N19 . . . . .13 C3
Lambeth SE11 . . . .135 B2
16 Stoke Newington
N16 . . . . .16 A4
Blake Mews 15
TW9 . . . . .44 C2
Blakemore Rd
SW16 . . . . .74 A1
Blakeney Cl
5 Camden Town
NW1 . . . . .13 C1
4 Dalston E8 . . . . .16 C3
Blakenham Ct
W12 . . . . .29 C1
Blaker Rd E15 . . . .27 B4
Blakes Cl W10 . . . .30 B4
Blake's Rd SE15 . . .49 B3
Blanca Ho 18 N1 . .24 A3
Blanchard Way E8 . .16 C2
Blanch Cl SE15 . . . .50 B3
Blanchedowne
SE5 . . . . .63 C3
Blandfield Rd
SW12 . . . . .72 C4
Blandford Ct
Brondesbury Pk
NW6 . . . . .10 A1
6 De Beauvoir Town
N1 . . . . .16 A1
Blandford Ho
SW8 . . . . .162 C2
Blandford Rd W4 . .38 A3
Blandford Sq NW1 .90 B1
Blandford St W1 . .103 B3
Bland Ho SE11 . . . .149 A2
Blantyre St SW10 .157 B2
Blantyre Twr
SW10 . . . . .157 B2
Blantyre Wlk
SW10 . . . . .157 B2
Blashford St SE13 . .12 B1
Blasker Wlk 3
E14 . . . . .42 A1
Blaxland Ho 12
W12 . . . . .30 A2
Blazer Ct NW8 . . . .89 C3
Blechynden St
W10 . . . . .30 C3

Blechynden St
W10 . . . . .30 C2
Bleeding Heart Yd
EC1 . . . . .107 C3
Blemundsbury
WC1 . . . . .106 C4
Blendworth Point 8
SW15 . . . . .69 A3
Blenheim 20 SW19 .69 C3
Blenheim Cres
Notting Hill W11 . . .31 A3
Notting Hill
W11 . . . .31 A2 112 B4
Blenheim Ct
Barnsbury N7 . . . . .14 A2
Richmond TW9 . . . .54 B4
17 Rotherhithe
SE16 . . . . .32 C1
Upper Holloway N19 . .5 A2
Blenheim Gdns
Clapham Pk SW2 . .62 B1
Dollis Hill NW2 . . . .9 B3
Blenheim Gr SE15 .49 C1
Blenheim Pas
NW8 . . . . .78 C2
Blenheim Rd
Acton W4 . . . . .38 A3
St John's Wood
NW8 . . . . .79 A2
Blenheim St W1 . .104 A1
Blenheim Terr
NW8 . . . . .78 C2
Blenkarne Rd
SW11 . . . . .60 B1
**Blessed Sacrament
RC Prim Sch** N1 . .84 C3
Blessington Cl
SE13 . . . . .67 C4
Blessington Rd
SE13 . . . . .67 C3
Bletchley Ct N1 . . .87 B1
Bletchley St N1 . . . .87 A1
Bletsoe Wlk N1 . . .87 A2
Blick Ho 5 SE16 . . .40 B3
Blincoe Cl SW19 . . .69 C2
Bliss Cres 3 SE13 . .52 A1
Blissett St SE10 . . . .52 B2
Bliss Mews 14
W10 . . . . .23 A2
Blisworth Ho 12
E2 . . . . .24 C4
Blithfield St W8 . . .128 A1
Bloemfontein Ave
W12 . . . . .30 A1
Bloemfontein Rd
W12 . . . . .30 A1
Blomfield Ct
Battersea SW11 . . .167 C4
Paddington W9 . . . .89 A2
Blomfield Ho 4
E14 . . . . .34 A2
Blomfield Mans 7
W12 . . . . .30 B1
Blomfield Rd W9 . .100 C4
Blomfield St EC2 . .109 C3
Blomfield Villas
W9 . . . . .100 C4
Blondel St SW11 . . .169 B2
Blondin St E3 . . . . .26 C3
Blondin Wy SE16 . .41 A4
Bloomberg Space
EC1 . . . . .109 C4
Bloomburg St
SW1 . . . . .147 A3
Bloomfield Ho 19
E1 . . . . .111 B3

Bloomfield Pl W1 . .118 B4
Bloomfield Terr
SW1 . . . . .145 C2
Bloom Gr SE27 . . . .75 A1
Bloom Park Rd
SW6 . . . . .154 C1
BLOOMSBURY . . .106 A4
Bloomsbury Ct
WC1 . . . . .106 B3
Bloomsbury Ho 10
SW4 . . . . .61 C1
**Bloomsbury
International
Language Sch**
WC1 . . . . .106 B3
Bloomsbury Pl
London SW18 . . . . .59 B2
St Giles WC1 . . . . .106 B3
Bloomsbury Sq
WC1 . . . . .106 B3
Bloomsbury St
WC1 . . . . .105 C3
Bloomsbury Way
WC1 . . . . .106 B3
Blore Cl SW8 . . . . .171 B3
Blore Ct W1 . . . . . .119 B4
Blore Ho SW10 . . . .156 B2
Blossom Cl W5 . . . .36 A4
Blossom Pl
E1 . . . . .24 A1 98 B1
Blossom St
E1 . . . . .24 A1 98 B1
Blount St E14 . . . . .33 A3
Blucher Rd SE5 . . . .48 B3
Blue Anchor Alley 4
TW9 . . . . .54 A3
Blue Anchor La
SE16 . . . . .40 A2
Blue Anchor Yd
E1 . . . . .125 B4
Blue Ball Yd SW1 . .118 C1
Bluebell Cl 10 E9 . . .25 B4
**Blue Gate Fields Jun
& Inf Schs** E1 . . . .32 B2
Bluegate Mews
E1 . . . . .32 A2
Blue Lion Pl SE1 . .138 A2
Blueprint Apartments
15 SW12 . . . . .73 A4
Blundell Cl E8 . . . . .16 C4
Blundell St N7 . . . . .14 A2
Blurton Rd E5 . . . . .17 C4
Blyth Cl 4 E14 . . . . .42 C2
Blythe Ho 8
SE11 . . . . .163 C4
Blythe Mews 2
W14 . . . . .39 C3
Blythendale Ho 36
E2 . . . . .24 C3
Blythe Rd W14 . . . .126 A1
Blythe St E2 . . . . . .25 A2
Blyth's Wharf E14 . .33 A2
Blythwood Rd N4 . . .5 A4
**BMI Fitzroy Square
Hospl 41** 92 C1
**Bnois Jerusalem Girls
Sch 2** N16 . . . . .6 C4
Boades Mews 3
NW3 . . . . .11 C4
Boadicea St N1 . . . .84 C4
Boardwalk Pl E14 . .34 B1
Boarley Ho SE17 . . .152 A3
Boathouse Ctr The
W10 . . . . .22 B1
Boathouse Wlk 24
SE15 . . . . .49 B3

Boat Lifter Way 19
SE16 . . . . .41 A2
Bobbin Cl SW4 . . . .61 B4
Bob Marley Way 10
SE24 . . . . .62 C3
Bocking St E8 . . . . .25 A4
Boddicott Cl SW19 .70 A3
Boddington Gdns
W3 . . . . .36 C4
Boddington Ho 2
SE14 . . . . .50 B2
Bodeney Ho 3
SE5 . . . . .49 A2
Boden Ho 4 1 . . . .111 B4
Bodington Ct 2
W12 . . . . .39 C4
Bodley Manor Way
SE24 . . . . .74 C4
Bodmin St SW18 . . .70 C3
Bodnant Gdns
SW20 . . . . .79 A1
Bogart Ct 11 E14 . .33 C3
Bohemia Pl 1 E8 . .17 A2
Bohn Rd E1 . . . . . . .33 A4
Boileau Rd SW13 . .47 A4
Boilerhouse SE1 . .124 C1
Boisseau Ho 31 E1 . .32 B4
Bolden St SE8 . . . . .52 A1
Boldero Pl NW8 . . . .90 A1
Boleyn Rd N16 . . . .16 A3
Bolina Rd SE16 . . . .40 B1
Bolingbroke Acad
SW11 . . . . .60 A2
Bolingbroke Gr
SW11 . . . . .60 B1
Bolingbroke Rd
W14 . . . . .39 C3
Bolingbroke Wlk
SW11 . . . . .168 A4
Bollo Bridge Rd
W3 . . . . .37 B4
Bollo Ct 3 W3 . . . .37 B3
Bollo La 3 W3 . . . .37 A3
Bolney Gate SW7 .130 A3
Bolney St SW8 . . . .162 C1
Bolsover St W1 . . . .92 B1
Bolt Ct EC4 . . . . . .107 C1
Bolton Cres SE5 . . .48 A3
Bolton Ct SW11 . . .169 C3
Bolton Gdns
Kensal Rise
NW10 . . . . .22 C3
South Kensington
SW5 . . . . .142 B2
Bolton Gdns Mews
SW10 . . . . .142 C2
Bolton Ho 8 SE10 . .43 A1
Bolton Pl SW5 . . . .142 C2
Bolton Rd
Chiswick W4 . . . . . .45 B3
Harlesden NW10 . . .21 A4
Kilburn NW8 . . . . . .78 B3
Boltons Ct SW5 . . .142 B2
Bolton St W1 . . . . .118 B2
Boltons The
SW10 . . . . .142 C2
Bolton Studios
SW10 . . . . .143 A1
Bolton Wlk N7 . . . . .5 B2
Bombay Ct 8
SE16 . . . . .40 B4
Bombay St SE16 . . .40 A2
Bomore Rd
W11 . . . . . . .31 A2 112 A4
Bonar Rd SE15 . . . .49 C3
Bonchurch Rd
W10 . . . . .31 A4

Bond Ct EC4...... 109 B1
Bond Ho 4 NW6..... 23 B3
Bonding Yard Wlk
SE16...............41 A3
Bond St W1.........37 C2
Bond Street Sta
W1.................103 C1
Bondway SW8.......162 C4
Bonfield Rd SE13...67 B3
Bonham Ho
W11...........31 B1 112 C2
Bonham Rd SW2....62 B2
Bonheur Rd W4......37 C4
Bonhill St EC2.......97 C1
Bonington Ho N1....84 C1
Bonita Mews SE15..65 C4
Bonner Ho 3
SW15...............56 C2
Bonner Prim Sch 50
E2.................25 B3
Bonner Rd E2.......25 B3
Bonner St E2........25 B3
Bonneville Gdns
SW4...............61 B1
Bonneville Prim Sch
SW4...............61 B1
Bonnington Sq
SW8.............162 C4
Bonny St NW1......13 B1
Bonsor Ho SW8....171 A4
Bonsor St SE5......49 A3
Bonthron Ho
SW15...............47 B1
Booker Cl III E3.....33 B4
Boord St SE10......43 A3
Boothby Rd N19......4 C2
Booth Cl III E9......25 A4
Booth Ho 2 SW2...74 C4
Booth La EC4......122 C4
Booth's Pl W1......105 A3
Boot St N1....24 A2 98 A3
Bordon Wlk 5
SW15...............68 C4
Boreas Wlk N1......86 B1
Boreham Ave E16..35 C3
Boreman Ho III
SE10...............52 B4
Borland Rd SE15...65 B3
Borneo St SW15....57 B4
Borough High St
SE1..............123 B2
Borough Mkt SE1..123 B2
Borough Rd SE1...136 B2
Borough Sq SE1...136 C2
Borough Sta SE1...137 B4
BOROUGH THE ..136 C4
Borrett Cl SE17....150 C1
Borrodaile Rd
SW18.............59 A1
Borrowdale NW1...92 C3
Borthwick St SE8...41 C1
Boscastle Rd NW5...4 A1
Boscobel Ho III
E8................17 A2
Boscobel Pl SW1..145 C4
Boscobel St NW8...89 C1
Boscombe Cl E5...18 A3
Boscombe Rd
W12...............38 C4
Boss Ho SE1......138 C4
Boss St SE1......138 C4
Boston Gdns W4...46 A4
Boston Ho
24 Camberwell 48 B1
Earl's Ct SW5....142 B3

Boston Ho continued
Lisson Gr NW1......90 C2
Boston Pl NW1......90 C1
Bosun Cl 21 E14....41 C4
Boswell Ct
Bloomsbury WC1..106 B4
III Hammersmith
W14..............39 C3
Boswell Ho III......106 B4
Boswell St WC1...106 B4
Bosworth Ho 4
W10...............23 A1
Bosworth Rd W10..23 A1
Bothwell Cl E16....35 B4
Bothwell St W6....47 C4
Botolph Alley EC3.124 A4
Botolph La EC3....124 A4
Bott's Mews W2...31 C3
Boughton Rd SE18.137 B3
Boulcott St E1......32 C3
Boulevard The
Chelsea SW6.....167 A3
4 Upper Tooting
SW17.............72 C2
Boulogne Ho SE1.138 C2
Boulter Ho 8
SE14.............50 B2
Boulton Ho 18 E3..26 C3
Boundaries Mans 3
SW12.............72 C3
Boundaries Rd
SW12.............72 C3
Boundary Ho
3 Balham SW12...73 A3
III Camberwell SE5..48 B3
III Notting Hill
W11..............30 C1
Boundary La SE17..48 B4
Boundary Pas
E2...........24 B1 98 C2
Boundary Rd NW8..79 A4
Boundary Road Est
NW8..............79 B3
Boundary Row
SE1.............136 A4
Boundary St
E2...........24 B1 98 C2
Bourbon Rd SW9..173 C3
Bourchier St W1...119 B4
Bourdon Pl W1....118 B3
Bourdon St W1....118 B3
Bourke Cl
London SW4......62 A1
Willesden NW10.....8 A2
Bourlet Cl W1.....104 C3
Bourne Cl W4.....45 B4
Bourne Ho 5 SW4.61 B3
Bourne Mews W1..104 A2
Bournemouth Cl
SE15..............49 C1
Bournemouth Rd
SE15..............49 C1
Bourne Pl W4.....37 C1
Bourne St SW1...145 B3
Bourne Terr W2...100 B3
Bousfield Prim Sch
SW10.............142 C2
Bousfield Rd SE14..50 C1
Boutcher CE Prim Sch
SE1.............152 C4
Boutflower Rd
SW11.............60 A3
Bouverie Mews
N16................7 A2
Bouverie Pl W2...101 C2
Bouverie Rd N16...7 A2

Bouverie St EC4...107 C1
Bovingdon Cl 4
N19................4 B2
Bovingdon Rd
SW6.............166 B3
BOW..............26 C3
Bowater Cl SW2...62 A1
Bowater Ho EC1...97 A1
Bow Brook The 20
E2................25 C3
Bow Church Sta
E3................26 C2
BOW COMMON ...34 A4
Bow Common La
E3................34 A4
Bowden Ho 22 E3...26 C2
Bowden St SE11..149 C1
Bowditch SE8.....41 B1
Bowen Ct 2 N5....15 A4
Bowen Dr SE21...76 A1
Bowen St E14....34 A3
Bower Ave SE3....53 A3
Bowerdean St
SW6.............166 A4
Bower Ho SE14...50 C2
Bowerman Ave
SE14..............51 A4
Bowerman Ct II
N19................4 C2
Bower St E1......32 C3
Bowes-Lyon Hall III
E16................35 C1
Bowfell Rd W6....47 B4
Bowhill Cl SW9...163 C2
Bow Ho II E3......26 C2
Bowie Cl SW4.....73 C4
Bow La EC2, EC4...109 A1
Bowland Ho N4....6 B4
Bowland Rd SW4..61 C3
Bowland Yd SW1..131 A3
Bowles Rd III SE1..49 C4
Bowley Ho 0
SE16..............139 B2
Bowling Green Cl
SW19..............69 A4
Bowling Green Ho
SW10............157 B2
Bowling Green La
EC1...............95 C2
Bowling Green Pl
SE1.............137 B4
Bowling Green St
SE11.............163 B4
Bowling Green Wlk
N1...........24 A2 98 A4
Bowman Ave E16..35 B2
Bowman Mews
St George in t East
Wandsworth SW18..70 B3
Bowman's Mews
N7................5 A1
Bowman's Pl N7...5 A1
Bowmore Wlk
NW1..............13 C1
Bowness Cl 5 E8..16 B2
Bowness Ho SE15..50 B3
Bowood Rd SW11..60 C2
Bow Rd E3......26 C2
Bow Road Sta E3..26 C2
Bowry Ho III E14..33 B4
Bow Sch
III E3.............26 C2

Bow Sch continued
Mill Meads E16.....27 B1
Bowsprit Point II
E14..............41 C3
Bow St WC2......106 B1
Bowstead Ct
SW11.............167 C3
Bow Triangle Bsns Ctr
III E3.............26 C2
Bowyer Ho
27 Shoreditch N1...24 A4
Wandsworth SW18..59 C3
Bowyer Pl SE5.....48 B3
Bowyer St III SE5...48 B3
Boxall Rd SE21....64 A1
Boxley Ho 8 E5...17 A3
Boxmoor Ho
III Hackney E2....24 C4
III Shepherd's Bush
W11..............30 C1
Box Tree Ho SE8...41 A1
Boxworth Gr N1....85 A4
Boyce Ho 9 W10..23 B2
Boyd Ct SW15.....57 B1
Boydell Ct NW8...11 C1
Boyd St E1......111 C1
Boyfield St SE1...136 B3
Boyle St W1......118 C4
Boyne Ct NW10....8 C1
Boyne Rd SE13....67 C4
Boyne Terr Mews
W11.........31 B1 112 C2
Boyson Rd III
SE17..............48 C4
Boyton Cl E1.....25 C1
Boyton Ho
Kennington SE11..149 B1
St John's Wood
NW8..............79 C2
Brabant Ct EC3...124 A4
Brabazon St E14...34 A3
Brabner Ho 9
E2...........24 C2 99 B4
Braburn Sq SE15..50 B1
Bracer Ho II N1...24 A3
Bracewell Rd W10..30 B4
Bracey Mews N4...5 A2
Bracey St N4......5 A2
Bracken Ave
SW12.............72 C4
Brackenbury N4....5 C3
Brackenbury Gdns
W6................39 A3
Brackenbury Prim Sch
4 W6.............39 A3
Brackenbury Rd
W6................39 A3
Bracken Gdns
SW13.............46 C1
Bracken Ho III E3..33 C4
Brackley Ave SE15..65 B4
Brackley Ct NW8...89 C2
Brackley Rd W4...38 A1
Brackley St EC1...109 A4
Brackley Terr II
W4................38 A1
Bracklyn Ct N1...87 B2
Bracklyn St N1...87 B2
Bracknell Gate
NW3.............11 A3
Bracknell Gdns
NW3.............11 A3
Bracknell Way
NW3.............11 A3
Bradbeer Ho 24
E2................25 B2

Bradbourne St
SW6.............165 C2
Bradbury Ct 2
SE3................53 C3
Bradbury Ho 4....111 A2
Bradbury St 28
N16...............16 A3
Bradby Ho NW8...78 B1
Braddon Rd TW9...54 B4
Braddyll St SE10...43 A1
Bradenham
SE17..............48 C4
Bradenham Cl
SE17..............48 C4
Braden St W9.....88 A1
Bradfield Ct III
NW1..............13 A1
Bradfield Ho 15
SW8.............171 B2
Bradford Ho 4
W14..............39 C3
Bradford Rd W3...38 A4
Bradgate Rd SE6...67 A1
Brading Rd SW2...74 B4
Brading Terr W12..38 C3
Bradiston Rd W9...23 B2
Bradley Cl N7.....14 B2
Bradley Ho
Bermondsey SE16..40 A2
Bromley E3....27 A2
Bradley Mews
SW12.............72 B3
Bradley's Cl N1...85 C2
Bradlord Ho SE21..76 A1
Bradmead SW8...160 C1
Bradmore Park Rd
W6................39 A2
Brad St SE1......121 C1
Bradstock Ho E9...18 A1
Bradstock Rd E9...18 A2
Bradwell Ho 3
NW6..............78 A3
Bradwell St 24 E1..25 C2
Brady Ho
London SW4......61 C2
South Lambeth
SW8.............171 A4
Brady St E1......25 A1
Braefoot Ct SW15..57 C2
Braemar SW15....57 C1
Braemar Ave SW18,
SW19..............70 C2
Braemar Ho W9...88 C3
Braemar Mans
W8..............128 B1
Braes St N1......15 A1
Braganza St SE17..150 A1
Braham Ho SE11..149 A1
Brahma Kumaris
World Spiritual Univ
NW10..............8 C4
Braid Ave W3.....29 A3
Braid Ho SE10....52 B2
Braidwood St SE1.124 A1
Brailsford Rd SW2..62 C1
Braintree Ho 3
E1................25 B1
Braintree St E2...25 B2
Braithwaite Ho
EC1..............97 B2
Braithwaite Twr
W2..............101 B4
Bramah Gn SW9...173 C4
Bramah Rd SW9...173 C3

Bramall Ct N7 . . . . . . 14 B2
Bramber W14 . . . . 44 A3
Bramber Ct TW8 . . . . . 36 A2
Bramber Rd W14 . . . . 154 C4
Brambledown

N4 . . . . .5 A4
Bramble Gdns

W12 . . . . 29 B2
Bramble Ho 18 E3 . . . . 33 C4
Brambling Ct 23

SE8 . . . . 51 B4
Bramcote Gr SE16 . .40 B1
Bramcote Rd

SW15 . . . . 9 C1
Bramerton NW6 . . . . . .9 C1
Bramerton St

SW3 . . . . 158 A4
Bramfield Ct N4 . . . . . .6 B2
Bramfield Rd

SW11 . . . . 60 B2
Bramford Rd

SW18 . . . . 59 B3
Bramham Gdns

SW5 . . . . 142 B2
Bramham Ho SE22 . .64 A3
Bramlands Cl

SW11 . . . . 60 A4
Bramley Cres

SW8 . . . . 161 C2
Bramley Ct SE13 . . . . 67 C2
Bramley Ho 11

W10 . . . . 30 C3
Roehampton SW15 . . .56 B1
Bramley Rd W10 . . . . .30 C3
Brampton WC1 . . . . . 106 C3
Bramshaw Rd E9 . . . .17 C2
Bramshill Gdns

NW5 . . . . .4 A1
Bramshill Rd

NW10 . . . . 21 B3
Bramshurst NW8 . . . . 78 B3
Bramston Rd

Harlesden NW10 . . . . .21 C3
Wandsworth SW17 . . .71 B1
Bramwell Ho

Borough The SE1 . . . 137 A1
Chelsea SW1 . . . . . . 160 C4
Bramwell Mews

N1 . . . . 85 A4
Brancaster Ho

22 Globe Town

E1 . . . . 25 C2
Islington N5 . . . . .15 A3
Brancaster Rd

SW16 . . . . 74 A1
Branch Hill NW3 . . . . .2 B1
Branch Pl N1 . . . . . . .87 C4
Branch St SE15 . . . . .49 A3
Brand Cl N4 . . . . .6 A3
Branden Lo 3 W4 . . .37 B1
Brandlehow Prim Sch

SW15 . . . . 58 B3
Brandlehow Rd

SW15 . . . . 58 B3
Brandon Mews

Barbican EC2 . . . . . 109 B4
Walworth SE17 . . . . 151 A3
Brandon St SE17 . . . 151 A3
Brandrams Wharf

SE16 . . . . 40 B4

Brandreth Rd

SW17 . . . . 73 A2
Brand St SE10 . . . . . .52 B3
Brangton Rd

SE11 . . . . 149 A1
Brangwyn Cn W14 . 126 A1
Branksea St SW6 . . 154 A1
Branksome Ho

SW8 . . . . 162 C2
Branksome Rd

SW2 . . . . 62 A2
Bransby Ct 4 N16 . .16 A4
Branscombe NW1 . . . 83 A3
Branscombe St

SE13 . . . . 67 A4
Bransdale Cl NW6 . . .23 C4
Branstone Ct 9

TW9 . . . . 44 B2
Branston Ho N7 . . . . .14 C3
Brantwood Ho 9

SE5 . . . . 48 B3
Brantwood Rd

SE24 . . . . 63 B2
Brasenose Dr

SW13 . . . . 47 B4
Brashley Road Cvn

Site NW10 . . . . .21 A2
Brassey Ho 1 E14 . .42 A2
Brassey Rd NW6 . . . .10 B2
Brassey Sq SW11 . . .60 C4
Brassie Ave W3 . . . . .29 A3
Brass Talley Alley 31

SE16 . . . . 40 C4
Brathay NW1 . . . . . . .83 A1
Brathway Rd

SW18 . . . . 70 C4
Bratley St 11

E1 . . . . 99 B1
Bravington Pl W9 . . .23 B1
Bravington Rd W9 . . .23 B2
Brawne Ho 12

SE17 . . . . 48 A4
Braxfield Rd SE4 . . . .66 B3
Bray NW3 . . . . .12 A1
Brayard's Rd SE15 . .50 A1
Braybrook St W12 . . .29 B3
Brayburne Ave

SW4 . . . . 171 A1
Bray Cres SE16 . . . . .40 C4
Braydon Rd N16 . . . . .7 C3
Bray Dr E16 . . . . .35 B2
Brayfield Terr N1 . . . .14 C1
Brayford Sq 2 E1 . . .32 B3
Bray Pl SW3 . . . . . . 144 C3
Bread St EC2, EC4 . 109 A1
Breakspeare SE21 . .76 B1
Breakspears Mews

SE4 . . . . 51 C1
Breakspears Rd

SE4 . . . . 66 C4
Breakwell Ct 16

W10 . . . . 23 A1
Breamore Cl

SW15 . . . . 68 C3
Breamore Ho 21

SE15 . . . . 49 C3
Bream's Bldgs

EC4 . . . . 107 B2
Bream St E3 . . . . .26 C4
Breasley Cl SW15 . . .57 A3
Brechin Pl SW7 . . . . 143 A3

Brecon Ho

Stamford Hill N16. . . . .7 B3
Wandsworth SW18 . . .70 C4
Brecon Mews 23

N7 . . . . 13 C3
Brecon Rd W6 . . . . . 154 B3
Bredel Ho 1 E14 . . . .33 C4
Bredgar SE13 . . . . . . .67 A2
Bredgar Rd N19 . . . . .4 B2
Bredinghurst SE22 . .76 C4
Bredin Ho SW10 . . . 156 B2
Breer St SW6 . . . . . . .59 A4
Breezer's Ct 23

E1 . . . . 125 C3
Breezer's Hill E1 . . . 125 C3
Brehon Ho NW1 . . . . .82 C3
Bremans Row 1

SW18 . . . . 71 B2
Bremner Rd SW7 . . 129 A2
Brenchley Gdns SE15,

SE22, SE23 . . . . . . 65 C1
Brenda Rd SW17 . . . .72 B2
Brendon Ave NW10 . .8 A4
Brendon Ho NW1 . . 103 B4
Brendon St W1 . . . 102 B2
Brenley Ho SE1 . . . 137 B4
Brennands Ct 14

N19 . . . . .4 B1
Brent Ct 5 W12 . . . .38 A3
Brentford Fountain L

Ctr W4 . . . . 36 C1
Brent Ho 18 E9 . . . . .17 B2
Brenthouse Rd E9 . . .17 B2
Brenthurst Rd

NW10 . . . . .8 B2
Brent Mus NW10 . . . . .9 A2
Brent New Ent Ctr

NW10 . . . . .8 B2
Brenton Ct E9 . . . . . .18 A3
Brenton St E14 . . . . .33 A3
Brent Rd E16 . . . . . . .35 C4
Brent Trad Est

NW10 . . . . .8 A3
Brentwick Gdns

TW8 . . . . 36 A2
Brereton Ho 4

SW2 . . . . 74 C4
Bressenden Pl

SW1 . . . . 132 C2
Breton Ho

Bermondsey SE1 . . . 138 C2
St Luke's EC2 . . . . . .97 A1
Brett Cl N16 . . . . .7 A2
Brett Cres NW10 . . . .20 C4
Brettell St SE17 . . . . 151 C1
Brett Ho SW15 . . . . . .69 C4
Brett House Cl 2

SW15 . . . . 69 C4
Brettinghurst 8

SE1 . . . . 153 B1
Bretton Ho N19 . . . . .5 A3
Brett Pas E8 . . . . . . .17 A3
Brett Rd E8 . . . . .17 A3
Brewers Bldgs EC1 . .96 A4
Brewers Ct W2 . . . . 100 C2
Brewer's Gn SW1 . . 133 B2
Brewers Hall Gdns

EC2 . . . . 109 A3
Brewer St W1 . . . . . 119 A4
Brewery Ind Est The

N1 . . . . 87 A1
Brewery Rd N7 . . . . . .14 A2
Brewery Sq

Bermondsey SE1 . . . 124 C1
Clerkenwell EC1 . . . . .96 B2

Brewhouse La

Putney SW15 . . . . . . .58 A4
Wapping E1 . . . . .32 A1
Brewhouse Wlk

SE16 . . . . 33 A1
Brewhouse Yd EC1 . .96 A2
Brewster Gdns

W10 . . . . 30 B4
Brewster Ho

Bermondsey SE1 . . . 153 A4
Poplar E14 . . . . .33 B2
Briant Ho SE1 . . . . . 135 A1
Briant St SE14 . . . . . .50 C3
Briar Ct

7 Bow E3 . . . . .26 C3
5 Dalston E8 . . . . . . .16 B1
Briardale SW19 . . . . .70 B3
Briardale Gdns

NW3 . . . . .1 C1
Briardale Ho 12

N16 . . . . .7 C3
Briar Rd NW2 . . . . . . .9 B4
Briar Wlk

Putney SW15 . . . . . . .57 A3
West Kilburn W10 . . .23 A1
Briarwood Rd

SW4 . . . . 61 C2
Briary Cl NW3 . . . . . .12 A1
Briary Ct 19 E16 . . . .35 B3
Brickbarn Cl

SW10 . . . . 157 A2
Brick Ct EC4 . . . . . . 107 B1
Brick Farm Cl

TW9 . . . . 45 A2
Brickfield Rd 14

SW4 . . . . 61 C1
Brick La

Shoreditch

E2 . . . . 24 B2 99 A3
Spitalfields

E1 . . . . 24 B1 99 A1
Brick Lane Mkt E2 . 99 A2
Bricklayers Arms

SE1 . . . . 137 C1
Brick St W1 . . . . 118 A1
Brickworth Ho 26

SW9 . . . . 173 C4
Brideale Cl SE15 . . . .49 B4
Bride Ct EC4 . . . . . . 108 A1
Bride La EC4 . . . . . . 108 A1
Bridel Mews N1 . . . . .86 A3
Bride St N7 . . . . .14 B2
Bridewain St SE1 . . 138 C2
Bridewell Pl

Holborn EC4 . . . . . . 108 A1
20 Wapping E1 . . . . .32 A1
Bridford Mews

W1 . . . . 104 B4
Bridge Acad The

51 Bethnal Green

E2 . . . . 24 B4
Bridge App NW3 . . . .11 C1
Bridge Ave W6 . . . . . .39 B1
Bridge Avenue Mans

7 W6 . . . . 39 B1
Bridge Cl 13 W10 . . .30 C3
Bridge Ct

9 Blackwall E14 . . . . .34 C2
7 Willesden NW10 . . .8 A4
Bridge Field Ho 7

W2 . . . . 100 A2
Bridgefoot SE1 . . . . 148 B1
Bridge Gdns N16 . . . .15 C4
Bridge Ho

Brockley SE4. . . . . . . .66 B3

Bridge Ho continued

11 Camden Town

NW1 . . . . 12 C1
Homerton E9 . . . . . . .17 C3
Bridge House Quay

E14 . . . . 34 B1
Bridge La SW11 . . . 168 B3
Bridgeland Rd

E16 . . . . 35 C2
Bridgeman Ho 19

E9 . . . . 17 B1
Bridgeman Rd N1 . . .14 B1
Bridgeman St

NW8 . . . . 80 A1
Bridge Meadows

SE14 . . . . 50 C4
Bridgemount Mews

N19 . . . . .5 A4
Bridgend Rd SW18 . .59 B3
Bridgen Ho 9 E1 . . .32 A3
Bridge Pk 7

SW18 . . . . 58 C2
Bridge Pl SW1 . . . . 146 B4
Bridgeport Pl 4

E1 . . . . 125 C2
Bridge Rd

Stratford Marsh

E15 . . . . 27 C4
Willesden NW10 . . . . .8 A2
Bridge Sch The

N7 . . . . 14 A3
Bridges Ct SW11 . . 167 B1
Bridges Ho 15 SE5 . .48 C3
Bridge St

Chiswick W4 . . . . . . .37 C2
Westminster SW1 . . 134 B3
Bridge Terr E15 . . . . .19 C1
Bridgeview 6 W6 . . .39 B1
Bridgewater Rd

E15 . . . . 27 B4
Bridgewater Sq

EC2 . . . . 108 C4
Bridgewater St

EC2 . . . . 108 C4
Bridgeway St NW1 . .83 A1
Bridge Wharf 18

E2 . . . . 25 C3
Bridge Yd SE1 . . . . 123 C2
Bridgford St SW17,

SW18 . . . . 71 B1
Bridgman Rd W4 . . . .37 B3
Bridgnorth Ho 10

SE15 . . . . 49 C4
Bridgwater Ho

W2 . . . . 100 C2
Bridle La W1 . . . . . . 119 A4
Bridlington Ho

SW18 . . . . 59 B3
Bridport SE17 . . . . . 151 A1
Bridport Ho N1 . . . . . .87 C3
Bridport Pl N1 . . . . . .87 C3
Bridstow Pl W2 . . . . .31 C3
Brief St SE5 . . . . .48 A2
Brierfield NW1 . . . . . .82 C3
Brierley Rd

Leyton E11 . . . . .19 C4
Upper Tooting

SW12 . . . . 73 B2
Brierly Gdns E2 . . . . .25 B3
Brigade St SE3 . . . . .53 B1
Briggeford Cl 5 E5 . .7 C2
Briggs Ho 20

E2 . . . . 24 B2 99 A4
Bright St E14 . . . . . . .34 A4
Brightling Rd SE4 . . .66 B1
Brightlingsea Pl 5

E14 . . . . 33 B2

Brightman Rd
SW18 . . . . .71 C3
Brighton Bldgs
SE1 . . . .**138** A1
Brighton Ct SW15 . . .**58** B1
Brighton Gr SE14 . . .51 A2
Brighton Ho **7**
SE5 . . . . .48 C2
Brighton Rd N16 . . . .16 A4
Brighton Terr
SW9 . . . . .62 B3
Brightside Rd
SE13 . . . . .67 C1
Bright St E14 . . . . . . .34 A4
Brightwell Ct N7 . . . .14 B3
Brightwells **1**
SW6 . . . .**166** A2
Brig Mews SE8 . . . . . .51 C4
Brigstock Ho SE5 . . .48 B1
Brill Pl NW1 . . . .**83** C1
Brimsdown Ho E3 . . .27 B1
Brindisi Green Sch
SE13 . . . . .67 C1
Brindley Ho
57 Notting Hill
W2 . . . . .31 C4
2 Streatham
SW2 . . . . .74 A4
Brindley St SE14 . . . .51 B2
Brine Ho **13** E3 . . . . .26 A3
Brinklow Ho W2 . . . .**100** A3
Brinkworth Way
E9 . . . . .18 B2
Brinsley Ho **7** E1 . . .32 B3
Brinsley St E1 . . . . . .32 A3
Brinton Wlk SE1 . . . .**122** A1
Brion Pl E14 . . . . .34 B4
Brisbane Ho **3**
W12 . . . . .30 A2
Brisbane St SE5 . . . .48 C3
Briset St EC1 . . . . . . .96 A1
Briset Way N7 . . . . . .5 B2
Bristol Gdns
Putney SW15 . . . . . . .69 B4
Westbourne Green
W9 . . . . .88 B1
Bristol Ho SE11 . . . .**135** B1
Bristol Mews W9 . . .88 B1
Bristowe Cl **2**
SW2 . . . . .62 C1
Britannia Bsns Ctr **5**
NW6 . . . . .9 C4
Britannia Building
N1 . . . .**97** B4
Britannia Cl SW4 . . .**61** C3
Britannia Gate **1**
E16 . . . . .35 C1
Britannia Junc
NW1 . . . .**82** B4
Britannia L Ctr N1 . .24 A4
Britannia Rd
23 Millwall E14 . . . .41 C2
Walham Green
SW6 . . . .**156** A1
Britannia Row N1 . . .86 C4
Britannia St WC1 . . .**94** C4
Britannia Way
NW10 . . . . .20 A1
Britannia Wlk N1 . . .**97** B4
British Coll of
Osteopathic
Medicine NW3 . . . .11 B2
British Dental
Association Mus
W1 . . . .**104** A3
British Gr W4 . . . .**38** B1

British Grove Pas **2**
W4 . . . .**38** B1
British Grove S **3**
W4 . . . .**38** B1
British Library The
WC1 . . . .**93** C4
British Mus WC1 . . .**106** A3
British Optical
Association Mus
SW1 . . . .**120** A2
British St E3 . . . .**26** B2
British Wharf Ind Est
SE14 . . . . .50 C4
Britley Ho **8** E14 . . . .33 B3
Brittage Rd **11**
Brittany Ho SW15 . . .57 B3
Brittany Point
SE11 . . . .**149** B3
Britten Cl NW11 . . . . .2 A3
Britten Ho SW3 . . . .**144** A2
Britten St SW3 . . . . .**144** A2
Britton St EC1 . . . . . .96 A1
BRIXTON 62 C4
Brixton Hill SW2 . . .62 B1
Brixton Hill Ct **5**
SW2 . . . . .62 B2
Brixton Hill Pl
SW2 . . . . .74 A4
Brixton Mkt SW9 . . .**173** B2
Brixton Rec Ctr
SW9 . . . . .62 C4
Brixton Sta SW9 . . . .62 C4
Brixton Station Rd
SW9 . . . . .62 C4
Brixton Water La
SW2 . . . . .62 B2
Broadbent Cl N6 . . . .4 A3
Broadbent St W1 . . .**118** A4
Broadbridge Cl
SE3 . . . . .53 C3
Broad Common Est
N16 . . . . .7 C3
Broad Ct WC2 . . . . .**106** B1
Broadfield NW6 . . . .11 A2
Broadfield La
NW1 . . . . .14 A1
Broadfields Way
NW10 . . . . .8 B3
Broadford Ho **12**
E1 . . . . .26 A1
BROADGATE **110** A4
Broadgate EC2 . . . .**110** A4
Broadgate Circ
EC2 . . . .**110** A3
Broadgates Ct
SE11 . . . .**149** C1
Broadgates Rd
SW18 . . . . .71 C3
Broadgate Twr The
EC2 . . . .**98** B1
Broadhinton Rd
SW4 . . . . .61 B4
Broadhurst Cl **3**
Hampstead NW6 . . .11 B2
2 Richmond TW10 . .54 B2
Broadhurst Gdns
NW6 . . . . .11 A2
Broadhurst Mans
NW6 . . . . .11 A2
Broadlands N6 . . . . . .3 C4
Broadlands Ave
SW16 . . . . .74 A2

Broadlands Cl
Highgate N6 . . . . .3 C4
Streatham SW16 . . . .74 A2
Broadlands Lo
TW9 . . . . .44 C2
Broadlands Lo **1** . . .51 A2
Broadlands Mans **2**
SW16 . . . . .74 A1
Broadlands Rd N6 . . .3 B4
Broadley St NW8 . . .**102** A4
Broadley Terr
NW1 . . . . .90 B1
Broadmayne SE17 . .**151** B2
Broadmead W14 . . . .**140** A3
Broadoak Ct **5**
SW9 . . . . .62 C4
Broadoak Ho **11**
NW6 . . . . .78 B3
Broad Passage **3**
W3 . . . . .29 B1
Broad St Ave EC2 . .**110** A3
Broad Sanctuary
SW1 . . . .**134** A3
Broadstone Ho **4**
SW8 . . . .**162** C1
Broadstone Pl
W1 . . . .**103** B3
Broad Street Pl
EC2 . . . .**109** C3
Broadwalk Ho
SW7 . . . .**128** C3
Broadwalk La NW11 .1 B4
Broadwall SE1 . . . . .**121** C2
Broadway
Stratford E15 . . . . . . .19 C1
Westminster SW1 . .**133** B2
Broadway Arc **3**
W6 . . . . .39 B2
Broadway Ho **2**
E8 . . . . .25 A4
Broadway Mans
SW6 . . . .**155** C1
Broadway Market
E8 . . . . .25 A4
Broadway Market
Mews **21** E8 . . . . . . .24 C4
Broadway Mews **5** . .7 A4
Broadway Mkt E8 . . .25 A4
Broadway Ret Pk . . .
Broadway Sh Ctr **6**
W6 . . . . .39 B2
Broadway The
Barnes SW13 . . . . . . .46 A1
South Acton W3 . . . .36 C4
Broadway Wlk **4**
E14 . . . . .41 C3
Broadwick St W1 . . .**105** A1
Broad Wlk
Mayfair W1 . . . .**117** B2
Regent's Pk NW1 . . .**81** C1
Richmond TW9 . . . . .44 B3
Broad Wlk The
W8 . . . .**114** B1
Broadwood Terr
W14 . . . .**141** A4
Broad Yd EC1 . . . . . . .96 A1
Brocas Cl NW3 . . . . .12 A1
Brockbridge Ho
SW15 . . . . .56 B1
Brocket Ho **16**
SW8 . . . .**171** B2
Brockham Dr SW2 . .74 B4
Brockham Ho
Camden Town
NW1 . . . .**83** A3

Brockham Ho continued
11 Streatham SW2 . .74 B4
Brockham St SE1 . .**137** A2
Brockhurst Ho N4 . . .6 C4
Brockill Cres SE4 . . .66 A3
Brocklebank Rd
SW18 . . . . .71 B4
Brocklebank Road Ind
Est SE7 . . . . .43 C2
Brockhurst St
SE14 . . . . .50 C3
BROCKLEY 66 B3
Brockley Cross
SE4 . . . . .66 B4
Brockley Cross Bsns
Ctr SE4 . . . . .66 A4
Brockley Gdns
SE4 . . . . .51 B1
Brockley Gr SE4 . . . .66 C2
Brockley Hall Rd
SE4 . . . . .66 A2
Brockley Ho SE17 . .**152** A2
Brockley Mews
SE4 . . . . .66 A2
Brockley Rd SE4 . . . .66 B2
Brockley Sta SE4 . . .66 B3
Brockley Way SE4 . .66 A3
Brockmer Ho **5**
E1 . . . . .32 A2
Brock Pl E3 . . . . .27 A1
Brock St SE15 . . . . . .65 B4
Brockweir **28** E2 . . .25 B3
Brockwell Ct **2**
SW2 . . . . .62 C2
Brockwell Ho
SE11 . . . .**163** A4
Brockwell Lido
SE24 . . . . .63 A1
Brockwell Park
Brockwell Park Gdns
SE24 . . . . .75 A4
Brockwell Park Row
SW2 . . . . .62 C1
Broderick Ho
SE21 . . . . .76 A1
Brodia Rd N16 . . . . . .7 A1
Brodick Ho **17** E3 . . .26 B3
Brodie Ho SE1 . . . . .**153** A2
Brodie St SE1 . . . . . .**153** A2
Brodlove La E1 . . . . .32 C2
Brodrick Rd SW17 . .72 A2
Brody Ho **1** SE1 . . .**110** C3
Broken Wharf
EC4 . . . .**122** C4
Brokesley St E3 . . . .26 B2
Broke Wlk
Hackney E8 . . . . .24 B4
1 Hackney E8 . . . . .24 C4
Bromar Rd SE5 . . . . .64 A4
Bromehead St **8**
E1 . . . . .32 B3
Bromell's Rd SW4 . .61 B3
Bromfelde Rd
SW4 . . . .**171** C1
Bromfield Ct **20**
SE16 . . . .**139** C2
Bromfield St N1 . . . .**85** C2
Bromleigh Ho
SE1 . . . .**138** C2
BROMLEY 27 A2
Bromley-by-Bow Sta
E3 . . . . .98 A4
Bromley Hall Rd
E14 . . . . .34 B4

Bromley High St
E3 . . . . .27 A2
Bromley Lo **2** W3 . .28 B3
Bromley Pl W1 . . . .**104** C4
Bromley St E1 . . . . . .32 C3
BROMPTON **130** A1
Brompton Arc
SW1 . . . .**131** A3
Brompton Oratory
SW3 . . . .**130** A1
Brompton Park Cres
SW6 . . . .**156** A3
Brompton Pl SW3 . .**130** B2
Brompton Rd
SW3 . . . .**130** A1
Brompton Sq
SW3 . . . .**130** A2
Bromstone Ho **19**
SW9 . . . .**173** B3
Bromwich Ave N6 . . .3 C2
Bromwich Ho **3**
TW10 . . . . .54 A1
Bromyard Ave W3 . .29 A2
Bromyard Ho
Acton W3 . . . . .29 A1
3 Peckham SE15 . .50 A3
Bron Ct NW6 . . . . . . .23 C4
BRONDESBURY 10 A2
Brondesbury College
Sch **10** NW6 . . . . . . .10 C1
Brondesbury Ct
NW2 . . . . .9 C2
Brondesbury Mews **11**
NW6 . . . . .10 C1
BRONDESBURY
PARK 22 C4
Brondesbury Park Sta
NW6 . . . . .23 A4
Brondesbury Pk
NW6 . . . . .9 C1
Brondesbury Sta
NW6 . . . . .10 B1
Brondesbury Villas
NW6 . . . . .23 C3
Bronsart Rd SW6 . . .**154** A1
Bronte Ct **3** W14 . . .39 C3
Bronte Ho
Kilburn NW6 . . . . . . .23 C2
8 Stoke Newington
N16 . . . . .16 A3
Bronti Cl SE17 . . . . .**151** A2
Bronwen Ct NW8 . . .**89** B3
Bronze St SE8 . . . . . .51 C3
Brookbank Rd
SE13 . . . . .67 A4
Brook Cl SW17 . . . . .72 C2
Brook Com Prim Sch
E8 . . . . .16 C3
Brook Ct SW14 . . . . .55 B4
Brookdale Rd SE6 . .67 A1
Brook Dr SE11 . . . . .**150** A4
Brooke Ct W10 . . . . .23 A3
Brooke Ho **4**
SE14 . . . . .51 A2
Brookes Ct EC1 . . . .**107** B4
Brooke's Mkt EC1 . .**107** C4
Brooke St EC1 . . . . .**107** C3
Brookfield
Dartmouth Pk N6 . . .3 C1
1 Finsbury Pk N4 . . .5 C2

Brookfield Ho 23
E2 . . . . .25 A3
Brookfield Pk NW5 . .4 A1
Brookfield Prim Sch
N19. . . . .
Brookfield Rd
Acton W4 . . . . .37 C4
Homerton E9 . . . . .18 A2
Brookgate N16 . . . . . .6 C2
Brook Gate W1 . . .117 A1
Brook Gdns SW13 . .56 B4
Brook Gn W6 . . . . .39 C2
BROOK GREEN 39 C2
Brook Green Flats 4
W14 . . . . .39 C3
Brook Ho 3
Clapham Pk
SW4 . . . . .61 B2
Ealing W3 . . . . .36 C4
4 Hammersmith
W6 . . . . .39 B2
Marylebone WC1 . . . .105 B4
Brook Hos NW1 . . . .83 A1
Brooklands Ave
SW18 . . . . .71 A3
Brooklands Court
Apartments 1
NW6 . . . . .10 C1
Brooklands Ct 2
NW6 . . . . .10 B1
Brooklyn Ct W12 . . .30 B1
Brookmarsh Ind Est
SE10 . . . . .52 A3
Brook Mews N
W2 . . . . .115 A4
Brookmill Rd SE8 . .51 C2
Brooksbank Ho 7
E9 . . . . .17 B2
Brooksbank St 9
E9 . . . . .17 B2
Brooksby Ho 9
N1 . . . . .14 C1
Brooksby Mews
N1 . . . . .14 C1
Brooksby St N1 . . . .14 C1
Brooksby's Wlk E9 .17 C3
Brooks Ct
3 London SW4 . . . .172 A2
New Elms SW8 . . . .161 A2
Brooks Ho 6 SW2 . .74 C3
Brookside Rd N19 . .4 C1
Brooks La W4 . . . . . .44 C4
Brook's Mews W1 .118 A4
Brooks Rd W4 . . . . . .36 C1
Brook St
Bayswater W2 . . . .115 C4
Mayfair W1 . . . . .118 A4
Brookstone Ct
SE15 . . . . .65 A3
Brooksville Ave
NW6 . . . . .23 A4
Brookville Rd
SW6 . . . . .154 C1
Brookwood Ave
SW13 . . . . .46 B1
Brookwood Ho
SE1 . . . . .136 B3
Brookwood Rd
SW18 . . . . .70 C3
Broome Ct 3
TW9 . . . . .44 C2
Broome Ho 7 E5 . . .17 A3
Broome Way SE5 . . .48 C3
Broom Farm SW6 .165 C2

Broomfield 7
NW1 . . . . .12 C1
Broomfield Ho
SE17 . . . . .152 A3
Broomfield House Sch
TW9 . . . . .44 B2
Broomfield Rd
TW9 . . . . .44 B2
Broomfield St E14 . .34 A4
Broomgrove Rd
SW9 . . . . .173 A1
Broomhill Rd
SW18 . . . . .58 C2
Broomhouse La
SW6 . . . . .58 C4
Broomhouse Rd
SW6 . . . . .165 B2
Broomsleigh St
NW6 . . . . .10 B3
Broomwood Hall
(Lower Sch) 5
SW12 . . . . .60 D1
Broomwood Hall Sch
(Lower Sch) 3
SW16 . . . . .73 C1
Broomwood Hall Sch
(Upper Sch) 3
SW12 . . . . .72 C4
Broomwood Rd
SW11 . . . . .60 C2
Brougham Rd
Acton W3 . . . . .28 B3
Hackney E8 . . . . .24 C4
Brougham St
SW11 . . . . .169 A2
Brough Cl SW8 . . . .162 B1
Broughton Dr 19
SW9 . . . . .63 A3
Broughton Rd
SW6 . . . . .166 B2
Broughton Road App
2 SW6 . . . . .166 A2
Broughton St
SW8 . . . . .170 A2
Brouncker Rd W3 . .37 B4
Browne Ho 6 SE8 . .51 C3
Brownfield E14 . . . .34 B3
Brownflete Ho
SE4 . . . . .66 A3
Brown Hart Gdns
W1 . . . . .117 C4
Browning Cl W9 . . . .89 A1
Browning Ct W14 . .154 C4
Browning Ho
2 London SE14 . . . .51 A2
7 Shepherd's Bush
W12 . . . . .30 B3
10 Stoke Newington
N16 . . . . .16 A4
Browning Mews
W1 . . . . .103 C3
Browning Ho SE17 .151 A3
Brownlow Ho 3
SE16 . . . . .139 B3
Brownlow Mews
WC1 . . . . .95 A1
Brownlow Rd
Hackney E8 . . . . .24 C4
Willesden NW10 . . . . . .8 A1
Brownlow St WC1 .107 A3
Brown's Bldgs
EC3 . . . . .110 B1
Brown St W1 . . . . . .102 C2
Brownswood Rd N4 .6 B2
Broxash Rd SW11 . . .60 C1

Broxbourne Ho 1
E3 . . . . .27 A1
Broxholme Ho
SW6 . . . . .166 A4
Broxholm Rd SE27,
SW16 . . . . .74 C1
Broxwood Way
NW8 . . . . .80 B3
Bruce Cl W10 . . . . . .30 C4
Bruce Glasier Ho 13
N19. . . . .
Bruce Ho
4 Clapham Pk
SW4 . . . . .61 C1
5 North Kensington
W10 . . . . .30 C4
Putney SW15 . . . . .57 A2
Bruce Rd E3 . . . . . . .27 A2
Bruckner St W10 . . .23 B2
Bruges Pl 16 NW1 . .13 B1
Brune Ho E1 . . . . . .110 C3
Brunei Gall The
WC1 . . . . .105 C4
Brunel Ct
3 Barnes SW13 . . . . .46 B1
College Park NW1 . . .21 C3
Brunel Est W2 . . . . .31 C4
Brunel Ho
Chelsea SW10 . . . . . .157 C2
4 Gospel Oak
NW5 . . . . .13 A4
Millwall E14 . . . . .42 A1
New Cross SE8 . . . . . .51 B3
25 Streatham SW2 . .74 A4
Brunel Mews
NW10 . . . . .22 C2
Brunel Mus SE16 . . .40 B4
Brunel Rd
Acton W3 . . . . .29 A4
Wapping SE16 . . . . . . .32 B1
Brunel St E16 . . . . . .35 B3
Brunlees Ho SE1 . . .137 A1
Bruno Ct 8 E8 . . . . .16 C2
Brunswick Ct
Bermondsey SE1 . . . .138 B4
Finsbury EC1 . . . . .96 A3
Westminster SW1 . . .147 C3
Brunswick Gdns
W8 . . . . .31 C1 113 C1
Brunswick Ho
4 Haggerston E2 . . . .24 B3
Lisson Gr NW1 . . . . . .90 C2
Brunswick Mews
W1 . . . . .103 A2
Brunswick Park Prim
Sch 22 SE5 . . . . .49 A3
Brunswick Pk SE5 . .49 A2
Brunswick Pl N1 . . . .97 C3
Brunswick Quay
SE16 . . . . .40 C3
Brunswick Rd E14 . .34 B3
Brunswick Sch Ctr
WC1 . . . . .94 B2
Brunswick Sq WC1 . .94 B2
Brunswick Villas 2
SE5 . . . . .49 A2
Brunton Pl E14 . . . . .33 A3
Brushfield St E1 . . .110 C4
Brussels Rd SW11 . .59 C3
Bruton La W1 . . . . . .118 B3
Bruton Pl W1 . . . . . .118 B3
Bruton St W1 . . . . . .118 B3
Brutus Ct SE11 . . . . .150 A3
Bryan Ave NW10 . . . .9 A1
Bryan Ct W1 . . . . . . .102 C2

Bryan Ho SE16 . . . . .41 B4
Bryan Rd SE16 . . . . .41 B4
Bryanston Ct W1 . .102 C2
Bryanston Ho 12
SE15 . . . . .49 B2
Bryanston Mans
W1 . . . . .102 C4
Bryanston Mews E
W1 . . . . .102 C3
Bryanston Mews W
W1 . . . . .102 C3
Bryanston Pl W1 . . .102 C3
Bryanston Sq W1 . .102 C2
Bryanston St W1 . . .103 A1
Bryant Ct
Acton W3 . . . . .28 C1
5 Haggerston E2 . . . .24 B3
Bryantwood Rd N5,
N7 . . . . .14 C3
Bryce Ho 22 SE14 . . .50 C4
Brydale Ho 2
SE16 . . . . .40 C2
Brydges Pl WC2 . . .120 A3
Brydges Rd E15 . . . .19 C3
Brydon Wlk N1 . . . . .84 B4
Bryer Ct EC2 . . . . . .108 C4
Bryett Rd N7 . . . . .5 A1
Bryher Ho W4 . . . . . .37 B1
Brymay Cl E3 . . . . . .26 C3
Brymon Ct W1 . . . . .103 A3
Brynmaer Ho
SW11 . . . . .169 A3
Brynmaer Rd
SW11 . . . . .169 A3
Bryony Rd W12 . . . . .29 C2
BT Twr W1 . . . . .104 C4
Buccleuch Ho E5 . . . .
SE16 . . . . .40 C2
Buchanan Gdns
NW10 . . . . .22 A3
Buchanan Ho
Dulwich SE21 . . . .
Wandsworth SW18 . . .70 C4
Buchan Ho W3 . . . . .37 A4
Buchan Rd SE15 . . . .65 B4
Bucharest Rd
SW18 . . . . .71 B4
Buckfast St
E2 . . . . .24 C2 99 C3
Buck Hill Wlk W2 . .115 C3
Buckhold Rd
SW18 . . . . .58 C1
Buckhurst Ho 6
N7 . . . . .13 C3
Buckhurst St E1 . . . .25 A1
Buckingham Ave
SW1 . . . . .120 B3
Buckingham Gate
SW1 . . . . .133 A2
Buckingham Ho
Finsbury Pk N4 . . . . . . .6 B3
Richmond TW10 . . . . .54 C2
Buckingham Mans
NW6 . . . . .11 A3
Buckingham Mews
Harlesden NW10 . . . . .21 B3
7 Kingsland N1 . . . . .16 A2
Westminster SW1 . . .132 C2
Buckingham Pal
SW1 . . . . .132 C2
Buckingham Palace
Rd SW1 . . . . .146 B4
Buckingham Pl
SW1 . . . . .132 C2

Buckingham Rd
Harlesden NW10 . . . . .21 B3
Kingsland N1 . . . . .16 A2
Buckingham St
WC2 . . . . .120 B3
Buckingham Yd
NW10 . . . . .21 B3
Buckland Cres
NW3 . . . . .11 C2
Buckland Ct 6 N1 . .24 A3
Buckland Ho 3
N1 . . . . .14 C1
Buckland St N1 . . . . .87 C1
Buckland Wlk 2
W3 . . . . .37 B4
Buckler's Alley
SW6 . . . . .155 A2
Bucklersbury EC2,
EC4 . . . . .109 B1
Buckle St
15 Whitechapel
E1 . . . . .111 B2
Whitechapel E1 . . . . .111 A2
Buckley Ct 5
NW6 . . . . .10 B1
Buckley Rd NW6 . . . .10 B1
Buckmaster Cl 1
SW9 . . . . .62 C4
Buckmaster Ho
N7 . . . . .14 B4
Buckmaster Rd
SW11 . . . . .60 A3
Bucknall St WC1 . . .106 A2
Bucknell Cl SW2 . . . .62 B3
Buckner Rd SW2 . . . .62 B3
Buckridge Bldg
EC1 . . . . .107 B4
Buckshead Ho 3
W2 . . . . .31 C4
Buck St NW1 . . . . . . .13 A1
Buckstone Cl SE23 . .65 B1
Buckters Rents
SE16 . . . . .33 A1
Buckthorne Rd
SE4 . . . . .66 A2
Budge Row EC4 . . .109 B1
Budge's Wlk W2 . . .115 A2
Budleigh Ho 19
SE15 . . . . .49 C3
Buer Rd SW6 . . . . . .164 B1
Bugsby's Way
SE10 . . . . .43 B2
Buick Ho 4 E3 . . . . .26 C1
Building Crafts Coll
E15 . . . .
Bulbarrow 8
NW8 . . . . .78 B3
Bulinga St SW1 . . . .147 C3
Bullace Row SE5 . . .48 C2
Bullards Pl 18 E2 . . .25 C2
Bulleid Way SW1 . .146 B3
Bullen Ho 13 E1 . . . .25 A1
Bullen St SW11 . . . .168 B2
Buller Cl SE15 . . . . . .49 C3
Buller Rd NW10 . . . . .22 C2
Bullfinch Ct 8
SE21 . . . . .75 C2
Bullingham Mans
W8 . . . . .127 C4
Bull Inn Ct WC2 . . .120 B3
Bullivant St 9
E14 . . . . .34 B2
Bulls Alley SW14 . . .45 C1
Bull's Gdns SW3 . . .144 B4
Bulls Head Pas
EC3 . . . . .110 A1
Bull Yd SE15 . . . . . . .49 C2

Bulmer Mews
W11 . . . . . 31 C1 113 B2
Bulow St SW6 . . . 166 B2
Bulstrode PI W1 . . 103 C3
Bulstrode St W1 . . 103 C2
Bulwer St W12 . . . . 30 B1
Bunbury Ho SE15 . . 49 C3
Bunhill Row EC1 . . . 97 B1
Bunhouse PI
  Chelsea SW1 . . . . 145 C2
  SW1 . . . . 145 C2
Bunkers Hill NW11 . . 2 A4
Bunning Ho N7 . . . . 14 A4
Bunning Way N7 . . . 14 B1
Bunsen St 3 E3 . . . 26 A3
Bunsen St 3 E3 . . . 26 A3
Bunyan Ct EC2 . . . 108 C4
Buonaparte Mews
  SW1 . . . . 147 B2
Burbage CI SE1 . . . 137 B1
Burbage Ho
  16 Deptford SE14 . . 50 C4
  Shoreditch N1 . . . . 87 C3
Burbage Rd SE21,
  SE24 . . . . 75 C2
Burcham St E14 . . . 34 B3
Burchell Ho SE11 . . 149 A2
Burchell Rd SE15 . . 50 A2
Burcher Gale Gr 5
  SE15 . . . . 49 B3
Burcote Rd SW18 . . 71 C4
Burden Ho SW8 . . . 162 A1
Burdenshott Ave
  TW10 . . . . 55 A3
Burder CI N1 . . . . . 16 A2
Burder Rd N1 . . . . . 16 A2
Burdett Coutts &
  Townshend CE Prim
  Sch SW1 . . . . . . 133 B1
Burdett Mews 4
  W2 . . . . 100 A2
Burdett Rd
  Richmond TW9 . . . . 54 B4
  Tower Hamlets E3 . . 33 B4
Burdon Ct 3 E8 . . . 16 C2
Burford Ct SE8 . . . . 51 C4
Burford Ho
  1 Brentford
  11 South Lambeth
  SW9 . . . . 173 A1
Burford Rd
  Brentford TW8 . . . . 36 A1
  5 Stratford Marsh
  E15 . . . . 27 C4
Burford Wlk SW6 . . 156 B1
Burgate Ct 2
  SW9 . . . . 62 C4
Burgas Gr SW13 . . . 47 A3
Burgess Bros Pk
  SE5 . . . . 48 B2
Burgess Hill NW2 . . 10 C4
Burgess Ho 3 SE5 . . 48 B3
Burgess Park Mans
  NW6 . . . . 10 C4
Burgess St E14 . . . . 33 C4
Burge St SE1 . . . . 137 C1
Burgh House &
  Hampstead Mus
  NW3 . . . . 11 C4
Burghley Hall CI
  SW19 . . . . 70 A3
Burghley Ho SW19 . . 70 A1
Burghley Rd NW5 . . 13 A4
Burghley Twr 3 W3 . 29 B2
Burgh St N1 . . . . . . 86 B2

Burgon St EC4 . . . 108 B1
Burgos Gr SE10 . . . . 52 A2
Burgoyne Rd SW9 . . 62 B4
Burhan Uddin Ho
  E1 . . . . . 24 B1 98 C1
Buriton Ho 9
  SW15 . . . . 69 A3
Burke CI SW15 . . . . 56 A3
Burke Ho 1 SW11 . . 59 C3
Burke St E16 . . . . . 35 B4
Burland Rd SW11 . . 60 B2
Burleigh Coll W6 . . . 39 B2
Burleigh Ho
  Chelsea SW3 . . . 157 C3
  5 North Kensington
  W10 . . . . 30 C4
Burleigh PI SW15 . . 57 C2
Burleigh St WC2 . . 120 C4
Burley Ho E1 . . . . . 32 C3
Burlington Arc
  W1 . . . . 118 C3
Burlington Ave
  TW9 . . . . 44 C2
Burlington CI W9 . . 23 C1
Burlington Ct
  Chiswick W4 . . . . . 45 B3
  Highgate N6 . . . . . 3 C3
Burlington Danes
  Acad W12 . . . . . 30 A3
Burlington Gdns
  Acton Green W4 . . . 37 B1
  Acton W3 . . . . . . 28 B1
  4 Fulham SW6 . . 164 B1
  Marylebone W1 . . 118 C3
Burlington Ho
  NW3 . . . . 11 C3
Burlington La W4 . . 45 C3
Burlington Lodge
  SW6 . . . . 164 B1
Burlington Mews
  Acton W3 . . . . . . 28 B1
  2 Putney SW15 . . 58 B2
Burlington PI
  SW6 . . . . 164 B1
Burlington Rd
  Acton Green W4 . . . 37 B1
  Fulham SW6 . . . . 164 B1
Burma Rd N16 . . . . 15 C4
Burmarsh 6 NW5 . . 12 C2
Burmester Ho
  SW17 . . . . 71 B1
Burmester Rd
  SW17 . . . . 71 B1
Burnaby Cres W4 . . 45 B4
Burnaby Ct 31
  SE16 . . . . 139 C3
Burnaby Gdns W4 . . 45 A4
Burnaby St SW10 . . 157 A1
Burnand Ho 3
  W14 . . . . 39 C3
Burnbury Rd SW12 . . 73 B3
Burne Jones Ho
  W14 . . . . 140 A3
Burnell Ho 18
  SW2 . . . . 74 C3
Burnell Wlk SE1 . . 153 A2
Burness CI N7 . . . . 14 B2
Burne St NW1 . . . 102 A4
Burnett Ct 7
  SW11 . . . . 168 A3
Burnett Ho 6
  SE13 . . . . 52 B1
Burney St SE10 . . . . 52 B3
Burnfoot Ave
  SW6 . . . . 164 B3
Burnham NW3 . . . . 12 A1

Burnham CI SE1 . . 153 A3
Burnham Ct W2 . . . 114 B4
Burnham Est 8
  E2 . . . . 25 B2
Burnham St E2 . . . . 25 B2
Burnhill Ho EC1 . . . 96 C3
Burnhill Ho EC1 . . . 96 C3
Burnley Rd
  London SW9 . . . . 172 C2
  Willesden NW10 . . . 8 C3
Burnsall St SW3 . . 144 B2
Burns Ho
  18 Bethnal Green
  E2 . . . . 25 B2
  2 Islington N7 . . . 14 B2
  Kennington SE17 . . 150 B1
  11 Stoke Newington
  N16 . . . . 16 A4
Burn's Ho NW10 . . . 21 A4
Burnside CI SE16 . . 32 C1
Burns Rd SW11 . . . 168 C2
Burn's Rd SW11 . . . 21 B4
Burnthwaite Rd
  SW6 . . . . 155 A1
Burntwood CI
  SW18 . . . . 72 A3
Burntwood Ct
  SW17 . . . . 71 B1
Burntwood Grange Rd
  SW18 . . . . 72 A3
Burntwood La
  SW17 . . . . 71 C2
Burntwood Sch
  SW17 . . . . 71 C2
Buross St E1 . . . . . 32 A3
Burrage PI 17
  SE16 . . . . 40 C2
Burrard Rd NW6 . . . 10 C4
Burr CI E1 . . . . . . 125 B2
Burrell St SE1 . . . 122 A2
Burrell's Wharf Sq
  E14 . . . . 42 A1
Burrhill Ct SE16 . . . 40 C3
Burrow Ho
  SW9 . . . . 173 A1
Burrow Rd SE22 . . . 64 A3
Burrows Mews
  SE1 . . . . 136 A4
Burrows Rd NW10 . . 22 B2
Burrow Wlk SE21 . . 75 B4
Burr Rd SW18 . . . . 70 C4
Bursar St SE1 . . . . 124 A1
Burslem St E1 . . . . 111 C1
Burstock Rd SW15 . . 58 A3
Burston Rd SW15 . . 57 C2
Burtley CI N4 . . . . . 6 B3
Burton Bank N1 . . . 15 C1
Burton Ct SW3 . . . 145 A2
Burton Gr SE17 . . . 151 B1
Burton Ho
  8 Bermondsey
  SE16 . . . . 40 A4
  Brixton SE5 . . . . . 48 A2
Burton Lo 6
  SW15 . . . . 58 B2
Burton Mews
  SW1 . . . . 145 C3
Burton PI WC1 . . . . 93 C3
Burton Rd
  7 Brixton SW9 . . 173 B2
  Brixton SW9 . . . . 48 A1
  Brondesbury NW6 . . 10 B1
Burtons Ct E15 . . . . 19 C1
Burton St WC1 . . . . 93 C2

Burtonwood Ho N4 . . 6 C4
Burtt Ho 6
  N1 . . . . . 24 A2 98 A4
Burwash Ho SE1 . . 137 C3
Burwell CI 21 E1 . . . 32 A3
Burwell Wlk 4 E3 . . 26 C1
Burwood Ho 11
  SW9 . . . . 63 A3
Burwood PI W2 . . . 102 B2
Bury CI SE16 . . . . . 32 C1
Bury Ct EC3 . . . . . 110 B2
Buryfield Ct 23
  SE8 . . . . 40 C2
Bury St
  St James SW1 . . . 119 A2
  Whitechapel C3 . . 110 B2
Bury Wlk SW3 . . . 144 A2
Busbridge Ho 20
  E14 . . . . 33 C4
Busby Mews 5
  NW1 . . . . 13 C2
Busby PI NW5 . . . . 13 C2
Bushaby CI SW1 . . 138 A1
Bushberry Rd E9 . . . 18 A2
Bush Cotts 12
  SW18 . . . . 58 C2
Bush CI 8 W12 . . . 39 C4
Bushell CI SW2 . . . 74 B2
Bushell St E1 . . . . 125 C2
Bushey Down
  SW12 . . . . 73 A2
Bushey Hall SE5 . . . 49 B2
Bushey Hill Rd
  SE5 . . . . 49 B2
Bushfield Ho N5 . . . 15 B3
Bush Ind Est
  London N19 . . . . . 20 C1
  Upper Holloway N19 . 4 C1
Bush La EC4 . . . . . 123 B4
Bushnell Rd SW17 . . 73 A1
Bush Rd
  Bermondsey SE8 . . . 40 C2
  Hackney E8 . . . . . 25 A4
  Richmond TW9 . . . . 44 B4
Bushwood Dr SE1 . . 153 A3
Bushwood Rd
  TW9 . . . . 44 C4
Business Design Ctr
  N1 . . . . 85 C3
Buspace Studios 3
  W10 . . . . 23 A1
Butcher Row E1 . . . 32 C3
Butcher Ho E6 . . . . 35 C3
Bute Gdns W6 . . . . 39 C2
Bute House Prep Sch
Bute St SW7 . . . . 143 B4
Bute Wlk 2 N1 . . . 15 C2
Butfield Ho 6 E9 . . . 17 B2
Butler Ho
  18 Bethnal Green
  E2 . . . . 25 B2
  5 Brixton SW9 . . . 48 A2
  11 Poplar E14 . . . . 33 B3
Butler PI SW1 . . . . 133 B2
Butlers & Colonial
  Wharf SE1 . . . . . 139 A4
Butler St SW3 . . . 144 C3
Butler's Wharf W
  SE1 . . . . 124 C1
Butley Ct 8 E3 . . . . 26 A3
Butterfield CI 1
  SE16 . . . . 40 A4

C

Cabanel Pl SE11 . . . . **149** A3
Cabbell St NW1 . . . . . **102** A3
Cabinet Off SW1 . . . . **134** A4
Cabinet War Rooms &
Churchill Mus
SW1 . . . . **133** C4
Cable Ho NW1 . . . . **95** B4
Cable Pl SE10 . . . . **52** B2
Cable St E1 . . . . **32** A2
Cabot Ct SE16 . . . . **40** C3
Cabot Sq E14 . . . . **33** C1
Cabul Rd SW11 . . . . . **168** B1
Cactus Cl SE5 . . . . **49** A1
Cactus Wlk W12 . . . . . **29** B3
Cadbury Way **4**
SE16 . . . . **153** B4
Caddington Rd
NW2 . . . . **1** A1
Cadell Cl E2 . . . . **24** B3
Cadell Ho **12** E2 . . . . . . **24** B3
Cade Rd SE10 . . . . **52** C2
Cader Rd SW18 . . . . . . **59** B1
Cadet Dr SE1 . . . . **153** A2
Cade Tyler Ho **10**
SE10 . . . . **52** B2
Cadiz St SE17 . . . . **151** A1
Cadman Cl SW9 . . . . . . **48** A3
Cadmore Ho **4**
N1 . . . . **15** A1
Cadmus Cl **9**
SW4 . . . . **61** C4
Cadmus Ct **5**
SW9 . . . . **173** B4
Cadnam Lo E14 . . . . . . **42** C3
Cadnam Point **15**
SW15 . . . . **69** A3
Cadogan Cl E9 . . . . **18** B1
Cadogan Ct SW3 . . . . **144** C3
Cadogan Ct Gdns
SW1 . . . . **145** B4
Cadogan Gate
SW1 . . . . **145** A4
Cadogan Gdns
SW3 . . . . **145** A3
Cadogan Hall
SW1 . . . . **145** B4
Cadogan Ho SW3 . . . **157** C3
Cadogan La SW1 . . . . **131** B1
Cadogan Pier
SW3 . . . . **158** B3
Cadogan Pl SW1 . . . . **131** A1
Cadogan Sq SW1 . . . . **131** A1
Cadogan St SW3 . . . . **144** C3
Cadogan Terr E9 . . . . . . **18** B1
Caedmon Rd N7 . . . . . . **14** B4
Caernarvon Ho
W2 . . . . **100** C2
Caesar Ct **22** E2 . . . . . . **25** C3
Cahill St EC1 . . . . **97** A1
Caine Ho W3 . . . . **37** A4
Caird St W10 . . . . **23** B2
Cairns Ho **3** N7 . . . . **14** B4
Cairns Rd SW11 . . . . . . **60** A2
Caister Ho N7 . . . . **14** B2
Caistor Ho **10**
SW12 . . . . **73** A4
Caistor Mews
SW12 . . . . **73** A4
Caistor Rd SW12 . . . . . **73** A4

Caithness Ho N1 . . . . . **84** C4
Caithness Rd W14 . . . . **39** C3
Calabria Rd N5 . . . . **15** A3
Calais Gate SE5 . . . . . . **48** A2
Calais St SE5 . . . . **48** A2
Calbourne Rd
SW12 . . . . **72** C4
Calcraft Ho **10** E2 . . . . . **25** B3
Caldecot Ct SE5 . . . . . . **48** B1
Caldecot Rd SE5 . . . . . . **48** B1
Calder Ct SE16 . . . . **33** B1
Calderon Ho NW8 . . . . **80** A2
Calderon Pl **20**
W10 . . . . **30** B4
Caldervale Rd
SW4 . . . . **61** C2
Caldew St SE5 . . . . **48** C3
Caldy Wlk **10** N1 . . . . . **15** B2
Caleb St SE1 . . . . **137** A4
Caledonia Ho **13**
E14 . . . . **33** A3
Caledonian Market
SE1 . . . . **138** B2
Caledonian Rd
Islington N1 . . . . **84** C3
Lower Holloway N7 . . . **14** B2
Caledonian Road &
Barnsbury Sta
N7 . . . . **14** B1
Caledonian Road Sta
N7 . . . . **14** B2
Caledonian Sq **6**
NW1 . . . . **13** C2
Caledonian Wharf Rd
E14 . . . . **42** C2
Caledonia St N1 . . . . . . **84** B1
Cale St SW3 . . . . **144** A2
Caletock Way
SE10 . . . . **43** B1
Calgarth NW1 . . . . **83** A1
Calgary Ct **30** SE16 . . . **40** B4
Caliban Twr **3** N1 . . . . . **24** A3
Calico Ho **4** SW11 . . . . **59** B4
Calico Row **5**
SW11 . . . . **59** B4
Calidore Cl SW2 . . . . . . **62** B1
California Bldg **2**
SE13 . . . . **52** A2
Callaby Terr **11**
N1 . . . . **15** C2
Callahan Cotts **8**
E1 . . . . **32** B4
Callcott Ho NW6 . . . . . **10** B1
Callcott Rd NW6 . . . . . **10** B1
Callcott St
W8 . . . . **31** C1 **113** B2
Callendar Rd
SW7 . . . . **129** B2
Callingham Cl **13**
E14 . . . . **33** B4
Callingham Ho **4**
SW4 . . . . **62** A4
Callow St SW3 . . . . . . **157** B4
Calmington Rd
SE5 . . . . **49** A4
Calshot Ho N1 . . . . **84** C2
Calshot St N1 . . . . **84** C1
Calstock NW1 . . . . **83** B3
Calstock Ho SE11 . . . **149** C2
Calthorpe St WC1 . . . . **95** A3
Calton Ave SE21 . . . . . . **64** A1
Calver **13** NW5 . . . . **13** A4
Calverley Gr N19 . . . . . . **4** C3
Calvert Ave
E2 . . . . **24** B2 **98** C3

Calvert Ct
1 London N19 . . . . **4** B3
5 Richmond TW9 . . . **54** B3
Calvert Ho **9** W12 . . . . **30** A2
Calverton SE5 . . . . **49** A4
Calvert Rd SE10 . . . . . . **43** B1
Calvert's Bldgs
SE1 . . . . **123** B1
Calvert St NW1 . . . . **81** B4
Calvin St E1, E2 . . . **98** C1
Calypso Cres **6**
SE15 . . . . **49** B3
Calypso Way SE8,
SE16 . . . . **41** B2
Cambalt Ho **3**
SW15 . . . . **57** C2
Cambalt Rd SW15 . . . . . **57** C2
Cambay Ho **7** E1 . . . . . **26** A1
Camber Ho **4**
SE15 . . . . **50** B4
Camberley Ho
NW1 . . . . **82** B1
CAMBERWELL **3**
SE5 . . . . **48** C2
Camberwell Bsns Ctr
SE5 . . . . **48** C3
Camberwell Church St
SE5 . . . . **48** C2
Camberwell Coll of
Arts
12 Camberwell
SE5 . . . . **49** A2
25 Camberwell
SE15 . . . . **49** B3
Camberwell Glebe
SE5 . . . . **49** A2
Camberwell Gn
SE5 . . . . **48** C2
Camberwell Gr
SE5 . . . . **48** C1 **49** A2
Camberwell Green
SE5 . . . . **48** C2
Camberwell New Rd
SW9 . . . . **48** A3
Camberwell Rd
SE5 . . . . **48** C3
Camberwell Station
Rd SE5 . . . . **48** B2
Camberwell Trad Est
SE5 . . . . **48** B2
Camborne Rd
SW18 . . . . **70** C4
Cambourne Mews **6**
W11 . . . . **31** A3
Cambray Rd SW12 . . . . **73** B3
Cambria Ho **14**
E14 . . . . **33** A3
Cambria Lo **3**
SW15 . . . . **58** B2
Cambrian Cl SE27 . . . . . **75** A1
Cambrian Rd
TW10 . . . . **54** B1
Cambria Rd SE5 . . . . . . **63** B4
Cambria St SW6 . . . . . **156** B1
Cambridge Ave
NW6 . . . . **23** C3
Cambridge Cir
WC2 . . . . **105** C1
Cambridge Cotts
TW9 . . . . **44** C4
Cambridge Cres **2**
E2 . . . . **25** A3

Cambridge Ct continued
2 Kilburn NW6 . . . . . **23** C3
Marylebone W2 . . . . **102** A3
Stamford Hill N16 . . . . . **7** A4
Cambridge Gate
NW1 . . . . **92** A2
Cambridge Gate
Mews NW1 . . . . **92** B2
Cambridge Gdns
Kilburn NW6 . . . . **23** C3
North Kensington
W10 . . . . **31** A3
Cambridge Gr W6 . . . . . **39** A2
Cambridge Grove Rd
NW6 . . . . **23** C3
Cambridge Heath Rd
E1, E2 . . . . **25** A2
Cambridge Heath Sta
E2 . . . . **25** A3
Cambridge Ho
SW6 . . . . **58** A4
Cambridge Mans
SW11 . . . . **168** C3
Cambridge Pas **2**
E9 . . . . **17** B1
Cambridge Pl W8 . . . . **128** B3
Cambridge Rd
Barnes SW13 . . . . **46** B1
Battersea SW11 . . . . **168** C3
Kilburn NW6 . . . . **23** C2
Kilburn NW6 . . . . **23** C3
Richmond TW9 . . . . . . **44** C3
Cambridge Rd N
W4 . . . . **37** A1
Cambridge Rd S **3**
W4 . . . . **37** A1
Cambridge Sch **2**
W6 . . . . **39** A2
Cambridge Sq
W2 . . . . **102** A2
Cambridge St
SW1 . . . . **146** C2
Cambridge Terr
NW1 . . . . **92** A3
Cambridge Terr Mews
NW1 . . . . **92** B3
Cambus Rd E16 . . . . **35** C4
Cam Ct **2** SE15 . . . . . . **49** B4
Camden Arts Ctr
NW3 . . . . **11** B3
Camden Gdns
NW1 . . . . **13** A1
Camden High St
NW1 . . . . **82** C3
Camden Ho **6**
SE8 . . . . **41** B2
Camdenhurst St
E14 . . . . **33** A3
Camden Lock Mkt
NW1 . . . . **13** A1
Camden Lock Pl
NW1 . . . . **13** A1
Camden Mews
NW1 . . . . **13** C2
Camden Mkt NW1 . . . . **82** B4
Camden Park Rd
NW1 . . . . **13** C2
Camden Pas N1 . . . . . . **86** A3
Camden Rd NW1 . . . . . **82** B4
Camden Road Sta
NW1 . . . . **13** B1
Camden Row SE3 . . . . . **53** A1
Camden Sch for Girls
The NW5 . . . . **13** B2
Camden Sq NW1 . . . . . **13** C2
Camden St NW1 . . . . . . **83** A3
Camden Studios
NW1 . . . . **83** A3

Camden Terr **17**
NW1 . . . . **13** C2
CAMDEN TOWN **13** A1
Camden Town Sta
NW1 . . . . **82** B4
Camden Wlk N1 . . . . . . **86** A3
Cameford Ct **20**
SW12 . . . . **74** A4
Camelford Ho **3**
SW1 . . . . **83** A3
Camelford Ct **18**
W11 . . . . **31** A3
Camelford Ho
SE11 . . . . **148** B1
Camelford Wlk **13**
W11 . . . . **31** A3
Camellia Ho SE8 . . . . . . **51** B3
Camellia St SW8 . . . . . **162** A1
Camelot Ho **18**
NW1 . . . . **13** C2
Camelot Prim Sch
SE15 . . . . **50** A4
Camera Pl SW10 . . . . . **157** B4
Camera Press Gall
SE1 . . . . **138** C3
Cameret Ct **6**
W11 . . . . **39** C4
Cameron Ct **3**
SW19 . . . . **70** A3
Cameron Ho
Camberwell SE5 . . . . . **48** B3
St John's Wood
NW8 . . . . **80** A2
Cameron House Sch
SW10 . . . . **157** C4
Cameron Pl SW16 . . . . **74** C2
Camerton Cl **8** E8 . . . . **16** B2
Camilla Rd SE16 . . . . . . **40** A2
Camlet St
E2 . . . . **24** B1 **98** C2
Camley St Natural Pk
NW1 . . . . **83** C3
Camley St NW1 . . . . **83** C2
Camomile St EC3 . . . . **110** B2
Campaign Ct W9 . . . . . . **23** B1
Campana Rd SW6 . . . **165** C4
Campbell Ct
Dulwich SE21 . . . . **76** C3
South Kensington
SW7 . . . . **128** C1
Campbell Gordon Way
NW2 . . . . **9** A4
Campbell Ho
Paddington W2 . . . . . . **89** B1
Pimlico SW1 . . . . **146** C1
30 Shepherd's Bush
W12 . . . . **30** A2
Campbell Rd E3 . . . . . . **26** C2
Campbell Wlk N1 . . . . . **84** B4
Campdale Rd N7 . . . . **4** C1
Campden Gr W8 . . . . . **127** C4
Campden Hill W8 . . . . **127** B4
Campden Hill Ct
W8 . . . . **127** C4
Campden Hill Gate
W8 . . . . **127** B4
Campden Hill Gdns
W8 . . . . **31** C1 **113** B2
Campden Hill Mans
W8 . . . . **31** C1 **113** C2
Campden Hill Pl
W14 . . . . **31** B1 **113** A2
Campden Hill Rd
W8 . . . . **127** B4
Campden Hill Sq
W14 . . . . **31** B1 **113** A2

Campden Ho 4
NW6 . . . . 11 C1
Campden Hos
W8 . . . . 31 C1 113 B1
Campden House Cl
W8 . . . . 127 C4
Campden St
W8 . . . . 31 C1 113 B1
Campen Cl SW19 . . . .70 A2
Camperdown St
E1 . . . . 111 A1
Campion Ho 13
N16 . . . . 16 A3
Campion Rd SW15 . .57 B2
Camplin St SE14 . . . .50 C3
Campshill Pl SE13 . .67 B2
Campshill Rd SE13 . .67 B2
Campton Hill Twrs
W8 . . . . 31 C1 113 B2
Cam Rd E15 . . . . .27 C4
Camsey Ho 8
SW2 . . . . .62 B2
Canada Cres W3 . . . .20 B1
Canada Est 35
SE16 . . . . .40 B4
Canada Gdns SE13 . .67 B2
Canada Memorial
SW1 . . . . 132 C4
Canada Rd W3 . . . . . .28 B4
Canada Sq E14 . . . . . .34 B1
Canada St SE16 . . . . .40 C4
Canada Water Sta
SE16 . . . . .40 C3
Canada Way W12 . . . .30 A2
Canal App SE8 . . . . . .51 A4
Canal Bldg N1 . . . . . .86 C2
Canal Bridge SE15 . .49 C4
Canal Bvd 7 NW1 . .13 C2
Canal Cl
  Mile End E1 . . . . . . .26 A1
  North Kensington
  W10 . . . . .22 C1
Canal Gr SE15 . . . . . .50 A4
Canal Head Public Sq
  1 SE15 . . . . .49 C2
Canal Path 22 E2 . . .24 B4
Canal Reach N1 . . . . .84 A4
Canalside Studios 24
N1 . . . . .24 A4
Canal St SE5 . . . . . . .48 C4
Canal Way W10 . . . . .22 C1
Canal Wlk N1 . . . . . .87 C4
CANARY WHARF 34 A1
Canary Wharf Coll
E14 . . . . .42 B2
Canary Wharf Pier
E14 . . . . .33 B1
Canary Wharf Sta
E14 . . . . .34 A1
Canary Wharf Sta
(DLR) E14 . . . . .33 C1
Canbury Mews
SE26 . . . . .76 C1
Cancell Rd SW9 . . .173 C4
Candahar Rd
SW11 . . . . .168 B1
Candida Ct 9
NW1 . . . . .13 A1
Candishe Ho 51 SE1 .138 C4
Candle Gr SE15 . . . . .65 A4
Candlemakers 24
SW11 . . . . .59 C4
Candle St E1 . . . . .33 A4
Candover St W1 . . . .104 C3
Candy St E3 . . . . .26 B4

Canfield Gdns
NW6 . . . . .11 A1
Canfield Pl NW6 . . . .11 B2
Canford Rd SW11 . . . .60 C2
Canham Rd W3 . . . . . .38 A4
Cann Ho W14 . . . . . . 126 B1
Canning Cross
SE5 . . . . .49 A1
Canning Ho 28
W12 . . . . .30 A2
Canning Pas W8 . . . 128 C2
Canning Pl W8 . . . . 128 C2
Canning Pl Mews
W8 . . . . 128 C2
Canning Rd N5 . . . . . .6 A1
Cannington 14
NW5 . . . . .12 C2
CANNING TOWN 35 B3
Canning Town
E16 . . . . .35 A3
Canning Town Sta
E16 . . . . .35 A3
Cannock Ho N4 . . . . . .6 C4
Cannon Dr 21 E14 . . .33 C2
Cannon Hill NW6 . . . . .1 A1
Cannon La NW3 . . . . . .2 C1
Cannon Pl NW3 . . . . . .2 C1
Cannon St EC4 . . . . 123 A4
Cannon Street Rd
E1 . . . . .32 A3
Cannon Street Sta
EC4 . . . . 123 B4
Cannon Wharf Bsns
  Ctr 12 SE8 . . . . .41 A2
Canon Barnett Prim
  Sch E1 . . . . 111 A2
Canon Beck Rd
SE16 . . . . .40 B4
CANONBURY 15 B2
Canonbury Bsns Ctr
N1 . . . . .87 A4
Canonbury Cres
N1 . . . . .15 B1
Canonbury Ct 21
N1 . . . . .15 A1
Canonbury Gr N1 . . .15 B1
Canonbury Hts 13
N1 . . . . .15 C2
Canonbury La N1 . . .15 A1
Canonbury Pk N
N1 . . . . .15 B2
Canonbury Pk S
N1 . . . . .15 B2
Canonbury Pl N1 . . .15 A2
Canonbury Prim Sch
  4 N1 . . . . .15 A2
Canonbury Rd N1 . . .15 A1
Canonbury Sq N1 . . .15 A1
Canonbury St N1 . . .15 B1
Canonbury Sta N1,
N5 . . . . .15 B3
Canonbury Villas
N1 . . . . .15 A1
Canonbury Yd E 28
N1 . . . . .15 B2
Canon Murnane Rd
SE1 . . . . 138 C1
Canon Row SW1 . . 134 A3
Canons Cl N2 . . . . . . .2 C4
Canon St N1 . . . . . . .86 C3
Canrobert St E2 . . . .25 A2
Cantelowes Rd
NW1 . . . . .13 C2
Canterbury SE13 . . . .67 B2

Canterbury Cl 10
SE5 . . . . .48 B1
Canterbury Cres
SW9 . . . . .62 C4
Canterbury Ct
  Acton W3 . . . . .29 A1
  Kilburn NW6 . . . . . . .23 C3
Canterbury Gr SE27,
SW16 . . . . .74 C1
Canterbury Ho
  8 Bromley E3 . . . . .27 A2
  Lambeth SE1 . . . . . 135 A2
Canterbury Ind Pk 15
SE15 . . . . .50 B4
Canterbury Mans
NW6 . . . . .11 A2
Canterbury Pl
SE17 . . . . 150 B3
Canterbury Rd
NW6 . . . . .23 C3
Canterbury Terr
NW6 . . . . .23 C3
Cantium Ret Pk
SE1 . . . . .49 C4
Canton St E14 . . . . . .33 C3
Cantrell Rd E3 . . . . . .26 C1
Canute Ct SW16 . . . .74 C1
Canute Gdns SE16 . .40 C2
Canvey St SE1 . . . . 122 C2
Cape Henry Ct 8
E14 . . . . .34 C2
Capel Ho 7 E9 . . . . . .17 B1
Capel Lo
  5 Richmond
  TW9 . . . . .44 B2
  12 Streatham SW2 . .74 B4
Capener's Cl SW1 131 B3
Capern Rd SW18 . . . .71 B3
Capital City Acad
NW10 . . . . .22 A4
Capital East Apts 3
E16 . . . . .35 C2
Capital Interchange
  Way TW8 . . . . .36 C1
Capital Sh Ctrs
SW1 . . . . 133 B3
Capital Wharf 14
E1 . . . . 125 C1
Capland Ho 3 NW8 . .89 C2
Capland St NW8 . . . .89 C2
Caple Ho SW10 . . . 157 A2
Caple Rd NW10 . . . . .21 B3
Capper St WC1 . . . . .93 A1
Capstan Ho 6 E14 . .42 B2
Capstan Sq E14 . . . . .42 B4
Capstan Way E14 . . .33 A1
Capulet Mews 1
E16 . . . . .35 C1
Caradoc Cl W2 . . . . . .31 C3
Caradoc St SE10 . . . .43 A1
Cara Ho 10 N1 . . . . . .14 C1
Caranday Villas 5
W11 . . . . .30 C1
Caravel Cl E14 . . . . . .41 C3
Caravel Mews 4
SE8 . . . . .51 C4
Caraway Hts E14 . . . .34 B2
Carbery Ave W3 . . . .36 B4
Carbis Rd E14 . . . . . .33 B3
Carbroke Ho 9
E9 . . . . .25 B4
Cardale St 1 E14 . . .42 B3
Carden Rd SE15 . . . . .65 A4
Cardiff Ho 9 SE15 . .49 C4

Cardigan Rd
  Barnes SW13 . . . . . .46 C1
  Bow E3 . . . . .26 B3
  Richmond TW10 . . . .54 A1
Cardigan St SE11 . . 149 B2
Cardigan Wlk 19
N1 . . . . .15 B1
Cardinal Bourne St
SE1 . . . . 137 C1
Cardinal Cap Alley
SE1 . . . . 122 C3
Cardinal Hinsley Cl
NW10 . . . . .21 C3
Cardinal Pl SW15 . . .57 C3
Cardinal Pl SW1 . . 132 C1
Cardinal Pole RC Sch
  51 Hackney E9 . . . . .17 C2
  London E9 . . . . .18 A3
Cardinals Way N19 . .4 C3
Cardinal Vaughan
  Meml Sch The
  W14 . . . . 126 A4
Cardinal Wlk
SW1 . . . . 132 C1
Cardine Mews
SE15 . . . . .50 A3
Cardington St
NW1 . . . . .93 A3
Cardozo Rd N7 . . . . .14 A3
Cardross St W6 . . . . .39 A3
Cardwell Rd 3
N7 . . . . .14 A4
Career Ct 11 SE16 . .40 C4
Carew Cl N7 . . . . .5 B2
Carew Ct 13 SE14 . . .50 C4
Carew Ho SW16 . . . .74 C1
Carew St SE5 . . . . . . .48 B1
Carey Gdns SW8 . . 171 B3
Carey La EC2 . . . . . 108 C2
Carey Pl SW1 . . . . . 147 B3
Carey St WC2 . . . . . 107 A1
Carfax Pl SW4 . . . . . .61 C3
Carfree Cl 5 N1 . . . .14 C1
Cargill Rd SW18 . . . .71 B3
Carinthia Ct 9
SE8 . . . . .41 A2
Carisbrooke Ct
  Acton W3 . . . . .37 B4
  1 Streatham
  SW16 . . . . .74 B1
Carisbrooke Gdns
SE15 . . . . .49 B3
Carisbrooke Ho
TW10 . . . . .54 C2
Carker's La
  Crouch End N19 . . . .4 C4
  Gospel Oak NW5 . . .13 A3
Carleton Gdns
N19 . . . . .13 B3
Carleton Rd N7 . . . .13 C4
Carlile Cl E3 . . . . .26 B3
Carlile Ho SE1 . . . . 137 C1
Carlingford Rd
NW3 . . . . .11 C4
Carlisle Ave
  Acton W3 . . . . .29 A3
  Whitechapel EC3 . . 110 C1
Carlisle Ho 6 NW5 . .4 B1
Carlisle La SE1 . . . . 135 A2
Carlisle Pl SW1 . . . . 132 C1
Carlisle Rd
  Finsbury Pk N4 . . . . .5 C4
  Kilburn NW6 . . . . . . .23 A4
  Willesden NW6 . . . . .9 A1
Carlisle St W1 . . . . . 105 B1
Carlisle Wlk 6 E8 . .16 B2

| Cam–Car | **193** |

Carlos Pl W1 . . . . . . 118 A3
Carlow St NW1 . . . . . .82 C2
Carlson Ct SW13 . . . .58 B3
Carlton Cl NW3 . . . . . .1 C1
Carlton Ct
  Brixton SW9 . . . . . . .48 A2
  Kilburn NW6 . . . . . . .78 B2
  4 Willesden NW2 . . .9 B2
Carlton Dr SW15 . . . .58 A2
Carlton Gdns
SW1 . . . . 119 B1
Carlton Gr SE15 . . . . .50 A2
Carlton Hill NW8 . . . .78 C2
Carlton Ho
  1 Kilburn NW6 . . . . .23 B3
  Kilburn NW6 . . . . . . .23 C3
  Marylebone W1 . . . 103 A2
Carlton House Terr
SW1 . . . . 119 C2
Carlton Lo N4 . . . . . . .5 C4
Carlton Mans
  Brixton SW9 . . . . . . .62 C3
  Cricklewood NW2 . . .9 C3
  Kensington W14 . . . 126 B4
  Maida Vale W9 . . . . .88 B4
  7 South Hampstead
  NW6 . . . . .10 C1
  Stamford Hill N16 . . .7 B3
Carlton Prim Sch
NW5 . . . . .12 C3
Carlton Rd
  Acton W4 . . . . .37 C4
  Finsbury Pk N4 . . . . .5 C4
  Mortlake SW14 . . . . .55 B3
  Carlton Sq E1 . . . . . .25 C1
  Carlton St SW1 . . . 119 B3
Carltons The 5
SW15 . . . . .58 A2
Carlton Tower Pl
SW1 . . . . 131 A2
Carlton Vale NW6 . . .23 C3
Carlton Vale Inf Sch
  12 NW6 . . . . .23 B2
Carlyle Ho
  Camberwell
  SE5 . . . . .48 B3
  Chelsea SW3 . . . . . 157 C4
  12 Stoke Newington
  N16 . . . . .7 A1
Carlyle Mans
SW3 . . . . 158 A3
Carlyle Mews 24
E1 . . . . .25 C1
Carlyle Pl SW15 . . . .57 C3
Carlyle Rd
NW10 . . . . .20 C4
Carlyle's Ho SW3 . .158 A3
Carlyle Sq SW3 . . . .143 C1
Carmalt Gdns
SW15 . . . . .57 B3
Carmarthen Ho 8
SE1 . . . . 138 A4
Carmarthen Pl
SE1 . . . . 138 A4
Carmel Ct W8 . . . . . 128 A4
Carmelite St EC4 . . 121 C4
Carmel Lo SW6 . . . . 155 B4
Carmen St E14 . . . . .34 A3
Carmichael Cl 6
SW11 . . . . .59 C4
Carmichael Ct 5
SW13 . . . . .46 B1
Carmichael Ho 6
E14 . . . . .34 B2

Carmichael Mews
SW18 . . . .**71** C4
Carminia Rd SW17 . .**73** A2
Carnaby St W1 . . . .**104** C1
Carnac St SE21,
SE27 . . . .**75** C1
Carna Ct TW9 . . . . . .**44** B2
Carnegie Ho NW3 . . . .**2** C1
Carnegie Pl SW19 . . . .**69** C1
Carnegie St N1 . . . .**85** A3
Carnicot Ho **9**
SE15 . . . .**50** A2
Carnoustie Dr N1 . . .**14** B1
Carnwath Ho SW6 . .**59** A4
Carnwath Rd SW6 . .**59** A4
Caroline Cl
Bayswater W2 . . . .**114** B3
Streatham SW16 . . .**74** B1

Caroline Ct
E2 . . . . .24 A2 **98** B4
Caroline Ho
Bayswater W2 . . . .**114** B3
20 Hammersmith
W6 . . . .**39** B1
Caroline Martyn Ho **8**
N19 . . . .**4** C4
Caroline Pl
Bayswater W2 . . . .**114** B3
Clapham SW11 . . . .**169** C1
Caroline Pl Mews
W2 . . . .**114** B3
Caroline St E1 . . . . .**32** C3
Caroline Terr
SW1 . . . .**145** B3
Caroline Wlk W6 . . .**154** A3
Carol St NW1 . . . . . .**82** C4
Caronia Ct **4**
SE16 . . . .**41** A2
Carpenter Ho
11 Tower Hamlets
E14 . . . .**33** C4
5 Tufnell Pk N19 . .**13** C4
Carpenters Ct
NW1 . . . .**82** C4
Carpenter's Pl
SW4 . . . .**61** C3
Carpenters Prim Sch
E15 . . . .**27** B4
Carpenter St W1 . . .**118** A3
Carradale Ho **2**
E14 . . . .**34** B3
Carrara Cl **18** SW9 . .**63** A3
Carrara Wharf
SW6 . . . .**58** A4
Carriage Dr E
SW11 . . . .**159** C2
Carriage Drive E
SW11 . . . .**159** C2
Carriage Drive N SW11,
SW8 . . . .**159** C3
Carriage Dr N
Battersea SW8,
SW11 . . . .**158** C2
Battersea SW8,
SW11 . . . .**159** C3
Carriage Dr S
SW11 . . . .**169** A4
Carriage Dr W
SW11 . . . .**158** C2
Carrick Ho
Islington N7 . . . . . .**14** B2
Kennington SE11 . . .**150** A2
Carrick Mews SE8 . .**51** C4

Carrington Ct
SW11 . . . .**60** A3
Carrington Ho
W1 . . . .**118** A1
Carrington Lo **3**
TW10 . . . .**54** A2
Carrington Rd
TW10 . . . .**54** C3
Carrington St W1 . .**118** A1
Carrol Cl NW5 . . . . .**13** A4
Carroll Ct
Acton W3 . . . .**37** A3
4 Shacklewell E5 . .**7** C1
Carroll Ho W2 . . . .**115** B4
Carron Cl E14 . . . . . .**34** A3
Carroun Rd SW8 . . .**162** C2
Carr St **5** E14 . . . . .**33** A3
Carslake Rd SW15 . .**57** B1
Carson Rd
Dulwich SE21 . . . . .**75** C2
Newham E16 . . . . . .**35** C4
Carter Ct EC4 . . . . .**108** B1
Carteret Ho **8**
W12 . . . .**30** A2
Carteret St SW1 . . .**133** B3
Carteret Way SE8 . . .**41** A2
Carter Ho
1 London SW2 . . .**62** C2
Spitalfields E1 . . . .**110** C3
Carter La EC4 . . . .**108** B1
Carter Pl SE17 . . . .**151** A1
Carters Cl NW5 . . . .**13** C2
Carter St SE17 . . . .**150** C1
Carter's Yd SW18 . . .**58** C2
Carthew Rd W6 . . . .**39** A3
Carthew Villas W6 . .**39** A3
Carthusian St EC1 .**108** C4
Cartier Circ E14 . . . .**34** B1
Carting La WC2 . . . .**120** B3
Cartmel NW1 . . . . . .**92** C4
Carton Ho
4 Bermondsey
SE16 . . . .**139** B2
12 Shepherd's Bush
W12 . . . .**38** B4
Cartoon Mus The
WC1 . . . .**106** A3
Cartwright Gdns
WC1 . . . .**94** A3
Cartwright Ho
SE1 . . . .**137** A1
Cartwright St E1 . . .**125** A3
Cartwright Way
SW13 . . . .**47** A3
Carvel Ho E14 . . . . .**42** B1
Carver Cl **13** W4 . . .**37** C3
Carver Rd SE24 . . . .**63** B1
Carville Cres TW8 . . .**36** A2
Caryl Ho **8** SW19 . .**69** C3
Carysfort Rd N16 . . .**15** C4
Casby Ho **5** SE16 . .**139** C2
Casella Rd SE14 . . . .**50** C3
Casey Cl NW8 . . . . . .**90** B3
Casino Ave SE24 . . . .**63** C2
Caspian Ho **10** E1 . .**32** C4
Caspian St SE5 . . . .**48** C3
Cassandra Ct **7**
NW2 . . . .**9** B2
Cass Bsns Sch EC1 . .**97** B1
Cassell Ho **21**
SW9 . . . .**172** B2
Casserley Ho W4 . . .**37** C3
Cass Ho **2** E9 . . . . .**17** C2
Cassidy Rd SW6 . . .**155** B1
Cassilis Rd E14 . . . . .**41** C4
Cassinghurst SE24 . .**63** C2

Cassland Rd **2** **17** C2
Casson Ho **11** E1 . .**111** B4
Casson St E1 . . . . .**111** B3
Castalia Sq **6** E14 . .**42** B4
Castellain Mans
W9 . . . .**88** A2
Castellain Rd W9 . . .**88** B2
Castello Ave SW15 . .**57** B2
Castelnau SW13 . . . .**47** A3
Castelnau Gdns
SW13 . . . .**47** A4
Castelnau Mans
SW13 . . . .**47** A4
Castelnau Row
SW13 . . . .**47** A4
Casterbridge
Kilburn NW6 . . . . . .**78** B4
8 Notting Hill W11 .**31** C3
Casterton St E8 . . . . .**17** A2
Castleacre W2 . . . . .**102** A1
Castle Baynard St
EC4 . . . .**122** C4
Castlebrook Cl
SE11 . . . .**150** A4
Castle Cl
5 Acton W3 . . . . .**37** B4
Homerton E9 . . . . . .**18** A3
Wimbledon SW19 . . .**69** C1
Castlecombe Dr
SW19 . . . .**69** C4
Castle Ct EC3 . . . . .**109** C1
Castleden Ho
NW6 . . . .**11** C1
Castleford Ct NW8 . . .**89** C2
Castlefrank Ho **20**
N1 . . . . .24 A2 **98** B4
Castlegate TW9 . . . . .**54** B4
Castlehaven Rd
NW1 . . . .**13** A1
Castle Ho
Newington SE1 . . . .**150** C4
South Lambeth
SW8 . . . .**162** B2
Castle Ind Est
SE17 . . . .**150** C4
Castle La SW1 . . . .**132** C2
Castleman Ho **3**
SW11 . . . .**169** A2
Castlemaine St **2**
E1 . . . .**32** B4
Castle Mead SE5 . . . .**48** B3
Castle Mews NW1 . . .**13** A2
Castle Pl
8 Acton W4 . . . . .**38** A2
Camden Town NW1 . .**13** A2
Castle Rd NW1 . . . . .**13** A2
Castlereagh St
W1 . . . .**102** C2
Castleton Ho **3**
E14 . . . .**42** B2
Castletown Rd
W14 . . . .**140** B1
Castleview Cl N4 . . . .**6** B2
Castle Way SW19 . . .**69** C1
Castlewood Ho
WC1 . . . .**105** C2
Castle Yd
Highgate N6 . . . .**3** C4
Lambeth SE1 . . . . .**122** B2
Castor La E14 . . . . . .**34** A2
Catalpa Ct SE13 . . . .**67** C1
Caterham Rd SE13 . .**67** B4
Catesby Ho **23** E9 . .**17** B1
Catesby St SE17 . . .**151** C3

Cathay Ho SE16 . . . .**40** A4
Cathay St **12** SE16 . .**40** A4
Cathcart Hill N19 . . . .**4** B1
Cathcart Rd
SW10 . . . .**156** C4
Cathcart St NW5 . . . .**13** A2
Cathedral Ct EC4 . . .**108** B1
Cathedral Lo EC1 . .**108** C4
Cathedral Sch of St
Saviour & St Mary
Overie The] SE1 . .**137** A4
Cathedral St SE1 . .**123** B2
Cathedral Wlk
SW1 . . . .**132** C2
Catherall Rd N5,
N16 . . . .**6** B1
Catherine Baird Ct **12**
SW12 . . . .**73** A4
Catherine Dr TW9 . . .**54** A3
Catherine Gr SE10 . .**52** A2
Catherine Griffiths Ct
EC1 . . . .**95** C2
Catherine Ho **18**
N1 . . . .**24** A4
Catherine St WC2 . .**120** C4
Catherine Wheel Alley
E1 . . . .**110** B3
Catherine Wheel Yd
SW1 . . . .**118** C1
Catherwood Ct N1 . . .**87** B1
Cathles Rd SW12 . . .**61** A1
Cathnor Rd W12 . . . .**39** A4
Catlin St SE16 . . . . .**40** A1
Catman Ho N4 . . . . . .**5** B3
Cato Rd SW4 . . . . . .**61** C3
Cator St
Camberwell SE15 . . .**49** B3
Camberwell SE15 . . .**49** B4
Cato St W1 . . . .**102** B2
Catton St WC1 . . . .**106** C3
Caughley Ho
SE11 . . . .**135** B1
Caulfield Ct **15**
NW1 . . . .**13** B1
Caulfield Rd
Gunnersbury W3 . . .**37** B3
London SE15 . . . . . .**50** A1
Causeway The
SW18 . . . .**59** A2
Causton Cotts **3**
E14 . . . .**33** A3
Causton Ho SE5 . . . .**48** B3
Causton Rd N6 . . . . . .**4** A4
Causton St SW1 . . .**147** C2
Cautley Ave SW4 . . .**61** B2
Cavalry Gdns
SW15 . . . .**58** B2
Cavaye Ho SW10 . . .**157** A4
Cavaye Pl SW10 . . .**143** A1
Cavell Ct **3** N19 . . . .**4** B2
Cavell Ho **8** N1 . . . .**24** A4
Cavell St E1 . . . .**32** B4
Cavendish Ave
NW8 . . . .**79** C1
Cavendish Cl
Brondesbury NW6 . .**10** B2
7 Putney SW15 . . .**58** A2
St John's Wood
NW8 . . . .**89** C4
Cavendish Coll
WC1 . . . .**105** B4
Cavendish Ct **2** . . .**110** B2
Cavendish Gdns
SW4 . . . .**61** B1

Cavendish Ho
South Lambeth
SW8 . . . .**172** A4
St John's Wood
NW8 . . . .**79** C1
Cavendish Mans
2 Clapham Pk
SW12 . . . .**61** B1
Hackney E5 . . . . . .**17** B3
6 West Hampstead
NW6 . . . .**10** C3
Cavendish Mews N
W1 . . . .**104** B4
Cavendish Mews S
W1 . . . .**104** B3
Cavendish Par
SW12 . . . .**61** A1
Cavendish Pl
Balham SW4 . . . . . .**61** A1
Brondesbury NW2 . . . .**9** C2
Marylebone W1 . . .**104** B2
Cavendish Prim Sch
W4 . . . .**46** A3
Cavendish Rd
Brondesbury NW6 . .**10** B1
Chiswick W4 . . . . . .**45** B2
Clapham Pk SW12 . .**61** B1
Cavendish Sch **14**
SE16 . . . .**40** B2
Cavendish Sch The
NW1 . . . .**82** B4
Cavendish Sq **14**
W1 . . . .**104** B2
Cavendish St N1 . . . .**87** B1
Cavendish Terr **11**
E3 . . . .**26** B2
Cavendish The
NW11 . . . .**2** A4
Cavenham Ho **7**
SE15 . . . .**49** C4
Caversham Rd
NW5 . . . .**13** B2
Caversham St
SW3 . . . .**158** C4
Caverswall St SW2 . .**62** B3
Cavour Ho SE17 . . . .**150** B2
Caxton Gr E3 . . . . . .**26** C2
Caxton Hall SW1 . . .**133** B2
Caxton Rd W12 . . . . .**39** C4
Caxton St N E16 . . . .**35** B3
Caxton St SW1 . . . .**133** B2
Caxton Wlk WC2 . . .**105** C1
Cayford Ho **1**
NW3 . . . .**12** B3
Cayley Prim Sch
E14 . . . .**33** A3
Cayton Pl EC1 . . . . .**97** B3
Cayton St EC1 . . . . .**97** B3
Cazenove Mans **1**
N16 . . . .**7** C2
Cazenove Rd N16 . . . .**7** C2
Cecil Ct
Chelsea SW10 . . . .**156** C4
South Hampstead
NW6 . . . .**11** A1
St James WC2 . . . .**120** A3
Cecil Gr NW8 . . . . . .**80** B3
Cecilia Rd E8 . . . . . .**16** C3
Cecil Mans **2**
SW17 . . . .**72** C2
Cecil Rd
Acton W3 . . . .**28** B4
Harlesden NW10 . . .**21** A4
Cecil Rhodes Ho
NW1 . . . .**83** B2

Cedar Cl
Old Ford E3 . . . . .26 B4
West Norwood
SE27 . . . . .75 B2
Cedar Ct
Islington N1 . . . . .15 B1
Marylebone W1 . .**102** B2
Mortlake SW14 . . . . .55 B3
Wimbledon SW19 . . .69 C1
Cedar Gr W5 . . . . . . .36 A3
Cedar Ho
5 Cubitt Town
E14 . . . . .42 B4
Kensington W8 . . . .**128** A2
New Cross Gate
SE14 . . . . .50 C2
5 Richmond TW9 . . .45 A2
10 Rotherhithe
SE16 . . . . .40 C4
Cedar La
Brondesbury NW2 . . .10 B2
Fulham SW6 . . . . . . .47 C2
Cedar Rd SW6 . . .**156** A1
Cedarne Rd NW2 . . . . .9 B4
Cedars Cl SE13 . . . . .67 C4
Cedars Ct SW15 . . . .56 C1
Cedars Ho **21** SW2 . .62 B3
Cedars Mews SW4 . .61 A3
Cedars Rd
Barnes SW13 . . . . . .46 C1
Clapham SW4 . . . . . .61 A3
Clapham Pk SW4 . . .61 C3
Cedar Terr TW9 . . . .54 A3
Cedar Way NW1 . . . .83 B4
Cedra Ct N16 . . . . . . .7 C3
Cedric Chambers
NW8 . . . . .89 B2
Celandine Cl E3,
E14 . . . . .33 C4
Celandine Dr E8 . .16 B1
Celbridge Mews
W2 . . . .**100** B2
Celebration Ave
E15 . . . . .19 C2
Celestial Gdns
SE13 . . . . .67 C3
Celia Blairman Ho
E1 . . . .**110** C4
Celia Ct **7** TW9 . . . .44 B2
Celia Fiennes Ho . .24 A3
Celia Rd N19 . . . . . . .34 A4
Cenacle Cl NW3 . . . . .1 C1
Cenotaph S1 . . . . .**134** A4
Centaur Ct **3**
TW8 . . . . .36 A1
Centaur St SE1 . . .**135** A2
Central Ave SW11 .**159** A1
Central Bsns Ctr
NW10 . . . . .8 A3
Central Foundation
Boys' Sch EC2 . . . .**97** C2
Central Foundation
Upper Girls Sch The
27 E3 . . . . .26 B2
Central Ho E15 . . . . .27 B3
Central Middlesex
Hospl NW10 . . . . . .20 B2
Central Par W3 . . . . .37 A4
Central St Martins
Coll EC1 . . . .**95** C1
Central St Martins
College of Art &
Design N1 . . . . . .**84** A3
Central Sch of Ballet
EC1 . . . .**95** C1

Central Sch of Speech
& Drama N3 . . . . . .11 C1
Central St EC1 . . . .**96** C3
Central Way NW10 . .20 B2
Centre Acad **4**
SW11 . . . . .59 C3
Centre Ave W3 . . . . .28 C1
Centre Bldg SE17 .**151** A4
Centre Hts **5**
NW3 . . . . .11 C1
Centre Point **3**
SE1 . . . .**153** B2
Centre Point Ho
WC2 . . . .**105** C2
Centre St E2 . . . . . . .25 A3
Centurion Bldg
SW8 . . . .**160** A3
Centurion Cl N7 . . . .14 B1
Centurion Ho **17** . . .94 B3
Century Ho SE13 . . .52 A1
Century Mews **6**
E5 . . . . .6 A1
Cephas Ave E1 . . . . .25 B1
Cephas Ho **5** E1 . . . .25 B1
Cephas St E1 . . . . . .25 B1
Cerise Rd SE15 . . . . .49 C2
Cerney Mews **4** . .**115** B4
Cervantes Ct **12**
W2 . . . .**100** B2
Cester St E2 . . . . . . .24 C4
Ceylon Rd
6 Hammersmith
W14 . . . . .39 C3
Kensington W14 . . . .39 C3
Chabot Dr SE15 . . . .65 A4
Chadacre Ho **10**
SW9 . . . . .63 A3
Chadbourn St E14 . .34 A4
Chadston Ho **17**
N1 . . . . .15 A1
Chadswell Wlk 94 B3
Chadwick St WC1 . . .95 C4
Chadwick CI SW15 . .68 B4
Chadwick Rd
Harlesden NW10 . . . .21 B3
Peckham SE15 . . . . .49 B1
Chadwick St SW1 .**133** B1
Chadworth Ho
Finsbury EC1 . . . . .**96** C3
Finsbury Pk N4 . . . . . .6 B3
Chagford Ho
30 Bromley E3 . . . .27 A2
Marylebone NW1 . .**90** C1
Chagford St NW1 . .**91** A1
Chalbury Ho **3**
SW9 . . . . .62 B3
Chalbury Wlk N1 . . .85 B2
Chalcot Cres NW1 . .81 A4
Chalcot Gdns NW3 . .12 B2
Chalcot Mews
SW16 . . . . .74 A1
Chalcot Rd NW1 . . . .81 C4
Chalcot Sq NW1 . . . .12 C1
Chaldon Rd SW6 . .**154** B2
Chale Rd SW2 . . . . . .62 A1
Chalfont Ct NW1 . . . .91 A1
Chalfont Ho **2**
SE16 . . . . .40 A3
Chalford **7** NW3 . . .11 B2
Chalford Ct **15**
SW15 . . . . .57 C1
Chalkers Cnr TW9 . .55 A4
Chalk Farm Sta
NW1 . . . . .12 C1
Chalk Hill Rd W6 . . .39 C2

Chalkwell Ho **10**
E1 . . . . .32 C3
Challenge Cl
NW10 . . . . .21 A4
Challenger Ho **7**
E14 . . . . .33 A2
Challice Way SW2 . .74 B3
Challoner Cres
W14 . . . .**140** C1
Challoner Mans
W14 . . . .**140** C1
Challoner St W14 .**140** C1
Chalmers Ho **16**
SW11 . . . . .59 B4
Chalmer's Wlk **24**
SE17 . . . . .48 A4
Chalner Ho SW2 . . . .74 C3
Chaloner Ct SE1 . .**137** B4
Chalsey Lodge
SE4 . . . . .66 B3
Chalsey Rd SE4 . . . .66 B3
Chalton St NW1 . . . .83 B1
Chamberlain Cotts
SE5 . . . . .48 C2
Chamberlain Ho **6**
E1 . . . . .32 B2
Chamberlain St **7**
NW1 . . . . .12 B1
Chamberlayne Mans
3 NW10 . . . . .22 C2
Chamberlayne Rd
NW10 . . . . .22 B4
Chambers La NW10 . .9 B1
Chambers Rd N7 . . .14 A4
Chambers St
SE16 . . . .**139** C3
Chamber St E1 . . .**125** A4
Chambon PI **7**
W6 . . . . .38 C2
Chambord Ho **6**
E2 . . . . .24 B2 **99** A3
Chambord St
E2 . . . . .24 B2 **99** A3
Champion Gr SE5 . . .63 C4
Champion Hill SE5 . .63 C4
Champion Pk SE5 . .48 C1
Champlain Ho **26**
W12 . . . . .30 A2
Chancel St SE1 . .**122** B1
Chancellor Gr
SE21 . . . . .75 B1
Chancellor Ho
South Kensington
SW7 . . . .**129** A2
26 Wapping E1 . . . .32 A1
Chancellor Pas
E14 . . . . .33 C1
Chancellors' Ct
WC1 . . . .**106** C4
Chancellor's Rd
W6 . . . . .39 B1
Chancellors St W6 . .39 B1
Chancellors Wharf **21**
W6 . . . . .39 B1
Chancel St SE1 . . .**122** A1
Chancery Bldgs **14**
E1 . . . . .32 B2
Chancery Ho
WC2 . . . .**107** B3
Chancery La WC4 .**107** B2
Chancery Lane Sta
WC1 . . . .**107** B3
Chancery Mews
SW17 . . . . .72 A2
Chance St
E2 . . . . .24 B1 **98** C2

Chandler Ave E16 . . .35 C4
Chandlers Mews
E14 . . . . .41 C4
Chandler St E1 . . . . .32 A1
Chandlers Way **11**
SE24 . . . . .74 C4
Chandler Way
SE15 . . . . .49 B3
Chandlery Ho **28**
E1 . . . .**111** B1
Chandos PI WC2 . .**120** A3
Chandos Rd
Cricklewood NW2 . . . .9 C3
Old Oak Comm
NW10 . . . . .21 A1
Stratford New Town
E15 . . . . .19 C3
Chandos St W1 . . .**104** B3
Chandos Way NW11 . .2 A3
Change Alley EC3 .**109** C1
Channel Gate Rd
NW10 . . . . .21 A2
Channel Ho E14 . . . .33 A4
Channel Sea Bsns Ctr
E15 . . . . .27 C3
Channelsea Rd
E15 . . . . .27 C3
Channing Jun Sch
N6 . . . . .3 C3
Channing Sch N6 . . . .4 A3
Chantrey Rd SW9 . . .62 B4
Chantry Cl W9 . . . . .23 B1
Chantry Cres NW10 . .8 B2
Chantry Ct SW6 . . .**58** A4
Chantry Sq W8 . . .**128** A1
Chantry St N1 . . . . . .86 B3
Chant Sq E15 . . . . . .19 C1
Chant St E15 . . . . . . .19 C1
Chapel CI NW10 . . . . .8 B2
Chapel Ct SE1 . . . .**137** B4
Chapel House St
E14 . . . . .42 A2
Chapel Mkt N1 . . . . .85 B2
Chapel PI
Islington N1 . . . . . .**85** C2
Marylebone W1 . . .**104** A1
12 Shoreditch
EC2 . . . . .24 A2 **98** A3
Chapel Side W2 . .**114** A3
Chapel St
Paddington NW1 . .**102** A3
Westminster SW1 .**131** C3
Chapleton Ho
SW2 . . . . .62 C2
Chaplin CI SE1 . . .**136** A4
Chaplin Ho **6**
SW9 . . . . .62 C3
Chaplin Rd NW2 . . . .8 C2
Chaplow CI SW6 . .**166** C1
Chapman Ho
2 Stepney E1 . . . . .32 A3
3 West Norwood
SE27 . . . . .75 A1
Chapman Rd E9 . . . .18 B2
Chapmans Park Ind
Est NW10 . . . . .8 B2
Chapman Sq
SW19 . . . . .69 C2
Chapman St E1 . . . .32 A2
Chaponie Pl W1 . . .**105** B1
Chapter Cl **18** W4 . .37 B3
Chapter House & Pyx
Chamber SW1 . . .**134** A2
Chapter Rd
Kennington SE17 . .**150** B1
Willesden NW2 . . . . .8 C3

Chapter St SW1 . . .**147** B3
Chara PI W4 . . . . . . .45 C4
Charcot Ho SW15 . .56 B1
Charcroft Ct **11**
W14 . . . . .39 C4
Chard Ho **7** N7 . . . .5 B2
Chardin Ho **30**
SW9 . . . .**173** C4
Chardin Rd **11** W4 . .38 A2
Chardmore Rd N16 . .7 C3
Charecroft Way
W12 . . . . .39 C4
Charfield Ct W9 . . . .88 B1
Charford Rd E16 . . . .35 C4
Chargrove Cl **24**
SE16 . . . . .40 C4
Charing Cross
SW1 . . . .**120** A2
Charing Cross Hospl
W6 . . . . .39 C1
Charing Cross Rd
WC2 . . . .**105** C1
Charing Cross Sta
WC2 . . . .**120** B2
Charing Ho SE1 . .**135** C4
Chariot Cl **3** E3 . . .26 C4
Charlbert Ct NW8 . .80 A2
Charlbert St NW8 . .80 A2
Charles Allen Ho
EC1 . . . . .96 A4
Charles Auffray Ho **30**
E1 . . . . .32 B4
Charles Barry Cl
SW4 . . . . .61 B4
Charles Burton Ct
E5 . . . . .18 A4
Charles Coveney Rd
SE15 . . . . .49 B2
Charles Darwin Ho **8**
E2 . . . . .25 A2
Charles Dickens Ho **21**
E2 . . . . .25 A2
Charles Dickens Mus
The WC1 . . . .**95** A1
Charles Dickens Prim
Sch SE1 . . . .**136** C3
Charles Edward
Brooke Sch **1**
SW9 . . . . .48 A2
Charles Flemwell
Mews **2** E16 . . . .35 C1
Charles Haller St **25**
SW2 . . . . .74 C4
Charles Harrod Ct
SW13 . . . . .47 B4
Charles Hobson Ho **4**
NW10 . . . . .8 A1
Charles Hocking Ho **8**
W3 . . . . .37 B4
Charles II PI SW3 .**144** C1
Charles II St SW1 .**119** B2
Charles La NW8 . . . .80 A2
Charles Lamb Ct
N1 . . . . .86 B2
Charles Mackenzie Ho
SE16 . . . .**153** C4
Charles PI NW1 . . . .93 A3
Charles Rowan Ho
WC1 . . . . .95 B3
Charles Sq N1 . . . .97 C3
Charles St
Barnes SW13 . . . . . .46 A1
Mayfair W1 . . . . . .**118** A2

Charles St continued
B Upper Holloway
N19 . . . . 5 A3
Charleston St
SE17 . . . . 151 A3
Charles Townsend Ho
EC1 . . . . 96 A2
Charles Utton Ct
E8 . . . . 16 C4
Charlesworth Ho B
E14 . . . . 33 C3
Charleville Ct
SW5 . . . . 140 C1
Charleville Mans
W14 . . . . 140 B1
Charleville Rd
W14 . . . . 140 C1
Charlotte Ct 10
W6 . . . . 38 C2
Charlotte Despard
Ave SW11 . . . . . . 169 C3
Charlotte Ho 12
W6 . . . . 39 B1
Charlotte Mews
Marylebone W1 . . . 105 A4
North Kensington
W10 . . . . 30 C3
West Kensington
W14 . . . . 140 A4
Charlotte Pl
Marylebone W1 . . . 105 A3
Westminster SW1 . 146 C3
Charlotte Rd
Barnes SW13 . . . . . . 46 A2
Shoreditch
EC2 . . . . . . 24 A1 98 A2
Charlotte Row
SW4 . . . . 61 B4
Charlotte Sharman
Prim Sch SE11 . . 136 A1
Charlotte Sq 5
TW10 . . . . 54 B1
Charlotte St W1 . . . 105 A4
Charlotte Terr N1 . . 85 A3
Charlton Ct
25 Hackney E2 . . . . . 24 B4
17 Kentish Town
N7 . . . . 13 C3
Charlton Ho
5 Brentford
TW8 . . . . 44 A4
Somers Town NW1. . 93 B4
Charlton King's Rd
NW5 . . . . 13 C3
Charlton Pl N1 . . . . 86 A2
Charlton Rd NW10 . . 21 A4
Charlton Terr
SE11 . . . . 163 C3
Charlton Way SE10,
SE3 . . . . 53 A2
Charlwood Ho
Richmond TW9 . . . . . 45 A3
1 Streatham SW2 . . 74 B3
Westminster SW1 . 147 B3
Charlwood Pl
SW1 . . . . 147 A3
Charlwood Rd
SW15 . . . . 57 C3
Charlwood St
SW1 . . . . 147 A2
Charlwood Terr 5
SW15 . . . . 57 C3
Charman Ho
18 London SW2 . . . . 62 C1

Charman Ho continued
South Lambeth
SW8 . . . . 162 A2
Charman Ho 10
N1 . . . . 24 A3
Charmouth Ct
TW10 . . . . 54 B2
Charmouth Ho
SW8 . . . . 162 C2
Charnock Ho 22
W12 . . . . 30 A2
Charnwood Gdns
E14 . . . . 41 C2
Charrington Ho 42
E1 . . . . 25 B1
Charrington St
NW1 . . . . 83 B2
Charter Bldgs 14
SE10 . . . . 52 A2
Charter Ct
Finsbury Pk N4 . . . . . 5 C3
Marylebone W1 . . . 102 B3
Charter Ho 42 . . . . 106 B1
W6 . . . . 38 C2
Charterhouse Bldgs
EC1 . . . . 96 C1
Charterhouse Mews
EC1 . . . . 108 B4
Charterhouse Rd
E8 . . . . 16 C3
Charterhouse Sq
EC1 . . . . 108 B4
Charterhouse Square
Sch The EC1 . . . . 108 B4
Charterhouse St
EC1 . . . . 108 A3
Charterhouse Works
SW18 . . . . 59 B3
Charteris Rd
Finsbury Pk N4 . . . . . 5 C3
Kilburn NW6 . . . . . . 23 B4
Charteris Sp Ctr
NW6 . . . . 23 C4
Charter Sch The
SE24 . . . . 63 C2
Chartes Ho SE1 . . . 138 B2
Chartfield Ave
SW15 . . . . 57 B2
Chartfield Sq
SW15 . . . . 57 C2
Chartham Ct 12
SW9 . . . . 62 C4
Chartham Gr SE27 . . 75 A1
Chartham Ho SE1 . 137 C2
Chart House The 5
E14 . . . . 42 A1
Chartridge SE17 . . . 48 C4
Chart St N1 . . . . . . 97 C4
Chartwell 28
SW19 . . . . 69 C3
Chase Ct SW3 . . . . 130 C1
Chase Ctr The
NW10 . . . . 20 C2
Chaseley Ct W4 . . . . 37 A1
Chaseley St E14 . . . . 33 A3
Chasemore Ho
SW6 . . . . 154 B2
Chase Rd NW10 . . . . 20 C1
Chase Road Trad Est
NW10 . . . . 20 C1
Chaseley St SW19 . . . 69 B4
Chater Ho 6 E2 . . . . 25 C2
Chatfield Rd SW11 . . 59 B4
Chatham Ho 7
SE5 . . . . 49 A1
Chatham Pl E9 . . . . 17 B2

Chatham Rd SW11 . . 60 B2
Chatham St SE17 . . 151 C4
Chatsworth Ct
Brondesbury NW2 . . . 9 C2
Clapton Pk E5 . . . . . 17 C4
Earl's Ct W8 . . . . . . 141 B4
Chatsworth Est E5 . . 17 C4
Chatsworth Gdns
W3 . . . . 28 B2
Chatsworth Lo 1
W4 . . . . 37 C1
Chatsworth Rd
Brondesbury NW2 . . . 9 C2
Chiswick W4 . . . . . . 45 B4
Clapton Pk E5 . . . . . 17 C4
Chatsworth Way
SE27 . . . . 75 B1
Chattenden Ho 8
N4 . . . . 6 C4
Chatterton Ct TW9 . . 44 B1
Chatterton Rd N4 . . . 6 A1
Chatto Rd SW11 . . . . 60 B2
Chaucer Ave TW9 . . . 44 C1
Chaucer Ct 11
N16 . . . . 16 A4
Chaucer Dr SE1 . . . 153 A3
Chaucer Ho SW1 . . 146 C1
Chaucer Rd
Acton W3 . . . . 28 B1
Herne Hill SE24 . . . . 63 A2
Chaulden Ho EC1 . . . 97 B3
Cheadle Ct NW8 . . . . 89 C2
Cheadle Ho 1
E14 . . . . 33 B3
Cheam St 8 SE15 . . . 65 A4
Cheapside EC2 . . . . 109 A1
Chearsley SE17 . . . . 151 A4
Cheddington Ho 9
E2 . . . . 24 C4
Chedworth Cl E16 . . . 35 B3
Chedworth Ho 2
E5 . . . . 7 C2
Cheering La E15, E9 . 19 B3
Cheesemans Terr
W14 . . . . 140 C1
Chelmer Rd E9 . . . . . 17 C3
Chelmsford Cl W6 . . . 47 C4
Chelmsford Ho 5
N7 . . . . 14 B4
Chelmsford Sq
NW10 . . . . 22 B4
CHELSEA 144 B1
Chelsea Acad
SW10 . . . . 157 A1
Chelsea Barracks
SW1 . . . . 145 C2
Chelsea Bridge
SW1 . . . . 160 A4
Chelsea Bridge Rd
SW1 . . . . 145 C1
Chelsea Cl NW10 . . . 20 C4
Chelsea Cloisters
SW3 . . . . 144 B3
Chelsea Coll of Arts
SW1 . . . . 148 A2
Chelsea Cres
Brondesbury NW2 . . 10 B2
Chelsea SW10 . . . . 167 A3
Chelsea SW3 . . . . . 159 B4
Chelsea Emb
SW3 . . . . 158 C3
Chelsea Est SW3 . . 158 A3
Chelsea Farm Ho
SW10 . . . . 157 C3
Chelsea Gate
SW1 . . . . 145 C1

Chelsea Gdns
SW1 . . . . 145 C1
Chelsea Harbour
Design Ctr
SW10 . . . . 167 A4
Chelsea Harbour Dr
SW10 . . . . 167 A4
Chelsea Harbour Pier
SW10 . . . . 167 A4
Chelsea Ind Coll
SW6 . . . . 156 A1
Chelsea Lo SW3 . . . 159 A4
Chelsea Manor Ct
SW3 . . . . 158 B4
Chelsea Manor Gdns
SW3 . . . . 144 B3
Chelsea Manor St
SW3 . . . . 144 B3
Chelsea Manor
Studios SW3 . . . 144 B1
Chelsea Park Gdns
SW3 . . . . 157 B4
Chelsea Physic Gdn
SW3 . . . . 158 C4
Chelsea Reach Twr
SW10 . . . . 157 B2
Chelsea Sp Ctr
SW3 . . . . 144 B1
Chelsea Sq SW3 . . . 143 C1
Chelsea Stad Tours &
Mus SW6 . . . . . . 156 B2
Chelsea Twrs
SW3 . . . . 158 B4
Chelsea &
Westminster Hospl
SW10 . . . . 157 A3
Chelsfield Ho
SE17 . . . . 152 A3
Chelsfield Point 3
E9 . . . . 17 C1
Chelsham Ho 1
SW4 . . . . 61 C4
Chelsham Rd SW4 . . 61 C4
Cheltenham Pl
10 Acton W3 . . . . . . 28 A1
1 South Acton W3 . . 37 B4
Cheltenham Rd
SE15 . . . . 65 B2
Cheltenham Terr
SW3 . . . . 145 A2
Chelverton Ct
SW15 . . . . 57 C3
Chelverton Rd
SW15 . . . . 57 C3
Chelwood Ho 5
W2 . . . . 101 C1
Chelwood Ct
SW11 . . . . 167 C4
Chelwood Gdns
TW9 . . . . 44 C1
Chenies Ho W2 . . . 114 A4
Chenies Mews
WC1 . . . . 93 B1
Chenies Pl NW1 . . . . 83 C2
Chenies St WC1 . . . 105 B4
Chenies The NW1 . . 83 C2
Cheniston Gdns
W8 . . . . 128 A2
Chepstow Cl
SW15 . . . . 58 A2
Chepstow Cres
W11 . . . . . 31 C2 113 B4
Chepstow Ct
W11 . . . . . 31 C2 113 B4

Chepstow Pl
W2 . . . . . 31 C3 113 C4
Chepstow Rd W2 . . . 31 C3
Chepstow Villas
W11 . . . . . 31 C2 113 B4
Chequers Ct EC1 . . . 97 B1
Chequers Ho NW8 . . 90 A2
Chequer St EC1 . . . . 97 A1
Cherbury Ct N1 . . . . 87 C1
Cherbury St N1 . . . . 87 C1
Cheriton Ho 5 E5 . . . 17 A3
Cheriton Sq SW17 . . 72 C2
Cheriton 7 SW2 . . . 74 C4
Cherry Ct
Acton W3 . . . . 29 A1
5 Rotherhithe
SE16 . . . . 33 A1
Cherry Garden Ho 7
SE16 . . . . 40 A4
Cherry Garden Sch **20**
SE16 . . . . 153 C3
Cherry Garden St
SE16 . . . . 40 A4
Cherry Laurel Wlk
1 SW2 . . . . 74 B4
Cherry Tree Cl E 11
E9 . . . . 25 B4
Cherry Tree Ct
1 Camden Town
NW1 . . . . 13 B1
3 Peckham SE15 . . 50 A2
Cherry Tree Dr
SW16 . . . . 74 A1
Cherrytree Ho 6
W10 . . . . 22 C2
Cherry Tree Ho
SE14 . . . . 51 B1
Cherry Trees Sch The
2 E3 . . . . 26 C2
Cherry Tree Terr
SE1 . . . . 138 B4
Cherry Tree Wlk
EC1 . . . . 97 A1
Cherrywood Cl E3 . . 26 A2
Cherrywood Dr
SW15 . . . . 57 C2
Chertsey Ct SW14 . . 55 A4
Chertsey Ho 37
E2 . . . . 24 B2 98 C3
Cherwell Ho NW8 . . 89 C1
Cherwell Mews
SW11 . . . . 60 A3
Cheryls Cl SW6 . . . 166 B4
Chesham Cl SW1 . . 131 B1
Chesham Ct SW18 . . 71 C4
Chesham Flats
W1 . . . . 117 C4
Chesham Ho SW1 . . 131 B1
Chesham Mews
SW1 . . . . 131 B2
Chesham Pl SW1 . . 131 B1
Chesham St SW1 . . 131 B1
Cheshire St
E2 . . . . 24 B1 99 A2
Chesholm Rd N16 . . . 7 A1
Cheshunt Ho 1
NW6 . . . . 78 A3
Chesil Ct
17 Bethnal Green
E2 . . . . 25 B3
Chelsea SW3 . . . . . 158 B4
Chesilton Rd SW6 . . 164 C4
Chesney Ct W9 . . . . 23 C1
Chesney Ho SE13 . . . 67 C3
Chesney St SW11 . . 169 B3

Chessington Ho
SW8 .... **171** B2
Chesson Rd W14 . **155** A4
Chessum Ho E8 ... **16** C2
Chester Ave TW10 . **54** B1
Chester CI
Barnes SW13 ..... **57** A4
Knightsbridge
SW1 .... **132** A3
1 Richmond TW10 . **54** B1
Chester Close N
NW1 .... **92** B4
Chester Close S
NW1 .... **92** B3
Chester Cres E8 .. **16** B3
Chester Ct
Bermondsey SE8 .. **40** C1
4 Camberwell SE5 . **48** C3
Gospel Oak NW5 .. **12** C4
Regent's Pk NW1 .. **92** B3
Chesterfield Ct
SE13 .... **67** B4
Chesterfield Gdns
Greenwich SE10 .. **52** C3
Mayfair W1 ..... **118** A2
Chesterfield Gr
SE22 .... **64** B2
Chesterfield Hill
W1 .... **118** A2
Chesterfield Ho
Highgate N6 ...... **4** A3
Mayfair W1 ..... **117** C2
Chesterfield Rd
W4 .... **45** B4
Chesterfield St
W1 .... **118** A2
Chesterfield Way
SE15 .... **50** B3
Chesterford Gdns
NW3 .... **11** A4
Chester Gate NW1 . **92** B3
Chester Ho
Dartmouth Pk N19 . **4** C2
1 Deptford SE8. .. **51** B4
Chesterman Ct
W4 .... **46** A3
Chester Mews
SW1 .... **132** A2
Chester Pl NW1 ... **92** A4
Chester Rd
Dartmouth Pk N19 . **4** A2
Regent's Pk NW1 .. **92** A4
Chester Row SW1 . **145** C4
Chester Sq SW1 .. **146** A4
Chester Sq Mews
SW1 .... **132** A1
Chester St
Bethnal Green
E2 .... **24** C1 **99** C2
Westminster SW1 . **131** C2
Chester Terr NW1 . **92** A4
Chesterton CI
SW18 .... **58** C2
Chesterton Ct W3 . **37** A3
Chesterton Ho
20 Battersea
SW11 .... **59** C4
3 Kensal Town
W10 .... **31** A4
Chesterton Prim Sch
SW11 .... **169** B3
Chesterton Rd
W10 .... **31** A4
Chesterton Sq
W8 .... **141** B3
Chester Way SE11 **149** C3

Chestnut Alley
SW6 .... **155** A3
Chestnut Ave **11**
SW14 .... **55** C4
Chestnut CI
New Cross Gate
SE14 .... **51** B2
1 Stoke Newington
N16 .... **6** C2
Chestnut Ct SW6 . **155** A4
Chestnut Gr SW12 . **72** C3
Chestnut Grove Sch
SW12 .... **72** C3
Chestnut Ho
1 Acton W4 .... **38** A2
Brockley SE4 .... **66** B4
7 Maitland Pk
NW3 .... **12** B2
West Norwood
SE27 .... **75** B1
Chestnut Mews
SW6 .... **155** B1
Chestnut Rd SE21,
SE27 .... **75** B1
Chestnuts The **1**
N5 .... **15** A4
Chettle CI SE1 ... **137** B2
Chetwode Ho NW8 . **90** A2
Chetwode Rd
SW17 .... **72** B1
Chetwynd Rd NW5 . **4** A1
Cheval Ct SW15 .. **57** A3
Cheval PI SW7 ... **130** B2
Cheval St E14 .... **41** C3
Chevening Rd
Cubitt Town SE10 . **43** B1
Kilburn NW6 ..... **23** A4
Cheverell Ho **29**
E2 .... **24** C3
Cheverton Rd N19 . **4** C3
Chevet St E9 .... **18** A3
Cheviot Ct **12** SE14 . **50** B3
Cheviot Gate NW2 . **1** A2
Cheviot Gdns NW2 . **1** A2
Cheviot Ho N16 ... **7** B3
Chevron CI E16 ... **35** C3
Cheylesmore Ho
SW1 .... **146** A2
Cheyne Ct **9** SW3 . **158** C4
Cheyne Gdns
SW3 .... **158** B3
Cheyne Mews
SW3 .... **158** B3
Cheyne PI SW3 ... **158** C4
Cheyne Row SW3 . **158** B3
Cheyne Wlk
SW10 .... **157** B2
Cheyney Ho **2** E9 . **17** C2
Chichele Mans
NW2 .... **9** C3
Chichele Rd NW2 .. **9** C3
Chicheley St SE1 . **135** A4
Chichester Ct
NW1 .... **13** B1
Chichester Ho
NW6 .... **23** C3
Chichester Rd
Bayswater W2 ... **100** B4
Kilburn NW6 ..... **23** C3
Chichester Rents
WC2 .... **107** B2
Chichester St
SW1 .... **147** A1
Chichester Way
E14 .... **42** C2

Chicksand Ho **14**
E1 .... **111** B4
Chicksand St E1. . **111** A3
Chicksand Street
E1 .... **111** B3
Chiddingstone
SE13 .... **67** B2
Chiddingstone St
SW6 .... **165** C2
Chigwell Ct **1** E9 . **18** A2
Chigwell Hill E1. .. **32** A2
Chiham Ho **5**
SE15 .... **50** B4
Chilcombe Ho **6**
SW15 .... **68** C4
Chilcot CI **13** E14 . **34** A3
Childebert Rd
SW17 .... **73** A2
Childeric Prim Sch
SE14 .... **51** A3
Childeric Rd SE14 . **51** A3
Childerley St
SW6 .... **164** A4
Childers St SE8. .. **51** A4
Child La SE10 .... **43** B3
Childrens House
Upper Sch **15** N1 . **16** A2
CHILD'S HILL **1** B2
Child's Hill Prim Sch
NW2 .... **1** A1
Child's Mews
SW5 .... **141** C3
Child's PI SW5 ... **141** C3
Child's St SW5 ... **141** C3
Child's Wlk SW5 .. **141** C3
Chilham Ct **13**
SW9 .... **62** C4
Chilham Ho SE1 .. **137** C2
Chillington Dr
SW11 .... **59** C3
Chillingworth Rd
N7 .... **14** C3
Chiltern Ct
15 Deptford SE14 . **50** B3
Marylebone NW1 .. **91** A1
Chiltern Ho
Camberwell SE17 . **48** C4
4 Kensal Town
W10 .... **31** A4
7 Stamford Hill N16 . **7** B3
Chiltern Rd E3 ... **26** C1
Chiltern St W1 ... **103** B4
Chilton Gr SE8 ... **41** A1
Chiltonian Mews
SE13 .... **67** C2
Chilton Rd TW9 ... **54** C4
Chilton St
E2 .... **24** B1 **99** A2
Chilver St SE10. .. **43** B1
Chilworth Ct **3**
SW19 .... **69** C3
Chilworth Mews
W2 .... **101** B1
Chilworth St W2 .. **101** A1
Chimney Ct **22** E1 . **32** A1
China Ct **1** E1 ... **32** A1
China Hall Mews **10**
SE16 .... **40** B3
China Mews **17**
SW2 .... **74** B4
Chindit Ho **10** N16 . **15** C4
Ching Ct WC2 ... **106** A1
Chinnocks Wharf
E14 .... **33** A2
Chipka St E14 .... **42** B4
Chipley St SE14. .. **51** A4

Chippendale Ho
SW1 .... **146** B1
Chippenham Gdns
NW6 .... **23** C2
Chippenham Mews
W9 .... **23** C1
Chippenham Rd
W9 .... **23** C1
Chip St SW4 ..... **61** C3
Chipstead Ho **2**
SW2 .... **74** A3
Chipstead St SW6 . **165** C2
Chirk Ct SE4 ..... **51** B1
Chisenhale Prim Sch
E3 .... **26** A3
Chisenhale Rd E3 . **26** A3
Chisholm Ct **1**
W6 .... **38** C1
Chisholm Rd **19**
TW10 .... **54** B1
Chisledon Wlk E9 . **18** B2
Chislehurst Rd
TW10 .... **54** A2
Chislet **5** NW5 ... **12** C2
Chiswell St
Barbican EC1 ... **109** B4
Camberwell SE5 .. **48** C3
CHISWICK **38** B1
Chiswick & Bedford
Park Prep Sch W4 . **38** A2
Chiswick Common Rd
W4 .... **38** A2
Chiswick Green
Studios **7** W4. ... **37** B2
Chiswick High Rd
W4 .... **38** A2
Chiswick High Road
(North Circular Rd)
Chiswick W4 ..... **36** C1
Chiswick La W4 ... **38** A1
Chiswick La S W4 . **46** A4
Chiswick Mall W4 . **38** A1
Chiswick Park Sta
W4 .... **37** B2
Chiswick Pier W4 . **46** A4
Chiswick Quay W4 . **45** B2
Chiswick Rd W4 .. **37** B2
Chiswick Rdbt W4 . **36** C1
Chiswick Sch W4 . **45** C3
Chiswick Sq W4 .. **46** A4
Chiswick Sta W4 .. **45** B3
Chiswick Staithe
W4 .... **45** B2
Chiswick Terr **6**
W4 .... **37** B2
Chiswick Village
W4 .... **45** A4
Chiswick Wharf
W4 .... **46** B4
Chitty St W1 .... **105** A4
Chivalry Rd SW11 . **60** A2
Chivelston **27**
SW19 .... **69** C3
Chobham Acad
E15 .... **19** B3
Chobham Gdns
SW19 .... **69** C2
Chobham Rd E15 . **19** C3
Cholmeley Cres N6 . **4** A4
Cholmeley Lo N6 .. **4** A3
Cholmeley Pk N6 .. **4** A4

Cholmley Gdns
NW6 .... **10** C3
Cholmondeley Ave
NW10 .... **21** C3
Chopin's Ct **13** E1 . **32** A1
Chopwell CI E15 .. **19** C1
Choumert Gr SE15 . **49** C1
Choumert Mews
SE15 .... **49** C1
Choumert Rd SE15 . **49** B1
Choumert Sq **25**
SE15 .... **49** C1
Chow Sq **2** E8 ... **16** B3
Chrisp Ho SE10 .. **53** A4
Chrisp St E14 .... **34** A3
Chris Pullen Wlg **6**
N1 .... **14** A2
Christ Church
TW9 .... **54** A4
Christchurch Ave
NW6 .... **10** A1
Christ Church
Bentinck CE Prim
Sch NW1 .... **102** B4
Christ Church CE
Prim Sch
Battersea SW11 .. **60** A4
Brondesbury NW6 . **10** B1
Cubitt Town SE10 . **43** A1
12 Greenwich SE10 . **43** A1
Christchurch CE Sch
E1 .... **111** A3
Christ Church CE Sch
1 Brondesbury Pk
NW6 .... **10** A1
Harlesden NW10 .. **21** A4
Christchurch Hill
NW3 .... **11** C4
Christchurch Ho **2**
SW2 .... **74** A3
Christchurch Pas
NW3 .... **2** B1
Christ Church Prim
Sch
Camberwell
SW9 .... **173** C4
Hampstead NW3 .. **2** C1
SW3 .... **158** C4
Christchurch Rd
Mortlake SW14 ... **55** B2
Streatham SW2 ... **74** C3
Christ Church Sch
NW1 .... **92** B4
Christchurch Sq **2**
E9 .... **25** B4
Christchurch St
SW3 .... **158** C4
Christ Church
Streatham CE Prim
Sch SW2 .... **74** B3
Christchurch Terr
SW3 .... **158** C4
Christchurch Way
SE10 .... **43** A1
Christian Ct SE16. . **33** B1
Christian Ct **1**
E1 .... **111** C1
Christie Ct
Maitland Pk NW3 . **12** A3
2 Upper Holloway
N19 .... **5** A2
Christie Ho **2**
SE10 .... **43** B1
Christie Rd E9 ... **18** A2
Christina Sq N4 ... **6** A3

Christina St
EC2 . . . . 24 A1 98 A2
Christopher Boone's
Almshouses
SE13 . . . . 67 C3
Christopher Cl
SE16 . . . . 40 C4
Christopher France
Ho 21 . . . . 26 A2
Christopher Hatton
Prim Sch EC1 . . . . 95 B1
Christopher Lo 2
N6 . . . . 4 C4
Christopher Pl
NW1 . . . . 93 C3
Christopher St EC2 . . . 97 C1
Christ's Sch TW10 . . . . 54 C2
Christ the King RC
Prim Sch 12 . . . . 114 A3
Christ the King Sixth
Form Coll SE13 . . . . . . 67 C4
Chryssell Rd SW9 . . 163 C1
Chubworthy St 5
SE14 . . . . 51 A4
Chudleigh Rd
Hampstead NW6 . . . . . . 9 C1
London SE4 . . . . 66 C2
Chudleigh St E1 . . . . . 32 C3
Chumleigh Gdns
SE5 . . . . 49 A4
Chumleigh St SE5 . . . . 49 A4
Church App SE21 . . . 75 C1
Church Ave
Camden Town
NW1 . . . . 13 A2
Mortlake SW14 . . . . 55 C4
Church Cl W8 . . . . 128 A4
Church Cres E9 . . . . . . 17 C1
Churchcroft Cl
SW12 . . . . 72 C4
Church Ct
Holborn EC4 . . . . 107 C1
Rotherhithe SE16 . . . . . 41 B4
Churchdale Ct 1
W4 . . . . 37 A1
CHURCH END NW10 . . 8 A2
Church Entry EC4 . . . 108 B1
Church Estate
Almshouses 8
TW9 . . . . 54 B3
Churchfield Ho
W2 . . . . 89 B1
Churchfield Mans 7
SW6 . . . . 165 A1
Churchfield Rd
W3 . . . . 28 B1
Churchfields SE10 . . 52 B4
Church Garth 4
N19 . . . . 4 C2
Church Gate SW6 . . . . 58 A4
Church Gn 4
SW9 . . . . 173 C2
Church Gr SE13 . . . . . 67 A2
Church Ho EC1 . . . . . 96 B2
Churchill Ct
Finsbury Pk N4 . . . . 5 C4
Peckham SE15 . . . . 49 C1
Willesden NW2 . . . . 9 A3
Churchill Gardens
Prim Sch SW1 . . . . . . 147 A1
Churchill Gdns
SW1 . . . . 160 C4
Churchill Gdns Rd
SW1 . . . . 160 C4

Churchill Pl E14 . . . . . 34 A1
Churchill Rd
Gospel Oak NW5 . . . . . 13 A4
Willesden NW2 . . . . 9 A2
Churchill Wlk E9 . . . . 17 B3
Church Mead SE5 . . 48 B3
Churchmead Rd
NW10 . . . . 8 C2
Church Path W4 . . . . 37 B3
Church Pl SW1 . . . . . 119 A3
Church Rd
Acton W3 . . . . 37 B4
Barnes SW13 . . . . 46 C2
Canonbury N1, N5 . . . . 15 B2
Richmond TW10,
TW9 . . . . 54 A2
Willesden NW10 . . . . 8 A1
Church Row NW3 . . 11 B4
Church St
Chiswick W4 . . . . 46 B4
Lisson Gr NW8 . . . . 90 A1
Church Street Est
NW8 . . . . 89 C1
Church Studios 16
NW1 . . . . 13 C2
Churchward Ho
Camberwell SE17 . . . . . 48 A4
West Kensington
SW5 . . . . 141 A1
Churchway NW1 . . . 93 C4
Church Wlk
Barnes SW13 . . . . 46 C2
Canonbury N16 . . . . . . 15 C4
Child's Hill NW2 . . . . 1 B1
Dartmouth Pk N6 . . . . . . 3 C1
Churchyard Row
SE11 . . . . 150 B4
Churnfield 2 N4 . . . . . . 5 C2
Churston Cl 18
SW2 . . . . 74 C3
Churston Mans
WC1 . . . . 95 A1
Churton Pl
Brentford W4 . . . . 45 A4
Pimlico SW1 . . . . 147 A3
Churton St SW1 . . . . 147 A3
Chute Ho 17 SW9 . . 173 B1
Chuter Ede Ho
SW6 . . . . 155 A3
Cicada Rd SW18 . . . . 59 B2
Cicely Ho NW8 . . . . . 79 C1
Cicely Rd SE15 . . . . . 49 C2
Cinema Mus The
SE11 . . . . 150 A3
Cinnabar Wharf
Central 11 E1 . . . . . 125 C2
Cinnabar Wharf East
13 E1 . . . . 125 C2
Cinnabar Wharf West
17 E1 . . . . 125 C2
Cinnamon Cl 8
SE15 . . . . 49 B3
Cinnamon Row 3
SW11 . . . . 59 B4
Cinnamon St E1 . . . . 32 A1
Cinnamon Wharf
SE1 . . . . 139 A4
Circle Ho 6 E14 . . . . 34 C3
Circle The SE1 . . . . . 139 A4
Circus Lo NW8 . . . . . 80 A3
Circus Mews W1 . . 102 C4
Circus Pl EC2 . . . . . 109 C3
Circus Rd NW8 . . . . . 79 B1
Circus St SE10 . . . . . 52 B3
Cirencester St
W2 . . . . 100 A4

Cissbury Ho 6
SE26 . . . . 76 C1
Citadel Pl SE11 . . . . 148 C2
Citizen Ho N7 . . . . . . 14 C4
Citizen Rd N7 . . . . . . 14 C4
Citron Terr 4
SE15 . . . . 65 A4
Citrus Ho 14 SE8 . . 41 B1
City Academy,
Hackney The 2
E9 . . . . 17 B3
City Bsns Coll EC1 . . 96 B3
City Bsns Ctr 30
SE16 . . . . 40 B4
City Central Est
EC1 . . . . 96 C3
City Coll of London
The WC1 . . . . 107 A3
City Forum EC1 . . . . . 96 C4
City Garden Row
N1 . . . . 86 B1
City Gate E1 . . . . 25 B1
City & Guilds of
London Art Sch
SE11 . . . . 149 C1
City Hall 11 . . . . 124 B1
City Harbour E14 . . 42 A3
City Heights Acad 7
SW2 . . . . 74 C4
City & Islington Coll
EC1 . . . . 94 B2
City & Islington Coll
(Ctr for Applied
Sciences) EC1 . . . . . . 96 A4
City & Islington Coll
(Ctr for Bsns, Arts &
Technology) 3
N7 . . . . 14 A4
City & Islington Coll
(Ctr for Health,
Social & Child Care)
7 N7 . . . . 14 A4
City & Islington Coll
(Ctr for Lifelong
Learning) 3 N4 . . . . . 5 C1
City Law Sch The
EC1 . . . . 107 A3
City Lights The
SE11 . . . . 149 C1
CITY OF
LONDON 122 B4
City of London Acad-
Islington N1 . . . . 86 C3
City of London Acad
The SE1 . . . . 153 C2
City of London
Information Ctr
EC4 . . . . 108 B1
City of London Sch
EC4 . . . . 122 C4
City of London Sch
for Girls EC2 . . . . . . 109 A4
City of Westminster
Coll W2 . . . . 101 B4
City of Westminster
Coll, Cosway Street
Ctr NW1 . . . . 102 B4
City of Westminster
Coll, Maida Vale Ctr
9 W9 . . . . 88 B3
City of Westminster
Coll, Queens Park
Ctr 10 W9 . . . . 23 C2
City Rd EC1 . . . . 97 A4
City Thameslink Sta
EC4 . . . . 108 A1

City, University of
London EC1 . . . . 96 A3
City Wlk SE1 . . . . . 138 A3
Clabon Mews
SW1 . . . . 144 C4
Clack St SE16 . . . . . . 40 B4
Claire Ct NW2 . . . . . . 10 A2
Claire Pl E14 . . . . 41 C3
Clancarty Rd SW6 165 C1
Clandon Cl W3 . . . . . . 37 A4
Clandon St SE8 . . . . . 51 C1
Clanfield Ho 12
SW15 . . . . 68 C3
Clanricarde Gdns
W2 . . . . 31 C2 113 C3
CLAPHAM 61 A4
Clapham Common . . . . .
SW4 . . . . 61 A3
Clapham Common
North Side SW4 . . . . 60 C3
Clapham Common
South Side SW4 . . . . 61 B2
Clapham Common Sta
SW4 . . . . 61 B3
Clapham Common
West Side
Clapham SW4,
SW11 . . . . 60 B3
Clapham SW4 . . . . 60 B3
Clapham Computer &
Secretarial Coll 18
SW11 . . . . 60 A4
Clapham Court Terr
2 SW4 . . . . 62 A2
Clapham Cres
SW4 . . . . 61 C3
Clapham Ct 3
SW4 . . . . 62 A3
Clapham High St
SW4 . . . . 61 C4
Clapham High Street
Sta SW4 . . . . 61 C4
Clapham Junction Est
SW11 . . . . 60 A3
Clapham Junction Sta
SW11 . . . . 60 A3
Clapham L Ctr
SW4 . . . . 61 C4
Clapham Manor Prim
Sch 3 SW4 . . . . 61 B4
Clapham Manor St
SW4 . . . . 61 C4
Clapham Mans
SW4 . . . . 61 A1
Clapham North Bsns
Ctr 10 SW4 . . . . 61 C4
Clapham North Sta
SW4 . . . . 62 A4
CLAPHAM PARK . . 61 C2
Clapham Park Rd
SW4 . . . . 61 C3
Clapham Park Terr 4
SW2 . . . . 62 A2
Clapham Rd
Brixton SW9 . . . . 173 A4
SW9 . . . . 163 A2
Clapham South Sta
SW4 . . . . 61 A2
Clapton Comm E5 . . 7 C4
Clapton Girls' Acad
E5 . . . . 17 B3
CLAPTON PARK . . 17 C4
Clapton Pas E5 . . . . . 17 B3
Clapton Sq E5 . . . . . 17 B3

Clapton Terr E5 . . . . . . 7 C3
Clapton Way E5 . . . . . 16 C4
Clara Grant Ho 10
E14 . . . . 41 C3
Clara Grant Prim Sch
The 18 E3 . . . . 26 C1
Clare Ct WC1 . . . . . . 94 B3
Claredale Ho 6
E2 . . . . 25 A3
Claredale St E2 . . . . 24 C3
Clare Gdns W11 . . . . 31 A3
Clare Ho
Bermondsey SE1 . . . . 153 A2
6 Old Ford E3 . . . . . . 26 B4
Clare La N1 . . . . 15 B1
Clare Lawn Ave
SW14 . . . . 55 C2
Clare Mews SW6 . . 156 A1
Clare Mkt WC2 . . . . 107 A1
Claremont 1
SW15 . . . . 58 A2
Claremont Cl
Finsbury N1 . . . . 85 C1
4 Streatham SW2 . . . 74 B3
Claremont Ct 1
W9 . . . . 23 B3
Claremont Gr W4 . . 46 A3
Claremont Rd
Highgate N6 . . . . 4 A4
West Kilburn W9 . . . . . 23 B3
Claremont Sq N1 . . 85 B1
Claremont St SE10 . . 52 A4
Claremont Way SW4 61 C1
Clarence Ave
SW4 . . . . 61 C1
Clarence Ct 10
W6 . . . . 39 A2
Clarence Gate
NW1 . . . . 91 A2
Clarence Gate Gdns
NW1 . . . . 91 A1
Clarence Gdns
NW1 . . . . 92 B4
Clarence Ho SE17 . . 48 B4
Clarence La SW15 . 119 A1
Clarence Mews
Balham SW12 . . . . 73 A4
Hackney E5 . . . . 17 A3
1 Rotherhithe
SE16 . . . . 32 C1
Clarence Pl 23 E5 . . 17 A3
Clarence Rd
Brentford W4 . . . . 36 C1
Brondesbury NW6 . . . . . 10 B1
Greenwich SE8 . . . . 52 A4
Lower Clapton E5 . . . . . 17 A4
Richmond TW9 . . . . 44 C2
Clarence St 5
TW9 . . . . 54 A3
Clarence Terr
NW1 . . . . 91 A2
Clarence Way
NW1 . . . . 13 A1
Clarence Wlk 3
SW4 . . . . 172 A2
Clarendon Cl
Bayswater W2 . . . . . . 116 A4
Hackney E9 . . . . 17 B1
Clarendon Cross
W11 . . . . 31 A2 112 B3
Clarendon Ct
Paddington W9 . . . . . . 89 A2
1 Richmond TW9 . . . . 44 C2
Willesden NW2 . . . . 9 B1

Clarendon Dr
SW15 . . . . .57 B3
Clarendon Flats
W1 . . . . .103 C1
Clarendon Gdns
W9 . . . . .89 A1
Clarendon Gr NW1 .93 B4
Clarendon Ho
NW1 . . . . .83 A1
Clarendon Mews
W2 . . . . .116 A4
Clarendon Pl W2 . .116 A4
Clarendon Rd
W11 . . . . .31 A2 112 B3
Clarendon Rise
SE13 . . . . .67 B3
Clarendon St
SW1 . . . . .146 B2
Clarendon Terr
W9 . . . . .89 A2
Clarendon Wlk **4**
W11 . . . . .31 A3
Clare Pl SW15 . . . . . .68 B4
Clare Rd
New Cross Gate
SE14 . . . . .51 B2
Willesden NW10 . . . . . .8 B1
Clare St E2 . . . . .25 A3
Clareville Ct SW7 .143 A3
Clareville Gr SW7 .143 A3
Clareville Grove Mews
SW7 . . . . .143 A3
Clareville St SW7 .143 A3
Clarewood Ct W1 .102 C3
Clarewood Wlk
SW9 . . . . .62 C3
Clarges Ho W1 . . . .118 B2
Clarges Mews
W1 . . . . .118 A2
Clarges St W1 . . . .118 B2
Clariat Ct W3 . . . . . . .36 C4
Claribel Rd SW9 . . . .48 A1
Claridge Ct SW6 . .164 C3
Clarissa Ho **7** E14 .34 A3
Clarissa St E8 . . . . . .24 B4
Clarke Ho **2** SW4 .61 B4
Clarke Path N16 . . . .7 C3
Clarkes Mews W1 .103 C4
Clark Ho SW10 . . . .156 C2
Clark Lawrence Ct
SW11 . . . . .59 C4
Clarkson Rd E16 . . . .35 B3
Clarkson Row
NW1 . . . . .82 C1
Clarkson St E2 . . . . .25 A2
Clark's Pl EC2 . . . . .110 A2
Clark St E1 . . . . .32 A4
Classic Mans **33**
E9 . . . . .17 B1
Classinghall Ho **14**
SW15 . . . . .57 C1
Claude Rd SE15 . . . .50 A1
Claude St E14 . . . . . .41 C2
Claudia Jones Way
SW2 . . . . .62 A1
Claudia Pl SW19 . . . .70 A3
Clavell St **8** SE10 . .52 B4
Claverdale Rd
SW2 . . . . .74 C4
Clavering Ave
SW13 . . . . .47 A4
Clavering Ho SE13 . .67 C3
Clavering Pl **6**
SW12 . . . . .60 C1
Claverton St SW1 .147 A1
Clave St E1 . . . . .32 B1

Claxton Gr
W6 . . . . .39 C1 140 A1
Claybank Gr SE13 . .67 A4
Claybrook Rd W6 . . .47 C4
Claydon SE17 . . . . . .150 C4
Clayhall St **20** E3 . . .26 B3
Claylands Pl SW8 . .163 A2
Claylands Rd
SW8 . . . . .163 A3
Claypole Rd E15 . . . .27 B3
Claypons Ave
TW8 . . . . .36 A2
Claypons Hospl
W5 . . . . .36 A4
Claypons Sq **1** TW8 .36 A1
Clays Ct N16 . . . . . . .7 B3
Clay St W1 . . . . .103 A3
Clayton Cres N1 . . . .84 C3
Clayton Ct N16 . . . . . .7 C4
Clayton Ho **2** E9 . . .17 B1
Clayton Mews
SE10 . . . . .52 C2
Clayton Rd SE15 . . . .49 C2
Clayton St SE11 . . .163 B4
Clearbrook Way **3**
E1 . . . . .32 B3
Clear Water Ho **9**
TW10 . . . . .54 A2
Clearwater Terr **4**
W11 . . . . .39 C4
Clearwell Dr W9 . . . .88 B1
Cleaver Ho **6**
NW3 . . . . .12 B1
Cleaver Sq SE11 . . .149 C1
Cleaver St SE11 . . .149 C2
Cleeve Ho **15**
E2 . . . . .24 A2 98 B3
Cleeve Way SW15 . .68 B4
Cleeve Workshops **5**
E2 . . . . .24 A2 98 B3
Clegg St **16** E1 . . . . .32 A1
Cleland Ho **22** E2 . . .25 B3
Clematis St W12 . . . .29 C2
Clem Atlee Par
SW6 . . . . .155 A3
Clem Attlee Ct
SW6 . . . . .155 A3
Clement Attlee Ho
NW10 . . . . .8 B1
Clement Ave SW4 . .61 C3
Clement Cl
Acton W4 . . . . .37 C2
Hampstead NW6 . . . . .9 B1
Clement Danes Ho **2**
W12 . . . . .30 A3
Clement Ho
14 Deptford SE8 . . . .41 A2
3 North Kensington
W10 . . . . .30 B4
Clements Ave SW4 .61 C3
Clement Cl
E16 . . . . .35 C4
Clements Inn
WC2 . . . . .107 A1
Clements Inn Pas
WC2 . . . . .107 A1
Clement's La EC2,
EC4 . . . . .123 C4
Clement's Rd SE16 .40 A3
Clemson Ho E8 . . . . .24 B4
Clennam St SE1 . . .137 A4
Clenston Mews
W1 . . . . .102 C2
Clent Ho **5** N16 . . . . .7 B3

Clephane Rd **13**
N1 . . . . .15 B2
Clephane Rd N N1 . .15 B2
Clephane Rd S N1 . .15 C2
Clere Pl EC2 . . . . . . .97 C2
Clere St EC2 . . . . . . .97 C2
CLERKENWELL 96 A1
Clerkenwell Cl
EC1 . . . . .95 C1
Clerkenwell Gn
EC1 . . . . .96 A1
Clerkenwell Parochial
CE Prim Sch EC1 .95 B3
Clerkenwell Rd
EC1 . . . . .96 A1
Clerkenwell
Workshops EC1 . .95 C2
Clermont Rd E9 . . . .25 B4
Clevedon Ct
Battersea SW11 . . . .168 A4
Dulwich SE21 . . . . . .75 C1
Clevedon Mans
NW5 . . . . .12 C4
Cleve Ho NW6 . . . . . .11 A1
Cleveland Ave W4 . .38 B2
Cleveland Ave W3 . . .1 A1
Cleveland Gdns
Barnes SW13 . . . . . . .46 B1
Paddington W2 . . . . . .100 C1
Cleveland Gr **30**
E1 . . . . .25 B1
Cleveland Mans
8 Brixton SW9 . . . .163 B1
4 Brondesbury
NW6 . . . . .10 B1
Paddington W9 . . . . . .23 C1
Cleveland Mews
W1 . . . . .104 C4
Cleveland Pl SW1 . .119 A2
Cleveland Rd
Barnes SW13 . . . . . . .46 B1
Islington N1 . . . . .15 C1
14 South Acton W4 . .37 B3
Cleveland Row
SW1 . . . . .119 A1
Cleveland Sq W2 . .100 C1
Cleveland St W1 . . . .92 C1
Cleveland Terr
W2 . . . . .101 A2
Cleveland Way E1 . .25 B1
Cleveley Est W12 . . .29 C2
Cley Ho SE4 . . . . . . .65 C3
Clichy Ho **52** E1 . . . .32 B4
Clifden Mews E5 . . .17 C3
Clifden Rd E5 . . . . . .17 C3
Cliff Ct 4 NW1 . . . .13 C2
Cliffe Ho **4** SE10 . . .43 B1
Clifford Ave
Mortlake SW14 . . . . .45 B1
Mortlake SW14,
TW9 . . . . .45 A1
Clifford Ct
Bayswater W2 . . . . . .100 A3
Wandsworth SW18 . . .71 C4
Willesden NW10 . . . . .8 A4
Clifford Dr SW9 . . . .63 A3
Clifford Gdns
NW10 . . . . .22 B3
Clifford Haigh Ho
SW6 . . . . .47 C3
Clifford Ho W14 . . .140 C3

Clifford's Inn Pas
EC4 . . . . .107 B1
Clifford St W1 . . . . .118 C3
Clifford Way NW10 . .8 B4
Cliff Rd NW1 . . . . . .13 C2
Cliff Road Studios **13**
NW1 . . . . .13 C2
Cliffsend Ho **23**
SW9 . . . . .173 C3
Cliff Terr SE8 . . . . . . .51 C1
Cliffview Rd SE13 . . .66 C4
Cliff Villas NW1 . . . .13 C2
Cliff Wlk E16 . . . . . . .35 B4
Clifton Ave W12 . . . .29 B1
Clifton Cres SE15 . .50 A3
Clifton Ct
Finsbury Pk N4 . . . . . .5 C2
Paddington NW8 . . . . .89 B2
Peckham SE15 . . . . . .50 A3
Putney SW15 . . . . . . .57 C2
Clifton Gate
SW10 . . . . .156 C4
Clifton Gdns
Chiswick W4 . . . . .37 C2
Paddington W9 . . . . . .88 C1
Clifton Gr E8 . . . . . . .16 C2
Clifton Hill NW8 . . . .78 C3
Clifton Ho
E2 . . . . .24 B1 98 C2
Clifton Mans **4**
SW9 . . . . .62 C3
Clifton Pl
Paddington W2 . . . .101 C1
Rotherhithe SE16 . . . .40 B4
Clifton Rd
Harlesden NW10 . . . .21 C3
Newham E16 . . . . . . .35 A4
Paddington W9 . . . . . .89 A2
Clifton Rise SE14 . . .51 A3
Clifton St
EC2 . . . . .24 A1 98 A1
Clifton Terr N4 . . . . . .5 C2
Clifton Villas W9 . .100 C4
Clifton Way SE15 . . .50 B3
Climsland Ho SE1 . .121 C2
Clinch Ct **11** E16 . . .35 C4
Cline Ho SW15 . . . . .56 C2
Clinger Ct N1 . . . . . . .24 A4
Clink Prison Mus The
SE1 . . . . .123 B2
Clink St SE1 . . . . . . .123 B2
Clinton Rd E3 . . . . . .26 A2
Clipper Appts **12**
SE10 . . . . .52 B4
Clipper Cl 3 SE16 . .40 C4
Clipper Ho E14 . . . . .42 B1
Clipper Way SE13 . .67 B3
Clipstone Ho **10**
SW15 . . . . .56 C2
Clipstone Mews
W1 . . . . .104 C4
Clipstone St W1 . . .104 C4
Clissold Cres N16 . .15 C4
Clissold Ct N4 . . . . . .6 B2
Clissold Ho **4** N16 . . .6 C3
Clissold Rd N16 . . . . .6 C1
Clitheroe Rd SW9 . .172 B1
Clive Ct W9 . . . . .89 A2
Cliveden Ho SW1 . .145 B4
Cliveden Pl SW1 . . .145 B4
Clive Ho
18 Clapham
SW8 . . . . .171 B2
Greenwich SE10 . . . .52 B4
Clive Rd SE21,
SE27 . . . . .75 C1

Cloak La EC4 . . . . . .123 B4
Clochar Ct NW10 . . .21 B4
Clock Ho N16 . . . . . . .7 B4
Clockhouse Cl
SW19 . . . . .69 B2
Clockhouse Pl
SW15 . . . . .58 A1
Clockhouse The
SW19 . . . . .69 B1
Clockmakers Mus
EC2 . . . . .109 A2
Clock Tower Mews
N1 . . . . .87 A3
Clock Tower Pl **1**
N7 . . . . .14 A2
Clock View Cres **2**
N7 . . . . .14 A2
Cloister Rd
Acton W3 . . . . .28 B4
Child's Hill NW2 . . . . .1 B2
Cloisters The **22**
SW9 . . . . .173 C3
Clonbrock Rd N16 . .16 A4
Cloncurry St SW6 . .47 C1
Clone Ct **4** W12 . . . .38 A3
Clonmel Rd SW6 . .165 A4
Clonmore St SW18 .70 B3
Clorane Gdns NW3 . .1 C1
Close The
Lewisham SE3 . . . . . .52 C1
Mortlake SW14 . . . . .55 A4
Cloth Ct EC1 . . . . . .108 B3
Cloth Fair EC1 . . . . .108 B3
Clothier St E1 . . . . . .110 B2
Cloth St EC1 . . . . . .108 C4
Cloudesdale Rd
SW17 . . . . .73 A2
Cloudesley Mans
N1 . . . . .85 C3
Cloudesley Pl N1 . . .85 C3
Cloudesley Rd N1 . .85 C3
Cloudesley Sq N1 . .85 C3
Cloudesley St N1 . . .85 C3
Clove Cres E14 . . . . .34 C2
Clovelly Ct NW2 . . . . .9 B3
Clovelly Ho W2 . . . .100 C2
Clovelly Rd W4 . . . . .37 C4
Clovelly Way E1 . . . .32 B3
Clover Mews
SW3 . . . . .159 A4
Clowes Ho 3
SW4 . . . . .62 A3
Cloysters Gn E1 . . .125 B2
Club Row E2 . . .24 B1 98 C2
Clunbury St N1 . . . . .87 C1
Clunie Ho SW1 . . . .131 A2
Cluny Mews SW5 . .141 B3
Cluny Pl SE1 . . . . . .138 A2
Cluse Ct N1 . . . . .86 C2
Clutton St E14 . . . . . .34 A4
Clyde Ct NW1 . . . . . .83 C2
Clyde Flats SW6 . . .154 C2
Clyde Rd
NW10 . . . . .55 A3
Clydesdale Ho 4
W11 . . . . .31 B3
Clydesdale Rd
W11 . . . . .31 B3
Clyde St SE8 . . . . . . .51 B4
Clynes Ho **3** E2 . . . .25 C2
Clyro Ct N4 . . . . .5 B3
Clyston St SW8 . . . .171 A2

Coach & Horses Yd
W1 . . . . **118** C2
Coach House La
Highbury N5 . . . . .15 A4
Wimbledon SW19 . . . . .**69** C1
Coach House Mews
SE23 . . . .**65** C1
Coach House Yd **5**
NW3 . . . . .2 C1
Coachmaker Mews **7**
SW9 . . . .**62** A4
Coalbrook Mans **3**
SW12 . . . .**73** A3
Coaldale Wlk SE11 .**75** B4
Coalecroft Rd
SW15 . . . .**57** B2
Coalport Ho SE11 .**149** B4
Coatbridge Ho **8**
N1 . . . .**14** B1
Coates Ave SW18 . .**60** A1
Coates St SW3 . . . . . .12 A3
Coate St E2 . . . . .24 C3
Coates Wlk TW8 . . . .36 A1
Cobalt Bldg E1 . . . .**167** C3
Cobbett St SW8 . .**163** A1
Cobble La N1 . . . . .5 C1
Cobble Mews N4,
N5 . . . . .6 B1
Cobbold Ct SW1 . . .**147** B4
Cobbold Ind Est
NW10 . . . . .8 B2
Cobbold Mews
W12 . . . . .38 B4
Cobbold Rd
Bedford Pk W12 . . . .38 B4
Willesden NW10 . . . . .8 B2
Cobb's Hall **7**
SW6 . . . . .47 C4
Cobb St E1 . . . .**110** C3
Cobden Bldgs
WC1 . . . .**94** C4
Cobden Ho
11 Bethnal Green
E2 . . . . .24 C2 **99** C4
Regent's Pk NW1 . .**82** C2
Cobham Cl SW11 . . . .60 A1
Cobham Mews **9**
NW1 . . . . .13 C1
Coborn Mews **9**
E3 . . . . .26 B2
Coborn Rd E3 . . . . . .26 B2
Coborn St E3 . . . . . . .26 B2
Cobourg Prim Sch
SE5 . . . . .49 B4
Cobourg Rd SE5 . . . .49 B4
Cobourg St NW1 . . . .**93** A3
Coburg Cl SW1 . . . .**147** A4
Coburg Cres SW2 . . .74 C3
Coburg Dwellings **9**
E1 . . . . .32 B2
Coca-Cola London
Eye WC2 . . . .**134** C4
Cochrane Cl NW8 . . .**79** C1
Cochrane Ho **18**
E14 . . . . .41 C4
Cochrane Mews
NW8 . . . .**79** C1
Cochrane St NW8 . . .**79** C1
Coci Ho W14 . . . . . .**141** A3
Cockburn Ho
SW1 . . . .**147** C1
Cock Hill E1 . . . . . .**110** B3
Cock La EC1 . . . .**108** A3
Cockpit Yd WC1 . . .**107** A4

Cockspur Ct SW1 . .**119** C2
Cockspur St SW1 . .**119** C2
Coda Ctr The **5**
SW6 . . . .**164** B4
Code St E1 . . . . .24 B1 **99** A1
Codicote Ho **22**
SE8 . . . . .40 C2
Codicote Terr N4 . . . .6 B2
Codling Ct E14 . . . .**125** C2
Codrington Ct **3**
SE16 . . . . .33 A1
Codrington Ho **7**
E1 . . . . .25 A1
Codrington Mews
W11 . . . . .31 A3
Cody Rd E16 . . . . . . .27 C1
Coffey St SE8 . . . . . .51 C3
Cohen Lo E5 . . . . . . .18 A3
Coin St SE1 . . . .**121** B2
Coity Rd NW5 . . . . . .12 C2
Cokers La SE21 . . . . .75 C3
Coke St E1 . . . .**111** C2
Colas Mews **7**
NW6 . . . . .23 C4
Colbeck Mews
SW5 . . . .**142** B3
Colberg Pl N16 . . . . .7 B4
Colbert **5** SE5 . . . . . .49 B2
Colborne Ho **8**
E14 . . . . .33 C2
Colchester Ho **17**
SW8 . . . .**171** B2
Colchester St E1 . .**111** A2
Coldbath Sq EC1 . . . .**95** B2
Coldbath St SE13 . . .52 A1
Cold Blow La SE14 . . .51 A3
Coldharbour E14 . . . .34 B1
Coldharbour Ind Est
SE5 . . . . .48 B1
Coldharbour La
SW9 . . . . .63 A4
Coldharbour Pl
SE5 . . . . .48 C1
Coldstream Gdns
SW18 . . . . .58 B1
Colebeck Mews
N1 . . . . .15 A2
Colebert Ave E1 . . . .25 B1
Colebert Ho **21** E1 . .25 B1
Colebrook Ct
SW3 . . . .**144** B3
Colebrooke Pl N1 . . .**86** B4
Colebrooke Row
Islington N1 . . . .**84** B4
Islington N1 . . . .**86** A2
Islington N1 . . . .**86** B1
Colebrook Ho **1**
E14 . . . . .34 A3
Coleby Path **21**
SE5 . . . . .48 C3
Colechurch Ho **1**
SE1 . . . .**153** B1
Colefax Bldg **12**
E1 . . . .**111** C2
Coleford Rd SW18 . .59 B2
Colegrave Prim Sch
E15 . . . . .19 C3
Colegrave Rd E15 . . .19 C3
Colegrove Rd
SE15 . . . . .49 B4
Coleherne Ct
SW5 . . . .**142** B1
Coleherne Mans
SW5 . . . .**142** B2

Coleherne Mews
SW10 . . . .**142** A1
Coleherne Rd
SW10 . . . .**142** A1
Colehill Gdns **5**
SW6 . . . .**164** A3
Colehill La SW6 . . .**164** A3
Cole Ho SE1 . . . . . .**135** C3
Coleman Ct SW18 . . .70 C4
Coleman Fields
N1 . . . .**87** A4
Coleman Mans N8 . . .5 A4
Coleman Rd SE5 . . . .49 A3
Coleman St EC2 . . .**109** B2
Coleman Street Bldgs
EC2 . . . .**109** B2
Colenso Rd E5 . . . . .17 B4
Coleraine Rd SE3 . . .53 B4
Coleridge Cl SW8 . .**170** B1
Coleridge Ct **14** . . .**39** C3
Coleridge Gdns
NW6 . . . . .11 B1
Coleridge Ho
Pimlico SW1 . . . . . .**147** A1
Walworth SE17 . . . .**151** A2
Coleridge Prim Sch
N8 . . . . .4 C4
Coleridge Rd N4,
N7 . . . . .5 C2
Coleridge Sq
SW10 . . . .**156** C2
Coles Ct SW11 . . . .**167** C3
Coleshill Flats
SW1 . . . .**145** C3
Cole St SE1 . . . .**137** A3
Colestown St **4**
SW11 . . . .**168** B2
Colet Gdns W14 . . . .39 C2
Colet Ho SE17 . . . .**150** B1
Colette Ct **5** SE16 . .40 C4
Coley St WC1 . . . . . .**95** A1
Colfe & Hatchcliffe's
Glebe SE13 . . . . .67 A2
Colgate Ho SE13 . . .52 A1
Colin Blanchard Ho
SE4 . . . . .51 C1
Colin Ct SW16 . . . . . .73 C2
Colinette Rd SW15 . .57 B3
Colin Rd NW10 . . . . . .8 C2
Colinsdale N1 . . . . . .**86** A3
Colin Winter Ho **11**
E1 . . . . .25 B1
Coliston Pas SW18 . .70 C4
Coliston Rd SW18 . . .70 C4
Collamore Ave
SW18 . . . . .72 B3
Collard Pl NW1 . . . . .13 A1
Collcutt Lo SW4 . . . .62 A3
College App SE10 . . .52 B4
College Cl E5 . . . . . . .17 B3
College Cres NW3 . .11 C2
College Cross N1 . . .14 C1
College Ct
Chelsea SW3 . . . . .**145** A1
3 Hammersmith
W6 . . . . .39 B1
College Francais
Bilingue de Londres
12 NW5 . . . . .13 A2
College Gdns
Dulwich SE21 . . . . . .76 A3
Upper Tooting
SW17 . . . . .72 A2
College Gr **11** NW1 . .83 B4

College Green Ct
SW9 . . . . .63 A4
College Hill EC4 . . .**123** A4
College La NW5 . . . .13 A4
College Mews **3**
SW18 . . . . .59 A2
COLLEGE PARK . . .22 A2
College Park Cl
SE13 . . . . .67 C3
College Park Sch **20**
W2 . . . .**100** A1
College Pl
Camden Town
NW1 . . . .**83** A3
Chelsea SW10 . . . .**156** C2
College Rd
Dulwich SE19,
SE21 . . . . .76 A2
Kensal Green
NW10 . . . . .22 B3
College St EC4 . . . .**123** A4
College Terr E3 . . . .26 B2
Collent Ho **12** E9 . . .17 B2
Collent St E9 . . . . . .17 B2
Collerston Ho
SE10 . . . . .43 B1
Collette Ho N16 . . . . .7 B3
Collett Ho SE13 . . . .67 A4
Collett Rd SE16 . . .**139** C2
Colley Ho **17** N7 . . .13 C3
Collier St N1 . . . .**84** C1
Collingbourne Rd
W12 . . . . .30 A1
Collingham Coll
SW5 . . . .**142** B3
Collingham Gdns
SW5 . . . .**142** B3
Collingham Pl
SW5 . . . .**142** B4
Collingham Rd
SW5 . . . .**142** B4
Collington St SE10 . .42 C1
Collingwood Ho
3 Bethnal Green
E1 . . . . .25 A1
Marylebone W1 . . .**104** C4
Collingwood St E1 . .25 A1
Collins Ct E8 . . . . . .16 C2
Collins Ho
5 Cubitt Town
SE10 . . . . .43 B1
4 Poplar E14 . . . .34 B2
Collinson Ct **3** **136** C3
Collinson Ho **14**
SE15 . . . . .49 C3
Collinson St SE1 . .**136** C3
Collinson Wlk
SE1 . . . .**136** C3
Collins Rd N5, N16 . .15 B4
Collins St SE3 . . . . . .53 A1
Collins Yd N1 . . . . . .**86** A3
Collison Pl N16 . . . . .7 A3
Coll of Arms EC4 . .**122** C4
Coll of Law The
(Bloomsbury)
EC1 . . . .**105** B4
Coll of Law The
(Moorgate) EC1 . . .**97** B1
Coll of NW London
NW6 . . . . .23 C4
Coll of NW London
(Willesden Centre)
NW10 . . . . .9 A2
Coll of Optometrists
The SW1 . . . .**120** A2

Coll Sharp Ct **42**
E2 . . . . .24 B2 **98** C3
Coll's Rd SE15 . . . . .50 B2
Collyer Pl SE15 . . . . .49 C2
Colmans Wharf **5**
E14 . . . . .34 A4
Colmar Cl **3** E1 . . . . .25 C1
Colmore Mews
SE15 . . . . .50 A2
Colnbrook St SE1 . .**136** A2
Colne Ho NW8 . . . . .**89** C1
Colne Rd E5 . . . . . . .18 A4
Colne St E13 . . . .**68** C3
Colombo St SE1 . . .**122** A1
Colomb St SE10 . . . .43 A1
Colonades The **4**
SE5 . . . . .48 C2
Colonial Dr W4 . . . . .37 B2
Colonnade WC1 . . . .**94** B1
Colonnade Ho SE3 . .53 B1
Colonnades The **6**
E8 . . . . .17 A2
Colonnade Tile **12**
SE8 . . . . .41 B2
Colorado Bldg **9**
SE13 . . . . .52 A2
Colosseum Terr
NW1 . . . .**92** B2
Colour Ho SE1 . . . .**138** B3
Colstead Ho **9** E1 . .32 A3
Colston Rd SW14 . . .55 B3
Colthurst Cres N4 . . .6 B2
Coltman Ho SE10 . . .52 B4
Coltman St E14 . . . .33 A4
Columba Ho SE14 . .51 B2
Columbas Dr NW3 . . .2 C1
Columbia Ho **13**
E3 . . . . .26 C2
Columbia Point **10**
SE16 . . . . .40 B3
Columbia Prim Sch **50**
E2 . . . . .24 B2 **99** A4
Columbia Rd
1 Hackney E2 . . . . .24 C3
Shoreditch
E2 . . . . .24 B2 **98** C4
Columbia Road
Flower Mkt
E2 . . . .**99** A4
Colverson Ho **14**
E1 . . . . .32 B4
Colvestone Cres
E8 . . . . .16 B3
Colvestone Prim Sch
E8 . . . . .16 B3
Colville Gdns W11 . .**31** B3
Colville Ho
Notting Hill W11 . . . .**31** B3
South Acton W3 . . . .37 A3
Colville Mews
W11 . . . .**31** B3
Colville Pl W1 . . . .**105** A3
Colville Prim Sch **8**
W11 . . . .**31** B3
Colville Rd
Notting Hill W11 . . . .**31** B3
South Acton W3 . . . .37 A3
Colville Sq W11 . . . .**31** B3
Colville Terr W11 . . .**31** B3
Colwall Ho **9**
SW9 . . . .**173** A1
Colwell Rd SE22 . . . .64 B2
Colwick Cl N6 . . . . . . .4 C4
Colwith Rd W6 . . . . .47 B4
Colworth Gr SE17 . .**151** A3

Colwyn Ho SE1... **135** B1
Colyton Rd SE22...**65** A2
Combe Ave SE3 ...**53** B3
Combedale Rd
  SE10 ...**43** C1
Combe Ho
  Mortlake SW14...**45** B1
  20 Paddington W2...**31** C4
Combemartin Rd
  SW18...**70** A3
Combe Mews 4
  SE3 ...**53** B3
Comber Gr SE5...**48** B3
Comber Grove Prim
  Sch 25 SE5 ...**48** B3
Comber Ho SE5...**48** B3
Combermere Rd
  SW9...**62** B4
Combe The NW1...**92** B3
Com Coll Hackney
  The 17 E8...**25** A4
Comeragh Mews
  W14...**140** B1
Comeragh Rd
  W14...**140** B1
Comerford Rd SE4..**66** B3
Comet Pl SE8 ...**51** C3
Comet St SE8 ...**51** C3
Comfort St 6
  SE15...**49** A4
Comins Ho SW4...**61** B2
Commercial Rd
  Stepney E1...**32** B3
  Whitechapel E1...**111** C2
Commercial St
  E1 ...**110** C4
Commercial Way
  Peckham SE15...**49** C3
  Wembley NW10...**20** A3
Commerell Pl
  SE10...**43** B1
Commerell St
  SE10...**43** A1
Commodity Quay
  E1 ...**125** A3
Commodore Ct
  SE8...**51** C2
Commodore Ho 7
  E14 ...**34** B2
Commodore St E1..**26** A1
Commondale
  SW15...**57** B4
Common Rd SW13..**56** C4
Common View
  SW15...**57** B4
Commonwealth Ave
  25 W12...**30** A2
Commonwealth Ho
  WC1...**106** B2
Community La N7...**13** C3
Community Rd
  E15...**19** C3
Comodore Ho
  SW18...**59** B3
Compania Bldg 12
  E1...**125** C3
Compass Ct SE1...**124** C1
Compass Ho
  Bayswater W2...**100** A1
  London SE8...**52** A1
Compass Point 10
  E14 ...**33** C2
Compass Sch 12
  SE16...**40** A3
Compayne Gdns
  NW6...**11** A1

Compton Ave
  Islington N1...**15** A2
  London N6 ...**3** A4
Compton Cl
  Camberwell SE15...**49** B3
  Regent's Pk NW1...**92** B3
Compton Cres W4...**45** B4
Compton Ho
  SW11...**168** A4
Compton Pas EC1...**96** B2
Compton Pl WC1...**94** A2
Compton Rd
  Islington N1...**15** A2
  Kensal Green
  NW10...**22** C2
Compton St EC1...**96** B3
Compton Terr N1...**15** A2
Comus Ho E17...**152** A3
Comus Pl SE17...**152** A3
Comyn Rd SW11...**60** A3
Comyns Cl E16...**35** B4
Conant Ho SE11...**48** A4
Conant Mews 1
  E1...**125** B4
Concanon Rd SW2,
  SW4 ...**62** B3
Concepts Univ Coll
  London SW8 ...**162** A1
Concert Hall App
  SE1 ...**121** A1
Concord Bsns Ctr
  W3 ...**28** A4
Concorde Way
  SE16...**40** C2
Concordia Wharf 11
  E14...**34** B1
Concord Rd W3...**20** A1
Condell Rd SW8...**171** A3
Conder St E14...**33** A3
Conduit Ct WC2...**120** A4
Conduit Ho SE10...**52** C2
Conduit Mews
  W2...**101** B1
Conduit Pas W2...**101** B1
Conduit Pl W2...**101** B1
Conduit St W1...**118** C4
Conewood St N5...**6** A1
Coney Acre SE21...**75** B3
Coney Way SW8...**163** A3
Congers Ho SE8...**51** C3
Congress Ho WC1...**105** C2
Congreve Ho 10
  N16...**16** A3
Congreve St SE17...**152** A3
Conifer Ct 28
  SW19...**69** C3
Conifer Gdns
  SW16...**74** B1
Conifer Ho SE4...**66** B3
Coniger Rd SW6...**165** B2
Coningham Ct
  SW10...**157** A2
Coningham Mews
  W12...**29** C1
Coningham Rd
  W12...**39** A4
Coningsby Rd N4...**6** A4
Conington Rd
  SE13...**67** B4
Conisbrough NW1...**82** C3
Coniston NW1...**92** C4
Coniston Cl
  Barnes SW13...**46** B3
  Chiswick W4...**45** B3

Coniston Ct
  Marylebone W2 ...**102** B1
  6 Rotherhithe
  SE16...**40** C4
Conistone Way N7..**14** A1
Coniston Ho
  14 Bow E3 ...**26** B2
  28 Camberwell SE5...**48** B3
Coniston Wlk E9 ...**17** B3
Conlan St W10 ...**23** A1
Conley Rd NW10...**8** A2
Conley St SE10...**43** A1
Connaught Ave
  SW14...**55** B3
Connaught Cl W2...**102** B1
Connaught Ho
  College Pk NW10...**22** A2
  Mayfair W1...**118** A3
Connaught House Sch
  W2 ...**102** C1
Connaught Lo N4...**5** C4
Connaught Mans
  Battersea SW11...**168** B3
  3 Brixton SW9 ...**62** C3
  15 Canonbury N16...**15** C4
  Fulham SW6 ...**164** A4
Connaught Pl W2...**102** C1
Connaught Rd
  Finsbury Pk N4...**5** C4
  Harlesden NW10...**21** B3
  8 Richmond TW10 ...**54** B2
Connaught Sq
  W2 ...**102** C1
Connaught St W2...**102** B1
Connaught Works
  E3 ...**26** A4
Connell Ct 6
  SE14...**50** C4
Connor Ct SW11...**170** A3
Connor St E9 ...**25** C4
Conrad Ho
  6 Limehouse
  SE16...**33** A2
  South Lambeth
  SW8 ...**162** A2
  15 Stoke Newington
  N16...**16** A3
Conrad Twr W3...**37** A3
Consort Ho W2...**114** B3
Consort Lo NW8...**80** C3
Consort Rd SE15...**50** A1
Cons St SE1 ...**135** C4
Constable Ct 11
  SE16...**40** A1
Constable Ho
  Millwall E14...**41** C4
  Primrose Hill NW3...**12** B1
Constable Wlk
  SE21...**76** A1
Constant Ho 12
  E14...**34** A2
Constantine Ho
  SW2...**75** A3
Constantine Rd
  NW3...**12** A4
Constitution Hill
  W1...**132** B4
10 Consul Ho E3...**26** C1
Content St SE17...**151** B3
Convent Gdns
  W11...**31** B3
Convent of Jesus &
  Mary Language Coll
  NW10...**21** B4

Convent of Jesus &
  Mary RC Inf Sch 9
  NW2...**9** B2
Conway Gr W3...**28** C4
Conway Ho
  Chelsea SW3 ...**145** A1
  5 Millwall E14 ...**42** A2
  8 Streatham SW2 ...**74** A3
Conway Mews W1...**92** C1
Conway St W1...**92** C1
Conybeare NW3...**12** A1
Conyer St 12 E3...**26** A3
Cookham Cres
  SE16...**40** C4
Cookham Ho
  E2...**24** B1 **98** C2
Cook's Rd
  Camberwell SE17...**48** A4
  Stratford Marsh
  E15...**27** A3
Coomassie Rd W9...**23** B1
Coombe Ho 15 N7...**13** C3
Coombe Rd W4...**38** A1
Coomber Ho SW6...**59** A4
Coombs St N1...**86** B1
Coomer Mews
  SW6 ...**155** A3
Coomer Pl SW6 ...**155** A3
Cooperage The
  SE1 ...**124** C1
Cooper Cl SE1 ...**135** C3
Cooper Ho NW8 ...**89** B1
Cooper Rd NW10...**8** C3
Coopersale Rd E9...**17** C3
Coopers Cl E1...**25** B1
Coopers Ct
  5 Acton W3 ...**28** B1
  Tower Hamlets E3 ...**26** B2
Coopers La NW1 ...**83** C1
Coopers Lo SE1 ...**138** C4
Cooper's Rd SE1 ...**153** A2
Cooper's Row
  EC3 ...**124** C4
Cooper St 10 E16...**35** B4
Coopers Yd N1 ...**15** A1
Cope Ho EC1 ...**97** A3
Copeland Dr E14...**41** C2
Copeland Ho
  SE11 ...**135** A1
Copeland Ind Pk 7
  SE15...**49** C1
Copeland Rd SE15..**50** A1
Copenhagen Gdns
  W4 ...**37** C4
Copenhagen Ho
  N1 ...**85** B3
Copenhagen Pl
  E14 ...**33** B3
Copenhagen Prim Sch
  N1 ...**84** C3
Copenhagen St N1...**84** C3
Cope Pl W8 ...**127** B1
Cope St SE16...**40** C2
Copford Wlk N1...**86** C4
Copleston Rd
  SE15...**64** B4
Copley Cl 17 SE17...**48** A4
Copley St 1 E1...**32** C4
Coppedhall 2
  SE21...**75** C2
Copperas St SE8...**52** A4
Copper Beech N6...**3** C4
Copperbeech Cl
  NW3...**11** C3
Copper Box Arena
  E15...**18** C2

Col–Cor **201**

Copperfield Ho SE1...**139** B3
Copperfield Rd E3...**33** A4
Copperfields Ct
  W3...**36** C4
Copperfield St
  SE1 ...**136** C4
Copper Lane 27 N16...**15** C4
Copper Mews 18
  W4 ...**37** B3
Copper Row SE1 ...**124** C1
Copperwood Pl 14
  SE1...**52** B2
Coppice Dr SW15...**57** A1
Coppin Ho SW2 ...**75** A3
Coppock Cl SW11 ...**168** A1
Copse Ct SW15 ...**58** A2
Copthall Ave EC2 ...**109** C2
Copthall Bldgs
  EC2...**109** C2
Copthall Cl EC2...**109** B2
Copthorne Ave
  SW12 ...**73** C4
Coptic St WC1 ...**106** A3
Copton Cl E3 ...**33** C4
Coral Apts 8 E16 ...**35** C2
Coral Row 14
  SW11 ...**59** B4
Coral St SE1 ...**135** C3
Coram Ho
  Bloomsbury WC1 ...**94** A2
  3 Chiswick W4 ...**38** A1
Coram Mans WC1 ...**94** C1
Coram St WC1 ...**94** A1
Corbden Cl SE15 ...**49** B2
Corbet Ct EC3 ...**109** C1
Corbet Ho N1 ...**85** B3
Corbet Pl E1 ...**110** C4
Corbin Ho 3 E3...**27** A2
Corbridge SE8 ...**52** A4
Corbridge Cres E2...**25** A3
Corbyn St N4, N19 ...**5** A3
Corby Rd NW10...**20** C3
Corby Way E3 ...**26** C1
Cordelia Cl SE24...**63** A3
Cordelia Ho 22 N1...**24** A3
Cordelia St E14...**34** A3
Cording St E14...**34** A4
Cordwainers Ct 18
  E9...**17** B1
Cordwell Rd SE13...**67** C2
Corfe Ho SW8...**162** C2
Corfe Lodge 15
  SE21...**75** C2
Corfe Twr 6 W3...**37** B4
Corfield St E2...**25** A2
Coriander Ave E14...**34** C3
Coriander Ct 14
  SE1...**139** A4
Corinne Rd N19...**13** B4
Corker Wlk N7...**5** B2
Cork Sq E1...**32** A1
Cork St W1 ...**118** C3
Corlett St NW1 ...**102** A4
Cormont Rd SE5...**48** A2
Cormorant Ct
  26 Deptford SE8 ...**51** B4
  13 Dulwich SE21 ...**75** C2

Cornbury Ho 🖲
SE8..................51 B4
Cornelia St N7....14 B2
Cornell Bldg 🖲
E1....................111 B2
Corner Fielde
SW2..................74 B3
Corner Gn SE3....53 C1
Corner House St
WC2................120 A2
Cornerstone Ct 🖲
E1..............24 C1 99 C1
Cornerways SW15..56 C3
Corney Rd W4......46 A4
Corney Reach Way
W4....................46 A3
Cornflower Terr
SE22..................65 A1
Cornford Gr SW12..73 A2
Cornhill EC3......109 C1
Cornick Ho 🖸
SE16..................40 A3
Cornish Ho
Brentford TW8......36 B1
🗓 Camberwell
SE17..................48 A4
Cornmill La SE13..67 B4
Cornmow Dr NW10..8 C3
Cornwall Ave E2..25 B2
Cornwall Cres
W11....................31 A3
Cornwall Flats
SE1..................135 C4
Cornwall Gdns
Kensington SW7..128 B1
Willesden NW10..9 A2
Cornwall Gdns Wlk
SW7................128 B1
Cornwall Gr W4..38 A1
Cornwall Ho
Marylebone NW1..91 A1
🗓 Putney SW15....69 B4
Cornwallis Ct
SW8..................172 A4
Cornwallis Ho 🖳
W12....................30 A2
Cornwallis Rd N19..5 A2
Cornwallis Sq
🖫 Finsbury Park
N4......................5 C2
London N19..........5 C2
Cornwall Mans
Chelsea SW10....157 A2
Marylebone NW1..91 A1
Cornwall Mews S
SW7..................128 C1
Cornwall Mews W
SW7..................128 B1
Cornwall Rd
Finsbury Pk N4......5 C4
Lambeth SE1......135 C4
Cornwall Sq SE11..150 A2
Cornwall St 🖪 E1..32 A2
Cornwall Terr
NW1....................91 A1
Cornwall Terrace
Mews NW1........91 A1
Cornwood Dr E1..32 B3
Coronation Ave 🖲
N16....................16 B4
Coronation Ct 🖫
W10....................30 B4
Coronet St
N1..............24 A2 98 A3

Corporation Row
EC1....................95 C2
Corporation St N7..14 A3
Corpus Christi RC
Prim Sch 🖽 SW2..62 B2
Corrance Rd SW2,
SW4....................62 A3
Corringham Ct
NW11..................1 C4
Corringham Ho 🗓
E1......................32 C3
Corringham Rd
NW11..................1 C4
Corringway NW11..2 A4
Corry Dr SW9......63 A3
Corry Ho 🗔 E14..34 A2
Corsham St N1....97 C3
Corsica St N5....15 A2
Corsley Way E9....18 B2
Cortayne Rd SW6 165 A2
Cortis Rd SW15....57 A1
Cortis Terr SW15..57 A1
Corunna Rd SW8 171 A4
Corunna Terr
SW8..................170 C4
Corvette Sq 🖲
SE10..................52 C4
Coryton Path W9..23 B1
Cosbycote Ave
SE24..................63 B2
Cosgrove Ho 🖩
E2......................24 C4
Cosmo Pl WC1..106 B4
Cosmur Cl W12....38 B3
Cossall Wlk SE15..50 A2
Cossar Mews 🗓
SW2....................62 C2
Cosser St SE1..135 C1
Costa St SE15....49 C1
Coston Wlk 🖪
SE4....................65 C3
Cosway Mans
NW1..................102 B4
Cosway St NW1..102 B4
Cotall St E14......33 C4
Cotes Ho NW8....90 A1
Cotham St SE17 151 A3
Cotherstone Rd
SW2....................74 B3
Cotleigh Rd NW6..10 C1
Cotman Cl SW15..57 C2
Cotman Ho NW8..89 A2
Cotrill Gdns E8..17 A2
Cotswold Ct EC1....96 C2
Cotswold Gate NW2..1 A3
Cotswold Ho N16..7 B3
Cotswold Mews
SW11................167 C3
Cottage Gn SE5..48 C3
Cottage Gr SW9..62 A4
Cottage Pl SW3 130 A1
Cottage Rd N7....14 B3
Cottage St E14....34 A2
Cottages The SE1 134 C1
Cottage Wlk 🖪 N16..7 B1
Cottenham Ho 🖲
N19....................5 A2
Cottesbrook St 🖫
SE14..................51 A3
Cottesloe Ho NW8..90 A2
Cottesloe Mews
SE1..................135 C2
Cottesmore Ct
W8..................128 B2
Cottesmore Gdns
W8..................128 B2

Cottingham Rd
SW8..................163 A2
Cottington St
SE11................150 A2
Cotton Ave W3....28 C3
Cotton Ho
Bedford Pk W12....38 B4
🖺 Streatham
SW12..................74 A4
Cotton Row SW11..59 C4
Cotton's Gdns
E2..............24 A2 98 B4
Cottons La SE1..123 C2
Cotton St E14......34 B2
Cottrell Ct SE10..43 B2
Couchman Ho 🖽
SW4....................61 B1
Coulgate St SE4..66 A4
Coulson Ho 🖲
SW2....................74 A3
Coulson St SW3 144 C2
Coulter Rd W6....39 A3
Coults Cres NW5..3 C1
Councillor St SE5..48 B3
Counters Ct W14 126 B2
Counter St SE1..124 A1
Countess Rd NW5..13 B3
Countisbury Ho
SE26..................76 C1
County Gr SE5....48 B2
County Ho
🗓 Herne Hill
SE24..................63 A3
🖲 South Lambeth
SW9..................173 B4
County St SE1....137 A1
Courier Ho 🖫
SW2....................74 C4
Courland Gr SW8 171 C3
Courland St SW8 171 C3
Courtauld Ho 🗓
E2......................24 C3
Courtauld Institute of
Art W1..............103 B2
Courtauld Inst of Art
WC2..................120 C4
Courtauld Rd N19..5 A3
Courtenay Ave N6..3 A4
Courtenay Sq
SE11................149 B1
Courtenay St
SE11................149 B2
Courtfield Gdns
SW5..................142 B3
Courtfield Ho EC1 107 B4
Courtfield Mews
SW5..................142 B3
Courtfield Rd
SW7..................142 C3
Court Gdns N7....14 C2
Courthill Rd SE13..67 B3
Courthope Ho
🗓 Rotherhithe
SE16..................40 B3
🖲 South Lambeth
SW8..................162 A1
Courthope Rd
NW3....................12 B4
Court La SE21......76 B4
Courtlands TW10..54 C2
Courtlands Ave
TW9....................45 A1
Court Lane Gdns
SE21..................76 A4
Court Mans 🖲 W6..38 C2

Courtmead Cl
SE24..................63 B1
Courtnell St W2..31 C3
Courtney Ct N7....14 C3
Courtney Ho W14 126 B2
Courtney Rd N7....14 C3
Courtrai Rd SE23..66 A1
Court Royal SW6..58 A2
Court St 🖪 E1......32 A4
Courtville Ho 🖸
W10....................23 A2
Court Way W3......28 B4
Courtyard The
Fulham SW6........164 A3
Islington N1........14 B1
🗓 Wandsworth
SW18..................59 C3
Cousin La EC4....123 B3
Couzens Ho 🖪 E3..33 B4
Coval Gdns SW14..55 A3
Coval La SW14....55 A3
Coval Pas SW14..55 B3
Coval Rd SW14....55 B3
Covell Ct 🗓 SE8..51 C3
Covent Garden Sta
WC2..................106 B1
Covent Gdn WC2... 120 B4
Coventry Cl NW6..23 C3
Coventry Rd E1....25 A1
Coventry St W1..119 B3
Coventry Univ London
EC2....................97 C2
Coverdale Rd
Brondesbury
NW2..................10 A2
Hammersmith W12..39 A4
Hampstead NW6....9 C1
Coverham Ho 🖲
SE4....................65 C3
Coverley Cl E1....111 C4
Coverley Point
SE11................148 C3
Cowcross St EC1 108 A4
Cowdenbeath Path
N1......................84 C4
Cowdray Hall Royal
Coll of Nursing
W1....................104 A2
Cowdray Ho 🖩
SE22..................64 A4
Cowdry Rd E9....18 B2
Cowley Ho
Brixton SW9......173 C4
East Acton W3......29 B1
Mortlake SW14....56 A4
Cowley St SW1....134 A1
Cowling Cl
W11..........31 A1 112 A2
Cowper Ho
Pimlico SW1......147 C1
Walworth SE17....151 A2
Cowper Rd
Acton W3............28 C1
Stoke Newington
N16....................16 A4
Cowper's Ct EC3 109 C1
Cowper St EC1,EC2..97 C2
Cowper Terr W10..30 C4
Cowthorpe Rd
SW8..................171 C4
Cox Ho W6........154 A4
Coxson Way SE1..138 C3
Coysh Ct 🖫 SW15..58 A2
Crabtree Cl E2....24 B3
Crabtree Hall SW6..47 B3
Crabtree La SW6..47 C3

Craddock St NW5..12 C2
Cragie Ho SE1....153 A3
Craigleith SW15..57 C1
Craignair Rd SW2..74 C4
Craigrossie Rd SW2..74 C4
Craig's Ct SW1..120 A2
Craik Ct NW6......23 B3
Crail Row SE17....151 C3
Cramer St W1....103 C3
Crammond Cl NW6 154 A3
Crampton Prim Sch
SE17..................150 B2
Crampton St SE17 150 C2
Cranbourn Alley
WC2..................119 C4
Cranbourne Ct
SW11................158 B2
Cranbourne Rd
E15....................19 B4
Cranbourn Ho 🖲
SE16..................40 A4
Cranbourn Pas 🖫
SE16..................40 A4
Cranbourn St
WC2..................119 C4
Cranbrook NW1....83 A3
Cranbrook Ho 🖫
E5......................17 A3
Cranbrook Rd
Chiswick W4........38 A1
St Johns SE8........51 C2
Cranbrook St E2..25 C3
Cranbury Rd SW6 166 B1
Crandale Ho 🖪
E5......................17 A3
Crandley Ct SE8..41 A2
Crane Ave W3......28 B2
Crane Ct
🗓 Acton W12........38 A4
Holborn EC4......107 C1
Crane Gr N7........14 C2
Crane Ho
🖪 Bow E3............26 A3
🖰 Peckham SE15..49 B2
Crane Mead SE16..40 C2
Crane St
Greenwich SE10....42 C1
🖰 Peckham SE15..49 B2
Cranfield Cl 🖪
SE27..................75 B1
Cranfield Ct NW1..102 B3
Cranfield Ho WC1 106 B4
Cranfield Rd SE4..66 B4
Cranford Cotts 🖪
E1......................32 C2
Cranford Lo SW19..69 C2
Cranford St E1....32 C2
Cranhurst Rd NW2..9 B3
Cranleigh
W11..........31 B1 112 C2
Cranleigh Ct
Richmond TW9....54 C4
🖲 Stamford Hill N16..7 A3
Cranleigh Hos
NW1....................83 A1
Cranleigh Mews
SW11................168 C1
Cranleigh St NW1..83 A1
Cranley Gdns
SW7..................143 B2
Cranley Mews
SW7..................143 A2
Cranley Pl SW7..143 B3
Cranmer Ct SW3 144 B3
Cranmer Ho
SW11................168 A4
Cranmer Rd SW9 163 C2

Cranswick Rd
SE16 ....40 A1
Cromwell Cl E3 ....27 A1
Cranwich Rd N16 .....14 A4
Cranwood Ct EC1 ....97 C3
Cranwood St EC1 ....97 C3
Cranworth Gdns
SW9 ....173 A4
Cranworth Ho **6**
N7 ....14 B4
Craster Rd SW2 ......74 B4
Craston Ho **2** SE5 ...49 A1
Craven Cl N16 ....7 C3
Craven Cottage
(Fulham FC)
SW6 ....47 C2
Craven Ct NW10 ......21 A4
Craven Hill W2 ....115 A4
Craven Hill Gdns
W2 ....115 A4
Craven Hill Mews
W2 ....115 A4
Craven Ho **2**
SW14 ....55 C4
Craven Lo
Bayswater W2 ....115 A4
Fulham NW6 ....47 C2
Craven Mews **6**
SW11 ....60 C4
Craven Park Mews
NW10 ....21 A4
Craven Park Rd
NW10 ....21 A4
Craven Pass SC2 ...120 A2
Craven Pk NW10 ......21 A4
Craven Rd
Paddington W2 ......101 A1
Stonebridge NW10 ...20 C4
Craven St SW2 ....47 C2
Craven Terr W2 ......115 A4
Craven Wlk E5, N16 ..7 C4
Crawford Bldgs
...............................102 B3
Crawford Mews
W1 ....102 C3
Crawford Pas EC1 ...95 C1
Crawford Pl W1 .....102 B3
Crawford Place
Dwellings NW1 ......102 B3
Crawford Point **4**
E16 ....35 B3
Crawford Prim Sch
11 Camberwell
SE5 ....48 B2
London SE5 ....48 B2
Crawford Rd SE5 ....48 B1
Crawford St W1 .....102 C3
Crawshay Ct SW9 ..173 C4
Crawshay Ho **13**
N16 ....15 C4
Crawthew Gr SE22 ..64 B3
Crayford Ho
Bermondsey SE1 ...137 C3
5 Lower Holloway
N7 ....14 A4
Crayford Rd N7........13 C4
Crayle Ho EC1 ....96 B2
Crealock St SW18 ...59 A1
Creasy Est SE1 .....138 A1
Crebor St SE22 ....64 C1
Credenhill Ho **2**
SE15 ....50 A3
Crediton Hill NW6 ..11 A3
Crediton Rd
Brondesbury Pk
NW10 ....22 C4

Crediton Rd continued
Newham E16 ....35 C3
Credon Rd E16 ....35 C3
Creechurch La
EC3 ....110 B1
Creechurch Pl
EC3 ....110 B1
Creed Ct **5** E1 ....26 A2
Creed Ho SE15 ....65 A4
Creed La EC4 ....108 B1
Creek Ho W14 ....126 B2
Creek Rd SE10,
SE8 ....52 A4
Creek Road Ind Est
.................................52 A4
Creekside SE8 ....52 A3
Creekside Foyer
SE8 ....52 A3
Crefeld Cl W6 ....154 A3
Creighton Cl W12 ...30 A2
Creighton Rd NW6 ..22 C3
Cremer Bsns Ctr **8**
E2 ....24 B3
Cremer Ho **9** SE8 .51 C3
Cremer St E2 ....24 B3
Cremorne Rd
SW10 ....157 B2
Creon Ct **3** SW9 ..173 B4
Crescent Arc **1**
SE10 ....52 B4
Crescent Court Bsns
Ctr **11** E16 ....27 C1
Crescent Gr SW4 ...61 C3
Crescent Gdns
SW19 ....70 C1
Crescent Ho SE13 ..52 A1
Crescent La SW4 ....61 C2
Crescent Mans
1 Islington N5 .....15 A3
2 Notting Hill
W11 ....31 A2 112 B4
Crescent Pl SW3 ...144 B4
Crescent Row EC1 ..96 C1
Crescent St N1 ......14 B1
Crescent Stables
SW15 ....58 A2
Crescent The
Acton W3 ....29 A3
Barnes SW13 ....56 C4
Wimbledon SW19 ...70 C1
Crescent Way SE4 ..66 C4
Crescent Wood Rd
SE21, SE26 ....76 C1
Cressage Ho **9**
TW8 ....44 A4
Cressall Ho **14**
E14 ....41 C3
Cresset Ho E9 ....17 B2
Cresset Rd E9 ....17 B2
Cresset St SW4 .....61 C4
Cressfield Cl NW5 ..12 C3
Cressida Rd N19 .....4 C3
Cressingham Rd
SE13 ....67 B4
Cressington Cl **4**
N16 ....16 A3
Cresswell Gdns
SW5 ....142 C2
Cresswell Pl
SW10 ....143 A2
Cressy Ct
Hammersmith W6 ...39 A3
36 Stepney E1 ......32 B4

Cressy Ct continued
6 Stepney E1 ....32 B4
Cressy Ho SW13 .....57 A4
Cressy Hos **5** E1 ..32 B4
Cressy Pl E1 ....32 B4
Cressy Rd NW3 ......12 B4
Cresta Ho
1 Bow E3 ....26 C1
Hampstead NW3 ....12 B1
Crestfield St N1,
WC1 ....94 B4
Crestview NW5 ....4 A1
Crestway SW15 ......57 A1
Creswick Ct W3 ......28 A2
Creswick Rd W3 .....28 A2
Creswick Wlk **7**
E3 ....26 C2
Crewdson Rd
SW9 ....163 B1
Crewe Pl NW10 ......21 B2
Crewkerne Ct
SW11 ....167 C4
Crews St E14 ....41 C2
Crewys Rd
Child's Hill NW2 ....1 B2
London SE15 ....50 A1
Crichton St SW8 ...170 C2
Cricketers Mews **4**
SW18 ....59 A2
Cricketfield Rd E5 ..17 A4
Cricklade Ave
SW2 ....74 B2
CRICKLEWOOD 9 B4
Cricklewood
Broadway NW2 ....9 C4
Cricklewood La
NW2 ....1 B1
Cricklewood Sta
NW2 ....9 C4
Crieff Rd SW18 ......59 B1
Criffel Ave SW2 .....73 C3
Crimscott St SE1 ..138 B1
Crimsworth Rd
SW8 ....161 C1
Crinan St N1 ....84 B2
Cringle St SW8 .....160 C2
Cripplegate St
EC1 ....109 A4
Crispe Ho N1 ....85 A3
Crispian Cl NW10 ....8 A4
Crispin Cl SE17 .....152 A3
Crispin Pl E1 ....110 C3
Crispin St E1 ....110 C3
Crisp Rd W6 ....39 B1
Cristowe Rd SW6 ..165 A1
Criterion Mews
N19 ....4 C2
Crockerton Rd
SW17 ....72 B2
Croft Ct SE13 ....67 B1
Croftdown Rd NW5 ..4 A1
Crofters Ct **9** SE8 .41 A2
Crofters Way NW1 ..83 B4
Croft Ho
Putney SW15 ....58 A1
11 West Kilburn
W10 ....23 A2
Crofton Ave W4 .....45 C3
Crofton Gate Way
SE4 ....66 A2
Crofton Park Rd
SE4 ....66 B1
Crofton Park Sta
SE4 ....66 B2
Crofton Rd SE5 .....49 A1

Crofton Terr
Homerton E5 ....18 A3
Richmond TW9 ....54 B3
Crofts Ho **2** E2 .....24 C3
Crofts St E1 ....125 B3
Croft St SE8 ....41 A2
Croft TW NW10 ......21 B3
Crogsland Rd
NW1 ....12 C1
Cromartie Rd N19 ...4 C4
Cromarty Ho **3**
E1 ....33 A4
Crombie Mews **5**
SW11 ....168 B2
Cromdale Ct N16 .....7 C4
Cromer Ct
Streatham SW16 ....74 A1
Wandsworth SW18 ..58 B1
Cromer Rd SW17 ...73 A2
Cromer St WC1 ....94 B3
Cromer Terr E8 ......16 C3
Cromer Villas Rd
SW18 ....58 B1
Cromford Path **1**
E5 ....17 C4
Cromford Rd
SW18 ....58 C2
Crompton Ct SW3 .144 A4
Crompton Ho
Borough The SE1 ...137 A1
Paddington W2 ....89 B1
South Lambeth
SW8 ....171 A3
Crompton St W2 .....89 B1
Cromwell Ave
Hammersmith W6 ...39 A2
Highgate N6 ....4 A3
Cromwell Cl
Acton W3 ....28 B1
2 Gunnersbury
W4 ....37 A1
Cromwell Cres
SW5 ....141 B4
Cromwell Ctr
NW10 ....20 C2
Cromwell Gdns
SW7 ....129 C1
Cromwell Gr W6 .....39 B3
Cromwell Ho
Battersea SW11 .....169 C3
Putney SW15 ....56 C3
Cromwell Hospl
(BUPA) SW5 ....142 A4
Cromwell Lo **40**
E1 ....25 B1
Cromwell Mans
SW5 ....141 C4
Cromwell Mews
SW7 ....143 C4
Cromwell Pl
5 Acton W3 ....28 B1
Barbican EC1 ....109 A4
Highgate N6 ....4 A3
Mortlake SW14 ......55 B4
South Kensington
SW7 ....143 C4
Cromwell Rd
Brixton SW9 ....48 A2
South Kensington
SW7 ....143 A4
Cromwell Twr
EC2 ....109 A4
Crondace Rd
SW6 ....165 C3
Crondall Ct **7** N1 ..24 A3
Crondall Ho SW15 ..68 C3

Crondall Pl **15** N1 ..24 A3
Crondall St N1 ....24 A3
Crone Ct **5** NW6 ...23 B3
Cronin St SE15 ....49 B3
Crooked Billet Yd **18**
E2 ....24 A2 98 B4
Crooke Rd SE8 ....41 A1
Crookham Rd
SW6 ....164 C3
Croom's Hill SE10 ..52 C3
Croom's Hill Gr
SE10 ....52 B3
Cropley Ct N1 ....87 B2
Cropley St N1 ....87 B2
Cropthorne Ct W9 ..89 A3
Crosby Ct SE1 ....137 B4
Crosby Ho **10** E14 ..42 B3
Crosby Row SE1 ...137 B4
Crosby Sq EC3 ......110 A2
Crosby Wlk
1 Dalston E8 ....16 B2
Streatham SE24 .....74 C4
Crosfield Ct **3**
W10 ....30 C3
Crosfield Ho
W11 ....31 A2 112 A3
Crosland Pl **5**
SW11 ....60 C4
Crossbow Ho **15**
N1 ....24 A4
Cross Cl SE15 ....50 A1
Cross Ct SE5 ....63 C4
Crossfield Rd
NW3 ....11 C2
Crossfield St SE8 ....51 C3
Crossford St SW9 ..172 C1
Crossharbour Sta
E14 ....42 A3
Cross Keys Cl W1 ..103 C3
Cross La EC3 ....124 A3
Crossleigh Ct **3**
SE14 ....51 B3
Crosslet St SE17 ...151 C4
Crosslet Vale SE10 ..52 A2
Crossman Hos **10**
SW12 ....74 A4
Crossmount Ho **13**
SE5 ....48 B3
Crossrail Pl E14 .....34 A1
Cross Rd SE5 ....49 A1
Cross St
Islington N1 ....86 B4
Mortlake SW13 ......56 A4
Crossthwaite Ave
SE24 ....63 C3
Crosstrees Ho **7**
E14 ....41 C3
Crosswall EC3 ....124 C4
Crossway E8, N16 ..16 A3
Crossway Ct SE4 ....51 A1
Crossways Acad
SE4 ....51 A1
Croston St E8 ....24 C4
Crouch End Hill N8 ..4 C4
Crouch Hall Ct N19 ..5 A3
Crouch Hill N4, N8,
N19 ....5 A4
Crouch Hill Sta N4 ..5 B4
Crouchmans Cl SE21,
SE26 ....76 C1
Crowder St E1 ....32 A2
Crowfield Ho N5 .....15 B3
Crowfoot Cl E9 ....18 B3

Crowhurst Cl
SW9 . . . . **173** C2
Crowhurst Ho 21
SW9 . . . . **173** A1
Crowland Ho NW8 . **78** C3
Crowland Terr N1 . . **15** C1
Crowline Wlk 1
N1 . . . . **15** B2
Crown Cl
Bow E3 . . . . **26** C4
Hampstead NW6 . . **11** A2
Crown Close Bsns Ctr
E3 . . . . **26** C4
Crown Ct
City of London
EC4 . . . . **109** A1
4 Putney SW15 . . **57** C3
St Giles WC2 . . . . **106** B1
St John's Wood
NW8 . . . . **90** B3
Crowndale Ct NW1 **83** B2
Crowndale Rd
NW1 . . . . **83** A2
Crowne Ho SE1 . . **123** A1
Crownfield Rd
E15 . . . . **19** C4
Crowngate Ho 23
E3 . . . . **26** B3
Crownhill Rd
NW10 . . . . **21** B4
Crownleigh Ct
SW2 . . . . **62** C2
Crown Lo SW3 . . **144** B3
Crown Mews 9
E1 . . . . **32** C4
Crown Office Row
EC4 . . . . **121** B4
Crown Pas SW1 . **119** A1
Crown Pl
Broadgate EC2 . . . **110** A4
Kentish Town NW5 . **13** A2
Crown Reach
SW1 . . . . **147** C1
Crown St
Acton W3 . . . . **28** A1
Camberwell SE5 . . . **48** B3
Crownstone Ct 1
SW2 . . . . **62** C2
Crownstone Rd
SW2 . . . . **62** C2
Crown Terr TW9 . . **54** B3
Crows Rd E3, E15 . . **27** C2
Crowther Ave
TW8 . . . . **36** A2
Crowther Cl SW6 **155** A3
Crowthorne Cl
SW18 . . . . **70** B3
Crowthorne Rd
W10 . . . . **30** C3
Croxley Rd W9 . . . **23** B2
Croxted Cl SE21 . . **75** B4
Croxted Rd SE21,
SE24 . . . . **75** C3
Croxteth Ho 8
SW8 . . . . **171** B2
Croydon Ho SE1 . **135** C4
Crozier Ho SW8 . **162** C1
Crozier Terr E9 . . . **17** C3
Crucifix La SE1 . . **138** A4
Cruden Ho
19 Bow E3 . . . . . . **26** B3
7 Camberwell
SE17 . . . . **48** A4
Cruden St N1 . . . . **86** B3

Cruickshank St
WC1 . . . . **95** B4
Cruikshank Ho
NW8 . . . . **80** B2
Crusader Ho EC1 . . **96** A1
Crusoe Mews N16 . . **6** C2
Crutched Friars
EC3 . . . . **124** B4
Crystal Palace Rd
SE22 . . . . **64** C2
Crystal Wharf N1 . . **86** B1
Cuba St E14 . . . . . **41** C4
Cubitt Bldg SW1 . **146** A1
Cubitt Ho 4 SW4 . . **61** B1
Cubitt St WC1 . . . **95** A3
Cubitt Terr SW4 . . . **61** B4
CUBITT TOWN . . . **42** B2
Cubitt Town Jun & Inf
Sch E14 . . . . **42** B3
Cuddington SE17 **151** A4
Cudworth Ho
SW8 . . . . **171** A3
Cudworth St E1 . . . **25** A1
Cuffley Ho 3 W10 . **30** B4
Cuff Point 12
E2 . . . . **24** B2 98 C4
Culand Ho SE17 . . **152** A3
Culford Gdns
SW3 . . . . **145** A3
Culford Gr N1 . . . . **16** A2
Culford Mans
SW3 . . . . **145** A3
Culford Mews N1 . . **16** A2
Culford Rd
Kingsland N1 . . . . . **16** A2
Shoreditch N1 . . . . **24** A4
Culham Ho
21 Paddington
W2 . . . . **31** C4
8 Shoreditch
E2 . . . . **24** B2 98 C3
Cullen Ho W9 . . . . **23** B3
Cullen Way NW10 . **20** B1
Culling Rd SE16 . . . **40** B3
Cullingworth Rd
NW10 . . . . **9** A3
Culloden Cl 2 1
SE16 . . . . **153** C1
Culloden Prim Sch 16
E14 . . . . **34** B3
Cullum St EC3 . . . **124** A4
Culmore Rd SE15 . . **50** B3
Culmstock Rd
SW11 . . . . **60** C2
Culpeper Ct
SE11 . . . . **149** B4
Culross Bldgs
NW1 . . . . **84** A2
Culross St W1 . . . **117** B3
Culver Ct SW18 . . . **59** A1
Culverden Rd
SW12 . . . . **73** B2
Culverhouse WC1 **106** C3
Culverhouse Gdns
SW16 . . . . **74** B1
Culverin Ct 1 N7 . . **14** B3
Culvert Ct SW11 . **169** B2
Culvert Pl SW11 . . **169** B1
Culvert Rd SW11 . **169** A2
Culworth Ho NW8 . **80** A1
Culworth St NW8 . . **80** A1
Culzean Cl 3
SE27 . . . . **75** A1
Cumber Ho SW18 . . **70** C3
Cumberland Ave
NW10 . . . . **20** A2

Cumberland Bsns Pk
NW10 . . . . **20** A2
Cumberland Cl E8 . . **16** B2
Cumberland Cres
W14 . . . . **140** B4
Cumberland Ct
W1 . . . . **103** A1
Cumberland Gate
W1 . . . . **117** A4
Cumberland Gdns
WC1 . . . . **95** B4
Cumberland Ho
Paddington W9 . . . . **88** C1
1 Putney SW15 . . **69** B4
Cumberland Mans
Marylebone W1 . . **102** C2
2 West Hampstead
NW6 . . . . **10** C3
Cumberland Market
NW1 . . . . **92** B4
Cumberland Mills Sq
E14 . . . . **42** C1
Cumberland Park Ind
Est NW10 . . . . **21** C2
Cumberland Pk
W3 . . . . **28** B2
Cumberland Pl
NW1 . . . . **92** A4
Cumberland Rd
Acton W3 . . . . **28** B2
Barnes SW13 . . . . . **46** C2
Richmond TW9 . . . . **44** C3
Cumberland St
SW1 . . . . **146** B2
Cumberland Terr
NW1 . . . . **92** A4
Cumberland Terrace
Mews NW1 . . . . . **82** A1
Cumberland Villas
W3 . . . . **28** B2
Cumberland Wharf 10
SE16 . . . . **40** B4
Cumbrian Gdns
NW2 . . . . **1** A2
Cuming Mus SE17 **150** C3
Cumming St N1 . . . **85** A1
Cumnor Cl 28
SW9 . . . . **173** A2
Cunard Pl EC3 . . . **110** B1
Cunard Rd NW10 . . **20** C2
Cunard Wlk 3
SE16 . . . . **41** A2
Cundy St SW1 . . . **145** C3
Cunningham Ct
W2 . . . . **89** B1
Cunningham Ho 16
SE5 . . . . **48** C3
Cunningham Pl
NW8 . . . . **89** B2
Cunnington St W4 . **37** B2
Cupar Rd SW11 . . **169** C4
Cureton St SW1 . . **147** C3
Curlew Ho
Brockley SE4 . . . . . **66** A3
7 Peckham SE15 . . **49** B2
Curlew St SE1 . . . **139** A4
Curness St SE13 . . . **67** B3
Curran Ho SW3 . . **144** A3
Curricle St SW3 . . . **29** A1
Currie Ho 13
SW12 . . . . **73** C4
Cursitor St EC4 . . **107** B2
Curtain Pl
EC2 . . . . **24** A1 98 B2
Curtain Rd
EC2 . . . . **24** A1 98 B2

Curtis Dr W3 . . . . . **28** C3
Curtis Ho SE17 . . **151** B2
Curtis St SE1 . . . . **152** C4
Curtis Way SE1 . . **152** C4
Curve Bldg The
SE4 . . . . **66** B2
Curve The W12 . . . **29** C2
Curwen Gall W1 . . **105** B3
Curwen Rd W12 . . . **38** C4
Curzon Cres NW10 . . **8** A1
Curzon Gate 4
W1 . . . . **117** C1
Curzon Sq
City of London
W1 . . . . **117** C1
Curzon St W1 . . . **117** C1
Curzon St W1 . . . **118** A2
Custance Ho N1 . . . **87** B1
Custance St N1 . . . **97** B4
Custom House
EC3 . . . . **124** A3
Custom House Reach
SE16 . . . . **41** B3
Cutbush Ho N7 . . . . **13** C3
Cutcombe Rd SE5 . . **48** B1
Cuthbert Harrowing
Ho EC1 . . . . **96** C1
Cuthbert Ho W2 . . **101** B4
Cuthbert St W2 . . . **89** B1
Cuthill Wlk 3 SE5 . . **48** C2
Cutlers Gdns EC2 . **110** B2
Cutlers Gdns Arc
EC2 . . . . **110** B2
Cutlers Sq E14 . . . . **41** C2
Cutler St EC2 . . . **110** B2
Cutler La SE10 . . . . **43** A4
Cutty Sark SE10 . . . **52** B4
Cut The SE1 . . . . **135** C4
Cutty Sark SE10 . . . **52** B4
Cutty Sark Ho 10
E14 . . . . **42** A2
Cutty Sark Sta
SE10 . . . . **52** B4
Cuxton Ho SE17 . . **152** B2
Cyclops Mews 22
E14 . . . . **41** C2
Cygnet Ho NW8 . . . **78** C4
Cygnet House N 18
E14 . . . . **34** A3
Cygnet House S 19
E14 . . . . **34** A3
Cygnet St
E1 . . . . **24** B1 99 A2
Cygnus Bsns Ctr
NW10 . . . . **8** B2
Cynthia St N1 . . . . **85** A1
Cyprus Pl 8 E8 . . . **17** A1
Cypress Cl 9 E5 . . . . **7** C2
Cypress Ct 3 E11 . . **19** C4
Cypress Gdns SE4 . . **66** A2
Cypress Ho SE14 . . **50** C2
Cypress Pl W1 . . . . **93** A1
Cyprus Pl 22 E2 . . . **25** B3
Cyprus St E2 . . . . . **25** B3
Cyrena Rd SE22 . . . **64** B2
Cyril Jackson Prim
Sch (North Bldg) 24
E14 . . . . **33** B2
Cyril Jackson Prim
Sch (South Bldg) 25
E14 . . . . **33** B2
Cyril Mans SW11 . **169** A3
Cyril Thatcher Ho
SW6 . . . . **165** C3
Cyrus Ho EC1 . . . . **96** B2
Cyrus St EC1 . . . . . **96** B2
Czar St SE8 . . . . . . **51** C4

D

Dabb's La EC1 . . . . **95** C1
Dabin Cres SE10 . . . **52** B2
Dacca St SE8 . . . . . **51** B4
Dace Rd E3 . . . . . . **26** C4
Dacre Ho SW3 . . . **157** C3
Dacre St SW1 . . . **133** B2
Daffodil St W12 . . . **29** B2
Dafforne Rd SW17 . **72** C1
Dagmar Ct E14 . . . . **42** B3
Dagmar Gdns
NW10 . . . . **22** C3
Dagmar Pas N1 . . . **86** B4
Dagmar Rd
Camberwell SE5 . . . **49** A2
Finsbury Pk N4 . . . . . **5** C4
Dagmar Terr N1 . . . **86** B4
Dagnall St SW11 . **169** B3
Dagnan Rd SW12 . . **73** B4
Dagobert Ho 27
E1 . . . . **32** B4
Daimler Ho 8 E3 . . **26** C1
Dainton Ho 22 W2 . **31** C4
Dainty Way E9 . . . . **18** B2
Dairy Cl NW10 . . . . **21** C4
Dairyman Ct W2 . . . . **1** A1
Daisy Dormer Ct 11
SW9 . . . . **62** B3
Daisy La SW6 . . . . **58** C4
Dakin Pl 2 E1 . . . . **33** A4
Dakota Bldg 6
SE13 . . . . **52** A2
Dalberg Rd SW2 . . . **62** C2
Dalbury Ho 6
SW9 . . . . **62** B3
Dalby Rd SW18 . . . **59** B3
Dalby St NW5 . . . . **13** A2
Dalebury Rd SW17 . **72** B2
Dale Croft N4 . . . . . **6** B1
Dalehead NW1 . . . . **82** C1
Dalehaven
NW3 . . . . **11** C2
Daleham Mews
NW3 . . . . **11** C2
Dale Ho
London SE4 . . . . . . **66** A3
St John's Wood
NW8 . . . . **78** C4
Dalemain Ho 5
E8 . . . . **171** C2
Dalemain Mews 12
E16 . . . . **35** C1
Dale Rd
Camberwell SE17 . . **48** A4
Gospel Oak NW5 . . **12** C3
Dale Row W11 . . . **31** A3
Dale St W4 . . . . . . **38** A1
Daley Ho 3 W12 . . . **30** A3
Daley St E9 . . . . . . **17** C2
Daley Thompson Way
7 SW8 . . . . **61** A4
Dalgarno Gdns
W10 . . . . **30** B4
Dalgarno Way
W10 . . . . **22** B1
Dalgleish St 24
E14 . . . . **33** A3
Daling Way E3 . . . **26** A3
Dalkeith Ct SW1 . **147** C3
Dalkeith Ho 5 SW9 . **48** A2
Dalkeith Rd SE21 . . **75** B4
Dalling Rd W6 . . . . **39** A2

Dallington Sch
  EC1 . . . . 96 B2
Dallington St EC1 . . 96 B2
Dalmeny Ave N7 . . . 13 C4
Dalmeny Avenue Est
  3 N7 . . . . 13 C4
Dalmeny Rd N7 . . . . 13 C4
Dalmeyer Rd N10 . . .8 B4
Dalmore Rd SE21 . . .75 B2
Dalrymple Rd SE4 . .66 A3
DALSTON 16 C2
Dalston Jct E8 . . . . .16 B2
Dalston Junction Sta
  E8 . . . . .16 A2
Dalston Kingsland Sta
  E8 . . . . .16 B3
Dalston La E8 . . . . . .16 C3
Dalton Ho
  7 Balham SW12 . .73 A4
  10 Bow E3 . . . . .26 A3
  13 Deptford SE14 . .50 C4
Dalton St SE27 . . . . .75 A1
Dalwood St SE5 . . . .49 A2
Dalyell Rd SW9 . . . .62 B4
Damascene Wlk
  SE21 . . . . .75 B3
Damer Ho 9
  TW10 . . . . .54 B1
Damer Terr SW10 . 157 A1
Dame St N1 . . . . . . .86 C2
Damien Ct 12 E1 . . .32 A3
Damien St E1 . . . . . .32 A3
Damory Ho 1
  SE16 . . . . .40 B2
Dan Bryant Ho 5
  SW12 . . . . .73 B4
Danbury St N1 . . . . .86 B2
Danby Ho
  23 Hackney E9 . . . .17 B1
  3 West Kilburn
  W10 . . . . .23 B2
Danby St SE15 . . . . .64 B4
Dancer Rd
  Fulham SW6 . . . . 164 C3
  Richmond TW9 . . . .54 C4
Dandridge Cl SE10 . .43 B1
Dandridge Ho E1 . 110 C4
Danebury 8 W10 . .30 B4
Danebury Ave
  SW15 . . . . .56 B1
Danecroft Rd
  SE24 . . . . .63 C2
Dane Ho 15 SE5 . . . .48 B1
Danehurst St
  SW6 . . . . 164 A4
Danemere St
  SW15 . . . . .57 B4
Dane Pl E3 . . . . .26 B3
Danes Ct NW8 . . . . .80 C3
Danesdale Rd E9 . . .18 A2
Danesfield SE5 . . . . .49 A4
Danes Ho W10 . . . . .30 B4
Dane St WC1 . . . . . 106 C3
Daneville Rd SE5 . . .48 C2
Daniel Bolt Cl E14 . .34 A4
Daniel Gdns SE15 . . .49 B3
Daniell Ho N1 . . . . .87 C2
Daniel's Rd SE15 . . .65 B4
Dan Leno Wlk
  SW6 . . . . 156 A1
Dansey Pl W1 . . . . 119 B4
Dante Pl SE11 . . . . 150 B3
Dante Rd SE11 . . . . 150 A4

Danube Ct 13
  SE15 . . . . .49 B3
Danube St SW3 . . . 144 B2
Danvers Ho 55 E1 . 111 C1
Danvers St SW3 . . 157 C3
Da Palma Ct SW6 . 155 B3
Daphne St SW18 . . .59 B1
Daplyn St 6 E1 . . . 111 B4
D'arblay St W1 . . . 105 A1
Darcy Ho E8 . . . . . .25 A4
Darell Prim Sch
  TW9 . . . . .54 C4
Darell Rd TW9 . . . . .54 C4
Daren Ct 7 N7 . . . . .14 A4
Darent Ho NW8 . . . 101 C4
Darenth Rd N16 . . . .7 B3
Darfield NW1 . . . . . .82 C3
Darfield Rd SE4 . . . .66 B2
Darfield Way W10 . .30 C3
Darfur St 2 SW15 . .57 C4
Darien Ho
  16 London SW11 . . .59 C4
  11 Stepney E1 . . . .32 C4
Darien Rd SW11 . . .59 C4
Daring Ho 23 E3 . . .26 A3
Darlan Rd SW6 . . . 155 A1
Darley Ho SE11 . . . 148 C1
Darley Rd SW11 . . .60 B1
Darling Rd SE4 . . . .66 C4
Darling Row E1 . . . .25 A1
Darlington Ho
  SW8 . . . . 161 C1
Darnall Ho 4
  SE10 . . . . .52 B2
Darnay Ho 3
  SE16 . . . . 139 B2
Darnell Ho 3
  SE10 . . . . .52 B3
Darnley Ho 7 E14 . .33 A3
Darnley Rd E9 . . . . .17 B2
Darnley Terr 12
  W11 . . . . .30 C1
Darrell Rd SE22 . . . .64 C2
Darren Cl N4 . . . . . . .5 B4
Darsley Dr SW8 . . . 172 A4
Dartford Ho SE1 . . 153 A4
Dartford St SE17 . . .48 B4
Dartington Ho
  Bayswater W2 . . . 100 A4
  2 London SW8 . . . 171 C2
Dartle Ct 29 SE16 139 C3
Dartmoor Wlk 18
  E14 . . . . .41 C2
Dartmouth Cl W11 . .31 C3
Dartmouth Ct
  SE10 . . . . .52 B2
Dartmouth Gr
  SE10 . . . . .52 B2
Dartmouth Hill
  SE10 . . . . .52 B2
Dartmouth Ho
  Dartmouth Pk N19 . .4 A2
  Lewisham SE10 . . . .52 B1
DARTMOUTH
  PARK 4 A4
Dartmouth Park Ave
  NW5 . . . . .4 A1
Dartmouth Park Hill
  N19 . . . . .4 A2
Dartmouth Park Rd
  NW5 . . . . .4 A1
Dartmouth Pl W4 . .46 A4
Dartmouth Rd NW2 . .9 C2
Dartmouth Row
  SE10 . . . . .52 B2

Dartmouth St
  SW1 . . . . 133 C3
Dartmouth Terr
  SE10 . . . . .52 C2
Darton Ct W3 . . . . .28 B1
Dartrey Twr
  SW10 . . . . 157 B2
Dartrey Wlk
  SW10 . . . . 157 A2
Dart St W10 . . . . . . .23 B2
Darville Rd N16 . . . .7 B1
Darwen Pl E2 . . . . . .25 A4
Darwin Ct NW1 . . . .81 C4
Darwin Ctr SW7 . . 129 B1
Darwin Ho 8
  SE13 . . . . .52 B1
Darwin St SE17 . . . 151 C4
Daryngton Ho
  SW8 . . . . 162 A1
Dashwood Ho
  SE21 . . . . .76 B1
Data Point Bsns Ctr
  E16 . . . . .27 C1
Datchelor Pl 4
  SE5 . . . . .48 C2
Datchet Ho NW1 . . .92 B4
Datchett Ho 40
  E2 . . . . .24 B2 98 C3
Datchwood St N4 . . .6 B1
Datchworth Ho 8
  N1 . . . . .15 A1
Daubeney Prim Sch
  E5 . . . . .18 A4
Daubeney Rd E5 . . .18 A4
Daubeney Twr 2
  SE8 . . . . .41 B1
Dault Rd SW18 . . . .59 B1
Dauney Ho SE1 . . . 136 A3
Dave Adams Ho 8
  E3 . . . . .26 B3
Davenant Ho 20
  E1 . . . . 111 C4
Davenant Rd N19 . . .4 C2
Davenant St E1 . . . 111 C3
Davenport Ho
  SE11 . . . . 135 B1
Davenport Mews 6
  W12 . . . . .30 A1
Davenport Rd SE6 . .67 B1
Daventry St NW1 . . 102 A4
Dave Porter Hts
  SW19 . . . . .70 A4
Davern Cl SE10 . . . .43 B2
Davey Cl N7 . . . . . . .14 B2
Davey Rd E9 . . . . . .18 C1
Davey's Ct WC2 . . 120 A4
Davey St SE15 . . . . .49 B4
David Devine Ho 7
  E8 . . . . .16 C3
David Game Coll
  Notting Hill W2 . . 113 C2
David Hewitt Ho 2
  E3 . . . . .34 A4
David Ho
  8 Putney SW15 . . .56 C2
  South Lambeth
  SW8 . . . . 162 A2
David Mews
  18 Greenwich
  SE10 . . . . .52 B3
  W1 . . . . 103 A4

Davidson Gdns
  SW8 . . . . 162 A2
Davidson Ho 7
  N19 . . . . .13 B4
David St E15 . . . . . .19 C3
Davies Mews W1 . . 118 A4
Davies St W1 . . . . . 118 A4
Davina Ho
  Brondesbury NW2 . .10 B2
  48 Hackney E5 . . . .17 A3
Da Vinci Ct 12
  SE16 . . . . .40 A1
Davis Ho 37 W12 . .30 A2
Davis Rd W3 . . . . . .38 B4
Davisville Rd W12 . .38 C4
Dawes Ho SE17 . . . 151 B3
Dawes Rd SW6 . . . 154 C2
Dawes St SE17 . . . 151 C2
Dawlish Ave SW18 . .71 A2
Dawlish Rd NW2 . . . .9 C2
Dawnay Gdns
  SW18 . . . . .71 C2
Dawnay Rd SW17,
  SW18 . . . . .71 C2
Dawn Cres E15 . . . .27 C4
Dawson Ho
  23 Bethnal Green
  E2 . . . . .25 B2
  5 Camberwell SE5 .49 A2
Dawson Pl
  W2 . . . . . . .31 C2 113 C4
Dawson Rd NW2 . . . .9 B4
Dawson St E2 . . . . . .24 B3
Day Ho 2 SE5 . . . . .48 B3
Daylesford Ave
  SW15 . . . . .56 C3
Daynor Ho 4
  NW6 . . . . .23 C4
Daysbrook Rd
  SW2 . . . . .74 B3
Dayton Gr SE15 . . . .50 B2
Deacon Ho SE11 . . 149 A3
Deacon Mews N1 . .15 C1
Deacon Rd NW2 . . . .8 C2
Deacon Way SE17 151 A4
Deal Ho
  Deptford SE15 . . . .50 C4
  Walworth SE17 . . . 152 B2
Deal Porters Way
  SE16 . . . . .40 C3
Deal St E1 . . . . 111 B4
Dealtry Rd SW15 . . .57 B3
Deal Wlk 3 SW9 . . 163 C1
Dean Bradley St
  SW1 . . . . 134 A1
Dean Ct
  Acton W3 . . . . .28 C3
  South Lambeth
  SW8 . . . . 162 A1
Deanery Mews
  W1 . . . . 117 C2
Deanery St W1 . . . 117 C2
Dean Farrar St
  SW1 . . . . 133 C2
Deanhill Ct 2
  SW14 . . . . .55 A3
Deanhill Rd SW14 . .55 A3
Dean Ho
  London N4 . . . . .6 B4
  New Cross SE14 . . .51 B3
  Stamford Hill N16 . . .7 B3
  18 Stepney E1 . . . .32 B3

Dean Rd NW2 . . . . . .9 B2
Dean Ryle St SW1 . 148 A4
Dean's Bldgs
  SE17 . . . . 151 C3
Deans Cl W4 . . . . . .45 A4
Dean's Ct EC4 . . . . 108 B1
Dean's Gateway 9
  SE10 . . . . .52 C3
Deanshanger Ho 21
  SE8 . . . . .40 C2
Dean's Mews W1 . . 104 B2
Dean St W1 . . . . . . 105 B1
Dean Stanley St
  SW1 . . . . 134 A1
Dean's Yd SW1 . . . 133 C2
Dean Trench St
  SW1 . . . . 134 A1
Dearmer Ho 6
  SW2 . . . . .74 C4
Deason St E15 . . . . .27 B4
Deauville Ct
  14 London SW4 . . .61 B1
  4 Rotherhithe
  SE16 . . . . .40 C4
Deauville Mans 13
  SW4 . . . . .61 B1
De Barowe Mews
  5 Highbury N5 . . . .15 A4
  1 London N5 . . . . .15 A3
Debdale Ho 20 E2 . .24 C4
De Beauvoir Cres
  N1 . . . . .24 A4
De Beauvoir Ct N1 .15 C1
De Beauvoir Pl 5
  N1 . . . . .16 A2
De Beauvoir Prim Sch
  N1 . . . . .16 A2
De Beauvoir Rd
  N1 . . . . .16 A1
De Beauvoir Sq
  N1 . . . . .16 A1
DE BEAUVOIR
  TOWN 16 A1
Debenham Ct E8 . . .24 C4
Debnams Rd SE16 . .40 B2
Decima St SE1 . . . . 138 A2
Deck Cl SE16 . . . . . .32 C1
De Coubertin St
  E15 . . . . .19 B2
De Crespigny Pk
  SE5 . . . . .48 C1
Deeley Rd SW8 . . . 171 B4
Deepdale N4 . . . . . . .6 A4
Deepdene Gdns
  SW2 . . . . .74 B4
Deepdene Ho N16 . . .6 C3
Deepdene Lo 5
  SW2 . . . . .74 B4
Deepdene Mans
  SW6 . . . . 164 C4
Deepdene Rd SE5,
  SE24 . . . . .63 C3
Deerbrook Rd SE24,
  SW2 . . . . .75 A3
Deerdale Rd SE24 . .63 B3
Deerhurst Ho 6
  SE15 . . . . .49 C4
Deerhurst Rd NW2 . .9 C2
Deer Lo SW6 . . . . . .58 A4
Deeside Rd SW17 . .71 C1
Dee St E14 . . . . .34 B3
Defoe Ave TW9 . . . .44 C3

Defoe Ho
Barbican EC2 . . . . . . **108** C4
5 Stoke Newington
N16. . . . . 7 A1
Defoe Pl EC2 . . . . . . **108** C4
Defoe Rd
Rotherhithe SE16. . . **41** B4
Stoke Newington
N16. . . . . 7 A1
De Gama Pl 3
E14 . . . . .41 C1
Dekker Ho E9 SE5 . . **48** C3
Dekker Rd SE21 . . . . **64** A1
Delafield Ho 2
E1 . . . . **111** C2
Delaford Rd SE16. . . **40** A1
Delaford St SW6. . . **154** B3
Delamere Ho 4 N4 . . .6 C4
Delamere Rd W5 . . . .36 A4
Delamere Terr
W2 . . . . **100** B4
Delancey Pas NW1 **82** B3
Delancey St NW1 . . . **82** B3
Delancey Studios
NW1 . . . . **82** B3
Delany Ho SE10 . . . . **52** B4
Delarch Ho SE1 . . . **136** A3
De Laune St SE17 . . **150** A1
Delaware Rd W9 . . . **88** A2
Delawyk Cres
SE24 . . . . .63 C1
Delft Way 2 SE22 . . .64 A2
Delhi St N1 . . . . **84** B3
Delia St SW18 . . . . . .71 A4
Delius Gr E15 . . . . . . **27** B3
Delius Ho 2
E2 . . . . **24** C2
Dellow Ho 6 E1 . . . . .32 A2
Dellow St E1 . . . . .32 A2
Dell's Mews SW1 . . **147** A3
Deloraine Ho 8
SE8 . . . . .51 C2
Deloraine St SE8 . . . .51 C2
Delorme St W6 . . . . . .47 C4
Delta Bldg 7 E14 . . . .34 B3
Delta Ho N1 . . . . .97 B4
Delta Pk SW18 . . . . . .59 A3
Delta Point 5
E2 . . . . **24** C2
Delta St 4
E2 . . . . **24** C2 **99** B4
Delverton Ho
SE17 . . . . **150** B2
Delverton Rd
SE17 . . . . **150** B2
Delvino Rd SW6 . . . **165** C3
De Montfort Ct 1
SW16 . . . . .74 A1
De Montfort Rd
SW16 . . . . .74 A2
De Morgan Rd
SW6 . . . . .59 A4
Dempster Rd
SW18 . . . . .59 B2
Denbigh Cl
W11 . . . . .31 B2 **113** A4
Denbigh Gdns
TW10 . . . . .54 B2
Denbigh Ho
Knightsbridge
SW1 . . . . **131** A2
7 Notting Hill W11 . .31 B3
Notting Hill
W11 . . . . . . .31 B2 **113** A4

Denbigh Mews
SW1 . . . . **146** C3
Denbigh Pl SW1 . . . **146** C2
Denbigh Rd
W11 . . . . . . .31 B2 **113** A4
Denbigh St SW1 . . . **147** A2
Denbigh Terr
W11 . . . . . . .31 B2 **113** A4
Denbury Ho 48 E3 . . **27** A2
Denby Ct SE11 . . . . **149** A4
Dence Ho 18
E2 . . . . **24** C2 **99** B3
Denchworth Ho 14
SW9 . . . . **173** B1
Dene Cl SE4 . . . . .66 A3
Denehurst Gdns
Acton W3 . . . . .28 A1
Richmond TW10. . . . .54 C3
Dene Mans 1
NW6 . . . . .10 C2
Denesmead SE24 . . .63 B2
Denewood Rd N6. . . . .3 B4
Dengie Wlk N1 . . . . . **86** C4
Denham Ho 32
W12 . . . . .30 A2
Denham St SE10 . . . . .43 C1
Denholme Rd W9 . . . .23 B2
Denland Ho SW8 . . . **163** A1
Denman Ho 2 N16 . . . .7 A2
Denman Rd SE15 . . . .49 B1
Denman St W1 . . . . . **119** B3
Denmark Gr N1 . . . . . **85** B2
Denmark Hill SE5. . . .48 C1
Denmark Hill Sta
SE5. . . . . .48 C1
Denmark Mans 14
SE5. . . . . .48 B1
Denmark Pl
24 Bow E3 . . . . **26** C2
2 Bromley E3 . . . . . **26** C2
Soho WC2 . . . . **105** C2
Denmark Rd
Camberwell SE5. . . . .48 B1
Kilburn NW6. . . . . . . .23 B3
Denmark St WC2 . . . **105** C2
Denmead Ho
SW15 . . . . .56 B1
Denne Terr E8 . . . . . . **24** B4
Dennett's Gr SE14 . . .50 C1
Dennett's Rd SE14 . . .50 B2
Denning Cl NW8. . . . . **89** A3
Denning Mews
SW12 . . . . .60 C1
Denning Point E1 . . **111** A2
Denning Rd NW3 . . . . .11 C4
**Dennington Park
Mansions 17**
NW6 . . . . .10 C2
Dennington Park Rd
NW6 . . . . .10 C2
Dennis Ct SE10 . . . . . .52 B2
Dennis Ho 8 E3 . . . . . **26** B3
Dennison Point
E15 . . . . **19** B1
Dennis Severs' House
E1 . . . . **110** B4
Dennis Way SW4 . . . .61 C4
Denny Cres SE11 . . . **149** C2
Denny St SE11 . . . . . **149** C2
Densham Ho NW8 . . . **79** C1
Denstone Ho 5
SE15 . . . . .49 C4
Den The (Millwall FC)
SE16 . . . . .40 B1
Dent Ho SE17 . . . . . **152** A3
Denton NW1 . . . . .12 C2

Denton Ho N1. . . . . . .15 A1
Denton St SW18 . . . . .59 A1
Dents Rd SW11 . . . . . .60 B1
Denver Rd N16 . . . . . . .7 A4
Denyer Ho 1
NW5 . . . . .13 A4
Denyer St SW3 . . . . **144** B4
Denzil Rd NW10 . . . . . .8 B3
Deodar Rd SW15 . . . . .58 A3
Depot App NW2 . . . . . .9 C4
Depot Rd W12 . . . . . . .30 B2
Depot St SE5 . . . . .48 C4
DEPTFORD 51 A4
Deptford Bridge
SE8 . . . . .51 C2
Deptford Bridge Sta
SE8 . . . . .51 C2
Deptford Broadway
SE8, SE14 . . . . .51 C2
Deptford Church St
SE8 . . . . .51 C3
Deptford Ferry Rd 24
E14 . . . . .41 C2
Deptford Gn SE8 . . . . .51 C3
**Deptford Green Sch
(Annex) 2** SE14 . . . .51 A3
Deptford High St
SE8 . . . . .51 C3
**Deptford Park Prim
Sch 2** SE8 . . . . .41 A1
Deptford Sta SE8 . . . .51 C3
Deptford Trad Est
SE8 . . . . .51 A4
Deptford Wharf
SE8 . . . . .41 B2
De Quincey Mews 3
E16 . . . . .35 C1
Derby Ct 8 E5 . . . . . . .17 C4
Derby Gate SW1 . . . **134** A4
Derby Ho SE11 . . . . . **149** B4
Derby Rd
Mortlake SW14 . . . . . .55 A3
South Hackney E9 . . .25 C4
Derby St W1 . . . . **117** C1
Dere Cl SW6 . . . . **164** A4
Dereham Ho 7
SE4 . . . . .65 C3
Dereham Pl
EC2 . . . . .24 A1 **98** B2
Derek Walcott Cl
SE24 . . . . .63 A2
Dericote St E8 . . . . . . **25** A4
Dering St W1 . . . . . . **104** B1
Dermody Gdns
SE13 . . . . .67 C2
Dermody Rd SE13 . . . .67 C2
Deronda Rd SE24,
SW2 . . . . .75 A3
Derrick Ho 13
SW2 . . . . .74 C3
Derrycombe Ho 18
W2 . . . . .31 C4
Derry St W8 . . . . **128** A3
Dersingham Rd
NW2 . . . . .1 A1
Derwent NW1 . . . . **92** C3
Derwent Ct
2 Hammersmith
W6. . . . . .38 C2
8 Rotherhithe
SE16 . . . . .40 C4

Derwent Gr SE22 . . . .64 B3
Derwent Ho
South Kensington
SW7 . . . . **143** A4
Tower Hamlets E3 . . .26 B1
Derwent St SE10 . . . . .43 A1
Derwentwater Mans
2 W3 . . . . .28 B1
**Derwentwater Prim
Sch** W3 . . . . .28 B1
Derwentwater Rd
W3 . . . . .28 B1
Desborough Cl
W2 . . . . **100** B4
Desborough Ho
W14 . . . . **155** A4
Desenfans Rd
SE21 . . . . .64 A1
Design Mus W8 . . . **127** B2
Desmond St SE14 . . . .51 A4
Despard Ho SW2 . . . . .74 C2
Despard Rd N19 . . . . . .4 B3
Desvignes Dr SE13 . . .67 C1
Dethick Ct 11 E3 . . . . **26** A4
Detling Ho SE17 . . . . **152** A3
Devas St E3 . . . . **27** A1
Deventer Cres 8
SE22 . . . . .64 A2
De Vere Cotts W8 . . **128** C2
De Vere Gdns W8 . . **128** C3
Deverell St SE1 . . . . **137** B1
De Vere Mews
W8 . . . . **128** C2
Devereux Ct WC2 . . **107** B1
Devereux Ho 7
SW15 . . . . .56 C2
Devereux La SW13 . . .47 A3
Devereux Rd
SW11 . . . . .60 B1
Devitt Ho 5 E14 . . . . . .34 A2
Devizes St N1 . . . . **87** C3
Devonhurst Pl 4
W4 . . . . .37 C1
Devonia Rd N1 . . . . . . **86** B2
Devon Mans SE1 . . . **138** B4
Devonport W2 . . . . . **102** A2
Devonport Ho
Greenwich SE10 . . . . .52 B4
8 Paddington W2 . . . .31 C4
Devonport Rd
W12 . . . . .39 A4
Devonport St E1 . . . . .32 C3
Devonshire Cl
W1 . . . . **104** A4
Devonshire Ct
14 Balham SW12 . . . .73 A4
2 Richmond TW9 . . . .44 B2
Devonshire Dr
SE10 . . . . .52 A2
Devonshire Gdns
W4 . . . . .45 B3
Devonshire Gr
SE15 . . . . .50 A4
Devonshire Hall 15
E9 . . . . **17** B2
Devonshire Ho
Brondesbury NW6 . . .10 B2
Newington SE1 . . . . . **136** C2
Paddington W2 . . . . **101** C4
3 Putney SW15 . . . . .69 B4
Westminster SW1 . . **147** C2
**Devonshire House
Prep Sch** NW3 . . . . . .11 B3
Devonshire Mews 3
W4 . . . . .38 A1

Devonshire Mews N
W1 . . . . **104** A4
Devonshire Mews S
W1 . . . . **104** A4
Devonshire Mews W
W1 . . . . **103** C4
Devonshire Pl
Child's Hill NW2 . . . . . .1 C1
Kensington W8 . . . . **128** A1
Marylebone W1 . . . **103** C4
**Devonshire Place
Mews** W1 . . . . **103** C4
Devonshire Rd
W4 . . . . .38 A1
Devonshire Row
EC2 . . . . **110** B3
**Devonshire Row
Mews** W1 . . . . **92** B1
Devonshire Sq
EC2 . . . . **110** B2
Devonshire St
Chiswick W4 . . . . .38 A1
Marylebone W1 . . . **104** A4
Devonshire Terr
W2 . . . . **101** A1
Devons Rd E3 . . . . **27** A1
Devons Road Sta
E3 . . . . **27** A1
Dewar St SE15 . . . . . . .64 C4
De Walden Ho
NW8 . . . . **80** A2
De Walden St W1 . . **103** C3
Dewberry St E14 . . . . **34** B4
Dewey Rd N1 . . . . **85** B2
Dewhurst Rd W14 . . . .39 C3
Dewsbury Ct 5
W4 . . . . .37 B2
Dewsbury Rd NW10 . . .8 C3
Dewsbury Terr
NW1 . . . . **82** B4
D'eynsford Rd SE5. . **48** C2
Dhonau Ho SE16 . . . **153** A4
Diadem Ct W1 . . . . . **105** B2
Dial Wlk The W8. . . **128** B4
Diamond Est
SW17 . . . . .72 A1
Diamond Ho 22
E3 . . . . **26** A3
Diamond St SE15 . . . . .49 A3
Diamond Terr
SE10 . . . . .52 B2
Diana Ho
Barnes SW13 . . . . .46 B2
4 Brixton SW2 . . . . . .62 B2
**Diana, Princess of
Wales Meml
Fountain** W2 . . . . . **129** C4
**Diana, Princess of
Wales Meml Wlk**
W2 . . . . **114** C1
Dibden Ho 5 SE5 . . . .49 A3
Dibden St N1 . . . . **86** C4
Dibdin Ho W9 . . . . . . **78** A1
Dibdin Row SE1 . . . . **135** C2
Dicey Ave NW2 . . . . . . .9 B4
Dickens Ct EC1 . . . . . **96** A1
Dickens Ho
Bloomsbury WC1 . . . **94** A2
Kensington NW6 . . . **23** C2
Kilburn NW6 . . . . **23** C2
Paddington NW8 . . . **89** C2
Dickenson Rd N8. . . . . .5 A4
Dickens Sq SE1 . . . . **137** A2
Dickens St SW8 . . . . **170** B1

Dickinson Ho 18
 E2 . . . . .24 C2 99 B3
Dicksee Ho NW8 . . . . 89 B1
Dick Shepherd Ct 17
 SW2 . . . . .74 C4
Dickson Ho 4 E1 . . .32 A1
Didbin Ho N7 . . . . 5 B2
Dieppe Cl W14 . . .140 C2
Digby Bsns Ctr 19 . .17 C2
Digby Cres N4 . . . . . .6 B2
Digby Mans W6 . . . . .39 B1
Digby Rd E9 . . . . .17 C2
Digby St E2 . . . . .25 B2
Diggon St EC1 . . . . . .96 A2
Dighton Ct SE17 . . . .48 B4
Dighton Rd SW18 . . .59 B3
Dignum St N1 . . . . . .85 B2
Digswell St N7 . . . . .14 C2
Dilke St SW3 . . . . . .159 A4
Dilston Gr SE16 . . . . .40 B2
Dilton Gdns SW15 . . .69 A3
Dimes Pl 9 W6 . . . . .39 A2
Dimson Cres 3 . . . . .26 C2
Dinerman Ho NW8 . .79 A4
Dingle Gdns E14 . . . .33 C2
Dingley La SW16 . . . .73 C2
Dingley Pl EC1 . . . . . .97 A3
Dingley Rd EC1 . . . . .96 C3
Dingwall Rd SW18 . .71 B4
Dinmont Ho 27 E2 . .24 C3
Dinmont St 2 E2 . . .25 A3
Dinmore Ho 6 E9 . . .25 B4
Dinnington Ho 17
 E1 . . . . .25 A1
Dinsdale Rd SE3 . . . .53 B4
Dinsmore Rd
 SW12 . . . . .73 A4
Dinton Ho NW8 . . . . .90 A2
Dinwiddy Ho N1 . . . .84 C1
Dionis Ho SW6 . . . . .165 B2
Disbrowe Rd W6 . . .154 B3
Discovery Bsns Pk 3
 SE16 . . . . .139 C1
Discovery Dock E
 E14 . . . . .42 A4
Discovery Ho 1
 . . . . .34 B2
Disney Pl SE1 . . . . . .137 A4
Disney St SE1 . . . . . .137 A4
Disraeli Cl 1 W4 . . . .37 C2
Disraeli Gdns
 SW15 . . . . .58 B3
Disraeli Rd
 Acton W3 . . . . .20 C3
 Putney SW15 . . . . . .58 A3
Diss St E2 . . . .24 B2 98 C4
Distaff La EC4 . . . . . .122 C4
Distillery La W6 . . . . .39 B1
Distillery Rd W6 . . . . .39 B1
Distillery Wlk 14
 TW8 . . . . .44 A4
Distin St SE11 . . . . .149 B3
Ditchburn St E14 . . . .34 B2
Ditton Ho 10 E5 . . . .17 A3
Divis Way SW15 . . . . .57 A1
Dixon Clark Ct N1 . . .15 A2
Dixon Ho 20 NW10 . .30 C3
Dixon Rd SE14 . . . . . .51 A2
Dixon's Alley 10
 SE16 . . . . .40 A4
Dixon Way 8 NW10 . .8 A1
DLD College London
 Marylebone Campus
 W1 . . . . .103 C2
DLD Coll London
 SE1 . . . . .135 A3

Dobree Ave NW10 . . .9 A1
Dobson Cl NW6 . . . . .11 C1
Dobson Ho 18
 . . . . .50 C4
Doby Ct EC4 . . . . . . .123 A4
Dockers Tanner Rd 26
 E14 . . . . .41 C2
Dockhead SE1 . . . . .139 A3
Dockhead Wharf
 SE1 . . . . .139 A4
Dock Hill Ave
 SE16 . . . . .40 C4
Docklands Acad
 London E14 . . . . . . .42 A3
Docklands Ct 20
 E14 . . . . .33 B3
Docklands Visitor Ctr
 . . . . .42 A4
Dockley Rd SE16 . . . .139 B1
Dockley Road Ind Est
 11 SE16 . . . . .139 B1
Dock Offices 12
 SE16 . . . . .40 B3
Dock Rd E16 . . . . . . .35 B2
Dock St E1 . . . . .125 B4
Doctor Spurstowe
 Almshouses 3
 E8 . . . . .17 A2
Docura Ho N7 . . . . . . 5 B2
Docwras Bldgs N1 . .16 A2
Dodbrooke Rd
 SE27 . . . . .75 A1
Dodd Ho 15 SE16 . . .40 A2
Doddington Gr
 SE17 . . . . .150 B1
Doddington Pl 4
 SE17 . . . . .48 A4
Dodson St SE1 . . . . .135 C3
Dod St E14 . . . . .33 C3
Dog & Duck Yd
 WC1 . . . . .106 A4
Dog Kennel Hill
 SE22 . . . . .64 A4
Dog Kennel Hill Sch
 22 SE22 . . . . .64 A4
Dolben Ct SW1 . . . .147 C3
Dolben St SE1 . . . . .122 B1
Dolby Rd SW6 . . . . .164 C1
Doleman Ho 19
 SE10 . . . . .52 A2
Dolland Ho SE11 . . .149 A1
Dolland St SE11 . . . .149 A1
Dollar Bay E14 . . . . . .42 B4
DOLLIS HILL 9 A4
Dollis Hill Sta NW2 . .8 C3
Dolman Rd W4 . . . . . .37 C2
Dolman St SW4 . . . . .62 B3
Dolphin Cl 2
 SE16 . . . . .40 C4
Dolphin Ct N7 . . . . . .13 C4
Dolphin La E14 . . . . .34 A2
Dolphin Sq SW1 . . .147 A1
Dolphin Twr 21
 SE8 . . . . .51 B4
Dombey Ho
 1 Bermondsey
 SE1 . . . . .139 B3
 4 Shepherd's Bush
 W11 . . . . .30 C2
Dombey St WC1 . . . .106 C4
Domelton Ho
 SW18 . . . . .59 A1
Domett Cl SE5 . . . . . .63 C3
Domfe Pl E5 . . . . .17 B4
Domingo St EC1 . . . . .96 C1

Dominie Sch The
 SW11 . . . . .169 B3
Dominion Dr 39 . . . . .40 C4
Dominion St
 EC2 . . . . .109 C4
Dominion Sch SE2 . .109 C4
Donaghue Cotts 11
 E14 . . . . .33 A4
Donaldson Rd
 NW6 . . . . .23 B4
Donegal Ho 2 E1 . . .25 B1
Donegal St N1 . . . . . .85 A1
Doneraile Ho
 SW1 . . . . .146 A1
Doneraile St SW6 . . . .47 C2
Dongola Rd E1 . . . . . .33 A4
Don Gratton Ho 22
 E1 . . . . .111 B3
Donkey Alley SE22 . .64 C1
Donkin Ho 16
 SE16 . . . . .40 A2
Donne Ct SE24 . . . . .63 B1
Donne Ho
 18 Canonbury
 N16 . . . . .15 C4
 14 Deptford SE14 . .50 C4
 10 Poplar E14 . . . . .33 C3
Donnelly Ct SW6 . . .154 B2
Donne Pl SW3 . . . . .144 B4
Donnington Ct
 11 Camden Town
 NW1 . . . . .13 A1
 Willesden NW10 . . .9 A1
Donnington Ho 12
 SW8 . . . . .171 B2
Donnington Prim Sch
 NW10 . . . . .22 A4
Donnington Rd
 NW10 . . . . .22 A4
Donovan Ct SW7 . . .143 B1
Donovan Ho 4 E1 . . .32 B2
Don Phelan Cl
 SE5 . . . . .48 C2
Doon St SE1 . . . . . .121 B2
Doradus Ct 20
 SW19 . . . . .69 C3
Dora Ho
 7 Shepherd's Bush
 W11 . . . . .30 C2
 1 Tower Hamlets
 E14 . . . . .33 B3
Dorando Cl W12 . . . .30 A2
Doran Wlk
 Stratford E15 . . . . .19 B1
 Stratford Marsh
 E15 . . . . .27 A4
Dora St E14 . . . . .33 B3
Dorcas Ct 9
 SW18 . . . . .59 C3
Dorchester Ct
 1 De Beauvoir Town
 N1 . . . . .16 A1
 Herne Hill SE24 . . .63 B2
 Knightsbridge
 SW1 . . . . .131 A1
 5 Streatham
 SW16 . . . . .74 A2
Dorchester Dr
 SE24 . . . . .63 B2
Dorchester Gr W4 . . .38 B1
Dorchester Ho
 TW9 . . . . .45 A3
Dordrecht Rd W3 . . . .29 A1
Doria Rd SW6 . . . . . .165 A2
Doric Ho 7 E2 . . . . . .25 C3
Doric Way NW1 . . . . .93 B4

Doris Emmerton Ct
 SW18 . . . . .59 B3
Dorking Cl SE8 . . . . .51 B4
Dorking Ho SE1 . . . .137 C2
Dorland Ct SW15 . . . .58 B1
Dorlcote Rd SW18 . . .72 A4
Dorleston Ct N1 . . . . .87 C4
Dorman Way NW8 . . .79 B4
Dorman Way SE5 . . . .59 A2
Dormstone Ho
 SE17 . . . . .152 A3
Dornberg Cl SE3 . . . .53 C3
Dorncliffe Rd
 SW6 . . . . .164 B2
Dorney NW3 . . . . . . .12 A1
Dorney Ct SW6 . . . . .58 A4
Dornfell St NW6 . . . .10 B3
Dornoch Ho 20 E3 . . .26 B3
Dornton Rd SW12,
 SW17 . . . . .73 B2
Dorothy Charrington
 SE5 . . . . .64 C2
Dorothy Rd SW11 . . .60 B4
Dorrell Pl 18 SW9 . . .62 C4
Dorrien Wlk SW16 . . .73 C2
Dorrington Point 20
 E3 . . . . .27 A2
Dorrington St
 EC1 . . . . .107 B4
Dorrit Ho 2 W11 . . .30 C1
Dorrit St SE1 . . . . . .137 A4
Dorset Bldgs EC4 . . .108 A1
Dorset Cl NW1 . . . . .102 C4
Dorset Ct 3 N1 . . . . .16 A1
Dorset Mans 2
 W6 . . . . .47 C4
Dorset Mews
 SW1 . . . . .132 A2
Dorset Pl E15 . . . . . . .19 C2
Dorset Rd SW8 . . . .162 C2
Dorset Rise EC4 . . . .108 A1
Dorset Sq NW1 . . . . .90 C1
Dorset St W1 . . . . . .103 A3
Dorton Cl 6 SE15 . . .49 A3
Dorville Cres W6 . . . .39 A3
Doughty Ct 1 E1 . . .32 A1
Doughty Mews
 WC1 . . . . .94 C1
Doughty St WC1 . . . .94 C1
Douglas Bldgs
 SE1 . . . . .137 A4
Douglas Ct 5
 NW6 . . . . .10 C1
Douglas Gracey Ho 1
 SW18 . . . . .70 A4
Douglas Ho
 Putney SW15 . . . . . .56 C1
 Westminster SW1 . .147 B3
Douglas Johnstone
 Ho SW6 . . . . .154 C3
Douglas Mews
 NW2 . . . . 1 A1
Douglas Path E14 . . .42 B1
Douglas Rd
 Islington N1 . . . . . . .15 B1
 Kilburn NW6 . . . . . .23 B4
 5 Newham E16 . . . . .35 C4
Douglas Rd N N1 . . .15 B2
Douglas Rd S N1 . . .15 B2
Douglas St SW1 . . . .147 B3
Douglas Waite Ho
 NW6 . . . . .11 A1
Douglas Way SE8 . . .51 B3
Doulton Ho SE11 . . .149 A4
Doulton Mews 4
 NW6 . . . . .11 A2

Dounesforth Gdns
 SW18 . . . . .71 A3
Douro Pl W8 . . . . . . .128 B2
Douro St E3 . . . . .26 C3
Douthwaite Sq 11
 E1 . . . . .125 C2
Dovecote Gdns 3
 SW14 . . . . .55 C4
Dovedale Cotts 6
 SW11 . . . . .168 C2
Dovedale Ho N16 . . . .6 C4
Dovedale Rd SE22 . . .65 A1
Dovehouse St
 SW3 . . . . .144 A1
Dove Mews SW7 . . .143 A2
Dovercourt Rd
 SE22 . . . . .64 B1
Dover Ct
 Clerkenwell EC1 . . . .96 A2
 17 Greenwich SE10 .52 A2
Dove Rd N1 . . . . .15 C2
Doverfield Rd
 SW2 . . . . .74 A4
Dover Flats SE1 . . . .152 B3
Dover Ho
 Brixton SE5 . . . . . . .48 A2
 14 Deptford SE15 . .50 B4
Dover House Rd
 SW15 . . . . .57 A2
Dover Mans 18
 SW9 . . . . .62 C4
Dover Park Dr
 SW15 . . . . .57 A1
Dover St W1 . . . . . . .118 C2
Dover Terr TW9 . . . . .44 C1
Dover Yd W1 . . . . . .118 C2
Doves Yd N1 . . . . . . .85 B3
Dovet Ct SW8 . . . . . .172 C4
Doveton Ho 7 E1 . . .25 B1
Doveton St 8 E1 . . . .25 B1
Dove Ley W14 . . . . .145 B2
Dove Lo E14 . . . . .14 C1
Dowdeny Cl 22
 NW5 . . . . .13 B3
Dowdeswell Cl
 SW15 . . . . .56 A3
Dowding Ho N6 . . . . .3 C4
Dowell Ho SE21 . . . .76 B1
Dowells St SE10 . . . .52 A4
Dowes Ho 10
 SW16 . . . . .74 A1
Dowgate Hill EC4 . . .123 B4
Dowland St W10 . . . .23 A2
Dowlas St SE5 . . . . . .49 A3
Dowlen Ct E14 . . . . . .41 C4
Dowler Ho 32 E1 . . .111 C1
Downbarton Ho 1
 SW9 . . . . .173 B4
Downbury Mews 10
 SW18 . . . . .58 C2
Downs Ct 2
 E5 . . . . .17 C4
Down's Cotts
 SW4 . . . . .61 B3
Downey Ho 6 E1 . . .25 C1
Downfield Cl W9 . . . .88 A1
Downham Ct 1
 N1 . . . . .15 C1
Downham Rd N1 . . . .15 C1
Downing Ho
 2 North Kensington
 W10 . . . . .30 C3

Downing Ho *continued*
4 Putney SW15 ....56 C2
Downing St W1 ..134 A4
Down Pl W6........39 A1
Down St Mews
W1 ....118 A1
Downs Ct E8 .....17 A3
Downsell Prim Sch
E15 ....19 C4
Downsell Rd E15 ...19 C4
Downshire Hill
NW3 ....11 C4
Downside 2
SW15 ....58 A2
Downside Cres
NW3 ....12 A3
Downs La 2 E5 ...17 A4
Downs Park Rd E5,
E8 ....16 C3
Downs Rd E5, N16 ..16 C4
Down St W1......118 A1
Downton Ave SW2 ..74 B2
Downtown Rd
SE16 ....41 A4
Dowrey St N1 ....85 B4
Dowson Cl SE5 ...63 C3
Dowson Ct SE13 ...67 C4
Dowson Ho 8 E1 ..32 C3
Doyce St SE1 .....136 C4
Doyle Gdns NW10 ..22 A4
Doyle Ho W3 ......37 A4
D'Oyley St SW1 ..145 B4
Doynton St N19 ...4 A2
Draco St SE17 ....48 B4
Dragmore St 18
SW4 ....61 C1
Dragon Ct WC2 ...106 B2
Dragonfly Pl 1
SE4 ....66 A4
Dragon Rd SE15 ..49 A4
Dragon Yd WC1 ...106 B2
Dragoon Rd SE8 ..41 B1
Dragor Rd NW10 ..20 C1
Drake Cl 30 SE16 ..40 C4
Drake Croft N16 ...6 C2
Drake Ct 5 W12 ...39 A4
Drakefell Rd SE4,
SE14 ....65 C4
Drakefield Rd
SW17 ....72 C1
Drake Ho
2 Limehouse
E14 ....33 A2
20 Stepney E1 ....32 B4
Drakeley Ct N5 ...15 A4
Drake Rd SE4 .....66 C4
Drakes Ctyd NW6 ..10 B1
Drake St WC1 ....106 C3
Drama Ctr London
EC1................95 C1
Draper Ho SE1 ...150 B4
Draper Pl N1 .....86 B4
Drapers Almhouses 5
E3 ....26 C2
Drapers Gdns
EC2 ....109 C2
Drapers Rd E15 ...19 C4
Drappers Way 8
SE16 ....153 C4
Draycott Ave
SW3 ....144 B3
Draycott Cl SE5 ...48 C3
Draycott Ct SW11 ..168 A4
Draycott Ho SW3 ..144 C3

Draycott Pl SW3 ...144 C3
Draycott Terr
SW3 ....145 A3
Drayford Cl W9 ...23 B1
Dray Gdns SW2 ...62 B2
Draymans Ct 4
SW9 ....62 B4
Draymans Mews
SE15 ....49 B1
Drayson Mews
W8 ....127 C3
Drayton Ct SW10 ..143 A1
Drayton Gdns
SW10 ....143 A1
Drayton Ho 14
SE5 ....48 C3
Drayton Park Mews 12
N5.................14 C3
Drayton Park Prim
Sch 15 N5........14 C3
Drayton Park Sta
N5.................14 C3
Drayton Pk N5, N1 ..14 C4
Drayton Rd NW10 ..21 B4
DRCA Business Ctr
SW11 ....169 C3
Dreadnought St
SE10 ....43 A3
Dresden Cl NW6 ..11 A2
Dresden Ho
5 Clapham
SW11 ....169 B2
Lambeth SE11 ...149 A4
Dresden Rd N19 ...4 C3
Dressington Ave
SE4 ....66 C1
Drewett Ho 6 E1 ..111 C1
Drew Ho 6 SW16 ..74 A1
Drewstead La
SW16 ....73 C2
Drewstead Rd
SW16 ....73 C2
Driffield Rd 8 E3 ..26 A3
Driftway Ho 19 E3 ..26 B3
Drinkwater Ho 8
SE5 ....48 C3
Drive Mans 1
SW6 ....164 B2
Drive The
Acton W3 ....28 B3
Harlesden NW10 ..21 B4
Islington N7 .....14 A3
Hendon NW11 ...1 A4
Dr Johnson's House
W17 ....73 A1
Dr Johnson's House
EC4 ....107 C1
Droitwich Cl SE26 ..76 C1
Dromore Rd SW15 ..58 A1
Dron Ho 8 E1 .....32 B4
Droop St W10 ....23 A1
Drovers Ct SE13 ..67 B4
Drovers Pl SE15 ..50 A3
Drovers Way 9 N7 ..14 A2
Druce Rd SE21 ...64 A1
Druid St SE1 .....138 C3
Drumbeat Sch
SE4 ....66 A4
Drummer Lo N7 ...5 B1
Drummond Cres
NW1 ....93 B4
Drummond Gate
SW1 ....147 C2
Drummond Ho 13
E2 ....24 C3

Drummond Rd
SE16 ....40 A3
Drummonds Pl
TW9 ....54 A3
Drummond St
NW1 ....92 C2
Drury La WC2 ....106 B1
Drury Ho SW8 ....170 C4
Dryad St SW15 ...57 C4
Dryburgh Ho SW1 ..146 B2
Dryburgh Mans
SW15 ....57 B4
Dryburgh Rd
SW15 ....57 B4
Dryden Bldg 10
E1 ....111 B2
Dryden Cl SW4 ...61 C2
Dryden Ct SE11 ...149 C3
Dryden Ho
6 Camberwell
SE5 ....49 A2
16 Stoke Newington
N16................7 A1
Dryden St WC2 ..106 B1
Dryfield Wlk 1
SE8 ....51 C4
Drysdale Flats 3
E8 ....16 B3
Drysdale Ho 19
E2 ....24 A2 98 B4
Drysdale Pl
N1 ....24 A2 98 B4
Drysdale St
N1 ....24 A2 98 B4
Dublin Ave E8 ....24 C4
Ducal St 28
E2 ....24 B2 99 A3
Ducane Cl 6 W12 ..30 B3
Du Cane Ct SW12 ..72 C3
Du Cane Rd W12 ..29 C3
Ducavel Ho SW2 ..74 B3
Duchess Mews
W1 ....104 B3
Duchess of Bedford
Ho W8 ....127 B4
Duchess of Bedford's
Wlk W8 ....127 B3
Duchess St W1 ...104 B3
Duchy St SE1 ....121 C2
Ducie Ho 2 SW15 ..57 B2
Ducie St SW4 ....62 B3
Duckett St E1 ....33 A4
Duck La W1 ......105 B1
Du Cros Rd W3 ...29 A1
DUDDEN HILL ...8 C3
Dudden Hill La
NW10 ....8 B3
Dudley Ct
Marylebone W1 ..102 C1
St Giles WC2 ...106 A2
Dudley Ho
13 Hereford Rd W2 ..173 B2
Paddington W2 ...101 B3
Dudley Mews 14
SW2 ....62 C1
Dudley Rd
Kilburn NW6 .....23 B3
Richmond TW9 ...44 B1
Dudley St W2 ....101 B3
Dudmaston Mews
SW3 ....143 C2
Duett Ho SE11 ...150 A3
Dufferin Ave EC1 ..97 B1
Dufferin Ct EC1 ...97 B1
Dufferin St EC1 ...97 A1

Duffield Ho N4 ...6 B4
Duff Miller Sixth Form
Coll SW7 ....129 A1
Duff St E14 ....34 A3
Dufour's Pl W1 ...105 A1
Dugard Way SE11 ..150 A3
Dugdale Ho 10 N7 ..13 C3
Duke Humphrey Rd
SE3 ....53 A1
Duke of Wellington Pl
SW1, W1 ....131 C4
Duke of York's Sq
SW3 ....145 A3
Duke of York St
SW1 ....119 A2
Duke Rd W4 ......37 C1
Duke St Hill SE1 ..123 C2
Duke St St James's
SW1 ....119 A2
Duke's Ave W4 ...37 C1
Dukes Ct
Dulwich SE22 ....76 C3
East Dulwich SE15 ..65 A3
Lewisham SE13 ...52 B1
Mortlake SW14 ...55 C4
Dukes Gate 4 W4 ..37 B2
Dukes Head Yd N6 ..4 A3
Duke's Ho SW1 ..147 C4
Duke Shore Wharf
E14 ....33 B2
Dukes La W8 .....128 A4
Duke's Mews W1 ..103 C2
Duke's Pl EC3 ....110 B1
Dukes Point N6 ...4 A3
Duke's Rd WC1 ...94 A3
Duke Street Mans
W1 ....103 C1
Duke's Yd W1 ....117 C4
Dulas St N4 ......5 B3
Dulford St
W11 ....31 A2 112 A4
Dulka Rd SW11 ...60 B2
Dulverton NW1 ...83 A3
Dulverton Mans
WC1 ....95 A1
DULWICH........76 A1
Dulwich Coll SE21 ..76 A1
Dulwich Coll Prep Sch
SE21 ....76 B1
Dulwich Com Hospl
SE22 ....64 A3
Dulwich Comm
SE21 ....76 A1
Dulwich Hamlet Jun
Sch SE21 ....63 C1
Dulwich Lawn Cl
SE22 ....64 B2
Dulwich L Ctr
SE22 ....64 B2
Dulwich Mead
SE24 ....63 B1
Dulwich Mews
1 East Dulwich
SE22 ....64 B2
East Dulwich SE22 ..64 B2
Dulwich Oaks The
SE21 ....76 B1
Dulwich Picture Gall
SE21 ....76 A1
Dulwich Prep Sch
SE21 ....76 C2
Dulwich Rd SE24 ..63 A1
DULWICH
VILLAGE.........76 A4

Dulwich Village
SE21 ....64 A1
Dulwich Village CE Inf
Sch
Dulwich SE21 ....64 A1
Dulwich SE21 ....64 A1
Dulwich Wood Prim
Sch SE21 ....76 A1
Dumain Ct SE11 ..150 A3
La Maurier Ho 2
NW3 ....12 B3
Dumbarton Ct 18
SW2 ....74 A4
Dumbarton Rd
SW2 ....62 A1
Dumont Rd N16 ...7 A1
Dumphreys Ho 5
SW4 ....73 C4
Dumpton Pl NW1 ..12 C1
Dunbar St SE27 ...75 B1
Dunbar Wharf 20
E14 ....33 B2
Dunboyne Rd NW3 ..12 B3
Dunbridge Ho
SW15 ....56 B1
Dunbridge St
Bethnal Green
E2 ....25 A1
Bethnal Green E2 ..25 A1
Duncan Ct 3 E14 ..34 B4
Duncan Gr W3 ...29 A3
Duncan Ho 3
NW3 ....12 B1
Duncan St N1 ....86 A2
Duncannon Ho
SW1 ....147 C1
Duncannon St
WC2 ....120 A3
Duncan Rd
Hackney E8 ......25 A4
Richmond TW9 ...54 A3
Duncan St N1 ....86 A2
Duncan Terr N1 ...86 A2
Dunch St 33 E1 ...32 A3
Duncombe Ho 7
SW19 ....69 C3
Duncombe Prim Sch
N19 ....5 A3
11 Upper Holloway
N19 ....4 C3
Duncombe Rd N19 ..4 C3
Duncrievie Rd
SE13 ....67 C1
Dundalk Ho 1 E1 ..32 B3
Dundalk Rd SE4 ..66 A4
Dundas Ho 12 E2 ..25 B3
Dundas Rd
Brixton SW9 .....173 C3
London SE15 .....50 B1
Dundee Ct 58 E1 ..32 A1
Dundee Ho W9 ...88 C4
Dundee St E1 ....32 A1
Dundee Wharf
E14 ....33 A2
Dundonald Rd
NW10 ....22 C4
Dundry Ho 8
SE26 ....76 C1
Dunelm Gr
Brixton SE27 .....75 B1
West Norwood
SE27 ....75 B1
Dunelm St E1 ....32 C3
Dunford Rd N7 ...14 B4
Dungarvan Ave
SW15 ....56 C3

Dungeness Ho
SW18 . . . . 59 B3

Dunhill Point 12
SW15 . . . . 69 A3

Dunkeld Ho 18
E14 . . . . 34 C3

Dunlace Rd E5 . . . . . . 17 C4

Dunlin Ct 12 SE21 . . . . 75 C2

Dunlin Ho 15 SE16 . . . 40 C2

Dunloe Ct 7 E2 . . . . . . 24 B3

Dunloe St E2 . . . . 24 B3

Dunlop Pl SE16 . . . . . 139 A1

Dunmore Point 18
E2 . . . . 24 B2 98 C3

Dunmore Rd NW6 . . . . 23 A4

Dunmow Ho SE11 . . . 149 A2

Dunmow Rd E15 . . . . . 76 B4

Dunmow Wlk N1 . . . . . 86 C4

Dunnage Cres
SE16 . . . . 41 A2

Dunne Mews 11
NW5 . . . . 13 B3

Dunnet Ho 27 E3 . . . . . 26 B3

Dunnico Ho SE17 . . . . 152 A2

Dunnock Ct 11
SE21 . . . . 75 C2

Dunn's Pas SW1 . . . . 106 B2

Dunn St E8 . . . . 16 B3

Dunollie Pl NW5 . . . . . 13 B3

Dunollie Rd NW5 . . . . . 13 B3

Dunoon Ho N1 . . . . . . 84 C3

Dunraven Ho 12
TW9 . . . . 44 B2

Dunraven Rd W12 . . 29 C1

Dunraven Sch
SW16 . . . . 74 B1

Dunraven St W1 . . . . 117 A4

Dunrobin Ct NW3 . . . . 11 A3

Dunsany Rd W14 . . . . 39 C3

Dunsfold Ho 4
SW2 . . . . 74 B4

Dunsford Way
SW15 . . . . 57 A1

Dunsmure Rd N16 . . . . 7 A3

Dunstable Ct 8
SE3 . . . . 53 C3

Dunstable Mews
W1 . . . . 103 C4

Dunstable Rd TW10,
TW9 . . . . 54 A3

Dunstall Ho 9
SE15 . . . . 49 C2

Dunstan Hos 6 E1 . . . 32 B4

Dunstan Hos 6
E1 . . . . 32 B4

Dunstan Rd NW11 . . . . 1 C3

Dunstan's Gr SE22 . . . 65 A1

Dunstan's Rd SE22 . . 64 C1

Dunster Ct E3 . . . . . 124 B4

Dunster Gdns
NW6 . . . . 10 B1

Dunsterville Way
SE1 . . . . 137 C3

Dunston Rd
Clapham SW11 . . . . . 169 C1
Hackney E8 . . . . 24 B4

Dunston St E8 . . . . . . 24 B4

Dunton Ho 14
SW16 . . . . 74 A1

Dunton Rd SE1 . . . . . 152 A4

Duntshill Rd SW18 . . 71 A3

Dunworth Mews
W11 . . . . 31 B3

Duplex Ride SW1 . . . 131 A3

Durand Acad
SW9 . . . . 173 A3

Durand Gdns
SW9 . . . . 173 A3

Durant St
E2 . . . . 24 C2 99 B4

Durban Ho 28
W12 . . . . 30 A2

Durdans Ho 8
NW1 . . . . 13 B1

Durfey Pl SE5 . . . . . . 48 C3

Durford Cres
SW15 . . . . 69 A3

Durham Ct
Brockley SE4 . . . . 66 C4
4 Kilburn NW6 . . . . . 23 C3

Durham Ho
7 Dartmouth Pk
NW5 . . . . 4 B1
Lisson Gr NW8 . . . . . 90 B3

Durham House St
WC2 . . . . 120 B3

Durham Pl SW3 . . . . 144 C1

Durham Rd N4, N7 . . . 5 B2

Durham Row E1 . . . . . 33 A4

Durham St SE11 . . . . 162 C4

Durham Terr W2 . . . . 100 A2

Durley Rd N16 . . . . 7 A4

Durlock Ho 16
SW9 . . . . 173 B4

Durlston Rd E5 . . . . . . 7 C2

Durnford St 4
SE10 . . . . 52 B4

Durnsford Ave SW18,
SW19 . . . . 70 C2

Durnsford Rd SW18,
SW19 . . . . 70 C1

Durnsford Rd Ind Est
SW19 . . . . 71 A1

Durrell Rd SW6 . . . . . 164 C3

Durrels Ho W14 . . . . 141 A4

Durrington Rd E5 . . . . 18 A4

Durrington Twr 3
SW8 . . . . 171 A2

Durrisdeer Ho
NW2 . . . . 10 B4

Durston Ho SW5 . . . . 142 A3

Durward St E1 . . . . . . 32 A4

Durweston Mews
W1 . . . . 103 A4

Durweston St W1 . . . 103 A3

Dutch Yd SW18 . . . . . 58 C2

Dutton Ho SW2 . . . . . 75 A3

Dutton St SE10 . . . . . 52 B2

Dwight Ct 8 SW6 . . . 164 B2

Dycer Ho 18 E9 . . . . . 17 C2

Dye House La E3 . . . . 26 C4

Dyer Ho SE4 . . . . 51 A1

Dyer's Bldgs EC1 . . . 107 B3

Dyer's La SW15 . . . . . 57 A3

Dykes Ct 11 SW2 . . . . 74 B3

Dylan Rd 8 SE24 . . . . 63 A3

Dylways SE5 . . . . 63 C3

Dymchurch Ho 12
E5 . . . . 17 A3

Dymes Path SW19 . . . 69 C2

Dymock St SW6 . . . . . 59 A4

Dyne Rd NW6 . . . . . . 10 B1

Dynevor Rd
Richmond TW10 . . . . 54 A2
Shacklewell N16 . . . . . 7 B1

Dynham Rd NW6 . . . . 10 C1

Dyott St
Soho WC1 . . . . 105 C2
St Giles WC1, WC2 . . 106 A2

Dysart St
EC2 . . . . 24 A1 98 A1

Dyson Ho 8 SE10 . . . 43 B1

E

Eade Rd N4 . . . . 6 B4

Eagle Cl SE16 . . . . . . 40 B1

Eagle Ct
12 Dulwich SE21 . . . . 75 C2
Holborn EC1 . . . . . . 108 A4

Eagle Dwellings
EC1 . . . . 97 A4

Eagle Ho
2 Bethnal Green
E1 . . . . 25 A1
Finsbury Pk N7 . . . . . . 5 B1

Eagle Hts 15 SW11 . . 60 A4

Eagle Lo NW11 . . . . . . 1 B4

Eagle Mans N16 . . . . . 16 B3

Eagle Mews N1 . . . . . 16 A2

Eagle Pl
South Kensington
SW7 . . . . 143 A2
St James SW1 . . . . . 119 A3

Eagle St WC1 . . . . . . 106 C3

Eagle Wharf SE1 . . . 124 C1

Eagle Wharf Rd
N1 . . . . 87 A2

Eagle Works
E1 . . . . 24 B1 99 A1

Eagling Cl 3 E3 . . . . . 26 C2

**Ealing, Hammersmith
and West London
Coll** 18 W3 . . . . 28 A1

**Ealing,
Hammersmith
& West London Coll**
W14 . . . . 140 A1

Eamann Casey Ho 16
SW9 . . . . 173 C3

Eamont St NW8 . . . . . 80 B2

Eamont St NW8 . . . . . 80 B2

Eardley Cres SW5 . . 141 C1

Earldom Rd SW15 . . . 57 B3

Earle Ho SW1 . . . . . . 147 C3

Earlham St WC2 . . . . 106 A1

Earl Ho NW1 . . . . 90 B1

Earlom Ho WC1 . . . . . 95 B3

Earl Rd SW14 . . . . 55 B3

EARL'S COURT 141 C3

Earl's Court Gdns
SW5 . . . . 142 A3

Earl's Court Rd SW5,
W8 . . . . 141 C3

Earl's Court Sq
SW5 . . . . 142 A2

Earl's Court Sta
SW5 . . . . 141 C3

Earlsferry Way N1 . . . 14 A1

EARLSFIELD 71 B3

Earlsfield Prim Sch
SW18 . . . . 71 B2

Earlsfield Rd
SW18 . . . . 71 B4

Earlsfield Sta
SW18 . . . . 71 B3

Earlsmead Rd
NW10 . . . . 22 B2

Earl St EC2 . . . . 110 A4

Earls Terr W8 . . . . . . 127 A1

Earlsthorpe Mews 3
SW12 . . . . 60 C1

Earlstoke St EC1 . . . . 96 A4

Earlston Gr E9 . . . . . . 25 A4

Earls Wlk W8 . . . . . . 127 B1

Earlswood Cl 10
SE10 . . . . 43 A1

Earlswood Ho 3
SW2 . . . . 74 B3

Earlswood St SE10 . . 43 A1

Early Mews NW1 . . . . 82 B4

Earnshaw Ho EC1 . . . 96 B3

Earnshaw St WC1,
WC2 . . . . 105 C2

Earsby St SW14 . . . . 140 B4

Earth Galleries
SW7 . . . . 129 C1

Eashing Point 5
SW15 . . . . 69 A3

Easleys Mews W1 . . 103 C2

EAST ACTON 29 B3

East Acton Arc
W3 . . . . 29 B3

East Acton Ct W3 . . . 29 A2

East Acton La W3 . . . 29 A2

East Acton Prim Sch
W3 . . . . 29 A3

East Acton Sta
W12 . . . . 29 B3

East Arbour St E1 . . . 32 C3

East Bank N16 . . . . 7 A4

East Block 5 E1 . . . . 152 C2

Eastbourne Ave
W3 . . . . 28 C3

Eastbourne Gdns
SW14 . . . . 55 B4

Eastbourne Mews
W2 . . . . 101 A2

Eastbourne Rd
W4 . . . . 45 B4

Eastbourne Terr
W2 . . . . 101 A2

Eastbury Gr W4 . . . . . 38 A1

Eastbury Terr E1 . . . . 25 C1

Eastcastle St W1 . . . 105 A2

Eastcheap EC3 . . . . . 124 A4

East Churchfield Rd
W3 . . . . 28 C1

Eastcote St SW9 . . . 172 C1

East Cross Route
Bow E3 . . . . 26 C4
Hackney Wick E9 . . . 18 B3

Eastdown Ho E8 . . . . . 16 C4

Eastdown Pk SE13 . . . 67 C3

EAST DULWICH 64 C2

East Dulwich Gr
SE22 . . . . 64 A2

East Dulwich Rd SE15,
SE22 . . . . 64 C3

East Dulwich Sta
SE22 . . . . 64 B3

Eastern Rd SE4 . . . . . 66 C3

East Ferry Rd E14 . . . 42 A2

Eastfields Ave
SW18 . . . . 58 C3

Eastfields Rd W3 . . . . 28 B4

Eastfield St E14 . . . . . 33 A4

East Harding St
EC4 . . . . 107 C2

East Heath Rd NW3 . . 2 C1

East Hill SW18 . . . . . . 59 B2

East India Bldgs 9
E14 . . . . 33 C2

East India Ct 7
SE16 . . . . 40 B4

East India Dock Basin
E14 . . . . 35 A2

East India Dock Rd
E14 . . . . 34 A2

**East India Dock Road
Tunnel** 8 E14 . . . . . 34 C3

East La 5 SE16 . . . . . 139 B3

East La 8 SE16 . . . . . 139 B3

Eastlake Ho NW8 . . . . 89 C1

Eastlake Rd SE5 . . . . 48 B1

Eastlands Cres
SE21 . . . . 64 B1

Eastleigh Wlk 9
SW15 . . . . 68 C4

Eastman Dental Hospl
WC1 . . . . 94 C2

Eastman Ho 7
SW4 . . . . 61 B1

Eastmearn Rd W3 . . . 37 C4

Eastmearn Rd SE21,
SE22 . . . . 75 B2

East Mount St E1 . . . . 32 A4

Eastney St SE10 . . . . 42 C1

Easton St WC1 . . . . . . 95 B3

Easton St WC1 . . . . . . 95 B2

East Parkside
SE10 . . . . 43 B4

East Pas EC1 . . . . . . 108 C4

East Point E14 . . . . . . 34 A1

East Point 4 SE1 . . . 153 B2

East Poultry Ave
EC1 . . . . 108 A3

East Putney Sta
SW15 . . . . 58 A2

East Rd
Chelsea SW1 . . . . . . 145 B1
Shoreditch N1 . . . . . . 97 C4

East Row W10 . . . . . . 23 A1

Eastry Ho SW8 . . . . 162 A1

EAST SHEEN 55 C3

East Sheen Ave
SW14 . . . . 55 C3

East Sheen Prim Sch
SW14 . . . . 56 A3

East Smithfield
E1 . . . . 125 A3

East St SE17 . . . . 151 B2

East Surrey Gr
SE15 . . . . 49 B3

East Tenter St E1 . . . 111 A1

Eastvale 1 W3 . . . . . . 29 B1

East View NW3 . . . . . . 2 C2

Eastway E3, E9 . . . . . 26 A4

Eastwell Ho SE1 . . . . 137 C2

Eastwick Ct 2
SW19 . . . . 69 C2

Eastwood Cl 2
N7 . . . . 14 C3

Eaton Cl SW1 . . . . . . 145 B3

Eaton Dr SW9 . . . . . . 63 A3

Eaton Gate SW1 . . . . 145 B4

Eaton Ho
Battersea SW11 . . . . 167 C3
2 Limehouse E14 . . . 33 B2

Eaton House Sch
SW1 . . . . 145 B4

**Eaton House The
Manor Sch** SW4 . . . 61 A3

Eaton La SW1 . . . . . . 132 B1

Eaton Mans SW1 . . . 145 B3

Eaton Mews N
SW1 . . . . 131 C1

Eaton Mews S
SW1 . . . . 132 A1

Eaton Mews W
SW1 . . . . 145 C4

Eaton Pl SW1 . . . . . . 131 C1

Eaton Row SW1 . . . . 132 A1

Eaton Sq SW1 . . . . . 131 C1

**Eaton Sq Pre-Prep
Sch** SW1 . . . . 146 A4

Eaton Square Sch
SW1 . . . . 146 C3

Eaton Terr
Belgravia SW1 . . . . . **145** C4
Bow E3 . . . . .26 A2
Eaton Terr Mews
SW1 . . . . .72 B2
Eatonville Rd
SW17 . . . . .72 B2
Eatonville Villas
SW17 . . . . .72 B2
Ebbisham Dr SW8 **162** C3
Ebbsfleet Rd NW2 . .10 A4
Ebenezer Ho
SE11 . . . . **150** A3
Ebenezer Mussel Ho
E2 . . . . .25 B3
Ebenezer St N1 . . . .97 B4
Ebley Cl SE15 . . . . . . .49 B4
Ebner St SW18 . . . . .59 A2
Ebony Cl NW10 . . . . . .8 B2
Ebony Ho
27 Bethnal Green
E2 . . . . .24 C2 **99** B3
26 West Hampstead
NW3 . . . . .11 A2
Ebor Cotts SW15 . .68 A1
Ebor St E1,
E2 . . . . .24 B1 **98** C2
Ebrahim Academy
E1 . . . . **111** C2
Ebrahim Coll E1 . . **111** C2
Eburne Rd N7 . . . . . . .5 A1
Ebury Bridge Rd
SW1 . . . . **145** C1
Ebury Mews
Belgravia SW1 . . . . **146** A4
West Norwood
SE27 . . . . .75 A1
Ebury Mews E
SW1 . . . . **132** A1
Ebury Sq SW1 . . . . . **145** C3
Ebury St SW1 . . . . . **146** A4
Ecclesbourne Rd
N1 . . . . .15 B1
Eccles Cl SE11 . . . . **149** A1
Eccles Rd SW11 . . . .60 B3
Eccleston Ho
SW2 . . . . .62 C1
Eccleston Mews
SW1 . . . . **131** C1
Eccleston Sq
SW1 . . . . **146** B3
Eccleston Sq Mews
SW1 . . . . **146** C3
Eccleston St SW1 . **146** A4
Eckford St N1 . . . . . .85 B2
Eckstein Rd
SW11 . . . . .60 A3
Ecole Française
Jacques Prévert 5
W6 . . . . .39 C2
Edans Ct W12 . . . . . .38 B3
Edbrooke Rd W9 . . .23 C1
Eddisbury Ho 7
SE26 . . . . .76 C1
Eddiscombe Rd
SW6 . . . . **165** A2
Eddison Ct N19 . . . . . .5 A2
Eddystone Rd SE4 . .66 A2
Eddystone Twr
SE8 . . . . .41 A1
Edenbridge Cl 28
SE16 . . . . .40 A1

Edenbridge Rd E9 . .17 C1
Eden Cl
Child's Hill NW3 . . . . . .1 C2
Kensington W8 . . . . . **127** C2
Eden Gr
Islington N7 . . . . .14 B3
Willesden NW10 . . . . . .9 A2
Edenham Way
W10 . . . . .31 B4
Eden Ho
11 Battersea
SW11 . . . . .60 A4
Lisson Gr NW8 . . . . . **90** A1
Edenhurst Ave
SW6 . . . . .58 B4
Eden Lodge NW6 . . . .9 C1
Eden Mews SW17 . .71 B1
Edensmuir Ct SE3 . .53 C3
Edensor Gdns W4 . .46 A3
Edensor Rd W4 . . . . .46 A3
Edenvale St SW6 . **166** C1
Eden Way E3 . . . . . . .26 B4
Edgar Ho
Homerton E9 . . . . .18 A3
South Lambeth
SW8 . . . . **162** A2
Edgar Kail Way
SE22 . . . . .64 A3
Edgarley Terr
SW6 . . . . **164** A3
Edgar Rd E3 . . . . .27 A2
Edgar Wallace Cl 4
SE15 . . . . .49 A3
Edgcott Ho 2
W10 . . . . .30 B4
Edgecombe Ho
4 London SE5 . . . . . . .49 A1
Putney SW19 . . . . .70 A4
Edgecote Cl 7
W3 . . . . .28 B1
Edgehill Ho 4
SW9 . . . . .48 A1
Edgeley La SW4 . . . .61 C4
Edgeley Rd SW4 . . . .61 C4
Edge St
W8 . . . . .31 C1 **113** C2
Edgeworth Ho
NW8 . . . . .78 C4
Edgson Ho SW1 . . . **146** A2
Edgware Acad
WC2 . . . . **106** B1
Edgware Rd W2,
NW1, NW8 . . . . **102** A3
Edgware Road Sta
(Bakerloo) NW1 . . **102** A3
Edgware Road Sta
(Met, Distr, Circle)
NW1 . . . . **102** B3
Edinburgh Cl 7
E2 . . . . .25 B3
Edinburgh Ct 10
SE16 . . . . .32 C1
Edinburgh Ho
3 Acton W3 . . . . .28 C3
Maida Vale W9 . . . . . . **88** B4
Edington 20 NW5 . . .12 C2
Edison Bldg 7
E14 . . . . .41 C4
Edison Ct SE10 . . . . .43 B3
Edison Ho SE1 . . . . **151** B4
Edis St NW1 . . . . .81 C4
Editha Mans
SW10 . . . . **156** C3

Edith Cavell Cl 2
N19 . . . . .5 A4
Edith Gr SW10 . . . . **157** A2
Edith Ho 6 W6 . . . . . .39 B1
Edithna St SW9 . . . . .62 A4
Edith Neville Cotts
NW1 . . . . .93 B4
Edith Neville Prim
Sch NW1 . . . . .83 B1
Edith Ramsay Ho 2
E1 . . . . .33 A4
Edith Rd
Stratford New Town
E15 . . . . .19 C3
West Kensington
W14 . . . . **140** B3
Edith Row SW6 . . . **166** A4
Edith St E2 . . . . .24 C3
Edith Summerskill Ho
6
SW6 . . . . **154** C2
Edith Terr SW10 . . **156** C2
Edith Villas W14 . . **140** C2
Edith Yd SW10 . . . . **157** A2
Edmeston Cl E9 . . . . .18 A2
Edmond Ct SE14 . . . .50 B2
Edmonton Ct 5
SE16 . . . . .40 B3
Edmund Halley Way
SE10 . . . . .43 A4
Edmund Ho
Kennington SE17 . . **150** B1
New Cross Gate
SE14 . . . . .51 A2
Edmundsbury Ct Est
10 SW9 . . . . .62 B3
Edmund St SE5 . . . . .48 C3
Edmund Waller Prim
Sch SE14 . . . . .50 C1
Ednam Ho SE15 . . . .49 C4
Edna St SW11 . . . . . **168** A3
Edred Ho E9 . . . . .18 A4
Edrich Ho SW4 . . . . **172** A3
Edric Ho SW1 . . . . . **147** C4
Edric Rd SE14 . . . . . .50 C3
Edridge Ho 9
SE27 . . . . .75 A1
Edward Alleyn Ho
SE21 . . . . .76 A4
Edward Ct 2 E16 . . .35 C4
Edward Dodd Ct
N1 . . . . .97 C4
Edward Edward's Ho
SE1 . . . . **122** A1
Edwardes Pl W8 . . **127** A1
Edwardes Sq W8 . **127** B1
Edward Friend Ho 6
N16 . . . . .7 A1
Edward Ho
Paddington W2 . . . . . . .89 B1
Vauxhall SE11 . . . . . . **149** A2
Edward Kennedy Ho
10 W10 . . . . .23 A1
Edward Mann Cl 13
E1 . . . . .32 C3
Edward Mews
NW1 . . . . .82 B1
Edward Mills Wy 23
E14 . . . . .33 C3
Edward Pl SE8 . . . . . .51 B4
Edward Robinson Ho
6
SE14 . . . . .50 C3
Edward's Cotts 11
N1 . . . . .15 A1
Edward's La N16 . . . . .7 A2
Edwards Mews
Islington N1 . . . . .14 C1

Edwards Mews
continued
Marylebone W1 . . . . . **103** B1
Edward Sq
Islington N1 . . . . . . **84** C3
1 Rotherhithe
SE16 . . . . .33 A1
Edward St SE14 . . . .51 B3
Edward VII Mans
NW10 . . . . .22 C2
Edward Wilson Prim
Sch 2 W2 . . . . **100** A4
Edwin Ho SE15 . . . . .49 C3
Edwin's Mead E9 . . .18 A4
Edwin St
Bethnal Green E1 . . . .25 B1
Newham E16 . . . . .35 C4
Edwy Ho E9 . . . . .18 B4
Edwyn Ho SW18 . . . .59 A1
Eel Brook Cl SW6 . **166** A4
Effie Pl SW6 . . . . . . **155** C1
Effie Rd SW6 . . . . . . **155** C1
Effingham Ho 37
SW8 . . . . **171** B1
Effra Ct SW2 . . . . . . .62 B2
Effra Mans SW2 . . . .62 C2
Effra Par SW2 . . . . . .62 C2
Effra Rd SW2 . . . . . . .62 C2
Effra Road Ret Pk
SW2 . . . . .62 C2
EF International
Language Sch
SE1 . . . . **121** C1
Egbert Ho E9 . . . . . . .18 A3
Egbert St NW1 . . . . . .81 B4
Egbury Ho SW15 . . .56 B1
Egerton Cres
SW3 . . . . **144** B4
Egerton Ct 5
TW10 . . . . .54 A2
Egerton Dr SE10 . . . .52 A2
Egerton Gdns
Knightsbridge
SW3 . . . . **130** B1
Willesden NW10 . . . . . .22 B4
Egerton Gdns Mews
SW3 . . . . **130** B1
Egerton Ho W4 . . . . .45 B4
Egerton Pl SW3 . . . **130** B1
Egerton Rd N16 . . . . . .7 B4
Egerton Terr SW3 . **130** B1
Egham Cl SW19 . . . . .70 A2
Eglantine Rd
SW18 . . . . .59 B2
Eglington Ct SE17 . .48 B4
Egliston Mews
SW15 . . . . .57 B4
Egliston Rd SW15 . . .57 B4
Egmont St SE14 . . . .50 C3
Egremont Ho SE13 . .52 A1
Egremont Rd SE27 . .74 C1
Egret Ho 15 SE16 . . .40 C2
Eider Ct 33 SE8 . . . . .51 B4
Elaine Ct 18 NW3 . . .12 B2
Elaine Gr NW5 . . . . . .12 C3
Elaine Ho N4 . . . . .5 A3
Elam Cl SE5 . . . . .48 A1
Elam St SE5 . . . . .48 A1
Elan Ct E1 . . . . .32 A4
Eland Rd SW11 . . . . .60 B4
Elba Pl SE17 . . . . . . **151** A4
Elbe St SW6 . . . . . . **166** C2
Elborough St
SW18 . . . . .70 C3
Elbury Dr E16 . . . . . . .35 C3
Elcho St SW11 . . . . **158** B1

Elcot Ave SE15 . . . . .50 A3
Elderberry Rd W5 . .36 A4
Elderfield Ho 4
E14 . . . . .33 C2
Elderfield Rd E5 . . . .17 B4
Elder St E1 . . . .24 B1 **98** C1
Elder Wlk
Islington N1 . . . . **86** B4
2 Lewisham SE13 . . .67 B4
Eldon Ct NW6 . . . . . .23 C4
Eldon Gr NW3 . . . . . .11 C3
Eldon Ho SW9 . . . . . .63 A4
Eldon Rd W8 . . . . . . **128** B1
Eldon St EC2 . . . . . . **109** C3
Eldon Way NW10 . . .20 A3
Eldridge Ct SE16 . . **139** B1
Eleanor Cl SE16 . . . .40 C4
Eleanor Ct 13 E2 . . .24 C4
Eleanor Gr SW13 . . .56 A4
Eleanor Ho
10 Hammersmith
W6 . . . . .39 B1
4 Kentish Town
NW5 . . . . .13 B3
Eleanor Palmer Prim
Sch 12 NW5 . . . . .13 B4
Eleanor Rathbone Ho
6 N6 . . . . .4 C4
Eleanor Rd
Brixton SW9 . . . . . . **173** C3
Hackney E8 . . . . .17 A1
Eleanor St E3 . . . . . . .26 C2
Electra Bsns Pk
E16 . . . . .34 C4
Electra Ct 9 SW2 . . . .9 B2
Electric Ave SW9 . . .62 C3
Electric Ho 13 E3 . . .26 C2
Electric La 2
SW9 . . . . .62 C3
Electric Mans 1
SW9 . . . . .62 C3
Elephant & Castle
Newington SE1 . . . . **136** B1
Newington SE11 . . . . **150** A4
Elephant & Castle Sh
Ctr SE1 . . . . **150** C4
Elephant & Castle Sta
Lambeth SE1 . . . . . . **136** B1
Newington SE17 . . . . **150** C4
Elephant La SE16 . . .40 B4
Elephant Rd SE17 . **150** C4
Elfindale Rd SE24 . . .63 B2
Elfort Rd N5 . . . . .14 C4
Elf Row E1 . . . . .32 B2
Elgar Ave W5 . . . . . . .36 A4
Elgar Cl SE8 . . . . .51 C3
Elgar Ct W14 . . . . . . **126** A1
Elgar Ho
Pimlico SW1 . . . . . . **146** B1
South Hampstead
NW6 . . . . .11 B1
Elgin Ave
Hammersmith
W12 . . . . .39 A3
Westbourne Green
W9 . . . . **88** B4
Elgin Cl W12 . . . . .39 A3
Elgin Cres
W11 . . . . .31 A2 **112** B4
Elgin Ct W9 . . . . **88** A2
Elgin Ho 8 E14 . . . . .34 A3
Elgin Mans W9 . . . . . **88** B3
Elgin Mews W11 . . . .31 A3
Elgin Mews N W9 . . **88** B4
Elgin Mews S W9 . . **88** B4

Elgood Cl
W11 . . . . 31 A1 112 A1
Elgood Ho NW6 . . . . 79 C1
Elham Ho 15 E5 . . . .17 A3
Elia Mews N1 . . . . . 86 A1
Elias Pl SW8 . . . . . 163 B3
Elia St N1 . . . . 86 A1
Elim Est SE1 . . . . . 138 A2
Elim St SE1 . . . . . . 138 A2
Eliot Cotts SE3 . . . . 53 A1
Eliot Ct SW18 . . . . . 59 A1
Eliot Gdns SW15 . . . 56 C3
Eliot Ho 10 TW10 . . . 54 B1
Eliot Hill SE13 . . . . 52 B1
Eliot Mews NW8 . . . 78 C1
Eliot Pk SE13 . . . . . 52 B1
Eliot Pl SE3 . . . . . . 53 A1
Eliot Vale SE3 . . . . 52 C1
Elis Wy E15 . . . . . . 19 B3
Elizabeth Ave
  Islington N1 . . . . . . 15 C1
  Shoreditch N1 . . . . 87 A4
Elizabeth Barnes Ct 5
  SW6 . . . . 166 B2
Elizabeth Blount Ct 4
  E14 . . . . 33 A3
Elizabeth Cl
  Paddington W9 . . . . 89 A1
  12 Poplar E14 . . . . 34 A3
Elizabeth Cooper Lo
  SW12 . . . . 60 C1
Elizabeth Cotts 5
  TW9 . . . . 44 C2
Elizabeth Ct
  Chelsea SW10 . . . . 157 C3
  East Dulwich SE22 . . 64 C3
  Marylebone NW8 . . . 90 B2
  Westminster SW1 . 133 C1
Elizabeth Finn Ho 8
  W12 . . . . 38 C3
Elizabeth Garrett
  Anderson Language
  Coll N1 . . . . 85 A1
Elizabeth Gdns
  W3 . . . . 29 B1
Elizabeth Ho 12
  12 Hammersmith
  W6 . . . . 39 B1
  Lambeth SE11 . . . 149 C3
Elizabeth Ind Est
  SE14 . . . . 50 C4
Elizabeth Kenny Ho
  N1 . . . . 15 B2
Elizabeth Mews
  20 Hackney E2 . . . . 24 C3
  Maitland Pk NW3 . . . 12 B2
Elizabeth Selby Inf
  Sch 51 E2 . . . 24 C2 99 C4
Elizabeth Sq 13
  SE16 . . . . 33 A2
Elizabeth St SW1 . 145 C4
Elkington Point
  SE11 . . . . 149 B3
Elkstone Rd W10 . . . 31 B4
Ellacombe Ho 1
  SW2 . . . . 74 C4
Ellaline Rd W6 . . . . 47 C4
Ella Mews NW3 . . . . 12 B4
Elland Ho 11 E14 . . . 33 B3
Elland Rd SE15 . . . . 65 B3
Ella Rd N4, N8 . . . . . 5 A4
Ellenborough Ho 5
  W12 . . . . 30 A2
Ellenborough Pl
  SW15 . . . . 56 C3
Ellen St E1 . . . . . . 111 C1

Ellen Wilkinson Ho
  7 Globe Town
  E2 . . . . 25 C2
  West Brompton
  SW6 . . . . 155 A3
Ellerby St SW6 . . . . 47 C2
Ellerdale Cl 18
  NW3 . . . . 11 B4
Ellerdale Rd NW3 . . 11 B3
Ellerdale St SE13 . . 67 A4
Ellerker Gdns
  TW10 . . . . 54 A1
Ellerslie Gdns
  NW10 . . . . 21 C4
Ellerslie Ind Est
  SW2 . . . . 62 A2
Ellerslie Rd W12 . . . 30 A1
Ellerton Ct W3 . . . . 37 A4
Ellerton Rd
  Barnes SW13 . . . . . 46 C2
  Wandsworth SW17,
  SW18 . . . . 71 C3
Ellery Cl 5 NW10 . . . 21 B3
Ellery Ho SE17 . . . 151 C3
Ellery St SE15 . . . . 50 A1
Ellesmere Ct W4 . . . 45 C4
Ellesmere Rd
  Bow E3 . . . . 26 A3
  Chiswick W4 . . . . . 45 C4
  Willesden NW10 . . . . 8 B2
Ellesmere St E14 . . 34 A3
Ellingfort Rd E8 . . . 17 A1
Ellingham Rd
  Leyton E15 . . . . . . 19 C4
  Shepherd's Bush
  W12 . . . . 38 C4
Ellington Ho SE1 . 137 A1
Ellington St N7 . . . . 14 C2
Elliott Rd
  Acton W4 . . . . 38 A2
  Brixton SW9 . . . . . 48 A2
Elliott's Pl N1 . . . . . 86 B3
Elliott Sq NW3 . . . . 12 A1
Elliott's Row SE11 . 150 B4
Ellis Cl NW10 . . . . . 9 B2
Ellisfield Dr SW15 . . 68 C4
Ellis Franklin Ct
  NW8 . . . . 78 C2
Ellis Ho SE17 . . . . 151 B2
Ellison Ho 1 SE13 . . 52 B1
Ellison Rd SW13 . . . 46 B1
Ellis St SW1 . . . . . 145 B4
Ellis Terr SE5 . . . . 163 C2
Ellsworth St E2 . . . . 25 A2
Ellwood Ct 11 W9 . . 88 B1
Elm Bank Gdns
  SW13 . . . . 46 A1
Elm Bank Mans
  SW13 . . . . 46 A1
Elmbourne Rd
  SW17 . . . . 73 A1
Elmbridge Wlk E8 . . 16 C1
Elm Cl N19 . . . . 4 B2
Elmcourt Rd SE21,
  SE27 . . . . 75 B2
Elm Cres W5 . . . . . 36 A4
Elmcroft N6 . . . . 4 B4
Elmcroft Ave NW11 . . 1 B4
Elmcroft Cres
  NW11 . . . . 1 A4
Elmcroft St E5 . . . . 17 B4
Elm Ct
  Brixton SW9 . . . . . 173 B4
  Lewisham SE13 . . . . 67 C4
  16 Notting Hill W2 . . 31 C4

Elm Ct continued
  Strand EC4 . . . . . 121 B4
Elm Ct Sch SE27 . . . 74 B4
Elmer Ho NW1 . . . 102 A4
Elmfield Ho
  6 Canonbury N5 . . . 15 B3
  Paddington W9 . . . . 23 C1
Elmfield Mans 5
  SW17 . . . . 72 C2
Elmfield Rd SW17 . . 73 A2
Elmfield Way W9 . . . 31 C4
Elm Friars Wlk
  NW1 . . . . 13 C1
Elm Gn W3 . . . . 29 A3
Elm Gr
  Cricklewood NW2 . . . 9 C4
  Peckham SE15 . . . 49 C1
Elm Green Sch The
  SE27 . . . . 75 A2
Elm Grove Rd
  Barnes SW13 . . . . . 46 C1
  Ealing W5 . . . . 36 A4
Elm Ho 6 E14 . . . . . 42 B4
Elmhurst Mans
  SW4 . . . . 61 C4
Elmhurst St SW4 . . . 61 C4
Elmhurst Villas
  SE15 . . . . 65 B3
Elmington Rd SE5 . . 48 C3
Elmira St SE13 . . . . 67 A4
Elm Lo SW6 . . . . . . 47 C2
Elmore Ho SW9 . . . 48 A1
Elmore St N1 . . . . . 15 C1
Elm Park Gdns
  SW10 . . . . 143 B1
Elm Park Ho
  SW10 . . . . 143 B1
Elm Park La SW3 . . 143 B1
Elm Park Mans
  SW10 . . . . 157 A4
Elm Pk SW2 . . . . . . 74 B4
Elm Pk SW7 . . . . . 143 B2
Elm Quay SW8 . . . . 161 B3
Elm Rd SW14 . . . . . 55 B3
Elm Row NW3 . . . . . 2 B1
Elms Cres SW4 . . . . 61 C1
Elmshaw Rd SW15 . . 56 C2
Elmslie Point 2
  E3 . . . . 33 B4
Elms Mews W2 . . . 115 B4
Elms Rd SW4 . . . . . 61 B2
Elm St WC1 . . . . . . 95 A1
Elms The
  Barnes SW13 . . . . . 56 B4
  8 Harlesden
  NW10 . . . . 21 A3
Elmstone Rd SW6 . 165 B4
Elm Terr NW2 . . . . . 1 C1
Elmton Ct NW8 . . . . 89 B2
Elm Tree Cl NW8 . . . 89 B4
Elm Tree Ct
  5 Camberwell
  SE5 . . . . 48 B2
  St John's Wood
  NW8 . . . . 89 B4
Elm Tree Rd NW8 . . 89 B4
Elm Way NW10 . . . . 8 A4
Elm Wlk NW3 . . . . . 1 C2
Elmwood Ct
  SW11 . . . . 170 A4
Elm Wood Prim Sch
  SE27 . . . . 75 C1
Elmwood Rd
  Chiswick W4 . . . . . 45 B4
  Herne Hill SE24 . . . 63 C2

Elmworth Gr SE21 . . 75 C2
Elnathan Mews
  W9 . . . . 88 B1
Elphinstone St N5 . . 15 A4
Elrington Rd E8 . . . 16 C2
Elsa St E1 . . . . 33 A4
Elsdale Ho 10 E9 . . . 17 B2
Elsdale St E9 . . . . . 17 B1
Elsden Mews E2 . . . 25 B3
Elsenham St SW18,
  SW19 . . . . 70 B2
Elsfield NW5 . . . . . 13 A3
Elsham Rd W14 . . . 126 A3
Elsham Terr W14 . . 126 A3
Else Lane Ct W12 . . 30 A3
Elsiemaud Rd SE4 . . 66 B2
Elsie Rd SE22 . . . . . 64 B3
Elsinore Gdns NW2 . . 1 A1
Elsinore Ho
  12 Camberwell
  SE5 . . . . 48 B1
  Islington N1 . . . . . . 85 B3
Elsinore Way TW9 . . 55 A4
Elsley Rd SW11 . . . . 60 C4
Elsley Sch 8
  SW17 . . . . 72 A2
Elspeth Rd SW11 . . 60 B3
Elstead Ho 8
  SW2 . . . . 74 B4
Elsted St SE17 . . . 151 C3
Elstow Grange
  NW6 . . . . 9 C1
Elswick Rd SE13 . . . 52 A1
Elswick St SW6 . . . 166 C2
Elsworthy Rd NW3 . . 80 A4
Elsworthy Rise
  NW3 . . . . 12 A1
Elsworthy Terr
  NW3 . . . . 12 A1
Elsynge Rd SW18 . . 59 C2
Elsynge Road Mans
  SW18 . . . . 59 C2
Elthiron Rd SW6 . . . 165 C3
Elthorne Rd N19 . . . 4 C2
Elthruda Rd SE13 . . 67 C1
Elton Ho 3 E3 . . . . 26 B4
Elton Pl N16 . . . . . 16 A3
Elton St 11 N16 . . . 16 A3
Eltringham St
  SW18 . . . . 59 B3
Elvaston Mews
  SW7 . . . . 129 A2
Elvaston Pl SW7 . . 129 A1
Elveden Ho 17
  SW9 . . . . 63 A3
Elver Gdns 10
  E2 . . . . 24 C2 99 C4
Elverson Rd SE8 . . . 52 A1
Elverson Rd Sta
  SE8 . . . . 52 A1
Elverton St 1 SW1 147 B4
Elvin Ho 2 E9 . . . . 17 B2
Elvis Rd NW2 . . . . . 9 B2
Elwin St E2 . . . 24 C2 99 B4
Elwood Ho N5 . . . . 6 A1
Elwood St N4, N5 . . 6 A1
Elworth Ho SW8 . . 163 A1
Ely Cotts SW8 . . . . 162 C1
Ely Court Flats
  SW6 . . . . 164 A3
Ely Ct
  Holborn EC1 . . . . 107 C3
  1 Maida Vale
  NW6 . . . . 23 C3
Ely Ho 22 SE15 . . . . 49 C3

Ely Pl
  EC1 . . . . 107 C3
  Kennington SE11 . . 162 C1
Elysium Gate 7
  SW6 . . . . 164 C2
Elysium Pl SW6 . . . 164 C1
Elysium St SW6 . . . 164 C1
Elystan Ct SW15 . . . 57 A2
Elystan Pl SW3 . . . 144 C2
Elystan St SW3 . . . 144 B3
Elystan Wlk N1 . . . . 85 B3
Emanuel Ave W3 . . . 28 B3
Emanuel Ct W3 . . . . 28 C3
Emanuel Sch
  SW11 . . . . 60 A2
Embankment
  SW15 . . . . 47 C1
Embankment Gdns
  SW3 . . . . 159 A4
Embankment Pier
  WC2 . . . . 120 B2
Embankment Pl
  WC2 . . . . 120 B2
Embankment Sta
  WC2 . . . . 120 B2
Embassy Ct NW8 . . 79 C1
Embassy Ho 2
  NW6 . . . . 10 C1
Emba St SE16 . . . . 139 C3
Ember Ct 2 W12 . . 38 A3
Emberton SE5 . . . . 49 A4
Emberton Ct EC1 . . 96 A3
Embleton Rd SE13 . . 67 A3
Emden St SW6 . . . . 166 B4
Emerald Rd NW10 . . 20 C4
Emerald Sq SW15 . . 56 C2
Emerald St WC1 . . . 106 C4
Emerson Ho N16 . . . 16 A3
Emerson St SE1 . . . 122 C2
Emery Hill St
  SW1 . . . . 133 A1
Emery St SE1 . . . . 135 C2
Emily St 1 E16 . . . . 35 B3
Emirates Airway
  SE10 . . . . 35 B1
Emirates Greenwich
  Peninsula Sta . . . 43 A4
Emirates Royal Dock
  E16 . . . . 35 C2
Emirates Stad
  (Arsenal FC) N7 . . 14 C4
Emlyn Gdns 3
  W12 . . . . 38 A3
Emlyn Rd W12 . . . . 38 B3
Emmanuel CE Prim
  Sch NW6 . . . . 10 C3
Emmanuel Ho
  Dulwich SE21 . . . . . 75 C1
  Lambeth SE11 . . . 149 B3
Emmanuel Rd
  SW12 . . . . 73 C3
Emma St E2 . . . . . . 25 A3
Emminster NW6 . . . 78 A4
Emmott Cl E1 . . . . . 26 A1
Emperor's Gate
  SW7 . . . . 142 C4
Empingham Ho 20
  SE8 . . . . 40 C2
Empire Ho SW3 . . . 130 A1
Empire Sq N19 . . . . 5 A1
Empire Wharf E3 . . . 26 A4
Empire Wharf Rd
  E14 . . . . 42 C2

Empress App
SW6 . . . . **155** B4
Empress Mews **4**
SW6 . . . . .48 B1
Empress Pl SW5 . . .141 B1
Empress St SE17 . . . .48 B4
Empress State
Building SW6 . . . .141 B1
Empson St E3 . . . . . . .27 A1
Emsworth St SW2 . .74 B2
Emu Rd SW8 . . . . . . .170 A1
Enard Rd E8 . . . . .26 B3
Enbrook St W10 . . . .23 A2
Enclave Ct EC1 . . . . . .96 B2
Endell St WC2 . . . . . .106 A1
Enderby St SE10 . . . .43 A1
Endlesham Ct **2**
SW12 . . . . .72 C4
Endlesham Rd
SW12 . . . . .72 C4
Endsleigh Gdns
WC1 . . . . .93 B2
Endsleigh Mans **4**
SW16 . . . . .74 A1
Endsleigh Pl WC1 . . .93 C2
Endsleigh St WC1 . . .93 C2
Endwell Rd SE4 . . . .51 A1
Endymion Rd
Harringay N4 . . . . .6 A4
Tulse Hill SW2 . . . . . . .62 B1
Energen Cl NW10 . . . .8 A2
Enfield Cloisters **7**
N1 . . . . .24 A2 **98** A4
Enfield Ho **24**
SW9 . . . . .172 B2
Enfield Rd
De Beauvoir Town E8,
N1 . . . . .16 A1
South Acton W3 . . . . .37 A4
Enford St W1 . . . . . .102 C4
Engadine St SW18 . .70 C3
Engate St SE13 . . . . .67 B3
England's La NW3 . .12 B2
Englefield NW1 . . . . .92 C3
Englefield Rd N1 . . . .16 A1
Englewood Rd
SW12 . . . . .61 B1
English Gardening
Sch The SW3 . . . .158 C4
English Grounds
SE1 . . . . .124 A1
English Martyrs RC
Prim Sch
Walworth SE17 . . . .151 C3
Whitechapel E1 . . . .111 A1
English St E3 . . . . . . .26 B1
Enid St SE16 . . . . . .139 A2
Enid Stacy Ho **11**
N19 . . . . .4 C4
Enmore Ct SW14 . . .55 C2
Enmore Gdns
SW14 . . . . .55 C2
Enmore Rd SW15 . . .57 B2
Ennerdale Ho **3**
N4 . . . . .6 C4
Ennerdale Rd TW9 . .44 B1
Ennersdale Rd
SE13 . . . . .67 C2
Ennis Ho **10** E14 . . . .34 A3
Ennismore Ave
W4 . . . . .38 B2
Ennismore Gdns
SW7 . . . . .130 A2

Ennismore Gdns
Mews SW7 . . . . . .130 A2
Ennismore Mews
SW7 . . . . .130 A2
Ennismore St
SW7 . . . . .130 A2
Ensign Ct **12** E1 . . .125 C3
Ensign Ho SW18 . . . .59 A3
Ensign St E1 . . . . . .125 B4
Ensor Mews SW7 . . .143 B2
Enterprise Ho **36**
E9 . . . . .17 B1
Enterprise Way
College Pk NW10 . . . .21 C2
Wandsworth SW18 . .58 C3
Enterprise Ho **7**
SE8 . . . . .41 B2
Epirus Mews SW6 . .155 B2
Epirus Rd SW6 . . . .155 A2
Epping Cl E14 . . . . .41 C2
Epping Ho **8** E5 . . . . .7 C2
Epping Pl N1 . . . . . .14 C2
Epple Rd SW6 . . . . .165 A4
Epstein Ct N1 . . . . . .86 B3
Epworth St
EC2 . . . . .24 B2 **99** A3
Erasmus St SW1 . . .147 C3
Erconwald St W12 . .29 B3
Eresby Ho SW7 . . . .130 B3
Eresby Pl NW6 . . . . .10 C1
Erica Ct SW4 . . . . . .172 B3
Erica Ho SE4 . . . . . . .66 B4
Erica St W12 . . . . . . .29 C2
Ericcson Cl SW18 . . .58 C2
Eric Fletcher Ct **15**
N1 . . . . .15 B1
Eric Macdonald Ho
SW6 . . . . .165 C3
Eric Rd NW10 . . . . . . .8 B2
Ericson Ho
London SE13 . . . . . . .67 C3
Stamford Hill N16 . . . .7 B3
Eric St E3 . . . . .26 B1
Eric Wilkins Ho **2**
SE1 . . . . .153 B1
Eridge Ho SE22 . . . .64 B4
Eridge House Prep
Sch **18** SW6 . . . . .164 C2
Eridge Rd W4 . . . . . .37 C3
Erin Cl SW6 . . . . . . .155 C1
Erin Ct NW2 . . . . .9 B2
Erlanger Rd SE14 . . .50 C1
Ermine Rd SE13 . . . .67 A3
Ernest Bevin Coll
SW17 . . . . .72 A2
Ernest Gdns W4 . . . .45 A4
Ernest Simmonds Ho
SE14 . . . . .50 B1
Ernest St E1 . . . . .25 C1
Ernshaw Pl SW15 . . .58 A2
Eros (Shaftesbury
Meml Fountain)
W1 . . . . .119 B3
Erpingham Rd
SW15 . . . . .57 B4
Errington Rd W9 . . . .23 B1
Errol St EC1 . . . . .97 A1
Erskine Ho SW1 . . .146 C1
Erskine Rd NW3 . . . .12 B1
Escuan Lo N5 . . . . . .15 B3
Esher Gdns SW19 . . .69 C2
Esher Ho **8** SW8 . . .171 C2
Esdaile St E8 . . . . . . .82 C1

Esk Ho E3 . . . . .26 B1
Esme Ho SW15 . . . . .56 B3
Esmeralda Rd
SE1 . . . . .153 C3
Esmond Ct W8 . . . .128 B2
Esmond Gdns W4 . . .37 C2
Esmond Rd
Acton W4 . . . . .37 C3
Kilburn NW6 . . . . .23 B4
Esmond St SW15 . . .58 A3
Esparto St SW18 . . . .71 A4
Espirit Ct E1 . . . . . . .110 C3
Espirit Ho **6**
SW15 . . . . .58 A2
Essendine Mans
W9 . . . . .23 C2
Essendine Prim Sch
11 W9 . . . . .23 C2
Essendine Rd W9 . . .23 C2
Essex Ct
Barnes SW13 . . . . . .46 B1
Hammersmith W6 . . .39 B3
Holborn EC4 . . . . . . .107 B1
Essex Ho **2** E14 . . . .34 A3
Essex Park Mews
W3 . . . . .29 A1
Essex Pl W4 . . . . .37 B2
Essex Place Sq **5**
W4 . . . . .37 C2
Essex Rd
Acton W3 . . . . .28 B2
Chiswick W4 . . . . .37 C2
Islington N1 . . . . .86 B4
Willesden NW10 . . . . .8 A1
Essex Road Sta N1 . .15 B1
Essex St WC2 . . . . . .121 B4
Essex Villas W8 . . . .127 B3
Essian St E1 . . . . .33 A4
Essington SW15 . . . .58 A1
Estcourt Rd SW6 . . .154 C2
Estella Ho **19** W11 . .30 C2
Estelle Rd NW3 . . . . .12 B4
Esterbrooke St
SW1 . . . . .147 B3
Este Rd SW11 . . . . . .60 A4
Estoria Cl **22** SW2 . .74 C4
Etal Ho N1 . . . . .15 A1
Etchingham Rd
E15 . . . . .19 B4
Eternit Wlk SW6 . . . .47 C2
Ethelbert Ho E9 . . . .18 A4
Ethelbert St SW12 . .73 A3
Ethelburga St
SW11 . . . . .168 B4
Ethelburga Twr
SW11 . . . . .168 B4
Ethelden Rd W12 . . .30 A1
Ethel Rankin Ct **8**
SW6 . . . . .164 C2
Ethel St SE17 . . . . . .151 A3
Ethelworth Ct **4**
SW2 . . . . .74 C3
Etherow St SE22 . . . .76 C4
Ethnard Rd SE15 . . . .50 A4
Eton Ave NW3 . . . . . .12 A1
Eton Cl SW18 . . . . . . .71 A4
Eton College Rd
NW3 . . . . .12 B2
Eton Ct NW3 . . . . . . .11 C1
Eton Garages **11**
NW3 . . . . .12 A2
Eton Hall NW3 . . . . . .12 B2
Eton Ho
Hackney E9 . . . . .18 B2
Highbury N5 . . . . .15 A4
Eton Pl NW1 . . . . . . .12 C1

Eton Rd NW3 . . . . . . .12 B2
Eton Rise NW3 . . . . . .12 B2
Eton St TW10 . . . . . .54 A2
Eton Villas NW3 . . . . .12 B2
Etta St SE8 . . . . .51 A4
Ettrick St E14 . . . . . . .34 B3
Eugene Cotter Ho
SE17 . . . . .151 C3
Eugenia Rd SE16 . . . .40 B2
Eurocentres SW1 . .146 B3
Euro Cl NW10 . . . . . . .8 C2
Eurolink Bsns Ctr
SW2 . . . . .62 C2
Europa Pl EC1 . . . . . .96 C3
European Coll **3**
E1 . . . . .111 B2
Eustace Bldg
SW8 . . . . .160 A3
Eustace Rd SW6 . . .155 B2
Euston Rd NW1 . . . . .93 A2
Euston Sq NW1 . . . . .93 B3
Euston Square Sta
NW1 . . . . .93 A2
Euston St NW1 . . . . . .93 A3
Euston St NW1 . . . . . .93 B3
Euston Underpass
NW1 . . . . .92 C2
Evan Cook Cl SE15 . .50 B2
Evandale Rd SW9 . .173 C2
Evangelist Rd
NW5 . . . . .13 A4
Evans Cl E8 . . . . .16 B2
Evans Ho
34 Shepherd's Bush
W12 . . . . .30 A2
South Lambeth
SW8 . . . . .161 C1
Evelina Childrens'
Hospl SE1 . . . . . . .134 C2
Evelina Mans **9**
SE5 . . . . .48 C3
Evelina Rd SE15 . . . .50 B1
Evelyn Ct
Marylebone W1 . . . .102 C1
Shacklewell E8 . . . . .16 C4
Shoreditch N1 . . . . . .87 B1
Evelyn Denington Ct
2 N1 . . . . .15 A1
Evelyn Fox Ct W10 . .30 B4
Evelyn Gdns
Richmond TW9 . . . . . .54 A3
South Kensington
SW7 . . . . .143 B1
Evelyn Grace Acad
SE24 . . . . .63 A3
Evelyn Ho
Bedford Pk W12 . . . .38 B4
3 Brixton SW2 . . . . .62 B2
18 Spitalfields E1 . .111 B3
Evelyn Rd
Acton W4 . . . . .37 C3
Richmond TW9 . . . . . .54 A4
Evelyn St
Greenwich SE10 . . . .52 B4
SE8 . . . . .41 A1
Evelyn Terr TW9 . . . .54 A4
Evelyn Wlk N1 . . . . . .87 B1
Evelyn Yd W1 . . . . . .105 B2
Evenwood Cl
SW15 . . . . .58 A2
Everard Ho **37** E1 . .111 C1
Everatt Cl SW18 . . . .58 B2
Everdon Rd SW13 . . .46 C4
Everest Pl E14 . . . . . .34 B4

Everett Ho
Islington N7 . . . . .14 C4
Walworth SE17 . . . .151 B2
Evergreen Sq **3**
E8 . . . . .16 B1
Everilda St N1 . . . . . .85 A3
Evering Rd E5, N16 . . .7 C1
Everington St W6 . . .47 C4
Everitt Rd NW10 . . . .20 C2
Everleigh St N4 . . . . . .5 B3
Eversfield Rd TW9 . .44 B1
Evershed Ho E1 . . . .111 A2
Evershed Wlk W4 . . .37 C2
Eversholt St NW1 . . . .93 B4
Evershot Rd N4 . . . . . .5 B3
Eversleigh Rd
SW11 . . . . .169 B1
Eversley Ho E2 . . . . . .24 C2 **99** B3
Everthorpe Rd
SE15 . . . . .64 B4
Everton Bldgs
NW1 . . . . .92 C3
Evesham Ct **2**
TW10 . . . . .54 B1
Evesham Ho
1 Bethnal Green
E2 . . . . .25 B3
Pimlico SW1 . . . . . . .146 B2
St John's Wood
NW8 . . . . .78 C3
Evesham St W11 . . . .30 C2
Evesham Way
SW11 . . . . .60 C4
Evesham Wlk
Brixton SW9 . . . . . . .173 B2
Camberwell SE5 . . . .48 C1
Ewald Rd SW6 . . . . .164 C1
Ewart Pl **18** E3 . . . . .26 B3
Ewe Cl N7 . . . . .14 A2
Ewen Cres SW2 . . . . .74 C4
Ewen Henderson Ct
10 SE14 . . . . .51 A3
Ewen Ho N1 . . . . .84 C3
Ewer St SE1 . . . . . . .122 C1
Ewhurst **15** SW15 . .57 C1
Ewhurst Cl E1 . . . . . .32 B4
Ewhurst Rd SE4 . . . .66 B1
Exbury Ho
Hackney E9 . . . . .17 B2
4 London SW9 . . . . .62 B3
Excel Ct WC2 . . . . . .119 C3
Excellence Prim Sch
18 E9 . . . . .25 A4
Excelsior Gdns
SE13 . . . . .52 B1
Excelsior Ind Est
SE16 . . . . .50 B4
Exchange Arc
EC2 . . . . .110 B4
Exchange Ct WC2 . .120 B3
Exchange Mans **2**
NW11 . . . . .1 B4
Exchange Pl EC2 . . .110 A4
Exchange Sq EC2 . .110 A4
Exeter Ct NW6 . . . . . .23 C3
Exeter Ho
Paddington W2 . . . .100 C2
11 Peckham SE15 . .49 C4
Putney SW15 . . . . . . .57 C1
Exeter Mans NW2 . . .10 A2
Exeter Mews
Fulham SW6 . . . . . . .155 B2
12 Hampstead
NW6 . . . . .11 A2

Exeter Rd
Brondesbury
NW2 . . . . .10 A2
Newham E16 . . . . .35 C4
Exeter St WC2 . . . . .120 C4
Exeter Way 2
SE14 . . . . .51 B3
Exford Ct SW11 . . . .167 C4
Exhibition Cl W12 . .30 B2
Exhibition Rd
SW7 . . . . .129 C2
Exmoor Ho 2 E3. .26 A3
Exmoor St W10 . . . . .30 C4
Exmouth Ho
Clerkenwell EC1 . . . . .95 C2
2 Millwall E14 . . . . . .42 A2
Exmouth Market
EC1 . . . . .95 C2
Exmouth Mews
NW1 . . . . .93 A3
Exmouth Pl E8 . . . . . .17 A1
Exmouth St E1 . . . . . .32 B3
Exonbury NW8 . . . . . .78 B3
Exon St SE17 . . . . . .152 A3
Explorers Ct 6
E14 . . . . .34 C2
Express Wharf 10
E14 . . . . .41 C4
Exton St SE1 . . . . . .121 B1
Eynella Rd SE21 . . . .76 B4
Eynham Rd W12 . . . . .30 B3
Eynsford Coll W1 . . .105 B2
Eynsford Ho
Borough The SE1 . . .137 B4
12 Deptford SE15 . . .50 B4
Walworth SE17 . . . . .152 A3
Eyot Gdns W6 . . . . . .38 B1
Eyot Gn W4 . . . . .38 B1
Eyre Ct NW8 . . . . . . .79 B2
Eyre St Hill EC1 . . . .95 B1
Eythorne Rd SW9 . . .173 C3
Ezra St E2 . . . .24 B2 99 A4

F

Fabian Rd SW6 . . . . .155 A2
Fabyc Ho TW9 . . . . . .44 C3
Fairacres SW15 . . . . .56 C3
Fairbairn Gn 1
SW9 . . . . .48 A2
Fairbourne Ho 10
SW4 . . . . .61 C1
Fairbriar Residence
SW7 . . . . .143 A4
Fairbridge Rd N19 . . .4 C2
Fairburn Ct SW15 . . .58 A2
Fairburn Ho
8 Stamford Hill
N16 . . . . .7 A3
West Kensington
SW5 . . . . .141 A1
Fairby Ho SE1 . . . . .153 A4
Faircharm Trad Est
SE8 . . . . .52 A3
Fairchild Cl 6
SW11 . . . . .167 C1
Fairchild Ho
13 Hackney E9 . . . . . .17 B1
Pimlico SW1 . . . . . . .147 A3
5 Shoreditch
N1 . . . . .24 A2 98 A4
Fairchild Pl
EC2 . . . . .24 A1 98 B1
Fairchild St
EC2 . . . . .24 A1 98 B1

Fairclough St E1 . . .111 C1
Faircourt 10 NW3 . . .12 B2
Faircroft N16 . . . . .6 C3
Fairdale Gdns
SW15 . . . . .57 A3
Fairdene Ct N7 . . . . .14 A3
Fairfax Ho
1 Brixton SW9 . . . . .173 C1
4 Putney SW15 . . . .56 C2
Fairfax Mews
W4 . . . . .37 C1
Fairfax Pl
Kensington W14 . . . .126 B1
South Hampstead
NW6 . . . . .11 B1
Fairfax Rd
Acton W4 . . . . .38 A3
South Hampstead
NW6 . . . . .11 B1
Fairfield
Camden Town
NW1 . . . . .82 C3
4 Stepney E1 . . . . . .32 B4
Fairfield Ct
Harlesden NW10 . . . .21 C4
1 London SW18 . . . .59 A2
Fairfield Dr SW18 . . .59 A2
Fairfield Rd E3 . . . . .26 C3
Fairfield St SW18 . . .59 A2
Fairfoot Rd E3 . . . . .26 C1
Fairford Ho SE11 . . .149 C3
Fairhazel Gdns
NW6 . . . . .11 B1
Fairheathe SW15 . . .57 C1
Fairholme Rd
W14 . . . . .140 B1
Fairholt Cl N16 . . . . . .7 A3
Fairholt Rd N16 . . . . .6 C3
Fairholt St SW7 . . . .130 B2
Fairhurst 3 NW6 . . . .11 A3
Fairlawn Ave W4 . . . .37 B2
Fairlawn Ct 3 W4 . . .37 B2
Fairlawn Gr W4 . . . . .37 B2
Fairlawn Mans
SE14 . . . . .50 C2
Fairlawns SW15 . . . . .57 C2
Fairlead Ho 6
E14 . . . . .41 C3
Fairley House Sch
SW1 . . . . .147 C2
Fairlie Ct
1 Bromley E3 . . . . . .27 A2
13 Tufnell Pk N7 . . . .13 C4
Fairlight Ave
NW10 . . . . .21 A3
Fairlight Ct 4
NW10 . . . . .21 A3
Fairlop Pl NW8 . . . . . .89 C3
Fairmead Ho E9 . . . .18 A4
Fairmead Rd N7 . . . .5 B1
N19 . . . . .5 A1
Fairmont Ave E14 . . .34 C1
Fairmont Ho 1
E3 . . . . .26 C1
Fairmont Rd
SW2 . . . . .62 B1
Fair St SE1 . . .138 C4
Fairstead Wlk N1 . . .86 C4
Fairthorn Rd SE7 . . . .
SE10 . . . . .43 C1
Fairview Ho 14
SW2 . . . . .74 B4
Fairview Pl SW2 . . . .74 B4
Fairwall Ho 9
SE5 . . . . .49 A2
Fairway Cl NW11 . . . .2 B4

Fairway Ct 13
SE16 . . . . .40 C4
Fairway The W3 . . . . .29 A3
Fairweather Ho
N7 . . . . .14 A4
Faith Ct NW2 . . . . .9 A2
Faithfull Ho N5 . . . . .15 B3
Fakruddin St
E1 . . . . .24 C1 99 C1
Falconberg Ct
W1 . . . . .105 C2
Falconberg Mews
W1 . . . . .105 C2
Falconbrook Prim Sch
20 SW11 . . . . .59 C4
Falcon Cl
Chiswick W4 . . . . .45 B4
Lambeth SE1 . . . . . .122 B2
Falcon Ct
8 Dulwich SE21 . . . . .75 C2
Holborn EC4 . . . . . . .107 B1
Islington N1 . . . . .86 B1
Falconer Wlk 12 N7 . .5 B2
Falcon Ho 6 SE15 . . .49 B2
Falcon La SW11 . . . . .60 A4
Falcon Lo
W Paddington
W9 . . . . .31 C4
West Hampstead
NW3 . . . . .11 A4
Falcon Pk Ind Est
NW10 . . . . .8 A3
Falcon Point SE1 . . .122 B3
Falcon Rd SW11 . . . . .60 A4
Falcons Pre-Prep Sch
for Boys The 7
W4 . . . . .45 A4
Falcons Prep Sch for
Boys The TW9 . . . . .54 A3
Falcon Terr SW11 . . . .60 A4
Falcon Way E14 . . . . .42 A2
Falconwood Ct
SE3 . . . . .53 B1
Falkener Ct SW11 . . .169 C3
Falkirk Ct 11 SE16 . . .32 C1
Falkirk Ho W9 . . . . . .88 B4
Falkirk St N1 . . . . . . .24 A3
Falkland Ho
Kensington W8 . . . . .128 A1
West Kensington
W14 . . . . .140 C2
Falkland Pl 2
NW5 . . . . .13 B3
Falkland Rd NW5 . . .13 B3
Fallodon Ho
6 London SW8 . . . . .171 C2
Paddington W11 . . . .31 B4
Fallow Ct 20 SE16 . .153 C1
Fallowfield N4 . . . . . . .5 B2
Falmouth Ho
Bayswater W2 . . . . . .116 A4
Kennington SE11 . . . .149 C2
Falmouth Rd SE1 . . .137 A1
Falmouth St E15 . . . .19 C3
Falstaff Ct SE11 . . . .150 A3
Falstaff Ho 18 N1 . . .24 A3
Fane St W14 . . . . . . .155 A4
Fan Mus The SE10 . .52 B3
Fann St EC1 . . . . .97 A1
Fanshaw St
N1 . . . . .24 A2 98 A4
Fanthorpe St
SW15 . . . . .57 B4

Faraday Cl N7 . . . . . .14 B2
Faraday Ho
2 Balham SW12 . . . .73 A4
6 Gospel Oak
NW5 . . . . .13 A4
Kensal Town W10 . . . .31 A4
6 Poplar E14 . . . . . .33 B2
Faraday Rd
Acton W3 . . . . .28 B2
Kensal Town W10 . . . .31 A4
Faraday Sch 1
E14 . . . . .35 A2
Fareham Ho 13
SW15 . . . . .68 C3
Fareham St W1 . . . . .105 B2
Farjeon Ho NW6 . . . . .11 C1
Farleigh Pl N16 . . . . .16 B4
Farleigh Rd N16 . . . .16 B4
Farley Ct
Kensington W14 . . . .126 C2
Marylebone NW1 . . . .91 B1
Farlington Pl
SW15 . . . . .69 A4
Farlow Rd SW15 . . . .57 C4
Farlton Rd SW18 . . . .71 A4
Farm Ave NW2 . . . . . .1 B1
Farm Cl SW6 . . . . . .155 C2
Farmdale Rd SE10 . .43 C1
Farmer Ho 4
SE16 . . . . .40 A3
Farmers Mkt 18
W8 . . . . .31 C1 113 C2
Farmers Rd SE5 . . . .48 A3
Farmer St
W8 . . . . .31 C1 113 B2
Farm La Trad Ctr
SW6 . . . . .155 C3
Farmleigh Ho
SW9 . . . . .63 A2
Farm Pl
W8 . . . . .31 C1 113 B2
Farm Rd NW10 . . . . .20 C4
Farm St W1 . . . . . . .118 A3
Farnaby Ho 2
W10 . . . . .23 B2
Farnborough Ho 1
SW15 . . . . .68 C3
Farncombe St
SE16 . . . . .139 C3
Farndale Ho 3
NW6 . . . . .78 A4
Farnell Mews
SW5 . . . . .142 A2
Farnell Pl W3 . . . . . .28 A2
Farnfield Ho 12
SW2 . . . . .74 C4
Farnham Ct 2 N16 . .7 A3
Farnham Ho
Borough The SE1 . . .122 C1
Marylebone NW1 . . . .90 B1
Farnham Pl SE1 . . . .122 B1
Farnham Royal
SE11 . . . . .149 A1
Farnhurst Ho 4
SW11 . . . . .169 B2
Farningham Ho 4
N4 . . . . .6 C4
Farnley Ho 13
SW8 . . . . .171 B2
Farnsworth Ct
SE10 . . . . .43 B3
Farnworth Ho 5
E14 . . . . .42 C2
Faroe Rd W14 . . . . . .39 C3
Farquhar Rd SW19 . .70 C1

Farrance St E14 . . . .33 C3
Farrant Ho 14
SW11 . . . . .59 C4
Farrell Ho E1 . . . . . . .32 B3
Farrer Ho SE8 . . . . . .51 C3
Farriers Mews
SE15 . . . . .65 B4
Farrier St NW1 . . . . . .13 B1
Farrier Wlk SW10 . . .156 C4
Farringdon La EC1 . . .95 C1
Farringdon Rd EC1 . .95 C1
Farringdon St
EC4 . . . . .108 A2
Farringdon Sta
EC1 . . . . .108 A4
Farrins Rents
SE16 . . . . .33 A1
Farrow La SE14 . . . . .50 B3
Farrow Pl SE16 . . . . .41 A3
Farthingale Wlk
E15 . . . . .19 C1
Farthing Alley 5
SE1 . . . . .139 B3
Farthing Fields 8
E1 . . . . .32 A1
Fashion Retail Acad
The W1 . . . . .105 B2
Fashion St E1 . . . . . .111 A3
Fashion & Textile Mus
SE1 . . . . .138 A4
Fassett Rd E8 . . . . . .16 C2
Fassett Sq E8 . . . . . .16 C2
Fauconberg Ct
W4 . . . . .45 B4
Fauconberg Rd
W4 . . . . .45 B4
Faulkner Ho SW15 . .47 B1
Faulkner's Alley
EC1 . . . . .108 A4
Faulkner St SE14 . . .50 B2
Faunce Ho 1
SE17 . . . . .48 A4
Faunce St SE17 . . . .150 A1
Favart Rd SW6 . . . . .165 C4
Faversham Ho
Camden Town
NW1 . . . . .83 A3
Walworth SE17 . . . . .152 A1
Fawcett Cl SW11 . .167 C1
Fawcett Est E5 . . . . . .7 C3
Fawcett Ho 25
SW9 . . . . .172 B2
Fawcett Rd NW10 . . . .8 B1
Fawcett St SW10 . . .156 C4
Fawe Park Rd
SW15 . . . . .58 B3
Fawe St E14 . . . . .34 A4
Fawkham Ho SE1 . . .153 A3
Fawley Ct SE27 . . . . .75 A2
Fawley Lo 2 E14 . . . .42 C2
Fawley Rd NW6 . . . . .11 A3
Fawnbrake Ave
SE24 . . . . .63 B2
Fayetville Ho 26
N19 . . . . .4 C4
Faygate Rd SW2 . . . .74 B2
Fazerley Ct 43 W2 . .31 C4
Fearnley Ho SE5 . . . .49 A1
Fearon St SE10 . . . . .43 C1
Feathers Pl SE10 . . .52 C4
Featherstone St
EC1 . . . . .97 B2
Featley Rd SW9 . . . . .63 A4

Felbridge Ho **21**
SE22 . . . . .64 A4
Felday Rd SE13 . . . . . .67 A1
Felden St SW6 . . . . .164 C3
Felgate Mews **4**
W6 . . . . .39 A2
Felix St E2 . . . . .25 A3
Felixstowe Rd
NW10 . . . . .22 A2
Fellbrigg Rd SE22 . . . .64 B2
Fellbrigg St E1 . . . . . . .25 A1
Fell Ho **11** N19 . . . . . .4 B1
Fellows Ct E2 . . . . .24 A3
Fellows Rd NW3 . . . . .12 A1
Fells Haugh **6**
W3 . . . . .28 B3
Felltram Way SE7 . . . .43 C1
Felmersham Cl **2**
SW4 . . . . .61 C3
Felsberg Rd SW2 . . . .74 A4
Felsham Ho **5**
SW15 . . . . .57 C4
Felsham Mews **14**
SW15 . . . . .57 C4
Felsham Rd SW15 . . . .57 C4
Felstead St E9 . . . . . . .18 B2
Felstead Wharf
E14 . . . . .42 B1
Felton Ho N1 . . . . .87 C3
Felton St N1 . . . . .87 C3
Fenchurch Ave
EC3 . . . . .110 A1
Fenchurch Bldgs **7**
EC3 . . . . .110 B1
Fenchurch Pl EC3 **2** . .124 B4
Fenchurch St EC3 . . .124 B4
Fenchurch Street Sta
EC3 . . . . .124 B4
Fen Ct EC3 . . . . .124 A4
Fendall St SE1 . . . . . .138 B1
Fenn St E9 . . . . .17 B3
Fen St E16 . . . . .35 B2
Fenstanton **3** N4 . . . . .5 B3
Fenstanton Prim Sch
20 SW2 . . . . .74 B3
Fentiman Rd SW8 . . .162 C2
Fenton Cl
16 Dalston E8 . . . . . .16 B2
South Lambeth
SW9 . . . . .172 C1
Fenton Ho SE14 . . . . .51 A4
Fenton House NW3 . . .2 B1
Fentons SE3 . . . . .53 B3
Fenton St E1 . . . . .32 A3
Fenwick Gr SE15 . . . .64 C4
Fenwick Pl SW9 . . . . .62 A4
Fenwick Rd SE15 . . . .64 C4
Ferdinand Ho **1**
NW1 . . . . .13 A1
Ferdinand Pl NW1 . . . .12 C1
Ferdinand St NW1 . . . .12 C1
Ferguson Dr W3 . . . . .28 C3

Ferguson Ho SE10 . . .52 B2
Ferguson's Cl E14 . . . .41 C2
Fergus Rd N5 . . . . .15 A3
Fermain Ct E N1 . . . . .24 A4
Fermain Ct N N1 . . . . .24 A4
Fermain Ct W N1 . . . . .24 A4
Fermoy Rd W9 . . . . . . .23 B1
Fernbank Mews
SW12 . . . . .61 B1
Fern Cl **3** N1 . . . . .24 A3
Ferncliff Rd E8 . . . . . . .16 C3
Ferncroft Ave
NW3 . . . . .10 C4
Fern Ct SE14 . . . . .50 C1
Ferndale Com Sp Ctr
SW9 . . . . .62 B3
Ferndale Ct **3**
SE3 . . . . .53 B3
Ferndale Ho N16 . . . . . .6 C3
Ferndale Rd SW4,
SW9 . . . . .62 B3
Ferndene Rd SE24 . . .63 B3
Ferndown Lo **17**
E14 . . . . .42 B3
Fernhead Rd W9 . . . . .23 B2
Fernholme Rd
SE15 . . . . .65 C2
Fernhurst Rd
SW6 . . . . .164 B4
Fernie Ho SE22 . . . . . .64 B4
Fernlea Rd SW12 . . . .73 A3
Fernleigh Cl W9 . . . . . .23 B2
Fernsbury St WC1 . . . .95 B3
Fernshaw Mans
SW10 . . . . .156 C3
Fernshaw Rd
SW10 . . . . .156 C3
Fernside NW11 . . . . . . .1 C3
Fernside Rd SW12 . . .72 C4
Fern St E3 . . . . .26 C1
Ferntower Rd N5 . . . . .15 C3
Fernwood SW19 . . . . . .70 B3
Ferrey Mews **18**
SW9 . . . . .173 C1
Ferriby Cl N1 . . . . .14 C1
Ferrier Ind Est
SW18 . . . . .59 A3
Ferrier Point **6**
E16 . . . . .35 C4
Ferrier St SW18 . . . . . .59 A3
Ferrings SE21 . . . . . . .76 A1
Ferrybridge Ho
SE11 . . . . .135 A1
Ferry La
Barnes SW13 . . . . . . .46 B4
Brentford TW8 . . . . . .44 A4
Richmond TW9 . . . . . .44 A4
Ferry Rd SW13 . . . . . .46 C2
Ferry Sq **1** TW8 . . . . .44 A4
Ferry St E14 . . . . .42 B1
Festing Rd SW15 . . . . .57 C4
Festival Ct **3** E8 . . . . .16 B1
Festival Pier SE1 . . . .121 A2
Fetter La EC4 . . . . . . .107 C2
Fettes Ho NW8 . . . . . .79 C1
Ffinch St SE8 . . . . .51 C3
Field Ct
Hampstead NW3 . . . . .11 B3
Holborn WC1 . . . . . . .107 A3
Lower Holloway N7 . . . .4 B4
Wimbledon SW19 . . . . .70 C1
Fieldgate Mans **5**
E1 . . . . .111 C3

Fieldgate St E1 . . . . . .111 C3
Field Ho NW10 . . . . . . .22 C2
Fieldhouse Rd
SW12 . . . . .73 B3
Fielding Ho
Chiswick W4 . . . . .46 A4
4 Kilburn NW6 . . . . .23 C2
St John's Wood
NW8 . . . . .78 C4
Fielding Mews
SW13 . . . . .47 A4
Fielding Rd
Acton W4 . . . . .38 A3
Hammersmith W14 . . .39 C3
Fielding St SE17 . . . . .48 B4
Field Lo NW10 . . . . .8 B2
Field Rd W6 . . . . .154 A4
Fields End E8 . . . . .17 C4
Field St WC1 . . . . .94 C4
Fieldsway Ho N5 . . . . .14 C3
Fieldview SW17,
SW18 . . . . .71 C3
Fieldview Ct **2**
N5 . . . . .15 A3
Fieldway Cres N5,
N7 . . . . .14 C3
Fieldwick Ho **14**
E9 . . . . .17 C2
Fife Rd
Mortlake SW14 . . . . . .55 B2
Newham E16 . . . . .35 C4
Fife Terr N1 . . . . .85 A2
Fifth Ave W10 . . . . .23 A2
Fig Tree Cl NW10 . . . .21 A4
Filey Ave N16 . . . . .7 C3
Filey Ho SW18 . . . . . . .59 B3
Filigree Ct SE16 . . . . .33 B1
Filmer Ho SW6 . . . . .164 B4
Filmer Mews
SW6 . . . . .164 B4
Filmer Rd SW6 . . . . .154 C1
Filton Ct **13** SE14 . . . .50 B3
Finborough Rd
SW10 . . . . .156 B4
Finchdean Ho
SW15 . . . . .68 B4
Finch La EC2, EC3 . . .109 C1
Finch Lo **8** W9 . . . . . .31 C4
Finchley Pl NW8 . . . . .79 B2
Finchley Rd
Hampstead NW3 . . . . .11 B2
St John's Wood
NW8 . . . . .79 B2
Finchley Road &
Frognal Sta NW3 . . . . .11 B3
Finchley Road Sta
NW3 . . . . .11 B2
Finch Lo **19** W9 . . . . .31 C4
Finch Mews **3**
SE15 . . . . .49 B2
Finch's Ct **10** E14 . . .34 A2
Findhorn St **8**
E14 . . . . .34 B3
Findon Cl SW18 . . . . .58 C1
Findon Rd W12 . . . . . .38 C4
Fine Arts Coll
NW3 . . . . .12 B2
Fineran Ct **18**
SW11 . . . . .59 C3
Fingal St SE10 . . . . . . .43 B1
Fingest Ho NW8 . . . . .90 A2
Finland Rd SE4 . . . . . .66 A4
Finland St SE16 . . . . . .41 A3
Finlay St SW6 . . . . . .47 C2
Finley Ct **23** SE5 . . . . .48 B3
Finley Ct **2** SE5 . . . . .48 B3
Finmere Ho **1** N4 . . . .6 B4

Finnemore Ho N1 . . . .86 C4
Finn Ho N1 . . . . .97 C4
Finnis St E2 . . . . .25 A1
FINSBURY 95 C4
Finsbury Ave EC2 . . .109 C3
Finsbury Cir EC2 . . . .109 C3
Finsbury Ct EC2 . . . .109 B3
Finsbury L Ctr EC1 . . .96 C3
Finsbury Market
EC2 . . . . .110 A4
Finsbury Mkt
EC2 . . . . .24 A1 98 A1
FINSBURY PARK 5 C2
Finsbury Park Rd N4,
N5 . . . . .6 A2
Finsbury Park Sta
N5 . . . . .5 C2
Finsbury Pavement
EC2 . . . . .109 C4
Finsbury Sq EC2 . . . .109 C4
Finsbury St EC2 . . . . .109 B4
Finsen Rd SE5 . . . . . . .63 B4
Finstock Rd W10 . . . . .30 C3
Finton House Sch
SW17 . . . . .72 B2
Finucane Ct TW9 . . . . .54 B4
Finwhale Ho E14 . . . . .42 A3
Fiona Ct **3** NW6 . . . . .23 B3
Firbank Rd SE15 . . . . .50 A1
Fircroft N1 . . . . .86 B4
Fircroft Prim Sch
SW17 . . . . .72 B1
Fircroft Rd SW17 . . . .72 B1
Fire Brigade Pier
SE1 . . . . .148 B4
Firecrest Dr NW3 . . . . .2 A1
Firle Ho **6** W10 . . . . .30 B4
Fir Lo SW15 . . . . .57 A3
Firmston Ho **9**
SW14 . . . . .55 C4
Firs Ave SW14 . . . . . . .55 B3
Firsby Rd N16 . . . . .7 C3
First Ave
East Acton W3 . . . . . . .29 B1
Mortlake SW14 . . . . . .56 A4
West Kilburn W10 . . . .23 B1
First St SW3 . . . . .144 B4
Firth Gdns SW6 . . . . .164 A3
Fir Tree Ho **11**
SE14 . . . . .50 B3
Fir Trees Cl SE16 . . . .33 A1
Fisher Cl SE16 . . . . . . .32 C1
Fisher Ho
Islington N1 . . . . .85 B3
2 Shadwell E1 . . . . .32 B2
2 Tufnell Pk N19 . . . .4 B1
Fishermans Dr
SE16 . . . . .40 C4
Fisherman's Wlk
E14 . . . . .33 C1
Fishers Cl SW16 . . . . .73 C1
Fishers Ct SE14 . . . . . .50 C2
Fisher's La W4 . . . . . . .37 C2
Fisher St
Holborn WC1 . . . . . . .106 C3
Newham E16 . . . . .35 C4
Fisherton St NW8 . . . .89 C2
Fisherton Street Est
NW8 . . . . .89 C1
Fishlock Ct **8**
SW4 . . . . .172 A2
Fish St Hill EC3 . . . . .123 C3
Fitch Ct SW2 . . . . .62 C2
Fitzalan St SE11 . . . .149 B4
Fitzclarence Ho
W11 . . . . .126 A4

Fitz-George Ave
W14 . . . . .140 A3
Fitzgerald Ave
SW14 . . . . .56 A4
Fitzgerald Ho
15 Brixton SW9 . . .173 B1
14 Poplar E14 . . . . .34 A3
Fitzgerald Rd
SW14 . . . . .55 C4
Fitzhardinge Ho
W1 . . . . .103 B2
Fitzhardinge St
W1 . . . . .103 B2
Fitzherbert Ho **11**
TW10 . . . . .54 B1
Fitzhugh Gr SW18 . . .59 C1
Fitzjames Ave
W14 . . . . .140 B3
Fitzjohn's Ave
NW3 . . . . .11 C3
Fitzjohns Mans
NW3 . . . . .11 B2
Fitzjohn's Prim Sch **4**
NW3 . . . . .11 C3
Fitzmaurice Ho **17**
SE16 . . . . .40 A2
Fitzmaurice Pl
W1 . . . . .118 B2
Fitzneal St W12 . . . . . .29 B3
FITZROVIA 104 A4
Fitzroy Cl N6 . . . . .3 B3
Fitzroy Cres W4 . . . . . .45 C3
Fitzroy Ct W1 . . . . .93 A1
Fitzroy Ho
Bermondsey SE1 . . . .153 A2
17 Tower Hamlets
E14 . . . . .33 B3
Fitzroy Mews W1 . . . . .92 C1
Fitzroy Pk N6 . . . . .3 B3
Fitzroy Rd NW1 . . . . . .81 B4
Fitzroy Sq W1 . . . . . . .92 C1
Fitzroy St W1 . . . . .92 C1
Fitzroy Yd NW1 . . . . . .81 B4
Fitzwarren Gdns
N19 . . . . .4 B3
Fitzwilliam Ave
TW9 . . . . .44 B1
Fitzwilliam Mews
E16 . . . . .35 C1
Fitzwilliam Rd
SW4 . . . . .61 B4
Fives Ct SE11 . . . . . . .136 A1
Fiveways Rd SW9 . . .173 C1
Flamborough Ho **12**
SE15 . . . . .49 C2
Flamborough St
E14 . . . . .33 A3
Flamingo Ct **2**
SE8 . . . . .51 C3
Flamsteed Ct **19**
SE13 . . . . .52 A2
Flamsteed Ho
SE10 . . . . .52 C3
Flanchford Rd
W12 . . . . .38 B3
Flanders Ho N16 . . . . . .7 A1
Flanders Mans **1**
W4 . . . . .38 B2
Flanders Rd W4 . . . . . .38 A2
Flanders Way E9 . . . . .17 C2
Flank St E1 . . . . .125 B4
Flansham Ho **2**
E14 . . . . .33 B3
Flask Cotts **4**
NW3 . . . . .11 C4
Flask Wlk NW3 . . . . . .11 C4

Flatiron Sq SE1.... **123** A1
Flatiron Yd SE1.... **123** A1
Flavell Mews SE10 . .43 A1
Flaxman Ct N1.... **105** B1
Flaxman Ho
🔟 Chiswick W4...... .38 A1
Newington SE1.... **136** B2
Flaxman Rd SE5....48 A1
Flaxman Sp Ctr
.... .48 B1
Flaxman Terr WC1 . .93 C3
Flecker Ho 🔟 SE5 . .48 C3
Fleece Wlk N7 ..... .14 A2
Fleet Ct W9......... .88 C3
Fleetfield WC1 .... **94** B4
Fleet Ho
🔟 Brixton SW2.... .62 C2
🛆 Limehouse E14 . .33 A2
Fleet Pl EC4...... **108** A2
Fleet Prim Sch 🔟
NW3............... .12 B3
Fleet Rd NW3 ..... .12 B2
Fleet St Hill E1 ....24 C1
Fleet Sq WC1...... **95** A3
Fleet St EC4...... **107** C1
Fleet Street Hill 🔟
E1............ .24 C1 **99** B1
Fleetway WC1 .... **94** B4
Fleet Wood 🔟 N16 . .7 B2
Fleetwood Rd
.... .8 C3
Fleetwood St N16 . . .7 A2
Fleming Cl 🛆 W9 . .23 C1
Fleming Ct W2.... **101** B4
Fleming Ho
🔟 Bermondsey
SE16............. **139** B3
Finsbury Pk N4..... .6 B3
Fleming Rd SE17...48 A4
Fletcher Bldgs
WC2............. **106** B1
Fletcher Ct 🛆
NW5............... .13 A4
Fletcher Ho 🔟
N16............... .16 A4
Fletcher Path 🛆
SE8............... .51 C3
Fletcher Rd W4.....37 B3
Fletcher St 🔟 E1...125 C4
Fleur De Lis St
.... .24 B1 **98** C1
Fleur Gates 🛆
SW19.............. .69 C4
Flinders Ho 🔟 E1 . .125 C2
Flinton St SE17.... **152** B2
Flint St SE17 ..... **151** C3
Flitcroft St WC2 . .105 C1
Flitton Ho 🔟 N1....15 A1
Flock Mill Pl
SW18.............. .71 A3
Flodden Rd SE5....48 B2
Flood St SW3.....158 B4
Flood Wlk SW3... **158** B4
Flora Cl E14........34 A3
Flora Gardens Prim
Sch 🔟 W6......... .39 A2
Flora Gdns 🛆 W6 . .39 A2
Floral St WC2.... **120** A4
Florence Gdns W4 . .45 B4
Florence Ho
🟦 Bermondsey
SE16............. .40 A1
🛆 Brixton SW2 ... .62 B2
🔟 Shepherd's Bush
W11.............. .30 C2

Florence Ho continued
🞄 Wandsworth
SW18............. .59 C3
Florence Mans
SW6............. **164** C4
Florence Nightingale
Ho 🛆 N1......... .15 B2
Florence Nightingale
Mus SE1......... **135** A3
Florence Rd
Acton W4......... .37 C3
Finsbury Pk N4 .... .5 C4
New Cross Gate
SE14............. .51 B2
Florence St N1......15 A1
Florence Terr
Kingston u T
SW15............. .68 A1
New Cross Gate
SE14............. .51 B2
Florence Way
SW12.............. .72 B3
Flores Ho 🔟 E1.....32 C4
Florfield Rd E8......17 A2
Florian SE5.........49 A2
Florian Rd SW15...58 A3
Florida St
E2............ .24 C2 **99** C3
Florida State Univ
WC1............. **105** C3
Florin Ct S E1.... **138** C3
Floris Pl 🔟 SW4...61 B4
Florys Ct 🛆 SW19 . .70 A3
Floss St SW15......57 B4
Flower & Dean Wlk
E1............... **111** A3
Flowersmead
SW17............. .72 C2
Flowers Mews 🛆
N19.............. .4 B2
Flower Wlk The
SW7.............. **129** A4
Floyer Cl T W10...54 B2
Flynn Ct 🞄 E14.....33 C2
Foley Ho 🔟 E1.....32 B3
Foley St W1...... **104** C3
Folgate St E1.... **110** C4
Foliot Ho N1..... **84** C2
Foliot St W12.......29 B3
Follett Ho SW10 . . **157** B2
Follett St E14......34 B3
Folly Wall E14.......42 B4
Fonda Ct 🛆 E14 ....33 C2
Fontarabia Rd
SW11............. .60 C3
Fontenelle SE5.....49 A2
Fontenoy Ho
SE11............. **150** A3
Fontenoy Rd SW12,
SW17............. .73 B2
Fonthill Ho
Kensington W14 . .126 B2
Pimlico SW1..... **146** B2
Fonthill Mews N4 ...5 B2
Fonthill Rd N4 ..... .5 C2
Fontley Way SW15 . .68 C4
Footpath The
SW15............. .56 C2
Forber Ho 🛆 E2.... **25** B2
Forbes Ho 🞄 W4...36 C1
Forbes St E1..... **111** C1
Forburg Rd N16 .... .7 C3
Ford Cl 🞄 E3.......26 A3
Fordcombe 🔟
NW5............. .12 C2

Fordham Ho 🔟
SE14............. .51 A3
Fordham St 🔟 E1 . .111 C2
Fordingley Rd W9 . .23 B2
Ford Rd E3..........26 B3
Fords Park Rd E16 . .35 C3
Ford Sq E1..........32 A4
Ford St
Bow E3............ .26 A3
Canning Town E16 . .35 B3
Fordwych Ct NW2...10 A2
Fordwych Rd NW2 . .10 A3
Fordyce Rd SE13 . . .67 B2
Forecastle Ct E14 . .41 C4
Foreign &
Commonwealth
Office SW1..... **134** A4
Foreland Ho
W11............. .31 A2 **112** A4
Foreshore SE8......41 B2
Fore St EC2...... **109** A3
Forest Ct Cl NW6.... .1 C2
Forester Rd SE15...65 A4
Forest Gr E8.......16 B2
Forest Hill Rd
SE22............. .65 A1
Forest Rd
Dalston E8......16 B2
Richmond TW9 ....44 C3
Fore Street Ave
EC2............. **109** B3
Forest Way 🔟 N19...4 B2
Forfar Rd SW11 . .169 C4
Forge Pl NW1......12 C2
Forman Ho SE4....65 C3
Forman Pl 🔟 N16...16 B4
Formby Ct 🛆 N7...14 C3
Formosa Ho E1.....26 A1
Formosa St W9.....88 B1
Forrest Ct N7......14 C2
Forrest Ho SW15 . .47 B1
Forset Ct W1..... **102** B2
Forset St W1..... **102** B2
Forster Rd SW2....74 A4
Forston St N1..... **87** A2
Forsyth Gdns SE17 . .48 A4
Forsyth Ho
🞄 Hackney E9..... .17 B1
Pimlico SW1..... **147** A3
Forsythia Ho SE4...66 A4
Fortescue Ave 🔟
E8............... .17 A1
Fortess Gr NW5....13 B3
Fortess Rd NW5....13 B4
Fortess Wlk NW5 . .13 A3
Fortess Yd 🔟
NW5............. .13 A4
Forthbridge Rd
SW11............. .60 C3
Forth Ho 🔟 E3.....26 B3
Forties The 🟠
NW5............. .13 B3
Fortior Ct N6........4 B4
Fortnam Rd N19......4 C2
Fort Rd SE1..... **153** A3
Fortrose Cl E14......34 C3
Fortrose Gdns SW2,
SW12............. .74 A3
Fort St E1........ **110** B3
Fortuna Cl N7......14 B2
Fortune Ct 🟦 E8 . .16 B1
Fortune Gate Rd
NW10............. .21 A4
Fortune Green Rd
NW6............. .10 C4

Fortune Ho
Lambeth SE11 .... **149** B3
St Luke's EC1..... **97** A1
Fortune St EC1.... **97** A1
Fortune Way
NW10............. .21 C2
Forty Acre La E16 . .35 C4
Forum Cl 🔟 E3.....26 C4
Forward Bsns Ctr The
🛆 E16............ .27 C1
Fosbrooke Ho
SW8............. **162** A1
Fosbury Ho 🔟
SW9.............. .62 B3
Fosbury Mews
W2............. **114** B3
Foscote Mews W9 . .31 C4
Foskett Rd SW6 . .165 A1
Fossil Rd SE13......66 C4
Foster Ct
🛆 Camden Town
NW1............. .13 B1
Canning Town E16 . .35 B2
Foster Ho SE14....51 B2
Foster La EC2.... **108** C2
Foster Rd
Acton W3.......... .29 A2
Chiswick W4....... .37 C1
Foubert's Pl W1 . .104 C1
Foulden Rd N16....16 B4
Foulden Terr N16 . .16 B4
Foulis Terr SW7 . .143 C2
Foundary Ho 🔟
E14............. .34 A4
Founders Ct EC2 . .109 B2
Founders Ho SW1 . .147 B2
Foundling Ct WC1 . .94 A3
Foundling Mus The
.... .94 B2
Foundry Bsns Ctr The
SE1............. **136** A3
Foundry Cl SE16 . .33 A1
Foundry Mews
NW1............. **93** A2
Foundry Pl
Stepney E1........ .32 B4
Wandsworth SW18 . .71 A4
Fountain & Colonnade
Sh Ctr SW1..... **146** A3
Fountain Ct
Belgravia SW1 .... **146** A3
🛆 Shepherd's Bush
W11.............. .39 C4
Strand EC4..... **121** B4
Fountain Green Sq 🞄 SE16............. .139 C3
Fountain Ho
🞄 Bermondsey
SE16............. **139** C3
🛆 Brondesbury Pk
NW6............. .10 A1
Mayfair W1...... **117** C2
Fountain Mews
🟠 Highbury N5 ... .15 B4
Maitland Pk NW3 . .12 B2
Fountain PI SW9 . .173 C3
Fountayne Rd N16 . .7 C2
Fount St SW8.... **161** C1
Fournier St E1.... **111** A4
Fourscore Mans
E8............... .16 B1
Four Seasons Cl
E3............... .26 C3
Fourth Ave W10 .....23 A2
Fovant Ct 🟦 SW8 . .170 C1

Fowey Cl E1.........32 A1
Fowey Ho SE11 . .149 C2
Fowler Cl SW11 ....59 C4
Fowler Ho
🟦 Camberwell
.... .49 A1
Islington N1....... .86 B4
South Lambeth
SW8............. **171** C3
Fowler Rd N1...... .86 B4
Fownes St SW11...60 A4
Fox and Knot St
EC1............. **108** B4
Foxberry Ct SE4....66 B3
Foxberry Rd SE4....66 A4
Foxborough Gdns
SE4.............. .66 C2
Foxbourne Rd
SW17............. .72 C2
Fox Cl
Bethnal Green E1 . .25 B1
🛆 E16............ .35 C4
Foxcombe SE6
SW15............. .68 C3
Foxcote SE5..... **152** B1
Foxcroft WC1..... **85** A1
Foxfield NW1...... .82 B3
Foxglove St W12 . .29 B2
Foxham Rd N19.....4 C1
Fox Ho 🛆 SW11 ....59 C3
Foxley Cl E8.......16 C3
Foxley Ho 🛆 E3 . .27 A2
Foxley Rd SW9 .....48 A3
Foxley Sq 🔟 SW9 . .48 A2
Foxmore St SW11 . .168 C3
Fox Prim Sch
.... .31 C1 **113** B1
Fox's Ho E16.......35 B4
Fox's Yd E2...24 B1 **99** A2
Foxwell Mews SE4 . .66 A4
Foxwell St SE4.....66 A4
Foyle Rd SE3......53 B4
Fradel Lo N16...... .6 C2
Framfield Rd N5.....15 A3
Frampton NW1.... .13 C1
Frampton Ct 🟦
W3............... .37 B4
Frampton Ho NW8. .89 C1
Frampton Park Rd
E9............... .17 B2
Frampton St NW8 . .89 C1
Francemary Rd
SW17............. .72 B2
Franche Court Rd
SW17............. .71 B1
Francis Chichester
Way SW11..... **169** C3
Francis Cl 🛆 E14...42 B2
Francis Ct 🔟 SE14 . .50 C4
Francis Ho
Harlesden NW10 . .21 B4
🟦 Shoreditch N1...24 A4
Walham Green
SW10............. **156** B2
Francis Holland Sch
Belgravia SW1 .... **145** C3
Marylebone NW1 . .90 C2
Francis Snary Lo 🔟
SW18............. **147** A4
Francis Terr N19.... .4 B1
Francis Terrace Mews
🔟 N19............ .4 B1

Francis Wlk N1..... **84** C4
Franconia Rd SW4..**61** C2
Frank Barnes Sch
N1.................... **83** C3
Frank Beswick Ho
SW6................. **155** A3
Frank Dixon Cl
SE21............... .76 A3
Frank Dixon Way
SE21............... .76 A3
Frankfurt Rd SE24..**63** B2
Frankham Ho **5**
SE8................. .51 C3
Frankham St SE8...51 C3
Frank Ho SW8.....**162** A2
Frankland Cl SE16..40 A2
Frankland Ho **4**
SW12............... .73 A4
Frankland Rd
SW7................ **129** B1
Franklin Bldg **5**
E14................. .41 C4
Franklin Cl
Greenwich SE13.....52 A2
West Norwood
SE27............... .75 A1
Franklin Ho
New Cross SE4......51 A1
28 Wapping E1......32 A1
Franklin Pl SE13....52 A2
Franklin Sq SW5 ..**141** A1
Franklin's Row
SW3................ **145** A2
Franklin St **3** E3..27 A2
Franklyn Rd NW10...8 A2
Frank Rowers **2**
SE1................. .40 A2
Frank Soskice Ho
SW6................. **155** A3
Frank Whymark Ho **4**
SE16................ .40 B4
Frans Hals Ct E14 ..42 C3
Fraserburgh Ho **29**
E3................... .26 B3
Fraser Ct SW11...**168** A4
Fraser Ho
Brentford TW8..... .36 B1
40 Clapham SW8 ..**171** B1
Fraser Regnart Ct **12**
NW5................ .12 B3
Fraser St W4........38 A1
Frazier St SE1.....**135** B3
Frean St SE16......**139** B2
Frearson Ho W1...**226** C4
Freda Corbett Cl **10**
SE15............... .49 C3
Frederica St **4**
N7................. .14 B1
Frederick Bldg N1 ..16 A2
Frederick Charrington
Ho **4** E1.........25 B1
Frederick Cl W2 ..**116** C4
Frederick Cres
SW9................ .48 A3
Frederick Ct SW6..58 A4
Frederick Hugh House
Sch SW3............**158** A4
Frederick Rd SW9 ..48 A4
Frederick's Pl
EC2................ **109** B1
Frederick Sq **1**
SE16............... .33 A2
Frederick's Row
EC1................. .96 A4

Frederick St WC1... **94** C3
Frederick Terr E8...16 B1
Frederic Mews
SW1............... **131** B3
Freedom St SW11 **169** A2
Freegrove Rd N7...14 A3
Freeling Ho NW8 .. **79** B4
Freeling St
Barnsbury N1.......14 A1
1 London N1.......14 B1
Freeman Ho **3**
SW2................ .74 A4
Freemantle St
SE17............... **152** A2
Freemens Hos **1**
SW9................ .62 B3
Freight La NW1.....13 C1
Freightliners City
Farm **1** N7......14 C2
Freke Rd SW11.....60 C4
Fremantle Ho **14**
E1................... .25 A1
Fremont St E9......25 B4
French Inst The
SW7................ **143** B4
French Pl
E1.......**24** A1 **98** B2
Frendsbury Rd
SE4................. .66 A3
Frensham Ct N5...15 B3
Frensham Dr
SW15............... .68 C2
Frensham St SE15..49 C4
Frere St **1** SW11 .**168** B2
Freshfield Ave E8..16 B1
Freshfield Cl SE13..67 C3
Freshford St SW17,
SW18............... .71 B1
Preston Rd W10,
W11................ .30 C2
Freswick Ho **6**
SE8................. .41 A2
Freud Mus The
NW3................ .11 B2
Frewell Bldg EC1..**107** B4
Frewin Rd SW18...71 C3
Friar Mews SE27 ..75 A1
Priars Ave
Roehampton SW15..58 A2
Roehampton SW15..68 B1
Friars Cl SE1.....**122** B1
Friars Gdns W3....28 C3
Friars Mead E14...42 B3
Friars Place La
W3................. .28 C2
Friars Prim
Foundation Sch
SE1................ **136** B3
Friars Stile Pl **9**
TW10............... .54 A1
Friars Stile Rd
TW10............... .54 A1
Friar St EC4......**108** B1
Friars Way W3.....28 C3
Friary Park Ct **12**
W3................. .28 B3
Friary Rd
Acton W3...........28 B3
Peckham SE15.....49 C3
Friday Grove Mews **11**
SW12............... .73 B4
Fridewide Pl
NW5................ .13 B3
Friendly Pl **18**
SE13............... .52 A2

Friendly St SE8.....51 C2
Friendly Street Mews
SE8................. .51 C1
Friendship Way
E15................ .27 C4
Friend St EC1.......96 A4
Frigate Ho **7** E14 .42 B2
Frigate Mews SE8..51 C4
Frimley Cl SW19...70 A2
Frimley Way **1**
E1................... .25 C1
Frinstead Ho **1**
W10................ .30 C2
Friston St SW6 ..**166** A1
Frith Ho
Bethnal Green
E2.......**24** C2 **99** B3
Paddington NW8 .. **89** C1
Frith Rd E11........19 C4
Frith St W1........**105** B1
Frithville Ct **2**
W12................ .30 B1
Frithville Gdns
W12................ .30 B1
Frobisher Ct
1 Greenwich
SE10............... .52 C4
3 Shepherd's Bush
W12................ .39 B4
Frobisher Ho **27**
E1................... .32 A1
Frobisher Pas E14..34 A1
Frobisher Pl SE14..50 B2
Frobisher St SE10 .53 A4
Frogley Rd SE22...64 B3
Frogmore SW18....58 C2
Frogmore Est
N5................. .15 B2
Frogmore Ind Est
N5.......**15** B2 **86** C3
Frognal NW3.......11 B3
Frognal Cl NW3....11 B2
Frognal Ct NW3...11 B2
Frognal Gdns
NW3................ .11 B3
Frognal La NW3....11 A3
Frognal Par NW3...11 B2
Frognal Rise NW3 .11 B3
Frognal Way NW3 .11 B4
Frome Ho SE15....65 B3
Frome St N1.......86 C2
Fromow's Cnr **14**
W4................. .37 B1
Frontenac NW10....9 A1
Frostic Wlk E1 ..**111** A3
Froude St SW8 ..**170** B1
Frowd Cl SE1.....**126** B2
Frying Pan Alley
E1................. **110** C3
Fry Rd NW10........21 A4
Fulbeck Ho N7.....14 B2
Fulbourne St E1...32 A4
Fulbrook Rd N19 ..13 B4
Fulcher Ct **15** SE8..51 B4
Fulcher Ho
18 Deptford SE8 ..41 B1
5 Shoreditch N1....24 A4
Fulford Mans **3**
N4................. .21 A4
Fulford St SE16....40 A4
FULHAM..............47 C1
Fulham Broadway
SW6................ **155** C1
Fulham Broadway Sh
Ctr SW6............ **155**

Fulham Broadway Sta
SW6................ **155** C2
Fulham Bsns
Exchange SW6 ..**167** A3
Fulham College Boys'
Sch SW6........... **164** A4
Fulham Cross Girls'
Sch SW6........... **154** A1
Fulham Ct SW6....**165** B4
Fulham High St
SW6................ **164** B1
Fulham Pal (Mus) ..47 C1
Fulham Palace Rd SW6,
W6................. .47 C4
Fulham Park Gdns
SW6................ **164** C1
Fulham Park Rd
SW6................ **164** C2
Fulham Prep Sch
9 Fulham SW6 ..**164** B1
Fulham SW6....... **154** B4
Fulham Prim Sch
SW6................ **155** B3
Fulham Rd
Chelsea SW10 .. **157** A4
Fulham SW6....... **165** A4
Fuller Cl **4**
E2.......**24** C1 **99** B2
Fullers Ho **5**
SW18............... .58 C2
Fullerton Rd SW18 .59 B2
Fullwood's Mews
N1................. .97 C4
Fulmar Ct **5** SE21..75 C2
Fulmar Ho
12 Bermondsey
SE16............... .40 C2
Marylebone NW8 .. **90** B1
Fulmead St SW6 ..**166** B3
Fulneck **1** E1.....32 B4
Fulthorp Rd SE3...53 C1
Fulton Mews W2 ..**114** C4
Fulwood Pl WC1 ..**107** A3
Fulwood Wlk
SW19............... .70 A3
Furber St W6.......39 A3
Furley Ho **7** SE15..49 C3
Furley Rd SE15....49 C3
Furlong Rd N7.....14 C2
Furmage St SW18..71 A4
Furness Ho SW1 ..**146** A2
Furness Lo **4**
SW14............... .55 A3
Furness Prim Sch
NW10............... .21 C3
Furness Rd
Harlesden NW10 ..21 C3
Sands End SW6 ..**166** B2
Furnival St EC4 ..**107** B2
Furrow La E9........17 B3
Fursecroft W1.....**102** C2
Furze St E3.........33 C4
Fusion Ct SW15....68 A1
Futters Ct **3**
NW10............... .20 C3
Fyfield N4...........5 C2
Fyfield Rd **5** SW9 .62 C4
Fynes St SW1 ..**147** B4

G

Gable Ho **12** W4...38 A2
Gables Cl SE5......49 A2
Gables The
3 Clapham SW4 ..61 B4

Gables The *continued*
Hampstead NW3 ....2 C2
Gabriel Ho SE11 ..**148** C4
Gabrielle Ct NW3...11 C2
Gabriel Mews NW2 ..1 B2
Gabriel's Wharf
SE1................ **121** B2
Gaddesden Ho EC1 **97** C3
Gadsden Ho
6 Homerton E9....17 C2
8 Kensal Town
W10................ .23 A1
Gagarin Ho SW11 ..59 C4
Gage Rd E16.......35 A4
Gage St WC1.....**106** B4
Gainford Ho E2 ..**25** A2
Gainford St N1.....85 B4
Gainsborough Ct
6 Bermondsey
SE16............... .40 A1
Dulwich SE21......76 A2
Shepherd's Bush
W12................ .39 B4
Gainsborough Gdns
Golders Green
NW11.............. .1 B4
Hampstead NW3 ....2 C1
Gainsborough Ho
Finsbury Pk N4.....5 B3
8 Hampstead
NW3................ .11 B4
5 Limehouse E14 .33 A2
Westminster SW1 .**147** C3
Gainsborough Prim
Sch E9.............18 C2
Gainsborough Rd
Bedford Pk W4....38 B2
Richmond TW9.....54 B4
Gainsborough St **3**
E9................. .18 B2
Gainsborough Studios
N1................. .87 B3
Gainsfd St SE1 ..**139** A4
Gairloch Ho **2**
NW1................ .13 C1
Gairloch Rd SE5...49 A1
Gaisford St NW5...13 B2
Gaitskell Ct SW11 **168** A2
Gaitskell Ho SE17..**48** C4
Gaitskell Way SE1 **136** C4
Galata Rd SW13 ..46 C3
Galatea Sq SE15 ..65 A4
Galaxy Bldg **6**
E14................ .41 C2
Galaxy Ho EC2....**97** C2
Galbraith St E14 ..42 B3
Gale Ho **10** SW2..62 B2
Galena Ho **4** W6 .39 A2
Galena Rd W6.....39 A2
Galen Pl WC1.....**106** B3
Galesbury Rd
SW18............... .59 B1
Gales Gdns E2.....25 A2
Gale St E3..........33 C4
Galgate Cl **4**
SW19............... .70 A3
Galleon Cl SE16....40 C4
Galleon Ho **5** E14 .42 B2
Gallery Ct SW10 ..**156** C3
Gallery Rd SE21 ..75 C3
Gallery The
SE16............... .40 A2
Galleywall Rd
SE16............... .40 A2
Galleywall Road Trad
Est **2** SE16.......40 A2
Galleywood Ho **1**
W10................ .30 B4

Gallia Rd N5 . . . . . .15 A3
Galloway Rd W12. . . .29 C1
Galsworthy Ave
E14. . . . . .33 A4
Galsworthy Ct W3 . .37 B3
Galsworthy Ho 4
W11 . . . . .31 A3
Galsworthy Rd
NW2. . . . . .10 A4
Galton St W10. . . . . .23 A2
Galveston Ho 2
E1. . . . . .26 A1
Galveston Rd
SW15 . . . . .58 B2
Galway Cl 28 SE16. .40 A1
Galway Ho
Finsbury EC1 . . . . . .97 A3
7 Stepney E1 . . . . . .32 C4
Galway St EC1. . . . . .97 A3
Gambetta St 3
SW8 . . . . .170 B1
Gambia St SE1 . . . . 122 B1
Gambier Ho EC1. . . . .97 A3
Gamlen Rd SW15. . . .57 C3
Gandolfi St 5
SE15 . . . . .49 A4
Ganley Ct 18
SW11 . . . . .59 B4
Gannet Ct 6 SE21. .75 C2
Gannet Ho SE15. . . .49 B2
Ganton St W1 . . . . .105 A1
Garand Ct 2 N7. . . .14 B3
Garbett Ho 2
SE17. . . . . .48 A4
Garbutt Pl W1. . . . .103 C3
Garden Cl SW15 . . . .69 A4
Garden Ct
4 Richmond
TW9 . . . . .44 B2
12 South Acton W4 .37 B3
St John's Wood
NW8 . . . . .89 B4
Strand EC4 . . . . . . .121 B4
Garden Flats
SW16 . . . . .74 A1
Garden Ho 12
SW9 . . . . .172 B2
Garden House Sch
SW3 . . . . .145 A2
Garden La SW2 . . . . .74 B3
Garden Mews
W2 . . . . .31 C2 113 C3
Garden Mus SE1. . .134 C1
Garden Pl 28 E2 . . . .24 B4
Garden Rd
Richmond TW9 . . . . .54 C4
St John's Wood
NW8 . . . . .89 A4
Garden Row SE1 . . .136 A2
SW15 . . . . .57 C1
Garden Sch The
N16. . . . . .16 B4
Garden St E1. . . . . . .32 C4
Gardens The
East Dulwich
SE22 . . . . .64 C3
Stamford Hill N16. . . .7 B4
Garden Terr
Knightsbridge
SW7 . . . . .130 B3
Pimlico SW1. . . . . . .147 B2
Garden Wlk
EC2 . . . . .24 A1 98 A2
Gardiner Ave NW2. . .9 B3
Gardiner Ct NW10 . .20 C4

Gardiner Ho
SW11 . . . . .168 A4
Gardner Ct N5. . . . . .15 B4
Gardners La EC4 . . .122 C4
Gardnor Mans 14
NW3. . . . . .11 B4
Gardnor Rd NW3 . . . .11 C4
Gard St EC1 . . . . . . .96 B4
Gareth Ct SW16 . . . .73 C1
Garfield Ho W2. . . . .102 C1
Garfield Mews 7
SW11 . . . . .60 C4
Garfield Rd SW11. . . .60 C4
Garford St E14 . . . . .33 C2
Garland Cl SE1 . . . . 137 A1
Garland Ho 12 E14 . .33 C2
Garland Rd N16. . . . .65 A4
Garlands Ho NW8 . . .78 B2
Garlick Hill EC4 . . . .123 A4
Garlinge Ho 10
SW9 . . . . .173 B4
Garnault Mews
EC1 . . . . .95 C3
Garnault Pl EC1 . . . .95 C3
Garner St E2 . . . . . . .24 C3
Garnet Rd NW10. . . . .8 A2
Garnet St E1 . . . . . . .32 B2
Garnett Ho 3
NW3. . . . . .12 B3
Garnett Rd NW3 . . . .12 B3
Garnham Cl 2 N16. . .7 B2
Garnham St 1 N16. . .7 B2
Garnies Cl SE15 . . . .49 B3
Garrad's Rd SW16 . . .73 C1
Garrard Wlk NW10. . .8 A2
Garratt Ho 8 N16. . . .7 A3
Garratt La SW18. . . . .71 A3
Garratt Park Sch 6
SW18 . . . . .71 B2
Garraway Ct SW13 . .47 B3
Garraway Ho SE21. . .76 B1
Garrett Cl W3 . . . . . .28 C4
Garrett Ho 8 W12. . .30 A3
Garrett St EC1 . . . . . .97 A2
Garrick Cl SW18. . . . .59 B3
Garrick Ho
Chiswick W4. . . . . . .46 A4
Mayfair W1. . . . . . . .118 A1
Garrick Rd TW9 . . . . .44 C1
Garrick St WC2 . . . . 120 A4
Garrick Yd WC2. . . . .120 A4
Garsdale Terr
SW5 . . . . .141 A2
Garsington Mews
SE4 . . . . .66 B4
Garson Ho 2 W2 . . .115 B4
Garston Ho 6 N1. . . .15 A1
Garter Way SE16 . . . .40 C4
Garth Ct W4 . . . . . . .45 C4
Garth Ho NW2 . . . . . .1 B2
Garth Rd
Child's Hill NW2 . . . . .1 B2
8 Chiswick W4 . . . . .37 C1
Gartmoor Gdns
SW19 . . . . .70 B3
Garton Ho 6 N6. . . . .4 C4
Gartons Way SW11. . .59 B1
Gartons Way
SW11 . . . . .59 B4
Garway Rd W2 . . . .100 A1
Gascoigne Pl 17
E2 . . . . .24 B2 98 C3
Gascony Ave NW6 . .10 C1
Gascoyne Ho 2
E9 . . . . .17 C1

Gascoyne Rd E9. . . . .17 C1
Gaselee St E14. . . . . .34 B2
Gasholder Pl
SE11. . . . . .149 A1
Gaskarth Rd SW12. . .61 A1
Gaskell St SW4 . . . . 172 A2
Gaskin Ho N16 . . . . . .6 C1
Gaskin St N1. . . . . . . .86 A4
Gaspar Cl SW7. . . . . 142 B4
Gaspar Mews
SW5 . . . . .142 B4
Gasson Ho 24
SE14 . . . . .50 C4
Gastein Rd W6 . . . . .47 C4
Gastigny Ho EC1. . . . .97 A3
Gaston Bell Cl
TW9 . . . . .54 B4
Gaston Gate SW8 . .172 C4
Gataker Ho 5
SE16 . . . . .40 A3
Gataker St 6
SE16 . . . . .40 A3
Gatcliff Cl SW1. . . . .145 C1
Gatcombe Ho 20
SE22 . . . . .64 A4
Gatcombe Rd
8 Newham E16 . . . . .35 C1
Tufnell Pk N19 . . . . . .4 C1
Gatefield Ct SE15. . . .64 C4
Gateforth St NW8 . . .90 A1
Gate Hill Ct
W11 . . . . .31 B1 113 A2
Gatehouse Sch 28
E2 . . . . .25 C3
Gatehouse Sq
SE1 . . . . .123 A2
Gateley Ho 6 SE4. . .65 C3
Gateley Rd SW9 . . . .62 B4
Gate Mews SW7 . . . .130 B3
Gatesborough St
EC2 . . . . .24 A1 98 A2
Gates Ct SE17 . . . . .150 C2
Gatesden WC1. . . . . .94 B3
Gateside Rd SW17. . .72 B1
Gate St WC2 . . . . . . 106 C2
Gateway SE17 . . . . . .48 B4
Gateway Arc N1 . . . .86 A2
Gateway Ho SW12. . .61 A1
Gateway Ind Est
NW10 . . . . .21 C1
Gateway Mews 4
E8 . . . . .16 B3
Gateway Prim Sch
NW8 . . . . .89 C2
Gateways The
SW3 . . . . .144 B3
Gateway Trad Est
NW10 . . . . .21 B2
Gathorne St 12 E2. . .25 C3
Gatliff Rd SW1 . . . . .146 A1
Gatonby St SE15 . . . .49 C2
Gatwick Ho 3 E14 . .33 B3
Gatwick Rd SW18. . . .70 B4
Gauden Cl SW4 . . . . .61 C4
Gauden Rd SW4 . . . .61 C4
Gaugin Ct 13 SE16. . .40 A1
Gaunt St SE1 . . . . . .136 C2
Gautrey Rd SE15. . . .50 B1
Gavel St SE17 . . . . . .151 C1
Gaverick Mews 3
E14 . . . . .41 C2
Gaviller Pl 3 E5 . . . .17 A4
Gawber St E2 . . . . . .25 B2
Gawthorne Ct E3. . . .26 C3
Gay Cl NW2 . . . . .9 A3
Gaydon Ho W2 . . . .100 A4

Gayfere St SW1. . . . .134 A1
Gayford Rd W12. . . . .38 B4
Gay Ho N16 . . . . .16 A3
Gayhurst SE17. . . . . .48 C4
Gayhurst Ho NW8 . . .90 B2
Gayhurst Prim Sch 1
E8 . . . . .16 C1
Gayhurst Rd E8 . . . .16 C1
Gaymead NW8 . . . . .78 B3
Gay Rd E15. . . . . . . .27 C3
Gaysley Ho SE11. . . 149 B3
Gay St SW15 . . . . . . .57 C4
Gayton Cres NW3. . . .11 C4
Gayton Ho E3 . . . . . .26 C1
Gayton Rd NW3 . . . .11 C4
Gayville Rd SW11. . . .60 B1
Gaywood Cl SW2 . . .74 C3
Gaywood St SE1 . . . 136 B1
Gaza St SE17 . . . . . .150 A1
Gaze Ho 11 E14 . . . .34 C3
Gean Ct 8 E11 . . . . .19 C4
Geary Ho N7 . . . . . . .14 B3
Geary Rd NW10 . . . . .8 C3
Geary St N7 . . . . . . .14 B3
Gedling Ho SE22 . . . .64 B4
Gedling Pl SE1 . . . . 139 A2
Gees Ct W1 . . . . . . .103 C1
Gee St EC1 . . . . .96 C2
Geffrye Ct N1 . . . . . .24 A3
Geffrye Mus 22 E2. . .24 B3
Geffrye St E2 . . . . . .24 B3
Geldart Rd SE15. . . . .50 A3
Geldeston Rd E5 . . . . .7 C2
Gellatly Rd SE14. . . . .50 C1
Gemini Bsns Ctr
E16 . . . . .27 C1
Gemini Ho 11 E3 . . . .26 C4
Gems Hampshire Sch
(Main Sch) SW7 . . . 144 A1
Gems Hampshire Sch
(The Early Years)
SW7 . . . . .143 A3
General Wolfe Rd
SE10 . . . . .52 C2
Genesis Bsns Pk
NW10 . . . . .20 A3
Geneva Ct
1 Putney SW15 . . . .57 C2
Stoke Newington
N16 . . . . .6 C3
Geneva Dr SW9 . . . . .62 C3
Genoa Ave SW15 . . .57 B2
Genoa Ho 10 E1 . . . .25 C1
Geoffrey Cl SE5 . . . .48 B1
Geoffrey Ct SE4 . . . .66 B4
Geoffrey Ho SE1. . . 137 C2
Geoffrey Jones Ct
NW10 . . . . .21 C4
Geoffrey Rd SE4 . . . .66 B4
George Beard Rd 11
SE8 . . . . .41 B2
George Belt Ho 8
E2 . . . . .25 C2
George Ct WC2 . . . .120 B3
George Downing Est
N16 . . . . .7 B2
George Eliot Ho
SW1 . . . . .147 A3
George Eliot Prim Sch
NW8 . . . . .79 B3
George Elliot Ho
SE17 . . . . .150 C2
George Elliston Ho 13
SE1 . . . . .153 B1

George Eyre Ho
NW8 . . . . .79 C1
George Green's Sch
E14 . . . . .42 B1
George Inn SE1 . . . .123 B1
George Inn Yd
SE1 . . . . .123 B1
George La SE13 . . . . .67 B1
George Lansbury Ho
7 Bow E3 . . . . .26 B2
8 Willesden NW10. . . .8 A1
George Lashwood Ct
12 SW9 . . . . .62 B3
George Leybourne Ho
15 E1 . . . . .125 C4
George Lindgren Ho
SW6 . . . . .155 A2
George Loveless Ho
4 E2 . . . . .24 B2 99 A4
George Mathers Rd
SE11 . . . . .150 A4
George Mews
27 Brixton SW9 . . . .173 B1
NW1 . . . . .92 C3
George Peabody Ct
NW1 . . . . .102 A4
George Potter Wy
SW11 . . . . .167 C1
George Row SE16 . . 139 B3
George's Rd N7 . . . .14 B3
George's Sq SW6 . . .155 A4
George St
6 Canning Town
E16 . . . . .35 B3
Marylebone W1 . . . .103 A2
George Tingle Ho
SE1 . . . . .139 A2
Georgette Pl SE10 . . .52 B3
George Vale Ho 55
E2 . . . . .24 C3
George Walter Ho 11
SE16 . . . . .40 B2
George Wyver Cl
SW18 . . . . .70 A4
George Yd
City of London
EC3 . . . . .109 C1
Mayfair W1 . . . . . . .117 C4
Georgiana St NW1. . .83 A4
Georgian Ct 12 E9 . .25 B4
Georgina Gdns 10
E2 . . . . .24 B2 99 A4
Geraldine Rd
Brentford W4 . . . . . .44 C4
Wandsworth SW18 . .59 B2
Geraldine St SE11 . .136 A1
Gerald Mews
SW1 . . . . .145 C4
Gerald Rd SW1 . . . .145 C4
Gerard Ct NW2 . . . . . .9 C3
Gerards Cl SE16 . . . .40 B1
Gernigan Ho
SW18 . . . . .59 C1
Gernon Rd E3 . . . . . .26 A3
Gerrard Ho 5
SE14 . . . . .50 C3
Gerrard Pl W1 . . . . .119 C4
Gerrard Rd N1 . . . . . .86 B2
Gerrard St W1 . . . . .119 C4
Gerridge Ct SE1 . . . .135 C2
Gerridge St SE1 . . . .135 C2
Gerry Raffles Sq
E15 . . . . .19 C2

Gertrude St SW10 . .**157** A3
Gervase St SE15 . . . . .**50** A3
Getters Talmud Torah
  3 N16 . . . .**6** C4
Getters Talmud Torah
  Sch 11 N16 . . . .**6** C4
Ghent Way E8 . . . .**16** B2
Gherkin The (30 St
  Mary Axe) EC2 . . **110** B2
Giant Arches Rd
  SE24 . . . .**63** B1
Gibbings Ho SE1 . . **136** B3
Gibbins Rd E15 . . . . . .**19** B1
Gibbon Ho NW8 . . . .**89** C1
Gibbon Rd
  Acton W3 . . . .**29** A2
  Nunhead SE15 . . . . . .**50** B1
Gibbons Rd NW10 . . .**8** A2
Gibbon's Rents
  SE1 . . . . **124** A1
Gibbs Ho SW15 . . . . .**56** C3
Gibbs Gn W14 . . . . **141** A2
Gibbs Green Cl
  W14 . . . . **141** A2
Gibbs Ho SW12 . . . . .**73** A4
Gibraltar Ho
  N10 . . . .**21** A3
Gibraltar Wlk 28
  E2 . . . .**24** B2 **99** A3
Gibson Cl E1 . . . .**25** B1
Gibson Gdns N16 . . . .**7** B2
Gibson Rd SE11 . . . **149** A3
Gibson Sq N1 . . . . . .**85** C4
Gibson St SE10 . . . . . .**43** A1
Gideon Rd SW11 . . . .**60** C4
Giesbach Rd N19 . . . . .**4** C2
Giffen Square Mkt
  SE8 . . . .**51** C3
Giffin St SE8 . . . .**51** C3
Gifford Ho
  5 Clapham SW4 . . .**61** C3
  Greenwich SE10 . . . .**42** C1
  Pimlico SW1 . . . . . **146** C1
Gifford Rd NW10 . . . .**8** A1
Gifford St N1 . . . .**14** A1
Gilbert Ho
  Barbican EC2 . . . . . **109** A3
  Deptford SE8 . . . . . .**51** C4
  5 Globe Town E2 . . .**25** C2
  Pimlico SW1 . . . . . **146** B1
  South Lambeth
  SW8 . . . . **162** A2
Gilbert Pl WC1 . . . . **106** A3
Gilbert Rd SE11 . . . **149** C2
Gilbert Sheldon Ho
  W2 . . . . **101** C4
Gilbertson Ho 11
  E14 . . . .**41** C3
Gilbert St W1 . . . . . **103** C1
Gilbeys Yd NW1 . . . .**12** C1
Gilby Ho 5 E9 . . . . . .**17** C2
Gilda Cres N16 . . . . . .**7** C3
Gildea St W1 . . . . . **104** B3
Gilden Cres NW5 . . . .**12** C3
Giles Ho
  7 Bermondsey
  SE16 . . . . **139** B2
  Notting Hill W11 . . . .**31** C3
Gilesmead SE5 . . . . . .**48** C2
Gilkes Cres SE21 . . . .**64** A1
Gilkes Pl SE21 . . . . . .**64** A1
Gillam Ho 9 SE16 . .**40** B2
Gill Ave E16 . . . .**35** C3
Gillender St E3 . . . . . .**27** B1

Gillespie Prim Sch
  N5 . . . .**6** A1
Gillespie Rd N4, N5 . . .**6** A1
Gillett Pl 27 E8 . . . . .**16** A3
Gillett St E8, E16, ...**16** A3
Gillfoot NW1 . . . .**82** C1
Gillian St SE13 . . . . . .**67** A2
Gillies St NW5 . . . . . .**12** C3
Gilling Ct 5 NW3 . . .**12** A2
Gillingham Ho
  SW1 . . . . **146** C4
Gillingham Mews
  SW1 . . . . **146** C4
Gillingham Rd NW2 . .**1** A1
Gillingham Row
  SW1 . . . . **146** C4
Gillingham St
  SW1 . . . . **146** C4
Gillison Wlk 19
  SE16 . . . . **139** C2
Gillis Sq 5 SW15 . . .**56** C1
Gilman Ho 11 E2 . . .**24** C3
Gillray Ho SW10 . . **157** B3
Gill St E14 . . . .**33** B2
Gilmore Ho SW4 . . . .**60** B3
Gilmore Rd SE13 . . . .**67** C3
Gilpin Ave SW14 . . . .**55** C3
Gilpin Cl W2 . . . . . **101** A4
Gilpin Rd E5 . . . .**18** A4
Gilray Ho W2 . . . . . **115** B4
Gilstead Rd SW6 . . **166** B2
Gilston Rd SW10 . . **143** A1
Giltspur St EC1 . . . . **108** B2
Gilwell Ct 7 E5 . . . . .**17** A4
Gipsy Cnr W3 . . . . . .**28** C4
Gipsy La SW15 . . . . . .**57** A4
Giraud St E14 . . . .**34** A3
Girdlers Rd W14 . . . .**39** C2
Girdlestone Wlk
  N19 . . . .**4** B2
Girdwood Rd SW18,
  SW19 . . . .**70** A4
Girling Ho 9 N1 . . . .**24** A4
Gironde Rd SW6 . . **155** A1
Girton Ho SW15 . . . .**57** C1
Girton Villas 6
  W10 . . . .**30** C3
Gisburn Ho 23
  SE15 . . . .**49** C3
Gissing Wlk N1 . . . . .**14** C1
Glade The W12 . . . . . .**39** A4
Glading Terr N16 . . . . .**7** B1
Gladsmuir Rd N19 . . . .**4** B3
Gladstone Ct
  Westminster
  SW1 . . . . **147** C3
  Willesden NW2 . . . . . .**9** A3
Gladstone Ho 18
  E14 . . . .**33** C3
Gladstone Park Sch
  NW10 . . . .**9** A3
Gladstone St SE1 . . **136** A2
Gladstone Terr
  SW8 . . . . **170** B4
Gladwin Ho NW1 . . .**83** A1
Gladwyn Rd SW15 . . .**57** C4
Gladys Rd NW6 . . . . .**10** C1
Glaisher St SE8 . . . . . .**52** A4
Glamis Ct W3 . . . .**37** A4
Glamis Est 3 E1 . . . .**32** C2
Glamis Pl E1 . . . .**32** B2
Glamis Rd E1 . . . .**32** B2
Glanville Ho 4
  SW12 . . . .**73** B4
Glanville Rd SW2 . . . .**62** A2

Glasbury Ho 5
  SW9 . . . .**62** B3
Glaserton Rd N16 . . . .**7** A4
Glasgow Ho W9 . . . .**78** B1
Glasgow Terr
  SW1 . . . . **146** C1
Glashill St SE1 . . . . **136** B4
Glasshouse Fields
  E1 . . . .**32** C2
Glasshouse St
  W1 . . . . **119** A3
Glasshouse The
  SE11 . . . .**67** B3
Glasshouse Wlk
  SE11 . . . . **148** C2
Glasshouse Yd
  EC1 . . . .**96** C1
Glass St 4 E2 . . . . . .**25** A1
Glastonbury Ct 12
  SE14 . . . .**50** B3
Glastonbury Ho
  SW1 . . . . **146** A2
Glastonbury Pl 2
  E1 . . . .**32** B3
Glastonbury St
  NW6 . . . .**10** B3
Glaucus St E3 . . . .**34** A4
Glazbury Rd W14 . . **140** B2
Glazebrook Cl
  SE21 . . . .**75** C2
Glebe Cl 1 W4 . . . . . .**38** A1
Glebe Ho 8 SE16 . . . .**40** A3
Glebelands Cl SE5 . . .**64** A4
Glebe Pl SW3 . . . . . **158** A4
Glebe Rd
  Barnes SW13 . . . . . .**46** C1
  Dalston E8 . . . .**16** B1
  Willesden NW10 . . . . .**8** C2
Glebe St W4 . . . .**38** A1
Gledhow Gdns
  SW5 . . . . **142** C3
Gledstanes Rd
  W14 . . . . **140** B1
Glegg Pl 3 SW15 . . .**57** C3
Glenaffric Ave E14 . . .**42** C2
Glen Albyn Rd
  SW19 . . . .**69** C2
Glenalmond Ho 2
  SW15 . . . .**57** C1
Glenarm Rd E5 . . . . . .**17** C4
Glenbrook Prim Sch
  SW4 . . . .**61** C1
Glenbrook Rd
  NW6 . . . .**10** C3
Glenburnie Rd
  SW17 . . . .**72** B1
Glencoe Mans 6
  SW9 . . . . **163** B1
Glendall St SW9 . . . .**62** B3
Glendarvon St
  SW15 . . . .**57** C4
Glendower Gdns 10
  SW14 . . . .**55** C4
Glendower Pl
  SW7 . . . . **143** B4
Glendower Prep Sch
  SW7 . . . . **143** B4
Glendown Ho 2
  E8 . . . .**16** C3
Glendun Ct W3 . . . . .**29** A2
Glendun Rd W3 . . . . .**29** A2
Gleneagles Cl 21
  SE16 . . . .**40** A1
Glenelg Rd SW2 . . . . .**62** A2

Glenfield Rd SW12. . .**73** B3
Glenfinlas Way
  SE5 . . . .**48** A3
Glenforth St SE10 . . .**43** B1
Glengall Gr E14 . . . . .**42** B3
Glengall Pass 2
  NW6 . . . .**23** C4
Glengall Rd
  Camberwell SE15 . . . .**49** B4
  Kilburn NW6 . . . .**23** B4
Glengall Terr SE15 . . .**49** B4
Glengarnock Ave
  E14 . . . .**42** B2
Glengarry Rd SE22 . .**64** B2
Glenhurst Ave
  NW5 . . . .**12** C4
Glenilla Rd NW3 . . . .**12** A2
Glenister Rd SE10 . . .**43** B1
Glenkerry Ho 1
  E14 . . . .**34** B3
Glenloch Ct 2
  NW3 . . . .**12** A2
Glenloch Rd NW3 . . .**12** A3
Glenluce Rd SE3 . . . . .**53** C4
Glenmore SW15 . . . . .**57** C1
Glenmore Ho 6
  TW10 . . . .**54** A1
Glenmore Rd NW3 . . .**12** A2
Glennie Ct SE21 . . . . .**76** C3
Glennie Ho SE10 . . . .**52** B2
Glennie Rd SE27,
  SW16 . . . .**74** C1
Glenridding NW1 . . . .**83** A1
Glenrosa St SW6 . . **166** C2
Glenroy St W12 . . . . .**30** B3
Glensdale Rd SE4 . . . .**66** B4
Glenshaw Mans 7
  SW9 . . . . **163** B1
Glentanner Way
  SW17 . . . .**71** C1
Glentham Gdns
  SW13 . . . .**47** A4
Glentham Rd
  SW13 . . . .**47** A4
Glenthorne Mews
  W6 . . . .**39** A2
Glenthorne Rd
  W6 . . . .**39** A2
Glenthorpe SW15. . . .**56** B3
Glentworth St
  NW1 . . . .**91** A1
Glenville Gr SE8 . . . . .**51** B3
Glenville Mews
  SW18 . . . .**70** C4
Glenworth Ave
  E14 . . . .**42** C2
Gliddon Rd W14 . . . **140** A2
Globe Pond Rd
  SE16 . . . .**33** A1
Globe Prim Sch 17
  E2 . . . .**25** B2
Globe St SE1 . . . . . . **137** B3
Globe Terr 9 E2 . . . . .**25** B2
Globe Theatre The
  SE1 . . . . **122** C2
GLOBE TOWN **25** C2
Globe View EC4 . . . **122** C4
Globe Yd W1 . . . . . **104** A1
Globe Ave 4 NW11 . . **141** A3
Gloucester Ave
  NW1 . . . .**81** C4
Gloucester Cir
  SE10 . . . .**52** B3

Gloucester Cres
  NW1 . . . .**82** A4
Gloucester Ct
  Borough The SE1 . . **137** A2
  City of London EC3 . **124** B3
  Dulwich SE22 . . . . . .**76** C3
  Golders Green NW11. . .**1** B4
  Richmond TW9 . . . . . .**44** C3
Gloucester Dr N4. . . . .**6** A2
Gloucester Gate
  NW1 . . . .**82** A2
Gloucester Gate
  Mews NW1 . . . .**82** A2
Gloucester Gdns
  Golders Green
  NW11 . . . .**1** B4
  Paddington W2. . . . **100** C2
Gloucester Ho
  Kilburn NW6 . . . .**23** C3
  Richmond TW10 . . . .**54** C2
Gloucester Mews
  W2 . . . . **101** A1
Gloucester Mews W
  W2 . . . . **101** A1
Gloucester Pk
  SW7 . . . . **142** C4
Gloucester Pl W1 **103** A4
Gloucester Pl Mews
  W1 . . . . **103** A3
Gloucester Rd
  Acton W3 . . . .**37** B4
  Richmond TW9 . . . . .**44** C3
  South Kensington
  SW7 . . . . **142** C4
Gloucester Road Sta
  SW7 . . . . **142** C4
Gloucester Sq
  6 Hackney E2. . . . . .**24** C4
  Paddington W2. . . . **102** A1
Gloucester St
  SW1 . . . . **146** C2
Gloucester Terr
  W2 . . . . **101** A1
Gloucester Way
  EC1 . . . .**95** C3
Gloucester Wlk
  W8 . . . . **127** C4
Glover Ho
  London SE15. . . . . . .**65** A3
  5 South Hampstead
  NW6 . . . .**11** B1
Glycena Rd SW11. . . .**60** B4
Glyn Ct SE27 . . . .**74** C1
Glynde Mews
  SW3 . . . . **130** B1
Glynde Reach WC1 . .**94** B3
Glynde St SE4 . . . .**66** B1
Glynfield Rd NW10. . . .**8** A1
Glyn Mans W14 . . . . .**40** B3
Glyn Rd E5 . . . .**17** C4
Glyn St SE11 . . . . . . **148** C1
Goater's Alley
  SW6 . . . . **155** A1
Goat Wharf TW8. . . . .**44** A4
Godalming Rd E14. . . .**34** A4
Goddard Ho SW19 . . .**69** C2
Goddard Pl N19 . . . . . .**4** B1
Godfrey Ho EC1 . . . . .**97** B3
Godfrey St
  Chelsea SW3 . . . . . **144** B2
  Mill Meads E15. . . . . .**27** B3
Goding St SE11. . . . **148** B1
Godley Rd SW18. . . . .**71** C3
Godliman St EC4 . . **122** C4
Godman Rd SE15 . . . .**50** A1

Godolphin Ho
Primrose Hill
NW3 . . . . .12 A1
7 Streatham SW2 . .74 C3
Godolphin & Latymer
Sch 10 W6 . . . . .39 A2
Godolphin Rd W3 . .28 C2

Godolphin Rd
W12 . . . . .39 A4
Godson St N1 . . . . . .85 B2
Godstone Ct 11 N16 .7 A3
Godstone Ho SE1 . .137 C2
Godwin Cl N1 . . . . . .87 A2
Godwin Cl NW1 . . . .83 A2

Godwin Ho
2 Haggerston E2 . .24 B3
Kilburn NW6 . . . . . . .78 A2
Goffers Ho SE3 . . . .53 A1
Goffers Rd SE3,
SE13 . . . . .53 A1
Goffton Ho 14
N1 . . . . .173 A1

Golborne Gdns
5 Kensal Town
W10 . . . . .23 A1
West Kilburn W10 . .23 B1
Golborne Mews 6
W10 . . . . .31 A4
Golborne Rd W10 . .31 A4
Golden Cross Mews
2 W11 . . . . .31 B3
Golden Hinde II The
SE1 . . . . .123 B2
Golden Hind Pl 5
SE8 . . . . .41 B2
Golden La EC1 . . . . .97 A1
Golden Lane L Ctr
EC1 . . . . .96 C1
Golden Plover Cl
E16 . . . . .35 C3
Golden Sq W1 . . . .119 A4
Golders Ct NW11 . . .1 B4
Golders Gdns NW11 .1 B4
GOLDERS GREEN . .1 C4
Golders Green Coll
NW11 . . . . .1 C4
Golders Green Cres
NW11 . . . . .1 C4
Golders Green Rd
NW11 . . . . .1 A4
Golders Green Sta
NW11 . . . . .1 C4
Golders Hill Sch
NW11 . . . . .1 C4
Golderslea NW11 . . .1 C3
Golders Park Cl
NW11 . . . . .1 C3
Golders Way NW11 . .1 C3
Goldhawk Ind Est
W6 . . . . .39 A3
Goldhawk Mews 2
W12 . . . . .39 A4
Goldhawk Rd W12 . .38 C3
Goldhawk Road Sta
W12 . . . . .39 B4
Goldhurst Terr
NW6 . . . . .11 B1
Goldie Ho N19 . . . . . .4 C4
Golding St E1 . . . . .111 C1
Goldington Cres
NW1 . . . . .83 B2
Goldington Ct
NW1 . . . . .83 B3
Goldington St
NW1 . . . . .83 B2

Goldman Cl
E2 . . . . .24 C1 99 B2
Goldney Rd W9 . . . .23 C1
Goldsboro Rd
SW8 . . . . .161 C1
Goldsborough Ho
SW8 . . . . .171 C3
Goldsmith Ave W3 . .28 C2
Goldsmith Ct
WC1 . . . . .106 B2
Goldsmith Ho W3 . .28 C1
Goldsmith Rd
Acton W3 . . . . .28 C1
Peckham SE15 . . . .49 C2
Goldsmith's Bldgs
W3 . . . . .28 C1
Goldsmiths Cl W3 . .28 C1
Goldsmith's Pl 6
NW6 . . . . .78 A3
Goldsmith's Row
E2 . . . . .24 C3
Goldsmith's Sq 17
E2 . . . . .24 C3
Goldsmith St EC2 . .109 A2
Goldsmiths Univ of
London SE14 . . . . . .51 A2
Goldsworthy Gdns
18 SE16 . . . . .40 B2
Goldthorpe NW1 . . .82 C3
Goldwell Ho SE22 . .64 A3
Goldwin Cl SE14 . . .50 B2
Goldwing Cl E16 . . .35 C3
Gomm Rd SE16 . . . .40 B3
Gondar Gdns NW6 . .10 B3
Gondar Mans NW6 . .10 B3
Gonson St SE8 . . . .52 A4
Gonston Cl SW19 . . .70 A2
Gonville Ho 6
SW15 . . . . .57 C1
Gonville St SW6 . . . .58 A4
Gooch Ho EC1 . . . .107 B4
Goodall Ho 10 SE4 . .65 C3
Goodenough Coll
WC1 . . . . .94 C2
Goodfaith Ho 18
E14 . . . . .34 A2
Goodge Pl W1 . . . .105 A3
Goodge St W1 . . . .105 A3
Goodge Street Sta
W1 . . . . .105 B4
Goodhall St NW10 . .21 B2
Good Hart Pl E14 . . .33 A2
Goodhope Ho 17
E14 . . . . .34 A2
Goodinge Cl N7 . . . .14 A2
Gooding Ho N7 . . . .14 A2
Goodman Cres
SW2 . . . . .73 C2
Goodman's Ct
E1 . . . . .124 C4
Goodman's Stile 7
E1 . . . . .111 B2
Goodman's Yd E1,
EC3 . . . . .124 C4
Goodrich Com Prim
Sch SE22 . . . . .64 C1
Goodrich Ct 9
W10 . . . . .30 C3
Goodrich Ho
20 Bethnal Green
E2 . . . . .25 B3
Stamford Hill N16 . . .7 A4
Goodrich Rd SE22 . .64 C1
Good Shepherd RC
Prim Sch The
W12 . . . . .38 B4

Goodson Rd NW10 . .8 A1
Goodspeed Ho 20
E14 . . . . .34 A2
Goodsway NW1 . . . .84 A2
Goodway Gdns
E14 . . . . .34 C3
Goodwill Ho 22
E14 . . . . .34 A2
Goodwin Cl SE16 . .139 A1
Goodwin Ho 22
SE15 . . . . .65 A4
Goodwin Rd W12 . . .38 C4
Goodwins Ct WC2 . .120 A4
Goodwood Ct W1 . .104 B4
Goodwood Ho 3
W4 . . . . .37 B1
Goodwood Mans 3
SW9 . . . . .62 C4
Goodwood Rd
SE14 . . . . .51 A3
Goose Green Prim
Sch SE22 . . . . .64 B3
Goose Green Trad Est
SE22 . . . . .64 C3
Gophir La EC4 . . . .123 B4
Gopsall St N1 . . . . . .87 C3
Gordon Ave SW14 . .56 A3
Gordonbrock Prim
Sch SE4 . . . . .66 C2
Gordonbrock Rd
SE4 . . . . .66 C2
Gordon Ct 5 W12 . .30 B3
Gordondale Rd SW18,
SW19 . . . . .70 C2
Gordon Gr SE5 . . . .48 A1
Gordon Ho 6 E1 . . .32 B2
Gordon Hospl
SW1 . . . . .147 B3
Gordon House Rd
NW5 . . . . .12 C4
Gordon Lo N16 . . . . .6 C2
Gordon Mans WC1 . .93 B1
Gordon Pl W8 . . . . .127 C4
Gordon Rd
Chiswick W4 . . . . . .45 A4
Leyton E15 . . . . .19 B4
Peckham SE15 . . . .50 A1
Richmond TW9 . . . . .44 B1
Gordon Sq WC1 . . . .93 C2
Gorefield Ho NW6 . .23 C3
Gorefield Pl NW6 . . .23 C3
Gore Rd E9 . . . . . . .25 B4
Gore St SW7 . . . . . .129 A2
Gorham Ho 10
SW4 . . . . .61 B1
Gorham Pl 21
W11 . . . . .31 A2 112 A3
Goring St EC3 . . . .110 B2
Gorleston St W14 . .140 B4
Gorse Cl E16 . . . . . .35 C3
Gorsefield Ho 6
E14 . . . . .33 C2
Gorst Rd
London SW11 . . . . . .60 B1
North Acton NW10 . .20 C4
Gorsuch Pl 11
E2 . . . . .24 B2 98 C4
Gorsuch St
E2 . . . . .24 B2 98 C4
Gosberton Rd
SW12 . . . . .72 C3
Gosfield St W1 . . . .104 C3
Gosford Ho 25 E3 . .26 B3
Goslett Yd WC2 . . . .105 C2

Gosling Ho 2 E1 . . .32 B2
Gosling Way SW9 . .173 B3
Gospatric Home Ho
SW14 . . . . .56 A4
GOSPEL OAK 12 C4
Gospel Oak Prim Sch
NW5 . . . . .12 C4
Gospel Oak Sta
NW5 . . . . .12 C4
Gosport Ho 9
SW15 . . . . .68 C3
Gosset St E2 . .24 C2 99 B4
Gosterwood St
SE8 . . . . .41 A1
Goswell Pl EC1 . . . . .96 B3
Goswell Rd EC1 . . . .96 B4
Gothic Ct 17 SE5 . . .48 B3
Gottfried Mews
NW5 . . . . .13 B4
Gough Ho N1 . . . . . .86 B4
Gough Sq EC4 . . . .107 C2
Gough St WC1 . . . . .95 A1
Gough Wlk 14 E14 . .33 C3
Goulden Ho SW11 .168 A2
Gouldman Ho 33
E1 . . . . .25 B1
Gould Terr 28 E8 . . .17 A3
Goulston St E1 . . . .110 C2
Goulton Rd E5 . . . . .17 A4
Govan St E2 . . . . . . .24 C4
Gover Ct 8 SW4 . . .172 B2
Gowan Ave SW6 . . .164 A4
Gowan Ho 2
E2 . . . . .24 B2 99 A3
Gowan Rd NW10 . . . .9 A2
Gower Cl SW4 . . . . .61 B1
Gower Ct WC1 . . . . .93 B2
Gower Ho SE17 . . . .151 A2
Gower Mews
WC1 . . . . .105 C4
Gower Pl NW1,
WC1 . . . . .93 B2
Gower Sch The 4
N7 . . . . .14 A2
Gower St WC1 . . . . .93 B1
Gower's Wlk E1 . . . .111 B1
Gowlett Rd SE15 . . .64 C4
Gowrie Rd SW11 . . .60 C4
Gracechurch St EC2,
EC4 . . . . .123 C4
Gracefield Gdns
SW16 . . . . .74 A1
Gracehill 2 E1 . . . . .32 B4
Grace Ho SE11 . . . .163 A4
Grace Jones Cl E8 . .16 C2
Grace Pl E3 . . . . . . .27 A2
Graces Mews NW8 . .79 A1
Grace's Mews SE5 . .49 A1
Grace's Rd SE5 . . . .49 A1
Grace St E3 . . . . . . .27 A2
Graemesdyke Ave
SW14 . . . . .55 A3
Grafton Cres NW1 . .13 A2
Grafton Ct 8 E8 . . . .16 C3
Grafton Ho
8 Bow E3 . . . . .26 C2
Deptford SE8 . . . . . .41 B1
Grafton Mans SW4 . .61 B3
Grafton Mews W1 . . .92 C1
Grafton Pl NW1 . . . .93 C3
Grafton Prim Sch
N7 . . . . .5 B1
Grafton Rd
Acton W3 . . . . .28 B2
Gospel Oak NW5 . . .12 C3
Grafton Sq SW4 . . . .61 B4

Grafton St W1 . . . .118 B3
Grafton Terr NW5 . .12 C3
Grafton Way W1 . . . .93 A1
Grafton Yd NW5 . . . .13 A2

Graham Ct 5
SE14 . . . . .50 C4
Graham Ho
6 Balham SW12 . . .73 A4
6 Tufnell Pk N19 . .13 C4
Graham Mans 2
E8 . . . . .17 A2
Graham Rd
Acton W4 . . . . .37 C3
Dalston E8 . . . . .16 C2
Graham St N1 . . . . . .86 B1
Graham Terr SW1 . .145 C3
Graham Twr W3 . . . .37 A3
Grainger Ct 2
SE5 . . . . .48 B3
Grampian Gdns
NW2 . . . . .1 A3
Grampians The 10
W14 . . . . .39 C4
Granard Ave SW15 . .57 A2
Granard Ho 20 E9 . .17 C2
Granard Prim Sch
SW15 . . . . .57 A1
Granard Rd SW11,
SW12 . . . . .72 B4
Granary Rd E1 . . . . .25 A1
Granary Sq
Islington N1 . . . . . . .14 C2
N1 . . . . .84 A3
Granary St NW1 . . . .83 B3
Granary The SE8 . . .51 C3
Granby Pl SE1 . . . .135 B3
Granby St
Bethnal Green
E2 . . . . .24 C1 99 B2
Shoreditch
E2 . . . . .24 B1 99 A2
Granby Terr NW1 . . .82 C1
Grand Ave EC1 . . . .108 B4
Grand Canal Ave
SE8 . . . . .51 C3
Grandfield Ct W4 . . .45 C4
Grandison Rd
SW11 . . . . .60 B2
Grand Junction Wharf
N1 . . . . .86 C1
Grand Par SW14 . . .55 B3
Grand Union Cl
W9 . . . . .31 B4
Grand Union Cres
E8 . . . . .24 C4
Grand Union Ind Est
NW10 . . . . .20 A3
Grand Vitesse Ind Est
SE1 . . . . .122 B1
Granfield St
SW11 . . . . .167 C3
Grangecourt Rd
N16 . . . . .7 A3
Grange Ct
Peckham SE15 . . . .49 B1
Strand WC2 . . . . . .107 A1
1 Willesden NW10 . .8 A4
Grangefield NW1 . . .14 A1
Grange Gdns NW3 . .2 A1
Grange Gr N1 . . . . . .15 B2
Grange Ho
Bermondsey SE1 . .138 C1
Willesden NW10 . . . .9 A1
Grange La SE21 . . . .76 B2

Grangemill 11
NW5 . . . . 13 A4
GRANGE MILLS . . 73 B3
Grange Mills
SW12 . . . . 3 B2
Grange Pl NW6 . . . . 10 C1
Grange Prim Sch
SE1 . . . . 138 A1
Grange Rd
Barnes SW13 . . . . . . 46 C2
Bermondsey SE1 . . . 138 C1
Gunnersbury W4 . . . 37 A1
Willesden NW10 . . . . 8 A4
Grange St N1 . . . . 87 C3
Grange The
Bermondsey SE1 . . . 138 C1
7 Gunnersbury
W4 . . . . 37 A1
Hammersmith W12 . . 39 A3
19 Maitland Pk
NW3 . . . . 12 B2
South Acton W3 . . . . 37 A4
West Kensington
W14 . . . . 140 C3
Grangeway NW6 . . 10 C1
Grange Wlk SE1 . . 138 C1
Grange Yd SE1 . . . 138 C1
Granite Apts E15 . . 19 C2
Grannary The 10
SE16 . . . . 40 B4
Gransden Ave E8 . . 17 A1
Gransden Ho 1
SE8 . . . . 41 B1
Gransden Rd W12 . . 38 B4
Grantbridge St N1 . 86 B2
Grantham Ct 3
SE16 . . . . 40 C4
Grantham Ho 12
SE15 . . . . 49 C4
Grantham Pl W1 . . 118 A1
Grantham Rd
Chiswick W4 . . . . . . 46 A3
South Lambeth
SW9 . . . . 172 B1
Grant Ho
3 Clapham
SW8 . . . . 171 B1
Clerkenwell EC1 . . . 108 B4
Grantley Ho
2 Deptford SE14 . . 50 C4
5 Putney SW19 . . . 69 C3
Grantley St E1 . . . . 25 C1
Grant Mus of Zoology
WC1 . . . . 93 B1
Grant Rd SW11 . . . . 60 A4
Grant St N1 . . . . . . 85 B2
Grantully Rd W9 . . . 88 A3
Granville Ct
6 Deptford SE14 . . 51 A4
Shoreditch N1 . . . . . 87 C4
Granville Gr SE13 . . 67 B4
Granville Ho 18
E14 . . . . 33 C3
Granville Ind Est
NW2 . . . . 1 B2
Granville Mans 8
W12 . . . . 39 B4
Granville Pk SE13 . . 67 C4
Granville Pl
Marylebone W1 . . . . 103 B1
Walham Green
SW6 . . . . 156 A1
Granville Point
NW2 . . . . 1 B2

Granville Rd
Child's Hill NW2 . . . . 1 B2
Kilburn NW6 . . . . . . 23 C3
Wandsworth SW18 . . 70 B4
Granville Sq
3 Camberwell
SE15 . . . . 49 A3
Finsbury WC1 . . . . . 95 A3
Granville St WC1 . . 95 A3
Grape St WC2 . . . . 106 A2
Grasgarth Cl W3 . . 28 B2
Grasmere NW1 . . . . 92 B3
Grasmere Ave W3 . . 37 A3
Grasmere Ct
SW13 . . . . 46 C4
Grasmere Ho 20
N16 . . . . 15 C4
Grasmere Point 2
SE15 . . . . 50 B3
Grasmere Prim Sch
N16 . . . . 15 C4
Grateley Ho 10
SW15 . . . . 69 A3
Gratton Rd W14 . . . 126 A1
Graveley Ho 7
SE8 . . . . 41 A2
Gravel La E1 . . . . . 110 C2
Gravesend Rd
W12 . . . . 29 C2
Grayfriars Pas
EC1 . . . . 108 B2
Gray Ho SE17 . . . . 151 A2
Grayland Ct WC1 . . 94 C3
Grayling Rd N16 . . . 6 C2
Grayling Sq
E2 . . . . 24 C2 99 C4
Grayshott Rd
SW11 . . . . 60 C4
Gray's Inn WC1 . . . 107 A3
Gray's Inn Pl WC1 . 107 A3
Gray's Inn Rd WC1 . 95 A2
Gray's Inn Sq
WC1 . . . . 107 B4
Grayson Ho EC1 . . . 97 A3
Gray St SE1 . . . . . . 135 C3
Grayswood Point 14
SW15 . . . . 68 C3
Gray's Yd W1 . . . . . 103 C2
Grazebrook Rd N16 . 6 C2
Great Arthur Ho
EC1 . . . . 96 C1
Great Bell Alley
EC2 . . . . 109 B2
Great Castle St
W1 . . . . 104 C2
Great Central St
NW1 . . . . 102 C4
Great Chapel St
W1 . . . . 105 B2
Great Chart St
SW11 . . . . 59 B3
Great Chertsey Rd
SW14,W4 . . . . . . 45 C2
Great Church La
W6 . . . . 39 C1
Great College St
SW1 . . . . 134 A2
Great Croft WC1 . . . 94 B3
Great Cross Ave
SE3 . . . . 53 A1
Great Cumberland
Mews W1 . . . . . 102 C1
Great Cumberland Pl
W1 . . . . 103 A1
Great Dover St
SE1 . . . . 137 B2

Great Eastern Bldgs
10 E8 . . . . 17 A2
Great Eastern Ent Ctr
E14 . . . . 42 A4
Great Eastern Pier
E14 . . . . 41 C1
Great Eastern Rd
E15 . . . . 19 C2
Great Eastern St
EC2 . . . . 24 A1 98 A2
Great Eastern Wharf
SW11 . . . . 158 B1
Great Field 1
NW5 . . . . 13 B3
Greatfield Cl
London SE4 . . . . . . 66 C3
4 Tufnell Pk N19 . . . 13 B4
Great George St
SW1 . . . . 134 A3
Great Guildford Bsns
Sq SE1 . . . . 122 C1
Great Guildford St
SE1 . . . . 122 C1
Greatham Wlk 8
SW15 . . . . 68 C3
Great James St
WC1 . . . . 106 C4
Great Marlborough St
W1 . . . . 104 C1
Great Maze Pond
SE1 . . . . 137 C4
Great Newport St
WC2 . . . . 120 A4
Greatorex Ho 13
E1 . . . . 111 B4
Greatorex St E1 . . . 111 B4
Great Ormond St
Hospl for Children
WC1 . . . . 94 C1
Great Ormond St
WC1 . . . . 94 C1
Great Percy St
WC1 . . . . 95 B4
Great Peter St
SW1 . . . . 133 C1
Great Portland St
W1 . . . . 104 B4
Great Portland Street
Sta W1 . . . . 92 B1
Great Pulteney St
W1 . . . . 119 A4
Great Queen St
WC2 . . . . 106 B2
Great Russell Mans
WC1 . . . . 106 A3
Great Russell St
WC1 . . . . 106 A3
Great St Helen's
EC3 . . . . 110 A2
Great St Thomas
Apostle EC4 . . . . . 123 A4
Great Scotland Yd
SW1,WC2 . . . . . . 120 A2
Great Smith St
SW1 . . . . 133 C2
Great Spilmans
SE22 . . . . 64 A2
Great Suffolk St
SE1 . . . . 122 B1
Great Sutton St
EC1 . . . . 96 B1
Great Swan Alley
EC2 . . . . 109 B2
Great Titchfield St
W1 . . . . 104 C3

Great Tower St
EC3 . . . . 124 A4
Great Trinity La
EC4 . . . . 123 A4
Great Turnstile
WC2 . . . . 107 A3
Great Western Rd W2,
W9 . . . . 31 B4
Great West Rd W4 . . 45 C4
Great West Road
Cedars Rd W4 . . . 45 A4
Great West Road
Hogarth La W4 . . . 46 A4
Great Winchester St
EC2 . . . . 109 C2
Great Windmill St
W1 . . . . 119 B4
Great Yd SE1 . . . . . 138 B4
Greaves Cotts 10
E14 . . . . 33 A4
Greaves Twr
SW10 . . . . 157 A2
Grebe Ct 16 E14 . . . 42 B4
Greek St W1 . . . . . 105 C1
Greek St W1 . . . . . 105 C1
Greenacre Cl SE6 . . 67 A1
Greenacre Sq 26
SE16 . . . . 40 C4
Green Arbour Ct
EC1 . . . . 108 A2
Greenaway Gdns
NW3 . . . . 11 A4
Greenaway Ho
Finsbury WC1 . . . . . 95 B3
St John's Wood
NW8 . . . . 78 C4
Green Bank E1 . . . . 32 A1
Greenbanks Ct
SE1 . . . . 67 A4
Greenberry St
NW8 . . . . 80 A1
Green Cl NW11 . . . . 2 A4
Greencoat Pl
SW1 . . . . 147 A4
Greencoat Row
SW1 . . . . 133 A1
Greencourt Ho 25
E1 . . . . 25 C1
Greencroft Gdns
NW6 . . . . 11 B1
Green Ct 2 NW10 . . 8 A4
Green Dale SE22 . . . 64 A2
Greendale Cl SE22 . . 64 A2
Green Dragon Ct
SE1 . . . . 123 B1
Green Dragon Ho
WC1 . . . . 106 B2
Green Dragon La
TW8 . . . . 36 B1
Green Dragon Prim
Sch TW8 . . . . 44 A4
Green Dragon Yd 24
E1 . . . . 111 B3
Greene Ct 20 SE14 . . 50 C4
Greene Ho SE1 . . . 137 B1
Greenend Rd W4 . . . 38 A4
Greener Ho 3
SW4 . . . . 61 C4
Greenfell Mans
SE8 . . . . 52 A4
Greenfield Gdns
NW2 . . . . 1 A1
Greenfield Ho 28
SW19 . . . . 69 C3
Greenfield Rd E1 . . 111 C2

Greenham Cl SE1 . . 135 B3
Greenham Ho 5
E9 . . . . 25 B4
Greenheath Bsns Ctr
3 E2 . . . . 25 A1
Greenhill NW3 . . . . 11 C4
Greenhill Pk
NW10 . . . . 21 A4
Greenhill Rd
NW10 . . . . 21 A4
Greenhill's Rents
EC1 . . . . 108 A4
Greenhills Terr 18
N1 . . . . 15 C2
Green Ho The 5
SW19 . . . . 70 A3
Green Hundred Rd
SE15 . . . . 49 C4
Greening Ho SE13 . . 67 C3
Greenland Ho
Bermondsey SE8 . . . 40 C1
4 Mile End E1 . . . . 26 A1
Greenland Mews
SE8 . . . . 40 C1
Greenland Pier
SE8 . . . . 41 B3
Greenland Quay
SE16 . . . . 40 C2
Greenland Rd
NW1 . . . . 82 C4
Greenland St NW1 . . 82 C4
Green Lanes N4, N8,
N15 . . . . 6 A4
Greenleaf Cl 5
SW2 . . . . 74 C4
Green Link Wlk
TW9 . . . . 45 A2
Greenman St N1 . . . 86 C4
Greenmead &
Paddock Schs
SW15 . . . . 57 A2
Green Mews N1 . . . 97 C4
Greenock Rd 11
W3 . . . . 37 B3
Greenroof Way
SE10 . . . . 43 B3
Green's Ct
W11 . . . . 31 B1 112 C1
Greenside Prim Sch
W12 . . . . 38 C4
Greenside Rd W12 . . 38 C4
Green Spring
Academy Shoreditch
E2 . . . . 24 B2 99 A3
Green St W1 . . . . . 117 B4
Greenstead Gdns
SW15 . . . . 57 A2
Greenstreet Hill
SE4 . . . . 65 C4
Greensward Ho
SW6 . . . . 166 C2
Green Terr EC1 . . . . 95 C3
Green The W3 . . . . 29 A3
Greenview Cl W3 . . . 29 A1
Greenview Ct
East Dulwich
SE22 . . . . 64 C3
Wandsworth SW18 . . 72 A4
Greenway Cl N4 . . . 6 B2
Greenwell St W1 . . . 92 B1

GREENWICH 43 C3
Greenwich Acad
SE10 . . . . .52 A2
Greenwich Bsns Ctr
SE10 . . . . .52 A3
Greenwich Bsns Pk
SE10 . . . . .52 A3
Greenwich Church St
SE10 . . . . .52 B4
Greenwich Com Coll
11 SE10 . . . . .52 B3
Greenwich Ct 11
E1 . . . . .52 A3
Greenwich High Rd
SE10 . . . . .52 A3
Greenwich Ho
SE13 . . . . .67 C1
Greenwich Ind Est
SE10 . . . . .52 A3
Greenwich Mkt 2
SE10 . . . . .52 B4
Greenwich Park
SE10 . . . . .53 C3
Greenwich Park St
SE10 . . . . .52 C3
Greenwich Pier
SE10 . . . . .42 B1
Greenwich Quay
SE8 . . . . .52 A4
Greenwich South St
SE10 . . . . .52 A2
Greenwich Sta
SE10 . . . . .52 A3
Greenwich Steiner
Sch SE3 . . . . .53 C4
Greenwich View Pl
E14 . . . . .42 A3
Green Wlk SE1 . . . . .138 A1
Greenwood 3
SW19 . . . . .69 C4
Green Wood NW5 . .13 B3
Greenwood Ho
Finsbury WC1 . . . . . . .95 B3
8 Nunhead SE4 . . . . .65 C3
Greenwood Pl
NW5 . . . . .13 A3
Greenwood Rd E8 . .16 C2
Greenwood Terr
NW10 . . . . .20 C3
Green Yd WC1 . . . . . .95 A2
Greet Ho SE1 . . . . . .135 C3
Greet St SE1 . . . . . . .121 C1
Gregor Mews SE3 . . .53 C3
Gregory Pl W8 . . . . .128 A4
Greig Terr SE17 . . . . .48 A4
Grenada Ho 18
E14 . . . . .33 B2
Grenade St E14 . . . . .33 B2
Grena Gdns TW9 . . .54 B3
Grena Rd TW10,
TW9 . . . . .54 B3
Grenard Cl SE15 . . . .49 C3
Grendon Ho
23 Hackney E9 . . . . . .17 B1
Pentonville N1 . . . . . .84 C1
Grendon St NW8 . . . .90 A2
Grenfell Ho SE5 . . . . .48 B3
Grenfell Rd W11 . . . .30 C2
Grenfell Twr 11
W11 . . . . .30 C2
Grenfell Wlk 4
W11 . . . . .30 C2
Grenier Apartments
11 SE15 . . . . .50 A3
Grenville Ho
20 Bow E3 . . . . .26 A3

Grenville Ho continued
4 Deptford SE8 . . . . .51 C4
Grenville Lo N6 . . . . .4 B4
Grenville Mans
WC1 . . . . .94 A2
Grenville Mews
SW7 . . . . .142 C3
Grenville Pl SW7 . . .142 C4
Grenville Rd N19 . . . .5 A3
Grenville St WC1 . . . .94 B1
Gresham Almshouses
3 SW9 . . . . .62 B3
Gresham Coll EC1 . . .107 C3
Gresham Gdns
NW11 . . . . .1 A3
Gresham Pl 2 N19 . . .4 C2
Gresham Rd SW9 . . .62 C4
Gresham St EC2 . . . .109 A2
Gresham Way
SW19 . . . . .70 C1
Gresham Way Est
SW19 . . . . .71 A1
Gresley Ho SW8 . . . .171 C4
Gresley Rd N19 . . . . .4 B4
Gressenhall Rd
SW18 . . . . .70 B4
Gresse St W1 . . . . . .105 B2
Greswell St SW6 . . . .47 C2
Greta Ho SE3 . . . . . . .53 B4
Gretton Ho 2 E2 . . . .25 B2
Greville Hall NW6 . . .78 B2
Greville Ho
Knightsbridge
SW1 . . . . .131 B2
Putney SW15 . . . . . . .57 C4
Greville Lo 5 SW2 . .100 A2
Greville Mews 1
NW6 . . . . .78 B2
Greville Pl W9 . . . . . .78 B2
Greville Rd
Kilburn NW6 . . . . .78 B2
Richmond TW10 . . . . .54 B1
Greville St EC1 . . . . .107 C4
Grey Coat Hospital
The (Sch)
SW1 . . . . .147 B3
SW1 . . . . .133 B1
Greycoat Pl SW1 . . .133 B1
Greycoat St SW1 . . .133 B1
Grey Eagle St
E1 . . . . .24 B1 99 A1
Greyfriars 16 SE26 . .76 C1
Greyfriars Ho SE3 . . .53 B4
Grey Ho 20 W12 . . . .30 A2
Greyhound Ct
WC2 . . . . .121 B4
Greyhound Rd
College Pk NW10 . . . .22 A2
Fulham W6 . . . . .154 A4
Greyladies Gdns
SE10 . . . . .52 B1
Greystoke Ho
SE15 . . . . .49 C4
Greystoke Pl EC4 . . .107 C2
Grey Turner Ho
W12 . . . . .29 C3
Grierson Ho E8 . . . . .16 B3
Grierson Rd SE23 . . .66 A1
Griffin Cl NW10 . . . . . .9 A3
Griffin Ct
3 Brentford
TW8 . . . . .44 A4
Chiswick W4 . . . . .38 B1
Shepherd's Bush
W12 . . . . .30 A1

Griffin Gate 1
SW15 . . . . .57 C4
Griffin Prim Sch
SW8 . . . . .171 A3
Griffon Ho 3
SW11 . . . . .60 A4
Grigg's Pl SE1 . . . . . .138 B2
Grimaldi Ho N1 . . . . .84 C2
Grimsby St
E2 . . . . .24 C1 99 A2
Grimsel Path SE5 . . .48 A3
Grimshaw Cl N6 . . . . .3 C4
Grimston Rd SW6 . . .164 C1
Grimthorpe Ho
EC1 . . . . .96 A2
Grimwade Cl SE15 . . .65 B4
Grindall Ho 25 E1 . . .25 A1
Grindal St SE1 . . . . . .135 B3
Grindley Ho 3 E3 . . .33 B4
Grinling Gibbons Prim
Sch 2 SE8 . . . . .51 B4
Grinling Pl SE8 . . . . .51 C4
Grinstead Rd SE8 . . . .41 A1
Grisedale NW1 . . . . .92 C4
Grittleton Rd W9 . . . .23 C1
Grocers' Hall Ct
EC2 . . . . .109 B1
Groombridge Rd
E9 . . . . .17 C1
Groom Cres SW18 . . .71 C4
Groome Ho SE11 . . . .149 A3
Groom Pl SW1 . . . . . .131 C2
Grosse Way SW15 . . .57 A1
Grosvenor Ave
Canonbury N5 . . . . . . .15 B3
Mortlake SW14 . . . . . .56 A4
Richmond TW10 . . . . .54 A2
Grosvenor Bridge
SW1 . . . . .160 B4
Grosvenor Cotts
SW1 . . . . .145 B4
Grosvenor Court Mans
W2 . . . . .102 C1
Grosvenor Cres
SW1 . . . . .131 C3
Grosvenor Cres Mews
SW1 . . . . .131 B3
Grosvenor Ct
Brondesbury Pk
NW6 . . . . .22 C4
Gunnersbury W4 . . . .37 A1
22 Poplar E14 . . . . . .33 B3
Putney SW15 . . . . . . .58 A2
Grosvenor Gdns
Cricklewood NW2 . . . . .9 B3
Mortlake SW14 . . . . . .56 A4
Westminster SW1 . . .132 B1
Grosvenor Gdns Mews
E SW1 . . . . .132 B1
Grosvenor Gdns Mews
N SW1 . . . . .132 A1
Grosvenor Gdns Mews
S SW1 . . . . .132 B1
Grosvenor Hill
W1 . . . . .118 A4
Grosvenor Ho E5 . . . . .7 C3
Grosvenor Park
SE5 . . . . .48 B3
Grosvenor Pier
SW1 . . . . .161 B4
Grosvenor Pk SE5 . . .48 B4

Grosvenor Pl
SW1 . . . . .132 A3
Grosvenor Rd
Acton Green W4 . . . . .37 B1
Pimlico SW1 . . . . .161 A4
Richmond TW10 . . . . .54 A2
Grosvenor Residences
1 W14 . . . . .39 C3
Grosvenor Sq W1 . . .117 C4
Grosvenor St W1 . . . .118 A4
Grosvenor Terr
SE5 . . . . .48 B4
Grosvenor The
SW1 . . . . .132 A4
Grosvenor Wy
SW17 . . . . .71 C1
Grosvenor Wharf Rd
E14 . . . . .42 C2
Grote's Bldgs SE3 . . .53 A1
Grote's Pl SE3 . . . . . .53 A1
Groton Rd SW18 . . . . .71 A2
Grotto Ct SE1 . . . . . .136 C4
Grotto Pass SE1 . . . .103 B4
Grove Crescent Rd
E15 . . . . .19 C2
Grove Ct
Camberwell SE5 . . . . .48 C3
Clapham SW4 . . . . . . .61 B4
South Kensington
SW3 . . . . .143 A1
St John's Wood
NW8 . . . . .89 B4
Grovedale Rd N19 . . . .4 C2
Grove Dwellings
E1 . . . . .32 B4
Grove End Ho NW5 . .13 A4
Grove End Gdns
NW8 . . . . .79 B1
Grove End Ho
NW8 . . . . .89 B3
Grove End Rd NW8 . . .89 B3
Grove Gdns NW8 . . . .90 B3
Grove Hall Ct
Bow E3 . . . . .26 C3
St John's Wood
NW8 . . . . .89 A4
Grove Hill Rd SE5 . . . .64 A4
Grove Ho
Blackheath SE3 . . . . . .53 B1
Chelsea SW3 . . . . . . .158 B4
Grove La SE5 . . . . . . .64 A4
Groveland Ct EC4 . . .109 A1
Grovelands Cl SE5 . . .49 A1
Grove Lane Terr
SE5 . . . . .48 C1
Groveley Ho 7 N4 . . . .6 B4
Grove Lo SW4 . . . . . . .61 B3
Grove Mans
London SW4 . . . . .60 B3
6 Shepherd's Bush
W6 . . . . .39 B4
3 Stamford Hill N16 . .7 C3
Grove Mews W6 . . . . .39 B3
GROVE PARK W4 . . . .45 B2
Grove Park Bridge
W4 . . . . .45 B3
Grove Park Gdns
W4 . . . . .45 A3
Grove Park Mews
W4 . . . . .45 B3
Grove Park Prim Sch
W4 . . . . .45 B3
Grove Park Rd W4 . . .45 A3
Grove Park Terr
W4 . . . . .45 A3
Grove Pk SE5 . . . . . . .49 A1

Grove Pl
Acton W3 . . . . .28 B1
Balham SW12 . . . . . . .61 A1
Hampstead NW3 . . . . . .2 C1
Grover Ct SE13 . . . . . .52 A1
Grove Rd
Acton W3 . . . . .28 B1
Barnes SW13 . . . . . . .46 B1
Bow E3 . . . . .26 A3
Richmond TW10 . . . . .54 B1
Willesden NW2 . . . . . . .9 B2
Grover Ho
4 London SW4 . . . . . .61 B2
Vauxhall SE11 . . . . . .149 A1
Groveside Ct
SW11 . . . . .167 B2
Grove St SE8 . . . . . . .41 B1
Grove Terr NW5 . . . . .13 A4
Grove Terrace Mews
NW5 . . . . .4 A1
Grove The
Dulwich SE21 . . . . . . .76 C3
Hendon NW11 . . . . .1 A4
Highgate N6 . . . . .3 C3
Stroud Green N4 . . . . . .5 B4
Grove Vale SE22 . . . .64 B3
Groveway SW9 . . . . .173 A3
Grovewood 9
TW9 . . . . .44 C2
Grovewood Ho
NW2 . . . . .1 B2
Grummant Rd
SE15 . . . . .49 B2
Grundy St E14 . . . . . .34 A3
Guardian Angels RC
Prim Sch **3** E3 . . . . .26 A2
Guards Mus The
SW1 . . . . .133 A3
Gubyon Ave SE24 . . . .63 A2
Gudden Dr E5 . . . . . . .17 A4
Guerin Sq E3 . . . . . . .26 B2
Guernsey Gr SE24 . . .75 B4
Guernsey Ho 10
N1 . . . . .15 B2
Guernsey Rd 11
N1 . . . . .15 B2
Guildford Gr SE10 . . .52 A2
Guildford Ho 2
SE5 . . . . .48 B1
Guildford Rd SW8 . . .172 B4
Guildhall Art Gall
EC2 . . . . .109 B2
Guildhall Ho EC2 . . . .109 B2
Guildhall Sch Music &
Drama EC2 . . . . .109 A4
Guildhall Yd EC2 . . . .109 A2
Guildhouse St
SW1 . . . . .146 C3
Guilford Pl WC1 . . . . .94 C1
Guilford St WC1 . . . . .94 B1
Guillemot Ct 28
SE8 . . . . .51 B4
Guinness Cl E9 . . . . . .18 A1
Guinness Ct
Chelsea SW3 . . . . . . .144 C3
Finsbury EC1 . . . . .97 A3
Primrose Hill NW8 . . . .80 B3
Whitechapel E1 . . . . .111 C1
Guinness Sq SE1 . . . .152 A4
Guinness Trust Bldgs
Bermondsey SE1 . . . .138 A4
7 Bethnal Green
E2 . . . . .24 C3
Chelsea SW3 . . . . . . .144 C3

Guinness Trust Bldgs
continued
Hammersmith W6 ... **39** B1
Kennington SE11 ... **150** A2
Guion Rd SW6 ... **165** A2
Gujarat Ho **1** E16 ... **7** A1
Gulland Wlk **2** N1 ... **15** B2
Gullane Ho **8** E3 ... **26** B3
Gulliver St SE16 ... **41** B3
Gulston Wlk SW3 ... **145** A4
Gunmakers La **1** E3 ... **26** A4
GUNNERSBURY ... **37** B2
Gunnersbury Avenue (North Circular Rd)
W3 ... **36** C3
Gunnersbury Cl **8**
W4 ... **37** B1
Gunnersbury Cres
W3 ... **36** B4
Gunnersbury Ct **8**
W3 ... **37** A4
Gunnersbury Dr
W5 ... **36** B4
Gunnersbury Gdns
W3 ... **36** B4
Gunnersbury La
W3 ... **36** C4
Gunnersbury Mews **6**
W4 ... **37** A1
Gunnersbury Park
W3 ... **36** C3
Gunnersbury Park
Mus W3 ... **36** C3
Gunnersbury Sta
W4 ... **37** A1
Gunnersbury Triangle
Nat Res W12 ... **37** B2
Gunners Rd SW18 ... **71** C2
Gunpowder Sq
EC4 ... **107** C2
Gun St E1 ... **110** C3
Gunstor Rd N16 ... **16** A4
Gunter Gr SW6 ... **156** C2
Gunterstone Rd
W14 ... **140** B2
Gunthorpe St E1 ... **111** A2
Gunton Mews
SE13 ... **67** C1
Gunwhale Cl SE16 ... **32** C1
Gun Wharf
Old Ford E3 ... **26** A4
Wapping E1 ... **32** B1
Gurdon Ho **7** E14 ... **33** C3
Gurdon Rd SE7 ... **43** C1
Gurney Ho
1 Bayswater
W2 ... **100** A2
14 Bethnal Green
E2 ... **24** C3
Gurney Rd SW6 ... **59** B4
Guthrie Ct SE1 ... **135** C3
Guthrie St SW3 ... **144** A2
Gutter La EC2 ... **108** C2
Guyscliff Rd SE13 ... **67** B2
Guy's Hospl SE1 ... **137** C4
Guy St SE1 ... **137** C4
Gwalior Rd SW15 ... **57** C4
Gwendolen Ave
SW15 ... **57** C2
Gwendolen Cl
SW15 ... **57** C2
Gwendwr Rd W14 ... **140** B2
Gwent Ct **13** SE16 ... **32** C1

Gwilym Maries Ho **11**
E2 ... **25** A2
Gwyn Cl SW6 ... **156** C1
Gwynne Cl W4 ... **46** B4
Gwynne Ho
Finsbury WC1 ... **95** B3
6 Streatham SW2 ... **74** B3
Whitechapel E1 ... **32** A4
Gwynne Pl WC1 ... **95** A3
Gwynne Rd SW11 ... **167** C2
Gye Ho **2** SW4 ... **62** A3
Gylcote Cl SE5 ... **63** C3

H

Haarlem Rd 12
W14 ... **39** C3
Haberdasher Pl **4**
N1 ... **24** A2 **98** A4
Haberdashers' Aske's Hatcham Coll
4 Deptford SE14 ... **51** A1
6 Deptford SE14 ... **51** A2
... SE4 ... **51** A1
Haberdasher St
N1 ... **97** C4
Hackford Rd SW9 ... **173** A4
Hackford Wlk
SW9 ... **173** B3
HACKNEY ... **17** A2
Hackney Central Sta
E8 ... **17** A2
Hackney City Farm
E2 ... **24** C3
Hackney Com Coll **33**
N1 ... **24** A2 **98** B4
Hackney Downs Sta
E8 ... **17** A3
Hackney Empire
E8 ... **17** A2
Hackney Gr E8 ... **17** A2
Hackney New Sch **35**
N1 ... **24** A3
HACKNEY WICK ... **18** C2
Hackney Rd E2 ... **24** C3
Hackney Wick E9 ... **18** B2
Hackney Wick Sta
E9 ... **18** C2
Hackworth Point **24**
E3 ... **27** A2
Hacon Sq **12** E8 ... **17** A1
Haddo Ho
Gospel Oak NW5 ... **13** A4
Greenwich SE10 ... **52** A4
Haddon Ct W3 ... **29** B2
Haddo St SE10 ... **52** A4
Haden Ct N4 ... **5** C2
Hadfield Ho **57**
E1 ... **111** C1
Hadleigh Cl **17** E1 ... **25** B1
Hadleigh Ho **10** E1 ... **25** B1
Hadleigh St E2 ... **25** B2
Hadley Ct N16 ... **7** C3
Hadley Gdns W4 ... **37** C1
Hadley St NW1 ... **13** A2
Hadlow Ho SE17 ... **152** B2
Hadrian Cl **5** E3 ... **26** C4
Hadrian Ct SE14 ... **66** C4
Hadrian Est **33** E2 ... **24** C3
Hadrian St SE10 ... **43** A1
Hadstock Ho NW1 ... **93** C4
Hadyn Park Ct **13**
W12 ... **38** C4
Hadyn Park Rd
W12 ... **38** C4

Hafer Rd SW11 ... **60** B3
HAGGERSTON ... **24** B3
Haggerston Rd E8 ... **24** B4
Haggerston Sch **15**
E2 ... **24** B3
Haggerston Sta
E8 ... **24** B3
Haggerston Studios
E8 ... **24** B4
Hague Prim Sch **21**
E2 ... **25** A1
Hague St **30**
E2 ... **24** C2 **99** C3
Haig Ho **6** E2 ... **24** C3
Hailsham Ave SW2 ... **74** B2
Hainford Cl SE4 ... **65** C3
Haining Cl **3** W4 ... **36** C1
Hainton Cl E1 ... **32** A3
Halcomb St N1 ... **24** A4
Halcrow St E1 ... **32** A4
Halcyon Cl SW13 ... **56** C4
Haldane Pl SW18 ... **71** A3
Haldane Rd SW6 ... **155** A3
Haldon Rd SW18 ... **58** B1
Hale Ho SW1 ... **147** C2
Hales Ho **3** SW12 ... **73** A4
Hales Prior N1 ... **84** C1
Hale St E14 ... **34** A2
Halesworth Rd
SE13 ... **67** A4
Half Moon Cres
N1 ... **85** A2
Half Moon Ct EC1 ... **108** C3
Half Moon La
SE24 ... **63** B1
Halfmoon Pas E1 ... **111** A1
Half Moon St SW1 ... **118** B1
Halford Ho **9**
SW15 ... **57** C2
Halford Rd
Richmond TW10 ... **54** A2
West Brompton
SW6 ... **155** B3
Haliday Ho N1 ... **15** C2
Haliday Wlk **4** N1 ... **15** C2
Halidon Cl E9 ... **17** B3
Haliwell Ho **10**
NW6 ... **78** A3
Halkett Ho **1** E2 ... **25** B4
Halkin Arc SW1 ... **131** A2
Halkin Mews SW1 ... **131** B2
Halkin Pl SW1 ... **131** B2
Halkin St SW1 ... **131** C3
Hallam Ct W1 ... **104** B4
Hallam Ho
17 London SW9 ... **173** B4
Pimlico SW1 ... **147** A1
Hallam Mews W1 ... **104** B4
Hallam Rd SW13 ... **57** A4
Hallam St W1 ... **104** B4
Halley Gdns SE13 ... **67** C3
Halley Ho
16 Bethnal Green
E2 ... **24** C3
8 Cubitt Town
SE10 ... **43** B1
Halley Prim Sch **24**
E14 ... **33** A4
Halley St E14 ... **33** A4
Hallfield Prim Sch **21**
W2 ... **100** B1
Hall Gate NW8 ... **89** A4
Halliday Ho **10** E1 ... **111** C1
Halliford St N1 ... **15** C1
Halling Ho SE1 ... **137** C3

Hallings Wharf
Studios **2** E15 ... **27** C4
Halliwell Ct **4**
SE22 ... **64** C2
Halliwell Rd SW2 ... **62** B1
Hall Oak Wlk NW6 ... **10** B2
Hall Pl W2 ... **89** B1
Hall Rd
Leyton E15 ... **19** C4
St John's Wood
NW8 ... **89** A4
Hall Sch The NW3 ... **11** C2
Hall Sch Wimbledon
SW15 ... **68** C1
Hall St EC1 ... **96** B4
Hallsville Prim Sch
E16 ... **35** C3
Hallsville Rd E16 ... **35** B3
Hall Twr W2 ... **101** C4
Halpin Pl SE17 ... **151** C3
Halsbury Ho **4** N7 ... **14** B4
Halsbury Rd W12 ... **30** A1
Halsey St SW3 ... **144** C4
Halsmere Rd SE5 ... **48** A2
Halstead Ct N1 ... **87** C1
Halston Cl SW11 ... **60** B1
Halstow NW5 ... **12** C2
Halstow Prim Sch **4**
SE10 ... **43** C1
Halstow Rd
Greenwich SE3,
SE10 ... **43** C1
Kensal Green
NW10 ... **22** C2
Halton Cross St
N1 ... **86** B4
Halton Ho
Halton Ho **22** N1 ... **15** A1
Halton Mans N1 ... **15** A1
Halton Pl N1 ... **86** C4
Halton Rd N1 ... **86** B4
Halyard Ho E14 ... **42** A3
Hambalt Rd SW4 ... **61** B2
Hambledon SE17 ... **48** C4
Hambledon Chase
N4 ... **5** A4
Hambledon Ho E5 ... **17** A4
Hambledon Pl
SE21 ... **76** B3
Hambledon Rd
SW18 ... **70** B4
Hamble St SW6 ... **59** A4
Hambley Ho **5**
SE16 ... **40** A2
Hamblyn Ct N16 ... **7** B4
Hambridge Way
SW2 ... **74** C4
Hambrook Ct **12**
NW5 ... **13** A4
Hamers Ho **5**
SW2 ... **74** C4
Hamilton Cl
Rotherhithe SE16 ... **41** A4
St John's Wood
NW8 ... **89** B3
Hamilton Ct **9** W9 ... **89** A3
Hamilton Gdns
NW8 ... **89** A4
Hamilton Hall
NW8 ... **78** C1
Hamilton Ho
21 Bow E3 ... **26** B2
Chiswick W4 ... **46** A4
Kensington W8 ... **128** A4
1 Poplar E14 ... **33** B2

Hamilton Ho *continued*
Putney SW15 ... **56** C2
10 Richmond TW9 ... **44** C2
St John's Wood
NW8 ... **89** B4
Hamilton La N5 ... **15** A4
Hamilton Lo **8** E1 ... **25** B1
Hamilton Mews
W1 ... **132** A4
Hamilton Pk N5 ... **15** A4
Hamilton Pk W N5 ... **15** A4
Hamilton Pl W1 ... **117** C1
Hamilton Rd
Acton W4 ... **38** A4
Hendon NW11 ... **1** A4
Willesden NW10 ... **8** C3
Hamilton Sq SE1 ... **137** C4
Hamilton St SE8 ... **51** C4
Hamilton Terr
NW8 ... **89** A4
Hamlet Ct
1 Hammersmith
W6 ... **38** C2
Kennington SE11 ... **150** A2
Hamlet Gdns W6 ... **38** C2
Hamlet Ind Ctr E9 ... **18** C1
Hamlets Way E3 ... **26** B1
Hamlet Sq NW2 ... **1** A1
Hamlet The SE5 ... **63** C4
Hamlet Way SE1 ... **137** C4
Hammelton Gn **2**
SW9 ... **48** A2
Hammersley Ho **8**
SE14 ... **50** B3
HAMMERSMITH ... **39** B2
Hammersmith Acad
W12 ... **39** A4
Hammersmith Bridge
Rd W6, SW13 ... **39** B1
Hammersmith Broadway
Hammersmith W6 ... **39** B2
5 Hammersmith
W6 ... **39** B2
Hammersmith Flyover
W6 ... **39** B1
Hammersmith Gr
W6 ... **39** B3
Hammersmith Hospl
W12 ... **30** A3
Hammersmith Rd
Hammersmith W6 ... **39** C2
Kensington W14 ... **140** B4
Hammersmith Sta
W6 ... **39** B2
Hammersmith Terr **6**
W6 ... **38** C1
Hammersmith & West
London Coll **18**
W6 ... **39** C1
Hammett St EC3 ... **124** C4
Hammond Ho
10 Deptford SE14 ... **50** B3
Millwall E14 ... **42** A3
Hammond Lo **6**
W9 ... **31** C4
Hammond St NW5 ... **13** B2
Hamond Sq N1 ... **24** A3
Hampden Cl NW1 ... **83** C2
Hampden Gurney CE
Prim Sch W1 ... **102** B2
Hampden Gurney St
W1 ... **102** C1
Hampden Rd N19 ... **4** C2
Hampshire Ct **6**
SW13 ... **46** B1

Hampshire Hog La
3 Hammersmith
W6 .... 39 A1
11 Hammersmith
W6 .... 39 A2
Hampshire St
NW5 .... 13 C2
Hampson Way
SW8 .... 172 C4
HAMPSTEAD 11 B2
Hampstead Coll of
Fine Arts &
Humanities **12**
NW3 .... 12 A2
Hampstead Com Mkt
NW3 .... 11 C4
Hampstead Gate
NW3 .... 11 B3
Hampstead Gn
NW3 .... 12 A3
Hampstead Gr NW3 .. 2 B1
Hampstead Heath
NW3 .... 2 B3
Hampstead Heath Sta
NW3 .... 12 A4
Hampstead High St
NW3 .... 11 C3
Hampstead Hill Gdns
NW3 .... 12 A4
Hampstead Hill Sch
1 NW3 .... 12 A4
Hampstead La N6 ..... 3 A4
Hampstead Parochial
CE Prim Sch **30**
NW3 .... 11 B4
Hampstead Rd
NW1 .... 92 C4
Hampstead Sch
NW2 .... 10 A4
Hampstead Sq **1**
NW3 .... 2 B1
Hampstead Sta
NW3 .... 11 B4
Hampstead Theatre
NW3 .... 11 C1
Hampstead West **1**
NW6 .... 10 C2
Hampstead Wlk **1**
E3 .... 26 B4
Hampton Ct
1 Islington N1 ..... 15 A2
19 Rotherhithe
SE16 .... 32 C1
Hampton Ho SE1 .. 150 B3
Hamstead Gates **11**
NW5 .... 13 A2
Ham Yd W1 .... 119 B4
Hana Mews E5 ..... 17 A4
Hanbury Ho
8 Bethnal Green
E1 .... 111 B4
South Lambeth
SW8 .... 162 B3
Hanbury Mews N1 .. 87 A3
Hanbury Rd W3 ... 37 A4
Hanbury St E1 .... 111 A4
Hancock Nunn Ho **1**
NW3 .... 12 B1
Hancock Rd E3 ... 27 B2
Handa Wlk **3** N1 .. 15 B2
Hand Ct WC1 ..... 107 A3
Handel & Hendrix in
London W1 ...... 118 B4
Handel Mans
Barnes SW13 ...... 47 B3

Handel Mans *continued*
Bloomsbury WC1 ... 94 B2
Handel St WC1 ..... 94 B2
Handforth Rd
SW9 .... 163 B2
Handley Rd E9 ... 25 B4
Hands Wlk E16 ... 35 C3
Handyside St N1 .. 84 A3
Hanford Cl SW18 .. 70 C3
Hankey Pl SE1 .. 137 C3
Hanley Ct N4 .... 5 B3
Hanley Gdns N4 ...... 5 B3
Hanley Rd N4, N19 ... 5 A3
Hanmer Wlk N7 ... 5 B2
Hannah Mary Way **17**
SE1 .... 153 C3
Hannay La N8 .... 4 C4
Hannay Wlk SW16 .. 73 C2
Hannell Rd SW6 .. 154 B2
Hannen Ho SE5 ... 63 C3
Hannen Rd SE27 .. 75 A1
Hannibal Rd E1 ... 32 B4
Hannington Rd
SW4 .... 61 A4
Hanover Ave E16 .. 35 C1
Hanover Cl TW9 .. 44 C3
Hanover Ct
Shepherd's Bush
W12 .... 29 C1
Stamford Hill N16 .. 7 A3
Hanover Gate Mans
NW1 .... 90 B2
Hanover Gdns
SE11 .... 163 B3
Hanover Mans **5**
SW2 .... 62 C2
Hanover Pk SE15 .. 49 C2
Hanover Pl
10 Bow E3 .... 26 B2
St Giles WC2 .... 106 B1
Hanover Prim Sch
N1 .... 86 C2
Hanover Rd NW10 .. 22 B4
Hanover Sq W1 ... 104 B1
Hanover St W1 ... 104 B1
Hanover Stps W2 .. 102 B1
Hanover Terr NW1 .. 90 C3
Hanover Terrace
Mews NW1 .... 90 C3
Hanover West Ind Est
NW10 .... 20 C2
Hanover Yd N1 ... 86 C2
Hansard Mews
W14 .... 39 C4
Hanscomb Mews
SW4 .... 61 B3
Hans Cres SW1 .. 130 C2
Hansler Ct **14**
SW19 .... 70 A3
Hansler Rd SE22 .. 64 B2
Hansom Mews
SE11 .... 149 A2
Hanson Cl
Balham SW12 ...... 73 A4
Mortlake SW14 ... 55 B4
Hanson Ho **2** E1 .. 125 C4
Hanson St W1 .... 104 C4
Hans Pl SW1 ..... 130 C2
Hans Rd SW3 .... 130 C2
Hans St SW1 ..... 131 A1
Hanway Ho **28**
SW9 .... 173 C4
Hanway Pl W1 ... 105 B2
Hanway St W1 ... 105 B2

Hanworth Ho SE5 .. 48 A3
Harben Rd NW6 ... 11 B1
Harberson Rd
SW12 .... 73 A3
Harberton Rd N19 .. 4 B3
Harbet Rd W2 .... 101 C3
Harbinger Prim Sch
1 E14 .... 42 A2
Harbinger Rd E14 .. 42 A2
Harbin Ho **5** SW2 .. 74 C3
Harbledown Ho
SE1 .... 137 B3
Harbledown Rd
SW6 .... 165 B4
Harbord Cl
Camberwell SE15 ... 49 A3
London SE5 ...... 48 C1
Harbord Ho **5**
SE16 .... 40 C2
Harbord St SW6 .. 47 C2
Harbour Ave
SW10 .... 167 A3
Harbour Exchange Sq
E14 .... 42 A4
Harbour Rd SE5 .. 63 B4
Harbridge Ave
SW15 .... 68 C4
Harbut Rd SW11 ... 59 C3
Harcombe Rd N16 .. 7 A1
Harcourt Ho
27 Clapham
SW8 .... 171 B2
Marylebone W1 .. 104 A2
4 Willesden NW10 .. 9 B2
Harcourt Rd E15 .. 54 C4
Harcourt St W1 .. 102 B3
Harcourt Terr
SW10 .... 142 B1
Hardcastle Ho
3 New Cross Gate
SE14 .... 51 A2
8 Peckham SE15 .. 49 C2
Hardel Rise SW2 .. 75 A3
Hardel Wlk SW24,
SW2 .... 74 C4
Harden Ho SE5 ... 49 A1
Harders Rd SE15 .. 50 A1
Hardess St SE24 .. 63 B4
Hardham Ho **5**
SE5 .... 48 C2
Harding Cl SE17 .. 48 B4
Hardinge Rd
NW10 .... 22 B4
Hardinge St E1 ... 32 B3
Harding Ho SW13 .. 47 A4
Hardington **2**
NW1 .... 12 C1
Hardwick Ho **14**
NW8 .... 90 B2
Hardwicke Mews
WC1 .... 95 A3
Hardwicke Rd W4 .. 37 C2
Hardwick Ho
14 London SW8 .. 171 B2
Hardwick St EC1 .. 95 C3
Hardwick's Way
SW18 .... 58 C2
Hardwidge St
SE1 .... 138 A4
Hardy Ave **4** E16 .. 35 C1
Hardy Cl SE16 ..... 40 C4
Hardy Cotts **2**
SE10 .... 52 C4
Hardy Ct SE3 ..... 53 B4
Hardy Rd SE3 .... 53 B4

Hare and Billet Rd
SE3 .... 52 C1
Harecourt Rd N1 .. 15 B2
Hare Ct EC4 ...... 107 B1
Haredale Ho **24**
SE16 .... 139 B3
Haredale Rd SE24 .. 63 B3
Harefield Mews
SE4 .... 66 B4
Harefield Rd SE4 .. 66 B4
Hare Marsh
E2 .... 24 C1 99 B2
Hare Pl EC4 ...... 107 C1
Hare Row E2 ...... 25 A3
Hare Wlk N1 .... 24 A3
Harewood Ave
NW1 .... 90 B1
Harewood Pl W1 .. 104 B1
Harewood Row
NW1 .... 102 B4
Harfield Gdns **1**
SE5 .... 64 A4
Harfleur Ct SE11 .. 150 A3
Harford Ho
Camberwell SE5 ... 48 B4
Notting Hill W11 .. 31 B4
Harford Mews **5**
N19 .... 4 C1
Harford St E1 ..... 26 A1
Hargrave Mans **3**
N19 .... 4 C2
Hargrave Park Sch
14 London N19 ..... 4 B2
10 Upper Holloway
N19 .... 4 C2
Hargrave Pl N7 ... 13 C3
Hargrave Rd N19 .. 4 B2
Hargraves Ho **14**
W12 .... 30 A2
Hargwyne St SW9 .. 62 B4
Harkness Ho **30**
E1 .... 111 C1
Harlech Twr **5**
W3 .... 37 B4
Harlescott Rd
SE15 .... 65 C3
HARLESDEN 21 B4
Harlesden Gdns
NW10 .... 21 B4
Harlesden Plaza **2**
NW10 .... 21 B4
Harlesden Prim Sch
NW10 .... 21 A3
Harlesden Rd
NW10 .... 21 C4
Harlesden Sta
NW10 .... 20 C3
Harleyford Ct
SW8 .... 162 C4
Harleyford Manor **3**
W3 .... 28 B1
Harleyford Rd
SE11 .... 162 C4
Harleyford St
SE11 .... 163 B3
Harley Gdns
SW10 .... 143 A1
Harley Gr **3** E3 .. 26 B2
Harley Ho NW1 ... 91 C1
Harley Pl W1 .... 104 A3
Harley Rd
Hampstead NW3 .. 11 C1
Harlesden NW10 .. 21 A3
Harley St Clinic The
W1 .... 104 A4

Harley St W1 ..... 104 A3
Harley Villas
NW10 .... 21 A3
Harling Ct **3**
SW11 .... 168 C2
Harlowe Ho **13** E8 .. 24 B4
Harlynwood **19**
SE5 .... 48 B3
Harman Cl
10 Bermondsey
SE1 .... 153 B1
Cricklewood NW2 ... 1 A1
Harman Dr NW2 ... 10 A4
Harmood Gr NW1 .. 13 A1
Harmood Ho **8**
NW1 .... 13 A1
Harmood St NW1 .. 13 A1
Harmsworth St
SE17 .... 150 A1
Harnage Ho TW8 .. 36 A1
Harney Ct SE14 ... 51 A2
Harold Ct SE16 ... 40 C4
Harold Est SE1 .. 138 B1
Harold Ho **15** E2 .. 25 C3
Harold Laski Ho
EC1 .... 96 B3
Harold Maddison Ho
SE17 .... 150 B2
Harold Rd NW10 .. 20 C2
Harold Wilson Ho
SW6 .... 155 A3
Harp Alley EC4 ... 108 A2
Harpenden Point
NW2 .... 1 B2
Harper Ho **3** SW9 .. 63 A4
Harper Mews
SW17 .... 71 B1
Harper Rd SE1 .. 137 A2
Harp La EC3 ..... 124 A3
Harpley Sq **1** E1 .. 25 C1
Harpsden St
SW11 .... 169 B3
Harpur Mews
WC1 .... 106 C4
Harpur St WC1 .. 106 C4
Harrier Ho **9**
SW11 .... 60 A4
Harriet Cl E8 ..... 24 C4
Harriet Ho SW6 .. 156 B1
Harriet St SW1 .. 131 A3
Harriet Tubman Cl **21**
SW2 .... 74 C4
Harriet Wlk SW1 .. 131 A3
Harrington Ct
South Kensington
SW7 .... 143 C4
9 West Kilburn
W9 .... 23 B2
Harrington Gdns
SW7 .... 142 C3
Harrington Ho
Regent's Pk NW1 .. 92 C4
Westminster SW1 .. 147 C2
Harrington Rd
SW7 .... 143 B4
Harrington Sq
NW1 .... 82 C1
Harrington St NW1 .. 92 C4
Harriott Cl SE10 .. 43 B2
Harriott Ho **11** E1 .. 32 B3

Harris Acad at
Peckham SE15 . . . . . .49 B2

Harris Acad
Bermondsey
SE1 . . . . .153 A4

Harris Academy
Battersea SW11 . . . .169 A3

Harris Boys' Academy
East Dulwich
SE22 . . . . .65 A2

Harris Girls' Acad East
Dulwich SE15 . . . . . .65 B2

Harris Ho
8 Bow E3 . . . . .26 C2
7 Brixton SW9 . . . . .62 C4
Harrison Ho SE17 . .151 B2
Harrison Rd NW10 . .20 C4
Harrisons Ct 1
SE14 . . . . .50 C4
Harrison St WC1 . . . .94 B3
Harris St SE5 . . . . . . .48 C3
Harrodian Sch The
SW13 . . . . .46 B3
Harrogate Ct 2
SE26 . . . . .76 C1
Harrold Ho 1
NW3 . . . . .11 B1
Harroway Rd
SW11 . . . . .167 C2
Harrowby St W1 . . .102 B2
Harrowgate Ho 22
E9 . . . . .17 C2
Harrowgate Rd E9 . .18 A1
Harrow La E14 . . . . . .34 B2
Harrow Pl E1 . . . . . .110 B2
Harrow St
Little Venice W2 . . . .101 A3
Westbourne Green W2,
W9 . . . . .23 C1
Harrow St 1 . . . . . .102 A4
Harry Gosling Prim
Sch E1 . . . . .111 C1
Harry Hinkins Ho
SE17 . . . . .151 A1
Harry Lambourn Ho
10 SE15 . . . . .50 A3
Harston Wlk E3 . . . . .27 A1
Hartfield Terr E3 . . .26 C2
Hartham Cl N7 . . . . .14 A3
Hartham Rd N7 . . . . .14 A3
Hart Ho SW2 . . . . . . .74 C3
Hartington Ct
Chiswick W4 . . . . .45 A3
South Lambeth
SW8 . . . . .172 A4
Hartington Rd
Chiswick W4 . . . . .45 A3
South Lambeth
SW8 . . . . .162 A1
Hartismere Rd
SW6 . . . . .155 A2
Hartlake Rd E9 . . . . .18 A2
Hartland NW1 . . . . . .83 A3
Hartland Rd
Camden Town
NW1 . . . . .13 A1
Kilburn NW6 . . . . .23 B4
Hartley Ho
Bermondsey SE1 . . . .153 A4
Putney SW15 . . . . . . .56 C2
Hartley St E2 . . . . . . .25 B2
Hartley St E2 . . . . . . .25 B2
Hartnoll Ho 2
Hartnoll St N7 . . . . . .14 B3

Harton Lodge 2
SE8 . . . . .51 C2
Harton St SE8 . . . . . .51 C2
Hartopp Ct 20 N16 . .7 A1
Hartopp Point
SW6 . . . . .154 B2
Hartshorn Alley
EC3 . . . . .110 B1
Hart's La SE14 . . . . .51 A2
Hart St EC3 . . . . . . .124 B4
Hartswood Ho 10
SW2 . . . . .74 A3
Hartswood Rd
W12 . . . . .38 B3
Hartwell Cl 12
SW2 . . . . .74 B3
Hartwell St E22 . . . . .16 A3
Hartwell St E8 . . . . . .16 B2
Harvard Ct NW6 . . . .11 A3
Harvard Hill W4 . . . .45 A4
Harvard Ho
3 Camberwell
SE17 . . . . .48 A4
Putney SW15 . . . . . . .57 C1
Harvard Mans 18
SW11 . . . . .59 C3
Harvard Rd
11 Acton Green
W4 . . . . .37 B1
Gunnersbury W4 . . . .37 A1
Lewisham SE13 . . . . .67 B1
Harvey Cl SW11 . . .168 B3
Harvey Ho
1 Bethnal Green
E1 . . . . .25 A1
Brentford TW8 . . . . . .36 A1
Pimlico SW1 . . . . . . .147 C1
Shoreditch N1 . . . . . .87 C3
Harvey Lo 9 W9 . . .31 C4
Harvey Point 7
E16 . . . . .35 C4
Harvey Rd 15 SE5 . .48 C2
Harvey St N1 . . . . . . .87 C3
Harvington Wlk
E8 . . . . .16 C1
Harvist Rd NW6 . . . .23 A3
Harwood Ct
Putney SW15 . . . . . . .57 B3
Shoreditch N1 . . . . . .87 C3
Harwood Point
SE16 . . . . .41 B4
Harwood Rd SW6 .156 A1
Harwood Terr
SW6 . . . . .166 A4
Hascombe Ho 11
SW15 . . . . .69 A3
Hascombe Terr 2
SE5 . . . . .48 C1
Haselrigge Rd
SW4 . . . . .61 C3
Hasker St SW3 . . . .144 B4
Haslam Cl N1 . . . . . .14 C1
Haslam Ho 10 N1 . . .15 B1
Haslam St SE15 . . . .49 B2
Haslemere Ave
SW18 . . . . .71 A2
Haslemere Ct 5
N16 . . . . .7 A3
Haslemere Ind Est
SW18 . . . . .71 A2
Haslemere Rd N8 . . .5 A4
Hassard St E2 . . . . . .24 B3
Hassett Rd E9 . . . . . .18 A2
Hassop Rd NW2 . . . . .9 C4
Hastings Cl 17
SE15 . . . . .49 C3

Hastings Ho 18
W12 . . . . .30 A2
Hastings Hos WC1 . .94 A3
Hastings St 1 . . . . . . .94 A3
Hatcham Mews Bsns
Ctr SE14 . . . . .50 C2
Hatcham Park Mews
SE14 . . . . .50 C2
Hatcham Park Rd
SE14 . . . . .50 C2
Hatcham Rd SE15 . .50 B4
Hatchard Rd N19 . . . .5 A2
Hatchers Mews
SE1 . . . . .138 B3
Hatcliffe Almshouses
SE10 . . . . .43 A1
Hatcliffe St SE10 . . .43 A1
Hatfield Cl SE14 . . . .50 C3
Hatfield Ct SE3 . . . . .53 C3
Hatfield Ho EC1 . . . .96 C1
Hatfield Rd W4 . . . . .37 C4
Hatfields SE1 . . . . . .121 C2
Hathaway Ho 3
N1 . . . . .24 A2 98 A4
Hatherley Ct 5
W2 . . . . .100 A2
Hatherley Gr W2 . .100 A2
Hatherley Rd TW9 . .44 B2
Hatherley St SW1 . .147 A3
Hathersage Ct N1 . .15 C3
Hathersley Ho 3
SW2 . . . . .74 C4
Hathorne Cl 3
SE15 . . . . .50 A1
Hathway Ho 3
SE15 . . . . .50 B1
Hathway St 5
SE15 . . . . .50 B1
Hatley Rd N4, N7 . . . .5 B2
Hat & Mitre Ct EC1 .96 B1
Hatstone Ct 2
N3 . . . . .11 B3
Hatteraick St 16
SE16 . . . . .40 B4
Hatton Gdn EC1 . . .107 C4
Hatton Ho 7 E1 . . . .125 C4
Hatton Pl EC1 . . . . .107 C4
Hatton Row NW8 . . .89 C1
Hatton St NW8 . . . . .89 C1
Hatton Wall EC1 . . .107 B4
Haunch of Venison Yd
W1 . . . . .104 A1
Hauteville Court Gdns
3 W6 . . . . .38 B3
Havana Rd SW18, . . .70 C2
Havannah St E14 . . .41 C4
Havelock Cl 13
W12 . . . . .30 A2
Havelock Ct 8
SE15 . . . . .50 A3
Havelock St N1 . . . . .84 B4
Havelock Terr
SW8 . . . . .160 B1
Haven Cl SW19 . . . . .69 C1
Havenpool NW8 . . . .78 B3
Haven St 10 NW1 . . .13 A1
Haven The TW9 . . . . .54 C4
Havercourt 3
NW3 . . . . .12 A2
Haverfield Gdns
TW9 . . . . .44 C3
Haverfield Rd E3 . . .26 A2
Haverhill Rd SW12 . .73 B3
Havering 8 NW1 . . . .13 A1
Havering Ho N4 . . . . .6 B4

Havering St E1 . . . . .32 C3
Haversham Lo NW2 . .9 C3
Haversham Pl N6 . . . .3 B2
Haverstock Hill
NW3 . . . . .12 B2
Haverstock Rd
NW5 . . . . .12 C3
Haverstock Sch 12
NW3 . . . . .12 C2
Haverstock St N1, 86 B1
Havilland Mews
W12 . . . . .39 A4
Havil St SE5 . . . . .49 A2
Havisham Ho 25
SE16 . . . . .139 B3
Hawarden Gr SE24 . .75 B4
Hawberry Lo N7 . . . .14 A2
Hawes St N1 . . . . . . .15 A1
Hawgood St E3 . . . . .33 C4
Hawke Ho 20 E1 . . . .25 C1
Hawke Pl 26 SE16 . .40 C4
Hawkesbury Rd
SW15 . . . . .57 A2
Hawkesdown House
Sch W2 . . . .31 C1 113 C1
Hawkesworth Ho 5
SW4 . . . . .61 B1
Hawke Twr 4
SE14 . . . . .51 A4
Hawk Ho 7 SW11 . . .60 A4
Hawkins Ho 3
SE8 . . . . .51 C4
Hawkins Rd NW10 . .8 A1
Hawkley Gdns
SE27 . . . . .75 A2
Hawkridge 1
NW5 . . . . .12 C2
Hawkshaw Cl 23
SW2 . . . . .74 A4
Hawkshead 4
NW1 . . . . .92 C4
Hawkshead Rd
Acton W4 . . . . .38 A4
Willesden NW10 . . . . .8 B1
Hawkslade Rd
SE15 . . . . .65 C2
Hawksley Rd N16 . . . .7 A1
Hawks Mews 10
SE10 . . . . .52 B3
Hawksmoor Mews
E1 . . . . .32 A2
Hawksmoor Pl 2
E2 . . . . .24 C1 99 B2
Hawksmoor St 5
W6 . . . . .47 C4
Hawkstone Rd
SE16 . . . . .40 B2
Hawkwell Wlk N1 . . .87 A4
Hawley Cres NW1 . .13 A1
Hawley Inf Sch 28
NW1 . . . . .13 A1
Hawley Mews 4
NW1 . . . . .13 A1
Hawley Rd 3 N1 . . .13 A1
Hawley St NW1 . . . . .13 A1
Haworth Ho 7
SW2 . . . . .62 C1
Hawstead Rd SE6 . . .67 A1
Hawthorn Ct
Putney SW15 . . . . . . .57 A4
Richmond TW9 . . . . . .45 A2
Hawthorne Ave E3 . .26 B4
Hawthorne Cl N1 . . .16 A2
Hawthorne Cres
SE10 . . . . .43 B1

Hawthorne Ho
SW1 . . . . .147 A1
Hawthorn Ho SE14 . .51 B2
Hawthorn Rd NW10 . .8 C1
Hawthorn Wlk
W10 . . . . .23 A1
Hawtrey Rd NW3 . . .12 A1
Haycroft Gdns
NW10 . . . . .22 A4
Haycroft Mans
NW10 . . . . .21 C4
Haycroft Rd SW2 . . .62 A2
Hay Currie St E14 . .34 A3
Hayday Rd E16 . . . . .35 C4
Hayden Piper Ho
SW3 . . . . .158 C4
Hayden's Pl W11 . . .31 B3
Haydon Ho 5 SW11 .60 A4
Haydon Way SW11 . .59 C3
Haydon Wlk E1 . . . .111 A1
Hayes Ct
2 Camberwell
SE5 . . . . .48 B3
Streatham SW12 . . . .74 A3
Hayes Gr SE15,
SE22 . . . . .64 B3
Hayes Pl NW1 . . . . . .90 B1
Hayes Pl NW1 . . . . . .90 B1
Hayfield Pass E1 . . . .25 B1
Hayfield Yd 18 E1 . .25 B1
Hay Hill W1 . . . . . . .118 B3
Hayhurst N1 . . . . . . .86 B4
Hayles Bldgs
SE11 . . . . .150 B4
Hayles St SE11 . . . .150 A4
Hayling Ct 21 N16 . .16 C3
Haymans Point
SE11 . . . . .148 C2
Haymarket SW1 . . .119 B3
Haymerle Ho 6
SE15 . . . . .49 C4
Haymerle Rd SE15 . .49 C4
Haymerle Sch 15
SE15 . . . . .49 C4
Hayne Ho
W11 . . . . .31 A1 112 A2
Haynes Ho 3 E9 . . . .17 C2
Hayne St EC1 . . . . . .108 B4
Hay's Galleria
SE1 . . . . .124 A2
Hay's La SE1 . . . . . .124 A2
Hay's Mews W1 . . .118 A2
Hay St E2 . . . . .24 C4
Hayter Ho W12 . . . . .29 C2
Hayter Rd SW2 . . . . .62 B2
Haythorn Ho
SW11 . . . . .167 C3
Hayton Cl 11 E8 . . . .16 B2
Hayward Ct 14
SW4 . . . . .172 B2
Hayward Gallery
SE1 . . . . .121 A2
Hayward Gdns
SW15 . . . . .57 B1
Hayward Ho N1 . . . .85 B2
Hayward Mews 1
SE4 . . . . .66 B2
Hayward's Pl EC1 . . .96 A2
Haywood Lo 23
N7 . . . . .14 C3
Hazelbourne Rd
SW12 . . . . .61 A1
Hazel Cl
Peckham SE15 . . . . . .49 C1
Upper Holloway N19 . .4 B2

Hazel Ct **8** SE16 . . . 33 A1
Hazeldon Rd SE4 . . . . 66 A2
Hazel Ho
London SE4 . . . . 66 B4
12 Maitland Pk
NW3 . . . . 12 B2
Hazel La SE10 . . . . . . 43 B1
Hazellville Rd N19 . . . 4 C3
Hazelmere Ct **10**
SW2 . . . . 74 B3
Hazelmere Rd
NW6 . . . . 23 B4
Hazel Rd NW10 . . . . . 22 B2
Hazel Way SE1 . . . . . 152 C4
Hazelwood Cl W5 . . . 36 A4
Hazelwood Ho **11**
SE8 . . . . 41 A2
Hazelwood Mans
SW6 . . . . 164 C4
Hazlebury Rd
SW6 . . . . 166 B2
Hazledene Rd W4 . . . 45 B4
Hazlewell Rd
SW15 . . . . 57 B2
Hazlewood Cres
W10 . . . . 23 A1
Hazlewood Mews
SW9 . . . . 62 A4
Hazlewood Twr
W10 . . . . 23 B1
Hazlitt Mews
W14 . . . . 126 A1
Hazlitt Rd W14 . . . . 126 A1
Headbourne Ho
SE1 . . . . 137 C2
Headcorn M N15 . . . 13 C4
Headfort Pl SW1 . . . 131 C3
Headington Rd
SW18 . . . . 71 C2
Headlam Rd SW4 . . . 73 C4
Headlam St E1 . . . . . 25 A1
Heads Mews N1 . . . . 31 C3
Head St E1 . . . . 32 C3
Heald St SE8, SE14 . . 51 C2
Healey St NW1 . . . . . 13 A2
Healy Ho **2** E3 . . . . . 26 C1
Heanor Ct **4** E5 . . . . 17 C4
Hearne Rd W4 . . . . . 44 C4
Hearn's Bldgs
SE17 . . . . 151 C3
Hearnshaw St **1**
E14 . . . . 33 A3
Hearn St
EC2 . . . . 24 A1 98 B1
Hearnville Rd
SW12 . . . . 72 C3
Heart Radio W11 . . . 30 C2
Heathbrook Prim Sch
3 SW4 . . . . 170 C1
Heath Brow NW3 . . . 2 B1
Heath Cl NW11 . . . . . 2 A4
Heathcote Gate
SW6 . . . . 58 C4
Heathcote Point **9**
E9 . . . . 17 C2
Heathcote St WC1 . . . 94 C3
Heathcroft NW11 . . . 2 A3
Heath Ct
2 Hampstead
NW3 . . . . 11 B2
Stoke Newington
N16 . . . . 6 C3
Heath Dr NW3 . . . . . 11 A4
Heather Cl
Clapham SW8 . . . . . . 61 A4
6 Finsbury Park N7 . . 5 B1

Heather Ct SW4 . . . 172 B3
Heather Ho **11** E14 . . 34 B3
Heatherley Ct N16 . . . 7 C1
Heatherley Sch of
Fine Art SW10 . . . . 156 C1
Heather Lo N16 . . . . . 7 A3
Heather Wlk W10 . . . 23 A1
Heathfield Ave
SW18 . . . . 71 C4
Heathfield Ct
1 Bow E3 . . . . 26 C3
5 Chiswick W4 . . . . 37 C1
Wandsworth SW18 . . 71 C4
Heathfield Gdns
Acton Green W4 . . . . 37 B1
Blackheath SE3 . . . . . 53 A1
Wandsworth SW18 . . 59 C1
Heathfield Ho SE3 . . . 53 A1
Heathfield House Sch
14 W4 . . . . 37 B1
Heathfield Pk NW2 . . 9 B2
Heathfield Rd
South Acton W3 . . . . 37 A4
Wandsworth SW18 . . 59 C1
Heathfield Sq
SW18 . . . . 71 C4
Heathfield Terr
W4 . . . . 37 C1
Heathgate Pl NW3 . . 12 B4
Heath House Prep
Sch **1** SE8 . . . . . . 53 B1
Heath Hurst Rd
NW3 . . . . 12 A4
Heath La SE3 . . . . . . 52 C1
Heathland Rd N16 . . . 7 A3
Heath Mans
5 Hampstead
NW3 . . . . 11 B4
Putney SW15 . . . . . . 57 C1
Heathman's Rd
SW6 . . . . 165 A3
Heath Mead SW19 . . 69 C1
Heathmere Prim Sch
SW15 . . . . 68 C3
Heath Park Gdns
NW3 . . . . 2 A1
Heathpool Ct **8**
E1 . . . . 25 A1
Heath Rd SW8 . . . . 170 B1
Heath Rise SW15 . . . 57 C1
Heath Royal SW15 . . 57 C1
Heathshott **8**
TW10 . . . . 54 A1
Heathside NW3 . . . . . 11 C4
Heathside Prep Sch
32 NW3 . . . . 11 B4
Heath St NW3 . . . . . 2 B1
Heathstan Rd W12 . . 29 C3
Heath View NW5 . . . 12 C4
Heathview Ct
SW19 . . . . 69 C2
Heathview Gdns
SW15 . . . . 69 B4
Heath Villas NW3 . . . 11 C4
Heathville Rd N4,
N19 . . . . 5 A4
Heathwall St
SW11 . . . . 60 B4
Heathway SE3 . . . . . 53 C3
Heathway Ct NW3 . . 1 C2
Heathwood Ct
SW12 . . . . 73 B3
Heaton Ho
Chelsea SW10 . . . . 157 A4
2 Peckham SE15 . . 50 A1
Heaton Rd SE15 . . . . 50 A1

Heaven Tree Cl
N1 . . . . 15 B3
Heaver Rd **23**
SW11 . . . . 59 C4
Hebden Ct **24** E2 . . . 24 B4
Hebdon Rd SW17 . . . 72 A1
Heber Prim Sch
SE22 . . . . 64 B1
Heber Rd
Cricklewood NW2 . . . 9 C3
East Dulwich SE22 . . 64 B1
Hebron Rd W6 . . . . . 39 A3
Heckfield Pl SW6 . . 155 B1
Heckford Ho E14 . . . 34 A3
Heckford St E1 . . . . . 32 C2
Hector Ct
1 London SW9 . . . 173 B4
Putney SW15 . . . . . . 57 C2
Hector Ho **02** E2 . . . 25 A3
Heddington Gr N7 . . . 14 B3
Heddon St W1 . . . . 118 C4
Hedger's Gr E9 . . . . . 18 A2
Hedger St SE11 . . . . 150 A4
Hedingham Cl **6**
N1 . . . . 15 B1
Hedley Ct SW15 . . . . 57 C1
Hedley Ho E14 . . . . . 42 B3
Hedley Row N5,
N7 . . . . 15 C3
Hedsor Ho
E2 . . . . 24 B1 98 C2
Heidegger Cres
SW13 . . . . 47 A3
Heights The NW3 . . . 11 B4
Heiron St SE17 . . . . . 48 A4
Helby Rd SW4 . . . . . 61 C1
Heldar Ct SE1 . . . . . 137 C3
Helena Pl E9 . . . . 25 B4
Helena Rd NW10 . . . 9 A3
Helena Sq **18** SE16 . . 33 A2
Helen Gladstone Ho
SE1 . . . . 136 A4
Helen Ho **2** E2 . . . . . 25 A3
Helen Mackay Ho **10**
E14 . . . . 34 C3
Helen Peele Cotts **10**
SE16 . . . . 40 B3
Helenslea Ave
NW11 . . . . 1 C3
Helen's Pl E2 . . . . . . 25 B2
Helen Taylor Ho **5**
SE16 . . . . 153 B4
Heliport Ind Est
SW11 . . . . 167 C1
Helix Ct **17** W11 . . . 30 C1
Helix Gdns SW2 . . . . 62 B1
Helix Rd SW2 . . . . . . 62 B1
Helix The SW19 . . . . 69 C2
Hellings St E1 . . . . . 125 C1
Helmet Row EC1 . . . . 97 A2
Helmsdale Ho
NW6 . . . . 78 A1
Helmsley Pl E8 . . . . . 17 A1
Helmsley St **7** E8 . . 17 A1
Helperby Rd NW10 . . 8 A1
Helsby Ct NW8 . . . . . 89 B2
Helsinki Sq SE16 . . . 41 A3
Helston NW1 . . . . . . 83 A2
Helston Ho SE11 . . . 149 C2
Hemans Est SW8 . . 161 C1
Hemans St SW8 . . . 161 C1
Hemberton Rd
SW9 . . . . 62 A4
Hemingford Rd N1 . . 85 A4
Hemlock Rd W12 . . . 29 B2

Hemming St
E1 . . . . 24 C1 99 C1
Hemmingway Cl
NW5 . . . . 12 C4
Hemp Wlk SE17 . . . 151 C4
Hemstal Rd NW6 . . . 10 C1
Hemsworth Ct N1 . . 24 A3
Hemsworth St N1 . . 24 A3
Hemus Pl SW3 . . . . 144 B1
Henchman St W12 . . 29 B3
Henderson Ct
8 Deptford SE14 . . . 50 C4
Hampstead NW3 . . . 11 C3
Wandsworth SW18 . . 72 A4
Henderson Dr
NW8 . . . . 89 B2
Henderson Rd
SW18 . . . . 72 A4
Hendham Rd
SW17 . . . . 72 B2
Hendre Ho SE1 . . . . 152 B3
Hendre Rd SE1 . . . . 152 B3
Hendrick Ave
SW12 . . . . 72 B4
Heneage La EC3 . . . 110 B1
Heneage Pl EC3 . . . 110 B1
Heneage St E1 . . . . 111 A4
Henfield Cl N19 . . . . 4 B3
Hengrave Rd SE23 . . 65 B1
Henley Ct
Brondesbury NW2 . . . 9 C2
Peckham SE15 . . . . . 64 C4
Henley Dr SE1 . . . . 153 A4
Henley Ho
E2 . . . . 24 B1 99 A2
Henley Prior N1 . . . . 84 C1
Henley Rd NW10 . . . 22 B4
Henley St SW11 . . . 169 C2
Henniker Mews
SW3 . . . . 157 B4
Henniker Rd E15 . . . 19 C3
Henning St SW11 . . 168 A3
Henrietta Cl SE8 . . . 51 C4
Henrietta Ho **11**
W6 . . . . 39 B1
Henrietta Mews
WC1 . . . . 94 B2
Henrietta Pl W1 . . . 104 A2
Henrietta St
Strand WC2 . . . . . . 120 B4
Stratford New Town
E15 . . . . 19 B3
Henriques St E1 . . . 111 C1
Henry Dent Cl SE5 . . 63 C4
Henry Dickens Ct
W11 . . . . 31 A2
Henry Fawcett Prim
Sch **8** SE11 . . . . 163 B4
Henry Ho
Lambeth SE1 . . . . . 121 C1
South Lambeth
SW8 . . . . 162 A2
St John's Wood
NW8 . . . . 90 A2
Henry Jackson Ho **4**
SW15 . . . . 57 C4
Henry Jackson Rd
SW15 . . . . 57 C4
Henry Rd N4 . . . . . . 6 B3
Henryson Rd SE4 . . . 66 C2
Henry Wise Ho
SW1 . . . . 147 A3
Henshall Point **19**
E3 . . . . 27 A2
Henshall St N1 . . . . . 15 C2
Henshaw St SE17 . . 151 B4

Hensley Point **20**
E9 . . . . 18 A2
Henslowe Rd SE22 . . 64 C2
Henslow Ho **12**
SE15 . . . . 49 C3
Henson Ave NW2 . . . 9 B3
Henson Ct **3** N5 . . . 15 B4
Henstridge Pl
NW8 . . . . 80 A3
Henty Cl SW11 . . . . 168 B4
Henty Wlk SW15 . . . 57 A2
Hepburn Mews
SW11 . . . . 60 B2
Hepburn Pl W3 . . . . . 28 A2
Hepplestone Cl
SW15 . . . . 57 A1
Hepscott Rd E9 . . . . 18 C1
Hepworth Ct
Chelsea SW1 . . . . . 146 A1
Islington N1 . . . . 86 A4
Hera Ct **15** E14 . . . . 41 C2
Heralds Pl SE11 . . . 150 A4
Herald St **5** E2 . . . . 25 A1
Herald Hill EC1 . . . . 95 C1
Herbert Chapman Ct
N5 . . . . 15 A4
Herbert Cres
SW1 . . . . 131 A2
Herbert Gdns
Chiswick W4 . . . . . . 45 A4
Willesden Green
NW10 . . . . 22 A3
Herbert Ho E1 . . . . . 110 C2
Herbert Mews **15**
SW2 . . . . 62 C1
Herbert Morrison Ho
SW6 . . . . 154 C3
Herbert Morrison
Prim Sch SW8 . . . 162 A1
Herbert St NW5 . . . . 12 C2
Herbrand Est WC1 . . 94 A2
Herbrand St WC1 . . . 94 A2
Hercules Ct **7**
SE14 . . . . 51 A4
Hercules Rd SE1 . . . 135 A1
Hercules St N7 . . . . . 5 A1
Here East E9 . . . . . . 18 C3
Hereford Bldgs
SW3 . . . . 157 C4
Hereford Ho
5 Brixton SW2 . . . . 62 C3
6 Camberwell SE5 . . 48 B1
Knightsbridge
SW1 . . . . 130 B2
Walham Green
SW10 . . . . 156 B2
Hereford Mans **10**
W2 . . . . 31 C3
Hereford Mews **11**
W2 . . . . 31 C3
Hereford Pl SE14 . . . 51 B3
Hereford Rd
Acton W3 . . . . 28 B2
Bayswater
W2 . . . . 31 C2 113 C4
Hereford Retreat **5**
SE15 . . . . 49 C3
Hereford Sq SW7 . . 143 A3
Hereford St
E2 . . . . 24 C1 99 B2
Hereward House Sch
NW3 . . . . 11 C2
Heritage Cl SW9 . . . 63 A4

Heritage Ct SE8 . . . . 40 C1
Heritage Ho 22
SW19 . . . . 69 C3
Hermes Cl 5 SW9 . . . .23 C1
Hermes Ct 4
SW9 . . . . 173 B4
Hermes St N1 . . . . 85 B1
Hermitage Ct
2 Child's Hill NW2 . . . .1 C1
1 Wapping E1 . . . . . 125 C1
Hermitage Gdns
NW2 . . . . 1 C1
Hermitage La NW2 . . . . 1 C1
Hermitage Prim Sch
18 E1 . . . . 125 C2
Hermitage Row 9
E8 . . . . .16 C3
Hermitage St W2 . . . 101 B3
Hermitage The
Barnes SW13 . . . . 46 B2
Richmond TW10 . . . . . . 54 A2
Hermitage Villas
SW6 . . . . 155 B4
Hermitage Wall
E1 . . . . 125 C1
Hermit Pl NW6 . . . . . 78 A3
Hermit St EC1 . . . . . . 96 A4
Herndon Rd SW18 . . . 59 B2
HERNE HILL 63 B2
Herne Hill SE24 . . . . . . 63 B3
Herne Hill Ho
SE24 . . . . 63 A1
Herne Hill Mans
SE24 . . . . 63 B1
Herne Hill Rd
SE24 . . . . 63 B3
Herne Hill Sch
SE24 . . . . 63 B2
Herne Hill Sta
SE24 . . . . 63 A1
Herne Hill Velodrome
SE24 . . . . 63 A1
Herne Pl SE24 . . . . 63 A2
Heron Cl NW10 . . . . . . 8 A2
Heron Ct
16 Cubitt Town
E14 . . . . 42 B3
7 Dulwich SE21 . . . 75 C2
Herondale Ave
SW18 . . . . 72 A3
Heron Dr N4 . . . . 6 B2
Herongate N1 . . . . . 87 A4
Heron Ho
Battersea SW11 . . . 168 B4
Peckham SE15 . . . . . . 49 B2
St John's Wood
NW8 . . . . 80 A1
Heron Pl
Marylebone W1 . . . 103 C2
Rotherhithe SE16 . . . . 33 A1
Heron Quays Sta
E14 . . . . 33 C1
Heron Rd SE24 . . . . . . 63 B3
Heron Trad Est
W3 . . . . 28 A4
Herrick Ho
18 Camberwell
SE5 . . . . 48 C3
17 Canonbury N16 . .15 C4
Herrick Rd N5 . . . . 6 B1
Herrick St SW1 . . . . 147 C3
Herries St W10 . . . . . . 23 A3
Hersant Cl NW10 . . . . 21 C4

Herschell's Mews
SE5 . . . . .63 B4
Hibbert St SW11 . . . . .59 C4
Herschell Cl 1
SE14 . . . . .55 A3
Hertford Ave
SW14 . . . . .56 A3
Hertford Ct 16
SW11 . . . . .60 A4
Hertford Lo 10
SW19 . . . . .70 A3
Hertford Pl W1 . . . . 93 A1
Hertford Rd N1 . . . . . .24 A4
Hertford St W1 . . . . 118 A1
Hertmitage The 5
SE13 . . . . .52 B1
Hertslet Rd N7 . . . . . . .5 B1
Hertswood Rd E14 . .33 C2
Hesewall Ct SW4 . . 171 A1
Hesketh Pl
W11 . . . . 31 A2 112 A3
Heslop Ct 1
SW12 . . . . .72 C3
Heslop Rd SW12 . . . . 72 B3
Hesper Mews
SW5 . . . . 142 A3
Hesperus Cres
E14 . . . . 42 A2
Hessel St E1 . . . . 32 A3
Hestercombe Ave
SW6 . . . . 164 B3
Hester Rd SW11 . . . . 158 A1
Hester Terr TW9 . . . . 54 C4
Hestia Ho SE1 . . . . . 138 A3
Heston Ho
Gunnersbury W4 . . . . 37 A1
St Johns SE8 . . . . 51 C2
Heston St SE14 . . . . . .51 C2
Hetherington Rd SW2,
SW4 . . . . 62 A3
Hethpool Ho W2 . . . 89 B1
Hetley Rd W12 . . . . . 39 A4
Hetty Rees Ct 6
N19 . . . . 5 A4
Hevelius Cl SE10 . . . . 43 B1
Hever Ho SE15 . . . . . .50 C4
Heversham Ho
SE15 . . . . .50 B4
Heward Ct SE13 . . . . 52 B1
Hewer Ho 4 SW4 . . 61 B2
Hewer St W10 . . . . . . 30 C4
Hewett Ho SW15 . . . . 47 B1
Hewett St
EC2 . . . . . . 24 A1 98 B1
Hewison St E3 . . . . . . 26 B3
Hewlett Rd E3 . . . . . . 26 A3
Hewling Ho 1
N16 . . . . .16 A3
Hexagon The N6 . . . . . .3 B3
Hexham Rd SE27 . . . .75 B2
Hexton Ct N4 . . . . 6 B2
Heybridge 9 NW1 . .13 A2
Heydon Ho 3
SE14 . . . . .50 B2
Heyford Ave SW8 . . 162 B2
Heyford Terr
SW8 . . . . 162 B2
Heygate St SE17 . . . 151 A4
Heylyn Sq E3 . . . . 26 B2
Heysham La NW3 . . . . 2 A1
Heythorp St SW18 . .70 A3
Heythorp Coll W8 128 A2
Heywood Ho
11 Deptford SE14 . . .50 C4
2 Tulse Hill SW2 . . . 62 C1
Heyworth Rd E5 . . . . 17 A4

Hibbert Ho 13 E14 . .41 C3
Highgate Ave N6 . . . . 4 A4
Hibbert St SW11 . . . . .59 C4
Highgate Cemetery
N19 . . . . 4 A2
Hichisson Rd SE15 . .65 B3
Highgate Cl N6 . . . . . 3 C4
Hicken Rd SW2 . . . . . .62 B2
Highgate High St
Hickes Ho 6 NW6 . .11 C1
N6 . . . . 4 A3
Hickey's Almshouses
Highgate Hill N19 . . . 4 B3
7 TW9 . . . . .54 B3
Highgate Ho 4
Hickin St 2 E14 . . . . . .42 B3
SE26 . . . . 76 C1
Hickleton NW1 . . . . . .83 A3
Highgate Pre-Prep &
Hickling Ho 10
Jun Sch N6 . . . . . . 3 B4
SE16 . . . . .40 A3
Highgate Rd NW5 . . 13 A4
Hickmore Wlk
Highgate Sch N6 . . . . 3 C4
SW4 . . . . .61 B4
Highgate West Hill
Hicks Cl SW11 . . . . . . .60 A4
Highgate N6 . . . . .3 C3
Hicks St SE8 . . . . 41 A1
London N6 . . . . 3 C2
Hide Pl SW1 . . . . 147 B3
Highgrove Point 2
Hide Twr SW1 . . . . . 147 B3
NW3 . . . . 11 B4
Hieover SE21 . . . . .75 B2
High Holborn
Higgins Ho 7 N1 . . . . 24 A4
WC1 . . . . 106 C3
Higginson Ho 2
High Holborn Ho
NW3 . . . . 12 B1
WC1 . . . . 107 A3
Higgs Ind Est 9
Highlands Ave W3 . .28 B2
SE24 . . . . .63 A4
Highlands Cl N4 . . . . . .5 A4
Highbridge Ct 13
Highlands Heath
SE14 . . . . .50 B3
SW15 . . . . 69 B4
High Bridge Wharf
Highlever Rd W10 . . 30 B4
SE10 . . . . .42 C1
High London N6 . . . . . 4 C4
Highbury Mans 2
High Mount 1 NW4 . . 1 A4
N1 . . . . .15 A1
High Park Ave
HIGHBURY 15 A3
TW9 . . . . 44 C2
Highbury Cnr N5 . . . .15 A2
High Park Rd TW9 . . 44 C2
Highbury Corner
High Par The
N5 . . . . .15 A2
SW16 . . . . 74 A1
Highbury Cres N5 . . . .14 C2
High Point N6 . . . . . . 3 C4
Highbury Fields Sch
High Rd NW10 . . . . . . .8 C2
4 N5 . . . . .15 A3
Highshore Rd
Highbury Gr N5 . . . . . .15 A3
SE15 . . . . 49 B1
Highbury Grange
Highshore Sch
N5 . . . . .15 B4
1 Camberwell
Highbury Grove Ct
SW6 . . . . 48 A3
N5 . . . . .6 B1
18 London SE15 . . . 49 B2
Highbury Grove Sch
High St
N5 . . . . .15 B3
Acton W3 . . . . .28 A1
Highbury Hill N5 . . . .15 A4
Brentford TW8 . . . . . .44 A4
Highbury & Islington
Stratford Marsh
Sta N1 . . . . .15 A1
E15 . . . . 27 B4
Highbury New Pk
High Street Harlesden
N5 . . . . .15 B4
NW10 . . . . 21 B3
Highbury Pk N5 . . . . . .15 A4
High Street
Highbury Pl N5 . . . . . .15 A3
Kensington Sta
Highbury Pool N5 . . . .15 A2
W8 . . . . 128 A3
Highbury Quadrant
High The SW16 . . . . . 74 A1
N5 . . . . .6 B1
High Timber St
Highbury Quadrant
EC4 . . . . 122 C4
Prim Sch N5 . . . . . . .15 A4
High Trees SW2 . . . . 74 C3
Highbury Station Rd
Hightrees Ho
N1 . . . . .14 C2
SW12 . . . . 60 C1
Highbury Terr N5 . . . .15 A3
Highview N8 . . . . .5 A4
Highbury Terrace
Highview Ct 2
Mews N5 . . . . .15 A3
SW19 . . . . 70 A3
Highcliffe Dr
High View Prim Sch
SW15 . . . . .56 B1
SW11 . . . . 59 C3
Highcroft Rd N19 . . . .5 A4
Highway Bsns Pk The
Highcross Way 4
7 E1 . . . . 32 C2
SW15 . . . . .68 C3
Highway The E1 . . . . 32 C2
Highdown Rd
Highway Trad Ctr The
SW15 . . . . .57 A1
6 E1 . . . . 32 C2
Highfield Ave NW11 . .1 A4
Highwood Cl SE22 . .76 C3
Highfield Cl SE13 . . .67 C1
Highwood Rd N19 . . . .5 A1
Highfield Mews
Highworth St
NW6 . . . . .11 A1
NW1 . . . . 102 B4
Highfield Rd W3 . . . . 28 B4
Hilary Cl SW6 . . . . . 156 A2
HIGHGATE 4 A3
Hilary Rd W12 . . . . . . 29 B2
Highgate Archway
N6 . . . . .4 B3

Hilborough Ct 1
E8 . . . . .24 B4
Hilborough Rd 1
E8 . . . . .16 B1
Hilda Terr 2
SW9 . . . . 173 C2
Hilditch Ho 7
TW10 . . . . .54 B1
Hildred Ho SW1 . . . .146 A4
Hildreth St 5
SW12 . . . . .73 A3
Hildreth Street Mews
2 SW12 . . . . .73 A3
Hildyard Rd SW6 . . 155 C4
Hiley Rd NW10 . . . . . .22 B2
Hilgrove Rd NW6 . . . .11 B1
Hillary Ct 13 W12 . . . .39 B4
Hillbeck Cl
Deptford SE15 . . . . . .50 B3
Deptford SE15 . . . . . .50 B4
Hillbrow 7 TW10 . . . .54 A1
Hillbury Rd SW17 . . . .73 A1
Hillcourt Rd SE22 . . . .65 A1
Hillcrest
Camberwell SE24 . . . .63 C3
Highgate N6 . . . . 3 C4
Notting Hill
W11 . . . . 31 B2 112 C3
Hillcrest Cl NW2 . . . . 10 A3
Hillcrest Rd W3 . . . . . .28 A1
Hill Ct
Hampstead NW3 . . . .12 A4
Putney SW15 . . . . . . .57 C2
Hilldrop Cres N7 . . . .13 C3
Hilldrop La N7 . . . . . .13 C3
Hilldrop Rd N7 . . . . . .13 C3
Hillersdon Ave
Barnes SW13 . . . . . . .46 C1
Hillersdon Ho
SW1 . . . . 146 A1
Hillery Cl SE17 . . . . 151 C3
Hill Farm Rd W10 . . .30 C4
Hillfield Ct NW3 . . . . .12 A3
Hillfield Ho N5 . . . . . .15 B3
Hillfield Mans
NW3 . . . . 11 A4
Hillfield Rd NW6 . . . .10 C3
Hillgate Pl
Balham SW12 . . . . . . .73 A4
Kensington
W8 . . . . . . 31 C1 113 B2
Hillgate St
W8 . . . . . . 31 C1 113 B2
Hill House Sch
SW1 . . . . 131 A1
Hilliard Ho 11 E1 . . .32 A1
Hilliard's Ct E1 . . . . . .32 B1
Hillier Ho 1 NW1 . . .13 C1
Hillier Rd SW11 . . . . .60 B1
Hillingdon St SE17 . .48 A4
Hill Lo SW11 . . . . .59 C3
Hillman Dr 12
NW10 . . . . .22 B1
Hillman St E8 . . . . . . .17 A2
Hillmarton Rd N7 . . . .14 A3
Hillmead Dr SW9 . . . .63 A3
Hill Mead Prim Sch 2
SW9 . . . . .63 A3
Hillmore Ct SE13 . . . .67 C4
Hill Rd NW8 . . . . 79 A1
Hillrise Mans N19 . . . .5 A4
Hillrise Rd N19 . . . . . . .5 A4
Hillsboro Rd SE22 . . .64 A2
Hillsborough Ct 13
NW6 . . . . 78 A3

Hillside
  Greenwich SE10 . . . . . 52 C3
  Stonebridge NW10 . . . 20 C4
Hillside Cl NW8 . . . . . . 78 B2
Hillside Ct NW3 . . . . . . 11 A3
Hillside Gdns SW2 . . . 74 C2
Hillside Rd SW2 . . . . . 74 C2
Hillsleigh Rd
  W14 . . . . 31 B1 113 A2
Hills Pl W1 . . . . 104 C1
Hill St W1 . . . . 118 A2
Hillstone Ct ❺ E3 . . . . 27 A1
Hilltop Ct
  ❷ London SW18 . . . . 59 C3
  South Hampstead
  NW8 . . . . 11 B1
Hilltop Ho ❼ N6 . . . . . . 4 C4
Hilltop Rd NW6 . . . . . . 10 C1
Hill View NW1 . . . . . . 81 A4
Hillway N6 . . . . 3 C2
Hill Wood Ho NW1 . . . 83 B1
Hillworth Rd SW2 . . . 74 C4
Hillyard St SW9 . . . . 173 B3
Hillyfield Cl E9 . . . . . . 18 A3
Hilly Fields Cres
  SE4 . . . . 66 C4
Hilsea Point ❼
  SW15 . . . . 69 A3
Hilsea St E5 . . . . 17 B4
Hilton Docklands Pier
  SE16 . . . . 33 B1
Hilton Ho
  Lower Holloway
  ❾ N7 . . . . 14 A4
  ❷ Nunhead SE4 . . . . 65 C3
Hilversum Cres ❿
  SE22 . . . . 64 A2
Hinckley Rd SE15 . . . . 64 C3
Hind Ct EC4 . . . . 107 C1
Hinde Mews W1 . . . . 103 C2
Hinde St W1 . . . . 103 C2
Hind Gr E14 . . . . 33 C3
Hindhead Point ❻
  SW15 . . . . 69 A3
Hind Ho
  ❸ Deptford SE14 . . . 50 C4
  Islington N7 . . . . 14 C4
Hindle Ho E8 . . . . 16 B3
Hindley Ho N7 . . . . 5 B1
Hindlip Ho SW8 . . . . . 171 B3
Hindmans Rd
  SE22 . . . . 64 C2
Hindmans Yd ❺
  SE22 . . . . 64 C2
Hindmarsh Cl E1 . . . . 125 C4
Hindrey Rd E5 . . . . . . 17 A3
Hinstock NW6 . . . . . . 78 A4
Hinton Rd SE24 . . . . . 63 A4
Hippodrome Mews
  W11 . . . . 31 A2 112 A3
Hippodrome Pl
  W11 . . . . 31 A2 112 B3
Hirst Ct SW1 . . . . 146 A1
Hitchcock La E15 . . . . 19 B1
Hitchin Sq E3 . . . . 26 A3
Hithe Gr ❶❺ SE16 . . . . 40 B3
Hitherfield Prim Sch
  SW16 . . . . 74 C2
Hitherfield Rd SW16,
  SW27 . . . . 74 C1
Hither Green La
  SE13 . . . . 67 C1
Hitherlands SW12 . . . 73 A2
HM Prison
  Wormwood Scrubs
  W12 . . . . 29 C3

HMS Belfast SE1 . 124 B2
HMS President
  EC4 . . . . 121 C4
Hoadly Rd SW16 . . . . . 73 C2
Hobart Pl SW1 . . . . . 132 A2
Hobbs Wlk SW15 . . . . . 57 A2
Hobbs' Pl N1 . . . . 24 A4
Hobday St E14 . . . . . . 34 A3
Hobhouse Ct SW1 . . . 119 C3
Hobsons Pl ❼ E1 . . . 111 B4
Hobury St SW10 . . . . 157 B3
Hocker St ❺ E2 . . . . . 24 B2 98 C3
Hockett Cl SE8 . . . . . . 41 B2
Hockley Ho ❹ E9 . . . . 17 B2
Hockliffe Ho ❺
  W10 . . . . 30 B4
Hockworth Ho ❼
  N16 . . . . 7 A3
Hocroft Ave NW2 . . . . 1 B1
Hocroft Ct NW2 . . . . . . 1 B1
Hocroft Rd NW2 . . . . . . 1 B1
Hocroft Wlk NW2 . . . . . 1 B1
Hodford Lo NW11 . . . . 1 C2
Hodford Rd NW11 . . . . 1 B3
Hodister Cl ❷❹ SE5 . . 48 B3
Hodnet Gr SE16 . . . . . 40 B2
Hoffman Sq N1 . . . . . . 97 C4
Hofland Rd W14 . . . . 126 A2
Hogan Mews W2 . . . . 101 B4
Hogan Way E5 . . . . 7 C2
Hogarth Bsns Pk
  W4 . . . . 46 A4
Hogarth Ct
  ❸ Camden Town
  NW1 . . . . 13 B1
  City of London EC3 . 124 B4
  ❷❹ Whitechapel E1 . 111 C1
Hogarth Ho SW1 . . . . 147 C3
Hogarth Ind Est
  NW10 . . . . 21 C1
Hogarth La W4 . . . . . . 46 A4
Hogarth Pl SW5 . . . . 142 A3
Hogarth Rd SW5 . . . . 142 A3
Hogarth Roundabout
  W4 . . . . 46 A4
Hogarth's House
  W4 . . . . 46 A4
Holbeach Mews ❶
  SW12 . . . . 73 A3
Holbeck Row SE15 . . . 49 C3
Holbein Ho SW1 . . . . 145 B2
Holbein Mews
  SW1 . . . . 145 B2
Holbein Pl SW1 . . . . . 145 B3
Holberton Gdns
  NW10 . . . . 22 A2
HOLBORN 107 C3
Holborn EC1 . . . . 107 C3
Holborn Cir EC1 . . . . 107 C3
Holborn Ho ❶
  W12 . . . . 30 A3
Holborn Pl WC1 . . . . 106 C3
Holborn Sta WC1 . . . 106 C3
Holborn Viaduct
  EC1 . . . . 108 A3
Holbrook Cl N19 . . . . . 4 A3
Holbrooke Ct N7 . . . . 14 A4
Holbrook Ho
  Acton W3 . . . . 28 C4
  ❸ Streatham SW2 . . 74 B3
Holcombe Ho
  SW9 . . . . 62 A4

Holcombe Pl SE4 . . . . 66 A4
Holcombe St W6 . . . . . 39 A2
Holcroft Ct W1 . . . . . 104 C4
Holcroft Ho
  Battersea SW11 . . . . 59 C4
  Lewisham SE13 . . . . 52 B2
Holcroft Rd E9 . . . . . . 17 B1
Holdenby Rd SE4 . . . . 66 A2
Holden Ho
  ❶❷ Deptford SE8 . . . 51 C3
  Islington N1 . . . . 86 C3
Holden Point E15 . . . . 19 C2
Holden St SW11 . . . . 169 B1
Holdernesse Rd ❺
  SW17 . . . . 72 C2
Holderness Ho
  SE5 . . . . 64 A4
Holdsworth Ho ❺
  SW2 . . . . 74 C4
Holford Ho
  ❻ Bermondsey
  SE16 . . . . 40 A2
  Finsbury WC1 . . . . . . 95 A4
Holford Pl WC1 . . . . . 95 A4
Holford Rd NW3 . . . . . . 2 C1
Holford St WC1 . . . . . 95 A4
Holford Way SW15 . . 56 C1
Holford Yd WC1 . . . . . 85 B1
Holgate Ave SW11 . . 59 C4
Holland Gdns
  Brentford TW8 . . . . . 44 A4
  Kensington W14 . . . . 126 B2
Holland Gr SW9 . . . . . 163 C1
Holland Park
  W11 . . . . 31 B1 112 C1
Holland Park Ave
  W11 . . . . 31 A1 112 B1
Holland Park Ct
  W14 . . . . 126 B4
Holland Park Gdns
  W14 . . . . 31 A1 112 B1
Holland Park Mews
  W11 . . . . 31 B1 112 B1
Holland Park Pre
  Prep Sch W14 . . . 126 C1
Holland Park Rd
  W14 . . . . 127 A1
Holland Park Rdbt
  W11 . . . . 31 A1
Holland Park Sch
  W8 . . . . 127 A4
Holland Park Sta
  W11 . . . . 31 B1 112 C1
Holland Pas N1 . . . . . 86 C4
Holland Pl W8 . . . . . . 128 A4
Holland Rd
  West Kensington
  W14 . . . . 126 B2
  Willesden Green
  NW10 . . . . 22 A3
Holland Rise Ho
  SW9 . . . . 163 A1
Holland St
  Kensington W8 . . . . 127 C4
  Lambeth SE1 . . . . . 122 B2
Holland Villas Rd
  W14 . . . . 126 B1
Holland Wlk
  Kensington W14 . . . . 127 A3
  Upper Holloway N19 . 4 C3
Hollar Rd N16 . . . . 7 B1
Hollen St W1 . . . . 105 B2
Holles St W1 . . . . 104 B2
Holley Rd W3 . . . . 38 A4

Holliday Sq ❻
  SW11 . . . . 59 C4
Hollies The SW12 . . . 73 B2
Hollies Way ❶
  SW12 . . . . 72 C4
Hollingbourne Rd
  SE24 . . . . 63 B2
Hollins Ho N7 . . . . 14 A4
Hollisfield WC1 . . . . . 94 B3
Holloway Rd
  Lower Holloway
  N7 . . . . 14 B2
  Upper Holloway N19 . 4 C1
Holloway Road Sta
  N7 . . . . 14 B3
Holloway Sch N7 . . . 13 C3
Holly Berry La ❺
  NW3 . . . . 11 B4
Hollybush Gdns
  E2 . . . . 25 A2
Holly Bush Hill ❹
  NW3 . . . . 11 B4
Hollybush Ho ❷❸
  E2 . . . . 25 A2
Hollybush Pl E2 . . . . . 25 A2
Holly Bush Steps ❺
  NW3 . . . . 11 B4
Holly Bush Vale ❿
  NW3 . . . . 11 B4
Holly Cl NW10 . . . . . . 8 A1
Hollycroft Ave NW3 . . 1 C1
Hollydale Prim Sch
  SE15 . . . . 50 B1
Hollydale Rd SE15 . . . 50 B1
Hollydene
  Hither Green
  SE13 . . . . 67 C1
  ❺ Peckham SE15 . . . 50 A2
Holly Gr SE15 . . . . . . 49 C1
Hollyhedge Ho
  SE3 . . . . 52 C1
Holly Hedge Terr
  SE13 . . . . 67 C2
Holly Hill NW3 . . . . . . 11 B4
Holly Lo W10 . . . . . . 127 B4
Holly Lodge SE13 . . . . 67 C4
Holly Lodge Gdns
  N6 . . . . 3 C3
Holly Lodge Mans
  N6 . . . . 3 C2
Holly Mews SW10 . . . 143 A1
Holly Mount NW3 . . . 11 B4
Hollymount Cl ❾
  SE10 . . . . 52 B2
Holly Park Est N4 . . . . 5 B4
Holly Park Montessori
  Sch ❶❹ N19 . . . . . . 4 C3
Holly Pk N4 . . . . 5 B4
Holly Rd ❻ W4 . . . . . . 37 C2
Holly St E8 . . . . 16 B1
Holly Terr N6 . . . . 3 C3
Hollytree Cl SW19 . . . 69 C3
Holly Tree Ho SE4 . . . 66 B4
Holly Village N6 . . . . . 4 A2
Holly Wlk NW3 . . . . . . 11 B4
Hollywood Lofts
  E1 . . . . 24 B1 98 C1
Hollywood Mews
  SW10 . . . . 156 C4
Hollywood Rd
  SW10 . . . . 156 C4
Holman Ho ❷ E2 . . . . 25 C2
Holman Hunt Ho
  W14 . . . . 140 A1
Holman Rd SW11 . . . 167 B1

Holmbrook NW1 . . . . 83 A1
Holmbury Ct SW17 . . 72 B1
Holmbury Ho SW9 . . . 63 A2
Holmbush Rd
  SW15 . . . . 58 A1
Holmcote Gdns
  N5 . . . . 15 B3
Holmdale Rd NW6 . . . 10 C3
Holmdene Ave
  SE24 . . . . 63 B2
Holmead Rd SW6 . 156 B1
Holmefield Ct ❹
  NW3 . . . . 12 A2
Holmefield Ho
  W10 . . . . 23 A1
Holmes Cl SE22 . . . . . 64 C3
Holmes Ct
  ❶❶ South Acton
  W4 . . . . 37 B3
  South Lambeth
  SW4 . . . . 172 A2
Holmesdale Ave
  SW14 . . . . 55 A3
Holmesdale Ho ❶❷
  NW6 . . . . 23 C4
Holmesdale Rd
  Highgate N6 . . . . 4 A4
  Richmond TW9 . . . . . 44 B2
Holmesley Rd
  SE23 . . . . 66 A1
Holmes Pl SW10 . . . . 157 A4
Holmes Rd NW5 . . . . . 13 A3
Holmes Terr SE1 . . . . 135 B4
Holmewood Gdns
  SW2 . . . . 74 B4
Holmewood Rd
  SW2 . . . . 74 B4
Holmhurst SE13 . . . . . 67 C1
Holmleigh Prim Sch
  N16 . . . . 7 A3
Holmleigh Rd N16 . . 7 A3
Holm Oak Cl SW15 . . 58 B1
Holm Oak Mews ❶❶
  SW4 . . . . 62 A2
Holmsbury Ho ❻
  N7 . . . . 13 C3
Holmsdale Ho ❷❹
  E14 . . . . 34 A2
Holmside Ct SW12 . . 60 C1
Holmside Rd
  SW12 . . . . 60 C1
Holmsley Ho
  SW15 . . . . 68 B4
Holm Wlk SE3 . . . . . . 53 C1
Holmwood Ct ❸
  WC1 . . . . 95 A1
Holt Ct SE10 . . . . 52 B4
Holt Ho SW2 . . . . 62 C1
Holton St E1 . . . . 25 C1
Holwood Pl ❼
  SW4 . . . . 61 C3
Holybourne Ave
  SW15 . . . . 68 C4
Holy Cross RC Prim
  Sch SW6 . . . . 165 B4

Holy Ghost RC Prim
Sch 4 SW12.....72 C4
Holyhead Cl E3.....26 C2
Holyoake Ct SE16...41 B4
Holyoak Rd SE11 . 150 B3
Holyport Rd SW6... 47 C2
Holyrood Ho N4.....6 B3
Holyrood Mews
6 Greenwich
SE7.............45 A1
10 Newham E16...35 C1
Holyrood St SE1 .. 124 A1
Holy Trinity CE Prim
Sch
Belgravia SW1 .... 145 B4
Chelsea SW3 .... 145 A4
Dalston E8........16 B2
2 Hampstead
NW3...........11 C4
Richmond TW10 ... 54 C3
Streatham SW2 ... 74 B4
Holy Trinity & Saint
Silas CE Prim Sch
NW1............13 A1
Holywell Cl
7 Bermondsey
SE16...........40 A1
2 Greenwich SE3 ...53 C4
Holywell La
EC2.........24 A1 98 B2
Holywell Row
EC2...........24 A1
Homan Ho 6 SW4 .73 C4
Homecross Ho 7
W4.............37 C2
Homefield Rd W4 . 38 B1
Homefield St 14
N1.............24 A3
Homeleigh Ct 8
SW16..........74 A1
Homeleigh Rd
SE15...........65 C2
Homemead SW12 ..73 A2
Home Office SW1 133 C1
Home Park Rd
SW19..........70 B1
Home Rd SW11...168 A2
Homer Dr E14.....41 C2
Homer Rd E9......18 A2
Homer Row W1 .. 102 B3
Homer St W1 ... 102 B3
HOMERTON.......17 C1
Homerton Gr E9....17 C3
Homerton High St
E9.............17 B3
Homerton Hospital
E9.............18 C3
Homerton Rd E9 .. 18 B3
Homerton Sta E9 ..17 C2
Homerton Terr E9..17 C2
Homerton University
Hospl E9.......18 C3
Homestall Rd
SE22...........65 B2
Homestead Rd
SW6...........155 A1
Homewoods 2
SW12...........73 B4
Homildon Ho 10
SE26...........76 C1
Honduras St EC1.. 96 C2
Honeybourne Rd
NW6...........11 A3
Honeybrook Rd SW12,
SW4...........73 B4

Honeyfield N4.....5 C2
Honey La EC2 ... 109 A1
Honey Lane Ho
SW10..........156 A4
Honeyman Cl NW6 ..9 C1
Honeywell Jun & Inf
Schs 3 SW11....60 B1
Honeywell Rd
SW11..........60 B1
Honeywood Ho 5
SE15...........49 C2
Honeywood Rd
NW10..........21 B3
Honiton Gdns 1
SE15...........50 B1
Honiton Ho 23 SE5 .48 B1
Honiton Rd NW6 ..23 B3
HONOR OAK.....65 B2
Honor Oak Park Sta
SE23...........65 C1
Honor Oak Pk
SE23...........65 C1
Honor Oak Rise
SE23...........65 C1
Honour Lea Ave
E15............19 A3
Honwell Ho 2
W2.............31 C4
Hood Ave SW14...55 B2
Hood Ct N7.......5 B1
Hood Ho 17 SE5...48 C3
Hooke Ct SE10....52 B2
Hooke Ho 23 E3...26 A3
Hookham Ct SW8. 171 B4
Hooks Cl SE15....50 A2
Hooper Ho 9
SW18..........58 B2
Hooper Rd E16 ...35 C3
Hooper's Ct SW1. 130 C3
Hooper's Mews 4
W3.............28 B1
Hooper St E1 .... 111 B1
Hoop La NW11 ....1 C4
Hope Cl
2 Brentford
TW8...........36 A1
Canonbury N1....15 B2
Hopefield Ave
NW6...........23 A3
Hope Gdns 10 W3 .37 A4
Hope St
London SW11....59 C4
Poplar E14......35 A3
Hopetown St E1 ..111 A3
Hopewell St SE5...48 C3
Hop Gdns WC2 .. 120 A3
Hopgood St 8
W12...........30 B1
Hopkins Ho 7
E14............33 C3
Hopkinson Ho 1
SW11..........169 B2
Hopkinson's Pl
NW1...........81 B4
Hopkins St W1 .. 105 B1
Hopping La N1....15 A2
Hops La SE10.....43 B2
Hopton Ho 5
SW9...........48 A1
Hopton's Gdns
SE1............122 B2
Hopton St SE1 ... 122 B2
Hopwood Cl SW17.71 B1
Hopwood Rd SE17. 48 C4
Hopwood Wlk E8 . 16 C1
Horatio Ho 13 E2..24 B3

Horatio Pl 9 E14..34 B1
Horatio St 1 E2...24 B3
Horbury Cres
W11........31 C2 113 B3
Horbury Mews
W11........31 A2 113 A3
Horder Rd SW6.. 164 B3
Hordle Prom E 15
SE15...........49 B3
Hordle Prom N 4
SE15...........49 B3
Hordle Prom S 7
SE15...........49 B3
Horizon Bldg 22
E14............33 C2
Horizon Ind Est
SE15...........49 C3
Horle Wlk SE5....48 A1
Hormead Rd W9...23 B1
Hornbeam Cl
SE11...........149 B4
Hornbeam Ho 2
NW3...........12 B2
Hornbeam Sq 8
E3.............26 B4
Hornblower Cl 2
SE16...........41 A2
Hornby Cl NW3...11 C1
Hornby Ho 6
SE11...........163 C4
Horndean Cl 3
SW15..........68 C3
Horner Hos 11 N1..24 A4
Horne Way SW15 ..47 B1
Horn La
Acton W3.......28 B3
Greenwich SE10...43 C2
Horn Link Way
SE10...........43 C2
Hornsby House Sch 7
SW12..........72 C3
Hornsey La N6....4 B4
Hornsey Lane Gdns
N6.............4 B4
Hornsey Rd N7, N19..5 B2
Hornsey Rise Gdns
N19............5 A4
Hornsey St N7.....14 B3
Hornshay St SE15..50 B4
Hornton Ct W8 .. 127 C3
Hornton Pl W8 .. 127 C3
Hornton St W8 .. 127 C4
Horrocks Ho
SW15..........57 A2
Horse & Dolphin Yd
W1............119 C4
Horseferry Pl 6
SE10...........52 B4
Horseferry Rd
Limehouse E14...33 A2
Westminster SW1 . 147 C4
Horseferry Rd Est
SW1...........133 B1
Horse Guards Ave
SW1...........120 A1
Horse Guards Par
SW1...........119 C1
Horse Guards Rd
SW1...........133 C4
Horsell Rd N5....14 C3
Horselydown La
SE1............124 C1
Horselydown Mans
SE1............138 C4
Horsemongers Mews
SE1............137 A3

Horsendon Ho 11
N7.............13 C3
Horseshoe Cl E14 .42 B1
Horse Yd N1......86 B4
Horsfield Ho 13
N1.............15 B1
Horsford Rd SW2..62 B2
Horsley Ct SW1 .. 147 C3
Horsley Ho 11 SE4..65 C3
Horsley St SE17...48 C4
Horsman Ho 5
SE5............48 B4
Horsman St SE5...48 B4
Horsmonden Rd
SE4............66 B1
Horston Ho N4....6 B4
Hortensia Ho
SW10..........156 C2
Hortensia Rd
SW10..........156 C2
Horticultural Pl 3
W4.............37 C1
Horton Ave NW2..10 A4
Horton Ho
13 Deptford SE15 .50 B4
South Lambeth
SW8...........162 C2
West Kensington
W14...........140 A1
Horton Rd E8.....17 A2
Horton St SE13...67 A4
Horwood Ho
24 Bethnal Green
E2.............25 A2
Marylebone NW8.. 90 B2
Hosack Rd SW12,
SW17..........72 C2
Hosier La EC1 ... 108 B3
Hoskins Cl E16...35 C2
Hospl for Tropical
Diseases NW1 .. 93 A1
Hospl of St John & St
Elizabeth NW8 ... 79 B1
Hotham Prim Sch
SW15..........57 C3
Hotham Rd SW15..57 B4
Hotfield Pl SE16...40 B3
Hotspur St SE11 . 149 B2
Houblon Rd TW10 .54 A2
Houghton Cl 10
E8............16 B2
Houghton Sq SW9..62 A4
Houghton St WC2. 107 A1
Houndsditch EC3 . 110 B2
Household Cavalry
Mus SW1.......80 A3
Houseman Way 20
SE5............48 C3
Houses of Parliament
SW1...........134 B2
Hoveden Rd NW2..10 A3
Howard Bldg
SW8...........160 A3
Howard Cl
Acton W3.......29 A3
Cricklewood NW2..10 A4
Howard Ct
Lewisham SE13...52 B2
Peckham SE15...64 C4
Howard Ho
2 Brixton SW9...62 C4
14 Deptford SE8...51 B4
Fitzrovia W1......92 B1
Howard Mews N5..15 A4
Howard Rd
Canonbury N16...15 C4

Howard Rd continued
Cricklewood NW2....9 C4
Howard's La SW15..57 B3
Howbury Rd SE15..65 B4
Howcroft Ho 3
E3.............26 B2
Howden St SE15...64 C4
Howell Ho 5 N7...13 C3
Howell Wlk SE1 .. 150 B3
Howgate Rd SW14..55 C4
Howick Pl SW1 .. 133 A1
Howie St SW11 .. 158 A1
Howitt Cl
6 Maitland Pk
NW3...........12 A2
Stoke Newington
N16............16 A4
Howitt Rd NW3...12 A2
Howland Ho 9
SW16..........74 A1
Howland Mews E
W1............105 A4
Howland St W1.. 105 A4
Howland Way
SE16...........41 A4
Howletts Rd SE24..63 B1
Howley Pl W2 ... 101 A4
Howsman Rd
SW13..........46 C4
Howson Rd SE4...66 A3
Howson Terr
TW10..........54 A1
How's St E2......24 B3
HOXTON..........24 A3
Hoxton Garden Prim
Sch 30 N1......24 A3
Hoxton Mkt 10
N1.........24 A2 98 A3
Hoxton Point
N1.........24 A2 98 A3
Hoxton Sq
N1.........24 A2 98 A3
Hoxton St N1.....24 A3
Hoxton Sta N1....24 B3
Hoyland Cl 4
SE15...........50 A3
Hoy St E16.......35 B3
Hub Buildings The 8
SW12..........73 A3
Hub E15 ....27 A3
Huberd Ho SE1 .. 137 C2
Hubert Gr SW9...62 A4
Hubert Ho NW8 .. 90 A1
Hub The NW1 ....81 A1
Hucknall Ct NW8..89 B2
Huddart St 6 E3...33 C4
Huddleston Cl E2..25 B3
Huddlestone Rd
NW2...........9 A2
Huddleston Rd N7..13 C4
Hudson Cl 18 W12..30 A2
Hudson Ct 1 E14..41 C1
Hudson Ho
Chelsea SW10 .. 156 C2
5 Notting Hill W11..31 A3
Hudsons Ho N1...97 C3
Hudson's Pl SW1. 146 C4
Huggin Ct EC4...123 A4
Huggin Hill EC4 . 123 A4
Huggins Ho 9 E3..26 C2
Huggins Pl SW2 ..74 B3
Hughan Rd E15...19 C3
Hugh Astor Ct
SE1............136 B2

Hugh Dalton Ave
SW6 . . . . **154** C3
Hughenden Ho
NW8 . . . . **90** A2
Hughendon Terr
E15 . . . . .19 B4
Hughes Ho
26 Bethnal Green
E2 . . . . .25 B2
Camberwell SE5 . . . .48 B2
9 Deptford SE8 . . . .51 C4
Newington SE17 . . .150 B3
Hughes Mans
E1 . . . . .24 C1 99 C1
Hughes Terr 6
E16 . . . . .35 B4
Hugh Gaitskell Cl
SW6 . . . . **154** B4
Hugh Gaitskell Ho
Stoke Newington
N16 . . . . .7 B2
Willesden NW10 . . . . .8 B1
Hugh Mews SW1 . .146 B3
Hugh Morgan Ho 5
SW4 . . . . .61 C4
Hugh Myddelton Prim
Sch EC1 . . . . .95 C3
Hugh Platt Ho 28
E2 . . . . .25 A3
Hugo Ho 5 SW1 . . .131 A2
Hugo Rd NW5 . . . .59 A4
Hugon Rd SW6 . . . .59 A4
Hugo Rd N19 . . . . .13 B4
Huguenot Ct 9
E1 . . . . .111 B4
Huguenot Ho 27
London SW18 . . . . . .59 B2
Spitalfields E1 . . . .111 A4
Huguenot Sq SE15. .65 A4
Hullbridge Mews
N1 . . . . .87 B4
Hull Cl SE16. . . . . . .32 C1
Hull Ct SE5. . . . . . .48 C1
Hull St EC1. . . . . . .96 C3
Hulme Pl SE1 . . . .137 A3
Humber Dr W10 . . . .22 C1
Humber Rd SE3 . . . .53 B4
Humberton Cl E9 . . .18 A3
Humbolt Rd W6 . . .154 A3
Hume Ct N1 . . . . . . .15 A1
Hume Ho 14 W11 . . .30 C1
Humphrey Ct
SW11 . . . . .167 C3
Humphrey St SE1 .152 C2
Humphry Ho 19
SW15 . . . . .57 C2
Hungerford Bridge
WC2 . . . . .120 C2
Hungerford Ho
SW1 . . . . .161 A4
Hungerford La
WC2 . . . . .120 B2
Hungerford Prim Sch
19 N7 . . . . .13 C2
Hungerford Rd
12 Camden Town
N7. . . . . .13 C2
Lower Holloway N7 . .14 A3
Hungerford St 9
E1 . . . . .32 A3
Hunsdon Rd SE14. . .50 C3
Hunslett St 28 E2. . .25 B3
Hunstanton Ho
NW1 . . . . .102 A4
Hunt Cl W11. . . . . . .30 C1

Hunter Cl
Borough The SE1 . . .137 C1
Upper Tooting
SW12 . . . . .72 C3
Huntercombe-
Roehampton Hospl
The SW15 . . . . .68 C4
Hunter Ct
8 London SE5. . . . . .63 C3
7 Streatham SW2 . . .74 C4
Hunter Ho
Bloomsbury WC1 . . . .94 B2
Lambeth SE1 . . . . . .136 B3
South Lambeth
SW8 . . . . .161 C1
1 Tufnell Pk N19 . . . .4 B1
West Brompton
SW5 . . . . .141 C1
Huntingdon Ct
SW14 . . . . .55 B4
Huntingdon Gdns
W4 . . . . .45 B3
Huntingdon Ho
SW5 . . . . .141 C4
Huntingdon St
Canning Town
E16 . . . . .35 B3
Islington N1 . . . . . . .14 B1
Huntingfield Rd
SW15 . . . . .56 C2
Huntingford Ho
SW15 . . . . .47 B1
Huntings Ho 37
E3 . . . . .27 A2
Hunt's La E15 . . . . .27 B3
Huntsman St
SE17 . . . . .152 A3
Huntspill St SW17 . .71 B1
Hunts Slip Rd
SE21 . . . . .76 A2
Huntsworth Mews
NW1 . . . . .90 C1
Hurdwick Ho NW1. .82 C2
Hurdwick Pl NW1. . .82 C2
Hurleston Ho 11
SE8 . . . . .41 B1
Hurley Cres SE16. . .40 C4
Hurley Ho
Lambeth SE11 . . . . .149 C3
2 Shoreditch
E2 . . . . . . .24 B2 98 C3
Hurley Lo SE22 . . . .65 B1
Hurlingham Bsns Pk
SW6 . . . . .58 C4
Hurlingham &
Chelsea Sec Sch
SW6 . . . . .58 A4
Hurlingham Court
Mans SW6 . . . . . . .165 B1
Hurlingham Ct
SW6 . . . . .58 B4
Hurlingham Gdns
SW6 . . . . .58 B4
Hurlingham Rd
SW6 . . . . .165 A1

Hurlingham Sch
SW15 . . . . .58 B3
Hurlingham Sq
SW6 . . . . .59 A4
Hurlock Ho 1 N5 . . . .6 A1
Hurlock St N5. . . . . . .6 A1
Huron Rd SW17 . . . .72 C1
Hurstbourne Ho
SW15 . . . . .56 B1
Hurst Ho WC1 . . . . .85 A1
Hurst St SE24 . . . . .63 A1
Hurstway Wlk 2
W11 . . . . .30 C2
Husbourne Ho 8
SE8 . . . . .41 A2
Huson Cl NW3. . . . .12 A1
Hutching's St E14 . .41 C4
Hutching's Wharf 1
E14 . . . . .41 C4
Hutchins Cl E15 . . . .19 B1
Hutchins Ho 3
SW4 . . . . .73 C4
Hutton Ct 4 N4. . . . .5 B3
Hutton Ho 19
E2 . . . . .24 C2 99 B3
Hutton St EC4 . . . .107 C1
Huxbear St SE4 . . . .66 B2
Huxley Ho
4 London SW9 . . . .172 C2
Paddington NW8 . . . .89 C1
Huxley St W10 . . . . .23 A2
Hyacinth Rd SW15. . .68 C3
Hyde Farm Mews
SW12 . . . . .73 C3
Hyde La SW11 . . . .168 A4
Hyde Park W 11
Hyde Park Cnr
SW1 . . . . .131 C4
Hyde Park Corner Sta
SW1 . . . . .131 C4
Hyde Park Cres
W2 . . . . .102 A1
Hyde Park Gate Mews
SW7 . . . . .129 A3
Hyde Park Gdns
W2 . . . . .116 A4
Hyde Park Gdns Mews
W2 . . . . .116 A4
Hyde Park Mans
NW1 . . . . .102 A3
Hyde Park Pl W2 . .116 B4
Hyde Park Sch
SW7 . . . . .129 A1
Hyde Park Sq W2 102 A1
Hyde Park Square
Mews W2 . . . . . .102 A1
Hyde Park Twrs
W2 . . . . .114 C3
Hyde Rd
Richmond TW10 . . . .54 B2
Shoreditch N1. . . . . .24 A4
Hyde's Pl 22 N1 . . . .15 A1
Hyde St SE8 . . . . . .51 C4
Hydethorpe Rd
SW12 . . . . .73 B3
Hyde Vale SE10. . . . .52 B3
Hylda Ct NW5 . . . . . .3 C1
Hyndman Ho 4
N19 . . . . .13 C4
Hyndman St SE15. . .50 A4

Hyperion Ho
17 Bow E3 . . . . . . .26 A3
Streatham SW2 . . . .74 B4
Hyson Rd SE16 . . . .40 A1
Hythe Ho 16 SE16 . .40 B4
Hythe Rd NW10. . . .21 C1
Hythe Road Ind Est
NW10 . . . . .21 C1

I

Ian Hamilton Ho
NW1 . . . . .93 B4
Ian Mikardo High Sch
E3 . . . . .27 A2
Ibberton Ho
Kensington W14. . . .126 B1
South Lambeth
SW8 . . . . .162 C2
Ibbotson Ave E16. . .35 B3
Ibbott St 22 E1 . . . .25 B1
Iberia Ho 17 N19 . . . .4 C4
Ibis Ct 18 SE8 . . . . .51 B4
Ibis La W4 . . . . .45 B2
Ibsley Gdns SW15 . .68 C3
Ibstock Place Sch
SW15 . . . . .56 A1
Icarus Ho 21 E3 . . . .26 B2
Iceland Rd E3 . . . . .26 C4
Iceland Wharf
SE16 . . . . .41 A2
Iceni Ct 28 E3 . . . . .26 B4
Ice Wharf NW1 . . . .84 B2
Ickburgh Sch 7
E9 . . . . .18 A3
Idaho Bldg 7
SE13 . . . . .52 A2
Ida St E14. . . . . .34 B3
Identity & Passport
Office SW1 . . . . .146 B4
Idmiston Rd SE21,
SE27 . . . . .75 B2
Idol La EC3 . . . . . .124 A3
Idonia St SE8 . . . . .51 C3
Iffley Ho 17
E2 . . . . .24 B2 98 C3
Iffley Rd W6. . . . . . .39 A3
Ifield Ho SE17 . . . .152 B2
Ifield Rd SW10 . . . .156 B4
Ifor Evans Pl E1 . . .25 C1
Ightham Ho SE17 . .152 A3
Ikon Ho 21 E1 . . . . .32 B2
Ilbert St W10 . . . . . .23 A2
Ilchester Gdns
W2 . . . . .114 A4
Ilchester Mans
W8 . . . . .127 B2
Ilchester Pl W14 . .127 A2
Ildersly Gr SE21 . . . .75 C2
Ilderton Prim Sch 15
SE16 . . . . .40 B1
Ilderton Rd SE15,
SE16 . . . . .40 B1
Ilex Rd NW10 . . . . . .8 B2
Ilford Ho 14 N1. . . . .15 C2
Ilfracombe Flats
SE1 . . . . .137 A4
Iliffe St SE17 . . . . .150 B2
Iliffe Yd SE17 . . . . .150 B2
Ilkeston Ct 7 E5 . . .17 C4
Ilminster Gdns
SW11 . . . . .60 A3
Ilsley Ct 8 SW8 . . .170 C1
Imber St N1 . . . . . . .87 B3

Imperial Ave 5
N16 . . . . .16 A4
Imperial Cl NW2. . . . .9 A3
Imperial College
London (Charing
Cross) W6. . . . . . .39 C1
Imperial College
London (Chelsea &
Westminster)
SW10 . . . . .157 A3
Imperial College
London
(Hammersmith)
W12 . . . . .30 A3
Imperial College
London (South
Kensington)
SW7 . . . . .129 B2
Imperial College
London (St Mary's)
W2 . . . . .101 C2
Imperial College Rd
SW7 . . . . .129 B2
Imperial Cres
SW6 . . . . .167 A1
Imperial Ct NW8. . . .80 B2
Imperial Ho
3 Bow E3 . . . . .26 A2
2 Poplar E14 . . . . . .33 B2
Strand WC2 . . . . . .106 C1
Imperial Rd SW6 . .166 B3
Imperial Sq SW6 . .166 B4
Imperial St E3 . . . . .27 B2
Imperial Twrs 3
NW3 . . . . .11 B2
Imperial War Mus SE1,
SE11 . . . . .135 C1
Imperial Wharf Sta
SW10 . . . . .167 A3
Imre Cl W12. . . . . . .30 A1
Inchbald Sch of
Design SW1 . . . . .145 B4
Independent Pl E8 . .16 B3
Indescon Ct E14. . . .42 A4
Indiana Bldg 7
SE8 . . . . .51 C2
India St EC3 . . . . . .110 C1
India Way W12 . . . . .30 A2
India Wy 4 SW15 . . .56 C1
Indigo Mews N16. . . .6 C1
Indus Ct 18 SE15. . .49 B3
Ingate Pl SW8 . . . .170 B3
Ingelow Ho W8. . . .128 A4
Ingersoll Rd W12 . . .30 A1
Ingestre Pl W1 . . . .105 A1
Ingestre Rd NW5 . . . .4 A1
Ingham Rd NW6. . . .10 C4
Inglebert St EC1 . . . .95 B4
Ingleborough St
SW9 . . . . .173 B2
Ingleby Rd N7 . . . . . .5 A1
Inglefield Sq 12
E1 . . . . .32 A1
Ingle Ho 3 SW12. . .73 C3
Inglesham Wlk E9 . .18 B2
Ingleside Gr SE3 . . . .53 B4
Inglethorpe Ho 6
E5 . . . . .7 C2
Inglethorpe St
SW6 . . . . .47 C2
Ingleton St SW9 . . .173 B2
Inglewood Cl E14 . . .41 C2

Inglewood Mans 11
NW6 . . . . .10 C3

Inglewood Rd
NW6 . . . . .10 C3

Inglis Ho 5 SW15 . .57 B2

Inglis St E5 . . . . . . .48 A2

Ingram Ave NW11 . . .2 A4

Ingram Cl SE11 . . .149 A4

Ingram Ho E3 . . . . . .26 A4

Ingram Lo 8 SW11 . .60 A4

Ingrave St SW11 . . . .60 A4

Ingrebourne Ho
NW8 . . . . .101 C4

Ingress St 4 W4 . . . .38 A1

Inigo Pl WC2 . . . . . .120 A4

Inkerman Rd NW5 . . .13 A2

Inkerman Terr
W8 . . . . .127 C1

Inkster Ho 8
SW11 . . . . .60 A4

Inman Rd
Harlesden NW10 . . . .21 A4
Wandsworth SW18 . .71 B4

Inner Circ NW1 . . . .91 B4

Inner Park Rd
SW19 . . . . .69 C2

Inner Temple EC4 . .121 B4

Inner Temple La
EC4 . . . . .107 B1

Innes Gdns SW15 . .57 A1

Innisfree Ho NW2 . . .9 C2

Innis Ho SE17 . . . .152 A2

Insley Ho 13 E3 . . . .27 A2

Institute of Cancer
Research The
SW7 . . . . .143 A2

Institute Pl 8 E8 . . . .17 A3

Instituto Espanol
Canada Blanch Sch
W10 . . . . .31 A4

Inst of Child Health
WC1 . . . . .94 C1

Inst of Neurology
Bloomsbury WC1 . . .106 B4
St Pancras WC1 . . . .94 B1

Int Coll of
Accountancy The
SW17 . . . . .72 B1

Interchange The
NW5 . . . . .12 C3

International Com Sch
W1 . . . . .91 C1

International House
Language Sch
WC2 . . . . .106 B2

International Sch of
London W3 . . . . . . .36 C2

International Sch of
Screen Acting
E15 . . . . .27 B2

International Wy
E15 . . . . .19 B1

Inver Ct
11 Bayswater
W2 . . . . .100 B1
4 Hammersmith
W6 . . . . .38 C3

Inverforth Cl NW3 . . .2 B3

Inverforth Ho NW3 . . .2 B3

Invergarry Ho
NW6 . . . . .78 A1

Invermead Cl W6 . . .38 C2

Inverness Gdns
W8 . . . . .114 A1

Inverness Mews
W2 . . . . .114 A4

Inverness Pl W2 . . .114 A4

Inverness Pl NW1 . . .82 B4

Inverness Terr
W2 . . . . .114 A4

Inverton Rd SE15 . .65 C3

Invicta Cl 2 E3 . . . .33 C4

Invicta Plaza SE1 . .122 A2

Invicta Prim Sch
SE3 . . . . .53 C3

Invicta Rd SE3, SE7 . .53 C4

Inville Rd SE17 . . . .151 C1

Inwen Ct SE8 . . . . . .41 A1

Inwood Ct 12 NW1 . .13 B1

Inwood Ho 19
SE22 . . . . .64 A4

Inworth St NW11 . . .86 B4

Inworth Wlk N1 . . . .86 C4

Ion Ct 2 E2 . . . . . .24 C3

Ionian Bldg 41
E14 . . . . .33 A2

Ionian Ho 22 E1 . . . .25 C1

Ipsden Bldgs SE1 . .135 C4

Ipswich Ho SE4 . . . .66 A2

Iqra Ind Sch SW9 . .62 C4

Irby Ho SW2 . . . . . .62 C1

Ireland Yd EC4 . . . .108 B1

Irene Rd SW6 . . . . .165 C3

Ireton Ho 22 SW9 . .173 C1

Ireton St 12 E3 . . . .26 C1

Iris Ct 8 SE15 . . . . .50 A1

Iroko Ho 7 NW3 . . .11 A2

Iron Bridge Cl
NW10 . . . . .8 A3

Iron Bridge Ho
NW3 . . . . .12 B1

Irongate Ho EC3 . . .110 B4

Iron Mill Pl SW18 . . .59 A1

Iron Mill Rd SW18 . .59 A1

Ironmonger La
EC2 . . . . .109 B1

Ironmonger Pas
EC1 . . . . .97 A3

Ironmonger Row
EC1 . . . . .97 A3

Ironmonger Row
Baths EC1 . . . . . . .97 A3

Ironmongers Pl
E14 . . . . .41 C2

Ironmonger's Pl 2
E14 . . . . .41 C2

Ironside Cl SE16 . . . .40 C4

Ironside Ho E9 . . . . .18 A4

Ironworks 1 E3 . . . .26 C4

Irvine Ct W1 . . . . . .93 A1

Irvine Ho N7 . . . . . .14 B2

Irving Gr SW9 . . . .172 C1

Irving Ho SE17 . . . .150 A1

Irving Mews N1 . . . .15 B2

Irving Rd W14 . . . . .39 C3

Irving St WC2 . . . . .119 C3

Irwell Est 30 SE16 . .40 B4

Irwin Gdns NW10 . . .22 A4

Isabella Ct 8
TW10 . . . . .54 B1

Isabella Ho
3 Hammersmith
W6 . . . . .39 B1
Kennington SE11 . . .150 A2

Isabella Mews 11
E8 . . . . .16 A2

Isabella Rd E9 . . . . .17 B3

Isabella St SE1 . . . .122 A1

Isabel St SW9 . . . . .173 A4

Isambard Mews
E14 . . . . .42 B3

Isambard Pl SE16 . . .32 B1

Iseldon Ct N7 . . . . . .14 A4

Isel Way 4 SE22 . . . .64 A2

Isis Cl SW15 . . . . . . .57 B3

Isis Ct W4 . . . . .45 A3

Isis Ho NW8 . . . . . . .89 C1

Isis St SW18 . . . . . . .71 B2

Islamia Prim & Girls
Sec Schs NW6 . . . .23 B4

Islamic Coll for
Advanced Studies 3
NW10 . . . . .9 A2

Island Gardens Sta
E14 . . . . .42 B1

Island Ho E14 . . . . .27 B2

Island Rd SE16 . . . . .40 C2

Island Row E14 . . . .33 B3

Islay Wlk 12 N1 . . . .15 B2

Isleden Ho N1 . . . . .86 C4

Isledon Rd N4, N7 . . .5 C1

ISLE OF DOGS 42 B2

ISLINGTON 14 C2

Islington Arts & Media
Sch 6 N4 . . . . .5 B3

Islington Bsns Ctr
N1 . . . . .87 A4

Islington Gn N1 . . . .86 A3

Islington Gn Sch
N1 . . . . .86 A3

Islington High St
N1 . . . . .86 A2

Islington Mus 9 N1 . .96 A3

Islington Park Mews
2 N1 . . . . .15 A1

Islington Park St
N1 . . . . .15 A1

Islington Tennis Ctr
N7 . . . . .14 A2

Islip St NW5 . . . . . .13 B3

Isokon Flats 3
NW3 . . . . .12 B3

Issac Way SE1 . . . .137 A4

Italia Conti Acad of
Theatre Arts EC1 . .96 C1

IUC Languages Sch
W1 . . . . .104 B3

Ivanhoe Ho
8 Balham SW12 . . .73 A4
2 Bow E3 . . . . .26 A3

Ivanhoe Rd SE5 . . . .64 B4

Ivatt Pl W14 . . . . . .141 A1

Iveagh Cl E9 . . . . . .25 C4

Iveagh Ct EC3 . . . . .110 C1

Iveagh Ho
2 Brixton SW9 . . . . .48 A1
Chelsea SW10 . . . .157 A2

Ivebury Ct 8 W10 . . .30 B3

Iveley Rd SW4 . . . .170 C1

Iver Ct N1 . . . . .15 B2

Iverna Ct W8 . . . . . .127 C2

Iverna Gdns W8 . . . .127 C2

Iverson Rd NW6 . . . .10 C2

Ives Rd E16 . . . . .35 A4

Ives St SW3 . . . . . .144 B4

Ivimey St E2 . .24 C2 99 C4

Ivinghoe Ho 10 N7 . .13 C3

Ivor Ct NW1 . . . . . . .90 C2

Ivories The N1 . . . . .15 B1

Ivor Mayor Lo
SW12 . . . . .60 C1

Ivor Pl NW1 . . . . . . .90 C1

Ivor St NW1 . . . . . . .13 B1

Ivory Ho
9 London SW11 . . . .59 B4

Ivory Ho continued
St George in t East
E1 . . . . .125 A2

Ivory Sq 13 SW18 . . .59 B4

Ivybridge Ho 18
SE22 . . . . .64 A4

Ivybridge La WC2, . .120 B3

Ivy Church La SE1, . .152 C2

Ivy Cres W4 . . . . . . .37 B2

Ivy Ct 17 SE16 . . . .153 C1

Ivydale Prim Sch
SE15 . . . . .65 C3

Ivydale Rd SE15 . . . .65 C3

Ivyday Gr SW16 . . . .74 B1

Ivy Lo W8 . . .31 C1 113 B2

Ivymount Rd SE27 . .74 C1

Ivy Rd
Brockley SE4 . . . . . .66 C3
Cricklewood NW2 . . . .9 B4
Newham E16 . . . . . .35 C3

Ivy St N1 . . . . .24 A3

Ixworth Pl SW3 . . . .144 A3

J

Jacaranda Gr E8 . . .16 B1

Jackman Ho 24
E1 . . . . .32 A1

Jackman St E8 . . . . .25 A4

Jackson Cl E9 . . . . . .17 C1

Jackson Ho 18
SW11 . . . . .59 C4

Jackson Rd N7 . . . . .14 B4

Jackson's La N6 . . . . .4 A4

Jack Taylor Sch
NW8 . . . . .78 C4

Jack Tizard Sch
W6 . . . . .39 C2

Jack Walker Ct
N5 . . . . .15 A4

Jacobin Lo N7 . . . . .14 A3

Jacob Mans 15 E1 . .32 A3

Jacobson Ct
SW11 . . . . .168 B3

Jacobson Ho E1 . . . .110 C2

Jacob St SE1 . . . . . .139 B4

Jacob's Well Mews
W1 . . . . .103 C2

Jacotts Ho W10 . . . .22 B1

Jacqueline Ho 8
E1 . . . . .32 C4

Jaggard Way
SW12 . . . . .72 B4

Jagger Ho SW11 . . .168 C4

Jago Wlk SE5 . . . . . .48 C3

Jamaica Rd
Bermondsey SE1 . . .138 B4
Bermondsey SE16 . . .40 A3

Jamaica St E1 . . . . . .32 B4

James Allen's Girls'
Sch (prep) 13
SE22 . . . . .64 A2

James Allen's Girls'
Sch (pre-prep)
SE22 . . . . .63 C1

James Allen's Girls'
Sch (senior) 12
SE22 . . . . .64 A2

James Anderson Ct 26
E2 . . . . .24 A3

James Ave NW2 . . . . .9 B3

James Brine Ho 11
E2 . . . . .24 B2 99 A4

James Campbell Ho
3 E2 . . . . .25 B3

James Collins Cl
W9 . . . . .23 B1

James Docherty Ho 4
E2 . . . . .25 B3

James Hammett Ho
9 E2 . . . . .24 B3

James Ho
Mile End E1 . . . . . . .26 A1
50 Rotherhithe
SE16 . . . . .40 C4

James Joyce Wlk 7
SE24 . . . . .63 A3

James Leicester Hall
of Residence N7 . . .14 A2

James Lind Ho 6
SE8 . . . . .41 B2

James Middleton Ho
2 E2 . . . . .25 A2

James Morgan Mews
N1 . . . . .87 A3

Jameson Ct 3 E2 . . .25 B3

Jameson Ho SE11 . .148 C2

Jameson Pl 6
W3 . . . . .37 B4

Jameson St
W8 . . . . . .31 C1 113 C2

James's Cotts
TW9 . . . . .44 C3

James St
Marylebone W1 . . . .103 C1
Strand WC2 . . . . . .120 B4

James Stewart Ho
NW6 . . . . .10 B1

James Stroud Ho
SE17 . . . . .151 A1

Jamestown Rd
NW1 . . . . .82 A4

Jamestown Way
E14 . . . . .34 C2

James Voller Way 30
E1 . . . . .32 B3

James Wolfe Prim
Sch 8 SE10 . . . . . .52 B3

Jamuna Cl E14 . . . . .33 A4

Jane St E1 . . . . .32 A3

Janet St E14 . . . . . .41 C3

Janeway Pl 2
SE16 . . . . .40 A4

Janeway St SE16 . .139 C3

Jansen Ho 5
SW15 . . . . .56 C2

Jansen Wlk SW11 . . .59 C3

Japan Cres N4 . . . . . .5 B3

Jardine Rd E1 . . . . . .32 C2

Jarman Ho
Bermondsey SE16 . . .40 C2
15 Stepney E1 . . . . .32 B4

Jarrett Cl SW2 . . . . .75 A3

Jarrow Rd SE16 . . . .40 B1

Jarrow Way E9 . . . . .18 B4

Jarvis Ho 3 SE15 . . .49 C2

Jarvis Rd SE22 . . . . .64 A3

Jasmin SE1 . . . . . . .125 A1

Jasmine Sq 13 E3 . . .26 B4

Jasmin Ho SE4 . . . . .66 B4

Jasmin Lo 17 SE16 . .40 A1

Jason Ct
2 London SW9 . . . .173 B4
Marylebone W1 . . . .103 C2

Jasper Wlk N1 . . . . .97 B4

Java Wharf SE1 . . . .139 A4

Jay Ho SW15 . . . . . .47 B1

Jay Mews SW7 . . . .129 A3

Jean Darling Ho
SW10 . . . . .157 B3

Jean Pardies Ho 23
  E1 . . . . .32 B4
Jebb Ave SW2 . . . . .62 A3
Jebb St E3 . . . . .26 C3
Jedburgh St SW11 . . . .60 C3
Jeddo Mews W12 . . . . .38 B4
Jeddo Rd W12 . . . . .38 B4
Jefferson Bldg 3
  E14 . . . . .41 C4
Jeffrey's Ct 2
Jeffrey's Ct SW4 . . . . 172 A2
Jeffrey's Pl NW1 . . . . .13 B1
Jeffrey's Rd SW4 . . . . 172 A2
Jeffrey's St NW1 . . . . .13 B1
Jeger Ave E2 . . . . .24 B4
Jelf Rd SW2 . . . . .62 C2
Jellicoe Ho
  5 Bethnal Green
  E2 . . . . .24 C3
  Fitzrovia NW1 . . . . . . .92 C3
  1 Putney SW15 . . . . .57 C2
Jemotts Ct 3
  SE14 . . . . .50 C4
Jenkins Ho SW8 . . . . 171 B4
Jenkinson Ho 12
  E2 . . . . .25 C2
Jenner Ave W3 . . . . . . .28 C4
Jenner Ho SE3 . . . . . . .53 A4
Jenner Pl SW13 . . . . . .47 A4
Jenner Rd N16 . . . . .7 B1
Jennifer Ho SE11 . . . 149 C3
Jennings Ho SE10 . . . .42 C1
Jennings Rd SE22 . . . .64 B1
Jensen Ho E13 . . . . . . .26 C1
Jephson Ct 17
  SW4 . . . . .172 B1
Jephson Ho 6
  SE17 . . . . .48 A4
Jephson St SE5 . . . . . .48 C2
Jephtha Rd SW18 . . . .58 C1
Jerdan Pl SW6 . . . . . 155 B2
Jeremiah St 11
  E14 . . . . .34 A3
Jeremy Bentham Ho
  24 E2 . . . . .24 C2
Jermyn St SW1 . . . . . 119 A2
Jerningham Ct
  SE14 . . . . .51 A2
Jerningham Rd
  SE14 . . . . .51 A2
Jerome Cres NW8 . . . .90 A2
Jerome Ho NW1 . . . . 102 B4
Jerome St
  E1 . . . . .24 B1 98 C1
Jerome Twr 5
  W3 . . . . .37 A4
Jerrard St SE13 . . . . . .67 A4
Jerrold Lo SW15 . . . . .57 B4
Jerrold St 25 N1 . . . . .24 A3
Jersey Ho N1 . . . . .15 B2
Jersey Rd N1 . . . . .15 B2
Jersey St E2 . . . . .25 A2
Jerusalem Pas
  EC1 . . . . .96 A1
Jervis Bay Ho 9
  E14 . . . . .34 C3
Jervis Ct
  1 Greenwich
  SE10 . . . . .52 B2
  Marylebone W1 . . . . 104 B1
Jervis Rd SW6 . . . . . 155 A3
Jessel Ho
  St Pancras WC1 . . . . .94 A3
  Westminster SW1 . . 147 C4
Jessica Rd SW18 . . . . .59 B2

Jessie Blythe La 4
  N19 . . . . .5 A4
Jessie Duffett Ho 11
  SE5 . . . . .48 B3
Jesson Ho SE17 . . . . 151 B3
Jessop Ct N1 . . . . .86 B1
Jessop Ho 4 W4 . . . . .37 C2
Jessop Prim Sch 24
  SE24 . . . . .63 B3
Jessop Sq E14 . . . . . . .33 C1
Jeston Ho 10 SE27 . . .75 A1
Jethou Ho 10 N1 . . . . .15 B2
Jevons Ho 8
  NW8 . . . . .11 C1
Jewell Ho 3
  SW12 . . . . .73 B4
Jewel Tower SW1 . . . 134 A2
Jewish Mus NW1 . . . . .82 A3
Jewry St EC3 . . . . 110 C1
Jews Row SW18 . . . . .59 B3
Jeymer Ave NW2 . . . . .9 B3
Jeypore Rd SW18 . . . .59 B1
Jim Griffiths Ho
  SW6 . . . . 155 A3
Jim Veal Dr 3
  N17 . . . . .14 A2
Joanna Ho 7 W6 . . . . .39 B1
Joan St SE1 . . . . 122 A1
Jocelin Ho N1 . . . . .85 A3
Jocelyn Rd TW9 . . . . . .54 A4
Jocelyn St SE15 . . . . .49 C2
Jockey's Fields
  WC1 . . . . 107 A4
Jodane Rd SE8 . . . . . .41 B2
Jodrell Rd E3 . . . . .18 B1
Johanna St SE1 . . . . 135 B3
John Adam St
  WC2 . . . . 120 B3
John Aird Ct W2 . . . . 101 A4
John Archer Way
  SW18 . . . . .59 C1
John Ashby Cl
  SW2 . . . . .62 B1
John Ball Prim Sch
  SE3 . . . . .53 A1
John Barker Ct
  NW6 . . . . .10 A1
John Betts' Ho
  W12 . . . . .38 C3
John Betts Prim Sch
  W6 . . . . .39 A3
John Bond Ho 2
  E3 . . . . .26 B3
John Brent Ho 8
  SE8 . . . . .40 C2
John Buck Ho
  NW10 . . . . .21 B4
John Burns Prim Sch
  SW11 . . . . 169 C1
John Campbell Rd 26
  N16 . . . . .16 A3
John Carpenter St
  EC4 . . . . 122 A4
John Cartwright Ho
  7 E2 . . . . .25 A2
John Clynes Ct
  SW15 . . . . .57 A3
John Conwey Ho 3
  SW2 . . . . .62 C1
John Dee Ho 3
  SW14 . . . . .55 C4
John Donne Prim Sch
  13 SE15 . . . . .50 A1
John Dwight Ho
  SW6 . . . . .59 A4

John Fearon Wlk 5
  W10 . . . . .23 A2
John Felton Rd 19
  SE16 . . . . 139 B3
John Fielden Ho 10
  E2 . . . . .25 A2
John Fisher St E1 . . . 125 B4
John F Kennedy Sch
  6 E15 . . . . .27 C4
John Harris Ho
  SE15 . . . . .64 C4
John Harrison Way
  SE10 . . . . .43 B3
John Howard Ctr The
  E9 . . . . .18 A3
John Islip St SW1 . . . 148 A3
John Keall Ho 3
  SW15 . . . . .57 C4
John Keble CE Prim
  Sch NW10 . . . . .21 B4
John Kennedy Ct 1
  N1 . . . . .15 C2
John Kennedy Ho 1
  SE16 . . . . .40 C2
John Kennedy Lo 2
  N1 . . . . .15 C2
John King Ct 5
  N19 . . . . .4 C2
John Kirk Ho
  18 Battersea
  SW11 . . . . .59 C4
  5 Streatham
  SW16 . . . . .74 A1
John Knight Lo
  SW6 . . . . 155 C2
John McDonald Ho 3
  E14 . . . . .42 B3
John McKenna Wlk 17
  SE16 . . . . 139 C2
John Maurice Cl
  SE17 . . . . 151 B4
John Nettleford Ho 14
  E2 . . . . .25 A2
John Orwell Sports
  Ctr E1 . . . . .32 A1
John Parker Sq 7
  SW11 . . . . .59 C4
John Parry Ct 28
  N1 . . . . .24 A3
John Penn Ho SE8 . . . .51 B3
John Penn St
  SE13 . . . . .52 A2
John Perryn Prim Sch
  W3 . . . . .29 A3
John Prince's St
  W1 . . . . 104 B2
John Pritchard Ho 16
  E1 . . . . .24 C1 99 C1
John Ratcliffe Ho 6
  NW6 . . . . .23 C2
John Rennie Wlk 1
  E1 . . . . .32 B1
John Roan Sch
  SE3 . . . . .53 A3
John Roll Way
  SE16 . . . . 139 C2
John Ruskin Prim Sch
  SE5 . . . . .48 B4
John Ruskin St
  SE5 . . . . .48 B4
John Scurr Ho 18
  E14 . . . . .33 A3
John Scurr Prim Sch
  40 E1 . . . . .25 B1
John Silkin La SE8 . . .40 C1
John's Mews WC1 . . .95 A1

John Smith Ave
  SW6 . . . . 154 C2
John Smith Mews
  E14 . . . . .34 C2
Johnson Cl E8 . . . . . . .24 C4
Johnson Ct 10
  SW18 . . . . .59 C3
Johnson Ho
  Belgravia SW1 . . . . 145 C3
  23 Bethnal Green
  E2 . . . . .24 C2 99 C3
  Somers Town NW1 . . .83 A1
  South Lambeth
  SW8 . . . . 161 C1
Johnson Lo 12 W9 . . .31 C4
Johnson Rd NW10 . . . .20 C4
Johnsons Ct EC4 . . . . 107 C1
Johnson's Pl SW1 . . . 146 C1
Johnson St E1 . . . . . . .32 B3
Johnsons Way
  NW10 . . . . .20 A1
John Spencer Sq
  N1 . . . . .15 A2
John's Pl E1 . . . . .32 A3
John St WC1 . . . . .95 A1
John Stainer Com
  Prim Sch SE4 . . . . .66 A4
Johnston Cl SW9 . . . 173 A3
Johnstone Ho
  SE13 . . . . .67 C4
John Strachey Ho
  SW6 . . . . 155 A3
John Trundle Ct
  EC4 . . . . 108 C4
John Tucker Ho 5
  E14 . . . . .41 C3
John Wesley's House
  & Mus of Methodism
  EC1 . . . . .97 C2
John Wheatley Ho
  14 London N19 . . . . . .4 C4
  West Brompton
  SW6 . . . . 155 A3
John Williams Cl
  SE14 . . . . .50 C4
Joiners Arms Yd 5
  SE5 . . . . .48 C2
Joiner St SE1 . . . . . . 123 C1
Joiners Yd N1 . . . . . . .84 B1
Joiles Ho 13 E3 . . . . . .27 A2
Jonathan Ct 9
  W4 . . . . .38 A2
Jonathan St SE11 . . . 148 C2
Jones Ho
  6 South Bromley
  E14 . . . . .34 C3
  Stamford Hill N16 . . . . .7 A3
Jones St W1 . . . . 118 A3
Jones Wlk 6
  TW10 . . . . .54 B1
Jonson Ho
  Borough The SE1 . . . 137 C1
  16 Canonbury N16 . . .15 C4
Jordan Ct SW15 . . . . .57 C3
Jordan Ho
  12 London SE4 . . . . .65 C3
  Shoreditch N1 . . . . . .87 C3
Jordans Ho NW8 . . . . .90 A1
Joscoyne Ho 5
  E1 . . . . .32 A3
Joseph Ave W3 . . . . . .28 C3
Joseph Conrad Ho
  SW1 . . . . 147 A3
Joseph Ct N16 . . . . .7 A4
Joseph Hardcastle Cl
  SE14 . . . . .50 C3

Josephine Ave
  SW2 . . . . .62 B2
Joseph Irwin Ho 11
  E14 . . . . .33 B2
Joseph Mews
  Islington N7 . . . . .14 C2
  Kennington SE15 . . . .65 C4
Joseph Powell Cl 1
  SW12 . . . . .61 B1
Joseph Priestley Ho
  12 E2 . . . . .25 A2
Joseph St E3 . . . . .26 B1
Joseph Trotter Cl
  EC1 . . . . .95 C3
Joshua St E14 . . . . . . .34 B3
Joslings Cl W12 . . . . . .29 C2
Josseline Ct 9 E3 . . . .26 A3
Joubert Mans
  SW3 . . . . 144 B2
Joubert St SW11 . . . . 169 A2
Jowett Ho 27
  SW9 . . . . 172 B1
Jowett St SE15 . . . . . .49 B3
Jubet Ho 9 N16 . . . . . .15 C4
Jubilee Bldgs NW8 . . .79 B2
Jubilee Cl 4
  NW10 . . . . .21 B3
Jubilee Cres E14 . . . . .42 B3
Jubilee Ct N1 . . . . .84 B4
Jubilee Ho SE11 . . . . 149 C3
Jubilee Hts NW2 . . . . .10 B2
Jubilee Mans 10
  E1 . . . . .32 B3
Jubilee Market
  WC2 . . . . 120 B4
Jubilee Pl SW3 . . . . . 144 B2
Jubilee Prim Sch
  SW2 . . . . .62 C1
Jubilee Sch N16 . . . . . .7 C3
Jubilee St E1 . . . . .32 B4
Jubilee The 2
  SE10 . . . . .52 A3
Jubilee Yd SE1 . . . . . 138 C4
Judd St WC1 . . . . .94 A3
Jude St E16 . . . . .35 B3
Judges' Wlk NW3 . . . . .2 B1
Juer St SW11 . . . . . . 158 B1
Julian Ave W3 . . . . . . .28 A2
Julian Ct SW13 . . . . . .46 B2
Julian Pl E14 . . . . .42 A1
Julia St NW5 . . . . .12 C3
Julius Ct TW8 . . . . . . .44 A3
Julius Ho 11 N1 . . . . . .24 A3
Julius Nyerere Cl
  N1 . . . . .84 C3
Junction App
  Battersea SW11 . . . . .60 A4
  Lewisham SE13 . . . . .67 B4
Junction Mews
  W2 . . . . 102 A2
Junction Pl W2 . . . . . 101 C2
Junction Rd N19 . . . . . .4 B1
Juniper Cres NW1 . . . .12 C1
Juniper Ct N16 . . . . .7 B3
Juniper Dr SW18 . . . . .59 B3
Juniper Ho
  6 Peckham SE14,
  SE15 . . . . .50 B3
  8 Richmond TW9 . . . .45 A2
Juniper St 16 E1 . . . . .32 B2
Juno Ct 11 SW9 . . . . 163 B1
Juno Ho 3 E3 . . . . .26 C4
Juno Way SE14 . . . . . .50 C4

Juno Way Ind Est
SE14 . . . . .50 C4
Jupiter Ct 10
SW9 . . . . .163 B1
Jupiter Way N7 . . . .14 B2
Jupp Rd E15 . . . . . .19 C1
Jupp Rd W E15 . . . .27 C4
Jura Ho SE16 . . . . . .41 A2
Jurston Ct SE1 . . . .135 C3
Justice Wlk SW3 . .158 A3
Justines Pl E2 . . . . .25 C2
Jutland Cl N19 . . . . .5 A3
Jutland Ho 4 SE5 . .48 B1
Juxon St SE11 . . . .149 A4

K

Kambala Rd SW11 . .59 C4
Kara Way NW2 . . . . . .9 C4
Karen Ct
 2 Camberwell
  SE5 . . . . .64 A4
 Forest Hill SE23 . . .66 A1
Karen Ho 7 N16 . . .15 C4
Kasmin Ct NW10 . . .8 C1
Kassala Rd SW11 169 A3
Katherine Cl 3
 SE16 . . . . .32 C1
Katherine Ho 15
  W10 . . . . .23 A1
Katherine Sq
  W11 . . . . . . .31 A1 112 A2
Kathleen Ave W3 . .28 B4
Kathleen Rd SW11 . .60 B4
Kayani Ave N4 . . . . . .6 B3
Kay Rd SW9 . . . . . .172 C1
Kay St E2 . . . . .24 C3
Kean Ho 6 SE17 . . .48 A4
Kean St WC2 . . . . .106 C1
Keates Est N16 . . . . .7 B2
Keats Cl
 Bermondsey SE1 . .152 C3
 Hampstead NW3 . . .12 A4
Keats Gr NW3 . . . . .12 A4
Keats Ho
 4 Bethnal Green
  E2 . . . . .25 B2
 30 Camberwell SE5 .48 B3
 Chelsea SW1 . . . . .161 A4
Keats House (Mus)
 NW3 . . . . .12 A4
Keats Pl EC2 . . . . .109 B3
Keble Ho 4 SW15 . .57 C1
Keble St SW13 . . . . .47 A4
Kedelston Ct E5 . . .18 A4
Kedge Ho 10 E14 . . .41 C3
Kedleston Wlk 21
  E2 . . . . .25 A2
Keel Cl SE16 . . . . . .32 C1
Keel Ct 3 E14 . . . . .34 C2
Keeley St WC2 . . . .106 C1
Keeling Ho 4 E2 . . .25 A3
Keelson Ho 4
  E14 . . . . .41 C3
Keen's Yd N1 . . . . . .15 A2
Keeper Wharf E1 . .32 C2
Keepier Wharf 18
  E1 . . . . .32 C2
Keep The SE3 . . . . .53 C1
Keeton's Rd SE16 . .40 A3
Keevil Dr SW19 . . . .70 A4
Keighley Cl N7 . . . .14 A4
Keildon Rd SW11 . . .60 B3

Keir Hardie Ho
 Fulham W6 . . . . . . .47 C4
 15 Newington Green
  N19 . . . . .4 C4
 Willesden NW10 . . . .8 B1
Keir Hardy Prim Sch
  E16 . . . . .35 C4
Keith Connor Cl 8
  SW8 . . . . .61 A4
Keith Gr W12 . . . . . .29 C1
Keith Ho NW6 . . . . .78 A1
Kelby Ho N7 . . . . . .14 B2
Kelfield Ct 1 W10 . .30 C3
Kelfield Gdns W10 . .30 C3
Kelfield Mews
  W10 . . . . .30 C3
Kellett Ho N1 . . . . . .87 C3
Kellett Rd SW2 . . . .62 C3
Kellow Ho SE1 . . . .137 B4
Kell St SE1 . . . . . . .136 B2
Kelly Ave SE15 . . . . .49 B2
Kelly Ct 18 E14 . . . . .33 C2
Kelly Mews 4 W9 . .23 B1
Kelly St NW1 . . . . . .13 A2
Kelman Cl SW4 . . . .171 C1
Kelmore Gr SE22 . . .64 C3
Kelmscott Gdns
  W12 . . . . .38 C3
Kelmscott House
  W6 . . . . .39 A1
Kelmscott Rd
  SW11 . . . . .60 B2
Kelross Rd N5 . . . . .15 B4
Kelsall Mews TW9 . .45 A2
Kelsey St E2 . . .24 C1 99 C2
Kelshall Ct N4 . . . . . .6 B2
Kelson Ho E14 . . . . .42 B3
Kelso Pl W8 . . . . . .128 B2
Kelvedon Ho SW8 .172 B4
Kelvedon Rd SW6 .155 A1
Kelvin Ct
 Chiswick W4 . . . . . .45 B3
 Notting Hill
  W11 . . . . . . .31 C2 113 B3
Kelvington Rd
  SE15 . . . . .65 C2
Kelvin Rd N5 . . . . . .15 B4
Kelyway Ho 20
  SW2 . . . . .74 C4
Kember St N1 . . . . . .14 B1
Kemble Ho SW9 . . . .63 A4
Kemble St WC2 . . . .106 C1
Kemerton Rd SE5 . . .63 B4
Kemey's St E9 . . . . .18 A3
Kemp Ct SW8 . . . . .162 A1
Kemp Ho 5 SE1 . . .137 C1
Kempe Rd NW6 . . . .22 C3
Kemp Ho
 Finsbury EC1 . . . . . .97 B3
 1 Globe Town 2
  E2 . . . . .25 C3
Kempis Way 5
  SE22 . . . . .64 A2
Kemplay Rd NW3 . . .11 C4
Kemp's Ct W1 . . . . .105 B1
Kemps Dr E14 . . . . .33 C2
Kempsford Gdns
  SW5 . . . . .141 C1
Kempsford Rd
 Lambeth SE11 . . . .149 C3
 Newington SE11 . . .150 A3
Kemps Gdns SE13 . .67 B2
Kempson Rd SW6 .155 C1
Kempthorne Rd
  SE8 . . . . .41 B2
Kempton Ct E1 . . . . .32 A4

Kempton Ho 13
  N1 . . . . .24 A4
Kemsing Ho SE1 . .137 C3
Kemsing Rd SE10 . .43 C1
Kemsley SE13 . . . . .67 A2
Kenbrook Ho
 Kensington W14 . .127 A1
 5 Kentish Town
  NW5 . . . . .13 B3
Kenbury Gdns 1
  SE5 . . . . .48 B1
Kenbury Mans 4
  SE5 . . . . .48 B1
Kenbury St SE5 . . . .48 B1
Kenchester Cl
  SW8 . . . . .162 B1
Kendal NW1 . . . . . . .92 B4
Kendal Ave W3 . . . .28 A4
Kendal Cl SE5 . . . . .48 A3
Kendal Ct NW2 . . . .10 A3
Kendal Ho
 8 Hackney E9 . . . .17 B1
 Islington N1 . . . . . . .85 A2
Kendall Ct 3
  SE22 . . . . .64 A2
Kendall Pl W1 . . . .103 B3
Kendal Pl SW15 . . . .58 B2
Kendal Rd NW10 . . . .8 C4
Kendal St W2 . . . . .102 B1
Kendal Stps W2 . . .102 B1
Kender Prim Sch
 7 Deptford SE14 . . .50 B2
 London SE14 . . . . . .50 B2
Kender St SE14 . . . .50 B2
Kendoa Rd 1
  SW4 . . . . .61 C3
Kendon Ho E15 . . . .19 C1
Kendrick Ct 4
  SE15 . . . . .50 A2
Kendrick Mews
  SW7 . . . . .143 B3
Kendrick Pl SW7 . .143 B3
Kenilford Rd
  SW12 . . . . .73 A4
Kenilworth Ct
  SW6 . . . . .58 A4
Kenilworth Rd
 Bow E3 . . . . .26 A3
 Kilburn NW6 . . . . .223 B4
Kenley Wlk
  W11 . . . . . . .31 A2 112 A3
Kenmont Gdns
  NW10 . . . . .22 A2
Kenmont Prim Sch
  NW10 . . . . .22 A2
Kenmore Cl TW9 . . .44 C3
Kenmore Ct NW6 . . .10 C1
Kenmure Rd E8 . . . .17 A3
Kenmure Yd E8 . . . .17 A3
Kennacraig Cl 6
  E16 . . . . .35 C1
Kennard Ho 12
  SW11 . . . . .169 C3
Kennard Rd E15 . . . .19 C1
Kennard St 9
  SW11 . . . . .169 B3
Kennedy Cox Ho 9
  E16 . . . . .35 B4
Kennedy Ho SE11 .148 C2
Kennedy Wlk
  SE17 . . . . .151 C3
Kennet Cl SW11 . . . .59 C3
Kennet Ct 47 W2 . . .31 C4
Kenneth Campbell Ho
  NW8 . . . . .89 C2
Kenneth Cres NW2 . .9 A3

Kenneth Ct SE11 . .149 C4
Kennet Ho NW8 . . . .89 C1
Kenneth Younger Ho
  SW6 . . . . .155 A3
Kennet Rd W9 . . . . .23 B1
Kennet St E1 . . . . .125 C2
Kennett Wharf La
  EC4 . . . . .123 A4
Kenning Ho 6 N1 . . .24 A4
Kenning St 18
  SE16 . . . . .40 B4
Kennings Way
  SE11 . . . . .149 C2
KENNINGTON . . .163 A3
Kennington Ent Ctr
  SE17 . . . . .150 B1
Kennington La
  SE11 . . . . .149 A1
Kennington Oval
  SE11 . . . . .163 A3
Kennington Palace Ct
  SE11 . . . . .149 B2
Kennington Park
 Gdns SE17 . . . . . . .48 A4
Kennington Park Ho
  SE11 . . . . .150 A3
Kennington Park Pl
  SE11 . . . . .48 A4
Kennington Park Rd
  SE11 . . . . .150 A2
Kennington Rd
  SE11 . . . . .149 B3
Kennington Sta
  SE17 . . . . .150 A2
Kennoldes SE21 . . . .75 C2
Kenrick Pl W1 . . . .103 B3
KENSAL GREEN . . .22 B2
Kensal Green Cemy
 (All Souls) NW10 . .22 B2
Kensal Green Sta
  NW10 . . . . .22 C2
Kensal Ho W10 . . . .22 C1
Kensal Rd W10 . . . .23 A1
KENSAL RISE 22 C3
Kensal Rise Prim Sch
  NW6 . . . . .22 C3
Kensal Rise Sta
  NW10 . . . . .22 C2
KENSAL TOWN . . .23 A1
KENSINGTON 127 C3
Kensington Aldridge
 Acad 22 W11 . . . . .30 C3
Kensington & Chelsea
 Coll
 Chelsea SW10 . . . .156 C2
 14 Kensal Town
  W10 . . . . .31 A4
Kensington Church Ct
  W8 . . . . .128 A3
Kensington Church St
  W8 . . . . . . .31 C1 113 C1
Kensington Church
 Wlk W8 . . . . .128 A3
Kensington Court
  W8 . . . . .128 B3
Kensington Court
 Mews W8 . . . . . . .128 B2
Kensington Court Pl
  W8 . . . . .128 B2
Kensington Ct
  W8 . . . . .128 B3
Kensington Ct Gdns
  W8 . . . . .128 B2

Kensington Gardens
  W2 . . . . .115 A1
Kensington Gate
  W8 . . . . .128 C2
Kensington Gdns Sq
  W2 . . . . .100 A1
Kensington Gore
  SW7 . . . . .129 B3
Kensington Hall Gdns
  W14 . . . . .140 C2
Kensington High St
  W8 . . . . .127 C2
Kensington Ho 8
  W8 . . . . .31 C1 113 B1
Kensington L Ctr
  W11 . . . . . . .31 A2 112 A4
Kensington Mall
  W8 . . . . .31 C1 113 C2
Kensington Mans
  SW5 . . . . .141 C2
Kensington Olympia
 Sta W14 . . . . .126 A2
Kensington Pal
  W8 . . . . .114 B1
Kensington Palace
 Gdns W8 . . . . . . .114 A2
Kensington Park
 Gdns W11 . . .31 B2 113 A3
Kensington Park
 Mews W11 . . . . . . .31 B3
Kensington Park Rd
  W11 . . . . . . .31 B2 113 A4
Kensington Pl
  W8 . . . . .31 C1 113 B2
Kensington Prep Sch
  SW6 . . . . .165 A4
Kensington Sq
  W8 . . . . .128 A3
Kensington Village
  W14 . . . . .141 A3
Kensington W
  W14 . . . . .140 A4
Kensworth Ho EC1 . .97 C3
Kent Ct 3 E2 . . . . . . .24 B3
Kent Ho
 Camberwell SE1 . . .153 A1
 13 Chiswick W4 . . . .38 A1
 Marylebone W1 . . .104 C2
 Pimlico SW1 . . . . .147 B1
 Richmond TW10 . . .54 C2
Kentish Bldgs
  SE1 . . . . .123 B1
KENTISH TOWN . . .13 B2
Kentish Town C of E Prim
 Sch 5 NW5 . . . . . .13 B3
Kentish Town City
 Farm NW5 . . . . . . .12 C3
Kentish Town Rd
  NW1 . . . . .13 A2
Kentish Town Sp Ctr
  NW5 . . . . .13 A2
Kentish Town Sta
  NW5 . . . . .13 B3
Kentish Town West
 Sta NW5 . . . . .13 A2
Kent Lo 9 SW19 . . .69 C3
Kentmere Ho SE15 . .50 B4
Kenton Ct W14 . . . .126 C1
Kenton Ho
 20 Globe Town
  E1 . . . . .25 B1
 Highbury N5 . . . . . . .5 C1

Kenton Rd E9 . . . . .17 C2
Kenton St WC1 . . . . .94 A2
Kent Pas NW1 . . . . .90 C2
Kent Pk Ind Est
SE15 . . . . .50 A4
Kent Rd
  Richmond TW9 . . . .44 C3
  South Acton W4 . . .37 B3
Kent St E2 . . . . .90 B3
Kent Terr NW1 . . . . . .90 B3
Kentwell Cl SE4 . . . .66 A3
Kentwode Gn
  SW13 . . . . .46 C3
Kent Yard SW7 . . . .130 B3
Kenway Rd SW5 . . .142 A3
Ken Wilson Ho **19**
  E2 . . . . .24 C3
Kenwood Cl NW3 . . .2 C3
Kenwood Ho
  SW9 . . . . .63 A3
Kenwood Ho NW3 . . .3 A3
Kenworthy Rd E9 . .18 A2
Kenwrick Ho N1 . . . .85 A3
Kenwyn Rd SW4 . . .61 C3
Kenyon Ho SE11 . . .149 B3
Kenyon St SW6 . . . .47 C2
Kepler Ho **9** SE10 . .43 B1
Kepler Rd SW2,
  SW4 . . . . .62 A3
Keppel Ho
  Brompton SW3 . . .144 A3
  3 Deptford SE8 . . .41 B1
Keppel Row SE1 . . .122 C1
Keppel St WC1 . . . . .105 C4
Kerbela St **8**
  E2 . . . . .24 C1 **99 B2**
Kerbey St E14 . . . . . .34 A3
Kerfield Cres SE5 . .48 C2
Kerfield Pl SE5 . . . . .48 C2
Kerin Ho E15 . . . . . . .19 A3
Kerridge Ct **10** N16 . .16 A2
Kerrier Ho **10** SW10 . .157 A1
Kerrington Ct **7**
  W12 . . . . .39 B4
Kerrison Rd
  Battersea SW11 . . .60 A4
  Mill Meads E15 . . . .27 C4
Kerry N7 . . . . .14 A2
Kerry Ho **5** E1 . . . . .32 B3
Kerry Path SE8 . . . . .51 B4
Kerry Rd SE8 . . . . . .51 B4
Kerscott Ho **30** E3 . .27 A2
Kersfield Ho SW15 .57 C1
Kersfield Rd SW15 .57 C1
Kershaw Cl SW18 . .59 C1
Kershaw Ho **7**
  SE27 . . . . .75 A1
Kersley Mews
  SW11 . . . . .168 C3
Kersley Rd N16 . . . .7 A1
Kersley St SW11 . . .168 C2
Kerwick Cl **11** N7 . .14 A1
Keslake Mans
  NW10 . . . . .22 C3
Keslake Rd NW6 . . .22 C3
Keston Ho SE17 . . .152 B2
Keston Rd SE15 . . . .64 C4
Kestrel Ave SE24 . .63 B2
Kestrel Ho
  4 Battersea
    SW11 . . . . .60 A4
  Finsbury EC1 . . . . .96 C4
Kestrel Pl SE14 . . . .51 A4
Keswick Broadway **1**
  SW15 . . . . .58 B2

Keswick Ct **2**
  SE22 . . . . .64 C2
Keswick Ho **8**
  SE5 . . . . .48 B2
Keswick Hts **9**
  SW15 . . . . .58 A2
Keswick Lo E8 . . . . . .16 B2
Keswick Rd SW15 . .58 A2
Kett Gdns SW2 . . . .62 B2
Kettleby Ho SW9 . . .63 A4
Ketton Ho **11** W10 . .22 B1
Kevan Ho SE5 . . . . . .48 B3
KEW 44 C4
Kew Bridge TW8 . . .36 B1
Kew Bridge Ct W4 . .36 C1
Kew Bridge
  Distribution Ctr
  TW8 . . . . .36 B1
Kew Bridge Rd
  TW8 . . . . .36 B1
Kew Bridge Sta
  TW8 . . . . .36 B1
Kew Coll TW9 . . . . . .44 C4
Kew Foot Rd TW9 . .54 A4
Kew Gardens Rd
  TW9 . . . . .44 C2
Kew Gardens (Royal
  Botanic) TW9 . . . . .44 B2
Kew Gardens Sta
  TW9 . . . . .44 B2
Kew Gn TW9 . . . . . . .44 B4
Kew Green TW9 . . . .44 B4
Kew Green Prep Sch
  TW9 . . . . .44 B4
Kew Lo **11** TW9 . . . .44 B4
Kew Pier TW9 . . . . . .44 A4
Kew Rd TW9, W4 . .44 B2
Kew Ret Pk TW9 . . .45 A2
Kew Riverside Prim
  Sch TW9 . . . . .45 A1
Key Cl E1 . . . . .25 A1
Keyes Ct SE22 . . . . .64 C2
Keyes Rd NW2 . . . . .9 C3
Keyham Ho **8** W2 .31 C4
Key Ho **9** SE11 . . .163 B4
Keymer Rd SW2 . . .74 B2
Keynsham Ho
  N4 . . . . .6 B4
Keystone Cres N1 . .84 B1
Keyworth Cl E5 . . . .18 A4
Keyworth Pl SE1 . . .136 B2
Keyworth Prim Sch
  SE17 . . . . .150 A2
Keyworth St SE1 . . .136 B2
Kezia St SE8 . . . . . . .41 A1
Khyber Rd SW11 . .168 A1
Kia Oval The (Surrey
  Cnty Crkt Club)
  SE11 . . . . .163 A4
Kibworth St SW8 . .162 C1
Kidbrooke Gdns
  SE3 . . . . .53 C2
Kidderpore Ave
  NW3 . . . . .10 C4
Kidderpore Gdns
  NW3 . . . . .10 C4
Kiffen St EC2 . . . . . .97 C2
Kilbrennan Ho **9**
  E14 . . . . .34 B3
KILBURN 23 C4
Kilburn Bridge **14**
  NW6 . . . . .23 C4
Kilburn Gate NW6 .78 A2
Kilburn High Rd
  NW6 . . . . .23 C4

Kilburn High Road Sta
  NW6 . . . . .78 A3
Kilburn Ho **11** W9 . .23 B2
Kilburn La W10 . . . .23 A3
Kilburn Park Rd
  NW6 . . . . .23 C2
Kilburn Park Sch The
  16 NW6 . . . . .23 B3
Kilburn Park Sta
  NW6 . . . . .23 C4
Kilburn Pl NW6 . . . .23 C4
Kilburn Priory
  NW6 . . . . .78 A3
Kilburn Sq NW6 . . .23 C4
Kilburn Sta NW2 . .10 B2
Kilburn Vale NW6 . .78 A3
Kilburn Vale Est **13**
  NW6 . . . . .23 C4
Kilby Ct SE10 . . . . . .43 B3
Kildare Ct W2 . . . . . .31 C3
Kildare Gdns W2 . . .31 C3
Kildare Rd E16 . . . .35 C4
Kildare Terr W2 . . . .31 C3
Kildare Wlk E14 . . .33 C3
Kildoran Rd SW2 . .62 A2
Kilgour Rd SE23 . . .66 A1
Kilkie St SW6 . . . . .166 C1
Killarney Rd SW18 .59 B1
Killick St N1 . . . . . . .84 C1
Killieser Ave SW2 . .74 A2
Killip Cl E16 . . . . . . .35 B3
Killoran Ho **9** E14 .42 B3
Killowen Rd E9 . . . .17 C2
Killyon Rd SW8 . . .171 B1
Kilmaine Rd SW6 . .154 B1
Kilmarsh Rd W6 . . .39 B2
Kilmington Rd
  SW13 . . . . .46 C4
Kilmore Ho **11** E14 .34 A3
Kilmuir Ho SW1 . . .145 C3
Kiln Ct E14 . . . . .33 B2
Kilner Ho **8** SE11 .163 B4
Kilner St E14 . . . . . . .33 C4
Kiln Pl NW5 . . . . . . .12 C3
Kiloh Ct **11** SW11 . .60 A4
Kilpatrick Ct N16 . .7 B3
Kilpeck Ho **8** N4 . .6 B4
Kilravock St W10 . .23 A2
Kilronan **5** W3 . . . .28 C3
Kimbell Gdns
  SW6 . . . . .164 A3
Kimber Ctr The
  SW18 . . . . .70 C4
Kimberley Ave
  SE15 . . . . .65 B4
Kimberley Ho **7**
  E14 . . . . .42 B3
Kimberley Rd
  Kilburn NW6 . . . . .23 A4
  Stockwell SW9 . . .62 A4
Kimber Rd SW18 . .71 A4
Kimble Ho
  Lisson Gr NW8 . . .90 B2
  1 Lower Holloway
    N7 . . . . .14 A3
Kimbolton Row
  SW3 . . . . .144 A3
Kimpton Ct **12** SE5 .48 C2
Kimpton Ho SW15 . .68 C4
Kimpton Rd SE5 . . .48 C2
Kinburn St SE16 . . .40 C4
Kincaid Rd SE15 . . .50 A3
Kincardine Gdns
  W9 . . . . .23 C1

Kindell Ho **4**
  SW14 . . . . .55 C4
Kinder Ho N1 . . . . .87 C2
Kindersley Ho **38**
  E1 . . . . .111 C1
Kinder St **10** E1 . . . .32 A3
Kinefold Ho N7 . . . .14 A2
Kinfauns Rd SW2 . .74 C2
King Alfred Sch
  NW11 . . . . .2 A3
King Arthur Cl
  SE15 . . . . .50 B3
King Charles Ct **16**
  SE17 . . . . .48 A4
King Charles Ho
  SW6 . . . . .156 B2
King Charles St
  SW1 . . . . .134 A4
King Charles Terr **11**
  E1 . . . . .32 A2
King Charles Wlk **6**
  SW19 . . . . .70 A3
King David La E1 . . .32 B2
Kingdom St W2 . . . .100 C3
Kingdon Ho
  E14 . . . . .42 B3
Kingdon Rd NW6 . .10 C2
Kingdown Cl W10 . .30 C3
King Edward Mews
  SW13 . . . . .46 C2
King Edward Mews
  SW13 . . . . .46 C2
King Edwards Mans
  SW6 . . . . .155 B1
King Edward's Rd
  E9 . . . . .25 B4
King Edward St
  EC1 . . . . .108 C2
King Edward The
  Third Mews **6**
  SE16 . . . . .40 A4
King Edward VII's
  Hospl W1 . . . . . . .103 C3
King Edward Wlk
  SE1 . . . . .135 C2
King Fahed Acad The
  W14 . . . . .126 C2
Kingfield St E14 . . .42 B2
Kingfisher Ct
  11 Battersea
    SW11 . . . . .60 A4
  17 Cubitt Town E14 .42 B4
  Putney SW19 . . . . .70 A2
Kingfisher Ho
  16 Battersea
    SW18 . . . . .59 B4
  Peckham SE15 . . . .49 B2
  West Kensington
    W14 . . . . .126 C2
Kingfisher Mews
  SE13 . . . . .67 A2
Kingfisher Sq **19**
  SE8 . . . . .51 B4
King Frederik IX Twr
  SE16 . . . . .41 B3
King George Sq
  TW10 . . . . .54 B1
King George St
  SE10 . . . . .52 B3
Kingham Cl
  5 Shepherd's Bush
    W11 . . . . .39 A3
  Wandsworth SW18 .71 B4
Kingham Ind Est
  NW10 . . . . .20 C2

King Henry's Rd
  NW3 . . . . .12 A1
King Henry's Reach
  W6 . . . . .47 B4
King Henry St N16 .16 A3
King Henry's Wlk
  N1 . . . . .16 A2
King Henry's Yd **5**
  N16 . . . . .16 A3
King Henry Terr **18**
  E1 . . . . .32 A2
King Ho **12** W12 . . . .30 A3
Kinghorn St EC1 . . .108 C3
King James Ct
  SE1 . . . . .136 B3
King James St
  SE1 . . . . .136 B3
King John Ct
  EC2 . . . . .24 A1 **98 B2**
King John St E1 . . . .32 C4
Kinglake St SE17 . . .152 B2
Kingly Ct W1 . . . . . .119 A4
Kingly St W1 . . . . . .118 C4
King & Queen St
  SE17 . . . . .151 A2
King's Arms Ct E1 .111 B3
King's Arms Yd
  EC2 . . . . .109 B2
Kings Ave SW4 . . . .62 A1
Kings Avenue Sch
  SW4 . . . . .62 A2
King's Bench St
  SE1 . . . . .136 B4
King's Bench Wlk
  EC4 . . . . .107 C1
King's Boulevard
  NW1 . . . . .84 A1
Kingsbridge N16 . . .6 C3
Kingsbridge Ave
  W3 . . . . .36 B4
Kingsbridge Ct
  E14 . . . . .41 C2
Kingsbridge Rd
  W10 . . . . .30 B3
Kingsbury Rd N1 . .16 A2
Kingsbury Terr N1 . .16 A2
Kingsclere Cl
  SW15 . . . . .68 C4
Kingscliffe Gdns
  SW19 . . . . .70 B3
King's Coll SE24 . . .63 C1
Kings College **11**
  NW3 . . . . .12 A1
King's College Hospl
  SE5 . . . . .48 C1
Kings College London
  NW3 . . . . .11 C1
King's Coll London
  (Denmark Hill
  Campus) SE5 . . . . .48 B1
King's Coll London
  School of Medicine
  SE1 . . . . .123 C1
King's Coll London
  (Strand Campus)
  WC2 . . . . .121 A4
King's Coll London (St
  Thomas' Campus)
  SE1 . . . . .134 C1
King's Coll London
  (Waterloo Campus)
  SE1 . . . . .121 B1
Kingscote NW11 . . .1 B3
Kingscote Rd W4 . .37 C3

Kingscote St EC4 . . **122** A4
King's Court N
SW3 . . . . **144** A1
Kingscourt Rd
SW16 . . . . .74 A1
King's Court S
SW3 . . . . **144** A1
King's Cres N4, N5 . . .6 B1
Kingscroft SW4 . . . . .62 A1
Kingscroft Rd
NW2 . . . . .10 B2
KING'S CROSS 84 C2
King's Cross WC1 . . .94 B4
King's Cross Acad
N1 . . . . **83** C3
King's Cross Bridge
WC1 . . . . **95** A3
King's Cross Rd
WC1 . . . . **94** B4
King's Cross, St
Pancras N1 . . . . . . **94** A4
King's Cross Sta
N1 . . . . **84** B1
Kings Ct
6 Barnsbury N1 . . .14 B1
Chiswick W6 . . . . . .38 C2
East Dulwich SE22 . . .64 C3
Primrose Hill NW8 . . **80** C3
10 Putney SW15 . . . .68 C4
King's Ct SE1 . . . . . **136** C4
Kingsdale Gdns
W11 . . . . .30 C1
Kingsdale Sch
SE21 . . . . .76 A1
Kingsdown Ave
W3 . . . . .29 A2
Kingsdown Cl
26 Deptford SE16 . . .40 A1
8 Notting Hill W11 . .31 A3
Kingsdown Ct
SW11 . . . . .60 A1
Kingsdown Ho **1**
E8 . . . . .16 C3
Kingsdown Rd **4**
N19 . . . . .5 A2
Kings Farm Ave
TW10 . . . . .54 C3
Kingsfield Ho
N16 . . . . .7 A1
Kingsford St NW5 . . .12 B3
Kingsgate Est N1 . . .16 A2
Kingsgate Ho **20**
SW9 . . . . **173** C4
Kingsgate Par
SW1 . . . . **133** A1
Kingsgate PI NW6 . .10 C1
Kingsgate Prim Sch
NW6 . . . . .10 C1
Kingsgate Rd
NW6 . . . . .10 C1
King's Gdns **6**
NW6 . . . . .10 C1
King's Gr
Peckham SE15 . . . . .50 A2
Peckham SE15 . . . . .50 A3
Kingshall Mews
SE13 . . . . .67 B4
King's Head Yd
SE1 . . . . **123** B1
Kingshill SE17 . . . . **151** A4
Kings Ho
10 Limehouse
E14 . . . . .33 B2

Kings Ho continued
South Lambeth
SW8 . . . . **162** B2
Kingshold Rd E9 . . .17 B1
Kings House Sch
TW10 . . . . .54 B2
Kings House Sch
(Jun) TW10 . . . . . . .54 B2
Kingshold Ho **5**
SW15 . . . . .57 C2
KINGSLAND 16 A2
Kingsland Basin
N1 . . . . .16 A2
Kingsland Gn **1** E8, . . .
N1 . . . . .16 A2
Kingsland High St
E8 . . . . .16 B3
Kingsland Pas **2**
E8 . . . . .16 B3
Kingsland Rd E2 . . . .24 A3
Kingsland Sh Ctr **2**
E8 . . . . .16 B3
Kingslawn Cl
SW15 . . . . .57 A2
Kingsley Cl NW2 . . . .9 C2
Kingsley Flats
SE1 . . . . **152** B3
Kingsley Ho
Chelsea SW3 . . . . . **157** C3
2 Clapham SW4 . . **171** C2
Kingsley Mews
Kensington W8 . . . . **128** B1
3 St George in East
E1 . . . . .32 A2
Kingsley PI N6 . . . . . .3 C4
Kingsley Rd NW6 . . .23 B4
Kings Mall SH Ctr
W6 . . . . .39 B2
King's Mans SW3 . . **158** A3
Kingsmead TW10 . . .54 B1
Kingsmead Ct N6 . . . .4 C4
Kingsmead Ho E9 . . .18 A4
Kingsmead Prim Sch
E9 . . . . .18 A4
Kingsmead Rd
SW2 . . . . .74 C2
King's Mead Way E5, . . .
E9 . . . . .18 A4
Kingsmere Cl **13**
SW15 . . . . .57 C4
Kingsmere PI N16 . . .6 C3
Kingsmere Rd
SW19 . . . . .69 C2
King's Mews
1 Clapham Pk
SW4 . . . . .62 A2
Gray's Inn WC1 . . . . **95** A1
Kingsmill NW8 . . . . **79** C2
Kingsmill Terr
NW8 . . . . **79** C2
Kingsnorth Ho **12**
W10 . . . . .30 C3
King Solomon Acad
NW1 . . . . **102** A4
Kings Pl **3** Hammersmith
W12 . . . . .38 C3
Willesden NW10 . . . .22 B4
Kings Pl N1 . . . . **84** B2
King's PI SE1 . . . . . **136** C3
King Sq EC1 . . . . .96 C3
King's Quay SW10 **167** A4
Kings Rd
Richmond TW10,
TW9 . . . . .54 B2

Kings Rd continued
Willesden NW10 . . . . .9 A1
King's Rd
Chelsea SW3 . . . . . **144** B1
Chelsea SW10 . . . . **157** A2
Mortlake SW14 . . . . .55 C4
Kings Ride Gate
TW10 . . . . .54 C3
Kingsridge SW19 . . .70 A2
King's Scholars' Pas
SW1 . . . . **146** C4
King St
Acton W3 . . . . .28 B1
Hammersmith W6 . . .38 C2
St James SW1 . . . . **119** A2
Strand WC2 . . . . . . **120** A4
Whitechapel EC2 . . **109** A1
King Stairs Cl **17**
SE16 . . . . .40 A4
King's Terr NW1 . . . . **82** C3
Kingston Ho **4**
NW6 . . . . .10 A1
Kingston Ho E
SW7 . . . . **130** A3
Kingston Ho N
SW7 . . . . **130** A3
Kingston Ho S
SW7 . . . . **130** A3
Kingston Ho SW15,
SW19 . . . . .69 A3
Kingston Univ
(Roehampton Vale)
SW15 . . . . .68 B1
Kingston Vale
SW15 . . . . .68 A1
Kingstown St NW1 . . **81** B4
King Street Cloisters
3 Hammersmith
W6 . . . . .39 A2
Kingswater Pl
SW11 . . . . **158** A1
Kingsway
Mortlake SW14,
TW9 . . . . .55 A4
St Giles WC2 . . . . . **106** C2
Kingsway Mans
WC1 . . . . **106** C4
Kingsway PI EC1 . . . .96 A2
Kingswear Rd NW5 . .4 B1
Kings Well **8**
NW3 . . . . .11 B4
Kings Wlk Sh Mall
SW3 . . . . **144** C2
Kingswood **31** E2 . . .25 B3
Kingswood Ave
NW6 . . . . .23 A3
Kingswood Cl
SW8 . . . . **162** B1
Kingswood Ct
Hither Green
SE13 . . . . .67 C1
7 Richmond TW10 . .54 B2
Kings Wood Ct **4**
NW6 . . . . .10 C1
Kingswood Rd
South Acton W4 . . . .37 B3
Streatham SW2 . . . . .74 A4
Kingswood Terr
W4 . . . . .37 B3
Kings Yd SE15 . . . . .18 C2
Kington Ho **18**
NW6 . . . . **78** B3
Kingward Ho E1 . . . **111** B4
Kingweston Cl NW2 .1 A1
King William La **3**
SE10 . . . . .43 A1

King William St
EC4 . . . . **123** C4
King William Wlk
SE10 . . . . .52 B4
Kingwood Rd
SW6 . . . . **154** A1
Kinloch St N7 . . . . . . .5 B1
Kinnaird Ave W4 . . . .45 B3
Kinnear Rd W12 . . . .38 B4
Kinnerton PI N
SW1 . . . . **131** A3
Kinnerton PI S
SW1 . . . . **131** A3
Kinnerton St SW1 . . **131** B3
Kinnerton Yd
SW1 . . . . **131** B3
Kinnoull Mans **10**
E5 . . . . .17 A4
Kinnoul Rd W6 . . . . **154** A4
Kinross Ho N1 . . . . . **84** C4
Kinsale Rd SE15 . . . .64 C4
Kinsham Ho **5**
E2 . . . . .24 C1
Kintore Way SE1 . . **152** C4
Kintyre Ct **17** SW2 . .74 A4
Kintyre Ho **6** E14 . . .34 B1
Kinver Ho N4 . . . . . . .6 C4
Kipling Ho **22** SE5 . . .48 B3
Kipling St SE1 . . . . **137** C4
Kipling Twr **8** W3 . . .37 B3
Kirby Est SE16 . . . . .40 A3
Kirby Gr SE1 . . . . . **138** A4
Kirby St EC1 . . . . . **107** C4
Kirkeby Bldg EC1 . . **107** B4
Kirkland Wlk **4**
E8 . . . . .16 B2
Kirkley Ho N16 . . . . . .7 A3
Kirkman Ho **16** . . **105** B3
Kirkman PI W1 . . . . **105** B3
Kirkmichael Rd
E14 . . . . .34 B3
Kirkside Rd SE3 . . . .53 C4
Kirk St WC1 . . . . . . **94** B1
Kirkstall Gdns
SW2 . . . . .74 A3
Kirkstall Ho SW1 . . **146** A2
Kirkstall Rd SW2 . . .74 A3
Kirkstead Ct E5 . . . .18 A4
Kirkstone NW1 . . . . . **92** C4
Kirkwall PI E2 . . . . . .25 B2
Kirkwood Rd SE15 . .50 A1
Kirtley Ho SW8 . . . **171** A4
Kirtling St SW8 . . . . **160** C2
Kirton Cl W4 . . . . . . .37 C2
Kirton Gdns **27** E2 . .24 B2 B3
Kirwin Way SE5 . . . .48 A3
Kitcat Terr **31** E3 . . .26 C2
Kite Ho **5** SW11 . . . .60 A4
Kite PI **9**
E2 . . . . .24 C2
Kitson Rd
Barnes SW13 . . . . . .46 C2
Camberwell SE5 . . . .48 B3
Kittiwake Ct **28**
SE8 . . . . .51 B4
Kitto Rd SE14 . . . . . .50 C1
Kiver Rd N19 . . . . . . .5 A2
Klea Ave SW4 . . . . . .61 B1
Kleffens Ct **12** SE3 . .53 B3
Kleine Wharf **30**
N1 . . . . .24 A4
Knapp Cl NW10 . . . . .8 A2
Knapp Rd E3 . . . . . . .26 C1
Knaresborough Dr
SW18 . . . . .71 A3

Knaresborough Ho **4**
N4 . . . . .6 B4
Knaresborough Pl
SW5 . . . . **142** A4
Knatchbull Rd
Brixton SE5 . . . . .48 A3
Stonebridge NW10 . .20 C4
Knebworth Ho
South Lambeth
SW8 . . . . **171** C3
2 Stoke Newington
N16 . . . . .16 A4
Knebworth Rd **3**
N16 . . . . .16 A4
Kneller Ho **9**
SW8 . . . . **171** C2
Kneller Rd SE4 . . . . .66 A3
Knighten St E1 . . . . .32 A1
Knighthead Point **23**
E14 . . . . .41 C4
Knight Ho SE17 . . . **152** A3
Knightleas Ct NW2 . .9 B2
Knightrider Ct
EC4 . . . . **122** C4
Knightrider St
EC4 . . . . **122** B4
Knights Arc SW1 . . **130** C3
Knight's Ave W5 . . . .36 A4
KNIGHTSBRIDGE . . . . . .
. . . . **130** A2
Knightsbridge SW1,
SW7 . . . . **130** C3
Knightsbridge Ct
SW1 . . . . **131** A3
Knightsbridge Gn
SW1 . . . . **130** C3
Knightsbridge Sch
SW11 . . . . **130** C1
Knightsbridge Sta
SW1 . . . . **131** A3
Knightsbridge Under
Sch SW7 . . . . **143** A3
Knights Cl **9**
Bermondsey SE1 . . **138** C4
South Lambeth
SW8 . . . . **162** B1
West Kensington
SW5 . . . . **140** C2
Knight's Ho SW10 **156** C2
Knights Rd E16 . . . . .43 C4
Knight's Wlk SE11 **150** A3
Knightswood Ct N6 . .4 C4
Knivet Rd SW6 . . . . **155** B3
Knoll Ho NW8 . . . . . **78** C2
Knoll Rd SW18 . . . . .59 B2
Knolly's Cl SE27, ...
SW16 . . . . .74 C1
Knolly's Rd SE27, ...
SW16 . . . . .74 C1
Knot Ho SE1 . . . . . **124** C1
Knottisford St E2 . . .25 B2
Knowlden Ho **5**
E1 . . . . .32 B2
Knowle Cl SW9 . . . . .62 C4
Knowledge Point Sch
3 N7 . . . . .14 B2
Knowles Hill Cres
SE13 . . . . .67 C2
Knowles Ho
Wandsworth
SW18 . . . . .59 A1
Willesden Green
NW10 . . . . .21 C4
Knowles Wlk SW4 . .61 B4

Knowlton Ho 32
SW9 . . . . 173 C4
Knowsley Rd
SW11 . . . . 168 C1
Knox Ct 16 SW4 . 172 B2
Knox Ho SW15. . . . 47 B1
Knox St W1 . . . . . 102 C4
Knoyle Ho W14 . . 126 B2
Knoyle St SE14 . . . 51 A4
Kobi Nazrul Prim Sch
E1 . . . . 111 C2
Koops Mill Mews
SE1 . . . . 139 A2
Kossuth St SE10 . 43 A1
Kotree Way 18
SE1 . . . . 153 C4
Kramer Mews
SW5 . . . . 142 A1
Kreedman Wlk 8
E8 . . . . 16 C3
Kreisel Wlk TW9. . . 44 B4
Kylemore Ct 4
W12 . . . . 38 C4
Kylemore Rd NW6. . 10 C1
Kylestrome Ho
SW1 . . . . 145 C3
Kynance Mews
SW7 . . . . 128 B1
Kynance Pl SW7 . 128 C1
Kynaston Ho 7
SW2 . . . . 74 B3
Kynaston Rd N16. . . 7 A1
Kyrle Rd SW11 . . . 60 C1
Kyverdale N16 . . . 7 B3

L

Laburnham Ct NW2. . 1 A3
Laburnum Cl 5
SE15 . . . . 50 B3
Laburnum Ct 20
E2 . . . . 24 B4
Laburnum Ho
New Cross SE4. . . 51 B1
6 Stoke Newington
N16 . . . . 6 C2
Laburnum St E2. . . 24 B4
Lacey Ho 7 SE13. . 52 B1
Lacey Mews 3 E3. 26 C3
Lacine Ct 15 SE16. 40 C4
Lackington St
EC2 . . . . 109 C4
Lackland Ho 1 SE1. 153 A2
Lacland Ho SW10. 157 B2
Lacon Rd SE22 . . . 64 C3
Lacy Rd SW15 . . . . 57 C3
Ladbroke Cres
W11 . . . . 31 A3
Ladbroke Gdns
W11 . . . 31 B2 112 C4
Ladbroke Gr
Kensal Town W10. . 31 A4
Notting Hill
W11 . . . 31 B2 112 C4
Ladbroke Grove Ho
W11 . . . 31 B2 112 C4
Ladbroke Grove Sta
W10 . . . . 31 A3
Ladbroke Ho 1
E1 . . . . 111 A3
Ladbroke Mews
W11 . . . 31 A1 112 B2
Ladbroke Rd
W11 . . . 31 B1 112 C2
Ladbroke Sq
W11 . . . 31 B2 113 A3

Ladbroke Terr
W11 . . . 31 B1 113 A2
Ladbroke Wlk
W11 . . . 31 B1 113 A2
Ladlands SE22. . . . 76 C4
Ladybower Ct 6
E5 . . . . 17 C4
Ladycroft Rd SE13. . 67 A4
Lady Elizabeth Ho
SW14 . . . . 55 B4
Lady Florence Ctyd 18
SE8 . . . . 51 C3
Lady Margaret Rd
NW5 . . . . 13 B3
Lady Margaret Sch
SW6 . . . . 165 B3
Lady Somerset Rd
NW5 . . . . 13 A4
LADYWELL 67 A1
Ladywell Arena
SE13 . . . . 67 A1
Ladywell Cl SE4 . . 66 B1
Ladywell Hts SE4. . 66 B1
Ladywell Rd SE13. . 67 A2
Ladywell Sta SE13. . 67 A2
Ladywell Water Twr
SE4 . . . . 66 C2
Lafitte Ho 20 N19. . 4 C4
Lafone Ho 13 SW2. 74 A4
Lafone St SE1 . . . 138 C4
Lagado Mews
SE16 . . . . 32 C1
Lagonda Ho 11 E3. 26 C1
Lagonier Ho EC1 . . 97 A3
Laindon Ho 6 N16. . 7 B3
Laing Ho SE5. . . . . 48 B3
Lainson St SW18 . . 70 C4
Lairdale Cl SE21. . . 75 B4
Laird Ho SE5 . . . . . 48 B3
Lairs Cl N7 . . . . 14 A2
Laitwood Rd SW12. 73 A3
Lakanal 14 SE5 . . . 49 A2
Lake Ho SE1 . . . . 136 C3
Laker Ct SW4 . . . . 172 B2
Laker Pl SW15. . . . . 58 A1
Lakeside Ct N4. . . . . 6 B3
Lakeside Rd W14. . 39 C3
Lakeview 23 E3. . . 26 C3
Lake View Ct
SW1 . . . . 132 B2
Lakis Cl NW3. . . . . . 11 B4
Laleham Ho
E2 . . . . . . 24 B1 98 C2
Lalor St SW6 . . . . 164 B2
Lambard Ho 4
SE10 . . . . 52 B3
Lamb Ct 14 E14. . . 33 A2
Lamberhurst Ho 16
SE15 . . . . 50 B4
Lambert Ho
16 Brixton SW9. . 173 B1
19 Crouch End N19. . 4 C4
Lambert Rd SW2. . . 62 B2
Lambert St N1 . . . . 14 C1
LAMBETH 134 C3
Lambeth Acad
SW4 . . . . 61 B2
Lambeth Coll (Brixton
Ctr) SW2. . . . . . . 62 B2
Lambeth Coll
(Clapham Ctr)
SW4 . . . . 61 B2

Lambeth Coll
(Vauxhall Ctr)
SW8 . . . . 171 B4
Lambeth Ct 8
Lambeth High St
SE1 . . . . 148 C4
Lambeth Hill EC4. 122 C4
Lambeth Hospl
SE11 . . . . 62 B4
Lambeth North Sta
SE1 . . . . 135 B2
Lambeth Pal SE1 . 134 C1
Lambeth Palace Rd
SE1 . . . . 134 C2
Lambeth Pier SE1. 134 B2
Lambeth Rd SE1 . 135 C1
Lambeth Twrs
SE11 . . . . 135 B1
Lambeth Wlk
SE11 . . . . 149 A4
Lambfold Ho N7. . . 14 A2
Lamb Ho
28 Camberwell
SE5 . . . . 48 B3
11 Camberwell SE5. . 48 C2
Greenwich SE10. . . 52 B4
Lamb La E8 . . . . . . 17 A1
Lamble St NW5 . . . 12 C4
Lamb Office Ct
WC1 . . . . 106 A4
Lambolle Pl NW3. . 12 A2
Lambolle Rd NW3. 12 A2
Lambourn Cl 9
NW5 . . . . 13 B4
Lambourne Gr
SE16 . . . . 40 C1
Lambourne Ho
NW8 . . . . 101 C4
Lambourn Rd SW4. 61 A4
Lambrook Ho 13
SE15 . . . . 49 C2
Lambrook Terr
SW6 . . . . 164 A4
Lamb's Bldgs EC1. 97 B1
Lamb's Conduit Pas
WC1 . . . . 106 C4
Lamb's Conduit St
WC1 . . . . 94 C1
Lamb's Mews N1 . . 86 A3
Lamb's Pass EC1 . . 97 B1
Lamb St E1 . . . . . . 110 C4
Lambton Ct 2 N19. . 5 A3
Lambton Mews 4
N19 . . . . 5 A3
Lambton Pl
W11 . . . 31 B2 113 A4
Lambton Rd N19 . . 5 A3
Lamb Wlk SE1 . . . 138 A3
Lamerton Lo 10
TW9 . . . . 44 B2
Lamerton St 8
SE8 . . . . 51 C4
Lamington St 3
W6 . . . . 39 A2
Lamlash St SE11. . 150 A4
Lamley Ho SE10 . . 52 A3
Lammas Rd E9 . . . 17 C1
Lammermoor Rd
SW12 . . . . 73 A4
Lamont Rd SW10. 157 B3
Lamont Rd Pas
SW10 . . . . 157 B3
Lampard Gr N16. . . 7 B3
Lampern Sq 8
E2 . . . . . . 24 C2 99 C4

Lampeter Sq W6 . 154 A3
Lamplighter Cl 34
E1 . . . . 25 B1
Lampson Ho 8
N19 . . . . 13 C4
Lanark Ho 8 SE1. 153 B1
Lanark Mans
Paddington W9 . . 89 A2
15 Shepherd's Bush
W12 . . . . 39 B4
Lanark Mews W9. 89 A3
Lanark Pl W9 . . . . 89 A2
Lanark Rd W9 . . . 88 C3
Lanark Sq E14. . . . 42 A3
Lanbury Rd SE15. . 65 C3
Lancashire Ct W1. 118 B4
Lancaster Ave SE21,
SE27 . . . . 75 B2
Lancaster Cl
10 De Beauvoir Town
N1 . . . . 16 A1
Kensington W2 . . 114 A3
Lancaster Cotts 1
TW10 . . . . 54 A1
Lancaster Ct
Bayswater W2 . . . 115 A4
Parsons Green
SW6 . . . . 155 A1
West Norwood
SE27 . . . . 75 A2
Lancaster Dr
Canary Wharf E14. . 34 B1
Maitland Pk NW3. . 12 A2
Lancaster Gate
W2 . . . . 115 B4
Lancaster Gate Sta
W2 . . . . 115 B4
Lancaster Gr NW3. 12 A2
Lancaster hall 14
E16 . . . . 35 C1
Lancaster Ho
SW15 . . . . 47 B1
Lancaster Ho
SW1 . . . . 132 C4
Lancaster Lo 2
W11 . . . . 31 A3
Lancaster Mews
Bayswater W2 . . . 115 A4
2 Richmond TW10. . 54 A1
3 Wandsworth
SW18 . . . . 59 A2
Lancaster Pk
TW10 . . . . 54 A2
Lancaster Pl WC2. 120 C3
Lancaster Rd
Dudden Hill NW10. . 8 C3
Finsbury Pk N4 . . . 5 C4
Notting Hill W11 . . 31 A3
Lancaster Stables 13
NW3 . . . . 12 A2
Lancaster Terr
W2 . . . . 115 B4
Lancaster Wlk
W2 . . . . 115 A2
Lancefield Ho
SE15 . . . . 65 A4
Lancefield St W10. 23 B2
Lancell St N16 . . . . 7 A2
Lancelot Pl SW7 . 130 C3
Lancer Sq W8 . . . 128 A4
Lanchester Ct W2. 102 C1
Lanchester Way
SE14 . . . . 50 C2

Lancing St NW1 . . 93 B3
Lancresse Ct N1. . . 24 A4
Landale Ct SE10 . . 52 B2
Landale Ho 13
SE16 . . . . 40 B3
Landcroft Rd SE22. 64 B1
Landells Rd SE22. . 64 C1
Landford Rd SW15. 57 B4
Landin Ho 1 E14. . . 33 C3
Landleys Field 2
N7 . . . . 13 C3
Landmann Ho 10
SE16 . . . . 40 A2
Landmann Way
SE14 . . . . 40 C1
Landmark Hts E5. . 18 A4
Landon Pl SW1 . . 130 C2
Landons Cl E14. . . . 34 B1
Landon Wlk 11
E14 . . . . 34 A2
Landor Ct N16 . . . . 16 A3
Landor Ho 7 SE5 . 48 C3
Landor Rd SW9. . . . 62 A4
Landor Wlk 11
W12 . . . . 38 C4
Landrake NW1 . . . 83 A3
Landridge Rd
SW6 . . . . 164 C2
Landseer Ct 10 N19. . 5 A2
Landseer Ho
Battersea SW11. . . 169 C3
Paddington NW8 . . 89 C2
Westminster SW1. 147 C3
Landseer Rd N19 . . 5 A2
Landulph Ho
SE11 . . . . 149 C2
Landward Ct W1 . 102 B2
Lane Ct SW11 . . . . 72 A4
Lanercost Cl SW2. 74 C2
Lanercost Rd SW2. 74 C2
Lane The NW8 . . . . 78 C1
Laneway SW15 . . . 57 A2
Laney Bldg EC1 . . 107 B4
Lanfranc Rd E3 . . . 26 A3
Lanfrey Pl W14 . . 140 C1
Langbourne Ave N6. . 3 C2
Langbourne Ho 7
SW2 . . . . 62 C2
Langbourne Mans
N6 . . . . 3 C2
Langbourne Pl
E14 . . . . 42 A1
Langdale NW1 . . . . 92 C4
Langdale Cl
Camberwell SE17. . . 48 B4
Mortlake SW14 . . . 55 A3
Langdale Ho SW1. 146 C1
Langdale Rd SE10. 52 B3
Langdale St 25 E1. 32 A3
Langdon Ct
Finsbury EC1 . . . . 86 B1
Harlesden NW10 . . 21 A4
Langdon Ho 3
E14 . . . . 34 B3
Langdon Park Rd
N6 . . . . 4 B4
Langdon Park Sch
E14 . . . . 34 B3
Langdon Park Sta
E14 . . . . 34 A4
Langdon Pk L Ctr
E14 . . . . 34 A4
Langdon Pk Sta
E3 . . . . 34 A4

Langdon Pl SW14....55 B4
Langdon Way 18
SE1..............153 C3
Langford Cl
Shacklewell E8.....16 C3
St John's Wood
NW8............79 A2
Langford Ct NW8...79 A1
Langford Gn SE5...64 A4
Langford Ho 5
SE8..............51 C4
Langford Pl NW8...79 A2
Langford Prim Sch
SW6............166 B2
Langford Rd 4
SW6............166 B2
Langham Ct 4
SW15...........57 C2
Langham Ho SW4..61 B2
Langham Mans
SW5............142 A4
Langham Pl
Chiswick W4......46 A4
Fitzrovia W1.....104 B3
Langham St W1...104 B3
Lang Ho
South Lambeth
SW8............162 A1
3 Tufnell Pk N19....4 B1
Langholm Cl
SW12............73 C4
Langhorne Ct 10
NW8............11 C1
Langhurst Ho 10
SW11...........169 B2
Langland Gdns
NW3............11 A3
Langland Ho 4
SE5.............48 C3
Langland Mans
NW3............11 A3
Langler Rd NW10..22 B3
Langley Ct
South Lambeth
SW8............172 A4
Strand WC2......120 A4
Langley Dr W3....37 A4
Langley Ho
11 Lower Clapton
E5..............17 B3
36 Paddington W2...31 C4
Langley La SW8...162 B4
Langley Mans
SW8............162 B4
Langley St WC2...106 A1
Langmead Ho 34
E3..............27 A2
Langmore Ho 36
E1.............111 C1
Langport Ho 1
SW9............48 A1
Langridge 15 NW5..12 C2
Langroyd Rd SW17 .72 B2
Langside Ave
SW15...........56 C3
Lang St E1.......25 B1
Langston Hughes Cl
5 SE24..........63 A3
Langthorn Ct EC2 .109 C2
Langthorne Lo 30
SW2............74 C4
Langthorne St
SW6............47 C3
Langton Cl WC1...95 A2

Langton Ct SW15...58 B1
Langton Ho SE11..149 A4
Langton Pl SW18...70 C3
Langton Rd SW9...48 A3
Langton St SW10..157 A3
Langton Way SE3..53 C3
Langtry Pl SW6...155 C4
Langtry Rd NW8...78 A3
Langtry Wlk NW8...78 C4
Lanhill Rd W9.....23 C1
Lanier Rd SE13....67 C1
Lanner Ho 2
SW11...........60 A4
Lannoy Point
SW6............154 B2
Lanrick Rd E14....35 A3
Lansbury Gdns 1
E14............114 A4
Lansbury Lawrence
Prim Sch 5 E14...34 A3
Lanscombe Wlk
SW8............162 A1
Lansdell Ho 9
SW2............62 C1
Lansdowne Coll
W2.............114 A3
Lansdowne Cres
W11.......31 A2 112 B3
Lansdowne Dr E8..16 C1
Lansdowne Gdns
SW8............172 A4
Lansdowne Gr
NW10............8 A4
Lansdowne Hill
SE27...........75 A1
Lansdowne Ho
W11.......31 B1 112 C2
Lansdowne Mews
W11.......31 B1 112 C2
Lansdowne Pl
SE1............137 C2
Lansdowne Rd
W11.......31 A2 112 B3
Lansdowne Rise
W11.......31 A2 112 B3
Lansdowne Row
W1............118 B2
Lansdowne Sch 8
SW9............62 B4
Lansdowne Terr
WC1............94 B1
Lansdowne Way SW4,
SW8............172 B3
Lansdowne Wlk
W11.......31 B1 112 C2
Lansdowne Wood Cl
7 SE27..........75 A1
Lansdown Ho 6
SE5.............48 B1
Lantern Cl SW15...56 C3
Lantern Ho E14....41 C4
Lanterns Ct E14....41 C3
Lanterns Wy E14...42 A4
Lant Ho SE1.....136 C3
Lantry Ct 1 W3....28 A1
Lant St SE1......137 A3
Lanvanor Rd SE15..50 B1
Lanyard Ho 8 SE8..41 B2
Lapford Cl W9....23 B1
Lapsang SE1.....125 A1
Lapwing Twr 31
SE8............51 B4
Lapworth Ct W2...100 B4
Lara Cl SE13.......67 B1
Larch Ave W3.....29 A1

Larch Cl
Balham SW12.....73 A2
2 Deptford SE8...51 B4
10 Upper Holloway
N19............4 B2
Larch Ct 11 W2....31 C4
Larches Ave SW14..55 C3
Larchfield Ho 2
N5.............15 B3
Larch Ho 25 SE16...40 B4
Larchmore Ct N19...5 A2
Larch Rd NW2.....9 B4
Larcom St SE17...151 A3
Larden Rd W3.....38 A4
La Retraite RC Girls
Sch SW12........73 B4
Larissa St SE17...151 C3
Larix Ct NW10....21 A1
Larkfield Rd TW9...54 A3
Larkhall La SW4...172 A3
Larkhall Rise
SW4...........171 B1
Lark Row E2......25 B4
Larmenier & Sacred
Heart RC Prim Sch
4 W6...........39 C2
Larnaca Ho SE1...138 C2
Larnach Rd W6....47 C4
Larpent Ave SW15..57 B2
La Saint Union RC Sec
Sch NW5.........3 C1
Lascelles Ho NW1..90 B1
Lassell St SE10....42 C1
Lasseter Pl SE3....53 B4
Latchmere Rd
SW11...........168 C1
Latchmere St 5
SW11...........168 C2
Latham Ho E1....32 C3
Latimer SE17....152 A1
Latimer Ho
11 Homerton E9....17 C2
Notting Hill
W11.......31 B2 113 A3
Latimer Ind Est 1
W10............30 B3
Latimer Pl W10....30 B3
Latimer Rd W10...30 B3
Latimer Road Sta
W10............30 B3
Latona Rd SE15....49 C4
Lattimer Pl W4....46 A4
Latvia Ct SE17....151 A1
Latymer Ct W6....39 C2
Latymer Upper Sch
6 W6...........38 C2
Lauderdale Mans
W9.............88 B3
Lauderdale Rd W9..88 B3
Lauderdale Twr
EC2...........108 C4
Laud St SE11.....148 C2
Laughton Ho 11
SW2............62 C1
Launcelot St SE1..135 B3
Launceston Pl
W8........31 C1 128 C4
Launch St E14....42 B3
Laundress La N16...7 C1
Laundry La N1....15 B1
Laundry Rd W6...154 A3
Laura Pl E5.......17 B4
Laurel Bank Gdns 1
SW6............165 A2
Laurel Cl 8 N19....4 B2

Laurel Ct
Dalston E8.......16 B1
5 Putney SW15...57 C2
6 Rotherhithe
SE16............33 A1
Laurel Ho
6 Deptford SE8...51 B4
5 Hamstead NW3 .11 A2
West Hampstead
NW3...........11 A2
Laurel Rd SW13...46 C1
Laurel St E8......16 B2
Laurence Mews 12
W12............38 B4
Laurence Pountney
Hill EC4........123 B4
Laurence Pountney La
EC4...........123 C4
Laurie Gr SE14....51 A2
Laurie Ho
Newington SE1...136 B1
Notting Hill
W8.......31 C1 113 B1
Laurier Rd NW5....4 A1
Lauriston Ho 6
E9..............17 C1
Lauriston Lo E9....17 B1
Lauriston Prim Sch 6
E9..............17 C1
Lauriston Rd E9....17 C1
Lausanne Rd SE15..50 B2
Lavell St N16......15 C4
Lavender Cl SW3..157 C3
Lavender Ct SW4..172 B3
Lavender Gdns
SW11...........60 C3
Lavender Gr E8....16 C1
Lavender Hill
SW11...........60 C4
Lavender Ho
20 Richmond
TW9............45 A2
14 Rotherhithe
SE16............32 C1
Lavender Rd
Battersea SW11...59 C4
Rotherhithe SE16...33 A1
Lavender Sweep
SW11...........60 B3
Lavender Terr 12
SW11...........60 A4
Lavender Wlk
SW11...........60 B3
Lavendon Ho NW8 .90 B3
Lavengro Rd SE27..75 B2
Lavenham Rd
SW18...........70 C3
Laverers Rd SE6....67 A1
Laverstoke Gdns
SW15...........68 C1
Laverton Mews
SW5............142 B3
Laverton Pl SW5..142 B3
Lavina Gr N1.....84 C2
Lavington Cl E9...18 B2
Lavington St SE1..122 B1
Lawdale Jun Sch
Bethnal Green E2..99 C4
2 E2......24 C2 99 C4
Lawford Rd
Chiswick W4......45 B3
De Beauvoir Town
N1.............16 A1
Kentish Town NW5..13 B2
Lawfords Wharf 18
NW1............13 B1
Lawless Ho 6 E14..34 B2
Lawless St 12 E14..34 A2

Lawley St E5......17 B4
Lawman Ct 2
TW9............44 B2
Lawn Cres TW9....44 C1
Lawnfield Ct NW6...9 C1
Lawn House Cl
E14............42 B4
Lawn La SW8....162 C4
Lawn Rd NW3....12 B3
Lawns The N16....16 A3
Lawrence Ave
NW10...........20 C4
Lawrence Bldgs 1
N16.............7 B1
Lawrence Cl
Bow E3.........26 C3
6 Shepherd's Bush
W12............30 A2
Lawrence Ct
4 South Acton
W3.............37 B3
Stoke Newington
N16.............7 B1
Lawrence Ho
20 Camden Town
NW1............13 A1
Westminster SW1..147 C3
Lawrence La EC2..109 A2
Lawrence Mans
SW3............158 A3
Lawrence Mews
SW15...........57 B3
Lawrence Pl N1....84 B4
Lawrence St
Canning Town
E16............35 B4
Chelsea SW3.....158 A3
Lawrence Trad Est
SE10...........43 A2
Lawrence Univ
SW7...........143 A3
Lawson Cl SW19...69 C1
Lawson Ct 1 N4....5 B3
Lawson Ho 17
W12............30 A2
Law St SE1......137 C2
Lawton Rd E3....26 A2
Laxfield Ct E8....24 C4
Laxley Cl SE5.....48 A3
Laxton Path 1
SE4.............65 C3
Laxton Pl NW1....92 B2
Layard Rd SE16...40 A2
Layard Sq SE16...40 A2
Laybourne Ho 18
E14............41 C4
Laycock Prim Sch 5
N1.............15 A2
Laycock St N1....14 C2
Layfield Ho 6
SE10...........43 C1
Laystall Ct EC1....95 B1
Laystall St EC1....95 B1
Layton Pl TW9....44 C2
Lazar Wlk 2 N7....5 B2
Leabank Sq E9....18 C2
Leabourne Rd N16 ..7 C4
Leacroft Ave
SW12...........72 B4
Lea Ct 3 W12......38 A4
Leadenhall Building
The EC3........110 A1
Leadenhall Mkt
EC3...........110 A1
Leadenhall Pl
EC3...........110 A1

Leadenhall St
EC3 . . . . **110** A1

Leadenham Ct **18**
E3 . . . . .18 B3

Lea Ho NW8 . . . . **90** A1

Leahurst Rd SE13. . .**67** C2

Lea Int E9 . . . . .18 C3

Leake St
Lambeth SE1 . . . . . **135** B3
South Bank SE1 . . . **135** A4

Leamington Ct
4 Forest Hill
SE26 . . . . .76 C1
North Acton W3 . . . .28 C4

Leamington Ho **4**
W11 . . . . .31 B4

Leamington Pk
W3 . . . . .28 C4

Leamington Rd Villas
W11 . . . . .31 B4

Leamore St W6 . . . . .39 B2

Leamouth Rd E14 . .34 C3

Leander Ct
27 Hackney E9 . . . . . .17 B1
St Johns SE8 . . . . . .51 C2

Leander Rd SW2 . . .62 C1

Leary Ho SE11 . . . .**149** A1

Leaside Bsns Ctr
E16 . . . . .34 B4

Lea Sq **22** E3 . . . . . .26 B4

Leatherdale St
32 Bethnal Green
E1 . . . . .25 B1
19 Globe Town E1 . .25 C2

Leatherhead Cl N16 .7 B3

Leather La EC1 . . .**107** C4

Leather La Mkt
EC1 . . . .**107** C4

Leathermarket Ct
SE1 . . . .**138** A3

Leathermarket St
SE1 . . . .**138** A3

Leather Rd SE16 . . .40 C2

Leathwaite Rd
SW11 . . . . .60 B2

Leathwell Rd SE8. .52 A1

Lebanon Gdns
SW18 . . . . .58 C1

Lebanon Rd SW18 .58 C2

Lebus Ho NW8 . . . . .80 A1

Lechmere Rd NW2. . .9 A2

Leckford Rd SW18. .71 B3

Leckhampton Pl **23**
SW2 . . . . .74 C4

Lecky Ho NW2. . . . . .9 A4

Lecky St SW7 . . . .**143** B2

L'Ecole de Battersea
SW11 . . . .**168** A3

L'Ecole des Petits Sch
SW6 . . . .**166** A2

L'Ecole du Parc **13**
SW11 . . . . .60 C4

Leconfield Ave SW13,
SW15 . . . . .56 B4

Leconfield Ho SE5. .64 A4

Leconfield Rd N5. . .15 C4

Lector Ct EC1 . . . . . .95 C1

Leda Ct **9** SW9 . . .**163** B1

Ledam Bldg EC1. . .**107** B4

Ledbury Ho **12**
SE22 . . . . .64 A4

Ledbury Mews N
W11 . . . . .31 C3

Ledbury Mews W
W11 . . . .31 C2 **113** B4

Ledbury Rd W11. . . .31 C3

Ledbury St SE15. . . .49 C3

Ledo Ho **1** N16 . . . .15 C4

Lee Conservancy Rd
E9 . . . . .18 B3

Lee Ct SE13 . . . . . . .67 C3

Lee Ho **3** N19. . . . . .13 C3

Leeke St WC1 . . . . . .94 C4

Leeland Way NW10. . .8 B4

Leerdam Dr E14 . . .42 B3

Lees Ct W1. . . . . . .**117** B4

Lees Ho SE17 . . . .**151** C1

Leeson Rd **11**
SE24 . . . . .62 C3

Lees Pl W1 . . . .**117** B4

Lee St E8 . . . . .24 B4

Leet Ct N16 . . . . . . .15 C4

Lee Valley Hockey &
Tennis Ctr E15 . . . .19 A4

Lee Valley Velo Pk
E15 . . . . .19 A3

Leeve Ho **9** W9 . . .23 B2

Leeward Ct **3** E1 . .**125** C2

Leeway SE8 . . . . . . .41 B1

Lefevre Wlk E3 . . . .26 C4

Leffern Rd W12. . . .38 C4

Leff Ho **9** NW6 . . . .10 A1

Lefroy Ho SW8 . . .**136** C3

Lefroy Rd W12 . . . . .38 B4

Legard Rd N5 . . . . . . .6 A1

Leggatt Rd E15. . . .27 B3

Legge St SE13 . . . . .67 B2

Leghorn Rd NW10 .21 C3

Legion Cl N1 . . . . . .14 C1

Legion Terr E3 . . . .26 C4

Leicester Ct
46 Paddington
W2 . . . . .31 C4
St James WC2 . . . .**119** C4

Leicester Ho
4 Brixton SW9 . . . .63 A4
5 Putney SW15 . . . .69 B4

Leicester Pl WC2 .**119** C4

Leicester Sq WC2 .**119** C3

Leicester Square Sta
WC2 . . . .**119** C3

Leigham Ave
SW16 . . . . .74 A1

Leigham Cl **5**
SW16 . . . . .74 B1

Leigham Court Rd
SW16 . . . . .74 B1

Leigham Hall **3**
SW16 . . . . .74 A1

Leigham Hall Par **2**
SW16 . . . . .74 A1

Leigham Vale SE27,
SW16, SW2 . . . . . . .74 C2

Leigh Ct **22** SW2. . .62 C1

Leighfield Ho **5** N4 . .6 B4

Leigh Gdns NW10 . .22 B3

Leigh Ho **9** SW15 . .56 C2

Leigh Orchard Cl
SW16 . . . . .74 B1

Leigh Pl EC1 . . . . .**107** B4

Leigh Rd N5. . . . . . .15 A4

Leigh St WC1 . . . . . .94 A3

Leighton Cres
NW5 . . . . .13 B3

Leighton Gdns
NW10 . . . . .22 B3

Leighton Gr NW5 . .13 B3

Leighton House Mus
W14 . . . .**127** A2

Leighton Pl NW5 . .13 B3

Leighton Rd NW5. . .13 B3

Leinster Ave SW14. .55 B3

Leinster Gdns W2 .**114** C4

Leinster Mews
W2 . . . .**114** C4

Leinster Pl W2 . . . .**100** C1

Leinster Sq W2 . . .**100** A1

Leinster Terr W2. . .**114** C4

Leitch Ho **8** NW8 . .11 C1

Leithcote Path
SW16 . . . . .74 B1

Leith Ho
7 Kentish Town
N7 . . . . .13 C3
13 Streatham SW2 . .74 B4

Leith Mans W9 . . . . .88 A3

Leith Yd **3** NW6 . . .10 C1

Lelitia Cl E8 . . . . . . .24 C4

Leman St E1 . . . . . .**111** B1

Lemmon Rd SE10. . .53 A4

Le Moal Ho **20** E1 . .32 B4

Lemsford Ct N4 . . . . .6 B2

Lena Gardens Prim
Sch W6 . . . . .39 B3

Lena Gdns W6. . . . . .39 B3

Lendal Terr **7**
SW4 . . . . .61 C4

Len Freeman Pl
SW6 . . . .**154** C3

Lenham **11** NW5 . . .12 C2

Lenham Ho SE1 . . .**137** C3

Lennon Rd NW2 . . . .9 B2

Lennox Gdns
Knightsbridge
SW1 . . . .**130** C1
Willesden NW10 . . . .8 B4

Lennox Gdns Mews
SW1 . . . .**144** C4

Lennox Ho **10** E9 . .17 B2

Lennox Rd
11 Camberwell
SW9 . . . . .48 A2
Finsbury Pk N4, N7. . .5 C2

Lenthal Ho **1** SW1 .**147** A1

Lenthall Rd E8 . . . .16 C1

Lenthorp Rd SE10 . .43 B2

Lenton Rise TW9 . . .54 A4

Len Williams Ct
NW6 . . . . .23 C3

Leonard Ct
Bloomsbury WC1 . . . .94 A2
Kensington W8. . . .**127** B2

Leonard Day Ho **3**
NW5 . . . . .13 A2

Leonard Pl **6** N16. .16 A4

Leonard St EC2 . . . .97 C2

Leonora Ho W9 . . . .88 C2

Leontine Cl SE15 . . .49 C3

Leopards Ct EC1. . .**107** B4

Leopold Bldgs **14**
E2 . . . . .24 B2 **98** C4

Leopold Mews E9 . .25 B4

Leopold Prim Sch
NW10 . . . . .8 B1

Leopold Rd NW10 . . .8 A1

Leopold St E3 . . . . .33 B4

Leopold Wlk SE11 .**148** C1

Leo St SE15 . . . . . . .50 A3

Leo Yd EC1 . . . . .96 B1

Leppoc Rd SW4 . . . .61 C2

Leroy St SE1 . . . . . .**152** A4

Lerry Cl W14 . . . . .**155** A4

Lerwick Ho SW18. . .59 B3

Lesley Ct SW1 . . . .**133** B1

Leslie Prince Ct **5**
SE5 . . . . .48 C3

Leslie Rd E11. . . . . . .19 C4

Lessar Ave SW4 . . . .61 B2

Lessar Ct SW4. . . . . .61 B1

Lester Ct **42** E3 . . . .27 A2

Leswin Pl N16. . . . . . .7 B1

Leswin Rd N16. . . . . .7 B1

Letchford Gdns
NW10 . . . . .21 C2

Letchford Mews
NW10 . . . . .21 C2

Letchmore Ho **7**
W10 . . . . .22 B1

Lethaby Ho **15**
SW4 . . . . .62 B3

Lethbridge Cl
SE13 . . . . .52 B1

Letterstone Rd
SW6 . . . .**154** C1

Lettice St SW6 . . . .**165** A3

Lett Rd
Brixton SW9 . . . . .**173** A4
London E15. . . . . . .19 C1

Lettsom St SE5 . . . .49 A1

Levana Cl SW19 . . . .70 A3

Levant Ho **17** E1. . .25 C1

Levehurst Way
SW9 . . . .**172** B2

Leven Rd E14 . . . . . .34 C3

Lever Ct **12** E9 . . . . .17 C2

Leverett St SW3 . .**144** B4

Leverington Pl N1. .**97** C3

Lever St EC1 . . . . . . .96 C3

Leverstock Ho
SW3 . . . .**144** B2

Leverton Pl NW5 . . .13 B3

Leverton St NW5 . . .13 B3

Levison Way **2**
N19 . . . . .4 C3

Levita Ho NW1 . . . . .93 C4

Levyne Ct EC1 . . . . .**95** B2

Lewesdon Cl **18**
SW19 . . . . .69 C3

Lewes Ho
Bermondsey SE1 . .**138** B4
Peckham SE15 . . . .49 C4

Leweston Pl N16 . . . .7 B4

Lewey Ho E3 . . . . . .26 B1

Lewin Rd SW14. . . . .55 C4

Lewis Ct **5** SE16 . . .40 A1

Lewis Gr SE13 . . . . .67 B4

LEWISHAM 67 B3

Lewisham Bsns Ctr
SE14 . . . . .50 C4

Lewisham Coll
(Deptford Campus)
SE8 . . . . .51 C2

Lewisham High St
SE13 . . . . .67 A2

Lewisham Hill
SE13 . . . . .52 B1

Lewisham Pk SE13 .52 B1

Lewisham Rd SE13 .52 B1

Lewisham Sh Ctr
SE13 . . . . .67 B4

Lewisham Southwark
Coll SE1 . . . .**136** A4

Lewisham Southwark
Coll (Tressillian
Building) SE4 . . . . .51 C1

Lewisham St SW1 .**133** C3

Lewisham Sta
SE13 . . . . .67 B4

Lewisham Way SE4,
SE14 . . . . .51 B2

Lewis Pl E8 . . . . .16 C3

Lewis Silkin Ho **9**
SE15 . . . . .50 B4

Lewis St NW1 . . . . . .13 A2

Lexden Rd W3 . . . . .28 A1

Lexfield Ho N5 . . . . .15 B4

Lexham Gardens
Mews W8 . . . .**128** B1

Lexham Gdns W8 .**142** A4

Lexham Mews
W8 . . . .**141** C4

Lexham Wlk W8 . .**128** B1

Lexington St W1. . .**119** A4

Lexton Gdns SW12. .73 C3

Leyborne Pk TW9. .44 C2

Leybourne Ho **20**
SE15 . . . . .50 B4

Leybourne Rd **11**
NW1 . . . . .13 A1

Leybourne St **5**
NW1 . . . . .13 A1

Leyden Mans **7**
N19 . . . . .5 A4

Leyden St E1 . . . . .**110** C3

Leydon Cl
Rotherhithe SE16 . . .32 C1
SE16 . . . . .32 C1

Ley Ho SE1 . . . . . .**136** C3

Leyland Ho **6** E14. .34 A2

Leylands SW18 . . . .58 B1

Leylang Rd SE14. . .50 C3

Leys Ct **9** SW9 . . .**173** B1

Leysdown **9** NW5 . .12 C2

Leysdown Ho
SE17 . . . .**152** B2

Leysfield Rd W12. .38 C4

Leythe Rd W3 . . . . . .37 B4

LEYTON 19 C4

Leyton Mill Ret Pk
E10 . . . . .19 B4

Leyton Rd E15. . . . . .19 C2

Liardet St SE14. . . . .51 A4

Liberia Rd N5 . . . . . .15 A2

Liberty Bridge Rd
E15 . . . . .19 B3

Liberty Mews
SW12 . . . . .61 A1

Liberty St SW9 . . .**173** A4

Libra Rd **7** E3 . . . . .26 B3

Library Mans **4**
W12 . . . . .39 B4

Library Par NW10. . .21 A4

Library Pl E1 . . . . . .32 A2

Library St SE1 . . . .**136** B3

Lichfield Ct TW9. . . .54 A3

Lichfield Gdns TW9,
TW9 . . . . .54 A2

Lichfield Ho **27**
SE5 . . . . .48 B1

Lichfield Rd
Mile End E3. . . . . . .26 A2
Richmond TW9 . . . .44 B2
West Hampstead
NW2 . . . . .10 A4

Lichfield Terr **1**
TW9 . . . . .54 A2

Lickey Ho W14 . . . .**155** A4

Lidcote Gdns **22**
SW9 . . . .**173** A1

Liddell Gdns
NW10 . . . . .22 B3

Liddell Rd NW6. . . .10 C2

Lidfield Rd N16. . . .15 C4

Lidgate Rd 22
SE15 . . . . 49 B3
Lidiard Rd SW12 . . . . . . 73 B2
Lidlington Pl NW1 . . 83 A1
Lido The W2 . . . . 116 A1
Lidyard Rd N19 . . . . 4 B3
Liffey Ct NW10 . . . . 8 C1
Liffords Pl SW13 . . . . . . 46 B1
Lifford St SW15 . . . . . . 57 C3
Lighter Cl 10 SE16 . . . . 41 A2
Lighterman Mews 15
E1 . . . . 32 C3
Lighterman's Rd
E14 . . . . 42 A4
Lighterman's Wlk
SW18 . . . . 58 B4
Light Horse Ct
SW1 . . . . 145 B1
Ligonier St
E2 . . . . 24 B1 98 C2
Lilac Ho SE4 . . . . 66 B4
Lilac Pl SE11 . . . . 148 C3
Lilac St W12 . . . . 29 C2
Lilestone Est NW8 . . 89 C1
Lilestone Ho NW8 . . 89 C2
Lilestone St NW8 . . 90 A2
Lilford Ho 図 SE5 . . . . 48 B1
Lilford Rd SE5 . . . . 48 A1
Lilian Baylis Ho
N1 . . . . 15 B2
Lilian Baylis Tech Sch
SE11 . . . . 149 A1
Lilley Cl E1 . . . . 125 C1
Lillian Ave W3 . . . . 36 C4
Lillian Cl 図 N16 . . . . . . 7 A1
Lillian Rd SW13 . . . . . . 47 A4
Lillie Ho N5 . . . . 14 C3
Lillie Rd SW6 . . . . . . 154 C3
Lillie Road Mans
SW6 . . . . 154 B3
Lillieshall Rd SW4 . . . 61 A4
Lillie Yd SW6 . . . . 155 B4
Lillingston Ho N7 . . . . 14 C4
Lily Cl W14 . . . . 39 C2
Lily Pl EC1 . . . . 107 C4
Lilyville Rd SW6 . . . . 164 C4
Limasol St SE1 . . . . . 139 A2
Limborough Ho 図
E14 . . . . 33 C4
Limburg Rd SW11 . . . 60 A3
Limeburner La
EC4 . . . . 108 A2
Lime Cl E1 . . . . 125 C2
Lime Ct SW15 . . . . 57 A4
Lime Gr W12 . . . . 39 B4
Limeharbour E14 . . . . 42 A4
Lime Ho 図 TW9 . . . . . 45 A2
LIMEHOUSE 33 A2
Limehouse Cswy
E14 . . . . 33 B2
Limehouse Ct 図
E14 . . . . 33 C3
Lime House Ct 図
E14 . . . . 33 B3
Limehouse Cut 4
E14 . . . . 34 A4
Limehouse Fields Est
14 E14 . . . . 33 A4
Limehouse Link
(Tunnel) E14 . . . . . 33 B2
Limehouse Sta
E14 . . . . 33 A3
Limekiln Wharf 21
E14 . . . . 33 B2

Limerick Cl SW12 . . . 73 B4
Limerick Ct 1
SW12 . . . . 73 B4
Limerston St
SW10 . . . . 157 A3
Lime St Pas EC3 . . 124 A4
Limes Ave
Barnes SW13 . . . . 46 B1
Golders Green NW11 . . 1 A4
Limes Ct NW6 . . . . 9 C1
Limes Field Rd
SW14 . . . . 56 A4
Limesford Rd
SE15 . . . . 65 C3
Limes Gdns SW18 . . . 58 C1
Limes Gr SE13 . . . . . . 67 B3
Lime St EC3 . . . . 110 A1
Limes The
Camberwell SE5 . . . . . . 64 A4
Kensington
W2 . . . . . . 31 C2 113 C3
Limes Wlk SE15 . . . . . 65 B3
Limetree Cl SW2 . . . . 74 B3
Lime Tree Ct 14
E3 . . . . 33 C4
Limpsfield Ave
SW19 . . . . 69 C2
Limscott Ho 図 E3 . . . 27 A2
Linacre Cl SE15 . . . . . 65 A4
Linacre Ct W6 . . . . 39 C1
Linacre Rd NW2 . . . . . . 9 A2
Linale Ho N1 . . . . 87 B1
Linberry Wlk 8
SE8 . . . . 41 B2
Lincoln Ave SW19 . . . 69 C1
Lincoln Ct N16 . . . . 6 C4
Lincoln Ho
Bloomsbury WC1 . . 107 A3
図 Dartmouth Pk
NW5 . . . . 4 B1
図 Islington N1 . . . . . 15 B1
Knightsbridge
SW1 . . . . 130 C3
Lincoln Mews
NW6 . . . . 23 B4
Lincoln's Inn WC2 107 A2
Lincoln's Inn Fields
WC2 . . . . 107 A2
Lincoln St SW3 . . . . 144 C3
Lindale SW19 . . . . 70 A2
Lindal Rd SE4 . . . . 66 B2
Linden Ave NW10 . . . 22 C3
Linden Ct
8 Battersea
SW18 . . . . 59 C3
图 Shepherd's Bush
W12 . . . . 30 B1
Linden Gdns
Chiswick W4 . . . . 37 C1
Notting Hill
W2 . . . . . . 31 C2 113 C3
Linden Gr SE15 . . . . . . 65 B4
Linden Ho 10 SE8 . . 51 B4
Linden Lodge Sch
SW19 . . . . 70 A3
Linden Mans N6 . . . . . 4 A3
Linden Mews
Kensington
W2 . . . . . . 31 C2 113 C3
Stoke Newington
N1 . . . . 15 C3
Lindens The W4 . . . . 45 B2
Lindfield Gdns
NW3 . . . . 11 B3
Lindfield Hts NW3 . . 11 B3
Lindfield St E14 . . . . . 33 C3

Lindisfarne Way
E9 . . . . 18 A4
Lindley Ho
13 Peckham SE15 . . . . 49 C3
図 Stepney E1 . . . . . 32 B4
Lindley Pl TW9 . . . . . . 44 C2
Lindley St E1 . . . . 32 B4
Lindop Ho 8 E1 . . . . . 26 A1
Lindore Rd SW11 . . . . 60 B3
Lindores Rd SW11 . . . 50 B1
Lindrop St SW6 . . . . 166 C2
Lindsay Ct SW11 . . . 167 C3
Lindsay Sq SW1 . . . 147 C2
Lindsell St 6
SE10 . . . . 52 B2
Lindsey Ho SW10 . 157 C2
Lindsey Mews 18
N1 . . . . 15 B1
Lindsey St EC1 . . . . 108 B4
Lind St SE8 . . . . 52 A1
Linfield WC1 . . . . 94 C3
Linford Christie
Stadium The
W12 . . . . 30 A4
Linford Ho 17 E2 . . . . 24 C4
Linford St SW8 . . . . 170 C3
Linford Street Bsns
Est SW8 . . . . 170 C4
Lingard Ho 図 E14 . . 42 B3
Lingards Rd SE13 . . . 67 B3
Lingfield Ho
図 Acton Green
W4 . . . . 37 B1
Lambeth SE1 . . . . . . 136 B3
Lingham St SW9 . . . 172 C1
Ling Rd E16 . . . . 35 C4
Ling's Coppice
SE21 . . . . 75 C2
Lingwell Rd SW17 . . . 72 A1
Lingwood Rd E5 . . . . . 7 C4
Linhope St NW1 . . . . 90 C1
Linkenholt Mans 3
W6 . . . . 38 B2
Link St E9 . . . . 17 B3
Links Yd
10 Spitalfields
E1 . . . . 111 A4
Spitalfields E1 . . . . 111 A4
Link The W3 . . . . 28 A3
Linkway N4 . . . . 6 B4
Linkwood Wlk
NW1 . . . . 13 C1
Linnell Ho
Spitalfields E1 . . . . 110 C4
St John's Wood
NW8 . . . . 78 C4
Linnell Rd SE5 . . . . . . 49 A1
Linnet Mews
SW12 . . . . 72 C4
Linom Rd SW4 . . . . . . 62 A3
Linscott Rd E5 . . . . . . 17 B4
Linsey St SE16 . . . . . 153 B4
Linslade Ho
10 Hackney E2 . . . . . 24 C4
Marylebone NW8 . . . 90 B2
Linstead St 1
NW6 . . . . 10 C1
Linstead Way SW18,
SW19 . . . . 70 A4
Lintaine Cl W6 . . . . 154 B3
Linthorpe Rd N16 . . . . 7 A4
Linton Ho
Lower Holloway
N7 . . . . 14 B4
2 Tower Hamlets
E3 . . . . 33 C4

Linton St N1 . . . . 87 A3
Linver Rd SW6 . . . . 165 B2
Linwood Cl SE5 . . . . . 49 B1
Lion Cl SE4 . . . . 66 C1
Lionel Ho 5 W10 . . . 31 A4
Lionel Mans 17
W14 . . . . 39 C3
Lionel Mews 13
W10 . . . . 31 A4
Lionel Prim Sch
TW8 . . . . 36 A2
Lionel Road N
TW8 . . . . 36 A2
Lionel Road S
TW8 . . . . 36 B1
Lion Gate Gdns
TW9 . . . . 54 B4
Lion Gate Mews
SW18 . . . . 70 C4
Lion Mills 2 E2 . . . . . 24 C3
Lion Yd SW4 . . . . 61 C3
Lipton Rd 8 E1 . . . . . 32 C3
Lisburne Rd NW3 . . . 12 B4
Lisford St SE15 . . . . . 49 B2
Lisgar Terr W14 . . . 140 C4
Liskeard Gdns SE3 . . 53 C2
Liskeard Ho SE11 . 149 C2
Lisle Ct NW2 . . . . 1 A1
Lisle St WC2 . . . . 119 C4
Lismore Circ NW5 . . . 12 C3
Lismore Wlk 4
N1 . . . . 15 B2
Lissenden Gdns
NW5 . . . . 12 C4
Lissenden Mans
NW5 . . . . 12 C4
Lisson Cotts NW1 . 102 B3
Lisson Gall W1 . . . . 102 C3
Lisson Gr NW1,
NW8 . . . . 90 A2
LISSON GROVE 90 B1
Lisson Ho NW1 . . . . 102 A4
Lisson St NW1 . . . . 102 A4
Lister Cl W3 . . . . 28 C4
Lister Ct N16 . . . . 7 A2
Lister Ho
Greenwich SE3 . . . . . 53 A4
Marylebone W1 . . . 104 A2
Spitalfields E1 . . . . 111 C4
Lister Hospl SW1 146 A1
Lister Mews N7 . . . . . 14 B4
Liston Rd SW4 . . . . . . 61 B4
Listowel Cl 2
SW9 . . . . 163 C2
Listria Lo N16 . . . . 7 B2
Listria Pk N16 . . . . 7 B2
Litchfield Gdns
NW10 . . . . 8 C2
Litchfield St WC2 119 C4
Lithos Rd NW3 . . . . . . 11 B2
Little Albany St
NW1 . . . . 92 B2
Little Argyll St
W1 . . . . 104 C1
Little Boltons The
SW10 . . . . 142 B1
Little Britain EC1 . 108 B3
Littlebury Rd SW4 . . 61 C4
Little Chelsea
Antiques Fair
SW3 . . . . 144 B1
Little Chelsea Ho
SW10 . . . . 157 A3
Little Chester St
SW1 . . . . 132 A2

Little Cloisters
SW1 . . . . 134 A2
Little College St
SW1 . . . . 134 A2
Little Combe Cl 13
SW15 . . . . 57 C1
Littlecote Cl SW19 . . 70 A4
Little Cottage Pl
SE10 . . . . 52 A3
Little Deans Yd
SW1 . . . . 134 A2
Little Dimocks
SW12 . . . . 73 A2
Little Dorrit Ct
SE1 . . . . 137 A4
Little Edward St
NW1 . . . . 92 B4
Little Essex St
WC2 . . . . 121 B4
Little George St
SW1 . . . . 134 A3
Little Green St
NW5 . . . . 13 A4
Little Marlborough St
W1 . . . . 104 C1
Little Newport St
WC2 . . . . 119 C4
Little New St EC4 107 C2
Little Portland St
W1 . . . . 104 C2
Little Russell St
WC1 . . . . 106 A3
Little St James's St
SW1 . . . . 118 C1
Little St Leonards
SW14 . . . . 55 B4
Little Sanctuary
SW1 . . . . 134 A3
Little Smith St
SW1 . . . . 133 C2
Little Somerset St
E1 . . . . 110 C1
Little Titchfield St
W1 . . . . 104 C3
Littleton St SW18 . . . 71 B2
Little Trinity La
EC4 . . . . 123 A4
Little Turnstile
WC1 . . . . 106 C3
LITTLE VENICE 101 A4
Little Venice W9 . . 100 C4
Littlewood SE13 . . . . 67 B1
Livermere Ct 8
E8 . . . . 24 B4
Livermere Rd E8 . . . . 24 B4
Liverpool Gr SE17 151 B1
Liverpool Ho N7 . . . . 14 C2
Liverpool Rd
Islington N1 . . . . 85 C3
Islington N1, N7 . . . 14 C1
Newham E16 . . . . 35 A4
Liverpool St EC2 . 110 A3
Liverpool Street Sta
EC2 . . . . 110 A3
Livesey Pl SE15 . . . . 49 C4
Livingstone Ho 10
SE5 . . . . 48 B3
Livingstone Lo 10
W9 . . . . 31 C4
Livingstone Pl E14 . 42 B1
Livingstone Rd
13 Battersea
SW11 . . . . 59 C4
Mill Meads E15 . . . . . 27 B4

Livity Sch The
  London SW2 . . . . 62 A2
    Streatham Hill
    SW16 . . . . 74 B2
Livonia St W1 . . . . 105 A1
Lizard St EC1 . . . . 97 A3
Llandovery Ho 🔟
  E14 . . . . 42 B4
Llanelly Rd NW2 . . . 1 B2
Llanvanor Rd NW2 . . 1 B2
Llewellyn Ho 🔟
  N19 . . . . 4 B1
Llewellyn St SE16 139 C3
Lloyd Baker St
  WC1 . . . . 95 B3
Lloyd Ct
    Ladywell SE13 . . . . . 67 A2
  6 West Norwood
    SE27 . . . . 75 A1
Lloyd Ho N16 . . . . 6 C1
Lloyd's Ave EC3 . . 110 B1
Lloyd's Bldg EC3 . . 110 A1
Lloyd's PI SE3 . . . . . . 53 A1
Lloyd Sq WC1 . . . . . . 95 B4
Lloyd's Row EC1 . . . 96 A3
Lloyd St WC1 . . . . 95 B4
Lloyd Villas SE4 . . . 51 C1
Lloyd Williamson Sch
  The 🔟 W10 . . . . 31 A4
Loampit Hill SE13 . . 52 A1
Loampit Vale SE13 . 67 B4
Loanda Cl 🔟 E8 . . . . 24 B4
Loats Rd SW2 . . . . 62 A1
Locarno Rd 6 W3 . . 28 B1
Lochaline St W6 . . . . 47 B4
Lochbie 🗟 N4 . . . . 5 A4
Lochinvar St
  SW12 . . . . 73 A4
Lochmore Ho
  SW1 . . . . 145 C3
Lochnagar St E14 . . 34 B4
Lockbridge Ct 🗟
  W9 . . . . 31 C4
Locke Ho
    Nine Elms SW8 . . . 170 C4
    Stamford Hill N16 . . 7 B3
Lockesfield PI E14 . . 42 A1
Lockgate Cl E9 . . . . . 18 B3
Lockhart Cl N7 . . . . . 14 B2
Lockhart St E3 . . . . . . 26 B1
Lockhurst St E5 . . . . 17 C4
Lockington Rd
  SW8 . . . . 170 B4
Lockmead Rd
  SE13 . . . . 67 B4
Lock Mews 🗟
  NW1 . . . . 13 C2
Lockside 🔟 E14 . . . . 33 A2
Lockside Est E14 . . . 33 B4
Lock View C1 🗟
  E14 . . . . 33 A2
Lockwood Ho 🔟
  SE11 . . . . 163 B3
Lockwood Sq
  SE16 . . . . 40 A3
Lockyer Est SE1 . . 137 C3
Lockyer Ho
  🗟 Greenwich
    SE10 . . . . 43 B1
  🔟 Putney SW15 . . 57 C4
    South Lambeth
    SW8 . . . . 162 A2
Lockyer St SE1 . . . 137 C3
Locton Gn 4 E3 . . . 26 B4
Loddiges Ho 🗟 E9 . 17 B1
Loddiges Rd E9 . . . . 17 B1

Loddon Ho NW8 . . . 89 C1
Loder St SE15 . . . . . . 50 B3
Lodge Ave SW14 . . 56 A4
Lodge Rd NW8 . . . . . 90 A3
Lodge The 🗟 W4 . . 38 A3
Lodore St E14 . . . . . . 34 B3
Lodsworth Ho
  SW11 . . . . 169 B3
Loftie St SE16 . . . . . 139 C3
Lofting Ho 🗟 N1 . . 14 C1
Lofting Rd N1 . . . . . . 14 C1
Lofts on the Park 🗟
  E9 . . . . 17 C2
Loftus Rd W12 . . . . . 30 A1
Loftus Rd (Queens
    Park Rangers FC)
  W12 . . . . 30 A1
Logan Cl E15 . . . . . . 19 A3
Logan Mews 🗟 . . 141 B4
Logan PI W8 . . . . . . 141 B4
Loggetts SE21 . . . . . 76 A2
Lohmann Ho 🗟
  SE11 . . . . 163 B4
Lolesworth Cl E1 . 111 A3
Lollard St SE11 . . . 149 B3
Lollards Twr SE1 . . 134 C1
Loman St SE1 . . . . . 136 B4
Lomas St E1 . . . . . . 111 C4
Lombard Ct
  5 Acton W3 . . . . . . 28 A1
    City of London EC3 123 C4
Lombard La EC4 . . 107 C1
Lombard Rd
  SW11 . . . . 167 B2
Lombard St EC3 . . 109 C1
Lombardy PI W2 . . 114 B3
Lomley Ho 🔟
  SW2 . . . . 62 C1
Lomond Gr SE5 . . . . 48 C3
Lomond Ho 🔟
  SE5 . . . . 48 C2
Loncroft Rd SE5 . . . 49 A4
Londesborough Ho 🗟
  N16 . . . . 16 A4
Londesborough Rd
  N16 . . . . 16 A4
London Acad for
    Higher Education
  The E15 . . . . 27 C4
London Acad of
    Computing &
    Electronics
  SW17 . . . . 72 B2
London Aquatics Ctr
  E15 . . . . 19 B1
London Bridge EC4,
  SE1 . . . . 123 C2
London Bridge City
    Pier
  SE1 . . . . 124 A2
  SE1 . . . . 124 A2
London Bridge
    Experience The
  SE1 . . . . 123 C2
London Bridge Hospl
  SE1 . . . . 123 C2
London Bridge St
  SE1 . . . . 123 C1
London Bridge Sta
  SE1 . . . . 123 C1
London Bridge Wlk
  SE1 . . . . 123 C2
London Britannia Coll
  N1 . . . . 97 B4

London Business Sch
  NW1 . . . . 90 C2
London Canal Mus
  N1 . . . . 84 B2
London Central
    Mosque NW8 . . . 90 B3
London Chest Hospl
  E2 . . . . 25 B3
London City Sch Ctr
  EC1 . . . . 97 A1
London Clinic The
    (Hospl) NW1 . . . 91 C1
London Coll of Beauty
    Therapy W1 . . . 105 A1
London Coll of Bsns &
    Computer Studies
  SW4 . . . . 61 C3
London Coll of
    Communication (Sch
    of Printing &
    Publishing)
  SE1 . . . . 136 B1
London Coll of
    Economics &
    Science NW10 . . 20 B1
London Coll of
    Fashion (Curtain Rd)
  EC2 . . . . 24 A1 98 B2
London Coll of
    Fashion (Golden La)
  EC1 . . . . 96 C1
London Coll of
    Fashion (John
    Prince's St) W1 . 104 A1
London Coll of
    Fashion (Mare St)
  E8 . . . . 17 B1
London Coll of
    International
    Business Studies
  WC2 . . . . 106 B3
London Ct 🗟
  SW18 . . . . 58 C2
London Ctr of
    Contemporary
    Music E1 . . . . . . 123 A1
London Cty Hall
  SE1 . . . . 134 C4
London Dungeon The
  SE1 . . . . 134 C4
London East Acad
  E1 . . . . 111 C2
London Eye Hospl
  W1 . . . . 104 A3
London Eye
    (Millennium Wheel)
  SE1 . . . . 134 C4
London Fields East
    Side E8 . . . . 17 A1
London Fields Prim
    Sch 🗟 E8 . . . . 25 A4
London Fields Sta
  E8 . . . . 17 A1
London Fields West
    Side 🗟 E8 . . . . . . 25 A4
London Film Mus
  SE1 . . . . 134 C4
London Film Sch The
  WC2 . . . . 106 A1
London Fire Brigade
    Pop-up Mus
  SE1 . . . . 148 C4
London Glassblowing
    Workshop SE1 . . 138 A4
London Ho 🗟 W6 . 38 C2
London Ho NW8 . . . 80 B2

London Ho NW8 . . . 80 B2
London Hospital
    Dental Inst 🗟 E1 . 32 A4
London Independent
    Hospl The E1 . . . 32 C4
London Irish Rifles
    Mus SW9 . . . . 48 B2
London Islamic Sch
  E1 . . . . 32 B4
London La E8 . . . . . . 17 A1
London Metropolitan
    Univ E1 . . . . 110 C1
London Metropolitan
    Univ (Central Ho)
  E1 . . . . 111 B2
London Metropolitan
    Univ (Commercial
    Rd) 🔟 E1 . . . . . 111 C2
London Metropolitan
    Univ (Ladbrook Ho)
  🗟 N5 . . . . 15 A3
London Metropolitan
    Univ (Moorgate)
  EC2 . . . . 109 C3
London Metropolitan
    Univ North Campus
  N7 . . . . 14 B4
London Mews W2 101 C2
London Mus of Water
    & Steam TW8 . . . 36 B1
London Nautical Sch
  SE1 . . . . 121 C2
London Oratory Sch
    The 🗟 SW6 . . . 155 C2
London Oratory The
  SW7 . . . . 130 A1
London Rd SE1 . . . 136 B2
London Sch of
    Economics &
    Political Science
  WC2 . . . . 107 A1
London South Bank
    Univ SE1 . . . . . . 136 B2
London St
    City of London
    EC3 . . . . 124 B4
    Paddington W2 . . . 101 B1
London Stadium
    (West Ham FC)
  E15 . . . . 19 A1
London Stile 🗟
  W4 . . . . 36 C1
London Stock
    Exchange EC2 . . 108 C2
London Terr 🗟 E2 . 24 C3
London Transport
    Mus WC2 . . . . . . 120 B4
London Trocadero
  W1 . . . . 119 B3
London Wall EC2 . 109 C3
London Wall Bldgs
  EC2 . . . . 109 C3
London Wharf 4
  E2 . . . . 25 A4
Long Acre WC2 . . 106 B1
Longbeach Rd
  SW11 . . . . 60 B4
Longberrys NW2 . . 1 B1
Longbridge Way
  SE13 . . . . 67 B2
Longcliffe Ho
  SW18 . . . . 59 A2
Long Dr W3 . . . . 29 A3
Longfellow Way
  SE1 . . . . 153 A3

Longfield Dr
  SW14 . . . . 55 A2
Longfield Est SE1 153 A3
Longfield St SW18 . 70 C4
Longford Ct
  🔟 Bedford Pk
    W12 . . . . 38 A4
  🗟 Clapton Pk E5 . 17 C4
Longford Ho 🔟
  E1 . . . . 32 B3
Longford St NW1 . . 92 B2
Longford Wlk 🗟
  SW2 . . . . 74 C4
Longhope CI SE15 . 49 B4
Longhurst Ho 🗟
  W9 . . . . 23 B2
Long La
    Bermondsey SE1 . 137 C3
    Holborn EC1 . . . . 108 B4
Longland Ct
    Bermondsey SE1 . 153 B2
    Hackney E9 . . . . . . 18 A3
Longlands Ct
  W11 . . . . 31 B2 113 A4
Longleat Ho SW1 . 147 B2
Longleigh Ho 🗟
  SE5 . . . . 49 A2
Longlents Ho 🗟
  NW10 . . . . 20 C4
Longley Ho 🗟
  N19 . . . . 13 B4
Longley St SE1 . . . 153 B4
Longman Ho
  🗟 Globe Town
    E2 . . . . 25 C3
  🔟 Shoreditch E8 . 24 B4
Long Meadow 🗟
  N7 . . . . 14 C3
Longmoor Point 🔟
  SW15 . . . . 69 A3
Longmore St
  SW1 . . . . 146 C3
Longnor Rd E1 . . . . 25 C2
Long Pond Rd SE3 . 53 A2
Longridge Ho
  SE1 . . . . 137 A1
Longridge Rd
  SW5 . . . . 141 C3
Long's Ct 🗟 TW9 . 54 B3
Longs Ct W1 . . . . . 119 C3
Longshore SE8 . . . . 41 B2
Long St E2 . . . . 24 B2 98 C4
Longstaff Cres
  SW18 . . . . 70 C4
Longstaff Rd
  SW18 . . . . 58 C1
Longstone Ave
  NW10 . . . . 21 B4
Longthorne Ho 🔟
  E3 . . . . 26 B2
Longthorpe Ct 🗟
  W6 . . . . 38 B2
Longville Rd SE11 150 B4
Long Wlk SE1 . . . . 138 B2
Longwood Dr
  SW15 . . . . 56 C1
Long Yd WC1 . . . . . 94 C1
Lonsdale Ho
    Fulham SW6 . . . . . 58 C4
  🗟 Stoke Newington
    N4 . . . . 6 B4
Lonsdale Mews
    Notting Hill W11 . . 31 B3

Lonsdale Mews
continued
4 Richmond TW9 . . . . 44 C2
Lonsdale Pl N1 . . . . . . 14 C1
Lonsdale Rd
Barnes SW13 . . . . 46 B3
Chiswick W4 . . . . 38 B2
Kilburn NW6 . . . . 23 B4
Notting Hill W11 . . . . . 31 B3
Lonsdale Sq
Islington N1 . . . . 14 C1
Islington N1 . . . . 5 C1
Lopez Ho 4 SW9 . . . 62 A4
Loraine Rd
Chiswick W4 . . . . 45 A4
Islington N7 . . . . 14 B3
Lord David Pitt Ho 7
SE24 . . . . 63 A3
Lorden Wlk 13
E2 . . . . 24 C2 99 B3
Lord Hills Rd W2 . 100 B4
Lord Holland La 5
SW9 . . . . 173 C2
Lord Napier Pl
W6 . . . . 38 C1
Lord North St
SW1 . . . . 134 A1
Lord Roberts Mews
SW6 . . . . 156 A1
Lords Cl SE21 . . . . . . 75 B2
Lord's Cricket Mus
NW8 . . . . 89 C3
Lordship Gr N16 . . . . . 6 C2
Lordship Ho 5 N16 . . 6 C2
Lordship La SE22 . . 64 B1
Lordship Park Mews
N16 . . . . 6 B2
Lordship Pk N16 . . . . . 6 C2
Lordship Pl SW3 . 158 A3
Lordship Rd N16 . . . . 6 C2
Lordship Terr N16 . . . 6 C2
Lord's Indoor Cricket
Sch NW8 . . . . 90 A4
Lord's (MCC &
Middlesex Cty
Cricket Ground)
NW8 . . . . 89 C4
Lord's View NW8 . . 89 C3
Loreburn Ho 2
N7 . . . . 14 B4
Lorenzo St N1,
WC1 . . . . 94 C4
Loris Rd W6 . . . . 39 B3
Lorn Ct SW9 . . . . . 173 B2
Lorne Cl SW1 . . . . . 57 C1
Lorne Gdns 5
W11 . . . . 39 C4
Lorne Ho
Hornsey N4 . . . . 5 B4
7 Tower Hamlets
E1 . . . . 33 A4
Lorne Rd
Finsbury Pk N4 . . . . . . 5 B3
3 Richmond TW10 . . 54 B2
Lorn Rd SW9 . . . . . 173 B2
Lorraine Ct 10
NW1 . . . . 13 A1
Lorrimore Rd
SE17 . . . . 48 A4
Lorrimore Sq
SE17 . . . . 48 A4
Lorton Ho 9 NW6 . 23 C4

Lostock Ho 10
SW8 . . . . 171 B2
Lothair Rd S N4 . . . . 6 A4
Lothbury EC2 . . . . . 109 B2
Lothian Rd SW9 . . 48 A2
Lothrop St W10 . . . . 23 A2
Lots Rd SW10 . . . . 157 A1
Loudoun Rd NW8 . . 79 A3
Loughborough Ct
SW9 . . . . 63 A4
Loughborough
Junction Sta
SW9 . . . . 63 A4
Loughborough Pk
SW9 . . . . 63 A3
Loughborough Prim
Sch SW9 . . . . 48 A1
Loughborough Rd SE5,
SW9 . . . . 48 A1
Loughborough St
SE11 . . . . 149 A1
Lough Rd N7 . . . . . . 14 B2
Louisa Gdns E1 . . . 25 C1
Louisa Ho SW15 . . 56 B3
Louisa St E1 . . . . . . 25 C1
Louise Bennett Cl 9
SE24 . . . . 63 A3
Louise De Marillac Ho
2 E1 . . . . 32 B4
Louise White Ho 1
N19 . . . . 4 C3
Louisville Rd
SW17 . . . . 72 C1
Louvaine Rd SW11 . 59 C3
Lovat La EC3 . . . . . 124 A3
Lovatt Ct SW12 . . . . 73 A3
Loveday Ho 2
SW2 . . . . 74 C3
Lovegrove St SE1 . 49 C4
Lovegrove Wlk
E14 . . . . 34 B1
Love La EC2 . . . . . . 109 A2
Lovelace Ho 12 E8 . 24 B4
Lovelace Rd SE21 . 75 B3
Lovelinch Cl SE15 . 50 B4
Lovell Ho E8 . . . . . . 24 C4
Lovell Pl SE16 . . . . . 41 A3
Loveridge Mews
NW6 . . . . 10 B2
Loveridge Rd NW6 . 10 B2
Lover's Wlk W1 . . . 117 B1
Lovette Ho 3 E3 . . 26 C2
Lovetts Pl SW18 . . 59 A3
Love Wlk SE5 . . . . . 48 C1
Low Cross Wood La
SE21 . . . . 76 B1
Lowden Rd SE24 . . 63 B3
Lowder Ho 6 E1 . . . 32 A1
Lowe Ave E16 . . . . . 35 C4
Lowell St E14 . . . . . 33 A3
Lower Addison Gdns
W14 . . . . 126 A3
Lower Belgrave St
SW1 . . . . 132 A1
LOWER CLAPTON . 17 B4
Lower Clapton Rd
E5 . . . . 17 B4
Lower Clarendon Wlk
9 W11 . . . . 31 A3
Lower Comm S
SW15 . . . . 57 A4
Lower Grosvenor Pl
SW1 . . . . 132 B2

Lower Grove Rd
TW10 . . . . 54 B2
LOWER
HOLLOWAY 14 A3
Lower James St
W1 . . . . 119 A4
Lower John St
W1 . . . . 119 A4
Lower Lea Crossing
E14, E16 . . . . 35 A2
Lower Mall W6 . . . . 39 A1
Lower Marsh SE1 . 135 B3
Lower Merton Rise
NW3 . . . . 12 A1
Lower Mortlake Rd
TW9 . . . . 54 B4
Lower Pk
Acton W3 . . . . 20 B1
5 Putney SW15 . . . . 57 C2
LOWER PLACE . . . 20 B3
Lower Place Bsns Ctr
NW10 . . . . 20 B3
Lower Rd SE16 . . . . 40 B4
Lower Richmond Rd
Mortlake SW14,
TW9 . . . . 55 A4
Putney SW15 . . . . . . 57 B4
Lower Robert St
WC2 . . . . 120 B3
Lower Sloane St
SW1 . . . . 145 B2
Lower Terr NW3 . . . . 2 B1
Lower Thames St
EC3 . . . . 124 A3
Lowerwood Ct
W11 . . . . 31 A3
Loweswater Ho 8
E3 . . . . 26 B1
Lowfield Rd
Dagenham W3 . . . . . . 28 B3
Hampstead NW6 . . . . . 10 C1
Lowlands NW3 . . . . 12 A2
Lowman Rd N7 . . . . 14 B4
Lowndes Cl SW1 . 131 C1
Lowndes Ct
Knightsbridge
SW1 . . . . 131 A2
Marylebone W1 . . . . 104 C1
Lowndes Lo SW1 . 131 A2
Lowndes Pl SW1 . 131 B1
Lowndes Sq SW1 . 131 A3
Lowndes St SW1 . 131 B2
Lowood Ho 6 E1 . . 32 B2
Lowry Ct 5 SE16 . . 40 A1
Lowther Ho
Pimlico SW1 . . . . . . 147 A1
11 Shoreditch E8 . . 24 B4
Lower Prim Sch
SW13 . . . . 46 C4
Lowther Rd
Barnes SW13 . . . . . . 46 B2
Islington N7 . . . . 14 C3
Lowth Rd SE5 . . . . . 48 B1
Loxford Gardens 1
N5 . . . . 15 A4
Loxford Ho SW1 . . 145 C3
Loxham St WC1 . . . 94 B3
Loxley Rd SW18 . . 71 C3
Lubavitch Boys Prim
Sch 6 E5 . . . . 7 B4
Lubavitch House Sch
(Jun Boys) 9 E5 . . 7 B4
Lubavitch Senior
Girls' Sch 3 N16 . . 7 B4
Lubbock Ho 21
E14 . . . . 34 A2

Lubbock St SE14 . . 50 B3
Lucan Ho N1 . . . . . . 87 C3
Lucan Pl SW3 . . . . 144 B3
Lucas Ct SW11 . . . 169 C3
Lucas Ho
2 Clapham SW8 . . 171 A2
Walham Green
SW10 . . . . 156 B2
Lucas St SE4, SE8 . 51 C2
Lucas Vale Prim Sch
SE8 . . . . 51 C2
Lucerne Mews
W8 . . . . 31 C1 113 C2
Lucerne Rd N5 . . . . 15 A4
Lucey Rd SE16 . . . 139 B1
Lucey Way SE16 . . 153 C4
Lucien Rd SW18 . . 71 A2
Lucraft Ho 13 SW2 . 74 A4
Lucy Ashe Ho
SE17 . . . . 150 B3
Lucy Brown Ho
SE1 . . . . 123 A1
Lucy Cres W3 . . . . . 20 B1
Ludgate Broadway
EC4 . . . . 108 B1
Ludgate Cir EC4 . . 108 A1
Ludgate Hill EC4 . 108 B1
Ludgate Sq EC4 . . 108 B1
Ludham NW5 . . . . . . 12 C3
Ludlow Ct W3 . . . . . 37 B4
Ludlow St EC1 . . . . 96 C2
Ludovick Wlk
SW15 . . . . 56 A3
Ludwell Ho W14 . . 126 B2
Ludwick Mews
SE14 . . . . 51 A3
Lugard Ho 2 W12 . 30 A1
Lugard Rd SE15 . . 50 A2
Luke Ho 22 E1 . . . . 32 A3
Luke St EC2 . . 24 A1 98 A2
Lukin St E1 . . . . 32 B3
Lullingstone Ho 27
SE15 . . . . 50 B4
Lullingstone La
SE13 . . . . 67 C1
Lulot Gdns N19 . . . . 4 A2
Lulworth
Camden Town
NW1 . . . . 13 C2
Walworth SE17 . . . . 151 B2
Lulworth Ho SW8 . 162 C1
Lulworth Rd SE15 . 50 A1
Lumiere Ct 7
SW17 . . . . 72 C2
Lumina Bldg 1
E14 . . . . 34 B1 124 C1
Lumley Ct WC2 . . . 120 B3
Lumley Flats SW1 . 145 B2
Lumley St W1 . . . . 103 C1
Lumsdon NW8 . . . . 78 B3
Lunan Ho 14 E3 . . 26 B3
Lund Point E15 . . . . 27 B4
Luntley Pl E1 . . . . . 111 B3
Lupin Cl SW2 . . . . . 75 A2
Lupino Ct SE11 . . . 149 A4
Lupin Point SE1 . . 139 A3
Lupton St NW5 . . . . 13 B4
Lupus St SW1 . . . . 147 A1
Luralda Gdns E14 . . 42 C1
Lurgan Ave W6 . . . . 47 C4
Lurline Gdns
SW11 . . . . 169 C4
Luscombe Ho
SW18 . . . . 58 B2

Luscombe Way
SW8 . . . . 162 A2
Lusher Ho SW15 . . 57 C1
Lushington Rd
NW10 . . . . 22 A3
Lushington Terr 11
E8 . . . . 16 C3
Luton Pl SE10 . . . . . 52 B3
Luton St NW8 . . . . . 89 C1
Luttrell Ave SW15 . 57 A2
Lutyens Ho SW1 . . 146 C1
Luxborough Ho
W1 . . . . 103 B4
Luxborough St
W1 . . . . 103 B4
Luxborough Twr
W1 . . . . 103 B4
Luxemburg Gdns
W6 . . . . 39 C2
Luxford St SE16 . . 40 C2
Luxmore St SE14 . 51 B2
Luxor St SE5 . . . . . 63 B4
Lyall Mews SW1 . . 131 B1
Lyall Mews W
SW1 . . . . 131 B1
Lyall St SW1 . . . . . 131 B1
Lyal Rd E3 . . . . 26 A3
Lycée Français
Charles de Gaulle
SW7 . . . . 143 B4
Lycett Ho 10 SW2 . 74 A4
Lycett Pl 3 W12 . . 38 C4
Lycott Gr SE22 . . . . 64 B2
Lydden Gr SW18 . . 71 A4
Lydden Rd SW18 . . 71 A4
Lydford NW1 . . . . . . 83 A3
Lydford Cl 2 N16 . 16 A3
Lydford Rd
Brondesbury NW2 . . . 9 C2
Paddington W9 . . . . . 23 B1
Lydgate Ho 8
N16 . . . . 16 A3
Lydhurst Ave SW2 . 74 B2
Lydney Cl
Camberwell SE15 . . . 49 A3
Putney SW19 . . . . . . 70 A2
Lydon Rd SW4 . . . . 61 B4
Lydwell Ho 20
SW8 . . . . 171 B1
Lyford Rd SW18 . . 72 A3
Lygoe Ho 18 N6 . . 4 C4
Lygon Ho 2
E2 . . . . 24 C2 99 B4
Lygon Pl SW1 . . . . 132 A1
Lyham Cl SW2 . . . . 62 A1
Lyham Rd SW2 . . . . 62 A2
Lyle St W1 . . . . 119 B4
Lyly Ho SE1 . . . . . . 137 C1
Lyme Gr E9 . . . . 17 B1
Lyme Grove Ho 2
E9 . . . . 17 B1
Lyme St NW1 . . . . . 82 C4
Lymington Gdns SW17,
SW18 . . . . 72 A3
Lymington Mans
NW6 . . . . 11 A2
Lymington Rd
NW6 . . . . 11 A2
Lympstone Gdns
SE15 . . . . 49 C3
Lynbrook Gr SE15 . 49 A3
Lynch Wlk 2 SE8 . 51 B4
Lyncott Cres SW4 . 61 A3
Lyncourt SE3 . . . . . 52 C1
Lyncroft Gdns
NW6 . . . . 10 C3

Lyncroft Mans 🔢
NW6 . . . . .10 C3
Lyndale NW2 . . . . . . .1 B1
Lyndale Ave NW2 . . . .1 B1
Lyndale CI SE3 . . . . .53 B4
Lynde Ho 🔢 SW4 . . . .61 C4
Lynden Gate SW15 .69 A4
Lyndhurst Gdns
NW3 . . . . .11 C3
Lyndhurst Gr SE5,
SE15 . . . . .49 B1
Lyndhurst Ho 🔢
SW15 . . . . .68 C4
Lyndhurst House Prep
Sch NW3 . . . . .11 C3
Lyndhurst Lo 🔢
E14 . . . . .42 C2
Lyndhurst Rd NW3 .11 C3
Lyndhurst Sch
SE5 . . . . .48 C1
Lyndhurst Sq SE15 .49 B2
Lyndhurst Terr
NW3 . . . . .11 C3
Lyndhurst Way
SE15 . . . . .49 B1
Lyneham Wlk E5 . .18 A3
Lynette Ave SW4 . .61 B1
Lynford French Ho
SE17 . . . . .150 C2
Lyngham Ct 🔢 N4 . .5 A4
Lynhurst Ct NW8 . .79 B3
Lyn Mews 🔢 E3 . . .26 B2
Lynmouth Rd N16 . .7 B3
Lynne Ct NW6 . . . . .11 A1
Lynnett Ct E9 . . . . . .18 A2
Lynn Ho SE15 . . . . .49 C4
Lynton CI NW10 . . . .8 B3
Lynton Est SE1 . . . .153 B3
Lynton Ho 🔢 W2 .100 C2
Lynton Lo N5 . . . . . .15 A3
Lynton Mans SE1 . .135 B2
Lynton Rd
Acton W3 . . . . .28 A1
Bermondsey SE1 . .153 A3
Paddington NW6 . . . .23 B3
Lynton Terr 🔢 W3 .28 B3
Lynx Terr SW19 . . . .70 C1
Lyon Ho NW8 . . . . . .90 A1
Lyons PI NW8 . . . . . .89 B1
Lyon St N1 . . . . .14 B1
Lyons Wlk W14 . . .140 A4
Lyric Rd SW13 . . . .46 B2
Lysander Gr N19 . . . .4 C3
Lysander Ho 🔢
E2 . . . . .25 A3
Lysander Mews N19 .4 B3
Lysia Ct SW6 . . . . . .47 C3
Lysias Rd SW12 . . . .61 A1
Lysia St SW6 . . . . . .47 C3
Lysons Wlk SW15 . .56 C2
Lytham St SE17 . . .151 B1
Lyttelton CI NW3 . . .12 A1
Lytten Ct 🔢 W12 . .38 C4
Lyttleton Ho 🔢 E9 .17 B1
Lytton Ct WC1 . . . .106 B3
Lytton Gr SW15 . . . .58 A1

M

Mabel Thornton Ho 🔢
N16 . . . . .15 C4
Mabledon PI NW1,
WC1 . . . . .93 C3

Mablethorpe Rd
SW6 . . . . .154 A1
Mabley St E9 . . . . . .18 A3
MacArthur Ho 🔢
SW2 . . . . .74 A4
Macartney Ho
SE10 . . . . .52 C3
Macaulay CE Prim
Sch SW4 . . . . .61 A3
Macaulay Ct SW4 . .61 A4
Macaulay Ho 🔢
🔢 Kensal Town
W10 . . . . .31 A4
🔢 Stoke Newington
N16 . . . . .7 A1
Macaulay Rd SW4 . .61 A3
Macaulay Sq SW4 . .61 A3
McAuley CI SE1 . . .135 B2
Macaulay Mews
SE13 . . . . .52 B1
McAusland Ho 🔢
E3 . . . . .26 B3
Macbeth Ho 🔢 N1 .24 A3
Macbeth St W6 . . . .39 A1
McBride Ho 🔢 E3 . .26 B3
McCall CI SW4 . . . .172 A2
McCall Ho N7 . . . . . .14 A4
Mccarthy Ct
SW11 . . . . .168 B3
Macclesfield Rd
EC1 . . . . .96 C4
Macclesfield St
W1 . . . . .119 C4
McCoid Way SE1 . .136 C3
Mcconnell Ho
SW8 . . . . .171 B3
McCormick Ho 🔢
SW2 . . . . .74 C3
McCrone Mews 🔢
NW3 . . . . .11 C2
McCullum Rd E3 . .26 B4
McDermott CI
SW11 . . . . .60 A4
McDermott Rd
SW11 . . . . .169 B2
Macdonald Ho 🔢
SW11 . . . . .169 B2
Macdonald Rd N19 . .4 B2
McDougall Ct
TW9 . . . . .44 C1
Mcdougall Ho
E2 . . . . .24 C2
McDowall CI E16 . . .35 B4
McDowall Rd SE5 . .48 B2
Macduff Rd SW11 .169 C4
Mace CI E1 . . . . . . .32 A1
Mace St E2 . . . . .25 C3
McEwan Way E15 . .27 C4
Macey Ho
Battersea SW11 . . .168 A3
🔢 Greenwich SE10 .52 B4
Macfarlane Rd
W12 . . . . .30 B1
Macfarren Ho 🔢
W10 . . . . .23 A2
MacFarren PI NW1 .91 C1
McGlashon Ho 🔢
E1 . . . . .C1 99 B1
MacGregor Ho 🔢
SW12 . . . . .73 C3
McGregor Rd W11 .31 B4
Machell Rd SE15 . . .65 B4
McIndoe Ct N1 . . . . .87 B4

McIntosh Ho 🔢
SE16 . . . . .40 B2
McIntyre Ct 🔢
SW4 . . . . .172 B2
Mackay Ho 🔢
W12 . . . . .30 A2
Mackay Rd SW4 . . .61 A4
McKenna Ho 🔢
E3 . . . . .26 B3
Mackennal St NW8 .80 B2
Mackenzie CI 🔢
W12 . . . . .30 A2
Mackenzie Rd N7 . .14 B2
Mackenzie Wlk
E14 . . . . .33 C1
McKerrell Rd SE15 .49 C2
Mackeson Rd
NW3 . . . . .12 B4
Mackie Ho 🔢
SW2 . . . . .74 C4
McKiernan Ct 🔢
SW11 . . . . .168 A2
McKinnon Wood Ho
🔢 E2 . . . . . . .C2 99 C3
Mackintosh La E9 . .17 C3
Macklin St WC2 . .106 C2
Mackonochie Ho
EC1 . . . . .107 B4
Mackrow Wlk 🔢
E14 . . . . .34 B2
Macks Rd SE16 . . .153 C4
Mackworth Ho
NW1 . . . . .92 C4
Mackworth St
NW1 . . . . .92 C4
Mac Laren Mews
SW15 . . . . .57 B3
Maclean Rd SE23 . .66 A1
Mcleod Ct SE21 . . . .75 C2
McLeod's Mews
SW7 . . . . .142 B4
Macleod St SE17 . .151 A1
Maclise Rd W14 . .126 A1
McManus Ho 🔢
SW11 . . . . .59 C4
Mcmillan Ho SE4 . .66 A4
Macmillan Ho
Cricklewood NW6 . . .9 A4
Lisson Gr NW8 . . . .90 B3
McMillan St SE8 . . .51 C4
Mcmorran Ho 🔢
N7 . . . . .14 A4
Macnamara Ho
SW10 . . . . .157 B2
Mcneil Rd SE5 . . . .49 A1
McNicol Dr NW10 . .20 B3
Maconochies Rd 🔢
E14 . . . . .42 A1
Macquarie Way
E14 . . . . .42 A2
Macready Ho W1 . .102 B3
Macready PI 🔢
N7 . . . . .14 A4
Macroom Ho W9 . . .23 B2
Macroom Rd W9 . . .23 B2
Mac's PI EC4 . . . . .107 C2
Madame Tussauds
NW1 . . . . .91 B1
Madani Girls' Sch 🔢
E1 . . . . .32 A3
Maddams St E3 . . . .27 A1
Maddocks Ho 🔢
E1 . . . . .32 A2
Maddock Way
SE17 . . . . .48 A4

Maddox Rd SW1 . .118 B4
Madinah Rd
🔢 Dalston E8 . . . .16 C2
London E8 . . . . . . .16 C3
Madison Ho E3 . . . .27 B2
Madoc CI NW2 . . . . .1 C2
Madras PI N7 . . . . .14 C2
Madrid Rd SW13 . . .46 C3
Madron St SE17 . . .152 B2
Mafeking Ave
TW8 . . . . .44 A4
Magdala Ave N19 . . .4 B2
Magdalen CI 🔢
SE15 . . . . .50 A1
Magdalene Ho 🔢
SW15 . . . . .57 C1
Magdalen Pas E1 .125 A4
Magdalen Rd
SW18 . . . . .71 C3
Magdalen St SE1 . .124 A1
Magee St SE11 . . .163 B4
Magellan Ho 🔢
E1 . . . . .25 C1
Magellan PI 🔢
E14 . . . . .41 C2
Magnin CI 🔢 E8 . . .24 C4
Magnolia Ct
Richmond TW9 . . . .45 A2
Wandsworth SW11 . .60 B1
Magnolia Ho 🔢
SE8 . . . . .51 B4
Magnolia PI SW4 . .62 A2
Magnolia Rd W4 . . .45 A4
Magnolia Wharf
W4 . . . . .45 A4
Magpie Ho 🔢 E3 . .26 B4
Magpie PI SE14 . . . .51 A4
Magri Wlk 🔢 E1 . . .32 B4
Maguire St SE1 . . .139 A4
Mahatma Gandhi Ind
Est 🔢 SE24 . . . . . .63 A3
Mahogany CI SE16 .33 A1
Mahoney Ho SE14 . .51 B2
Maida Ave W2 . . . . .89 A1
MAIDA VALE 88 A4
Maida Vale W9 . . . .88 C3
Maida Vale Sta
W9 . . . . .88 B4
Maiden La
Borough The SE1 . .123 A2
Camden Town NW1 . .13 C1
Strand WC2 . . . . . .120 B4
Maidenstone Hill
SE10 . . . . .52 B2
Maidstone Bldgs
SE1 . . . . .123 B1
Maidstone Ho 🔢
E14 . . . . .34 A3
Mail Coach Yd 🔢
E2 . . . . .24 A2 98 B4
Main Yd E9 . . . . . . .18 C2
Maismore St SE15 . .49 C4
Maitland CI 🔢
SE10 . . . . .52 A3
Maitland Ct W2 . . .115 B4
Maitland Ho
Chelsea SW1 . . . .160 C4
🔢 South Hackney
E2 . . . . .25 B3
MAITLAND PARK . . .12 B2
Maitland Park Rd
NW3 . . . . .12 B2
Maitland Park Villas
NW3 . . . . .12 B2
Maitland PI E5 . . . . .17 B4
Majestic Ct N4 . . . . .6 A3

Major CI SW9 . . . . .63 A4
Majorie Mews 🔢
E1 . . . . .32 C3
Major Rd E15 . . . . .19 C3
Makepeace Ave N6 . .3 C2
Makepeace Mans
N6 . . . . .3 C2
Makins St SW3 . . .144 B3
Malabar Ct 🔢
W12 . . . . .30 A2
Malabar St E14 . . . .41 C4
Malam Ct SE11 . . .149 B3
Malam Gdns 🔢
E14 . . . . .34 A2
Malay Ho 🔢 E1 . . .32 B1
Malbrook Rd
SW15 . . . . .57 A3
Malcolm Ho 🔢 N1 .24 A3
Malcolm PI E2 . . . . .25 B1
Malcolm Rd E1 . . . .25 B1
Malcolmson Ho
SW1 . . . . .147 C1
Malden Cres NW1 . .12 C2
Malden PI NW5 . . . .12 C3
Malden Rd NW5 . . . .12 C2
Maldon CI
Camberwell SE5 . . .64 A4
Shoreditch N1 . . . . .87 A4
Stratford New Town
E15 . . . . .19 C3
Maldon Rd W3 . . . . .28 B2
Malet PI WC1 . . . . . .93 B1
Malet St WC1 . . . .105 C4
Maley Ave SE27 . . . .75 A2
Malfort Rd SE5 . . . .64 A4
Malins Ct SW12 . . . .60 C1
Mallams Mews 🔢
SW9 . . . . .63 A4
Mallard CI
🔢 Hackney E9 . . . .18 B2
Kilburn NW6 . . . . . .23 C4
Mallard Ho
🔢 Camberwell
SE15 . . . . .49 B2
St John's Wood
NW8 . . . . .80 A1
Mallard Point 🔢
E3 . . . . .26 C2
Mallet Ho 🔢
SW15 . . . . .56 C2
Mallet Rd SE13 . . . .67 C1
Mall Galleries
SW1 . . . . .119 C2
Malling SE13 . . . . . .67 A2
Mallinson Rd
SW11 . . . . .60 B2
Mallinson Sp Ctr
N6 . . . . .3 B4
Mallon Gdns E1 . . .111 A3
Mallord St SW3 . . .157 C4
Mallory Bldgs EC1 . .96 A1
Mallory CI SE4 . . . .66 A3
Mallory St NW8 . . . .90 B2
Mallow Ct SE13 . . . .52 B1
Mallow St EC1 . . . . .97 B2
Mall Rd W6 . . . . . . .39 A1
Mall Studios 🔢
NW3 . . . . .12 B3
Mall The
Mortlake SW14 . . . .55 B2
St James SW1 . . . .119 B1
Malmesbury 🔢
E2 . . . . .26 B2
Malmesbury Prim Sch
🔢 E3 . . . . .26 B2

Malmesbury Rd
Bow E3 .... 26 B3
Newham E16 .... 35 A4
Malmesbury Terr
E16 .... 35 B4
Malmsey Ho SE11 149 A2
Malmsmead Ho
E9 .... 18 A3
Malorees Jun & Inf
Schs NW6 .... 9 C1
Malpas Rd
Hackney E8 .... 17 A2
New Cross SE4 ...... 51 B1
Malta St EC1 .... 96 B2
Maltby St Mkt
SE1 .... 138 C3
Maltby St SE1 ... 138 C3
Malthouse Dr W4 .. 46 B4
Malthouse Pas
SW13 .... 46 A1
Malting Ho E14 .... 33 B2
Maltings W4 .... 36 C1
Maltings Cl SW13 .. 46 A1
Maltings Lo W4 .... 46 A1
Maltings Pl
Bermondsey SE1 .. 138 B4
Parsons Green
SW6 .... 166 B3
Malt Mill SE1 .... 124 C1
Malton Mews [1]
W10 .... 31 A3
Malton Rd W10 .... 31 A3
Maltravers St
WC2 .... 121 B4
Malt St SE1 .... 49 C4
Malva Cl SW18 .... 59 A2
Malvern Cl W10 .. 31 B4
Malvern Ct
[15] Shepherd's Bush
W12 .... 38 C4
South Kensington
SW7 .... 143 C4
Malvern Gdns NW2 ..1 A2
Malvern Ho
London N16 .... 7 B3
SE17 .... 151 A1
Malvern Mews
NW6 .... 23 C2
Malvern Pl NW6 .. 23 B2
Malvern Rd
Dalston E8 .... 16 C1
Maida Vale NW6 .... 23 C2
Upper Holloway N19 .. 4 C3
Malvern Terr N1 ... 85 B4
Malwood Rd SW12 .61 A1
Malyons Rd SE13 ..67 A2
Malyons Terr SE13 .67 A2
Managers St [8]
E14 .... 34 B1
Manaton Cl SE15 .. 65 A4
Manbre Rd W6 .... 47 B4
Manchester Dr
W10 .... 23 A1
Manchester Gr
E14 .... 42 B1
Manchester Mans
N19 .... 4 C4
Manchester Mews
W1 .... 103 B3
Manchester Rd
E14 .... 42 B3

Manchester Sq
W1 .... 103 C2
Manchester St
W1 .... 103 B3
Manchuria Rd
SW11 .... 60 C1
Manciple St SE1 .. 137 C2
Mandalay Ho [6]
N16 .... 15 C4
Mandalay Rd SW4 .61 B2
Mandarin Ct [6]
SE8 .... 51 C4
Mandela Cl [36]
W12 .... 30 A2
Mandela Ho [18]
E2 .... 24 B2 98 C4
Mandela Rd E16 ... 35 C3
Mandela St
Camden Town
NW1 .... 83 A4
Kennington SW9 .. 163 B1
Mandela Way SE1 152 B4
Mander Portman
Woodward Sch
SW7 .... 143 B3
Manderville Ho
SE1 .... 153 A2
Mandeville Cl [5]
SE3 .... 53 B3
Mandeville Ct
NW3 .... 11 A3
Mandeville Ctyd
SW11 .... 169 B3
Mandeville Ho [6]
SW4 .... 61 B2
Mandeville Pl W1 103 C2
Mandrake Rd
SW17 .... 72 B1
Mandrell Rd SW2 ..62 A2
Manette St W1 ... 105 C1
Manfred Ct [7]
SW15 .... 58 A2
Manfred Rd SW15 .58 B2
Manger Rd N7 .... 14 A2
Manilla St E14 .... 41 C4
Manilla Wk SE10 ..43 A2
Manitoba Ct [29]
SE16 .... 40 B4
Manley Ct N16 ...... 7 B1
Manley Ho SE11 .. 149 B2
Manley St NW1 .... 81 B4
Manneby Prior N1 .. 85 A1
Mannering Ho [16]
SW2 .... 62 B2
Manning Ho [3]
W11 .... 31 A3
Manning Pl TW10 ..54 B1
Manningtree Cl
SW19 .... 70 A3
Manningtree St [2]
E1 .... 111 B2
Manny Shinwell Ho
SW6 .... 155 A3
Manor Ave SE4 .... 51 B1
Manor Circus TW9 .54 C4
Manor Ct
[7] Brixton SW2 ...... 62 B2
Camberwell SE15 .. 49 B3
Gunnersbury W3 .. 36 C2
Parsons Green
SW6 .... 166 B3
Streatham SW16 ....74 A1
Manorfield Cl [3]
N19 .... 13 B4

Manorfield Prim Sch
[6] E14 .... 34 A4
Manor Gdns
[8] Chiswick W4 .... 38 A1
Clapham SW4 ...... 171 A1
Gunnersbury W3 .. 36 C2
Richmond TW10,
TW9 .... 54 B3
Upper Holloway N7 .. 5 A1
Manor Gr
Deptford SE15 ...... 50 B4
Richmond TW9 ..... 54 C4
SW15 .... 58 A2
Manor Ho NW1 ... 102 A4
Manor House Ct
W9 .... 88 C1
Manor House Dr
NW6 .... 9 B1
Manor House Sta
N4 .... 6 A4
Manor Lo NW2 ...... 9 C2
Manor Mans
[7] Hampstead
NW3 .... 12 A2
Tufnell Pk N7 .... 5 A1
Manor Mews
New Cross SE4 ...... 51 B1
Paddington NW6 .. 23 C3
Manor Oak Mans
SE22 .... 65 A1
Manor Par N16 ...... 7 B2
Manor Park Par
SE13 .... 67 C3
Manor Park Rd
NW10 .... 21 B4
Manor Pk TW9 ..... 54 B3
Manor Pl SE17 ... 150 C2
Manor Rd
Richmond TW10,
TW9 .... 54 B3
Stamford Hill N16 ....7 A3
Manor Sch
Brondesbury
NW6 .... 10 A1
Willesden NW10 ... 22 B4
Manor Street Est
SW3 .... 158 B4
Manor The W1 ... 118 A3
Manor Way W3 .... 36 C2
Manresa Rd SW3 144 A1
Mansel Ct SW11 .. 168 B3
Mansell Ho SW8 .. 171 A4
Mansell Rd W3 .... 37 C4
Mansell St E1 ..... 111 A1
Manse Rd N16 ...... 7 B1
Mansfield Ct [27]
E2 .... 24 B4
Mansfield Ho
SW15 .... 57 C1
Mansfield Mews
W1 .... 104 A3
Mansfield Pl [28]
NW3 .... 11 B4
Mansfield Rd
Acton W3 .... 20 A1
Maitland Pk NW3 .. 12 B4
Mansfield St W1 .. 104 A3
Mansford St E2 .... 24 C3
Mansion Cl SW9 .. 173 C4
Mansion Gdns NW3 ..2 A1
Mansion House EC4 109 B1
Mansion House Pl EC3,
EC4 .... 109 B1
Mansion House St
EC2 .... 109 B1

Mansion House Sta
EC4 .... 123 A4
Mansions The
NW6 .... 10 B3
Manson Mews
SW7 .... 143 B3
Manson Pl SW7 .. 143 B3
Manston Ho W14 .. 126 B1
Manstone Rd NW2 ..10 A3
Manston NW1 ...... 13 B1
Manthorp Rd SE18 .83 A1
Mantle Rd SE4 .... 66 A4
Manton Ho N16 ..... 6 C1
Mantua St [22]
SW11 .... 59 C4
Mantus Cl E1 ...... 25 B1
Mantus Rd E1 ..... 25 B1
Manville Gdns
SW17 .... 73 A1
Manville Rd SW17 .73 A1
Manwood Rd SE4 .. 66 B1
Many Gates SW12 .73 A2
Mapesbury Ct
NW2 .... 10 A3
Mapesbury Rd
NW2 .... 10 A2
Mapeshill Pl NW2 ...9 B2
Mapes Ho [7] NW6 .10 A1
Mape St E2 .... 25 A1
Maple Ave W3 .... 29 A1
Maple Cl SW4 ..... 61 C1
Maple Ct [3] NW2 ...9 C4
Mapledene Est E8 .16 C1
Mapledene Rd E8 .16 C1
Maple Ho
[11] Maitland Pk
NW3 .... 12 B2
[5] New Cross SE8 ...51 B3
[4] Richmond TW9 .. 45 A2
Maple Leaf Sq [20]
SE16 .... 40 C4
Maple Lo SW15 ... 58 A1
Maple Mews NW6 .78 A2
Maple Pl W1 .... 93 A1
Maples Pl E1 ...... 32 A4
Maple St
[2] Bethnal Green
E2 .... 25 A3
Fitzrovia W1 .... 93 A1
Maplestead Rd
SW2 .... 74 B4
Mapleton Cres
SW18 .... 59 A1
Mapleton Rd
SW18 .... 59 A1
Maple Wlk W10 ... 22 C1
Maplin St E3 .... 26 B2
Marada Ho NW6 ... 10 A1
Marais W4 .... 45 B3
Marathon Science
Sch of Excellence [2]
SE8 .... 41 A2
Marban Rd W9 .... 23 B2
Marble Arch W1 .. 117 A4
Marble Arch Sta
W1 .... 103 A1
Marble Cl W3 ..... 28 A1
Marbleford Ct [4]
N6 .... 4 C4
Marble Ho W9 .... 23 B1
Marcella Rd SW9 . 173 B1
Marchant Ho [13]
SW2 .... 62 B2
Marchant St SE14 .51 A4

Marchbank Rd
W14 .... 155 A4
March Ct SW15 .... 57 A3
Marchmont Rd
TW10 .... 54 B2
Marchmont St
WC1 .... 94 A2
Marchwood Cl [9]
SE5 .... 49 A3
Marcia Rd SE1 ... 152 B3
Marcilly Rd SW18 .59 C2
Marcol Ho W1 ..... 104 A2
Marcon Ct [8] E8 .. 17 A3
Marcon Pl E8 ...... 17 A3
Marco Rd W6 ...... 39 B3
Marcus Ct TW8 .... 44 A3
Marcus Garvey Mews
SE22 .... 65 A2
Marcus Garvey Way
[8] SE24 .... 62 C3
Marcus Ho [4]
SE15 .... 49 B2
Marcus St SW18 ... 59 A1
Marcus Terr SW18 .59 A1
Marden Ho [8] E8 .. 17 A3
Marden Sq SE16 ... 40 A3
Mardyke Ho SE17 151 C4
Maresfield Gdns
NW3 .... 11 B2
Mare St E8 .... 17 A1
Margaret Bondfield
Ho
[6] Bow E3 .... 26 A3
[22] Kentish Town
N7 .... 13 C3
Margaret Ct W1 .. 104 C2
Margaret Herbison Ho
SW6 .... 155 A3
Margaret Ho [6]
W6 .... 39 B1
Margaret Ingram Cl
SW6 .... 154 C3
Margaret Mcmillan
Ho [10] N19 .... 4 C4
Margaret Rd N16 ...7 B3
Margaret Rutherford
Pl [3] SW12 .... 73 B3
Margaret St W1 .. 104 C2
Margaretta Terr
SW3 .... 158 B4
Margaret White Ho
NW1 .... 93 B4
Margate Rd SW2 .. 62 A2
Margery Fry Ct N7 ..5 A1
Margery St WC1 ... 95 B3
Margravine Gdns
Hammersmith W6 ...39 C1
West Kensington
W14 .... 140 A2
Margravine Rd
W6 .... 154 A4
Marham Gdns SW17,
SW18 .... 72 A3
Maria Cl [13] SE1 . 153 C4
Maria Fidelis Catholic
Sch (Lower)
NW1 .... 93 B4
Maria Fidelis Catholic
Sch (Upper) NW1 .93 B4
Maria Montessori Sch
[6] NW3 .... 11 B2
Marian Ct E9 ...... 17 B3
Marian Pl E2 ...... 25 A3
Marian Sq E2 ..... 25 A3
Marian St [2] E2 .. 25 A3
Marian Way NW10 .8 B1

Maria Terr E1 . . . . . . 25 C1
Maribor 15 SE10 . . . 52 B3
Marie Curie SE1. . . . . 49 A2
Marie Lloyd Ct 13
  SW9 . . . . 62 B3
  N19 . . . . 5 A4
Marie Lloyd Gdns 1
  N19 . . . . 5 A4
Marie Stopes Ct 3
  N19 . . . . 5 A4
Marigold St SE16 . . . 40 A4
Marina Ct 12 E3 . . . 26 C2
Marina Point 4
  E14 . . . . 42 A3
Marinefield Rd
  SW6 . . . . 166 B2
Marinel Ho 22 SE5. . 48 B3
Mariners Mews
  E14 . . . . 42 C2
Marine St SE16 . . . 139 B2
Marine Twr 20
  SE8 . . . . 51 B4
Marion Richardson
  Prim Sch 17 E1. . . 32 C3
Marischal Rd SE13 . 67 C4
Maritime Ho 5
  SW4 . . . . 61 C4
Maritime Quay 5
  E14 . . . . 41 C1
Maritime St E3 . . . . 26 B1
Marius Mans 3
  SW17 . . . . 72 C2
Marius Rd SW17 . . . 72 C2
Marjorie Gr SW11 . . 60 B3
Market Ct W1 . . . . . 104 C2
Market La W12 . . . . . 39 B4
Market Mews W1 . . 118 A1
Market PI
  3 Acton W3 . . . . . . 28 B1
  1 Bermondsey
  SE16 . . . . 40 A2
  Marylebone W1 . . . 104 C2
Market Rd
  Barnsbury N7 . . . . . 14 A2
  Richmond TW9 . . . . 54 C4
Market Sq E14 . . . . . 34 A3
Market St E1. . . . . . 110 C4
Market Studios 14
  W12 . . . . 39 B4
Market Way E14 . . . . 34 A3
Market Yd Mews
  SE1. . . . . 138 A2
Markham PI SW3 . . 144 C2
Markham Sq SW3 . . 144 C2
Markham St SW3 . . 144 B2
Mark Ho 33 E2 . . . . . 25 C3
Mark La EC3 . . . . . . 124 B4
Markland Ho W10 . . 30 C2
Mark Mans W12. . . . 38 C4
Marksbury Ave
  TW9 . . . . 54 C4
Mark Sq EC2. 24 A1 98 A2
Mark St EC2.24 A1 98 A2
Markstone Ho
  SE1. . . . . 136 A3
Markyate Ho 6
  W10 . . . . 22 B1
Marland Ho SW1 . . 131 A2
Marlborough
  1 Putney SW15 . . . .57 C2
  St John's Wood W9 . 88 C4
Marlborough Ave 3
  E8 . . . . 24 C4
Marlborough CI
  SE17 . . . . 150 B3

Marlborough Cres
  W4 . . . . 38 A3
Marlborough Ct
  Kensington W8. . . . 141 B4
  Marylebone W1 . . . 104 C1
Marlborough Flats
  SW3 . . . . 144 B4
Marlborough Gr
  SE1. . . . . 153 B1
Marlborough Hill
  NW8 . . . . 79 A3
Marlborough Ho
  Marylebone NW1. . . 92 B2
  Richmond TW10 . . . 54 C2
  Stoke Newington N4 . 6 B3
Marlborough House
  SW1 . . . . 119 A1
Marlborough Mans 5
  NW6 . . . . 10 C3
Marlborough Mews 3
  SW2 . . . . 62 B3
Marlborough PI
  NW8 . . . . 79 A2
Marlborough Prim
  Sch SW3 . . . . 144 B3
Marlborough Rd
  Acton Green W4. . . . 37 B1
  Richmond TW10 . . . 54 B1
  St James SW1 . . . . 119 A1
  Upper Holloway N19 . 4 C2
Marlborough St
  SW3 . . . . 144 B3
Marlborough Trad Est
  TW9 . . . . 45 A2
Marlborough Yd
  N19 . . . . 4 C2
Marley Ho 14 W11. . 30 C2
Marley Wlk NW2 . . . . 9 B3
Marloes Rd W8 . . . 128 A1
Marlow Ct NW6 . . . . 9 C1
Marlowe Bsns Ctr 2
  SE14 . . . . 51 A3
Marlowe Ct SW3 . . 144 B3
Marlowe Ho 15
  N16 . . . . 16 A4
Marlowes The
  NW8 . . . . 79 B4
Marlow Ho
  Bermondsey SE1 . . 138 C2
  15 Kensington W2 . 100 B1
  44 Spitalfields
  E2 . . . . 24 B2 98 C3
Marlow Studio
  Workshops 13
  E2 . . . . 24 B2 98 C3
Marlow Way SE16 . . 40 C4
Marl Rd SW18 . . . . . 59 B3
Marlton St SE10 . . . 43 B1
Marmion Ho 3
  SW12 . . . . 73 A4
Marmion Mews 4
  SW11 . . . . 60 C4
Marmion Rd SW11. . 60 C3
Marmont Rd SE15 . . 49 C3
Marmora Ho E1 . . . 33 A4

Marmora Rd SE22 . . 65 B1
Marner Prim Sch 6
  E3 . . . . 27 A1
Marne St W10. . . . . . 23 A2
Marney Rd SW11 . . . 60 C3
Marnfield Cres
  SW2 . . . . 74 B3
Marnham Ave
  NW2. . . . . 10 A4
Marnock Ho SE17 . 151 B2
Marnock Rd SE4. . . . 66 B2
Maroon St E14 . . . . . 33 A4
Marquess Rd N1 . . . 15 C2
Marquess Rd S
  N1 . . . . 5 B3
Marquis Rd
  Finsbury Pk N4. . . . . 5 C4
  Kentish Town NW1 . 13 C2
Marrick CI SW15 . . . 56 C3
Marrick Ho 10
  NW6 . . . . 78 B3
Marriott Rd N4 . . . . . 5 B3
Marryat Ct 12 W6. . . 39 A2
Marryat Ho SW1 . . 146 C1
Marryat Sq SW6 . . 164 A4
Marsala Rd SE13 . . . 67 A3
Marsalis Ho 3 E3 . . 26 C2
Marsden Rd SE15. . . 64 B4
Marsden St NW5 . . . 12 C2
Marshall Ct SW18 . . 59 B1
Marshall Ct SW4 . . 172 B3
Marshall Ho
  Paddington NW6 . . 23 B3
  Shoreditch N1. . . . . 87 C2
  Walworth SE17. . . . 151 B2
Marshall Rd E10. . . . 19 A4
Marshall St W1 . . . 105 A1
Marshall's PI
  SE16 . . . . 139 A1
Marshalsea Rd
  SE1. . . . . 137 A4
Marsham Ct
  18 Putney SW15 . . . 69 C3
  Westminster SW1 . 147 C4
Marsham St SW1 . . 147 C4
Marsh Ct E8 . . . . . . 16 C2
Marshfield St E14 . . 42 B3
Marshgate Bsns Ctr
  E15 . . . . 27 B3
Marshgate Primary
  Sch TW10 . . . . 54 B2
Marsh Hill E9 . . . . . 18 A3
Marsh St E14 . . . . . . 42 A2
Marsh Wall E14 . . . . 42 A4
Marshwood Ho 10
  NW6 . . . . 23 C4
Marsland CI SE17. . 150 B1
Marsom Ho N1 . . . . 87 B1
Marston SE17 . . . . . 151 A4
Marston CI NW6. . . . 11 B1
Marsworth Ho 8
  E2 . . . . 24 C4
Martaban Rd N16. . . 7 B2
Martello St E8. . . . . 17 A1
Martello Terr E8 . . . 17 A1
Martel PI E8 . . . . . . 16 B2
Martha's Bldgs
  EC1. . . . . 97 B2
Martha St E1 . . . . . 32 B3

Martin Ct 15 E14 . . . 42 B4
Martindale SW14. . . 55 B2
Martindale Ave 2
  E16 . . . . 35 C2
Martindale Ho 23
  E14 . . . . 34 A2
Martindale Rd
  SW12 . . . . 73 A4
Martineau Ho
  SW1 . . . . 146 C1
Martineau Mews
  N5 . . . . 15 A4
Martineau Rd N5 . . . 15 A4
Martin Ho
  Newington SE1 . . . 137 A1
  South Lambeth
  SW8 . . . . 162 A2
Martin La EC4 . . . . 123 C4
Martlett Ct WC2 . . 106 B1
Martlett Lo NW3 . . . 11 A4
Martley Ho SW8 . . 171 A4
Martock Ct 10
  SE15 . . . . 50 A2
Marton Rd 2 N16 . . . 7 A1
Marvel Ho 5 SE5 . . 48 C3
Marville Rd SW6 . . 154 C1
Marvin St 8 E8 . . . . 17 A2
Marwell Ct SE3 . . . . 52 C1
Mary Adelaide CI
  SW15 . . . . 68 A1
Mary Adelaide Ho
  W2 . . . . 101 C4
Mary Ann Bldgs
  SE8 . . . . 51 C4
Mary Datchelor CI
  SE5 . . . . 48 C2
Mary Dine Ct
  SW8 . . . . 163 A1
Mary Gn NW8 . . . . . 78 B4
Mary Ho
  6 Stockwell SW9 . 172 C1
Mary James Ho 32
  E2 . . . . 24 C3
Mary Jones Ho 20
  E14 . . . . 33 C2
Maryland Rd
  Paddington W9. . . . 23 C1
  Stratford New Town
  E15 . . . . 19 C3
Marylands Rd W9 . . 23 C1
Maryland Wlk N1. . . 86 C4
Mary Lawrenson PI 1
  SE3 . . . . 53 C3
MARYLEBONE 104 B2
Marylebone Flyover
  NW1 . . . . 102 A3
Marylebone High St
  W1 . . . . 103 C4
Marylebone La
  W1 . . . . 103 C2
Marylebone Mews
  W1 . . . . 104 A3
Marylebone Pas
  W1 . . . . 105 A2
Marylebone Rd
  NW1 . . . . 103 C4
Marylebone St
  W1 . . . . 103 C3
Marylebone Sta
  NW1 . . . . 90 C1
Marylee Way
  SE11 . . . . 149 A3
Mary McArthur Ho 12
  N19 . . . . 4 C4

Mary Macarthur Ho
  15 Globe Town
  E2 . . . . 25 C2
  W14 . . . . 154 A4
Maryon Mews
  NW3 . . . . 12 A4
Mary PI
  W11 . . . . 31 A2 112 A3
Mary's Ct NW8 . . . . 90 B2
Mary Secole Ct 21
  E8 . . . . 24 B4
Mary Smith Ct
  SW5 . . . . 141 C3
Mary St
  8 Canning Town
  E16 . . . . 35 B4
  Shoreditch N1. . . . . 87 A3
Mary Terr NW1 . . . . 82 C3
Mary Wharrie Ho 3
  NW3 . . . . 12 B1
Masbro' Rd W14 . . . 39 C3
Mascotte Rd 2
  SW15 . . . . 57 C3
Masefield Ct N5 . . . 15 C3
Masefield Ho 4
  NW6 . . . . 23 C2
Mashie Rd W3. . . . . 29 A3
Maskall CI SW2. . . . 74 C3
Maskell Rd SW17. . . 71 B1
Maskelyne CI
  SW11 . . . . 168 B4
Mason CI
  Bermondsey
  SE16 . . . . 153 C2
  Newham E16 . . . . . 35 C2
Mason Ho
  15 Bermondsey
  SE1. . . . . 153 C3
  16 Hackney E9. . . . 17 B1
Mason's Arms Mews
  W1 . . . . 118 B4
Mason's Ave EC2 . 109 B2
Mason's PI EC1. . . . 96 C4
Mason's Yd
  Finsbury EC1 . . . . . 96 B4
  St James SW1 . . . . 119 A2
Massie Rd E8 . . . . . 16 C2
Massinger St SE1,
  SE17 . . . . 152 A3
Massingham St E1 . 25 C1
Mast Ct 17 SE16 . . . 41 A2
Masterman Ho 5
  SE5 . . . . 48 C3
Masters Dr SE16 . . . 40 A1
Masters Lo 24 E1. . . 32 B3
Master's St 18 E1 . . 32 C4
Mast House Terr
  E14 . . . . 41 C2
Masthouse Terrace
  Pier SE8 . . . . 41 C1
Mastin Ho SW18. . . 70 C3
Mast L Ctr The
  SE16 . . . . 40 C2
Mastmaker Rd
  E14 . . . . 41 C4
Matara Mews
  SE17 . . . . 150 C1
Matching Ct 13 E3. . 26 C2
Matham Sq SE22 . . 64 B3
Matheson Lang Ho
  SE1. . . . . 135 B3
Matheson Rd
  W14 . . . . 140 C3

Mathews Yd WC2 ....106 A1
Mathieson Ct SE1 136 B3
Mathison Ho
SW10 ....156 C2
Matilda Gdns 🔟
E3 ....26 A3
Matilda Ho E1....125 B2
Matilda St N1......85 A4
Matlock Ct SE24....63 B3
Matlock Ct
❼ Herne Hill SE5....63 C3
St John's Wood
NW8 ....78 C2
Matlock St E14 ....33 A3
Maton Ho SW6 ...154 C2
Matrix Ind Pk
NW10 ....20 A2
Matson Ho
9 Bermondsey
SE16 ....40 A3
🔟 Homerton E9....17 B2
Matthew Cl W10....22 C1
Matthew Parker St
SW1 ....133 C3
Matthews Ct N5....15 B4
Matthews Ho 3
E14 ....33 C4
Matthews St
SW11 ....168 C2
Matthias Ct 🔢
TW10 ....54 A1
Matthias Ho 2
N16 ....16 A3
Matthias Rd N16 ..16 A3
Mattingly Way 🔟
SE15 ....49 B3
Maude Ho 🔢 2....24 A3
Maude Rd SE5......49 A2
Maudlins Gn E1 ...125 B2
Maudsley Ho TW8 ..36 A1
Maudsley Hospl
SE5 ....48 C1
Maud St E16 ....35 C2
Maud Wilkes Cl 🔟
NW5 ....13 B3
Maugham Ct 5
W3 ....37 B3
Maugham Wy 🔢
W3 ....37 B3
Mauleverer Rd
SW2 ....62 A2
Maundeby Wlk
NW10 ....8 A2
Maunsel St SW1..147 B4
Maurer Ct 2 SE10..43 B3
Mauretania Bldg 🔟
E1 ....32 C2
Maurice Ct 🔢 E1..26 A2
Maurice Ho 🔟
SW9 ....172 C2
Maurice St W12....30 A3
Mauritius Rd SE10..43 A2
Maury Rd N16......7 C1
Maverton Rd E3....26 C4
Mavor Ho N1......85 A3
Mawbey Ho SE1...153 A1
Mawbey Pl SE1....153 A1
Mawbey Rd SE1...153 A1
Mawbey St SW8...162 A1
Mawdley Ho SE1..135 C3
Mawson Ct N1......87 C3
Mawson Ho EC1..107 B4
Mawson La W4......46 B4
Maxden Ct SE15....64 C4

Maxted Rd SE15....64 B4
Maxwell Ct SE21...76 C3
Maxwell Rd SW6..156 B1
Maya Cl SE15........50 A1
Mayall Rd SE24....63 A2
Maybury Ct W1....103 C3
Maybury Gdns
NW10 ....9 A2
Maybury Mews N6..4 B4
Maydew Ho SE16..40 B2
Maydwell Ho 6
E14 ....33 C4
MAYFAIR 118 A3
Mayfair Pl W1....118 B2
Mayfield Ave W4....38 A2
Mayfield Cl
Clapham Pk SW4..61 C2
Dalston E8 ....16 B2
Mayfield Ho
🔟 Bethnal Green
E2 ....25 A3
Stamford Hill N16....7 A4
Mayfield Mans
SW15 ....58 B2
Mayfield Rd
Acton W3 ....28 A2
Bedford Pk W12....38 A4
Dalston E8 ....16 B1
Mayflower Cl SE16..40 C2
Mayflower Prim Sch
22 E14 ....34 A3
Mayflower Rd
SW9 ....62 A4
Mayflower St 🔟
SE16 ....40 B4
Mayford NW1......83 A2
Mayford Cl SW12 ..72 B4
Mayford Rd SW12 ..72 C4
Maygood Ho N1....85 B2
Maygood St N1....85 B2
Maygrove Rd NW6..10 B2
Mayhew Ct 2 SE5..63 C3
Maylands Ho
SW3 ....144 B3
Maylie Ho 4 SE16..40 A4
Maynard Ct 4....156 B1
Maynard Ho E1....26 A2
Maynards Quay E1 .32 B2
Mayne Ct E8 ....16 C4
Mayo Ho 🔟 E1......32 B4
Mayola Rd E5 ......17 B4
Mayo Rd NW10......8 A2
May's Buildings Mews
SE10 ....52 C3
Mays Ct WC2 ....120 A3
May's Ct SE10......52 C3
Maysoule Rd
SW11 ....59 C3
May St
Kensington W14..140 C1
W14 ....141 A1
Mayston Mews 3
SE10 ....43 C1
Maythorne Cotts
SE13 ....67 C1
Mayton St N7......5 B1
May Tree Ho SE4..66 B4
Maytree Wlk SW2 .74 C2
Mayward Ho 7
SE5 ....49 A2
Mazahirul Uloom
London 28 E15 ....25 C1
Maze Hill SE10,
SE3 ....53 A4
Maze Hill Lodge 7
SE10 ....52 C4

Maze Hill Sta
SE10 ....53 A4
Mazenod Ave
NW6 ....10 C1
Maze Ho N1........14 C2
Mead Cl 3 NW1....12 C1
Meadcroft Rd
SE17 ....48 A4
Hackney E5 ....16 A4
Meader Ct SE14....50 C3
Mead Ho
W11 ....31 B1
Mead Lo W4 ......37 C4
Meadowbank NW3 .12 B1
Meadow Bank 5
SW15 ....58 B2
Meadow Cl
🔟 E9 ....18 B3
Meadowcroft 8
W4 ....36 C1
Meadow Mews
SW8 ....162 C3
Meadow Pl
Chiswick W4 ......46 A3
South Lambeth
SW8 ....162 B2
Meadow Rd SW8 .162 C2
Meadow Row SE1 .136 C1
Meadows Wy SE4...66 A4
Mead Pl E9 ....17 B2
Mead Row SE1....135 B2
Meadway The SE3 .52 C1
Meakin Est SE1....138 A2
Meakin Ho N7......14 B3
Meard St W1........105 B1
Meath Cres E1, E2..25 C2
Meath Ho SE24....63 A1
Meath St SW11....170 A4
Mecklenburgh Pl
WC1 ....94 C2
Mecklenburgh Sq
WC1 ....94 C2
Mecklenburgh St
WC1 ....94 C2
Medburn St NW1..83 B2
Medcroft Gdns
SW14 ....55 B3
Medfield St SW15..69 A4
Medhurst Cl 🔢 E3..26 A3
Median Rd E5......17 B3
Medina Ct N7......5 C1
Medina Gr N7......5 C1
Medina Ho SE15...65 B3
Medina Rd N7......5 C1
Medlar St SE5......48 B2
Medley Rd NW6...10 C2
Medora Rd SW2...74 B4
Medresco Ho
NW3 ....11 C3
Medusa Rd SE6,
SE13 ....67 A1
Medway Bldgs E3..26 A3
Medway Ct WC1...94 A3
Medway Ho
Bermondsey SE1 .137 C3
Paddington NW8 .102 A4
Stoke Newington
N16 ....15 C4
Medway Mews 35
E3 ....26 A3
Medway Rd E3....26 A3
Medway St SW1...133 C1
Medwin St SW4....62 B3
Meecham Ct 1
SW11 ....168 A2

Meeson St E5 ......18 A4
Meeting House Alley
🔟 E1 ....32 A1
Meeting House La
SE15 ....50 A3
Mehetabel Rd E9...17 B3
Melba Way SE13...52 A2
Melbourne Ct
Hackney E5 ....18 A4
Paddington W9 ....89 A2
Melbourne Gr
SE22 ....64 B3
Melbourne Ho
W8 ....31 C1 113 B1
Melbourne Mews
SW9 ....173 B3
Melbourne Pl
WC2 ....107 A1
Melbourne Sq 9
SW9 ....173 B3
Melbray Mews 🔟
SW6 ....164 C1
Melbreak Ho 🔟
SE22 ....64 A4
Melbury Ct W8 ...127 A2
Melbury Dr SE5 ...49 A3
Melbury Ho SW8 .162 C2
Melbury Rd W14..127 A2
Melchester 6
W11 ....31 B3
Melchester Ho 🔟
N19 ....4 C1
Melcombe Ct
NW1 ....102 C4
Melcombe Ho
SW8 ....162 C1
Melcombe Pl
NW1 ....102 C4
Melcombe Prim Sch
6 W6 ....47 C4
Melcombe St NW1..91 A1
Meldon Cl SW6 ...166 B4
Melford Ct
Bermondsey SE1 ..138 B2
Dulwich SE22 ......76 C4
Melford Rd SE21,
SE22 ....76 C3
Melgund Rd N5 ...14 C3
Melina Ct
Putney SW15 ......56 C4
St John's Wood
NW8 ....89 B3
Melina Pl NW8 ...89 B3
Melina Rd W12....39 A4
Melior Pl SE1 .....138 A4
Melior St SE1 .....138 A4
Melisa Ct N6 ......4 C4
Mellington Ct 2
N16 ....7 C1
Mellis Ave TW9 ...45 A2
Mellish Ho 🔟 2....32 A3
Mellish St E14......41 C3
Mellitus St W12....29 B3
Mell St 5 SE10....43 A1
Melody La N5 ......15 B3
Melody Rd SW18..59 B2
Melon Pl W8 ......127 C4
Melon Rd SE15 ....49 C2
Melrose Ave
Cricklewood NW2...9 B3
Wimbledon SW19..70 C1
Melrose Cl SE12....73 A4
Melrose Gdns W6..39 B3
Melrose Ho
Maida Vale NW6...23 C2
Pimlico SW1 .....146 B2

Melrose Rd
🔟 Barnes SW13...46 B1
Wandsworth SW18 .58 B1
Melrose Terr W6....39 B3
Melton Ct SW7 ...143 C3
Melton Ho E5 ......7 C2
Melton St NW1....93 B3
Melville Court Flats 🔟
W12 ....39 A4
Melville Ct
🔟 4 Brentford W4..36 C1
Rotherhithe SE8 ...41 A2
Melville Ho SE10...52 B2
Melville Pl 4 N1...15 B1
Melville Rd SW13 .46 C2
Melville Villas Rd
W3 ....28 C1
Melvin Ct 🔟 TW9..44 C2
Melwood Ho 🔟
E1 ....32 A3
Melyn Cl N7 ....13 B4
Memel Ct EC1 .....96 C1
Memel St EC1 .....96 C1
Menai Pl 2 E3.....26 C3
Menard Ct EC1 ....97 A3
Mendez Wy 🔟
SW15 ....56 C1
Mendham Ho SE1 .138 A2
Mendip Ct
🔟 Battersea
SW11 ....59 B4
Deptford SE14 ....50 B4
Mendip Dr NW2,
NW11 ....1 A2
Mendip Ho 2 N4....6 C4
Mendip Hos 🔢 E2 .25 B2
Mendip Rd SW11..59 B4
Mendora Rd SW6 .154 C2
Mendip Rd NW2....9 C4
Menelik Rd NW2...10 A4
Menorah Prim Sch
🔟 NW11 ....1 A4
Menotti St 🔟
E2 ....24 C1 99 C2
Menteath Ho 9
E14 ....33 C3
Mentmore Terr E8 .17 A1
Mentone Ct SW8 .172 B4
Meon Rd W3 ......37 B4
Mepham St SE1...121 B1
Merbury Cl SE13...67 C2
Mercator Pl 4
E14 ....41 C1
Mercator Rd SE13..67 C3
Merceron Ho 🔟
E2 ....25 B2
Merceron St E1....25 A1
Mercers Cl SE10...43 B2
Mercer's Cotts 🔟
E3 ....33 A4
Mercers Mews N7..13 C4
Mercers Pl W6 ....39 C2
Mercers Rd N19....4 C1
Mercer St WC2 ...106 A1
Merchant Ct E1....32 B1
Merchants Ho
SE10 ....42 C1
Merchant Sq W2 .101 B3
Merchant St E3....26 B2
Merchant Taylors'
Hall EC3 ....109 C1
Merchon Ho N7....13 B4
Mercia Gr SE13....67 B3
Mercia Ho 🔢 SE5...48 B1
Mercie Ct SE22.....76 C3
Mercier Rd SW15..58 A2

Mercury Ct
8 Brixton SW9 . . . **173 B4**
10 Millwall E14 . . . . . . 41 C2
Mercury Ho **6** E3 . .26 C4
Mercury Way SE14 . .50 C4
Mercy Terr SE13 . . . .67 A2
Mere Cl SW15,
SW19 . . . . .69 C4
Meredith Ave NW2 . . 9 B3
Meredith Ho **17**
N16 . . . . .16 A3
Meredith Mews
SE4 . . . . .66 B3
Meredith St EC1 . . .96 A3
Meredith Twr W3 . . .37 A3
Meredyth Rd
SW13 . . . . .46 C1
Meretone Cl SE4 . . .66 A3
Mereton Mans **6**
SE8 . . . . .51 C2
Mereworth Ho **3**
SE15 . . . . .50 B4
Merganser Ct **17**
SE8 . . . . .51 B4
Meridan St EC1 . . . .67 C3
Meriden Ct SW3 . .144 A1
Meriden Ho **28** N1 . .24 A4
Meridian Courtyard
SE10 . . . . .52 C3
Meridian Ho SE10 . .43 A2
Meridian Pl E14 . . . .42 B4
Meridian Prim Sch
SE10 . . . . .52 C4
Meridian Sq E15 . . .19 C1
Merivale Rd SW15 . .58 A3
Merlin Ho
7 Chiswick W4 . . . .37 C1
West Hampstead
NW3 . . . . .11 A4
Merlin Sch The **11**
SW15 . . . . .58 A2
Merlins St WC1 . . . .95 B3
Merlin St EC1 . . . . .95 B3
Mermaid Ct
2 Bermondsey SE1 . **137 B4**
Rotherhithe SE16 . . .33 B1
Mermaid Ho **6**
E14 . . . . .34 B2
Mermaid Twr **22**
SE8 . . . . .51 B4
Meroe Ct N16 . . . . . .7 A2
Merredene St
SW2 . . . . .62 B1
Merriam Ave **2**
E9 . . . . .18 B2
Merricks Ct **5**
SW14 . . . . .55 A3
Merrick Sq SE1 . . .137 B2
Merrington Rd
SW6 . . . . .155 C4
Merritt Rd SE4 . . . .66 B2
Merrivale NW1 . . . .83 A3
Merrow St SE17 . .151 C1
Merrow Wlk SE17 . **151 C2**
Merryfield SE3 . . . . .53 B1
Merryweather Ct **18**
N19 . . . . .4 B1
Merryweather Pl **6**
SE10 . . . . .52 A3
Mersey Ho **10** N7 . . .14 C3
Merstone Ho
SW18 . . . . .59 A1
Merthyr Terr
SW13 . . . . .47 A4
Merton Ave W4 . . . .38 B2
Merton Ho SW18 . . .70 C3

Merton La N6 . . . . . . .3 B2
Merton Rd SW18 . . .70 C4
Merton Rise NW3 . .12 A1
Merton Road Ind Est
SW18 . . . . .70 C4
Mertins Rd SE15 . . .65 C2
Merttins Rd SE15 . .65 C2
Mervan Cl NW5 . . . .12 C3
Mervan Rd SW2 . . . .62 C3
Messaline Ave W3 . .28 B3
Messina Ave NW6 . .10 C1
Messiter Ho N1 . . . .85 A3
Metcalfe Ho **28**
SW8 . . . . .171 B2
Meteor St SW11 . . . .60 C3
Methley Ho **8** N7 . . . .5 B2
Methley St SE11 . .149 C1
Methodist Central
Hall SW1 . . . . **133 C3**
Methwold Rd W10 . .30 C4
Met Police Heritage
Ctr SW6 . . . . **141 B1**
Metropolis
Apartments **5**
SW12 . . . . .73 A3
Metropolitan Benefit
Societies
Almshouses **3**
N1 . . . . .16 A2
Metropolitan Bsns Ctr
9 N1 . . . . .16 A1
Metropolitan Cl **23**
E14 . . . . .33 C4
Mews St E1 . . . . . **125 B2**
Mews The
Shoreditch N1 . . . . .87 A4
6 Upper Holloway
N19 . . . . .5 A3
Mexborough N1 . . . .82 C3
Mexfield Rd SW18 . .58 B2
Meyer Ho **1**
SW12 . . . . .73 A4
Meymott St SE1 . .122 A1
Meynell Cres E9 . . .17 C1
Meynell Gdns E9 . . .17 C1
Meynell Rd E9 . . . . .17 C1
Meyrick Ho **3**
E14 . . . . .33 C4
Meyrick Rd
Battersea SW11 . . . .60 A4
Willesden NW10 . . . . 8 C2
Miah Terr **9** E1 . . . **125 C1**
Micawber Ct N1 . . . .97 A4
Micawber Ho **27**
SE16 . . . . **139 C3**
Micawber St N1 . . . .97 A4
Michael Cl **1** E3 . . . .26 B1
Michael Cliffe Ho
EC1 . . . . .95 C3
Michael Faraday Ho
SE17 . . . . **151 C1**
Michael Faraday Prim
Sch SE17 . . . . **151 C1**
Michael Manley Ind
Est **12** SW8 . . . **171 A2**
Michael Rd SW6 . .166 B4
Michael Tippett Sch
The SE24 . . . . .63 B3
Michelangelo Ct **3**
SE16 . . . . .40 A1
Michelle Ct W3 . . . .28 C2
Michels Almshouses
11 NW10 . . . . .22 A3
Michelsdale Dr **3**
TW9 . . . . .54 A3
Michelson Ho
SE11 . . . . **149 A3**

Michel's Row **2**
TW9 . . . . .54 A3
Michigan Ho E14 . . .41 C3
Mickledore NW1 . . . .83 A1
Micklethwaite Rd
SW6 . . . . .155 C3
Mickleton Ho **30**
W2 . . . . .31 C4
Middlefield NW8 . . .79 B4
Middle Row W10 . . .23 A1
Middlesex Ct **5**
W4 . . . . .38 B2
Middlesex Ho W1 . **105 A4**
Middlesex Pas
EC1 . . . . **108 B3**
Middlesex Pl **13**
E9 . . . . .17 B2
Middlesex St E1 . . .110 C2
Middle St EC1 . . . .108 C4
Middle Temple
EC4 . . . . **121 B4**
Middle Temple La
EC4 . . . . **121 B4**
Middleton Dr
SE16 . . . . .40 C4
Middleton Gr N7 . . .14 A3
Middleton Ho
Dalston E8 . . . . .16 B1
Newington SE1 . . . **137 B1**
Middleton Mews
N7 . . . . .14 A3
Middleton Pl W1 . **104 C3**
Middleton Rd
Dalston E8 . . . . .16 B1
Golders Green NW11 . .1 C4
Middleton Way
SE13 . . . . .67 C3
Midford Pl W1 . . . . .93 A1
Midhope Ho WC1 . . .94 B3
Midhope St WC1 . . .94 B3
Midhurst Ct N8 . . . . .5 A4
Midhurst Ho **6**
E14 . . . . .33 B3
Midhurst Way E5 . . .16 C4
Midland Pl E14 . . . . .42 B1
Midland Rd NW1 . . .94 A4
Midland Terr
NW10 . . . . .21 A1
Midlothian Ho NW2 . .9 A4
Midlothian Rd E3 . . .26 B1
Midmoor Rd SW12 . .73 B3
Midnight Ave **2**
SE8 . . . . .51 A4
Midship Cl SE16 . . . .32 C1
Midship Point E14 . .41 C4
Midstrath Rd NW10 . .8 A4
Midway Ho EC1 . . . .96 B4
Milborne Ho
SW10 . . . . **143 A1**
Milborne Ho **11** E9 . .17 B2
Milborne St E9 . . . . .17 B2
Milbrook Ct NW3 . . . 2 B3
Milcote St SE1 . . . .136 B3
Mildmay Ave N1 . . .15 C2
Mildmay Ct N1 . . . . .15 C3
Mildmay Gr N N1 . . .15 C3
Mildmay Gr S N1 . . .15 C3
Mildmay Ho **6**
SW15 . . . . .57 B2
Mildmay Mission
Hospl E2 . . .24 B2 98 C3
Mildmay Pk N1 . . . .15 C3
Mildmay Rd N1 . . . .16 A3
Mildmay St N1 . . . . .15 C2

MILE END 26 A1
Mile End Hospl E2 . .25 C2
Mile End Park L Ctr &
Stad E3 . . . . .33 B4
Mile End Pl E1 . . . . .25 C1
Mile End Rd E1, E3 . .25 C1
Mile End Sta E3 . . . .26 B2
Miles Bldgs NW1 . .102 A4
Miles Coverdale Prim
Sch **7** W12 . . . . . . .39 B4
Miles Ct E1 . . . . .32 A3
Miles Ho **5** SE10 . . .43 A1
Miles Lo E15 . . . . . .19 C3
Miles Pl NW8, ...101 C4
Miles St SW8 . . . . .162 B3
Milestone Green
SW14 . . . . .55 C3
Milfoil St W12 . . . . .29 C2
Milford Ct **3** N11 . . .19 C4
Milford La WC2 . . .121 B4
Milford Mews
SW16 . . . . .74 B1
Milk St E1 . . . . .109 A2
Milkwell Yd **7**
SE5 . . . . .48 B2
Milkwood Rd SE24 . .63 A3
Milk Yd E1 . . . . .32 B2
Millais Rd E11 . . . . .19 C4
Milland Ho **11**
SW15 . . . . .68 C3
Millard Cl **21** N16 . . .16 A3
Millard Rd SE8 . . . . .41 B1
Millbank SW1 . . . .148 A3
Millbank Acad
SW1 . . . . .147 C3
Millbank Millennium
Pier SW1 . . . . .148 B3
Millbrooke Ct **7**
SW15 . . . . .58 A2
Millbrook Ho **4**
SE15 . . . . .49 C4
Millbrook Pl NW1 . . .82 C2
Millbrook Rd SW9 . .63 A4
Millender Wlk
SE16 . . . . .40 B2
Millennium Bridge **5**,
EC4 . . . . **122 C3**
Millennium City Acad
W1 . . . . **104 B3**
Millennium Dr
E14 . . . . .42 C2
Millennium Harbour
E14 . . . . .41 C4
Millennium Pl **27**
E2 . . . . .25 A3
Millennium Prim Sch
SE10 . . . . .43 B3
Millennium Sq
SE1 . . . . **139 A4**
Millennium Way
SE10 . . . . .43 B3
Miller Ho **9** SW2 . . .74 A4
Miller's Ave E8,
N16 . . . . .16 B3
Miller's Ct **3** W4 . . .38 B1
Miller's Ho **6**
SW18 . . . . .59 A2
Miller St NW1 . . . . .82 C2
Miller's Terr **1** E8 . .16 B3
Miller's Way W6 . . .39 B4
Millers Wharf Ho
E1 . . . . .125 B1
Miller Wlk SE1 . . .121 C1
Millfield N4 . . . . .5 C2
Millfield La N6 . . . . . 3 B2
Millfield Pl N6 . . . . . .3 C2
Millfields Com Sch
E5 . . . . .17 B4

Millgrove St **6**
SW11 . . . . **169 B2**
Millharbour E14 . . . .42 A4
Mill Hill SW13 . . . . .56 C4
Mill Hill Gr **11** W3 . .28 A1
Mill Hill Rd
Barnes SW13 . . . . . .46 C1
South Acton W3 . . . .37 A4
Mill Hill Terr **9**
W3 . . . . .28 A1
Mill Ho **4** SE13 . . . .67 B4
Milligan St E14 . . . .33 B2
Milliners Ho SW18 . .58 C3
Millington Ho N16 . . .6 C1
Mill La NW6 . . . . . . .10 B3
Millman Ct WC1 . . . .94 C1
Millman Mews
WC1 . . . . .94 C1
Millman Pl WC1 . . . .95 A1
Millman St WC1 . . . .94 C1
Millmark Gr SE14 . . .51 A1
MILL MEADS 27 C3
Millner Ct SE4 . . . . .51 B1
Mill Pl E14 . . . . .33 A3
Mill Pond Cl SW8 . .161 C1
Millpond Est SE16 . .40 A4
Mill Row N1 . . . . . . .24 A4
Mills Ct EC2 . . .24 A2 98 A3
Mills Gr **1** E14 . . . . .34 B4
Mills Ho SW8 . . . . .171 A3
Millshott Cl SW6 . . .47 B2
Mills Row W4 . . . . . .37 C2
Mill St
Bermondsey SE1 . . .139 A4
Mayfair W1 . . . . . .118 C4
Millstone Cl E15 . . . .19 C2
Millstream Ho **14**
SE16 . . . . .40 A4
Millstream Rd
SE1 . . . . **138 C3**
Mill Trad Est The
NW10 . . . . .20 B2
MILLWALL 41 C3
Millwall Dock Rd
E14 . . . . .41 C3
Millwood St **10**
W10 . . . . .31 A4
Mill Yd E1 . . . . .125 B4
Milman Rd NW6 . . . .23 A3
Milman's Ho
SW10 . . . . **157 B3**
Milman's St SW10 . **157 B3**
Milner Bldg N16 . . . .6 C1
Milner Ho **1**
SW11 . . . . .59 C4
Milner Pl N1 . . . . . . .85 C4
Milner Sq N1 . . . . . .15 A1
Milner St SW3 . . . .144 C4
Milnthorpe Rd W4 . .45 C4
Milo Rd SE22 . . . . . .64 B1
Milrood Ho **5** E1 . . .32 C4
Milroy Wlk SE1 . . .122 A2
Milson Rd W14 . . . .126 A2
Milsted Ho **22** E5 . . .17 A3
Milton Ave
Becontree NW10 . . . .20 C4
Crouch End N6 . . . . . .4 B4
Stonebridge NW10 . . .20 B4
Milton Cl SE1 . . . . .152 C3
Milton Court Rd
SE14 . . . . .51 A4
Milton Ct
Fulham SW6 . . . . . .58 A4
St Luke's EC2 . . . . .109 B4

Milton Ct *continued*
9 Wandsworth
SW18 . . . . .58 C2
Milton Ho
10 Bethnal Green
E2 . . . . .25 B2
2 Camberwell SE5 . .48 C3
Milton House Mans
E8 . . . . .16 B4
Milton Pk N6 . . . . .4 A4
Milton Pl **3** N7 . . . . .14 C3
Milton Rd
Acton W3 . . . . .28 C1
Crouch End N6 . . . . . . .4 B4
Mortlake SW14 . . . . . .55 C4
Tulse Hill SE24 . . . . . .63 A2
Milton St EC1, EC2 **109** B4
Milverton NW5 . . . . . .12 C3
Milverton Rd NW6 . . . .9 B1
Milverton St SE11 **149** C1
Milward St E1 . . . . . . .32 A4
Mimosa Ct SW4 . . . .172 B3
Mimosa St SW6 . . . . .165 A3
Mina Rd SE17 . . . . . .152 B2
Minchin Ho **10**
E14 . . . . .33 C3
Mincing La EC3 . . . .124 A4
Minera Mews
SW1 . . . . .145 C4
Minerva Cl SW9 . . . .163 C2
Minerva Rd NW10 . . .20 C2
Minerva St E2 . . . . . . .25 A3
Minerva Wlk EC1 . . .108 B2
Minet Ave NW10 . . . . .21 A3
Minet Gdns NW10 . . .21 A3
Minet Ho **20** E1 . . . .111 B1
Minet Rd SE5, SW9 . .48 A1
Minford Gdns
W14 . . . . .39 C4
Mingard Wlk N7 . . . . . .5 B1
Ming St E14 . . . . .33 C2
Minnow Wlk SE17 **152** B3
Minories EC3 . . . . . . .124 C4
Minshull St SW8 . . . .171 B3
Minson Rd E9 . . . . . . .25 C4
Minstead Gdns
SW15 . . . . .68 B4
Minster Ct EC3 . . . . .124 B4
Minster Rd NW2 . . . . .10 A3
Mint Bsns Pk **12**
E16 . . . . .35 C4
Mintern St N1 . . . . . . .87 C2
Minton Ho SE11 . . . .149 B4
Minton Mews **3**
NW6 . . . . .11 A2
Mint St SE1 . . . . .137 A4
Mirabelle Gardens
E15 . . . . .19 B4
Mirabel Rd SW6 . . . .155 A2
Miranda Cl **6** E1 . . . .32 B4
Miranda Ho **17** N1 . . .24 A3
Miranda Rd N19 . . . . . .4 B3
Missenden SE17 . . . .151 C1
Missenden Ho
NW8 . . . . .90 A2
Mission Pl SE15 . . . . .49 C2
Mission Sq **13**
TW8 . . . . .44 A4
Mission The
13 Bermondsey
SE16 . . . . .40 A4
14 Poplar E14 . . . . .33 B3

Misterton Ct
SW11 . . . . .167 C4
Mistral SE5 . . . . .49 A2
Mitali Pas **21** E1 . . . .111 B1
Mitcham Ho **9**
SE5 . . . . .48 B2
Mitchell Brook Prim
Sch NW10 . . . . .8 A2
Mitchell Ct SW14 . . . .56 A3
Mitchell Ho
Gunnersbury W4 . . . . .37 A1
8 Islington N1 . . . . .14 C1
31 Shepherd's Bush
W12 . . . . .30 A1
Mitchell's Pl SE21 . . .76 A4
Mitchell St EC1 . . . . . .97 A2
Mitchison Rd N1 . . . . .15 C2
Mitford Rd N19 . . . . . . .5 A2
Mitre Bridge Ind Pk
W10 . . . . .22 A1
Mitre Rd SE1 . . . . . . .135 C4
Mitre Sq EC3 . . . . . . .110 B1
Mitre St EC3 . . . . .110 B1
Mitre The **4** E14 . . . .33 B2
Mitre Way W10 . . . . . .30 A4
Mizzen Ct E14 . . . . . . .41 C4
Moatfield NW6 . . . . . . .10 A1
Moat Pl
Acton W3 . . . . .28 A3
Stockwell SW9 . . . . . .62 B4
Moat Sch The **7**
SW6 . . . . .164 A2
Moberly Rd SW4 . . . . .73 C4
Mobey Ct SW4 . . . . . .172 A3
Mocatta Ho **4** E1 . . .25 A1
Modbury Gdns
NW5 . . . . .12 C2
Modder Pl SW15 . . . . .57 C3
Model Cotts SW14 . . .55 B4
Modling Ho **8** E2 . . . .25 C3
Moelwyn Hughes Ct
N7 . . . . .13 C3
Moffat Ho **24** SE5 . . .48 B3
Mohawk Ho **33** E3 . . .26 A3
Moiety Rd E14 . . . . . . .41 C4
Moira Ct SW17 . . . . . .72 C2
Moira Ho **11** SW9 . .173 B4
Molasses Ho **1**
SW11 . . . . .59 B4
Molasses Row **2**
SW11 . . . . .59 B4
Mole Ct **2** W12 . . . . .38 A4
Mole Ho NW8 . . . . .89 C1
Molesey Ho
E2 . . . . .24 B1 **98** C2
Molesford Rd
SW6 . . . . .165 B3
Molesworth Ho **9**
SE17 . . . . .48 A4
Molesworth St
SE13 . . . . .67 B3
Molly Huggins Cl
SW12 . . . . .73 B4
Molton Ho N1 . . . . . . .85 A3
Molyneux Ho W1 . . .102 B2
Molyneux St W1 . . . .102 B3
Mona Rd SE15 . . . . . .50 B1
Mona St E16 . . . . .35 B4
Monck's Row
SW18 . . . . .58 B1
Monck St SW1 . . . . . .133 C1
Monckton Ct W14 . .126 C2
Monclar Rd SE5 . . . . .63 C3
Moncorvo Cl SW7 **130** A3
Moncrieff St SE15 . . .49 C1

Mondragon Ho
SW8 . . . . .172 B4
Monet Ct **15** SE16 . . .40 A1
Moneyer Ho N1 . . . . . .97 B4
Monica Shaw Ct
NW1 . . . . .83 C1
Monier Rd E3 . . . . . . .18 C1
Monkbretton Ho
E2 . . . . .24 C2 **99** B3
Monk Ct W12 . . . . . . .29 C1
Monk Dr E16 . . . . .35 C2
Monkridge **3** N8 . . . .4 C4
Monksfield N4 . . . . . . .5 C2
Monkswell Ho
E2 . . . . .24 C2 **99** B3
Monkton Ho
SE16 . . . . .40 C4
2 Hackney E5 . . . . .17 A3
Monkton St SE11 . . .149 C4
Monkwell Sq EC2 . . .109 A3
Monmouth Cl W4 . . . .37 C3
Monmouth Gr
TW8 . . . . .36 A2
Monmouth Ho
3 Camden Town
NW5 . . . . .13 A2
Wandsworth SW18 . . .58 C1
Monmouth Pl W2 **100** A1
Monmouth Rd W2 . . .31 C3
Monmouth St
WC2 . . . . .106 A1
Monnery Rd N19 . . . . .4 B1
Monnow Rd SE1 . . . .153 B3
Monro Dr SW14 . . . . .55 A2
Monroe Ho
10 Crouch End N19 . . .4 C4
Lisson Gr NW8 . . . . . .90 B3
Monro Ho
16 Hampstead
NW3 . . . . .11 B4
Putney SW15 . . . . . . .57 A2
Monro Way E5 . . . . . .16 C4
Monsal Ct E5 . . . . . . .18 A4
Monsell Ct **4** N4 . . . . .6 A1
Monsell Rd N4, N5 . . . .6 A1
Monson Rd
Deptford SE14 . . . . . .50 C3
Willesden Green
NW10 . . . . .22 A2
Montagu Ct W1 . . . .103 A3
Montague Ave
SE4 . . . . .66 C3
Montagu Cl SE1 . . . .123 B2
Montagu Mans W1 .103 A4
Montague Rd
Richmond TW10 . . . . .54 A1
Shacklewell E8 . . . . . .16 C3
Montague Sq SE15 **50** B3
Montague St
Bloomsbury WC1 . . .106 A4
City of London EC1 . .108 C3
Montagu Mans
W1 . . . . .103 A3
Montagu Mews N
W1 . . . . .103 A3
Montagu Mews S
W1 . . . . .103 A2
Montagu Mews W
W1 . . . . .103 A2
Montagu Pl W1 . . . .103 A3
Montagu Row W1 . .103 A3
Montagu Sq W1 . . . .103 A3
Montagu St W1 . . . .103 A2
Montaigne Cl
SW1 . . . . .147 C3

Montana Bldg **4**
SE13 . . . . .52 A2
Montana Rd SW17 . .72 C1
Montcalm Ho E14 . . .41 C3
Montclare St
E2 . . . . .24 B1 **98** C2
Monteagle Ct **27**
N1 . . . . .24 A3
Monteagle Way
Nunhead SE15 . . . . . .65 A4
Shacklewell E5 . . . . . . .7 C1
Montefiore Ct **2**
N16 . . . . .7 B3
Montefiore St **2**
SW8 . . . . .170 B1
Montego Cl **9**
SW2 . . . . .62 C3
Montem Prim Sch **8**
N7 . . . . .5 B1
Montem St N4 . . . . . . .5 B3
Monteray Studios
W10 . . . . .23 A3
Montesquieu Terr **3**
E16 . . . . .35 B3
Montfichet Rd E15, .19 B2
Montford Pl SE11 . . .149 B1
Montfort Ho
4 Bethnal Green
E2 . . . . .25 B2
Cubitt Town E14 . . . . .42 B3
Montfort Pl SW19 . . .69 C3
Montgomery Ct
W4 . . . . .45 B4
Montgomery Ho **5**
SW14 . . . . .55 C4
Montgomery Lo **28**
E1 . . . . .25 B1
Montgomery Rd
W4 . . . . .37 B2
Montgomery St
E14 . . . . .34 A1
Montholme Rd
SW11 . . . . .60 B1
Monthope Rd **17**
E1 . . . . .111 B3
Montolieu Gdns
SW15 . . . . .57 A2
Montpelier Gr
NW5 . . . . .13 B3
Montpelier Mews
SW7 . . . . .130 B2
Montpelier Pl
Knightsbridge
SW7 . . . . .130 B2
2 Stepney E1 . . . . .32 B3
Montpelier Rd
SE15 . . . . .50 A2
Montpelier Rise
NW11 . . . . .1 A4
Montpelier Row
SE3 . . . . .53 B1
Montpelier Sq
SW7 . . . . .130 B3
Montpelier St
SW7 . . . . .130 B2
Montpelier Terr
SW7 . . . . .130 B3
Montpelier Vale
SE3 . . . . .53 B1
Montpelier Way
NW11 . . . . .1 A4
Montpelier Wlk
SW7 . . . . .130 B2
Montreal Pl WC2 . . . .120 C4
Montrell Rd SW2 . . . .74 A3

Montrose Ave
NW6 . . . . .23 A3
Montrose Ct SW7 . . .129 C3
Montrose Ho
Belgravia SW1 . . . . . .131 C3
Millwall E14 . . . . .41 C3
Montrose Pl SW1 . . .131 C3
Montrose Villas **3**
W6 . . . . .38 C1
Montserrat Rd
SW15 . . . . .58 A3
Monument Gdns
SE13 . . . . .67 B2
Monument St EC3 . .123 C4
Monument Sta
EC3 . . . . .123 C4
Monument The
EC3 . . . . .123 C4
Monza Bldg The
E1 . . . . .32 B2
Monza St E1 . . . . .32 B2
Moodkee St SE16 . . .40 B3
Moody Rd SE15 . . . . .49 B2
Moody St E1 . . . . .25 C2
Moon St N1 . . . . .86 A4
Moorcroft Rd
SW16 . . . . .74 A1
Moore Ct N1 . . . . .55 B4
Moore Ct N1 . . . . .86 A3
Moore Ho
10 Bethnal Green
E2 . . . . .25 B2
5 Greenwich SE10 . .43 B1
7 Shadwell E1 . . . . .32 B2
Wandsworth SW17 . . .71 C1
Moore Park Ct
SW6 . . . . .156 B2
Moore Park Rd
SW6 . . . . .156 A1
Moore St SW3 . . . . .144 C4
Moorfields EC2 . . . . .109 B3
Moorfields Eye Hospl
EC1 . . . . .97 B3
Moorfields Highwalk
EC2 . . . . .109 B3
Moorgate EC2 . . . . . .109 B3
Moorgate PI EC2 . . .109 B2
Moorgate Sta
EC2 . . . . .109 B3
Moorgreen Ho
EC1 . . . . .96 A4
Moorhouse Rd W2 .109 B3
Moorhouse Rd
W2 . . . . .31 C3
Moor La EC2 . . . . . . .109 B3
Moorland Rd SW9 . . .63 A3
Moor PI EC2 . . . . .109 B3
Moor St W1 . . . . .105 C1
Morant St E14 . . . . . .33 C2
Morant St E14 . . . . . .33 C2
Mora Prim Sch
NW2 . . . . .9 B4
Mora Rd NW2 . . . . . . .9 B4
Mora St EC1 . . . . .97 A3
Morat St SW9 . . . . . .173 A4
Moravian Ct SW3 . .157 C3
Moravian Pl
SW10 . . . . .157 C3
Moravian St **10** E2 . .25 B2
Moray Ho **8** E1 . . . . .26 A1
Moray Mews N4, N7 . . .5 B2
Moray Rd N4, N7 . . . . .5 B2
Mordaunt Ho
3 Becontree
NW10 . . . . .20 C4
34 Clapham SW8 . .171 B1

Mordaunt Rd
NW10 . . . . .20 C4
Mordaunt St SW9 . .62 B4
Morden Hill SE13 . .52 B1
Morden Ho 🔢
SW2 . . . . .62 C1
Morden La SE13 . . .52 B2
Morden Mount Prim
Sch 🔢 SE13 . . . . . . .52 A1
Morden Rd SE3 . . . .53 C1
Morden Road Mews
SE3 . . . . .53 C1
Morden St SE13 . . .52 A2
Morden Wharf Rd
SE10 . . . . .43 A3
Mordern Ho NW1 . .90 B1
Morecambe Cl 🔢
E1 . . . . .32 C4
Morecambe St
SE17 . . . . .151 A2
More Cl
Canning Town
E16 . . . . .35 B3
West Kensington
W14 . . . . .140 A3
Moredown Ho 🔢
E8 . . . . .16 C3
More House Sch
SW1 . . . . .131 A1
Moreland Ct 🔢
NW2 . . . . .1 C1
Moreland Prim Sch
EC1 . . . . .96 B3
Moreland St EC1 . . .96 B4
Morella Rd SW11,
SW12 . . . . .72 B4
Morell Ho 🔢 SW9 172 C1
More London Pl
SE1 . . . . .124 A1
Moresby Wlk 🔢
SW8 . . . . .170 B1
More's Gdn SW3 .157 C3
Moreton Ho SE16 . .40 A3
Moreton Pl SW1 . .147 A2
Moreton St SW1 . .147 B2
Moreton Terr
SW1 . . . . .147 A2
Moreton Terr Mews N
SW1 . . . . .147 A2
Moreton Terr Mews S
SW1 . . . . .147 A2
Moreton Twr 🔢
W3 . . . . .28 A1
Morgan Ct 🔢
SW11 . . . . .167 C2
Morgan Rd
Nine Elms SW8 . . . .171 A4
Pimlico SW1 . . . . . . .147 A3
Morgan Rd
Islington N7 . . . . .14 C3
Notting Hill W10 . . . . .31 B4
Morgans La SE1 . . .124 A1
Morgan St
Canning Town
E16 . . . . .35 B4
Globe Town E3 . . . . . .25 C2
Morgan's Wlk
SW11 . . . . .158 A1
Moriatry Cl N7 . . . . .14 A4
Morie St SW18 . . . . .59 A2
Morkyns Wlk SE21 . .76 A1
Morland Cl NW11 . . . .2 A4
Morland Ct W12 . . . .39 A4
Morland Est E8 . . . . .16 C1
Morland Ho
Kilburn NW6 . . . . .23 C4

Morland Ho continued
Notting Hill W11 . . . . .31 A3
Somers Town NW1 . . .83 A1
Westminster SW1 . . .148 A4
Morland Mews N1 . .14 C1
Morley Coll SE1 . . .135 C2
Morley Ct SE13 . . . . .67 B3
Morley Ho
Stoke Newington
N16 . . . . .7 C2
Streatham SW2 . . . . . .74 A4
West Norwood
SE27 . . . . .75 A1
Morley Rd SE13 . . . .67 B3
Morley St SE1 . . . .135 C3
Morna St SE5 . . . . . .48 B1
Morning La E9 . . . . . .17 B2
Morningside Prim Sch
🔢 E9 . . . . .17 C2
Mornington Ave
W14 . . . . .140 C3
Mornington Avenue
Mans W14 . . . . . . .140 C3
Mornington Cres
Camden Town
NW1 . . . . .82 C2
NW1 . . . . .82 C2
Mornington Crescent
Sta NW1 . . . . .82 C2
Mornington Ct
NW1 . . . . .82 C2
Mornington Gr E3 . .26 C2
Mornington Mews 🔢
SE5 . . . . .48 B2
Mornington Pl
🔢 New Cross
SE8 . . . . .51 B3
Regent's Pk NW1 . . . .82 C2
Mornington Rd SE14,
SE8 . . . . .51 B3
Mornington St
NW1 . . . . .82 B2
Mornington Terr
NW1 . . . . .82 B2
Morocco St SE1 . . .138 A3
Morpeth Gr E9 . . . . .25 C4
Morpeth Rd E9 . . . . .25 C4
Morpeth Sch E2 . . . .25 B2
Morpeth St E2 . . . . .25 C2
Morpeth Terr
SW1 . . . . .146 C4
Morrel Ct 🔢 E2 . . . .24 C3
Morris Blitz Ct 🔢
N16 . . . . .16 B4
Morris Ct 🔢 SE5 . . .63 C3
Morris Gdns SW18 . .70 C4
Morris Ho
🔢 Bethnal Green
E2 . . . . .25 B2
Lisson Gr NW8 . . . . . .90 A1
🔢 Stockwell SW4 . . .62 A3
🔢 Tufnell Pk N19 . . .13 B4
Morrish Rd SW2 . . . .74 A4
Morrison Bldgs 🔢
E1 . . . . .111 B2
Morrison Ho SW2 . . .74 C3
Morrison St SW11 . .60 C4
Morris Pl N4 . . . . .5 C2
Morris Rd E14 . . . . . .34 A4
Morris Ho 🔢
E2 . . . . .25 B2
Morris St E1 . . . . . . .32 A3
Morshead Mans
W9 . . . . .23 C2
Mortain Ho 🔢
SE16 . . . . .40 A2

Morten Cl SW4 . . . . .61 C1
Mortimer Cl
🔢 Child's Hill NW2 . . .1 B1
Streatham SW16 . . . .73 C2
Mortimer Cres
NW6 . . . . .78 B3
Mortimer Ct NW8 . .79 A1
Mortimer Est NW6 . .78 B3
Mortimer Ho
🔢 Shepherd's Bush
W11 . . . . .30 C1
West Kensington
W14 . . . . .140 B3
Mortimer Lo 🔢
SW19 . . . . .70 A3
Mortimer Market
WC1 . . . . .93 A1
Mortimer Pl NW6 . . .78 A3
Mortimer Rd
De Beauvoir Town
N1 . . . . .16 A1
Kensal Green
NW10 . . . . .22 C2
Mortimer Sq W11 . . .30 C2
Mortimer St W1 . . . .104 C3
Mortimer Terr
NW5 . . . . .13 A4
MORTLAKE 55 B4
Mortlake High St
SW14 . . . . .55 C4
Mortlake Ho 🔢
W4 . . . . .37 B2
Mortlake Rd SW14,
TW9 . . . . .44 C2
Mortlake Sta
SW14 . . . . .55 B4
Mortlake Terr
TW9 . . . . .44 C3
Mortlock Cl SE15 . . .50 A2
Morton Cl 🔢 E1 . . . .32 B3
Morton Ho SE17 . . . .48 A4
Morton Mews
SW5 . . . . .142 A3
Morton Pl SE1 . . . . .135 B1
Morton Rd N1 . . . . . .15 B1
Morval Rd SW2 . . . . .62 C2
Morven Rd SW17 . . . .72 B1
Morville Ho SW18 . . .59 C1
Morville St E3 . . . . . .26 C3
Morwell St WC1 . . . .105 C3
Moscow Pl W2 . . . .114 A4
Moscow Rd W2 . . . .114 A4
Mosedale NW1 . . . . .92 B3
Moseley Row SE10 . .43 B2
Mosque Tower 🔢
E1 . . . . .111 C3
Mossbourne Com
Acad E8 . . . . .16 C3
Mossbourne Victoria
Park Acad 🔢 E9 . . .17 C1
Mossbury Rd
SW11 . . . . .60 A4
Moss Cl E1 . . . . .111 C4
Mossford St E3 . . . . .26 B1
Mossington Gdns
SE16 . . . . .40 B2
Mossop St SW3 . . . .144 B4
Mostyn Gdns
NW10 . . . . .22 C3
Mostyn Gr E3 . . . . . .26 C3
Mostyn Lo N5 . . . . . .15 B4
Mostyn Rd SW9 . . . .173 C3
Motcomb St SW1 . .131 B2
Mothers Sq The 🔢
E5 . . . . .17 A4

Motley Ave
EC2 . . . . .24 A1 98 A2
Motley St SW8 . . . .170 C2
Moules Ct SE5 . . . . .48 B3
Moulins Rd E9 . . . . . .17 B1
Moulsford Ho
🔢 Lower Holloway
N7 . . . . .13 C3
🔢 Paddington W2 . . .31 C4
Mounsey Ho 🔢
W10 . . . . .23 A2
Mount Adon Pk SE1,
SE22 . . . . .76 C4
Mountague Pl 🔢
E14 . . . . .34 B2
Mountain Ho
SE11 . . . . .148 C2
Mount Angelus Rd
SW15 . . . . .68 B4
Mount Ararat Rd
TW10 . . . . .54 A2
Mountbatten Ho
N6 . . . . .3 C4
Mountbatten Mews
SW18 . . . . .71 B3
Mount Carmel 🔢
N7 . . . . .14 B3
Mount Carmel RC
Tech Coll for Girls
🔢 N19 . . . . .4 C4
Mountearl Gdns SW16,
SW2 . . . . .74 B1
Mount Ephraim La
SW16 . . . . .73 C1
Mount Ephraim Rd
SW16 . . . . .73 C1
Mountfield NW2 . . . .1 B2
Mountfield Ct
SE13 . . . . .67 C1
Mount Ford St E1 . .111 B2
Mountfort Cres
N1 . . . . .14 C1
Mountfort Terr 🔢
N1 . . . . .14 C1
Mountgrove Rd N5 . . .6 B1
Mountjoy Ho EC2 . .108 C3
Mount Lodge SW4 . .61 C3
Mount Mills EC1 . . . .96 B3
Mount Nod Rd SW16,
SW2 . . . . .74 B1
Mount Pl 🔢 W3 . . . . .28 A1
Mount Pleasant
WC1 . . . . .95 B1
Mount Pleasant Cres
N4 . . . . .5 B4
Mount Pleasant Rd
Lewisham SE13 . . . . . .67 B1
Willesden NW10 . . . . .22 B5
Mount Pleasant Villas
N4 . . . . .5 B4
Mount Rd SW18,
SW19 . . . . .71 A2
Mount Row W1 . . . .118 A3
Mount St Mews
W1 . . . . .118 A3
Mounts Pond Rd SE3,
SE13 . . . . .52 C1
Mount Sq The 🔢
NW3 . . . . .2 B1
Mount St W1 . . . . . .117 C3
Mount Terr E1 . . . . . .32 A4
Mount The
Hampstead NW3 . . . . .2 B1
Kensington
W8 . . . . . . .31 C1 113 B1
Mount Tyndall NW3 . .2 C3

Mount Vernon
NW3 . . . . .11 B4
Mountview 🔢
SW16 . . . . .74 B1
Mountview Cl
NW11 . . . . .2 B3
Mount Villas SE27 . . .75 A1
Mourne Ho NW3 . . . .11 B2
Mowatt Cl N19 . . . . . .4 C3
Mowbray Rd NW6 . . .10 A1
Mowlem Prim Sch 🔢
E2 . . . . .25 B3
Mowlem St E2 . . . . . .25 A3
Mowll St SW9 . . . . .163 B1
Moxon St W1 . . . . . .103 B3
Moye Cl 🔢 E2 . . . . . .24 C3
Moylan Rd W6 . . . . .154 A3
Moyle Ho SW1 . . . .161 A4
Moyne Ho 🔢 SW9 . . .63 A3
Mozart St W10 . . . . .23 B2
Mudchute Pk & Farm
E14 . . . . .42 B2
Mudchute Sta E14 . . .42 A2
Mudie Ho 🔢 SW2 . . .74 A4
Mudlarks Blvd 🔢
SE10 . . . . .43 B3
Muirdown Ave
SW14 . . . . .55 C3
Muir Dr SW18 . . . . . .60 A1
Muirfield W3 . . . . . . .29 A3
Muirfield Cl 🔢
SE16 . . . . .40 A1
Muirfield Cres
🔢 E14 . . . . .42 A3
Muir Rd E5 . . . . .7 C1
Mulberry Bsns Ctr
SE16 . . . . .40 C4
Mulberry Cl
Chelsea SW3 . . . . . .157 C3
East Dulwich SE22 . . .64 C1
Hampstead NW3 . . . .11 C4
Mulberry Ct
Finsbury EC1 . . . . . . .96 B3
Islington N5 . . . . .15 A3
🔢 Leyton E11 . . . . . .19 C4
🔢 Paddington W9 . . .23 B2
Mulberry Ho
🔢 Bethnal Green
E2 . . . . .25 B2
🔢 Deptford SE8 . . . .51 B4
Mulberry House Sch
The NW2 . . . . .10 A3
Mulberry Mews
SE14 . . . . .51 B2
Mulberry Pl W6 . . . . .38 C1
Mulberry Rd E8 . . . . .16 B1
Mulberry Sch for Girls
🔢 Stepney E1 . . . . . .32 A3
🔢 St George in E1 . .32 A2
Mulberry St 🔢
E1 . . . . .111 B2
Mulberry Wlk
SW3 . . . . .157 C4
Mulgrave Rd
West Kensington
W14 . . . . .154 C4
Willesden NW10 . . . . . .8 B4
Mulkern Rd N19 . . . . .4 C3
Mullard Ho WC1 . . .105 B4
Mullens Ho 🔢
SW15 . . . . .57 B2
Mullen Twr EC1 . . . . .95 B1
Muller Rd SW4 . . . . .61 C1

Mullet Gdns 7
E2 . . . . .24 C2
Mulletsfield WC1 . . 94 B3
Mull Ho 17 E3 . . . . . .26 B3
Mullins Path
SW14 . . . . .55 C4
Mulready St NW8 . . 90 A2
Multi Way W3 . . . . . .38 A4
Multon Ho E9 . . . . . .17 C1
Multon Rd SW18 . . .71 C4
Mulvaney Way
SE1 . . . . .137 C3
Mumford Rd SE24 . .63 A2
Muncaster Rd
SW11 . . . . .60 C2
Mundania Ct SE2 . .65 A3
Mundania Rd SE22 . .65 A3
Munday Ho SE1 . . .137 B1
Munday Rd E16 . . . .35 C3
Munden Ho 5 E3 . . .27 A2
Munden St W14 . . . .140 A4
Mund St W14 . . . . .141 A1
Mundy Ho W10 . . . .23 A2
Mundy St
N1 . . . . .24 A2 98 B4
Munro Ho
Bermondsey SE1 . .137 C3
Lambeth SE1 . . . . .135 B3
Munro Mews W10 . .31 A4
Munster Ct SW6 . . .164 C2
Munster Rd SW6 . .154 B2
Munster Residences
SW6 . . . . .164 B4
Munster Sq NW1 . . .92 B2
Munton Rd SE1,
SE17 . . . . .151 A4
Murchison Ho 1
W10 . . . . .31 A4
Murdoch Ho 4
SE16 . . . . .40 B3
Murdock Cl E16 . . . .35 B3
Murdock St SE15 . . .50 A4
Murfett Cl SW19 . . .70 A2
Muriel St N1 . . . . . .85 A4
Murphy Ho SE1 . . .136 B2
Murphy St SE1 . . . .135 B3
Murray Gr N1 . . . . . .87 C1
Murray Mews
NW1 . . . . .13 C1
Murray St NW1 . . . .13 C1
Murray Terr NW3 . . .11 C4
Musard Rd W6 . . . .154 B4
Musbury St E1 . . . . .32 B3
Muscal W6 . . . . . . .154 A4
Muscatel Pl SE5 . . .49 A2
Muschamp Rd
SE15 . . . . .64 B4
Muscott Ho 18 E2 . .24 C4
Muscovy St EC3 . .124 A4
Museum & Galleries
of Modern London
EC2 . . . . .108 C3
Museum Ho 6 E2 . . .25 B2
Museum La SW7 . .129 B1
Museum Mans
WC1 . . . . .106 A3
Museum of Brands,
Packaging &
Advertising W11. . .31 B3
Museum of Childhood
(V&A) E2 . . . . . . .25 B2
Museum of
Instruments
SW7 . . . . .129 B2

Museum of London
EC2 . . . . .108 C3
Museum of London
Docklands E14 . . .33 C2
Museum of the Order
of St John EC1 . . .96 A1
Museum St WC1 . .106 A2
Museum Way W3 . .36 C4
Musgrave Cres
SW6 . . . . .165 C4
Musgrave Ct
SW11 . . . . .168 A4
Musgrave Ho 1
E9 . . . . .17 C2
Musgrove Rd SE14 . .51 A2
Musical Mus The
TW8 . . . . .44 B4
Musjid Rd 2
SW11 . . . . .167 C1
Mustow Pl 2
SW6 . . . . .165 A2
Mutrix Rd NW6 . . . .23 C4
Mutton Pl NW1 . . . .12 C2
Myatt Garden Prim
Sch SE4 . . . . .51 B1
Myatt Ho SE5 . . . . .48 A1
Myatt Rd SW9 . . . . .48 A1
Myatts Field Ct
SE5 . . . . .48 B2
Mycenae Rd SE3 . .53 C4
Myddelton Pas
EC1 . . . . .95 C4
Myddelton Sq EC1 . .95 C4
Myddelton St EC1 . .95 C3
Myddleton Ave N4. .6 B2
Myers Ho 5 SE5 . . .48 B3
Myers La SE14 . . . .50 C4
Mylius Cl SE14 . . . .50 B2
Mylne Cl W6 . . . . . .38 C1
Mylne St EC1 . . . . .85 B1
Mynterne Ct 16
SW19 . . . . .69 C3
Myrdle Ct 14 E1 . . .111 C2
Myrdle St E1 . . . . .111 C2
Myron Pl SE13 . . . . .67 B4
Myrtle Ho SE14 . . . .50 C2
Myrtle Rd W3 . . . . .28 B1
Myrtle Wlk 20 N1 . .24 A3
Mysore Rd SW11 . .60 B3
Myton Rd SE21 . . . .75 C1
Mytton Ho SW8 . . .162 C1

N

N1 Sh Ctr N1 . . . . .85 C2
Nags Head N7 . . . . .14 B4
Nags Head Ct EC1 . .97 A1
Nags Head Sh Ctr The
N7 . . . . .14 B4
Naima Jewish Prep
Sch 4 NW6 . . . . .78 A2
Nainby Ho SE11 . . .149 B3
Nairne Gr SE5,
SE24 . . . . .63 C3
Nairn St E14 . . . . . .34 B4
Naldera Gdns SE3 . .53 C4
Nalton Ho 4 NW6 . .11 B1
Namco Funscape
SE1 . . . . .134 C4
Nankin St E14 . . . . .33 C3
Nansen Rd SW11 . .60 C4
Nant Ct NW2 . . . . . . .1 B2
Nantes Cl SW18 . . .59 B3
Nant Rd NW2 . . . . . .1 B2
Nant St E2 . . . . . . .25 A2

Naoroji St WC1 . . . .95 B3
Napa Cl E15 . . . . . .19 B3
Napier Ave
Deptford E14 . . . . .41 C1
Fulham SW6 . . . . . .58 B4
Napier Cl
New Cross SE14,
SE8 . . . . .51 B3
West Kensington
W14 . . . . .126 C2
Napier Ct
Fulham SW6 . . . . . .58 B4
Shoreditch N1 . . . . .87 B2
Napier Gr N1 . . . . . .87 A2
Napier Ho SE17 . . . .48 A4
Napier Pl W14 . . . .126 C1
Napier Rd
College Pk NW10 . .22 A2
Kensington W14 . .126 C1
Napier Terr N1 . . . .15 A1
Narbonne Ave
SW4 . . . . .61 B2
Narborough St
SW6 . . . . .166 A1
Narcissus Rd NW6 .10 C3
Narford Rd E5 . . . . . .7 C2
Narrow St
6 Acton W3 . . . . . .28 A1
Limehouse E14 . . . .33 A2
Nascot St W12 . . . . .30 B3
Naseby Cl NW6 . . . .11 B1
Nashe Ho SE1 . . . .137 B1
Nash Ho
5 Millwall E14 . . . .41 C3
Pimlico SW1 . . . . .146 B1
Nash Rd SE4 . . . . . .66 A2
Nash St NW1 . . . . . .92 B4
Nasmyth St W6 . . . .39 A3
Nassau Rd SW13 . . .46 B2
Nassau St W1 . . . .104 C3
Nassington Rd
NW3 . . . . .12 B4
Nathan Ho SE11 . . .149 C3
Nathaniel Cl E1 . . .111 A3
National Archives The
TW9 . . . . .45 A3
National Army Mus
SW3 . . . . .159 A4
National Gallery
W1 . . . . .119 C3
National Hospl for
Neurology &
Neurosurgery
WC1 . . . . .94 B1
National Maritime
Mus SE10 . . . . . .52 C4
National Portrait
Gallery W1 . . . . .119 C3
National Tennis Ctr
SW15 . . . . .56 A2
National Theatre
SE1 . . . . .121 A2
Natural History Mus
SW7 . . . . .129 B1
Nautilus Bldg The
EC1 . . . . .95 C4
Naval Row E14 . . . . .34 B2
Navarino Gr E8 . . . .16 C2
Navarino Mans E8 . .16 C2
Navarino Rd E8 . . . .16 C2
Navarre St
E2 . . . . .24 B1 98 C2
Navenby Wlk 13
E3 . . . . .26 C1
Navy St SW4 . . . . . .61 C4

Naxos Bldg 9 E14 .41 C4
Naylor Bldg W 4
E1 . . . . .111 B2
Naylor Ho
53 Clapham
SW8 . . . . .171 B1
Walworth SE17 . . .151 C2
3 West Kilburn
W10 . . . . .23 B2
Naylor Rd SE15 . . . .50 A3
Nayor Bdg E 6
E1 . . . . .111 B2
Nazareth Cl SE15 . . .50 A1
Nazrul St E2 . .24 B2 98 C4
Nealden St SW9 . . .62 B4
Neal St WC2 . . . . . .106 A1
Neal's Yd WC2 . . . .106 A1
Neasden Cl NW10 . .8 A3
Neasden Junc
NW10 . . . . .8 A4
Neasden La NW10 . .8 A3
Neasden Sta NW10 . .8 A3
Neathouse Pl
SW1 . . . . .146 C4
Nebraska Bldg 11
SE13 . . . . .52 A2
Nebraska St SE1 . .137 B3
Neckinger SE16 . . . .139 A2
Neckinger Est
SE16 . . . . .139 A2
Neckinger St SE1 . .139 A2
Nectarine Way
SE13 . . . . .52 A1
Nedahall Ct 4
NW11 . . . . .1 B4
Needham Ho
SE11 . . . . .149 B3
Needham Rd W11 . .31 C3
Needleman St
SE16 . . . . .40 C4
Needwood Ho N4 . .6 B3
Neilson-Terry Ct 9
SW9 . . . . .62 B3
Neil Wates Cres 1
SW2 . . . . .74 C3
Nella Rd W6 . . . . . .47 C4
Nelldale Rd SE16 . . .40 B2
Nell Gwynn Ho
SW3 . . . . .144 B3
Nelson Cl 2 NW6 . .23 C2
Nelson Ct SE16 . . . .33 B1
Nelson Docks
SE16 . . . . .33 B1
Nelson Gdns
E2 . . . . .24 C2 99 C4
Nelson Pas EC1 . . . .97 A4
Nelson Pl N1 . . . . . .86 B1
Nelson Rd SE10 . . . .52 B4
Nelson's Column
WC2 . . . . .120 A2
Nelson Sq SE1 . . . .136 A4
Nelsons Row SW4 . .61 C3
Nelson St
Canning Town
E16 . . . . .35 B2
Stepney E1 . . . . . .32 A3
Nelsons Yd NW1 . . .82 C2
Nelson Terr N1 . . . .86 B1
Nemoure Rd W3 . . .28 B2
Nepaul Rd 17
SW11 . . . . .60 A4
Nepean St SW15 . . .68 C4
Neptune Ct 13 E14 . .41 C2
Neptune Ho
2 Rotherhithe
SE16 . . . . .40 B3

Neptune Ho continued
14 Stoke Newington
N16 . . . . .16 A3
Neptune St SE16 . . .40 B3
Nesham Ho N1 . . . .24 A4
Nesham St E1 . . . .125 B2
Ness St 12 SE16 . . .139 B2
Nestor Ho 8 E2 . . . .25 A3
Netheravon Rd
W4 . . . . .38 B1
Netheravon Rd S
W4 . . . . .38 B1
Netherby Ho 23
SW8 . . . . .171 B1
Nethercombe Ho 1
SE3 . . . . .53 C4
Nethercott Ho 27
E3 . . . . .27 A2
Netherfield Rd
SW17 . . . . .72 C1
Netherford Rd
SW4 . . . . .171 A1
Netherhall Gdns
NW3 . . . . .11 B3
Netherhall Way
NW3 . . . . .11 B3
Netherleigh Cl N6 . .4 A3
Netherton Gr
SW10 . . . . .157 A3
Netherwood Rd
W14 . . . . .39 C4
Netherwood St
NW6 . . . . .10 C2
Netley 15 SE5 . . . . .49 A2
Netley Prim Sch
N1 . . . . .92 C3
Netley Rd TW8 . . . .44 A4
Netley St NW1 . . . . .92 C3
Nettlecombe NW1 . .13 C1
Nettleden Ho
SW3 . . . . .144 B3
Nettlefold Pl SE27 . .75 A1
Nettleton Rd SE14 . .50 C2
Nevada St SE10 . . . .52 B4
Nevena Ct 3 SW2 . .62 C2
Nevern Mans
SW5 . . . . .141 B2
Nevern Pl SW5 . . . .141 C3
Nevern Rd SW5 . . .141 B3
Nevern Sq SW5 . . .141 C3
Nevil Ho 7 SW9 . . .48 A1
Nevill Ct SW10 . . . .156 C2
Neville Cl
Acton W3 . . . . .37 B4
Paddington NW6 . . .23 B3
Peckham SE15 . . . .49 C2
Somers Town NW1 . .83 C1
Neville Ct 10
SW12 . . . . .73 B4
Neville Gill Cl
SW18 . . . . .59 A1
Neville Rd NW6 . . . .23 B3
Neville St SW7 . . . .143 B2
Neville Terr SW7 . .143 B2
Nevill Rd N16 . . . . . .7 A1
Nevinson Cl SW18 . .59 C1
Nevis Rd SW17 . . . .72 C2
Nevitt Ho N1 . . . . . .87 C1
Newall Ho SE1 . . . .137 A2
Newark Cres
NW10 . . . . .20 C2
Newark Ho 3
SW9 . . . . .48 A1
Newark St E1 . . . . . .32 A4
New Atlas Wharf
E14 . . . . .41 C3

New Bentham Ct **10**
N1.................15 B1
Newberry Ho N1....15 B1
Newbold Cotts **4**
E1.................32 B3
Newbolt Ho SE17 .151 B2
New Bond St W1 .118 B4
New Bridge St
EC4...............108 A1
New Broad St
EC2...............110 A3
New Bsns Ctr The
NW10.............21 B2
Newburgh Rd W3 ..28 B1
Newburgh St W1 .105 A1
New Burlington Mews
W1................118 C4
New Burlington Pl
W1................118 C4
New Burlington St
W1................118 C4
Newburn Ho SE11 149 A2
Newburn St SE11 149 A2
Newbury Ct E5 ....18 A3
Newbury Ho
Brixton SW9.......48 A1
14 Kensington W2 .100 B1
Newbury Mews
NW5...............12 C2
Newbury St EC1 ..108 C4
New Butt La SE8 ...52 C3
Newby NW1........92 C4
Newby Pl E14 .....34 B2
Newby St SW8 .....61 A4
New Caledonian Mkt
SE1 ....138 B2
New Caledonian
Wharf SE16 ....41 B3
New Campden Ct **1**
NW3 ....11 B4
Newcastle Cl EC4 108 A2
Newcastle Ct EC4 123 A4
Newcastle Ho W1 103 B4
Newcastle Pl W2 .101 C4
Newcastle Row
EC1................95 C1
New Cavendish St
W1................104 A3
New Change EC4 108 C1
New Charles St
EC1................96 B4
New Church Rd
32 Camberwell
SE5...............48 C4
Camberwell SE5....48 C4
New College Ct **6**
NW3 ....11 B2
New College Mews **7**
N1.................14 C1
New College Par **1**
NW3...............11 C1
Newcombe Ho N5 ..15 B3
Newcombe St
W8 ....31 C1/113 C2
Newcomen Ho **5**
NW5...............13 A4
Newcomen Rd
SW11..............59 C4
Newcomen St
SE1 ....137 B4
New Compton St
WC2..............106 A1
New Concordia Wharf
SE1 ....139 A4
Newcourt Ho **26**
E2.................25 A2

Newcourt St NW8 . **80** A1
New Covent Garden
Flower Market
SW8 ....162 A3
New Covent Garden
Fruit & Vegetable
Mkt SW8.........162 B3
New Crane Pl E1 ..32 B1
New Crescent Yd **1**
NW10.............21 B3
NEW CROSS........51 B2
New Cross SE14 ...51 B3
NEW CROSS
GATE 50 C2
New Cross Gate
SE14 ....50 C2
New Cross Gate Sta
SE14 ....51 A3
New Cross Rd
SE14 ....51 A2
New Cross Sta
SE14 ....51 B3
New Ct
City of London
EC4..............107 B1
26 Hampstead
NW3 ....11 B4
Stoke Newington
N16................6 C4
Newdigate Ho **5**
E14................33 B3
Newell St E14 ......33 B3
New End NW3 ....2 B1
New End Prim Sch **33**
NW3 ....11 C4
New End Sq NW3 ..11 C4
Newent Cl SE15 ...49 A3
New Fetter La
EC4..............107 C2
Newfield Prim Sch
NW10.............22 B4
Newgate St EC1 ..108 B2
New Globe Wlk
SE1 ....122 C2
New Goulston St
E1................110 C2
Newham Sixth Form
Coll (Stratford Ctr)
7 E15.........19 C1/C2
Newham's Row
SE1 ....138 B3
Newhaven La **3**
E16................35 C4
New Hope Christian
Acad **1** SE22....64 B3
NEWINGTON......150 B4
Newington Barrow
Way N7..............5 B1
Newington Butts SE1,
SE11.............150 B3
Newington Cswy
SE1 ....136 C2
Newington Gn
N16................15 C3
Newington Green
Mans N16.........15 C3
Newington Green
Prim Sch **11** N16 .15 C3
Newington Green Rd
N1.................15 C2
Newington Ind Est
SE17..............150 C3
New Inn Broadway
EC2........24 A1/98 B2
New Inn Sq
EC2........24 A1/98 B2

New Inn St
EC2........24 A1 98 B2
New Inn Yd
EC2........24 A1 98 B2
New James Ct
SE15..............65 A4
New Kent Rd SE1 151 A4
New King's Prim Sch
12 SW6 ....165 A4
New King's Rd SW6 .165 C3
New King St SE8 ..51 C4
Newland Ct EC1....97 B2
Newland Ho **17**
SE14..............50 C4
Newlands NW1.....92 C4
Newlands Acad
SE15..............49 C3
Newlands Quay E1 .32 B2
New London St
EC3..............124 B4
Newlyn NW1......83 A3
Newman Catholic Coll
NW10.............21 C4
Newman Pas W1 ..105 A3
Newman St W1....105 A3
Newmill Ho E3 ....27 B1
Newmount St E15 ..11 C3
New Mount St E15 ..19 C1
Newnes Path
SW15..............57 A3
Newnham Ho **9**
SW15..............57 A3
Newnham Terr
SE1 ....135 B2
Newnton Cl N4.....6 C4
New North Com Sch
N1................86 C4
New North Pl
EC2........24 A1 98 A2
New North Rd N1 .87 B3
New North Road
Bridge N1........87 A3
New North St
WC1..............106 C4
Newnton Cl N4.....6 C4
New Oxford St
WC1..............106 A2
New Palace Yd
SW1..............134 A3
New Park St **20**
SW2...............74 A4
New Park Par **14**
SW2...............74 A4
New Park Rd SW2 .74 A4
New Place Sq
SE16..............40 A3
Newport Ave E14 ..34 C2
Newport Ct WC2 ..119 C4
Newport Ho **2** E3 ..26 A2
Newport Pl WC2 ..119 C4
Newport Rd SW13 .46 C2
Newport St SE11 ..149 A4
Newport St SE11 ..149 A4
New Priory Ct **9**
NW6...............10 C1
New Providence
Wharf E14........34 C1
Newquay Ho SE11 149 B2
New Quebec St
W1................103 A1
New Rd E1.........32 A4
New River Ct N5 ..15 C4

New River Way N4 ..6 C4
New Row WC2 ....120 A4
New St Sq EC4 ...107 C2
New Scotland Yard
SW1..............134 B4
New Shepherd's Bush
Mkt **6** W12.......39 B4
New Spring Gdns Wlk
SE11..............148 B1
New Sq WC2 ......107 A2
New Square Pas
WC2..............107 A2
Newstead Ho N1 ..85 C2
Newton Ave W3 ...37 B4
Newton Gr W4 .....38 A2
Newton Ho
22 Clapham
SW8 ....171 B2
Paddington NW8 .78 B4
1 Stepney E1 ...32 A2
Newton Pl E14 ....41 C2
Newton Point **1**
E16................35 B3
Newton Prep Sch
SW8 ....170 B4
Newton Rd
Acton W3 ....37 B4
Kensington W2....100 B1
Stratford New Town
E15................19 C3
Newton St WC2 ..106 B2
Newton's Yd **14**
SW18.............58 C2
New Tower Bldgs **21**
E1.................32 A1
Newtown Ct
Battersea SW11...170 A3
Clapham SW4......61 A2
New Union Cl E14 .42 B3
New Union St
EC2..............109 B3
New Wharf Rd N1 .84 B2
Niagara Cl N1 .....87 A2
Niagara Ct **6**
SE16..............40 B3
Nicholas Ct
Chiswick W4......46 A3
Golders Green NW11..1 C4
Nicholas Ho **2**
SW15..............56 C2
Nicholas La EC2,
EC4..............123 C4
Nicholas Pas EC3 123 C4
Nicholas Rd
Bethnal Green E1 ..25 B1
20 Shepherd's Bush
W11...............30 C2
Nicholay Rd N19 ...4 C3
Nicholl Ho N4......6 B3
Nicholl St E2.......24 C4
Nichols Cl N4......5 C3
Nichols Ct E2......24 B3
Nicholson Ho
SE17..............151 B2
Nicholson St SE1 122 A1
Nickleby Ho
18 Bermondsey
SE1 ....139 B3
7 Shepherd's Bush
W11...............30 C1
Nickols Wlk SW18 ..59 A3
Nicoll Ct NW10....21 A4
Nicoll Rd NW10....21 A4
Nicosia Rd SW18 ..72 A4
Nigel Bldg EC1 ...107 B4

Nigel Playfair Ave
W6 ....39 A1
Nigel Rd SE15 ....64 C4
Nightingale Cl W4 ..45 B3
Nightingale Ct
14 Cubitt Town
E14................42 B3
Finsbury Pk N4.....5 B2
Nightingale Gr
SE13..............67 C2
Nightingale Ho
10 Hoxton E1.....24 A4
4 North Kensington
W12...............30 B3
7 St George in t East
E1................125 B2
Nightingale Hospl
NW1..............102 B4
Nightingale La SW11,
SW12.............60 C1
Nightingale Lo **5**
W9 ....31 C4
Nightingale Mans **4**
SW12.............60 C1
Nightingale Mews
1 Bow E3 ....26 A3
Newington SE11 ..150 A4
Nightingale Pl
SW10 ....157 A4
Nightingale Prim Sch
E5................16 C4
Nightingale Rd
2 Canonbury N1 ..15 B2
Dagenham NW10 ..21 A3
Nightingale Sch
SW17..............72 A2
Nightingale Sq
SW12..............72 C4
Nightingale Wlk SW18,
SW4...............61 A1
Nile Cl N16..........7 B1
Nile Ho N1.........97 B4
Nile St N1..........97 B4
Nile Terr SE1,
SE15..............153 A1
Nimegen Way **9**
SE22..............64 A2
Nimrod Pas **4** N1..16 A2
NINE ELMS.......160 C2
Nine Elms La
SW8 ....161 B3
Nisbet Ho E9......17 C3
Niton Rd TW9 .....54 C4
Niton St SW6.....47 C3
Nobel Ho **8** SE5 ...48 B1
Noble Ct E1........32 A2
Noble St EC2......108 C2
Noel Coward Ho
SW1 ....147 A3
Noel Ho **3** NW3 ..11 C1
Noel Rd
Acton W3 ....28 A3
Islington N1.......86 B2
Noel St W1 ....105 A1
Noko NW10 ....22 C2
Nolan Way E5 .....16 C4
Noll Ho N7..........5 B2
Norbiton Rd E14 ..33 B3
Norbroke St W12 ..29 B2
Norburn St W10 ...31 A4
Norcombe Ho **2**
N19.................4 C1
Norcott Rd N16.....7 C1

Norcroft Gdns
SE22 . . . . .76 C4
Norden Ho 22 E2 . . . . .25 A2
Nore Ct NW10 . . . . .8 C1
Norfolk Cres W2 . . .102 B2
Norfolk Ho
City of London
EC4 . . . . .122 C4
Greenwich SE3 . . . . . . .53 A4
4 Putney SW15 . . . . . .69 B4
Richmond TW10 . . . . . .54 C2
Shacklewell E8 . . . . . . .16 B4
St Johns SE8 . . . . .51 C2
Westminster SW1 . .147 C4
Norfolk House Rd
SW16 . . . . .74 A1
Norfolk Mans
Battersea SW11 . . .169 A3
10 Wandsworth
SW18 . . . . .58 C2
Norfolk Mews 12
W10 . . . . .31 A4
Norfolk Pl W2 . . . . .101 C2
Norfolk Rd
St John's Wood
NW8 . . . . .79 C3
Willesden NW10 . . . . . .8 C1
Norfolk Row SE1,
SE11 . . . . .148 C4
Norfolk Sq W2 . . . .101 C2
Norfolk Sq Mews
W2 . . . . .101 C2
Norgrove St SW12 . .72 C4
Norland Ho 13
W11 . . . . .30 C1
Norland Pl
W11 . . . . . .31 A1 112 B1
Norland Place Sch
W11 . . . . . .31 A1 112 A1
Norland Sq
W11 . . . . . .31 A1 112 A1
Norley Vale SW15 . . .68 C3
Norman Butler Ho 6
W10 . . . . .23 A1
Normanby Cl
SW15 . . . . .58 B2
Normanby Rd NW10 . .8 B4
Norman Ct
Dulwich SE22 . . . . . . .76 C4
Finsbury Pk N4 . . . . . . .5 C4
Willesden NW10 . . . . . .8 C1
Normand Croft Com
Sch W14 . . . . .155 A4
Normand Mews
W14 . . . . .154 B4
Normand Rd W14 .154 C4
Normandy Ho 8
E14 . . . . .42 B4
Normandy Rd
SW9 . . . . .173 B3
Norman Gr E3 . . . . . .26 A3
Norman Ho SW8 . .162 A2
Normanhurst Rd
SW2 . . . . .74 B2
Norman Rd SE10 . . .52 A3
Norman St EC1 . . . .97 A3
Normanton Ave SW18,
SW19 . . . . .70 C2
Normanton Ho 6
SW4 . . . . .61 B1
Norman Way W3 . . .28 A3

Norris Ho
10 Hoxton N1 . . . . . . .24 A4
18 South Hackney
E9 . . . . .25 B4
Norris St SW1 . . . .119 B3
Norroy Rd SW15 . . .57 C3
Norse Ho 13 SE5 . . .48 B3
Norstead Pl SW15 . .68 C2
NORTH ACTON 20 C2
North Acton Rd
NW10 . . . . .20 C2
North Acton Sta
W3 . . . . .28 C4
Northampton Gr
N1 . . . . .15 C3
Northampton Pk
N1 . . . . .15 C2
Northampton Rd
EC1 . . . . .95 C2
Northampton Sq
EC1 . . . . .96 A3
Northampton St
N1 . . . . .15 B1
North Audley St
W1 . . . . .117 B4
North Ave 8 TW9 . . .44 C2
Northaw Ho 4
W10 . . . . .22 B1
North Bank NW8 . . .90 A3
North Block 19 E1 . .32 B2
Northbourne Ho 7
E5 . . . . .17 A3
Northbourne Rd
SW4 . . . . .61 C2
North Bridge House
Sch 11 NW3 . . . . .11 B2
North Bridge House
School Prep Sch
NW1 . . . . .82 A3
North Bridge House
Senior Sch 8
NW3 . . . . .11 C4
Northburgh St EC1 .96 B2
North Carriage Dr
W2 . . . . .116 B4
North Chiswick Bsns
Pk W3 . . . . .37 B3
Northchurch
SE17 . . . . .151 C2
Northchurch Ho 11
E2 . . . . .24 C4
Northchurch Rd
N1 . . . . .15 C1
Northchurch Terr
N1 . . . . .16 A1
North Circular Rd NW2,
NW10 . . . . .8 A3
North Colonnade The
E14 . . . . .34 A1
Northcote Lodge Sch
SW11 . . . . .60 B1
Northcote Rd
Wandsworth
SW11 . . . . .60 B2
Willesden NW10 . . . . . .8 A1
Northcourt W1 . . . .105 A4
North Cres
Marylebone WC1 . . .105 B4
Newham E16 . . . . . . .27 C1
W12 . . . . .38 C4
North Cross Rd
SE22 . . . . .64 C2
North Ct SW1 . . . . .134 A1
Northdown St N1 . . .84 C1

North Dulwich Sta
SE21 . . . . .63 C2
NORTH END 2 B2
North End NW3 . . . . .2 B2
North End Cres
W14 . . . . .140 C3
North End Ho
W14 . . . . .140 B3
North End Par
W14 . . . . .140 B3
North End Rd
Golders Green
NW11 . . . . .2 A3
West Kensington
W14 . . . . .141 A1
North End Way
NW3 . . . . .2 B2
Northern Hts N8 . . . .4 C4
Northesk Ho 6
E1 . . . . .25 A1
North Eyot Gdns 1
W6 . . . . .38 B1
Northey St E14 . . . . .33 A2
Northfield Hall N6 . . .3 C4
Northfield Ho 5
SE15 . . . . .49 C4
Northfield Rd N16 . . .7 A4
Northfields SW18 . . .58 C3
Northfields Prospect
SW18 . . . . .58 C3
Northfields Rd W3 . .28 B4
Northfleet Ho
SE1 . . . . .137 B4
North Flower Wlk
W2 . . . . .115 B3
North Gate NW8 . . .80 A1
Northgate Ct 14
SW9 . . . . .62 C4
North Gower St
NW1 . . . . .93 A3
North Gr N6 . . . . .3 C4
North Greenwich Pier
SE10 . . . . .35 B1
North Greenwich Sta
SE10 . . . . .43 A4
North Hill Ct N6 . . . .3 C4
North Ho 5 SE8 . . . .41 B1
Northiam WC1 . . . . .94 B3
Northiam St E9 . . . . .25 B4
Northington St
WC1 . . . . .95 A1
NORTH
KENSINGTON 31 A4
Northlands St SE5 . .48 B1
Northleigh Ho 38
E3 . . . . .27 A2
North Lo SW4 . . . . . .61 A3
North Lodge Cl
SW15 . . . . .57 C2
North Mews WC1 . . .95 A1
Northolme Rd N5 . . . .5 C2
North Pas SW18 . . . .58 C2
Northpoint Sq 8
NW1 . . . . .13 C2
North Pole Rd
W10 . . . . .30 B4
Northport St N1 . . . .87 C3
North Rd
Barnsbury N7 . . . . . . .14 A2
Brentford TW8 . . . . . .44 A4
Highgate N6 . . . . .3 C4
Richmond TW9 . . . . . .44 C1
North Ride W2 . . . . .116 A3
North Rise W2 . . . .102 B1
North Row W1 . . . .117 B4

North Sheen 44 C1
North Sheen Sta
TW10 . . . . .54 C3
North Side
Wandsworth Comm
SW18 . . . . .59 C2
North St SW4 . . . . . .61 B4
Northstead Rd
SW2 . . . . .74 C2
North Tenter St
E1 . . . . .111 A1
North Terr SW3 . . .130 A1
Northumberland Alley
EC3 . . . . .110 B1
Northumberland Ave
WC2 . . . . .120 A2
Northumberland Ho
NW5 . . . . .13 B2
Northumberland
Mans E5 . . . . .17 B4
Northumberland Pl
W2 . . . . .31 C3
Northumberland St
WC2 . . . . .120 A2
Northumbria Ct 10
TW9 . . . . .54 A3
Northumbria St
E14 . . . . .33 C3
North Verbena Gdns
2 W6 . . . . .38 C1
Northview 1 N7 . . . . .5 A1
Northview Cres
NW10 . . . . .8 B4
Northview Jun & Inf
Sch NW10 . . . . .8 B4
North Villas NW1 . . .13 C2
Northway Rd SE5 . . .63 B4
Northways Par 2
NW3 . . . . .11 C1
North West London
Jewish Day Sch
NW6 . . . . .10 A1
Northwest Pl N1 . . .85 C2
North Wharf Rd
W2 . . . . .101 B3
Northwick Cl NW8 . .89 B2
Northwick Ho
NW8 . . . . .89 A2
Northwick Terr
NW8 . . . . .89 B2
North Wlk W2 . . . .114 C3
Northwold Prim Sch
E5 . . . . .7 C2
Northwold Rd E5,
N16 . . . . .7 C2
North Wood Lo
NW3 . . . . .11 A4
Northwood Rd N6 . . .4 A4
North Worple Way
SW14 . . . . .55 C4
Norton Folgate
E1 . . . . .110 B4
Norton Ho
16 Globe Town
E2 . . . . .25 C3
30 Stepney E1 . . . . . .32 A3
16 Stockwell SW9 . .173 C1
Norval Gn 8 SW9 . .173 C2
Norvic Ho 5 SE5 . . .48 B1
Norway Gate SE16 . .41 A3
Norway Pl E14 . . . . .33 B3
Norway St SE10 . . . .52 A4
Norwich Ho 3
E14 . . . . .34 A3
Norwich St EC4 . . .107 B2
Norwood Cl NW2 . . . .1 A1

Norwood Ho 25
E14 . . . . .34 A2
Norwood NHS Ctr
SE27 . . . . .75 A1
Norwood Rd SE24,
SE27 . . . . .75 A3
Notley Pl 8 SW4 . . .62 A1
Notley St SE5 . . . . . .48 C3
Notre Dame RC Sec
Girls' Sch SE1 . . . .136 A2
Notting Barn Rd
W10 . . . . .22 C1
Nottingdale Sq
W11 . . . . . .31 A1 112 A2
Nottingham Ct
WC2 . . . . .106 A1
Nottingham Ho
33 Camberwell
SE5 . . . . .48 B1
Stoke Newington N4 . .6 B3
Nottingham Pl
W1 . . . . .103 B4
Nottingham Rd
SW17 . . . . .72 B3
Nottingham St
W1 . . . . .103 B4
Nottingham Terr
NW1 . . . . .91 B1
NOTTING HILL 112 C3
Notting Hill Gate
W11 . . . . . .31 C1 113 B2
Notting Hill Gate Sta
W11 . . . . . .31 C1 113 A2
Notting Hill Prep Sch
7 W11 . . . . .31 A3
Nottingwood Ho
W11 . . . . . .31 A2 112 A4
Nova Bldg 1 E14 . . .41 C2
Nova Ct E 3 E14 . . .34 B1
Nova Ct W 2 E14 . . .34 B1
Novello St SW6 . . .165 B4
Nowell Rd SW13 . . . .46 C4
Noyna Rd SW17 . . . .72 B1
Nucleus NW10 . . . . . .20 B2
Nuding Cl SE13 . . . . .66 C4
Nuffield Lo 14 W9 . . .31 C4
Nugent Ct 3 N19 . . . .5 A3
Nugent Rd N19 . . . . . .5 A3
Nugent Terr NW8 . . .79 A1
Nun Ct EC2 . . . . . . .109 B2
NUNHEAD 65 B3
Nunhead Cres
SE15 . . . . .65 A4
Nunhead Gn SE15 . .65 A4
Nunhead Gr SE15 . .65 B4
Nunhead La SE15 . . .65 A4
Nunhead Sta SE15 . .50 B1
Nursery Cl
New Cross SE4 . . . . . .51 B1
Putney SW15 . . . . . . .57 C3
Nursery La
North Kensington
W10 . . . . .30 B4
Shoreditch E2 . . . . . . .24 B4
Nursery Rd
Hackney E9 . . . . .17 B2
Stockwell SW9 . . . . . .62 B3
Nursery Row
SE17 . . . . .151 B3
Nutbourne St W10 . .23 A2
Nutbrook St SE15 . . .64 C4
Nutcroft Rd SE15 . . .50 A3
Nutfield Rd
East Dulwich
SE22 . . . . .64 B3
Leyton E15 . . . . .19 B4

Nutford Pl W1.....**102** C2
Nuthurst Ave SW2..74 B2
Nutley Terr NW3....11 C2
Nutmeg La E14.....34 C3
Nuttall St N1.......24 A3
Nutt St SE15.......49 B3
Nye Bevan Ho
  SW6 ....**154** C2
Nye's Wharf SE1,
  SE15 ....49 C4
Nylands Ave TW9 ..44 C1
Nynehead St SE14 .51 A3
Nyton Cl 7 N19.....5 A3

O

O2 Arena The
  SE10.............35 A1
O2 Ctr NW6 ....11 B2
Oakbank Ct SE22..63 B3
Oakbury Rd SW6..**166** B1
Oakcourt 17 SE15..49 B3
Oak Cres E16......35 A4
Oakcroft Ct SE3 ...53 C2
Oakcroft Rd SE13..52 C1
Oakdale Ct N19.....5 A2
Oakdale Rd SE15...65 B4
Oakdene 3 SE15...50 A2
Oakdene Ho 4 N16..7 A3
Oakden St SE11 ...**149** C4
Oakeford Ho W14.**126** B1
Oakend Ho 10 N4...6 C4
Oakeshott Ave N6 ..3 C2
Oakey La SE1......**135** B2
Oakfield Ct
  Clapham Pk SW4 ...62 A1
  Finsbury Pk N8.....5 A4
Oakfield Prep Sch
  SE21..............75 C3
Oakfield Rd
  Finsbury Pk N4.....5 C4
  Wimbledon SW19....69 C1
Oakfield St SW10 .**156** C4
Oakford Rd NW5 ...13 B4
Oak Gr NW2........10 A4
Oakham Ho 5
  W10 ....22 B1
Oakhill Ave NW3 ...11 A4
Oakhill Ct
  Honor Oak SE23....65 B1
  Putney SW15 ......58 B2
Oak Hill Lo NW3 ...11 A4
Oak Hill Park Mews
  NW3 ....11 B4
Oak Hill Pk NW3 ...11 A4
Oakhill Pl SW15 ...58 C2
Oakhill Rd SW15...58 C2
Oak Hill Way NW3..11 A4
Oak Ho
  7 Cubitt Town
  E14...............42 B4
  8 Maitland Pk
  NW3 ....12 B2
  2 Richmond TW9 ..45 A2
  5 Stoke Newington
  N16 ....7 A3
Oakhurst Ct SE22..64 C3
Oakington Rd W9 ..23 C1
Oakington Way N8 ..5 A4
Oak La E14.........33 B2
Oaklands Ct
  Dagenham NW10....21 A4
  6 Shepherd's Bush
  W12 ....30 A1
Oaklands Gr W12...29 C1

Oaklands Ho SE4...66 B4
Oaklands Mews 1
  NW2 ....9 C4
Oaklands Pas NW2 ..9 C4
Oaklands Pl 8
  SW4 ....61 C3
Oaklands Rd
  Cricklewood NW2....9 C4
  Mortlake SW14 ....55 B3
Oaklands Sch 51..
  E2................25 A2
Oakley Cres EC1....86 B1
Oakley Dr SE13....67 C1
Oakley Gdns SW3.**158** B4
Oakley Ho SW1 ...**145** A4
Oakley Pl SE1.....**152** C1
Oakley Rd N1 ......15 C1
Oakley Sq NW1....83 A2
Oakley St SW3 ...**158** A4
Oak Lock Mews 16
  W4 ....38 A1
Oak Lodge 14
  SE21..............75 C2
Oak Lodge Sch
  SW12.............72 C4
Oakman Ho 23
  SW19.............69 C3
Oak Park Gdns
  SW19.............69 C3
Oak Park Mews
  N16 ....7 B1
Oakshaw Rd SW18..71 A4
Oakshott Ct NW1...83 B1
Oak Sq SW4.......**172** C1
Oaks Sh Ctr The
  W3 ....28 B1
Oaks The
  Brondesbury Pk
  NW6 ....9 C4
  Willesden NW10....9 A1
Oak Tree Ct
  Acton W3 ....28 A2
  8 Clapham Pk
  SW4 ....62 A2
Oak Tree Ho W9 ...88 A2
Oak Tree Rd NW8 ..90 A3
Oakview Lo NW11 ..1 B4
Oak Village NW5...12 C4
Oak Way W3 ....29 A1
Oakwell Ho 24
  SW8 ....11 C3
Oakwood Bsns Pk
  NW10.............20 C1
Oakwood Ct SE13..67 C1
Oakwood Ct W14 ..**126** C2
Oakwood La W14 ..**126** C2
Oakworth Rd W10..30 C4
Oasis Academy
  Johanna SE1.....**135** B3
Oast Ct 8 E14......33 B2
Oast Lo W4.........46 A3
Oat La EC2.......**109** A2
Oatlands Ct 8
  SW19.............69 C3
Oatwell Ho SW3..**144** B3
Oban Ho E14.......34 C3
Oban St E14........34 C3
Oberon Ho 5 N1...24 A3
Oberstein Rd 1
  SW11.............59 C3
Oborne Cl SE24....63 A2
O'Brian Ho 11 E1..25 C2

Observatory Gdns
  W8 ....**127** C4
Observatory Mews
  E14...............42 C1
Observatory Rd
  Kensington SW7...**129** B1
  Mortlake SW14 ....55 B3
Occupation Rd
  SE17.............**150** C2
Ocean St E1........32 C4
Ocean Wharf E14...41 C4
Ockbrook 3 E1.....32 B4
Ockendon Rd N1 ..15 C2
Ockley Rd SW16...74 A1
Octagon Arc EC2 .**110** A3
Octagon The W10 ..3 A1
Octavia Ho W10 ...23 A1
Octavia Mews 1
  W9 ....23 B1
Octavia St SW11..**168** B3
Octavia St SE8 .....51 C3
Odell Wlk SE13....67 B4
Odeon Ct
  Dagenham NW10....21 A4
  1 Newham E16....35 C4
Odessa Rd NW10 ..21 C3
Odessa St SE16....41 B3
Odette Duval Ho 3
  E1................32 B4
Odger St SW11 ...**169** A2
Odhams Wlk WC2 .**106** B1
Odin Ho 5 SE5......48 B1
O'Donnell Ct WC1 ..94 B2
O'Driscoll Ho 4
  W12 ....30 A3
Offa's Mead E9 ....18 A4
Offenbach Ho 1
  E2................25 C3
Offerton Rd SW4...61 B4
Offham Ho SE17 .**152** A3
Offley Ho 10 E9 ...17 C2
Offley Rd SW9 ...**163** B2
Offord Rd N1.......14 B1
Offord St N1........14 B1
Ogilvie Ho 12 E1 ..32 C3
Oglander Rd SE15 ..64 B4
Ogle St W1.......**104** C4
O'Gorman Ho
  SW10 ....**157** A2
Ohio Bldg 13 SE13..52 A2
Oil Mill La W6......38 C1
Okehampton Rd
  NW10.............22 C4
Okeover Manor
  SW4 ....61 A3
Olaf St W11 ....30 C2
Old Bailey EC4 ...**108** B1
Old Bailey (Central
  Criminal Court)
  EC4.............**108** B2
Old Barrack Yd
  SW1 ....**131** B3
Old Bellgate Wharf
  E14...............41 C3
Old Bethnal Green Rd
  E2................25 A2
Old Billingsgate Wlk
  EC3................27 C2
Old Bldgs WC2 ...**107** B2
Old Bond St W1 ..**118** C3
Old Brewery Mews
  NW3 ....11 C4
Old Broad St EC2 **109** C2
Old Brompton Rd SW5,
  SW7 ....**143** A3

Old Burlington St
  W1 ....**118** C3
Oldbury Ct E9......18 A3
Oldbury Pl W1 ....**103** C4
Old Canal Mews
  SE15.............**153** A1
Old Castle St E1 ..**111** A2
Old Cavendish St
  W1 ....**104** A1
Old Change Ct
  EC4.............**108** C1
Old Chiswick Yd
  W4 ....46 A4
Old Church La E1 ..32 C3
Old Church St
  SW3 ....**143** C1
Old Compton St
  W1 ....**105** B1
Old Court Ho W8 .**128** A3
Old Court Pl W8..**128** A3
Old Curiosity Shop
  The WC2 ....**106** C2
Old Dairy Ct 3 N19 ..5 B3
Old Dairy Mews
  5 Balham SW12 ...72 C3
  4 Camden Town
  NW5 ....12 C2
Old Deer Park Gdns
  TW9 ....54 A4
Old Devonshire Rd
  SW12.............73 A4
Old Dock Cl TW9 ..44 C4
Oldfield Gr SE16...40 C2
Oldfield Ho 14 W4..38 A1
Oldfield Mews N6 ..4 B4
Oldfield Rd
  Bedford Pk W3,
  W12 ....38 B4
  Stoke Newington
  N16 ....7 A1
  Willesden NW10....8 B1
Old Fish St Hill
  EC4.............**122** C4
Old Fleet La EC4 .**108** A2
OLD FORD...........26 B3
Old Ford Prim Sch 38
  E3................26 B3
Old Ford Rd E2, E3..25 C3
Old Ford Trad Est
  E3................26 C4
Old Forge Mews
  W12 ....39 A4
Old Forge Rd N19 ..4 C2
Old Gloucester St
  WC1 ....**106** B4
Oldham Terr W3 ...28 B1
Oldhill St N16.......7 C3
Old Hospital Cl SW12,
  SW17.............72 B3
Olding Ho 9
  SW12.............73 B4
Old Jamaica Bsns Est
  23 SE16.........**139** B1
Old Jamaica Rd
  SE16.............**139** B2
Old James St SE15 ..65 A4
Old Jewry EC2....**109** B1
Old Kent Rd
  Deptford SE1,
  SE15.............**150** B4
  Walworth SE1....**152** B2
Old Laundry The 14
  SW18.............59 C3
Old Manor Ct NW8 ..79 A2
Old Manor Yd
  SW5 ....**142** A3

Old Market St 11
  E2...............24 B2
Old Marylebone Rd
  NW1.............**102** B3
Old Mitre Ct EC4 .**107** C1
Old Montague St
  E1................**111** B3
Old Nichol St
  E2................98 C2
Old North St WC1.**106** C4
OLD OAK
  COMMON.........21 B1
Old Oak Common La
  NW10.............21 A1
Old Oak La NW10 ..21 C2
Old Oak Prim Sch
  W12 ....29 B3
Old Oak Rd W3 ....29 B2
Old Orch The W3 ..29 B2
Old Palace Prim Sch
  5 E3..............27 A2
Old Paradise St
  SE11.............**148** C3
Old Park Ave
  SW12..............60 C1
Old Park La W1 ..**118** A1
Old Pearson St
  SE10..............52 A3
Old Pye St Est
  SW1 ....**133** B2
Old Quebec St
  W1 ....**103** A1
Old Queen St
  SW1 ....**133** C3
Oldridge Rd SW12..73 A4
Old Royal Free Pl
  N1................85 C3
Old Royal Free Sq
  N1................85 C3
Old School Cl
  SE10..............43 A3
Old School Sq 12
  E14...............33 C3
Old Seacoal La
  EC4.............**108** A1
Old South Lambeth
  Rd SW8..........**162** B2
Old Spitalfields Mkt
  E1................**110** C4
Old Sq WC2 ......**107** B2
Old St EC1.........97 C2
Old Stable Mews
  N5.................6 B1
Old Station Wy 12
  SW4 ....61 C4
Old Street Sta EC1..97 C2
Old Sun Wharf
  E14...............33 A2
Old Swan Wharf
  SW11.............**167** C4
Old Theatre Ct
  SE1 ....**123** A2
Old Town SW4.....61 B4
Old Vicarage Sch 37
  TW10..............54 A1
Old Woolwich Rd
  SE10..............42 C1
Old York Rd SW18..59 A2
O'Leary Sq E1......32 B4
Olga Prim Sch 37
  E3................26 A3

Olga St 20 E3 . . . . 26 A3
Oliphant St W10 . . . . . . 23 A3
Olive Blythe Ho 14
  W10 . . . . 23 A1
Oliver Bsns Pk
  NW10 . . . . 20 B3
Oliver Cl W4 . . . . 45 A4
Olive Rd NW2 . . . . 9 B4
Oliver Goldsmith Prim
  Sch 49 B2
Oliver Ho
  22 Bermondsey
  SE16 . . . . 139 B3
  Notting Hill
  W11 . . . . 31 A2 112 A3
  South Lambeth
  SW8 . . . . 162 A2
Oliver House Prep
  Sch 1 SW4 . . . . 61 A1
Oliver Mews SE15 . . . . 49 C1
Oliver's Yd EC1 . . . . . . 97 C2
Olive Tree Ho 7
  SE15 . . . . 50 B4
Olive Tree Sch The
  SE13 . . . . 67 A1
Olivette St 1
  SW15 . . . . 57 C4
Olympian Ct 2
  E14 . . . . 41 C2
Olympia Way
  W14 . . . . 126 B1
Olympia Yd W2 . . . . . 114 B3
Olympic Ho 10
  W10 . . . . 30 B3
Olympic Park Ave
  E15 . . . . 19 A3
Olympus Sq E5 . . . . 7 C1
Oman Ave NW2 . . . . 9 B4
Oman Ct NW4 . . . . 9 A4
Ombersley Ho H4 . . . . 6 B4
Omeara St SE1 . . . . . 123 A1
Omega Cl E14 . . . . 42 A2
Omega Ho SW10 . . . . 157 A2
Omega Pl N1 . . . . 84 B1
Omega St SE14 . . . . . . 51 C2
Omega Works E3 . . . . . 18 C1
Ommaney Rd
  SE14 . . . . 51 A2
Omnibus Bsns Ctr
  N7 . . . . 14 A3
Ondine Rd SE15 . . . . . 64 B4
Onedin Point 10
  E1 . . . . 125 C3
Onega Gate SE16 . . . . 41 A3
O'Neill Ho NW8 . . . . . . 79 C1
One New Change Sh
  Ctr EC4 . . . . 108 C1
One Tree Cl SE23 . . . . 65 B1
Ongar Ho 15 N1 . . . . . 15 C2
Ongar Rd SW6 . . . . . . 155 C4
Onslow Ave TW10 . . . . 54 A2
Onslow Avenue Mans
  10 TW10 . . . . 54 A2
Onslow Cl W9 . . . . 23 B2

Onslow Ct SW10 . . . . 143 A1
Onslow Gdns
  SW7 . . . . 143 B2
Onslow Lo 28 SW2 . . . 74 C4
Onslow Mews E
  SW7 . . . . 143 B3
Onslow Mews W
  SW7 . . . . 143 B3
Onslow Rd TW10 . . . . . 54 A1
Onslow Sq SW7 . . . . . 143 C3
Onslow St EC1 . . . . . . 95 C1
Ontario St SE1 . . . . . . 136 B2
Ontario Way E14 . . . . . 33 C2
Opal St SE11 . . . . 150 A2
Open Air Theatre,
  Regent's Pk NW1 . . . . 91 B3
Openview SW17,
  SW18 . . . . 71 C2
Opera Ct 7 N19 . . . . . . 4 C1
Operating Theatre
  Mus & Herb Garret
  The SE1 . . . . 123 C1
Ophelia Gdns NW2 . . . . 1 A1
Ophir Terr SE15 . . . . . 49 C2
Opie Ho NW8 . . . . 80 B2
Oppenheim Rd
  SE13 . . . . 52 B1
Oppidan Apartments
  NW6 . . . . 10 C1
Oppidans Rd NW3 . . . . 12 B1
Orange Gr E11 . . . . 40 B3
Orange Pl 16 SE16 . . . . 40 B3
Orangery Gallery The
  W8 . . . . 114 A1
Orange St WC2 . . . . . 119 C3
Orange Yd WC2 . . . . . 105 C1
Oransay Rd 25 N1 . . . . 15 B2
Oratory La SW3 . . . . . 143 C2
Oratory RC Prim Sch
  SW3 . . . . 144 A2
Orbain Rd SW6 . . . . . 154 B1
Orbel St SW11 . . . . . . 168 A3
Orb St SE17 . . . . 151 B3
Orchard Cl
  Honor Oak SE23 . . . . . 65 B1
  21 Islington N1 . . . . . 15 B1
  Kensal Town W10 . . . . 31 A4
Orchard Ct
  Barnes SW13 . . . . 56 B4
  Marylebone W1 . . . . . 103 B2
Orchard Dr SE3 . . . . . . 53 A1
Orchard Hill SE13 . . . . 52 A2
Orchard Ho
  Camberwell SE5 . . . . . 48 B2
  11 Rotherhithe
  SE16 . . . . 40 B3
  Shepherd's Bush
  W12 . . . . 29 C1
Orchard Ho Sch 15
  W4 . . . . 38 A2
Orchard Mead Ho
  NW11 . . . . 1 C2
Orchard Mews
  Lewisham SE13 . . . . . 67 B1
  London N1 . . . . 15 C1
Orchard Pl E14 . . . . . . 35 A2
Orchard Prim Sch 14
  E9 . . . . 17 B1
Orchard Rd
  Highgate N6 . . . . 4 A4
  Richmond TW9 . . . . . 54 C1
Orchard Rise
  TW10 . . . . 55 A3
Orchardson Ho
  NW8 . . . . 89 C1

Orchardson St
  NW8 . . . . 89 C1
Orchard Sq W14 . . . . 140 C1
Orchard St W1 . . . . . . 103 C2
Orchard The
  Acton Green W4 . . . . . 37 C2
  Lewisham SE3 . . . . . . 52 C1
Orchid Cl SE13 . . . . . . 67 C2
Orchid Mews 10
  NW10 . . . . 20 C4
Orchid St W12 . . . . . . 29 C2
Orde Hall St WC1 . . . . 106 C4
Orde Ho 10 N16 . . . . . . 6 C1
Ordell Ct 23 E3 . . . . . 26 B3
Ordell Rd E3 . . . . 26 B3
Ordnance Cres
  SE10 . . . . 43 A4
Ordnance Hill
  NW8 . . . . 79 C3
Ordnance Mews
  NW8 . . . . 79 C2
Ordnance Rd E16 . . . . 35 B4
Oregano Dr E14 . . . . . 34 C3
Oregon Bldg 3
  SE13 . . . . 52 A2
O'Reilly St SE17 . . . . . 152 C4
Orestes Mews 1
  NW6 . . . . 10 C3
Orford Ct SE27 . . . . . . 75 A2
Oriana Ho 3 E14 . . . . . 33 B2
Oriel Ct NW3 . . . . 11 B4
Oriel Ho NW6 . . . . 78 A2
Oriel Dr SW13 . . . . . . 47 B4
Oriel Rd
  Hackney E9 . . . . 18 A2
  Homerton E9 . . . . 17 C2
Oriens Mews E15 . . . . 19 B2
Orient St SE11 . . . . . . 150 A4
Orion Bsns Ctr
  SE14 . . . . 40 C1
Orion Ho 3 E1 . . . . . . 25 A1
Orion Point 3
  E14 . . . . 41 C2
Orkney Ho N1 . . . . 84 C4
Orkney St SW11 . . . . . 169 B2
Orlando Rd SW4 . . . . . 61 B4
Orleston Mews N7 . . . . 14 C2
Orleston Rd N7 . . . . . . 14 C2
Orlop St SE10 . . . . 43 A1
Orme Ct W2 . . . . 114 A3
Orme Ct Mews
  W2 . . . . 114 B3
Orme Ho 8 E8 . . . . . . 24 B4
Orme La W2 . . . . 114 A3
Ormeley Rd SW12 . . . . 73 A3
Ormerod Ho 3
  SW9 . . . . 62 A4
Orme Sq W2 . . . . 114 A3
Ormiston Gr W12 . . . . 30 A1
Ormiston Rd SE10 . . . 43 C1
Ormond Cl WC1 . . . . . 106 B4
Ormonde Ct SW15 . . . 57 B3
Ormonde Gate
  SW3 . . . . 145 A1
Ormonde Mans
  WC1 . . . . 106 B4
Ormonde Pl SW1 . . . . 145 C3
Ormonde Rd SW14 . . . 55 B4
Ormonde Terr
  NW8 . . . . 80 C3
Ormond Ho 7 N16 . . . 6 C2
Ormond Mans
  WC1 . . . . 94 B1
Ormond Mews
  WC1 . . . . 94 B1
Ormond Rd N4, N19 . . . 5 A3
Ormond Yd SW1 . . . . 119 A2

Ormrod Ct W11 . . . . . . 31 B3
Ormsby Cl 7 W4 . . . . . 38 A3
Ormsby Pl N16 . . . . 7 B1
Ormsby St E2 . . . . 24 B3
Ormside St SE15 . . . . . 50 B4
Ornan Rd NW3 . . . . . . 12 A3
Orpen Ho SW5 . . . . . . 141 C3
Orpen Wlk N16 . . . . 7 A1
Orpheus Ho 25 N19 . . . 4 C4
Orpheus St SE5 . . . . . . 48 C2
Orsett Mews W2 . . . . 100 C2
Orsett St SE11 . . . . . . 149 A2
Orsett Terr W2 . . . . . . 100 C2
Orsman Rd N1 . . . . . . 24 A4
Orton St E1 . . . . 125 B1
Orville Rd SW11 . . . . . 167 C2
Orwell Ct
  Hackney E8 . . . . 24 C4
  Highbury N5 . . . . 15 B4
Orwell Ho W12 . . . . . . 29 C2
Osbaldeston Rd
  N16 . . . . 7 C3
Osbert St SW1 . . . . . . 147 B3
Osborn Cl E8 . . . . 24 C4
Osborne Rd
  Finsbury Pk N4 . . . . . 5 C3
  Hackney E9 . . . . 18 B2
  South Acton W3 . . . . . 37 A4
Osborn St E1 . . . . 111 A4
Osbourne Ho
  TW10 . . . . 54 C2
Oscar Faber Pl 8
  N1 . . . . 16 A1
Oscar St SE8 . . . . 51 C1
Oseney Cres NW5 . . . . 13 C2
Osier Ct E1 . . . . 25 C1
Osier La SE10 . . . . 43 B3
Osier Mews W4 . . . . . 46 B4
Osier St E1 . . . . 25 B1
Oslo Ct NW8 . . . . 80 A1
Oslo Ho 2 SE5 . . . . . . 48 B1
Oslo Sq SE16 . . . . 41 A3
Oslow Cl W10 . . . . 23 B2
Osman Rd W6 . . . . 39 B3
Osmani Prim Sch
  E1 . . . . 111 C4
Osmington Ho
  SW8 . . . . 163 A1
Osmund St W12 . . . . . 29 B4
Osnaburgh St NW1 . . . 92 B2
Osnaburgh Terr
  NW1 . . . . 92 B2
Osprey Ct NW3 . . . . . . 11 A3
Osprey Ho
  Camberwell SE5 . . . . . 49 B2
  3 Limehouse E14 . . . . 33 A2
Ospringe Ho SE1 . . . . 121 C1
Ospringe Rd NW5 . . . . 13 B4
Osram Ct W6 . . . . 39 B3
Osric Path 5 N1 . . . . . 24 A3
Ossian Mews N4 . . . . . 5 B4
Ossian Rd N4 . . . . 5 B4
Ossington Bldgs
  W1 . . . . 103 B3
Ossington Cl
  W2 . . . . 31 C2 113 C3
Ossington St W2 . . . . 114 A3
Ossory Rd SE1 . . . . . . 49 C4
Ossulston St NW1 . . . 83 C2
Ostade Rd SW2 . . . . . . 74 B4
Osten Mews SW7 . . . . 128 B1
Osterley Ho 5
  E14 . . . . 34 A3
Osterley Rd N16 . . . . . 16 A4

Oswald Bldg SW8 . . . 160 A3
Oswald's Mead E9 . . . 18 A4
Osward Rd SW12,
  SW17 . . . . 72 B2
Oswell Ho 3 E1 . . . . . 32 A1
Oswin St SE11 . . . . . . 150 B4
Oswyth Rd SE5 . . . . . . 49 A1
Otford Cres SE4 . . . . . 66 B1
Otford Ho
  Bermondsey SE1 . . . . 137 C3
  4 Deptford SE15 . . . . . 50 B4
Otha Ho 3 SW9 . . . . . 172 B2
Othello Cl SE11 . . . . . 150 A2
Otis St E3 . . . . 27 B2
Otley Ho N5 . . . . 6 A1
Ottaway Ct E5 . . . . 7 C1
Ottaway St E5 . . . . 7 C1
Otterburn Ho 12
  SE5 . . . . 48 B3
Otter Cl E15 . . . . 27 B4
Otto St SE17 . . . . 48 A4
Our Lady of Dolours
  RC Prim Sch 1
  W2 . . . . 100 A4
Our Lady of Lourdes
  RC Prim Sch
  NW10 . . . . 8 B2
Our Lady of Victories
  RC Prim Sch
  7 Putney SW15 . . . . . 57 C3
  South Kensington
  SW7 . . . . 143 A3
Our Lady Queen of
  Heaven Primary Sch
  SW19 . . . . 69 C3
Our Lady RC Prim Sch
  Camden Town
  NW1 . . . . 83 A4
  20 Poplar E14 . . . . . . 33 B3
Our Lady & St Joseph
  Catholic Prim Sch 1
  N1 . . . . 16 A2
Our Lady & St Joseph
  RC Prim Sch 12
  N1 . . . . 33 C2
Our Lady's Convent
  High Sch N15 . . . . 7 A4
Ouseley Rd SW12 . . . . 72 B3
Outer Circ NW8 . . . . . . 81 A1
Outgate Rd NW10 . . . . 8 B1
Outram Pl N1 . . . . 84 B4
Outwich St EC3 . . . . . 110 B2
Outwood Ho 3
  SW2 . . . . 74 B4
Oval Mans SE11 . . . . . 163 A4
Oval Pl SW8 . . . . 163 A2
Oval Rd NW1 . . . . 82 A4
Oval Sta SE11 . . . . . . 163 B3
Oval The E2 . . . . 25 A3
Oval Way SE11 . . . . . 149 A1
Overbury Ho 3
  E5 . . . . 17 C4
Overbury St E5 . . . . . . 17 C4
Overcliff Rd SE13 . . . . 66 C4
Overhill Rd SE21,
  SE22 . . . . 76 C4
Overlea Rd E5 . . . . 7 C4
Oversley Ho 17
  W2 . . . . 31 C4
Overstone Ho 10
  E14 . . . . 33 C3
Overstone Rd W6 . . . . 39 B2
Overstrand Mans
  SW11 . . . . 169 B3
Overton Ho SW15 . . . . 68 B4
Overton Rd SW9 . . . . 173 C2

Overy Ho SE1..... **136** A3
Ovex CI E14 .... **42** B4
Ovington Ct SW3. **130** B1
Ovington Gdns
SW3 .... **130** B1
Ovington Mews
SW3 .... **130** B1
Ovington Sq SW3. **130** B1
Ovington St SW3. **130** B1
Owen Ho N19 .... **13** B4
Owen's Ct EC1 .... **96** A4
Owen's Row EC1.. **96** A4
Owen St EC1 ...... **86** A1
Owgan Cl SE5 ..... **48** C3
Oxberry Ave SW6. **164** B2
Oxbridge Ct **4**
W4 .... **37** A1
Oxendon St SW1,
W1 .... **119** B3
Oxenford St SE15.. **64** B4
Oxenham Ho **13**
SE8 .... **51** C4
Oxenholme NW1.. **83** A1
Oxestalls Rd SE8 .. **41** A1
Oxford & Cambridge
Mans NW1 .... **102** B3
Oxford Cir W1 ..... **104** C1
Oxford Circus Sta
W1 .... **104** C1
Oxford Circus Sta
W1 .... **104** C1
Oxford Ct
City of London
EC4 .... **123** B4
Gunnersbury W4 ... **37** A1
4B Paddington W2 .. **31** C4
Oxford Dr SE1..... **124** A1
Oxford Gardens Prim
Sch **10** W10 ..... **30** C3
Oxford Gate W6 .. **39** C2
Oxford Gdns
Brentford W4 ..... **44** C4
North Kensington
W10 .... **30** C3
Oxford Ho N4 .... **5** C3
Oxford Rd
Finsbury Pk N4..... **5** C3
Paddington NW6 .. **23** C3
Putney SW15 ..... **58** A3
Stratford E15 ..... **19** C2
Oxford Rd N W4 .. **37** A1
Oxford Rd S W4 .. **37** A1
Oxford Sq W2 .... **102** B1
Oxford St W1 ..... **104** B1
Oxley Cl SE1 ...... **153** A2
Oxonian St SE22... **64** B3
OXO Tower Wharf
SE1 .... **121** C3
Oxted St N16 ...... **7** A3
Oyster Row E1 .... **32** B3
Ozolins Sq E16....**35** C3

P

Pablo Neruda Cl **4**
SE24 .... **63** A3
Pace Pl E1 .... **32** A3
Pacific Ho **15** E1... **25** C1
Pacific Rd E16.... **35** C3
Pacific Wharf
SE16 .... **32** C1
Packenham Ho
24 Crouch End N19 .. **4** C4

Packenham Ho
continued
21 Spitalfields
...... **24** B2 **99** A4
Packington Rd **20**
W3 .... **37** B3
Packington Sq N1. **86** C4
Packington St N1 . **86** B3
Padbury SE17 .... **152** B1
Padbury Ct
E2 .... **24** B2 **99** A4
Padbury Ho NW8.. **90** B2
Paddenswick Ct **2**
W6 .... **39** A3
Paddenswick Rd
W6 .... **38** C3
PADDINGTON **100** C3
Paddington Acad **7**
W9 .... **23** C1
Paddington Gn
W2 .... **101** B4
Paddington Green
Prim Sch NW8 ... **89** B1
Paddington St
W1 .... **103** B4
Paddington Sta
W2 .... **101** B2
Paddock CI SE3 .. **53** C1
Paddock Sch
SW15 .... **56** B3
Paddock Way **11**
SW15 .... **69** B4
Padfield Rd SE5 .. **63** B4
Padstone Ho **50**
E3 .... **27** A2
Padstow Ho **22**
E14 .... **33** B2
Pagden St SW8 .. **170** B4
Pageant Cres
SE16 .... **33** B1
Pageantmaster Ct
EC4 .... **108** A1
Page Ho SE10 .... **52** B4
Page Mews SW11 **169** C3
Page's St SW1 ... **147** C4
Page's Wlk SE1 .. **138** B1
Page's Yd W4 .... **46** A4
Paget Ho **18** E2.. **25** B3
Paget Rd N16 .... **6** C3
Paget St EC1 ..... **96** A4
Pagham Ho **8**
W10 .... **22** B1
Pagnell St SE14 .. **51** B3
Pagoda Ave TW9 .. **54** B4
Pagoda Gdns SE3 . **52** C1
Pagoda Gr
Brixton SE27.... **75** B2
West Dulwich SE27 . **75** B2
Paine Ct SE3 ..... **53** B4
Painsthorpe Rd **3**
N16 .... **7** A1
Painswick Ct **1**
SE15 .... **49** B3
Painters Mews
SE16 .... **153** C4
Pakefield Mews
SW3 .... **74** B3
Pakeman Ho SE1 . **136** B4
Pakeman Prim Sch **1**
N7................... **5** B1
Pakeman St N7... **5** B1
Pakenham Cl
SW12 .... **72** C3
Pakenham St WC1. **95** A2
Palace Ave W8 ... **128** B4
Palace Cl **4** E9 ... **18** B2

Palace Ct
Hampstead NW3 .. **11** A3
Kensington NW2 .. **114** A3
Streatham SW2 ... **74** C2
Palace Garden Mews
W8 .... **31** C1 **113** C2
Palace Gate W8 .. **128** C3
Palace Gdns Mews
W8 .... **114** B1
Palace Mans W14 **140** B4
Palace Mews
Belgravia SW1 ... **145** C3
Fulham SW6..... **155** A2
Palace of
Westminster
SW1 .... **134** B3
Palace Pl SW1 ... **132** C2
Palace Rd SE27, SW16,
SW2 .... **74** C2
Palace St SW1 ... **132** C2
Palatine Ave N16.. **16** A4
Palatine Rd N16 .. **16** A4
Palazzo Apartments
11 N1................. **16** A1
Palemead Cl SW6 . **47** C2
Palermo Rd NW10.. **21** C3
Palewell Common Dr
SW14 .... **55** C2
Palewell Pk SW14 . **55** C3
Palfrey Pl SW8 ... **163** A2
Palgrave Gdns
NW1 .... **90** B2
Palgrave Ho
7 Camberwell
SE5 .... **48** B3
4 Maitland Pk
NW3 .... **12** B3
Palgrave Rd W12 . **38** B3
Palissy St **8**
E2 .... **24** B2 **98** C3
Pallant Ho SE1 .. **137** C1
Pallester Ct NW11 ... **1** A3
Palliser Ct W14 .. **140** A1
Palliser Ho
3 Greenwich
SE10 .... **52** C4
4 Stepney E1 ... **25** C1
Palliser Rd W14 .. **140** A1
Pallister Terr
SW15 .... **68** B2
Pall Mall SW1 ... **119** B1
Pall Mall E SW1 . **119** C2
Pall Mall Pl SW1 . **119** A1
Palm Ct
18 Camberwell
SE15 .... **49** B3
Stoke Newington
N16 .... **6** C2
Palmer Ho
6 Deptford SE14 .. **50** C3
8 Kentish Town
NW5 .... **13** B4
5 Tufnell Pk N19... **4** B1
Palmer Pl N7 .... **14** C3
Palmers Rd
Globe Town E2 ... **25** C3
Mortlake SW14 ... **55** B4
Palmer St SW1 .. **133** B2
Palmerston Ct **22**
E3 .... **25** C3
Palmerston Ho
Battersea SW11... **169** C3
Kensington
W8 .... **31** C1 **113** B1

Palmerston Rd
Acton Green W3... **37** B3
Brondesbury NW6.. **10** B1
Hampstead NW6 .. **10** C1
Mortlake SW14 ... **55** B3
Palmerston Way
SW8 .... **160** B1
Palm Gr W5....... **36** A3
Palm Tree Ho **2**
SE14 .... **50** C3
Pamela Ct NW10 .. **8** C1
Pamela Ho **13** E8.. **24** B4
Pamlion Ct N4 .... **5** A4
Panama Ho **6** E1 . **32** C4
Pancras La EC2... **109** B1
Pancras Rd NW1 . **83** C2
Pancras Square
NW1 .... **84** A2
Pancras Way E3.. **26** C3
Pandian Way **4**
NW5 .... **13** C2
Pandora Rd NW6.. **10** C2
Pangbourne Ho **4**
N7.................. **14** A3
Pangbourne Ave
W10 .... **30** B4
Pankhurst Cl **7**
SE14 .... **50** C3
Pankhurst Ho **2**
NW10 .... **22** C2
Panmure Cl N5... **15** A4
Pan Penisula Sq
E14 .... **42** A4
Pansy Gdns W12.. **29** C2
Panton St SW1 .. **119** B3
Panyer Alley EC2 . **108** C2
Paper Mill Wharf
E14 .... **33** A2
Papworth Gdns
N7.................. **14** B3
Papworth Way
SW9 .... **74** C4
Parade Mans **19**
SE5 .... **48** B1
Parade Mews SE27,
SW2 .... **75** B2
Parade The SW11 **159** A2
Paradise Pas N7.. **14** C3
Paradise Rd
Richmond TW10 ... **54** A2
South Lambeth
SW4 .... **172** A2
Paradise Row E2.. **25** A3
Paradise St SE16 . **40** A4
Paradise Wlk
SW3 .... **159** A4
Paragon Christian
Acad E5 .... **17** C4
Paragon Cl E16... **35** C3
Paragon Ho SE3 .. **53** B1
Paragon Mews
SE1 .... **151** C4
Paragon Pl SE3.... **53** B1
Paragon Rd E9 ... **17** B2
Paragon The
Kidbrooke SE3 .... **53** C1
Walworth SE17 ... **151** C4
Paramount Bldg
EC1 .... **96** A2
Paramount Ct
WC1 .... **93** A1
Parbury Rd SE23 .. **66** A1
Pardoner St SE1.. **137** C2
Pardon St EC1.... **96** B2
Parfett St E1 ..... **111** C2

Parfitt Cl NW11.... **2** B3
Parfrey St W6 .... **47** B4
Paris Gdn SE1.... **122** A2
Paris Ho **12** E2 ... **25** A3
Parison Cl **1** TW9 .. **54** C4
Park Ave
Golders Green
NW11............. **2** A3
Mortlake SW14 ... **55** C3
Willesden NW2.... **9** B2
Park Ave N NW10... **9** A3
Park Cl
Kensington W14... **127** A2
Knightsbridge
SW1 .... **130** C3
13 South Hackney
E9 .... **25** B4
Park Cres W1 .... **92** A1
Park Crescent Mews
E W1 .... **92** B1
Park Crescent Mews
W W1 .... **92** A1
Park Ct
Battersea SW11... **170** A4
Clapham Pk SW4 .. **61** C2
Dulwich SE21 .... **75** C1
7 Hammersmith
W6................. **38** C2
Upper Tooting
SW12 .... **72** C3
Park Dr
Acton W3 .... **36** C3
Golders Green NW11.. **2** A3
Mortlake SW14 ... **55** C3
Park Dwellings **7**
NW3 .... **12** B3
Park End NW3.... **12** A4
Parker Ct
Shoreditch N1..... **87** A4
South Lambeth
SW4 .... **172** B3
Parke Rd SW13... **46** C2
Parker Mews
WC2 .... **106** B2
Parkers Row **15**
SE16 .... **139** B3
Parker's Row SE1 **139** A3
Parker St WC2.... **106** B2
Parkfield Ave
SW14 .... **56** A3
Parkfield Ct SE14.. **51** B2
Parkfield Ind Est
SW11 .... **169** C2
Parkfield Rd
13 Clapham Park
SW4 .... **61** C1
New Cross SE14... **51** B2
Willesden NW10... **9** A1
Parkfields SW15... **57** B3
Parkfield St N1 ... **85** C2
Park Flats N6 .... **3** A4
Parkgate Gdns
SW14 .... **55** C2
Parkgate House Sch
SW11 .... **60** C3
Parkgate Mews N6 .. **4** B4
Parkgate Rd
SW11 .... **158** B1
Park Hall SE10 ... **52** C3
Park Hall Rd SE21.. **75** C1
Park Hall Road Trad
Est SE21.......... **75** C1
Parkham St SW11 **168** A3

Park Heights Ct 21
E14 . . . . .33 B3
Park Hill
Clapham Pk SW4 . . . . .61 C2
Richmond TW10 . . . . . .54 B1
Park Hill E3
Park Hill Ct SW17 . . . .72 B1
Parkhill Rd N7 . . . . . . .14 A4
Park Hill Wlk 10
NW3 . . . . .12 B3
Park Ho
8 Camberwell
SE5 . . . . .48 C2
Finsbury Pk N4 . . . . .6 A2
39 Hackney E9 . . . . . . .17 B1
Richmond TW10 . . . . . .54 A1
Parkholme Rd E8 . . . .16 C2
Parkhouse St SE5 . . .48 C3
Parkhurst Ct N7 . . . .14 A4
Parkhurst Rd N7 . . . .14 A4
Parkinson Ct
Finsbury N1 . . . . .97 B3
Shoreditch EC1 . . . . . . .97 C4
Parkinson Ho 6
E9 . . . . .17 B1
Park La
Mayfair W1 . . . . .117 B3
Mill Meads E15 . . . . . . .27 C4
Parkland Ct W14 . . . .126 A4
Parkland Gdns 12
SW19 . . . . .69 C3
Parklands
East Dulwich
SE22 . . . . .65 A2
Highgate N6 . . . . .4 A4
Parklands Cl
SW14 . . . . .55 B2
Park Lea Ct N16 . . . . . .7 A4
Park Lo 1
11 South Hampstead
NW8 . . . . .11 C1
10 Wapping E1 . . . . . . .32 A1
Willesden NW2 . . . . .9 B4
Park Lofts 9 SW4 . .62 A2
Park Lorne 8 NW8 . .90 B3
Park Mans
Battersea SW11 . . . . .168 C3
Bedford Pk W6 . . . . . . .38 B3
Fulham SW6 . . . . .164 B3
Knightsbridge
SW1 . . . . .130 C3
St John's Wood
NW8 . . . . .80 A1
Vauxhall SW8 . . . . . . .162 B4
Parkmead SW15 . . . .57 A1
Park Mews
Greenwich SE10 . . . . . .43 B1
Kensal Rise W10 . . . . . .23 A3
Park Par
Acton W3 . . . . .36 C3
Dagenham NW10 . . . . .21 B3
Park Piazza 3
SE13 . . . . .67 C1
Park Pl
Canary Wharf
E14 . . . . .33 C1
Gunnersbury W3 . . . . . .36 C2
Shoreditch N1 . . . . .87 C4
St James SW1 . . . . . . .118 C2
Park Place Dr W3 . . . .36 C3
Park Place Ho 8
SE10 . . . . .52 C4
Park Place Villas
W2 . . . . .101 A4

Park Rd
Chiswick W4 . . . . .45 C4
Dagenham NW10 . . . . .21 A4
Lisson Gr NW1,
NW8 . . . . .90 B2
Richmond TW10 . . . . . .54 B1
Park Rd E W3 . . . . . . .37 B4
Park Rd N
Chiswick W4 . . . . .37 C1
South Acton W3 . . . . . .37 A4
Park Road E 11
W3 . . . . .37 A4
Park Row SE10 . . . . . .52 C4
PARK ROYAL 20 A2
Park Royal NW10 . . . .20 A4
Park Royal Bsns Ctr
NW10 . . . . .20 B1
Park Royal Metro Ctr
NW10 . . . . .20 A1
Park Royal Rd NW10,
W3 . . . . .20 B1
Park Sheen 3
SW14 . . . . .55 A3
Parkshot TW9 . . . . . . .54 A3
Parkside
East Acton W3 . . . . .29 A1
Greenwich SE3 . . . . . . .53 B3
Park Side NW2 . . . . . . .9 A4
Parkside Ave 18
SE10 . . . . .52 B2
Parkside Bsns Est
SE8 . . . . .51 A4
Parkside Cres N7 . . . . .5 C1
Parkside Est E9 . . . . .25 C4
Parkside (Private)
Hospl SW19 . . . . .69 C1
Parkside St SW11 . . .169 B3
Park Sq E NW1 . . . . . . .92 A1
Park Square Mews
NW1 . . . . .92 A1
Park Sq W NW1 . . . . . .92 A1
Park St
Borough The SE1 . . . . .123 A2
Mayfair W1 . . . . .117 B3
Parkstead Rd
SW15 . . . . .57 A2
Parkstone Rd 5
SE15 . . . . .49 C1
Park Stps W2 . . . . . . .116 B4
Park The NW11 . . . . . . .1 C4
Parkthorne Rd
SW12 . . . . .73 C4
Park Twrs W1 . . . . . . .118 A1
Park View
Dagenham W3 . . . . .28 B4
Highbury N5 . . . . .15 B4
Willesden NW2 . . . . .9 B4
Parkview Ct SW6 . . . .164 B1
Park View Ct
SW18 . . . . .58 C1
Park View Ho
SE24 . . . . .63 A1
Park View Mans N4 . . .6 A4
Park View Mews 26
SW9 . . . . .172 C2
Park View Rd NW10 . . .8 B4
Park Village E
NW1 . . . . .82 B1
Park Village W
NW1 . . . . .82 A2
Parkville Rd SW6 . . .154 C1

Park Vista SE10 . . . . .52 C4
Park Walk Prim Sch
SW10 . . . . .157 B3
Parkwat Cres E15 . . .19 B3
Parkway NW1 . . . . . . .82 A3
Park Way W3 . . . . .36 C2
Parkway Ho SW14 . . .55 C3
Park West W2 . . . . . .102 B1
Park West Pl W1,
W2 . . . . .102 B2
Park Wlk 1 SE10 . . . . .52 C4
Park Wlk
Chelsea SW10 . . . . . . .157 B4
Highgate N6 . . . . .3 C4
Parkwood NW8 . . . . . .80 C3
Parkwood Prim Sch
1 N4 . . . . .6 A2
Parliament Ct
NW3 . . . . .12 A4
Parliament Hill
NW3 . . . . .12 A4
Parliament Hill Mans
NW5 . . . . .12 C4
Parliament Hill Sch
NW5 . . . . .12 C4
Parliament Mews
SW14 . . . . .45 B1
Parliament Sq
SW1 . . . . .134 A3
Parliament St
SW1 . . . . .134 A4
Parliament View
Apartments
SE11 . . . . .148 C4
Parma Cres SW11 . . . .60 B3
Parminter Ind Est 28
E2 . . . . .25 A3
Parmiter St E2 . . . . . . .25 A3
Parmoor Ct EC1 . . . . . .96 C2
Parnell Cl W12 . . . . . .39 A3
Parnell Ho WC1 . . . . .105 C2
Parnell Rd E3 . . . . .26 B4
Parnham St E14 . . . . .33 A3
Parolles Rd N19 . . . . . .4 B3
Parr Ct N1 . . . . .87 B2
Parrington Ho 1
SW4 . . . . .61 C1
Parr Pl W4 . . . . .38 B2
Parr St N1 . . . . .87 B2
Parry Ho 8 E1 . . . . . . .32 A1
Parry Rd W10 . . . . .23 A2
Parry St SW8 . . . . . . .162 B4
Parsifal Ho NW3 . . . . .10 C4
Parsifal Rd NW6 . . . . .10 C3
Parsonage St E14 . . . .42 B2
Parsons Gn SW6 . . . .165 B3
PARSONS
GREEN 165 B4
Parsons Green La
SW6 . . . . .165 B4
Parsons Green Sta
SW6 . . . . .165 B3
Parsons Ho
Paddington W2 . . . . . . .89 B1
21 Streatham
SW12 . . . . .74 A4
Parsons Lo NW6 . . . . .11 A1
Parthenia Rd
SW6 . . . . .165 C3
Partington Cl N19 . . . .4 C3
Parton Lo 14 E8 . . . . .16 B2
Partridge Ct EC1 . . . . .96 A2
Partridge Ho 22
E3 . . . . .26 B3
Pascall Ho SE17 . . . . .48 B4
Pascal St SW8 . . . . . .161 C2

Pascoe Rd SE13 . . . . .67 C2
Pasley Cl SE17 . . . . . .150 C1
Passfield Dr E14 . . . . .34 A4
Passfields W14 . . . . .140 C1
Passing Alley EC1 . . . .96 B1
Passmore St SW1 . . .145 B2
Pastor St SE1,
SE11 . . . . .150 B4
Patcham Terr
SW8 . . . . .170 B4
Patent Ho E14 . . . . . . .34 A4
Paternoster La
EC4 . . . . .108 B2
Paternoster Row
EC4 . . . . .108 B2
Pater St W8 . . . . .127 B1
Patience Rd
SW11 . . . . .168 A1
Patience Villas
SE13 . . . . .67 C4
Patmore Ho 8
N16 . . . . .16 A3
Patmore St SW8 . . . .171 A4
Patmos Rd SW9 . . . . .48 A2
Paton Cl E3 . . . . .26 C2
Paton Ho 3 SW9 . . . .172 C2
Paton St EC1 . . . . .96 C3
Patrick Coman Ho
EC1 . . . . .96 A3
Patrick Connolly Gdns
4 E3 . . . . .27 A2
Patriot Sq E2 . . . . .25 A3
Patrol Pl SE6 . . . . .67 A1
Pat Shaw Ho 2
E1 . . . . .25 C1
Patshull Pl NW5 . . . . .13 B2
Patshull Rd NW5 . . . .13 B2
Patten Ho N4 . . . . .6 B3
Patten Rd SW18 . . . . .72 A4
Patterdale NW1 . . . . . .92 B3
Patterdale Rd
SE15 . . . . .50 B3
Pattina Wlk SE16 . . . .33 A1
Pattinson Point 10
E16 . . . . .35 C4
Pattison Ho
Borough The SE1 . . . . .137 A4
2 Stepney E1 . . . . .32 C3
Pattison Rd NW2 . . . . .1 C1
Pat Williams Ho
SE27 . . . . .75 B1
Paul Daisley Ct 2
NW6 . . . . .10 A1
Paulet Rd SE5 . . . . . . .48 A2
Paul Ho 10 W10 . . . . . .23 A1
Pauline Ho 21 E1 . . . .111 C4
Paul Julius Cl E14 . . .34 C2
Paul St EC2 . . . . .24 A1 98 A2
Paultons Ho SW3 . . . .157 C4
Paultons Sq SW3 . . . .157 C4
Paultons St SW3 . . . .157 C3
Pauntley Ho 6 N19 . . .4 B3
Pauntley St 4 N19 . . .4 B3
Pavan Ct 29 E2 . . . . . .25 B2
Paveley Dr SW11 . . . .158 A1
Paveley Ho N1 . . . . . . .84 C1
Paveley St NW8 . . . . . .90 B2
Pavement The
Brentford W5 . . . . .36 A3
Clapham SW4 . . . . .61 B3
Pavilion Ct
1 Hampstead
NW3 . . . . .11 B4
Hampstead NW3 . . . . . .11 C3

Pavilion Ct continued
3 Paddington
NW6 . . . . .23 C2
Pavilion Mans 10
SW9 . . . . .62 B3
Pavilion Rd SW1 . . . .131 A1
Pavilion Sq SW17 . . . .72 B1
Pavilion St SW1 . . . . .131 A1
Pavilion Terr 8
W12 . . . . .30 B3
Pavilion Cl SE10 . . . . .43 B2
Pavilion La SE10 . . . . .43 A4
Pavitt Ct NW10 . . . . . . .8 C1
Paxton Cl TW9 . . . . . . .44 B1
Paxton Ho SE17 . . . . .151 A2
Paxton Rd W4 . . . . . . .46 A4
Paxton Terr SW1 . . . .160 B4
Paymal Ho 33 E1 . . . . .32 B4
Payne Ho N1 . . . . .85 A3
Payne Rd E3 . . . . .27 A3
Paynesfield Ave
SW14 . . . . .55 C4
Payne St SE8 . . . . .51 B4
Paynes Wlk W6 . . . . .154 A3
Peabody Ave
SW1 . . . . .146 B1
Peabody Bldgs
6 Camberwell
SE5 . . . . .48 C2
Walworth SE17 . . . . . . .151 B3
Peabody Cl SW1 . . . .160 B4
Peabody Ct
5 Camberwell
SE5 . . . . .48 C2
St Luke's EC1 . . . . .97 A1
Peabody Est
18 Bethnal Green
E2 . . . . .25 A3
Borough The SE1 . . . . .122 C1
Fulham SW6 . . . . .155 A4
6 Hammersmith
W6 . . . . .39 B1
Holborn EC1 . . . . .95 C1
Lambeth SE1 . . . . .121 C1
North Kensington
W10 . . . . .30 B4
4 Ratcliff E1 . . . . .32 C2
7 St George in t East
E1 . . . . .125 B4
St Luke's EC1 . . . . .97 A1
Strand WC2 . . . . .106 C1
Streatham SE24 . . . . . .75 B4
Westminster SW1 . . . .147 A4
Peabody Sq SE1 . . . . .75 B3
Peabody Sq SE1 . . . .136 A3
Peabody Twr EC1 . . . .97 A1
Peabody Yd N1 . . . . . .86 C4
Peace Pagoda
SW1 . . . . .159 A2
Peach Rd W10 . . . . . . .22 C2
Peachum Rd SE3 . . . . .53 B4
Peach Walk Mews 24
E3 . . . . .25 C3
Peacock St SE17 . . . .150 B3
Peacock Yd SE17 . . . .150 B3
Peak Ho N4 . . . . .6 B3
Pearce Ho
Camden Town N19 . . . .4 B1
7 Streatham SW2 . . . . .74 A4
Westminster SW1 . . . .147 C3
Pear Cl SE14 . . . . .51 A3
Pear Ct 27 SE15 . . . . .49 B3
Peardon St SW8 . . . .170 B1
Pearfield Ho 1
N5 . . . . .15 B3
Pearl St E1 . . . . .32 A1

Pearmain Ho 9
SE16 . . . .**52 B1**
Pearman St SE1 . . .**135 C3**
Pear Pl SE1 . . . . . .**135 B4**
Pearscroft Ct
SW6 . . . .**166 B3**
Pearscroft Rd
SW6 . . . .**166 B3**
Pearse St 8 SE15 . .**49 A4**
Pearson Ct 4 SW15 .**48 B2**
Pearson Ho SW15 . .**57 B2**
Pearson's Ave SE8,
SE14 . . . .**51 A2**
Pearson St E2 . . . . .**24 B3**
Peartree Ave
SW17 . . . .**71 B1**
Pear Tree Cl 2
E2 . . . .**24 B4**
Pear Tree Ct
Holborn EC1 . . . . .**95 C1**
Putney SW15 . . . . . .**57 A3**
Pear Tree Ho SE4 . .**66 B3**
Peartree La E1 . . . . .**32 B2**
Peartree St EC1 . . . .**96 C2**
Peartree Way
SE10 . . . .**43 C2**
Peary Pl E2 . . . .**25 B2**
Peckarmans Wood
SE21, SE26 . . . . . .**76 C1**
Pecket Sq 8 N5 . . . .**15 A4**
Peckford Pl SW9 . . .**173 C1**
PECKHAM **49 C2**
Peckham Gr SE15 . .**49 A3**
Peckham High St
SE15 . . . .**49 C2**
Peckham Hill St
SE15 . . . .**49 C3**
Peckham Park Prim
Sch 82 SE15 . . . . .**49 C3**
Peckham Park Rd
SE15 . . . .**49 C3**
Peckham Rd SE5 . . .**49 A2**
Peckham Rye
East Dulwich
SE22 . . . .**64 C3**
Peckham SE15,
SE22 . . . .**65 A3**
Peckham Rye Sta
SE15 . . . .**49 C1**
Peckwater Ho 2
NW5 . . . .**13 C2**
Peckwater St NW5 .**13 B3**
Pedlars Wlk N7 . . . .**14 A3**
Pedley St E1 **84 B1 99 A1**
Pedro St E5 . . . .**17 C4**
Pedworth Gdns 4
SE16 . . . .**40 B2**
Peel Gr E2 . . . .**25 B3**
Peel Pass
W8 . . . . . .**31 C1 113 B1**
Peel Pl SW6 . . . . . .**155 B4**
Peel Prec NW6 . . . . .**23 C3**
Peel St W8 . .**31 C1 113 B1**
Peerless St EC1 . . . .**97 B3**
Pegasus Cl N16 . . . .**15 C4**
Pegasus Ct
11 Acton W3 . . . . . .**28 B3**
Brentford TW8 . . . . .**36 B1**
College Pk NW10 . . .**22 A2**
Pegasus Ho 9 E1 . . .**25 C1**
Pegwell Ho 15 E5 . .**17 A3**
Pekin St E14 . . . . . .**33 C3**
Pekoe SE1 . . . .**125 A1**
Peldon Ct TW10 . . . .**54 B2**
Pelham Cl SE5 . . . . .**64 A4**
Pelham Cres SW7 .**144 A3**

Pelham Ct SW3 . . .**144 A3**
Pelham Ho W14 . . .**140 C3**
Pelham Pl SW7 . . . .**144 A3**
Pelham St SW7 . . . .**143 C4**
Pelican Ho 8 SE8 . .**41 B2**
Pelican Pas 3 E1 . .**25 B1**
Pelier St SE17 . . . . .**48 B4**
Pella Ho SE11 . . . .**149 A2**
Pellant Rd SW6 . . .**154 B2**
Pellatt Rd SE22 . . . .**64 B2**
Pellerin Rd N16 . . . .**16 A3**
Pellew Ho 15 E1 . . .**25 A1**
Pelling St E14 . . . . .**33 C3**
Pell St 21 SE8 . . . . .**41 B2**
Pelter St E2 . .**24 B2 98 C4**
Pelton Rd SE10 . . . .**43 A1**
Pember Rd NW10 . .**22 C2**
Pemberton Ct 18
E1 . . . .**25 C2**
Pemberton Gdns
N19 . . . .**4 B1**
Pemberton Pl 2
E8 . . . .**17 A1**
Pemberton Row
EC4 . . . .**107 C2**
Pemberton Terr
N19 . . . .**4 B1**
Pembridge Cres
W11 . . . . . .**31 C2 113 B4**
Pembridge Gdns
W2 . . . .**31 C2 113 B4**
Pembridge Hall Sch
W2 . . . .**31 C2 113 B4**
Pembridge Mews
W11 . . . . . .**31 C2 113 B4**
Pembridge Pl
Notting Hill
W2 . . . .**31 C2 113 C4**
Wandsworth
SW18 . . . .**58 C2**
Pembridge Rd
W11 . . . . . .**31 C2 113 B4**
Pembridge Sq
W2 . . . .**31 C2 113 C3**
Pembridge Villas
W11 . . . . . .**31 C2 113 B4**
Pembroke W14 . . .**141 A3**
Pembroke Ave N1 . .**84 B4**
Pembroke Bldgs
NW10 . . . .**21 C2**
Pembroke Cl
SW1 . . . .**131 C3**
Pembroke Gardens
SW14 . . . .**55 B1**
Pembroke Gdns
W8 . . . .**141 A4**
Pembroke Gdns Cl
W8 . . . .**127 B1**
Pembroke Ho
Acton W3 . . . .**37 B4**
Chelsea SW1 . . . . .**131 B1**
5 Clapham Pk
SW2 . . . .**62 A2**
17 Kensington W2 .**100 B1**
Putney SW15 . . . . . .**56 C2**
Pembroke Lo 2
SW16 . . . .**74 A1**
Pembroke Mews
8 Bow E3 . . . .**26 A2**
Kensington W8 . . . .**127 B1**
Pembroke Pl W8 . .**127 B1**
Pembroke Rd W8 .**141 B4**
Pembroke Sq W8 .**127 B1**
Pembroke St N1 . . .**84 B4**
Pembroke Studios
W8 . . . .**127 A1**

Pembroke Terr
NW8 . . . .**79 B1**
Pembroke Villas
W8 . . . .**141 B4**
Pembroke Wlk
W8 . . . .**141 B4**
Pembury Cl E5 . . . . .**17 A3**
Pembury Ho SE5 . . .**49 A1**
Pembury Pl 15 E5,
E8 . . . .**17 A3**
Pembury Rd E5 . . . .**17 A3**
Pemell Cl 5 E1 . . . .**25 B1**
Pemell Ho 6 E1 . . . .**25 B1**
Penally Pl N1 . . . . . .**87 C4**
Penang St E1 . . . . . .**32 A1**
Penarth Ctr The
SE15 . . . .**50 B4**
Penarth St SE15 . . .**50 B4**
Pencombe Mews
W11 . . . . . .**31 B2 113 A4**
Pencraig Way
SE15 . . . .**50 A4**
Penda's Mead E9 . .**18 A4**
Pendennis Ho 15
SE8 . . . .**41 A2**
Pendergast Ladywell
Sch SE4 . . . .**66 C1**
Penderyn Way N7 . .**13 C4**
Pendle Ho 16
SE26 . . . .**76 C1**
Pendley Ho 18 E2 . .**24 C4**
Pendrell Ho WC2 . .**105 C1**
Pendrell Rd SE4 . . .**51 A1**
Penelope Ho 20
SW9 . . . .**173 B3**
Penfield Lo 7 W9 . .**31 C4**
Penfields Ho N7 . . . .**14 A2**
Penfold Pl NW1 . . .**102 A4**
Penfold St NW8 . . . .**89 C1**
Penford St SE5 . . . . .**48 A1**
Penhurst Mans
SW6 . . . .**164 C4**
Peninsula Ct E14 . . .**42 A3**
Peninsula Ret Pk
TW9 . . . .**44 C3**
Peninsular Park Rd
SE7 . . . .**43 C2**
Pennack Rd SE15 . .**49 B4**
Penn Almshouses 9
SE10 . . . .**52 B3**
Pennant Mews
W8 . . . .**142 A4**
Pennard Mans 5
W12 . . . .**39 B4**
Pennard Rd W12 . . .**39 B4**
Pennefather Ho
N1 . . . .**15 C2**
Penner Cl SW19 . . . .**70 A2**
Pennethorne Cl
E9 . . . .**25 B4**
Pennethorne Ho
SW11 . . . .**59 C4**
Pennethorne Rd
SE15 . . . .**50 A3**
Penn Ho NW8 . . . . .**90 A1**
Pennine La NW2 . . . .**1 A2**
Pennine Mans NW2 . .**1 A2**
Pennine Par NW2 . . .**1 A2**
Pennington St
E1 . . . .**125 C3**
23 St George in East
E1 . . . .**125 C3**
Pennington St E1 . . .**32 A2**

Penn Rd N7 . . . .**14 A4**
Penn St N1 . . . .**87 C3**
Penny Brookes St
E15 . . . .**19 B2**
Penny Ct SW10 . . .**157 A4**
Pennyfields E14 . . . .**33 C2**
Pennyford Ct NW8 . .**89 B2**
Penny Mews
SW12 . . . .**73 A4**
Pennymore Wlk
W9 . . . .**23 B1**
Penny Rd NW10 . . . .**20 A2**
Penpoll Rd E8 . . . . .**17 A2**
Penrhyn Cres
SW14 . . . .**55 B3**
Penrith Cl SW15 . . .**58 A2**
Penrith Pl SE27 . . . .**75 A2**
Penrose Gr SE17 . .**150 C1**
Penrose Ho SE17 . .**150 C1**
Penrose St SE17 . .**150 C1**
Penryn Ho SE11 . . .**150 A2**
Penryn St NW1 . . . .**83 B2**
Penry St SE1 . . . . .**152 B3**
Pensbury Pl SW8 . .**171 A2**
Pensbury St SW8 . .**171 A2**
Pensford Ave TW9 . .**44 C1**
Penshurst 2 NW5 . .**12 C2**
Penshurst Ho 15
SE15 . . . .**50 B4**
Penshurst Rd E9 . . .**17 C1**
Pentland Cl NW11 . .**1 A2**
Pentland Gdns
SW18 . . . .**59 B1**
Pentland Ho
17 Camden Town
NW5 . . . .**12 C2**
7 Stamford Hill N16 . .**7 B3**
Pentland Rd 1
NW8 . . . .**78 C4**
Pentlow St SW15 . . .**57 B4**
Pentney Rd SW12 . .**73 B3**
Penton Gr N1 . . . . . .**85 B1**
Penton Ho N1 . . . . . .**85 B1**
Penton Pl SE17 . . .**150 B2**
Penton Rise WC1 . . .**95 A4**
Penton St N1 . . . . . .**85 B1**
PENTONVILLE **85 A1**
Pentonville Rd
WC1 . . . .**84 C1**
Pentridge St SE15 . .**49 B3**
Penwith Rd SW18 . .**71 A2**
Penwood Ho
SW15 . . . .**56 B1**
Penywern Rd
SW5 . . . .**141 C2**
Penzance Ho
SE11 . . . .**149 C2**
Penzance Pl
W11 . . . . . .**31 A1 112 B2**
Penzance St
W11 . . . . . .**31 A1 112 A2**
Peony Gdns W12 . . .**29 C2**
Peperfield WC1 . . . . .**94 C3**
Pepler Ho 17 W10 . .**23 A1**
Pepler Mews SE1 . .**152 C1**
Peploe Rd NW6 . . . .**22 C3**
Peppermead Sq
SE13 . . . .**66 C2**
Pepper St
Borough The SE1 . .**136 C4**
Millwall E14 . . . .**42 A3**
Peppie Cl N16 . . . . . .**7 A2**
Pepys Cres 2 E16 . .**35 C1**
Pepys Ent Ctr 13
SE8 . . . .**41 B2**

Pepys Ho
14 Bethnal Green
E2 . . . .**25 B2**
Clapham Pk SW4 . . .**61 C2**
Pepys Rd SE14 . . . .**50 C1**
Pepys St EC3 . . . . .**124 B4**
Perceval Ave NW3 . .**12 A3**
Percheron Ct 3
SW9 . . . .**62 B4**
Perch St E8 . . . .**16 B4**
Percival Mews
SW8 . . . .**162 C4**
Percival Rd SW14 . .**55 B3**
Percival St EC1 . . . . .**96 B3**
Percy Cir WC1 . . . . .**95 A4**
Percy Laurie Ho 6
SW15 . . . .**57 C3**
Percy Mews W1 . . .**105 B3**
Percy Pas W1 . . . . .**105 B3**
Percy Rd
Newham E16 . . . . . .**35 A4**
Shepherd's Bush
W12 . . . .**38 C4**
Percy St W1 . . . . . .**105 B3**
Peregrine Ho
6 Battersea
SW11 . . . .**60 A4**
Finsbury EC1 . . . . . .**96 B4**
Perham Rd W14 . . .**140 B1**
Perifield SE21 . . . . .**75 B3**
Perkins Ho 13 E14 . .**33 B4**
Perkins Rents
SW1 . . . .**133 B1**
Perkins Sq SE1 . . . .**123 A2**
Perley Ho 8 E3 . . . . .**33 B4**
Perotti Ho SW6 . . . . .**54 A4**
Perran Rd SE24,
SW2 . . . .**75 A2**
Perren St NW5 . . . . .**13 A2**
Perrers Rd W6 . . . . .**39 A2**
Perring Est E3 . . . . .**33 C4**
Perrin's Ct 20
NW3 . . . .**11 B4**
Perrin's La NW3 . . . .**11 B4**
Perrin's Wlk NW3 . .**11 B4**
Perronet Ho SE1 . .**136 B1**
Perry Ave W3 . . . . .**28 C3**
Perry Ct 18 E14 . . . .**41 C1**
Perry Ho 20 SW2 . . .**74 A4**
Perrymead St
SW6 . . . .**166 A3**
Perryn Ho W3 . . . . .**29 A2**
Perryn Rd
Acton W3 . . . .**28 C2**
6 Bermondsey
SE16 . . . .**40 A3**
Perry's Pl W1 . . . . .**105 B2**
Perrywood Ho 17
E5 . . . .**17 A3**
Perseverance Works
17 E2 . . . . . .**24 A2 98 B4**
Perth Ct 5 SE5 . . . .**63 C3**
Perth Ho N1 . . . . . .**14 B1**
Perth Rd N4 . . . .**5 C3**
Petchey Acad The
E8 . . . .**16 A3**
Peter Ave NW10 . . . .**9 A1**
Peter Best Ho 1
E1 . . . .**32 A3**
Peterboat Cl SE10 . .**43 A2**
Peterborough Ct
EC4 . . . .**107 C1**
Peterborough Mews
SW6 . . . .**165 B2**

Peterborough Rd
SW6 . . . . .58 C4
Peterborough Villas
SW6 . . . . .166 A4
Peter Butler Ho 9
SE1 . . . . .139 B3
Peterchurch Ho
SE15 . . . . .50 A4
Petergate SW11 . . . .59 B3
**Peter Harrison
Planetarium**
SE10 . . . . .52 C3
Peter Heathfield Ho
4 E15 . . . . .27 C4
Peter Hills Ho 6
SE16 . . . . .153 B4
**Peter Hills with St
Mary's & St Paul's CE
Sch 25** SE16 . . . . . . .32 C1
Peter Ho SW8 . . . . .162 A2
Peter James Ent Ctr
NW10 . . . . .20 B2
Peterley Bsns Ctr 8
E2 . . . . .25 A3
Peter Scott Visitor
Centre SW13 . . . . . .47 A2
Peters Ct 30 W2 . . .100 B2
Peter's Ct SW4 . . . .171 B4
Petersfield Rd W3 . .37 B4
Petersfield Rise
SW15 . . . . .69 A3
Petersham Ho
SW7 . . . . .143 B4
Petersham La
SW7 . . . . .128 C2
Petersham Mews
SW7 . . . . .129 A1
Petersham Pl
SW7 . . . . .129 A2
Peter's La EC1 . . . .108 B4
Peter St W1 . . . . . . .119 B4
Peterstow Cl
SW19 . . . . .70 A2
Petherton Ct
NW10 . . . . .22 C4
Petherton Ho N4 . . . .6 B3
Petherton Rd N5 . . .15 B3
Petiver Cl 25 E9 . . .17 B1
Petley Rd W6 . . . . . .47 C3
Peto Pl NW1 . . . . . . .92 B2
Peto St N E16 . . . . . .35 B3
Petrel Ct 8 SE21 . . .75 C2
Petrie Cl NW2 . . . . .10 A2
Petrie Mus of
Egyptian
Archaeology
WC1 . . . . .93 B1
Petros Gdns 1
NW3 . . . . .11 B2
Petticoat Lane Mkt
EC2 . . . . .110 C3
Petticoat Sq E1 . . . .110 C2
Petticoat Twr E1 . . .110 C2
Pettiward Cl SW15 . .57 B3
Petty France SW1 .133 B2
Petty Wales EC3 . . .124 B3
Petworth Ho 16
SE22 . . . . .64 A4
Petworth St
SW11 . . . . .168 B4
Petyt Pl SW3 . . . . . .158 A3
Petyward SW3 . . . . .144 B3

Pevensey Ct
4 South Acton
W3 . . . . .37 A4
West Norwood
SW16 . . . . .74 C1
Pevensey Ho 5
E1 . . . . .33 A4
Peveril Ho SE1 . . . .137 C1
Pewsham Ho N4 . . . .6 B3
Peyton Pl SE10 . . . .52 B3
Pharamond NW2 . . . . .9 C2
Phelps Ho 11
SW15 . . . . .57 C4
Phelp St SE17 . . . . . .48 C4
Phene St SW3 . . . . .158 B4
Philadelphia Ct
SW10 . . . . .157 A1
Philbeach Gdns
SW5 . . . . .141 B2
Phil Brown Pl 3
SW8 . . . . .61 A4
Philchurch Pl 38
E1 . . . . .111 C1
Philia Ho 4 NW1 . . .13 B1
Philip Blairman Ho
E1 . . . . .24 B1 98 C1
Philip Ct W2 . . . . . . .101 B4
Philip Ho 17 NW6 . . .78 A3
Philip Turner Est 28
E9 . . . . .17 B1
Philip Wlk SE15 . . . .64 C4
Phillimore Ct W8 . . .127 C3
Phillimore Gardens Cl
W8 . . . . .127 B2
Phillimore Gdns
Kensington W8 . . . . .127 B3
Willesden NW10 . . . . .22 B4
Phillimore Pl
W8 . . . . .127 B3
Phillimore Terr
W8 . . . . .127 C2
Phillimore Wlk
W8 . . . . .127 C2
Phillip Ho 11 E1 . . .111 A3
Phillipp St N1 . . . . . .24 A4
Philpot La EC3 . . . .124 A4
Philpot Sq SW6 . . . .59 A4
Philpot St E1 . . . . . .32 A3
Philson Mans 16
E1 . . . . .111 C2
Phipps Ho 16 W12 . .30 A2
Phipps Mews
SW1 . . . . .132 B1
Phipp St
EC2 . . . . .24 A1 98 A2
Phoebeth Rd SE4 . . .66 C2
Phoenix Bsns Ctr 25
E3 . . . . .33 C4
Phoenix Cl 18 E8 . .24 B4
Phoenix Ct
Brentford
TW8 . . . . .36 A1
2 Deptford SE14 . . .51 A4
Millwall E14 . . . . .41 C2
Phoenix High Sch
W12 . . . . .29 C2
Phoenix Ho SW1 . . .145 B4
Phoenix Lodge Mans
1 W6 . . . . .39 B2
Phoenix Pl WC1 . . . .95 A2
Phoenix Prim Sch
26 E3 . . . . .26 B2
Phoenix Rd NW1 . . . .93 B4
Phoenix Sch The 23
NW3 . . . . .11 C2
Phoenix St WC2 . . . .105 C1
Phoenix Wharf Rd
SE1 . . . . .139 A3

Phyllis Hodges Ho
NW1 . . . . .83 B1
Physic Pl SW3 . . . . .158 C4
Piano La 2 N16 . . . . .6 C1
Piccadilly W1 . . . . . .118 C2
Piccadilly Arc
SW1 . . . . .118 C2
Piccadilly Cir W1 . . . .119 B3
Piccadilly Circus Sta
SW1 . . . . .119 B3
Piccadilly Pl W1 . . . .119 A3
Pickard St EC1 . . . . . .96 B4
Pickering Cl E9 . . . . .17 C1
Pickering Ho
18 Kensington
W2 . . . . .100 B1
Stoke Newington N4 . . .6 C4
Pickering Mews 9
W2 . . . . .100 B2
Pickering Pl SW1 . . .119 A1
Pickering St N1 . . . . .86 B4
Pickets St SW12 . . . .73 A4
Pickfords Wharf
N1 . . . . .86 C1
Pickwick Ho
21 Bermondsey
SE16 . . . . .139 B3
7 Shepherd's Bush
W11 . . . . .30 C1
Pickwick Rd SE21 . . .76 A4
Pickwick St SE1 . . . .136 C3
Pickworth Cl
SW8 . . . . .162 B1
Picton Ho 6 SW4 . .74 A4
Picton Pl W1 . . . . . . .103 C1
Picton St SE5 . . . . . .48 C3
Picture Ho 6
SW16 . . . . .74 A2
Pied Bull Ct WC1 . . .106 B3
Pied Bull Yd WC1 . . .106 B3
Pier Head E1 . . . . . . .32 A1
Pierhead Wharf 37
E1 . . . . .32 A1
Pier Ho SW3 . . . . . .158 B3
Piermont Rd SE22 . . .65 A2
Pierpoint Bldg 4
E14 . . . . .41 C4
Pierrepont Rd
W3 . . . . .28 A2
Pierrepont Row
N1 . . . . .86 A3
Pier St E14 . . . . .42 B2
Pier Terr SW18 . . . . .59 B3
Piggott Ho 2 E2 . . . .25 C3
Pigott St E14 . . . . . . .33 C3
Pilgrimage St
SE1 . . . . .137 B3
Pilgrim Ho SE1 . . . .137 C1
Pilgrims Cloisters 10
SE5 . . . . .49 A3
Pilgrim's La NW3 . . .11 C4
Pilgrims Mews 12
E14 . . . . .34 C2
Pilgrim's Pl 6
NW3 . . . . .11 C4
Pilgrims Way N19 . . . .5 A3
**Pilgrims Way Prim
Sch 22** SE15 . . . . . . .50 B4
Pilkington Rd 4
SE15 . . . . .50 A1
Pilot Cl 13 SE8 . . . . .51 B4
Pilot Ind Ctr NW10 . .21 A1

Pilot Wk SE10 . . . . . .43 B3
Pilsden Cl SW19 . . . .69 C3
Pilton Pl SE17 . . . . .151 A2
Pimlico Sta SW1 . . .147 B2
PIMLICO 146 C1
Pimlico Acad
SW1 . . . . .147 A1
Pimlico Rd SW1 . . . .145 C2
Pimlico Wlk 1
N1 . . . . .24 A2 98 A4
Pinchin St E1 . . . . . .125 C4
Pincombe Ho
SE17 . . . . .151 B2
Pincott Pl SE4 . . . . . .65 C4
Pindar St EC2 . . . . . .110 A4
Pindock Mews W9 . .88 B1
Pine Apple Ct
SW1 . . . . .132 C2
Pine Ave E15 . . . . . . .19 C3
Pine Cl 11 N19 . . . . . .4 B2
Pinedene 2 SE15 . . . .50 A2
Pinefield Cl E14 . . . . .33 C2
Pine Gr N4, N19 . . . . . .5 B2
Pine Ho
Bow E3 . . . . .26 A4
21 Rotherhithe
SE16 . . . . .40 B4
Pinehurst Ct 6
W11 . . . . .31 B3
Pinelands Cl 7
SE3 . . . . .53 B3
Pine Lo SW15 . . . . . .58 A1
Pine Rd NW2 . . . . .9 C4
Pines Ct 18 SW19 . . .69 C3
Pine St EC1 . . . . .95 B2
Pine Tree Ho SE14 . .50 C3
Pine Tree Way 1
SE13 . . . . .67 A4
Pinewood Sch SW4 .61 C1
Pinkham Mans
W4 . . . . .36 B1
Pinnacle Ho E14 . . . .42 B3
Pinnacle Ho EC3 . . .124 A3
Pinnacle The 2
N1 . . . . .15 C2
Pinner Ct NW8 . . . . . .89 B2
Pinner Ho 30 SE5 . . .48 B1
Pintail Ct 30 SE8 . . . .51 B4
Pinter Ho 30 SW9 . .172 B1
Pioneer Cl
16 Bow Comm
E14 . . . . .34 A4
London W12 . . . . .30 A3
Pioneer St SE15 . . . .49 C2
Pioneer Way W12 . . .30 B3
Piper Cl N7 . . . . .14 B3
Pipers Ho SE10 . . . . .42 C1
Pipit Dr SW15 . . . . . .57 B1
Pippin Ho 17 W10 . . .30 C2
Pirate Castle The
NW1 . . . . .82 A4
Pirbright Rd SW18 . .70 C3
Pitcairn Ho 1 E9 . . . .17 B1
Pitfield Ho N5 . . . . . .15 B3
Pitfield St N1 . . . . . . .24 A3
Pitman Ho 8 SE8 . . . .51 C2
Pitman St SE5 . . . . . .48 B3
Pitmaston Ho 2
SE13 . . . . .52 B1
Pitsea Pl E1 . . . . .32 C3
Pitsea St E1 . . . . .32 C3
Pitt Ho 4 SW11 . . . . .59 C3
Pitt's Head Mews
W1 . . . . .117 C1
Pitt St W8 . . . . .127 C4

Pitwell Mews 8
E8 . . . . .16 C2
Pixley St E14 . . . . . . .33 B3
Planetree Ct W6 . . . .39 C2
Plane Tree Ho
SE8 . . . . .51 A4
Plantain Pl SE1 . . . .137 B4
Plantation La EC3 . .124 A4
Plantation The
SE3 . . . . .53 C1
Platanos Coll
SW9 . . . . .172 C3
Platehouse The 3
E14 . . . . .42 A1
Platina St EC2 . . . . . .97 C2
Plato Pl 1 SW6 . . . . .165 A2
Plato Rd SW2 . . . . . .62 A3
Platt's La NW3 . . . . . .1 C1
Platt St NW1 . . . . . . .83 B2
Plaxdale Ho SE17 . .152 A3
Playfair St W6 . . . . . .39 B1
Playfield Cres
SE22 . . . . .64 B2
Playford Rd
Finsbury Pk N4 . . . . . . .5 B2
Finsbury Pk N4 . . . . . . .5 C2
Playhouse Yd
EC4 . . . . .108 A1
Playon (Canary Wharf
Indoor Sports)
E14 . . . . .34 B1
Plaza Sh Ctr W1 . . . .105 A2
Pleasance Rd
SW15 . . . . .57 A2
Pleasance The
SW15 . . . . .57 A3
Pleasant Pl N1 . . . . .15 A1
Pleasant Row NW1 . .82 B3
Plender Ct NW1 . . . . .83 A3
Plender St NW1 . . . . .83 A3
Pleshey Rd N7 . . . . . .13 C4
Plevna St E14 . . . . . .42 B3
Pleydell Ave W6 . . . .38 B2
Pleydell Ct EC4 . . . .107 C1
Pleydell St EC4 . . . .107 C1
Plimsoll Cl E14 . . . . .34 A3
Plimsoll Rd N4 . . . . . .6 A1
Plough Cl NW10 . . . . .22 A2
Plough Ct EC3 . . . . . .123 C4
Plough La SE22 . . . . .64 B1
Ploughmans Cl
NW1 . . . . .83 B4
Plough Mews 19
SW11 . . . . .59 C3
Plough Pl EC4 . . . . . .107 C2
Plough Rd SW11 . . . .59 C3
Plough St 18 E1 . . . .111 B2
Plough Terr SW11 . . .59 C3
Plough Way SE16 . . .41 A2
Plough Yd
EC2 . . . . .24 A1 98 B1
Plover Ho 4 SW9 . . .163 B2
Plover Way SE16 . . . .41 A3
Plowman Ho
SW19 . . . . .69 C2
Plumbers Row E1 . .111 C2
Plumbridge St 7
SE10 . . . . .52 B2
Plume Ho SE10 . . . . .52 A4
Plummer Ct SE13 . . .67 A1
Plummer Rd SW4 . . .73 C4
Plumtree Ct EC4 . . . .108 A2
Plymouth Ho 20
SE10 . . . . .52 A4
Plymouth Rd E16 . . . .35 C4

Plymouth Wharf
E14 . . . . .42 C2
Plympton Ave
NW6 . . . . .10 B1
Plympton Pl NW1. .90 A1
Plympton Rd NW6. .10 B1
Plympton St NW8 . .90 A1
Pocklington Lo 6
SW15 . . . . .68 C3
Pocock St SE1. . . .136 B4
Podmore Rd SW18 .59 B3
Poets Cnr SW1 . . .134 A2
Poets Mews 3
SE24 . . . . .63 A2
Poet's Rd N5. . . . .15 C2
Point Cl SE10. . . . .52 B2
Pointer Sch The
SE3 . . . . .53 C3
Pointers Cl E14. . . .42 A1
Point Hill SE10 . . . .52 B2
Point Ho SE10 . . . .52 B2
Point Pleasant
SW18 . . . . .58 B3
Point Wharf La
TW8 . . . . .44 A3
Poland Ho 8 E15 . .27 C4
Poland St W1. . . .105 A1
Polesworth Ho 16
W2 . . . . .31 C4
Polish Inst & Sikorski
Mus SW7. . . . . . . .129 C3
Polish Univ Abroad 6
W6 . . . . .38 C2
Pollard Ct
Islington N7 . . . . . .14 B4
Newham E16 . . . . .35 C2
Pollard Ho N1. . . .84 C1
Pollard Row
E2 . . . . .24 C2 99 C4
Pollard St
E2 . . . . .24 C2 99 C4
Pollen St W1 . . . .104 B1
Pollitt Dr NW8. . . .89 C2
Pollock Ho W10 . . .23 A1
Pollock's Toy Mus
W1 . . . . .105 A4
Polperro Mans 3
NW6 . . . . .10 C3
Polperro Mews
SE11 . . . . .150 A4
Polygon Rd NW1 . .83 B1
Polygon The
1 Clapham SW4. . . .61 B3
St John's Wood
NW8 . . . . .79 C2
Pomell Way E1 . . .111 A2
Pomeroy Ct W11 . .31 A3
Pomeroy Ho 5 E2 .25 C3
Pomeroy St SE14 . .50 B2
Pomfret Rd SE5 . . .63 A4
Pomoja La N19 . . . .5 A2
Pomona Ho 10
SE8 . . . . .41 A2
Pond Cl SE3. . . . . .53 C1
Pond Cotts SE21. . .76 A3
Ponder St 5 N7 . . .14 B1
Pondfield Ho 4
N5. . . . . .15 B3
Pond Ho SW3 . . . .144 A3
Pond Mead SE21 . .63 C1
Pond Pl SW3. . . . .144 A3
Pond Rd SE3 . . . . .53 B1
Pond Sq N6 . . . . . . .3 C3
Pond St NW3. . . . . .12 A3

Ponler St E1. . . . . .32 A3
Ponsard Rd NW10 .22 A2
Ponsford St E9. . . .17 B2
Ponsonby Ho 13
E2 . . . . .25 B3
Ponsonby Pl SW1 .147 C2
Ponsonby Rd
SW15 . . . . .69 A4
Ponsonby Terr
SW1 . . . . .147 C2
Ponton Ho SW2 . . .74 C3
Ponton Rd SW8 . .161 C3
Pont St Mews
SW1 . . . . .130 C1
Pont St SW1 . . . . .131 A1
Pontypool Pl SE1 .136 A4
Poole Ct N1. . . . . .16 A1
Poole Ho NW8. . . .135 A1
Poole Rd E9 . . . . . .17 C2
Pooles Bldgs EC1. .95 B1
Pooles La SW10 . . .156 C2
Pooles Park Prim Sch
16 N4 . . . . .5 B2
Pooles Pk N4 . . . . .5 B2
Poole St N1. . . . . .87 B3
Pooley Ho E1 . . . . .25 C2
Pool Ho NW8. . . . .101 C4
Poolmans St SE16 . .40 C4
Poonah St E1 . . . . .32 B3
Pope Ho
7 Bermondsey
SE16 . . . . .40 A2
3 Camberwell SE5 . .48 C3
Pope John RC Prim
Sch W12 . . . . .30 A2
Pope's Head Alley
EC3 . . . . .109 C1
Pope's La W5. . . . .36 A3
Pope's Rd SW9. . . .62 C4
Pope St SE1. . . . . .138 B3
Popham Ct N16 . . . .7 A1
Popham Gdns
TW9 . . . . .55 A4
Popham Rd N1 . . . .86 C4
Popham St
Islington N1 . . . . . .86 B4
Shoreditch N1. . . . .86 C4
POPLAR 33 C3
Poplar Bath St 11
E14 . . . . .34 A2
Poplar Bsns Pk
E14 . . . . .34 B2
Poplar Cl E9 . . . . .18 B3
Poplar Ct 4 SW16 .74 B1
Poplar Gr W6 . . . . .39 B4
Poplar High St
E14 . . . . .34 A2
Poplar Ho
Brockley SE4. . . . . .66 B3
19 Rotherhithe
SE16 . . . . .40 C4
Poplar Mews 4
W12 . . . . .30 B1
Poplar Pl W2 . . . .114 B4
Poplar Rd SE24. . . .63 B3
Poplar Sta E14 . . . .34 A2
Poplars The NW5. . .13 B3
Poplar Wlk SE24 . .63 B3
Poppins Ct EC4. . .108 A1
Porchester Ct W2 .100 B1
Porchester Gate
W2 . . . . .100 B1
Porchester Gdn Mews
W2 . . . . .100 B1
Porchester Gdns
W2 . . . . .114 B4

Porchester Ho 3
E1 . . . . .32 A3
Porchester Mews
W2 . . . . .100 B2
Porchester Pl W2 .102 B1
Porchester Rd W2 .100 B2
Porchester Sq
W2 . . . . .100 B2
Porchester Terr
W2 . . . . .114 C4
Porchester Terr N
W2 . . . . .100 B2
Porden Rd SW2 . . .62 B3
Porland Rd SE1 . .137 B2
Porlock Ho 5
SE26 . . . . .76 C1
Porlock St SE1. . . .137 C4
Porson Ct SE13 . . .67 A4
Portal Cl SE27. . . . .74 C1
Portal Way W3 . . . .28 C4
Portbury Cl 17
SE15 . . . . .49 C2
Portchester Cl
SE24 . . . . .63 C3
Portelet Ct 1 N1. .24 A4
Portelet Rd E1 . . . .25 C2
Porten Hos W14. .126 A1
Porten Rd W14. . .126 A1
Porter Sq N19. . . . .5 A3
Porter St
Borough The SE1 . .123 A2
Marylebone W1 . . .103 A4
Porteus Pl 6 SW4..61 B3
Porteus Rd W2 . . .101 A4
Portgate Cl W9 . . .23 B1
Port Ho 6 SW11 . .59 B4
Port House The 6
E14 . . . . .42 A1
Portia Way E3 . . . .26 B1
Porticos The SW3 .157 B3
Portinscale Rd
SW15 . . . . .58 B2
Portishead Ho 29
W2 . . . . .31 C4
Portland Ave
N1 . . . . .16 A1
1 Deptford SE14. . .51 A4
Portland Gr SW8 .172 C4
Portland Ho 19
SW2 . . . . .74 C2
Portland Hospl for
Women & Children
The W1 . . . . .92 B1
Portland Mews
W1 . . . . .105 A1
Portland Pl W1 . . .104 B3
Portland Place Sch
W1 . . . . .104 B4
Portland Rd
Notting Hill
W11 . . . . .31 A1 112 B2
Notting Hill
W11 . . . . .31 A2 112 A3
Portland Rise N4. . . .6 B3
Portland Sq 4 E1. .32 A1
Portland St SE17 . .151 B1
Portland Village
W6 . . . . .39 B3
Portman Ave
SW14 . . . . .55 C4
Portman Cl W1. . . .103 B2

Portman Gate
NW1 . . . . .90 B1
Portman Hts 1
NW3 . . . . .1 C1
Portman Mews S
W1 . . . . .103 B1
Portman Pl E2 . . . .25 B2
Portman Sq W1 . .103 B2
Portman St W1. . . .103 B1
Portman Twrs
NW1 The NW1. . . .102 C1
Portman Twrs
W1 . . . . .103 B1
Portnall Rd W9. . . .23 B2
Portobello Ct Est
W11 . . . . .31 B3
Portobello Mews
W11 . . . . .31 B2 113 B3
Portobello Rd
W11 . . . . .31 B2 113 A4
Portobello Road Mkt
W10 . . . . .31 A4
Portpool La EC1. . .107 B4
Portree St E14 . . . .34 C3
Port Royal Pl 3
N16 . . . . .16 A3
Portsea Hall W2 . .102 B1
Portsea Ho 8
SW15 . . . . .69 A3
Portsea Mews
W2 . . . . .102 B1
Portsea Pl W2. . . .102 B1
Portslade Rd
SW8 . . . . .170 C2
Portsmouth Rd
SW15 . . . . .69 B4
Portsmouth St
WC2 . . . . .107 A1
Portsoken St E1,
EC3 . . . . .124 C4
Portswood Pl
SW15 . . . . .56 B1
Portugal St WC2. . .107 A1
Poseidon Ct 9
E14 . . . . .41 C2
Postal Museum The
WC1 . . . . .95 B2
Postern The EC2. .109 A3
Post Office Way
SW8 . . . . .161 B2
Potier St SE1 . . . .137 C1
Potterne Cl 5
SW19 . . . . .69 C4
Potters Cl 6 SE15. .49 A3
Potters Fields
SE1 . . . . .124 B1
Potters Lo E14 . . . .42 B1
Potters Rd SW6 . .166 C1
Pottery La
W11 . . . . .31 A1 112 B2
Pottery Rd TW8. . . .44 A4
Pottery St SE16. . . .40 A4
Pott St E2. . . . . . . .25 A2
Poullett Ho SW2. . .75 A3
Poulton Cl E8 . . . .17 A2
Poultry EC2 . . . . . .109 B1
Pound La NW10 . . . .8 C2
Pountney Rd
SW11 . . . . .60 C4
Povey Ho
Tulse Hill SW2 . . . .62 C1
Walworth SE17. . . .152 A3
Powell's Wlk W4 . .46 B4
Powergate Bsns Pk
NW10 . . . . .20 C2
Power Ho 13 TW9 . .44 C2
Power Ho The W4 . .38 B2

Power Rd W4 . . . .36 C2
Powerscroft Rd
E5 . . . . .17 B4
Powis Gdns
Golders Green
NW11 . . . . .1 B4
Notting Hill W11 . .31 B3
Powis Ho WC2. . . .106 B2
Powis Mews W11. .31 B3
Powis Pl WC1. . . . .94 B1
Powis Rd E3 . . . . . .27 A2
Powis Sq W11. . . . .31 B3
Powis Terr W11. . . .31 B3
Powlesland Ct 21
E14 . . . . .33 A3
Powlett Ho NW1 . .13 A2
Powlett Pl NW1 . . .13 A1
Pownall Rd E8 . . . .24 C4
Pownall Terr
SE11 . . . . .163 C3
Powrie Ho 4
SW11 . . . . .167 C3
Poynder Ct 3 N7 . .14 A3
Poynders Ct
SW4 . . . . .61 B1
Poynders Gdns
SW12 . . . . .73 B4
Poynders Rd SW12,
SW4 . . . . .73 C4
Poynings Rd N19 . . .4 B1
Poynter Ho
Paddington NW8 . .89 B2
9 Shepherd's Bush
W11 . . . . .30 C1
Poynton Rd N17 . .168 C1
Poyser St E2 . . . . .25 A3
Praed Mews W2 . .101 C2
Praed St W2 . . . . .101 C2
Prague Pl SW2 . . . .62 A2
Prah Rd N4 . . . . . . .5 C2
Prairie St SW8 . . .170 A1
Pratt Mews NW1 . .82 C3
Pratt St NW1 . . . . .82 C4
Pratt Wlk SE1,
SE11 . . . . .149 A4
Preachers Ct EC1. .96 B1
Prebend Gdns W4,
W6 . . . . .38 B2
Prebend Mans 4
W4 . . . . .38 B2
Prebend St N1 . . . .86 C4
Precinct The
Islington N1 . . . . . .86 C3
Islington N5 . . . . . .15 A3
Premier Corner
NW6 . . . . .23 B3
Premier Ho 25 N1. .15 A1
Premier Park Rd
NW10 . . . . .20 A3
Premier Pk NW10 . .20 A3
Premier Pl 17 E14. .33 C2
Prendergast Ho 7
SW4 . . . . .73 C4
Prendergast Prim Sch
SE4 . . . . .66 C3
Prendergast Rd
SE3 . . . . .53 A4
Prendergast Vale Sch
3 SE13 . . . . .67 A4
Prescot St E1 . . . .125 A4
Prescott Ho 13
SE17 . . . . .48 A4
Prescott Pl SW4. . .61 C3

Presentation Mews
SW2 . . . . 74 B3
President Dr E1 . . . . . 32 A1
President Ho EC1 . . . 96 B3
President St EC1 . . . 96 C4
Prestage Way 13
E14 . . . . 34 B2
Prested Rd SW11 . . . 60 A3
Preston Cl SE1 . . . . 152 A4
Preston Gdns NW10 . 8 A2
Preston Ho
Bermondsey SE1 . . 138 C2
Walworth SE1 . . . . 152 A4
Preston Pl
Richmond TW10 . . . . 54 A2
Willesden NW2 . . . . . 8 C2
Preston's Rd E14 . . . 34 B1
Prestwich Terr
SW4 . . . . 61 C2
Prestwood Ho 3
SE16 . . . . 40 A3
Prestwood St N1 . . . 87 A1
Priam Ho E2 . . . . 25 A3
Price Cl SW17 . . . . . 72 B1
Price Ho N1 . . . . 86 C3
Prices Ct SW11 . . . . 59 C4
Price's St SE1 . . . . 122 B2
Price's Yd N1 . . . . . . 85 A3
Prichard Ct
Battersea SW11 . . . 167 C3
Islington N7 . . . . 14 B3
Prideaux Ho WC1 . . . 95 A4
Prideaux Pl
Acton W3 . . . . 28 C2
St Pancras WC1 . . . . 95 A4
Prideaux Rd SW9 . . . 62 A4
Pride Ct N1 . . . . 85 C2
Priestley Ho N16 . . . . 7 B4
Priestley Ho
2 Camden Town
NW5 . . . . 13 A2
St Luke's EC1 . . . . . . 97 A2
Priestman Point 25
E3 . . . . 27 A2
Priests Bridge
SW14 . . . . 56 A4
Priest's Ct EC2 . . . . 108 C2
Prima Rd SW9 . . . . . 163 B2
Primrose Cl 6 E3 . . . 26 C3
Primrose Ct
2 Child's Hill NW2 . . 1 B1
Primrose Hill NW8 . . 80 C3
11 Streatham
SW12 . . . . 73 C4
Primrose Gdns
NW3 . . . . 12 A2
PRIMROSE HILL NW8 12 B1
Primrose Hill EC4 107 C1
Primrose Hill Ct
NW3 . . . . 12 B1
Primrose Hill Prim
Sch NW1 . . . . 81 C4
Primrose Hill Rd NW1,
NW3 . . . . 12 B1
Primrose Hill Studios
NW1 . . . . 81 B4
Primrose Ho
7 Peckham SE15 . . . 49 C2
1 Richmond TW9 . . . 44 B2
Primrose Mans
SW11 . . . . 169 B4
Primrose Mews 12
NW1 . . . . 12 B1
Primrose Sq E9 . . . . 25 B4

Primrose St EC2 . . . 110 B4
Primrose Wlk 6
SE14 . . . . 51 A3
Primrose Wy 10
SE15 . . . . 49 C4
Primula St W12 . . . . 29 C3
Prince Albert Ct
NW8 . . . . 80 C3
Prince Albert Rd
NW8 . . . . 80 C3
Prince Arthur Ct 18
NW3 . . . . 11 B4
Prince Arthur Mews
17 NW3 . . . . 11 B4
Prince Arthur Rd
NW3 . . . . 11 B4
Prince Charles Rd
SE3 . . . . 53 B2
Prince Consort Ho
SW7 . . . . 129 B2
Prince Consort Rd
SW7 . . . . 129 B2
Princedale Rd
W11 . . . . 31 A1 112 B2
Prince Edward Mans
W2 . . . . 31 C2 113 C4
Prince Edward Rd
E9 . . . . 18 B2
Prince George Rd
N16 . . . . 16 A4
Prince St EC1 . . . . . 111 A4
Prince of Orange La
3 SE10 . . . . 52 B3
Prince of Wales Dr
SW11 . . . . 169 B4
Prince of Wales Mans
Battersea SW11 . . . 169 C4
Clapham SW4 . . . . . 61 A2
Prince of Wales Pas
18 NW1 . . . . 92 C3
Prince of Wales Rd
Blackheath Vale
SE3 . . . . 53 B1
Camden Town NW5 . 12 C2
Prince of Wales Terr
Chiswick W4 . . . . . . 38 A1
Kensington W8 . . . . 128 B3
Prince Regent Ct 2
SE16 . . . . 33 A1
Prince Regent Mews
NW1 . . . . 92 C3
Princes Arc SW1 . . . 119 A2
Princes Ave W3 . . . . 36 C3
Princes Cl N4 . . . . . . 6 A3
Princes Coll WC1 . . . 106 A2
Princes Court Bsns
Cir 10 E1 . . . . 32 A2
Princes Ct
Brondesbury
NW2 . . . . 10 A3
Hampstead NW3 . . . 11 C4
Stepney E1 . . . . 32 A2
Prince's Ct SE16 . . . 41 B3
Princes Gate SW7 . . 129 C3
Prince's Gate
SW7 . . . . 130 A3
Princes Gate Ct
SW7 . . . . 129 C3
Princes Gate Mews
SW7 . . . . 129 C2
Princes Gdns
SW7 . . . . 129 C2
Princes Ho
W11 . . . . 31 C2 113 B3

Prince's Mews
1 Hammersmith
W6 . . . . 39 A1
Islington N1 . . . . 85 A3
Kensington W2 . . . . 114 A4
Princes Pl
Notting Hill
W11 . . . . 31 A1 112 A2
St James SW1 . . . . . 119 A2
Princes Rd
Kew TW9 . . . . 44 B2
Richmond TW10 . . . . 54 B2
Prince's Rd SW14 . . 55 C4
Princes Rise SE13 . . 67 B4
Princes Riverside Rd
7 SE16 . . . . 32 C1
Princess Alexandra
School of Nursing
The **13** E1 . . . . 32 A4
Princess Alice Ho 7
W10 . . . . 22 B1
Princess Beatrice Ho
SW10 . . . . 142 A1
Princess Cres N4 . . . 6 A2
Princess Ct
Hampstead NW6 . . . 11 A1
Kensington W2 . . . . 114 B4
Marylebone W1 . . . . 102 C3
Princess Frederica CE
VA Prim Sch
NW10 . . . . 22 B3
Princess Grace Hospl
The W1 . . . . 91 B1
Princess Louise Cl
W2 . . . . 101 C4
Princess Louise Wk 22
W10 . . . . 30 B4
Princess Mary Ho
SW1 . . . . 147 C3
Princess May Prim
Sch 18 N16 . . . . 16 B4
Princess May Rd
N16 . . . . 16 A4
Princess Mews
NW3 . . . . 11 C2
Prince's Sq W2 . . . . 114 A4
Princess Rd
Camden Town
NW1 . . . . 81 C4
Paddington NW6 . . . 23 C3
Princess St SE1 . . . 136 B1
Princes St W1 . . . . . 104 B1
Prince's St
City of London
EC2 . . . . 109 B1
Richmond TW10,
TW9 . . . . 54 A2
Prince St SE8 . . . . . . 51 B4
Princes Way
Acton W3 . . . . 36 C3
Putney SW15,
SW19 . . . . 70 A3
Princes Yd
W11 . . . . 31 A1 112 B2
Princethorpe Ho
W2 . . . . 100 A4
Princeton Mans
WC1 . . . . 106 C3
Princeton St WC1 . . 106 C4
Principal Sq E9 . . . . 17 C3
Printers Mews E3 . . 26 A4
Printers Rd SW9 . . . 173 A4
Printer St EC4 . . . . . 107 C2

Printing House Yd 16
E2 . . . . 24 A2 98 B3
Printon Ho 18 E3 . . . 33 B4
Print Village Ind Est
SE15 . . . . 49 B1
Prior Bolton St N1 . 15 A2
Prioress Ho 2 E3 . . . 27 A2
Prioress Rd SE27 . . 75 A1
Prioress St SE1 . . . 137 C1
Priors Lo 4 TW10 . . 54 A1
Prior St SE10 . . . . . . 52 B3
Prior Weston Prim
Sch
Broadgate EC1 . . . . 97 B2
St Luke's EC1 . . . . . 97 A1
Priory Ave W4 . . . . . 38 A3
Priory Ct
City of London
EC4 . . . . 108 B1
Homerton E9 . . . . . . 17 C3
Nunhead SE15 . . . . . 65 B3
Roehampton SW15 . . 56 B3
South Lambeth
SW8 . . . . 171 C4
Priory Gdns
Barnes SW13 . . . . . . 56 B4
6 Chiswick W4 . . . . 38 A2
Priory Gn N1 . . . . . . 84 C2
Priory Gr SW8 . . . . 172 A3
Priory Ho
Clerkenwell EC1 . . . 96 A2
Pimlico SW1 . . . . . . 147 B2
Spitalfields E1 . . . . . 110 C4
Priory Hospl
Roehampton The
SW15 . . . . 56 B3
Priory Hts N1 . . . . . . 85 A2
Priory La SW15 . . . . 56 B2
Priory Lo 7 W4 . . . . 36 C1
Priory Lodge Sch
SW15 . . . . 56 B3
Priory Mans
17 Maitland Pk
NW3 . . . . 12 B2
South Kensington
SW10 . . . . 143 A1
Priory Park Rd
NW6 . . . . 23 B4
Priory Rd
Bedford Pk W4 . . . . 37 C3
Hampstead NW6 . . . 11 A1
Richmond TW9 . . . . . 44 C3
Priory St 16 E3 . . . . 27 A2
Priory Terr NW6 . . . 78 A4
Priory The SE1 . . . . 136 A3
Priory Wlk SW10 . . 143 A1
Pritchard Ho 38
E2 . . . . 24 C3
Pritchard's Rd E2 . . 24 C4
Priter Rd SE16 . . . . 139 C1
Priter Road Hostel 14
SE16 . . . . 139 C1
Probert Rd SW2 . . . 62 C2
Probyn Ho SW1 . . . 147 C4
Probyn Rd SW2 . . . . 75 A2
Procter Ho 2 SE5 . . 48 C3
Procter St WC1 . . . 106 C3
Proctor Ho 5
SE1 . . . . 153 B1
Prologis Bsns Pk
E16 . . . . 27 B1
Prome Ho 3 N16 . . . . 7 A1
Promenade Approach
Rd W4 . . . . 46 A3
Promenade The
W4 . . . . 46 A2

Prospect Cotts
SW18 . . . . 58 C3
Prospect Ho
1 Dalston E8 . . . . . 16 B2
Islington N1 . . . . 85 B1
Newington SE1 . . . 136 B1
14 North Kensington
W10 . . . . 30 C3
Prospect House Sch
SW15 . . . . 69 C4
Prospect Pl
1 Child's Hill NW2 . 1 B1
2 Chiswick W4 . . . . 37 C1
4 Deptford SE8 . . . 51 B4
13 Hampstead
NW3 . . . . 11 B4
1 Lower Holloway
N7 . . . . 14 A4
Wapping E1 . . . . 32 B1
Prospect Quay
SW18 . . . . 58 C3
Prospect Rd NW2 . . . 1 C1
Prospect St SE16 . . . 40 A4
Prospect Wharf
E1 . . . . 32 B2
Prospero Rd N19 . . . 4 C3
Prothero Rd SW6 . . 154 C2
Proud Ho 10 E1 . . . . 32 A3
Proud Ct NW10 . . . . . 8 B4
Provence St N1 . . . . 86 C2
Providence Ct
Islington N1 . . . . 86 A3
Mayfair W1 . . . . 117 C4
Providence Pl N1 . . . 86 A3
Providence Row
N1 . . . . 84 C1
Providence Row Cl 10
E2 . . . . 25 A2
Providence Sq 11
SE1 . . . . 139 B4
Providence Yd 5
E2 . . . . 24 C2 99 A4
Province Dr 38
SE16 . . . . 40 C4
Provost Ct NW3 . . . . 12 B2
Provost Rd NW3 . . . . 12 B1
Provost St N1 . . . . . . 97 B4
Prowse Pl NW1 . . . . . 13 B1
Prudent Pas EC2 . . . 109 A1
Prusom's Island 8
E1 . . . . 32 B1
Prusom St E1 . . . . . . 32 A1
Pryors The NW3 . . . . 2 C1
Pudding La EC3 . . . 123 C4
Pudding Mill La
E15 . . . . 27 A4
Pudding Mill Lane Sta
E15 . . . . 27 A4
Puddle Dock EC4 . . . 122 B4
Pugin Ct N1 . . . . 14 C1
Pulborough Rd
SW18 . . . . 70 B4
Pulham Ho SW8 . . . 162 C1
Pullman Ct SW2 . . . 74 B3
Pullman Gdns
SW15 . . . . 57 B1
Pulross Rd SW9 . . . . 62 B4
Pulteney Cl 20 E3 . . 26 B4
Pulteney Terr N1 . . . 85 A4
Pulton Ho SE4 . . . . . 66 A3
Pulton Pl SW6 . . . . 155 B1
Puma Ct E1 . . . . 110 C4
Pump Ct EC4 . . . . . . 107 B1
Pump House Cl
SE16 . . . . 40 B4

Pump House Cres
TW8 . . . . 44 B4
Pumphouse
Educational Mus The
SE16 . . . . 33 A1
Pump House Gall
SW11 . . . . 159 B1
Pumping Ho 3
E14 . . . . 34 C2
Pumping Station Rd
W4 . . . . 46 A4
Pump La SE14 . . . . . . 50 B3
Punderson's Gdns
E2 . . . . 25 A2
Purbeck Ho SW8 . . 162 C1
Purbrook Est SE1 . . 138 B3
Purbrook Ho 2
SW15 . . . . 69 A3
Purbrook St SE1 . . 138 B2
Purcell Cres SW6 . . 154 A2
Purcell Ho SW10 . . 157 B3
Purcell Mews 2
NW10 . . . . 8 A1
Purcell St N1 . . . . . . 24 A3
Purchese St NW1 . . . 83 A1
Purday Ho 4 W10 . . 23 B2
Purdon Ho 11
SE15 . . . . 49 C2
Purdy St E3 . . . . 27 A1
Purley Ave NW2 . . . . 1 A2
Purley PI N1 . . . . 15 A1
Purser Ho 3 SW2 . . 62 C1
Pursers Cross Rd
SW6 . . . . 165 A4
Purves Rd NW10 . . . . 22 B3
Pusey Ho 20 E14 . . . . 33 C3
Puteaux Ho 6 E2 . . 25 C3
PUTNEY 57 C2
Putney Bridge App
SW6 . . . . 58 A4
Putney Bridge Rd
SW15 . . . . 58 B3
Putney Bridge Sta
SW6 . . . . 58 B4
Putney Comm
SW15 . . . . 57 B4
Putney Exchange
Shopping Ctr
SW15 . . . . 57 C3
PUTNEY HEATH . . 57 B1
Putney Heath
SW15 . . . . 57 B1
Putney Heath La
SW15 . . . . 57 C1
Putney High Sch
SW15 . . . . 57 C2
Putney High St
SW15 . . . . 58 A4
Putney Hill
12 Putney SW15 . . . . 69 B4
Putney SW15 . . . . 57 C2
Putney L Ctr SW15 . . 57 B3
Putney Park Ave
SW15 . . . . 56 C3
Putney Park La
SW15 . . . . 57 A2
Putney Pier SW15 . . 58 A4
Putney School of Art
& Design SW15 . . . . 58 A3
Putney Sta SW15 . . . 58 A3
PUTNEY VALE 68 C1
Putney Wharf Twr
SW15 . . . . 58 A4
Pykewell Lo 18 E8 . . 16 C3
Pylon Trad Est
E16 . . . . 34 C4

Pymers Mead
SE21 . . . . 75 B3
Pynfolds SE16 . . . . . . 40 A4
Pynnersmead
SE24 . . . . 63 B2
Pyrford Ho 12
SW9 . . . . 63 A3
Pyrland Rd
Richmond TW10 . . . . 54 B1
Stoke Newington
N5 . . . . 15 C3
Pyrmont Gr SE27 . . . 75 A1
Pyrmont Rd W4 . . . . 44 C4
Pytchley Rd SE22 . . 64 A4

Q

Quadrangle CI
SE1 . . . . 152 A4
Quadrangle The
Chelsea SW10 . . . . . 167 A4
Fulham SW6 . . . . . . 154 A1
Herne Hill SE24 . . . . 63 B2
3 North Kensington
W12 . . . . 30 B3
Paddington W2 . . . . 102 A2
Quadrant Arc W1 . . 119 A3
Quadrant Bsns Ctr
NW6 . . . . 23 A4
Quadrant Gr NW5 . . 12 B3
Quadrant The
4 Kensal Green
W10 . . . . 22 C2
Richmond TW9 . . . . . 54 A3
Quaker Ct EC1 . . . . . . 97 A2
Quaker St
E1 . . . . 24 B1 98 C1
Quality Ct WC2 . . . . 107 B2
Quantock Ho N16 . . . 7 B3
Quantock Mews 3
SE15 . . . . 49 C1
Quarrendon St
SW6 . . . . 165 C2
Quarry Rd SW18 . . . . 59 B1
Quarterdeck The
E14 . . . . 41 C4
Quayside Ct 6
SE16 . . . . 32 C1
Quebec & Crown
Wharves E1 . . . . . . 33 B3
Quebec Ind Est
SE16 . . . . 41 A3
Quebec Mews
W1 . . . . 103 A1
Quebec Way SE16 . . 41 A4
Quebec Wharf 32
E8 . . . . 24 A4
Quedgeley Ct 3
SE15 . . . . 49 B4
Queen Alexandra
Mans WC1 . . . . 94 A3
Queen Anne Mews
W1 . . . . 104 B3
Queen Anne Rd
E9 . . . . 17 C2
Queen Anne's Gate
SW1 . . . . 133 B3
Queen Anne's Gdns
Bedford Pk W4 . . . . 38 A3
Ealing W5 . . . . 36 A4
Queen Anne's Gr
Bedford Pk W4 . . . . 38 A3
Ealing W5 . . . . 36 A4
Queen Annes Sq
SE1 . . . . 153 B4

Queen Anne St
W1 . . . . 104 A3
Queen Anne Terr 9
E1 . . . . 32 A2
Queen Caroline St
W6 . . . . 39 B1
Queen Charlotte's &
Chelsea Hospl
W12 . . . . 29 C3
Queen Coll W1 . . . . 94 B1
Queen Elizabeth Ct 5
N1 . . . . 15 C2
Queen Elizabeth Hall
& Purcell Room
SE1 . . . . 121 A2
Queen Elizabeth Ho
SW12 . . . . 72 C4
Queen Elizabeth II
Con Ctr SW1 . . . . 133 C3
Queen Elizabeth II
Jubilee Sch 5
W9 . . . . 23 B1
Queen Elizabeth
Olympic Pk E15 . . 19 A2
Queen Elizabeth's CI
N16 . . . . 6 C2
Queen Elizabeth's Coll
10 SE10 . . . . 52 B3
Queen Elizabeth St
SE1 . . . . 138 C4
Queen Elizabeth's Wlk
SW13 . . . . 47 A3
Queen Elizabeth Wlk
N16 . . . . 6 C2
Queenhithe EC4 . . . 123 A4
Queen Isabella Way
EC1 . . . . 108 C2
Queen Margaret Flats
22 E2 . . . . 25 A2
Queen Margarets Ct
N1 . . . . 16 A1
Queen Margaret's Gr
N1 . . . . 16 A2
Queen Mary's Gdns
NW1 . . . . 91 B3
Queen Mary's Univ
Hospl SW15 . . . . . . 56 C1
Queen Mary Univ of
London E1 . . . . 26 A1
Queen Mary, Univ of
London E1 . . . . 26 A1
Queen Mother Sp Ctr
SW1 . . . . 146 C4
Queen of Denmark Ct
SE16 . . . . 41 B3
Queen St PI EC4 . . . 123 A4
Queensberry Mews W
SW7 . . . . 143 B4
Queensberry PI
SW7 . . . . 143 B4
Queensberry Way
SW7 . . . . 143 B4
Queensborough Mews
W2 . . . . 114 C4
Queensborough Pas
W2 . . . . 114 C4
Queensborough Terr
W2 . . . . 114 C4
Queensbridge Ct 11
E2 . . . . 24 B3
Queensbridge Inf Sch
11 E8 . . . . 16 B1
Queensbridge Rd
Dalston E8 . . . . 16 B1
Shoreditch E2, E8 . . 24 B4

Queensbury St 22
N1 . . . . 15 B1
Queen's CE Prim Sch
The TW9 . . . . 44 C3
Queen's Cir SW11 160 A1
Queen's Club Gdns
W14 . . . . 154 B4
Queen's Club The
W14 . . . . 140 B1
Queen's Coll W1 . . . 104 A3
Queen's Coll Prep Sch
W1 . . . . 104 A4
Queens Cres TW10 . . 54 B2
Queen's Cres NW5 . . 12 C2
Queens Ct
Battersea SW11 . . . 170 A4
Camberwell SE5 . . . 49 A1
4 Limehouse E14 . . 33 B2
Queen's Ct
Barnes SW13 . . . . . 56 C4
Kensington W2 . . . . 114 B3
8 Richmond TW10 . . 54 B3
St John's Wood
NW8 . . . . 79 B2
Queensdale Cres
W11 . . . . 30 C1
Queensdale PI
W11 . . . . 31 A1 112 A1
Queensdale Rd
Notting Hill W11 . . . 30 C1
Notting Hill
W11 . . . . 31 A1 112 A1
Queensdale Wlk
W11 . . . . 31 A1 112 A1
Queensdown Rd
E5 . . . . 17 A4
Queen's Dr N4 . . . . . . 6 A2
Queen's Elm Par
SW3 . . . . 143 C2
Queen's Elm Sq
SW3 . . . . 143 C1
Queen's Gallery
SW1 . . . . 132 B3
Queen's Gate
SW7 . . . . 129 A1
Queensgate Gdns
SW15 . . . . 57 A3
Queen's Gate Gdns
SW7 . . . . 129 A1
Queensgate Ho 34
E3 . . . . 26 B3
Queen's Gate Mews
SW7 . . . . 129 A2
Queensgate PI 10
NW6 . . . . 10 C1
Queen's Gate PI
SW7 . . . . 129 A1
Queen's Gate PI Mews
SW7 . . . . 129 A1
Queen's Gate Sch
SW7 . . . . 143 B4
Queen's Gate Terr
SW7 . . . . 129 A2
Queen's Gate Villas
E9 . . . . 18 A1
Queen's Gdns W2 . 114 C4
Queen's Gr NW8 . . . . 79 C2
Queen's Head Pas
EC2 . . . . 108 C2
Queen's Head St
N1 . . . . 86 B3
Queen's Head Yd
SE1 . . . . 123 B1
Queens Ho 11
SE17 . . . . 48 C4

Queen's House The
SE10 . . . . 52 C4
Queensland Rd
N7 . . . . 14 C4
Queen's Manor Prim
Sch SW6 . . . . 47 C3
Queens Mans
NW6 . . . . 11 A3
Queen's Mans W6 . . 39 C2
Queensmead NW8 . . 79 C4
Queensmere CI
SW19 . . . . 69 C2
Queensmere Ct
SW13 . . . . 46 C4
Queensmere Rd
SW19 . . . . 69 C2
Queen's Mews
W2 . . . . 114 A4
Queensmill Rd
SW6 . . . . 47 C3
Queensmill Sch
1 East Acton
W12 . . . . 29 C1
London SW6 . . . . . . 165 C1
Queensmill Sec Sch
W14 . . . . 141 A2
Queens Par 3 NW2 . 9 B2
Queens Park Com Sch
NW6 . . . . 10 A1
Queen's Park Ct 5
W10 . . . . 22 C2
Queen's Park Prim
Sch 20 W10 . . . . 23 A1
Queens Park Sta
NW6 . . . . 23 B3
Queen Sq WC1 . . . . . 106 B4
Queen's Quay EC4 123 A4
Queen's Rd
Mortlake SW14 . . . . 55 C4
New Cross Gate SE14,
SE15 . . . . 50 B2
Richmond TW10 . . . 54 B1
Queen's Rise
TW10 . . . . 54 B1
Queen's Road
Peckham Sta
SE15 . . . . 50 B2
Queen's Row SE17 . . 48 C4
Queen St
City of London
EC4 . . . . 123 A4
Mayfair W1 . . . . 118 A2
Queens Terr NW8 . . 79 B2
Queenstown Mews
SW8 . . . . 170 A3
Queenstown Rd
SW8 . . . . 160 A2
Queenstown Road
(Battersea) Sta
SW8 . . . . 170 B2
Queensville Rd SW12,
SW4 . . . . 73 C4
Queensway W2 . . . . 114 B4
Queensway Sta
W2 . . . . 114 B3
Queen's Wlk SW1 118 C1
Queenswood Ct 7
SW4 . . . . 62 A2
Queens Yd E9 . . . . . . 18 C2
Queen's Yd W1 . . . . . 93 A1
Queen Victoria Meml
SW1 . . . . 132 C4

Queen Victoria St
EC4 . . . . 122 C2
Queen Victoria Terr
12 E1 . . . . 32 A2
Quelch Ho 2 N19 . .13 C3
Quemerford Rd
N7 . . . . .14 B3
Quendon Ho 9
W10 . . . . .22 B1
Quenington Ct 5
SE15 . . . . .49 B4
Quenington Mans
SW6 . . . . 164 C4
Quennel Ho 7
SW12 . . . . .73 B4
Querrin St SW6 . .166 C1
Quested Ct 27 E8 . .17 A3
Quex Mews NW6 . .23 C4
Quex Rd NW6 . . . . .23 C4
Quick St N1 . . . . . .86 B1
Quick Street Mews
N1 . . . . .86 B1
Quickswood NW3 . .12 A1
Quill La SW15 . . . . .57 C3
Quill St N4 . . . . .5 C1
Quilp St SE1 . . . . 136 C4
Quilter St
E2 . . . . .24 C2 99 B4
Quilting Ct 2
SE16 . . . . .40 C4
Quince Rd SE13 . . .52 A1
Quinn Cl E2 . . . . . .25 B3
Quintin Cl W4 . . . . .45 B3
Quintin Kynaston Sch
NW8 . . . . .79 B3
Quintock Ho 2
TW9 . . . . .44 C2
Quinton Ho SW8 .162 A2
Quinton St SW18 . .71 B2
Quixley St E14 . . . .34 C2
Quorn Rd SE22 . . . .64 A4

R

Rabbit Row
W8 . . . . . .31 C1 113 C2
Raby St E14 . . . . . . .33 A3
Racine SE5 . . . . . . .49 A2
Racton Rd SW6 . .155 B3
Radbourne Cl E5 . .17 C4
Radbourne Rd
SW12 . . . . .73 C3
Radcliff Bldg EC1. 107 B4
Radcliffe Ave
NW10 . . . . .21 C3
Radcliffe Coll
Marylebone W1 . . . .104 C1
Soho W1 . . . . 105 B2
Radcliffe Ho 10
SE16 . . . . .40 A2
Radcliffe Path 5
SW8 . . . . 170 B1
Radcliffe Rd SE1 138 B2
Radcliffe Sq SW15. .57 C1
Radcot St SE11 . . .149 C1
Raddington Rd
W10 . . . . .31 A4
Radford Ho
7 Bow Comm
E14 . . . . .34 A4
Islington N7 . . . . . .14 B3
Radford Rd SE13 . .67 B1

Radipole Rd SW6 164 C4
Radland Rd E16 . . . .35 C3
Radlett Pl NW8 . . . .80 A4
Radley Cl 25 SE16 . .40 C4
Radley Ct SE16 . . . .90 C2
Radley Lo 50
SW19 . . . . .69 C3
Radley Mews W8 127 C1
Radley Terr 1
E16 . . . . .35 B4
Radnor Lo W2 . . . .101 C1
Radnor Mews W2 101 C1
Radnor Pl W2 . . . .102 A1
Radnor Rd
Kensal Rise NW6 . .23 A4
Peckham SE15 . . . .49 C3
Radnor St EC1 . . . .97 A3
Radnor Terr W14 .140 C4
Radnor Way NW10 . .20 A1
Radnor Wlk
Chelsea SW3 . . . .144 C1
22 Millwall E14 . . . .41 C2
Radstock St
SW11 . . . . .158 A1
Radway Ho 33 W2 . .31 C4
Radwell Ho SW2 . . .62 C2
Raebern Ct 6
SW2 . . . . .62 C2
Raeburn St SW2 . . .62 A3
RAF Bomber
Command Memorial
SW1 . . . . 132 A4
Ragged School Mus
E3 . . . . .26 A2
Raglan Ct SW16 . . .74 A1
Raglan St NW5 . . . .13 A2
Ragley Cl W3 . . . . . .37 B4
Rahere Ho EC1 . . . .96 C4
Railey Mews NW5 . .13 B3
Rail Sidings Rd
SE16 . . . . .139 C1
Railton Rd SE24 . .63 A2
Railway App SE1 .123 C2
Railway Ave SE16 . .40 B4
Railway Cotts W6 . .39 B4
Railway Rise SE22 . .64 B3
Railway Side
SW13 . . . . .56 A4
Railway St N1 . . . . .84 B1
Railway Terr SE13 . .67 A2
Rainbow Ave E14 . .42 A1
Rainbow Ct 8
SE14 . . . . .51 A4
Rainbow Montessori
Sch NW6 . . . . .11 A1
Rainbow Quay
SE16 . . . . .41 A3
Rainbow Sch 5
SW17 . . . . .71 B2
Rainbow St SE5 . . . .49 A3
Raines Ct N16 . . . . . .7 B2
Raine's Foundation
Lower Sch E2 . . . .25 A2
Raine's Foundation
Sch 34 E2 . . . . . . .25 B3
Raine St E1 . . . . . . .32 A1
Rainford Ho 9 N7 . . .5 B2
Rainham Cl SW11 . .60 A1
Rainham Rd NW10 . .22 B2
Rainhill Way E3 . . .26 C2
Rainsborough Ave
SE8 . . . . .41 A2
Rainsford Ct
NW10 . . . . .20 A3

Rainsford Ho 14
SW2 . . . . .62 B2
Rainsford Rd
NW10 . . . . .20 A3
Rainsford St W2 .102 A2
Rainton Rd SE7 . . . .43 C1
Rainville Rd W6 . . .47 C4
Raleigh Ct
7 Hammersmith
W12 . . . . .39 A4
2 Rotherhithe
SE16 . . . . .32 C1
Raleigh Gdns SW2 . .62 B1
Raleigh Ho
5 Clapham
SW8 . . . . 171 B2
Isle of Dogs E14 . . .42 A4
Raleigh Mews
N1 . . . . .86 B3
Raleigh Rd TW9 . . .54 B4
Raleigh St N1 . . . . . .86 B3
Ralph Ct 8 W2 . . . .100 B2
Ralston St SW3 . . .144 C1
Ramar Ho 10 E1 . .111 B4
Ramilles Cl SW2 . . . .62 A2
Ramillies Ho 4 W1 . .105 A1
Ramillies Pl W1 . . .104 C1
Ramillies Rd W4 . . . .37 C2
Ramillies St W1 . .104 C1
Rampart St E1 . . . . . .32 A3
Rampayne St
SW1 . . . . 147 B2
Ramsay Ho NW8 . . .80 A2
Ramsay Mews
SW3 . . . . 158 A4
Ramsay Rd W3 . . . . .37 B4
Ramsdean Ho 1
SW15 . . . . .69 A3
Ramsden Rd
SW12 . . . . .72 C4
Ramsey Ct
Putney SW15 . . . . . .57 B1
6 Upper Holloway
N19 . . . . .4 C4
Ramsey Ho
5 Battersea
SW8 . . . . 171 A4
14 Kennington
SW9 . . . . 163 C1
Ramsey St
E2 . . . . .24 C1 99 C2
Ramsey Wlk N1 . . . .15 C2
Ramsfort Ho
SE16 . . . . .40 A2
Ramsgate St E8 . . .16 B2
Ram St SW18 . . . . .59 A2
Randall Cl SW11 .168 A4
Randall Pl SE10 . . .52 B3
Randall Rd SE11 .148 C3
Randall Row SE11 148 C3
Randell's Rd N1 . . . .84 B4
Randolf Ct
Paddington NW6 . . .78 A1
St John's Wood
NW8 . . . . .78 C2
Randolph Ave W9 . .88 C3
Randolph Cres W9 88 C3
Randolph Gdns
NW6 . . . . .78 A1
Randolph Mews
W9 . . . . .89 A1
Randolph Rd W9 . .89 A1
Randolph St NW1 . .13 B1
Ranelagh Ave
Barnes SW13 . . . . .46 C1

Ranelagh Ave continued
Fulham SW6 . . . . . . .58 B4
Ranelagh Gardens
Mans SW6 . . . . . . .58 A4
Ranelagh Gardens
(site of Chelsea
Flower Show)
SW1 . . . . 145 C1
Ranelagh Gdns
3 Bedford Pk
W6 . . . . .38 B3
Chiswick W4 . . . . . .45 B3
Fulham SW6 . . . . . .58 B4
Ranelagh Gr SW1 145 C2
Ranelagh Ho SW3 144 C2
Ranelagh Mans 4
SW6 . . . . 165 A2
Ranelagh Rd
Dagenham NW10 . . .21 B3
Pimlico SW1 . . . . . .147 A1
Rangdon St EC3 . .110 C1
Ranger's House (The
Wernher Collection)
SE10 . . . . .52 C2
Rangers Sq SE10 . .52 C2
Rangoon Ho 5
N16 . . . . .15 C4
Rankine Ho SE1 . .136 C1
Ranmere St SW12 . .73 A3
Rann Ho 1 SW14 . .55 C4
Rannoch Rd W6 . . .47 C4
Ransomes Dock Bsns
Ctr SW11 . . . . . . .158 B1
Ransomes Mews
SW11 . . . . .158 B2
Ranston St NW1 . .102 A4
Ranulf Rd NW2 . . . .10 B4
Ranwell Cl 18 E3 . .26 B4
Ranwell Ho 17 E3 . .26 B4
Raphael Ct 9
SE16 . . . . .40 A1
Raphael St SW7 . .130 C3
Rapley Ho 9
E2 . . . . .24 C2 99 B3
Rashleigh Ct 3
SW8 . . . . .61 A4
Rashleigh Ho WC1. 94 A3
Rastell Ave SW12 . .73 C3
RATCLIFF 32 C2
Ratcliffe Cross St
E1 . . . . .32 C3
Ratcliffe Ho 10
E14 . . . . .33 A3
Ratcliffe La 10
E14 . . . . .33 A3
Ratcliffe Orch 9
E1 . . . . .32 C2
Rathbone Ho
5 Canning Town
E16 . . . . .35 B3
Kilburn NW6 . . . . . .23 C4
Rathbone Mkt 8
E16 . . . . .35 B4
Rathbone Pl W1 . .105 B2
Rathbone St
Canning Town
E16 . . . . .35 B3
Fitzrovia W1 . . . . . .105 A3
Rathgar Rd SW9 . . .63 A4
Rathmell Dr SW4 . .61 C1
Rattray Rd SW2 . . .62 C2
Raul Rd SE15 . . . . . .49 C2
Raveley St NW5 . . .13 B4
Ravenet Ct
Battersea SW11 . . .170 A3
Clapham SW4 . . . . .61 A2

Ravenet St SW11. .170 A3
Ravenfield Rd
SW17 . . . . .72 B1
Raven Ho 10 SE16 . .40 C2
Ravenna Rd SW15 . .57 C2
Raven Row E1 . . . . . .32 A4
Ravensbourne
SE10 . . . . .43 A4
Ravensbourne Ho
NW8 . . . . 102 A4
Ravensbourne Mans
9 SE8 . . . . .51 C4
Ravensbourne Pl 2
SE13 . . . . .51 B1
Ravensbury Rd
SW18 . . . . .71 A2
Ravenscar NW1 . . .82 C3
Ravenscort 1
N16 . . . . .7 C1
Ravenscourt Ave
W6 . . . . .38 C2
Ravenscourt Gdns
W6 . . . . .38 C2
Ravenscourt Ho 18
W6 . . . . .38 C2
Ravenscourt Park
W6 . . . . .39 A2
Ravenscourt Park
Prep Sch W6 . . . . .38 C2
Ravenscourt Park Sta
W6 . . . . .39 A2
Ravenscourt Pk
W6 . . . . .38 C2
Ravenscourt Pl
W6 . . . . .39 A2
Ravenscourt Rd
W6 . . . . .39 A2
Ravenscourt Sq
W6 . . . . .38 C3
Ravenscourt Theatre
Sch W6 . . . . .39 A2
Ravenscroft Ave
NW11 . . . . .1 B4
Ravenscroft Cl 4
E16 . . . . .35 C4
Ravenscroft
NW11 . . . . .1 B4
Ravenscroft Point 6
E9 . . . . .17 C2
Ravenscroft Rd
Acton W4 . . . . .37 B2
Newham E16 . . . . . .35 C4
Ravenscroft St
E2 . . . . .24 B2 99 A4
Ravensdon St
SE11 . . . . 149 C1
Ravenshaw St
NW6 . . . . .10 B3
Ravenslea Rd SW11,
SW12 . . . . .72 B4
Ravenstone SE17. 152 B1
Ravenstone Prim Sch
SW12 . . . . .72 C2
Ravenstone St
SW12 . . . . .72 C3
Ravenswood Rd
SW12 . . . . .73 A4
Ravensworth Ct
SW6 . . . . 155 B1
Ravensworth Rd
NW10 . . . . .22 A2
Raven Wharf SE1 138 C4

Ravey St
EC2 . . . . .24 A1 98 A2
Rav Pinter Cl N16 . . . .7 A4
Rawlings St SW3 . .144 C4
Rawlinson Ho
SE13 . . . . .67 C3
Rawlinson Point 8
E16 . . . . .35 B4
Rawreth Wlk N1 . . . .87 A4
Rawson Ct SW11 . .169 C3
Rawson St SW11 . .170 A3
Rawstone Pl EC1 . . .96 A4
Rawstone St EC1 . . .96 A4
Rayburne Ct W14 .126 A2
Raydon St N19 . . . . . .4 A2
Ray Ho
7 North Kensington
W10 . . . . .30 C3
Shoreditch N1 . . . . . .87 C3
Raymede Twr 2
W10 . . . . .30 C4
Raymond Bldgs
WC1 . . . . .107 A4
Raymouth Rd
SE16 . . . . .40 A2
Raynald Ho 15
SW16 . . . . .74 A1
Rayne Ct SE1 . . . .138 C4
Rayne Ho
1 Balham SW12 . . .60 C1
Paddington W9 . . . . .88 A2
Rayner Ct 10 W12 . .39 B4
Rayner's Rd SW15 . .58 A2
Raynes Ct NW2 . . . .10 A4
Raynham Ho 1
E1 . . . . .25 C1
Raynham Rd W6 . . .39 A2
Raynor Pl
22 Canonbury N1 . .15 B1
N1 . . . . .87 A4
Ray St EC1 . . . . .95 C1
Ray Wlk N7 . . . . .5 B2
Reachview Cl 17
NW1 . . . . .13 B1
Reade Ct 6 W3 . . . .37 B3
Reade Wlk 5
NW10 . . . . .8 A1
Read Ho 4 SE11 . .163 B4
Reading Ho
Paddington W2 . . .100 C1
Peckham SE15 . . . . .49 C4
Reading La E8 . . . . .17 A2
Reapers Cl NW1 . . .83 B4
Reardon Ho 6 E1 . .32 A1
Reardon Path 31
E1 . . . . .32 A1
Reardon St E1 . . . . .32 A1
Reaston St SE14 . . .50 C3
Reay Prim Sch
SW9 . . . . .163 A1
Reckitt Rd W4 . . . . .38 A1
Record St SE16 . . . .50 B4
Rector St N1 . . . . . .86 C3
Rectory Gdns 6
SW4 . . . . .61 B4
Rectory Gr SW4 . . .61 B4
Rectory Rd
Barnes SW13 . . . . . .46 C1
1 London W3 . . . . . .28 B1
Shacklewell N16 . . . . .7 B1
N16 . . . . .7 B1
Rectory Rd Sta
N16 . . . . .7 B1
Rectory Sq E1 . . . . .32 C4
Reculver Ho 2
SE15 . . . . .50 B4

Reculver Rd SE16 . .40 C1
Red Anchor Cl
SW3 . . . . .158 A3
Redan Pl W2 . . . . .100 A1
Redan St W14 . . . . .39 C3
Redan Terr SE5 . . . .48 A1
Redbourne Ho 7
E14 . . . . .33 B3
Redbourn Ho 10
W10 . . . . .22 B1
Redbridge Gdns
SE5 . . . . .49 A3
Redburn St SW3 . .158 C4
Redcar St SE5 . . . . .48 B3
Redcastle Cl E1 . . . .32 B2
Redchurch St
E2 . . . . .24 B1 98 C2
Redcliffe Cl SW5 . .142 A1
Redcliffe Gdns
Chiswick W4 . . . . . . .45 A3
Fulham SW10 . . . .156 B4
Redcliffe Mews
SW10 . . . . .142 B2
Redcliffe Pl SW10 .156 C3
Redcliffe Rd
SW10 . . . . .157 A4
Redcliffe Sch
SW10 . . . . .156 C4
Redcliffe Sq
SW10 . . . . .142 B1
Redcliffe St SW10 .156 B4
Redclyffe Ho 6 E2 .25 B2
Redcroft 5 NW6 . . .10 C2
Red Cross Cotts
SE1 . . . . .137 A4
Redcross Way
SE1 . . . . .123 A1
Reddins Rd SE15 . . .49 C4
Rede Pl
W2 . . . . .31 C2 113 C4
Redesdale St
SW3 . . . . .158 C4
Redfern Rd NW10 . . .8 A1
Redfield La SW5 . .142 A4
Redfield Mews
SW5 . . . . .141 C4
Redfiff Est SE16 . . .41 B3
Redford Wlk N1 . . . .86 C4
Redgate Terr
SW15 . . . . .57 C1
Redgrave Rd
SW15 . . . . .57 C4
Redhill Ct SW2 . . . .74 C2
Redhill St NW1 . . . .92 B4
Red House Sq 20
N1 . . . . .15 B1
Redington Gdns
NW3 . . . . .11 A4
Redington Ho N1 . .85 A2
Redington Rd
NW3 . . . . .11 A4
Redlands Prim Sch 55
E1 . . . . .32 B4
Redlands Way
SW2 . . . . .74 B4
Red Lion Cl 9
SE17 . . . . .48 C4
Red Lion Ct EC4 . .107 C1
Red Lion Row
SE17 . . . . .48 B4
Red Lion Sq WC1 .106 C3
Red Lion St WC1 . .106 C3
Red Lion Yd W1 . .117 C2
Redlynch Ct W14 . .126 B3
Redlynch Ho 27
SW9 . . . . .173 C4

Redman Bldg EC1 .107 B4
Redman Ho SE1 . . .137 A3
Redman's Rd E1 . . .32 B4
Redmayne Ho 16
SW9 . . . . .173 A2
Redmead La E1 . . .125 B1
Redmill Ho 24 E1 . .25 A1
Redmond Ho N1 . . .85 A3
Redmore Rd W6 . . .39 A2
Red Pl W1 . . . . .117 B4
Red Post Hill SE21,
SE24 . . . . .63 C2
Redriff Prim Sch
SE16 . . . . .41 A4
Redriff Rd SE16 . . . .41 A3
Red Rover SW13 . . .56 C4
Redrup Ho 21
SE14 . . . . .50 C4
Redruth Rd E9 . . . . .25 B4
Red Sq The N16 . . . .6 C1
Redstart Cl SE14 . . .51 A3
Redvers St
E2 . . . . .24 A2 98 B4
Redwald Rd E5 . . . .17 C4
Redwood Cl
4 Bow E3 . . . . .26 C3
Rotherhithe SE16 . . .33 A1
Redwood Ct
Brondesbury
NW6 . . . . .10 A1
Crouch End N19 . . . .4 C4
Redwood Mews 2
SW4 . . . . .61 A4
Redwoods SW15 . . .68 C3
Reece Mews SW7 .143 B4
Reed Cl E16 . . . . . . .35 C4
Reedham St SE15 . .64 C4
Reed Ho SW15 . . . .56 C1
Reedholm Villas
N16 . . . . .6 C1
Reed Pl
Battersea SW11 . . . .60 A3
Clapham SW4 . . . . . .61 C3
Reed's Pl NW1 . . . . .13 B1
Reedworth St
SE11 . . . . .149 C3
Reef Ho E14 . . . . . . .42 B3
Rees St N1 . . . . .87 A3
Reeves Ho
Lambeth SE1 . . . . .135 B3
Mayfair W1 . . . . . . .117 B3
Reeves Mews W1 .117 C3
Reeves Rd E3 . . . . . .27 A1
Reflection Ho 3
E2 . . . . .24 C1 99 B2
Reform St SW11 . .169 A2
Regal Cl E1 . . . . . . .111 C4
Regal La NW1 . . . . .81 C3
Regal Pl
3 Tower Hamlets
E3 . . . . .26 B2
Walham Green
SW6 . . . . .156 B2
Regan Way N1 . . . . .24 A3
Regatta Point
TW8 . . . . .44 B4
Regency Ct
3 Bow E3 . . . . .26 B3
14 South Hackney
E9 . . . . .25 B4
Regency Ho NW1 . . .92 B2
Regency Lo NW3 . . .11 C1
Regency Mews
Camberwell SW9 . . .48 A3
1 Willesden NW10 . . .8 C3
Regency Pl SW1 . .147 C4

Regency St SW1 . .147 C3
Regency Terr
SW7 . . . . .143 B2
Regency Wlk 8
TW10 . . . . .54 A2
Regeneration Rd
SE16 . . . . .40 C1
Regent Ct
Lisson Gr NW8 . . . . .90 A3
1 Stamford Hill N16 . .7 B4
Regent High Sch
NW1 . . . . .83 B2
Regent Ho W14 . . .140 A4
Regent Pl W11 . . . . .31 A4
Regent Rd SE24 . . .63 A2
Regents Bridge Gdns
SW8 . . . . .162 B2
Regents Canal Ho 8
E14 . . . . .33 A3
Regents Ct E8 . . . . .24 C4
Regents Gate Ho 20
E14 . . . . .33 A2
Regents Lo 9
SW2 . . . . .74 B3
Regents Mews
NW8 . . . . .79 A2
REGENT'S PARK . . .91 B1
Regent's Park
NW1 . . . . .82 B1
Regent's Park
Barracks NW1 . . . . .82 B1
Regent's Park Rd
Camden Town
NW1 . . . . .81 B4
Primrose Hill NW3 . .12 C1
Regent's Park Sta
NW1 . . . . .92 A1
Regent's Park Terr
NW1 . . . . .82 A4
Regent's Pl 5 SE3 . .53 C1
Regents Plaza 2
NW6 . . . . .78 A2
Regent Sq
23 Bromley E3 . . . . .27 A2
St Pancras WC1 . . . .94 B3
Regent's Row E8 . . .24 C4
Regent St
Brentford W4 . . . . . .36 C1
7 Kensal Green
NW10 . . . . .22 C2
Mayfair W1 . . . . . . .118 C4
Regent's University
London NW1 . . . . . .91 B2
Regents Wharf
3 Hackney E2 . . . . .25 A4
Islington N1 . . . . . . .84 C2
Reginald Pl 6
SE8 . . . . .51 C3
Reginald Rd SE8 . . .51 C3
Reginald Sq SE8 . . .51 C3
Regina Point SE16 . .40 B3
Regina Rd N4 . . . . . . .5 B3
Regis Ct NW1 . . . . .102 C4
Regis Pl 17 SW2 . . .62 B3
Regis Rd NW5 . . . . .13 A3
Regnart Bldgs
NW1 . . . . .93 A3
Reid Ct SW14 . . . . .45 B1
Reighton Rd E5 . . . . .7 C2
Reizel Cl N16 . . . . . . .7 B3
Relay Rd W12 . . . . .30 B1
Relf Rd SE15 . . . . . .64 C4
Reliance Sq
E2 . . . . .24 A1 98 B2
Relton Ct W3 . . . . . .36 C4

Relton Mews
SW7 . . . . .130 B2
Rembrandt Cl E14 . .42 C3
Rembrandt Ct
SE16 . . . . .40 A1
Rembrant Cl SW1 .145 B3
Remington St N1 . . .86 B1
Remnant St WC2 . .106 C2
Remsted Ho 7
NW6 . . . . .78 A3
Remus Rd E3 . . . . . .18 C1
Renaissance Wlk 4
SE10 . . . . .43 B3
Renbold Ho 5
SE10 . . . . .52 B2
Rendlesham Ho 3 E5,
N16 . . . . .7 C1
Rendlesham Rd E5 . .7 C1
Renforth St SE16 . . .40 B4
Renfrew Ho NW6 . . .78 A1
Renfrew Rd SE11 . .150 A3
Rennell Ho 18 E9 . .17 C2
Rennell St SE13 . . . .67 B4
Rennie Cotts 29
E1 . . . . .25 B1
Rennie Ct SE1 . . . .122 A2
Rennie Ho SE1 . . . .136 C1
Rennie St SE1 . . . .122 A2
Renoir Ct 22 SE16 . .40 A1
Renton Cl SW2 . . . .62 B1
Rephidim St SE1 . .138 A1
Replingham Rd
SW18 . . . . .70 C3
Reporton Rd SW6 .154 B1
Repton Ho SW1 . . .147 A3
Repton St E14 . . . . .33 A3
Reservoir Rd SE4 . . .51 A1
Reservoir Studios 10
E1 . . . . .33 A3
Resolution Way 4
SE8 . . . . .51 C3
Restell Cl SE3 . . . . .53 A4
Reston Pl SW7 . . . .128 C3
Restoration Sq
SW11 . . . . .167 C3
Retcar Pl N19 . . . . . .4 A2
Retford St E2 . . . . . .24 A3
Retreat Ho 6 E9 . . .17 B2
Retreat Pl E9 . . . . . .17 B2
Retreat The SW14 . .56 A4
Reunion Row 1 E1 . .32 A2
Reveley Sq SE16 . . .41 A4
Revelon Rd SE4 . . . .66 A4
Revelstoke Rd SW18,
SW19 . . . . .70 C2
Reverdy Rd SE1 . . .153 B3
Rewell St SW6 . . . .156 C1
Rex Pl W1 . . . . .117 C2
Reynard Cl SE4 . . . .66 A4
Reynard Pl SE14 . . .51 A4
Reynolds Cl NW11 . . .2 A4
Reynolds Ho
Finsbury Pk N4 . . . . . .5 A3
16 South Hackney
E2 . . . . .25 B3
St John's Wood
NW8 . . . . .79 C1
Westminster SW1 . .147 C3
Reynolds Pl 12
TW10 . . . . .54 B1
Reynolds Rd
Acton Green W4 . . . .37 B3
Nunhead SE15 . . . . .65 B3

Reynolds Sp Ctr
W3 . . . . .36 C4
Rffra Rd Ret Pk
SW2 . . . . .62 C2
Rheidol Mews N1 . .86 C2
Rheidol Terr N1 . . . .86 C3
Rhizotron & Xstrata
Treetop Walkway
TW9 . . . . .44 A2
Rhoda St E2. .24 B1 99 A2
Rhodes Ho
Shepherd's Bush
W12 . . . . .30 A1
Shoreditch N1 . . . . .97 B4
Rhodesia Rd SW9 172 B1
Rhodes St N7 . . . . .14 B3
Rhodeswell Rd
E14 . . . . .33 B3
Rhondda Gr E3. .26 B2
Rhyl Prim Sch 21
NW5 . . . . .12 C2
Rhyl St NW5. . . . . .12 C2
Ribblesdale Ho 7
NW6 . . . . .23 C4
Ribbon Dance Mews
SE5 . . . . .48 C2
Ribstone Ho E9. .17 C2
Ricardo St E14 . . . .34 A3
Riceyman Ho WC1 . .95 B3
Richard Anderson Ct
1 SE14 . . . . .50 C3
Richard Atkins Prim
Sch 20 SW2 . . . . .74 A4
Richard Burbidge
Mans SW13 . . . . .47 B4
Richard Cloudesley
Sch
Shoreditch N1 . . . .86 C3
St Luke's EC1 . . . . .97 A1
Richard Cloudesley
Sch (Prim Dept)
EC1 . . . . .97 A1
Richard Cobden Prim
Sch NW1 . . . . .83 A3
Richard Fox Ho N4 . .6 B1
Richard Ho 10
SE16 . . . . .40 B2
Richard Knight Ho
SW6 . . . . .165 C4
Richard Neale Ho 2
E1 . . . . .32 A2
Richardson Cl 10
E8 . . . . .24 B4
Richardson Ho 10
SW4 . . . . .172 B2
Richardson Ho 10
E14 . . . . .33 A4
Richardson's Mews
W1 . . . . .92 C1
Richard's Pl SW3 . .144 B4
Richard St 20 E1 . . .32 A3
Richbell WC1 . . . . .106 B4
Richbell Pl WC1 . . .106 C4
Richborne Terr
SW8 . . . . .163 A2
Richborough Ho
10 Deptford SE15 . .50 B4
15 Hackney E5 . . . .17 A4
Richborough Rd
NW2 . . . . .10 A4
Richbourne Ct
W1 . . . . .102 B2
Richford Gate W6 . .39 B3
Richford St W6. .39 B3

Rich Ind Est SE15. . .50 A4
Rich La SW5 . . . . .142 A2
Richland Ho 4
SE15 . . . . .49 C2
Richman Ho 10
SE8 . . . . .41 B1
Rich Mix E1 . . . . . .99 A2
RICHMOND 54 B3
Richmond Ave
Islington N1 . . . . . .85 A4
Willesden NW10. . . .9 B2
Richmond Bldgs
W1 . . . . .105 B1
Richmond Circus
TW9 . . . . .54 A3
Richmond Cres N1 .85 B4
Richmond Ct
SW1 . . . . .131 A3
Richmond Gr N1 . . .15 A1
Richmond Healthcare
Hamlet Hospl
TW9 . . . . .54 A4
RICHMOND HILL. . .54 A1
Richmond Hill
TW10 . . . . .54 A1
Richmond Hill Ct 5
TW10 . . . . .54 A1
Richmond Ho
12 Forest Hill
SE26 . . . . .76 C1
Regent's Pk NW1 . . .82 B1
Walworth SE17 . . . .151 B2
Richmond
International Bsns
Ctr 2 TW9 . . . . . . .54 B3
Richmond Mans
Earl's Ct SW5 . . . . .142 A2
Putney SW15 . . . . .58 A4
Richmond Mews
W1 . . . . .105 B1
Richmond Park Acad
SW14 . . . . .55 C3
Richmond Park Rd
SW14 . . . . .55 C3
Richmond Rd
Dalston E8 . . . . . . .16 C1
Ealing W5 . . . . .36 A4
Richmond Sta
TW9 . . . . .54 A3
Richmond Terr
SW1 . . . . .134 A4
Richmond Univ
Kensington W8 . . . .128 B2
Richmond Way W12,
W14 . . . . .39 C4
Rich St E14 . . . . . . .33 B2
Rickard Cl SW2 . . . .74 C3
Rickett St SW6 . . . .155 C4
Rickman Ho 23 E2. .25 B1
Rickman St 24 E1 . .25 B1
Rick Roberts Way
E15 . . . . .27 C3
Rickthorne Rd 7
N19 . . . . .5 A2
Riddell Ct SE1 . .152 C2
Ridgdale St E3 . . . .27 A3
Ridge Hill NW11. . . .1 A3
Ridge Rd NW2 . . . . .1 B1
Ridgeway 11
TW10 . . . . .54 A1
Ridgeway Dr W3 . .36 C3
Ridgeway Gdns N6. .4 B4
Ridgeway The
Acton W3 . . . . .36 C3
Golders Green NW11. .1 B3

Ridgewell Cl N1 . . . .87 A4
Ridgmount Gdns
WC1 . . . . .105 B4
Ridgmount Pl
WC1 . . . . .105 B4
Ridgmount Rd
SW18 . . . . .59 A2
Ridgmount St
WC1 . . . . .105 B4
Ridgway Rd SW9 . .63 A4
Riding House St
W1 . . . . .104 C3
Ridings Cl N6 . . . . . .4 B4
Riding The N1 . . . . .1 B4
Ridley Ho 14
SW11 . . . . .60 A4
Ridley Rd
Dalston E8 . . . . . . .16 B3
Willesden Green
NW10 . . . . .21 C3
Ridley Road Mkt
E8 . . . . .16 B3
Rifle Ct SE11 . . . . .163 C4
Rifle Pl W11. . . . . . .30 C1
Rifle St E14 . . . . . .34 A4
Riga Ho 10 E1 . .32 C4
Rigault Rd SW6 . . .164 B1
Rigden St E14 . . . . .34 A3
Rigeley Rd NW10 . .21 C2
Rigge Pl SW4 . . . . .61 C3
Rigg Ho 2 SW4 . . .74 A4
Rignold Ho 6 SE5. .49 A1
Riley Ho
9 Bow E3 . . . . .26 C1
Chelsea SW10 . . . .157 B3
4 Streatham SW4 . .73 C4
Riley Rd SE1 . . . . .138 C2
Riley St SW10 . . . .157 B2
Rill Ho 10 SE5 . . . .49 A3
Rimini Ct SW12 . . . .72 B3
Rinaldo Rd SW12 . .73 A4
Ringcroft St N7 . . . .14 C3
Ringford Ho SW18 . .58 B1
Ringford Rd SW18. .58 C1
Ring Ho 15 E1 . . . . .32 B2
Ringmer Ave SW6 164 B3
Ringmer Gdns 3
N19 . . . . .5 A2
Ringmer Ho 15
SE22 . . . . .64 A4
Ring Rd W12 . . . . . .30 B1
Ringsfield Ho
SE17 . . . . .151 A1
Ringwood Gdns
E14 Millwall E14 . . .41 C2
Roehampton SW15. .68 C3
Ripley Gdns SW14 . .55 C4
Ripley Ho
Mortlake SW14 . . . .56 A4
Nine Elms SW11. . .160 C4
Ripley's Believe It or
Not! SW1. . . . . .119 B3
Riplington Ct
SW15 . . . . .69 A4
Ripplevale Gr N1 . . .14 B1
Risborough SE17 . .150 C4
Risborough Ho
NW8 . . . . .90 B2
Risborough St
SE1 . . . . .136 B4
Risdon Ho 20 SE16 . .40 B4
Risdon St 27 SE16 . .40 B4
Riseholme Ct E9 . . .18 B2
Riseholme Ho 4
SE22 . . . . .64 A4

Riseldine Rd SE23 . .66 A1
Risinghill St N1 . . . .85 B2
Rising Sun Ct EC1 108 B3
Risley Ho 7 E9 . . . .17 C2
Rita Rd SW8 . . . . .162 C2
Ritchie Ho
Crouch End N19 . . . .4 C4
8 Rotherhithe
SE16 . . . . .40 B3
12 South Bromley
E14 . . . . .34 C3
Ritchie St N1 . . . . . .85 C2
Ritherdon Rd
SW17 . . . . .73 A2
Ritson Ho N1 . . . . .84 C3
Ritson Rd E8 . . . . . .16 C2
Riva Pl E9 . . . . .17 B2
Riven Ct 3 W2. . . .100 B1
Riverains The
SW11 . . . . .167 B3
River Barge Cl
E14 . . . . .42 B4
Rivercourt Rd W6 . .39 A1
River Ct SE1 . . . . .122 A3
Riverdale Dr
SW18 . . . . .71 A3
Riverfleet WC1. . . .94 B4
Riverford Ho 28
W2 . . . . .31 C4
River Ho SW13 . . . .46 A1
River House
Montessori Sch
E14 . . . . .42 A4
Rivermead Ct SW6 .58 B4
Rivermead Ho E9. .18 A3
River Pl N1 . . . . . . .15 B1
River Plate Ho
EC2 . . . . .109 C3
River Reach Bsns Pk
SW11 . . . . .59 B4
River St Mews EC1 .95 B4
Riversdale Prim Sch
SW18 . . . . .70 C3
Riversdale Rd N5. . .6 B1
Riversdene N5 . . . . .6 B1
Rivers Ho NW8 . .36 C1
Riverside
Battersea SW11 . . .158 B2
11 Rotherhithe
SE16 . . . . .40 B4
St Pancras WC1 . . . .94 B4
Riverside Bsns Ctr
SW18 . . . . .71 A3
Riverside Ct
Clapham SW4 . . . . .171 C1
Fulham SW6 . . . . . .47 A2
Riverside Dr
W6 . . . . .39 A1
Riverside Gdns
W6 . . . . .39 A1
Riverside Health &
Racquets Club
Chiswick The
W4 . . . . .46 A2
Riverside Ho 14
N1 . . . . .15 B1
Riverside Mans 4
E1 . . . . .32 B1
Riverside Prim Sch 27
SE16 . . . . .139 C3
Riverside Rd
Mill Meads E15. . . .27 B3
Wandsworth SW17,
SW19 . . . . .71 B1
Riverside Wlk Mkt
WC2 . . . . .121 A2
Riverside Workshops
SE1 . . . . .123 A2
River St EC1 . . . . . .95 B4

River Terr
London W6 . . . . . . .39 B1
St James SW1 . . . .120 C3
Riverton Cl W9 . . . .23 B2
Riverview Gdns
SW13 . . . . .47 A4
Riverview Gr W4 . . .45 A4
Riverview Rd W4 . . .45 A4
River Way SE10. . . .43 B3
Rivet Ho SE1 . . . . .153 A2
Rivington Ct
NW10 . . . . .21 C4
Rivington Pl
EC2 . . . . .24 A2 98 B3
Rivington St
EC2 . . . . .24 A2 98 A3
Rivington Wlk 4
E8 . . . . .24 C4
Rixon St N7 . . . . . . .5 C1
Roach Rd E3 . . . . . .18 C1
Roads End N19. . . . .5 A2
Roan St SE10. . . . . .52 B4
Robert Adam St
W1 . . . . .103 B2
Roberta St
E2 . . . . .24 C2 99 C3
Robert Bell Ho 2
SE16 . . . . .153 B4
Robert Blair Prim Sch
N7 . . . . .14 A2
Robert Browning Prim
Sch SE17 . . . . . .151 B2
Robert Cl W9 . . . . .89 A1
Robert Dashwood
Way SE17 . . . . . .150 C3
Robert Gentry Ho
W14 . . . . .140 B1
Robert Jones Ho 3
SE16 . . . . .153 B4
Robert Keen Cl 18
SE15 . . . . .49 C2
Robert Lowe Cl
SE14 . . . . .50 C3
Robert Owen Ho
Fulham SW6. . . . . .47 C2
6 Spitalfields
E2 . . . . .24 B2 99 A4
Robert Owen Lo 4
E5 . . . . .17 A4
Roberts Ct
Islington N1 . . . . . .86 B3
Willesden NW10. . . .8 A2
Roberts Ho 5
SE27 . . . . .75 A1
Roberts Mews
SW1 . . . . .131 B1
Robertson Ho 11
SE10 . . . . .52 B2
Robertson St
SW8 . . . . .170 B1
Robert's Pl EC1. . . .95 C2
Robert St
Regent's Pk NW1 . .92 C3
Strand WC2 . . . . . .120 B3
Robert Sutton Ho 20
E1 . . . . .32 B3
Robeson St 1 E3 . . .33 B4
Robin Ct E13 SE14 . .42 B3
Robin Gr
Dartmouth Pk N6 . . .3 C2
Highgate N6 . . . . . . .3 C2
Robin Ho NW8 . . . . .80 A1
Robin Hood SW15 . .68 A1
Robin Hood Gdns 4
E14 . . . . .34 B2

Robin Hood La
E14 . . . . 34 B2
Robinscroft Mews 18
SE10 . . . . 52 A2
Robins Ct TW10 . . . . 54 A1
Robin's Ct SW4 . . . . . 62 A1
Robinsfield Inf Sch
NW8 . . . . 80 A2
Robinson Ct
Islington N1 . . . . 86 B1
4 Richmond TW9 . . 54 B3
Robinson Ho
4 North Kensington
W10 . . . . 30 C3
15 Tower Hamlets
E14 . . . . 33 C4
Robinson Rd E2 . . . . 25 B3
Robinson St SW3 . . 158 C4
Robinson Wy 8
SE14 . . . . 50 C3
Robinswood Mews 6
N5 . . . . 15 A3
Robsart St SW9 . . 173 B2
Robson Ave NW10 . . 8 C1
Robson Rd SE21,
SE27 . . . . 75 B1
Roby Ho EC1 . . . . . . 96 C2
Rochdale Way 4
SE8 . . . . 51 C3
Roche Ho 19 E14 . . 33 B2
Rochelle Cl SW11 . . 59 C3
Rochelle Ct 1 E1 . . 32 B3
Rochelle St 31
E2 . . . . 24 B2 98 C3
Rochemont Wlk 2
E8 . . . . 24 C4
Roche Sch The 16
SW18 . . . . 58 C2
Rochester Ct
1 Bethnal Green
E2 . . . . 25 A1
6 Camden Town
NW1 . . . . 13 B1
Rochester Ho
Bermondsey SE1 . . 137 C3
18 Deptford SE15 . . 50 B4
Rochester Mews
NW1 . . . . 13 B1
Rochester Pl NW1 . . 13 B1
Rochester Rd
NW1 . . . . 13 B2
Rochester Row
SW1 . . . . 147 A4
Rochester Sq NW1 . . 13 B1
Rochester St
SW1 . . . . 133 B1
Rochester Terr
NW1 . . . . 13 B2
Rochester Wlk
SE1 . . . . 123 B2
Rochfort Wlk 3
E8 . . . . 16 C1
Rochfort Ho 4
SE8 . . . . 41 B1
Rock Ave 18 SW14 . . 55 C4
Rockell's Pl SE22 . . . 65 A1
Rockfield Ho SE10 . . 52 B4
Rock Grove Way
SE16 . . . . 153 C4
Rockhall Rd NW2 . . . 9 C4
Rockingham Cl
SW15 . . . . 56 B3
Rockingham St
SE1 . . . . 136 C1
Rockland Rd
SW15 . . . . 58 A3

Rockley Ct 9
W14 . . . . 39 C4
Rockley Rd W14 . . . 39 C4
Rocks La SW13 . . . . 56 C4
Rock St N4 . . . . 5 C2
Rockstraw Ho 5
NW3 . . . . 12 B1
Rockwood Ct N16 . . 7 C4
Rocliffe St N1 . . . . . 86 B1
Rocque Ho SW6 . 154 C2
Rodborough Rd
NW11 . . . . 1 C3
Rodenhurst Ct
SW4 . . . . 61 C2
Rodenhurst Rd
SW4 . . . . 61 C1
Roden St N7 . . . . 5 B1
Roderick Ho 3
SE16 . . . . 40 B2
Roderick Rd NW3 . . 12 B4
Rodgers Ho 4
SW4 . . . . 73 C4
Rodin Ct N1 . . . . . . 86 A3
Roding Ct 8 W12 . . 38 A4
Roding Ho 1
N1 . . . . 85 B2
Roding Mews E1 . . 125 C2
Roding Rd E5 . . . . . 18 A3
Rodmarton St W1 . 103 A3
Rodmell WC1 . . . . . . 94 B3
Rodmere St SE10 . . 43 A1
Rodmill La
SW2 . . . . 74 A4
Rodney Ct NW8 . . . 89 A2
Rodney Ho
4 Cubitt Town
E14 . . . . 42 A2
Islington N1 . . . . 85 A1
Notting Hill
W11 . . . . . . 31 C2 113 B4
Rodney Pl SE17 . . 151 A4
Rodney Rd SE17 . . 151 B3
Rodney St N1 . . . . . 85 A1
Rodway Rd SW15 . . 68 C4
Rodwell Rd SE22 . . 64 B1
Roedean Cres
SW15 . . . . 56 A2
ROEHAMPTON 68 A4
Roehampton Church
Sch SW15 . . . . 69 A4
Roehampton Cl
SW15 . . . . 56 C3
Roehampton Ct
SW13 . . . . 56 C4
Roehampton Gate
SW15 . . . . 56 A1
Roehampton High St
SW15 . . . . 68 C4
Roehampton La
Putney SW15 . . . . . . 56 C1
Roehampton SW15 . . 69 A3
Roehampton Vale
SW15 . . . . 68 B2
Roffey St E14 . . . . . . 42 B4
Rogate Ho E5 . . . . . . 7 C1
Roger Dowley Ct 3
E2 . . . . 25 B3
Roger's Almshouses
2 SW9 . . . . 62 B3
Rogers Ct 10 E14 . . 33 C2
Rogers Est 28 E2 . . 25 B2
Rogers Ho SW1 . . 147 C4
Rogers Rd E16 . . . . 35 B3
Roger St WC1 . . . . . 95 A1
Rokeby Ho
9 Balham SW12 . . . 73 A4
Bloomsbury WC1 . . . 94 C1

Rokeby Rd SE4 . . . . 51 B1
Rokeby Sch
11 Canning Town
E16 . . . . 35 B4
Stratford E15 . . . . . . 19 C1
Rokeland Ho SE4 . . 66 A3
Roland Gdns SW7 . 143 A2
Roland Ho SW7 . . 143 A2
Roland Mews 1
E1 . . . . 32 C4
Roland Way
South Kensington
SW7 . . . . 143 A2
Walworth SE17 . . . 151 C1
Rollins St SE15 . . . . 50 B4
Rollit Ho N7 . . . . . . 14 C3
Rollit St N7 . . . . 14 C3
Rollo Ct SW11 . . . 170 A3
Rolls Bldgs EC4 . . 107 C2
Rollscourt Ave
SE24 . . . . 63 B2
Rolls Pas EC4 . . . 107 B2
Rolls Rd SE1 . . . . . 153 A2
Rolt St SE8 . . . . 51 A4
Roman Ho 3 SW4 . . 37 A4
Roman Ct 4 N7 . . . . 14 B2
Romanfield Rd
SW2 . . . . 74 B4
Roman Rd
Chiswick W4 . . . . 38 B2
Globe Town E2, E3 . . 25 C3
25 Old Ford E3 . . . . 26 B4
Roman Road Mkt 1
E3 . . . . 26 B3
Roman Way
Barnsbury N7 . . . . . . 14 B2
4 Deptford SE15 . . . 50 B3
Roma Read Cl
SW15 . . . . 69 A4
Romayne Ho SW4 . . 61 C4
Romberg Rd SW17 . . 72 C1
Romborough Gdns
SE13 . . . . 67 B2
Romborough Way
SE13 . . . . 67 B2
Romer Ho 9 SW2 . . 62 B2
Romero Cl SW9 . . . 62 B4
Romeyn Rd SW16 . . 74 B1
Romford Ho 17
N1 . . . . 15 C2
Romford St E1 . . . . 32 A4
Romilly Rd N4 . . . . . . 6 A2
Romilly St W1 . . . 119 C4
Romily Ct 2 SW6 164 B2
Romney Ct
7 Deptford SE14 . . 50 B3
North End NW11 . . . . 2 B3
Romney Ct
9 Hammersmith
W12 . . . . 39 B4
8 Hampstead
NW3 . . . . 12 A2
Romney Mews
W1 . . . . 103 B4
Romney Rd SE10 . . 52 C4
Romney St SW1 . . 134 A1
Romola Rd SE24,
SW2 . . . . 75 B3
Ronald Ross Prim Sch
8 SW19 . . . . 70 A4
Ronaldshay N4 . . . . . 5 C3
Ronalds Rd N5 . . . . 14 C3
Ronald St E1 . . . . . . 32 B3
Rona Rd NW3 . . . . . 12 C4

Rona Wlk 20 N1 . . . . 15 C2
Rondu Rd NW2 . . . . . 10 A3
Rood La EC3 . . . . . 124 A4
Rookery Rd SW4 . . . 61 B3
Rooke Way SE10 . . . 43 B1
Rookwood Rd N16 . . 7 C4
Roosevelt Ct 15
SW19 . . . . 70 A3
Rootes Dr W10 . . . . 30 C4
Ropemaker Rd
SE16 . . . . 41 A3
Ropemaker's Fields 7
E14 . . . . 33 B2
Ropemaker St
EC2 . . . . 109 B4
Roper La SE1 . . . . . 138 B3
Roper's Orch
SW3 . . . . 158 A3
Ropers Wlk 19
SE24 . . . . 74 C4
Ropery St E3 . . . . . . 26 B1
Rope St SE16 . . . . . . 41 A3
Ropewalk Gdns 18
E1 . . . . 111 C2
Ropley St 4 E2 . . . . 24 C3
Rosa Alba Mews
N5 . . . . 15 B4
Rosalind Ho 26 N1 . . 24 A3
Rosaline Rd SW6 . . 154 B1
Rosaline Terr
SW6 . . . . 154 B1
Rosa Parks Ho 8
SW9 . . . . 172 C1
Rosary Gdns SW7 . 143 A3
Rosary RC Prim Sch
NW3 . . . . 12 B3
Rosaville Rd SW6 . 154 C1
Roscastle Rd SE4 . . 66 A2
Roscoe St EC1 . . . . 97 A1
Roscommon Ho 2
NW3 . . . . 11 C3
Rose Alley
Borough The SE1 . . 123 A2
Broadgate EC2 . . . 110 B3
Rosebank
3 Dagenham W3 . . 28 C3
Fulham SW6 . . . . . . 47 C3
Rosebank Gdns
Bow E3 . . . . 26 B3
1 Dagenham W3 . . 28 C3
Rosebank Way
W3 . . . . 28 C3
Rosebank Wlk
NW1 . . . . 13 C1
Rosebay Ho 23 E3 . . 33 C4
Roseberry Pl E8 . . . 16 B2
Roseberry St SE16 . . 40 A2
Rosebery Ave EC1 . . 95 C3
Rosebery Ct
Holborn EC1 . . . . . . 95 B1
Mayfair W1 . . . . . . 118 A2
Rosebery Ho 21
E2 . . . . 25 B3
Rosebery Rd Bsns Ctr
EC1 . . . . 95 C2
Rosebery Rd SW2 . . 62 A1
Rosebery Sq EC1 . . 95 B1
Rosebery Way SW6 166 B1
Rose Bush Ct NW3 . 12 B3
Rosecroft Ave NW3 . . 1 C1
Rose & Crown Ct
EC2 . . . . 108 C2
Rose & Crown Yd
SW1 . . . . 119 A1

Rose Ct
7 Dalston E8 . . . . . . 16 B1
Islington N1 . . . . 86 A3
Spitalfields E1 . . . . 111 A3
Rosedale Ct N5 . . . . 15 A4
Rosedale Ho N16 . . . 6 C3
Rosedale Rd TW9 . . 54 A3
Rosedale Terr W6 . . 39 A3
Rosedene NW6 . . . . 22 C4
Rosedene Ave
SW16 . . . . 74 B1
Rosedew Rd W6 . . . 47 C4
Rosefield Gdns
E14 . . . . 33 C2
Roseford Ct 15
W12 . . . . 39 C4
Rosegate Ho 82
E3 . . . . 26 B3
Rosehart Mews 3
W11 . . . . 31 C3
Rosehill Rd SW18 . . 59 B2
Rose Joan Mews
NW6 . . . . 10 C4
Roseland Ho SW6 . . 58 A4
Roseleigh Ave N5 . . 15 A4
Rosemary Branch
Bridge N1 . . . . 87 C4
Rosemary Ct 19
SE8 . . . . 51 B4
Rosemary Dr 16
E14 . . . . 34 C3
Rosemary Gdns
SW14 . . . . 55 B4
Rosemary Ho
Shoreditch N1 . . . . 87 C3
Willesden NW10 . . . . 22 A4
Rosemary La
SW14 . . . . 55 B4
Rosemary Rd
Camberwell SE15 . . . 49 B3
Wandsworth SW17 . . 71 B1
Rosemary St N1 . . . 87 C4
Rosemary Works Sch
N1 . . . . 87 C3
Rosemead Prep Sch
SE27 . . . . 75 B2
Rosemont Mans 11
NW3 . . . . 11 A2
Rosemont Rd
Acton W3 . . . . 28 A2
Richmond TW10 . . . 54 A1
South Hampstead
NW3 . . . . 11 B2
Rosemoor St
SW3 . . . . 144 C3
Rosemount Ct 2
W3 . . . . 28 A1
Rosemount Lo W3 . . 28 A2
Rosenau Cres
SW11 . . . . 168 C3
Rosenau Rd
SW11 . . . . 168 C4
Rosendale Prim Sch
SE21 . . . . 75 B4
Rosendale Rd SE21,
SE24 . . . . 75 C3
Roseneath Rd
SW11 . . . . 60 C1
Rosenthal Ho SE6 . . 67 A1
Rosenthal Rd SE6 . . 67 B1
Rosenthorpe Rd
SE15 . . . . 65 C2
Roserton St E14 . . . 42 B4
Rose Sq SW7 . . . . 143 C2

Rose St
Holborn EC4 . . . . . **108** B2
Strand WC2 . . . . . . **120** A4
Rose Theatre SE1 . . **122** C2

Rosethorn Cl
SW12 . . . .**73** C4
Rosetta Cl SW8 . .**162** B1
Roseway SE21 . . . .**63** C1
Rosewood Ct 2
E11 . . . .**19** C4

Rosewood Gdns
SE13 . . . .**52** B1
Rosewood Ho 9
NW3 . . . .**11** A2
Rosewood Sq
W12 . . . .**29** C3
Rosher Cl E15 . . . . .**19** C1
Rosina St E9 . . . . . .**17** C2
Roskell Rd SW15 . .**57** C4
Roslin Ho 2 E1 . . .**32** C2
Roslin Rd W3 . . . . .**37** A3
Rosmead Rd
W11 . . . . . **31** A2 **112** B4
Rosoman Pl EC1. . . .**95** C2
Rosoman St EC1 . . .**95** C2
Ross Ct
1 Hackney E5 . . . . . .**17** A4
4 Putney SW15 . . . . .**69** C4
Rossdale Rd SW15 . .**57** B3
Rosse Gdns SE13 . . .**67** C1
Rossendale Way
NW1 . . . .**83** A4
Rossetti Ct WC1 . . .**105** B4
Rossetti Gdns Mans
SW3 . . . . **158** C4
Rossetti Ho NW1 . .**147** C3
Rossetti Mews
NW8 . . . .**79** C3
Rossetti Rd SE16 . .**40** A1
Rossetti Studios
SW3 . . . . **158** B4
Ross Ho 18 E1 . . . . .**32** A1
Rossington St E5 . . .**7** C2
Rossiter Gr 1
SW9 . . . .**62** C4
Rossiter Rd SW12 . .**73** A3
Rosslyn Ave SW13 . .**56** B4
Rosslyn Ct NW3 . . .**12** A3
Rosslyn Hill NW3 . .**11** C3
Rosslyn Ho 8
TW9 . . . .**44** B2
Rosslyn Mans
1 Hampstead
NW3 . . . .**11** B2
South Hampstead
NW6 . . . .**11** B2
Rosslyn Mews 7
NW3 . . . .**11** C4
Rosslyn Park Mews
NW3 . . . .**11** C3
Rossmore Ct NW1 . .**90** C2
Rossmore Rd NW1 . .**90** B2
Ross Way 23 SE14 . .**51** A4
Rostrevor Mans
SW6 . . . . **164** C4
Rostrevor Mews
SW6 . . . . **164** C3
Rostrevor Rd
SW6 . . . . **164** C4
Rotary Lo 12 SE27 . .**75** A1
Rotary St SE1 . . . . **136** B2
Rothay NW1 . . . .**92** B4
Rothbury Rd E9 . . . .**18** C1
Rotheley Ho 38 E9 . .**17** B1

Rotherfield Ct
De Beauvoir Town
N1 . . . .**15** C1
Shoreditch N1 . . . . . .**87** A4
Rotherfield Prim Sch
N1 . . . .**87** A4
Rotherfield St
Islington N1 . . . .**15** B1
Shoreditch N1 . . . . . .**87** A4
Rotherham Wlk
SE1 . . . . **122** A1
ROTHERHITHE 2
SE16 . . . .**40** B4
Rotherhithe Bsns Est
2 SE16 . . . .**40** B2
Rotherhithe New Rd
SE16 . . . .**40** A1
Rotherhithe Old Rd
SE16 . . . .**40** C2
Rotherhithe Prim Sch
SE16 . . . .**40** C2
Rotherhithe St
SE16 . . . .**40** B4
Rotherhithe Sta
SE16 . . . .**40** B4
Rotherhithe Tunnel
SE16 . . . .**32** C1
Rother Ho SE15 . . . .**65** A3
Rotherwick Rd
NW11 . . . . **1** C4
Rotherwood Rd
SW15 . . . .**57** C4
Rothery St N1 . . . . .**86** B4
Rothesay Ave SW14 . .**56** A3
Rothesay Ct 13
SE11 . . . . **163** B3
Rothley Ct NW8 . . .**89** B2
Rothsay St SE1 . . . **138** A1
Rothsay Wlk 10
E14 . . . .**41** C2
Rothschild Rd W4 . .**37** B3
Rothwell St
10 Hampstead
NW1 . . . .**12** B1
Primrose Hill NW1 . . .**81** A4
Roth Wlk N7 . . . .**5** B2
Rotten Row SW1 . **130** C4
Rotterdam Dr E14 . .**42** B3
Rouel Rd
Bermondsey
SE16 . . . . **153** B4
Bermondsey SE16 . . **139** B1
Roundacre SW19 . . .**69** C2
Roundel Cl SE4 . . . .**66** B3
Roundhouse La
NW1 . . . .**83** A2
Roundhouse Theatre
NW1 . . . .**12** C1
Roundwood Rd
NW10 . . . .**8** B1
Rounton Rd E3 . . . .**26** C1
Roupell Rd SW2 . . . .**74** B3
Roupell St SE1 . . . **121** C1
Rousden St NW1 . . .**13** B1
Rouse Gdns SE21 . . .**76** C4
Rover Ho 23 N1 . . . .**24** A4
Rowallan Rd SW6 . **154** A1
Rowan Ct
19 Camberwell
SE15 . . . .**49** B3
Wandsworth SW11 . . .**60** B1
Rowan Ho
1 Bow E3 . . . .**26** B4
Dagenham NW10 . . . .**21** A1

Rowan Ho continued
5 Maitland Pk
NW3 . . . .**12** B2
Rowan Rd W6 . . . . . .**39** C2
Rowan Terr W6 . . . .**39** C2
Rowan Wlk
7 Dartmouth Pk
N19 . . . .**4** B2
Kensal Town W10 . . . .**23** A1
Rowberry Cl SW6 . . .**47** B3
Rowcross St SE1 . . **153** A2
Rowditch La
SW11 . . . . **169** B2
Rowdon Ave NW10 . . .**9** A1
Rowe Ho E9 . . . .**17** B2
Rowe La E9 . . . .**17** B3
Rowena Cres
SW11 . . . . **168** B1
Rowfant Rd SW12,
SW17 . . . .**72** C2
Rowhill Mans 11
E5 . . . .**17** A4
Rowhill Rd E5 . . . . . .**17** A4
Rowington Cl W2 . **100** A4
Rowland Hill Ho
SE1 . . . . **136** A4
Rowland Hill St
NW3 . . . .**12** A3
Rowley Gdns N4 . . . .**6** B4
Rowley Ho SE8 . . . . .**51** C4
Rowley Ind Pk W3 . .**37** A3
Rowley Way NW8 . . .**78** C4
Rowntree Cl NW6 . . .**10** C2
Rowse Cl E15 . . . . . .**27** B4
Rowstock 1 NW5 . . .**13** C2
Rowstock Gdns
N7 . . . .**13** C3
Roxby Pl SW6 . . . . **155** C4
Roxford Ho 2 E3 . . .**27** A1
Roxley Rd SE13 . . . .**67** A1
Roxwell 10 NW1 . . . .**13** A2
Roxwell Rd W12 . . . .**38** C4
Royal Academy of
Dramatic Art
WC1 . . . . **105** B4
Royal Acad of Arts
W1 . . . . **118** C3
Royal Acad of Dance
SW11 . . . . **167** C3
Royal Acad of Music
NW1 . . . .**91** C1
Royal Albert Hall
SW7 . . . . **129** B3
Royal Arc W1 . . . . . **118** C3
Royal Armouries The
E1 . . . . **124** C3
Royal Ave SW3 . . . **144** C2
Royal Avenue Ho
SW3 . . . . **144** C2
Royal Ballet Upper
Sch The WC2 . . . . . **106** B1
Royal Brompton Hospl
Chelsea SW3 . . . . . **143** B2
Chelsea SW3 . . . . . **144** A2
Royal Cir SE27 . . . . .**75** A1
Royal Cl
Deptford SE8 . . . . . .**51** B4
Putney SW19 . . . . . .**69** C2
Stamford Hill N16 . . . .**7** A4
Royal College of Art,
Battersea SW11 . . . **158** A1
Royal College of
Physicians Libry
NW1 . . . .**92** B2
Royal College St
NW1 . . . .**83** A4

Royal Coll of
Anaesthetists
WC1 . . . . **106** C3
Royal Coll of
Midwives W1 . . . . **104** C3
Royal Coll of Music
SW7 . . . . **129** B2
Royal Coll of
Obstetricians &
Gynaecologists
NW1 . . . .**90** C3
Royal Coll of
Paediatrics & Child
Health W1 . . . . . . **107** A4
Royal Coll of
Physicians NW1 . . .**92** B2
Royal Coll of
Radiologists W1. . **104** B4
Royal Coll of Science
SW7 . . . . **129** B2
Royal Coll of Speech
Language Therapists
SE1 . . . . **123** B1
Royal Coll of
Surgeons WC2 . . . **107** A2
Royal Coll of
Veterinary Surgeons
SW1 . . . . **134** A1
Royal Courts of
Justice WC2 . . . . . **107** B1
Royal Cres
W11 . . . .**31** A1
Royal Crescent Mews
W11 . . . .**30** C1
Royal Ct
City of London
EC3 . . . . **109** C1
Rotherhithe SE16 . . .**41** B3
Royal Duchess Mews
16 SW12 . . . .**73** A4
Royal Exchange
EC3 . . . . **109** C1
Royal Exchange Bldgs
EC3 . . . . **109** C1
Royal Festival Hall
SE1 . . . . **121** A1
Royal Free Hospl
NW3 . . . .**12** A3
Royal Fusiliers Mus
E1 . . . . **124** C3
Royal Geographical
Society SW7 . . . . **129** B3
Royal George Mews
16 SE5 . . . .**63** C3
Royal Hill SE10 . . . .**52** B3
Royal Hill Ct 2
SE10 . . . .**52** B3
Royal Horticultural
Society (Lawrence
Hall & Conf Ctr)
SW1 . . . . **133** B1
Royal Horticultural
Society (Lindley
Hall) SW1 . . . . . . **147** B4
Royal Hospital
Chelsea The
SW1 . . . . **145** B1
Royal Hospital Rd
SW3 . . . . **145** A1
Royal Hospl for Neuro-
Disability The
SW15 . . . .**58** A1
Royal Hospl Mus
SW3 . . . . **145** A1

Royal Institute of
British Architects
W1 . . . . **104** B4
Royal Institution
Faraday Mus The
SW1 . . . . **118** C3
Royal Langford
Apartments 3
NW6 . . . .**78** A2
Royal London Est The
NW10 . . . .**20** C3
Royal London Hospl
for Integrated
Medicine WC1. . . . **106** B3
Royal London Hospl
Mus E1 . . . .**32** A4
Royal London Hospl
(Whitechapel) The
E1 . . . .**32** A4
Royal Marsden Hospl
SW3 . . . . **143** C2
Royal Mews The
SW1 . . . . **132** B2
Royal Mint Pl 6
E1 . . . . **125** B4
Royal Mint St E1 . . **125** A4
Royal National
Orthopaedic Hospl
W1 . . . .**92** B1
Royal National TNE
Hospl The WC1 . . . . .**94** C4
Royal Naval Pl
SE14 . . . .**51** B3
Royal Oak Ct 9
N1 . . . . **24** A2 **98** A4
Royal Oak Pl SE22 . .**65** A1
Royal Oak Rd 8
E8 . . . .**17** A2
Royal Oak Sta
W2 . . . . **100** B3
Royal Oak Yd SE1 . . **138** A3
Royal Observatory
The SE10 . . . .**52** C3
Royal Opera Arc
SW1 . . . . **119** B3
Royal Orchard Cl
SW18 . . . .**70** A4
Royal Par
Blackheath Vale
SE3 . . . .**53** B1
Fulham SW6 . . . . . . **154** A2
12 Richmond TW9 . . .**44** C2
Royal Pharmaceutical
Society Mus E1. . . **125** B3
Royal Pl 11 SE10 . . .**52** B3
Royal Rd SE17 . . . . .**48** A4
Royal St SE1 . . . . . **135** A2
Royalty Ho W1 . . . . **105** B1
Royalty Mews W1 . . **105** B1
Royalty Studios
W11 . . . .**31** A3
Royal United Services
Institute SW1 . . . . **120** A1
Royal Veterinary Coll
The NW1 . . . .**83** B3
Royal Victoria Sta
E16 . . . .**35** C2
Royal Victor Pl E3 . .**25** C3
Roycroft Cl SW2 . . .**74** C3
Roydon Cl 7
SW11 . . . . **168** C2
Roy Ridley Ho 6
SW4 . . . .**61** C4
Roy Sq E14 . . . .**33** A2
Royston Ct
New Cross SE4 . . . . . .**51** B1

Royston Ct *continued*
3 Richmond TW9 . . . . 44 B2
Royston Ho 14
SE15 . . . . 49 C4
Royston Rd TW10 . . . 54 A2
Royston St 22 E2 . . . . 25 B3
Rozel Ct 3 N1 . . . . . 24 A4
Rozel Rd SW4 . . . . . . 61 B4
Ruby St SE15 . . . . . . 50 A4
Ruby Triangle
SE15 . . . . 50 A4
Ruckholt Rd E9,
E10 . . . . 18 C4
Rucklidge Ave
NW10 . . . . 21 C3
Rudall Cres NW3 . . . 11 C4
Rudbeck Ho 11
SE15 . . . . 49 C3
Ruddington Cl E5 . . . 18 A4
Rudge Ho 1
SE16 . . . . 139 C2
Rudgwick Terr
NW8 . . . . 80 B3
Rudhall Ho 4
SW2 . . . . 62 C1
Rudloe Rd SW12 . . . . 73 B4
Rudolf Pl SW8 . . . . 162 B3
Rudolph Rd NW6 . . . 23 C3
Rudstone Ho 10
E3 . . . . 27 A2
Rudyard Ct SE1 . . . 137 C3
Rufford St N1 . . . . . 84 B4
Rufford Street Mews
N1 . . . . 14 A1
Rufford Terr 5
W3 . . . . 28 B3
Rufus Bsns Ctr
SW18 . . . . 71 A2
Rufus Ho SE1 . . . . . 139 A2
Rufus St N1 . . 24 A2 98 A3
Rugby Mans W14 . 140 B4
Rugby Rd W4 . . . . . . 38 A4
Rugby St WC1 . . . . . 94 C1
Rugg St E14 . . . . 33 C2
Rugless Ho 2 E14 . . 42 B4
Rugmere 4 NW1 . . . 12 C1
Rumball Ho 14
SE5 . . . . 49 A3
Rumbold Rd SW6 . 156 B1
Rum Cl E1 . . . . 32 B2
Rumford Ho SE1 . . 136 C1
Rumsey Rd SW9 . . . 62 B4
Runacres Ct SE17 . 150 C1
Runcorn Pl
W11 . . . . 31 A2 112 A4
Rundell Twr 5 SW8 . 172 C4
Running Horse Yd 12
TW8 . . . . 44 A4
Runnymede Ct
SW15 . . . . 68 C3
Runnymede Ho
Hackney E9 . . . . 18 A4
Richmond TW10 . . . 54 C2
Rupack St 3 SE16 . . 40 B4
Rupert Ct W1 . . . . . 119 B4
Rupert Gdns SW9 . . 48 A1
Rupert Ho
SE11 . . . . 149 C3
3 Upper Holloway
N19 . . . . 4 C1
Rupert Rd
Bedford Pk W4 . . . . . 38 A3
Paddington NW6 . . . 23 B3
Upper Holloway N19 . 4 C2
Rupert St W1 . . . . . 119 B4
Rusbridge Cl E8 . . . 16 C3

Ruscoe Rd E16 . . . . . 35 B3
Rusham Rd SW12 . . 72 B4
Rushbrook Ho 8
SW8 . . . . 171 B2
Rushby Ct SW4 . . . . 172 A3
Rush Common Mews
11 SW2 . . . . 74 B4
Rushcroft Rd SW2,
SW9 . . . . 62 C3
Rushcutters Ct 18
SE16 . . . . 41 A2
Rushey Mead SE4 . . 66 C2
Rushford Rd SE4 . . . 66 B1
Rush Hill Mews 3
SW11 . . . . 60 C4
Rush Hill Rd SW11 . 60 C4
Rushlake Ho 3
SW11 . . . . 169 B2
Rushmead 5 E2 . . . . 25 A2
Rushmere Ho 2
SW15 . . . . 68 C3
Rushmore Cres 2
E5 . . . . 17 C4
Rushmore Ho
4 Kentish Town
N7 . . . . 13 C3
W14 . . . . 126 B1
Rushmore Prim Sch
12 E5 . . . . 17 C4
Rushmore Rd
Clapton Pk E5 . . . . . 17 C4
Hackney E5 . . . . 18 A4
Rusholme Rd
SW15 . . . . 58 A1
Rushton Ho 28
SW8 . . . . 171 B1
Rushton St N1 . . . . . 87 C2
Rushworth St SE1 . 136 B3
Ruskin Ave TW9 . . . 44 C3
Ruskin Ct SE5 . . . . . 63 C4
Ruskin Ho SW1 . . . 147 C3
Ruskin Park Ho
SE5 . . . . 63 C4
Ruskin Wlk SE24 . . . 63 B2
Rusper Ct SW9 . . . 172 B1
Russell Cl W4 . . . . . 46 B4
Russell Ct
Battersea SW11 . . . 169 C3
Bloomsbury WC1 . . . 94 A1
5 Peckham SE15 . . . 50 A1
St James SW1 . . . . 119 A1
Russell Gdns W14 . 126 A2
Russell Gdns Mews
W14 . . . . 126 A2
Russell Gr 33
SW9 . . . . 173 C4
Russell Ho
21 Poplar E14 . . . . . 33 C3
SW1 . . . . 146 C2
Russell Kerr Cl
W4 . . . . 45 B3
Russell Lo SE1 . . . . 137 B2
Russell Mans
WC1 . . . . 106 B4
Russell Pickering Ho
2 SW4 . . . . 62 A4
Russell Pl
Hampstead NW3 . . . 12 A3
Rotherhithe SE16 . . 41 A3
Russell Rd W14 . . . 126 B1
Russell Sq WC1 . . . . 94 A1
Russell Square Ho
WC1 . . . . 106 A4

Russell Square Sta
WC1 . . . . 94 A1
Russell St WC2 . . . 120 B4
Russell's Wharf 7
W9 . . . . 23 B1
Russell Wlk 4
TW10 . . . . 54 B1
Russell Yd SW15 . . . 58 A3
Russet Cres N7 . . . . 14 B3
Russett Way SE13 . . 52 A1
Russia Dock Rd
SE16 . . . . 33 A1
Russia La E2 . . . . . . 25 B3
Russia Row EC2 . . . 109 A1
Rusthall Ave W4 . . . 37 C3
Rusthall Mans 3
W4 . . . . 37 C2
Ruston Mews W11 . . 31 A3
Ruston St E3 . . . . . . 26 B4
Rust Sq SE5 . . . . 48 C3
Ruth Ct 8 E3 . . . . . . 26 A3
Rutherford Ho 12
E1 . . . . 25 A1
Rutherford House Sch
8 SW17 . . . . 72 C2
Rutherford St
SW1 . . . . 147 B4
Ruth Ho W10 . . . . . . 23 A1
Ruthin Rd SE3 . . . . . 53 C4
Ruthven St E9 . . . . . 25 C4
Rutland Cl SW14 . . . 55 A4
Rutland Ct
Herne Hill SE5 . . . . . 63 C3
SW7 . . . . 130 B3
Rutland Gate
SW7 . . . . 130 B3
Rutland Gate Mews
SW7 . . . . 130 A3
Rutland Gdns
SW7 . . . . 130 B3
Rutland Gdns Mews
SW7 . . . . 130 B3
Rutland Ho
W8 Putney SW15 . . . 69 B4
W8 . . . . 128 A1
Rutland Mews 21
NW8 . . . . 78 B3
Rutland Mews E
SW7 . . . . 130 B2
Rutland Mews S
SW7 . . . . 130 A2
Rutland Mews W
SW7 . . . . 130 A2
Rutland Park Gdns 1
NW2 . . . . 9 B2
Rutland Park Mans 2
NW2 . . . . 9 B2
Rutland Pk NW2 . . . . 9 B2
Rutland Pl EC1 . . . . 108 B4
Rutland Rd E9 . . . . . 25 C4
Rutland St SW7 . . . 130 B2
Rutland Studios
NW10 . . . . 21 C2
Rutley Cl SE11 . . . . 48 A4
Rutt's Terr SE14 . . . 50 C2
Ruvigny Gdns
SW15 . . . . 57 C4
Ruvigny Mans 1
SW15 . . . . 57 C4
Rycott Path SE22 . . 76 C4
Rycullf Sq SE3 . . . . 53 C1
Rydal Ho 23 SW8 . . 171 B1
Rydal Water NW1 . . 92 C3
Ryde Ho 1 NW6 . . . 23 C4
Ryder Ct SW1 . . . . . 119 A2

Ryder Dr SE16 . . . . . 40 A1
Ryder Ho 11 E1 . . . . 25 B1
Ryder St SW1 . . . . . 119 A2
Ryder's Terr NW8 . . 78 C2
Ryder Yd SW1 . . . . . 119 A2
Ryde Vale Rd
SW12 . . . . 73 B2
Rydon St N1 . . . . . . 87 A4
Rydston Cl 2 N7 . . . 14 B1
Ryecotes Mead
SE21 . . . . 76 A3
Ryecroft Rd SE13 . . 67 B2
Ryecroft St SW6 . . 166 A3
Ryedale SE22 . . . . . . 65 A1
Ryefield Path 7
SW15 . . . . 68 C3
Ryegates 2 SE15 . . . 50 A1
Rye Hill Pk SE15 . . . 65 B3
Rye Ho 11 SE16 . . . 40 B4
Rye La SE15 . . . . 49 C1
Rye Lane Mkt
SE15 . . . . 49 C1
Rye Oak Prim Sch 7
SE15 . . . . 65 A4
Rye Passage 6
SE15 . . . . 64 C4
Rye Rd SE15 . . . . . . 65 C3
Rye Wlk SW15 . . . . . 57 C2
Ryfold Rd SW19 . . . 70 C1
Ryland Rd NW5 . . . . 13 A2
Rylett Cres W12 . . . 38 B3
Rylett Rd W12 . . . . . 38 B3
Rylston Rd SW6 . . . 154 C3
Rymer St SE24 . . . . 63 A1
Rysbrack St SW1 . . 130 C2

Saatchi Gallery
SW3 . . . . 145 A2
Sabbarton St 8
E16 . . . . 35 B3
Sabella Ct E3 . . . . . . 26 B3
Sabine Rd SW11 . . . 60 C4
Sable St N1 . . . . 15 A1
Sacketts Ho 24
SW9 . . . . 173 C4
Sackville Ho 16
SW16 . . . . 74 A1
Sackville St W1 . . . 119 A3
Sacred Heart Catholic
Prim Sch SW11 . . 168 B1
Sacred Heart Catholic
Sch 18 SE5 . . . . . . 48 B2
Sacred Heart High
Sch 8 W6 . . . . 39 B2
Sacred Heart RC Prim
Sch SW15 . . . . 56 C2
Sacred Heart Sch
N7 . . . . 14 B3
Saddlers Mews
SW8 . . . . 172 B4
Sadler Ho
17 Bromley E3 . . . . . 27 A2
EC1 . . . . 96 A4
Sadler Pl E9 . . . . 18 A3
Saffron Ave E14 . . . . 34 C2
Saffron Ct 10 N1 . . . 15 C2
Saffron Hill EC1 . . . 107 C4
Saffron Ho 6
TW9 . . . . 45 A2
Saffron St EC1 . . . . 107 C4
Saffron Wharf
SE1 . . . . 139 A4
Sage Mews SE22 . . 64 B2

Sage St E1 . . . . 32 B2
Sage Way WC1 . . . . 94 C3
Sailacre Ho 10
SE10 . . . . 43 B1
Sail Ct 10 E14 . . . . . 34 C2
Sailmakers Ct
SW6 . . . . 59 B4
Sail St SE11 . . . . . . 149 A4
Sainfoin Rd SW17 . . 72 C2
St Agnes Cl E9 . . . . 25 B4
St Agnes Pl SE11 . . 48 A4
St Agnes RC Prim Sch
15 E3 . . . . 27 A2
St Agnes RC Sch
NW2 . . . . 1 A1
St Aidan's Prim Sch
N4 . . . . 5 C4
St Aidan's Rd SE22 . 65 A2
St Albans Ave W4 . . 37 C3
St Alban's CE Prim
Sch EC1 . . . . 107 B4
St Alban's Cl NW11 . 1 C3
St Albans Gr W8 . . 128 B2
St Albans La NW11 . 1 C3
St Albans Mans
W8 . . . . 128 B2
St Alban's Pl N1 . . . 86 A3
St Alban's Rd
Dagenham NW10 . . . 21 A4
Dartmouth Pk NW5 . . 4 A1
St Alban's St SW1 . 119 B3
St Albans Studios
W8 . . . . 128 B2
St Albans Terr
W6 . . . . 154 A4
St Alban's Villas
NW5 . . . . 3 C1
St Alfege Pas
SE10 . . . . 52 B4
St Alfege with St
Peter's CE Prim Sch
SE10 . . . . 52 C4
St Aloysius Convent
NW1 . . . . 93 B4
St Aloysius RC Coll 8
N19 . . . . 4 B3
St Aloysius RC Inf Sch
NW1 . . . . 93 B4
St Aloysius RC Jun
Sch NW1 . . . . 83 B1
St Alphage Gdn
EC2 . . . . 109 A3
St Alphage Highwalk
EC2 . . . . 109 A3
St Alphonsus Rd
SW4 . . . . 61 C3
St Andrew's
(Barnsbury) CE Prim
Sch N1 . . . . 85 A4
St Andrews Chambers
W1 . . . . 105 A2
St Andrews Cl 25
SE16 . . . . 40 A1
St Andrew's Ct 4
SW18 . . . . 71 B2
St Andrew's Gr N16 . 6 C3
St Andrew's Hill
EC4 . . . . 108 B1
St Andrews Ho 11
SE16 . . . . 40 A3
St Andrews Mans 9
E5 . . . . 17 A4

St Andrew's Mans
W1 . . . . **103** B3
St Andrews Mews
Greenwich SE3 . . . . . . **53** C3
4 Streatham
SW12 . . . . **73** C3
St Andrew's Mews
N16 . . . . **7** A3
St Andrew's Pl
NW1 . . . . **92** B2
St Andrew's Prim Sch
SW9 . . . . **172** B1
St Andrews Rd
W3 . . . . **29** A3
St Andrew's Rd
W14 . . . . **154** B4
Willesden NW2 . . . . . . **9** A2
St Andrews & St
Francis CE Prim Sch
6 NW2 . . . . **8** C2
St Andrew's Sq
W11 . . . . **31** A3
St Andrew St EC4 **107** C3
St Andrews Way
E3 . . . . **27** A1
St Andrew's Wharf
SE1 . . . . **139** A4
St Anne's CE Prim Sch
6 SW18 . . . . **59** A2
St Anne's Cl N6 . . . **3** C1
St Anne's Ct
Kensal Rise NW6 . . . . **23** A4
1 W1 . . . . **105** B1
St Anne's Flats
NW1 . . . . **93** B4
St Anne's Pas E14 . **33** B3
St Anne's RC Prim Sch
11 E1 . . . . **24** C1 **99** B1
SE11 . . . . **162** C4
St Anne's Row E14 **33** B3
St Anne St E14 . . . . **33** B3
St Anne's Trad Est 25
E14 . . . . **33** B3
St Ann's Cres
SW18 . . . . **59** B1
St Ann's Gdns
NW5 . . . . **12** C2
St Ann's Hill SW18 . **59** B1
St Ann's Ho WC1 . . . **95** B3
St Ann's La SW1 . . . **133** C1
St Ann's Park Rd
SW18 . . . . **59** B1
St Anns Rd
Barnes SW13 . . . . **46** B2
Shepherd's Bush
W11 . . . . **30** C2
St Ann's St SW1 . . . **133** C2
St Ann's Terr NW8 . **79** C2
St Ann's Villas
W11 . . . . . . **31** A1 **112** A1
St Anselm's Pl
W1 . . . . **118** A4
St Anselm's RC Prim
Sch SW17 . . . . **72** A2
St Anthonys Cl 5
SW17 . . . . **72** A2
St Anthony's Cl
6 E1 . . . . **125** B2
5 Hackney Wick
E9 . . . . **18** B2
St Anthony's Ct
2 Balham SW12 . . . **60** C1
Upper Tooting
SW17 . . . . **72** C2

St Anthony's Flats
NW1 . . . . **83** B1
St Anthony's RC Prim
Sch SE22 . . . . **64** C1
St Anthony's Sch 8
NW3 . . . . **11** C3
St Asaph Ct SE4 . . . **65** C4
St Asaph Rd SE4 . . . **65** C4
St Aubins Ct N1 . . . **87** C4
St Augustine's CE
High Sch **5**
NW6 . . . . **23** C3
St Augustine's Ho
NW1 . . . . **93** B4
St Augustine's Prim
Sch **5** NW6 . . . . . . **78** A2
St Augustine's RC
Prim Sch W6 . . . . . **154** B3
St Augustine's Rd
NW1 . . . . **13** C1
St Austell Rd SE13 . **52** C1
St Barnabas' CE Prim
Sch SW1 . . . . **145** C2
St Barnabas Cl 11
SE22 . . . . **65** A2
St Barnabas Mews
SW1 . . . . **145** C2
St Barnabas & St
Philip's CE Prim Sch
W8 . . . . **127** B2
St Barnabas St
SW1 . . . . **145** C2
St Barnabas Terr
E9 . . . . **17** C3
St Barnabas Villas
SW8 . . . . **172** B4
St Bartholomew's
Hospl EC1 . . . . **108** B3
St Bartholomew's Mus
EC1 . . . . **108** B3
St Bede's RC Inf Sch
SW12 . . . . **73** C3
St Benets Cl 8
SW17 . . . . **72** A2
St Benet's Pl EC3 **123** C4
St Bernadette RC Jun
Sch **12** SW12 . . . . . **73** B4
St Bernard Ho 6
E14 . . . . **42** B3
St Botolph St E1,
EC3 . . . . **110** C2
St Brelades Ct N1 . **87** C4
St Bride's EC4 . . . . **108** A1
St Bride's Ave
EC4 . . . . **108** A1
St Bride's Pas
EC4 . . . . **108** A1
St Bride St EC4 . . . **108** A2
St Catherines Cl 7
SW17 . . . . **72** A2
St Catherine's Ct 8
W4 . . . . **38** A3
St Catherine's Dr
SE14 . . . . **50** C1
St Catherines Mews
SW3 . . . . **144** C4
St Cecilia's CE Sch
SW18 . . . . **58** B3
St Chad's Pl WC1 . . **94** C4
St Chad's St WC1 . . **94** B4
St Charles' Hospl
W10 . . . . **30** C4
St Charles Pl W10 . **31** A4
St Charles RC Prim
Sch **7** W10 . . . . . . **30** C4

St Charles RC Sixth
Form Coll 8
W10 . . . . **30** C4
St Charles Sq W10 . **30** C4
St Christina's Sch
NW8 . . . . **80** B2
St Christophers Ct 15
N19 . . . . **4** B1
St Christopher's Ho
NW1 . . . . **83** B1
St Christopher's Pl
W1 . . . . **103** C2
St Christopher's Sch
5 NW3 . . . . **11** C3
St Clair Ho 17 E3 . . **26** C2
St Clare St EC3 . . . **110** C1
St Clement Danes CE
Prim Sch WC2 . . . . **106** C1
St Clement & St
James CE Prim Sch
W11 . . . . . **31** A1 **112** A2
St Clements Ct
Barnsbury N7 . . . . . . **14** B2
7 SE14 . . . . **50** C4
6 Shepherd's Bush
W11 . . . . **30** C2
St Clement's Ct
EC3 . . . . **123** C4
St Clements Ho
E1 . . . . **110** C3
St Clement's La
WC2 . . . . **107** A1
St Clements Mans 7
SW6 . . . . **47** C4
St Clements St N7 . **14** C1
St Columb's Ho 1
W10 . . . . **31** A4
St Crispins Ct
NW3 . . . . **12** A4
St Cross St EC1 . . . **107** C4
St Cuthbert's Rd
NW2 . . . . **10** B2
St Cuthbert with St
Matthias CE Prim
Sch SW5 . . . . **142** A2
St Davids Ct 27
SE16 . . . . **40** A1
St David's Sq E14 . **42** A1
St Dionis Rd SW6 . **165** A2
St Dominic's Catholic
Prim Sch **6** E9 . . . . **18** A2
St Dominic's RC Prim
Sch **14** NW5 . . . . . . **12** B3
St Donatt's Rd
London SE14 . . . . **51** B2
New Cross Gate
SE4 . . . . **51** B1
St Dunstan Ave
W3 . . . . **28** C2
St Dunstan Gdns
W3 . . . . **28** C2
St Dunstan's Alley
EC3 . . . . **123** C4
St Dunstan's Ct
EC4 . . . . **107** C1
St Dunstan's Hill
EC3 . . . . **124** A3
St Dunstan's La
EC3 . . . . **124** A3
St Dunstan's Rd
W6 . . . . **39** C1
St Edmund's Catholic
Prim Sch E14 . . . . . . **41** C2
St Edmunds Cl 3
SW17 . . . . **72** A2

St Edmund's Cl
NW8 . . . . **80** C3
St Edmund's Ct
NW8 . . . . **80** C3
St Edmund's Sq
SW13 . . . . **47** B4
St Edmund's Terr
NW8 . . . . **80** C3
St Edward's RC Prim
Sch NW1 . . . . **90** B1
St Elizabeth RC Prim
Sch **33** E2 . . . . **25** A3
St Elizabeth's RC Prim
Sch TW10 . . . . **54** B1
St Elmo Rd W12 . . . **38** B4
St Elmos Rd SE16 . . **41** A4
St Ermin's Hill
SW1 . . . . **133** B2
St Ervan's Rd W10 . **31** B4
St Eugene de
Mazenod RC Prim
Sch **12** NW6 . . . . . . **10** C1
St Faith's CE Prim Sch
1 SW18 . . . . **59** B2
St Faith's Rd SE24 **75** A3
St Francesca Cabrini
RC Prim Sch
SE23 . . . . **65** B1
St Francis' Ho
NW1 . . . . **83** B1
St Francis of Assisi RC
Prim Sch **9** W11 . . **30** C2
St Francis Pl
SW12 . . . . **61** A1
St Francis RC Prim
Sch **32** SE15 . . . . . . **49** C3
St Francis Rd
SE22 . . . . **64** A3
St Francis Xavier Coll
SW12 . . . . **61** A1
St Frideswides Mews
6 E14 . . . . **34** B3
St Gabriel's CE Prim
Sch SW1 . . . . **146** C1
St Gabriels Cl 3
E14 . . . . **34** A4
St Gabriel's Coll
(Dennen Site) **10**
SE5 . . . . **48** A2
St Gabriel's Rd
NW2 . . . . **9** C3
St George Ho
SW11 . . . . **169** C3
ST GEORGE IN THE
EAST **32** A2
St George's Ave
N7 . . . . **13** C4
St George's Bldgs
SE11 . . . . **136** B1
St George's Cath
NW1 . . . . **92** B4
St George's Cath RC
Prim Sch SE1 . . . . . **136** A2
St George's CE Prim
Sch
18 SE5 . . . . **49** A3
SW8 . . . . **161** A1
St George's Circ
SE1 . . . . **136** A2
St Georges Cl SW8 **171** A4
St Georges Coll N7 . . **5** C1
St George's Ct
SW15 . . . . **58** B3
St George's Ct
Brompton SW3 . . . . **144** A4

St George's Ct
continued
Kensington SW7 . . . **128** C1
Newington SE1 . . . . **136** A1
St George's Dr
SW1 . . . . **146** C2
St George's Field
W2 . . . . **102** B1
St George's Gr
SW17 . . . . **71** C1
St George's Hanover
Square CE Sch
W1 . . . . **117** C3
St George's Ho
NW1 . . . . **83** A1
St George's La
EC3 . . . . **124** A4
St George's Mews
1 NW1 . . . . **12** B1
2 Rotherhithe SE8 . . **41** B2
SE1 . . . . **135** C2
St Georges Pl N7 . . **13** C4
St George's Pools
E1 . . . . **32** A2
St George's RC Cath
SE1 . . . . **135** C2
St Georges Rd W4 . **37** C4
St George's Rd
Newington SE1 . . . . **136** A1
Richmond TW9 . . . . . . **54** B4
St George's
Residences 4
SW2 . . . . **62** C2
St Georges Sq 1
E14 . . . . **33** A2
St George's Sq
Rotherhithe SE8 . . . . . **41** B2
SW1 . . . . **147** B1
St George's Square
Mews SW1 . . . . . . **147** B1
St George St W1 . . **118** C4
St Georges Terr
NW1 . . . . **81** A4
St George's Terr
NW1 . . . . **12** B1
St George's Way
SE15 . . . . **49** A4
St George the Martyr
CE Prim Sch
WC1 . . . . **95** A1
St George Wharf
SW8 . . . . **162** A4
St George Wharf Pier
SW8 . . . . **162** A4
St Gerards Cl SW4 . **61** B2
St German's Pl
SE3 . . . . **53** C2
St Gildas' RC Jun Sch
18 N8 . . . . **5** A4
St Giles Cir WC1 . . **106** A2
St Giles Cir WC1 . . **105** C2
St Giles Ct WC2 . . **106** A2
St Giles High St
WC2 . . . . **105** C2
St Giles Ho SW16 . . **74** A1
St Giles International
WC1 . . . . **106** B4
St Giles Pas SW1 . . **105** C1
St Giles Rd SE5 . . . **49** A2
St Giles Terr EC1 . . **109** A3
St Giles Twr 3
SE5 . . . . **49** A2

St Gilles Ho 15 E2 . . . .25 C3

St Helena Ho WC1 . . . . 95 B3

St Helena Rd SE16 . .40 C2

St Helena St WC1 . . . 95 B3

St Helens Gdns
W10 . . . . .30 C3

St Helen's Pl EC3 110 A2

St Helen's RC Primary
Sch 17 SW9 . . . . .62 C4

St Helier Ct 4 N1 . .24 A4

St Hildas Cl 2
SW17 . . . . .72 A2

St Hilda's Cl NW6 . . . .9 C1

St Hilda's Rd
SW13 . . . . .47 A4

St Hildas Wharf
E1 . . . . .32 B1

St Hubert's Ho 2
E14 . . . . .41 C3

St Hughes Cl 8
SW17 . . . . .72 A2

St Ives Ct NW2 . . . . . .10 A2

St Ives Pl E14 . . . . . . .34 B4

ST JAMES 119 B2

St James' CE Prim
Sch
Bermondsey
SE16 . . . . .153 C4
SE1 . . . . . . 139 B2 125 C4

St James Ct
26 Bethnal Green
E2 . . . . .24 C2 99 C3
9 Brentford W4 . . . . .36 C1

St James' Ct
Bedford Pk W4 . . . . . .37 C3
SW1 . . . . .133 A2

St James Ho N5 . . . .14 C3

St James Ind Mews 18
SE1 . . . . .153 C4

St James Jun &
Senior Girls Schs
W14 . . . . .140 B4

St James' Mans
NW6 . . . . .10 C1

St James Mews
E14 . . . . .42 B3

St James's SE14 . . . .51 A2

St James & St
Michael's CE Prim
Sch W2 . . . . .115 A4

St James's App
EC2 . . . . .24 A1 98 A1

St James's Ave E2 . . .25 B3

St James's CE Prim
Sch SE14 . . . . .51 A2

St James School Flats
1 N7 . . . . .14 C3

St James's Cl
NW8 . . . . .80 C3
Upper Tooting
SW17 . . . . .72 B2

St James's Cloisters
2 SE22 . . . . .64 B3

St James's Cres
SW9 . . . . .62 C4

St James's Dr
Balham SW12,
SW17 . . . . .72 A4
Upper Tooting
SW17 . . . . .72 B3

St James's Gdns
W11 . . . . . . .31 A1 112 A2

St James's Gr
SW11 . . . . .169 A2

St James's Market
SW1 . . . . .119 B3

St James's Pal
SW1 . . . . .119 A1

St James's Park Sta
SW1 . . . . .133 B2

St James's Pas
EC3 . . . . .110 B1

St James's Pk 133 B4

St James's Pl
SW1 . . . . .118 C1

St James's Rd
Bermondsey SE1,
SE16 . . . . .153 C4
Peckham SE1 . . . . . . .49 C4

St James's Sq
SW1 . . . . .119 A2

St James's St
SW1 . . . . .118 C2

St James's Terr
NW8 . . . . .80 C4
2 Upper Tooting
SW12 . . . . .72 C3

St James's Terrace
Mews NW8 . . . . .80 C3

St James The Great
RC Prim Sch 17
SE15 . . . . .49 B2

St James the Less
Prim Sch SW1 . . . .147 C2

St James Wlk EC1 . . .96 A2

St Joan of Arc RC
Prim Sch N5 . . . . . .15 B4

St John Bosco Coll
SW11 . . . . .168 A3

St John of Jerusalem
CE Prim Sch 42
E9 . . . . .17 B1

ST JOHN'S 51 C1

St John & St James
CE Prim Sch 1
E9 . . . . .17 B3

St John's Angell Town
CE Prim Sch
12 Brixton SW8 . . . . .62 C3
23 London SW9 . . . .173 B1

St John's Ave
Dagenham NW10 . .21 B4
Putney SW15 . . . . . . .57 C2

St John's CE Prim Sch
33 E2 . . . . .25 B3

St John's Church Rd
E9 . . . . .17 B3

St John's Cl SW6 .155 B2

St John's Cres
SW9 . . . . .62 C4

St John's Ct EC1 . . .32 A1

St John's Dr
Finsbury Pk N4 . . . . . . .6 A2
Hammersmith W6 . . .39 A2
Lewisham SE13 . . . . .52 B1
5 South Hampstead
NW3 . . . . .11 B2

Saint John's Ct N5 .15 A4

St John's Dr SW18 .71 A3

St John's Est SE1 138 C3

St John's Gdns
W11 . . . . . . .31 B2 112 C3

St John's Gr
3 Barnes SW13 . . . .46 B1
1 Richmond TW9 . . .54 A3
Upper Holloway N19 . . .4 B2

St John's Highbury
Vale CE Prim Sch
N5 . . . . .6 A1

St John's Hill
SW11 . . . . .59 C3

St John's Hill Gr
SW11 . . . . .59 C3

St Johns Ho 5
SE17 . . . . .48 C4

St John's Ho 1
E14 . . . . .42 B3

St John's La EC1 . .108 B4

St John's Lodge 8
SE8 . . . . .51 C2

St John's Mans E5 .17 B3

St John's Park Mans
N19 . . . . .4 B1

St John's Path EC1 96 A1

St John's Pk SE3 . . .53 C3

St John's Pl EC1 . . .96 A1

St John's RC Prim Sch
SE16 . . . . .41 A4

St John's Rd
Battersea SW11 . . . .60 A3
Canning Town E16 . . .35 C3
Richmond TW9 . . . . .54 A3

St John's & St
Clement's CE Prim
Sch 4 SE15 . . . . . . .64 C4

St John's Smith Sq
Concert Hall
SW1 . . . . .134 A1

St John's Sq EC1 . . .96 A1

St Johns Sta SE8 . . .51 C1

St John St EC1 . . . . .96 A2

St John's Terr
W10 . . . . .22 C1

St John's Therapy Ctr
SW11 . . . . .59 C3

St John's Upper
Holloway CE Prim
Sch 3 N19 . . . . .4 C2

St John's Vale SE8 .51 C1

St John's Villas
Upper Holloway
N19 . . . . .4 C2
W8 . . . . .128 B1

St John's Walham
Green CE Prim Sch
SW6 . . . . .164 B4

St John's Walworth
CE Prim Sch
SE17 . . . . .151 A3

St John's Way N19 . . .4 C2

ST JOHN'S WOOD .79 B1

St John's Wood Ct
NW8 . . . . .89 C3

St John's Wood High
St NW8 . . . . .80 A1

St John's Wood Park
NW8 . . . . .79 B4

St John's Wood Pre-
Prep Sch NW8 . . . . .90 A4

St John's Wood Rd
NW8 . . . . .89 C3

St John's Wood Sta
NW8 . . . . .79 B2

St John's Wood Terr
NW8 . . . . .80 A2

St John the Baptist
VA CE Prim Sch
N1 . . . . .87 C1

St John the Divine CE
Jun & Inf Sch
SE5 . . . . .48 A3

St John the Evangelist
RC Prim Sch N1 . . .86 A2

St Joseph's
Camberwell RC
Schools' Federation
38 SE5 . . . . .48 B3

St Joseph's Cl
W10 . . . . .31 A4

St Joseph's Ct 8
NW10 . . . . .21 B3

St Joseph's Flats
NW1 . . . . .93 B4

St Joseph's Ho
W6 . . . . .39 C2

St Joseph's Hospice E9,
E2 . . . . .25 C4

St Joseph's RC Prim
Sch
Chelsea SW3 . . . . . . .144 C3
12 Deptford SE8 . . . .51 C3
11 Greenwich SE10 . .43 A1
Paddington W9 . . . . .88 C3
Rotherhithe SE16 . . . .40 B3
St Giles WC2 . . . . . . .106 B2
Upper Holloway N19 . . .4 A3
16 Wandsworth
SW18 . . . . .58 C2
9 Willesden NW10 . . .8 A1

St Joseph's St
SW8 . . . . .170 B4

St Joseph's Vale
SE3 . . . . .67 C4

St Jude & St Paul's CE
Prim Sch 11 N1 . . .16 A2

St Jude's CE Prim Sch
4 London SE24 . . . . .63 A2

St Jude's Ho 6
W10 . . . . .23 B2

St Jude's Rd E2 . . . .25 A3

St Jude St N16 . . . . .16 A3

St Julian's Rd
NW6 . . . . .23 C4

St Katharine's Ho
N1 . . . . .85 B2

St Katharine's Prec
NW1 . . . . .82 A2

St Katharine's Way
E1 . . . . .125 A2

St Katherine's Pier
E1 . . . . .125 A2

St Katherine's Row
EC3 . . . . .110 B1

St Katherine's Wlk 2
W11 . . . . .30 C1

St Kilda's Rd N16 . . . .7 A3

St Laurence's Cl
NW6 . . . . .22 C4

St Lawrence Ct N1 .87 C4

St Lawrence Ho
SE1 . . . . .138 B2

St Lawrence St
E14 . . . . .34 B1

St Lawrence Terr
W10 . . . . .31 A4

St Lawrence Way
SW9 . . . . .173 C2

St Leonards Ct
SW14 . . . . .55 B4

St Leonard's Ct N1 .97 C4

St Leonard's Hospl
N1 . . . . .24 A3

St Leonards Rd
SW14 . . . . .55 B4

St Leonard's Rd
Becontree NW10 . . . .20 C1
South Bromley E14 . . .34 B4

St Leonard's Sq
NW5 . . . . .12 C2

St Leonard's Terr
SW3 . . . . .145 A1

St Loo Ave SW3 . . .158 B4

St Loo Ct SW3 . . . .158 C4

ST LUKE'S 97 A2

St Luke's Ave SW4 .61 C3

St Luke's CE Prim Sch
7 Cubitt Town
E14 . . . . .42 C2
North Sheen TW9 . . . .44 C1
Paddington W9 . . . . . .23 B2
Shoreditch EC1 . . . . . .97 A3
1 West Hampstead
NW6 . . . . .10 C4

St Luke's Cl EC1 . . .97 A2

St Luke's Ct W11 . . .31 B3

St Luke's Mews
W11 . . . . .31 B3

St Luke's Prim Sch
E16 . . . . .35 B3

St Luke's Rd W11 . . .31 B4

St Luke's Sq E16 . . .35 B3

St Luke's St SW3 . .144 B2

St Margaret's Cres
SW15 . . . . .57 A2

St Margaret's Ct
Putney SW15 . . . . . . .57 A3
SE1 . . . . .123 B1

St Margaret's La
W8 . . . . .128 A1

St Margarets Lo
W3 . . . . .37 A4

St Margaret's Rd
Brockley SE4 . . . . . . .66 B3
Kensal Green
NW10 . . . . .22 B2

St Margaret's Sch
NW3 . . . . .11 A4

St Margaret St
SW1 . . . . .134 A3

St Mark's CE Prim Sch
Kennington SE11 . . . .163 A4
11 Upper Holloway
N19 . . . . .5 A2

St Marks Cl 5
SE10 . . . . .52 B3

St Mark's Cres
NW1 . . . . .81 C4

St Marks Gate E9 . . .18 B1

St Mark's Gr SW10 . .156 B2

St Marks Ho 6
SE17 . . . . .48 C4

St Mark's Mans 14
N4 . . . . .5 B2

St Mark's Pl W11 . . .31 A3

St Marks Rd
15 North Kensington
NW10 . . . . .30 C3
North Kensington
W10 . . . . .30 C4

St Mark's Rd W11 . .31 A3

St Mark's Rise E8 . . .16 C3

St Mark's Sq NW1 . .81 B3

St Mark St E1 . . . . .111 A1

St Martin-in-the-
Fields High Sch 21
SW2 . . . . .74 C3

St Martin's
Almshouses NW1 . .82 C4

St Martin's Cl NW1 .82 C4

St Martins Ct N1 ....24 A4
St Martin's Ct
WC2 ....**120** A4
  West Norwood
  SE27 ....75 A2
St Martin's La
WC2 ....**120** A3
St Martin's Le Grand
EC1 ....**108** C2
St Martin's Pl
WC2 ....**120** A3
St Martin's Rd
SW9 ....**172** C2
St Martin's St
WC2 ....**119** C3
St Martin's Way
SW17 ....71 B1
St Mary Abbots Ct
  Prim Sch W8....**128** A3
St Mary Abbot's Ct
  W14 ....**126** C1
St Mary Abbot's Pl
  W8 ....**127** A1
St Mary Abbots Terr
  W14 ....**127** A1
St Mary at Hill
  EC3 ....**124** A3
St Mary Axe EC3..**110** B2
St Marychurch St
  SE16 ....40 B4
St Mary Graces Ct
  E1 ....**125** A3
St Marylebone CE Sch
  The W1 ....**103** C4
St Mary le Bow
  Church EC2 .....**109** A1
St Mary– le-Park Ct
  SW11 ....**158** B1
St Mary Magdalene
  Acad N7 ....14 C2
St Mary Magdalene
  CE Prim Sch
  6 Greenwich
  SE10 ....43 B3
  3 Paddington W2 **100** A4
  2 Peckham SE15 ...50 U3
St Mary Magdalen's
  RC Prim Sch
  Brockley SE4......66 A3
  4 Mortlake SW14...55 C4
St Mary Magdelen's
  RC Jun Sch 1
  NW2 ....9 A2
St Mary Newington Cl
  SE17 ....**152** B3
St Mary of the Angels
  RC Prim Sch 12
  W2 ....31 C3
St Mary & St Michael
  Prim Sch E1 ...32 B3
St Mary & St Pancras
  CE Prim Sch
  NW1 ....83 B1
St Mary's Bryanston
  Square CE Sch
  W1 ....**102** C4
St Mary's CE Prim Sch
  Islington N1 ......86 B4
  2 London N16.......7 A2
  London SE13.......67 A2
  11 Putney SW15...57 C4
  Willesden NW10....8 A2
  St Mary's Ct W6....38 B3

St Mary's Est 2
  SE16 ....40 B4
St Mary's Flats
  NW1 ....93 B4
St Mary's Gate
  W8 ....**128** A1
St Mary's Gdns
  SE11 ....**149** C4
St Mary's Gr
  Barnes SW13 ......57 A4
  Chiswick W4 ....45 A4
  Islington N1 ......15 A2
  Richmond TW10,
  TW9 ....54 B3
St Mary's Ho N1...86 B4
St Mary's Hospl
  W2 ....**101** C2
St Mary's Hospl
  Medical Sch W2 **101** C2
St Mary's Kilburn CE
  Prim Sch 16
  NW6 ....23 C4
St Mary's Mans
  Dagenham NW10 ..21 A4
  Paddington W2 ...**101** B4
St Mary's Mews
  NW6 ....11 A1
St Mary's Path N1..86 B4
St Mary's Pl W8 ...**128** A1
St Mary's RC Prim Sch
  Chiswick W4 ....46 A4
  10 Clapham Pk
  SW4 ....61 B2
  Clapham SW8 ....**170** B4
  Hammersmith W14 .39 C2
  Paddington NW6 ..23 C3
  2 W10 ....23 A1
St Mary's Rd
  Golders Green
  NW11 ....1 A4
  Harlesden NW10 ...21 A4
  Nunhead SE15 .....50 B1
St Mary's Sch
  Hampstead NW3 ..11 C3
St Mary's Sq W2...**101** B4
St Mary's Terr
  W2 ....**101** B4
St Mary's Twr EC1 .97 A1
St Mary's Wlk
  SE11 ....**149** C4
St Matthews Ct
  SE1 ....**136** C1
St Matthew's Ho 8
  SE17 ....48 C4
St Matthew's Lo
  NW1 ....83 A2
St Matthew's Prim
  Sch SW1 ....**133** C2
St Matthew's Rd
  SW2 ....62 B2
St Matthew's Row
  E2 ....24 C1 99 B2
St Matthew St
  SW1 ....**133** B1
St Matthias CE Prim
  Sch E2.......24 B1 99 A2
St Matthias's CE Prim
  Sch N16 ....16 A4
St Mauritius Ho
  SE14 ....51 A2
St Maur Rd SW6...**165** A3
St Michael & All
  Angels CE Acad 15
  SE5 ....48 A3
St Michael's Alley
  EC3 ....**109** C1

St Michael's Cath Coll
  38 SE16 ....**139** B3
St Michael's CE Prim
  Sch
  Camden Town
  NW1 ....82 C4
  Highgate N6 ....3 C4
  Wandsworth SW18 .70 B4
St Michaels Ct 2
  E14 ....34 B4
St Michael's Ct
  NW11 ....1 B4
St Michael's Flats
  NW1 ....83 B1
St Michael's Gdns
  W10 ....31 A4
St Michael's Rd
  Cricklewood NW2 ...9 B4
  Stockwell SW9 ...**172** C2
St Michael's St
  W2 ....**102** A2
St Mildred's Ct
  EC2 ....**109** B1
St Monica's RC Prim
  Sch 20 N1...24 A2 98 B4
St Nicholas' Flats
  NW1 ....83 B1
St Nicholas Ho
  SE8 ....51 C4
St Nicholas Mans
  SW17 ....72 B2
St Nicholas St SE8..51 C2
St Norbert Gn SE4..66 A3
St Norbert Rd SE4..66 A3
St Olaf's Rd SW6..**154** B1
St Olaves Ct EC2..**114** A3
St Olave's Ct EC2 .**109** B1
St Olave's Est SE1 **138** B4
St Olave's Gdns
  SE11 ....**149** B4
St Olave's Mans
  SE11 ....**149** B4
St Olav's Sq 32
  SE16 ....40 B4
St Osmund's RC Prim
  Sch SW13.........46 B2
St Oswald's Pl
  SE11 ....**148** C1
St Oswulf St SW1 .**147** C3
St Owen Ho SE1 ..**138** B2
ST PANCRAS 94 B4
St Pancras
  Almshouses 13
  NW1 ....12 B3
St Pancras
  Commercial Ctr
  NW1 ....83 A4
St Pancras Hospl
  NW1 ....83 B3
St Pancras
  International Sta
  WC1 ....94 A4
St Pancras Way
  NW1 ....83 B4
St Patrick's RC Prim
  Sch NW5 ....13 A3
St Paul's Ave
  Rotherhithe SE16...32 C1
  Willesden NW2 .....9 B1
St Paul's Cath
  EC4 ....**108** C1
St Paul's Cath Sch
  EC4 ....**108** C1
St Paul's CE Jun Sch
  W6 ....39 B1

St Paul's CE Prim Sch
  continued
  Hampstead NW3 ...12 B4
  SE17 ....**150** C2
St Paul's Church Yd
  EC4 ....**108** C1
St Pauls Cl W5 ....36 B4
St Pauls Cres
  NW1 ....14 A1
St Paul's Ct
  Clapham SW4 .....61 C3
  6 Upper Holloway
  N19 ....5 A2
St Paul's Dr E15...19 C3
St Paul's Girls' Sch 1
  W6 ....38 C1
St Pauls Mews
  NW1 ....13 C1
St Pauls Pl N1 ....15 C2
St Pauls Rd TW9...54 B4
St Paul's Rd N1 ...15 B2
St Paul's Sch
  SW13 ....38 C1
St Paul's Sta EC2 .**108** C2
St Pauls Steiner Sch
  N1 ....15 C1
St Paul St N1......**87** A3
St Paul's Terr
  SE17 ....48 A4
St Pauls View WC1 .95 B3
St Paul's Way E3 ..33 C4
  St Paul's Way Com
  Sch 23 E3 ....33 C4
St Paul's Whitechapel
  CE Prim Sch 1 ..**125** C4
St Paul's with St
  Michael's CE Prim
  Sch 24 E8 ....24 C4
St Paul with St Luke
  CE Prim Sch 18
  E3 ....33 B4
St Peter & St Paul RC
  Prim Sch EC1 .....96 B2
St Peter's Alley
  EC3 ....**109** C1
St Peter's Ave 37
  E2 ....24 C3
St Petersburg Mews
  W2 ....23 A4
St Petersburgh Pl
  W2 ....**114** A3
St Peter's CE Prim
  Sch
  11 Chiswick W6 ...39 A1
  8 Paddington W9 ..23 C1
  SE17 ....**151** B1
St Peter's Church Ct
  N1 ....86 B3
St Peters Cl 1
  SW17 ....72 A2
St Peters Ct
  New Cross SE4 ....51 B1
  2 Stepney E1 .....25 B1
St Peter's Eaton Sq CE
  Prim Sch SW1...**132** B1
St Peter's Gdns
  SE27 ....74 C1
St Peter's Gr W6 ..38 C2
St Peters Ho W1 ..94 B3
St Peter's Ho
  4 SE17 ....48 C4
  Stamford Hill N16..7 A4
St Peter's London
  Docks CE Prim Sch
  5 E1 ....32 B1

St Peter's Pl W9...**88** A1
St Peter's Rd W6..38 C1
St Peter's Sq
  Chiswick W6 ......38 B1
  Hackney E2 ....25 A3
St Peter's St N1...86 B3
St Peter's Street
  Mews N1.........86 B2
St Peter's Terr
  SW6 ....**154** B1
St Peter's Villas 5
  W6 ....38 C2
St Peter's Way N1..16 A1
St Peter's Wharf 8
  W6 ....38 C1
St Philip Ho WC1 ..95 B3
St Philip Sq 1
  SW8 ....**170** A1
St Philip's Rd E8 ..16 C2
St Philip's Sch
  SW7 ....**143** A3
St Philip St SW8..**170** A1
St Philip's Way N1..87 A3
St Quentin Ho
  SW18 ....59 C1
St Quintin Ave
  W10 ....30 C4
St Quintin Gdns 21
  W10 ....30 B4
St Regis Hts NW3 ...2 A1
St Richard's Ho
  NW1 ....93 B4
St Rule St SW8 ...**170** C1
St Saviours SW4...61 A3
St Saviour & St Olaves
  CE Sch SE1 .....**137** C1
St Saviour's CE Prim
  Sch
  8 Bow Comm
  E14 ....34 A4
  Camberwell SE24 ...63 B4
  22 Paddington W9 .88 B1
St Saviours Ho 35
  SE1 ....**139** B3
St Saviour's RC Prim
  Sch SE13 ....67 B3
St Saviour's Rd
  SW2 ....62 B2
St Saviour's Wharf
  SE1 ....**139** A4
St Scholastica's RC
  Prim Sch E5 .....7 C1
St Silas Pl NW5....12 C2
St Simon's Ave
  SW15 ....57 B2
St Stephen's Ave
  W12 ....39 A4
St Stephen's CE Prim
  Sch
  16 London W12 ....39 B4
  Paddington W2 ....31 C4
  2 St Johns SE8....51 C1
  SW8 ....**162** C2
St Stephen's Cl
  Maitland Pk NW5...12 B3
  NW8 ....80 B3
St Stephen's Cres
  W2 ....31 C3
St Stephen's Gdns
  Notting Hill W2 ....31 C3
  4 Putney SW15 ...58 B2
St Stephen's Gr
  SE13 ....67 B4
St Stephens Ho 7
  SE17 ....48 C4

St Stephen's Mews 🈸
W2 . . . . .31 C4
St Stephen's Rd
E3 . . . . 26 B3
St Stephen's Row
EC4 . . . . 109 B1
St Stephen's Terr
SW8 . . . . 162 C1
St Stephen's Wlk
SW7 . . . . 142 C4
St Swithin's La
EC4 . . . . 123 B4
St Swithun's Rd
SE13 . . . . 67 C2
St Theresas Cl E9. .18 C4
St Thomas' CE Prim
Sch 🈸 W10 . . . . 23 A1
St Thomas Ct 🈔
NW1 . . . . 13 B1
St Thomas Ho 🈔
E1 . . . . 25 C2
St Thomas More
Language Coll
SW3 . . . . 144 C3
St Thomas of
Canterbury RC Prim
Sch SW6 . . . . 154 C2
St Thomas Rd E16 . .35 C3
St Thomas' Rd W4. .45 B4
St Thomas's Gdns
NW5 . . . . 12 C2
St Thomas's Hospl
SE1 . . . . 134 C2
St Thomas's Pl 🈳
E9 . . . . 17 B1
St Thomas's Rd
Dagenham NW10 . . .21 A4
Highbury N4, N5. . . .5 C4
St Thomas's Sq E9. .17 B1
St Thomas St SE1 . 123 C1
St Thomas's Way
SW6 . . . . 155 A2
St Thomas the
Apostle Coll
SE15 . . . . 50 B2
St Ursula's Convent
Sch SE10 . . . . 52 C3
St Vincent De Paul Ho
🈡 E1 . . . . 132 C4
St Vincent de Paul RC
Prim Sch SW1. . 133 A2
St Vincent Ho
SE1 . . . . 138 C2
St Vincent's Catholic
Prim Sch W3 . . . . . .28 A1
St Vincent's RC Prim
Sch W1 . . . . 103 C3
St Vincent St W1 . 103 C3
Salamanca Pl SE1 148 C3
Salamanca St SE1,
SE11 . . . . 148 C3
Salcombe Gdns
SW4 . . . . 61 A3
Salcombe Lo NW5. .12 C4
Salcombe Rd 🈷
N16 . . . . 16 A3
Salcombe Villas 🈚
TW10 . . . . .54 A2
Salcot N4 . . . . .5 B2
Salcott Rd SW11. . . .60 B2
Salehurst Rd SE4. . .66 B1
Salem Ho 🈘 E9 . . . . .17 C2
Salem Rd W2. . . . . . 114 B4
Sale Pl W2 . . . . 102 A3
Sale St E2. . . . .24 C1 99 C2
Salford Ho 🈟 E14. .42 B2

Salford Rd SW12,
SW2 . . . . .73 C3
Salisbury Cl SE17. 151 B4
Salisbury Ct
🈛 Bermondsey
SE16 . . . . 139 C1
Chiswick W4. . . . . . .38 A2
EC4 . . . . 108 A1
Hackney E9. . . . . . . .18 A3
Salisbury Ho
🈔 Islington N1 . . .15 A2
Islington N1 . . . . . . .86 A4
🈠 Poplar E14 . . . . .34 A3
Westminster SW1. 147 C2
Wimbledon SW19. . . .69 C1
Salisbury Mews
SW6 . . . . 154 C1
Salisbury Pl
🈙 Acton W3 . . . . . .37 B4
NW8 . . . . 90 A1
Salisbury Terr
SE15 . . . . .65 B4
Salisbury Wlk N19. . .4 B2
Salisbury Yd 🈚
SE13 . . . . .67 B4
Salmon La E14 . . . . .33 A3
Salmon St 🈗 E14. . .33 B3
Saltcoats Rd W4. . . .38 A4
Saltdene N4. . . . . 5 B3
Salter Rd
Rotherhithe SE16. . . .32 C1
SE16 . . . . .33 A1
Salters' Hall Ct
EC4 . . . . 123 B4
Salters Rd W10 . . . .22 C1
Salter St
College Pk NW10 . . . .21 C2
🈗 Poplar E14 . . . . .33 C2
Salterton Rd N7 . . . .5 B1
Saltoun Rd SW2,
SW9 . . . . .62 C3
Saltram Cres W9 . . .23 C2
Saltwell St E14 . . . .33 C2
Saltwood Gr SE17 151 B1
Saltwood Ho 🈙
SE15 . . . . .50 B4
Salusbury Prim Sch
NW6 . . . . .23 A4
Salusbury Rd NW6. .23 A4
Salutation Rd
SE10 . . . . .43 A2
Salvin Rd SW15. . . .57 C4
Salway Rd E15 . . . .19 C2
Salween Ho 🈔
N16. . . . . 15 C4
Sambrook Ho 🈔
E1 . . . . 32 B4
Samels Ct W6. . . . . .38 C1
Samford Ho N1. . . . .85 B3
Samford St NW8. . . .90 A1
Sam Manners Ho 🈚
SE10 . . . . .43 A1
Sam March Ho 🈛
E14 . . . . .34 C3
Sampson St E1. . . 125 C1
Samuel Cl
SE14 . . . . .50 C4
Shoreditch E8. . . . . .24 B4
Samuel Ct
N1. . . . . . . .24 A2 98 A3
Samuel Ho 🈘 E8. . .24 B4

Samuel Jones Ind Est
🈖 SE15 . . . . .49 A3
Samuel Lewis Bldgs
N1 . . . . 14 C1
Samuel Lewis Trust
Dwellings
🈕 Camberwell
SE5 . . . . 48 B2
Chelsea SW3 . . . . . 144 A3
Walham Green
SW6 . . . . 155 C2
West Kensington
W14 . . . . 140 B4
Samuel Rhodes Sch
🈘 Finsbury Pk N7 . .5 B1
🈖 Islington N5 . . . .15 B3
N1 . . . . 85 B4
Samuel Richardson
Ho W14 . . . . 140 C3
Samuel's Cl 🈔 W6 . .39 B2
Samuel Rhodes Sch
🈖 SE11. . . . . 149 A2
Sancroft Ct SW11. 168 B4
Sancroft Ho SE11. 149 A2
Sancroft St SE11. . 149 A2
Sanctuary Mews 🈘
E8 . . . . 16 B2
Sanctuary St SE1 . 137 B4
Sanctuary The
🈕 Wapping E1. . . .32 A1
Westminster SW1. 133 C2
Sandall Cl N16. . . . . .6 C1
Sandall Ho 🈔 E3 . .26 A3
Sandall Rd NW5 . . . .13 B2
Sandalwood Cl 🈚
E1 . . . . 26 A1
Sandalwood Ho 🈘
NW3 . . . . 11 A2
Sandbourne
🈕 Kensington
W11 . . . . .31 C3
🈖 Paddington NW8. .78 B4
Sandbourne Rd
SE14 . . . . .50 C4
Sandbrook Rd N16. .7 A1
Sandby Ho
🈕 Camberwell
SE5 . . . . 49 A2
🈖 Kilburn NW6 . . . .23 C4
Sandell St SE1 . . . 135 B4
Sanderling Ct 🈳
SE8 . . . . 51 B4
Sanders Ho W.C1. . . .95 B4
Sanderson Cl
NW5 . . . . .13 A4
Sanderson Ho 🈘
SE10 . . . . .43 B1
Sanderstead Ave
NW2 . . . . 1 A2
Sanderstead Cl
SW12 . . . . .73 B4
Sanders Way 🈖
N19 . . . . .4 C3
Sandfield WC1 . . . . . .94 B3
Sandford Ct N16. . . .7 A3
Sandford Row
SE17 . . . . 151 C2
Sandford St SW6 156 B1
Sandgate Ho 🈛
E5 . . . . 17 A4
Sandgate La SW17,
SW18 . . . . .72 A3
Sandgate St SE15. . .50 A4
Sandgate Trad Est
SE15 . . . . .50 A4
Sandham Ct SW4. 172 B3

Sandhills The
SW10 . . . . 157 A4
Sandhurst Ct SW2. .62 A3
Sandhurst Ho 🈗
E1 . . . . 32 B4
Sandilands Rd
SW6 . . . . 166 A3
Sandison St SE15. . .64 C4
Sandland St WC1 107 A3
Sandlings Cl SE15. .50 A1
Sandmere Rd SW4 .62 A3
Sandon Ho 🈘
SW2 . . . . .74 A4
Sandow Ho 🈔
W4 . . . . 37 B1
Sandpiper Cl SE16. .41 B4
Sandpiper Ct
🈔 Cubitt Town
E14 . . . . .42 B3
🈚 SE8 . . . . .51 C3
Sandridge St 🈘
N19 . . . . .4 B2
Sandringham Cl 🈚
SW19 . . . . .69 C3
Sandringham Ct
Marylebone W1 . . . 105 A1
Putney SW15. . . . . . .57 C1
🈐 Rotherhithe
SE16 . . . . .32 C1
St John's Wood W9 .89 A3
Sandringham Flats
WC2 . . . . 119 C4
Sandringham Ho
Richmond TW10 . . . .54 C2
W14 . . . . 140 A4
Sandringham Rd
Dalston E8 . . . . .16 B3
Golders Green NW11. .1 A4
Willesden NW2 . . . . . .9 A2
Sandrock Rd SE13. .66 C4
SANDS END 59 B4
Sands End La
SW6 . . . . 166 B4
Sandstone TW9. . . . .44 C3
Sandstone Pl N19 . . .4 A2
Sandways 🈘 TW9 . .44 C2
Sandwell Cres 🈚
NW6 . . . . .10 C2
Sandwell Mans 🈘
NW6 . . . . .10 C2
Sandwich Ho
🈐 Rotherhithe
SE16 . . . . .40 B4
WC1 . . . . .94 A3
Sandwich St WC1. . .94 A3
Sandycombe Ctr
TW9 . . . . .54 C4
Sandycombe Rd
TW9 . . . . .44 C1
Sandy La N6 . . . . 4 A4
Sandy Rd NW3 . . . . . .2 A2
Sandy's Row E1 . . . 110 B3
Sanford La 🈙 N16. . .7 B2
Sanford St SE14,
SE8 . . . . 51 A4
Sanford Terr N16 . . .7 B1
Sanford Wlk
🈘 Stoke Newington
N16. . . . . .7 B2
Sangora Rd 🈗
SW11 . . . . .59 C3
San Ho 🈕 E9. . . . . .17 C2
Sankey Ho 🈔 E2 . . .25 B3
Sansom St
Camberwell SE5. . . .48 C2

Sansom St continued
SE5 . . . . 48 C3
Sans Wlk EC1 . . . . . .96 A2
Santley Ho SE1. . . 135 C3
Santley St SW4. . . . .62 B3
Santos Rd SW18. . . .58 C2
Sapcote Trad Ctr
NW10 . . . . .8 B2
Saperton Wlk 🈘
SE11 . . . . 149 A4
Sapperton Ct EC1 . .96 C2
Sapphire Ct 🈡
E1 . . . . 125 B4
Sapphire Rd SE8 . . .41 A2
Saracen's Head Yd
EC2 . . . . 110 B2
Saracen St E14. . . . .33 C3
Sarah Ho
Roehampton
SW15 . . . . .56 B3
🈐 Stepney E1. . . . .32 A3
Sarah Swift Ho
SE1 . . . . 137 C4
Sara Lane Ct 🈛
N1 . . . . 24 A3
Saratoga Rd E5 . . . .17 B4
Sardinia Ho W.C2 . 106 C1
Sardinia St WC2 . . 106 C2
Sarjant Path SW19. .69 C2
Sark Ho 🈘 N1 . . . . .15 B2
Sarnersfield Ho
SE15 . . . . .50 A4
Sarratt Ho 🈐 W10. .30 B4
Sarre Rd NW2 . . . . . .10 B3
Sarsden Bldgs
W1 . . . . 103 C1
Sarsfeld Rd SW12,
SW17 . . . . .72 B3
Sartor Rd SE15 . . . .65 C3
Sarum Hall Sch
NW3 . . . . 12 A1
Sarum Ho
W11 . . . . . . .31 B2 113 A3
Sassoon Ho SE15. . .50 B1
Satchwell Rd 🈖
E2 . . . . .24 C2 99 B3
Saturn Ho 🈗 E3 . . .26 C4
Saul Ct 🈙 SE15. . . .49 B4
Saunders Cl 🈔
E14 . . . . .33 B2
Saunders Ho 🈚
SW2 . . . . .74 C4
Saunders Ness Rd
E14 . . . . .42 C2
Saunders St SE11. 149 B4
Savage Gdns EC3. 124 B4
Savana N16 . . . . .7 A2
Savannah Cl 🈘
SE15 . . . . .49 B3
Savernake Ho N4. . . .6 C4
Savernake Rd
NW3 . . . . 12 B4
Saville Rd W4 . . . . . .37 C3
Saville Row W11. . . 118 C4
Savill Ho 🈘 SW4 . . .61 C1
Savona St SW8 . . . 160 C1
Savoy Circus W3 . . .29 B2
Savoy Ct
Earl's Ct SW5 . . . . . 141 C4
Strand WC2 . . . . . . 120 B3
Savoy Hill WC2 . . . 120 C3
Savoy Mews SW9. . .62 A4
Savoy Pier WC2 . . . 120 C3
Savoy Pl WC2. . . . . 120 C3

Savoy Row WC2 . . . . . **120** C4
Savoy St WC2 . . . . . . **120** C3
Savoy Stps WC2 . . . . **120** C3
Savoy Way WC2 . . . . **120** C3
Sawkins Cl SW19 . . . . 70 A2
Sawley Rd W12 . . . . . . 29 C1
Sawmill Yd E3 . . . . 26 A4
Sawyer St SE1 . . . . . . **136** C4
Saxby Rd SW2 . . . . . . 74 A4
Saxonbury Ct
16 Kentish Town
N7 . . . . 13 C3
2 Lower Holloway
N7 . . . . 14 A3
Saxoncroft Ho
SW16 . . . . 73 C1
Saxon Dr W3 . . . . 28 A4
Saxonfield Cl SW2 . . . 74 B4
Saxon Hall W2 . . . . . . **114** A3
Saxon Ho **4** SW4 . . . 61 C3
Saxon Rd E3 . . . . 26 B3
Saxton Cl SE13 . . . . . 67 C4
Sayer Ho SE4 . . . . 66 A3
Sayes Court St
SE8 . . . . 51 B4
Sayes Ct SE8 . . . . 51 B4
Scafell NW1 . . . . **92** C4
Scala St W1 . . . . **105** A4
Scampston Mews **5**
W10 . . . . 30 C3
Scandrett St **18**
E1 . . . . 32 A1
Scarba Wlk N1 . . . . . . 15 C2
Scarborough Rd N4 . 5 C3
Scarborough St
E1 . . . . **111** A1
Scarlet Cl E15 . . . . . . 19 A3
Scarlette Manor Wlk
10 SE24 . . . . 74 C4
Scarsbrook Ho **2**
SW2 . . . . 62 B2
Scarsdale Pl W8 . . . **128** A2
Scarsdale Villas
W8 . . . . **127** C1
Scarth Rd SW13 . . . . 56 B4
Scawen Rd SE8 . . . . . 41 A1
Scawfell St E2 . . . . . . 24 B3
Sceptre Ho **10** E1 . . . 25 B1
Sceptre Rd E2 . . . . . . 25 B2
Schiller Univ SE1 . . **121** B1
Schofield Wlk SE3 . . 53 C3
Sch of Pharmacy
WC1 . . . . **94** B2
Sch of the Islamic
Republic of Iran The
6 NW6 . . . . 23 C3
Scholars Ct **5** N19 . . 4 C4
Scholars Pl **1** N16 . . 7 A1
Scholars Rd SW12 . . 73 B3
Scholefield Rd N19 . . 4 C2
Scholey Ho SW11 . . . 60 A4
Schomberg Ho
SW1 . . . . **147** C4
Schonfeld Sq N16 . . . 6 C3
School App **2**
E2 . . . . 24 A2 **98** B4
Schoolbank Rd
SE10 . . . . 43 B2
School Bell Cloisters
17 E3 . . . . 26 A3
Schoolbell Mews **12**
E3 . . . . 26 A3
School Flats SW8 . . **172** A3
School Ho SE1 . . . . **152** A4

Schoolhouse La
E1 . . . . 32 C2
School of Economic
Science W1 . . . . . . **103** C2
School Rd NW10 . . . . 20 C1
School Sq SE10 . . . . . 43 B3
Schooner Cl
Cubitt Town E14 . . . . 42 C3
1 Rotherhithe
SE16 . . . . 40 C4
Schubert Rd SE15 . . . 50 B1
Science Mus SW7 **129** B1
Sclater St
E1 . . . . 24 B1 **99** A2
Scoles Cres SW2 . . . 74 C3
Scoresby St SE1 . . . **122** A1
Scorton Ho **2** N1 . . . 24 A3
Scotch Ho SW1 . . . . **130** C3
Scoter Ct **28** SE8 . . . 51 B4
Scotia Bldg **10** E1 . . 32 C2
Scotia Ct **3** SE16 . . 40 B3
Scotia Rd **2** SW2 . . 74 C4
Scotland Pl SW1 . . . **120** A1
Scotney Ho E9 . . . . . . 17 B2
Scotson Ho SE11 . . . **149** B3
Scotswood St EC1 . . **95** C2
Scott Ave SW15,
SW18 . . . . 58 A1
Scott Ellis Gdns
NW8 . . . . **89** B3
Scott Ho
2 Barnsbury N7 . . . 14 B2
Islington N1 . . . . **87** B4
Lisson Gr NW8 . . . . . **90** A1
17 Millwall E14 . . . . 41 C4
Scott Lidgett Cres
SE16 . . . . **139** C3
Scotts Ct **6** W12 . . . 39 A4
Scott's Rd W12 . . . . . 39 A4
Scott's Sufferance
Wharf SE1 . . . . **139** A3
Scott St E1 . . . . 25 A1
Scott's Yd EC4 . . . . . **123** B4
Scoulding Ho **2**
E14 . . . . 41 C3
Scoulding Rd E16 . . . 35 C3
Scouler St E14 . . . . . . 34 C2
Scout App NW10 . . . . 8 A4
Scout La SW4 . . . . . . 61 B4
Scovell Cres SE1 . . . **136** C3
Scovell Rd SE1 . . . . **136** C3
Scrimgeour Pl N4 . . . 5 B2
Scriven Ct **5** E8 . . . . 24 B4
Scriven St E8 . . . . 24 B4
Scrooby St SE6 . . . . . 67 A1
Scrope Bldg EC1 . . . **107** B4
Scrubs La NW10, W10,
W12 . . . . 22 A1
Scrutton Cl SW12 . . . 73 C4
Scrutton St
EC2 . . . . 24 A1 **98** A1
Scutari Rd SE22 . . . . 65 B2
Scylla Rd SE15 . . . . . 65 A4
Seabright St **27**
E2 . . . . 25 A2
Seacole Cl W3 . . . . . . 28 C4
Seacon Twr **8**
E14 . . . . 41 C4
Seaford Ho **13**
SE16 . . . . 40 B4
Seaford St WC1 . . . . **94** B3

Seaforth Cres N5 . . . 15 B3
Seaforth Lo **2**
SW13 . . . . 46 B1
Seaforth Pl SW1 . . . **133** A2
Seager Pl E3 . . . . 33 B4
Seagrave Cl **5** E1 . . . 32 C4
Seagrave Lo SW6 . . **155** C4
Seagrave Rd SW6 . . **155** C4
Seagrove Cl E1 . . . . . 32 C4
Seagull La E16 . . . . . . 35 C2
Seal Ho SE1 . . . . **137** C2
SEA LIFE London
Aquarium SE1 . . . . **134** C3
Seal St E8 . . . . 16 B4
Searle Pl N4 . . . . 5 B3
Searles Cl SW11 . . . **158** B1
Searles Rd SE1 . . . . **151** C4
Searson Ho SE17 . . **150** B3
Sears St SE5 . . . . 48 C3
Seasalter Ho **1**
SW9 . . . . **173** B4
Seaton Cl SW15 . . . . 69 A4
Seaton Point E5 . . . . 16 C4
Seavington Ho **3**
SE5 . . . . 48 B1
Sebastian Ho **22**
N1 . . . . 24 A3
Sebastian St EC1 . . . **96** B3
Sebbon St N1 . . . . . . 15 A1
Sebright Ho **22** E2 . . 24 C3
Sebright Pas **30**
E2 . . . . 24 C3
Sebright Sch **30** . . . . .
Secker Ho SW9 . . . . . 48 A1
Secker St SE1 . . . . . **121** B1
Second Ave
East Acton W3 . . . . . . 29 B1
Kensal Town W10 . . . 23 A1
Mortlake SW14 . . . . . 56 A4
Sedan Way SE17 . . . **152** A2
Sedding St SW1 . . . **145** B4
Seddon Ho EC2 . . . . **109** A4
Seddon St WC1 . . . . **95** A3
Sedgeford Rd
W12 . . . . 29 B1
Sedgewick Ho
SW19 . . . . 69 C2
Sedgley Ho N4 . . . . . . 5 B2
Sedgmoor Pl SE5 . . . 49 A3
Sedgwick St E9 . . . . . 17 C3
Sedleigh Rd SW18 . . 58 B1
Sedlescombe Rd
SW6 . . . . **155** B4
Sedley Ho SE11 . . . . **149** A2
Sedley Pl W1 . . . . . . **104** A1
Seething La EC3 . . . **124** B4
Sefton St SW15 . . . . . 57 B4
Sekforde St EC1 . . . . **96** A2
Selbie Ave NW10 . . . . 8 B3
Selborne **2** SW11 . . 60 C4
Selborne Ho
SE1 . . . . **137** B3
Selborne Rd **1**
SE5 . . . . 48 C1
Selby Ho **10** SW4 . . . 61 B1
Selby Sq **11** W10 . . . 23 A2
Selby St E1 . . . . 25 C1
Selden Ho **2** SE15 . . 50 B1
Selden Rd SE15 . . . . 50 B1
Selden Wlk N7 . . . . . . 5 B2
Seldon Ho
Nine Elms SW8 . . . . **160** C1
Pimlico SW1 . . . . . . **146** C1
Selhurst Cl SW19 . . . 69 C3
Selina Ho NW8 . . . . . **89** C2

Selkirk Ho
N1 . . . . **84** C4
3 Stoke Newington
N16 . . . . 7 A1
Sellons Ave NW10 . . . 21 B4
Selma Ho **7** W12 . . . 30 A3
Selman Ho **9** E9 . . . 18 A2
Selsdon Way E14 . . . 42 A3
Selsea Pl N16 . . . . . . 16 A3
Selsey St E14 . . . . . . 33 C4
Selway Ho SW8 . . . **172** B4
Selwood Ho **10** N4 . . 6 B4
Selwood Pl SW7 . . . **143** B2
Selwood Terr
SW7 . . . . **143** B2
Selworthy Ho
SW11 . . . . **167** C4
Selwyn Ave TW9 . . . . 54 B4
Selwyn Ct **3**
TW10 . . . . 54 B2
Selwyn Ho **2**
SW15 . . . . 57 C1
Selwyn Rd
Bow E3 . . . . 26 B3
Willesden NW10 . . . . . 8 A1
Semley Gate E9 . . . . 18 B2
Semley Ho SW1 . . . **146** A3
Semley Pl SW1 . . . . **146** A3
Senate St SE15 . . . . . 50 B1
Senators Lo **3** E3 . . 26 A3
Sendall Ct **7**
SW11 . . . . 59 C4
Senior St W2 . . . . . . **100** A4
Senrab St E1 . . . . 32 C3
Sentamu Cl **5**
SE24 . . . . 75 A3
Seraph Ct EC1 . . . . . **96** C4
Serenaders Rd **20**
SW9 . . . . **173** B1
Sergeant Ind Est The
SW18 . . . . 59 A1
Serica Ct **14** SE10 . . 52 B3
Serjeants' Inn
EC4 . . . . **107** C1
Serlby Ct W14 . . . . . **126** C2
Serle St WC2 . . . . . . **107** A2
Sermon La EC4 . . . . **108** C1
Serpentine Ct **10**
SE16 . . . . 40 C4
Serpentine Gallery
W2 . . . . **129** C4
Serpentine Rd
W2 . . . . **116** C1
Serpentine Sackler
Gallery W2 . . . . . . **116** A3
Serpentine The
W2 . . . . **116** B1
Service Route No 1
E15 . . . . 19 C1
Service Route No 2 **1**
E15 . . . . 19 C1
Service Route No 3 **2**
E15 . . . . 19 C1
Servite Ho SE13 . . . . 52 A2
Servite RC Prim Sch
SW10 . . . . **156** C4
Setchell Rd SE1 . . . . **152** C4
Setchell Way SE1 . . . **152** C4
Seth St **29** SE16 . . . 40 B4
Settlers Ct **11** E14 . . 34 C2
Settles St E1 . . . . . . **111** C2
Settrington Rd
SW6 . . . . **166** A1
Seven Dials WC2 . . . **106** A1
Seven Islands L Ctr
SE16 . . . . 40 B3

Seven Mills Prim Sch
7 E14 . . . . 41 C4
Sevenoaks Rd SE4 . . 66 B1
Seven Sisters Rd
Finsbury Pk N4 . . . . . 6 A2
Stoke Newington N4, N7,
N15 . . . . 6 B4
Seven Stars Cnr
W12 . . . . 38 C3
Seven Stars Yd
E1 . . . . **111** A4
Severnake Cl E14 . . . 41 C2
Severn Ave **2**
W10 . . . . 23 A2
Severn Way NW10 . . . 8 B3
Severus Rd SW11 . . . 60 A3
Seville Ho **10** E1 . . . **125** C1
Seville Mews N1 . . . . 16 A1
Seville St SW1 . . . . . **131** A3
Sevington St W9 . . . . **88** A1
Seward St EC1 . . . . . **96** C3
Sewardstone Rd
E2 . . . . 25 B3
Sewell Ho **7** N16 . . . 16 A3
Sextant Ave E14 . . . . 42 C2
Sexton Ct **7** E14 . . . 34 C2
Sexton's Ho **5**
SE13 . . . . 52 B4
Seymour Ct
Putney SW15 . . . . . . 57 A3
Upper Clapton N16 . . . 7 C3
Seymour Gdns
SE4 . . . . 66 A4
Seymour Ho
Bloomsbury WC1 . . . **94** A2
1 Clapham SW8 . . **171** A2
Somers Town NW1 . . **93** C3
Seymour Mews
W1 . . . . **103** B2
Seymour Pl W1 . . . . **102** C2
Seymour Rd
Acton W4 . . . . 37 B2
Wandsworth SW18 . . 58 B1
Wimbledon SW19 . . . 69 C1
Seymour St W1 . . . . **103** A1
Seymour Wlk
SW10 . . . . **156** C4
Seyssel St E14 . . . . . 42 B2
Shaa Rd W3 . . . . 28 C2
Shabana Ct **3**
W12 . . . . 30 A1
Shacklewell Ct
5 Dulwich SE21 . . . 75 C2
2 Isle of Dogs E14 . 41 C1
4 Shepherd's Bush
W12 . . . . 39 A4
Shackleton Ho
E1 . . . . 32 B1
SHACKLEWELL 16 B4
Shacklewell Ho **3**
E8 . . . . 16 B4
Shacklewell La E8 . . 16 B3
Shacklewell Prim Sch
5 E8 . . . . 16 B4
Shacklewell Rd
N16 . . . . 16 B4
Shacklewell Row
E8 . . . . 16 B4
Shacklewell St **10**
E2 . . . . 24 B2 **99** A3
Shad Thames SE1 **139** A4
SHADWELL 32 B2
Shadwell Gdns E1 . . 32 B2
Shadwell Pierhead
E1 . . . . 32 B2
Shadwell Pl **1** E1 . . 32 B2

Shadwell Sta E1 . . . . 32 A2
Shaftesbury Ave
W1 . . . . 119 C4
Shaftesbury Ct
  Borough The SE1 . . . 137 B2
  1 Herne Hill SE5 . . . 63 C3
  Shoreditch N1 . . . . . 87 B1
  Streatham SW16 . . . . 73 C1
Shaftesbury Ctr
SW10 . . . . 22 C1
Shaftesbury Gdns
NW10 . . . . 21 A1
Shaftesbury Ho
  11 Canning Town
  E16 . . . . 35 B3
  13 Stoke Newington
  N16 . . . . 7 A1
  W2 . . . . 114 B4
Shaftesbury Lo 9
E14 . . . . 34 A3
Shaftesbury Mews
  8 Clapham Pk
  SW4 . . . . 61 B2
  W8 . . . . 127 C1
Shaftesbury Park
Chambers 1
SW11 . . . . 60 C4
Shaftesbury Rd
  Finsbury Pk N4,
  N19 . . . . 5 A3
  Richmond TW9 . . . . . 54 A4
Shaftesbury St N1 . . . 87 B1
Shafteswood Ct
SW17 . . . . 72 B1
Shafto Mews
SW1 . . . . 131 A1
Shafton Rd E9 . . . . . . 25 C4
Shaftsbury Park Prim
  Sch 18 SW11 . . . . . 169 B1
Shafts Ct EC3 . . . . . . 110 A1
Shahjalal Ho 10
E2 . . . . 24 C3
Shakespeare Ave 7
NW10 . . . . 20 C4
Shakespeare Ho 8
E9 . . . . 17 B1
Shakespeare Rd
  Acton W3 . . . . 28 B3
  Brixton SE24 . . . . . . 63 A3
  Stonebridge NW10 . . 20 C4
Shakespeare's Globe
Theatre (site of)
SE1 . . . . 123 A2
Shakespeare Twr
EC2 . . . . 109 A4
Shakspeare Mews 7
N16 . . . . 16 A4
Shakspeare Wlk
N16 . . . . 16 A4
Shalbourne Sq E9 . . . 18 B2
Shalcomb St
SW10 . . . . 157 A3
Shalden Ho SW15 . . . 56 B1
Shalfleet Dr W10 . . . . 30 C2
Shalford Ho SE1 . . . . 137 C2
Shalford Ct N1 . . . . . . 86 A2
Shalford Ho SE1 . . . . 137 C2
Shalimar Gdns W3 . . . 28 B2
Shalimar Lo W3 . . . . . 28 B2
Shalimar Rd W3 . . . . . 28 B2
Shalstone Rd SW14,
TW9 . . . . 55 A4
Shamrock St SW4 . . . 61 C4
Shandon Ct SE4 . . . . 51 A1
Shandon Rd SW4 . . . . 61 B1
Shand St SE1 . . . . . . 138 B4

Shandy St E1 . . . . 25 C1
Shan Ho WC1 . . . . 94 C1
Shannon Ct
  11 Peckham SE15 . . . 49 B3
  Stoke Newington
  N16 . . . . 7 A1
  Willesden NW10 . . . . 8 C2
Shannon Gr SW9 . . . . 62 B3
Shannon Pl NW8 . . . . 80 B2
Shanti Ct SW18 . . . . . 70 C3
Shapla Prim Sch 25
E1 . . . . 125 C3
Shardcroft Ave
SE24 . . . . 63 A2
Shardeloes Rd
SE14 . . . . 51 B1
Shard's Sq SE15 . . . . 49 C4
Shard The SE1 . . . . . 123 C1
Sharebourne Ho
SW2 . . . . 62 C2
Sharman Ho 10
E14 . . . . 34 B3
Sharnbrook Ho
W6 . . . . 155 B4
Sharon Gdns E9 . . . . 25 B4
Sharon Rd W4 . . . . . . 37 C1
Sharp Ho SW8 . . . . . . 61 A4
Sharples Hall St 8
NW1 . . . . 12 B1
Sharpness Ct 2
SE15 . . . . 49 B3
Sharratt St SE15 . . . . 50 B4
Sharsted St SE17 . . . 150 A1
Sharwood WC1 . . . . . 85 A1
Shaver's Pl SW1 . . . . 119 B3
Shawbury Ct SE22 . . . 64 B2
Shawbury Rd SE22 . . . 64 B2
Shaw Cres E14 . . . . . . 33 A3
Shaw Ct
  5 Acton Green
  W3 . . . . 37 B3
  11 Battersea SW11 . . 59 C4
  Upper Holloway N19 . . 5 A2
Shawfield St SW3 . . . 144 B1
Shawford Ct 9
SW15 . . . . 68 C4
Shaw Rd SE22 . . . . . . 64 A3
Shearling Way N7 . . . 14 A2
Shearsmith Ho 18
E1 . . . . 125 C4
Shearwater Ct 24
SE8 . . . . 51 B4
Sheba Pl E1 . . 24 B1 99 A1
Sheen Common Dr
SW14, TW10 . . . . 54 C2
Sheen Court Rd
TW10 . . . . 54 C3
Sheen Ct TW10 . . . . . 54 C3
Sheendale Rd
TW9 . . . . 54 B3
Sheen Gate Gdns
SW14 . . . . 55 B3
Sheengate Mans
SW14 . . . . 55 C3
Sheen Gr N1 . . . . 85 B4
Sheen La SW14 . . . . . 55 B3
Sheen Mount Prim
  Sch SW14 . . . . 55 A2
Sheen Pk TW10,
TW9 . . . . 54 B3
Sheen Rd TW10,
TW9 . . . . 54 B3
Sheen Wood
SW14 . . . . 55 B2
Sheepcote La
SW11 . . . . 169 A1

Sheep La E8 . . . . 25 A4
Sheffield Ho 16
SE15 . . . . 49 B2
Sheffield Sq 2 E3 . . 26 B2
Sheffield St WC2 . . . 106 C1
Sheffield Terr
W8 . . . . . 31 C1 113 C1
Shelbourne Ho 10
SW2 . . . . 57 C2
Shelburne Ct
SW15 . . . . 57 C2
Shelburne Rd N7 . . . . 14 B4
Shelbury Rd SE22 . . . 65 A2
Sheldon Ct SW8 . . . . 162 A1
Sheldon Ho 6 N1 . . . 15 B2
Sheldon Pl E2 . . . . . . 25 A3
Sheldon Rd NW2 . . . . 9 C4
Sheldon Sq W2 . . . . . 101 A3
Sheldrake Ho 16
SE16 . . . . 40 C2
Sheldrake Pl W8 . . . . 127 B4
Shelduck Ct 27
SE8 . . . . 51 B4
Shelford Pl N16 . . . . . 6 C1
Shelgate Rd SW11 . . . 60 B2
Shell Ctr SE1 . . . . . . 121 A1
Shelley Cl SE15 . . . . 50 A1
Shelley Ct
  Finsbury Pk N4 . . . . 5 B3
  SW3 . . . . 159 A4
Shelley Ho
  21 Bethnal Green
  E2 . . . . 25 B2
  Chelsea SW1 . . . . . 160 C4
  5 Stoke Newington
  N16 . . . . 16 A4
  Walworth SE17 . . . . 151 A2
Shelley Rd NW10 . . . . 20 C4
Shellgrove Rd 1
N16 . . . . 16 A3
Shell Rd SE13 . . . . . . 67 A4
Shellwood Rd
SW11 . . . . 168 C1
Shelmerdine Cl
E3 . . . . 33 C4
Shelton St WC2 . . . . 106 A1
Shene Bldg EC1 . . . . 107 B4
Shenfield St N1 . . . . . 24 A3
Shenley Rd SE5 . . . . 49 A2
Shepard Ho 17
SW11 . . . . 59 C4
Sheperdess Pl N1 . . . 97 A4
Shepherd Cl W1 . . . . 117 B4
Shepherdess Wlk
N1 . . . . 87 A1
Shepherd Ho
  Barnsbury N7 . . . . . 14 A2
  10 Poplar E14 . . . . . 34 A3
Shepherd Mkt
W1 . . . . 118 A1
SHEPHERD'S
BUSH 30 B1
Shepherd's Bush Gn
W12 . . . . 39 B4
Shepherd's Bush
  Market W12 . . . . . . 39 B4
Shepherd's Bush Mkt
  Sta W12 . . . . 30 B1
Shepherd's Bush
  Overground Sta
  W12 . . . . 39 C4
Shepherd's Bush Pl
W12 . . . . 39 C4
Shepherd's Bush Rd
W6 . . . . 39 B3

Shepherd's Bush Sta
W12 . . . . 39 C4
Shepherds Ct 8
W12 . . . . 39 C4
Shepherd's La E2 . . . 25 C3
Shepherds Pl W1 . . . 117 B4
Shepherd St W1 . . . . 118 A1
Shepherd's Wlk
NW3 . . . . 11 C4
Sheppard Dr SE16 . . . 40 A1
Sheppard Ho
  13 Hackney E2 . . . . 24 C3
  8 Streatham SW2 . . 74 C3
Shepperton Rd N1 . . 87 B4
Sheppey Ho E5 . . . . . 17 A4
Shepton Hos SW11 . . 167 C4
Shepton Hos 11
SW11 . . . . 167 C4
Sherard Ct N19 . . . . . 5 A1
Sherard Ho 21 E9 . . 17 B1
Sheraton Ho SW1 . . . 160 B4
Sheraton St W1 . . . . 105 B1
Sherborne Ho
  Pimlico SW1 . . . . . 146 B2
  South Lambeth
  SW8 . . . . 162 C1
Sherborne La EC4 . . 123 C4
Sherborne St N1 . . . . 87 B4
Sherbrooke Ho 6
E2 . . . . 25 B3
Sherbrooke Rd
SW6 . . . . 154 B1
Sherbrooke Terr
SW6 . . . . 154 B1
Shere Ho SE1 . . . . . . 137 B2
Sherfield Gdns
SW15 . . . . 56 B1
Sheridan Bldgs
WC2 . . . . 106 B1
Sheridan Ct
  Earl's Ct SW5 . . . . . 142 A3
  South Hampstead
  NW6 . . . . 11 B1
  South Lambeth
  SW9 . . . . 173 A3
Sheridan Ho
  SE11 . . . . 149 C3
  7 Stoke Newington
  N16 . . . . 7 A1
Sheridan Pl SW13 . . . 56 B4
Sheridan St 2 E1 . . 32 A3
Sheringdale Prim Sch
SW18 . . . . 70 B3
Sheringham NW8 . . . 79 C4
Sheringham Ho
NW1 . . . . 102 B4
Sheringham Mews 4
SW18 . . . . 71 B2
Sheringham Rd
N7 . . . . 14 C2
Sherlock Ct NW8 . . . 79 B4
Sherlock Holmes Mus
W1 . . . . 91 A1
Sherlock Mews
W1 . . . . 103 B4
Sherren Ho 16 E1 . . 25 B1
Sherrick Green Rd
NW10 . . . . 9 A3
Sherriff Ct NW6 . . . . 10 C2
Sherriff Rd NW6 . . . . 10 C2
Sherrin Rd E10 . . . . . 19 A4
Sherston Ct
  Finsbury WC1 . . . . . 95 B3
  Newington SE1 . . . . 150 B4

Sha–Sho 271

Sherwin Ho 1
SE11 . . . . 163 B4
Sherwin Rd SE14 . . . 50 C2
Sherwood NW6 . . . . . 10 A1
Sherwood Cl
SW13 . . . . 57 A4
Sherwood Ct
  1 Battersea
  SW11 . . . . 59 B4
  St Johns SE13 . . . . 52 A1
  W1 . . . . 102 C3
Sherwood Gdns
  Bermondsey SE16 . . 40 A1
  Millwall E14 . . . . . . 41 C2
Sherwood Ho N4 . . . . 6 B4
Sherwood St W1 . . . 119 A4
Shetland Rd E3 . . . . . 26 B3
Shillaker Ct W3 . . . . . 29 B1
Shillibeer Pl W1 . . . . 102 B3
Shillingford Ho 40
E3 . . . . 27 A2
Shillingford St 23
N1 . . . . 15 A1
Shillingstone Ho
W14 . . . . 126 B1
Shinfield St W12 . . . . 30 B3
Shipka Rd SW12 . . . . 73 A3
Ship La SW14 . . . . . . 45 B1
Shiplake Ho 48
E2 . . . . 24 B2 98 C3
Shipley Ho 32
SW8 . . . . 171 B1
Ship & Mermaid Row
SE1 . . . . 138 A4
Ship St SE8 . . . . 51 C2
Ship Tavern Pas
EC3 . . . . 124 A4
Shipton Ho
  7 Camden Town
  NW5 . . . . 12 C2
  14 Haggerston E2 . . 24 B3
Shipton St
E2 . . . . 24 B2 99 A4
Shipwright Rd
SE16 . . . . 41 A3
Shipwright Yd
SE1 . . . . 124 A1
Shirburt St E14 . . . . . 34 A2
Shire Pl SW18 . . . . . . 71 B4
Shirland Mews
W9 . . . . 23 B2
Shirland Rd W9 . . . . . 23 C1
Shirley Gr SW11 . . . . 60 C4
Shirley Ho 19 SE5 . . 48 C3
Shirley Rd W4 . . . . . . 37 C4
Shirley St E16 . . . . . . 35 B3
Shirlock Rd NW3 . . . . 12 B4
Shoe La EC4 . . . . . . 107 C2
Shooters Hill Rd SE3,
SE10 . . . . 53 A2
Shoot-Up Hill
NW2 . . . . 10 A2
Shopstop SW11 . . . . 60 A3
Shore Bsns Ctr 31
E9 . . . . 17 B1
SHOREDITCH 87 C1
Shoreditch Ct 2
E8 . . . . 16 B1
Shoreditch High St
E1 . . . . 24 A1 98 B2
Shoreditch High St
Sta E1 . . . . 24 A1

Shoreham Cl
SW18 . . . . .59 A2
Shore Ho SW8 . . . . . .61 A4
Shore Mews [30] E9. .17 B1
Shore Pl E9 . . . . .17 B1
Shore Rd E9 . . . . .17 B1
Shorncliffe Rd
SE1 . . . . .152 C2
Shorrolds Rd
SW6 . . . . .155 A2
Shortcroft Mead Ct
NW10 . . . . .8 B3
Shorter St EC3 . . . .125 A4
Shortlands W6 . . . . . .39 C2
Short Rd W4 . . . . .46 A4
Shorts Gdns WC2 .106 A1
Short St SE1 . . . . . .135 C4
Shottendane Rd
SW6 . . . . .165 B4
Shottfield Ave
SW14 . . . . .56 A3
Shottsford [1] W11. .31 C3
**Shoulder of Mutton
Alley** [16] E14 . . . . . . .33 A2
Shouldham St
W1 . . . . .102 B3
Shrek's Adventure!
London SE1 . . . . .134 C3
Shrewsbury Ho [2]
N19 . . . . .4 C4
Shrewsbury Ave
SW14 . . . . .55 C3
Shrewsbury Cres
NW10 . . . . .20 C4
Shrewsbury Ho
Chelsea SW3 . . . . . .158 A3
Kennington SE11 .163 A3
Shrewsbury Mews [8]
W2 . . . . .31 C4
Shrewsbury Rd
Notting Hill W2 . . .31 C3
[9] *Stonebridge*
NW10 . . . . .20 C4
Shrewsbury St
W10 . . . . .22 B1
Shropshire Ho
WC1 . . . . .93 A1
Shroton St NW1 . . .102 B4
Shrubbery Cl N1 . . . .87 A3
Shrubland Rd E8 . . .24 C4
Shrubs Ho SW1 . . .147 C3
Shurland Gdns
SE15 . . . . .49 B3
Shushan Cl [4] N16 . .7 A4
Shuters Sq W14 . . .140 C1
Shuttle St
E1 . . . . .24 C1 99 B1
Shuttleworth Rd
SW11 . . . . .168 A2
Sibella Rd SW4 . . . .171 C1
Sicilian Ave WC1 . .106 B3
Sidbury St SW6 . . .164 A4
Siddons Ct WC2 . . .106 C1
Siddons Ho [8]
NW3 . . . . .12 B3
Siddons La NW1 . . . .91 A1
Sidford Ho SE1 . . . .135 A1
Sidford Pl SE1 . . . . .135 A1
Sidgwick Ho [28]
SW9 . . . . .172 B1
Sidings Mews N7. . .14 C4
Sidlaw Ho N16 . . . . . .7 B3

Sidmouth Ho
[18] *Camberwell*
SE15 . . . . .49 C3
Marylebone W1 . . .102 B2
[26] *Streatham* SW2 .74 C4
Sidmouth Mews
WC1 . . . . .94 C3
Sidmouth Par NW2 . .9 B1
Sidmouth Rd NW2 . . .9 B1
Sidmouth St WC1 . . .94 C3
Sidney Boyd Ct
NW6 . . . . .10 C1
**Sidney Godley (VC)
Ho** [11] E2 . . . . .25 B2
Sidney Gr EC1 . . . . . .86 A1
Sidney Ho [2] E2. . . .25 C3
Sidney Miller Ct [8]
W3 . . . . .28 A1
Sidney Rd SW9 . . . .173 A1
Sidney Sq E1 . . . . . . .32 B4
Sidney St E1 . . . . . . .32 B4
Sidworth St [6] E8 . .17 A1
Siebert Rd SE3 . . . . .53 C4
Siege Ho [4] E1 . . . . .32 A3
Sienna Pl [1] SE23 . .66 A1
Sigdon Rd E8 . . . . . . .16 C3
Signal Ho
[9] *London* E8 . . . . .17 A1
SE1 . . . . .136 C3
Sigismunds Yd
NW1 . . . . .82 B3
Silbury Ho [8]
SE26 . . . . .76 C1
Silbury St N1 . . . . . . .97 B4
Silchester Rd W10. .30 C3
Silesia Bldgs E8 . . .17 A1
Silex St SE1 . . . . . .136 B3
Silkin Mews [24]
SE15 . . . . .49 C4
Silk Mews SE11 . . .149 C1
Silk Mills Path
SE13 . . . . .67 B4
Silk Mills Sq E9 . . . .18 B2
Silk St EC2 . . . . .109 A4
Sillitoe Ho N1 . . . . . .87 C3
Silsoe Ho NW1 . . . . .82 B1
Silverbirch Wlk [1]
NW3 . . . . .12 C2
Silverburn Ho [4]
SW9 . . . . .48 A2
Silver Cl SE14 . . . . . .51 A3
Silver Cres W4 . . . . .37 A2
Silver Ct N19 . . . . .4 B1
Silverdale NW1 . . . . .92 C4
Silverdale Ct EC1 . . .96 B2
Silvermere Rd SE6. .67 A1
Silver Pl W1 . . . . . . .119 A4
Silver Rd
Shepherd's Bush
W12 . . . . .30 C2
St Johns SE13 . . . . .67 A4
Silver Wlk
SE16 . . . . .33 B1
Silvertown Way
E16 . . . . .35 C2
Silver Wlk SE16 . . . .33 B1
Silverwood Pl [6]
SE10 . . . . .52 B2
Silvester Ho
[27] *Bethnal Green*
E2 . . . . .25 B2
[1] *Notting Hill* W11 . .31 B3
[6] *Stepney* E1 . . . . .32 A3

Silvester Rd SE22. . .64 B2
Silvester St SE1 . . .137 B3
Silwex Ho
E1 . . . . .24 B1 98 C1
Silwood St SE16. . . .40 B1
Simla Ho SE1 . . . . .137 C3
Simmonds Ct
SW5 . . . . .142 A3
Simmons Ho
[20] *Bethnal Green*
E2 . . . . .24 C2 99 B3
Finsbury Pk N7 . . . .5 B2
Simms Ct SW6 . . . . .58 A4
Simms Rd SE1 . . . .153 C3
Simon Cl
W11 . . . . .31 B2 113 A4
Simon Ct W9 . . . . . . .23 C2
Simon Lo [31] SW19 .69 C3
**Simon Marks Jewish
Prim Sch** N16 . . . . . .7 B2
Simons Wlk E15 . . . .19 C3
Simpson Dr W3 . . . .28 C3
Simpson Ho
Lisson Gr NW8 . . . .90 A3
Vauxhall SE11 . . . .149 A1
Simpson's Rd E14 . .34 A2
Simpson St SW11 . .168 A1
Sinclair Ct N5 . . . . .15 B2
Sinclair Gdns W14. .39 C4
Sinclair Ho [9]
SW12 . . . . .73 C3
Sinclair Ho *Sch*
SW6 . . . . .164 B4
Sinclair Mans [13]
W12 . . . . .39 C4
Sinclair Pl SE4 . . . . .66 C1
Sinclair Rd W14 . . .126 A2
Sinclairs Ho [18] E3. .26 B3
Singer Mews
SW4 . . . . .172 A1
Singer St EC2 . . . . . .97 C3
Sion Ho SE13 . . . . . .67 B3
**Sion-Manning RC Sch
for Girls**
[16] *Kensal Town*
W10 . . . . .31 A4
[9] *North Kensington*
W10 . . . . .30 C4
**Sir Abraham Dawes
Cotts** SW15. . . . . . . .58 A3
Sir Alexander Cl
W3 . . . . .29 B1
Sir Alexander Rd
W3 . . . . .29 B1
Sirdar Rd
W11 . . . . .31 A2 112 A3
**Sir Francis Drake
Prim Sch** [1] SE8. .41 A1
Sirinham Point
SW8 . . . . .163 A3
Sirius Bldg [1] E14. .34 B2
**Sir John Cass
Foundation &
Redcoat CE Sec Sch**
[19] E1 . . . . .32 C4
**Sir John Cass's
Foundation Prim
Sch** E3 . . . . .110 B1
Sir John Kirk Cl [5]
SE5 . . . . .48 B3
**Sir John Lillie Prim
Sch** SW6 . . . . .154 B3
Sir John Soane's Mus
WC2 . . . . .106 C2

**Sir Oswald Stoll
Foundation The**
SW6 . . . . .156 A2
Sir Thomas Abney
Prim Sch N16 . . . . . .6 C3
Sir Thomas More Est
SW3 . . . . .157 C3
Sir William Burrough
Prim Sch [27] E14. .33 B3
**Sir William Powell's
Almshos** SW6 . . . . .58 A4
Sise La EC4 . . . . .109 B1
Siskin Ho [20] SE16 . .40 C2
Sispara Gdns
SW18 . . . . .58 B1
Sissinghurst Ho [17]
SE15 . . . . .50 B4
Sister Mabel's Way [18]
SE15 . . . . .49 C3
Sistova Rd SW12 . . .73 A3
Sisulu Pl SW9 . . . . . .62 C4
Sitarey Ct [4] W12 . .30 A1
**Site of Changing of
the Guard** SW1 . . .132 C3
Sivill Ho [1]
E2 . . . . .24 B2 99 A4
Siward Rd SW17. . . .71 B1
Six Bridges Ind Est [8]
SE1 . . . . .153 C1
Sixth Ave W10 . . . . . .23 A2
Skardu Rd NW2 . . . .10 A3
Skeena Hill SW18,
SW19 . . . . .70 A4
Skeggs Ho [5] E14 . .42 B3
Skegness Ho [3]
N7 . . . . .14 B1
Skelbrook St
SW18 . . . . .71 B2
Skelgill Rd SW15 . . .58 B3
Skelton Cl [7] E8. . . .16 B2
Skelton Ho N16 . . . .16 A3
Skelwith Rd W6 . . . .47 B4
Skenfrith Ho SE15 . .50 A4
Sketchley Gdns
SE16 . . . . .40 C1
Skiffington Cl
SW2 . . . . .74 C3
Skinner Pl SW1 . . . .145 B3
Skinners' Acad [10]
N4 . . . . .6 B4
**Skinners Company
Sch (Upper)** [10]
N16 . . . . .7 B4
Skinners La EC4 . . .123 A4
Skinner St EC1 . . . . .95 C2
Skipsea Ho SW18. . .59 C1
Skipton Ho SE4 . . . .66 A3
Skipwith Bldg
EC1 . . . . .107 B4
Skipworth Rd E9 . . .25 B4
Skua Ct [33] SE8 . . . .51 B4
Skyline Ct SE1 . . . .138 C1
Skyline Plaza Bldg [19]
E1 . . . . .111 C2
Skylines E14 . . . . . . .42 B4
Slade Ct NW2 . . . . . .10 A3
Sladen Pl [25] E5. . . .17 A4
Slagrove Pl SE13 . . .67 A2
Slaidburn St
SW10 . . . . .157 A3
Slaithwaite Rd
SE13 . . . . .67 B3
Slaney Ct NW10 . . . . .9 B1
Slaney Pl [7] N7 . . . . .14 C3
Sleaford Ho [16] E3. .26 C1

Sleaford Ind Est
SW8 . . . . .161 A3
Sleaford St SW8. . .161 A1
Slee Ho [3] E3 . . . . . . .26 B3
Slievemore Cl [3]
SW4 . . . . .61 C4
Sligo Ho [8] E1 . . . . .25 C1
Slingsby Pl WC2. . .120 A4
Slippers Pl SE16 . . . .40 A3
Slipway Ho [1] E14. .42 A1
Sloane Ave SW1 . . .144 B3
Sloane Avenue Mans
SW1 . . . . .144 C3
Sloane Ct E SW3 . . .145 B2
Sloane Ct W SW3 . .145 B2
Sloane Gate Mans
SW1 . . . . .145 B4
Sloane Gdns SW1 .145 B3
Sloane Ho [7] E9 . . . .17 B1
Sloane Sq SW1 . . . .145 B3
Sloane Square Sta
SW1 . . . . .145 B3
Sloane St SW1 . . . .131 A1
Sloane Terr SW1 . . .145 B4
Sloane Terr Mans
SW1 . . . . .145 B4
Sly St [17] E1 . . . . . . .32 A3
Smallbrook Mews
W2 . . . . .101 B1
Smalley Cl N16 . . . . . .7 B1
Smart's Pl WC1,
WC2 . . . . .106 B2
Smart St E2 . . . . .25 C2
Smeaton Ct SE1 . . .136 C1
Smeaton Rd SW18. .70 C4
Smeaton St E1 . . . . .32 A1
Smedley St SW4. . . .171 C2
Smeed Rd E3 . . . . . . .18 C1
Smiles Pl SE13 . . . . .52 B1
Smith Cl SE16 . . . . . .32 C1
Smithfield Mkt
EC1 . . . . .108 B3
Smithfield St EC1 . .108 A3
Smith's Ct W1 . . . . .119 B4
Smith Sq SW1 . . . . .134 A1
Smith St SW3 . . . . . .144 C1
Smith's Yd SW18 . . .71 B2
Smithwood Cl
SW19 . . . . .70 A2
Smithy St E1 . . . . . . .32 B4
Smithy Street Sch [34]
E1 . . . . .32 B4
Smugglers Way
SW18 . . . . .59 A3
Smyrk's Rd SE17 . .152 B1
Smyrna Mans [3]
NW6 . . . . .10 C1
Smyrna Rd NW6 . . .10 C1
Smythe St E14 . . . . .34 A2
Snarsgate St W10 . .30 B4
Sneath Ave NW11. . . .1 B4
Sneyd Rd NW2 . . . . . .9 B4
Snowberry Cl E11 . .19 C4
Snowbury Rd [6]
SW6 . . . . .166 B1
Snowden St
EC2 . . . . .24 A1 98 A1
Snow Ho SE27 . . . . . .75 A1
Snow Hill EC1 . . . . .108 A3
Snowman Ho NW6 . .78 B4
Snowsfields SE1 . .137 C4
Snowsfields Prim Sch
SE1 . . . . .138 A4
Soames St SE15 . . . .64 B4
Soane Ct [10] NW1. .13 B1

Soane Ho SE17 . . . 151 C1
Soaphouse La
TW8 . . . . .44 A3
Sobell L Ctr N7 . . . . . 5 B1
SOHO 105 B1
Soho W1 . . . . 105 B2
Soho Parish CE Prim
Sch W1 . . . . 119 B4
Soho Sq W1 . . . . . . 105 B2
Soho St W1 . . . . 105 B2
Sojourner-Truth Cl 11
E8 . . . . 17 A2
Solander Gdns
13 Shadwell E1 . . . . 32 B2
Stepney E1 . . . . 32 A2
Solebay St E1 . . . . . . 26 A1
Solent Ho 6 E1 . . . . . 33 A4
Solent Rd NW6 . . . . . 10 C3
Soley Mews WC1 . . . 95 B4
Solidarity Ho 5
NW10 . . . . 9 B2
Solna Ave SW15 . . . . 57 B2
Solomon's Pas
SE15 . . . . 65 A3
Solon New Rd
SW4 . . . . 62 A3
Solon Rd SW2 . . . . . 62 A3
Solway Ho 12 E1 . . . 25 C1
Solway Rd SE22 . . . . 64 C3
Somali Rd NW2 . . . . 10 B3
Somborne Ho 11
SW15 . . . . 68 C4
Sombrook Ho
SE11 . . . . 149 B3
Somer Ct SW6 . . . . 155 B3
Somerfield Rd N4 . . . 6 A2
Somerfield St
SE16 . . . . 40 C1
Somerford Gr N16 . . 16 B4
Somerford Grove Est
N16 . . . . 16 B4
Somerford St E1 . . . 25 A1
Somerford Way
SE16 . . . . 41 A4
Somerleyton Rd
SW9 . . . . 62 C3
Somers Cl NW1 . . . . 83 B2
Somers Cres W2 . . . 102 A1
Somerset Gdns
Highgate N6 . . . . . . 3 C4
St Johns SE13 . . . . 52 A1
Somerset Ho
WC2 . . . . 121 A4
Somerset Ho
SW19 . . . . 70 A1
Somerset Lo
SW15 . . . . 57 A3
Somerset Rd
Bedford Pk W4 . . . . 37 C3
Wimbledon SW19 . . . 70 A1
Somerset Sq W14 . . 126 C3
Somers Pl SW2 . . . . 74 B4
Somers Rd SW2 . . . . 62 B1
SOMERS TOWN 93 C4
Somers Town Est
NW1 . . . . 83 A1
Somerton Ave
TW9 . . . . 55 A4
Somerton Rd
Cricklewood NW2 . . . 1 A1
Nunhead SE15 . . . . 65 A3
Somerville Ave
SW13 . . . . 47 B4
Somerville Cl
SW9 . . . . 173 A2

Somerville Ho 10
SW15 . . . . 57 C1
Somerville Point
SE16 . . . . 41 B4
Sonderburg Rd 13
N7 . . . . 5 B2
Sondes St SE17 . . . . 48 C4
Sonia Gdns NW10 . . . 8 B4
Sonning Ho 82
E2 . . . . 24 B2 98 C3
Sophia Cl N7 . . . . . . 14 B2
Sophia Ho 10 W6 . . 39 B1
Sophia Sq 4 SE16 . . 33 A2
Sopwith Way
SW8 . . . . 160 A2
Sorrel La 17 E14 . . . 34 C3
Sorrell Cl
6 Brixton SW9 . . . 173 C2
SE14 . . . . 51 A3
Sotheby Rd N5 . . . . 15 B4
Sotheran Cl E8 . . . . 24 C4
Sotheron Pl SW6 . . 156 B1
Soudan Rd SW11 . . 168 C3
Souldern Rd 10
W14 . . . . 39 C3
SOUTH ACTON 37 A3
South Acton Sta W3,
W4 . . . . 37 B3
South Africa Rd
W12 . . . . 30 A2
Southall Pl SE1 . . . 137 B3
Southam Ho 9
W10 . . . . 23 A1
Southampton Bldgs
WC2 . . . . 107 B3
Southampton Pl
WC1 . . . . 106 B3
Southampton Rd
NW5 . . . . 12 B3
Southampton Row
WC1 . . . . 106 B4
Southampton St
WC2 . . . . 120 B4
Southampton Way
SE5 . . . . 49 A3
Southam St W10 . . . 23 A1
South Audley St
W1 . . . . 117 C2
South Ave TW9 . . . . 44 C1
SOUTH BANK 120 C1
South Bank Bsns Ctr
SW8 . . . . 161 C3
Southbank Ctr
SE1 . . . . 121 A1
Southbank
International Sch 14
NW3 . . . . 11 B2
Southbank
International Sch
(Westminster
Campus) W1 . . . . 104 A4
Southbank Int Sch
W11 . . . . . 31 C2 113 B3
South Bermondsey
Sta SE16 . . . . 40 B1
South Black Lion La
7 W6 . . . . 38 C1
South Bldg SW1 . . 133 A2
South Block 2 E1 . . 32 B2
South Bolton Gdns
SW10 . . . . 142 B2
Southborough Ho
SE17 . . . . 152 B2
Southborough Rd
E9 . . . . 25 C4
SOUTH BROMLEY . 34 C4

South Building
SE10 . . . . 52 C3
Southbury NW8 . . . . 79 A4
South Carriage Dr SW1,
SW7 . . . . 130 C4
South Chelsea Coll 22
SW9 . . . . 62 B3
South Colonnade The
E14 . . . . 34 A1
Southcombe St
W14 . . . . 140 A4
Southcote Rd N19 . . 13 B4
Southcott Ho
17 Bromley E3 . . . . 27 A2
W9 . . . . 89 A1
South Cres
Newham E16 . . . . . 27 C1
WC1 . . . . 105 B3
Southcroft 8
NW10 . . . . 20 C4
South Ct 17 SW15 . . 57 C1
Southdean Gdns
SW19 . . . . 70 B2
Southdown N7 . . . . . 14 A2
South Eastern Univ 3
N7 . . . . 5 B1
South Eaton Pl
SW1 . . . . 145 C4
South Edwardes Sq
W8 . . . . 127 B1
South End W8 . . . . 128 B2
South End Cl NW3 . . 12 A4
South End Gn
NW3 . . . . 12 A4
South End Rd
NW3 . . . . 12 A4
South End Row
W8 . . . . 128 B2
Southerngate Way
SE14 . . . . 51 A3
Southern Gr E3 . . . . 26 B1
Southern Row
W10 . . . . 23 A1
Southern St N1 . . . . 84 C2
Southern Way
SE10 . . . . 43 B3
Southernwood Ret Pk
SE1 . . . . 153 A2
Southerton Rd W6 . . 39 B2
Southey Ho SE17 . . 151 A2
Southey Mews
E16 . . . . 35 C1
Southey Rd SW9 . . 173 B4
Southfield Lo W4 . . 37 C4
Southfield Prim Sch
W4 . . . . 38 A4
Southfield Rd W4 . . 37 C4
SOUTHFIELDS 71 A3
Southfields Acad
SW18 . . . . 70 C3
Southfields Rd
SW18 . . . . 58 C1
Southfields Sta
SW18 . . . . 70 B3
Southgate Ct N1 . . . 15 C1
Southgate Gr N1 . . . 15 C1
Southgate Rd N1 . . . 87 C4
South Gr N6 . . . . 3 C3
South Grove Ho N6 . . 3 C3
SOUTH HACKNEY . . 25 B4
SOUTH
HAMPSTEAD 11 B1
South Hampstead
High Sch
15 Hampstead
NW6 . . . . 11 B2

South Hampstead
High Sch continued
11 London NW3 . . . 11 C2
South Hampstead Sta
NW8 . . . . 11 B1
South Hill Pk NW3 . . 12 A4
South Hill Pk Gdns
NW3 . . . . 12 A4
Southill St E14 . . . . 34 A3
South Island Pl
SW9 . . . . 163 B1
SOUTH
KENSINGTON . 143 A3
South Kensington Sta
SW7 . . . . 143 C4
South Kensington
Station Arc SW7 143 C4
SOUTH
LAMBETH 172 B3
South Lambeth Pl
SW8 . . . . 162 B4
South Lambeth Rd
SW8 . . . . 162 B2
Southlands Dr
SW19 . . . . 69 C2
South Lo NW8 . . . . . 89 B4
South London Gall
SE5 . . . . 49 A2
South London
Montessori Sch
SW11 . . . . 168 A3
Southmead Prim Sch
SW19 . . . . 70 A3
Southmead Rd
SW19 . . . . 70 A3
South Molton La
W1 . . . . 104 A1
South Molton Rd
E16 . . . . 35 C3
South Molton St
W1 . . . . 104 A1
Southmoor Way
E9 . . . . 18 B3
Southolm St
SW11 . . . . 170 B3
South Par W4 . . . . . 37 C2
South Parade
SW3 . . . . 143 C2
South Park Mews
SW6 . . . . 59 A4
South Pl EC2 . . . . . 109 C3
South Pl Mews
EC2 . . . . 109 C3
South Quay Plaza
E14 . . . . 42 A4
South Quay Sta
E14 . . . . 42 A4
South Rise W2 . . . . 116 B4
South Sea St SE16 . . 41 B3
Southside W6 . . . . . 38 B3
Southside Ind Est
SW8 . . . . 170 C4
Southside Quarter 4
SW11 . . . . 168 C2
Southside Sh Ctr
SW18 . . . . 59 A1
South Sq WC1 . . . . 107 B3
South St W1 . . . . . . 117 C2
South Tenter St
E1 . . . . 111 A1
South Terr SW7 . . . 144 A4
South Thames Coll
(Roehampton Ctr)
SW15 . . . . 56 C1

South Thames Coll
(Wandsworth Ctr) 7
SW18 . . . . 59 A2
Southvale Rd SE3 . . 53 A1
Southview Ave
NW10 . . . . 8 B3
South Villas NW1 . . 13 C2
Southville
London SW8 . . . . 171 C3
South Lambeth
SW8 . . . . 172 A3
SOUTHWARK 40 B2
Southwark Bridge SE1,
EC4 . . . . 123 A3
Southwark Bridge Rd
SE1 . . . . 123 A1
Southwark Cath
SE1 . . . . 123 B2
Southwark Coll
(Blackfriars Ctr)
SE1 . . . . 122 A1
Southwark Coll
(Camberwell Ctr) 17
SE5 . . . . 49 A3
Southwark Park Est
11 SE16 . . . . 40 A2
Southwark Park Prim
Sch 10 SE16 . . . . . 40 A3
Southwark Park Rd
SE16 . . . . 153 B4
Southwark Park Sch
13 SE16 . . . . 40 A3
Southwark PE Sports
Complex SE16 . . . . 40 B2
Southwark St SE1 122 C1
Southwark Sta
SE1 . . . . 122 A1
Southwater Cl 8
E14 . . . . 33 B3
Southway Cl 9
W12 . . . . 39 A4
Southwell Gdns
SW7 . . . . 142 C3
Southwell Ho
8 Bermondsey
SE16 . . . . 40 A2
13 Stoke Newington
N16 . . . . 16 A3
Southwell Rd SE5 . . 63 B4
South Wharf Rd
W2 . . . . 101 C2
Southwick Mews
W2 . . . . 101 C2
Southwick Pl W2 . . 102 A1
Southwick St W2 . . 102 A2
Southwick Yd W2 . . 102 A1
Southwold Mans
W9 . . . . 23 C2
Southwood Ave N6 . . 4 A4
Southwood Ct EC1 . . 96 A3
Southwood Ho
W11 . . . . . 31 A2 112 A4
Southwood Hts N6 . . 4 A4
Southwood La N6 . . . 4 A4
Southwood Lawn Rd
N6 . . . . 4 A4
Southwood Park
N6 . . . . 4 A4
Southwood Smith Ho
4 E2 . . . . 25 A2
Southwood Smith St
N1 . . . . 86 A3
South Worple Ave
SW14 . . . . 56 A4

Southwyck Ho
SW9 . . . . .62 C3
South Yd EC1 . . . . . 109 B4
Sovereign Cl E1 . . . . 32 A2
Sovereign Cres
SE16 . . . . .33 A2
Sovereign Ct
3 Richmond
TW9 . . . . .54 B3
13 Stepney E1 . . . . . 32 A2
Sovereign Ho 23
E1 . . . . .25 A1
Sovereign Mews 6
E2 . . . . .24 B3
Sovereign Pk
NW10 . . . . .20 A1
Space Bsns Pk
NW10 . . . . .20 A2
Spa Ct 12 SE16 . . . . .18 B4
Spafield St EC1 . . . . .95 B2
Spalding Ho NE4 . . . .66 A2
Spanby Rd E3 . . . . . .26 C1
Spaniards EN11 . . . . .2 C1
Spaniards End NW3 . .2 B1
Spaniards Rd NW3 . . .2 B2
Spanish Pl W1 . . . .103 C2
Spanish Rd SW18 . . .59 B2
Spa Rd SE16 . . . . . .139 A1
Spare St SE17 . . . . .150 C3
Sparke Terr 2
E16 . . . . .35 B3
Sparkford Ho
SW11 . . . . .167 C4
Sparks Cl W3 . . . . . . .28 C3
Sparsholt Rd N19 . . . .5 A3
Sparta St 12 SE10 . . .52 B2
Spa Sch SE1 . . . . . .153 A4
Spa View 6 SW16 . . .74 B1
Speakers' Corner
W1 . . . . .117 A4
Speakman Ho SE4 . . .66 A4
Spear Mews SW5 . . 141 C3
Spears Rd N19 . . . . . . .5 A3
Spectrum Ho NW5 . .12 C4
Spectrum Wy 19
SW18 . . . . .58 C2
Spedan Cl NW3 . . . . . .2 A1
Speechly Mews
E8 . . . . .16 B3
Speed Ho EC2 . . . . .109 B4
Speedwell St 8
SE8 . . . . .51 C3
Speedy Pl WC1 . . . . .94 A3
Speldhurst Rd
Bedford Pk W4 . . . . . .37 C3
Homerton E9 . . . . .17 C1
Spellbrook Wlk N1 **87** A4
Spelman Ho 19
E1 . . . . .111 B3
Spelman St E1 . . . . .111 B4
Spence Cl SE16 . . . . .41 B4
Spencer Gdns
SW14 . . . . .55 B2
Spencer Ho
31 Clapham
SW8 . . . . .171 B1
24 Putney SW19 . . . .69 C3
Vale of Health NW3 . .2 C1
Wimbledon SW19 . . . .69 C1
Spencer House Mus
SW1 . . . . .118 C1
Spencer Mews
Fulham W6 . . . . .154 A4

Spencer Mews
continued
South Lambeth
SW9 . . . . .172 C3
Spencer Park Ct
SW18 . . . . .59 C2
Spencer Pk SW18 . . .59 C2
Spencer Pl
16 Islington N1 . . . . . .15 A1
SW1 . . . . .133 A1
Spencer Rd
Acton W3 . . . . .28 B1
Chiswick W4 . . . . .45 B3
Wandsworth SW18 . . .59 C2
Spencer Rise NW5 . .4 A1
Spencer St EC1 . . . . .96 A3
Spencer Way 8
E1 . . . . .32 A3
Spencer Wlk
23 Hampstead
NW3 . . . . .11 B4
Putney SW15 . . . . . . .57 C3
Spencer Yd SE3 . . . . .53 B1
Spenlow Ho 2
SE16 . . . . .139 C2
Spenser Gr N16 . . . . .16 A4
Spenser Mews
SE21 . . . . .75 C3
Spenser Rd SE24 . . . .63 A2
Spenser St SW1 . . .133 A2
Spens Ho WC1 . . . . . .94 C1
Spensley Wlk N16 . . .6 C1
Spert St E14 . . . . .33 A2
Spey St E14 . . . . .34 B4
Spezia Rd NW10 . . . .21 C3
Spice Ct
8 Battersea
SW11 . . . . .167 C3
2 St George in East
E1 . . . . .125 C2
Spice Quay Htss
SE1 . . . . .125 A1
Spicer Cl SE5, SW9 . .48 A1
Spicer Ho
E2 . . . . .24 C2 99 B3
Spindrift Ave E14 . . .42 A2
Spinnaker Ho 21
E14 . . . . .41 C4
Spinney The
Barnes SW13 . . . . .47 A4
Streatham SW16 . . . . .73 C1
Spire Cl 10 TW10 . . .54 A1
Spire Ho W2 . . . . . .115 A4
Spirit Quay E1 . . . . .32 A1
SPITALFIELDS 11 A4
Spitalfields City Farm
E1 . . . . .99 B1
Spital Sq E1 . . . . . . .110 B4
Spital St E1 . . . . . . .111 B4
Spital Yd E1 . . . . . . .110 B4
Splendour Wlk
SE16 . . . . .40 B1
Spode Ho SE1 . . . . .135 B1
Spode Wlk NW3 . . . .11 A3
Sporle Ct 5 SW11 . . .59 C4
Sprewell SW15 . . . . .58 A1
Spriggs Ho 14 N1 . . .15 A1
Sprimont Pl SW3 . . 144 C2
Springall St 9
SE15 . . . . .50 A3
Springalls Wharf 2
SE16 . . . . .139 B4
Springbank Wlk
NW1 . . . . .13 C1
Spring Cott 10
W12 . . . . .38 C4

Spring Ct NW2 . . . . .10 B2
Springdale Rd
N16 . . . . .15 C4
Springett Ho 19
SW2 . . . . .62 B2
Springfield Ct
7 Dagenham W3 . . . .28 B3
Hampstead NW3 . . . . .12 A1
Springfield Ho
Acton W3 . . . . .28 B3
1 Camberwell SE5 . . .49 A1
13 Dalston E8 . . . . . .16 B2
Springfield La
NW6 . . . . .78 A3
Springfield Rd
NW8 . . . . .79 A3
Springfield University
Hospl SW17 . . . . .72 A1
Springfield Wlk
NW6 . . . . .78 A3
Spring Gdns
Islington N5 . . . . .15 B3
SW1 . . . . .120 A2
Spring Gr W4 . . . . . . .44 C4
Spring Grove Rd
TW10 . . . . .54 B2
Spring Hill E5 . . . . . . .7 C4
Springhill Cl SE5 . . .63 C4
Spring Ho WC1 . . . . .95 B3
Spring Mews W1 . . 103 A4
Springpark Dr N4 . . .6 B3
Spring Pl NW5 . . . . . .13 A3
Springrice Rd
SE13 . . . . .67 C1
Spring St W2 . . . . . .101 B1
Spring Terr TW10 . . .54 A2
Springtide Cl 10
SE15 . . . . .49 C2
Springvale Ave
TW8 . . . . .36 A1
Springvale Terr 5
W14 . . . . .39 C3
Springwater WC1 . .106 C4
Springwell Ave
NW10 . . . . .21 B4
Spring Wlk E1 . . . . .111 C4
Springwood Cl 8
E3 . . . . .26 C3
Spruce Ct W5 . . . . . .36 A3
Spruce Ho 15
SE16 . . . . .40 C4
Sprules Rd SE4 . . . . .51 A1
Spurgeon St SE1 . . 137 B2
Spurling Rd SE22 . . .64 B3
Spur Rd SE1 . . . . . . .135 B4
Spurstowe Rd E8 . . .17 A2
Spurstowe Terr
E8 . . . . .17 A3
Square Rigger Row 7
SW11 . . . . .59 B4
Square The
Hammersmith W6 . . . .39 B1
SW6 . . . . .165 B3
Squarey St SW17 . . .71 B1
Squire Gdns NW8 . . .89 B3
Squires Ct SW4 . . . .172 B3
Squire's Mount
NW3 . . . . .2 C1
Squirrels The
SE13 . . . . .67 C4
Squirries St
E2 . . . . .24 C2 99 C3
Stable Rd 8 SE16 . . .40 B4
Stable St N1 . . . . . . .84 A3
Stables Way SE11 . .149 B2
Stable Way W10 . . . .30 B3

Stable Yd Rd
SW1 . . . . .133 A4
Stacey St
Highbury N7 . . . . .5 C1
Soho WC2 . . . . .105 C1
Stack Ho SW1 . . . . .145 C3
Stackhouse St
SW1 . . . . .130 C2
Stacy Path 18 SE5 . .49 A3
Stadium St SW10 . .157 A1
Stafford Cl NW6 . . . .23 C2
Stafford Cripps Ho
30 Bethnal Green
E2 . . . . .25 B2
SW6 . . . . .155 A3
Stafford Ct
Kensington W8 . . . . .127 C2
SW8 . . . . .172 A4
Stafford Ho SE1 . . .153 A2
Stafford Mans
13 Hammersmith
W14 . . . . .39 C3
14 Stockwell SW4 . . .62 A3
SW11 . . . . .158 C1
Stafford Pl SW1 . . .132 C2
Stafford Rd
Bow E3 . . . . .26 B3
Maida Vale NW6 . . . . .23 C2
Staffordshire St
Peckham SE15 . . . . . .49 C2
Peckham SE15 . . . . . .50 A2
Stafford St W1 . . . . .118 C2
Stafford Terr W8 . . .127 B2
Stag La SW15 . . . . . .68 B2
Stagshaw Ho 17
SE22 . . . . .64 A4
Stainer St SE1 . . . . .123 C1
Staining La EC2 . . . .109 A2
Stainsbury St 28
E2 . . . . .25 B3
Stainsby Rd E14 . . . .33 C3
Stalbridge Flats
W1 . . . . .103 C1
Stalbridge Ho
NW1 . . . . .82 C1
Stalham St SE16 . . . .40 A3
Stambourne Ho
SW8 . . . . .172 B4
Stamford Bridge
Stadium (Chelsea
FC) SW6 . . . . .156 A2
Stamford Brook Ave
1 W6 . . . . .38 B3
Stamford Brook Gdns
2 W6 . . . . .38 B3
Stamford Brook Mans
2 W6 . . . . .38 B3
Stamford Brook Rd
W6 . . . . .38 B3
Stamford Brook Sta
W6 . . . . .38 B2
Stamford Cl 2
NW3 . . . . .2 B1
Stamford Cotts
SW10 . . . . .156 B2
Stamford Ct SW6 . . .38 C2
Stamford Gr E 1
N16 . . . . .7 C3
Stamford Gr W 4
N16 . . . . .7 C3
STAMFORD HILL N16 .7 A3
Stamford Hill N16 . . .7 A3

Stamford Hill Mans 1
N16 . . . . .7 B3
Stamford Hill Sta
N16 . . . . .7 A4
Stamford Lo 2 N16 . .7 B4
Stamford Mans 2
N16 . . . . .7 B4
Stamford Rd N1 . . . .16 A2
Stamford St SE1 . . .121 C2
Stamp Pl E2 . .24 B2 99 A4
Stanard Cl N16 . . . . . .7 A4
Stanborough Ho 4
E3 . . . . .27 A1
Stanborough Pas
E8 . . . . .16 B2
Stanbridge Mans
SW15 . . . . .57 B4
Stanbridge Rd
SW15 . . . . .57 B4
Stanbrook Ct W1 . . 118 C2
Stanbury Ct 10
NW3 . . . . .12 B2
Stanbury Rd
Nunhead SE15 . . . . . . .50 B1
Peckham SE15 . . . . . .50 A1
Standard Pl 13
EC2 . . . . .24 A2 98 B3
Standard Rd
NW10 . . . . .20 C1
Standen Rd SW18 . . .70 C4
Standish Ho 6
W6 . . . . .38 C2
Standish Rd W6 . . . . .38 C2
Stanesgate Ho 20
SE15 . . . . .49 C3
Stanfield Ho NW8 . . .89 C2
Stanfield Rd E14 . . . .26 A3
Stanford Ct
Kensington W8 . . . . .128 B1
Walham Green
SW6 . . . . .166 B3
Stanford Pl SE1 . . . .152 A3
Stanford Rd W8 . . . .128 B2
Stanford St SW1 . . .147 B3
Stangate SE1 . . . . . .135 A2
Stanhope Cl 28
SE16 . . . . .40 C4
Stanhope Gate
W1 . . . . .117 C2
Stanhope Gdns
SW7 . . . . .143 A4
Stanhope Ho
4 Putney SW15 . . . . .57 B2
SE8 . . . . .51 B3
Stanhope Mews E 7
SW7 . . . . .143 A4
Stanhope Mews S 5
SW7 . . . . .143 A3
Stanhope Mews W
SW7 . . . . .143 A4
Stanhope Par NW1 . .92 C4
Stanhope Pl W2 . . . .102 C1
Stanhope Rd N6 . . . . .4 B4
Stanhope Row
W1 . . . . .118 A1
Stanhope St NW1 . . .92 C3
Stanhope Terr
W2 . . . . .115 C4
Stanier Cl SW5 . . . .141 A1
Stanlake Mews 7
W12 . . . . .30 B1
Stanlake Rd W12 . . . .30 B1
Stanlake Villas 8
W12 . . . . .30 B1
Stanley Cl SW8 . . . .162 C3

Stanley Cohen Ho
EC1 . . . . **96 C1**
Stanley Cres
W11 . . . . . . **31 B2 112 C4**
Stanley Gdns
Bedford Pk W3 . . . . . . **38** A4
Cricklewood NW2. . . . . **9** B3
W11 . . . . . . **31 B2 112** C4
Stanley Gr SW11. . **169** C1
Stanley Ho
28 Clapham
SW8 . . . . **171** B1
2 Poplar E14 . . . . . **33** C3
Stanley Holloway Ct
E16 . . . . **35** C3
Stanley Mans
SW10 . . . . **157** A4
Upper Tooting
SW17 . . . . **72** B2
Stanley Rd
Acton Green W3 . . . . **37** B3
Mill Meads E15. . . . . **27** C4
Mortlake SW14 . . . . . **55** A3
Stanley St SE14,
SE8 . . . . **51** B3
Stanley Studios
SW10 . . . . **157** A4
Stanley Terr 1 N19. . **5** A2
Stanliff Ho 1 E14 . .**41** C3
Stanmer St SW11. **168** B2
Stanmore Gdns
TW9 . . . . **54** B4
Stanmore Ho 21
SW8 . . . . **171** C2
Stanmore Pl NW1 . **82** B4
Stanmore Rd TW9 . **54** B4
Stanmore St N1. . . **84** C4
Stannard Cotts 7
E1 . . . . **25** B1
Stannard Mews
E8 . . . . **16** C2
Stannard Rd E8 . . . **16** C2
Stannary Pl SE11. **149** C1
Stannary St SE11. **149** C1
Stansbury Sq 3
W10 . . . . **23** A2
Stansfeld Ho SE1 . **153** A3
Stansfield Rd SW9. **62** B4
Stanstead Ho 3E3. . **27** B1
Stansted Express
Terminal EC2. . . . . **110** A4
Stanswood Gdns
SE5 . . . . **49** A3
Stanton Ct N16. . . . . **6** C4
Stanton Ho 9
SE10 . . . . **52** B4
Stanton Rd SW13. . **46** B1
Stanway Ct 2 N1. . **24** A3
Stanway St N1. . . . . **24** A3
Stanwick Rd W14 **140** C3
Stanworth St SE1 **139** A3
Stapleford Cl 3
SW2 . . . . **74** A3
Stapleford Cl
SW19 . . . . **70** A4
Staplehurst Ct 1
SW11 . . . . **60** B1
Staplehurst Ho 18
E5 . . . . **17** A3
Staple Inn WC2. . . **107** B3
Staple Inn Bldgs
WC2 . . . . **107** B3
Staples Cl SE16. . . . **33** A1
Staple St SE1. . . . **137** C3
Stapleton Hall N4 . . **5** B4

Stapleton Hall Rd
N4 . . . . **5** B4
Stapleton Ho 19
E2 . . . . **25** A2
Stapleton Rd
SW17 . . . . **72** C1
Star Alley EC3 . . . **124** B4
Starboard Way
E14 . . . . **41** C3
Starcross St NW1 . **93** A3
Starfield Rd W12 . . **38** C4
Star & Garter Mans 8
SW15 . . . . **57** C4
Star Lane Sta E16 . . **35** A4
Starliner Ct N7 . . . . **14** C2
Starling Ho NW8 . . **80** A2
Star Pl E1 . . . . . . **125** A3
Star Rd W14. . . . . **140** C1
Star St W2 . . . . . **102** A2
Star Works NW10. . **21** C2
Star Yd WC2. . . . . **107** B2
Statham St 7 N7 . . . **5** A1
Statham Gr N16. . . . **6** C1
Statham Ho SW8 . **170** C4
Station App
Dagenham NW10. . . **21** B2
Fulham SW6. . . . . . . **58** A4
Richmond TW9 . . . . . **44** C2
Station Approach Rd
W4 . . . . **45** B3
Station Approach
Road SE1 . . . . . **135** B4
Station Ave
5 Brixton SW9 . . . . **63** A4
14 Richmond TW9 . . **44** C2
Station Cres SE3 . . **43** C1
Station Ct 3 SE15. . **50** B1
Stationers Hall Ct
EC4 . . . . **108** B1
Station Gdns W4 . . **45** B3
Station Mews Terr 4
SE3 . . . . **43** C1
Station Par
Cricklewood NW2. . . . **9** B2
Richmond TW9 . . . . . **44** C2
4 Upper Tooting
SW12 . . . . **72** C3
Station Pas SE15 . . **50** B2
Station Pl N4 . . . . . . **5** C2
Station Rd
Barnes SW13 . . . . . **46** B1
Camden Town N19 . . . **4** B1
Harlesden NW10 . . . **21** B3
Lewisham SE13 . . . . **67** B4
New Cross Gate
SE14 . . . . **50** B2
Willesden NW10 . . . **22** A2
Station Rise SE27. . **75** A2
Station St E15 . . . . **19** C1
Station Terr
Camberwell SE5. . . . **48** B2
Kensal Rise NW10 . . **22** C2
Staunton Ho SE17 **152** A3
Staunton St SE8. . . **51** B4
Staveley NW1 . . . . **92** C4
Staveley Cl
Hackney E9. . . . . . . **17** B3
Lower Holloway N7 . .**14** A4
5 Peckham SE15 . . . **50** B2
Staveley Gdns W4 . **45** C2
Staveley Ho SE4 . . . **65** C4
Staveley Rd W4 . . . **45** C3
Stavers Ho 31 E3. . . **26** B3
Staverton Rd NW2 . . **9** B1
Stave Yard Rd
SE16 . . . . **33** A1

Stavordale Lo
W14 . . . . **127** A2
Stavordale Rd N5. . **15** A4
Stayner's Rd E1 . . **25** C1
Steadman Ct EC1. . **97** A2
Stead St SE17 . . . **151** B3
Stean St E8 . . . . . **24** B4
Stebbing Ho 8
W11 . . . . **30** C1
Stebondale St E14. **42** B2
Stebon Prim Sch 22
E14 . . . . **33** C4
Stedham Pl WC1 . **106** A2
Steedman St
SE17 . . . . **150** C3
Steele Rd
Acton Green W4. . . . **37** B3
Becontree NW10 . . . **20** C2
Steele's Mews N
NW3 . . . . **12** B2
Steele's Mews S
NW3 . . . . **12** B2
Steel's La 23 E1 . . . **32** B3
Steen Way 7
SE22 . . . . **64** A2
Steep Hill SW16 . . **73** C1
Steeple Cl SW6. . . **164** B1
Steeple Ct 6 E1. . . **25** A1
Steeple Wlk N1 . . . **87** A4
Steerforth St
SW18 . . . . **71** B2
Steers Way SE16 . . **41** A4
Stelfax Ho WC1. . . **95** A4
Stellman Cl E5 . . . . . **7** C1
Stephan Cl E8 . . . . **24** C4
Stephen Ct 18
SW18 . . . . **69** C3
Stephendale Rd
SW6 . . . . **166** C2
Stephen Fox Ho 7
W4 . . . . **38** A1
Stephen Hawking Sch
22 E14 . . . . **33** A3
Stephen Mews
W1 . . . . **105** B3
Stephen Pl SW4 . . . **61** B4
Stephen Saunders Ct
SW11 . . . . **60** A2
Stephens Ct SE4 . . **66** A4
Stephenson Ho
2 Gospel Oak
NW5 . . . . **13** A4
6 Maitland Pk
NW3 . . . . **12** B3
Newington SE1 . . . **136** C2
Stephenson St
Dagenham NW10. . . **21** B2
Newham E16 . . . . . **35** A4
Stephenson Way
NW1 . . . . **93** A2
Stephen St W1 . . . **105** B3
STEPNEY **32** C4
Stepney City E1 . . **32** B4
Stepney City Farm . .
E1 . . . . **32** C4
Stepney Cswy E1. . **32** C3
Stepney Gn E1 . . . **32** C4
**Stepney Greencoat CE
Prim Sch The 28** . . .
E14 . . . . **33** B3
Stepney Green Ct 4
E1 . . . . **32** C4

**Stepney Green Maths
& Computing Coll 18** . .
E1 . . . . **32** C4
Stepney Green Sta . .
E1 . . . . **32** C4
Stepney High St
E1 . . . . **32** C4
Stepney Way E1 . . **32** B4
Sterling Cl NW10 . . **8** C1
Sterling Gdns
SE14 . . . . **51** A4
Sterling Pl W5 . . . **36** A3
Sterling St SW7 . . **130** B2
Sterndale Rd W14 . **39** C3
Sterne St W12. . . . . **39** C4
Sternhall La SE15. . **64** C4
Sternhold Ave SW12, . .
SW2 . . . . **73** C2
Sterry St SE1. . . . **137** B3
Steve Biko Ct N10. . **22** C1
Steve Biko Rd N7. . . **5** C1
Stevedore St 3
E1 . . . . **32** A1
Stevenage Rd
SW6 . . . . **47** C2
Stevens Ave E9. . . . **17** B2
Stevenson Cres
SE16 . . . . **40** A1
Stevenson Ho
1 Battersea
SW11 . . . . **168** C1
6 Clapham Pk
SW2 . . . . **62** A2
NW8 . . . . **78** C4
Stevens St SE1 . . **138** B2
Steventon Rd W12. **29** B2
Steward St E1 . . . . **110** B3
**Stewart Headlam
Prim Sch 28** E1. . . **25** A1
Stewart Ho SE1 . . **138** A1
Stewart Rd E15. . . . **19** C4
Stewart's Gr SW3 **144** A2
Stewart's Pl E1 . . . . .
SW2 . . . . **62** B1
Stewart's Rd SW8 **170** C4
Stewart St E14 . . . **42** B4
Stew La EC4 . . . . . **122** C4
Steyne Ho
13 Acton W3 . . . . . **28** A1
11 Acton W3. . . . . **28** B1
Steyne Rd W3 . . . . **28** A1
Stifford Ho E1. . . . **32** B4
Stile Hall Gdns
W4 . . . . **36** C1
Stile Hall Par 6
W4 . . . . **36** C1
Stillingfleet Rd
SW13 . . . . **46** C4
Stillington St
SW1 . . . . **147** A4
Stillness Jun & Inf
Sch SE23 . . . . **66** A1
Stillness Rd SE23. . **66** B1
Stirling Ct
Clerkenwell EC1. . . **96** A2
Strand WC2 . . . . . **106** C1
Stirling Mans NW6 .**11** B2
Stirling Rd
South Acton W3 . . . . **37** A3
Stockwell SW9 . . . . **172** B1
Stoatley Ho 10
SW15 . . . . **68** C3
Stockbeck NW1 . . . **83** A1
Stockfield Rd
SW16 . . . . **74** B1

Stockholm Ho E1 **125** C4
Stockholm Rd
SE16 . . . . **40** B1
Stockholm Way
E1 . . . . **125** B2
Stockhurst Cl
SW15 . . . . **47** C1
Stockleigh Hall
NW8 . . . . **80** B2
Stock Orchard Cres
N7 . . . . **14** B3
Stock Orchard St
N7 . . . . **14** B3
Stocks Ct 8 E1 . . . **25** C1
Stocks Pl 15 E14 . . **33** B2
Stockton Ho 17 E2 . **25** A2
STOCKWELL **62** A4
Stockwell Ave
SW9 . . . . **62** B4
Stockwell Gdns
SW9 . . . . **172** C3
Stockwell Gn
SW9 . . . . **172** C1
Stockwell La SW9 **172** C1
Stockwell Park Cres
SW9 . . . . **173** A2
Stockwell Park Rd
SW9 . . . . **173** A3
Stockwell Park Wlk
SW9 . . . . **62** C4
Stockwell Prim Sch 6
SW9 . . . . **62** B4
Stockwell St SE10 . .**52** B4
Stockwell Sta
SW4 . . . . **172** B2
Stockwell Terr
SW9 . . . . **172** B2
Stoddart Ho SW8 **163** A3
Stodmarsh Ho 26
SW9 . . . . **173** C2
Stoford Cl 4
SW19 . . . . **70** A4
Stokenchurch St
SW6 . . . . **166** A3
**STOKE
NEWINGTON** **7** A2
**Stoke Newington
Church St** N16. . . .**7** A2
**Stoke Newington
Comm** N16. . . . . . . **7** B2
**Stoke Newington
High St** N16 . . . . . . **7** B1
Stoke Newington Rd
N16 . . . . **16** B4
Stoke Newington Sch
N16 . . . . **6** C1
Stoke Newington Sta
N16. . . . . **7** B2
Stoke Pl NW10 . . . **21** B2
Stokesley St W12. . **29** B3
Stondon Pk SE23 . . **66** A1
Stonhouse St SW4. **61** C3
STONEBRIDGE . . . **20** C4
Stonebridge Ctr 6 . . .
NW10 . . . . **20** C4
Stonebridge Prim Sch
NW10 . . . . **20** C4
Stone Cl SW4 . . . . **171** A1
Stonecutter St
EC4 . . . . **108** A2
Stonefield N4 . . . . **5** B2
Stonefield Mans
N1. . . . . **85** B3
Stonefield St N1. . . **85** C4

Stonegate **8** NW5 . .12 C2
Stonehill Cl SW14 . .55 C2
Stonehill Rd
  Brentford W4 . . . . . .36 C1
  Mortlake SW14 . . . . . .55 C2
Stonehills Ct SE21. .76 A1
Stonehill's Mans **3**
  SW16 . . . . .74 A2
Stonehouse NW1 . .83 A3
Stonehouse Ct
  EC2 . . . . .110 B2
Stonehouse Ho **7**
  W2 . . . . .31 C4
Stoneleigh Lo **13**
  TW9 . . . . .44 B2
Stoneleigh Mews **15**
  E3 . . . . .26 A3
Stoneleigh Pl W11. .30 C2
Stoneleigh St W11. .30 C2
Stoneleigh Terr
  N19 . . . . .4 A2
Stonell's Rd SW11. .60 B2
Stonenmasons Yd
  SW18 . . . . .71 C4
Stonenest St N4. . . . .5 B3
Stones End St
  SE1 . . . . .136 C3
Stoneyard La E14. . .34 A2
Stoney La EC3. . . . .110 B2
Stoney St SE1 . . . . .123 B2
Stonhouse St SW4. .61 C3
Stonor Rd W14 . . . .140 C3
Stopes St SE15 . . . . .49 B3
Stopford Rd SE17. .150 B1
Stopher Ho SE1 . . . .136 B3
Storace Ho **6**
  SW4 . . . . .62 A3
Storers Quay E14. . .42 C2
Store St
  Bloomsbury WC1 . .105 B4
  Stratford New Town
   E15 . . . . .19 C4
Storey Ct NW8. . . . .89 B3
Storey Ho **8** E14. . .34 A2
Storey's Gate
  SW1 . . . . .133 C3
Stories Mews SE5 . .49 A1
Stories Rd SE5 . . . . .64 A4
Storks Rd SE16. . . .139 C1
Stormont House Sch
  E5 . . . . .17 A4
Stormont Rd
  Clapham SW11. . . . .60 C3
  Highgate N6. . . . . . . .3 B4
Storrington WC1 . . .94 B3
Story St N1 . . . . . . .14 B1
Stothard Ho **8** E1. .25 B1
Stothard Pl E2 . . . .110 B4
Stothard St **12** E1. .25 B1
Stott Cl SW18 . . . . .59 C1
Stoughton Cl
  Roehampton
   SW15 . . . . .68 C3
  SE11 . . . . .149 A3
Stourcliffe Cl W1 . .102 C2
Stourcliffe St W1 . .102 C1
Stourhead Cl **6**
  SW19 . . . . .69 C4
Stour Rd E3. . . . . . . .18 C1
Stowage SE8 . . . . . .52 A4
Stowe Ho **11** N16. . .7 A1
Stowe Rd W12. . . . . .39 A4
Stracey Rd NW10. . .20 C4
Stradbroke Rd N5 . .15 B4

Stradella Rd SE24 . .63 B1
Straffan Lo **8**
  NW3 . . . . .12 A2
Strafford Ho **9**
  SE8 . . . . .41 B1
Strafford Rd W3. . . .37 B4
Strafford St E14. . . .41 C4
Strahan Rd E3. . . . .26 A2
Straightsmouth
  SE10 . . . . .52 B3
Straker's Rd SE15 . .65 A3
Strale Ho **17** N1 . . .24 A4
STRAND 120 C4
Strand
  Strand WC2 . . . . . .120 C4
  Strand WC2 . . . . . .107 A1
Strand Dr TW9 . . . . .45 A3
Strand La WC2 . . . .121 A4
STRAND ON THE
  GREEN 44 C4
Strand-on-the-Green
  W4 . . . . .44 C4
Strand on the Green
  Jun & Inf Sch **5**
  W4 . . . . .44 C4
Strang Ho N1 . . . . . .86 C3
Strangways Terr
  W14 . . . . .126 C1
Stranraer Way N1 . .14 A1
Strasburg Rd
  SW11 . . . . .170 A3
Stratford Bus Sta
  E15 . . . . .19 C1
Stratford Gr SW15. .57 C3
Stratford High St Site
  E15 . . . . .27 C4
STRATFORD
INTERNATIONAL
  Sta
  E15 . . . . .19 C4
STRATFORD
  MARSH. 27 A4
STRATFORD NEW
  TOWN 19 B3
Stratford Pl W1 . . .104 A1
Stratford Rd W8. . .127 C1
Stratford Sh Ctr
  E15 . . . . .19 C1
Stratford Sta E15 . .19 C1
Stratford Studios
  W8 . . . . .128 A1
Stratford Villas
  NW1 . . . . .13 C1
Stratford Workshops
  E15 . . . . .27 C4
Strathan Cl SW18. .58 A1
Strathblaine Rd
  SW11 . . . . .59 C3
Strathdon Dr
  SW17 . . . . .71 C1
Strathearn Ho
  W2 . . . . .116 A4
Strathearn Pl W2 . .116 A4
Stratheden Par
  SE3 . . . . .53 C3
Stratheden Rd
  SE3 . . . . .53 C3
Strathleven Rd
  SW2 . . . . .62 A2
Strathmore Ct
  NW8 . . . . .90 A4
Strathmore Gdns
  W8 . . . . .31 C1 113 C2

Strathmore Rd
  SW19 . . . . .70 C1
Strathnairn St
  SE1 . . . . .153 C3
Strathray Gdns
  NW3 . . . . .12 A2
Strath Terr SW11. . .60 A3
Strathville Rd
  SW18 . . . . .71 A2
Stratton Cl **3** N1. . .16 A1
Strattondale St
  E14 . . . . .42 B3
Stratton St W1 . . . .118 B2
Strauss Rd W4 . . . . .37 C4
Streamline Mews
  SE22 . . . . .76 C3
Streatham Cl
  SW16 . . . . .74 A2
Streatham & Clapham
  High Sch SW16. . .73 C1
Streatham Ct
  SW16 . . . . .74 A1
STREATHAM HILL. .74 A3
Streatham Hill
  SW2 . . . . .74 A3
Streatham Hill &
  Clapham High Sch
  14 SW2 . . . . .74 A2
Streatham Hill Sta
  SW2 . . . . .74 B2
Streatham Pl SW2. .74 A4
Streatham St
  WC1 . . . . .106 A2
Streathbourne Rd
  SW17 . . . . .72 C2
Streatham Wells Prim
  Sch SW2 . . . . .74 C2
Streatleigh Par **4**
  SW16 . . . . .74 A2
Streatley Pl
  27 Hampstead
   NW3 . . . . .11 B4
  Hampstead NW3 . . .11 C4
Streatley Rd NW6. . .10 B1
Streimer Rd E15. . . .27 B3
Strelley Way W3. . . .29 A2
Stretton Mans **16**
  SE8 . . . . .51 C4
Strickland Ct SE15. .64 C4
Strickland Ho **26**
  E2 . . . . .24 B2 99 A3
Strickland Row
  SW18 . . . . .71 C4
Strickland St SE8. . .51 C2
Stringer Hos **19**
  N1 . . . . .24 A4
Strode Ho **3** SW2. .74 C3
Strode Rd
  SW6 . . . . .154 A2
  Willesden NW10. . . . .8 C2
Strome Ho NW6. . . .78 A1
Stronsa Rd W12 . . . .38 B4
Strood Ho SE1. . . . .137 C3
Stroud Cres SW15. .68 C1
Stroud Green Prim
  Sch N4 . . . . .5 C3
Stroud Green Rd
  N4 . . . . .5 C3
Stroudley Ho
  SW8 . . . . .171 A4
Stroudley Wlk E3. . .27 A2
Stroud Rd SW19 . . . .70 C1
Strout's Pl **2**
  E2 . . . . .24 B2 98 C4
Strudwick Ct
  SW4 . . . . .172 B3

Strutton Ground
  SW1 . . . . .133 B1
Strype St E1. . . . . . .110 C3
Stuart Ave W5 . . . . .36 B4
Stuart Ho
  Hammersmith W6 . .39 B3
  1 Homerton E9. . . .17 C1
  5 Stockwell SW4. .62 A3
  W14 . . . . .140 A4
Stuart Mill Ho N1 . .84 C1
Stuart Rd
  Acton W3 . . . . .28 B1
  Maida Vale NW6. . . .23 C2
  Nunhead SE15 . . . . .65 B3
  Wimbledon SW19. . .70 C1
Stubbs Dr SE16. . . .40 A1
Stubbs Ho
  Finsbury Pk N4. . . . .5 B3
  1 Globe Town E2 . .25 C2
Stucley Pl **19** NW1. .13 A1
Studdridge St
  SW6 . . . . .165 C2
Studd St N1. . . . . . . .86 A4
Studholme Ct
  NW3 . . . . .10 C4
Studholme St
  SE15 . . . . .50 A3
Studio Pl SW1. . . . .131 A3
Studios NW8 . . . . . .78 C2
Studios The
  8 Clapham SW4. . .61 B3
  SW8 . . . . .171 C3
Studland SE17. . . . .151 B2
Studland Ho E14 . . .33 A3
Studland St W6 . . . .39 A2
Studley Cl E5 . . . . . .18 A3
Studley Ct **13** E14. .34 C2
Studley Rd SW4 . . .172 B2
Stukeley St WC2. . .106 B2
Stunell Ho **23**
  SE14 . . . . .50 C4
Sturdee Ho **2** E2. . .24 C3
Sturdy Ho **20** E3. . .26 A3
Sturdy Rd SE15. . . . .50 A1
Sturgeon Rd SE17 . .150 C1
Sturge St SE1. . . . .136 C4
Sturmer Way N7 . . .14 B3
Sturminster Ho
  SW8 . . . . .163 A1
Sturry St **14** E14. . .34 A3
Sturt St N1. . . . . . . .87 A1
Stutfield St E1 . . . . .111 C1
Stuttle Ho **14**
  E1 . . . . .24 C1 99 B1
Styles Gdns SW9 . . .63 A4
Styles Ho SE1 . . . . .122 A1
Stylus Apartments **25**
  E1 . . . . .32 B3
Sudbourne Prim Sch
  12 SW2 . . . . .62 B2
Sudbourne Rd
  SW2 . . . . .62 B2
Sudbrooke Rd
  SW12 . . . . .60 C1
Sudbury Ct SW8. . .171 C4
Sudbury Ho SW18 . .59 A2
Sudeley St N1. . . . . .86 B1
Sudlow Rd SW18 . . .58 C2
Sudrey St SE1 . . . . .136 C3
Suffield Ho SE17 . . .150 B2
Suffolk Ho **8** NW5. .4 B1
Suffolk La EC4. . . . .123 B4
Suffolk Pl SW1 . . . .119 C2
Suffolk Rd
  Barnes SW13. . . . . .46 C3
  Willesden NW10. . . . .8 A1

Suffolk St SW1 . . . .119 C2
Sugar House La
  E15 . . . . .27 B3
Sugar Loaf Wlk **6**
  E2 . . . . .25 B2
Sugden Rd SW11. . . .60 C3
Sulby Ho SE4. . . . . .66 A3
Sulgrave Gdns **11**
  W6 . . . . .39 B4
Sulgrave Rd W6. . . .39 B3
Sulina Rd SW2 . . . . .74 A4
Sulivan Ct SW6. . . .165 B1
Sulivan Ent Ctr
  SW6 . . . . .58 C4
Sulivan Prim Sch
  SW6 . . . . .165 B1
Sulivan Rd SW6. . . .58 C4
Sulkin Ho **11** E2. . . .25 C2
Sullivan Cl SW11 . . .60 A4
Sullivan Ct
  Stamford Hill N16. . .7 B3
  SW5 . . . . .141 C4
Sullivan Ho
  Chelsea SW1 . . . . .160 B4
  Vauxhall SE11. . . . .149 A3
Sullivan Rd SE11 . .149 C4
Sultan St SE5. . . . . .48 B3
Sumatra Rd NW6. . .10 C2
Sumburgh Rd
  SW12 . . . . .60 C1
Summercourt Rd
  E1 . . . . .32 B3
Summerfield Ave
  NW6 . . . . .23 A3
Summer Ho SE13. . .67 C3
Summerhouse Rd
  N16 . . . . .7 A2
Summerlands Ave
  W3 . . . . .28 B2
Summerley St
  SW18 . . . . .71 A2
Summers St EC1. . . .95 B1
SUMMERSTOWN . . .71 B1
Summit Ct NW2 . . . .10 A3
Summit Est N16. . . . .7 C4
Sumner Ave SE15. . .49 B2
Sumner Bldgs
  SE1 . . . . .122 C2
Sumner Ct SW8 . . .172 A4
Sumner Ho **1** E3. . .34 A4
Sumner Pl SW7 . . . .143 C3
Sumner Place Mews
  SW7 . . . . .143 C3
Sumner Rd SE15 . . .49 B3
Sumner St SE1 . . . .122 C2
Sumpter Cl NW3 . . .11 B2
Sun Alley **6** TW9. . .54 A3
Sun Alliance Ho
  WC2 . . . . .107 B2
Sunbeam Cres
  W10 . . . . .22 B1
Sunbeam Rd
  NW10 . . . . .20 C1
Sunbury Ave
  SW14 . . . . .55 C3
Sunbury Ct **3**
  SE14 . . . . .50 C4
Sunbury Ho **38**
  E2 . . . . .24 B2 98 C3
Sunbury La SW11 . .167 C4
Sunbury Workshops
  59 E2 . . . . .24 B2 98 C3
Sun Ct EC3. . . . . . .109 C1
Sunderland Ct
  SE22 . . . . .76 C4

Sunderland Ho 28
W2 . . . . .31 C4
Sunderland Terr
W2 . . . . .100 A2
Sundew Ave W12. .29 C2
Sundra Wlk 20 E1. .25 C1
Sundridge Ho 4
E9 . . . . .17 C1
Sunley Ho E1. . . . .111 A3
Sunlight Sq 28 E2. .25 A2
Sunningdale Ave
W3 . . . . .29 A2
Sunningdale Cl 22
SE16 . . . . .40 A1
Sunningdale Gdns
W8 . . . . .127 C1
Sunninghill Ct 9
W3 . . . . .37 B4
Sunninghill Rd
SE13 . . . . .52 A1
Sunnyhill Cl E5. . . .18 A4
Sunnymead Rd
SW15 . . . . .57 A2
Sunnyside 4 NW2. . .1 B1
Sunnyside Ho 3
NW2 . . . . .1 B1
Sunnyside Rd N19. . .4 C4
Sun Pas 8 SE16. .139 B2
Sunray Ave SE5,
SE24. . . . . .63 C3
Sun Rd W14. . . . . .140 C1
Sunrise Cl E15 . . . . .19 B3
Sun St Pas EC2. . . .110 A3
Sunset Rd SE5. . . . .63 C3
Sun St EC2 . . . . . . .109 C4
Sunwell Cl SE15 . . . .50 A2
Surcot Ho 2
SW4 . . . . .171 C1
Surrendale Pl W9 . .23 C1
Surrey Canal Rd SE14,
SE8 . . . . .50 C4
Surrey Cres
1 Brentford W4 . . . .36 C1
1 London W4 . . . . . .36 C1
Surrey Docks Farm
SE16. . . . . .41 B4
Surrey Docks
Watersports Ctr
SE8 . . . . .41 B2
Surrey Gr SE17 . . .152 A1
Surrey Ho 8 SE16. .32 C1
Surrey La SW11 . . .168 B3
Surrey Quays Rd
SE16. . . . . .40 C4
Surrey Quays Sh Ctr
SE16. . . . . .40 C3
Surrey Quays Sta
SE16. . . . . .40 C2
Surrey Rd SE15. . . . .65 C2
Surrey Row SE1. . .136 B4
Surrey Sq SE17. . . .152 B2
Surrey Square Prim
Sch SE17. . . . . .152 A2
Surrey St WC2. . . .121 A4
Surrey Terr SE17. . .152 B2
Surrey Water Rd
SE16. . . . . .32 C1
Surrey Wharf SE1. .49 C4
Surridge Ct 13
SW9 . . . . .172 B2
Surr St N7 . . . . .14 A3
Susan Constant Ct 18
E14 . . . . .34 C2
Susannah St E14 . . .34 B3
Sussex Cl N19. . . . . .5 A2

Sussex Ct
4 Barnes SW13 . . .46 B1
Greenwich SE10. . . .52 B4
Paddington W2 . . .101 B1
Sussex Gdns W2. . .101 C1
Sussex Ho
Hampstead NW3 . . .12 A2
Richmond TW9 . . . . .44 B1
Sussex House Sch
SW3 . . . . .144 C4
Sussex Lo W2 . . . .101 C1
Sussex Mans
South Kensington
SW7 . . . . .143 B3
Strand WC2 . . . . . .120 B4
Sussex Mews E
W2 . . . . .101 C1
Sussex Mews W
W2 . . . . .115 C4
Sussex Pl
22 Hammersmith
W6 . . . . .39 B1
Lisson Gr NW1. . . . .90 C2
Paddington W2 . . .101 C1
Sussex Sq W2 . . . .115 C4
Sussex St SW1 . . .146 B2
Sussex Way
Upper Holloway N7 . . .5 B1
Upper Holloway N7,
N19. . . . . .5 A2
Upper Holloway N19 . .4 C3
Sutherland Ave
W9 . . . . .88 C2
Sutherland Ct
1 Paddington
W9 . . . . .23 C1
Stoke Newington
N16. . . . . .6 C1
Sutherland Gdns
SW14 . . . . .56 A4
Sutherland Gr SW18,
SW19 . . . . .70 B4
Sutherland Ho
Kensington W8. . . .128 A1
2 Putney SW15 . . . .69 B4
8 South Hampstead
NW6 . . . . .11 B1
Sutherland Pl W2 . .31 C3
Sutherland Rd
Bow E3 . . . . .26 B3
Chiswick W4. . . . . . .46 A4
Sutherland Row
SW1 . . . . .146 B2
Sutherland Sq
SE17 . . . . .150 C1
Sutherland St
SW1 . . . . .146 B2
Sutherland Wlk
SE17 . . . . .151 A1
Sutton Court Mans
W4 . . . . .45 B4
Sutton Court Rd
W4 . . . . .45 B4
Sutton Ct
Chiswick W4 . . . . . . .45 B4
8 Hackney E5. . . . . .17 A4
Sutton Est SW3. . .144 B2
Sutton Est The 8
W10 . . . . .30 C4
Sutton Ho 8 Breaker's
Yd E9 . . . . .17 B3
Sutton La EC1. . . . . .96 B1
Sutton La N W4 . . . .37 B1
Sutton La S W4. . . . .45 B4
Sutton Pl E9 . . . . . .17 B3

Sutton Row W1. . .105 C2
Sutton Sq E9. . . . . .17 B3
Sutton St E1 . . . . . . .32 B3
Sutton Way EC1 . . . .97 A1
Sutton Way W10. . . .30 B4
Sutton Wlk SE1. . . .121 A1
Swaby Rd SW17,
SW18 . . . . .71 B2
Swaffield Prim Sch
SW18 . . . . .71 B4
Swaffield Rd
SW18 . . . . .71 B4
Swain's La N6. . . . . . .4 A2
Swainson Ho N7 . . .14 C4
Swainson Rd W3 . . .38 B4
Swain St NW8. . . . . .90 A2
Swallow Cl SE14. . . .50 C2
Swallow Ct 4 W9 . .31 C4
Swallowfield NW1. . .92 B3
Swallow Ho NW8. . . .80 A2
Swallow Pl
22 Poplar E14 . . . . .33 B3
W1 . . . . .104 B1
Swallow St W1 . . . .119 A3
Swanage Ct 5 N1. .16 A1
Swanage Ho SW8 .162 C1
Swanage Rd SW18. .59 B1
Swanbourne 17 .150 C3
Swanbourne Ho
NW8 . . . . .90 A2
Swan Ct
Chelsea SW3 . . . . .144 B1
Parsons Green
SW6 . . . . .155 B1
Poplar E14 . . . . .33 B3
Swan Ctr SW17. . . . .71 B1
Swandon Way
SW18 . . . . .59 A3
Swanfield St
E2 . . . . .24 B2 99 A3
Swan Ho N1. . . . . . .15 C1
Swan La EC4 . . . . . .123 C3
Swan Lane Pier
EC4. . . . . .123 B3
Swanlea Sch E1 . . . .25 A1
Swanley Ho SE17. .152 B2
Swan Mead SE1. . .138 A1
Swan Mews
Stockwell SW9 . . . .172 C2
SW6 . . . . .165 B4
Swanmore Ct
SW18 . . . . .59 B1
Swanne Ho 12
SE10 . . . . .52 B3
Swan Pl SW13. . . . . .46 B1
Swan Rd SE16 . . . . .40 B4
Swanscombe Ho 7
E16 . . . . .35 B4
Swanscombe Rd
5 Chiswick W4 . . . . .38 A1
Shepherd's Bush
W11 . . . . .30 C1
Swan St SE1. . . . . .137 A3
Swanton Gdns
SW19 . . . . .69 C3
Swanwick Cl
SW15 . . . . .68 B4
Swan Wlk SW3 . . .158 C4
Swan Yd N1 . . . . . . .15 A2
Swaton Rd E3 . . . . . .26 C1

Swaythling Ho
SW15 . . . . .56 B1
Swedenborg Gdns
E1. . . . . .32 A2
Sweden Gate SE16. .41 A2
Swedish Quays
SE16 . . . . .41 A3
Swedish Sch The
SW13. . . . . .47 A4
Sweeney Cres
SE1 . . . . .139 A3
Sweyn Pl SE3. . . . . .53 C1
Swift Ho
16 Stepney E1 . . . . .32 B3
2 Stoke Newington
N16. . . . . .7 A1
1 SW9 . . . . .163 C2
Swift St SW6 . . . . .164 C4
Swinbrook Rd
W10 . . . . .31 A4
Swinburne Ct 4
SE5. . . . . .63 C3
Swinburne Ho 19
E2 . . . . .25 B2
Swinburne Rd
SW15 . . . . .56 C3
Swindon St W12. . . .30 B1
Swinford Gdns
SW9 . . . . .63 A4
Swingfield Ho 4
E9 . . . . .25 B4
Swinley Ho NW1. . . .92 B4
Swinnerton St E9. . .18 A3
Swinton Ho 21
E2 . . . . .24 C2 99 B3
Swinton Pl WC1 . . . .94 C4
Swinton St WC1 . . . .94 C4
Swiss Cottage
NW3 . . . . .11 C1
Swiss Cottage La 7
NW3 . . . . .11 C1
Swiss Cottage Sch
3 South Hampstead
NW8 . . . . .11 C1
St John's Wood
NW8 . . . . .79 C4
Swiss Cottage Sta
NW3 . . . . .11 C1
Swiss Ct SW1 . . . .119 C3
Swiss Terr 7
NW3 . . . . .11 C1
Switch Ho 4 E14. . . .34 C2
Sybil Phoenix Cl
SE8 . . . . .40 C1
Sybil Thorndike
Casson Ho SW5 .141 C1
Sybil Thorndike Ho 12
N1 . . . . .15 B2
Sycamore Ave E3. . .26 B4
Sycamore Cl W3. . . .29 A1
Sycamore Ct
Kilburn NW6. . . . . . .23 C4
Tufnell Pk N19 . . . . . .4 C1
Sycamore Gdns W6,
W12 . . . . .39 A3
Sycamore Gr SE6. . .67 B1
Sycamore Ho
10 Maitland Pk
NW3 . . . . .12 B2
12 Rotherhithe
SE16 . . . . .40 C4
3 Shepherd's Bush
W6 . . . . .39 A4
2 Stoke Newington
N16. . . . . .6 C2

Sycamore Lo
SW15 . . . . .57 A4
Sycamore Mews 4
SW4 . . . . .61 B4
Sycamore St EC1. . .96 C1
Sycamore Wlk 1
W10 . . . . .23 A1
Sydcote SE21. . . . . .75 B3
Sydenham Hill SE21,
SE22, SE23, SE26,
SE19. . . . . .76 C1
Sydenham Hill Sta
SE21 . . . . .76 B1
Sydenham Hill Wood
Nature Reserve
SE26 . . . . .76 C1
Sydner Mews N16 . .16 B4
Sydner Rd N16 . . . . .16 B4
Sydney Cl SW3 . . .143 C2
Sydney Ho 4 W4. . .38 A2
Sydney Mews
SW3 . . . . .143 C2
Sydney Pl SW7 . . .144 A3
Sydney Rd TW10,
TW9 . . . . .54 A3
Sydney St SW3 . . .144 A2
Sylva Cotts 3 SE8 . .51 C2
Sylva Ct 8 SW15 . . .69 C4
Sylvan Ct 8 NW6. . .78 A4
Sylvan Gr
Hampstead NW2 . . . .9 C4
SE15. . . . . .50 A4
Sylvester Ho 7
E8 . . . . .17 A2
Sylvester Path 8
E8 . . . . .17 A2
Sylvester Rd E8 . . . .17 A2
Sylvia Ct N1. . . . . . . .87 B1
Sylvia Pankhurst Ho
14 E2. . . . . .25 C2
Symes Mews NW1. .82 C2
Symington Ho
SE1 . . . . .137 B1
Symington Mews
E9 . . . . .17 C3
Symister Mews
N1. . . . . .24 A2 98 A3
22 Shoreditch
N1. . . . . .24 A2 98 A3
Symons Cl 6 SE15 .50 B1
Symons St SW3 . . .145 A3
Symphony Mews 15
W10 . . . . .23 A2
Syringa Ho SE4. . . . .66 B4

T

Tabard Ct 6 E14 . . .34 B3
Tabard Ho SE1. . . .137 C2
Tabard Sq SE1. . . .137 B3
Tabard St SE1 . . . .137 B2
Tabernacle St EC2. .97 C2
Tableer Ave SW4 . . .61 C2
Tabley Rd N7. . . . . . .14 A4
Tabor Rd W6 . . . . . .39 A3
Tachbrook Est
SW1 . . . . .147 C1
Tachbrook Mews
SW1 . . . . .146 C4
Tachbrook St
SW1 . . . . .147 A3
Tack Mews SE4. . . . .66 C4
Tadema Ho NW8 . . .89 C1

Tadema Rd SW10 .... **157** A1
Tadmor St W12 ...... **30** C1
Tadworth Ho SE1 .. **136** B3
Taeping St E14 ...... **42** A2
Taffrail Ho ☑ E14 .. **42** A1
Taft Way ☑ E3 ...... **27** A2
Tailworth St ☑
E1 .... **111** B3
Tait Ct
☑ Old Ford E3 .... **26** A4
SW8 .... **171** C4
Tait Ho
SE1 .... **121** C1
☑ Tufnell Pk N19 .. **13** B4
Takhar Mews
SW11 .... **168** B1
Talacre Com Sp Ctr
NW5 .... **13** A2
Talacre Rd NW5 .... **12** C2
Talbot Ct EC3 ..... **123** C4
W11 .... **31** A3
Talbot Grove Ho ☑
W11 .... **31** A3
Talbot Ho
Highbury N7 .... **5** C1
Poplar E14 .... **34** A3
Talbot Pl SE3 ...... **53** A1
Talbot Rd
Camberwell SE22 ... **64** A3
Notting Hill W2 .... **31** C3
Notting Hill W11 ... **31** B3
Talbot Sq W2 ...... **101** B1
Talbot Wlk
Notting Hill W11 ... **31** A3
Willesden NW10 .... **8** A2
Talbot Yd SE1 ..... **123** B1
Talcott Path ☑
SW2 .... **74** C3
Talfourd Pl SE15 ... **49** B2
Talfourd Rd SE15 .. **49** B2
Talgarth Rd
Hammersmith W6 ... **39** B1
W14 .... **140** B2
Talia Ho E14 .... **42** B3
Talleyrand Ho SE5 . **48** B1
Tallis St EC4 ...... **121** C4
Talma Rd SW2 ..... **62** C3
Talmud Torah Bobov
Prim Sch ☑ N16 .. **7** B4
Talmud Torah
Machzikei Hadass
Sch E5 .... **7** C4
Talmud Torah Toldas
Yakov Yosef Sch
N16 .... **7** A3
Talmud Torah Yetev
Lev ☑ N16 .... **7** C2
Talwin St E3 .... **27** A2
Tamar Cl ☑ E3 ..... **26** B4
Tamar Ho
☑ Cubitt Town
E14 .... **42** B4
SE11 .... **149** C2
Tamarind Ct ☑
W3 .... **28** B3
Tamarind Ho ☑
SE15 .... **49** C3
Tamarind Yd ☑
E1 .... **125** C2
Tamarisk Sq W12 .. **29** B2
Tamworth St N7 .... **14** A2
Tamworth St
SW6 .... **155** B3
Tangier Rd TW10 ... **55** A4
Tangley Gr SW15 ... **68** B4

Tangmere WC1 ..... **94** C3
Tanhurst Ho ☑
SW2 .... **74** A4
Tankerton St WC1 .. **94** B3
Tanner Ho SE1 .... **138** B3
Tanner's Hill SE8 .. **51** C2
Tanners Mews
SE8 .... **51** B2
Tanner St SE1 ..... **138** B3
Tanners Yd ☑ E2 .. **25** A3
Tannery Ho ☑ E1 . **111** B4
Tannington Terr
N5 .... **5** C1
Tansley Cl N7 ...... **13** C3
Tanswell St SE1 ... **135** B3
Tantallon Rd
SW12 .... **72** C3
Tant Ave E16 .... **35** B3
Tanza Rd NW3 ...... **12** B4
Tapley Ho ☑ SE1 .. **139** B3
Taplow NW3 .... **11** C1
Taplow Ho ☑
E2 .... **24** B2 98
Taplow St N1 ...... **87** A1
Tappesfield Rd
SE15 .... **65** B4
Tapp St E1 .... **25** A1
Taranto Ho ☑ E1 .. **32** C4
Tarbert Rd SE22 ... **64** A2
Tarbert Wlk E1 ..... **32** B2
Tarling Rd E16 ..... **35** B3
Tarling St E1 ...... **32** A3
Tarnbrook Ct
SW1 .... **145** B3
Tarn St SE1 .... **136** C1
Tarns The NW1 ..... **92** C4
Tarplett Ho ☑
SE14 .... **50** C4
Tarragon Cl SE14 .. **51** A3
Tarranbrae NW6 ... **10** A1
Tarrant Ho E2 ..... **25** B2
Tarrant Pl W1 ..... **102** C3
Tarrantt Ho W14 .. **126** A2
Tarriff Cres SE8 ... **41** B2
Tarrington Cl
SW16 .... **73** C1
Tartan Ho ☑ E14 .. **34** B3
Tarver Rd SE17 ... **150** B2
Tarves Way SE10 .. **52** A3
Tasker Ho ☑ E14 .. **33** B4
Tasker Rd NW3 .... **12** B3
Tasman Ct ☑ E14 . **42** A2
Tasman Ho ☑ E1 .. **32** A1
Tasman Rd SW9 ... **62** A4
Tasso Rd W6 ...... **154** A4
Tasso Yd W6 ...... **154** A3
Tatchbury Ho ☑
SW15 .... **56** B1
Tate Britain SW1 . **148** A3
Tate Ho ☑ E2 ..... **25** C3
Tate Modern EC4 . **122** B2
Tatham Pl NW8 ... **79** C2
Tatton Cres E5, N16 . **7** B4
Tatum St SE17 .... **151** C3
Tauheed Cl N4 ..... **6** B2
Taunton Ho W2 ... **100** C1
Taunton Mews
NW1 .... **90** C1
Taunton Pl NW1 ... **90** C2
Tavern Cl SE1 .... **137** A1
Taverner Ho N16 ... **6** C1
Taverners Cl
W11 .... **31** A1 **112** A1
Taverner Sq ☑ N5 . **15** B4

Tavern La SW9 .... **173** C2
Tavistock Cl N16 ... **16** A3
Tavistock Cres
W11 .... **31** B4
Tavistock Ct WC2 . **93** C2
Tavistock Ho ☑
W11 .... **31** B4
Tavistock Mews ☑
W11 .... **31** B3
Tavistock Pl WC1 .. **94** A2
Tavistock Rd
Dagenham NW10 ... **21** B3
Notting Hill W11 ... **31** B4
Tavistock Sq WC1 . **93** C2
Tavistock St WC2 . **120** B4
Tavistock Terr N19 . **4** C1
Tavistock Twr
SE16 .... **41** A3
Taviton St WC1 ... **93** B2
Tavy Cl SE11 ..... **149** C2
Tawhid Boys Sch
N16 .... **7** B2
Tawny Way SE16 ... **40** C2
Taybridge Rd
SW11 .... **60** C3
Tayburn Cl E14 .... **34** B3
Tay Ho ☑ E3 ...... **26** B3
Tayler Ct NW8 ..... **79** B4
Taylor Ave TW9 .... **45** A1
Taylor Cl SE8 ...... **51** B4
Taylor Ho ☑ SW2 . **74** C3
Taylor's Grn W3 ... **29** A3
Taylor's La NW10 .. **8** A1
Tayport Cl N1 ...... **14** A1
Tayside Ct ☑ SE5 . **63** C3
Tayyibah Girls Sch ☑
E5 .... **7** C2
Teak Cl SE16 .... **33** A1
Tealby Ct N7 .... **14** B2
Teal Ct ☑ SE8 ..... **51** B4
Teale St E2 .... **24** C3
Teal St ☑ SE10 .... **43** B3
Teather St ☑ SE5 . **49** A3
Tebbs Ho ☑ SW2 . **74** C4
Tedman Ct SE13 ... **67** B3
Ted Roberts Ho ☑
E2 .... **25** A3
Tedworth Gdns
SW3 .... **144** C1
Tedworth Sq SW3 **144** C1
Teesdale Cl E2 ..... **25** A3
Teesdale St E2 ..... **25** A3
Teesdale Yd ☑ E2 . **25** A3
Tee The W3 .... **29** A3
Teignmouth Cl ☑
SW4 .... **61** C3
Teignmouth Rd
NW2 .... **9** C2
Telcon Wy SE10 ... **43** A2
Telegraph Hill NW3 . **2** A1
Telegraph Pl E14 .. **42** A2
Telegraph Rd
SW15 .... **69** B4
Telegraph St EC2 . **109** B2
Telephone Pl
SW6 .... **155** A4
Telfer Cl ☑ W3 .... **37** B4
Telfer Ho EC1 ...... **96** B3
Telferscot Prim Sch
☑ SW12 .... **73** C3
Telferscot Rd
SW12 .... **73** C3
Telford Ave SW12,
SW2 .... **74** A3

Telford Avenue Mans
☑ SW2 .... **74** A3
Telford Ho
☑ Kensal Town
W10 .... **31** A4
SE1 .... **136** C2
Telford Parade Mans
☑ SW2 .... **74** A3
Telford Rd W10 .... **31** A4
Telford Terr SW1 . **160** C4
Telford Way W3 ... **29** A4
Tell Gr SE22 .... **64** B3
Telscombe Ho
SW11 .... **169** B3
Temair Ho ☑
SE10 .... **52** B3
Temeraire Pl TW8 . **36** B1
Temeraire St SE16 . **40** B4
Temperley Rd
SW12 .... **72** C4
Templar Ho NW2 .. **10** B2
Templar St SE5 .... **48** A1
Temple Ave EC4 .. **121** C4
Temple Bar EC4 .. **108** B1
Temple Bar EC4 .. **108** B1
Templecombe Rd
E9 .... **25** B4
Temple Ct
Stepney E1 .... **32** C4
SW8 .... **162** A1
Temple Dwellings ☑
E2 .... **25** A3
Temple Gr Hatcham
Sch SE14 .... **50** C2
Temple Ho
☑ Battersea
SW11 .... **60** A4
☑ Tufnell Pk N7 ... **4** B1
Temple La EC4 ... **107** C1
Templemead Cl
W3 .... **29** A3
Templemead Ho
E9 .... **18** A4
TEMPLE MILLS **19** A3
Temple Mills La
London E10, E15 .... **19** B4
Stratford E15 .... **19** A4
Temple Mills Rd
E9 .... **18** C4
Temple Pl WC2 ... **121** A4
Temple Rd
Acton Green W4 ... **37** B3
Richmond TW9 .... **54** B4
Temple Sheen
SW14 .... **55** B2
Temple Sheen Rd
SW14 .... **55** A3
Temple St E2 ...... **25** A3
Temple Sta WC2 .. **121** B4
Templeton Cl ☑
N16 .... **16** A3
Templeton Pl
SW5 .... **141** C3
Temple West Mews
SE11 .... **136** A1
Templewood Ave
NW3 .... **2** A1
Templewood Gdns
NW3 .... **2** A1
Templewood Point
NW2 .... **1** B2
Tenbury Ct SW12 .. **73** C3
Tenby Ho
Islington N7 .... **14** C4
W2 .... **100** C1
Tench St E1 .... **32** A1

Tenda Rd SE16 .... **40** A2
Tendring Ho SW2 .. **62** C1
Tenham Ave SW2 .. **73** C2
Tenison Ct W1 .... **118** C4
Tenison Way SE1 . **121** B1
Tenniel Cl W2 .... **114** B4
Tennis St SE1 .... **137** B4
Tennyson Ho
SE17 .... **151** A2
Tennyson Rd NW6 . **23** B4
Tennyson St SW8 . **170** A1
Tensing Ho N1 ..... **15** A2
Tenterden Ho
SE17 .... **152** B2
Tenterden St W1 .. **104** B1
Tent Ground
E15 .... **110** C3
Tenterden St W1 .. **25** A1
Tequila Wharf E14 . **33** A3
Terborch Way ☑
SE22 .... **64** A3
Tercelet Terr NW3 . **11** B4
Teredo St SE16 .... **40** C3
Terling Ho ☑ W10 . **30** B4
Terling Wlk N1 .... **86** C4
Terminus Pl SW1 . **132** B1
Tern Ho ☑ SE15 ... **49** B2
Terrace Gdns
SW13 .... **46** B1
Terrace La TW10 .. **54** A1
Terrace Rd E9 ..... **17** B1
Terrace The
Barnes SW13,
SW14 .... **46** A1
EC4 .... **107** C1
Kilburn NW6 .... **23** C4
☑ Rotherhithe SE8 . **41** B2
Terrano Ho ☑
TW9 .... **45** A2
Terrapin Ct SW17 . **73** A1
Terrapin Rd SW17 . **73** A1
Terrick St W12 ..... **30** A3
Territorial Ho
SE11 .... **149** C3
Terry Ho SW2 ..... **74** C3
Tersha St TW9 .... **54** B3
Tessa Sanderson Pl ☑
SW8 .... **61** A4
Testerton Wlk ☑
W11 .... **30** C2
Testcott Rd SW10 **156** C1
Teversham La
SW8 .... **172** B4
Teviot St E14 ...... **34** B4
Teyham Ct ☑
SW11 .... **60** B1
Thackeray Ct
Chelsea SW3 ..... **144** C2
West Kensington
W14 .... **126** A1
Thackeray Ho
College Pk NW10 .. **21** C2
WC1 .... **94** A2
Thackeray Mews ☑
E8 .... **16** C2
Thackeray Rd
SW8 .... **170** B1
Thackeray's
Almshouses SE6.. **67** A1
Thackeray St W8 . **128** B2
Thalia Cl SE10 .... **52** C4
Tham Cl ☑ SE24 .. **63** A3
Thame Rd SE16 ... **40** C4
Thames Ave
SW10 .... **167** A4

Thames Bank
SW14 . . . . 45 B1
Thames Christian Coll
25 SW11 . . . . 59 C4
Thames Circ E14 . . . . 41 C2
Thames Cres W4 . . . . 46 A3
Thames Ct 10
SE15 . . . . 49 B3
Thames Hts SE1 . . . 138 C4
Thameside Ctr
TW8 . . . . 44 B4
Thames Link Ho 7
TW9 . . . . 54 A3
Thames Pl SW15 . . . 57 C4
Thames Quay
Millwall E14 . . . . 42 A4
SW10 . . . . 167 A3
Thames Rd W4 . . . . . 45 A4
Thames Reach W6 . . 47 B4
Thames Row TW9 . . . 44 B4
Thames St SE10 . . . . 52 A4
Thames Village
W4 . . . . 45 B2
Thames Wlk
SW11 . . . . 158 A2
Thane Mans N7 . . . . . 5 B1
Thanet Ho
WC1 . . . . 94 A3
1 West Norwood
SE27 . . . . 75 A1
Thanet Lo NW2 . . . . . 10 A2
Thanet St WC1 . . . . . 94 A3
Thane Villas N7 . . . . . 5 B1
Thane Works N7 . . . . 5 B1
Thavies Inn EC4 . . . 107 C2
Thaxted Ct N1 . . . . . 87 C1
Thaxted Ho SE16 . . . 40 B2
Thaxton Rd W14 . . . 155 A4
Thayer St W1 . . . . . 103 C2
Theatre Royal E10 . . 19 C2
Theatre Sq E15 . . . . 19 C2
Theatre St SW11 . . . 60 B4
Theberton St N1 . . . . 86 A4
Theed St SE1 . . . . . 121 C1
Thelbridge Ho 28
E3 . . . . 27 A2
Theobalds Ct N4 . . . . 6 B2
Theobald's Rd
WC1 . . . . 106 C4
Theobald St SE1 . . . 137 B1
Theodore Ct SE13 . . 67 C1
Theodore Ho 1
SW15 . . . . 56 C2
Theodore Rd SE13 . . 67 C1
Therapia Rd SE22 . . . 65 B1
Theresa Rd W6 . . . . . 38 C2
Therfield Ct N4 . . . . . 6 B2
Thermopylae Gate
E14 . . . . 42 A2
Theseus Ho 2
E14 . . . . 34 C3
Theseus Wlk N1 . . . . 86 B1
Thessaly Ho SW8 . . 160 C1
Thessaly Rd SW8 . . 171 A4
Thetford Ho SE1 . . . 138 C2
Thetis Terr TW9 . . . . 44 C4
Third Ave
East Acton W3 . . . . . 29 B1
West Kilburn W10 . . 23 A2
Thirleby Rd SW1 . . . 133 A1
Thirlmere NW1 . . . . . 92 B4
Thirlmere Ho 19
N16 . . . . 15 C4
Thirsk Rd SW11 . . . . 60 C3
Thistle Gr SW7 . . . . 143 A1
Thistle Ho 10 E14 . . 34 B3

Thistlewood Cl 3
N7 . . . . 5 B2
Thistly Ct SE8 . . . . . 52 A4
Thomas Baines Rd
SW11 . . . . 59 C4
Thomas Burt Ho 9
E2 . . . . 25 A2
Thomas Buxton Prim
Sch 17 E1 . . 24 C1 99 C1
Thomas Crowell Ct 26
N1 . . . . 16 A3
Thomas Doyle St
SE1 . . . . 136 B2
Thomas Fairchild
Com Sch N1 . . . . . 87 A2
Thomas Ho
3 Hackney E9 . . . . . 17 B2
4 Stockwell SW4 . . 62 A3
Thomas Hollywood Ho
2 E2 . . . . 25 B3
Thomas Jone Sch 16
W11 . . . . 31 A3
Thomas Milner Ho 8
SE15 . . . . 49 C3
Thomas More Ho
EC2 . . . . 108 C3
Thomas More Sq
E1 . . . . 125 B3
Thomas More St
E1 . . . . 125 B2
Thomas Neal's Ctr
WC1 . . . . 106 A1
Thomas North Terr 4
E16 . . . . 35 B4
Thomas Pl W8 . . . . . 128 A1
Thomas Rd E14 . . . . 33 C4
Thomas Road Ind Est
2 E14 . . . . 34 A3
Thomas's, Battersea
SW11 . . . . 167 C3
Thomas's London Day
Sch SW6 . . . . 59 A4
Thomas's London Ind
Day Sch W8 . . . . 128 B2
Thomas's Prep Sch
Clapham SW11 . . . . 60 B2
Thompson Ave
Richmond TW9 . . . . 54 C4
SW18 . . . . 48 B3
Thompson Ho
10 Kensal Town
W10 . . . . 23 A1
SE14 . . . . 50 C4
Thompson Rd
SE22 . . . . 64 B1
Thomson Ct 4 E8 . . 16 C2
Thomson Ho
Pimlico SW1 . . . . . 147 C1
Walworth SE17 . . . 152 A3
Thomson House Sch
SW14 . . . . 55 C4
Thorburn Ho SW1 . . 131 B3
Thorburn Sq SE1 . . 153 B3
Thoresby Ho N16 . . . 6 C1
Thoresby St N1 . . . . 97 A4
Thornaby Ho 15
E2 . . . . 25 A2
Thornbill Ho 1
SE15 . . . . 49 C3
Thornbury Cl N16 . . 16 A3
Thornbury Ct
W11 . . . . . . 31 C2 113 B4
Thornbury Ho N6 . . . 4 B3
Thornbury Rd
SW2 . . . . 62 A1

Thornbury Sq
London N6 . . . . 4 B3
7 Upper Holloway
N19 . . . . 4 B3
Thorncliffe Ct
SW2 . . . . 62 A1
Thorncliffe Rd
SW2 . . . . 62 A1
Thorncombe Rd
SE22 . . . . 64 A2
Thorncroft St
SW8 . . . . 162 A1
Thorndale Ho 10
N16 . . . . 7 A3
Thorndean St
SW18 . . . . 71 B2
Thorndike Cl
SW10 . . . . 156 C2
Thorndike Ho
SW1 . . . . 147 B2
Thorndike Rd 21
N1 . . . . 15 C2
Thorndike St
SW1 . . . . 147 B3
Thorne Cl E16 . . . . . 35 C3
Thorne Ho
24 Bethnal Green
E2 . . . . 25 B2
4 Cubitt Town E14 . 42 B3
Thorne Pas 5
SW13 . . . . 46 B1
Thorne Rd SW8 . . . 162 B1
Thorness Ct SW18 . 59 B1
Thorne St SW13 . . . . . .
SW14 . . . . 56 A4
Thornewill Ho 8
E1 . . . . 32 B2
Thorney Cres
SW11 . . . . 157 C1
Thorneycroft Ho 11
W4 . . . . 38 A1
Thorney Ct W8 . . . . 128 C3
Thorney Hedge Rd
W4 . . . . 37 A2
Thorney St SW1 . . . 148 A4
Thornfield Ho 5
E14 . . . . 33 C2
Thornfield Rd
W12 . . . . 39 A4
Thornford Rd
SE13 . . . . 67 B2
Thorngate Rd W9 . . 23 C1
Thornham Gr E15 . . 19 C3
Thorn Ham Ho
SE1 . . . . 137 C2
Thornham St SE10 . 52 A4
Thornhaugh St
WC1 . . . . 93 C1
Thornhill Bridge
Wharf N1 . . . . 84 C3
Thornhill Cres N1 . . 14 B1
Thornhill Gr N1 . . . . 14 C1
Thornhill Ho
12 Chiswick W4 . . . 38 A1
Islington N1 . . . . . . 14 C1
Thornhill Mews
SW15 . . . . 58 B3
Thornhill Prim Sch 13
N1 . . . . 14 C1
Thornhill Rd N1 . . . . 85 A4
Thornhill Sq N1 . . . . 14 B1
Thornicroft Ho 12
SW9 . . . . 173 A1
Thornley Pl 2
SE10 . . . . 43 A1

Thornsett Rd
SW18 . . . . 71 A3
Thornton Ave
Chiswick W4 . . . . . . 38 A2
Streatham SW2 . . . . 73 C3
Thornton Ct N7 . . . . 14 A3
Thornton Gdns
SW12 . . . . 73 C3
Thornton Ho
SE17 . . . . 152 A3
Thornton Pl W1 . . . 103 A4
Thornton Rd
Mortlake SW14 . . . . 55 C4
Streatham SW12,
SW2 . . . . 73 C3
Thornton St SW9 . . 173 B2
Thornville St SE8 . . . 51 C2
Thornwood Gdns
W8 . . . . 127 B4
Thornwood Lo
W8 . . . . 127 B4
Thornycroft Ct
TW9 . . . . 44 B1
Thorold Ho
SE1 . . . . 136 C4
6 Streatham SW2 . . 74 A4
Thorparch Rd
SW8 . . . . 161 C1
Thorpebank Rd
W12 . . . . 29 C1
Thorpe Cl W10 . . . . 31 A3
Thorpedale Rd N4 . . 5 B3
Thorpe Ho N1 . . . . . 85 A3
Thorverton Rd NW2 . 1 A1
Thoydon Rd E3 . . . . 26 A3
Thrale St SE1 . . . . . 123 A1
Thrasher Cl 20 E8 . . 24 B4
Thrawl St E1 . . . . . . 111 A3
Thrayle Ho 2
SW9 . . . . 62 B4
Threadgold Ho 8
N1 . . . . 15 C2
Threadneedle St EC2,
EC3 . . . . 109 C1
Three Colts La E2 . . 25 A1
Three Colt St E14 . . 33 B2
Three Cups Yd
WC1 . . . . 107 A3
Three Kings Yd
W1 . . . . 118 A4
Three Mill La E3 . . . 27 B2
Three Nun Ct EC2 . . 109 B2
Three Oak La SE1 . . 138 C4
Threshers Pl
W11 . . . . 31 A2 112 A4
Thring Ho 2
SW9 . . . . 172 C2
Throgmorton Ave
EC2 . . . . 109 C2
Throgmorton St
EC2 . . . . 109 C2
Thrush St SE17 . . . 150 C2
Thurland Ho 3
SE16 . . . . 40 A2
Thurland Rd SE16 . 139 B2
Thurleigh Ave
SW12 . . . . 60 C1
Thurleigh Ct
SW12 . . . . 60 C1
Thurleigh Rd
SW12 . . . . 60 C1
Thurloe Cl SW7 . . . 144 A3
Thurloe Ct SW3 . . . 144 A3
Thurloe Place Mews
SW7 . . . . 143 C4

Thurloe Sq SW7 . . . 144 A4
Thurloe St SW7 . . . 143 C4
Thurlow Hill SE21 . . 75 B2
Thurlow Ho 17
SW16 . . . . 74 A1
Thurlow Park Rd SE21,
SE24 . . . . 75 B2
Thurlow Rd NW3 . . . 11 C3
Thurlow St SE17 . . . 152 A1
Thurlow Terr NW5 . . 12 C3
Thurlow Twrs
SE27 . . . . 74 C1
Thurlow Wlk
SE17 . . . . 152 A1
Thurnscoe NW1 . . . 82 C3
Thursley Gdns
SW19 . . . . 69 C2
Thursley Ho 10
SW2 . . . . 74 B4
Thurso Ho NW6 . . . 78 A1
Thurston Ind Est
SE13 . . . . 67 A4
Thurston Rd SE8,
SE13 . . . . 52 A1
Thurtle Rd E2 . . . . . 24 B3
Tibbatts Rd E3 . . . . 27 A1
Tibberton Sq N1 . . . 86 C4
Tibbets Cl SW19 . . . 69 C2
Tibbet's Corner
SW19 . . . . 69 C4
Tibbet's Ride
SW19 . . . . 69 C4
Tiber Cl 10 E3 . . . . . 26 C4
Tiber Gdns N1 . . . . . 84 B3
Tickford Ho NW8 . . . 90 A3
Tidal Basin Rd
E16 . . . . 35 B2
Tidbury Ct SW8 . . . 160 C1
Tidemill Acad 20
SE8 . . . . 51 C3
Tideswell 10 NW5 . . 13 A4
Tideswell Rd
SW15 . . . . 57 B3
Tideway Ct 9
SE16 . . . . 32 C1
Tideway Ho E14 . . . 41 C4
Tideway Ind Est
SW8 . . . . 161 A3
Tideway Wharf
SW13 . . . . 46 A1
Tideway Yd SW13 . . 46 A1
Tidey St E3 . . . . 33 C4
Tidworth Ho 13
SE22 . . . . 64 A4
Tidworth Rd E3 . . . . 26 C1
Tierney Rd SW2 . . . 74 A3
Tierney Terr SW2 . . 74 A3
Tiger Ho WC1 . . . . . 93 C3
Tiger Way E5 . . . . . . 17 A4
Tignel Ct W3 . . . . . . 36 C4
Tilbury Cl 14 SE15 . 49 B3
Tilbury Ho 4
SE14 . . . . 50 C4
Tildesley Rd SW15 . 57 B1
Tilehurst NW1 . . . . . 92 B3
Tilehurst Rd SW17,
SW18 . . . . 71 C3
Tile Kiln La N6 . . . . . 4 B3
Tileyard Rd N7 . . . . 14 A1
Tilford Gdns SW19 . 69 C2
Tilford Ho 8 SW2 . . 74 B4
Tilia Rd E5 . . . . 17 A4
Tilia Wlk 21 SW9 . . 63 A3
Tiller Ho 26 N1 . . . . 24 A4

Tiller L Ctr E14.....41 C3
Tiller Rd E14.....41 C3
Tillet Sq SE16.....41 A4
Tillet Way 8
E2.....24 C2 99 B4
Tilling Ho 1 SE15..65 A4
Tillman Ho 8
SW2.....74 A3
Tillman St E1.....32 A3
Tilloch St 9 N1.....14 B1
Tillotson Ct SW8..161 C1
Tilney Ct EC1.....97 A2
Tilney Gdns 12 N1..15 C2
Tilney St W1.....117 C2
Tilson Cl 2 SE15...49 A3
Tilson Gdns SW2
SW4.....74 A4
Tilson Ho SW2.....74 A4
Tilton St SW6.....154 B3
Tiltwood The W3...28 B2
Timberland Ct 18
SE15.....49 C3
Timberland Rd E1..32 A3
Timber Mill Way
SW4.....61 C4
Timber Pond Rd
SE16.....40 C4
Timber St EC1.....96 C2
Time Sq E8.....16 B3
Timothy Cl 1
SW4.....61 B2
Timsbury Wlk 5
SW15.....68 C3
Tina Ct SW16.....74 C1
Tindal St SW9.....48 A2
Tinniswood Cl N5..14 C3
Tinsley Rd E1.....32 B4
Tintagel Cres
SE22.....64 B3
Tintagel Ct 6 EC1..96 A2
Tintern Cl SW15...58 A2
Tintern Ho
Belgravia NW1.....146 A3
Regent's Pk NW1...82 B1
Tintern St SW4.....62 A3
Tinworth St SE11..148 B2
Tipthorpe Rd
SW11.....60 C4
Tiptree 7 NW1.....13 A1
Tisbury Ct W1.....119 B4
Tisdall Pl SE17.....151 C3
Tissington Ct 4
SE16.....40 C2
Titan Bsns Est 3
SE8.....51 C3
Titan Ct TW8.....36 B1
Titchborne Row
W2.....102 B1
Titchfield Rd NW8..80 C4
Titchwell Rd
SW18.....71 C3
Tite St SW3.....158 C4
Titmuss St W12.....39 B4
Tiverton Rd NW6,
NW10.....22 C4
Tiverton St SE1.....136 C2
Tivoli Ct SE16.....33 B1
Tivoli Wy E14.....33 B3
Tobago St 12 E14..41 C4
Tobin Cl NW3.....12 A1
Toby La E1.....26 A1
Todber Ho W14...126 A2
Todds Wlk N7.....5 B2

Tokenhouse Yd
EC2.....109 B2
Token Yd SW15.....58 A3
Toland Sq SW15...56 C2
Tolchurch 2 W11...31 C3
Tolhurst Dr 4
W10.....23 A1
Tollbridge Cl W10..23 A1
Tollet St E1.....25 C1
Tollgate Dr SE21...76 A2
Tollgate Ho 1
NW6.....78 A2
Tollhouse Way N19..4 B2
Tollington Ct N4.....5 B2
Tollington Ho 1
N19.....5 A1
Tollington Pk N4.....5 B2
Tollington Pl N4.....5 B2
Tollington Rd N7...14 B4
Tollington Way N7...5 A1
Tolmers Sq NW1...93 A2
Tolpaide Ho SE11.149 B3
Tolpuddle St N1.....85 B2
Tolsford Rd E5.....17 A3
Tom Groves Cl
E15.....19 C3
Tom Hood Cl E15..19 C3
Tom Jenkinson Rd 5
E16.....35 C1
Tomkyns Ho SE11.149 B3
Tomline Ho SE1...122 C1
Tomlin's Gr E3.....26 C2
Tomlinson Cl
5 Gunnersbury
W4.....37 A1
Spitalfields
E2.....24 B2 99 A3
Tomlin's Terr E14..33 A3
Tomlins Wlk 4 N7...5 B2
Tompion Ho EC1...96 B2
Tompion St
EC1.....96 B3
Tom Smith Cl
SE10.....53 A4
Tomson Ho SE1...138 C2
Tom Williams Ho
SW6.....154 C3
Tonbridge Hos
WC1.....94 A3
Tonbridge St WC1..94 A3
Tonborough 18
NW8.....78 B3
Tonsley Hill SW18.59 A2
Tonsley Pl SW18...59 A2
Tonsley Rd SW18..59 A2
Tonsley St SW18...59 A2
Took's Ct EC4.....107 B2
Tooley St SE1.....124 A1
Tooting Bec Sta
SW17.....72 C1
Topham Ho 8
SE10.....52 B3
Topham St EC1.....95 B2
Topiary Sq TW9....54 B4
Topmast Point 2
E14.....41 C4
Tora Temimah Prim
Sch NW2.....9 C2
Torbay Ct 13 NW1..13 A1
Torbay Mans NW6..23 B4
Torbay Rd NW6.....10 B1
Torbay St 15 NW1..13 A1
Tor Ct W8.....127 C4
Tor Gdns W8.....127 B4

Tornay Ho
Hackney E9.....17 B1
N1.....84 C2
Torquay St W2.....100 A3
Torrence Ho 6
N19.....4 B2
Torrens Ct SE5.....63 C4
Torrens Rd SW2...62 B2
Torrens St EC1.....86 A1
Torres Sq E14.....41 C1
Torriano Ave NW5..13 C3
Torriano Cotts
NW5.....13 B3
Torriano Mews
NW5.....13 B3
Torriano Sch 24
NW5.....13 C3
Torridge Gdns
SE15.....65 B3
Torrington Ho 1
SE15.....50 A3
Torrington Pl
Bloomsbury WC1...105 B4
St George in t East
E1.....125 C2
Torrington Sq
WC1.....93 C1
Tortington Ho 1
SE15.....50 A3
Torwood Rd SW15..56 C2
Tothill Ho SW1...147 C4
Tothill St SW1.....133 C3
Totland Ho SW18..58 C4
Tottan Terr E1.....32 C3
Tottenhall 5 NW1..12 C1
Tottenham Court Rd
W1.....105 A2
Tottenham Court
Road Sta W1.....105 C2
Tottenham Mews
W1.....105 A4
Tottenham Rd N1..16 A2
Tottenham St W1..105 A4
Totteridge Ho
SW11.....167 C2
Touchard Ho N1.....97 C3
Toulmin St SE1...136 C3
Toulon St SE5.....48 B3
Toulouse Ct 2
SE16.....40 A1
Tounson Ct SW1..147 C3
Tournay Rd SW6..155 A2
Toussaint Wlk 18
SE16.....139 C2
Tovy Ho 6 SE1.....153 B1
Towcester Rd E3...27 B1
Tower 42 EC2.....110 A2
Tower Bldgs 22
E1.....32 A1
Tower Br App E1,
EC3.....124 C3
Tower Bridge EC3,
SE1.....124 C2
Tower Bridge Bsns
Complex SE16.....40 A3
Tower Bridge Bsns Sq
SE16.....40 A2
Tower Bridge Ex
E1.....124 C2
Tower Bridge Piazza
SE1.....124 C4
Tower Bridge Prim
Sch SE1.....138 C4
Tower Bridge Rd
SE1.....138 A3
Tower Bridge Sq
SE1.....138 C4

Tower Cl NW3.....11 C3
Tower Ct
Brockley SE4.....66 A3
Stamford Hill E5.....7 C3
St Giles WC2.....106 A1
St John's Wood
NW8.....80 B2
Towergate SE1...152 A4
Towergate Ho 35
E3.....26 B3
Tower Gateway Sta
EC3.....124 C4
Tower Hill Sta
EC3.....124 C4
Tower House Sch
SW14.....55 B3
Tower Mans SE1..138 C1
Tower Mews E5.....18 A3
Tower Millennium
Pier EC3.....124 B2
Tower Mill Rd
7 Camberwell
SE15.....49 A4
8 SE15.....49 A3
Tower of London The
EC3.....124 C3
Tower Pl E EC3...124 B3
Tower Pl W EC3...124 B3
Tower Rd NW10....8 C1
Tower Rise 9 TW9..54 A4
Tower Royal EC4..123 B4
Tower St WC2.....106 A1
Towers The
Dartmouth Pk NW5.4 A1
1 Richmond TW9..54 B3
Tower Terr SE4.....66 A3
Tower Wharf SE1.138 C4
Tower Wlk SE1...152 A4
Tower Workshops
SE1.....138 C3
Townhall Ave 3
W4.....37 C1
Town Hall Rd
SW11.....60 B4
Town Hos EC1.....96 B1
Townley Rd SE22..64 A2
Townley St 1 SE17.151 B2
Townmead Bsns Ctr
SW6.....59 B4
Townmead Rd
Richmond TW9.....45 A1
Sands End SE6....166 C1
Townsend Ho 14
SE1.....153 C3
Townsend Ind Est
NW10.....20 B3
Townsend Mews
SW18.....71 B2
Townsend Prim Sch
SE17.....152 A4
Townsend Rd NW8.80 B2
Townsend St SE17.152 A4
Townshend Ct
NW8.....80 B2

Townshend Est
NW8.....80 A2
Townshend Rd
Primrose Hill
NW8.....80 A3
Richmond TW9.....54 B3
Townshend Terr
TW9.....54 B3
Towns Ho 4 SW4..61 C4
Towpath Wlk E9...18 B3
Towton Rd SE27...75 B2
Toxteth Ho N4.....6 B4
Toynbee St E1.....110 C3
Toynbee Studios
E1.....111 A3
Tracey Ave NW2....9 B3
Tracy Ho 15 E3.....26 B2
Tradescant Ho 16
E9.....17 B1
Tradescant Rd
SW8.....162 B1
Trade Twr 8
SW11.....59 B4
Trade Winds Ct 1
E1.....125 C2
Trading Estate Rd
NW10.....20 B1
Traemore Ct
SW16.....74 C1
Trafalgar Ave
SE15.....49 B4
Trafalgar Cl 1
SE16.....41 A2
Trafalgar Gdns
Stepney E1.....32 C4
W8.....128 B2
Trafalgar Gr 10
SE10.....52 C4
Trafalgar Ho
SE17.....151 A2
Trafalgar Mews
E9.....18 B2
Trafalgar Point 2
N1.....15 C1
Trafalgar Rd SE10.43 A1
Trafalgar Sq SW1..119 C2
Trafalgar St SE17.151 C2
Trafalgar Way E14.34 B1
Trafford Ho N1.....87 C2
Trafford St SW11..158 A2
Trahorn Cl E1.....25 A1
Traitors Gate EC3.124 C2
Tralee Ct 31 SE16..40 A1
Tramway Ave E15..19 C1
Trance Way W3.....36 C3
Tranmere Ho 7
N7.....14 C3
Tranmere Rd SW17,
SW18.....71 B2
Tranquil Pas SE3...53 B1
Tranquil Vale SE3..53 A1
Transept St NW1..102 B3
Transom Cl SE16..41 A2
Transom Sq E14...42 A1
Tranton Rd SE16..40 A3
Trappes Ho 2
SE16.....40 A2
Travers Ho 6
SE10.....52 C4
Travers Rd N7.....5 C1
Travis Ho SE10.....52 B2
Treadgold Ho 7
W11.....30 C2
Treadgold St W11..30 C2
Treadway St E2.....25 A3
Treasury Bldgs
SW1.....134 A4

Treaty St N1 . . . . 84 C3
Trebeck St W1 . . . . . . 118 A1
Treborough Ho
  W1 . . . . 103 B4
Trebovir Rd SW5 . 141 C3
Treby St E3 . . . . 26 B1
Trecastle Way **2**
  N7 . . . . 13 C4
Tredegar Mews **10**
  E3 . . . . 26 B3
Tredegar Rd E3 . . . . . 26 B3
Tredegar Sq E3 . . . . . 26 B2
Tredegar Terr E3 . . . 26 B2
Trederwen Rd E8 . . 24 C4
Treen Ave SW13 . . 56 B4
Trees The N16 . . . . . . 6 C4
Trefil Wlk N7 . . . . . . 14 A4
Trefoil Rd SW18 . . . 59 B2
Tregarvon Rd
  SW11 . . . . 60 C3
Trego Rd E9 . . . . 18 C1
Tregothnan Rd
  SW9 . . . . 62 A4
Tregunter Rd
  SW10 . . . . 142 C1
Treherne Ct SW9 . . 48 A2
Trehern Rd **1**
  SW14 . . . . 55 C4
Trehurst St E5 . . . . . 18 A3
Trelawney Est E9 . . 17 B2
Trelawney Ho
  SE1 . . . . 136 C4
Trelawn Rd SW2 . . 62 C2
Trellis Sq **1** E3 . . . . . 26 B2
Tremadoc Rd SW4 . 61 C3
Tremaine Cl SE4 . . . 51 C1
Trematon Ho
  SE11 . . . . 149 C2
Tremlett Gr N19 . . . . 4 B1
Tremlett Mews **17**
  N19 . . . . 4 B1
Trenchard St SE10 . 42 C1
Trenchold St
  SW8 . . . . 162 A3
Trendell Ho **8**
  E14 . . . . 33 C3
Trenmar Gdns
  NW10 . . . . 22 A2
Trentham Ct W3 . . 28 C4
Trentham St SW18 . 70 C3
Trent Ho SE15 . . . . . 65 B3
Trent Rd SW2 . . . . . . 62 B2
Treport St SW18 . . . 71 A4
Tresco Ho SE11 . . . 149 B2
Tresco Rd SE15 . . . 65 A3
Tresham Cres
  NW8 . . . . 90 A2
Tresham Wlk E9 . . 17 B3
Tressider Ho **10**
  SW4 . . . . 73 C4
Tressel Cl **20** N1 . . . 15 A1
Tressillian Cres
  SE4 . . . . 66 C4
Tressillian Rd SE4 . 66 C4
Trevanion Rd
  W14 . . . . 140 B2
Trevelyan Gdns
  NW10 . . . . 22 B4
Trevelyan Ho
  16 Globe Town
  E2 . . . . 25 C2
  SE5 . . . . 48 A3
Treveris St SE1 . . . 122 B1
Treverton St W10 . 30 C4
Treverton Twr **1**
  W10 . . . . 30 C4

Treves Ho
  E1 . . . . 24 C1 99 C1
Treville St SW15 . . 69 A4
Trevithick Ho **13** Bermondsey
  SE16 . . . . 40 A2
  3 Gospel Oak
  NW5 . . . . 13 A4
  SW8 . . . . 171 B4
Trevithick St SE8 . . 51 C4
Trevithick Wy **28**
  E3 . . . . 26 C2
Trevor Pl SW7 . . . . 130 B3
Trevor-Roberts Sch
  NW8 . . . . 11 C1
Trevor Sq SW7 . . . 130 B3
Trevor St SW7 . . . . 130 B3
Trevose Ho SE11 . . 149 A2
Trewint St SW18 . . 71 B2
Triangle Ct E3 . . . . 123 A1
Triangle Est The
  SE11 . . . . 149 B1
Triangle Ho SE1 . . 138 C4
Triangle Pl SW4 . . . 61 C3
Triangle Rd **7** E8 . . 25 A4
Triangle The
  Crouch End N19 . . . 4 C4
  EC1 . . . . 96 B2
  18 Hackney E8 . . . 25 A4
Trident Ho E14 . . . . 34 B3
Trident St SE16 . . . . 40 C2
Trieste Ct SW12 . . . 72 B3
Trig La EC4 . . . . 122 C4
Trigon Rd SW8 . . . 163 A2
Trillington Ho
  W12 . . . . 29 C1
Trimdon NW1 . . . . . 83 A3
Trimmer Wlk **11**
  TW8 . . . . 44 A4
Trim St SE8 . . . . 51 B4
Trinder Gdns N19 . . 5 A3
Trinder Rd N4, N19 . 5 A3
Trinidad Ho **17**
  E14 . . . . 33 B2
Trinidad St E14 . . . 33 B2
Trinity Church Rd
  SW13 . . . . 47 A4
Trinity Church Sq
  SE1 . . . . 137 A2
Trinity Cl
  3 Clapham SW4 . . 61 B3
  Lewisham SE13 . . . 67 C3
Trinity Coll of Music
  SE10 . . . . 52 C3
Trinity Cotts TW9 . 54 B4
Trinity Cres SW17 . 72 C2
Trinity Ct
  Finsbury WC1 . . . . 94 C2
  2 Hoxton N1 . . . . . 24 A3
  Rotherhithe SE16 . . 41 A4
  Willesden NW2 . . . . 9 B3
Trinity Gdns
  E16 . . . . 35 B4
  Stockwell SW2,
  SW9 . . . . 62 B3
Trinity Gn **1** E1 . . . . 32 B4
Trinity Gr **8** SE10 . . 52 B2
Trinity Ho SE1 . . . . 137 A2
Trinity Homes **14**
  SW2 . . . . 62 B3
Trinity Laban
  Conservatoire of
  Music & Dance **7**
  SL8 . . . . 52 A4
Trinity Mews
  SW18 . . . . 70 C3

Trinity Pl EC3 . . . . 124 C3
Trinity Rd
  Richmond TW9 . . . 54 B4
  Wandsworth SW17,
  SW18 . . . . 72 A4
Trinity Rise SE24,
  SW2 . . . . 75 A4
Trinity St Mary's CE
  Prim Sch **8**
  SW12 . . . . 72 C3
Trinity Sq EC3 . . . . 124 B4
Trinity St
  3 Newham E16 . . . 35 C4
  SE1 . . . . 137 B2
Trinity Way W3 . . . 29 B2
Trio Pl SE1 . . . . 137 A3
Tristan Ct **34** SE8 . . 51 B4
Triton Ct EC2 . . . . . . 97 C1
Triton Ho **2** E14 . . . 42 A2
Triton Sq NW1 . . . . 92 B2
Tritton Rd SE21,
  SE27 . . . . 75 C1
Trocette Mans
  SE1 . . . . 138 B2
Trojan Ind Est
  NW10 . . . . 10 A1
Troon Cl **33** SE16 . . 40 A1
Troon Ho **8** E14 . . . 33 A3
Troon St E1 . . . . 33 A3
Tropical Ct **2**
  W10 . . . . 22 C2
Trossachs Rd
  SE22 . . . . 64 A2
Trothy Rd SE1 . . . . 153 C3
Trotman Ho **8**
  SE14 . . . . 50 B2
Trott St SW11 . . . . 168 A3
Trotwood Ho **3**
  SE16 . . . . 40 A4
Troubridge Ct **12**
  W4 . . . . 37 B1
Troutbeck NW1 . . . 92 B3
Troutbeck Rd
  SE14 . . . . 51 A2
Trouville Rd SW4 . 61 B1
Trowbridge Est **8**
  E15 . . . . 18 B2
Trowbridge Rd E9 . 18 B2
Trower Ho **5** E9 . . . 18 A2
Troy Ct W8 . . . . 127 B2
Troyes Ho NW3 . . 12 B3
Troy Town SE15 . . . 64 C4
Troy Town Flats
  SE15 . . . . 64 C4
Truman's Rd **24**
  N16 . . . . 16 A3
Trump St EC2 . . . . 109 A1
Trundle St SE1 . . . . 136 C4
Trundleys Rd SE8 . 51 A4
Trundley's Rd SE8 . 40 C1
Trundley's Terr
  SE8 . . . . 40 C2
Truro Ho **29** W2 . . . 31 C4
Truro St NW5 . . . . 12 C2
Trussley Rd W6 . . . 39 B3
Trust Wlk SE21 . . . 75 A3
Tryon Cres E9 . . . . 25 B4
Tryon St SW3 . . . . 144 C2
Tubbs Rd NW10 . . 21 B3
Tudor Cl
  Crouch End N4 . . . . 4 B4
  Hampstead NW3 . . 12 A2
  Tulse Hill SW2 . . . . 62 B1
Tudor Coll WC1 . . . 94 A3

Tudor Ct
  Kingsland N1 . . . . . 16 A2
  5 Rotherhithe
  SE16 . . . . 32 C1
  South Acton W5 . . 36 C4
Tudor Est NW10 . . 20 A3
Tudor Gdns SW14 . 56 A4
Tudor Gr E9 . . . . . . 17 B1
Tudor Ho
  Brook Green W14 . 39 C2
  34 Hackney E9 . . . 17 B1
Tudor Mews **2**
  NW10 . . . . 8 C2
Tudor Rd E9 . . . . . . 25 A4
Tudor St EC4 . . . . . 121 C4
Tudor Way W3 . . . . 36 C4
Tufnell Ct **19** E3 . . . 26 B2
Tufnell Mans **7**
  N7 . . . . 13 C4
TUFNELL PARK . . 13 C4
Tufnell Park Mans **3**
  N7 . . . . 5 A1
Tufnell Park Prim Sch
  N7 . . . . 13 B4
Tufnell Park Rd N19,
  N7 . . . . 13 B4
Tufnell Park Sta
  N19 . . . . 13 B4
Tufton Ct SW1 . . . 134 A1
Tufton St SW1 . . . . 134 A1
Tuke Sch SE15 . . . . 49 B4
Tullis Ho **2** E9 . . . . 17 B1
TULSE HILL 75 A4
Tulse Hill
  Tulse Hill SW2 . . . 74 C4
  Tulse Hill SW2 . . . 75 A4
Tulse Hill Sta
  SE27 . . . . 75 A2
Tulse Ho SW2 . . . . 62 C1
Tulsemere Rd SE21,
  SE27 . . . . 75 B2
Tunbridge Ct **1**
  SE26 . . . . 76 C1
Tunbridge Ho EC1 . 96 A4
Tunis Rd W12 . . . . 30 A1
Tunley Gn **12** E14 . . 33 B4
Tunley Rd
  Dagenham NW10 . 21 A4
  Upper Tooting SW12,
  SW17 . . . . 72 C3
Tunnel Avenue Trad
  Est SE10 . . . . 42 C4
Tunnel Rd SE16 . . . 40 B4
Tunstall Ct **14**
  TW9 . . . . 44 B2
Tunstall Rd SW9 . . 62 B3
Tunstall Wlk **11**
  TW8 . . . . 44 A4
Tunworth Cres
  SW15 . . . . 56 B1
Tun Yd SW8 . . . . . . 61 A4
Tupman Ho **26**
  SE16 . . . . 139 B3
Turberville Ho **1**
  SW8 . . . . 162 B2
Turenne Cl **14** SW8 59 B3
Turin St E2 . . . . 24 C2 99 B3
Turk's Head Yd
  EC1 . . . . 108 A4
Turks Row SW3 . . 145 A2
Turle Rd N4 . . . . 5 B2
Turlewray Cl N4 . . . 5 B3
Turnagain La EC4 . 108 A2
Turnberry Cl **24**
  SE16 . . . . 40 A1

Tre–Twy **281**

Turnberry Quay **1**
  E14 . . . . 42 A3
Turnbull Ho N1 . . . 86 B4
Turnchapel Mews **1**
  SW4 . . . . 61 A4
Turner Cl **7** SW9 . . 48 A2
Turner Ct
  5 Herne Hill SE5 . 63 C3
  6 Rotherhithe
  SE16 . . . . 40 B4
Turner Ho
  Finsbury Pk N4 . . . 5 B3
  22 Millwall E14 . . 41 C4
  St John's Wood
  NW8 . . . . 80 A2
  Strand WC2 . . . . . 120 B3
  Westminster SW1 . 147 C3
Turner Pl SW11 . . . 60 A2
Turners Ct E15 . . . . 19 B4
Turner's Rd E3 . . . 33 B4
Turner St
  Canning Town
  E16 . . . . 35 B3
  Stepney E1 . . . . . . 32 A4
Turneville Rd
  W14 . . . . 154 C4
Turney Rd SE21 . . . 75 C4
Turney Sch SE21 . . 75 C4
Turnham Green Sta
  W4 . . . . 38 A2
Turnham Green Terr
  W4 . . . . 38 A2
Turnham Ho SE4 . . 66 A3
Turnham Prim Sch **11**
  SE4 . . . . 66 A3
Turnmill Ho **8**
  SW2 . . . . 62 C2
Turnmill St EC1 . . 108 A4
Turnour Ho **31** E1 . . 32 A3
Turnpike Cl SE8 . . 51 B3
Turnpike Ho EC1 . . 96 B3
Turpentine La
  SW1 . . . . 146 B1
Turpin Ho SW11 . . 170 A4
Turpin Way N19 . . . 4 C3
Turquand St SE17 . 151 A3
Turret Gr SW4 . . . . 61 B4
Turville Ho NW8 . . 90 A2
Turville St
  E2 . . . . 24 B1 98 C2
Tuscan Ho **28** E2 . . 25 B2
Tuskar St SE10 . . . . 43 A1
Tuttle Ho SW1 . . . 147 C1
Tweed Ho E14 . . . . 34 B1
Tweezer's Alley
  WC2 . . . . 121 B4
Twelvetrees Bsns Pk
  E16 . . . . 27 C1
Twelvetrees Cres
  E3 . . . . 27 B2
Twig Folly Cl **21**
  E2 . . . . 25 C3
Twilley St SW18 . . 71 A4
Twine Ct E1 . . . . . . 32 B2
Twinings Mus
  WC2 . . . . 107 B1
Twisden Rd NW5 . 13 A4
Twycross Mews
  SE10 . . . . 43 A2

Twyford CE High Sch
W3 . . . . 28 A1
Twyford Ho N5 . . . . . 6 A1
Twyford Sp Ctr
W3 . . . . 28 A1
Twyford St N1 . . . . 84 C4
Twynholm Mans
SW6 . . . . 154 A2
Tyburn Tree (site of)
W2 . . . . 116 C3
Tyburn Way W1 . . 117 A4
Tyer's Est SE1 . . . 138 A3
Tyers Gate SE1 . . 138 A3
Tyers St SE11 . . . 148 C2
Tyers Terr SE11 . . 149 A1
Tyler Cl E2 . . . . . . 24 B3
Tyler Ho SE3 . . . . . 52 C1
Tyler St
Greenwich SE10 . . . 43 A1
SE10 . . . . 53 A4
Tylney Ho E1 . . . . . 32 A3
Tymperley Ct
SW19 . . . . 70 A3
Tyndale La N1 . . . . 15 A1
Tyndale Mans N1 . . 15 A1
Tyndale Terr 13
N1 . . . . 15 A1
Tyneham Cl 10
SW11 . . . . 60 C4
Tyneham Rd SW11 . 60 C4
Tynemouth St
SW6 . . . . 166 C2
Tyne St E1 . . . . . 111 A2
Tynsdale Rd NW10 . . 8 A2
Tynte Ct E9 . . . . . . 18 A3
Tynwald Ho 14
SE26 . . . . 76 C1
Type St E2 . . . . . . 25 C3
Tyrawley Rd SW6 . 166 A4
Tyrells Ct 3 SE15 . . 65 A4
Tyrrell Ho SW1 . . 161 A4
Tyrrell Rd SE22 . . . 64 C3
Tyrwhitt Rd SE4 . . . 66 C4
Tysoe St EC1 . . . . 95 C3
Tyssen Com Prim Sch
N16 . . . . 7 C3
Tyssen Rd N16 . . . . 7 B1
Tyssen St
Dalston E8 . . . . . . 16 B2
Hoxton N1 . . . . . . 24 A3
Tysson Ho E9 . . . . 18 A1
Tytherton 25 E2 . . 25 B3
Tytherton Rd N19 . . 4 C1

U

Uamvar St E14 . . . 34 A4
UCL Acad 13 NW3 . 11 C1
UCL Elizabeth Garrett
Anderson Wing
NW1 . . . . 93 A1
Udall St SW1 . . . 147 A3
Udimore Ho
W10 . . . . 30 B4
Uffington Rd
NW10 . . . . 22 A4
Ufford St SE1 . . . 135 C4
Ufton Gr N1 . . . . . 15 C1
Ufton Rd N1 . . . . . 16 A1
Uhura Sq 18 N16 . . . 7 A1
Ujima Ct N19 . . . . . 5 A3
Ullin St E14 . . . . . 34 B4
Ullswater SW15 . . . 57 C1

Ullswater Ho SE15 . 50 B4
Ullswater Rd
Barnes SW13 . . . . 46 C3
West Norwood SE27,
SW16 . . . . 75 A2
Ulster Pl NW1 . . . . 92 A1
Ulster Terr NW1 . . . 92 A2
Ulundi Rd SE3 . . . . 53 A4
Ulva Rd SW15 . . . . 57 C3
Ulverscroft Rd
SE22 . . . . 64 C2
Ulverstone Rd
SE27 . . . . 75 A2
Ulysses Rd NW6 . . 10 B3
Umberston St E1 . . 32 A3
Umbria St SW15 . . . 56 C1
Una Ho 7 NW5 . . . 13 A2
Undercliff SE10 . . . 52 B2
Undercliff Rd
SE13 . . . . 67 A4
Underhill Ho 7
E14 . . . . 33 C4
Underhill Pas NW1 . 82 B4
Underhill St NW1 . . 82 B3
Undershaft EC3 . . 110 A1
Underwood Ho
W6 . . . . 39 A3
Underwood Rd
E1 . . . . 24 C1 99 C1
Underwood Row
N1 . . . . 97 A4
Underwood St N1 . . 97 A4
Undine Rd E14 . . . . 42 A2
Unicorn Bldg 14
E1 . . . . 32 C2
Unicorn Sch TW9 . . 44 B2
Union Cl E11 . . . . . 19 C4
Union Ct
Paddington
W2 . . . . 31 C4
2 Richmond TW10 . 54 A2
South Lambeth
SW4 . . . . 172 A1
Whitechapel EC2 . . 110 A2
Union Dr E1 . . . . . 26 A1
Union Gr SW8 . . . 171 C2
Union Mews 32
SW9 . . . . 172 A1
Union Pk 8 SE10 . . 43 B1
Union Rd SW8 . . . 171 C1
Union Sq N1 . . . . . 87 A3
Union St
Mill Meads E15 . . . 27 C4
SE1 . . . . 122 C1
Union Wharf N1 . . 87 A2
Union Wlk
E2 . . . . 24 A2 98 B4
Union Yd W1 . . . 104 B1
Unity Cl NW10 . . . . 8 C2
Unity Mews NW1 . . 83 B2
Univ Coll Hospl at
Westmoreland St
W1 . . . . 103 C3
Univ Coll London
Bloomsbury WC1 . . 93 B2
Bloomsbury WC1 . . 94 B2
Univ Coll London
(Windeyer Inst)
W1 . . . . 105 A4
Univ Coll London
(Wolfson Ho)
NW1 . . . . 93 A3
Univ Coll Sch Junior
Branch 31 NW3 . . 11 B4
University College
London WC1 . . . 93 C1

University Coll Hospl
WC1 . . . . 93 A2
University Coll Sch
NW3 . . . . 11 B3
University Mans 9
SW15 . . . . 57 C4
University of Cumbria
London 25 E14 . . 33 C2
University St WC1 . 93 A1
Univ Hospl Lewisham
SE13 . . . . 67 A2
Univ of California
WC1 . . . . 105 C3
Univ of Greenwich
SE10 . . . . 52 C4
Univ of London
Birkbeck College
WC1 . . . . 105 C4
Univ of Notre Dame
(King's Coll Hall)
SE5 . . . . 63 C4
Univ of Notre Dame
W1 . . . . 119 C3
Univ of Notre Dame
W1 . . . . 119 C2
Univ of Roehampton
(Digby Stuart Coll)
SW15 . . . . 56 C2
Univ of Roehampton
(Froebel Coll)
SW15 . . . . 56 B1
Univ of Roehampton
(Southlands Coll)
SW15 . . . . 56 C2
Univ of Roehampton
(Whitelands Coll)
SW15 . . . . 68 C4
Univ of Wales Trinity
St David SW9 . . . 163 C2
Univ of Westminster
(Cavendish Campus)
W1 . . . . 104 C4
Univ of Westminster
(Marylebone
Campus) W1 . . . 103 B4
Univ of Westminster
(Regent Campus)
W1 . . . . 104 C3
Univ of Westminster
(Regent Campus,
Univ HQ) W1 . . . 104 B2
Univ of Westminster
(Wigram House
Halls of Residence)
SW1 . . . . 133 A1
Unwin Cl SE15 . . . . 49 C4
Unwin Rd SW7 . . . 129 C2
Upbrook Mews
W2 . . . . 101 A1
Upcerne Rd SW10 . 157 A1
Upcott Ho
53 Bromley E3 . . . . 27 A2
4 Hackney E9 . . . 17 B1
Upgrove Manor Way
16 SE24 . . . . 74 C4
Upham Park Rd
W4 . . . . 38 A2
Upland Rd SE22 . . . 64 C1
Uplands Cl SW14 . . 55 A2
Upnall Ho 16 SE15 . 50 B4
Upnor Way SE17 . . 152 B2
Upper Addison Gdns
W14 . . . . 126 A4
Upper Bank St
E14 . . . . 34 A1

Upper Bardsey Wlk 7
N1 . . . . 15 B2
Upper Belgrave St
SW1 . . . . 131 C2
Upper Berkeley St
W1 . . . . 103 A1
Upper Brockley Rd
SE4 . . . . 51 B1
Upper Brook St
W1 . . . . 117 B4
Upper Caldy Wlk 8
N1 . . . . 15 B2
Upper Camelford Wlk
14 W10 . . . . 31 A3
Upper Cheyne Row
SW3 . . . . 158 A4
Upper Clarendon Wlk
6 W11 . . . . 31 A3
Upper Dengie Wlk
N1 . . . . 86 C4
Upper Grosvenor St
W1 . . . . 117 B3
Upper Ground
SE1 . . . . 121 B2
Upper Gulland Wlk 2
N1 . . . . 15 B2
Upper Hampstead Wlk
25 NW3 . . . . 2 B1
Upper Handa Wlk 3
N1 . . . . 15 B2
Upper Harley St
NW1 . . . . 91 C1
Upper Hawkwell Wlk
N1 . . . . 87 A4
**UPPER
HOLLOWAY** 4 C2
Upper Holloway Sta
N19 . . . . 4 C2
Upper James St
W1 . . . . 119 A4
Upper John St
W1 . . . . 119 A4
Upper Lismore Wlk 8
N1 . . . . 15 B2
Upper Mall W6 . . . 39 A1
Upper Marsh SE1 . 135 A2
Upper Montague St
W1 . . . . 102 C3
Upper North St E3,
E14 . . . . 33 C4
Upper Park Rd
NW3 . . . . 12 B3
Upper Phillimore
Gdns W8 . . . . . 127 B3
Upper Ramsey Wlk 15
N1 . . . . 15 C2
Upper Rawreth Wlk
N1 . . . . 87 A4
Upper Richmond Rd
SW15 . . . . 57 B3
Upper Richmond Rd
W TW10, SW14,
SW15 . . . . 55 B3
Upper St Martin's La
WC2 . . . . 120 A4
Upper St N1 . . . . . 86 A3
Upper Tachbrook St
SW1 . . . . 147 A4
Upper Talbot Wlk 7
W10 . . . . 31 A3
Upper Terr NW3 . . . 2 B1
Upper Thames St
EC4 . . . . 123 A4
Upper Tollington Pk
N4 . . . . 5 C3
UPPER TOOTING . . 72 B1

Upper Tooting Park
Mans 1 SW17 . . . 72 C2
Upper Tooting Pk
SW17 . . . . 72 B2
Upper Tooting Rd
SW17 . . . . 72 B1
Upper Tulse Hill
SW2 . . . . 74 B3
Upper Wimpole St
W1 . . . . 103 C4
Upper Woburn Pl NW1,
WC1 . . . . 93 C3
Upstall St SE5 . . . . 48 A2
Upton Cl NW2 . . . . 1 A1
Urban Mews N4 . . . 6 A4
Urlwin St SE5 . . . . 48 B4
Urlwin Wlk SW9 . . 48 A2
Urmston Dr SW19 . 70 A3
Urmston Ho 4
E14 . . . . 42 B2
Ursula Gould Wy 27
E14 . . . . 33 C4
Ursula Mews N4 . . . 6 B3
Ursula St SW11 . . 168 A3
Urswick Rd E5, E9 . 17 B3
Urswick Sch The 18
E9 . . . . 17 B2
Usborne Mews
SW8 . . . . 163 A2
Usher Rd E3 . . . . . 26 B3
Usk Rd SW11 . . . . 59 B3
Usk St E2 . . . . . . 25 C2
Utah Bldg 3 SE13 . 52 A2
Utopia Ho 3 NW2 . . 8 C2
Utopia Village
NW1 . . . . 81 B4
Uverdale Rd
SW10 . . . . 157 A1
Uxbridge Rd W12 . . 30 A1
Uxbridge St
W8 . . . . 31 C1 113 B2

V

Vadnie Bish Ho
NW5 . . . . 13 B2
Vaine Ho 4 E9 . . . 18 A2
Vale Ct
2 Hammersmith
W3 . . . . 29 B1
St John's Wood W9 . 88 C3
Vale End SE22 . . . . 64 B3
Vale Est The 3 W3 . 29 A1
Vale Gr
Acton W3 . . . . . . 28 C1
Stoke Newington N4 . 6 B4
Valens Ho 1 SW2 . . 74 C3
Valentia Pl SW9 . . 62 C3
Valentine Ho
11 Clapham Pk
SW4 . . . . 61 B1
28 Old Ford E3 . . . 26 B4
Valentine Pl SE1 . 136 A4
Valentine Rd E9 . . . 17 C2
Valentine Row
SE1 . . . . 136 A3
VALE OF HEALTH . . 2 C1
Vale of Health NW3 . 2 C1
Vale Rd N4 . . . . . . 6 B4
Vale Rise NW11 . . . 1 B3
Vale Row N5 . . . . . 6 A1
Vale Royal N7 . . . 14 A1
Vale Sch The
SW7 . . . . 128 C1

Vale The
Cricklewood NW11 . . . . . 1 A2
East Acton W3 . . . . 29 A1
SW3 . . . . 157 C4
Valetta Rd W3 . . . . 38 B4
Valette Ho E9 . . . . 17 B2
Valette St E8 . . . . 17 A2
Valiant Ho
9 Cubitt Town
E14 . . . . 42 B4
SW11 . . . . 167 C3
Vallance Rd
E1 . . . . 24 C1 99 C5
Vallière Rd NW10 . . . . . 21 C2
Val McKenzie Ave
N7 . . . . 5 C1
Valmar Rd SE5 . . . . 48 B2
Valmar Trad Est
SE5 . . . . 48 B2
Valois Ho SE1 . . . . . . 138 C2
Valonia Gdns
SW18 . . . . 58 B1
Vanbern Ho NW5 . . . . . 12 C2
Vanbrugh Ct SE11 149 C3
Vanbrugh Fields
SE3 . . . . 53 B3
Vanbrugh Hill SE10,
SE3 . . . . 53 B4
Vanbrugh Ho 8
E9 . . . . 17 B1
Vanbrugh Park Rd
SE3 . . . . 53 B3
Vanbrugh Park Rd W
SE3 . . . . 53 B3
Vanbrugh Pk SE3 . . 53 B3
Vanbrugh Rd W4 . . 37 C3
Vanbrugh Terr
SE3 . . . . 53 B2
Vanburgh Ho E1 . . . . 110 C4
Vancover Ho 59
E1 . . . . 32 A1
Vanderbilt Rd
SW18 . . . . 71 B3
Vanderbilt Villas 1
W12 . . . . 39 C4
Vandon Ct SW1 . . . . 133 A2
Vandon Pas SW1 . . . 133 A2
Vandon St SW1 . . . . 133 A2
Vandyke Cl SW15 . . . 57 C1
Vandy St
EC2 . . . . 24 A1 98 A1
Vane Cl NW3 . . . . 11 C4
Vane St SW1 . . . . . . 147 A4
Vange Ho 15 W10 . . . 30 B4
Van Gogh Ct E14 . . . . 42 C3
Vanguard Bldg 6
E14 . . . . 41 C4
Vanguard Ho 77
E8 . . . . 17 A1
Vanguard St SE8 . . . 51 C2
Vanneck Sq SW15 . . . 56 C2
Vanner Point 27
E9 . . . . 17 C2
Vansittart St 7
SE14 . . . . 51 A3
Vanston Pl SW6 . . . . 155 C2
Vantage Mews 7
E14 . . . . 34 B1
Vantage Pl W8 . . . . . 127 C1
Vantrey Ho SE11 . . . 149 B3
Varcoe Rd SE16 . . . . . 40 B1
Vardens Rd SW11 . . 59 C3
Varden St E1 . . . . 32 A3
Vardon Cl W3 . . . . 28 C3
Vardon Ho SE10 . . . . . 52 B2
Varey Ho E1 . . . . 26 A2

Varley Ho 5 NW6 . . 23 C4
Varma Ct SE3 . . . . 53 C2
Varna Rd SW6 . . . . . 154 C1
Varndell St NW1 . . . 92 C4
Varnishers Yard
N1 . . . . 84 B1
Varsity Row SW14 . . 45 B1
Vascroft Est NW10 . . 20 A1
Vassall Ho 3 E3 . . . . 26 A2
Vassall Rd SW9 . . . . 163 C1
Vat Ho SW8 . . . . 162 B2
Vauban St SE16 . . . . 139 A1
Vauban St SE16 . . . . 139 A1
Vaudeville Ct N4 . . . . . 5 C2
Vaughan Ave W6 . . . 38 B2
Vaughan Est 8
E2 . . . . 24 B2 98 C4
Vaughan Ho SE1 . . . 136 A4
Vaughan Rd SE5 . . . . 63 B4
Vaughan St SE16 . . . . 41 B4
Vaughan Way E1 . . . 125 C2
Vaughan Williams Cl 7
SE8 . . . . 51 C3
VAUXHALL 148 B1
Vauxhall Bridge Rd
SW1 . . . . 147 A3
Vauxhall City Farm
SE1 . . . . 148 C1
Vauxhall Cross SE1,
SW8 . . . . 148 B1
Vauxhall Gr SW8 . . 162 C4
Vauxhall Prim Sch
SE11 . . . . 149 A2
Vauxhall St SE11 . . . 149 A2
Vauxhall Sta SE11 . . 148 B1
Vauxhall Wlk
SE11 . . . . 148 C2
Vawdrey Cl E1 . . . . . . 25 B1
Vaynor Ho N7 . . . . 14 A4
Vectis Ct SW18 . . . . . . 59 A1
Veda Rd SE13 . . . . 66 C3
Velde Way 1
SE22 . . . . 64 A2
Vellacott Ho 3
W12 . . . . 30 A3
Velletri Ho 17 E2 . . . 25 C3
Venables St NW8 . . 101 C4
Vencourt Pl W6 . . . . . 38 C2
Venetian Rd SE5 . . . . 48 B1
Venice Ct 14 SE5 . . . 48 B3
Venn Ho N1 . . . . 85 A3
Venn St SW4 . . . . 61 B3
Ventnor Rd SE14 . . . . 50 C3
Ventura Ho 12
SW2 . . . . 62 A3
Venue St E14 . . . . 34 B4
Venus Ho
7 Millwall E14 . . . . 41 C2
8 Old Ford E3 . . . . . 26 C4
Vera Ct 8 W2 . . . . . 100 A2
Vera Rd SW6 . . . . . . 164 B4
Verbena Gdns 4
W6 . . . . 38 C1
Verdun Rd SW13 . . . . 46 C3
Vere Bank SW19 . . . . 70 B3
Vereker Rd W14 . . . 140 B1
Vere St W1 . . . . 104 A1
Verity Cl W11 . . . . 31 A3
Verity Ho 20 E3 . . . . . 26 B2
Vermeer Ct E14 . . . . . 42 C3
Vermont Rd SW18 . . . 59 A1
Verne Ct 3 W3 . . . . . 37 B3
Verneer Gdns
SE15 . . . . 65 B3
Verney Ho
Lisson Gr NW8 . . . . 90 A2

Verney Ho continued
South Kensington
SW10 . . . . 156 C4
Verney Rd SE16 . . . . . 40 A1
Verney Way SE16 . . . . 40 A1
Vernon Ct NW2 . . . . 1 B1
Vernon Ho SE11 . . . . 149 A1
Vernon Mews
W14 . . . . 140 B3
Vernon Pl WC1 . . . . . 106 B3
Vernon Rd
Bow E3 . . . . 26 B3
Mortlake SW14 . . . . 55 C4
Vernon Rise WC1 . . . . 95 A4
Vernon Sq WC1 . . . . . 95 A4
Vernon St W14 . . . . . 140 B3
Vernon Yd
W11 . . . . 31 B2 112 C4
Verona Ct
Chiswick W4 . . . . . . 38 A1
10 SE14 . . . . 50 C4
Veronica Ho
Brockley SE4 . . . . . . 66 B4
28 Bromley E3 . . . . 27 A2
Veronica Rd SW17 . . 73 A2
Verran Rd SW12 . . . . 73 A4
Verulam Bldgs
WC1 . . . . 107 A4
Verulam Ho 1
W6 . . . . 39 B4
Verulam St EC1 . . . . 107 B4
Verwin Ho 5
SE15 . . . . 49 C3
Verwood Ho SW8 163 A1
Verwood Lo 1
E14 . . . . 42 C2
Vesage Ct EC1 . . . . . 107 C3
Vesey Path 15 E14 . 34 A3
Vespan Rd W12 . . . . . 38 C4
Vesta Ct SE1 . . . . . 138 A3
Vesta Ho 3 E3 . . . . . 26 C4
Vesta Rd SE4, SE14 . . 51 A1
Vestry Mews 12
SE5 . . . . 49 A2
Vestry Rd SE5 . . . . . 49 A2
Vestry St N1 . . . . 97 B4
Viaduct Pl 20 E2 . . . 25 A2
Viaduct St E2 . . . . 25 A2
Vian St SE13 . . . . 67 A4
Vibart Gdns SW2 . . . . 74 B4
Vicarage Ave SE3 . . . . 53 C3
Vicarage Cres
SW11 . . . . 167 B3
Vicarage Ct
8 Putney SW15 . . . . 68 C4
W8 . . . . 128 A4
Vicarage Dr SW14 . . . 55 C2
Vicarage Gate
W8 . . . . 114 A1
Vicarage Gdns
Mortlake SW14 . . . . 55 C2
W8 . . . . 31 C1 113 C1
Vicarage Gr SE5 . . . . 48 C2
Vicarage Rd SW14 . . . 55 C2
Vicarage Wlk
SW11 . . . . 167 C4
Vicar's Cl E9 . . . . . . 25 B4
Vicars Hill SE13 . . . . . 67 A3
Vicar's Rd NW5 . . . . . 12 C3
Viceroy Ct NW8 . . . . . 80 B2
Viceroy Rd SW8 . . . . 172 A4
Vic Johnson Ho 2
E3 . . . . 26 B4
Vickery Ct EC1 . . . . . . 97 A2

Vickery Ho 13
SW4 . . . . 62 A3
Vickery's Wharf 3
E14 . . . . 33 C3
Victor Cazalet Ho
N1 . . . . 86 A4
Victoria & Albert Mus
SW7 . . . . 129 C1
Victoria Arc SW1 . . 132 B1
Victoria Ave EC2 . . . 110 B3
Victoria Bldgs 13
E8 . . . . 25 A4
Victoria Chambers
EC2 . . . . 24 A1 98 A2
Victoria Coach Sta
SW1 . . . . 146 A3
Victoria Cotts
7 Richmond
TW9 . . . . 44 C2
3 Spitalfields E1 . . 111 B4
Victoria Ct
5 Clapham Pk
SW4 . . . . 61 C1
South Acton W3 . . . . 36 C4
St George in t East
E1 . . . . 125 B3
Victoria Dr SW19 . . . . 69 C3
Victoria Emb
WC2 . . . . 121 B3
Victoria Gate Gardens
SW7 . . . . 132 A3
Victoria Gdns
W11 . . . . . . 31 C1 113 B2
Victoria Gr Mews
W2 . . . . 114 A3
Victoria Hall 15
E16 . . . . 35 C1
Victoria Ho
6 Clapham Pk
SW4 . . . . 61 C1
2 Shepherd's Bush
W12 . . . . 38 C4
SW1 . . . . 146 A2
Victoria Ind Est
W3 . . . . 29 A4
Victoria Mans
8 Islington N7 . . . . 14 C3
Willesden NW10 . . . 9 A1
Victoria Mews
Kilburn NW6 . . . . . . 23 C4
Wandsworth SW18 . 71 B3
Victoria Mills 1
E15 . . . . 27 C4
Victorian Gr N16 . . . 7 A1
Victorian Rd N16 . . . 7 B1
Victoria Park Ct 11
E9 . . . . 17 B1
Victoria Park Ind Ctr
E9 . . . . 18 C2
Victoria Park Lofts
E9 . . . . 25 C4
Victoria Park Rd
E9 . . . . 17 C1
Victoria Park Sq
E2 . . . . 25 B2
Victoria Pas NW8 . . . 89 C2
Victoria Place Sh Ctr
SW1 . . . . 146 B4
Victoria Rd
Finsbury Pk N4 . . . . . 5 B3
Kensington W8 . . . 128 C2
Kilburn NW6 . . . . . 23 B4
Mortlake SW14 . . . . 55 C4

Val–Vin 283

Victoria Rd continued
North Acton NW10 . . 21 A1
Victoria Rise SW4 . . . 61 A4
Victoria Sq SW1 . . . 132 B2
Victoria St SW1 . . . 133 A1
Victoria Sta SW1 . . 146 B4
Victoria Terr
Dagenham NW10 . . 21 A1
Finsbury Pk N4 . . . . . 5 C3
Victoria
(Underground)
SW1 . . . . 132 B1
Victoria Villas
TW9 . . . . 54 B3
Victoria Wharf
E14 . . . . 33 A2
Victoria Yd 28 E1 . . . 111 C1
Victor Rd NW10 . . . . . 22 A2
Victory Pl
6 Limehouse
E14 . . . . 33 A2
SE17 . . . . 151 B4
Victory Prim Sch
SE17 . . . . 151 A4
Victory Way SE16 . . . 41 A4
Victory Wlk SE8 . . . . . 51 C2
Video Ct N4 . . . . 5 A4
View Cl N6 . . . . 3 B4
Viewfield Rd
SW18 . . . . 58 B1
Viewpoint 8 N5 . . . 15 A3
Vigo St W1 . . . . 118 C3
Viking Cl 13 E3 . . . . . 26 A3
Viking Ho 3 SE5 . . . 48 B1
Village Cl NW3 . . . . 11 C3
Village Mount 19
NW3 . . . . 11 B4
Village Sch The
NW3 . . . . 12 B2
Village The SW11 . . 60 B4
Village Way SE21 . . . 63 C1
Villa Rd SW9 . . . . 62 C4
Villa Sch The 1
SE15 . . . . 49 B1
Villas On The Heath
NW3 . . . . 2 B1
Villa St SE17 . . . . . . 151 C1
Villiers Ct SW11 . . . 168 B4
Villiers Gardens
E15 . . . . 19 A3
Villiers Rd NW2 . . . . . . 8 C2
Villiers St WC2 . . . . . 120 B2
Vince Ct N1 . . . . 97 C3
Vincent Ct
Finsbury Pk N4 . . . . . 5 A3
Marylebone W1 . . . 102 C2
South Lambeth
SW9 . . . . 173 A3
Vincent Mews 1
E3 . . . . 26 C3
Vincent Rd W3 . . . . . 37 B3
Vincent Sq SW1 . . . 147 B4
Vincent St
Canning Town
E16 . . . . 35 B4
Westminster SW1 . 147 C4
Vincent Terr N1 . . . . . 86 B2
Vince St EC1 . . . . 97 C3
Vine Cl E5 . . . . 16 C4
Vine Ct E1 . . . . 111 C3
Vinegar St E1 . . . . 32 A1
Vinegar Yd SE1 . . . . 138 A4
Vine Hill EC1 . . . . 95 B1

Vine La SE1 . . . . 124 B1
Vine Rd SW13 . . . . 56 B4
Vinery Wy W6 . . . . 39 A3
Vine St Bridge EC1 95 C1
Vine Sq W14 . . . . . . 141 A1
Vine St
W1 . . . . 119 A3
Whitechapel EC3 . . . 110 C1
Vineyard Path
SW14 . . . . 55 C4
Vineyard Sch The
TW10 . . . . 54 A1
Vineyard The
TW10 . . . . 54 A1
Vineyard Wlk EC1 . 95 B2
Viney Ct 9 SW4 . . . . 61 C1
Vine Yd SE1 . . . . 137 A4
Viney Rd SE13 . . . . . . 67 A4
Vining St SW2,
SW9 . . . . 62 C3
Vinson Ho 1 . . . . 94 A4
Vintners Ct EC4 . . 123 A4
Viola Sq W12 . . . . 29 B2
Violet Cl 32 SE8 . . . . . 51 B4
Violet Hill NW8 . . . . . 78 C1
Violet Hill Ho NW8 . 78 C1
Violet Rd E3 . . . . 27 A1
Violet St E2 . . . . 25 A1
Virgil Pl W1 . . . . 102 C3
Virgil St SE1 . . . . . . 135 A2
Virginia Ct 7
SE16 . . . . 40 C4
Virginia Ho 3 E14 . 34 B2
Virginia Prim Sch 48
E2 . . . . 24 B2 98 C3
Virginia Rd 19
E2 . . . . 24 B2 98 C3
Virginia St E1 . . . . . 125 C3
Virginia Wlk SW2 . . 62 B1
Viscount Ct 2
W11 . . . . 31 C3
Viscount St EC1 . . 108 C4
Vision Coll of
Theology E9 . . . . . . 18 B2
Vision Terr SE22 . . . 64 C2
Vista Bldgs 19 E3 . . 26 B2
Vitae Apartments 7
W6 . . . . 118 B3
Vitali Cl SW15 . . . . . 56 C1
Vittoria Ho N1 . . . . . 85 A3
Vittoria Prim Sch
N1 . . . . 85 B2
Vivian Comma Cl 3
N4 . . . . 6 A1
Vivian Ct NW6 . . . . . 78 A2
Vivian Ho N4 . . . . 6 C4
Vivian Rd E3 . . . . 26 A3
Vivian Sq SE15 . . . . . 65 A4
Vogans Mill SE1 . . 139 A4
Vogler Ho 3 E1 . . . . 32 B2
Vollasky Ho 5
E1 . . . . 111 B4
Voltaire
2 Camberwell
SE5 . . . . 49 B2
13 Richmond TW9 . . 44 B2
Voltaire Ct 13
SW11 . . . . 169 C2
Voltaire Rd SW4 . . . 61 C4
Volt Ave NW10 . . . . . 21 A2
Vorley Rd N19 . . . . 4 B2
Voss St E2 . . . . 24 C2 99 C3
Voyager Bsns Est 10
SE16 . . . . 139 B2

W

Wadcroft Ct SE4 . . . . 66 B4
Wadding St SE17 . . 151 B3
Waddington St
E15 . . . . 19 C2
Waddington St
E15 . . . . 19 C2
Wade Ho 16 SE1 . . 139 B3
Wadeson St E2 . . . . 25 A3
Wade's Pl E14 . . . . . . 34 A2
Wadham Gdns
NW3 . . . . 80 A4
Wadham Mews
SW14 . . . . 45 B1
Wadham Rd SW15 . . 58 A3
Wadhurst Rd
Battersea SW8 . . . 170 C4
London W4 . . . . 37 C3
Wager St E3 . . . . 26 B1
Waghorn St SE15 . . . 64 C4
Wagner St SE15 . . . 50 B3
Wainford Cl SW19 . . 69 C3
Wainwright Ho 3
E1 . . . . 32 B1
Waite St SE15 . . . . . . 49 B4
Waithman St EC4 . 108 A1
Wakefield Ho 6
SE15 . . . . 49 C2
Wakefield Mews
WC1 . . . . 94 B3
Wakefield St N1 . . . . 94 B3
Wakeford Cl SW4 . . 61 B2
Wakeham St 6
N1 . . . . 15 C2
Wakehurst Rd
SW11 . . . . 60 B2
Wakeling Ho 6
SE27 . . . . 75 A1
Wakeling St 11
E14 . . . . 33 A3
Wakelin Ho 10 N1 . . 15 A1
Wakeman Rd
NW10 . . . . 22 C2
Wakley St EC1 . . . . . 96 A4
Walberswick St
SW8 . . . . 162 B1
Walbrook EC4 . . . . 123 B4
Walbrook Ct 32
N1 . . . . 24 A3
Walbrook Wharf
EC4 . . . . 123 B4
Walburgh St 1
E1 . . . . 32 A3
Walcorde Ave
SE17 . . . . 151 A3
Walcot Gdns
SE11 . . . . 149 B6
Walcot Ho 7
SE22 . . . . 64 A4
Walcot Sq SE11 . . . 149 C4
Walcott St SW1 . . . 147 A4
Waldeck Gr SE27 . . 75 A1
Waldeck Rd
Brentford W4 . . . . . 44 C4
Mortlake SW14 . . . . 55 B4
Waldeck Terr
SW14 . . . . 55 B4

Waldegrave Ho 5
SW15 . . . . 57 B2
Waldemar Ave
SW6 . . . . 164 B2
Waldemar Avenue
Mans SW6 . . . . 164 A3
Walden Ct SW8 . . . 171 C4
Walden Ho
8 Clapham
SW11 . . . . 169 B2
SW1 . . . . 145 C3
Walden St E1 . . . . . . 32 A3
Waldo Cl SW4 . . . . . . 61 B2
Waldo Rd NW10 . . . . 22 A2
Waldron Ho 17
SW2 . . . . 62 B2
Waldron Mews
SW3 . . . . 157 C4
Waldron Rd SW18 . . 71 B1
Walerand Rd SE13 . 52 B1
Waleran Flats
SE1 . . . . 152 A4
Wales Cl SE15 . . . . . . 50 A4
Wales Farm Rd
W3 . . . . 28 C4
Waley St 1 E1 . . . . . . 33 A4
Walford Ho 20 E1 . . 32 A3
Walford Rd N16 . . . . 16 A4
Walham Ct 18
NW3 . . . . 12 B2
Walham Gr SW6 . . . 155 B2

WALHAM
GREEN 156 A1

Walham Green Arc
SW6 . . . . 155 C2
Walham Yd SW6 . . 155 B2
Walker Ho NW1 . . . . 83 B1
Walker Mews 9
SW2 . . . . 62 C2
Walkerscroft Mead
SE21 . . . . 75 B3
Walker's Ct W1 . . . 119 B4
Walkers Lo 18 E14 . 42 B4
Walker's Pl SW15 . . 58 A3
Walkinshaw Ct 9
N1 . . . . 15 B1
Walkynscroft 1
SE15 . . . . 50 A1
Wallace Collection*
W1 . . . . 103 B2
Wallace Ct NW1 . . 102 B3
Wallace Ho N7 . . . . . 14 B2
Wallace Lo N4 . . . . 5 C3
Wallace Rd N1, N5 . 15 B2
Wallbutton Rd
SE4 . . . . 51 A1
Wall Ct N4 . . . . 5 B3
Waller Rd SE14 . . . . 50 C1
Waller Wy 8 SE10 . 52 A3
Wallett Ct 11 NW1 . 13 B1
Wallflower St W12 . 29 B2
Wallgrave Rd
SW5 . . . . 142 A3
Wallingford Ave
W10 . . . . 30 C3
Wallis Alley SE1 . . 137 A4
Wallis Cl SW11 . . . . 59 C4
Wallis Ho 5 SE14 . . 51 A2
Wallis Rd E9 . . . . 18 C2
Wallis's Cottages
SW2 . . . . 74 A4
Wallorton Gdns
SW14 . . . . 55 C3
Wallside EC2 . . . . . 109 A3
Wall St N1 . . . . 15 C2
Wallwood St E14 . . 33 B4

Walmer Ho 8
W10 . . . . 30 C3
Walmer Pl W1 . . . . 102 C4
Walmer Rd
North Kensington
W10 . . . . 30 B3
W11 . . . . . . 31 A2 112 A4
Walmer Road Sch The
W11 . . . . 112 A4
Walm La NW2 . . . . 9 B2
Walney Wlk 6 N1 . . 15 B2
Walnut Cl SE8 . . . . . 51 B4
Walnut Ho 11 E3 . . . 26 B4
Walnut Tree Cl
SW13 . . . . 46 B2
Walnut Tree Ho
SW10 . . . . 156 B4
Walnut Tree Rd
Brentford TW8 . . . . 44 A4
Greenwich SE10 . . . 43 A1
Walnut Tree Walk
Prim Sch SE11 . . . 149 B4
Walnut Tree Wlk
SE11 . . . . 149 B4
Walpole Ave TW9 . . 44 B1
Walpole Ct
7 Hammersmith
W14 . . . . 39 C3
South Hampstead
NW6 . . . . 11 B1
Walpole Gdns W4 . . 37 B1
Walpole Mews
NW8 . . . . 79 B3
Walpole St SW3 . . 145 A2
Walsham Cl N16 . . . . 7 C3
Walsham Ho
New Cross Gate
SE14 . . . . 50 C1
SE17 . . . . 151 B2
Walsham Rd SE14 . 50 C1
Walsingham NW8 . . 79 C4
Walsingham Lo
SW13 . . . . 46 C2
Walsingham Mans
SW6 . . . . 156 B2
Walsingham Pl
SW11 . . . . 60 C1
Walsingham Rd E5 . . 7 C1
Walter Besant Ho 20
E1 . . . . 25 C2
Walter Ct 3 W3 . . . 28 B3
Walter Green Ho
SE15 . . . . 50 B2
Walter Ho SW10 . . 157 B2
Walter Northcott Ho
2 NW6 . . . . 10 C3
Walters Cl SE17 . . 151 A3
Walters Ho
6 Camberwell
SE5 . . . . 49 A1
Islington N1 . . . . . . 86 B4
10 Kennington
SE17 . . . . 48 A4
Walter Sickert Hall
N1 . . . . 86 C1
Walter St E2 . . . . 25 C2
Walters Way SE23 . 65 C1
Walter Taylor Ct
SE4 . . . . 66 B3
Walter Terr E1 . . . . . 32 C3
Walterton Rd W9 . . 23 C1
Waltham Green Ct
SW6 . . . . 156 A1
Waltham Ho
NW8 . . . . 78 C4
10 Stockwell SW9 . 173 A1

Walton Cl SW8 . . . 162 B2
Walton Gdns W3 . . . 28 A4
Walton Ho
E2 . . . . 24 B1 99 A2
Upper Holloway N7 . . 5 B1
Wandsworth SW18 . 58 C1
Walton Pl SW3 . . . 130 C2
Walton St SW3 . . . 130 B1
Walton Way W3 . . . 28 A4
Walt Whitman Cl 6
SE24 . . . . 63 A3
WALWORTH 151 C2
Walworth Acad
SE17 . . . . 152 B1
Walworth Pl SE17 151 A1
Walworth Rd
SE17 . . . . 151 A2
Wanborough Dr
SW15 . . . . 69 A3
Wandle Ct 4 W12 . 38 A4
Wandle Ho
NW8 . . . . 102 A4
Wandsworth SW18 . 71 A4
Wandle Rd SW17 . . 72 A2
Wandle Way SW18 . 71 A3
Wandon Rd SW6 . . 156 B1
WANDSWORTH . . 58 C1
Wandsworth Bridge
Rd SW6 . . . . 166 A3
Wandsworth Common
Sta SW12 . . . . 72 B4
Wandsworth Common
West Side SW18 . . 59 B2
Wandsworth Gyratory
SW18 . . . . 59 A2
Wandsworth High St
SW18 . . . . 59 A2
Wandsworth Plain
SW18 . . . . 59 A2
Wandsworth Prep Sch
8 SW18 . . . . 59 B2
Wandsworth Rd
SW8 . . . . 162 A4
Wandsworth Road Sta
SW4 . . . . 171 A1
Wandsworth Town
Sta SW18 . . . . 59 A3
Wangford Ho 13
SW9 . . . . 63 A3
Wanless Rd SE24 . . 63 B3
Wanley Rd SE5 . . . . 63 C3
Wansbeck Rd E3,
E9 . . . . 18 B1
Wansdown Pl
SW6 . . . . 156 A2
Wandsworth Riverside
Quarter Pier
SW6 . . . . 58 C4
Wansey St SE17 . . 151 A3
WAPPING 32 A1
Wapping Dock St 18
E1 . . . . 32 A1
Wapping High St
E1 . . . . 32 A1
Wapping La E1 . . . . . 32 B1
Wapping Sta E1 . . . . 32 B1
Wapping Wall E1 . . 32 B1
Warbeck Rd W12 . . 39 A4
Warburg Ho
E2 . . . . 24 C2 99 B3
Warburton Cl 6
N1 . . . . 16 A2
Warburton Ct
SE15 . . . . 64 C4
Warburton Ho 5
E8 . . . . 25 A4

Warburton Rd 🎇
E8 . . . . .25 A4
Warburton St 🖽
E8 . . . . .25 A4
Wardalls Gr SE14 . . . .50 B3
Wardalls Ho 🖽
SE8 . . . . .51 B4
Wardell Ho 🖽
SE10 . . . . .52 B4
Wardell Mews 🖽
SW4 . . . . .61 A4
Warden Rd NW5 . . . .12 C2
Wardens Gr SE1 . . .122 C1
Ward La E9 . . . . .18 A3
Wardle St E9 . . . . .17 C3
Wardley St SW18 . . . .71 A4
Wardlow Ho NW5 . . . .13 A4
Wardo Ave SW6 . . . .164 A4
Wardour Mews
W1 . . . . .105 A1
Wardour St W1 . . . .105 B1
Ward Point SE11 . .149 B3
Ward Rd
  Camden Town N19 . . . .4 B1
  Mill Meads E15 . . . . . .27 C4
Wardrobe Pl EC4 . .108 B1
Wardrobe Terr
EC4 . . . . .122 B4
Wareham Ct 🖽
N1 . . . . .16 A1
Wareham Ho
SW8 . . . . .162 C2
Warfield Rd NW10 . .22 C2
Warfield Yd 🖽
NW10 . . . . .22 C2
Wargrave Ho 🖽
E2 . . . . .24 B2 98 C3
Warham St SE5 . . . . . .48 A3
Waring Ho 🖽
E2 . . . . .24 C2 99 C3
Warley Ho N1 . . . . . . .15 C2
Warley St E2 . . . . .25 C2
Warlock Rd W9 . . . . .23 C1
Warlters Cl N7 . . . . . .14 A4
Warlters Rd N7 . . . . .14 A4
Warltersville Mans
N19 . . . . .5 A4
Warltersville Rd N4, N8,
N19 . . . . .5 A4
War Meml Homes
W4 . . . . .45 C3
Warmington Rd
SE24 . . . . .63 B1
Warmsworth NW1 . .82 C4
Warndon St SE16 . . .40 B2
Warneford St E9 . . . .25 A4
Warner Ho
  🟦 Homerton E9 . . . . . .17 C2
  Lewisham SE13 . . . . . .52 A1
  NW8 . . . . .88 C4
Warner Pl
E2 . . . . .24 C2 99 C4
Warner Rd SE5 . . . . . .48 B2
Warner St EC1 . . . . . .95 B1
Warner Yd EC1 . . . . . .95 B1
Warnford Ho
SW15 . . . . .56 A1
Warnham WC1 . . . . .94 C3
Warnham Ho 🖽
SW2 . . . . .74 B4
Warple Mews W3 . . .38 A4
Warple Way W3,
W12 . . . . .38 A4
Warren Ave SW14,
TW10 . . . . .55 A3
Warren Cl SE21 . . . . .75 B4

Warren Ct N1 . . . . . .85 B2
Warrender Rd N19 . .13 B4
Warren Gdns E15 . . .19 C3
Warren Ho 🖽 E3 . . . .27 A2
Warren Mews W1 . . .92 C1
Warren St W1 . . . . . .92 C1
Warren Street Sta
NW1 . . . . .93 A2
Warriner Gdns
SW11 . . . . .169 B3
Warrington Cres
W9 . . . . .88 C2
Warrington Gdns
W9 . . . . .88 C1
Warspite Ho 🔟
E14 . . . . .42 A2
Warton Rd E15 . . . . . .27 B4
Warwick W14 . . . . . .141 A3
Warwick Ave W9 . . . .88 C1
Warwick Avenue Sta
W9 . . . . .88 C1
Warwick Bldg
SW8 . . . . .160 A3
Warwick Chambers
W8 . . . . .127 B2
Warwick Cres W2 .100 C4
Warwick Ct WC1 . . .107 A3
Warwick Dr SW15 . . .57 A4
Warwick Ho
  🟦 Brixton SW9 . . . . .173 B1
  🟦 Putney SW15 . . . . .69 B4
  Stoke Newington N4 . . .6 B3
Warwick House St
SW1 . . . . .119 C2
Warwick La EC4 . . .108 B1
Warwick Lo NW2 . . .10 A3
Warwick Mans
SW5 . . . . .141 B4
Warwick Pas EC4 . .108 B2
Warwick Pl W9 . . . .100 C4
Warwick Pl N
SW1 . . . . .146 C3
Warwick Rd W14,
SW5 . . . . .141 A4
Warwick Row
SW1 . . . . .132 B2
Warwickshire Path
SE8 . . . . .51 B3
Warwick Sq
  Holborn EC4 . . . . .108 B2
  Pimlico SW1 . . . . .146 C2
Warwick Sq Mews
SW1 . . . . .146 C3
Warwick Way
SW1 . . . . .146 B4
Warwick Yd EC1 . . . .97 A1
Wasdale NW1 . . . . . .92 B3
Washbrook Ho
SW2 . . . . .62 C1
Washington Bldg 🔟
SE13 . . . . .52 A2
Washington Cl 🔟
E3 . . . . .27 A2
Washington Ho
SW1 . . . . .130 C3
Washington Rd
SW13 . . . . .46 C3
Watchfield Ct 🔽
W4 . . . . .37 B1
Watcombe Cotts
TW9 . . . . .44 C4
Watercress Pl 🔟
N1 . . . . .16 A1

Waterford Rd
SW6 . . . . .156 A1
Waterford Way
NW10 . . . . .8 C3
Water Gardens The
W2 . . . . .102 B2
Watergate EC4 . . . .122 A4
Watergate St SE8 . . .51 C4
Watergate Wlk
WC2 . . . . .120 B2
Waterhead NW1 . . . .92 C4
Waterhouse Cl
  Hammersmith W6 . . . .39 C1
  Hampstead NW3 . . . . .11 C3
Waterhouse Sq
EC1 . . . . .107 B3
Wateridge Cl E14 . . .41 C3
Water La
  Bermondsey EC3 . . . .124 B3
  🟦 Camden Town
  NW1 . . . . .13 A1
  SE14 . . . . .50 B3
Waterloo Bridge SE1,
WC2 . . . . .121 A3
Waterloo Cl E9 . . . . .17 B3
Waterloo East Sta
SE1 . . . . .121 C1
Waterloo Gdns
  🟦 Islington N1 . . . . . . .15 A1
  South Hackney E2 . . . .25 B3
Waterloo Millennium
  Pier SE1 . . . . .134 C4
Waterloo Pl
  Kew TW9 . . . . .44 C4
  🟦 Richmond TW9 . . . .54 A3
  SW1 . . . . .119 B2
Waterloo Rd SE1 . . .135 C4
Waterloo Sta SE1 . .135 B4
Waterloo Terr N1 . . .15 A1
Waterlow Rd N19 . . . .4 B3
Waterlow Rd N19 . . . .4 B3
Waterman Bldg 🔟
E14 . . . . .41 C4
Watermans Arts Ctr
TW8 . . . . .44 A4
Watermans Ct 🔟
TW8 . . . . .44 A4
Waterman St
SW15 . . . . .57 C4
Waterman Way E1 . .32 A1
Watermark Pl
EC4 . . . . .123 B3
Watermead Ho E9 . .18 B3
Watermeadow La
SW6 . . . . .166 C1
Watermill Ct SE13 . .67 A4
Watermint Quay
N16 . . . . .7 C4
Water's Edge SW6 . .47 B2
Waterside N1 . . . . . .86 C1
Waterside Cl
  🟦 Bermondsey
  SE16 . . . . .139 C3
  Old Ford E3 . . . . .26 B4
Waterside Ct SE13 . .67 C3
Waterside Pl NW1 . .81 C4
Waterside Point
SW11 . . . . .158 B2
Waterson St
E2 . . . . .24 B2 98 C4
Waters Pl SW15 . . . .47 B1
Water St WC2 . . . . . .121 B4
Water Tower Pl
N1 . . . . .86 A3

Waterview Ho 🔟
E14 . . . . .33 A4
Waterway Ave 🔟
SE13 . . . . .67 A4
Waterworks Rd
SW2 . . . . .62 B1
Watford Cl SW11 . .168 B4
Watford Rd E16 . . . . .35 C4
Watkins Ho 🔟 E14 . .42 B4
Watkinson Rd N7 . . .14 B2
Watling Ct EC4 . . . .109 A1
Watling Gdns
NW2 . . . . .10 A2
Watling St
  🟦 Camberwell
  SE15 . . . . .49 A4
  City of London EC4 . .109 A1
Watney Cotts
SW14 . . . . .55 B4
Watney Mkt E1 . . . . .32 A3
Watney Rd SW14 . . .55 B4
Watney St E1 . . . . . . .32 A3
Watson Cl N16 . . . . . .15 C3
Watson Ho 🔟
SW2 . . . . .74 A4
Watsons Mews
W1 . . . . .102 B3
Watson's St SE8 . . . .51 C3
Watts Gr E3 . . . . .34 A4
Watts Ho 🔟 W10 . . .31 A4
Watts St
  E1 . . . . .32 A1
  Wapping E1 . . . . .32 A1
Wat Tyler Rd SE10 . .52 C2
Wavel Ct
  🔽 Streatham
  SW16 . . . . .74 A1
  🟦 Wapping E1 . . . . . . .32 B1
Wavel Mews NW6 . .11 A1
Wavendon Ave
W4 . . . . .37 C1
Waveney Ave SE15 . .65 A3
Waveney Cl 🟦 E1 . .125 C2
Waveney Ho SE15 . . .65 A3
Waverley Ct
  🔽 Brondesbury
  NW6 . . . . .10 A1
  W1 . . . . .103 C4
Waverley Pl
  Finsbury Pk N4 . . . . . . .6 A3
  St John's Wood
  NW8 . . . . .79 B2
Waverley Rd N8 . . . . .5 A4
Waverly St NW3 . . . .12 B2
Waverton Ho 🔟
E3 . . . . .26 B4
Waverton Rd
SW18 . . . . .71 B4
Waverton St W1 . . .118 A2
Wavertree Ct 🔟
SW2 . . . . .74 A3
Wavertree Rd
SW2 . . . . .74 B3
Waxham NW5 . . . . . .12 B3
Waxlow Rd NW10 . . .20 C3
Wayford St SW11 . .168 B1
Wayland Ave E8 . . . .16 C3
Wayland Ho 🔟
SW9 . . . . .173 B2
Waylett Ho SE11 . . .149 B1
Waylett Pl SE27 . . . .75 A1
Wayman Ct E8 . . . . . .17 A2
Waynflete Sq
  🔟 North Kensington
  W10 . . . . .30 C3

Waynflete Sq continued
  🔟 Shepherd's Bush
  W10 . . . . .30 C2
Waynflete St
SW18 . . . . .71 B2
Wayside
  Golders Green
  NW11 . . . . .1 A3
  Mortlake SW14 . . . . . .55 A3
Weald Cl 🔟 SE16 . . .40 A1
Weald Sq E5 . . . . .7 C2
Weardale Ho N4 . . . . .6 B4
Weardale Rd SE13 . .67 C3
Wearmouth Ho 🔟
E3 . . . . .33 B4
Wear Pl 🖽 E2 . . . . . .25 A2
Wearside Rd SE13 . .67 A3
Weatherbury 🖽
W2 . . . . .31 C3
Weatherbury Ho 🖽
N19 . . . . .4 C1
Weatherley Cl E3 . . .33 B4
Weaver Ct 🖽 E2 . . . .25 A1
Weaver Ho 🔟
E1 . . . . .24 C1 99 B1
Weaver's La SE1 . . .124 B1
Weaver St
E1 . . . . .24 C1 99 B1
Weavers Way
  🟦 Camden Town
  NW1 . . . . .13 C1
  NW1 . . . . .83 B4
Webb Cl NW10 . . . . .22 B1
Webb Ct W3 . . . . .37 A4
Webber Row SE1 . .136 A3
Webber St SE1 . . . . .136 A3
Webb Est E5 . . . . .7 C4
Webb Ho SW8 . . . . .161 C1
Webb Pl NW10 . . . . .21 B2
Webb Rd SE3 . . . . . . .53 B4
Webb's Rd SW11 . . . .60 B2
Webb St SE1 . . . . . . .138 A1
Webheath 🔟 NW6 . .10 B1
Webster Ho 🔟
N16 . . . . .16 A3
Webster Rd SE16 . .139 C1
Weddell Ho 🔟 E1 . . .25 C1
Wedderburn Rd
NW3 . . . . .11 C3
Wedgewood Ho 🔟
SW1 . . . . .146 C1
Wedgewood Mews
W1 . . . . .105 C1
Wedgwood Wlk
NW3 . . . . .11 A3
Wedgwood Ho
  🔟 Globe Town
  E2 . . . . .25 C2
  SE11 . . . . .135 B1
Wedlake St W10 . . . .23 A1
Wedmore Gdns
N19 . . . . .4 C2
Wedmore Mews
N19 . . . . .4 C1
Wedmore St N19 . . . .4 C1
Weech Rd NW6 . . . . .10 C4
Weedington Rd
NW5 . . . . .12 C3
Weedon Ho W12 . . . .29 C3
Weekley Sq SW11 . . .59 C4
Weighhouse St
W1 . . . . .103 C1
Weimar St SW15 . . . .58 A4
Weir Ho 🔟 SW12 . . .73 B4

Weir Rd
Streatham SW12 ...73 B4
Wimbledon SW18,
SW19 ....71 A1
Weiss Rd SW15 ....57 C4
Welbeck Ct W14 ..140 C4
Welbeck Mans 10
NW6 ....10 C3
Welbeck St W1 ...104 A2
Welbeck Way W1 .104 A2
Welbury Ct E8 .....16 A1
Welby Ho W10 ......4 C4
Welby St SE5 ....48 A2
Weldon Ct SE8 .....51 C1
Weld Works Mews 2
SW2 ....62 B1
Welford Ct
Camden Town
NW1 ....13 A1
7 Clapham SW8 ..170 C1
Welland Ho SE15 ..65 B3
Welland Mews 21
E1 ....125 C2
Welland St SE10 ...52 B4
Wellclose Sq E1 ...125 C4
Wellclose St 20
E1 ....125 C3
Well Ct EC4 ....109 A1
Wellday Ho 2 E9 ..18 A2
Welldon Ct 1
SE21 ....75 C2
Weller Ho 28
SE16 ....139 B3
Weller St SE1 .....136 C4
Welles Ct 13 E14 ..33 C2
Wellesley Ave W6 ..39 A3
Wellesley Ct W9 ....88 C4
Wellesley Ho NW1 ..93 B3
Wellesley Pl
Camden Town
NW5 ....12 C3
NW1 ....93 B3
Wellesley Rd
Gospel Oak NW5 ..12 C3
Gunnersbury W4 ..37 A1
Wellesley St E1 ....32 C4
Wellesley Terr N1 ..97 A4
Wellfit St 8 SE24 ..63 A4
Wellgarth Rd NW11 ..2 A3
Wellington Arch
SW1 ....131 C4
Wellington Bldgs
18 Bow E3 ....26 C2
SW1 ....145 C1
Wellington Cl
Kensington W11 ..31 C3
New Cross Gate
SE14 ....50 C2
Wellington Ct
Knightsbridge
SW1 ....130 C3
St John's Wood
NW8 ....79 C1
Strand WC2 .....120 A4
Wandsworth SW18 ..60 A2
Wellington Gr
SE10 ....52 C3
Wellington Ho 19
NW3 ....12 B2
Wellington Hospl The
NW8 ....79 C1
Wellington Mans
N16 ....16 B4

Wellington Mews
East Dulwich
SE22 ....64 C3
3 Islington N7 ...14 B2
Streatham SW16 ..73 C1
Wellington Pl NW8 ..89 C4
Wellington Prim Sch
13 E3 ....26 C2
Wellington Rd
Kensal Green
NW10 ....22 C2
St John's Wood
NW8 ....79 C1
Wimbledon SW19 ..70 C2
Wellington Row
E2 ....24 C2 99 B4
Wellington Sq
Islington N1 .....84 B4
SW3 ....144 C2
Wellington St
WC2 ....120 C4
Wellington Terr 2
E1 ....32 A1
Wellington Way
E3 ....26 C2
Well La SW14 ......55 B2
Well Rd NW3 ....2 C1
Wells Ct
1 Hampstead
NW3 ....11 B4
1 Paddington
NW6 ....23 C3
Stoke Newington
N1 ....16 A3
Wells Ho
Finsbury EC1 .....96 A4
12 Kensal Town
W10 ....23 A1
New Cross Gate
SE4 ....51 A1
4 Rotherhithe
SE16 ....40 B3
Wells Ho The 2
NW3 ....11 C4
Wells House Rd
NW10 ....29 A4
Wells Mews W1 ...105 A2
Wells Pl SW18 .....71 B4
Wells Rd W12 ......39 B4
Wells Rise NW8 ....80 C3
Wells Sq WC1 ......95 A3
Wells St W1 ....105 A2
Well St E9 ....17 B1
Wells Terr N4 ....5 C2
Wells Way
Brompton SW7 ...129 B2
Camberwell SE5 ..49 A4
Well Wlk NW3 ....2 C1
Wellwood Ct
SW15 ....57 B3
Welmar Mews 13
SW4 ....61 C3
Welmar Works
SW4 ....153 B3
Welsh Ho 41 E1 ....32 A1
Welshpool Ho 22
E8 ....24 C4
Welshpool St
22 Hackney E8 ...24 C4
Welstead Ho 29
E1 ....32 A3
Welstead Way W4 ..38 B2

Weltje Rd W6 ....38 C1
Welton Ct SE5 ......49 A2
Welton Ho E1 ......32 C4
Welwyn St E2 ......25 B2
Wembury Mews N6 ..4 B4
Wembury Rd N6 .....4 A4
Wemyss Rd SE3 ....53 B1
Wendell Park Prim
Sch W12 ....38 B4
Wendell Rd W12 ...38 B4
Wendle Ct SW8 ...162 A3
Wendling NW5 .....12 B3
Wendon St E3 ......26 B4
Wendover SE17 ...152 A1
Wendover Ct
Acton W3 ....20 A1
Becontree W3 ....20 B1
4 Child's Hill NW2 ..1 C1
W1 ....103 B3
Wendover Rd
NW10 ....21 B3
Wengham Ho W12 ..29 C2
Wenham Ho SW8 ..160 C1
Wenlake Ho EC1 ...96 C2
Wenlock Ct N1 .....87 C1
Wenlock Rd N1 ....87 A1
Wenlock St N1 .....87 B1
Wennington Rd
E3 ....25 C3
Wensdale Ho E5 ....7 C2
Wensleydale Ho 8
N4 ....6 B4
Wentworth Cres
SE15 ....49 C3
Wentworth Ct
W6 ....154 A3
Wandsworth SW18 ..59 A1
Wentworth Dwellings
E1 ....110 C2
Wentworth Ho 4
SE3 ....53 C3
Wentworth Mews
E3 ....26 B2
Wentworth St E1 ..111 A3
Werrington St
NW1 ....83 A1
Werter Rd SW15 ...58 A3
Wesleyan Pl NW5 ...13 A4
Wesley Ave NW10 ..20 C2
Wesley Cl
Finsbury Pk N7 ....5 B2
SE17 ....150 B3
Wesley Ho SE24 ...63 C1
Wesley Rd NW10 ..20 B4
Wesley Sq W11 ....31 A3
Wesley St W1 .....103 C3
Wessex Ct SW11 ..167 C2
Wessex St E2 ......25 B2
Wessex Gardens Prim
Sch NW11 ....1 A3
Wessex Gdns NW11 ..1 A3
Wessex Ho
SE1 ....153 A1
4 Tufnell Pk N19 ..4 C1
Wessex St E2 ......25 B2
West 12 Sh Ctr
W12 ....39 C4
Westacott Cl N19 ...4 C3
West Acton Prim Sch
E3 ....32 C3
West Arbour St
E1 ....32 C3
West Bank N16 .....7 A4
Westbere Rd NW2 ..10 A3

West Block 18 E11 ..32 B2
Westbourne Ave
W3 ....28 C3
Westbourne Cres
W2 ....115 B4
Westbourne Ct
W2 ....100 A2
Westbourne Gdns
W2 ....100 A2
Westbourne Gr
Notting Hill W2 ..31 C3
W11 ....31 B3 113 A4
WESTBOURNE
GREEN 88 A2
Westbourne Gr Mews
7 W11 ....31 C3
Westbourne Gr Terr
W2 ....100 A1
Westbourne Ho
SW1 ....146 A2
Westbourne Park Rd
Notting Hill W2 ..31 C3
Notting Hill W11 ..31 B3
Westbourne Park Sta
W11 ....31 B4
Westbourne Park
Villas W2 ....100 A3
Westbourne Rd
N7 ....14 B2
N7 ....5 B1
Westbourne Terr
W2 ....101 A2
Westbourne Terrace
Mews W2 ....100 C2
Westbourne Terrace
Rd W2 ....100 C3
Westbridge Cl
W12 ....29 C1
Westbridge Rd
SW11 ....168 A3
WEST
BROMPTON 156 A4
West Brompton Sta
SW5 ....141 C1
Westbrook Ho
6 Bethnal Green
E2 ....25 B2
5 Clapham Pk
SW4 ....61 B2
Westbury Ct SW4 ..61 A1
Westbury Ho 6
NW10 ....8 A4
Westbush Ct 1
W12 ....39 A4
West Carriage Dr
W2 ....116 A2
West Central St
WC1 ....106 A2
Westchester Ho
W2 ....102 C1
Westcliff Ho 13
N1 ....15 C2
Westcombe Ct 1
SE3 ....53 B3
Westcombe Hill SE3,
SE10 ....53 C4
Westcombe Park Rd
SE3 ....53 A3
Westcombe Park Sta
SE3 ....43 C1
Westcott Ho 1
E14 ....34 A2
Westcott Rd SE17 ..48 A4
West Cotts NW6 ....10 C3

Westcroft Cl NW2 ..10 A4
Westcroft 3
W6 ....38 C2
Westcroft Sq W6 ...38 C2
Westcroft Way
NW2 ....10 A4
West Cromwell Rd
W14 ....141 A2
West Cross Route W10,
W11 ....30 C2
Westdean Cl
SW18 ....59 A1
Westdown Rd E15 ..19 B4
WEST DULWICH ...75 B2
West Dulwich Sta
SE21 ....75 C2
West Eaton Pl
SW1 ....145 B4
West Eaton Pl Mews
SW1 ....145 B4
West Ella Rd NW10 ..8 A1
West End Ct NW6 ..11 A1
West End La NW6 ..11 B2
Westerdale Ct N5 ..15 A4
Westerdale Rd 2
SE10 ....43 C1
Westerham NW1 ...82 C3
Westerham Ho
SE1 ....137 C2
Western Ave W3, ...20 A1
Western Avenue Bsns
Pk W3 ....20 A1
Western Beach Apts
E16 ....35 C1
Western Ct
4 Dagenham W3 ..28 C3
8 Kilburn W9 ....23 B3
Western Eye Hospl
The NW1 ....102 C4
Western Gateway
E16 ....35 C2
Western Ho 5
W9 ....23 B1
Western La SW12 ..72 C4
Western Mews
W9 ....23 B1
Western Pl 17
SE16 ....40 B4
19 SE16 ....40 B4
Western Rd
Becontree NW10 ..20 B2
Brixton SW9 .....62 C4
Western Terr 3
W6 ....38 C1
Westferry Cir E14 ..33 C1
Westferry Rd E14 ..41 C3
Westferry Sta E14 ..33 C2
Westfield NW3 .....10 C4
Westfield Ave E15 ..19 B2
Westfield Cl
SW10 ....156 C1
Westfield Ct 5
W10 ....22 C2
Westfield Ho 6
SE16 ....40 C2
Westfield London Sh
Ctr W12 ....30 B3
Westfields SW13 ...56 B4
Westfields Ave
SW13 ....56 A4
Westfields Rd W3 ..28 A4
Westfield Stratford Sh
Ctr EH15 ....19 B2

Westfield Way E1... 26 A1
West Garden Pl
W2 .... 102 B1
Westgate Bsns Ctr
2 Kensal Town
W10 ....23 A1
Westgate Ind Estate
W10 ....22 C1
Westgate Ct 15
SW9 ....62 C4
Westgate St E8....25 A4
Westgate Terr
SW10 .... 156 B4
West Gdns E1 ....32 A2
West Gr SE10....52 C2
Westgrove La
SE10 ....52 B2
West Halkin St
SW1 .... 131 B2
West Hall Rd TW9 ..45 A2
WEST
HAMPSTEAD 10 C4
West Hampstead
Mews NW6.......11 A2
West Hampstead Sta
NW6 ....10 C2
West Hampstead
Thameslink Sta
NW6 ....10 C2
West Harding St
EC4 .... 107 C2
Westhay Gdns
SW14 ....55 A2
West Heath Ave
NW11 .... 1 C3
West Heath Cl NW3 .1 C1
West Heath Ct
NW11 .... 1 C3
West Heath Dr
NW11 .... 1 C3
West Heath Gdns
NW3 .... 1 C1
West Heath Rd
NW3 .... 2 A1
WEST HILL 58 B1
West Hill SW15...58 A1
Westhill Ct
W11 ....31 B2 113 A4
West Hill Ct N6.... 3 C1
Westhill Pk
Dartmouth Pk N6 .3 C2
Highgate N6 ...... 3 C2
West Hill Prim Sch 17
West Ho 9 SW12 ..73 A4
Westhope Ho 20
E2 ....24 C2 99 C3
Westhorpe Rd
SW15 ....57 B4
West House Cl
SW19 ....70 A3
West India Ave
E14 ....33 C1
West India Dock Rd
E14 ....33 C2
West India Ho 1
E14 ....33 C2
West India Quay Sta
E14 ....33 C2
WEST
KENSINGTON ...140 B3
West Kensington Ct
W14 .... 140 C2
West Kensington
Mans W14........ 140 C1

West Kensington Sta
W14 .... 140 C2
WEST KILBURN ...23 A2
West La SE16.....40 A4
Westlake 12 SE16..40 B2
Westland Pl N1...97 B4
Westlands Terr 3
SW12 ....61 B1
Westleigh Ave
SW15 ....57 B2
West London Free
Sch 17 W6 ......38 C2
Westly Ct NW2 ....9 C2
Westmacott Ho
NW8 ....89 C1
West Mall
W11 ......31 C1 113 C2
Westmark Point 10
SW15 ....69 A3
Westmead SW15 ..57 A1
West Mews SW1 ..146 C3
Westmill Ct N4 .... 6 B2
WESTMINSTER ...133 A1
Westminster Abbey
SW1 .... 134 A2
Westminster Abbey
Choir Sch SW1...133 C2
Westminster Acad
W2 ....31 C4
Westminster Acad
(Sch of English)
W1 .... 105 A2
Westminster Boating
Base SW1 ...... 161 B4
Westminster Bridge
SE1, SW1 ...... 134 B3
Westminster Bridge
Rd SE1......... 134 C3
Westminster Cath
SW1 .... 132 C1
Westminster Cath
Choir Sch SW1 ..147 A4
Westminster Cath RC
Prim Sch SW1...147 C2
Westminster City Hall
SW1 .... 133 A2
Westminster City Sch
SW1 .... 133 A2
Westminster Coll
W1 .... 119 B4
Westminster Ct
22 Rotherhithe
SE16 ....32 C1
5 Wandsworth
SW18 ....58 C2
Westminster
Dragoons Mus
SW6 ....58 A4
Westminster Gdns
SW1 .... 148 A4
Westminster
Kingsway Coll
(King's Cross
Centre) WC1 .....94 C3
Westminster
Kingsway Coll
(Regent's Park Ctr)
NW1 ....92 C2
Westminster
Kingsway Coll
(Victoria Centre)
SW1 .... 147 B4
Westminster
Millennium Pier
SW1 .... 134 B3

Westminster Pier
SW1 .... 134 B3
Westminster Sch
SW1 .... 134 A2
Westminster Sta
SW1 .... 134 B3
Westminster Under
Sch SW1 .... 147 B3
Westmore Ct
SW15 ....58 A2
Westmoreland Ho
NW10 ....21 C2
Westmoreland Ho
SW1 .... 146 B1
Westmoreland Rd
Barnes SW13 .....46 C2
Camberwell SE17 ...48 C4
Westmoreland St
W1 .... 103 C3
Westmoreland Terr
SW1 .... 146 B1
WEST NORWOOD..75 B1
West Norwood Sta
SE27 ....75 A1
Westonbirt Ct 6
SE15 ....49 B4
Weston Ct N4 .... 6 B1
West One Ho NW1 ..104 C3
West One Sh Ctr
W1 .... 104 A1
Weston Ho
6 Brondesbury
NW6 ....10 A1
8 South Hackney
E9 ....25 B4
Weston Rise N4....4 W3
Weston Rise N1,
WC1 ....95 A4
Weston St SE1 ..137 C4
Weston Wlk 3 E8,
E9 ....17 A1
Westover Hill NW3 ..1 C2
Westover Rd
SW18 ....59 B1
West Park Ave
TW9 ....45 A2
West Park Rd
TW9 ....44 C2
West Parkside
Greenwich SE10 ...43 B3
Greenwich SE10 ...43 C2
West Plaza E14...34 A1
Westpoint SW15 ..57 C1
West Point 2
SE1 .... 153 B2
Westpoint Trad Est
W3 ....28 A4
Westport St E1...32 C3
West Poultry Ave
EC1 .... 108 A3
West Quarters
W12 ....29 C3
West Rd
Chelsea SW3 ....159 A4
Clapham Pk SW4 ..61 C2
Westrow SW15 ....57 B1
West Row W10 ....23 A1
West Sheen Vale
TW9 ....54 B3
Westside 11 W6..38 C2
Westside St 1
W9 ....23 C1
West Silvertown Sta
E16 ....35 C1
West Smithfield
EC1 .... 108 A3

West Sq SE11.... 136 A1
West St
30 Bethnal Green
E2 ....25 A3
Soho WC2.......105 C1
West Temple Sheen
SW14 ....55 A2
West Tenter St
E1 .... 111 A1
Westvale Mews
W3 ....38 A4
Westview Cl
North Kensington
W10 ....30 B3
Willesden NW10....8 B4
Westville Rd W12 ..38 C4
West Warwick Pl
SW1 .... 146 C3
Westway W10,
W12 ....29 C2
Westway (Elevated
Rd) W10 ....31 B4
Westway Lo 35
W2 ....31 C4
Westwell 4 NW5 ..12 C2
Westwick Gdns
W14 ....39 C4
Westwood Bsns Ctr
NW10 ....21 A1
Westwood Gdns
SW13 ....56 B4
Westwood Ho
6 Shepherd's Bush
W12 ....30 B1
3 Stoke Newington
N4 ....6 C4
Westwood Park Trad
Est W3 ....20 A1
Westwood Rd
SW13 ....56 B4
Wetherby Gdns
SW5 .... 142 C3
Wetherby Mans
SW5 .... 142 A2
Wetherby Mews
SW5 .... 142 A2
Wetherby Pl SW7 ..143 A3
Wetherby Sch
(Reception & Little
Wetherby)
W11 ....31 C2 113 B4
Wetherby Sch (Years
1, 2 & 3) W2 ....113 C3
Wetherell Rd E9 ..25 C4
Wevco Wharf
SE15 ....50 A4
Wexford Ho 11 E1..32 B4
Wexford Rd SW12 ..72 B4
Weybourne St
SW18 ....71 B2
Weybridge Ct 19
SE16 ....40 A1
Weybridge Point 11
SW11 .... 169 A2
Weydown Cl SW19..70 A3
Weyhill Ho 26 SE5 ..48 B1
Weyhill Rd 11 E1 ..111 C2
Wey Ho NW8 .....89 C1
Weymouth Ct
5 Haggerston E2 ..24 B3
15 Streatham SW2 ..74 B4
Weymouth Ho
Fitzrovia W1 ..... 104 B4
South Lambeth
SW8 .... 162 C1

Weymouth Mews
W1 .... 104 A4
Weymouth St W1 ..104 A4
Weymouth Terr
E2 ....24 B3
Whadcoat St N4 ...5 C2
Whaddon Ho
10 Camberwell
SE5 ....64 A4
SW1 .... 131 A3
Wharfdale Rd N1..84 B2
Wharfedale Ct 5
E5 ....17 C4
Wharfedale St
SW10 .... 142 A1
Wharf La 12 E14 ..33 B3
Wharf Pl E2 ......25 A4
Wharf Rd N1 .....86 C1
Wharfside Rd E16 ..35 A4
Wharf St
E16 ....35 A4
Isle of Dogs SE8 ..41 C1
Wharf View Ct 18
E14 ....34 B3
Wharncliffe Ho 8
SW15 ....57 B2
Wharton Cl NW10 ..8 A2
Wharton Ho SE1...138 C2
Wharton St WC1 ..95 A3
Whateley Rd SE22 ..64 B2
Whatman Ho 10
E14 ....33 B3
Wheatland Ho 7
SE22 ....64 A4
Wheatlands Rd
SW17 ....72 C1
Wheatley Ho
Gospel Oak NW5 ..13 A4
3 Putney SW15 ...68 C4
Wheatley St W1 ..103 C3
Wheat Sheaf Cl
E14 ....42 A2
Wheatsheaf La
Fulham SW6 .....47 B3
SW8 .... 162 B2
Wheatsheaf Terr
SW6 .... 155 A1
Wheatstone Ho 7
W10 ....31 A4
Wheatstone Rd
W10 ....31 A4
Wheeler Ct 4
SW11 ....59 C4
Wheeler Gdns 1 ..84 B4
Wheeler La E1 ...110 C4
Wheelhouse The 4
E14 ....42 A1
Wheelwright St
N7 ....14 B1
Wheldon Ct SE1...138 C4
Wheler Ho
E1 ....24 B1 98 C1
Wheler St
E1 ....24 B1 98 C1
Whellock Rd W4 ..38 A3
Whetstone Park
WC2 .... 106 C2
Whewell Rd N19....5 A2
Whichcote St SE1 ..121 B1
Whidborne Bldgs
NW1 ....94 A3
Whidborne Cl
SE8 ....51 C1
Whidborne St WC1 ..94 B3

Whippingham Ho
E3 . . . . .26 B2
Whiskin St E1 . . . . . 96 A3
Whistler Mews 2
SE15 . . . . .49 B3
Whistlers Ave
SW11 . . . . 157 C1
Whistler St N5 . . . .15 A3
Whistler Twr
SW10 . . . . 156 C1
Whistler Wlk
SW10 . . . . 157 A2
Whiston Ho 10 N1 . .15 A1
Whiston Rd E2 . . . . .24 C4
Whitbread Ctr EC1. . 97 B1
Whitbread Rd SE4. . 66 B3
Whitburn Rd SE13 . . 67 B3
Whitby Ave NW10 . .20 A2
Whitby Ct 6 N7 . . . .14 A4
Whitby Ho NW8 . . . 78 C3
Whitby St
E1 . . . . .24 B1 98 C2
Whitcher Cl SE14. . .51 A4
Whitcher Pl NW1 . . .13 B2
Whitchurch Ho 6
W10 . . . . .30 C3
Whitchurch Rd
W11 . . . . .30 C2
Whitcomb Ct W1 . 119 C3
Whitcomb St
WC2 . . . . 119 C3
Whitcome Mews
TW9 . . . . .45 A2
Whiteacre Mews
SE11 . . . . 149 C1
Whiteadder Way
E14 . . . . .42 A2
Whitear Wlk E15 . . .19 C2
Whitebeam Cl
SW9 . . . . 163 A1
Whitebeam Ho 3
NW3 . . . . .12 B2
White Bear Pl 1
NW3 . . . . .11 C4
White Bear Yd EC1 . 95 B1
WHITECHAPEL . 110 C1
Whitechapel Gall
E1 . . . . 111 A2
Whitechapel High St
E1 . . . . 111 A2
Whitechapel Mkt
E1 . . . . 111 C3
Whitechapel Rd
E1 . . . . .32 A4
Whitechapel Sta
E1 . . . . .32 A4
Whitechurch La 3
E1 . . . . 111 B2
Whitechurch Pas 5
E1 . . . . 111 B2
White City W10. . . .30 B3
White City Cl W12 . .30 B4
White City Est
W12 . . . . .30 A2
White City Rd
W12 . . . . .30 A2
White City Sta
W12 . . . . .30 B4
Whitecliff Ho
SW18 . . . . .59 A1
White Conduit St
N1 . . . . 85 C2
Whitecross Pl
EC2 . . . . 109 C4

Whitecross St EC1 . 97 A1
White Cube (Gall)
SE1 . . . . 138 A3
SW1 . . . . 119 A2
Whitefield Cl
SW18 . . . . .58 A1
Whitefriars St
EC4 . . . . 107 C1
Whitehall SW1 . . . 134 A4
Whitehall Ct SW1. . 120 B1
Whitehall Gdns
Chiswick W4. . . . . .45 A4
SW1 . . . . 120 A1
Whitehall Mans 4
N19 . . . . .4 B3
Whitehall Park Rd
W4 . . . . .45 A4
Whitehall Pk N19 . . .4 B3
Whitehall Pl W1 WC2,
SW1 . . . . 120 A1
White Hart Ct
EC2 . . . . 110 A3
White Hart La
Mortlake SW13 . . . .56 A4
Willesden NW10. . . . 8 B3
White Hart St
Holborn EC4. . . . . 108 B2
Kennington SE11 . . 149 C2
White Hart Yd
SE1 . . . . 123 B1
Whitehaven St
NW8 . . . . 90 A1
Whitehead Cl
SW18 . . . . .71 B4
Whitehead Ho 8
SW15 . . . . .57 C2
Whitehead's Gr
SW3 . . . . 144 B3
White Ho
2 Battersea
SW11 . . . . 167 C2
3 Streatham SW4 . .73 C4
Whitehorn Ho 6
E1 . . . . .32 B1
White Horse La
E1 . . . . .32 C4
Whitehorse Mews
SE1 . . . . 136 A2
Whitehorse Rd E1 . .33 A4
White Horse Rd
E1 . . . . .33 A3
White Horse St
W1 . . . . 118 B1
White Horse Yd
EC2 . . . . 109 B2
White Ho The
NW1 . . . . 92 B2
White House Prep Sch
SW12 . . . . .73 C3
White Kennett St
E1 . . . . 110 B2
Whitelands Cres
SW18 . . . . .70 A4
Whitelands Ho
SW3 . . . . 145 A2
Whiteley Ho 9
SW4 . . . . .73 C4
Whiteleys Ctr 10
W2 . . . . 100 B1
White Lion Ct
EC3 . . . . 110 A1
White Lion Hill
EC4 . . . . 122 B4
White Lion St N1. . . 85 C1
White Lo NW11. . . . 1 B3

Whitelock Ho 8
E9 . . . . .17 C2
White Lyon Ct
EC2 . . . . 108 C4
Whiteness Ho 18
SW9 . . . . 173 B4
White Post La E9 . .18 C2
White Post St SE14,
SE15 . . . . 50 B3
White Rd E2 . . . . . 110 A3
White's Grounds
SE1 . . . . 138 B4
White's Grounds Est
SE1 . . . . 138 B4
White's Row E1 . . . 110 C3
White's Sq SW4 . . . .61 C3
Whitestone La NW3 .2 B1
Whitestone Wlk
NW3 . . . . .2 B1
Whitethorn St E3. . .33 C4
White Twr Way E1 . .33 A4
Whitfield Ct SW4 . . 172 A3
Whitfield Gdns
W1 . . . . 105 A4
Whitfield Ho NW8 . . 90 A1
Whitfield Pl W1 . . . 93 A1
Whitfield St W1. . . . 105 A4
Whitgift Ho
Battersea SW11 . . . 168 A4
Lambeth SE11 . . . . 148 C4
Whitgift St SE11 . . . 148 C4
Whitington Ave
EC3 . . . . 110 A1
Whiting Wy SE8 . . . .41 A2
Whitley Ho 1 SW1 . 161 A4
Whitlock Dr SW19 . .70 A3
Whitman Ho 20 E2 . .25 B2
Whitman Rd E3. . . . .26 A1
Whitmore Gdns
NW10 . . . . .22 B3
Whitmore Ho 20
E1 . . . . .24 A4
Whitmore Prim Sch
N1 . . . . 87 C3
Whitmore Rd N1 . . .24 A4
Whitnell Ct 7
SW15 . . . . .57 C2
Whitnell Way
SW15 . . . . .57 C2
Whitney Ho 6
SE22 . . . . .64 A4
Whitstable Ho 11
W10 . . . . .30 C3
Whitsters Ho SE1 . 138 C4
Whittaker Ct SW4 . 172 B3
Whittaker St SW1 . 145 B3
Whittaker Way 19
SE1 . . . . 153 C4
Whittingham Ct
W4 . . . . .46 A3
Whittingstall Mans
SW6 . . . . 165 A3
Whittingstall Rd
SW6 . . . . 165 A3
Whittington Hospl
The N19. . . . . .4 B2
Whittlebury Ho N4 . .6 B4
Whittlesey St SE1 . 121 C1
Whitton NW3 . . . . . . 12 B1
Whitton Wlk E3 . . . .26 C2
Whitworth Ho
SE1 . . . . 137 A1
Whitworth St
SE10 . . . . .43 A1
Whorlton Rd SE15. . .65 A4
Whytlaw Ho 10 E3. . .33 B4

Wicker St E1 . . . . . .32 A3
Wickfield Ho 32
SE16 . . . . 139 C3
Wickford Ho 5
E1 . . . . .25 B1
Wickford St E1. . . . .25 B1
Wickham Cl E1. . . . .32 B3
Wickham Gdns
SE4 . . . . 66 B4
Wickham Ho
SW15 . . . . .57 C1
Wickham Mews
SE4 . . . . .51 B1
Wickham Rd SE4 . . 66 B4
Wickham St SE11 . 148 C2
Wick La
Hackney E3. . . . . . .18 B1
Stratford Marsh E3 . 26 C4
Wicklow Ho N16. . . .7 B3
Wicklow St WC1 . . . 94 C4
Wick Rd
Hackney E9. . . . . . .17 C2
Hackney E9. . . . . . .18 A2
Wickstead Ho
TW8 . . . . .36 B1
Wicksteed Ho
SE1 . . . . 137 A1
Wick Village 7
E9 . . . . .18 B3
Wickway Ct 7
SE15 . . . . 49 B4
Wickwood St SE5. . .48 A1
Widdenham Rd
N7 . . . . .14 B4
Widecombe Ho 32
SE5 . . . . 48 B1
Widegate St E1. . . . 110 B3
Widford 8 NW1. . . . .13 A2
Widford Ho N1 . . . . 86 A1
Widley Rd W9 . . . . .23 C1
Widnes Ho 6 N7 . . . .14 C3
Wigmore Hall 4 . . . 104 A2
Wigmore Pl W1 . . . 104 A2
Wigmore St W1 . . . 103 C2
Wigram Ct SW11 . . 168 A4
Wigram Ho 7 E14. . .34 A2
Wigton Pl SE11 . . . 149 C1
Wilberforce Ho 7
SW11 . . . . .59 C4
Wilberforce Mews 9
SW4 . . . . .61 C3
Wilberforce Prim Sch
W10 . . . . .23 A2
Wilberforce Rd
Finsbury Pk N4 . . . . 6 A2
Highbury N4, N5 . . . 6 B1
Wilbraham Ho
SW8 . . . . 162 A1
Wilbraham Pl
SW1 . . . . 145 B4
Wilby Mews
W11 . . . . .31 B1 113 A2
Wilcox Cl SW8 . . . . 162 B2
Wilcox Ho 5 E3. . . .33 B4
Wilcox Pl SW1. . . . 133 A1
Wilcox Rd SW8 . . . 162 A2
Wildcroft Manor
SW15 . . . . .69 B4
Wildcroft Rd
SW15 . . . . .69 B4
Wild Ct WC2 . . . . . 106 C2
Wilde Cl E8 . . . . . . .24 C4
Wilde Pl SW18 . . . .71 C4
Wilderness Mews
SW4 . . . . .61 A3
Wilderton Rd N16 . . .7 A4

Wild Goose Dr
SE14 . . . . .50 B2
Wilding Ho 17 E9 . . .17 C2
Wild's Rents SE1 . 138 A2
Wild St WC2. . . . . 106 C1
Wildwood Gr NW3. . .2 B3
Wildwood Rd NW11 . 2 B4
Wildwood Rise
NW11 . . . . 2 B4
Wildwood Terr NW3,
NW11 . . . . 2 B3
Wilfred Fienburgh Ho
N7 . . . . .13 C4
Wilfred St SW1 . . . 132 C2
Wilfrid Gdns W3. . . .28 B1
Wilkes Rd 3 TW8 . .44 A4
Wilkes St E1 . . . . . 111 A4
Wilkie Ho SW1 . . . 147 C2
Wilkin St Mews
NW5 . . . . .13 A2
Wilkins Ho SW1. . . 160 C4
Wilkinson Ho N1 . . 87 C1
Wilkinson St SW8 . 162 C1
Wilkinson Way
W4 . . . . .37 C4
Wilkin St NW5. . . . .13 A2
Wilks Pl N1 . . . . . . .24 A3
Willan Wall E16 . . . .35 B2
Willard St SW8 . . . .61 A4
Willbury Ho 4 N7 . . .13 C3
Willcott Rd W3 . . . .28 A1
Willenfield Rd
NW10 . . . . .20 B3
WILLESDEN 8 B1
Willesden Community
Hospl The NW10. . . .8 C3
WILLESDEN
GREEN 22 A4
Willesden Green Sta
NW2 . . . . 9 B2
Willesden Junction
Sta NW10 . . . . . . .21 B2
Willesden La NW2,
NW6 . . . . 9 C2
Willesden Sports Ctr
NW10 . . . . .22 A4
Willes Rd NW5 . . . .13 A2
Willett Ho SW9 . . . .62 A4
William Banfield Ho
10 SW6 . . . . 164 C2
William Blake Ho 2
SE15 . . . . .49 C1
William Bonney Est 10
SW4 . . . . .61 C3
William Booth Meml
Training Coll
SE5 . . . . .48 C1
William Brown Ct
SE27 . . . . .75 A2
William Caslon Ho 5
E2 . . . . .25 A3
William Channing Ho
6 E2 . . . . .25 A2
William Cl SE13 . . . .67 B4
William Congreve
Mews N1 . . . . . . 86 C3
William Davis Primary
Sch E2 . . . . 99 B2
William Davis Prim
Sch 12 E2 . . .24 C1 99 B2
William Dromey Ct
NW6 . . . . .10 B1
William Dunbar Ho
NW6 . . . . .23 B3
William Ellis Sch
NW5 . . . . .3 C1

William Ellis Way 16
SE16 . . . . 139 C1
William Evans Ho 9
SE8 . . . . 40 C2
William Gdns
SW15 . . . . 57 A2
William Guy Gdns 12
E3 . . . . 27 A2
William Harvey Ho 1
SW19 . . . . 70 A3
William Hogarth Sch
The 15 W4 . . . . 38 A1
William Hunt Mans
SW13 . . . . 47 B4
William IV St
WC2 . . . . 120 A3
William Margrie Cl 1
SE15 . . . . 49 C1
William Mews
SW1 . . . . 131 A3
William Morris Ho
W6 . . . . 47 C4
William Morris Sixth
Form W6 . . . . 39 C1
William Morris Way
SW6 . . . . 166 C1
William Patten Prim
Sch 8 N16 . . . . . . 7 B2
William Pl 17 E3 . . 26 B3
William Rathbone Ho
3 E2 . . . . 25 A2
William Rd N1 . . 92 C3
William Rushbrooke
Ho 4 SE16 . . . . 153 B4
William Saville Ho 2
NW6 . . . . 23 B3
William's Bldgs 1
E2 . . . . 25 B1
Williams Cl SW6 . 154 B2
Williams Coll EC1 107 C3
Williams Ho
10 Bow E3 . . . . . . 26 C2
3 Hackney E9 . . . 25 A4
14 Streatham SW2 . 74 C3
Williams La SW14 . 45 B1
Williamson Cl
SE10 . . . . 43 B1
Williamson Ct
SE17 . . . . 150 C1
Williamson St N7 . . 14 A4
William Sq 15
SE16 . . . . 33 A2
William St SW1 . . 131 A3
William Tyndale Prim
Sch 20 N1 . . . . . . 15 A1
William Winter Ct 2
SW2 . . . . 74 C4
Willingham Cl 4
NW5 . . . . 13 B3
Willingham Terr
NW5 . . . . 13 B3
Willington Rd
SW9 . . . . 62 A4
Willis Ho 8 E14 . . 34 A2
Willis St E14 . . . . 34 A3
Willoughby Ho
EC2 . . . . 109 B3
34 Wapping E1 . . 32 A1
Willoughby Rd
NW3 . . . . 11 C4
Willoughby St
WC1 . . . . 106 A3
Willoughbys The
SW14 . . . . 56 A3
Willow Ave SW13 . 46 B1
Willowbank SW6 . 58 A4

Willowbank Rd
SE15 . . . . 49 B4
Willow Bridge Rd
N1 . . . . 15 B2
Willow Cotts TW9 . . 44 C4
Willow Ct
Brixton SW9 . . . . 173 B3
Chiswick W4 . . . . . 46 A3
EC2 . . . . . . 24 A1 98 A2
Islington N7 . . . . . 14 B3
40 Paddington W2 . 31 C4
3 Streatham
SW16 . . . . 74 B1
Willowdene
Highgate N6 . . . . . . 3 B4
3 Peckham SE15 . . 50 A2
Willow Farm La
SW15 . . . . 57 A4
Willow Hall NW3 . 11 C4
Willow Ho
5 Maitland Pk
NW3 . . . . 12 B2
North Kensington
W10 . . . . 22 C1
Willow Lo
Fulham SW6 . . . . . 47 C2
Putney SW15 . . . . . 57 A4
Willow Lodge 10
SW8 . . . . 61 A4
Willowmere SE13 . 67 A2
Willow Pl SW1 . . 147 A4
Willow Rd
Ealing W5 . . . . 36 A4
Hampstead NW3 . . 11 C4
Willow St
EC2 . . . . . . 24 A1 98 A2
Willows Terr
NW10 . . . . 21 B3
Willow Tree Cl
14 Old Ford E3 . . . 26 B4
Wandsworth SW18 . 71 A3
Willow Vale W12 . . 29 C1
Willow Way 9
W11 . . . . 30 C2
Willow Wlk SE1 . 152 C4
Willsbridge Ct 1
SE15 . . . . 49 B4
Wilman Gr E8 . . . 16 C1
Wilmcote Ho W2 . 100 A4
Wilmer Gdns 22
N1 . . . . 24 A4
Wilmer Ho 6 E3 . . 26 A3
Wilmer Lea Cl E15 . 19 C1
Wilmer Pl N16 . . . . 7 B2
Wilmers Ct 8
NW10 . . . . 20 C4
Wilmington Ave
W4 . . . . 45 C3
Wilmington Sq
WC1 . . . . 95 B3
Wilmington St
WC1 . . . . 95 B3
Wilmot Cl SE15 . . 49 C3
Wilmot Pl NW1 . . 13 B1
Wilmot St E2 . . . . 25 A1
Wilna Rd SW18 . . 71 B4
Wilsham St
W11 . . . . . 31 A1 112 A2
Wilshaw Ho 10
SE8 . . . . 51 C3
Wilshaw St SE14 . 51 C2
Wilson Gr SE16 . . 40 A4
Wilson Ho
3 Clapham
SW8 . . . . 171 B1

Wilson Ho continued
South Hampstead
NW6 . . . . 11 B1
Wilson Rd SE5 . . . . 49 A2
Wilson's Pl E14 . . . 33 B3
Wilson's Rd W6 . . . 39 C1
Wilson St EC2 . . . 109 C4
Wiltern Ct NW2 . . 10 A2
Wilton Ave W4 . . . 38 A1
Wilton Cres SW1 . 131 B3
Wilton Ct
4 Richmond
TW10 . . . . 54 A2
17 Stepney E1 . . . 32 A3
Wilton Est E8 . . . . 16 C2
Wilton Ho 8 SE22 . 64 A4
Wilton Mews
SW1 . . . . 131 C2
Wilton Pl SW1 . . . 131 B3
Wilton Rd SW1 . . 146 C4
Wilton Row SW1 . 131 B3
Wilton Sq N1 . . . . 87 B4
Wilton St SW1 . . . 132 A2
Wilton Terr SW1 . 131 B2
Wilton Villas N1 . . 87 A3
Wilton Way E8 . . . 16 C2
Wiltshire Cl SW3 . 144 C3
Wiltshire Ct N4 . . . 5 B3
Wiltshire Rd SW9 . 62 C4
Wiltshire Row N1 . . 87 C3
Wimbart Rd SW2 . 74 B4
Wimbledon Lawn
Tennis Mus & Tours
SW19 . . . . 70 A1
Wimbledon Park Ct
SW19 . . . . 70 B3
Wimbledon Park
Montessori Sch
SW18 . . . . 70 C4
Wimbledon Park Prim
Sch SW19 . . . . 71 A2
Wimbledon Park Rd
SW18, SW19 . . . . . 70 B3
Wimbledon Park Side
SW19 . . . . 69 C3
Wimbledon Park Sta
SW19 . . . . 70 C1
Wimbledon Stadium
Bsns Ctr SW17 . . . 71 A1
Wimbledon Windmill
Mus SW19 . . . . 69 B1
Wimbolt St
E2 . . . . . . 24 C2 99 B4
Wimborne Ho
Canning Town
E16 . . . . 35 B2
Marylebone NW1 . . 90 B1
8 South Lambeth
SW8 . . . . 163 A1
Upper Tooting
SW17 . . . . 73 B1
Wimborne Ho N1 . 87 B2
Wimbourne St N1 . 87 B2
Wimpole Mews
W1 . . . . 104 A3
Wimpole St W1 . . 104 A2
Winans Wlk SW9 . 173 B1
Winant Ho 19 E14 . 34 A2
Wincanton Rd
SW18 . . . . 70 B4
Winchelsea Cl
SW15 . . . . 57 C2
Winchelsea Ho 16
SE16 . . . . 40 B4
Winchelsea Rd
NW10 . . . . 20 C4

Winchendon Rd
SW6 . . . . 165 A4
Winchester Ave
NW6 . . . . 10 A1
Winchester Cl
SE17 . . . . 150 B3
Winchester Ct
Richmond TW9 . . . 54 B4
8 W8 . . . . 128 A4
Winchester Ho
Bayswater W2 . . . 100 C1
Chelsea SW3 . . . . 157 C3
24 Tower Hamlets
E3 . . . . 26 B2
Winchester Pal
Winchester Pl
6 Dalston E8 . . . . . 16 B3
Highgate N6 . . . . . . 4 A3
Winchester Rd
Highgate N6 . . . . . . 4 A3
South Hampstead
NW3 . . . . 11 C1
Winchester Sq
SE1 . . . . 123 B2
Winchester St
Acton W3 . . . . 37 B4
SW1 . . . . 146 B2
Winchester Wlk
SE1 . . . . 123 B2
Winchfield Ho
SW15 . . . . 56 B1
Winch Ho
Isle of Dogs E14 . . 42 A3
SW10 . . . . 157 A2
Winchilsea Ho
NW8 . . . . 89 C3
Wincott St SE11 . . 149 C3
Windermere
NW1 . . . . 92 B4
12 Putney SW15 . . 57 C1
Windermere Ave
NW6 . . . . 23 A4
Windermere Ct
SW13 . . . . 46 B4
Windermere Ho
E3 . . . . 26 B1
Windermere Point 3
SE15 . . . . 50 B3
Windermere Rd
N19 . . . . 4 B2
Winders Rd SW11 . 168 A2
Windham Rd TW9 . 54 B4
Windlass Pl SE8 . . 41 A2
Windlesham Gr
SW19 . . . . 69 C3
Windmill WC1 . . . 106 C4
Windmill Alley 7
W4 . . . . 38 A2
Windmill Cl
12 Bermondsey
SE1 . . . . 153 C4
4 Lewisham SE13 . 52 B1
Windmill Ct NW2 . 10 A2
Windmill Dr
Clapham SW4 . . . . 61 A2
Cricklewood NW2 . . 1 A1
Windmill Gdns
SW2 . . . . 62 B1
Windmill Hill
1 Hampstead
NW3 . . . . 11 B4
Hampstead NW3 . . 2 B1
Windmill Ho
4 Millwall E14 . . . 41 C2
SE1 . . . . 121 C1

Windmill La E15 . . 19 C2
Windmill Pas 10
W4 . . . . 38 A2
Windmill Rd
Chiswick W4 . . . . . 38 A2
Roehampton SW19 . 69 A1
Wandsworth SW18 . 59 C1
Windmill Row
SE11 . . . . 149 B1
Windmill St W1 . . 105 B3
Windmill Wlk SE1 135 C4
Windrose Cl SE16 . 40 C4
Windrush Cl
Battersea SW11 . . . 59 C3
Chiswick W4 . . . . . 45 B3
4 Hackney E8 . . . . 16 C1
Windrush Ho
NW8 . . . . 101 C4
Windrush Rd
NW10 . . . . 20 C4
Windrush Sq
Brixton SW9 . . . . . 62 C3
SW2 . . . . 62 C3
Windsock Cl 1
SE16 . . . . 41 B2
Windsor Ct
Battersea SW11 . . 167 C2
Bayswater W2 . . . 114 A4
2 Clapham SW4 . . 61 B3
Fulham SW6 . . . . . 58 A4
20 Rotherhithe
SE16 . . . . 32 C1
4 Wandsworth
SW18 . . . . 58 C2
West Hampstead
NW3 . . . . 11 A4
Windsor Gdns W9 . 23 C1
Windsor Ho
4 Acton Green
W4 . . . . 37 B1
Brondesbury NW2 . 10 A2
42 Globe Town E2 . 25 C2
Regent's Pk NW1 . . 92 B4
Shoreditch N1 . . . . 87 A2
14 Stoke Newington N4 . 6 B3
Windsor Pl SW1 . . 147 A4
Windsor Rd
Richmond TW9 . . . 44 B1
Upper Holloway N7 . 5 A1
Willesden NW2 . . . . 9 A2
Windsor St N1 . . . 86 B4
Windsor Terr N1 . . 97 A4
Windsor Way
W14 . . . . 140 A4
Windsor Wharf E9 . 18 B3
Windsor Wlk SE5 . 48 C1
Windspoint Dr
SE15 . . . . 50 A4
Windus Rd N16 . . . 7 B3
Windus Wlk N16 . . 7 B3
Wine Cl E1 . . . . . . 32 B2
Wine Office Ct
EC4 . . . . 107 C2
Winfield Ho 3
SW11 . . . . 167 C2
Winford Ct 16
SE15 . . . . 49 C2
Winford Ho E3 . . . 18 B1
Winforton St SE10 . 52 B2
Winfrith Rd SW18 . 71 B3
Wingate Ho
26 Bromley E3 . . . 27 A2

Wingate Ho continued

[8] Stoke Newington
N16 . . . . 15 C4
Wingate Rd W6 . . . . . 39 A3
Wingfield Ct [5]
E14 . . . . 34 C2
Wingfield Ho
Paddington NW6 . . . 78 A2
[1] Spitalfields
E2 . . . . 24 B2 98 C5
Wingfield Mews
SE15 . . . . 64 C4
Wingfield St SE15 . . . 64 C4
Wingford Rd SW2 . . . 62 A1
Wingham [3] NW5 . . 12 C2
Wingmore Rd
SE24 . . . . 63 B4
Wingrad Ho [10] E1 . . 32 B4
Wingrave SE17 . . . 151 B3
Wingrave Rd W6 . . . . 47 B4
Wingreen [10] NW8 . . 78 B4
Winicotte Ho W2 . . 101 C4
Winifrede Paul Ho [9]
NW5 . . . . 13 A4
Winkley St [6] E2 . . . 25 A3
Winkworth Cotts [14]
E1 . . . . 25 B1
Winnett St W1 . . . . 119 B4
Winnington Ho
[11] Kensal Town
W10 . . . . 23 A1
[8] SE5 . . . . 48 B3
Winscombe St N19 . . 4 A2
Winsham Gr SW11 . . 60 C2
Winsham Ho NW1 . . . 93 C4
Winslade Rd SW2 . . . 62 A2
Winsland Mews
W2 . . . . 101 B2
Winsland St W2 . . . 101 B2
Winsley St W1 . . . . . 105 A2
Winslow SE17 . . . . 152 A1
Winslow Rd W6 . . . . 47 B4
Winstanley Rd
SW11 . . . . 59 C4
Winston Ho NW1 . . . 93 C2
Winston Rd N16 . . . . 15 C4
Winston Wlk [2]
W4 . . . . 37 C2
Winterbourne Ho
W11 . . . . . 31 A2 112 A3
Winter Box Wlk
TW10 . . . . 54 B2
Winterbrook Rd
SE24 . . . . 63 B1
Winterfold Cl
SW19 . . . . 70 A2
Winterleys [7]
NW6 . . . . 23 B3
Winter Lo [17]
SE16 . . . . 153 C1
Winterslow Ho [20]
SE5 . . . . 48 B1
Winterton Ho [18]
E1 . . . . 32 B3
Winterton Pl
SW10 . . . . 157 A4
Winterwell Rd
SW2 . . . . 62 A2
Winthorpe Rd
SW15 . . . . 58 A3
Winthrop Ho [10]
W12 . . . . 30 A2
Winthrop St E1 . . . . . 32 A4

Winton Prim Sch
N1 . . . . 84 C1
Wirrall Ho [15]
SE26 . . . . 76 C1
Wisbech [5] N4 . . . . . 5 B3
Wisden Ho SW8 . . . 163 A3
Wise Rd E15 . . . . 27 C4
Wiseton Rd SW17 . . . 72 B3
Wisley Ho SW1 . . . . 147 B2
Wisley Rd SW11 . . . . 60 C2
Wisteria Ho SE4 . . . . 66 A4
Wisteria Rd SE13 . . . 67 C3
Wistow Ho [14] E2 . . 24 C4
Witanhurst La N6 . . . . 3 C3
Witan St E2 . . . . 25 A2
Witchwood Ho [10]
SW9 . . . . 62 C4
Witcombe Point [14]
SE15 . . . . 49 C2
Witechapel Sp Ctr
Witham Ct SW17 . . . . 72 B1
Witham Ho [24] SE5 . . 48 B1
Witherington Rd
N5 . . . . 14 C3
Withers Pl EC1 . . . . . 97 A2
Withycombe Rd
SW19 . . . . 69 C4
Withy Ho [3] E1 . . . . 25 C1
Witley Ct WC1 . . . . . 94 A1
Witley Ho [3] SW2 . . 74 A4
Witley Point [8]
SW15 . . . . 69 A3
Witley Rd N19 . . . . . . 4 B2
Wittering Ho [9]
SW11 . . . . 169 A2
Wivenhoe Cl SE15 . . 65 A4
Wix Prim Sch SW4 . . 61 A3
Wix's La SW4 . . . . . . 61 A3
Woburn Ct
[32] Bermondsey
SE16 . . . . 40 A1
[1] Richmond TW9 . . 54 B4
Woburn Pl WC1 . . . . 94 A1
Woburn Sq WC1 . . . . 93 C1
Woburn Wlk WC1 . . . 93 C3
Wodeham Gardens [7]
E1 . . . . 32 A4
Wodehouse Ave
SE15 . . . . 49 B2
Wodehouse Ho [8]
W3 . . . . 37 B3
Woking Cl SW15 . . . . 56 B3
Wolcot Ho NW1 . . . . 83 A1
Wolfe Cres
[8] Bermondsey
SE16 . . . . 40 C4
[34] Rotherhithe
SE16 . . . . 40 C4
Wolfe Ho [15] W12 . . 30 A2
Wolfson Ct
Golders Green
NW11 . . . . 1 A4
Wolftencroft Cl
SW11 . . . . 59 C4
Wollaston Cl SE1 . . 150 C4
Wollstonecraft St
N1 . . . . 84 A3
Wolsey Ave SW18,
SW19 . . . . 70 C2
Wolsey Gdns

Wolseley Rd W4 . . . . 37 B2
Wolseley St SE1 . . . 139 A3
Wolsey Ct NW6 . . . . . 11 B1
Wolsey Ho [3]
NW5 . . . . 13 C2
Wolsey Mews
NW5 . . . . 13 B2
Wolsey Rd N1 . . . . . . 15 C3
Wolsey St E1 . . . . 32 B4
Wolverley St [2]
E2 . . . . 25 A2
Wolverton SE17 . . . 152 A2
Wolverton Gdns
W6 . . . . 39 C2
Wontner Cl [5] N1 . . 15 B1
Wontner Rd SW12,
SW17 . . . . 72 B2
Woodall Cl [15] E14 . . 34 A2
Woodberry Down
N4 . . . . 6 B4
Woodberry Down
Com Prim Sch N4 . . . 6 B4
Woodberry Gr N4 . . . . 6 B4
Woodbine Terr [9] E9 . 17 B2
Woodborough Rd
SW15 . . . . 57 A3
Woodbourne Ave
SW16 . . . . 73 C1
Woodbourne Cl
SW16 . . . . 74 A1
Woodbridge Cl [10]
N7 . . . . 5 B2
Woodbridge St
EC1 . . . . 96 A2
Woodchester Sq
W2 . . . . 100 A4
Woodchurch Ho [5]
SW9 . . . . 173 B4
Woodchurch Rd
NW6 . . . . 11 A1
Wood Cl E2 . . . 24 C1 99 B2
Woodcock Ho [4]
E14 . . . . 33 C4
Woodcote Ho [4]
SE8 . . . . 51 B4
Woodcott Ho [1]
SW15 . . . . 68 C4
Woodcroft Mews
SE8 . . . . 41 A2
Wood Dene [6]
SE15 . . . . 50 A2
Woodfall Rd N4 . . . . . 5 C2
Woodfall St SW3 . . . 144 C1
Woodfarrs SE5 . . . . . 63 C3
Wood Field NW3 . . . 12 B3
Woodfield Ave
SW16 . . . . 73 C1
Woodfield Ct
SW16 . . . . 73 C1
Woodfield Gr
SW16 . . . . 73 C1
Woodfield La
SW16 . . . . 73 C1
Woodfield Pl W9 . . . . 23 B1
Woodfield Rd W9 . . . 31 B4
Woodford Ct [1]
W12 . . . . 39 C4
Woodger Rd W12 . . . 39 B4
Woodhall NW1 . . . . . 92 C3
Woodhall Ave
SE21 . . . . 76 B1
Woodhall Dr SE21 . . . 76 B1
Woodhall Ho
SW18 . . . . 59 C1
Woodheyes Rd
NW10 . . . . 8 A3

Wood Ho
[4] Clapham SW4 . . 171 C2
[6] Paddington
NW6 . . . . 23 B3
Woodhurst Rd W3 . . . 28 C2
Woodison St E3 . . . . . 26 A1
Wood La W12 . . . . . . 30 B2
Woodland Cres
[5] Rotherhithe
SE16 . . . . 40 C4
SE10 . . . . 53 A4
Woodland Gr SE10 . . 43 A1
Woodland Hts SE3 . . 53 A4
Woodland Mews
SW16 . . . . 74 A1
Woodlands SW4 . . . . 61 A3
Woodlands Ave
W3 . . . . 28 A1
Woodlands Ct
NW10 . . . . 9 A2
Woodlands Gt
SW15 . . . . 58 B2
Woodlands Park Rd
SE10 . . . . 53 A4
Woodlands Rd
SW13 . . . . 56 B4
Woodland St [2]
E8 . . . . 16 B2
Woodlands The
Highbury N5 . . . . 15 B4
[12] Hornsey N8 . . . . . 5 A4
Woodlands Way
SW15 . . . . 58 B2
Woodland Wlk
[9] Greenwich
SE10 . . . . 43 A1
Hampstead NW3 . . . 12 A3
Wood Lane High Sch
W12 . . . . 30 A3
Wood Lane Sta
W12 . . . . 30 B2
Woodlawn Cl
SW15 . . . . 58 B2
Woodlawn Rd
SW6 . . . . 47 C2
Woodlea Rd N16 . . . . 7 A1
Woodleigh Gdns
SW16 . . . . 74 A1
Woodman Mews
TW9 . . . . 45 A2
Woodmans Gr
NW10 . . . . 8 B3
Woodmans Mews
W12 . . . . 30 A4
Woodmere Cl [11]
SW11 . . . . 60 C4
Woodmill Cl
SW15 . . . . 56 C1
Woodmill Rd SE1 . . 139 A2
Woodpecker Mews
SE13 . . . . 67 C3
Woodpecker Rd [5]
SE14 . . . . 51 A4
Wood Point [8]
E16 . . . . 35 C4
Woodquest Ave
SE24 . . . . 63 B2
Woodruff Ho [12]
SW2 . . . . 62 C1
Woodrush Cl [4]
SE14 . . . . 51 A3
Woodseer St E1 . . . . 111 A4
Woodsford SE17 . . . 151 B1
Woodsford Sq
W14 . . . . 126 B4
Woods Ho SW8 . . . . 170 C4

Wood's Mews W1 . . 117 B4
Woodsome Rd NW5 . . 4 A1
Wood's Pl SE1 . . . . . 138 B1
Woodspring Rd
SW19 . . . . 70 A2
Wood's Rd SE15 . . . . 50 A2
Wood St
Chiswick W4 . . . . 38 B1
City of London EC2 . 109 A2
Woodstar Ho [3]
SE15 . . . . 49 C3
Woodstock Ave
NW11 . . . . 1 A4
Woodstock Ct
SE11 . . . . 149 A2
Woodstock Gr
W12 . . . . 39 C4
Woodstock Ho [2]
N5 . . . . 15 B4
Woodstock Mews
W1 . . . . 103 C3
Woodstock Rd
Bedford Pk W4 . . . . . 38 A3
Finsbury Pk N4 . . . . . 5 C3
Golders Green NW11 . 1 B3
Woodstock St W11 . 104 A1
Woodstock Studios [7]
W12 . . . . 39 C4
Woodstock Terr
E14 . . . . 34 A2
Woodthorpe Rd
SW15 . . . . 57 A3
Woodview Cl N4 . . . . . 6 A4
Woodville Ct [3]
SE10 . . . . 52 B2
Woodville Ho SE1 . . 138 C2
Woodville Rd
Golders Green
NW11 . . . . 1 A4
Paddington NW6 . . . . 23 B3
Stoke Newington
N16 . . . . 16 A3
Woodwarde Rd
SE22 . . . . 64 A1
Woodwell St
SW18 . . . . 59 B2
Wood Wharf SE10 . . . 52 B4
Woodyard Cl NW5 . . 12 C3
Woodyard La SE21 . . 76 A4
Woolcombes Ct [4]
SE16 . . . . 32 C1
Wooler St SE17 . . . . 151 C2
Woolf Ct [7] W3 . . . . 37 B3
Woolf Mews WC1 . . . 94 A2
Woollon Ho [1] E1 . . 32 B3
Woolmore Prim Sch
E14 . . . . 34 B2
Woolmore St E14 . . . 34 B2
Woolneigh St
SW6 . . . . 166 A1
Woolpack Ho [1]
E9 . . . . 17 B2
Woolridge Way E9 . . 17 B1
Woolstaplers Way
SE16 . . . . 153 B4
Woolstone Ho [7]
E2 . . . . 25 C4
Woolven Ho SE3 . . . . 53 B4
WoolYd SE17 . . . . . 138 A4
Wooster Gdns E14 . . 34 C3
Wooster Pl SE1 . . . . 151 C4
Wootton St SE1 . . . 121 C1
Worcester Ct [44]
W2 . . . . 31 C4
Worcester Dr W4 . . . 38 A4

Worcester Gdns
  SW11 . . . . .60 B2
Worcester Ho
  Bayswater W2 . . . . **100** C1
  3 Islington N1 . . . . .15 B1
  Lambeth SE11 . . . . .**135** B1
  6 Putney SW15 . . . .69 B4
Worcester Mews **2**
  NW6 . . . . .11 A2
Wordsworth Ho
  NW6 . . . . .23 C2
Wordsworth Pl **11**
  NW5 . . . . .12 B3
Wordsworth Rd
  Bermondsey SE1 . . .**153** A3
  Stoke Newington
  N16 . . . . .16 A4
Worfield St SW11 . .**158** B1
Worgan St
  Rotherhithe SE16 . . .40 C2
  SE11 . . . .**148** C2
Working Men's Coll
  The NW1 . . . .**83** A2
World's End Pas
  SW10 . . . .**157** B2
World's End Pl
  SW10 . . . .**157** A2
World Trade Ctr
  London E14 . . . . . . .42 A4
Worlidge St W6 . . .39 B1
Worlingham Rd
  SE22 . . . . .64 B3
Wormholt Park Prim
  Sch W12 . . . . .29 C2
Wormholt Rd W12 . .29 C1
Wormwood St
  EC2 . . . .**110** A2
Wornington Rd
  W10 . . . . .31 A4
Woronzow Rd
  NW8 . . . .**80** A3
Worple St SW14 . . . .55 C4
Worple Way TW10 . .54 A3
Worship St
  EC2 . . . . .24 A1 **98** A1
Worsley Gr E5 . . . . .16 C4
Worsopp Dr SW4 . .61 B2
Worth Gr SE17 . . . .**151** B1
Worthington Ho
  EC1 . . . .**95** C4
  18 Streatham SW2 . . .74 C4
Wotton Ct **14** E14 . .34 C2
Wotton Rd **18** SE8 . .51 B4
Wouldham Rd E16 . .35 B3
Wraxall Rd **2** E3 . .26 B1
Wrayburn Ho **28**
  SE16 . . . .**139** C3
Wray Cres N4 . . . . . .5 B2
Wray Ct N4 . . . . .5 B2
Wray Ho **11** SW2 . . .74 A3
Wren Ave NW2 . . . . .9 B4
Wren Cl E16 . . . . .35 B3
Wren Ho
  28 Bow E3 . . . . .26 A3
  SW1 . . . .**147** B1

Wren Landing E14 . .33 C1
Wrenn Ho SW13 . . . .47 B4
Wren Rd SE5 . . . . . . .48 C2
Wren St WC1 . . . . . .**95** A2
Wrentham Ave
  NW10 . . . . .22 C3
Wren View N6 . . . . . . .4 B3
Wrestlers Ct EC3 . .**110** A2
Wresham Rd E3 . . . .26 C3
Wrigglesworth St
  SE14 . . . . .50 C3
Wright Cl SE13 . . . .67 C3
Wright Ho SW15 . . . .57 A2
Wright's Gn SW4 . . .61 C3
Wright's La W8 . . . .**128** A2
Wright's Rd E3 . . . . .26 B3
Wrights Wlk SW14 . .55 C4
Wrotham Ho SE1 . .**137** C2
Wrotham Rd **18**
  NW1 . . . . .13 B1
Wrottesley Rd
  NW10 . . . . .21 C3
Wroughton Rd
  SW11 . . . . .60 B1
Wroxton Rd SE15 . . .50 B1
Wulfstan St W12 . . . .29 B3
WWT London Wetland
  Ctr SW13 . . . . .47 A3
Wyatt Cl SE16 . . . . .41 B4
Wyatt Dr SW13 . . . . .47 A3
Wyatt Ho
  Blackheath Vale SE3 . .53 B1
  NW8 . . . .**89** C1
Wyatt Park Mans **1**
  SW2 . . . . .74 A2
Wyatt Park Rd
  SW2 . . . . .74 B2
Wybert St NW1 . . . .**92** C2
Wycherley Cl SE3 . .53 B3
Wychwood End N6 . . .4 B4
Wychwood Ho N4 . . . .6 B4
Wyclif Ct EC1 . . . . . .**96** A3
Wycliffe Ho **13**
  N16 . . . . .16 A4
Wyclif St EC1 . . . . . .**96** A3
Wycombe Ct SE3 . .53 C3
Wycombe Gdns
  NW11 . . . . .1 C2
Wycombe Ho NW8 .**90** A2
Wycombe Pl SW18 .59 B1
Wycombe Sq
  W8 . . . . .31 C1 **113** B1
Wyersdale Ho N4 . . .6 B4
Wye St SW11 . . . . . .**167** C1
Wyfold Rd SW6 . . .**154** A1
Wyke Rd E3 . . . . . . .18 C1
Wyldes Cl NW11 . . . .2 B3
Wyllen Cl E1 . . . . . .25 B1
Wymering Mans **9**
  W9 . . . . .23 C2
Wymering Rd W9 . .23 C2
Wymondham Ct
  NW8 . . . .**79** C4
Wymond St SW15 . .57 B4

Wynan Rd E14 . . . . . .42 A1
Wyndham Cres N19 . .4 B1
Wyndham Deedes Ho
  30 E2 . . . . .24 C3
Wyndham Ho
  SW1 . . . .**145** B3
Wyndham Mews
  W1 . . . .**102** C3
Wyndham Pl W1 . . .**102** C3
Wyndham Rd SE5 . .48 B3
Wyndhams Ct **4**
  E8 . . . . .16 B1
Wyndham St W1 . . .**102** C4
Wyndham Yd W1 . . .**102** C3
Wyneham Rd SE24 . .63 C2
Wynford Rd N1 . . . . .**85** A2
Wynne Ho SE14 . . . .50 C2
Wynne Rd SW9 . . . .**173** B1
Wynnstay Gdns
  W8 . . . .**127** C2
Wynter Ho **20**
  SW9 . . . .**173** A1
Wynter St SW11 . . . .59 B3
Wynton Pl W3 . . . . . .28 A3
Wynyard Ho SE11 . .**149** A2
Wynyard Terr
  SE11 . . . .**149** A2
Wynyatt Ho EC1 . . .**96** A4
Wynyatt St EC1 . . . .**96** A4
Wythburn Ho W1 . .**89** C1
Wythburn Pl W1 . .**102** C2
Wythes Rd E16 . . . .**102** C2
Wyvil Prim Sch
  SW8 . . . .**162** B2
Wyvil Rd SW8 . . . . .**162** A2
Wyvis St E14 . . . . . .34 A4

Y

Yabsley St E14 . . . . .34 B1
Yaldam Ho SE1 . . . .**152** A3
Yalding Ho **20** E5 . .17 A3
Yalding Rd SE16 . .**153** B4
Yale Ct NW6 . . . . . . .11 A3
Yardley St WC1 . . . .**95** B3
Yard The N1 . . . .**84** B1
Yarmouth Pl W1 . . .**118** C1
Yarnfield Sq **15**
  SE15 . . . . .49 C2
Yarrow Ho
  12 Cubitt Town
  E14 . . . . .42 B3
  10 North Kensington
  W10 . . . . .30 B4
Yatesbury Ct E5 . . .18 A3
Yates Ct NW2 . . . . . . .9 C2
Yates Ho **22**
  E2 . . . . .24 C2 **99** C4
Yatton Ho **10** W10 . .30 B4
Yeadon Ho **14**
  W10 . . . . .30 B4
Yearby Ho W10 . . . .22 B1
Yeate St N1 . . . . . . .15 C1
Yeats Cl NW10 . . . . . .8 A2
Yeldham Ho W6 . . . .39 C1

Yeldham Rd W6 . . . .39 C1
Yelverton Rd
  SW11 . . . .**167** C1
Yeoman Cl SE27 . . .75 A1
Yeoman's Row
  SW3 . . . .**130** B1
Yeoman St SE8 . . . .41 A2
Yeoman's Yd E1 . . .**125** A4
Yeo St **13** E3 . . . . . .34 A4
Yeovil Ho
  Finsbury Pk N7 . . . . .5 B2
  North Kensington
  W10 . . . . .22 B1
Yerbury Prim Sch
  N19 . . . . .4 C2
Yerbury Rd N19 . . . .4 C1
Yesoday Hatorah
  Senior Girls Sch **5**
  N16 . . . . .7 B4
Yet Lev Ct E5 . . . . . . .7 C3
Yewfield Rd NW10 . . .8 B2
Yew Gr NW2 . . . . .9 C4
Yew Ho SE14 . . . . . .51 B1
Yew Tree Cl **3**
  SE13 . . . . .67 B4
Yew Tree Ct **6** N16 . .6 C2
Yew Tree Rd W12 . .29 B2
Yoakley Rd N16 . . . . .7 A2
Yoke Cl N7 . . . . .14 A2
Yonge Pk N4, N7 . . . .5 C1
York Ave
  Mortlake SW14 . . . . .55 B2
  Walworth SE17 . . . .**151** A2
York Bldgs WC2 . . .**120** B3
York Bridge NW1 . . .**91** B2
York Cl **17** SE5 . . . . .48 B1
York Gate NW1 . . . . .**91** C1
York Gr SE15 . . . . . .50 B2
York Hall L Ctr E2 . .25 B3
York Hill SE27,
  SW16 . . . . .75 A1
York Ho
  Acton W3 . . . . .28 B2
  Chelsea SW3 . . . . . .**145** A2
  Islington N5 . . . . .14 C3
  Kensington W8 . . . .**128** A4
  11 Kentish Town
  N7 . . . . .13 C2
  Kew TW9 . . . . .44 C2
  Lambeth SE1 . . . . . .**135** A1
  Marylebone W1 . . . .**102** C4
  Pentonville N1 . . . . .**84** C1
  Richmond TW10 . . . . .54 C2
York House Pl
  W8 . . . .**128** A4
York Mans
  Battersea SW11 . . . .**169** C4
  Marylebone W1 . . . .**103** B4
  Walworth SE17 . . . .**151** A2
York Mews NW5 . . . .13 A3
York Pl
  Battersea SW11 . . . .59 C4
  WC2 . . . .**120** B3

Wor–ZSL 291

York Place Mans
  NW1 . . . .**103** A4
York Rd
  Battersea SW11,
  SW18 . . . . .59 C4
  2 Dagenham W3 . . .28 C3
  4 Richmond TW10 . .54 B2
  SE1 . . . .**135** A4
York Rise NW5 . . . . .4 A1
York Road Bsns Ctr
  SW11 . . . .**167** B1
York St Chambers
  W1 . . . .**103** A4
Yorkshire Cl N16 . . .7 A1
Yorkshire Grey Pl **13**
  NW3 . . . . .11 B4
Yorkshire Grey Yd
  WC1 . . . .**106** C3
Yorkshire Rd E14 . .33 A3
York Sq **12** E14 . . . .33 A3
York St W1 . . . .**103** A4
York Terr E NW1 . . .**91** C1
York Terr W NW1 . .**91** B1
Yorkton St E2 . . . . .24 C3
York Water Gate The
  SW1 . . . .**120** B2
York Way
  Barnsbury N1, N7,
  NW1 . . . . .14 A1
  N1 . . . .**84** B3
York Way Ct
  Islington N1 . . . .**84** B3
  Islington N1 . . . .**84** C3
Young's Bldgs EC1 . .**97** A2
Youngs Ct SW11 . .**169** C3
Young St W8 . . . . . .**128** A3
Yoxall Ho **2** W10 . .22 B1
Yukon Rd SW12 . . . .73 A4

Z

Zabludowicz
  Collection NW5 . . . .12 C2
Zampa Rd SE16 . . . .40 B1
Zander Ct
  E2 . . . . .24 C2 **99** C4
Zangwill Ho NW6 . . .23 B3
Zealand Ho **11** SE5 .48 B1
Zealand Rd E3 . . . . .26 A3
Zennor Rd SW12 . . .73 B3
Zennor Trade Pk **2**
  SW12 . . . . .73 B3
Zenoria St SE22 . . . .64 B3
Zetland Ho W8 . . . .**128** A2
Zetland St E14 . . . . .34 B4
Zeus Ho N1 . . . .**97** B3
Zion Ho **6** E1 . . . . .32 B3
Zoar St SE1 . . . .**122** C2
Zodiac Ho **3** E3 . . .26 C1
Zoffany St N19 . . . . .4 C2
ZSL London Zoo
  NW1 . . . .**81** B2

List of numbered locations

This atlas shows thousands more place names than any other London street atlas. In some busy areas it is impossible to fit the name of every place.

Where not all names will fit, some smaller places are shown by a number. If you wish to find out the name associated with a number, use this listing.

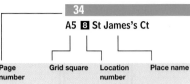

34

A5 **8** St James's Ct

Page number — Grid square — Location number — Place name

1

B1
1 Mortimer Ct
2 Primrose Ct
3 Sunnyside Ho
4 Sunnyside
5 Prospect Pl
B4 1 Berkeley Ct
2 Exchange Mans
3 Beechcroft Ct
4 Nedahall Ct
C1 1 Portman Hts
2 Hermitage Ct
3 Moreland Ct
4 Wendover Ct

2

B1 1 Hampstead Sq
2 Stamford Cl
3 Mount Sq The

4

B1 1 Hunter Ho
2 Fisher Ho
3 Lang Ho
4 Temple Ho
5 Palmer Ho
6 Carlisle Ho
7 Durham Ho
8 Suffolk Ho
9 Lincoln Ho
10 Llewellyn Ho
11 Fell Ho
12 Aveling Ho
13 Merryweather Ct
14 Brennands Ct
15 St Christophers Ct
16 Francis Terrace Mews
17 Tremlett Mews
B2 1 Flowers Mews
2 Archway Cl
3 Sandridge St
4 Bovingdon Cl
5 Cavell Ct
6 Torrence Ho
7 Rowan Wlk
8 Laurel Cl
9 Forest Way
10 Larch Cl
11 Pine Cl
12 Alder Mews
13 Aspen Cl
14 Hargrave Park Sch

B3 1 Calvert Ct
2 Academy The
3 Whitehall Mans
4 Pauntley St
5 Archway Hts
6 Pauntley Ho
7 Thornbury Sq
8 St Aloysius RC Coll
C1 1 Melchester Ho
2 Norcombe Ho
3 Weatherbury Ho
4 Wessex Ho
5 Archway Bsns Ctr
6 Harford Mews
7 Opera Ct
8 Rupert Ho
9 All Saints Church
C2 1 Bowerman Ct
2 Gresham Pl
3 Hargrave Mans
4 Church Garth
5 Ramsey Ct
6 St John's Upper Holloway CE Prim Sch
7 Hargrave Park Sch
C3 1 Louise White Ho
2 Levison Way
3 Sanders Way
4 Birbeck Ho
5 Scholars Ct
6 Mount Carmel RC Tech Coll for Girls
C4 1 Eleanor Rathbone House
2 Christopher Lo
3 Monkridge
4 Marbleford Ct
5 High London
6 Garton Ho
7 Hilltop Ho
8 Caroline Martyn Ho
9 Arthur Henderson House
10 Margaret Mcmillan House
11 Enid Stacy Ho
12 Mary McArthur Ho
13 Bruce Glasier Ho
14 John Wheatley Ho
15 Keir Hardie Ho
16 Monroe Ho

17 Iberia Ho
18 Lygoe Ho
19 Lambert Ho
20 Shelbourne Ho
21 Arkansas Ho
22 Lafitte Ho
23 Shreveport Ho
24 Packenham Ho
25 Orpheus Ho
26 Fayetville Ho
27 Bayon Ho

5

A1 1 Northview
2 Tufnell Park Mans
3 Fulford Mans
4 Tollington Ho
5 Grafton Prim Sch
A2 1 Bracey Mews
2 Christie Ct
3 Ringmer Gdns
4 Kingsdown Ho
5 Cottenham Ho
6 St Paul's Ct
7 Rickthorne Rd
8 Stanley Terr
9 Arundel Lo
10 Landseer Ct
11 St Mark's CE Prim Sch
A3 1 Beeches The
2 Lambton Ct
3 Nugent Ct
4 Lambton Mews
5 Mews The
6 Duncombe Prim Sch
7 Nyton Cl
8 Charles St
A4 1 Marie Lloyd Gdns
2 Edith Cavell Cl
3 Marie Stopes Ct
4 Jessie Blythe La
5 Barbara Rudolph Ct
6 Hetty Rees Ct
7 Leyden Mans
8 Brambledown
9 Lochbie
10 Lyngham Ct
11 High Mount
12 Woodlands The
13 St Gildas' RC Jun Sch

14 Holly Park Montessori Sch
B1 1 Pakeman Prim Sch
2 South Eastern Univ
3 Samuel Rhodes Sch
4 Montem Prim Sch
5 Heather Cl
B2 1 Berkeley Wlk
2 Lazar Wlk
3 Thistlewood Cl
4 Tomlins Wlk
5 Andover Ho
6 Barmouth Ho
7 Chard Ho
8 Christ the King RC Prim Sch
9 Methley Ho
10 Rainford Ho
11 Allerton Wlk
12 Falconer Wlk
13 Sonderburg Rd
14 St Mark's Mans
15 Athol Ct
16 Pooles Park Prim Sch
B3 1 Lawson Ct
2 Wiltshire Ct
3 Fenstanton
4 Hutton Ct
5 Wisbech
6 Islington Arts & Media Sch
7 Old Dairy Ct
C2 1 Brookfield
2 Churnfield
3 Cornwallis Sq

6

A1 1 Hurlock Ho
2 Blackstock Ho
3 Vivian Comma Cl
4 Monsell Ct
5 Century Mews
A2 1 Parkwood Prim Sch
2 Ambler Prim Sch
3 City & Islington Coll (Ctr for Life-long Learning)
B4 1 Finmere Ho
2 Keynsham Ho
3 Kilpeck Ho
4 Knaresborough Ho

5 Leighfield Ho
6 Lonsdale Ho
7 Groveley Ho
8 Wensleydale Ho
9 Badminton Ho
10 Skinners' Acad
C1 1 Betty Layward Prim Sch
2 Piano La
C2 1 Chestnut Cl
2 Sycamore Ho
3 Lordship Ho
4 Clissold Ho
5 Beech Ho
6 Laburnum Ho
7 Ormond Ho
8 Yew Tree Ct
9 Oak Ho
10 Beis Yaakov Girls Sch
C4 1 Selwood Ho
2 Bnois Jerusalem Girls Sch
3 Mendip Ho
4 Ennerdale Ho
5 Getters Talmud Torah
6 Delamere Ho
7 Westwood Ho
8 Bernwood Ho
9 Allerdale Ho
10 Chattenden Ho
11 Farningham Ho
12 Oakend Ho
13 Getters Talmud Torah Sch

7

A1 1 Gujarat Ho
2 Marton Rd
3 Painsthorpe Rd
4 Selkirk Ho
5 Defoe Ho
6 Edward Friend Ho
7 Sheridan Ho
8 Barrie Ho
9 Arnold Ho
10 Macaulay Ho
11 Stowe Ho
12 Carlyle Ho
13 Shaftesbury Ho
14 Lillian Cl
15 Swift Ho

17 Romford Ho
18 Bute Wlk
19 Upper Ramsey Wlk
20 Rona Wlk
21 Thorndike Rd
22 St Pauls Steiner Sch
C3 1 Newington Green Prim Sch
C4 1 Ledo Ho
2 Salween Ho
3 Prome Ho
4 Arakan Ho
5 Rangoon Ho
6 Mandalay Ho
7 Karen Ho
8 Wingate Ho
9 Jubet Ho
10 Orde Ho
11 Chindit Ho
12 Mabel Thornton Ho
13 Crawshay Ho
14 Avon Ho
15 Connaught Mans
16 Jonson Ho
17 Herrick Ho
18 Donne Ho
19 Thirlmere Ho
20 Grasmere Ho
21 Copper La

16

A1 1 Dorchester Ct
2 Wareham Ho
3 Dorset Ct
4 Stratton Ct
5 Swanage Ct
6 Blandford Ct
7 Portland Ct
8 Oscar Faber Pl
9 Metropolitan Bsns Ctr
10 Lancaster Cl
11 Palazzo Apartments
12 Watercress Pl
A2 1 Kingsland Gn
2 Kingsland Pas
3 Metropolitan Benefit Societies Almshouses
4 Nimrod Pas
5 De Beauvoir Pl
6 Warburton Cl
7 Buckingham Mews
8 Aztec Ct
9 Kerridge Ct
10 Isabella Mews
11 St Jude & St Paul's CE Prim Sch
12 De Beauvoir Prim Sch
13 Our Lady & St Joseph RC Prim Sch
14 Childrens House Upper Sch
A3 1 Hewling Ho
2 Matthias Ho
3 Port Royal Pl
4 Cressington Cl
5 King Henry's Yd
6 Bronte Ho
7 Sewell Ho
8 Lydgate Ho
9 Patmore Ho
10 Congreve Ho

11 Elton St
12 Conrad Ho
13 Southwell Ho
14 Neptune Ho
15 Campion Ho
16 Webster Ho
17 Meredith Ho
18 Beckford Ho
19 Ashley Ct
20 Hayling Cl
21 Millard Cl
22 Lydford Cl
23 Salcombe Rd
24 Truman's Rd
25 Templeton Cl
26 John Campbell Rd
27 Gillett Pl
28 Bradbury St
29 Thomas Crowell Ct
30 Shellgrove Rd
A4 1 Londesborough Ho
2 Knebworth Ho
3 Knebworth Rd
4 Bransby Ct
5 Imperial Ave
6 Leonard Pl
7 Shakspeare Mews
8 Binyon Ho
9 Shelley Ho
10 Browning Ho
11 Burns Ho
12 Andrew Marvell Ho
13 Wycliffe Ho
14 Blake Ho
15 Marlowe Ho
16 Fletcher Ho
17 Chaucer Ct
18 St Matthias's CE Prim Sch
B1 1 Hilborough Rd
2 Shoreditch Ct
3 Evergreen Sq
4 Wyndhams Ct
5 Festival Ct
6 Fortune Ct
7 Rose Ct
8 Ability Plaza
9 Briar Ct
10 Lomas Dr
11 Queensbridge Inf Sch
B2 1 Prospect Ho
2 Woodland St
3 Crosby Wlk
4 Kirkland Wlk
5 Bowness Cl
6 Carlisle Wlk
7 Skelton Cl
8 Camerton Cl
9 Buttermere Wlk
10 Houghton Cl
11 Hayton Cl
12 Kingsland Sh Ctr
13 Springfield Ho
14 Parton Lo
15 Sanctuary Mews
16 Fenton Cl
B3 1 Miller's Terr
2 Chow Sq
3 Drysdale Flats
4 Gateway Mews
5 Birkbeck Mews
6 Winchester Pl
B4 1 Coronation Ave
2 Morris Blitz Ct
3 Shacklewell Ho
4 Alexandra Ct

5 Shacklewell Prim Sch
6 Forman Pl
7 Princess May Prim Sch
C1 1 Aldington Ct
2 Bayton Ct
3 Rochford Wlk
4 Windrush Ct
5 Gayhurst Prim Sch
C2 1 Burdon Ct
2 Thomson Ct
3 Bruno Ct
4 Thackeray Mews
5 Madinah Rd
6 Pitwell Mews
C3 1 Kingsdown Ho
2 Glendown Ho
3 Moredown Ho
4 Blakeney Cl
5 Beeston Cl
6 Benabo Ct
7 David Devine Ho
8 Kreedman Wlk
9 Hermitage Row
10 Grafton Ct
11 Lushington Terr
12 Aspen Ct
13 Pykewell Lo
14 Albion Works Studios

17

A1 1 Fortescue Ave
2 Pemberton Pl
3 Weston Wlk
4 Bayford St Ind Ctr
5 Bayford St
6 Sidworth St
7 Helmsley St
8 Cyntra Pl
9 Signal Ho
10 All Nations Ho
11 Vanguard Ho
12 Hacon Sq
A2 1 Bohemia Pl
2 Graham Mans
3 Marvin St
4 Boscobel Ho
5 Royal Oak Ct
6 Colonnades The
7 Sylvester Ho
8 Sylvester Path
9 Doctor Spurstowe Almshouses
10 Great Eastern Bldgs
11 Sojourner-Truth Cl
A3 1 Birchington Ho
2 Bicknor Ho
3 Boxley Ho
4 Adisham Ho
5 Cranbrook Ho
6 Marden Ho
7 Broome Ho
8 Crandale Ho
9 Cheriton Ho
10 Ditton Ho
11 Langley Ho
12 Dymchurch Ho
13 Elham Ho
14 Davina Ho
15 Pembury Ct
16 Downs Ct
17 Perrywood Ho
18 Staplehurst Ho
19 Pegwell Ho
20 Yalding Ho

21 Northbourne Ho
22 Monkton Ho
23 Milsted Ho
24 Athlone Cl
25 Clarence Pl
26 Gould Terr
27 Quested Ct
28 Brett Pas
29 Marcon Ct
30 Appleton Ct
31 Institute Pl
A4 1 Ross Ct
2 Downs La
3 Gaviller Pl
4 Robert Owen Lo
5 Apprentice Way
6 Arrowe Ct
7 Gilwell Ct
8 Sutton Ct
9 St Andrews Mans
10 Kinnoull Mans
11 Rowhill Mans
12 Sladen Pl
13 Mothers Sq The
14 Richborough Ho
15 Sandgate Ho
16 Sheppey Ho
B1 1 Pitcairn Ho
2 Lyme Grove Ho
3 Shakespeare Ho
4 Upcott Ho
5 Loddiges Ho
6 Parkinson Ho
7 Sloane Ho
8 Vanbrugh Ho
9 Cambridge Pas
10 Lyttleton Ho
11 Victoria Park Ct
12 Tuilis Ho
13 Fairchild Ho
14 Forsyth Ho
15 Tradescant Ho
16 Mason Ho
17 Capel Ho
18 Cordwainers Ct
19 Bridgeman Ho
20 St Thomas's Pl
21 Barclay Ho
22 Clayton Ho
23 Danby Ho
24 Sherard Ho
25 Catesby Ho
26 Petiver Ct
27 Leander Ct
28 Philip Turner Est
29 Grendon Ho
30 Shore Mews
31 Shore Bsns Ctr
32 Kendal Ho
33 Classic Mans
34 Tudor Ho
35 Park Ho
36 Enterprise Ho
37 Alpine Gr
38 Clarendon Cl
39 Rotheley Ho
40 Bernie Grant Ho
41 Orchard Prim Sch
42 St John of Jerusalem CE Prim Sch
B2 1 Woolpack Ho
2 Elvin Ho
3 Thomas Ho
4 Hockley Ho
5 Retreat Ho
6 Butfield Ho

7 Brooksbank Ho
8 Cresset Ho
9 Brooksbank St
10 Lennox Ho
11 Milborne Ho
12 Collent Ho
13 Middlesex Pl
14 Elsdale Ho
15 Devonshire Hall
16 Brent Ho
17 Morningside Prim Sch
18 Urswick Sch The
B3 1 St John & St James CE Prim Sch
2 City Academy, Hackney The
C1 1 Stuart Ho
2 Gascoyne Ho
3 Chelsfield Point
4 Sundridge Ho
5 Banbury Ho
6 Lauriston Ho
7 Mossbourne Victoria Park Acad
C2 1 Musgrove Ho
2 Cheyney Ho
3 Haynes Ho
4 Warner Ho
5 Gilby Ho
6 Gadsden Ho
7 Risley Ho
8 Baycliffe Ho
9 Sheldon Ho
10 Offley Ho
11 Latimer Ho
12 Ribstone Ho
13 Salem Ho
14 Fieldwick Ho
15 Lever Ct
16 Matson Ho
17 Wilding Ho
18 Rennell Ho
19 Dycer Ho
20 Granard Ho
21 Whitelock Ho
22 Harrowgate Ho
23 Cass Ho
24 Lofts on the Park
25 Heathcote Point
26 Ravenscroft Point
27 Vanner Point
28 Hensley Point
29 San Ho
30 Berger Prim Sch
31 Cardinal Pole RC Sch
C4 1 Cromford Path
2 Longford Ct
3 Overbury Ho
4 Heanor Ct
5 Wharfedale Ct
6 Ladybower Ct
7 Ilkeston Ct
8 Derby Ct
9 Rushmore Cres
10 Blackwell Cl
11 Belper Ct
12 Rushmore Prim Sch

18

A2 1 Chigwell Ct
2 Wellday Ho

3 Selman Ho
4 Vaine Ho
5 Trower Ho
6 St Dominic's Catholic Prim Sch
A3 **7** Ickburgh Sch
B2 **1** Mallard Cl
2 Merriam Ave
3 Gainsborough St
4 Palace Cl
5 St Anthony's Cl
6 Trowbridge Est
B3 **7** Wick Village

19

C1 **1** Service Route No 2
2 Service Route No 3
3 Newham Sixth Form Coll (Stratford Ctr)
C4 **1** Mulberry Ct
2 Rosewood Ct
3 Gean Ct
4 Blackthorn Ct
5 Cypress Ct

20

C4 **1** Carlyle Rd
2 Bernard Shaw Ho
3 Longlents Ho
4 Mordaunt Ho
5 Wilmers Ct
6 Stonebridge Ctr
7 Shakespeare Ave
8 Southcroft
9 Shrewsbury Rd
10 Orchid Mews

21

A3 **1** Futters Ct
2 Barrett Ct
3 Elms The
4 Fairlight Ct
B3 **1** New Crescent Yd
2 Harlesden Plaza
3 St Josephs Ct
4 Jubilee Cl
5 Ellery Cl

22

B1 **1** Princess Alice Ho
2 Yoxall Ho
3 Yorkley Ho
4 Northaw Ho
5 Oakham Ho
6 Markyate Ho
7 Letchmore Ho
8 Pagham Ho
9 Quendon Ho
10 Redbourn Ho
11 Ketton Ho
12 Hillman Dr
C2 **1** Westfield Ct
2 Tropical Ct
3 Chamberlayne Mans
4 Quadrant The
5 Queens Park Ct
6 Warfield Yd
7 Regent St
8 Cherrytree Ho

9 Artisan Mews
10 Artisan Quarter

23

A1 **1** Sycamore Wlk
2 Westgate Bsns Ctr
3 Buspace Studios
4 Bosworth Ho
5 Golborne Gdns
6 Appleford Ho
7 Adair Twr
8 Gadsden Ho
9 Southam Ho
10 Norman Butler Ho
11 Thompson Ho
12 Wells Ho
13 Paul Ho
14 Olive Blythe Ho
15 Katherine Ho
16 Breakwell Ct
17 Pepler Ho
18 Edward Kennedy Ho
19 Winnington Ho
20 Queen's Park Prim Sch
21 Ark Brunel Prim Acad
22 St Mary's RC Prim Sch
23 St Thomas' CE Prim Sch
A2 **1** Selby Sq
2 Severn Ave
3 Stansbury Sq
4 Tolhurst Dr
5 John Fearon Wlk
6 Mundy Ho
7 Macfarren Ho
8 Bantock Ho
9 Banister Ho
10 Batten Ho
11 Croft Ho
12 Courtville Ho
13 Mounsey Ho
14 Bliss Mews
15 Symphony Mews
B1 **1** Octavia Mews
2 Russell's Wharf
3 Western Ho
4 Kelly Mews
5 Queen Elizabeth II Jubilee Sch
B2 **1** Boyce Ho
2 Farnaby Ho
3 Danby Ho
4 Purday Ho
5 Naylor Ho
6 St Judes Ho
7 Leeve Ho
8 Longhurst Ho
9 Harrington Ct
10 Mulberry Ct
11 Kilburn Ho
12 Carlton Vale Inf Sch
B3 **1** Claremont Ct
2 William Saville Ho
3 Western Ct
4 Bond Ho
5 Crone Ct
6 Wood Ho
7 Winterleys
8 Carlton Ho
9 Fiona Ct
10 Kilburn Park Sch The
C1 **1** Westside Ct

2 Byron Mews
3 Sutherland Ct
4 Fleming Cl
5 Hermes Cl
6 St Peter's CE Prim Sch
7 Paddington Acad
C2 **1** Pentland Rd
2 Nelson Cl
3 Pavilion Ct
4 Masefield Ho
5 Austen Ho
6 Fielding Ho
7 Argo Bsns Ctr
8 John Ratcliffe Ho
9 Wymering Mans
10 City of Westminster Coll, Queens Park Ctr
11 Essendine Prim Sch
12 Wells Ct
13 Cambridge Ct
14 Ely Ct
15 Durham Ct
16 St Augustine's CE High Sch
17 Sch of the Islamic Republic of Iran The
C4 **1** Ryde Ho
2 Glengall Pass
3 Leith Yd
4 Daynor Ho
5 Varley Ho
6 Sandby Ho
7 Colas Mews
8 Bishopsdale Ho
9 Lorton Ho
10 Marshwood Ho
11 Ribblesdale Ho
12 Holmesdale Ho
13 Kilburn Vale Est
14 Kilburn Bridge
15 Coll of NW London
16 St Mary's Kilburn CE Prim Sch

24

A2 **1** Pimlico Wlk
2 Aske Ho
3 Hathaway Ho
4 Haberdasher Pl
5 Fairchild Ho
6 Burtt Ho
7 Enfield Cloisters
8 McGregor Ct
9 Royal Oak Ct
10 Hoxton Mkt
11 Bath Pl
12 Chapel Pl
13 Standard Pl
14 Cleeve Workshops
15 Cleeve Ho
16 Printing House Yd
17 Perseverance Works
18 Crooked Billet Yd
19 Drysdale Ho
20 Castlefrank Ho
21 School App
22 Basing House Yd
23 Mail Coach Yd
24 St Monica's RC Prim Sch
25 Symister Mews
26 Hackney Com Coll

A3 **1** Bracer Ho
2 Scorton Ho
3 Fern Cl
4 Macbeth Ho
5 Oberon Ho
6 Buckland Ct
7 Crondall Ct
8 Osric Path
9 Caliban Twr
10 Celia Ho
11 Juliet Ho
12 Bacchus Wlk
13 Malcolm Ho
14 Homefield St
15 Crondall Pl
16 Blanca Ho
17 Miranda Ho
18 Falstaff Ho
19 Charmian Ho
20 Myrtle Wlk
21 Arden Ho
22 Sebastian Ho
23 Stanway Ct
24 Jerrold St
25 Rosalind Ho
26 Cordelia Ho
27 Monteagle Ct
28 John Parry Ct
29 James Anderson Ct
30 Ben Jonson Ct
31 Sara Lane Ct
32 Walbrook Ct
33 Hoxton Garden Prim Sch
A4 **1** Portelet Ct
2 Trinity Ct
3 Rozel Ct
4 St Helier Ct
5 Corbiere Ho
6 Kenning Ho
7 Higgins Ho
8 Cavell Ho
9 Girling Ho
10 Fulcher Ho
11 Francis Ho
12 Norris Ho
13 Kempton Ho
14 Nesham Ho
15 Crossbow Ho
16 Catherine Ho
17 Strale Ho
18 Horner Hos
19 Stringer Hos
20 Whitmore Ho
21 Nightingale Ho
22 Wilmer Gdns
23 Arrow Ho
24 Archer Ho
25 Meriden Ho
26 Rover Ho
27 Bowyer Ho
28 Tiller Ho
29 Canalside Studios
30 Kleine Wharf
31 Benyon Wharf
32 Quebec Wharf
33 Belvedere Ct
34 Portfleet Pl
35 Hackney New Sch
B2 **1** Gorsuch Pl
2 Strout's Pl
3 Vaughan Est
4 George Loveless Ho
5 Baroness Rd
6 James Brine Ho
7 Arthur Wade Ho
8 Robert Owen Ho

9 Sivill Ho
10 Georgina Gdns
11 Old Market Sq
12 Cuff Point
13 Bakers Rents
14 Leopold Bldgs
15 Dunmore Point
16 Wingfield Ho
17 Gascoigne Pl
18 Mandela Ho
19 Virginia Rd
20 Briggs Ho
21 Packenham Ho
22 Gowan Ho
23 Kirton Gdns
24 Chambord Ho
25 Ducal St
26 Strickland Ho
27 Alliston Ho
28 Gibraltar Wlk
29 Equity Sq
30 Shacklewell St
31 Rochelle St
32 Sonning Ho
33 Culham Ho
34 Hurley Ho
35 Palissy St
36 Taplow Ho
37 Chertsey Ho
38 Sunbury Ho
39 Sunbury Workshops
40 Datchett Ho
41 Hocker St
42 Coll Sharp Ct
43 Marlow Studio Workshops
44 Marlow Ho
45 Shiplake Ho
46 Wargrave Ho
47 Iffley Ho
48 Virginia Prim Sch
49 Green Spring Academy Shoreditch
50 Columbia Prim Sch
B3 **1** Queensbridge Ct
2 Godwin Ho
3 Kent Ct
4 Brunswick Ct
5 Weymouth Ct
6 Sovereign Mews
7 Dunloe Ct
8 Cremer Bsns Ctr
9 James Hammett Ho
10 Allgood St
11 Horatio St
12 Cadell Ho
13 Horatio Ho
14 Shipton Ho
15 Haggerston Sch
16 Randal Cremer Prim Sch
B4 **1** Hilborough Ct
2 Scriven Ct
3 Livermere Ct
4 Angrave Ct
5 Angrave Pas
6 Benfleet Ct
7 Belford Ho
8 Orme Ho
9 Clemson Ho
10 Longman Ho
11 Lowther Ho
12 Lovelace Ho
13 Harlowe Ho
14 Pamela Ho

21 Rosebery Ho
22 Sankey Ho
23 Cyprus Pl
24 Royston St
25 Stainsbury St
26 Hunslett St
27 Baildon
28 Brockweir
29 Tytherton
30 Malmesbury
31 Kingswood
32 Colville Ho
33 St Elizabeth RC
  Prim Sch
34 Raine's
  Foundation Sch
35 Mowlem Prim Sch

B4 1 Halkett Ho
2 Christchurch Sq
3 Helena Pl
4 Swingfield Ho
5 Greenham Ho
6 Dinmore Ho
7 Anstey Ho
8 Weston Ho
9 Carbroke Ho
10 Bluebell Cl
11 Cherry Tree Cl
12 Georgian Ct
13 Park Cl
14 Regency Ct
15 Norris Ho

C1 1 Raynham Ho
2 Pat Shaw Ho
3 Colmar Ct
4 Withy Ho
5 Stocks Ct
6 Downey Ho
7 Bay Ct
8 Sligo Ho
9 Pegasus Ho
10 Barents Ho
11 Biscay Ho
12 Solway Ho
13 Bantry Ho
14 Aral Ho
15 Pacific Ho
16 Magellan Ho
17 Levant Ho
18 Adriatic Ho
19 Genoa Ho
20 Hawke Ho
21 Palliser Ho
22 Ionian Ho
23 Weddell Ho
24 Carlyle Mews
25 Greencourt Ho
26 Mazahirul Uloom
  London
27 Sundra Wlk

C2 1 Stubbs Ho
2 Holman Ho
3 Clynes Ho
4 Windsor Ho
5 Gilbert Ho
6 Chater Ho
7 Ellen Wilkinson Ho
8 George Belt Ho
9 Ayrton Gould Ho
10 O'Brian Ho
11 Sulkin Ho
12 Jenkinson Ho

13 Bullards Pl
14 Sylvia Pankhurst
  House
15 Mary Macarthur Ho
16 Trevelyan Ho
17 Wedgwood Ho
18 Pemberton Ct
19 Leatherdale St
20 Walter Besant Ho
21 Barber Beaumont
  House
22 Brancaster Ho
23 Litcham Ho
24 Bradwell St

C3 1 Kemp Ho
2 Piggott Ho
3 Mark Ho
4 Sidney Ho
5 Pomeroy Ho
6 Puteaux Ho
7 Boding Ho
8 Modling Ho
9 Longman Ho
10 Ames Ho
11 Alzette Ho
12 Offenbach Ho
13 Tate Ho
14 Norton Ho
15 St Gilles Ho
16 Harold Ho
17 Velletri Ho
18 Bridge Wharf
19 Gathorne St
20 Bow Brook The
21 Twig Folly Cl
22 Palmerston St
23 Lakeview
24 Peach Walk Mews
25 Caesar Ct
26 Gatehouse Sch

C4 6 Lauriston Prim Sch

26

A1 1 Formosa Ho
2 Galveston Ho
3 Arabian Ho
4 Greenland Ho
5 Coral Ho
6 Anson Ho
7 Cambay Ho
8 Lindop Ho
9 Moray Ho
10 Azov Ho
11 Sandalwood Cl
12 Broadford Ho

A2 1 Imperial Ho
2 Newport Ho
3 Vassall Ho
4 Maurice Ct
5 Creed Ct
6 Christopher
  France House
7 Beaumont Ct
8 Pembrake Mews
9 Guardian Angels
  RC Prim Sch

A3 1 Nightingale Mews
2 Bunsen Ho
3 Bunsen St
4 Beatrice Webb Ho
5 Margaret Bondfield
  House
6 Wilmer Ho
7 Sandall Ho
8 Butley Ct
9 Josseline Ct
10 Dalton Ho

11 Brine Ho
12 Ford Cl
13 Viking Cl
14 Stanfield Rd
15 Stoneleigh Mews
16 Ruth Ct
17 School Bell
  Cloisters
18 Schoolbell Mews
19 Medhurst Ct
20 Olga St
21 Conyer St
22 Diamond Ho
23 Daring Ho
24 Crane Ho
25 Exmoor Ho
26 Grenville Ho
27 Hyperion Ho
28 Sturdy Ho
29 Wren Ho
30 Ardent Ho
31 Senators Lo
32 Hooke Ho
33 Mohawk Ho
34 Ivanhoe Ho
35 Medway Mews
36 Chisenhale
  Prim Sch

B1 1 Michael Cl
2 Wraxall Rd

B2 1 Trellis Sq
2 Sheffield Sq
3 Howcroft Ho
4 Astra Ho
5 Frye Ct
6 Byas Ho
7 George Lansbury
  House
8 Regal Pl
9 Coborn Mews
10 Tredegar Mews
11 Cavendish Terr
12 Lyn Mews
13 Buttermere Ho
14 Coniston Ho
15 Tracy Ho
16 Hanover Pl
17 St Clair Ho
18 Longthorne Ho
19 Vista Bldgs
20 Verity Ho
21 Icarus Ho
22 Whippingham Ho
23 Hamilton Ho
24 Winchester Ho
25 Malmesbury
  Prim Sch
26 Phoenix Prim Sch
27 Central Foundation
  Upper Girls Sch The

B3 1 Roman Road Mkt
2 John Bond Ho
3 McKenna Ho
4 Dennis Ho
5 McAusland Ho
6 McBride Ho
7 Libra Rd
8 Dave Adams Ho
9 Regency Ct
10 Tay Ho
11 Sleat Ho
12 Brodick Ho
13 Ewart Pl
14 Lunan Ho
15 Cruden Ho
16 Anglo Rd

17 Mull Ho
18 Sinclairs Ho
19 Driftway Ho
20 Clayhall Ct
21 Berebinder Ho
22 Partridge Ho
23 Barford Ho
24 Gullane Ho
25 Gosford Ho
26 Dornoch Ho
27 Dunnet Ho
28 Enard Ho
29 Fraserburgh Ho
30 Forth Ho
31 Stavers Ho
32 Rosegate Ho
33 Crowngate Ho
34 Queensgate Ho
35 Towergate Ho
36 Ordell Ct
37 William Pl
38 Old Ford Prim Sch

B4 1 Hampstead Wlk
2 Waverton Ho
3 Elton Ho
4 Locton Gn
5 Birtwhistle Ho
6 Clare Ho
7 Magpie Ho
8 Hornbeam Sq
9 Rowan Ho
10 Barge La
11 Walnut Ho
12 Birdsfield La
13 Atkins Ct
14 Willow Tree Cl
15 Jasmine Sq
16 Tait Ct
17 Ranwell Ho
18 Ranwell Cl
19 Tufnell Ct
20 Pulteney Cl
21 Vic Johnson Ho
22 Lea Sq
23 Iceni Ct
24 Tamar Cl
25 Roman Rd
26 Valentine Ho

C1 1 Fairmont Ho
2 Healy Ho
3 Zodiac Ho
4 Buick Ho
5 Consul Ho
6 Bentley Ho
7 Cresta Ho
8 Daimler Ho
9 Riley Ho
10 Jensen Ho
11 Lagonda Ho
12 Ireton St
13 Navenby Wlk
14 Burwell Wlk
15 Leadenham Ct
16 Sleaford Ho
17 Bow Triangle
  Bsns Ctr

C2 1 Bow Ho
2 Denmark Pl
3 Marsalis Ho
4 Lovette Ho
5 Drapers Almshouses
6 Mallard Point
7 Creswick Wlk
8 Bevin Ho
9 Huggins Ho

10 Williams Ho
11 Harris Ho
12 Marina Ct
13 Electric Ho
14 Matching Ct
15 Wellington Bldgs
16 Grafton Ho
17 Berkeley Ho
18 Columbia Ho
19 Bow Sch
20 Wellington
  Prim Sch
21 Cherry Trees
  Sch The
22 Trevithick Wy
23 Denmark Pl

C3 1 Vincent Mews
2 Menai Pl
3 Heathfield Ct
4 Redwood Cl
5 Acorn Ct
6 Primrose Cl
7 Briar Ct
8 Springwood Cl
9 Lacey Mews
10 Matilda Gdns

C4 1 Ironworks
2 Juno Ho
3 Chariot Cl
4 Saturn Ho
5 Hadrian Cl
6 Mercury Ho
7 Forum Cl
8 Venus Ho
9 Vesta Ho
10 Tiber Cl
11 Gemini Ho
12 Crown Close
  Bsns Ctr

27

A1 1 Broxbourne Ho
2 Roxford Ho
3 Biscott Ho
4 Stanborough Ho
5 Hillstone Ct
6 Marner Prim Sch

A2 1 Bradley Ho
2 Prioress Ho
3 Alton Ho
4 Foxley Ho
5 Munden Ho
6 Canterbury Ho
7 Corbin Ho
8 Barton Ho
9 Jolles Ho
10 Rudstone Ho
11 Baxter Ho
12 Baker Ho
13 Insley Ho
14 Hardwicke Ho
15 St Agnes RC
  Prim Sch
16 Priory St
17 Sadler Ho
18 Ballinger Point
19 Henshall Point
20 Dorrington Point
21 Warren Ho
22 Fairlie Ct
23 Regent Sq
24 Hackworth Point
25 Priestman Point
26 Wingate Ho
27 Nethercott Ho
28 Thelbridge Ho
29 Bowden Ho

47 Kennet Ct
48 Oxford St
49 Fazerley Ct

32

A1 1 China Ct
2 Wellington Terr
3 Stevedore St
4 Portland Sq
5 Reardon Ho
6 Lowder Ho
7 Meeting House Alley
8 Farthing Fields
9 Oswell Ho
10 Park Lo
11 Doughty Ct
12 Inglefield Sq
13 Chopin's Ct
14 Welsh Ho
15 Hilliard Ho
16 Clegg St
17 Tasman Ho
18 Ross Ho
19 Wapping Dock St
20 Bridewell Pl
21 New Tower Bldgs
22 Tower Bldgs
23 Chimney Ct
24 Jackman Ho
25 Fenner Ho
26 Franklin Ho
27 Frobisher Ho
28 Flinders Ho
29 Chancellor Ho
30 Beechey Ho
31 Reardon Path
32 Parry Ho
33 Vancover Ho
34 Willoughby Ho
35 Sanctuary The
36 Dundee Ct
37 Pierhead Wharf
38 Scandrett St
39 St Johns Ct
A2 1 Newton Ho
2 Richard Neale Ho
3 Maddocks Ho
4 Cornwall St
5 Brockmer Ho
6 Dellow Ho
7 Bewley Ho
8 Artichoke Hill
9 Queen Anne Terr
10 King Henry Terr
11 King Charles Terr
12 Queen Victoria Terr
13 Sovereign Ct
14 Princes Court Bsns Ctr
15 Kingsley Mews
16 Mulberry Sch for Girls
A3 1 Peter Best Ho
2 Mellish Ho
3 Porchester Ho
4 Dickson Ho
5 Joscoyne Ho
6 Silvester Ho
7 Wilton Ct
8 Sarah Ho
9 Bridgen Ho
10 Tylney Ho
11 Greenwich Ct

12 Damien Ct
13 Philson Mans
14 Siege Ho
15 Jacob Mans
16 Proud Ho
17 Sly St
18 Barnett St
19 Kinder St
20 Richard St
21 Hungerford St
22 Colstead Ho
23 Melwood Ho
24 Wicker St
25 Langdale St
26 Chapman Ho
27 Burwell Cl
28 Walford Ho
29 Welstead Ho
30 Norton Ho
31 Turnour Ho
32 Luke Ho
33 Dunch St
34 Sheridan St
35 Brinsley St
36 Spencer Way
37 Madani Girls' Sch
38 Mulberry Sch for Girls
A4 1 Wodeham Gdns
2 Castlemaine St
3 Court St
4 Ashfield St
5 London Hospital Dental Inst
6 Princess Alexandra School of Nursing The
7 Wodeham Gardens
B1 1 John Rennie Wlk
2 Malay Ho
3 Wainwright Ho
4 Riverside Mans
5 Shackleton Ho
6 Whitehorn Ho
7 Wavel Ct
8 Prusom's Island
9 St Peter's London Docks CE Prim Sch
B2 1 Shadwell Pl
2 Gosling Ho
3 Vogler Ho
4 Donovan Ho
5 Knowlden Ho
6 Chamberlain Ho
7 Moore Ho
8 Thornewill Ho
9 Fisher Ho
10 All Saints Ct
11 Coburg Dwellings
12 Lowood Ho
13 Solander Gdns
14 Chancery Bldgs
15 Ring Ho
16 Juniper St
17 Gordon Ho
18 West Block
19 North Block
20 South Block
21 Ikon Ho
22 Blue Gate Fields Jun & Inf Schs
B3 1 Woollon Ho
2 Dundalk Ho
3 Anne Goodman Ho

4 Newbold Cotts
5 Kerry Ho
6 Zion Ho
7 Longford Ho
8 Bromehead St
9 Athlone Ho
10 Jubilee Mans
11 Harriott Ho
12 Brayford Sq
13 Clearbrook Way
14 Rochelle Ct
15 Winterton Ho
16 Swift Ho
17 Brinsley Ho
18 Dean Ho
19 Foley Ho
20 Robert Sutton Ho
21 Montpelier Pl
22 Glastonbury Pl
23 Steel's La
24 Masters Lo
25 Stylus Apartments
26 Arta Ho
27 St Mary & St Michael Prim Sch
28 Bishop Challoner Catholic Federation of Schools
29 Morton Cl
30 James Voller Way
B4 1 Fulneck
2 Gracehill
3 Ockbrook
4 Fairfield
5 Dunstan Hos
6 Cressy Ct
7 Cressy Hos
8 Callahan Cotts
9 Lindley Ho
10 Mayo Ho
11 Wexford Ho
12 Sandhurst Ho
13 Addis Ho
14 Colverson Ho
15 Beckett Ho
16 Jarman Ho
17 Armsby Ho
18 Wingrad Ho
19 Miranda Cl
20 Drake Ho
21 Ashfield Yd
22 Magri Wlk
23 Jean Pardies Ho
24 St Vincent De Paul House
25 Sambrook Ho
26 Louise De Marillac House
27 Dagobert Ho
28 Le Moal Ho
29 Odette Duval Ho
30 Charles Auffray Ho
31 Boisseau Ho
32 Clichy Ho
33 Paymal Ho
34 Smithy Street Sch
35 Redlands Prim Sch
36 Cressy Ct
C1 1 Clarence Mews
2 Raleigh Ct
3 Katherine Ct
4 Woollcombes Ct
5 Tudor Ct
6 Quayside Ct
7 Princes Riverside Rd

8 Surrey Ho
9 Tideway Ct
10 Edinburgh Ct
11 Falkirk Ct
12 Byelands Ct
13 Gwent Ct
14 Lavender Ho
15 Abbotshade Rd
16 Bellamy's Ct
17 Blenheim Ct
18 Sandringham Ct
19 Hampton Ct
20 Windsor Ct
21 Balmoral Ct
22 Westminster Ct
23 Beatson Wlk
24 Peter Hills with St Mary's & St Paul's CE Sch
C2 1 Barnardo Gdns
2 Roslin Ho
3 Glamis Est
4 Peabody Est
5 East Block
6 Highway Trad Ctr The
7 Highway Bsns Pk The
8 Cranford Cotts
9 Ratcliffe Orch
10 Scotia Bldg
11 Mauretania Bldg
12 Compania Bldg
13 Sirius Bldg
14 Unicorn Bldg
15 Keeper Wharf
C3 1 Pattison Ho
2 St Thomas Ho
3 Arbour Ho
4 Bladen Ho
5 Antill Terr
6 Marjorie Mews
7 Billing Ho
8 Dowson Ho
9 Lipton Rd
10 Chalkwell Ho
11 Corringham Ho
12 Ogilvie Ho
13 Edward Mann Cl
14 Reservoir Studios
15 Lighterman Mews
16 Tower Hamlets Coll
17 Marion Richardson Prim Sch
C4 1 Roland Mews
2 Beatrice Ho
3 Morecambe Cl
4 Stepney Green Ct
5 Milrood Ho
6 Panama Ho
7 Galway Ho
8 Jacqueline Ho
9 Crown Mews
10 Caspian Ho
11 Darien Ho
12 Riga Ho
13 Flores Ho
14 Taranto Ho
15 Aden Ho
16 Master's St
17 Rosary Ct
18 Stepney Green Maths & Computing Coll

19 Sir John Cass Foundation & Redcoat CE Sec Sch
20 Seagrave Cl

33

A1 1 Edward Sq
2 Prince Regent Ct
3 Codrington Ct
4 Pennington Ct
5 Cherry Ct
6 Ash Ct
7 Beech Ct
8 Hazel Ct
9 Laurel Ct
A2 1 St Georges Sq
2 Drake Ho
3 Osprey Ho
4 Fleet Ho
5 Gainsborough Ho
6 Victory Pl
7 Challenger Ho
8 Conrad Ho
9 Lock View Ct
10 Shoulder of Mutton Alley
11 Frederick Sq
12 Helena Sq
13 Elizabeth Sq
14 Sophia Sq
15 William Sq
16 Lamb Ct
17 Lockside
18 Adriatic Bldg
19 Ionian Bldg
20 Regents Gate Ho
A3 1 Hearnshaw St
2 Berry Cotts
3 Causton Cotts
4 Elizabeth Blount Ct
5 Carr St
6 Shaw Cres
7 Darnley Ho
8 Mercer's Cotts
9 Troon Ho
10 Ratcliffe Ho
11 Wakeling St
12 York Sq
13 Anglia Ho
14 Cambria Ho
15 Caledonia Ho
16 Ratcliffe La
17 Bekesbourne St
18 John Scurr Ho
19 Regents Canal Ho
20 Basin App
21 Powlesland Ct
22 Cayley Prim Sch
23 Stephen Hawking Sch
24 Dalgleish St
25 Ross Wy
A4 1 Waley St
2 Edith Ramsay Ho
3 Andaman St
4 Atlantic Ho
5 Pevensey Ho
6 Solent Ho
7 Lorne Ho
8 Cromarty Ho
9 Dakin Pl
10 Greaves Cotts
11 Donaghue Cotts
12 Ames Cotts
13 Waterview Ho

14 Limehouse Fields Est
B2 1 Hamilton Ho
2 Imperial Ho
3 Oriana Ho
4 Queens Ct
5 Brightlingsea Pl
6 Faraday Ho
7 Ropemaker's Fields
8 Oast Ct
9 Mitre The
10 Bate St
11 Joseph Irwin Ho
12 Padstow Ho
13 Bethlehem Ho
14 Saunders Cl
15 Roche Ho
16 Stocks Pl
17 Trinidad Ho
18 Grenada Ho
19 Kings Ho
20 Dunbar Wharf
21 Limekiln Wharf
22 Belgrave St
23 Eaton Ho
24 Cyril Jackson Prim Sch (North Bldg)
25 Cyril Jackson Prim Sch (South Bldg)
B3 1 Dora Ho
2 Flansham Ho
3 Gatwick Ho
4 Ashpark Ho
5 Newdigate Ho
6 Midhurst Ho
7 Redbourne Ho
8 Southwater Cl
9 Andersens Wharf
10 Whatman Ho
11 Butler Ho
12 Fitzroy Ho
13 Salmon St
14 Mission The
15 Aithan Ho
16 Britley Ho
17 Cheadle Ho
18 Elland Ho
19 Wharf La
20 Docklands Ct
21 Park Heights Ct
22 Grosvenor Ct
23 Lime House Ct
24 Swallow Pl
25 St Anne's Trad Est
26 Stepney Greencoat CE Prim Sch The
27 Sir William Burrough Prim Sch
28 Our Lady RC Prim Sch
B4 1 Wearmouth Ho
2 Elmslie Point
3 Grindley Ho
4 Stileman Ho
5 Wilcox Ho
6 Huddart St
7 Robeson St
8 Couzens Ho
9 Perley Ho
10 Whytlaw Ho
11 Booker Cl
12 Tunley Gn
13 Callingham Cl
14 Bowry Ho
15 Perkins Ho
16 Printon Ho
17 Tasker Ho

18 St Paul with St Luke CE Prim Sch
C2 1 West India Ho
2 Berber Pl
3 Birchfield Ho
4 Elderfield Ho
5 Thornfield Ho
6 Gorsefield Ho
7 Arborfield Ho
8 Colborne Ho
9 East India Bldgs
10 Compass Point
11 Salter St
12 Garland Ct
13 Bogart Ct
14 Fonda Ct
15 Welles Ct
16 Rogers Ct
17 Premier Pl
18 Kelly Ct
19 Flynn Ct
20 Mary Jones Ho
21 Cannon Dr
22 Horizon Bldg
23 Our Lady & St Joseph Catholic Prim Sch
24 University of Cumbria London
C3 1 Landin Ho
2 Thomas Road Ind Est
3 Vickery's Wharf
4 Abbotts Wharf
5 Limehouse Ct
6 Charlesworth Ho
7 Gurdon Ho
8 Trendell Ho
9 Menteath Ho
10 Minchin Ho
11 Donne Ho
12 Old School Sq
13 Anglesey Ho
14 Gough Wlk
15 Baring Ho
16 Gladstone Ho
17 Hopkins Ho
18 Granville Ho
19 Overstone Ho
20 Pusey Ho
21 Russell Ho
22 Stanley Ho
23 Edward Mills Wy
C4 1 Bredel Ho
2 Linton Ho
3 Matthews Ho
4 Woodcock Ho
5 Limborough Ho
6 Maydwell Ho
7 Underhill Ho
8 Meyrick Ho
9 Ambrose Ho
10 Richardson Ho
11 Carpenter Ho
12 Robinson Ho
13 Bellmaker Ct
14 Lime Tree Ct
15 Bracken Ho
16 Bramble Ho
17 Berberis Ho
18 Bilberry Ho
19 Ladyfern Ho
20 Rosebay Ho
21 Invicta Cl
22 Phoenix Bsns Ctr
23 Metropolitan Cl
24 Busbridge Ho

25 St Paul's Way Com Sch
26 Stebon Prim Sch
27 Ursula Gould Wy

34
A2 1 Westcott Ho
2 Corry Ho
3 Malam Gdns
4 Blomfield Ho
5 Devitt Ho
6 Leyland Ho
7 Wigram Ho
8 Willis Ho
9 Balsam Ho
10 Finch's Ct
11 Poplar Bath St
12 Lawless St
13 Storey Ho
14 Abbot Ho
15 Woodall Cl
16 Landon Wlk
17 Goodhope Ho
18 Goodfaith Ho
19 Winant Ho
20 Goodspeed Ho
21 Lubbock Ho
22 Goodwill Ho
23 Martindale Ho
24 Holmsdale Ho
25 Norwood Ho
26 Constant Ho
27 Tower Hamlets Coll
A3 1 Colebrook Ho
2 Essex Ho
3 Salisbury Ho
4 Maidstone Ho
5 Osterley Ho
6 Norwich Ho
7 Clarissa Ho
8 Elgin Ho
9 Shaftesbury Lo
10 Shepherd Ho
11 Jeremiah St
12 Elizabeth Ct
13 Chilcot Cl
14 Fitzgerald Ho
15 Vesey Path
16 Ennis Ho
17 Kilmore Ho
18 Cygnet House N
19 Cygnet House S
20 Lansbury Lawrence Prim Sch
21 Bygrove Prim Sch
22 Mayflower Prim Sch
23 Tower Hamlets Coll
A4 1 Sumner Ho
2 David Hewitt Ho
3 St Gabriels Ct
4 Limehouse Cut
5 Colmans Wharf
6 Foundary Ho
7 Radford Ho
8 Manorfield Prim Sch
9 St Saviour's CE Prim Sch
10 Pioneer Cl
B1 1 Lumina Bldg
2 Nova Ct W
3 Nova Ct E
4 Aurora Bldg
5 Arran Ho
6 Kintyre Ho
7 Vantage Mews

8 Managers St
9 Horatio Pl
10 Concordia Wharf
B2 1 Discovery Ho
2 Mountague Pl
3 Virginia Ho
4 Collins Ho
5 Lawless Ho
6 Carmichael Ho
7 Commodore Ho
8 Mermaid Ho
9 Bullivant St
10 Anderson Ho
11 Mackrow Wlk
12 Robin Hood Gdns
13 Prestage Way
14 Woolmore Prim Sch
B3 1 Glenkerry Ho
2 Carradale Ho
3 Langdon Ho
4 Balfron Twr
5 St Frideswides Mews
6 Tabard Ct
7 Delta Bldg
8 Findhorn St
9 Kilbrennan Ho
10 Thistle Ho
11 Heather Ho
12 Tartan Ho
13 Sharman Ho
14 Trident Ho
15 Wharf View Ct
16 Culloden Prim Sch
B4 1 Mills Gr
2 St Michaels Ct
3 Duncan Ct
C2 1 Quixley St
2 Romney Ho
3 Pumping Ho
4 Switch Ho
5 Wingfield Ct
6 Explorers Ct
7 Sexton Ct
8 Keel Ct
9 Bridge Ct
10 Sail Ct
11 Settlers Ct
12 Pilgrims Mews
13 Studley Ct
14 Wotton Ct
15 Cape Henry Ct
16 Bartholomew Ct
17 Adventurers Ct
18 Susan Constant Ct
19 Atlantic Ct
C3 1 Lansbury Gdns
2 Theseus Ho
3 Adams Ho
4 Jones Ho
5 Sam March Ho
6 Arapiles Ho
7 Athenia Ho
8 Julius Ho
9 Jervis Bay Ho
10 Helen Mackay Ho
11 Gaze Ho
12 Ritchie Ho
13 Blairgowrie Ct
14 Circle Ho
15 Dunkeld Ho
16 Rosemary Dr
17 Sorrel La
18 East India Dock Road Tunnel

35
A2 1 Faraday Sch
B3 1 Newton Point
2 Sparke Terr
3 Montesquieu Terr
4 Crawford Point
5 Rathbone Ho
6 George St
7 Emily St
8 Fendt Cl
9 Sabbarton St
10 St Luke's Prim Sch
11 Briary Ct
11 Shaftesbury Ho
B4 1 Radley Terr
2 Bernard Cassidy St
3 Rathbone Mkt
4 Thomas North Terr
5 Mary St
6 Hughes Terr
7 Swanscombe Point
8 Rawlinson Point
9 Kennedy Cox Ho
10 Cooper St
11 Rokeby Sch
C1 1 Capulet Mews
2 Pepys Cres
3 De Quincey Mews
4 Hardy Ave
5 Tom Jenkinson Rd
6 Kennacraig Cl
7 Charles Flemwell Mews
8 Gatcombe Rd
9 Badminton Mews
10 Holyrood Mews
11 Britannia Gate
12 Dalemain Mews
13 Bowes-Lyon Hall
14 Lancaster Hall
15 Victoria Hall
C2 1 Clements Ave
2 Martindale Ave
3 Balearic Apts
4 Marmara Apts
5 Baltic Apts
6 Coral Apts
7 Aegean Apts
8 Capital East Apts
C4 1 Odeon Ct
2 Edward Ct
3 Newhaven La
4 Ravenscroft Cl
5 Douglas Rd
6 Ferrier Point
7 Harvey Point
8 Wood Point
9 Trinity St
10 Pattinson Point
11 Clinch Ct
12 Mint Bsns Pk
13 Keir Hardy Prim Sch

36
A1 1 Burford Ho
2 Hope Cl
3 Centaur Ct
4 Phoenix Ct
C1 1 Surrey Cres
2 Forbes Ho
3 Haining Cl
4 Melville Ct
5 London Stile

6 Stile Hall Par
7 Priory Lo
8 Meadowcroft
9 St James Ct
10 Rivers Ho
11 Surrey Cres

37

A1 1 Churchdale Ct
2 Cromwell Ct
3 Cambridge Rd S
4 Oxbridge Ct
5 Tomlinson Cl
6 Gunnersbury Mews
7 Grange The
8 Gunnersbury Cl
9 Bellgrave Lo
A2 10 Orchard House Sch
A4 1 Cheltenham Pl
2 Beaumaris Twr
3 Arundel Ho
4 Pevensey Ct
5 Jerome Twr
6 Anstey Ct
7 Bennett Ct
8 Gunnersbury Ct
9 Barrington Ct
10 Hope Gdns
11 Park Road E
B1 1 Arlington
   Park Mans
2 Sandown Ho
3 Goodwood Ho
4 Windsor Ho
5 Lingfield Ho
6 Ascot Ho
7 Watchfield Ct
8 Belgrave Ct
9 Beverley Ct
10 Beaumont Ct
11 Harvard Rd
12 Troubridge Ct
13 Branden Lo
14 Fromow's Cnr
15 Heathfield House Sch
B2 1 Chiswick Green Studios
2 Bell Ind Est
3 Fairlawn Ct
4 Dukes Gate
5 Dewsbury Ct
6 Chiswick Terr
7 Mortlake Ho
B3 1 Blackmore Twr
2 Bollo Ct
3 Kipling Twr
4 Lawrence Ct
5 Maugham Ct
6 Reade Ct
7 Woolf Ct
8 Shaw Ct
9 Verne Ct
10 Wodehouse Ct
11 Greenock Rd
12 Garden Ct
13 Barons Gate
14 Cleveland Rd
15 Carver Cl
16 Chapter Cl
17 Beauchamp Cl
18 Holmes Ct
19 Copper Mews
20 Packington Rd

21 Maugham Wy
B4 1 Belgrave Cl
2 Buckland Wlk
3 Frampton Ct
4 Telfer Cl
5 Harlech Twr
6 Corfe Twr
7 Barwick Ho
8 Charles Hocking House
9 Sunninghill Ct
10 Salisbury St
11 Jameson Pl
12 Castle Cl
13 Ark Priory
   Prim Acad
C1 1 Chatsworth Lo
2 Prospect Pl
3 Townhall Ave
4 Devonhurst Pl
5 Heathfield Ct
6 Horticultural Pl
7 Merlin Ho
8 Garth Rd
9 Autumn Rise
C2 1 Disraeli Ct
2 Winston Wlk
3 Rusthall Mans
4 Bedford Park Mans
5 Essex Place Sq
6 Holly Rd
7 Homecross Ho
8 Swan Bsns Ctr
9 Jessop Ho
10 Belmont Prim Sch

38

A1 1 Glebe Cl
2 Devonshire Mews
3 Binns Terr
4 Ingress St
5 Swanscombe Rd
6 Brackley Terr
7 Stephen Fox Ho
8 Manor Gdns
9 Coram Ho
10 Flaxman Ho
11 Thorneycroft Ho
12 Thornhill Ho
13 Kent Ho
14 Oldfield Ho
15 William Hogarth Sch The
16 Oak Lock Mews
A2 1 Chestnut Ho
2 Bedford Ho
3 Bedford Cnr
4 Sydney Ho
5 Bedford Park Cnr
6 Priory Gdns
7 Windmill Alley
8 Castle Pl
9 Jonathan Ct
10 Windmill Pas
11 Chardin Rd
12 Gable Ho
13 Chiswick & Bedford Park Prep Sch
14 Arts Educational Schools London
15 Orchard Ho Sch
A3 1 Fleet Ct
2 Ember Ct
3 Emlyn Gdns
4 Clone Ct
5 Brent Ct
6 Abbey Ct

7 Ormsby Lo
8 St Catherine's Ct
9 Lodge The
A4 1 Longford Ct
2 Mole Ct
3 Lea Ct
4 Wandle Ct
5 Beverley Ct
6 Roding Ct
7 Crane Ct
B1 1 Miller's Ct
2 British Grove Pas
3 British Grove S
4 Berestede Rd
5 North Eyot Gdns
B2 1 Flanders Mans
2 Stamford Brook Mans
3 Linkenholt Mans
4 Prebend Mans
5 Middlesex Ct
B3 1 Stamford Brook Gdns
2 Hauteville Court Gdns
3 Ranelagh Gdns
C1 1 Chisholm Ct
2 North Verbena Gdns
3 Western Terr
4 Verbena Gdns
5 Montrose Villas
6 Hammersmith Terr
7 South Black Lion La
8 St Peter's Wharf
9 St Peter's CE Prim Sch
C2 1 Hamlet Ct
2 Derwent Ct
3 Westcroft Ct
4 Black Lion Mews
5 St Peter's Villas
6 Standish Ho
7 Chambon Pl
8 Court Mans
9 Longthorpe Ct
10 Charlotte Ct
11 Westside
12 Park Ct
13 London Ho
14 Latymer Upper Sch
15 Polish Univ Abroad
16 West London Free Sch
C3 1 Elizabeth Finn Ho
2 Ashchurch Ct
3 King's Par
4 Inver Ct
5 Ariel Ct
6 Pocklington Lo
7 Vitae Apartments
C4 1 Becklow Gdns
2 Victoria Ho
3 Lycett Pl
4 Kylemore Ct
5 Alexandra Ct
6 Lytten Ct
7 Becklow Mews
8 Northcroft Ct
9 Bailey Ct
10 Spring Cott
11 Landor Wlk
12 Laurence Mews
13 Hadyn Park Ct
14 Askew Mans
15 Malvern Ct

39

A1 1 Prince's Mews
2 Aspen Gdns
3 Hampshire Hog La
4 Blades Ct
A2 1 Albion Gdns
2 Flora Gdns
3 Kingston Ho
4 Felgate Mews
5 Galena Ho
6 Albion Mews
7 Albion Ct
8 King Street Cloisters
9 Dimes Pl
10 Clarence Ct
11 Hampshire Hog La
12 Marryat Ct
13 Ravenscourt Ho
14 Ravenscourt Theatre Sch
15 Cambridge Sch
16 Godolphin & Latymer Sch
17 Flora Gardens Prim Sch
A3 1 Ravenscourt Park Mans
2 Paddenswick Ct
3 Ashbridge Ct
4 Brackenbury Prim Sch
A4 1 Westbush Ct
2 Goldhawk Mews
3 Sycamore Ho
4 Shackleton Ct
5 Drake Ct
6 Scotts Ct
7 Raleigh Ct
8 Melville Court Flats
9 Southway Cl
10 Hammersmith Acad
B1 1 Bridge Avenue Mans
2 Bridgeview
3 College Ct
4 Beatrice Ho
5 Amelia Ho
6 Edith Ho
7 Joanna Ho
8 Mary Ho
9 Adela Ho
10 Sophia Ho
11 Henrietta Ho
12 Charlotte Ho
13 Alexandra Ho
14 Bath Pl
15 Elizabeth Ho
16 Margaret Ho
17 Peabody Est
18 Eleanor Ho
19 Isabella Ho
20 Caroline Ho
21 Chancellors Wharf
22 Sussex Pl
23 St Paul's CE Prim Sch
B2 1 Phoenix Lodge Mans
2 Samuel's Cl
3 Broadway Arc
4 Brook Ho
5 Hammersmith Broadway
6 Broadway Sh Ctr
7 Cambridge Ct

8 Ashcroft Sq
9 Sacred Heart High Sch
B4 1 Verulam Ho
2 Grove Mans
3 Frobisher Ct
4 Library Mans
5 Pennard Mans
6 New Shepherd's Bush Mkt
7 Kerrington Ct
8 Granville Mans
9 Romney Ct
10 Rayner Ct
11 Sulgrave Gdns
12 Bamborough Gdns
13 Hillary Ct
14 Market Studios
15 Lanark Mans
16 St Stephen's CE Prim Sch
17 Miles Coverdale Prim Sch
18 Hammersmith & West London Coll
C2 1 St Paul's Girls' Sch
2 Bute House Prep Sch
3 Ecole Francaise Jacques Prevert
4 Larmenier & Sacred Heart RC Prim Sch
C3 1 Grosvenor Residences
2 Blythe Mews
3 Burnand Ho
4 Bradford Ho
5 Springvale Terr
6 Ceylon Rd
7 Walpole Ct
8 Bronte Ct
9 Boswell Ct
10 Souldern Rd
11 Brook Green Flats
12 Haarlem Rd
13 Stafford Mans
14 Lionel Mans
15 Barradell Ho
C4 1 Vanderbilt Villas
2 Bodington Ct
3 Kingham Ct
4 Clearwater Terr
5 Lorne Gdns
6 Cameret Ct
7 Bush Ct
8 Shepherds Ct
9 Rockley Ct
10 Grampians The
11 Charcroft Ct
12 Addison Park Mans
13 Sinclair Mans
14 Fountain Ct
15 Woodford Ct
16 Roseford Ct
17 Woodstock Studios

40

A1 1 Hockney Ct
2 Toulouse Ct
3 Lowry Ct
4 Barry Ho
5 Lewis Ct
6 Gainsborough Ct
7 Renoir Ct
8 Blake Ct
9 Raphael Ct

10 Rembrandt Ct
11 Constable Ct
12 Da Vinci Ct
13 Gaugin Ct
14 Michelangelo Ct
15 Monet Ct
16 Weald Cl
17 Jasmin Lo
18 Birchmere Lo
19 Weybridge Ct
20 Florence Ho
21 Gleneagles Cl
22 Sunningdale Cl
23 Muirfield Cl
24 Turnberry Cl
25 St Andrews Cl
26 Kingsdown Cl
27 St Davids Cl
28 Galway Cl
29 Edenbridge Cl
30 Birkdale Cl
31 Tralee Ct
32 Woburn Ct
33 Belfry Cl
34 Troon Cl
35 Holywell Cl
A2 1 Market Pl
2 Trappes Ho
3 Thurland Ho
4 Ramsfort Ho
5 Hambley Ho
6 Holford Ho
7 Pope Ho
8 Southwell Ho
9 Mortain Ho
10 Radcliffe Ho
11 Southwark Park Est
12 Galleywall Road Trad Est
13 Trevithick Ho
14 Barlow Ho
15 Donkin Ho
16 Landmann Ho
17 Fitzmaurice Ho
18 Dodd Ho
20 Frank Mews
A3 1 Perryn Rd
2 Chalfont Ho
3 Prestwood Ho
4 Farmer Ho
5 Gataker Ho
6 Gataker St
7 Cornick Ho
8 Glebe Ho
9 Matson Ho
10 Hickling Ho
11 St Andrews Ho
12 Compass Sch
13 Southwark Park Sch
15 Southwark Park Prim Sch
A4 1 Butterfield Cl
2 Janeway Pl
3 Trotwood Ho
4 Maylie Ho
5 Cranbourn Pas
6 Cranbourn Ho
7 Cherry Garden Ho
8 Burton Ho
9 Morriss Ho
10 Dixon's Alley
11 King Edward The Third Mews
12 Cathay St
13 Mission The
14 Millstream Ho

B1 10 Ilderton Prim Sch
B2 1 Damory Ho
2 Antony Ho
3 Roderick Ho
4 Pedworth Gdns
5 Banner Ct
6 Rotherhithe Bsns Est
7 Beamish Ho
8 Corbetts Pas
9 Gillam Ho
10 Richard Ho
11 George Walter Ho
12 Westlake
13 Adron Ho
14 Cavendish Sch
15 McIntosh Ho
16 Goldsworthy Gardens
B3 1 Blick Ho
2 Neptune Ho
3 Scotia Ct
4 Murdoch Ho
5 Edmonton Ct
6 Niagara Ct
7 Columbia Point
8 Ritchie Ho
9 Wells Ho
10 Helen Peele Cotts
11 Orchard Ho
12 Dock Offices
13 Landale Ho
14 Courthope Ho
15 Hithe Gr
16 China Hall Mews
B4 1 Mayflower St
2 St Mary's Est
3 Rupack St
4 Frank Whymark Ho
5 Adams Gardens Est
6 Hatteraick St
7 East India Ct
8 Bombay Ct
9 Stable Ho
10 Grannary The
11 Riverside
12 Cumberland Wharf
13 Seaford Ho
14 Hythe Ho
15 Sandwich Ho
16 Winchelsea Ho
17 Rye Ho
18 Kenning St
19 Western Pl
20 Ainsty St
21 Pine Ho
22 Beech Ho
23 Larch Ho
24 Turner Ct
25 Seth St
26 Risdon Ho
27 Risdon St
28 Aylton Est
29 Manitoba Ct
30 Calgary Ct
31 Irwell Est
32 St Olav's Sq
33 City Bsns Ctr
34 Albion Prim Sch
35 Canada Est
36 Western Pl
C2 1 John Kennedy Ho
2 Brydale Ho
3 Balman Ho
4 Tissington Ct
5 Harbord Ho
6 Westfield Ho

7 Albert Starr Ho
8 John Brent Ho
9 William Evans Ho
10 Raven Ho
11 Egret Ho
12 Fulmar Ho
13 Dunlin Ho
14 Siskin Ho
15 Sheldrake Ho
16 Buchanan Ct
17 Burrage Ct
18 Biddenham Ho
19 Ayston Ho
20 Empingham Ho
21 Deanshanger Ho
22 Codicote Ho
23 Buryfield Ct
24 Rotherhithe Prim Sch
C4 1 Schooner Cl
2 Dolphin Ct
3 Clipper Cl
4 Deauville Ct
5 Colette Ct
6 Coniston Ct
7 Virginia Ct
8 Derwent Ct
9 Grantham Ct
10 Serpentine Ct
11 Career Ct
12 Lacine Ct
13 Fairway Ct
14 Harold Ct
15 Spruce Ho
16 Cedar Ho
17 Sycamore Ho
18 Woodland Cres
19 Poplar Ho
20 Adelphi Ct
21 Basque Ct
22 Aberdale Ct
23 Quilting Ct
24 Chargrove Ct
25 Radley Ct
26 Greenacre Sq
27 Maple Leaf Sq
28 Stanhope Ct
29 Hawke Pl
30 Drake Cl
31 Brass Talley Alley
32 Monkton Ho
33 James Ho
34 Wolfe Cres
35 Dominion Dr
36 Province Dr
37 Wolfe Cres

41
A1 1 Sir Francis Drake Prim Sch
2 Deptford Park Prim Sch
A2 1 Trafalgar Ct
2 Hornblower Cl
3 Cunard Wlk
4 Caronia Ct
5 Carinthia Ct
6 Freswick Ho
7 Graveley Ho
8 Husbourne Ho
9 Crofters Ct
10 Pomona Ho
11 Hazelwood Ho
12 Cannon Wharf Bsns Ctr
13 Bence Ho
14 Clement Ho

9 Pendennis Ho
10 Lighter Cl
11 Mast Ct
12 Rushcutters Ct
13 Boat Lifter Way
14 Naomi St
15 Pell St
16 Marathon Science Sch of Excellence
B1 1 Gransden Ho
2 Daubeney Twr
3 North Ho
4 Rochfort Ho
5 Keppel Ho
6 Camden Ho
7 Sanderson Ho
8 Berkeley Ho
9 Strafford Ho
10 Richman Ho
11 Hurleston Ho
12 Grafton Ho
13 Fulcher Ho
14 Citrus Ho
B2 1 Windsock Cl
2 St George's Mews
3 Linberry Wlk
4 Lanyard Ho
5 Golden Hind Pl
6 James Lind Ho
7 Harmon Ho
8 Pelican Ho
9 Bembridge Ho
10 Terrace The
11 George Beard Ho
12 Colonnade The
13 Pepys Ent Ctr
C1 1 Hudson Ct
2 Shackleton Ct
3 De Gama Pl
4 Mercator Pl
5 Maritime Quay
6 Perry Ct
7 Amundsen Ct
C2 1 Nova Bldg
2 Apollo Bldg
3 Gaverick Mews
4 Windmill Ho
5 Orion Point
6 Galaxy Bldg
7 Venus Ho
8 Olympian Ct
9 Poseidon Ct
10 Mercury Ct
11 Aphrodite Ct
12 Cyclops Mews
13 Neptune Ct
14 Artemis Ct
15 Hera Ct
16 Ares Ct
17 Ringwood Gdns
18 Dartmoor Wlk
19 Rothsay Wlk
20 Ashdown Wlk
21 Radnor Wlk
22 Ironmonger's Pl
23 Britannia Rd
24 Deptford Ferry Rd
25 Magellan Pl
26 Dockers Tanner Rd
C3 1 Bowsprit Point
2 St Hubert's Ho
3 John Tucker Ho
4 Broadway Wlk
5 Nash Ho
6 Fairlead Ho
7 Crosstrees Ho
8 Stanliff Ho

42 B3 303
9 Keelson Ho
10 Clara Grant Ho
11 Gilbertson Ho
12 Scouding Ho
13 Hibbert Ho
14 Cressall Ho
15 Alexander Ho
16 Kedge Ho
C4 1 Anchorage Point
2 Waterman Bldg
3 Jefferson Bldg
4 Pierpoint Bldg
5 Franklin Bldg
6 Vanguard Bldg
7 Edison Bldg
8 Seacon Twr
9 Naxos Bldg
10 Express Wharf
11 Hutching's Wharf
12 Tobago St
13 Bellamy Cl
14 Dowlen Ct
15 Cochrane Ho
16 Beatty Ho
17 Scott Ho
18 Laybourne Ho
19 Ensign Ho
20 Beaufort Ho
21 Spinnaker Ho
22 Bosun Cl
23 Topmast Point
24 Turner Ho
25 Constable Ho
26 Knighthead Point
27 Seven Mills Prim Sch

42
A1 1 Slipway
2 Taffrail Ho
3 Platehouse The
4 Wheelhouse The
5 Chart House The
6 Port House The
7 Beacon Ho
8 Blasker Wlk
9 Maconochies Rd
A2 1 Brassey Ho
2 Triton Ho
3 Warspite Ho
4 Rodney Ho
5 Conway Ho
6 Exmouth Ho
7 Akbar Ho
8 Arethusa Ho
9 Tasman Ct
10 Cutty Sark Ho
11 Harbinger Prim Sch
A3 1 Turnberry Quay
2 Balmoral Ho
3 Aegon Ho
4 Marina Point
B2 1 Betty May Gray Ho
2 Castleton Ho
3 Urmston Ho
4 Salford Ho
5 Capstan Ho
6 Frigate Ho
7 Galleon Ho
B3 1 Cardale St
2 Hickin St
3 John McDonald Ho

4 Thorne Ho
5 Skeggs Ho
6 St Bernard Ho
7 Kimberley Ho
8 Kingdon Ho
9 Killoran Ho
10 Alastor Ho
11 Lingard Ho
12 Yarrow Ho
13 Sandpiper Ct
14 Nightingale Ct
15 Robin Ct
16 Heron Ct
17 Ferndown Lo
18 Crosby Ho
B4 1 Llandovery Ho
2 Rugless Ho
3 Ash Ho
4 Elm Ho
5 Cedar Ho
6 Castalia Sq
7 Aspect Ho
8 Normandy Ho
9 Valiant Ho
10 Tamar Ho
11 Watkins Ho
12 Alice Shepherd Ho
13 Oak Ho
14 Ballin Ct
15 Martin Ct
16 Grebe Ct
17 Kingfisher Ct
18 Walkers Lo
19 Antilles Bay
C2 1 Verwood Lo
2 Fawley Lo
3 Lyndhurst Lo
4 Blyth Cl
5 Farnworth Ho
6 Francis Cl
7 St Luke's CE
Prim Sch

43
A1 1 Bellot Gdns
2 Thornley Pl
3 King William La
4 Bolton Ho
5 Miles Ho
6 Mell St
7 Sam Manners Ho
8 Hatcliffe
Almshouses
9 Woodland Wlk
10 Earlswood Cl
11 St Joseph's RC
Prim Sch
12 Christ Church CE
Prim Sch
B1 1 Baldrey Ho
2 Christie Ho
3 Dyson Ho
4 Cliffe Ho
5 Moore Ho
6 Collins Ho
7 Lockyer Ho
8 Halley Ho
9 Kepler Ho
10 Sailacre Ho
11 Union Pk
B3 1 Teal St
2 Maurer Ct
3 Mudlarks Blvd
4 Renaissance Wlk

5 Alamaro Lo
6 St Mary Magdalene
CE Prim Sch
C1 1 Layfield Ho
2 Westerdale Rd
3 Mayston Mews
4 Station Mews Terr
5 Halstow Prim Sch
6 Holyrood Mews

44
A4 1 Ferry Sq
2 Watermans Ct
3 Wilkes Rd
4 Albany Par
5 Charlton Ho
6 Albany Ho
7 Alma Ho
8 Griffin Ct
9 Cressage Ho
10 Tunstall Wlk
11 Trimmer Wlk
12 Running Horse Yd
13 Mission Sq
14 Distillery Wlk
B2 1 Primrose Ho
2 Lawman Ct
3 Royston Ct
4 Garden Ct
5 Capel Lo
6 Devonshire Ct
7 Celia Ct
8 Rosslyn Ho
9 Branstone Ct
10 Lamerton Lo
11 Kew Lo
12 Dunraven Ho
13 Stoneleigh Lo
14 Tunstall Ct
15 Voltaire
C2 1 Clarendon Ct
2 Quintock Ho
3 Broome Ct
4 Lonsdale Mews
5 Elizabeth Cotts
6 Sandwick
7 Victoria Cotts
8 North Ave
9 Grovewood
10 Hamilton Ho
11 Melvin Ct
12 Royal Par
13 Power Ho
14 Station Ave
15 Blake Mews
C4 5 Strand on the
Green Jun &
Inf Sch

45
A2 1 Terrano Ho
2 Oak Ho
3 Aura Ho
4 Maple Ho
5 Cedar Ho
6 Saffron Ho
7 Lime Ho
8 Lavender Ho
9 Juniper Ho
A4 1 Falcons Pre-Prep
Sch for Boys The

46
B1 1 Melrose Rd
2 Seaforth Lo
3 St John's Gr
4 Sussex Ct

5 Carmichael Ct
6 Hampshire Ct
7 Thorne Pas
8 Brunel Ct
9 Beverley Path
10 Birch Yd

47
C4 1 Cobb's Hall
2 Dorset Mans
3 St Clements Mans
4 Bothwell St
5 Hawksmoor St
6 Melcombe Prim
Sch

48
A1 1 Langport Ho
2 Iveagh Ho
3 Newark Ho
4 Edgehill Ho
5 Hopton Ho
6 Ashby Ho
7 Nevil Ho
A2 1 Fairbairn Gn
2 Hammelton Gn
3 Foxley Sq
4 Silverburn Ho
5 Butler Ho
6 Dalkeith Ho
7 Turner Cl
8 Bathgate Ho
9 Black Roof Ho
10 St Gabriel's Coll
(Dennen Site)
11 Charles Edward
Brooke Sch
12 Lennox Rd
A3 1 Highshore Sch
2 Midnight Ave
3 St Michael & All
Angels CE Acad
A4 1 Faunce Ho
2 Garbett Ho
3 Harvard Ho
4 Doddington Pl
5 Kean Ho
6 Jephson Ho
7 Cornish Ho
8 Bateman Ho
9 Molesworth Ho
10 Walters Ho
11 Cruden Ho
12 Brawne Ho
13 Prescott Ho
14 Chalmer's Wlk
15 Copley Cl
16 King Charles Ct
B1 1 Bergen Ho
2 Oslo Ho
3 Viking Ho
4 Jutland Ho
5 Norvic Ho
6 Odin Ho
7 Baltic Ho
8 Nobel Ho
9 Mercia Ho
10 Kenbury Gdns
11 Zealand Ho
12 Elsinore Ho
13 Norse Ho
14 Denmark Mans
15 Dane Ho
16 Canterbury Cl
17 York Cl
18 Kenbury Mans
19 Parade Mans

20 Winterslow Ho
21 Lilford Ho
22 Bartholomew Ho
23 Guildford Ho
24 Boston Ho
25 Hereford Ho
26 Weyhill Ho
27 Lichfield Ho
28 Lansdown Ho
29 Honiton Ho
30 Pinner Ho
31 Baldock Ho
32 Widecombe Ho
33 Nottingham Ho
34 Witham Ho
35 Barnet Ho
36 Empress Mews
B2 1 Bertha Neubergh
House
2 Mornington Mews
3 Badsworth Rd
4 Pearson Cl
5 Elm Tree Ct
6 Samuel Lewis Trust
Dwellings
7 Milkwell Yd
8 Keswick Ho
9 Mitcham Ho
10 Sacred Heart
Catholic Sch
11 Crawford Prim Sch
B3 1 Boundary Ho
2 Day Ho
3 Burgess Ho
4 Carlyle Ho
5 Myers Ho
6 Thompson Ave
7 Palgrave Ho
8 Winnington Ho
9 Brantwood Ho
10 Lowell Ho
11 Jessie Duffett Ho
12 Otterburn Ho
13 Crossmount Ho
14 Venice Ct
15 Bowyer St
16 Livingstone Ho
17 Gothic Ct
18 Coniston Ho
19 Harlynwood
20 Carey Ct
21 Finley Ct
22 Grainger Ct
23 Hayes Ct
24 Moffat Ho
25 Marinel Ho
26 Hodister Cl
27 Arnot Ho
28 Lamb Ho
29 Kipling Ho
30 Keats Ho
31 Kenyon Ho
32 New Church Rd
33 Sir John Kirk Cl
34 Comber Grove
Prim Sch
35 Ark All Saints Acad
36 St Joseph's
Camberwell
RC Schools'
Federation
C1 1 Selborne Rd
2 Hascombe Terr
C2 1 Joiners Arms Yd
2 Butterfly Wlk
3 Cuthill Wlk
4 Colonades The

5 Artichoke Mews
6 Peabody Bldgs
7 Brighton Ho
8 Park Ho
9 Peabody Ct
10 Lomond Ho
11 Lamb Ho
12 Kimpton Ct
13 Belham Wlk
14 Datchelor Pl
15 Harvey Rd
C3 1 Masterman Ho
2 Milton Ho
3 Pope Ho
4 Chester Ct
5 Marvel Ho
6 Flecker Ho
7 Landor Ho
8 Leslie Prince Ct
9 Evelina Mans
10 Langland Ho
11 Drinkwater Ho
12 Procter Ho
13 Shirley Ho
14 Drayton Ho
15 Bridges Ho
16 Cunningham Ho
17 Hood Ho
18 Herrick Ho
19 Dekker Ho
20 Houseman Way
21 Coleby Path
22 Brunswick Park
Prim Sch
C4 1 Queens Ho
2 Arnside Ho
3 Horsley St
4 St Peter's Ho
5 St Johns Ho
6 St Marks Ho
7 St Stephens Ho
8 St Matthew's Ho
9 Red Lion Cl
10 Boyson Rd
11 Bradenham

49
A1 1 Springfield Ho
2 Craston Ho
3 Walters Ho
4 Edgecombe Ho
5 Fowler Ho
6 Rignold Ho
7 Chatham Ho
A2 1 Barnwell Ho
2 Brunswick Villas
3 St Giles Twr
4 Bentley Ho
5 Dawson Ho
6 Dryden Ho
7 Mayward Ho
8 Longleigh Ho
9 Fairwall Ho
10 Bodeney Ho
11 Sandby Ho
12 Vestry Mews
13 Netley
14 Lakanal
15 Racine
16 Camberwell
Coll of Arts
A3 1 Tower Mill Rd
2 Tilson Cl
3 Granville Sq
4 Edgar Wallace Cl
5 Potters Cl
6 Dorton Cl

7 Samuel Jones Ind Est
8 Dibden Ho
9 Marchwood Cl
10 Pilgrims Cloisters
11 Beacon Ho
12 Teather St
13 Stacy Path
14 Rumball Ho
15 Ballow Cl
16 Rill Ho
17 Southwark Coll (Camberwell Ctr)
18 St George's CE Prim Sch
A4 1 Downend Ct
2 Andoversford Ct
3 Pearse St
4 Watling St
5 Gandolfi St
6 Comfort St
7 Tower Mill Rd
B1 1 Villa Sch The
B2 1 Colbert
2 Voltaire
3 Finch Mews
4 Charles Coveney Rd
5 Bamber Rd
6 Crane St
7 Curlew Ho
8 Mallard Ho
9 Tern Ho
10 Crane Ho
11 Falcon Ho
12 Bryanston Ho
13 Basing Ct
14 Marcus Ho
15 Sheffield Ho
16 Highshore Sch
17 St James The Great RC Prim Sch
18 Oliver Goldsmith Prim Sch
B3 1 Painswick Ct
2 Sharpness Ct
3 Mattingly Way
4 Hordle Prom N
5 Burcher Gale Gr
6 Calypso Cres
7 Hordle Prom S
8 Cinnamon Cl
9 Savannah Ct
10 Thames Ct
11 Shannon Ct
12 Amstel Ct
13 Danube Ct
14 Tilbury Ct
15 Hordle Prom E
16 Indus Ct
17 Oakcourt
18 Palm Ct
19 Rowan Ct
20 Blackthorn Ct
21 Pear Ct
22 Lidgate Rd
23 Whistler Mews
24 Boathouse Wlk
25 Camberwell Coll of Arts
B4 1 Willsbridge Ct
2 Cam Ct
3 Quedgeley Ct
4 Saul Ct
5 Quenington Ct
6 Westonbirt Ct
7 Wickway Ct
C1 1 William Margrie Cl

2 William Blake Ho
3 Quantock Mews
4 Choumert Sq
5 Parkstone Rd
6 Atwell Rd
7 Copeland Ind Pk
C2 1 Canal Head Public Sq
2 Angelina Ho
3 Jarvis Ho
4 Richland Ho
5 Honeywood Ho
6 Wakefield Ho
7 Primrose Ho
8 Hardcastle Ho
9 Dunstall Ho
10 Springtide Cl
11 Purdon Ho
12 Flamborough Ho
13 Lambrook Ho
14 Witcombe Point
15 Yarnfield Sq
16 Winford Ct
17 Portbury Cl
18 Robert Keen Cl
C3 1 Thornhill Ho
2 Vervain Ho
3 Woodstar Ho
4 Tamarind Ho
5 Hereford Retreat
6 Haymerle Ho
7 Furley Ho
8 Thomas Milner Ho
9 Applegarth Ho
10 Freda Corbett Cl
11 Rudbeck Ho
12 Henslow Ho
13 Lindley Ho
14 Collinson Ho
15 Sister Mabel's Way
16 Timberland Cl
17 Hastings Cl
18 Sidmouth Ho
19 Budleigh Ho
20 Stanesgate Ho
21 Breamore Ho
22 Ely Ho
23 Gisburn Ho
24 Silkin Mews
25 Peckham Park Prim Sch
26 St Francis RC Prim Sch
C4 1 Bowles Rd
2 Western Wharf
3 Northfield Ho
4 Millbrook Ho
5 Denstone Ho
6 Deerhurst Ho
7 Caversham Ho
8 Battle Ho
9 Cardiff Ho
10 Bridgnorth Ho
11 Exeter Ho
12 Grantham Ho
13 Aylesbury Ho
14 Royston Ho
15 Haymerle Sch

50
A1 1 Walkynscroft
2 Ryegates
3 Hathorne Cl
4 Pilkington Rd
5 Russell Ct
6 Heaton Ho
7 Magdalene Cl

2 Iris Ct
3 St Mary Magdalene CE Prim Sch
A2 1 Willowdene
2 Pinedene
3 Oakdene
4 Beechdene
5 Hollydene
6 Wood Dene
7 Staveley Cl
8 Carnicot Ho
9 Martock Ct
10 Cherry Tree Ct
11 Kendrick Ct
12 John Donne Prim Sch
A3 1 Tortington Ho
2 Credenhill Ho
3 Bromyard Ho
4 Hoyland Cl
5 Willowdene
6 Ashdene
7 Acorn Par
8 Havelock Ct
9 Springall St
10 Harry Lambourn Ho
11 Grenier Apartments
12 Burnhill Cl
B1 1 Honiton Gdns
2 Selden Ho
3 Hathway Ho
4 Hathway St
5 Station Ct
6 Symons Cl
7 Hollydale Prim Sch
B2 1 Trotman Ho
2 Boddington Ho
3 Heydon Ho
4 Boulter Ho
5 Astbury Bsns Pk
6 Kender Prim Sch
B3 1 Ambleside Point
2 Grasmere Point
3 Windermere Point
4 Roman Way
5 Laburnum Cl
6 Juniper Ho
7 Romney Cl
8 Hammersley Ho
9 Hutchinson Ho
10 Hammond Ho
11 Fir Tree Ho
12 Glastonbury Ct
13 Highbridge Ct
14 Filton Ct
15 Chiltern Ct
16 Cheviot Ct
B4 1 Penshurst Ho
2 Reculver Ho
3 Mereworth Ho
4 Camber Ho
5 Chiham Ho
6 Otford Ho
7 Olive Tree Ho
8 Aspen Ho
9 Lewis Silkin Ho
10 Richborough Ho
11 Dover Ho
12 Eynsford Ho
13 Horton Ho
14 Lamberhurst Ho
15 Canterbury Ind Pk
16 Upnall Ho
17 Sissinghurst Ho
18 Rochester Ho
19 Saltwood Ho
20 Leybourne Ho

21 Lullingstone Ho
22 Pilgrims Way Prim Sch
C3 1 Richard Anderson Ct
2 Palm Tree Ho
3 Edward Robinson House
4 Antony Ho
5 Gerrard Ho
6 Palmer Ho
7 Pankhurst Ct
8 Robinson Wy
9 Eckington La
C4 1 Harrisons Ct
2 Grantley Ho
3 Sunbury Ct
4 Tilbury Ho
5 Graham Ct
6 Connell Ct
7 St Clements Ct
8 Henderson Ct
9 Jemotts Ct
10 Verona Ct
11 Heywood Ho
12 Francis Ct
13 Hind Ho
14 Donne Ho
15 Carew Ct
16 Burbage Ho
17 Newland Ho
18 Dobson Ho
19 Dalton Ho
20 Greene Ct
21 Redrup Ho
22 Tarplett Ho
23 Stunell Ho
24 Gasson Ho
25 Bryce Ho
26 Barnes Ho
27 Barkwith Ho
28 Bannister Ho
29 Apollo Ind Bsns Ctr

51
A1 4 Haberdashers' Aske's Hatcham College
A2 1 Archer Ho
2 Browning Ho
3 Hardcastle Ho
4 Brooke Ho
5 Wallis Ho
6 Haberdashers' Aske's Hatcham College
A3 1 Batavia Ho
2 Marlowe Bsns Ctr
3 Batavia Mews
4 Woodrush Cl
5 Alexandra St
6 Primrose Wlk
7 Vansittart St
8 Granville Ct
9 Cottesbrook St
10 Ewen Henderson Ct
11 Fordham Ho
12 Deptford Green Sch (Annex)
A4 1 Portland Ct
2 Phoenix Ct
3 Rainbow Ct
4 Hawke Twr
5 Chubworthy St
6 Woodpecker Rd
7 Hercules Ct
B3 1 Austin Ho

2 Exeter Way
3 Crossleigh Ct
4 Mornington Pl
5 Maple Ho
B4 1 Chester Ho
2 Lynch Wlk
3 Arlington Ho
4 Woodcote Ho
5 Cornbury Ho
6 Prospect Pl
7 Akintaro Ho
8 Mulberry Ho
9 Laurel Ho
10 Linden Ho
11 Ashford Ho
12 Wardalls Ho
13 Magnolia Ho
14 Howard Ho
15 Larch Cl
16 Ibis Ct
17 Merganser Ct
18 Wotton Rd
19 Kingfisher Sq
20 Sanderling Ct
21 Dolphin Twr
22 Mermaid Twr
23 Scoter Ct
24 Shearwater Ct
25 Brambling Ct
26 Kittiwake Ct
27 Diana Cl
28 Guillemot Ct
29 Marine Twr
30 Teal Ct
31 Lapwing Twr
32 Violet Cl
33 Skua Ct
34 Tristan Ct
35 Rosemary Ct
36 Cormorant Ct
37 Shelduck Ct
38 Eider Ct
39 Pintail Ct
40 Fulcher Ct
Grinling Gibbons Prim Sch
Pilot Cl
C1 1 Ashmead Mews
2 St Stephen's CE Prim Sch
C2 1 Admiralty Cl
2 Harton Lodge
3 Sylva Cotts
4 Pitman Ho
5 Heston Ho
6 Mereton Mans
7 Indiana Bldg
8 St John's Lodge
9 Dean's Gateway
10 Lucas Vale Prim Sch
11 Addey & Stanhope Sch
12 Lewisham Coll (Deptford Campus)
C3 1 Sandpiper Ct
2 Flamingo Ct
3 Titan Bsns Est
4 Rochdale Way
5 Speedwell St
6 Reginald Pl
7 Fletcher Path
8 Frankham Ho
9 Cremer Ho

10 Wilshaw Ho
11 Castell Ho
12 Holden Ho
13 Browne Ho
14 Resolution Way
15 Lady Florence Ctyd
16 Covell Ct
17 Albion Ho
18 St Joseph's RC
   Prim Sch
20 Tidemill Acad
C4 1 Dryfield Wlk
2 Blake Ho
3 Hawkins Ho
4 Grenville Ho
5 Langford Ho
6 Mandarin Ct
7 Bittern Ct
8 Lamerton St
9 Ravensbourne
   Mans
10 Armada St
11 Armada Ct
12 Benbow Ho
13 Oxenham Ho
14 Caravel Mews
15 Hughes Ho
16 Stretton Mans

52
A1 1 Morden Mount
   Prim Sch
2 Ravensbourne Pl
3 Bliss Cres
A2 1 Washington Bldg
2 California Bldg
3 Utah Bldg
4 Montana Bldg
5 Oregon Bldg
6 Dakota bldg
7 Idaho Bldg
8 Atlanta Bldg
9 Colorado Bldg
10 Arizona Bldg
11 Nebraska Bldg
12 Alaska Bldg
13 Ohio Bldg
14 Charter Bldgs
15 Flamsteed Ct
16 Friendly Pl
17 Dover Ct
18 Robinscroft Mews
19 Doleman Ho
20 Plymouth Ho
A3 1 Finch Ho
2 Jubilee The
3 Maitland Cl
4 Ashburnham
   Retreat
5 Waller Wy
6 Merryweather Pl
7 Victoria Gate
   Gardens
A4 7 Trinity Laban
   Conservatoire of
   Music & Dance
B1 1 Ellison Ho
2 Pitmaston Ho
3 Aster Ho
4 Windmill Cl
5 Hertmitagge The
6 Burnett Ho
7 Lacey Ho
8 Darwin Ho

9 Pearmain Ho
10 Primrose Wy
B2 1 Penn Almshouses
2 Jervis Ct
3 Woodville Ct
4 Darnall Ho
5 Renbold Ho
6 Lindsell St
7 Plumbridge St
8 Trinity Gr
9 Hollymount Cl
10 Cade Tyler Ho
11 Robertson Ho
12 Sparta St
13 Parkside Sq
14 Copperwood Pl
15 Parkside Ave
16 Silverwood Pl
B3 1 Temair Ho
2 Royal Hill Ct
3 Prince of
   Orange La
4 Lambard Ho
5 St Marks Cl
6 Ada Kennedy Ct
7 Arlington Pl
8 Topham Ho
9 Darnell Ho
10 Hawks Mews
11 Royal Pl
12 Swanne Ho
13 Maribor
14 Serica Ct
15 Queen Elizabeth's
   College
16 James Wolfe
   Prim Sch
17 Greenwich Com
   Coll
18 David Mews
19 Arlington Pl
B4 1 Crescent Arc
2 Greenwich Mkt
3 Turnpin La
4 Durnford St
5 Sexton's Ho
6 Bardsley Ho
7 Wardell Ho
8 Clavell St
9 Stanton Ho
10 Macey Ho
11 Boreman Ho
12 Clipper Appts
C3 1 Park Wlk
C4 1 Frobisher Ct
2 Hardy Cotts
3 Palliser Ho
4 Bernard Angell Ho
5 Corvette Sq
6 Travers Ho
7 Maze Hill Lodge
8 Park Place Ho
9 Meridian Prim Sch

53
B1 1 Heath House
   Prep Sch
B3 1 Westcombe Ct
2 Kleffens Ct
3 Ferndale Ct
4 Combe Mews
5 Mandeville Cl
6 Pinelands Cl
C3 3 Mary Lawrenson Pl
2 Bradbury Ct
3 Dunstable Ct
4 Wentworth Ho

C4 1 Nethercombe Ho
2 Holywell Cl

54
A1 1 Lancaster Cotts
2 Lancaster Mews
3 Bromwich Ho
4 Priors Lo
5 Richmond Hill Ct
6 Glenmore Ho
7 Hillbrow
8 Heathshott
9 Friars Stile Pl
10 Spire Ct
11 Ridgeway
12 Matthias Ct
13 Old Vicarage Sch
A2 1 Lichfield Terr
2 Union Ct
3 Carrington Lo
4 Wilton Ct
5 Egerton Ct
6 Beverley Lo
7 Bishop Duppa's
   Almshouses
8 Regency Wlk
9 Clear Water Ho
10 Onslow Avenue
   Mans
11 Michels
   Almshouses
12 Albany Pas
13 Salcombe Villas
A3 1 St John's Gr
2 Michel's Row
3 Micheldale Dr
4 Blue Anchor Alley
5 Clarence St
6 Sun Alley
7 Thames Link Ho
8 Benns Wlk
9 Waterloo Pl
10 Northumbria Ct
B1 1 Chester Ct
2 Queen's Ct
3 Russell Wlk
4 Charlotte Sq
5 Jones Wlk
6 Hilditch Ho
7 Isabella Ct
8 Damer Ho
9 Eliot Ho
10 Herbert Ho
11 Reynolds Pl
12 Chisholm Rd
B2 1 Alberta Ct
2 Beatrice Rd
3 Lorne Rd
4 York Rd
5 Connaught Rd
6 Albany Terr
7 Kingswood Ct
8 Selwyn Ct
9 Broadhurst Cl
B3 1 Towers The
2 Longs Ct
3 Sovereign Ct
4 Robinson Ct
5 Calvert Ct
6 Bedford Ct
7 Hickey's
   Almshouses
8 Church Estate
C2 1 Geneva Ct

9 Richmond
   International
   Bsns Ctr
10 Abercorn Mews
C4 1 Parison Cl

55
A3 1 Hershell Ct
2 Deanhill Ct
3 Park Sheen
4 Furness Lo
5 Merricks Ct
C4 1 Rann Ho
2 Craven Ho
3 John Dee Ho
4 Kindell Ho
5 Montgomery Ho
6 Avondale Ho
7 Addington Ct
8 Dovecote Gdns
9 Firmston Ho
10 Glendower Gdns
11 Chestnut Ave
12 Trehern Rd
13 Rock Ave
14 St Mary Magdalen's
   RC Prim Sch

56
C1 1 Woodmill Cl
2 Bader Wy
3 Mendez Wy
4 India Wy
5 Gillis Sq
6 Benkart Mews
7 Drury Cl
C2 1 Theodore Ho
2 Nicholas Ho
3 Bonner Ho
4 Downing Ho
5 Jansen Ho
6 Fairfax Ho
7 Devereux Ho
8 David Ho
9 Leigh Ho
10 Clipstone Ho
11 Mallet Ho
12 Arton Wilson Ho

57
B2 1 Inglis Ho
2 Ducie Ho
3 Wharncliffe Ho
4 Stanhope Ho
5 Waldegrave Ho
6 Mildmay Ho
7 Mullens Ho
C1 1 Balmoral Cl
2 Glenalmond Ho
3 Selwyn Ho
4 Keble Ho
5 Bede Ho
6 Gonville Ho
7 Magdalene Ho
8 Armstrong Ho
9 Newnham Ho
10 Somerville Ho
11 Balliol Ho
12 Windermere
13 Little Combe Cl
14 Classinghall Ho
15 Chalford Ct
16 Garden Royal
17 South Ct
18 Anne Kerr Ct
19 Ewhurst

2 Laurel Ct
3 Cambalt Ho
4 Langham Ct
5 Lower Pk
6 King's Keep
7 Whitnell Ct
8 Whitehead Ho
9 Halford Ho
10 Humphry Ho
11 Jellicoe Ho
C3 1 Olivette St
2 Mascotte Rd
3 Glegg Pl
4 Crown Ct
5 Charlwood Terr
6 Percy Laurie Ho
7 Our Lady of
   Victories RC
   Prim Sch
C4 1 Griffin Gate
2 Darfur St
3 John Keall Ho
4 Henry Jackson Ho
5 Felsham Ho
6 Ardshiel Cl
7 Ruvigny Mans
8 Star & Garter
   Mans
9 University Mans
10 Lockyer Ho
11 Phelps Ho
12 Princeton Ct
13 Kingsmere Cl
14 Felsham Mews
15 St Mary's CE
   Prim Sch

58
A2 1 Claremont
2 Downside
3 Cavendish Ct
4 Ashcombe Ct
5 Carltons The
6 Espirit Ho
7 Millbrooke Ct
8 Coysh Ct
9 Keswick Hts
10 Avon Ct
11 Merlin Sch The
B2 1 Keswick Broadway
2 Burlington Mews
3 Cambria Lo
4 St Stephen's Gdns
5 Atlantic Ho
6 Burton Lo
7 Manfred Ct
8 Meadow Bank
9 Hooper Ho
10 Aspire Bld
C2 1 Pembridge Pl
2 Adelaide Rd
3 London Ct
4 Windsor Ct
5 Westminster Ct
6 Fullers Ho
7 Bridge Pk
8 Lambeth Ct
9 Milton Ct
10 Norfolk Mans
11 Francis Snary Lo
12 Bush Cotts
13 Downbury Mews
14 Newton's Yd
15 Roche Sch The
16 St Joseph's RC
   Prim Sch

- 17 West Hill Prim Sch
- 19 Spectrum Wy

59

A2 1 Fairfield Ct
2 Blackmore Ho
3 Lancaster Mews
4 Cricketers Mews
5 College Mews
6 Arndale Wlk
6 St Anne's CE Prim Sch
7 South Thames Coll (Wandsworth Ctr)
B1 1 Wandsworth Prep Sch
B2 1 St Faith's CE Prim Sch
B4 1 Molasses Ho
2 Molasses Row
3 Cinnamon Row
4 Calico Ho
5 Calico Row
6 Port Ho
7 Square Rigger Row
8 Trade Twr
9 Ivory Ho
10 Spice Ct
11 Sherwood Ct
12 Mendip Ct
13 Chalmers Ho
14 Coral Row
15 Ivory Sq
16 Kingfisher Ho
C3 1 Burke Ho
2 High View Prim Sch
3 Centre Acad
4 Fox Ho
5 Buxton Ho
6 Pitt Ho
7 Ramsey Ho
8 Beverley Cl
9 Florence Ho
10 Linden Ct
11 Dorcas Ct
12 Johnson Ct
13 Agnes Ct
14 Hilltop Ct
15 Courtyard The
16 Old Laundry The
17 Oberstein Rd
18 Fineran Ct
19 Sangora Rd
18 Harvard Mans
19 Plough Mews
C4 1 Milner Ho
2 McManus Ho
3 Wilberforce Ho
4 Wheeler Ct
5 Sporle Ct
6 Holliday Sq
7 John Parker Sq
8 Carmichael Cl
9 Fenner Sq
10 Clark Lawrence Ct
11 Shaw Ct
12 Sendall Ct
13 Livingstone Rd
14 Farrant Ho
15 Jackson Ho
16 Darien Ho
17 Shepard Ho
18 Ganley Ct
19 Arthur Newton Ho
20 Chesterton Ho
21 John Kirk Ho

22 Mantua St
23 Heaver Rd
24 Candlemakers
25 Thames Christian Coll
26 Falconbrook Prim Sch
27 Benham Cl

60

A4 1 Kiloh Ct
2 Lanner Ho
3 Griffon Ho
4 Kestrel Ho
5 Kite Ho
6 Peregrine Ho
7 Hawk Ho
8 Inkster Ho
9 Harrier Ho
10 Eagle Hts
11 Kingfisher Ct
12 Lavender Terr
13 Temple Ho
14 Ridley Ho
15 Eden Ho
16 Hertford Ct
17 Nepaul Rd
B1 1 Staplehurst Ct
2 Teyham Ct
3 Honeywell Jun & Inf Schs
B2 1 Clapham Computer & Secretarial Coll
C1 1 Rayne Ho
2 St Anthony's Ct
3 Earlsthorpe Mews
4 Nightingale Mans
5 Clavering Pl
C4 1 Shaftesbury Park Chambers
2 Selborne
3 Rush Hill Mews
4 Marmion Mews
5 Crosland Pl
6 Craven Mews
7 Garfield Mews
8 Audley Cl
9 Basnett Rd
10 Tyneham Cl
11 Woodmere Cl
12 L'Ecole du Parc
D1 1 Broomwood Hall (Lower Sch)

61

A1 1 Oliver House Prep Sch
A4 1 Turnchapel Mews
2 Redwood Mews
3 Phil Brown Pl
4 Bev Callender Cl
5 Keith Connor Cl
6 Tessa Sanderson Pl
7 Daley Thompson Way
8 Rashleigh Ct
9 Abberley Mews
10 Willow Lodge
11 Beaufoy Rd
12 Wardell Mews
B1 1 Joseph Powell Cl
2 Cavendish Mans
3 Westlands Terr
4 Cubitt Ho
5 Hawkesworth Ho
6 Normanton Ho
7 Eastman Ho

8 Couchman Ho
9 Poynders Ct
10 Selby Ho
11 Valentine Ho
12 Gorham Ho
13 Deauville Mans
14 Deauville St
B2 1 Timothy Ct
2 Shaftesbury Mews
3 Brook Ho
4 Grover Ho
5 Westbrook Ho
6 Hewer Ho
7 Batten Ho
8 Mandeville Ho
9 George Beare Lo
10 St Mary's RC Prim Sch
B3 1 Polygon The
2 Windsor Ct
3 Trinity Cl
4 Studios The
5 Bourne Ho
6 Porteus Pl
B4 1 Clapham Manor Ct
2 Clarke Ho
3 Gables The
4 Sycamore Mews
5 Maritime Ho
6 Rectory Gdns
7 Floris Pl
8 Clapham Manor Prim Sch
C1 1 Parrington Ho
2 Savill Ho
3 Blackwell Ho
4 Bruce Ho
5 Victoria Ct
6 Victoria Ho
7 Belvedere Ct
8 Ingram Lo
9 Viney Ct
10 Bloomsbury Ho
11 Belgravia Ho
12 Barnsbury Ho
13 Parkfield Rd
14 Brickfield Rd
15 Dragmore St
16 Fairbourne Rd
17 Fennings Rd
C3 1 Kendoa Rd
2 Felmersham Cl
3 Abbeville Mews
4 Saxon Ho
5 Gifford Ho
6 Teignmouth Cl
7 Holwood Pl
8 Oaklands Pl
9 Wilberforce Mews
10 William Bonney Estate
11 London Coll of Bsns & Computer Studies
12 Welmar Mews
C4 1 Chelsham Ho
2 Lynde Ho
3 Greener Ho
4 Towns Ho
5 Hugh Morgan Ho
6 Roy Ridley Ho
7 Lendal Terr
8 Slievemore Cl
9 Cadmus Cl
10 Clapham North Bsns Ctr

11 Bicycle Mews
12 Old Station Wy

62

A1 3 Notley Pl
A2 1 King's Mews
2 Clapham Court Terr
3 Clapham Ct
4 Clapham Park Terr
5 Pembroke Ho
6 Stevenson Ho
7 Queenswood Ct
8 Oak Tree Ct
9 Park Lofts
10 Ashby Mews
11 Holm Oak Mews
A3 1 Morris Ho
2 Gye Ho
3 Clowes Ho
4 Thomas Ho
5 Stuart Ho
6 Storace Ho
7 Bedford Ho
8 Ascot Ct
9 Ascot Par
10 Ashmere Ho
11 Ashmere Gr
12 Ventura Ho
13 Vickery Ho
14 Stafford Mans
15 Beresford Ho
A4 1 Callingham Ho
2 Russell Pickering Ho
3 Ormerod Ho
4 Lopez Ho
5 Coachmaker Mews
B1 1 Stewart's Ct
2 Wild Works Mews
B2 1 Beatrice Ho
2 Florence Ho
3 Evelyn Ho
4 Diana Ho
5 Brixton Hill Ct
6 Austin Ho
7 Manor Ct
8 Camsey Ho
9 Romer Ho
10 Gale Ho
11 Byrne Ho
12 Farnfield Ho
13 Marchant Ho
14 Rainsford Ho
15 Springett Ho
16 Mannering Ho
17 Waldron Ho
18 Sudbourne Prim Sch
19 Corpus Christi RC Prim Sch
B3 1 Freemens Hos
2 Roger's Almshouses
3 Gresham Almshouses
4 Exbury Ho
5 Glasbury Ho
6 Dalbury Ho
7 Fosbury Ho
8 Chalbury Ho
9 Neilson-Terry Ct
10 Pavilion Mans
11 Daisy Dormer Ct
12 George Lashwood Ct
13 Marie Lloyd Ct
14 Trinity Homes

15 Lethaby Ho
16 Edmundsbury Ct Est
17 Regis Pl
18 Marlborough Mews
19 Alpha Ho
20 Beta Pl
21 Cedars Ho
22 South Chelsea Coll
B4 1 Turberville Ho
2 Thrayle Ho
3 Percheron Ct
4 Draymans Ct
5 Lansdowne Sch
6 Stockwell Prim Sch
C1 1 Eccleston Ho
2 Scarsbrook Ho
3 Purser Ho
4 Rudhall Ho
5 Hardham Ho
6 Heywood Ho
7 Haworth Ho
8 Birch Ho
9 Lansdell Ho
10 Lomley Ho
11 Laughton Ho
12 Woodruff Ho
13 Bascome St
14 Dudley Mews
15 Herbert Mews
16 Blades Lo
17 Dick Shepherd Ct
18 Charman Ho
19 Morden Ho
20 Bishop Ct
21 Blackburn Ct
22 Leigh Ct
23 John Conwey Ho
24 Bristowe Ct
C2 1 Crownstone Ct
2 Brockwell Ct
3 Nevena Ct
4 St George's Residences
5 Hanover Mans
6 Fleet Ho
7 Langbourne Ho
8 Turnmill Ho
9 Walker Mews
10 Cossar Mews
11 Carter Ho
12 Arungford Mews
C3 1 Electric Mans
2 Electric La
3 Connaught Mans
4 Clifton Mans
5 Hereford Ho
6 Chaplin Ho
7 Lord David Pitt Ho
8 Marcus Garvey Way
9 Montego Cl
10 Bob Marley Way
11 Leeson Rd
12 St John's Angell Town CE Prim Sch
C4 1 Buckmaster Cl
2 Albemarle Ho
3 Goodwood Mans
4 Angell Park Gdns
5 Fyfield Rd
6 Howard Ho
7 Harris Ho
8 Broadoak Ct
9 Burgate Ct

10 Witchwood Ho
11 Blacktree Mews
12 Chartham Ct
13 Chilham Ct
14 Northgate Ct
15 Westgate Ct
16 Dover Mans
17 St Helen's RC Primary Sch
18 Dorrell Pl
19 Rossiter Gr

63
A2 2 Poets Mews
4 St Jude's CE Prim Sch
A3 1 Mahatma Gandhi Ind Est
2 Dylan Rd
3 Bessemer Park Ind Est
4 Pablo Neruda Cl
5 Langston Hughes Cl
6 Walt Whitman Cl
7 James Joyce Wlk
8 Alice Walker Cl
9 Louise Bennett Cl
10 Chadacre Ho
11 Burwood Ho
12 Pyrford Ho
13 Wangford Ho
14 Ashford Ho
15 Kenwood Ho
16 Moyne Ho
17 Elveden Ho
18 Carrara Cl
19 Broughton Dr
20 Angela Davis Ind Est
21 Tilia Wlk
22 County Ho
23 Hill Mead Prim Sch
24 Jessop Prim Sch
A4 1 Mallams Mews
2 Amberley Ct
3 Harper Ho
4 Leicester Ho
5 Station Ave
6 Wellfit St
7 Loughborough Ct
8 Belinda Rd
9 Higgs Ind Est
10 Tham Ho
C3 1 Shaftesbury Ct
2 Mayhew Ct
3 Morris Ct
4 Swinburne Ct
5 Perth Ct
6 Tayside Ct
7 Matlock Ct
8 Hunter Ct
9 Turner Ct
10 Royal George Mews

64
A2 1 Velde Way
2 Delft Way
3 Arnhem Way
4 Isel Way
5 Kempis Way
6 Terborch Way
7 Steen Way
8 Deventer Cres

9 Nimegen Way
10 Hilversum Cres
11 St Barnabas Ct
12 James Allen's Girls' Sch (senior)
13 James Allen's Girls' Sch (prep)
A4 1 Harfield Gdns
2 Karen Ct
3 Seavington Ho
4 Appleshaw Ho
5 Birdsall Ho
6 Whitney Ho
7 Wheatland Ho
8 Wilton Ho
9 Walcot Ho
10 Whaddon Ho
11 Melbreak Ho
12 Ledbury Ho
13 Tidworth Ho
14 Riseholme Ho
15 Ringmer Ho
16 Petworth Ho
17 Stagshaw Ho
18 Ivybridge Ho
19 Inwood Ho
20 Gatcombe Ho
21 Felbridge Ho
22 Cowdray Ho
23 Dog Kennel Hill Sch
B3 1 Dulwich Mews
2 New Hope Christian Acad
3 St James's Cloisters
C2 1 Dorothy Charrington Ho
2 Keswick Ct
3 Kendall Ct
4 Halliwell Ct
5 Hindmans Yd
C4 1 St John's & St Clement's CE Prim Sch
2 Bellenden Prim Sch
3 Rye Passage

65
A4 1 Tilling Ho
2 Goodwin Ho
3 Tyrells Ct
4 Citron Terr
5 Basswood Ct
6 Cheam St
7 Rye Oak Prim Sch
C3 1 Laxton Path
2 Barlings Ho
3 Bayfield Ho
4 Coston Wlk
5 Coverham Ho
6 Gateley Ho
7 Dereham Ho
8 Greenwood Ho
9 Hilton Ho
10 Goodall Ho
11 Horsley Ho
12 Jordan Ho

66
A1 1 Sienna Pl
A3 1 Turnham Prim Sch
A4 1 Dragonfly Pl
B2 1 Hayward Mews

67
A4 1 Pine Tree Way

2 Waterway Ave
3 Prendergast Vale Sch
B4 1 Bankside Ave
2 Elder Wlk
3 Yew Tree Cl
4 Mill Ho
5 Salisbury Yd
C1 3 Park Piazza
4 Birdwood Ave
C3 1 Atlas Mews

68
C3 1 Farnborough Ho
2 Rushmere Ho
3 Horndean Cl
4 Highcross Way
5 Timsbury Wlk
6 Foxcombe Rd
7 Ryefield Path
8 Greatham Wlk
9 Gosport Ho
10 Stoatley Ho
11 Milland Ho
12 Clanfield Ho
13 Fareham Ho
14 Grayswood Point
C4 1 Woodcott Ho
2 Lyndhurst Ho
3 Wheatley Ho
4 Allbrook Ho
5 Bordon Wlk
6 Chilcombe Ho
7 Vicarage Ct
8 Shawford Ct
9 Eastleigh Wlk
10 Kings Ct
11 Somborne Ho

69
A3 1 Ramsdean Ho
2 Purbrook Ho
3 Portsea Ho
4 Blendworth Point
5 Eashing Point
6 Hindhead Point
7 Hilsea Point
8 Witley Point
9 Buriton Ho
10 Grateley Ho
11 Hascombe Ho
12 Dunhill Point
13 Westmark Point
14 Longmoor Point
15 Cadnam Point
B4 1 Cumberland Ho
2 Devonshire Ho
3 Cornwall Ho
4 Norfolk Ho
5 Leicester Ho
6 Warwick Ho
7 Sutherland Ho
8 Carmarthen Ho
9 Worcester Ho
10 Rutland Ho
11 Paddock Way
12 Putney Hill
C3 1 Sandringham Cl
2 Eastwick Ct
3 Oatlands Ct
4 Banning Ho
5 Grantley Ho
6 Caryl Ho
7 Duncombe Ho
8 Chilworth Ct
9 Kent Lo
10 Turner Lo

11 Marlborough
12 Parkland Gdns
13 Lewesdon Cl
14 Pines Ct
15 Ashtead Ct
16 Mynterne Ct
17 Arden
18 Stephen Ct
19 Marsham Ct
20 Doradus Ct
21 Acris Ct
22 Heritage Ho
23 Conifer Ct
24 Spencer Ho
25 Chartwell
26 Blenheim
27 Chivelston
28 Greenfield Ho
29 Oakman Ho
30 Radley Lo
31 Simon Lo
32 Admirals Ct
33 Augustus Rd
C4 1 Brett Ho
2 Brett House Cl
3 Sylva Ct
4 Ross Ct
5 Potterne Cl
6 Stourhead Cl
7 Fleur Gates
8 Greenwood
9 Our Lady Queen of Heaven Primary Sch
10 Prospect House Sch

70
A3 1 William Harvey Ho
2 Highview Ct
3 Cameron Ct
4 Galgate Cl
5 Green Ho The
6 King Charles Wlk
7 Florys Ct
8 Augustus Ct
9 Albert Ct
10 Hertford Lo
11 Mortimer Lo
12 Allenswood
13 Ambleside
14 Hansler Ct
15 Roosevelt Ct
16 Southmead Prim Sch
A4 1 Douglas Gracey Ho
2 Aman Dalvi Ho
3 Andrew Reed Ho
4 Stoford Ct
5 Ronald Ross Prim Sch

71
B2 1 Bremans Row
2 St Andrew's Ct
3 Townsend Mews
4 Sheringham Mews
5 Rainbow Sch
6 Garratt Park Sch

72
A2 1 St Peters Cl
2 St Hildas Cl
3 St Edmunds Cl
4 St Hughes Cl
5 St Anthonys Cl
6 St Benets Cl

7 St Catherines Cl
8 Elsley Sch
C2 1 Upper Tooting Park Mans
2 Cecil Mans
3 Marius Mans
4 Boulevard The
5 Elmfield Mans
6 Holdernesse Rd
7 Lumiere Ct
8 Rutherford House Sch
C3 6 Heslop Ct
2 St James's Terr
3 Boundaries Mans
4 Station Par
5 Old Dairy Mews
6 Chestnut Grove Sch
7 Hornsby House Sch
8 Trinity St Mary's CE Prim Sch
C4 1 Hollies Way
2 Endlesham Ct
3 Broomwood Hall Sch (Upper Sch)
4 Holy Ghost RC Prim Sch

73
A3 1 Holbeach Mews
2 Hildreth Street Mews
3 Coalbrook Mans
4 Hub Buildings The
5 Metropolis Apartments
6 Hildreth St
A4 1 Meyer Ho
2 Faraday Ho
3 Hales Ho
4 Frankland Ho
5 Graham Ho
6 Gibbs Ho
7 Dalton Ho
8 Ainslie Wlk
9 Rokeby Ho
10 Caistor Ho
11 Ivanhoe Ho
12 Catherine Baird Ct
13 Marmion Ho
14 Devonshire Ct
15 Blueprint Apartments
16 Royal Duchess Mews
17 Alderbrook Prim Sch
B3 1 Zennor Trade Pk
2 Margaret Rutherford Pl
B4 1 Limerick Ct
2 Homewoods
3 Jewell Ho
4 Glanville Ho
5 Dan Bryant Ho
6 Olding Ho
7 Quennel Ho
8 Weir Ho
9 West Ho
10 Neville Ct
11 Friday Grove Mews
12 St Bernadette RC Jun Sch
C3 1 Sinclair Ho
2 MacGregor Ho
3 Ingle Ho
4 St Andrews Mews

5 Telferscot Prim Sch
C4 1 Riley Ho
2 Bennett Ho
3 White Ho
4 Rodgers Ho
5 Dumphreys Ho
6 Homan Ho
7 Prendergast Ho
8 Hutchins Ho
9 Whiteley Ho
10 Tresidder Ho
11 Primrose Ct
12 Angus Ho
13 Currie Ho

74
A1 1 De Montfort Ct
2 Leigham Hall Par
3 Leigham Hall
4 Endsleigh Mans
5 John Kirk Ho
6 Raebarn Ct
7 Wavel Ct
8 Homeleigh Ct
9 Howland Ho
10 Beauclerk Ho
11 Bertrand Ho
12 Drew Ho
13 Dowes Ho
14 Dunton Ho
15 Raynald Ho
16 Sackville Ho
17 Thurlow Ho
18 Astoria Mans
A2 1 Wyatt Park Mans
2 Broadlands Mans
3 Stonehill's Mans
4 Streatleigh Par
5 Dorchester Ct
6 Picture Ho
A3 1 Beaumont Ho
2 Christchurch Ho
3 Staplefield Cl
4 Chipstead Ho
5 Coulsdon Ho
6 Conway Ho
7 Telford Avenue Mans

8 Telford Parade Mans
9 Wavertree Ct
10 Hartswood Ho
11 Wray Ho
A4 1 Picton Ho
2 Rigg Ho
3 Watson Ho
4 MacArthur Ho
5 Sandon Ho
6 Thorold Ho
7 Pearce Ho
8 Mudie Ho
9 Miller Ho
10 Lycett Ho
11 Lafone Ho
12 Lucraft Ho
13 Freeman Ho
14 New Park Par
15 Argyll Ct
16 Dumbarton Ct
17 Kintyre Ct
18 Cotton Ho
19 Crossman Hos
20 Cameford Ct
21 Parsons Ho
22 Brindley Ho
23 Arkwright Ho
24 Perry Ho
25 Brunel Ho
26 New Park Ct
27 Tanhurst Ho
28 Hawkshaw Cl
29 Richard Atkins Prim Sch
30 Rodmill La
31 Wallis's Cottages
B1 1 Carisbrooke Ct
2 Pembroke Lo
3 Willow Ct
4 Poplar Ct
5 Leigham Cl
6 Mountview
B3 1 Charlwood Ho
2 Earlswood Ho
3 Balcombe Ho
4 Claremont Cl

5 Holbrook Ho
6 Gwynne Ho
7 Kynaston Ho
8 Tillman Ho
9 Regents Lo
10 Hazelmere Ct
11 Dykes Ct
12 Hartwell Ct
13 Christ Church Streatham CE Prim Sch
14 Streatham Hill & Clapham High Sch
B4 1 Archbishop's Pl
2 Witley Ho
3 Outwood Ho
4 Dunsfold Ho
5 Deepdene Lo
6 Warnham Ho
7 Albury Lo
8 Tilford Ho
9 Elstead Ho
10 Thursley Ho
11 Brockham Ho
12 Capel Lo
13 Leith Ho
14 Fairview Ho
15 Weymouth Ct
16 Ascalon Ct
17 China Mews
18 Rush Common Mews
C3 1 Valens Ho
2 Loveday Ho
3 Strode Ho
4 Ethelworth Ct
5 Harbin Ho
6 Brooks Ho
7 Godolphin Ho
8 Sheppard Ho
9 McCormick Ho
10 Taylor Ho
11 Saunders Ho
12 Talcott Path
13 Derrick Ho
14 Williams Ho
15 Baldwin Ho
16 Churston Cl

17 Neil Wates Cres
18 Burnell Ho
19 Portland Ho
20 Fenstanton Prim Sch
21 St Martin-in-the-Fields High Sch
22 City Heights Acad
C4 1 Ellacombe Ho
2 Booth Ho
3 Hathersley Ho
4 Brereton Ho
5 Holdsworth Ho
6 Dearmer Ho
7 Cherry Cl
8 Greenleaf Cl
9 Longford Wlk
10 Scarlette Manor Wlk
11 Chandlers Way
12 Upgrove Manor Way
13 Ropers Wlk
14 Tebbs Ho
15 Bell Ho
16 Worthington Ho
17 Courier Ho
18 Mackie Ho
19 Hamers Ho
20 Kelyway Ho
21 Harriet Tubman Cl
22 Estoria Cl
23 Leckhampton Pl
24 Scotia Rd
25 Charles Haller St
26 Sidmouth Ho
27 Hunter Ct
28 Onslow Lo
29 William Winter Ct
30 Langthorne Lo

75
A1 1 Thanet Ho
2 Chapman Ho
3 Beaufoy Ho
4 Easton Ho
5 Roberts Ho
6 Lloyd Ct

7 Kershaw Ho
8 Wakeling Ho
9 Edridge Ho
10 Jeston Ho
11 Lansdowne Wood Cl
12 Rotary Lo
13 Culzean Cl
A3 5 Sentamu Cl
B1 1 Cranfield Cl
C2 1 Welldon Ct
2 Coppedhall
3 Shackleton Ct
4 Bullfinch Ct
5 Gannet Ct
6 Fulmar Ct
7 Heron Ct
8 Petrel Ct
9 Falcon Ct
10 Eagle Ct
11 Dunnock Ct
12 Dunlin Ct
13 Cormorant Ct
14 Oak Lodge
15 Corfe Lodge

76
C1 1 Tunbridge Ct
2 Harrogate Ct
3 Bath Ct
4 Leamington Ct
5 Porlock Ho
6 Cissbury Ho
7 Eddisbury Ho
8 Dundry Ho
9 Silbury Ho
10 Homildon Ho
11 Highgate Ho
12 Richmond Ho
13 Pendle Ho
14 Tynwald Ho
15 Wirrall Ho
16 Greyfriars

NOTES

Key to lines and symbols

Bakerloo	Victoria	○ Interchange stations
Central	Waterloo & City	Ⓢ Step-free access from street to train
Circle	DLR	Ⓢ Step-free access from street to platform
District	Emirates Air Line cable car (Special fares apply)	⊖ National Rail
Hammersmith & City	London Overground	✈ Airport
Jubilee	TfL Rail	⛴ Riverboat services
Metropolitan	London Trams	Ⓥ Victoria Coach Station
Northern	District open at weekends and on some public holidays	⬤ Emirates Air Line cable car
Piccadilly		

MAYOR OF LONDON

tfl.gov.uk

24 hour travel information
0343 222 1234*

Sign up for email updates
tfl.gov.uk/emailupdates

*Service and network charges may apply. See tfl.gov.uk/terms for details.

© Transport for London

Improvement works may affect your journey, please check before you travel

UNDERGROUND

TRANSPORT FOR LONDON

EVERY JOURNEY MATTERS

Version A TfL 3.2017   Correct at time of going to print

www.philips-maps.co.uk

First published in 2001 by Philip's, a division of
Octopus Publishing Group Ltd
www.octopusbooks.co.uk
Carmelite House, 50 Victoria Embankment, London, EC4Y 0DZ
An Hachette UK Company
www.hachette.co.uk

Sixth edition with interim revision 2017
First impression 2017
LONFA

© Philip's 2017

Spiral-bound
ISBN 978-1-84907-453-7

Perfect-bound
ISBN 978-1-84907-454-4

Hardback (Union Jack)
ISBN 978-1-84907-455-1

This product includes mapping data licensed
from Ordnance Survey® with the permission of
the Controller of Her Majesty's Stationery Office.
© Crown copyright 2017.
All rights reserved. Licence number 100011710.